Published in the United States of America by
    IGI Global
    Business Science Reference (an imprint of IGI Global)
    701 E. Chocolate Avenue
    Hershey PA, USA 17033
    Tel: 717-533-8845
    Fax: 717-533-8661
    E-mail: cust@igi-global.com
    Web site: http://www.igi-global.com

Library of Congress Cataloging-in-Publication Data

Names: Information Resources Management Association, editor.
Title: Social media marketing: breakthroughs in research and practice
  / Information Resources Management Association, editor.
Description: Hershey : Business Science Reference, [2018]
Identifiers: LCCN 2017051838| ISBN 9781522556374 (hardcover) | ISBN
  9781522556381 (ebook)
Subjects: LCSH: Social media. | Mass media and business.. | Relationship
  marketing. | Customer relations.
Classification: LCC HD59 .S626 2018 | DDC 651.8--dc23 LC record available at https://lccn.loc.gov/2017051838

British Cataloguing in Publication Data
A Cataloguing in Publication record for this book is available from the British Library.

All work contributed to this book is new, previously-unpublished material. The views expressed in this book are those of the authors, but not necessarily of the publisher.

For electronic access to this publication, please contact: eresources@igi-global.com.

Social Media Marketing:

Breakthroughs in Research and Practice

Information Resources Management Association
USA

Volume II

List of Contributors

Table of Contents

Section 2
Branding, Consumer Engagement, and CRM

Volume II

Section 3
Information Management and Analysis

Section 4
Industry-Specific

Section 5
Politics and Government Organizations

Preface

The constant advancement of new business strategies, especially those centered around technology, can make it very difficult to stay competitive in the modern business era. That is why IGI Global is pleased to offer this two-volume comprehensive reference that will empower students, researchers, practitioners, consultants, and academicians in a variety of industries with a stronger understanding of one of these very important strategies, social media marketing.

This compilation is designed to act as a single reference source on conceptual, methodological, and technical aspects, and will provide insight into emerging topics including but not limited to consumer behavior, popularity prediction, social media campaigns, strategic planning, and emotional branding. The chapters within this publication are sure to provide readers with the tools necessary to brainstorm and execute robust marketing campaigns that will effectively engage their customer base. Through a variety of outlined techniques, their organizations can benefit from long-term market sustainability.

Social Media Marketing: Breakthroughs in Research and Practice is organized into five sections that provide comprehensive coverage of important topics. The sections are:

1. Adoption, Implementation, and Strategy;
2. Branding, Consumer Engagement, and CRM;
3. Information Management Analysis;
4. Industry-Specific; and
5. Politics and Government Organizations.

The following paragraphs provide a summary of what to expect from each of these designated sections within this invaluable reference source:

Section 1, "Adoption, Implementation, and Strategy," opens this extensive reference source by highlighting the latest trends in marketing communications and consumer-generated media. Through perspectives on viral marketing, social networking sites, and brand awareness, this section demonstrates the importance of advertising and branding for business performance and success. The presented research facilitates a better understanding of how the use of electronic word-of-mouth is shaping business audience outreach.

Section 2, "Branding, Consumer Engagement, and CRM," includes chapters on emerging innovations in brand management and engaging social media audiences. Including discussions on customer retention, purchase intention, and social media intelligence, this section presents research on the impact of competitive intelligence and social networking in building brand loyalty. This inclusive information assists in advancing current practices in consumer and strategic online engagement.

Section 3, "Information Management Analysis," presents coverage on social media metrics to enhance business intelligence and management. Through innovative discussions on demographic data, competitive intelligence, and big data analytics, this section highlights the changing landscape of social media mining and networking. These inclusive perspectives contribute to the available knowledge on the use of social sharing content analysis to predict trends and build brand equity.

Section 4, "Industry-Specific," discusses coverage and research perspectives on the use of social media marketing strategy across different industries such as educational institutions, the fashion industry, the airline industry, banking, and tourism. The presented research facilitates a comprehensive understanding of areas including but not limited to tourism destination marketing, customer influence, and user-centered museums.

Section 5, "Politics and Government Organizations," includes chapters on the use of political marketing in various regions. Including discussions on online petitions, web campaigns, and political public relations, this section presents research on the implementation of social media in political campaigns to promote political awareness and alleviate political scandals. This inclusive information assists in advancing current government social media practices.

Although the primary organization of the contents in this work is based on its five sections, offering a progression of coverage of the important concepts, methodologies, technologies, applications, social issues, and emerging trends, the reader can also identify specific contents by utilizing the extensive indexing system listed at the end.

Section 3
Information Management and Analysis

Chapter 40
Social Media Metrics

S. K. Sudarsanam
VIT Business School, VIT University Chennai, India

ABSTRACT

Concepts and the theories related to social media are discussed in this chapter. This chapter talks about the various frameworks of social media for the use of organizations in developing social media framework with the business objectives. Definitions and guidelines in respect of social media metrics are mentioned in this chapter. Further it suggests the methods in choosing the right metrics for the key social media objectives in respect of canvassing or product launches. A new Social media metrics framework has been suggested and also the metrics have been identified for each framework group. This Chapter will help Organizations in identifying the key social media metrics for tracking and monitoring the measurement of the performance of one's brands, products, and services in the social media channels. Once the key social media metrics are identified, organizations can choose the right tool to measure the metrics defined. This would help Organizations to improve or enhance their marketing and operational business strategies by leveraging the power and reach of the social media channels. The future directions for research and the references indicated in this chapter would be of great help to researchers in the area of social media metrics.

INTRODUCTION

Buettner (2016) defines Social media as a computer-mediated tool that allow people to create, share or exchange information, career interests, ideas, and pictures/videos in virtual communities and networks. Accordingly to Kaplan and Michael (2010), Social media is "a group of Internet-based applications that build on the ideological and technological foundations of Web 2.0, and that allow the creation and exchange of user-generated content". Furthermore, social media depends on mobile and web-based technologies to create highly interactive platforms through which individuals and communities share, co-create, discuss, and modify user-generated content. They introduce substantial and pervasive changes to communication between businesses, organizations, communities, and individuals (Kietzmann & Hermkens, 2011). These changes are the focus of the emerging field of technoself studies. Social media differ from traditional or industrial media in many ways, including quality, reach, frequency, usability,

DOI: 10.4018/978-1-5225-5637-4.ch040

immediacy and permanence (Agichtein, Castillo, Donato, Gionis, & Mishne, 2008). Social media operates in a dialogic transmission system, many sources to many receivers (Pavlik & MacIntoch, 2015). This is in contrast to traditional media that operates under a monologic transmission model (one source to many receivers). "Social media has been broadly defined to refer to 'the many relatively inexpensive and widely accessible electronic tools that enable anyone to publish and access information, collaborate on a common effort, or build relationships'" (Murthy, 2013). Many Organizations use Social Media to Market their products and services and also use Social Media to communicate with customers or potential customers. Many customers use Social Media to share their experience of using a product or service. So, there is a need for Organizations to track Social Media content on their product and services. Organizations need to analyze Big data and measure certain key metrics. Many Organizations tend to apply the concepts of traditional metrics for measuring the Social Media Metrics. Social Media is defined as a group of organisms which are dynamic, interconnected, egalitarian and interactive and which are beyond the control of any organization (Peters, Chen, Kaplan, Ognibeni, & Pauwels, 2013). The Social media requires a distinct approach to measurement, analysis, and subsequently management. This Chapter discusses in detail the Framework for establishing the key objectives of Organizations, defining the key Social Media Metrics and Benchmarking the metrics with the industry best practices.

THE FRAMEWORK FOR SOCIAL MEDIA

Peters et al. (2013) defined a new theoretical framework for Social Media Metrics. In this framework, the social media constitutes a new kind of organism compared to traditional media. This is explained in Figure 1.

Figure 1. Social media metrics framework

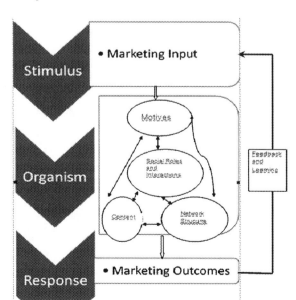

Motives, Content, Social Roles and interactions and Network Structure the four key elements of the SOR (Stimuli-Organism-Response) framework. Actors are the key ingradients of the system and they have dyadic ties with the community. They have motives, create and share content through their social roles and interactions using the network structure they have built in the Social Media over a period of time. So, any organization defining their own Social media metrics, first need to identify the metrics for each of the elements of the SOR framework. The metrics for each of the element of SOR framework are listed in Peters et al. (2013).

Models and frameworks play a key role in going from standard social media definitions and metrics to robust social media measurement. Bagnall and Bartholomew (2013) defines a five-step social media metrics measurement process:

1. Social media measurement starts with measurable objectives that are aligned with desired business outcomes and KPIs.
2. Define the specific metrics necessary to assess performance against the measurable social media objectives. A necessary and important step is setting performance targets for each metric.
3. Populate the Social media model with the metrics defined
4. Gather and analyze the data and evaluate the performance against the objectives and targets.
5. Report the results regularly on dashboards, to stakeholders and interested parties

A new type of framework (Bagnall & Bartholomew, 2013) integrates the Marketing Communication Phases with the Marketing Stages. This framework is elaborated in Table 1: AMEC Social Media Framework.

Some of the most positive aspects of the Framework are that it:

- Provides a mechanism to link activities to outputs to outcomes
- Tracks through the familiar sales funnel
- The framework is flexible and comprehends several PR use-cases – media relations, reputation, internal communications.
- Helps create a focus on outcomes and business impact.

While using the AMEC Framework in Social Media, two issues were noticed

Table 1. AMEC social media framework

Communications / Marketing Stages					
Key Area of Communication	**Awarenss**	**Knowledge/ Understanding**	**Interest/ Consideration**	**Support/ Preference**	**Action**
Public Relations Activity					
Intermediary Effect					
Target Audience Effect					Organization/ Business Results

- The intermediary effect, which in traditional public relations is the impact on the media, seemed at odds with the social world of direct interaction between consumers and brands, and consumers with each other.
- Use of the marketing sales funnel was only relevant in a percentage of social media use-cases and was found to be not the best way to model customer relations and stakeholder relationships

Forrester Research and McKinsey & Company had noted the traditional communications funnel was not necessarily funnel-shaped in social media. They described the discovery process that occurs when investigating companies and brands that often cause the consideration set to expand rather than be reduced, and the fact that a lot of engagement around brands happens post-conversion event.

To overcome these issues a new framework is proposed by AMEC. AMEC team (Bagnall & Bartholomew, 2013) developed the following model They divided Social media metrics into the following groups:

1. Program metrics. These metrics are directly tied to your campaign objectives or program;
2. Channel metrics. Metrics that are unique to specific social media channels – Twitter, Facebook, YouTube, Vimeo, LinkedIn, etc.;
3. Business metrics. Metrics that are designed to measure the impact of the campaign or initiative

Forrester Research has defined the channels as follows:

- Paid are social channels you pay to leverage (e.g. promoted tweets, display ads)
- Owned are channels you own and control (e.g. website, Facebook page)
- Earned is where customers become the channel (e.g. WOM, viral)

Pentin (2010) developed a framework for measuring social media metrics. This is elaborated further in Table 2: IAB Framework.

I - Intent: The following are some sample KPIs identified

To build brand awareness, To generate buzz, advocacy or WOM, To generate brand engagement, To shift consumer perceptions, To influence key opinion formers, To generate leads or build prospect base, To stimulate dialogue or relationship with pros, To encourage participation for social event etc

Table 2. IAB framework

I Intent	A Awareness Appreciation Action Advocacy	b Benchmark
Establish Intentions and Objectives	Define Core KPI metrics by Social Media Platform (Soft Metrics and Hard Financials)	Compare Benchmark with other Social media activity, channels and industry averages

The 4 A's: awareness of social media, appreciation, action and advocacy

The KPIs can be assigned to one or more of the above 4 As. The importance placed on the 4 As depends on the original intent. For example, the activity related to buzz and WOM will focus more on awareness, appreciation and advocacy

B – benchmark

Social media activity benchmarking:

a. First you need to compare the social media platform with other social media platforms your product or brand uses.
b. Compare how your objectives perform with other marketing channels which share similar objectives.
c. Compare how your competitors use social media activity to promote their products or brands.
d. Compare the social media activity with historical data (trend over a period of time).

Guidelines to define KPIs:
The following three parameters can be used to define KPI (key performance indicators)

- Social media platform (e.g. blog, microblogging, community forum, social network, fanpage, video forum, social network, fanpage, video sharing site, branded channel widget/application etc).
- 4As
- Soft metrics AND hard financials

Mavis, Stephanie and Charles (2010) offers following social media metric grouping method. According to them, the social media metrics should be divided into following groups:

1. Community health group. This group is divided in following four subgroups:
   1.1. Engagement;
   1.2. Customer satisfaction;
   1.3. Social content mobility;
2. Market perception group. This group is divided in following subgroups:
   2.1. Thought leadership;
   2.2. Message resonance;
   2.3. Market awareness;
   2.4. Market position;
3. Quantitative group. This group is divided into:
   3.1. Leads/sales/market share;
   3.2. Efficiency of communications

Elliott (2011) offers us to look at social media metrics from following perspective:
The first group is digital, this group is divided in smaller groups such as:

1.1. Social opportunity group. Following social media metrics belong to this group: fans, members, visitors, readers, friends and followers;

1.2. Social health group, this group includes following social media metrics: posts, comments and sentiment;

The second main group is brand group, this group is divided into following subgroups:

2.1. Branding group, following social media metrics are included in this group: awareness, brand attributes, purchase intent;

2.2. Product trial group, following metrics belong to this group: lead generation, coupon redemption and sampling;

Third main group is financial group. Following metrics belong in this group: conversions, revenue and lifetime value (Elliott, 2011).

Pangaro and Wenzek (2015) offers us to divide social media metrics in 5 groups while using CLEAT-framework. The author divides social media metrics into following groups:

1. Context group;
2. Language group;
3. Exchange group;
4. Agreement group;
5. Transaction group.

Next each of these groups are divided into following subgroups: 1. Primary metrics: consumer actions; 2. Secondary metrics: outcome (new & historical); 3. Supporting metrics: group statistics.

Murdough (2009) offers to divide the social media metrics based on the social media campaign aim: First group is named "Deepen relationship with customers".

In this group following metrics are included: numbers of advocates and numbers of comments posted;

The second groups name is "Learn from the community". Following metrics belong to this group: rank of topics discussed; decipher of positive and negative sentiments;

The third groups name is "Drive purchase intent". Following metrics are in this group: leads to ecommerce partners; retail locater results activity and product brochure downloads.

Praude and Skulme (2015) has proposed a social media channel grouping which divides the metrics into the following five groups.

1. Social networks
2. Micromedia
3. Blogs
4. Media Sharing
5. Widgets and social media applications

The Social media metrics are evaluated during each of the consumer purchase decision stages. The purchase decision stages are Need recognition, Information search, Alternative evaluation, Purchase Decision and Post Purchase Behaviour.

Based on the study of all frameworks defined above, a new framework covering groups like Brand Management, Channel Management, Financials and Benchmarks is proposed. The new framework is depicted in Figure 3.

The metrics will be captured and evaluated during the social media campaign initiation, planning, execution and closure phases (for each of the product of the organization).

The Brand Management and Channel management metrics will be tracked continuously throughout the lifecycle of an Organization during the product lifecycle all the release of the new products and service offerings of an Organization.

SOCIAL MEDIA METRICS DEVELOPMENT

Peters et al. (2013) linked theories, framework elements with guidelines for Social media metrics and Dashboards, The pictorial representation of the framework is given in Table 3.

Figure 2. AMEC social media metrics framework

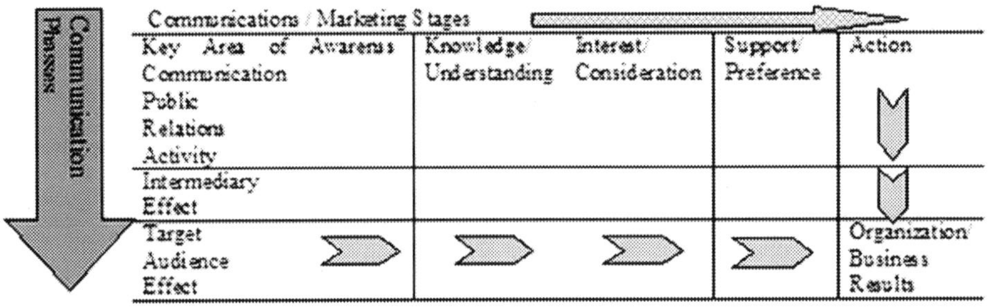

Table 3. Social media metrics theoretical framework and guidelines

Theoretical Framework Theories and Elements			Guidelines for Social Media Metrics and Dashboards	
Motives (M)	Social Roles and Interactions (SR & SI)	a)	Transition from Control to Influence	
		b)	Shift from States and Means to Processes and Distributions	
		c)	Shift from Convergence to Divergence	
Content (C)		d)	Shift from Quantity to Quality	
		e)	Leverage Transparency and Feedback loops on Metrics	
		f)	Balance the Metrics	
Network Structure (N)		g)	Cover general to specific	
		h)	Shift from Urgency to Importance	
		i)	Balance Theory and Pragmatism	

Figure 3. Proposed Social Media Metrics Framework

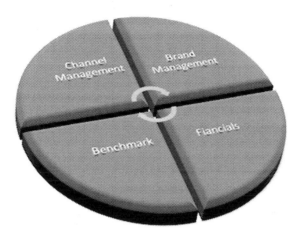

1. Transition from Control to influence: Organizations lose their control over brands or campaigns in social media and they need to use the influence of their engaged customers to promote their social media activities. The key metrics that could be measured are influencers, engaged users, listening and responsiveness of brand managers.

2. Shift from states and means to processes and distributions: In Social media, distribution and network is more important than states, so metrics that capture network dynamics is more relevant for social media metric dashboards

3. Shift from convergence to divergence: Brands need to capture adversity and positive sentiment in the network. The dashboards need to include heterogeneity and contingency in case of content relevancy of targeted segments.

4. Shift from Quantity to Quality: Metrics should focus on quality of engaged users rather than the number of users who liked or shared the contents.

5. Leverage Transparency and feedback loops on metrics: Metrics that measure user's influence over a social media or network e.g. Kloutscore (captures the influence of a user, ability to derive an action in social media), edgerank, google rank. The organizations need to be careful while measuring these metrics as they may be skewed over a period of time as they are gamed in social media network.

6. Balance the metrics: Need to develop metrics that balances both quality and quantity to remove the skewed quality metrics. Also, the metrics need to capture the dynamics over a period of time as well.

7. Cover general to specific: Need to have metrics that are general across social media and also metrics that are specific to each of the social media. Also, metrics to take care of level of social media activity (eg likes, shares, comments).

8. Shift from Urgency to importance: Organizations need to develop metrics that capture the essence of discussions, comments, sentiments in social media and need to respond at the right moment to the users to keep them engaged in their brands or products or services. The measurements need to factor the dynamics and heterogeneity of the network.

9. Balance theory and pragmatism: Metrics to be built with theoretical rigor and also of practical relevance. Metrics to be built in dashboards that both meet organizational objectives and also relevance for the organization.

The above nine guidelines need to be kept in mind while developing the social media metrics.

SOCIAL MEDIA METRICS

The following are the best social media metrics used by most of the organizations (Kaushik, 2012)

1. Conversion Rate
2. Amplification
3. Applause
4. Economic Value

Let us know discuss about the each of the above metrics in detail.

Conversion Rate

It is measured as no. of comments per post. This can be measured for any social media network. Many organizations promote their brand in social media. To achieve a higher conversion rate, organizations need to understand the target audience, brand attributes, strength of brands and value additions to followers and ecosystem. Organizations would be required to use a tool which will measure conversion rates across all social media networks and this would require buying or developing such tools.

The six principles of persuasion mentioned by Cialdini are reciprocity, consistency, social proof, authority, scarcity and liking. They serve to boost conversions in social media marketing if correctly used.

1. **Reciprocity:** Conversion rate improves quite significantly if quality content is offered to the customer and customer turns influencers for the brand. In Inbound Marketing there are many companies offering at the beginning free quality content and then informing their clients that if they want more detailed reports they can collaborate. Organizations also reach out to influencers in network or communities to increase their conversion rates.
2. **Consistency:** This principle is encountered in social media marketing as offering for a free license of a product for a month or so to a potential customer and then if the customer is happy with the product he will buy the product. The e-mail address of a potential customer is the most valuable for the company, so it is willing to offer trial versions of the product to obtain the contact details of interested customers.
3. **Social Proof:** The social proof principle in online social media can be proved by the number of fans/ followers in networks like Facebook or Twitter, by the number of visualization of YouTube videos or simply, by the number of likes and shares of posts. Another way in which this principle is used is by informing potential customers about best sold products, which might convince the customers to make a decision based on the number of other customers that made the same decision in the past.

4. **Authority:** Cialdini explains that people follow the advice of those with authority and expertise in a particular domain or business. They can be roped in as brand ambassadors to increase the conversion rate of the brand among his or her followers.
5. **Liking:** Some people tend to have similar interests as certain set of people who may represent a brand or a customer of a certain product. This enables them to be engaged more with the brand and in turn increase the conversion rate.
6. **Scarcity:** This principle is meant to show customers that product offerings are for a limited amount of time and for a limited quantity. Amazon and Flipkart offer products with discounts for a limited period of time and quantity.

Amplification Rate

It is measured as the rate at which the user's followers consume content and share it across their networks. For example, in twitter its measured as no. of retweets per tweet. Once the user's 1st network friends or followers find the shared content valuable, they will share it across to their network and the contents start to reach bigger group of customers

On Facebook, Google Plus: Amplification = # of Shares per Post

On a blog, YouTube: Amplification = # of Share Clicks per Post (or Video)

Applause Rate

Is measured as no. of likes per post (in facebook) or no. of favourite clicks per post (in twitter). The applause rate helps organizations to find out what the social media users like and what they like to view etc. Facebooks insights will measure the applause rate.

Economic Value

can be derived from micro and macro conversions (eg order of a catalogue, review of the product, an enquiry phone call). It is the sum of long term and short term revenue and cost savings. Organizations would require tools to measure macro and micro conversions across B2C, B2B and other channels. Google analytics will help capture the economic value metrics from all the participating social media channels. There are other tools also which help capture the economic value metrics.

Social Media Framework (With Metrics)

The Channel Management Metrics, Brand Management Metrics, Financial Metrics and Benchmark are proposed for the new framework. These metrics are elaborated in detail in Figure 5.

Figure 4. Social Media Metrics Framework with guidelines

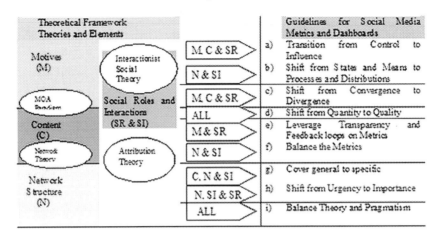

Figure 5. Proposed Framework with Social Media Metrics

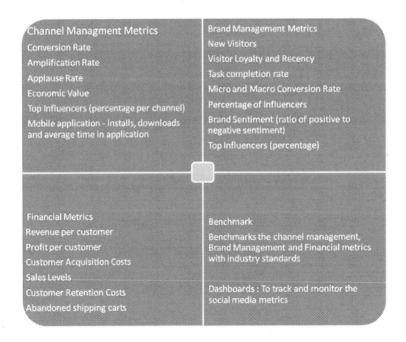

FUTURE RESEARCH DIRECTIONS

There is a need to improve the existing social media frameworks which could be used by Organizations to map their business objectives into metrics that could measure the success of the campaigns or product launch or customer feedback on the product and services offered by an organization. The future research need to focus on metrics focused on a particular social media for a particular objective. For example if you need to measure customer satisfaction twitter and facebook are the right social media to focus on. The tools used to measure and report metrics are focused mostly on a particular social media. There is a need to have an integrated tool which would measure all the metrics across all the social media channels. This would greatly reduce the cost of social media performance measuring and reporting for organizations. Organizations also could direct the user traffic from their websites to social media networks to gather customer feedback on their brands, products and services.

CONCLUSION

In this chapter the social media frameworks, guidelines to develop metrics, metric definitions and key social media metrics have been discussed in detail. The key social metrics which can be used for measuring the marketing campaigns and product launches are Conversion rate, amplification rate, applause rate, economic value, social value, engagement rate, percentage of influencers, Kloutscore, Edgerank, Google rank. Organizations need to measure the dynamism and heterogeneity of metrics over a period of time and also they need to respond at the right time with the right response and not very early in the discussion threads. Also, the focus should be on quality of metrics than the quantity. Organizations would need to research on social media frameworks, theories, develop guidelines for defining and measuring metrics, develop ability and tools to trace business objectives with metrics and measure the success of their objectives in the social media networks. Such an integrated approach would help CMOs to justify the investment made in Social media networks and also help businesses reach and service wider range of customers faster. In Business speed is the key and leveraging the power of social media would help businesses to grow faster and outsmart the competition in this dynamic and ever changing landscape.

REFERENCES

Agichtein, E., Castillo, C., Donato, D., Gionis, A., & Mishne, G. (2008). Finding high-quality content in social media. In *Proceedings of the 2008 International Conference on Web Search and Data Mining*. New York, NY: ACM Digital Library.

Baer, J. (2012). *A field guide to the 4 types of content marketing metrics* [PowerPoint slides]. Retrieved from http://www.slideshare.net/jaybaer/a-field-guide-to-the-4-types-of-content-marketing-metrics

Bagnall, R., & Bartholomew, D. (2013). *AMEC Social Media Measurement Framework* [PDF document]. Retrieved from Lecture Notes Online Web site: http://www.social-media-measurement-framework.org/wp-content/uploads/2014/06/Social-Media-Measurement-Framework.pdf

Buettner, R. (2016). *Getting a Job via Career-oriented Social Networking Sites: The Weakness of Ties*. Paper presented at the 49th Annual Hawaii International Conference on System Sciences, Kauai, HI. doi:10.1109/HICSS.2016.272

Cialdini, R. B. (1993). *Influence: The psychology of persuasion*. New York, NY: Harper Business.

Cialdini, R. B., & Goldstein, N. J. (2004). Social influence: Compliance and conformity. *Annual Review of Psychology*, 55(1), 591–621. doi:10.1146/annurev.psych.55.090902.142015

Cialdini, R. B., Wosinska, W., Barrett, D. W., Butner, J., & Gornik-Durose, M. (1999). Compliance with a request in two cultures: The differential influence of social proof and commitment/consistency on collectivists and individualists. *Personality and Social Psychology Bulletin*, *25*(10), 1242–1253. doi:10.1177/0146167299258006

Elliott, N. (2011), *Which Social Media Marketing Metrics Really Matter? (And To Whom?)*. Retrieved from http://blogs.forrester.com/nate_elliott/11-02-23-which_social_media_marketing_metrics_really_matter_and_to_whom

Ioanid, A., Militaru, G., & Mihai, P. (2015). Social Media Strategies for Organizations using influencer's power. *European Scientific Journal*. Retrieved from http://eujournal.org/index.php/esj/article/view/6144

Kaplan, A. M., & Michael, H. (2010). Users of the world, unite! The challenges and opportunities of social media. *Business Horizons*, *53*(1), 59–68. doi:10.1016/j.bushor.2009.09.003

Kaushik, A. (2012). Best Social Media Metrics: Conversation, Amplification, Applause, Economic Value. *Vikalpa*, *37*(4), 92–97. Retrieved from http://www.vikalpa.com/pdf/articles/2012/Pages-from-Vikalpa374-69-111.pdf

Kietzmann, J. H., Hermkens, K., McCarthy, I. P., & Silvestre, B. S. (2011). Social media? Get serious! Understanding the functional building blocks of social media. *Business Horizons*, *54*(3), 241–251. doi:10.1016/j.bushor.2011.01.005

Lee, K. (2014). *Know What's Working on Social Media: 19 Free Social Media Analytics Tools*. Retrieved May 22, 2016 from https://blog.bufferapp.com/social-media-analytics-tools

Marx, S. (2010). *Measuring Social Media and Its Impact on Your Brand*. Cisco.

Murdough, C. (2009). Social Media Measurement: It's Not Impossible. *Journal of Interactive Advertising*, *10*(1), 94–99. doi:10.1080/15252019.2009.10722165

Murthy, D. (2013). *Twitter: Social Communication in the Twitter Age*. Cambridge, MA: Polity.

Pangaro, P., & Wenzek, H. (2015). Engaging consumers through conversations: A management framework to get it right across converged channels. *Procedia: Social and Behavioral Sciences*, *213*, 628–634.

Pavlik, J. V., & MacIntoch, S. (2015). *Converging Media* (4th ed.). New York, NY: Oxford University Press.

Pentin, R. (2010). *A new framework for measuring social media activity* [PowerPoint slides]. Retrieved from http://www.slideshare.net/Ifonlyblog/iab-measurement-framework-for-social-media-final4-3

Peters, K., Chen, Y., Kaplan, A. M., Ognibeni, B., & Pauwels, K. (2013). Social Media Metrics —A Framework and Guidelines for Managing Social Media. *Journal of Interactive Marketing*, *27*(4), 281–298. doi:10.1016/j.intmar.2013.09.007

Praude, V., & Skulme, R. (2015). Social Media Campaign Metrics in Lativia. *Procedia: Social and Behavioral Sciences*, *213*, 628–634. doi:10.1016/j.sbspro.2015.11.462

ADDITIONAL READING

Alba, J. W. A., Lynch, J., Weitz, B., Janiszewski, C., Lutz, R., Sawyer, A., & Wood, S. (1997). Interactive Home Shopping: Consumer, Retailer, and Manufacturer Incentives to Participate in Electronic Marketplaces. *Journal of Marketing, 61*(3), 38–53. doi:10.2307/1251788

Ambler, T. (2003). *Marketing and the Bottom Line*. London: FT Press.

Ansari, A., Koenigsberg, O., & Stahl, F. (2011). Modeling Multiple Relationships in Social Networks. *JMR, Journal of Marketing Research, 48*(4), 713–728. doi:10.1509/jmkr.48.4.713

Arora, R. (1982). Validation of an S–O–R Model for Situation. Enduring, and Response Components of Involvement. *JMR, Journal of Marketing Research, 19*(6), 505–516.

Bandura, A. (1971). *Social Learning Theory*. New York: General Learning Press.

Batra, R., & Ray, M. (1985). How Advertising Works at Contact. In L. F. Alwitt & A. A. Mitchell (Eds.), *Psychological Processes and Advertising Effects* (pp. 13–44). Hillsdale, NJ: Lawrence Erlbaum Associates.

Belk, R. W. (1975). Situational Variables and Consumer Behavior. *The Journal of Consumer Research, 2*(3), 157–164. doi:10.1086/208627

Berger, J., & Milkman, K. L. (2012). What Makes Online Content Viral? *JMR, Journal of Marketing Research, 49*(2), 192–205. doi:10.1509/jmr.10.0353

Berger, J., Sorensen, A. T., & Rasmussen, S. J. (2010). Positive Effects of Negative Publicity:When Negative Reviews Increase Sales. *Marketing Science, 29*(5), 815–827. doi:10.1287/mksc.1090.0557

Blau, P. M. (1974). Presidential Address: Parameters of Social Structure. *American Sociological Review, 39*(5), 615–635. doi:10.2307/2094309

Burt, R. S. (1980). Models of Network Structure. *Annual Review of Sociology, 6*(1), 79–141. doi:10.1146/annurev.so.06.080180.000455

Burt, R. S. (2011). An Experimental Study of Homophily in the Adoption of Health Behavior. *Science, 334*(6060), 1269–1272. doi:10.1126/science.1207055

Chen, Y., Fay, S., & Wang, Q. (2011). The Role of Marketing in Social Media: How Online Consumer Reviews Evolve. *Journal of Interactive Marketing, 25*(2), 85–94. doi:10.1016/j.intmar.2011.01.003

Chintagunta, P. K., Gopinath, S., & Venkataraman, S. (2010). The Effects of Online User Reviews on Movie Box Office Performance: Accounting for Sequential Rollout and Aggregation Across Local Markets. *Marketing Science, 29*(5), 944–957. doi:10.1287/mksc.1100.0572

Coralio, B., Calvó-Armengol, A., & Zenou, Y. (2006). Who's Who in Networks Wanted: The Key Player. *Econometrica, 74*(5), 1403–1417. doi:10.1111/j.1468-0262.2006.00709.x

Damon (2010). The Spread of Behavior in an Online Social Network Experiment. *Science, 329*(5996), 1194–1197. doi:.10.1126/science.1185231

Edvardsson, B., Tronvoll, B., & Gruber, T. (2011). Expanding Understanding of Service Exchange and Value Co-creation: A Social Construction Approach. *Journal of the Academy of Marketing Science, 39*(2), 327–339. doi:10.1007/s11747-010-0200-y

Eisenbeiss, M., Blechschmidt, B., Backhaus, K., & Freund, P. A. (2012). The (Real) World Is Not Enough: Motivational Drivers and User Behavior in Virtual Worlds. *Journal of Interactive Marketing, 26*(1), 4–20. doi:10.1016/j.intmar.2011.06.002

Fader, P. S., & Winer, R. S. (2012). Introduction to the Special Issue on the Emergence and Impact of User-generated Content. *Marketing Science, 31*(3), 369–371. doi:10.1287/mksc.1120.0715

Farris, P.W., Bendle, N.T., Pfeifer, P.E., & Reibstein, D.J. (2006). *Marketing Metrics:*

Folkes, V.S. (1988). Recent attribution research in consumer behavior: A review and new directions. *The Journal of Consumer Research, 14*(1), 548–565.

Freeman, L. (2006). *The Development of Social Network Analysis.* Vancouver: Empirical Press.

Galeotti, A., & Goyal, S. (2010). The Law of the Few. *The American Economic Review, 100*(4), 1468–1492. doi:10.1257/aer.100.4.1468

Gensler, S., Völckner, F., Liu-Thompkins, Y., & Wiertz, C. (2013). Managing Brands in the Social Media Environment. *Journal of Interactive Marketing, 27*(4), 242–256. doi:10.1016/j.intmar.2013.09.004

Godes, D., Mayzlin, D., Chen, Y., Das, S., Dellarocas, C., Pfeiffer, B., & Verlegh, P. et al. (2005). The Firm's Management of Social Interactions. *Marketing Letters, 16*(3), 415–428.

Granovetter, M. (1973). The Strength of Weak Ties. *American Journal of Sociology, 78*(1), 1360–1380. doi:10.1086/225469

Hanneman, R.A., & Riddle, M. (2011). *Concepts and Measures for Basic Network Analysis.*

Hartmann, W. R. (2010). Demand Estimation with Social Interactions and the Implications for Targeted Marketing. *Marketing Science, 29*(4), 585–601. doi:10.1287/mksc.1100.0559

Hennig-Thurau, T., Malthouse, E. C., Friege, C., Gensler, S., Lobschat, L., Rangaswamy, A., & Skiera, B. (2010). The Impact of New Media on Customer Relationships. *Journal of Service Research, 13*(3), 311–330. doi:10.1177/1094670510375460

Hoffman, D. L., & Fodor, M. (2010). Can You Measure the ROI of Social Media Marketing? *MIT Sloan Management Review, 52*(1), 41–49.

Joseph, W. A., & Hutchinson, J. W. (1987). Dimensions of Consumer Expertise. *The Journal of Consumer Research, 13*(2), 411–454.

Kadushin, C. (2012). *Understanding Social Networks: Theories, Concepts, and Findings.* Oxford University Press.

Katona, Z., Zubcsek, P. P., & Sarvary, M. (2011). Network Effects and Personal Influences: The Diffusion of an Online Social Network. *JMR, Journal of Marketing Research, 48*(3), 425–443. doi:10.1509/jmkr.48.3.425

Kelley, H. H. (1967), Attribution Theory in Social Psychology. In David Levine (Ed.). *Nebraska Symposium on Motivation* (pp: 192-238). Lincoln, NE: University of Nebraska Press.

Kozinets, R. V., Valck, K., Wojnicki, A. C., & Wilner, S. J. S. (2010). Networked Narratives: Understanding Word-of-mouth Marketing in Online Communities. *Journal of Marketing, 74*(2), 71–89. doi:10.1509/jmkg.74.2.71

Kusum, L. A., Donald, R. L., & Scott, A. N. (2003). Revenue Premium as an Outcome Measure of Brand Equity. *Journal of Marketing, 67*(5), 1–17.

Labrecque, L., Esche, J., Mathwick, C., Novak, T. P., & Hofacker, C. F. (2013). Consumer Power: Evolution in the Digital Age. *Journal of Interactive Marketing, 27*(4), 257–269. doi:10.1016/j.intmar.2013.09.002

Liu-Thompkins, Y., & Rogerson, M. (2012). Rising to Stardom: An Empirical Investigation of the Diffusion of User-generated Content. *Journal of Interactive Marketing, 26*(2), 71–82. doi:10.1016/j.intmar.2011.11.003

MacInnis, D. J., Moorman, C., & Jaworski, B. J. (1991). Enhancing and Measuring Consumers' Motivation, Opportunity, and Ability to Process Brand Information from Ads. *Journal of Marketing, 55*(4), 32–53. doi:10.2307/1251955

Mallapragada, G., Grewal, R., & Lilien, G. (2012). User-generated Open Source Products: Founder's Social Capital and Time to Product Release. *Marketing Science, 31*(3), 474–492. doi:10.1287/mksc.1110.0690

Malthouse, E. C., Haenlein, M., Skiera, B., Wege, E., & Zhang, M. (2013). Managing Customer Relationships in the Social Media Era: Introducing the Social CRM House. *Journal of Interactive Marketing, 27*(4), 270–280. doi:10.1016/j.intmar.2013.09.008

Mavis, T. A., Stephanie, M. N., & Charles, H. N. (2010). The Influence of C2C Communications in Online Brand Communities on Third, our literature review reveals many disjoint studies on Customer Purchase Behavior. *Journal of the Academy of Marketing, 38*(5), 634–653. doi:10.1007/s11747-009-0178-5

Mead, G. (1934). *Mind, Self and Society*. Chicago, IL: University of Chicago Press.

50+ Metrics Every Executive Should Master. Upper Saddle River, NJ: Prentice Hall.

Mizerski, R. W., Golden, L. L., & Kernan, J. B. (1979). The Attribution Process in Consumer Decision Making. *The Journal of Consumer Research, 6*(3), 123–140. doi:10.1086/208756

Moe, W. W., & Trusov, M. (2011). The Value of Social Dynamics in Online Product Ratings Forums. *JMR, Journal of Marketing Research, 48*(3), 444–456. doi:10.1509/jmkr.48.3.444

Netzer, O., Feldman, R., Goldenberg, J., & Fresko, M. (2012). Mine Your Own Business: Market-structure Surveillance Through Text Mining. *Marketing Science, 31*(3), 521–543. doi:10.1287/mksc.1120.0713

Noort, V., Guda, H., Voorveld, A. M., & Reijmersdal, E. A. V. (2012). Interactivity in Brand Web Sites: Cognitive, Affective, and Behavioral Responses Explained by Consumers' Online Flow Experience. *Journal of Interactive Marketing, 26*(4), 223–234. doi:10.1016/j.intmar.2011.11.002

Park, C. W., & Mittal, B. (1985). A Theory of Involvement in Consumer Behavior: Problems and Issues. In J. N. Sheth (Ed.), *Research in Consumer Behavior* (pp. 201–231). Greenwich, CT: JAI Press Inc.

Paulo, A., Pavlidis, P., Chatow, U., Chen, K., & Jamal, Z. (2012). Evaluating Promotional Activities in an Online Two-sided Market of User-generated Content. *Marketing Science, 31*(3), 406–432. doi:10.1287/mksc.1110.0685

Pauwels, K., Ambler, T., Clark, B., La Pointe, P., Reibstein, D., Skiera, B., . . . Wiesel, T. (2008). Dashboards and Marketing: Why, What, How and What Research Is Needed? MSI Working Paper, Marketing Science Institute, Report 08-203.

Ransbotham, S., Kane, G. C., & Lurie, N. H. (2012). Network Characteristics and the Value of Collaborative User-generated Content. *Marketing Science, 31*(3), 387–405. doi:10.1287/mksc.1110.0684

Reibstein, D., & Srivastava, R. (2005). Metrics for Linking Marketing to Financial Performance. *Marketing Science Institute Special Report* 85–109.

Seraj, M. (2012). We Create, We Connect, We Respect, Therefore We Are: Intellectual, Social, and Cultural Value in Online Communities. *Journal of Interactive Marketing, 26*(4), 209–222. doi:10.1016/j.intmar.2012.03.002

Sinan, A., & Walker, D. (2011). Creating Social Contagion Through Viral Product Design: A Randomized Trial of Peer Influence in Networks. *Management Science, 57*(9), 1623–1639. doi:10.1287/mnsc.1110.1421

Sonnier, G. P., McAlister, L., & Rutz, O. J. (2011). A Dynamic Model of the Effect of Online Communications on Firm Sales. *Marketing Science, 30*(4), 702–716. doi:10.1287/mksc.1110.0642

Sridhar, S., & Srinivasan, R. (2012). Social Influence Effects in Online Product Ratings. *Journal of Marketing, 76*(5), 70–88. doi:10.1509/jm.10.0377

Stephen, A. T., & Toubia, O. (2010). Deriving Value from Social Commerce Networks. *JMR, Journal of Marketing Research, 47*(2), 215–228. doi:10.1509/jmkr.47.2.215

Stewart, D. W., & Pavlou, P. A. (2002). From Consumer Response to Active Consumer: Measuring the Effectiveness of Interactive Media. *Journal of the Academy of Marketing Science, 30*(4), 376–396. doi:10.1177/009207002236912

Sun, M. (2012). How Does the Variance of Product Ratings Matter? *Management Science, 58*(4), 696–707. doi:10.1287/mnsc.1110.1458

The SAGE Handbook of Social Network Analysis. John Scott, Peter J. Carrington, editors. SAGE Ltd., 364–367.

Tirunillai, S., & Tellis, G. J. (2012). Does Chatter Really Matter? Dynamics of User-generated Content and Stock Performance. *Marketing Science, 31*(2), 198–215. doi:10.1287/mksc.1110.0682

Trusov, M., Bodapati, A. V., & Bucklin, R. E. (2010). Determining Influential Users in Internet Social Networks. *JMR, Journal of Marketing Research, 47*(4), 643–658. doi:10.1509/jmkr.47.4.643

Vries, De., Lisette, S.G., & Leeflang, P.S.H. (2012). Popularity of Brand Posts on Brand Fan Pages: An Investigation of the Effects of Social Media Marketing. *Journal of Interactive Marketing, 26*(2), 83–91.

Wang, X., Yu, C., & Wei, Y. (2012). Social Media Peer Communication and Impacts on Purchase Intentions: A Consumer Socialization Framework. *Journal of Interactive Marketing*, *26*(4), 198–208. doi:10.1016/j.intmar.2011.11.004

Weinberg, B. D., Ruyter, K., Dellarocas, C., Buck, M., & Keeling, D. I. (2013). Destination Social Business: Exploring an Organization's Journey with Social Media, Collaborative Community and Expressive Individuality. *Journal of Interactive Marketing*, *27*(4), 299–310. doi:10.1016/j.intmar.2013.09.006

Wiesel, T., Pauwels, K., & Arts, J. (2011). Marketing's Profit Impact: Quantifying Online and Offline Funnel Progression. *Marketing Science*, *30*(4), 604–611. doi:10.1287/mksc.1100.0612

Yadav, M., Valck, K., Henning-Thurau, T., Hoffman, D. L., & Spann, M. (2013). Social Commerce: A Contingency Framework for Assessing Marketing Potential. *Journal of Interactive Marketing*, *27*(4), 311–323. doi:10.1016/j.intmar.2013.09.001

Zhang, K., Evgeniou, T., Padmanabhan, V., & Richard, E. (2012). Content Contributor Management and Network Effects in a UGC Environment. *Marketing Science*, *31*(3), 433–447. doi:10.1287/mksc.1110.0639

Zhang, X., & Zhu, F. (2011). Group Size and Incentives to Contribute: A Natural Experiment at Chinese Wikipedia. *The American Economic Review*, *101*(4), 1601–1615. doi:10.1257/aer.101.4.1601

Zhang, Z., Li, X., & Chen, Y. (2012). Deciphering Word-of-Mouth in Social Media: Text-based Metrics of Consumer Reviews. *ACM Transactions on Management. Information Systems*, *3*(1), 1–22.

KEYWORDS AND DEFINITIONS

AMEC: International Association for Measurement and Evaluation of Communication.

Audience Growth Rate: A comparison of your audience today to your audience yesterday, last week, last month, etc.

Average Engagement Rate: Individual post engagement compared to overall followers.

Bounce Rate: The percentage of people who land on your page and immediately leave, without viewing any other pages rate at which people leave your site after viewing only one page.

Conversions: The number of people who achieved a desired result. This could be paying for a product, signing up for a trial, completing a form, or any other goal you've set up for your campaign.

CPC: Cost per click.

Dashboard: It is a user interface that resembles an automobile's dashboard, organizes and presents information in a way that is easy to read.

Engagement: The total number of likes, shares, and comments on a post.

Exit Rate: The percentage of people who leave your site from a given page. It's possible these people have browsed other pages of your site before exiting.

Funnels: The paths that visitors take toward converting.

Impressions: A look at how many people saw your post.

Inbound Links: The number of sites linking back to your website or page.

Leads: Potential conversions. These include anyone with the need or interest to pursue your product or service.

Metrics: Standards of measurement by which efficiency, performance, progress, or quality of a plan, process or product can be assessed.

Metrics Framework: A set of definitions of metrics.

Metric Theory: A metric theory is a combination of a metric framework, a set of definitions of attributes (qualitative or quantitative) and a mapping from the framework to the set of attributes, representing the hypothesis that each metric is a good predictor of the associated attribute.

M-O-A: Motivation, Opportunity and Ability.

Reach: A measurement of the size of audience you are communicating with.

Response Rates: These can be measured in two ways, either as the speed with which you respond to comments and replies on social media, or how quickly your marketing or sales department follows up with leads from social.

Social Marketing Analytics: The discipline that helps companies measure, assess and explain the performance of Social Media initiatives in the context of specific Business objectives.

Social Media: Websites and applications that enable users to create and share content or to participate in social networking.

Social Media Metrics: The use of data to gauge the impact of social media activity on a company's revenue.

Time on Site: A measure in minutes and seconds of how long a visitor stays on your site before exiting.

Valid Metrics Framework: A Framework that provides a mechanism to link activities to outputs to outcomes, tracks through the familiar sales funnel and helps create a focus on outcomes.

Visits vs. Unique Visits: Visits count each time a person visits your site or page, regardless of whether or not they have visited before. Uniques count each person only once.

WOM: Word of Mouth.

This research was previously published in Social Media Listening and Monitoring for Business Applications edited by N. Raghavendra Rao, pages 131-149, copyright year 2017 by Business Science Reference (an imprint of IGI Global).

Chapter 41
The Primer of Social Media Analytics

Samuel Fosso Wamba
NEOMA Business School, France

Shahriar Akter
University of Wollongong, Australia

Hyunjin Kang
George Washington University, USA

Mithu Bhattacharya
University of Detroit Mercy, USA

Mohammed Upal
WebHawks IT, Japan

ABSTRACT

This article is intended to serve as a primer of social media analytics. The paper explores different dimensions of social media analytics by drawing on a review of the literature. Specifically, the paper sheds light on the definitional aspects, types of social media data and types of analytics to improve firm performance. The findings of the paper will help the reader to grasp the fundamentals of social media analytics.

INTRODUCTION

Social media is at the core of the so called "social commerce", which represents a new form of "Internet-based social media that allows people to participate in the marketing, selling, comparing, and buying of products and services in online marketplaces and communities" (Stephen & Toubia, 2010). Driven by the widespread adoption and diffusion of social media platforms such as Facebook, Twitter and Pinterest as well as mobile devices, social commerce is expected to generate tremendous business value in terms of operational efficiency and improved revenues in the incoming years. Some analysts estimated

DOI: 10.4018/978-1-5225-5637-4.ch041

that the social commerce market will grow from about US$5 billion in 2011, to almost US$30 billion by 2016 (Zhou, Zhang, & Zimmerman, 2011). In a McKinsey Global Institute report, the consulting firm foresaw that in 2012 only, "$900 billion to $1.3 trillion in annual value could be unlocked in just four sectors by products and services that enable social interactions in the digital realm". According to the same report, "[t]here's no doubt organizations have begun to realize significant value from largely external uses of social [media]. Yet internal applications have barely begun to tap their full potential, even though about two-thirds of social's estimated economic value stems from improved collaboration and communication within enterprises. Although more than 80 percent of executives say their companies deploy social technologies, few have figured out how to use them in ways that could have a large-scale, replicable, and measurable impact at an enterprise level" (Chui, Dewhurst, & Pollak, 2013). While business value from social media is emerging as an important field of research (Fosso Wamba, S. & Carter, L. 2014), very few empirical studies have been devoted to how to actually co-create and capture value from social media and relevant analytics.

Social media analytics (SMA) has emerged as an innovative research field after years of rapid and increasing adoption of social networks across the entire business. Due to the richness and the most dynamic evidence of social data, there are clear opportunities for theoretical and practical inquiry to create new knowledge and scientific possibilities by leveraging data, technology, analytics, business and society (Culnan, McHugh, & Zubillaga, 2010). There is growing evidence that SMA provides a broader view of consumers, groups and society and creates business value by identifying new patterns and opportunities (Batrinca & Treleaven, 2015; Kaplan & Haenlein, 2010). However, very few studies provide a general taxonomy to explore the types of social media data and analytics. Therefore, this paper identifies different conceptual dimensions of social media data, analytics and their relevance to business value.

The special issue on "Unveiling the Impact of Social Media: Importance of the Co-creation of Business Value during the Adoption and Use Process" of the Journal of Organizational and End User Computing (JOEUC) presents this position paper to encourage more frequent and knowledgeable use of social media analytics. The remainder of this paper is structured as follows. First, the concept of social media analytics is discussed. Second, types of social media data are explained. Third, types of social media analytics are illuminated. Finally, future research directions are provided as well as a conclusion.

DEFINING SOCIAL MEDIA ANALYTICS

The use of social media to engage with customers has increased dramatically in recent years. According to the Pew Research Center (Sheet, 2014), more than 74% of online adults in the U.S use social media to connect, interact, collaborate or engage with others. Social media based recommendations influenced an average of 26 percent purchases across 30 product area and more than 100 brands (Bughin, 2015). The widespread influence of social media as a source of information and marketplace has sparked research interests for social media analytics (SMA) (A. Chen, Lu, Chau, & Gupta, 2014; Qiu, Rui, & Whinston, 2014). Although the impact of social media continues to increase, its measurement remains a challenge.

Social media refers to communication technology platforms where people share information and opinions (Agrawal, Budak, & El Abbadi, 2011), which can connect both existing and potential customers not only with each other but also with companies and organizations (Mangold & Faulds, 2009). Hansen, Shneiderman, and Smith (2010) defined social media as a set of online tools that support social interaction between users that involves monologue (one to one) to dialogue (many to many). Zeng, Chen, Lusch, and Li (2010, p.13) identified social media as "a conversational, distributed mode of content genera-tion, dissemination, and communication among communities". A. Chen et al. (2014) put forward social media as a form of online community to get connected with people from internal and external circles. Such social media platforms let users entertain, learn, and even to make social and political changes through interacting with others on online social connection and networks (Agrawal et al., 2011). All opportunities for various aspects of business lie in the fact that virtually every social interaction among the consumers on social media can be observed and analyzed.

People in various businesses now can derive useful information from social network data to understand their consumers more comprehensively and precisely by utilizing various types of social media analytic tools. H. Chen, Chiang, and Storey (2012) defined Social Media Analytics (SMA) as a method to uncover what customers think and feel by analyzing structured and unstructured online data dispersed across a vast array of online sources. Zeng et al. (2010) highlighted SMA as informatics tools and frameworks to collect, monitor, analyze, summarize and visualize social media data to facilitate conversations and interactions to extract useful patterns and intelligence. Fan and Gordon (2014) identified SMA as inter-disciplinary modelling and analytical paradigm consisting of three steps: 1) capturing data from various courses; 2) understanding data using various analytics and models; and 3) summarizing and presenting the findings for decision making. SMA shares similarity with Big Data Analytics (BDA) in that both SMA and BDA involve analysis, management and visualization of the similar types of datasets—ac-cumulated traces of consumers' online activities (Kiron, Perguson, & Prentice, 2013). Also, SMA can be similar to social network analysis as both can aim to understand underlying relational components of consumer activities on social media.

SMA includes various analyses including sentiment analysis or opinion mining—the analytic tech-niques that analyzes people's opinions, sentiment, evaluation, attitude, judgments and emotions towards various objects, including issues, products, services, organizations, individuals, and so on (Liu, 2012). Thus, SMA can provide organizations with broad senses of customers' current needs (Mosley Jr, 2012), opinions (Eysenbach, 2009), public sentiments and future demands (Lee, Moon, & Salamatian, 2010; Szabo & Huberman, 2010), by incorporating big data and social network analytic tools. Therefore, we identify SMA as more comprehensive analysis tool than BDA social network or sentiment analysis, as SMA can encompass BDA, social network analysis and sentiment analysis to understand consumers.

TYPES OF SOCIAL MEDIA DATA

Different online social media generate different types of data. Data can be in many different forms, such as text, image, audio, video, click data, mouse movement data, deleted non-posted content, etc. (Batrinca & Treleaven, 2015). Social media data can be broadly categorized into seven categories: 1) Demographic Data, 2) Product Data, 3) Psychographic Data, 4) Behavioral Data, 5) Referrals Data, 6) Location Data and 7) Intention Data (see Table 1). First, demographic data are the publicly open and shared informa-tion, including age, race or ethnicity, gender, education, income, and geography (Kaplan & Haenlein, 2010). These data are available in profile information of individuals' social media profile. Although an individual's profile information may not be enough to understand the bigger picture, aggregated informa-tion can create a strong direction to make business decision. Second, product data are generated through social media users' mentioning of a particular brand or product on social media (Mangold & Faulds, 2009). This mentioning or discussion of a particular brand or product can appear either in any particular brand's social media page or in personal area of social media user. Third, consumers also share their problems and expectation with a product, and product value and features on social media (Heinonen, 2011). Psychographic data refer to such data that can inform consumers' personality, values, attitude, interests and lifestyle related to a product or a brand. Fourth, behavioral data represent consumers' past buying behavior, such as buying record, in social media platform (Kietzmann, Hermkens, McCarthy, & Silvestre, 2011). By analyzing behavioral data from social media pages, companies can identity their target customers and predict future intention. Fifth, referrals data are data from ratings and reviews shared on social media platforms. This type of data comes from positive or negative word of mouth on social media (Trusov, Bucklin, & Pauwels, 2009). Referrals data give a clearer picture that helps organizations or companies to identify reason for sharing the information. In order to generate positive word-of-mouth, analysis on consumers' referral data is crucial. Sixth, location data inform consumers' real time or current information regarding their geographical location (Wagner et al., 2010). Twitter and Facebook both have such features that enable users to share their current location while sharing certain information on social networking sites. Such location data provide a great opportunity for companies to build effective strategies that link virtual and real world. For instance, location data analysis can be helpful for hotel and resort and event management organization to better organize the business by targeting consumers based on their current geographical locations. Finally, intention data are those data that can help organizations and companies to predict consumers' expectation with a product or a brand and future activities related to them (Ballings & Van den Poel, 2015).

As the nature and type of social data represent the unique attributes of big data (i.e., volume, variety, velocity, veracity) (Fosso Wamba, S., Akter, S., Edwards, A., Chopin, G., & Gnanzou, D. 2015), there is possibility of new theory enquiring new challenging problems on better algorithms, infrastructure and data management to create business value and improve firm performance. The emerging social media analytics also indicate that social media data are "relational" and "networked", thus this stream necessitates new developments in system and data quality, privacy and ethical implications, strategic alignment and corporate culture.

TYPES OF SOCIAL MEDIA ANALYTICS

Table 2 shows that Social Media Analytics (SMA) can be classified into many types based on the objectives. First, topic modeling can be used to detect dominant topics from a large body of texts captured from social media platforms such as web usage including social media sites (e.g. Facebook, Twitter, Flicker) (Bollen, Mao, & Zeng, 2011; J. Chen, Nairn, Nelson, Bernstein, & Chi, 2010; Dou, Wang, Chang, & Ribarsky, 2011), news article reading (Teitler et al., 2008) and purchase behaviors (Hennig-Thurau, Gwinner, Walsh, & Gremler, 2004; Kozinets, 1999). Topic modeling can be used to identify user interests and key topics in forums or social media postings (Aggarwal & Wang, 2011; Lariscy, Avery, Sweetser, & Howes, 2009; Taboada, Brooke, Tofiloski, Voll, & Stede, 2011; Zailskaite-Jakste & Kuvykaite, 2012). Second, opinion mining or sentiment analysis plays a vital role in SMA which uses computational linguistics and natural language processing to extract insights from text data. They are typically used to determine brand image, track stock market, identify trends and manage crises (Fan & Gordon, 2014). Third, social network analysis is used to model connections, growth and dynamics of networks and activities in social media platforms, such as Facebook and Twitter. Opinion mining or sentiment analysis is a critical tool for viral marketing because it enables identification of influential groups or predictive modelling that

Table 1. Types of social media data for analytics

Types	Descriptions	Applications
Demographic Data	Consumers' demographic information in social media, which includes age, gender, education, geography etc.	• Amazon provides customized offer by name to its customers with specific product suggestions that ultimately lead to a long run relationship (Nemschoff, 2013). • Honda Japan offered login name to 63,000 people to their site to have a chance a newly launching vehicle CR-Z and the data collected from social media information where people asked for new product CR-Z's information. That ultimately took the prelaunch order to 4,500 units with 10,000 unit sales in first month (Edelman & Salsberg, 2010)
Product Data	Product data in social media, which are generated when a particular brand or product name is mentioned.	• Coca-Cola gained significant sales uplift by broadcasting a consumer made video, which was initially shared in YouTube and was gaining popularity there. The title of the video was, "The Extreme Diet Coke and Mentos Experiments" (Kaplan & Haenlein, 2010). • Just two weeks before launching iPhone5, Apple used various media channels to share products features with attractive commercials and media communication. With the help of social media conversation data, Apple found some most popular topics for promotion and to increase consumers' purchase intention (Moore, 2014). • Using Twitter, the car company Ford directly interacts with the consumers and responds in real time which ultimately helps the company to understand what's happening around the brand and helps to stop negative word-of-mouth before it gets viral (Balwani, 2009). • BBVA sets their communication strategy for responding to positive or negative comments in the Facebook, Twitter, blogs, online forums etc. Using this system, BBVA has increased customers' positive feedback more than one percent and decreased negative feedback by 1.5 percent with more delighted consumer experience (IBM, 2014). • Car Company Ford initiated a social media campaign while launching a new car, Fiesta Model, through which they received 50,000 requests for information regarding Fiesta Model and those were initially from non-Ford drivers. Later, after product lunching in late 2010, within first 6 days they sold around 10,000 cars. One of the major parts of the campaign was providing a European model of the car to 100 social media influencers completing "missions" and telling themselves to documenting and sharing experience to different social media sites. Only in YouTube the videos received 6.5 million views (Muñoz & Strotmeyer, 2010). • McDonald's sets an example of protecting brand image by regularly monitoring social media. They did it by responding to a hoax through quick social media response and responding individuals' tweets in some cases. The hoax was, the company was charging additional charging from African-Americans and that majorly appeared in Twitter. The reward of responding that hoax attack successfully in social media was, five percent stock price rise of McDonald's (Muñoz & Strotmeyer, 2010).
Psychographic Data	The type of social media data that indicate consumers' personality, interest and lifestyle.	• Helps to build content strategy with proper understanding of what consumers like and dislike. • Based on tracking information of consumers' web visiting device whether it is PC, mobile or Tablet, companies can take decision whether to go for technical update of their website for mobile friendly version (Schlagwein, 2014) • Based on the understanding of behavioral information, Starbucks has developed "My Starbucks Idea" platform where consumers provide new ideas for the company and the best ideas are voted by other members (Kaplan & Haenlein, 2010). • The research company Nielsen considers real-time Twitter data to build TV Audience Rating using its 140 million members. It helps to give more accurate TV rating information to its clients (Kiron, Palmer, Phillips, & Berkman, 2013). • Through DEWmocracy promotion, PepsiCo gathered customer insight from Social Media to create new verities of Mountain Dew brand which has been sold 36 million cases since 2008(Muñoz & Strotmeyer, 2010). • PepsiCo's sports drink Gatorade regularly started monitoring social media with major focus to various related terms including their brand, competitors and sportsmen they sponsored through real time customized data visualization and console. They analyze emotional responses around launched products and promotions, and they integrate all these findings to the product and marketing. To maintain all these, the company made a "war room" in their marketing department at Chicago. The visit to online resources of the brand, visitors' length of interaction and sharing from campaign - all have turned doubled due to all these monitoring and integration done by the company (Muñoz & Strotmeyer, 2010). • The software company Intuit made important changes in their Quicken and QuickBooks personal finance software based on direct consumer experience collected from online forum. The company initially made that forum so that one user can help another, and the company utilized and implemented the learning gained from consumers' comments in the forum (Muñoz & Strotmeyer, 2010).
Behavioral Data	Past behavioral information in social media that supports to predict future action.	• UBank in Australia maintains a dedicated team which monitors non-consumers' dissatisfaction on rival banks in social media and based on that information they make them their customer (Schlagwein, 2014) • Pursway, a social media monitoring company provides helpful consumer insights to its client firms. Pursway identifies 10-25 closest individuals of client companies' clients and monitor their transactions based on their spending pattern and provide insights through building social graph on that data (Technologies, 2013). • Using IBM Business Analytics Solutions, a global financial group BBVA analyses social data to monitor brand perception, find opportunities to make new clients, monitor existing clients' activities to retain them and create delighted customers(IBM, 2014)

continued on following page

Table 1. Continued

Types	Descriptions	Applications
Referrals Data	Ratings, reviews and non-verbal attitudes generate referral data.	• A radio station in Australia, "triple j" uses its Twitter data to understand whether listeners like their programs or not by monitoring the rate of re-tweets and responses (Schlagwein, 2014) • IKEA uses interactive catalogue to engage potential customers who share posts of relevant products within their social media circle. It resulted into a big spike into its sales figure (Scott, 2013). • McDonald's Japan promotes new products through utilizing fan base in blog and Twitter. These fans talk about their preferences of foods and the company and occasionally receive offers of free food (Edelman & Salsberg, 2010)
Location Data	Real time location data of consumer.	• Using social media, Levi Strauss offered location specific deals by generating word-of-mouth by their customers. And in one particular case, 400 customers' word-of-mouth brought 1600 people to the stores (Muñoz & Strotmeyer, 2010).
Intention Data	Data in social media that indicate consumers' future buying intentions and activity.	• By semantic analysis of Facebook status updates, Shift (an American company) measures people's purchase intent and shares the data with their client companies as service (Beckland, 2011). • Hornall Anderson, a marketing company, generates purchase intention score for their client companies through analyzing social media data; clients include a big number of retail and consumer companies (Gleanster, 2013). • By analyzing intention data, companies can design better offer and plan for consumers, better example can be set for real estate, bank, insurance etc.

identifies customer groups who have high purchase intentions. Fourth, trend analysis is used to uncover industry trends, such as product demands, consumer insights, and service quality of an industry. SMA can help business managers or decision makers to predict the future behaviors or trend of an entity (e.g. individual, group, community, events etc) based on historical data. For instance, e-commerce companies such as Amazon, e-Bay, Pandora, Last.fm, iLike, and many others predict the customer side demand based on frequency and sentiments of customers' recommendations and reviews left on the commercial sites. Fifth, popularity prediction is also becoming an important analytics tool because it predicts future demands of products and services analyzing, likes, comments and shares. Sixth, consumer engagement analysis has become another key practice in SMA since consumers increasingly interact with organizations, brands, and product through various social media channels. It can be used to assess consumers' engagement with a brand (Baird & Parasnis, 2011), advertising (Phillips & McQuarrie, 2010), service development process (Claycomb, Lengnick-Hall, & Inks, 2001; Graf, 2007), and online brand communities (Algesheimer, Dholakia, & Herrmann, 2005). Finally, Visual analytics can be defined as "the science of analytical reasoning facilitated by interactive visual interfaces" (Thomas & Cook, 2006). The ultimate goal of this analysis is to gain insights by identifying patterns, structures and trends through analysis of a vast amount of data aggregated from social media platforms. Overall, firms in the digital economy increasingly extract value from social commerce either by identifying opportunities or solving problems. This new development in the realm of data driven social commerce paves the path for innovative, nontraditional research.

FUTURE RESEARCH DIRECTIONS

Social media represents an embryonic and fascinating field of research for both practitioners and academics. Even if the emergent literature on the topic has identified various contributions of social media in transforming customers experiences, marketing processes (Bianchi & Andrews, 2015; Chang, Yu, & Lu, 2015; Hall-Phillips, Park, Chung, Anaza, & Rathod, 2015; Michaelidou, Siamagka, & Christodoulides,

Table 2. Types of Social Media Analytics (SMA)

Study	Area of Influenced Discussed	Definition	Purpose
Topic Modelling (Aggarwal & Wang, 2011; Claycomb et al., 2001; Fan & Gordon, 2014)	Politics (e.g., measuring and managing public opinion), Public Health (e.g. health related awareness) and Business (e.g. brand mentioned, product recommendation etc.)	Detecting dominant themes or topics by sifting through large body of captured text.	Using advanced statistics and machine learning, it helps to identify latent themes/topics.
Opinion Mining (Pang & Lee, 2008; Saggion & Funk, 2009)	E-commerce (e.g., forecasting demand and future event), Finance (e.g. stock market prediction) HR (hiring, retain and promotion of the right person), marketing (brand recognition, share of voice) etc.	Opinion mining is similar to Sentiment analysis, but it more focuses on the views, believes and judgment rather considering positive or negative sentiment at first place.	Opinion Analysis measures the views, and beliefs based on the criteria that depend on the purpose of analysis.
Sentiment analysis (Taboada et al., 2011; Weichselbraun, Gindl, & Scharl, 2010)	E–commerce (e.g., product/brand recommendation, product improvement needs), PR (e.g., public opinion and emotion), Politics (public sentiments and appraisal, popularity, new idea acceptance etc.), Marketing (consumer insights and emotions, share of voice, campaign design), service (e.g., service recommendation and word of mouth, service improvement), Supply chain (e.g., product demand forecast), Finance (e.g., stock market price).	Sentiment analysis is similar to opinion mining but its refers to more in-depth interpretation of data of public/consumer/ user sentiments, evaluations, appraisals, attitudes, and emotions towards entities such as products, services, organizations, Individuals, issues, events, topics, and their attributes.	Sentiment analysis measures the individual, group, communities emotions towards any types of events, products, services, brand etc.
Social Network Analysis (Hanneman & Riddle, 2005; Hansen et al., 2010; Sarner et al., 2011; Weinstein, Campbell, Delaney, & O'Leary, 2009)	CRM (e.g., relationship between groups and other community and brands), Politics (e.g., relationship between groups and community), Marketing (e.g., Brand influencer or sentiment influencer or community leader identification), Functional areas including production and operations (sales forecast, operation forecast, delivery channels etc.).	Analysis of the social network that made up of individuals call nodes and connected with other nodes with similar interest, knowledge, opinion, etc. Data analysis technique includes number of nodes, frequency of edges and eigenvectors (i.e., page rank algorithm).	Social Network Analysis measures the types and depth of relationship between the networks. Many scholars considered Social Network analysis as foundation of Social Media analytics.
Trend analysis (Fan & Gordon, 2014)	Customer or sales number, effectiveness of ad campaign, Shifts in consumer sentiment, stock markets etc.	Predicting market trends or customer behavior using historical data.	Forecasting sales, market share, customer growth or movements in stock market based on time series and regression analysis.
Popularity Prediction (Lee et al., 2010; Szabo & Huberman, 2010)	Business (e.g. forecasting demands and new product), Marketing (e.g. brand awareness, brand recognition, Brand popularity, consumer insights), PR (e.g. e- word of mouth), Entertainment (e.g. movie and record popularity, buzz marketing etc.), Politics (e.g. candidate selection, modifying election manifesto, awareness etc.) e-Governance (e.g. awareness and public reaction)	Popularity prediction is the methods of collecting positive and negative opinion/ ranks/feedbacks, shares and likes on certain subjects or events and to understand the level of current popularity and forecast the future based on the current evidence.	The popularity prediction allows organization to forecast the future demand of product, services, or events.
Customer engagement analysis (Greenberg, 2010; Kim, 2014; Zailskaite-Jakste & Kuvykaite, 2012)	E- commerce and Marketing (e.g. campaign development, new sells channel development, new product development etc.), Business (e.g. new customer segment development, new area/ distribution channel development etc.), politics (e.g. share of voice, information dissemination, opinion and concept testing, popularity measurement and increase etc.), e-Government (e.g. public awareness creation, public sentiments management etc.), Entertainment (e.g. movie or records e-word of mouth and promotion etc.)	Consumer engagement is the process to prolong the conversation or events or activities with social media participants or users. Without proper incentives it difficult to create engagement for long time, thus proper incentives and understanding the online consumer insights/behavior is very important.	The purpose of the consumer engagement is to measure the success of the online activities whether it is a commercial campaign on non-profit activities. It helps organization to understand the current situation and next action needed to be successful in online environment.
Visual analytics (Fan & Gordon, 2014; Keim, Mansmann, Schneidewind, Thomas, & Ziegler, 2008; Thomas & Cook, 2006)	Marketing, Sales, E-commerce, Big data etc.	Visual analytics is very popular in the era of big data. It is an iterative process that involves information gathering, processing and decision making.	The purpose of visual analytics is to use graphical interfaces (e.g., dashboards) to present, explore and confirm relationships among variables.

2011; Kevin J. Trainor, Andzulis, Rapp, & Agnihotri, 2014), information diffusion (Park, Lim, & Park, 2015; Zhang, 2015), government practices and government-citizen relationship (Klischewski, 2014; Pieri, 2014; Stamati, Papadopoulos, & Anagnostopoulos, 2015), firm performance (Kevin J. Trainor et al., 2014), many research questions are still unanswered, and thus justifying more research on social media.

The importance of IT in facilitating information sharing has been echoed by many scholars, including from the emerging literature on social media regarding information diffusion using Twitter and YouTube (Park et al., 2015) and firm's voluntary information disclosure (Zhang, 2015) . However, exploring the role of social media in information diffusion within organisation, industry and society, as well as across these entities is still interesting valuables for future research. Since social media tools are diverse and varied, it will be interesting to explore the best mechanism to be used for each type of social media (e.g., Twitter vs YouTube or Twitter vs Facebook, or Facebook vs YouTube) for improved information sharing for competitive advantage.

While traditional IT adoption research theories (e.g., TAM, UTAUT) have advanced our understanding of studying the adoption and use of IT at various levels, it will be interesting to see if these theories are still relevant in the context of social media adoption at the individual, organizational, and inter-organizational levels. Indeed, the emerging literature on social media points to a different direction. For example, when studying the adoption of social media in general by small and medium sized enterprises (SMEs), Fosso Wamba and Carter (2014) found that "firms' geographic location does not impact the adoption of social media tools by SMEs" (p. 8). However, the same authors found a significant positive relationship between firms' geographic location and the SMEs intention to adopt Twitter (S. Fosso Wamba & L. Carter, 2013). Considering that social media research is highly inter-disciplinary investigating different theoretical bases, the foundation of such research will be valuable to academics in general and more relevant findings from the research will then also eventually impact practitioners. It will also shed light on methodological trends in this stream of research. It will be interesting to see whether the trend in social media research is data driven or theory driven analyzing existing research.

In addition, social media-enabled business analytics at the individual, organizational and interorganizational levels is an interesting future research avenue. Additionally future research on developing roadmaps and frameworks towards better design, technical, and financial decision to appropriate social media technologies is the current demand. Finally, one of the most important future research directions is in the area of privacy, security, and trust issues involved in the use of social media technologies.

CONCLUSION

When different types of analyses are properly applied, SMA can deliver transactional, strategic and transformative business values to firms. SMA can be a very useful tool to understand and build relationships with customers based on their real-time activity and location data collected and shared through various social media channels (Greenberg, 2010; Sarner et al., 2011; Kevin J Trainor, 2012). Also, because SMA help firms to map the needs of the broader market, it will ultimately help them to improve market intelligence, scale and speed of production, flexibility of distribution, and effectiveness of supply chain and promotion (Chamlertwat, Bhattarakosol, Rungkasiri, & Haruechaiyasak, 2012; Kiron, Palmer, Phillips, & Kruschwitz, 2012; Zeng et al., 2010). Thus, SMA can provide sustainable business values to different areas of business, such as marketing, e-commerce, public relations, supply chain, and finance.

REFERENCES

Aggarwal, C. C., & Wang, H. (2011). *Text mining in social networks Social Network Data Analytics* (pp. 353–378). Springer. doi:10.1007/978-1-4419-8462-3_13

Agrawal, D., Budak, C., & El Abbadi, A. (2011). Information Diffusion in Social Networks: Observing and Influencing Societal Interests.

Algesheimer, R., Dholakia, U. M., & Herrmann, A. (2005). The social influence of brand community: Evidence from European car clubs. *Journal of Marketing, 69*(3), 19–34. doi:10.1509/jmkg.69.3.19.66363

Baird, C. H., & Parasnis, G. (2011). From social media to social customer relationship management. *Strategy and Leadership, 39*(5), 30–37. doi:10.1108/10878571111161507

Ballings, M., & Van den Poel, D. (2015). CRM in social media: Predicting increases in Facebook usage frequency. *European Journal of Operational Research, 244*(1), 248–260. doi:10.1016/j.ejor.2015.01.001

Balwani, S. (2009). Presenting: 10 of the Smartest Big Brands in Social Media. *Mashable.com*. Retrieved from http://mashable.com/2009/02/06/social-media-smartest-brands

Batrinca, B., & Treleaven, P. C. (2015). Social media analytics: A survey of techniques, tools and platforms. *AI & Society, 30*(1), 89–116. doi:10.1007/s00146-014-0549-4

Beckland, J. (2011). The End of Demographics: How Marketers Are Going Deeper With Personal Data. Retrieved from http://mashable.com/2011/06/30/psychographics-marketing/

Bianchi, C., & Andrews, L. (2015). Investigating marketing managers' perspectives on social media in Chile. *Journal of Business Research*. doi:10.1016/j.jbusres.2015.06.026

Bollen, J., Mao, H., & Zeng, X. (2011). Twitter mood predicts the stock market. *Journal of Computational Science, 2*(1), 1–8. doi:10.1016/j.jocs.2010.12.007

Bughin, J. (2015). Getting a sharper picture of social media's influence. *The McKinsey Quarterly*, (July): 1–4.

Chamlertwat, W., Bhattarakosol, P., Rungkasiri, T., & Haruechaiyasak, C. (2012). Discovering Consumer Insight from Twitter via Sentiment Analysis. *J. UCS, 18*(8), 973–992.

Chang, Y.-T., Yu, H., & Lu, H.-P. (2015). Persuasive messages, popularity cohesion, and message diffusion in social media marketing. *Journal of Business Research, 68*(4), 777–782. doi:10.1016/j.jbusres.2014.11.027

Chen, A., Lu, Y., Chau, P. Y. K., & Gupta, S. (2014). Classifying, Measuring, and Predicting Users' Overall Active Behavior on Social Networking Sites. *Journal of Management Information Systems, 31*(3), 213–253. doi:10.1080/07421222.2014.995557

Chen, H., Chiang, R. H., & Storey, V. C. (2012). Business intelligence and analytics: From big data to big impact. *Management Information Systems Quarterly, 36*, 1165–1188.

Chen, J., Nairn, R., Nelson, L., Bernstein, M., & Chi, E. (2010). *Short and tweet: experiments on recommending content from information streams.* Paper presented at the Proceedings of the SIGCHI Conference on Human Factors in Computing Systems. doi:10.1145/1753326.1753503

Chui, M., Dewhurst, M., & Pollak, L. (2013). Building the social enterprise. *The McKinsey Quarterly*, 1–4.

Claycomb, C., Lengnick-Hall, C. A., & Inks, L. W. (2001). The customer as a productive resource: A pilot study and strategic implications. *The Journal of Business Strategy*, *18*(1), 47–69.

Culnan, M. J., McHugh, P. J., & Zubillaga, J. I. (2010). How large US companies can use Twitter and other social media to gain business value. *MIS Quarterly Executive*, *9*(4), 243–259.

Dou, W., Wang, X., Chang, R., & Ribarsky, W. (2011). *Paralleltopics: A probabilistic approach to exploring document collections.* Paper presented at the 2011 IEEE Conference on Visual Analytics Science and Technology (VAST). doi:10.1109/VAST.2011.6102461

Edelman, D., & Salsberg, B. (2010). Beyond paid media: Marketing's new vocabulary. *The McKinsey Quarterly*, 1–8.

Eysenbach, G. (2009). Infodemiology and infoveillance: Framework for an emerging set of public health informatics methods to analyze search, communication and publication behavior on the Internet. *Journal of Medical Internet Research*, *11*(1), e11. doi:10.2196/jmir.1157 PMID:19329408

Fan, W., & Gordon, M. D. (2014). The Power of Social Media Analytics. *Association for Computing Machinery. Communications of the ACM*, *57*(6), 74–81. doi:10.1145/2602574

Fosso Wamba, S. & Carter, L. (2014). Social Media Tools Adoption and Use by SMES: An Empirical Study. [JOEUC]. *Journal of Organizational and End User Computing*, *26*(2), 1–17. doi:10.4018/joeuc.2014040101

Fosso Wamba, S., & Carter, L. (2014). Social Media Tools Adoption and Use by SMES: An Empirical Study. [JOEUC]. *Journal of Organizational and End User Computing*, *26*(2), 1–17. doi:10.4018/joeuc.2014040101

Fosso Wamba, S., Akter, S., Edwards, A., Chopin, G., & Gnanzou, D. (2015). How 'big data' can make big impact: Findings from a systematic review and a longitudinal case study. *International Journal of Production Economics*, *165*, 234–246. doi:10.1016/j.ijpe.2014.12.031

Gleanster. (2013). Harnessing the Power of Social Data to Predict (and Improve) Consumer Buying Behavior. Retrieved from http://help.sdl.com/download/harnessing-the-power-of-social-data-to-predict-consumer-buying-behavior/36451/

Graf, A. (2007). Changing roles of customers: Consequences for HRM. *International Journal of Service Industry Management*, *18*(5), 491–509. doi:10.1108/09564230710826269

Greenberg, P. (2010). The impact of CRM 2.0 on customer insight. *Journal of Business and Industrial Marketing*, *25*(6), 410–419. doi:10.1108/08858621011066008

Hall-Phillips, A., Park, J., Chung, T.-L., Anaza, N. A., & Rathod, S. R. (2015). I (heart) social ventures: Identification and social media engagement. *Journal of Business Research*. doi:10.1016/j.jbusres.2015.05.005

Hanneman, R. A., & Riddle, M. (2005). *Introduction to social network methods*. University of California Riverside.

Hansen, D. Shneiderman, B., & Smith, M.A. (2010). Analyzing social media networks with NodeXL: Insights from a connected world: Morgan Kaufmann.

Heinonen, K. (2011). Consumer activity in social media: Managerial approaches to consumers' social media behavior. *Journal of Consumer Behaviour*, *10*(6), 356–364. doi:10.1002/cb.376

Hennig-Thurau, T., Gwinner, K. P., Walsh, G., & Gremler, D. D. (2004). Electronic word-of-mouth via consumer-opinion platforms: What motivates consumers to articulate themselves on the Internet? *Journal of Interactive Marketing*, *18*(1), 38–52. doi:10.1002/dir.10073

IBM. (2014). BBVA seamlessly monitors and improves its online reputation. Retrieved from http://www.ibm.com/smarterplanet/global/files/sweden__none__banking__BBVA.pdf

Kaplan, A. M., & Haenlein, M. (2010). Users of the world, unite! The challenges and opportunities of Social Media. *Business Horizons*, *53*(1), 59–68. doi:10.1016/j.bushor.2009.09.003

Keim, D. A., Mansmann, F., Schneidewind, J., Thomas, J., & Ziegler, H. (2008). *Visual analytics: Scope and challenges*. Springer.

Kietzmann, J. H., Hermkens, K., McCarthy, I. P., & Silvestre, B. S. (2011). Social media? Get serious! Understanding the functional building blocks of social media. *Business Horizons*, *54*(3), 241–251. doi:10.1016/j.bushor.2011.01.005

Kim, K. Y. (2014). Business Intelligence and Marketing Insights in an Era of Big Data: The Q-sorting Approach. *Transactions on Internet and Information Systems (Seoul)*, *8*(2), 567–582. doi:10.3837/tiis.2014.02.014

Kiron, D., Palmer, D., Phillips, A. N., & Berkman, R. (2013). Social business: Shifting out of first gear. *MIT Sloan Management Review*, *55*(1), 1.

Kiron, D., Palmer, D., Phillips, A. N., & Kruschwitz, N. (2012). What managers really think about social business. *MIT Sloan Management Review*, *53*(4), 51.

Kiron, D., Perguson, R. B., & Prentice, P. K. (2013). *From Value to Vision: Reimagining the Possible with Data Analytics*. MIT Sloan Management Review.

Klischewski, R. (2014). When virtual reality meets realpolitik: Social media shaping the Arab government–citizen relationship. *Government Information Quarterly*, *31*(3), 358–364. doi:10.1016/j.giq.2013.10.015

Kozinets, R. V. (1999). E-tribalized marketing?: The strategic implications of virtual communities of consumption. *European Management Journal*, *17*(3), 252–264. doi:10.1016/S0263-2373(99)00004-3

Lariscy, R. W., Avery, E. J., Sweetser, K. D., & Howes, P. (2009). Monitoring public opinion in cyberspace: How corporate public relations is facing the challenge. *The Public Relations Journal*, *3*(4), 1–17.

Lee, J. G., Moon, S., & Salamatian, K. (2010). *An approach to model and predict the popularity of online contents with explanatory factors*. Paper presented at the 2010 IEEE/WIC/ACM International Conference on Web Intelligence and Intelligent Agent Technology (WI-IAT). doi:10.1109/WI-IAT.2010.209

Liu, B. (2012). Sentiment analysis and opinion mining. *Synthesis Lectures on Human Language Technologies*, *5*(1), 1–167. doi:10.2200/S00416ED1V01Y201204HLT016

Mangold, W., & Faulds, D. J. (2009). Social media: The new hybrid element of the promotion mix. *Business Horizons*, *52*(4), 357–365. doi:10.1016/j.bushor.2009.03.002

Michaelidou, N., Siamagka, N. T., & Christodoulides, G. (2011). Usage, barriers and measurement of social media marketing: An exploratory investigation of small and medium B2B brands. *Industrial Marketing Management*, *40*(7), 1153–1159. doi:10.1016/j.indmarman.2011.09.009

Moore, L. (2014). Fourth Source. Is your Advertising Campaign Driving Intent to Purchase? Retrieved from http://www.fourthsource.com/social-media/advertising-campaign-driving-intent-purchase-16868

Mosley, R.C. Jr. (2012). *Social media analytics: Data mining applied to insurance Twitter posts.* Paper presented at the Casualty Actuarial Society E-Forum, Winter 2012 (Vol. 2).

Muñoz, F. M., & Strotmeyer, K. C. (2010). Demystifying social media. *Journal of Student Affairs Research and Practice*, *47*(1), 123–127. doi:10.2202/1949-6605.6132

Nemschoff, M. (2013). Social Media Marketing: How Big Data is Changing Everything. Retrieved from http://www.cmswire.com/cms/customer-experience/social-media-marketing-how-big-data-is-changing-everything-022488.php

Pang, B., & Lee, L. (2008). Opinion mining and sentiment analysis. *Foundations and trends in information retrieval, 2*(1-2), 1-135.

Park, S. J., Lim, Y. S., & Park, H. W. (2015). Comparing Twitter and YouTube networks in information diffusion: The case of the "Occupy Wall Street" movement. *Technological Forecasting and Social Change*, *95*, 208–217. doi:10.1016/j.techfore.2015.02.003

Phillips, B. J., & McQuarrie, E. F. (2010). Narrative and persuasion in fashion advertising. *The Journal of Consumer Research*, *37*(3), 368–392. doi:10.1086/653087

Pieri, E. (2014). Emergent policing practices: Operation Shop a Looter and urban space securitisation in the aftermath of the Manchester 2011 riots. *Surveillance & Society*, *12*(1), 38–54.

Qiu, L., Rui, H., & Whinston, A. B. (2014). Effects of Social Networks on Prediction Markets: Examination in a Controlled Experiment. *Journal of Management Information Systems*, *30*(4), 235–268. doi:10.2753/MIS0742-1222300409

Saggion, H., & Funk, A. (2009). Extracting opinions and facts for business intelligence. *RNTI Journal. E (Norwalk, Conn.), 119*(17), 146.

Sarner, A., Thompson, J. D., Drakos, N., Fletcher, C., Mann, J., & Maoz, M. (2011). *Magic quadrant for social CRM*. Stamford: Gartner.

Schlagwein, D. (2014). Strategic tools: how firms successfully use social media. *Smart Company.* Retrieved from http://www.smartcompany.com.au/leadership/management/41115-strategic-tools-how-firms-successfully-use-social-media.html

Scott, M. (2013). With a Little Help from Social Media: Top 10 Business Success Stories. *Socialmediatoday*. Retrieved from http://www.socialmediatoday.com/content/little-help-social-media-top-10-business-success-stories

Sheet, Social Networking Fact. (2014). Pew Research Internet Project.

Stamati, T., Papadopoulos, T., & Anagnostopoulos, D. (2015). Social media for openness and accountability in the public sector: Cases in the Greek context. *Government Information Quarterly, 32*(1), 12–29. doi:10.1016/j.giq.2014.11.004

Stephen, A. T., & Toubia, O. (2010). Deriving Value from Social Commerce Networks. *JMR, Journal of Marketing Research, 47*(2), 215–222. doi:10.1509/jmkr.47.2.215

Szabo, G., & Huberman, B. A. (2010). Predicting the popularity of online content. *Communications of the ACM, 53*(8), 80–88. doi:10.1145/1787234.1787254

Taboada, M., Brooke, J., Tofiloski, M., Voll, K., & Stede, M. (2011). Lexicon-based methods for sentiment analysis. *Computational Linguistics, 37*(2), 267–307. doi:10.1162/COLI_a_00049

Technologies, SQream. (2013). Big Data & Social Media Insights are Bringing More Customers to Telcos. from http://sqream.com/social-media-insights-costumer-growth-for-telecommunication-companies-2/

Teitler, B. E., Lieberman, M. D., Panozzo, D., Sankaranarayanan, J., Samet, H., & Sperling, J. (2008). *NewsStand: A new view on news.* Paper presented at the Proceedings of the 16th ACM SIGSPATIAL international conference on Advances in geographic information systems.

Thomas, J. J., & Cook, K. (2006). A visual analytics agenda. *Computer Graphics and Applications, IEEE, 26*(1), 10–13. doi:10.1109/MCG.2006.5 PMID:16463473

Trainor, K. J. (2012). Relating social media technologies to performance: A capabilities-based perspective. *Journal of Personal Selling & Sales Management, 32*(3), 317–331. doi:10.2753/PSS0885-3134320303

Trainor, K. J., Andzulis, J., Rapp, A., & Agnihotri, R. (2014). Social media technology usage and customer relationship performance: A capabilities-based examination of social CRM. *Journal of Business Research, 67*(6), 1201–1208. doi:10.1016/j.jbusres.2013.05.002

Trusov, M., Bucklin, R. E., & Pauwels, K. (2009). Effects of word-of-mouth versus traditional marketing: Findings from an internet social networking site. *Journal of Marketing, 73*(5), 90–102. doi:10.1509/jmkg.73.5.90

Wagner, D., Lopez, M., Doria, A., Pavlyshak, I., Kostakos, V., Oakley, I., & Spiliotopoulos, T. (2010). *Hide and seek: location sharing practices with social media.* Paper presented at the Proceedings of the 12th international conference on Human computer interaction with mobile devices and services. doi:10.1145/1851600.1851612

Weichselbraun, A., Gindl, S., & Scharl, A. (2010). A context-dependent supervised learning approach to sentiment detection in large textual databases. *Journal of Information and Data Management, 1*(3), 329.

Weinstein, C., Campbell, W., Delaney, B., & O'Leary, G. (2009). *Modeling and detection techniques for counter-terror social network analysis and intent recognition.* Paper presented at the Aerospace conference. IEEE. doi:10.1109/AERO.2009.4839642

Zailskaite-Jakste, Ligita, & Kuvykaite, Rita. (2012). Consumer Engagement in Social Media by Building the Brand.

Zeng, D., Chen, H., Lusch, R., & Li, S.-H. (2010). Social media analytics and intelligence. *IEEE Intelligent Systems*, *25*(6), 13–16. doi:10.1109/MIS.2010.151

Zhang, J. (2015). Voluntary information disclosure on social media. *Decision Support Systems*, *73*, 28–36. doi:10.1016/j.dss.2015.02.018

Zhou, L., Zhang, P., & Zimmerman, H.-D. (2011). Call for Papers for a Series of Special Issues: Social Commerce. *Electronic Commerce Research and Applications*.

This research was previously published in the Journal of Organizational and End User Computing (JOEUC), 28(2); edited by Steven Walczak, pages 1-12, copyright year 2016 by IGI Publishing (an imprint of IGI Global).

Chapter 42
Predictive Analytics of Social Networks:
A Survey of Tasks and Techniques

Ming Yang
Kansas State University, USA

William H. Hsu
Kansas State University, USA

Surya Teja Kallumadi
Kansas State University, USA

ABSTRACT

In this chapter, the authors survey the general problem of analyzing a social network in order to make predictions about its behavior, content, or the systems and phenomena that generated it. They begin by defining five basic tasks that can be performed using social networks: (1) link prediction; (2) pathway and community formation; (3) recommendation and decision support; (4) risk analysis; and (5) planning, especially causal interventional planning. Next, they discuss frameworks for using predictive analytics, availability of annotation, text associated with (or produced within) a social network, information propagation history (e.g., upvotes and shares), trust, and reputation data. They also review challenges such as imbalanced and partial data, concept drift especially as it manifests within social media, and the need for active learning, online learning, and transfer learning. They then discuss general methodologies for predictive analytics involving network topology and dynamics, heterogeneous information network analysis, stochastic simulation, and topic modeling using the abovementioned text corpora. They continue by describing applications such as predicting "who will follow whom?" in a social network, making entity-to-entity recommendations (person-to-person, business-to-business [B2B], consumer-to-business [C2B], or business-to-consumer [B2C]), and analyzing big data (especially transactional data) for Customer Relationship Management (CRM) applications. Finally, the authors examine a few specific recommender systems and systems for interaction discovery, as part of brief case studies.

DOI: 10.4018/978-1-5225-5637-4.ch042

1. INTRODUCTION: PREDICTION IN SOCIAL NETWORKS

Social networks provide a way to anticipate, build, and make use of links, by representing relationships and propagation of phenomena between pairs of entities that can be extended to large-scale dynamical systems. In its most general form, a social network can capture individuals, communities or other organizations, and propagation of everything from information (documents, memes, rumors) to infectious pathogens. This representation facilitates the study of patterns in the formation, persistence, evolution, and decay of relationships, which in itself forms a type of dynamical system, and also supports modeling of temporal dynamics for events that propagate across a network.

In this first section, we survey goals of predictive analytics using a social network, outline the specific tasks that motivate the use of graph-based models of social networks, and discuss the general state-of-the-field in data science as applied to prediction.

1.1 Overview: Goals of Prediction

In general, time series prediction aims to generate estimates for variables of interest that are associated with future states of some domain. These variables frequently represent a continuation of the input data, modeled under some assumptions about how the future data are distributed as a function of the history of past input, plus exogenous factors such as noise. The term *forecasting* refers to this specific type of predictive task. (Gershenfeld & Weigend, 1994) Acquiring the information to support this operation is known as *modeling* and frequently involves the application of machine learning and statistical inference. A further goal of the analytical process that informs this model is *understanding* the way in which a generative process changes over time; in some scenarios, this means estimating high level parameters or especially structural elements of the time series model.

Getoor (2003) introduces the term *link mining* to describe a specialized form of data mining: analyzing a network structure to discover novel, useful, and comprehensible relationships that are often latent, *i.e.,* not explicitly described. Prototypical link mining tasks, as typified by the three domains that Getoor surveys, include modeling collections of web pages, bibliographies, and the spread of diseases. Each member of such a collection represents one entity. In the case of web page networks, links can be *outlinks* directed from a member page to another page, *inlinks* directed from another page to a member page, or *co-citation* links indicating that some page contains outlinks to both endpoints of a link. Bibliography or *citation networks* model paper-to-paper citations, co-author sets, author-to-institution links, and paper-to-publication relationships. Epidemiological domains are often represented using *contact networks*, which represent individual organisms (especially humans or other animals) using nodes and habitual or incidental contact using links. *Spread models* extend this graphical representation by adding information about incubation and other rates and time-dependent events.

Getoor and Diehl (2005) further survey the task of link mining, taxonomizing tasks into abstract categories such as *object-based*, *link-based*, and *graph-based*. Object-based tasks, used often in information retrieval and visualization, include ranking, classification, group detection (one instance of which is community detection), and identification (including disambiguation and deduplication). Link-based tasks, which we discuss in depth in this article, include the modeling task of *link prediction* – deducing or calculating the likelihood of a future link between two candidate entities, based on their individual attributes and mutual associations. Graph-based tasks include modeling tasks such as discovering subgraphs, as well as characterization or understanding tasks such as classifying an entire graph as a small-world network or being governed by a random generative model – *e.g.*, some type of Erdős–Rényi graph (Erdős & Rényi, 1960).

Social media have proliferated and gained in user population, bandwidth consumed, and volume of content produced since the early 2000s. A brief history and broad survey of social network sites is given by boyd and Ellison (2007), documenting different mechanisms by which online social identity is maintained and computer-mediated communication practiced. This article also introduces contemporary work on characterization and visualization of network structure, modeling offline and online social networks using a combined model, and preservation of privacy on social network sites (SNSs). Many of the modeling tools referenced in this survey paper admit direct application or extension to predictive analytics tasks for SNSs. (Yu, Han, & Faloutsos, 2010)

1.2 Tasks

Predictive analytics refers to the application of statistical and other computational tools to historical data, towards achieving goals of prediction listed in Section 1.1, with the purpose of identifying actionable patterns. These may be positive patterns that the end user wishes to promote and leverage, such as frequent web browsing sequences or social communities, or negative patterns representing phenomena to be counteracted, such as incipient epidemics and criminal networks. Link mining and prediction in social media exist as outgrowths and extensions of predictive analytics in general, but the applications thereof are formulated in service to specific goals. This section gives an overview of these goals and their supporting technical objectives. These are expressed in terms of task definitions: performance elements such as decision support, recommender systems, and risk management, to which the methodology of predictive analytics is applicable. In decision support systems, the goal is to provide assistive technology for generating and explaining a recommended course of action to a human user or users. We will see how decision support tasks for social networks can be understood in terms of link, pathway, and community prediction, giving rise to more specialized tasks such as the detection of at-risk groups and modeling the dynamics of information propagation to recognize and act on patterns in social networks.

1.2.1 Link Prediction

Liben-Nowell and Kleinberg (2007) formalize the *link prediction problem* as that of answering the question:

Given a snapshot of a social network, can we infer which new interactions among its members are likely to occur in the near future?

They relate this task to the atemporal problem of inferring missing links from a partially observed network and characterize solution approaches as being based upon node neighborhoods, existing paths in the known network, and "meta-approaches" that are compatible with node and path-based methods. *Node-based scores* that are positively correlated with the existence of a link (u, v) between nodes and v include: the count of their common neighbors in an undirected graph model; multiplicative or other nonlinear functions of their respective graph degrees, such as *preferential attachment*; and similarity measures used in information retrieval such as inverse log frequency of feature co-occurrence. *Path-based scores* are often based on the count or a parametrically weighted sum of alternative path lengths between u and v. Stochastic sampling-based variants of this type of score include the expected time for a random walk originating from *u* to reach *v* (the *hitting time*). Liben-Nowell and Kleinberg discuss Markov chain Monte Carlo approaches, including random walk with restart (Al Hasan, Ahmed, & Neville, 2013), towards estimation of path-based scores for the link prediction task. They also discuss how meta-level approximation methods, such as those resembling latent semantic analysis (Deerwester, Dumais, Furnas, Landauer, & Harshman, 1990), can be used to estimate the score for a candidate link (u,v).

Link prediction tasks may apply to graphs that are treated as unchanging over time (static) or dynamic. (Salem, 2009) In the case of static graphs, the task is to discover possibly hidden links from partial information. In the case of dynamic graphs, social network data is treated as a historical snapshot (Barabási, et al., 2002) and the task is to predict a continuation of the data, as in traditional time series. Recovering these missing links in the graph may be viewed as a reconstruction task for a hierarchical structure (Clauset, Moore, & Newman, 2008). This can be done by analyzing local structure or through transformations of the spectral density of edges across the graph (Kunegis & Lommatzsch, 2009). The local structure itself can represent general relationships in an entity-relational data model (Taskar, Wong, Abbeel, & Koller, 2004) or friendship and trust in social media (Hsu, Lancaster, Paradesi, & Weninger, 2007).

The existence of a relationship existing between two users in a social network can be identified by an inference process or by simple classification. Although the inference steps may be probabilistic, logical, or both, the links themselves tend to be categorical. They can be dependent purely on single nodes, local topology, or exogenous information. In addition to using the structure of the known graph, common features of candidates for link existence (friendship, trust, or mutual community membership) include text-based similarity measures such as the number of common interests or some semantically-weighted sum thereof. (Caragea, Bahirwani, Aljandal, & Hsu, 2009) Al Hasan and Zaki (2011) provide a broad survey of extant link prediction techniques, emphasizing the feature types surveyed earlier by Liben-Nowell and Kleinberg (2007). Recent work has focused on topic modelling approaches to the existence of friendship links in social networks (Parimi & Caragea, 2011) and to the development and use of spatial features in location-based social media (Scellato, Noulas, & Mascolo, 2011). Though these networks can theoretically contain hundreds of millions to billions of vertices, most empirical scientific studies to date have focused on data sets containing thousands to tens of millions of vertices. (Caragea, Bahirwani, Aljandal, & Hsu, 2009)

1.2.2 Degrees of Separation: Pathway and Community Formation

The task of link prediction can be extended to the general problem of finding paths and subgraphs (communities), a general class of problems which may involve the systematic application of local analytical techniques (Abrams, 2003; Backstrom, Huttenlocher, Kleinberg, & Lan, 2006) or holistic analysis of the entire social network. Nonlocal analysis is often based on having a global topic model that is used as a similarity measure between users to detect community structure, (Qian, Zhang, & Yang, 2006) This is a case of the general observed phenomenon and theory of homophily, the tendency of similar individuals to associate with one another. (McPherson, Smith-Lovin, & Cook, 2001) The purpose and typical performance elements of such a system are to understand the likely participation profiles of users: how long, how often, and with what frequency and volume of information propagation they are likely to participate. (Nov, Naaman, & Ye, 2009) Recent studies on computer-mediated communication have indicated that both internal observable factors such as a user's tenure (longevity of membership and role), and external ones such as a user's motivation for using a photo-sharing site, are relevant to these usage statistics. (Nov, Naaman, & Ye, 2010)

Meanwhile, techniques for predicting the formation of links such as follower linkage in social media are largely based on graph structure, *i.e.*, topology. (Romero & Kleinberg, 2010) Other features that are not purely topological may be overlaid on or otherwise combined with an existing social network. (Brown, Nicosia, Scellato, Noulas, & Mascolo, 2012) In addition, the basic tonal quality of posts by social network users, particularly sentiments expressed about topics of mutual interest, are a commonly-used basis for community formation. (Nguyen, Phung, Adams, & Venkatesh, 2012)

1.2.3 Prediction With Recommendation

One important function of a social network that is of particular importance to third-party providers of information and services is *recommendation*, the identification to users of information, services, and merchandise which they may be interested in. Recommender systems in social media are most often based on a model of intrinsic and tacit trust among users associated with the recipient of recommendations. Insofar as association is an indication of similarity of interests and preferences, this leads to a natural mechanism for collaborative filtering and ranking of recommendations. (O'Donovan & Smyth, 2005) This idea has subsequently been extended to systematic analyses of sparse user-item ratings matrices, weighted by similarity measures between users that are computed using these matrices, in order to make use of this normalization mechanism, a type of social regularization. (Ma, Zhou, Liu, Lyu, & King, 2011) This can also be used to recommend explicit association between users, especially a recommendation to follow another user's postings. (Ma, Yang, Wang, & Yuan, 2014)

In this article, we will introduce predictive methods based solely on this type of behavior within a social network and those that are based on, or augmented using, user profile information.

1.2.4 Risk Prediction and Identifying Risk Groups

Another important function of link prediction in social networks is the systematic identification of at-risk groups based on exposures that can be inferred from social contacts and known features. This often takes the form of contagious disease exposure, a topic that is heavily studied in the literature and which we will examine in this article; however, graph structure can reveal other information such as the support structure available to aged persons and their level of isolation. (Wenger, 1997)

This type of information can further be used to understand the intrinsic properties and identifying characteristics of risk groups. Furthermore, it can in some cases, such as in Wenger's study, provide some basic quantitative measures of risk levels and early-warning criteria for emergent problems, such as in elder care and community health.

1.2.5 Planning and Intervention

Once a mechanism exists for identifying groups that exhibit or admit elevated risk, it may be possible to use social network structure and content in order to plan for, and act during, emergencies. This includes disaster preparedness and intervention planning (National Research Council (S. L. Magsino, Rapporteur), 2009), as well as social mobilization for "time-critical feats, ranging from mapping crises in real time, to organizing mass rallies, to conducting search- and-rescue operations over large geographies".

(Rutherford, et al., 2013) The limiting factor here is proximity, which differentiates most interventional models for social crisis management from flash mobs, which in turn constrain the recruitment potential and response time.

Predictive analytics also provides a data-driven basis for optimization of coordination strategies, such as assignment and scheduling of rescue units in a natural disaster scenario such as a flood or landslide. (Wex, 2013) The prediction targets include early crisis warning metrics for such specific risks, extracted from social text and message propagation. The emerging field of computational disaster management includes time-critical aspects of preparation, response, rescue, relief, and repair or cleanup effort in the aftermath of a disaster. Optimization and intelligent systems tasks exist at all stages of this process. (Van Hentenryck, 2013)

1.3 Approaches: Prediction in Data Science

Because of the large scale of social networks, the largest of which currently number in the hundreds of millions to low billions of users, each with as many as several thousand relationships, the general problem area of prediction in social media falls under the rubric of "analytics using big data". Users of predictive analytics technology are often interested in decision support approaches that beyond the crisis intervention, risk management, and recommendation systems listed above. This presents new challenges to developers of analytics systems. (LaValle, Lesser, Shockley, Hopkins, & Kruschwitz, 2011)

In this article, we will delve into the data sciences and specific methodologies (Davenport & Patil, 2012) behind presently used and emerging systems for prediction in social media. The methodologies for big data tend to be more enterprise-wide than limited to analytics or information technology units of the client organization. (Davenport, Barth, & Bean, 2012) Additionally, scalable data integration from heterogeneous sources, such as are prevalent in big data, presents more data management issues than traditional analytics – particularly with respect to data definitions (metadata and ontologies). (Chen, Chiang, & Storey, 2012; Davenport, Barth, & Bean, 2012)

2. BACKGROUND

2.1 Predictive Analytics in Social Networks

The term *predictive analytics* generally refers to the development and federated display of models for the future state of a system based on observed data. As Wex (2013) notes, digital media outlets such as online news provide knowledge sources and a mechanism by which historical data (and text corpora) can help improve understanding on the emergence of crises:

With a main focus on online news and a ubiquitous information overload, crisis managers are constantly confronted to masses of publicly available, yet unstructured data sources. Online news cannot be clearly characterized as being "real-time" unlike e.g. ad-hoc messages, thus making it difficult to explain the latency between the occurrence of an event and its proclamation. Yet, news stories often possess meta-data such as geographical tagging, an accumulation of similar reports, keywords, or subjective author belief which calls for the application of superior analytical methods, i.e. text mining, to investigate hidden statistical relationships between the gradual emergence of a crisis and its medial proclamation.

However, expertise and knowledge of how to transform this data into machine-readable information and how to engage in prediction methods is frequently non-existent.

The challenges of predictive analytics applied to social media include data integration, cleaning, and visualization. (Thomas & Kielman, 2009) Thomas and Kielman identify the following ten needs of visual analytics technologies and systems:

1. **Whole-part relationships:** the ability to represent hierarchies in a scale-independent way
2. **Relationship discovery:** the capability to discover interrelationships among people, places, times, and other attributes and features, using techniques from information retrieval (indexing for phrase-based search), relational databases (query by example), and data mining (clustering and classification)
3. **Combined exploratory and confirmatory interaction**: a cognitive model for interactive hypothesis testing
4. **Multiple data types**: adaptive hypermedia and multimedia, task-adaptive views and representations, and a content repurposing capability
5. **Temporal views and interactions**: the ability to represent temporal dynamics of processes, including (causal) flows, timelines, and event and milestone visualizations
6. **Groupings and outlier identification:** labeling and annotation of clusters, and the application of clustering to outlier detection
7. **Multiple linked views**: materialized views supporting the application of data transformation actions committed on one view to data displayed using other views
8. **Labeling**: user-controllable, contextualized views for dynamic visualization and data modeling
9. **Reporting**: the ability to save and reproduce analytical operations and results for publication
10. **Interdisciplinary science**: accessibility by users and subject matter experts with different expertise and background

Predictive analytics applications that deal with social media are numerous, especially in business, and tend to focus around assistive technologies for customers as users, or decision support systems for customer relationship management and business intelligence. (Taylor, 2011)

2.1.1 Foundational Graph Theory and Link Analytics

Much of the methodology that supports link mining is based on analytical graph algorithms as the basis of predicting the existence or behavior of a link. (Washio & Motoda, 2003) The function of algorithms includes compilation of frequent pattern bases, in a manner similar to frequent itemset mining; *gSpan* (Yan & Han, 2002) is one of the earliest such algorithms and *CloseGraph* (Yan & Han, 2003) is its closed subgraph analogue. Some relational data mining systems use only such graph-based algorithms, while some also use logical constraints and properties as expressed using inductive logic programming. (Ketkar, Holder, & Cook, 2005) Ketkar *et al.* report results of experimental evaluation that illustrates tradeoffs: these results indicate that graph-based multirelational data mining algorithms perform better that logic-based ones on structurally complex networks, while the logic-based is best for semantically complex content, and the accuracy of relationship prediction is comparable for generic, semantically shallow, medium-sized networks.

Getoor (2003) introduced a catalog of link mining applications in the earliest survey of extant machine learning and data mining research applied to graph structure. Methodological advances since then have included both visual analytics and statistical analytics, and have focused on generalizing over both structure and content to recover network structure. (Shen, Ma, & Eliassi-Rad, 2006) Some of this early work on heterogeneous information network structure focuses semantic graphs with different entity types – hence the term "heterogeneous" – and the need to account for these semantics through some type of quantitative or formal ontology in estimating link strength.

Link analytics is an informal term that refers to the systematic analysis of graph topology and statistics in order to build a holistic predictive model. Algorithmic subtasks of link analytics include enumeration maximal cliques, a parallelizable task (Du, Wu, Xu, Wang, & Pei, 2006) and using large matrix factorization (Acar, Dunlavy, & Kolda, 2009). More recently Olsman, Roxendal, and Åkerblom (2013) have adapted network models of organizational theory to capture the behavior of organizational social networks.

2.1.2 Time Series Analysis: Forecasting, Modeling, and Understanding

Section 1 introduced the notions of forecasting, modeling, and understanding – terms from the literature of the time series analysis community, subareas such as signal identification, and related areas such as signal processing. We refer the interested reader to seminal references on the topic, especialy: Box, Jenkins, and Reinsel (2008), Chatfield (2004), and the introduction to time series modeling by Gershenfeld and Weigend (1994) in the anthology of time series analytics papers based on the Santa Fe Time Series Competition.

2.1.3 Statistical Modeling of Network Dynamics

Besides network topology, the task of predicting the behavior and output of a social network may involve network dynamics and thus fall under the purview of dynamical systems modeling. The mathematical foundations for this modeling include chaos theory (Gregersen & Sailer, 1993) and both statistical and graph-theoretic analysis of network topology as a determinant of dynamics (Borgatti, Mehra, Brass, & Labianca, 2009).

2.2 Using Network-Associated Content

Much of the early domain literature in content-based social network modeling and prediction originates from collaboration graphs and in particular citation graphs, where nodes represent papers and sometimes authors, and links represent citations. The *CiteSeer* system is one of the first of these (Giles, Bollacker, & Lawrence, 1998). The original system included an autonomous web agent that crawled and digested publication pages of academic authors in computer science (Bollacker, Lawrence, & Giles, 1998), extracting the local web of citations for all papers and linked preprints or reprints it identified. This autonomous citation indexing mechanism (Lawrence, Giles, & Bollacker, 1999) represents a broader class of document-based information federation (*aka* data integration or information integration) and information extraction systems based on web crawling and scraping. The resultant network modeling algorithms that emerged from this work support collaborative filtering of search results based on personality diagnosis of search engine users using memory-based and model-based inductive learning systems (Pennock, Horvitz, Lawrence, & Giles, 2000), and were later shown to be compatible with content-based filtering in data-sparse environments (Popescul, Ungar, Pennock, & Lawrence, 2001). Achieving high-recall link mining systems was shown to require more than simply maximizing scores in a system where publications competed for citations or other links (Pennock, Flake, Lawrence, Glover, & Giles, 2002).

More recently, the method of combining both content-based and collaborative filtering approaches has been applied to document categorization in scientific domains (Cao & Gao, 2005) and to online text in general (Angelova & Weikum, 2006). A profile of relevant work to date appears in a survey on web data mining research by Singh and Singh (2010).

2.2.1 User Profile Data

Web mining systems, going beyond simple link mining, often use user profile data (Cooley, Mobasher, & Srivastava, 1997). One application of this approach is towards user modeling, personalization, and adaptive synthesis of hypermedia (Mobasher, Cooley, & Srivastava, 2000); another is to use node-specific data (*i.e.,* single user data) in the link existence prediction task (Hsu, King, Paradesi, Pydimarri, & Weninger, 2006) and in understanding characteristic content-based features of their own accord, and in relation to subgraph patterns in social networks (Thelwall, 2008). This approach has been used to develop and refine data models for crawled social network data (Catanese, De Meo, Ferrara, Fiumara, & Provetti, 2011), to annotate user features with social relationships (Sun, Lin, Chen, & Liu, 2013), and to capture user self-description in microblogging sites such as *Twitter* (Semertzidis, Pitoura, & Tsaparas, 2013).

2.2.2 Temporal Event Data

Besides graph structure and content related to users or other individual nodes, we may consider identifiable events associated with originating nodes, which may propagate through the network structure. These events, which are often spatiotemporal in nature or can be associated with location and time, can in turn yield detected social network structure (Lauw, Lim, Pang, & Tan, 2011), and can be used to predict subsequent events and rank predictions (O'Madadhain, Hutchins, & Smyth, 2005). We refer the reader to Aggarwal (2011) for a general introduction to this type of data analytics.

2.2.3 Free Text Corpora

The idea of a semantic network dates back to work by Woods (1975), who considered the heterogeneity of nodes and links, and discussed ways in which link structure can be inferred from data and observations. Later researchers explored the use of free text corpora – *i.e.,* collections of documents for natural language text in unrestricted form – in this task (Mladenic, 1999). Blog and forum posts are often published online but are sometimes available only to registered users, limiting their general use as test beds. By the middle of the 2000s, a surge in formation of social network sites (SNSs) led to increased interest in e-mail corpora (Culotta, Bekkerman, & McCallum, 2004), especially author-recipient-topic models that could be built from public corpora such as the Enron e-mail corpus (McCallum, Corrada-Emmanuel, & Wang, 2005). The problem of discovering the roles of author and recipient in a behavioral rubric or schema then gained interest (McCallum, Wang, & Corrada-Emmanuel, 2007), both as a means of extracting social computing models from free text corpora but as a way to augment topic modeling (Chang, Boyd-Graber, & Blei, 2009). By 2010, the use of social media as a test bed for political sentiment analysis had become a popular topic of experimental and applied research (Tumasjan, Sprenger, Sandner, & Welpe, 2010).

Meanwhile, the named entities and relationships in free text corpora facilitated the development of document-topic hierarchies that used the organizational structure of the document collection itself. (Weninger, Bisk, & Han, 2012) This augmented the methodology of identifying and tracking actors to form a timeline of relationships using social networks and text (Danowski & Cepela, 2010) and the "news feed" approach of selecting items of relevance to a user (Berkovsky, Freyne, Kimani, & Smith, 2011).

The current state of the field in free text-augmented predictive analytics using social networks makes use of self-description (Semertzidis, Pitoura, & Tsaparas, 2013) and integrates sentiment, which may be dynamic, with detected topics (He, Lin, Gao, & Wong, 2013).

2.2.4 Decision History: Selections and Ratings

One key application of analytics using social data is helping users track their communications and history of relationships. Recently this has taken the form of a decision history, which users occasionally search through, but often review only for recent or significant events. The technique of personality diagnosis has been used to provide a topical filter for recommendation of such items (Pennock, Horvitz, Lawrence, & Giles, 2000). For more information, we refer the reader to a survey by Cacheda, Carneiro, Fernández, and Formoso (2011) on collaborative filtering systems.

2.2.5 Trust and Reputation

Trust and reputation systems can be based on ties indicated by social networks (Levin & Cross, 2004) and other forms of computer-mediated communication (CMC). A KDD 2006 panel (Piatetsky-Shapiro, et al., 2006) indicated that link mining applications such as trust networks represented one of the grand challenge problems in knowledge discovery in databases. More recent work has yielded approaches based on mutual influence within communities (Matsuo & Yamamoto, 2009). King, Li, and Chan (2009) survey these techniques in relation to data mining problems in social computing.

Some research on collaborative recommendation has looked at adversarial and remedial aspects (Mobasher, Burke, Bhaumik, & Sandvig, 2007). The evolution of trust networks is an important recent topic of interest to which supervised machine learning techniques have been applied (Zolfaghar & Aghaie, 2011).

2.3 Challenges

Link mining, especially social network mining, has frequently come up in the past decade as a major challenge in data mining research. (Yang & Wu, 2006) Challenging aspects of prediction in social networks include their large scale, the existence of partial data (especially due to having incomplete graphs at the time of application), hidden user information, heterogeneous structure and semantics, and multiple types and provenance of data such as free text that are associated with the network. (Gao, 2012)

2.3.1 Imbalanced Data

An additional challenge is that social networks can be sparse, which means that a candidate link may be unlikely to exist, and presenting imbalanced class labels in prediction data. Differences in link distribution have been observed in real-world applications (Al Hasan, Chaoji, Salem, & Zaki, 2006), including large-scale networks (Wakita & Tsurumi, 2007) and time series compiled by periodically crawling social network sites (Hsu, Weninger, & Paradesi, 2008). This property is particularly challenging in scale-free networks and in some multirelational, large-scale global networks (Szell, Lambiotte, & Thurner, 2010).

2.3.2 Partial Data

Partial data is also particularly challenging due to nuanced properties of social structure in some application domains such as prisons and other closed societies. (Zheng, Salganik, & Gelman, 2006) This is borne out in looking at the topology of huge SNSs (Ahn, Han, Kwak, Moon, & Jeong, 2007) and those that emerge episodically based on both online and in-person friend recommendations (Caragea, Bahirwani, Aljandal, & Hsu, 2009).

Links can also propagate gradually in a social network that publishes upvotes and likes. Modeling this in phenomenon in a fast and scalable way can be highly challenging. (Kashima, Kato, Yamanishi, Sugiyama, & Tsuda, 2009; Raymond & Kashima, 2010)

2.3.3 Social Concept Drift

In addition to partial observability, social networks are subject to other changes, such as gradual or sudden episodic changes in organizational structure. This can be thought of as a graph-based variation of concept drift. The problem of community detection is made more challenging by this temporal aspect. (Zhou, Councill, Zha, & Giles, 2007); recent work on time-aware link prediction has focused on this problem (Tylenda, Angelova, & Bedathur, 2009). The general problem of learning under concept drift is surveyed by Žliobaitė (2009).

2.3.4 Active Learning

Link prediction may be seen as a passive or active machine learning and classification task. The active variant may involve querying a source of information such as eliciting user annotation; this is appropriate for some tasks, such as deduplication, that are already intrinsically interactive. (Sarawagi & Bhamidipaty, 2002) Active learning can help to focus and speed up search over candidate network structures when the hypothesis space is very complex (Newman, 2003) and especially when a statistical risk minimization criterion is available (Macskassy, 2009). Recent applications of active learning to networked data include some clustering algorithms in both unsupervised and semi-supervised learning scenarios (Bilgic, Mihalkova, & Getoor, 2010).

Active learning in structured domains is an active research topic (Dietterich, Domingos, Getoor, Muggleton, & Tadepalli, 2008). One application of particular interest is interactivity in community formation, where users can provide individual feedback on the fly. (Amershi, Fogarty, & Weld, 2012)

2.3.5 Online Learning and Incrementality

Online learning is that which occurs during the application of the performance element of learning, such as recommendation or classification. The requirement that this be achieved without significant retraining is called *incremental learning*. Apart from potentially having an interactive setting, online learning can make use of conversations in progress (Glance, et al., 2005), search (Davitz, Yu, Basu, Gutelius, & Harris, 2007), semantic social media such as status updates and tweets (Barbieri, et al., 2010), and events between which some measure of similarity exists (Becker, Naaman, & Gravano, 2010).

2.3.6 Transfer Learning

Transfer learning allows learned models, produced using training data from one domain, to be applied to another domain that is either sufficiently similar or admits some analogical transformation or derivation. Pan and Yang (2010) provide a general survey of the task. In social networks, collective link prediction can be a very data-intensive problem, and so the application of multiple heterogeneous domains is one way to bootstrap the data mining task, when feasible. (Cao, Liu, & Yang, 2010) Some text-based approaches to transfer learning look at inferring implicit opinion from linguistic biases (Guerra, Veloso, Meira Jr., & Almeida, 2011). Finally, some social network mining systems attempt to infer social ties across heterogeneous networks. (Tang, Lou, & Kleinberg, 2012)

3. TECHNIQUES

3.1 Topological Analysis

As outlined in Section 1.2.1 and 2.1.1, the most basic and general link prediction algorithms are based purely on graph structure. (Huang, 2006) This has given rise to models of hierarchical structure (Clauset, Moore, & Newman, 2008), collective classification (Sen, et al., 2008), clique structure in social networks (Caragea, Bahirwani, Aljandal, & Hsu, 2009), and parameter estimation tasks that depend on the underlying graph structure, such as: learning influence probabilities between nodes (Goyal, Bonchi, & Lakshmanan, 2010); predicting positive and negative links (Leskovec, Huttenlocher, & Kleinberg, 2010); using supervised random walks over the network to predict and recommend links (Backstrom & Leskovec, 2011); performing feature construction using low-level topological features to predict links (Fire, et al., 2011); and performing structural role extraction and mining in large graphs (Henderson, et al., 2012).

3.2 Network Dynamics

Beyond topological structure lie statistics on the dynamics of networks: frequencies of link formation, deletion, and transformation, plus information propagation events. The latent structure of a social network can be learned in part using data about this dynamic behavior. (Myers & Leskovec, 2010) Some models are based on analysis of the network formation process according to a predictive process, such a power law process. (Clauset, Shalizi, & Newman, 2009)

3.3 Information Propagation in Heterogeneous Information Network

A central approach to social network mining is to examine the way that information propagates through events. In SNSs, these include sharing events such as posts, comments, shares (and retweets), likes (upvotes), and dislikes (downvotes).

Some organizational social networks, especially multiunit organizations, admit a hybrid cooperation and competition model of knowledge sharing. (Tsai, 2002) Some knowledge propagates purely by the sharing of links (Han, 2009). In networks where link evolution leads to a fixed structure such as a star schema, ranking information can be captured using graph clustering algorithms (Sun, Yu, & Han, 2009) More generally, heterogeneous information networks can be used to perform collective classification by graph-based transduction. (Ji, Sun, Danilevsky, Han, & Gao, 2010)

This general approach of tracking information propagation can be implemented using simple author-recipient tagging, even on public social media such as Twitter (Wu, Hofman, Mason, & Watts, 2011). The result of this type of addressing, as well as that of social tagging, can be applied to detect communities (Murata, 2011). By a similar token, observed sharing events can be used to infer topological features (Ohara, Saito, Kimura, & Motoda, 2011) and predict catastrophic propagation events in the case of an epidemiological spread model for a contact network (Boman, 2011). When teams in an organizational network are large and decentralized, heterogeneous information network analysis provides a means of performing efficient sharing and resolution of conflicting opinions (Pryymak, Rogers, & Jennings, 2011), biased propagation (Deng, Han, Zhao, Yu, & Lin, 2011) and ranking-based collective classification (Ji, Han, & Danilevsky, 2011), and top-k similarity search (Sun, Han, Yan, Yu, & Wu, 2011).

Network-wide dynamic properties can be estimated from similar observation data (Sycara, 2012), as can clustering of nodes based on relation strength (Sun, Aggarwal, & Han, 2012), and time-localized prediction of relationship links (Sun, Han, Aggarwal, & Chawla, 2012). This approach to clustering also supports path selection, *i.e.*, selection of entity type sequences in a directed graph, with user guidance (Gupta, Gao, Sun, & Han, 2012), giving rise to a general mechanism for using structural analysis to mine heterogeneous information networks (Sun & Han, 2012).

Specific applications of topological and statistical analysis of heterogeneous graphs include identification of important individuals (Schulte, Riahi, & Li, 2013), weighted collaborative filtering based on entity similarity (Yu, Ren, Gu, Sun, & Han, 2013), development of topic modeling similarity measures for collaborative classification and filtering (Hsu, Koduru, & Zhai, 2013), and identifying individuals in a cybercriminal network by probable role (Lau, 2013). The applicable clustering mechanisms include large matrix factorization (Liu & Han, 2013) and statistical relational learning (Schulte & Qian, 2013).

In addition, pairwise co-occurrence relationships such as label and instance correlations can add additional information for collective classification (Wang & Sukthankar, 2013), as can meta-path selection, *e.g.*, sequences such as **Author$_1$-Paper$_1$-Conference-Paper$_2$-Author$_2$**, when combined with the abovementioned user guidance (Sun, et al., 2013).

3.4 Predicting Events: Stochastic Processes and Other Time Series Models

Berendt *et al.* (2003) give a roadmap to web mining methods that were extant or under development at the time when the Semantic Web was first emerging. Since then, developments have been published that focus specifically on prediction of events. These include prediction and ranking algorithms (O'Madadhain, Hutchins, & Smyth, 2005), learning similarity metrics (Becker, Naaman, & Gravano, 2010), monitoring sharing events and user tags (Mathioudakis & Koudas, 2010), relating social media events to physical-world behavior (Abbasi, Chai, Liu, & Sagoo, 2012), analyzing responses to microblog posts (Artzi, Pantel, & Gamon, 2012), and performing aggregate sentiment analysis of Twitter (Hu, Wang, & Kambhampati, 2013).

3.5 Topic Modeling and Text Analytics

Text analytics adds a further dimension of complexity and richness to prediction in social networks. The literature is sparser on topic modeling as related to prediction in social networks than text mining *from* social network posts. A general survey is provided by Hu and Liu (2012), the first author of whom has published recent work on topic modeling to align events with Twitter feedback (Hu, John, Wang, & Kambhampati, 2012) and perform aggregate sentiment analysis over tweets from multiple users (Hu, Wang, & Kambhampati, 2013).

4. APPLICATIONS

This section surveys selected popular applications of predictive analytics in social network domains. These are: predicting which users will follow whom; making entity-to-entity recommendations (product-to-user, business-to-business, *etc.*); managing risk; analyzing big data in a scientific or engineering setting; and performing information management.

4.1 Follow Prediction

The problem of predicting and recommending followers can be addressed using scoring functions and latent factor analysis (Zhao, 2012), and may further involve the semantics of links and nodes by capturing which users are paying attention to what information from others (Rowe, Stankovic, & Alani, 2012). Factor models over social graphs may be asymmetric. (Ma, Yang, Wang, & Yuan, 2014)

4.2 Recommender Systems

Entity-to-entity recommendation in social media is based on a tacit model of trust between associated users, representing the idea that if another user or company is directly connected to the user or the user's company, then its recommendations should carry some positive weight. In social networks where trust and reputation (which puts a nonlocal bias on trust) is not only fluid but can affect whether links persist or are removed, the dynamics of trust in the network itself are important. Aula (2010) examines mechanisms of reputation risk and publicity management for users making recommendations. In trust networks, quantitative indicators of trust can be transmitted, by word of mouth or the equivalent in CMC. Studies of trust propagation have shown that it can be modeled predictively from observations just as recommendations themselves are: using large matrix factorization. (Jamali & Ester, 2010)

As discussed in Section 1.2.3, social networks can provide a regularization mechanism for recommendations that reweights them based on connectivity. (Ma, Zhou, Liu, Lyu, & King, 2011) A similar mechanism can be used to generate news article or topic recommendations based on retweets (Abel, Gao, Houben, & Tao, 2013) or other reshares. Analogous mechanisms extend this property to the general domain of social recommendation. (Sun, Lin, Chen, & Liu, 2013)

4.2.1 Collaborative Filtering and Collaborative Recommendation

Konstas, Stathopoulos, and Jose (2009) review the state of the field in collaborative recommendation using social networks. Some of the more recent work focuses on temporal dynamics as mentioned in Sections 2.2.2 and 3.2 (Koren, 2009); other approaches incorporate content-based personalization (Berkovsky, Freyne, & Smith, 2012) and attentional factors (Rowe, Stankovic, & Alani, 2012).

4.2.2 Coping With and Using Time

Fluctuations and the frequency and amplitude of concept drift are critical factors in predictive systems. In some intelligent systems, such as recommender systems, variation is deliberately induced to keep material fresh; some recommender systems are specifically designed to avoid redundant or stale (over-similar) recommendations within a set period of time. (Lathia, Hailes, Capra, & Amatriain, 2010) Many such systems (Koenigstein, Dror, & Koren, 2011) use an explicit "avoid this item for a while" or "avoid this category for a while" control; others (Baltrunas & Amatriain, 2009) use implicit feedback and perform time-dependent recommendation. Time-awareness is also important in link prediction. (Tylenda, Angelova, & Bedathur, 2009)

4.2.3 Using Location in Spatiotemporal Prediction

Some SNSs use geolocation as a feature for predicting user behavior such as visiting physical locales or frequenting local establishments. (Scellato, Noulas, & Mascolo, 2011; Brown, Nicosia, Scellato, Noulas, & Mascolo, 2012) Other social network-based user modeling systems maintain actual proximity networks to predict interactions between users. (Do & Gatica-Perez, 2013)

4.3 Risk Management and Assistive Technologies

Risk management is a key application of social networks, and includes concrete applications ranging from large scale disaster management (Wex, 2013; Van Hentenryck, 2013) to predicting runaways and isolated seniors at greater risk in case of medical emergencies.

4.3.1 Identifying At-Risk Groups in Epidemology and Health Care

Social networks for epidemiology date back to long before the current generation of contact network models. Berkman and Syme (1978) conducted a nine-year study of host resistance and mortality among Alameda County residents. Since then, graphical models of disease spread, including causal interventional models, have been used to predict the propagation of foot-and-mouth disease (Ferguson, Donnelly, & Anderson, 2001), tuberculosis (Getoor, Rhee, Koller, & Small, 2004), SARS (Meyers, Pourbohloul, Newman, Skowronski, & Brunham, 2005), and more generally individuals at higher risk of infection of communicable diseases, especially airborne diseases, due to social interactions (Christley, et al., 2005).

Risk management modeling using social networks is not limited to epidemiology; interaction networks have been used in applications such as antiterrorism and intelligence analytics (McCue, 2005), or combating obesity (Arteaga, Kudeki, & Woodworth, 2009). Also, not all epidemiological models built using social media are based on contact networks; some are based on geotagged mentions (*e.g.*, of influenza) in social media (Corley, Cook, Mikler, & Singh, 2009) and hybrid mining of free text and network structure for the same (Corley, Cook, Mikler, & Singh, 2010). Some epidemiological models admit mitigation strategies (Hsu, Roy Chowdhury, & Scoglio, 2011), while others are purely predictive and provide decision support or visual analytics capabilities.

The state of the field in predictive analytics for consumer health focuses on usability and accessibility of social media (Goldberg, et al., 2011), the mining of electronic health records (Silow-Carroll, Edwards, & Rodin, 2012), accounting for seasonal trends in abnormal event detection (Chae, et al., 2012), and spatiotemporal anomaly detection (Thom, Bosch, Koch, Worner, & Ertl, 2012).

4.3.2 Fraud Detection, Anomaly Detection, and Prediction of Risks

Anomaly detection is another major risk management area where social networks and prediction can often be of use. High-visibility applications include fraud detection, especially in internet banking (Aggelis, 2006), econometrics and market analytics (May, Levin, & Sugihara, 2008), supply chain integration (Cruz, Nagurney, & Wakolbinger, 2006), predictive analytics for marketing (Hair Jr,, 2007), decision management (Taylor, 2011), and automated power systems or "smart grid" systems (Li, Fang, Mahatma, & Hampapur, 2011).

4.4 Big Data Analytics

The term *big data analytics* currently refers to terascale to petascale computation applied to generate novel, valid, useful (actionable), and human-comprehensible models from data. As of 2014, "big data" usually connotes datasets that are multiple terabytes to petabytes in size or of a commensurately high complexity in terms of the complexity of analysis. Many issues facing analysts who work with big data, such as distributed backup, high bandwidth consumption for data federation and warehousing, and reliability (Russom, 2011) are beyond the scope of this article. Russom refers to the size as *volume* and bandwidth as *velocity* in reference to the "three Vs: volume, velocity, and variety". The issues of variety (semantic heterogeneity, especially a mixture of unstructured and structured data), on the other hand, have been highly relevant to this article, and figure prominently in the list of new challenges presented by terascale to petascale data sets, new metadata standards, and heterogeneous data sources. (Davenport, Barth, & Bean, 2012)

4.4.1 Business Intelligence (BI) and Decision Support

Business intelligence (BI), the application of data sciences to decision making, planning, and automation in domains such as management, marketing, and e-commerce, is another critical and very commonly-encountered application of predictive analytics, especially in organizational management (Horn, 2005). Recent work on monetizing BI has focused on using visual analytics and web analytics in an enterprise-wide context (Chen, Chiang, & Storey, 2012), on leveraging the results of data mining, and on decision support (Zaraté, 2012).

4.4.2 Customer Relationship Management (CRM)

Customer relationship management (CRM) refers to the use of technology to manage and support a company's interaction with its current and potential customers. It is facilitated directly by means of customer analytics (Stodder, 2012). In particular, recruitment, retention, and recommendation are supported by social media analytics, especially predictive analytics applied to customer feedback (Kannan & Vijayaraghavan, 2013) and collective sentiment analysis (Hu, Wang, & Kambhampati, 2013).

4.4.3 Scientific Applications

While social networks are used in sociological and anthropological domains to model human behavior – a very narrow and mostly commercial aspect of which is discussed in this article – there are numerous applications of quasi-social networks to scientific domains. These include general analysis of covariance over events using autocorrelation matrices (Krackhardt, 1988), text mining of scientific literature (Bollacker, Lawrence, & Giles, 2000), and annotation of learning conversations using argumentation theory, discourse analytics based on text and social graphs (De Liddo, Shum, Quinto, Bachler, & Cannavacciuolo, 2011).

4.5 Computational Information and Knowledge Management (CIKM)

Computational information and knowledge management (CIKM) refers to data sciences applied to the development, collection, maintenance, annotation, and distribution of information resources such as document collections, data sets, audiovisual recordings, multimedia, and their associated metadata. One way in which CIKM is augmented by the use of predictive analytics is through user analytics for personalized and user-centered resource management, such as in the domains of education (Zhang, et al., 2010), public health and security informatics (Boulos, Sanfilippo, Corley, & Wheeler, 2010), information systems research (Shmueli & Koppius, 2011), and to categorize and present human resource (HR) data such as performance assessment data (Kendrena, Donchetz, & Istre, 2012).

5. SYSTEMS

Fielded systems for social network-augmented decision support technology, including recommender systems and analytics systems for policymakers, are beginning to make increasing use of prediction techniques. This section surveys current and future research, fielded applications, and systems engineering competitions for three main purposes: for discovery informatics, for item-to-person and B2C (business-to-consumer *aka* targeted marketing) recommendation, and for citation and follow prediction, which is also a form of person-to-person (P2P) recommendation.

5.1 Interaction Discovery

Interaction discovery is a form of *discovery informatics* – that is, analyzing observed data to discover patterns and relationships that are interesting according to some specifiable criterion. It is frequently equated with discovery of interpersonal relationships in social networks, but is not limited to domains of human interaction.

For example, protein-protein interaction (PPI) is an important modeling problem in bioinformatics, specifically, proteomics (Rual, et al., 2005). PPI networks are quasi-social in the sense of Section 4.4.3, and as such have been represented using graphical models of probability such as Bayesian networks (Jansen, et al., 2003). More generally, some subfields of systems biology are centered around interacting members of some family of large molecules or molecular sequences (nucleotide sequences in the case of genomics, proteins in the case of proteomics, cellular lipids in the case of lipidomics, metabolic products and enzymes in the case of metabolomics); sets of mutually interacting molecules across one of these categories, and especially across multiple categories, are referred to as *interactomes* and present a general quasi-social network modeling and prediction problem. (Soler-López, Zanzoni, Lluís, Stelzl, & Aloy, 2011) Domains to which this type of predictive analytics is applicable include drug discovery. (Pujol, Mosca, Farrés, & Aloy, 2010)

Outside of systems biology but within the realm of computational sociology, classification of human interactions based on smartphone proximity data (Do & Gatica-Perez, 2011), localized prediction of human mobile phone-based interactions (Do & Gatica-Perez, 2013), and classifying social relationships by applicable life-facet based on smartphone data (Min, Wiese, Hong, & Zimmerman, 2013) also constitute interaction discovery applications.

5.2 Entity-to-Entity Recommendation

Entity-to-entity recommendation generally falls under the rubric of item-to-person, or business-to-consumer (B2C), or person-to-person (P2P). Most recommender systems that are reported as being for e-commerce (Driskill & Riedl, 1999) fall under the rubric of item-to-person or B2C. As such, they are subject to criteria such as trust and reputation that are commonly ascribed to vendor brands or the companies they represent, or less frequently to marketing agencies. Wang and Vassileva (2007) survey trust and reputation systems such as *Epinions*, *eBay*, *Amazon*, and *Google* for XML-based web services in a service-oriented architecture (SOA).

P2P recommendations include social network follow recommendation and friendship and dating sites (Pizzato, et al., 2013). In the next section, we focus on follow prediction and recommendation (a frequent side effect) as a special case of P2P prediction.

5.3 KDD Cup Competitions

5.3.1 KDD Cup 2003: Citation Prediction in arXiv

Section 2.2 introduces the concept of link mining using citation graphs and indexing data, an approach first popularized by systems such as *CiteSeer* (Giles, Bollacker, & Lawrence, 1998). Since the debut of the "web of citation" and the advent of methods for constructing and analyzing it, data mining competitions have been created to encourage the advancement of these methods and evaluate their effectiveness. One of the most prominent of these was the *KDD Cup 2003* competition (Gehrke, Ginsparg, & Kleinberg, 2003), which challenged competitors to predict citations between articles in the reprint repository *arXiv*.

One of the top-ranked systems (Manjunatha, Sivaramakrishnan, Pandey, & Murthy, 2003) processed the timestamped citation data to form a time series and used *k*-nearest neighbor regression-based classification to predict the existence of a candidate citation in a paper. The authors reported comparable results using *k*-nearest neighbor (an instance-based learning method) and support vector machines. A decade later, meta-path selection methods such as the type described by Sun *et al.* (2013), and for which an example is given in Section 3.3, were shown to outperform classification-based approaches. (Yu, Gu, Zhou, & Han, 2012)

5.3.2 KDD Cup 2012: Follow Prediction in Tencent Weibo

One of the more recent P2P prediction tasks is *follow prediction*, the problem of identifying, for a celebrity or other user of interest in a social network, whether a candidate follower will in fact follow them. This is related to the problem of developing a recommender system for suggesting people to follow, but such a system is just one possible application; these tasks are not identical. The acceptance rate of suggestions is typically low (less than 10%). (Wu, Sorathia, & Prasanna, 2012)

The top-performing system (Chen, et al., 2012) in Track 1 of the *KDD Cup 2012* competition, which was organized around the Chinese microblogging service *Tencent Weibo*, used a hybrid approach combining matrix factorization with an additive forest. In related work, the authors relate a technique for applying a multifaceted version of the factorization model part to a general recommender system task (Chen, et al., 2012).

Another system that achieves good performance on this task (Wu, Sorathia, & Prasanna, 2012) uses a five-term scoring function for ranking:

1. Recommended item category.
2. Recommended item popularity.
3. Followee acceptance (how many people one follows who in turn follow the recommended item or person).
4. Semantic keyword matching score.
5. A normalized additive bonus for information sharing events.

REFERENCES

Abbasi, M.-A., Chai, S.-K., Liu, H., & Sagoo, K. (2012). Real-World Behavior Analysis through a Social Media Lens. In S. J. Yang, A. M. Greenberg, & M. Endsley (Ed.), *Proceedings of the 5th International Conference on Social Computing, Behavioral-Cultural Modeling and Prediction (SBP 2012) - College Park, MD, USA, April 3-5, 2012. Lecture Notes in Computer Science (LNCS) 7227*, pp. 18-26. New York, NY, USA: Springer. doi:10.1007/978-3-642-29047-3_3

Abel, F., Gao, Q., Houben, G.-J., & Tao, K. (2013). Twitter-Based User Modeling for News Recommendations. In F. Rossi (Ed.), *Proceedings of the 23rd International Joint Conference on Artificial Intelligence (IJCAI 2013) - Beijing, China, August 3-9, 2013*. Menlo Park, CA, USA: AAAI Press / International Joint Conferences on Artificial Intelligence.

Abrams, J. H. (2003). *Patent No. US 7069308*. USA. Retrieved March 9, 2014, from http://www.google.com/patents/US7069308

Acar, E., Dunlavy, D. M., & Kolda, T. G. (2009). Link Prediction on Evolving Data Using Matrix and Tensor Factorizations. In Y. Saygin, J. X. Yu, H. Kargupta, W. Wang, S. Ranka, P. S. Yu, & X. Wu (Ed.), *Workshops Proceedings of the 9th IEEE International Conference on Data Mining (ICDM 2009)* (pp. 262-269). Los Alamitos, CA, USA: IEEE Computer Society.

Aggarwal, C. C. (2011). An Introduction to Social Network Data Analytics. In C. C. Aggarwal (Ed.), *Social Network Data Analytics* (pp. 1–15). New York, NY, USA: Springer. doi:10.1007/978-1-4419-8462-3_1

Aggelis, V. (2006). Offline Internet banking fraud detection. *Proceedings of the 1st International Conference on Availability, Reliability and Security (ARES 2006): The International Dependability Conference, Bridging Theory and Practice - Vienna, Austria, April 20-22, 2006* (pp. 904-905). Los Alamitos, CA, USA: IEEE Computer Society. Retrieved from doi:10.1109/ARES.2006.89

Ahn, Y.-Y., Han, S., Kwak, H., Moon, S. B., & Jeong, H. (2007). Analysis of topological characteristics of huge online social networking services. In C. L. Williamson, M. E. Zurko, P. F. Patel-Schneider, & P. J. Shenoy (Ed.), *Proceedings of the 16th International World Wide Web Conference (WWW 2007) - Banff, AB, Canada, May 8-12, 2007* (pp. 835-844). New York, NY, USA: ACM Press. doi:10.1145/1242572.1242685

Al Hasan, M., Ahmed, N., & Neville, J. (2013). Network Sampling: Methods and Applications - KDD 2013 Tutorial. In I. S. Dhillon, Y. Koren, R. Ghani, T. E. Senator, P. Bradley, R. Parekh, . . . R. Uthurusamy (Ed.), *Proceedings of the 19th ACM SIGKDD International Conference on Knowledge Discovery and Data Mining (KDD 2013) - Chicago, IL, USA, August 11-14, 2013* (p. 1528). New York, NY, USA: ACM Press. doi:10.1145/2487575.2506180

Al Hasan, M., Chaoji, V., Salem, S., & Zaki, M. J. (2006). Link Prediction using Supervised Learning. In C. C. Aggarwal (Ed.), *Social Network Data Analytics* (pp. 243–275). New York, NY, USA: Springer.

Al Hasan, M., & Zaki, M. J. (2011). A Survey of Link Prediction in Social Networks. In C. C. Aggarwal (Ed.), *Social Network Data Analytics* (pp. 243–275). New York, NY, USA: Springer. doi:10.1007/978-1-4419-8462-3_9

Amershi, S., Fogarty, J., & Weld, D. S. (2012). Regroup: interactive machine learning for on-demand group creation in social networks. In J. A. Konstan, E. H. Chi, & K. Höök (Ed.), *Proceedings of the 2012 ACM SIGCHI Conference on Human Factors in Computing Systems (CHI 2012) - Austin, TX, USA, May 5-10, 2012* (pp. 21-30). New York, NY, USA: ACM Press. doi:10.1145/2207676.2207680

Angelova, R., & Weikum, G. (2006). Graph-based text classification: learn from your neighbors. *Proceedings of the 29th Annual International ACM SIGIR Conference on Research and Development in Information Retrieval (SIGIR 2006) - Seattle, Washington, USA, August 6-11, 2006* (pp. 485-492). New York, NY, USA: ACM Press.

Arteaga, S. M., Kudeki, M., & Woodworth, A. (2009). Combating obesity trends in teenagers through persuasive mobile technology. *ACM SIGACCESS Accessibility and Computing* (94), 17-25. doi:10.1145/1595061.1595064

Artzi, Y., Pantel, P., & Gamon, M. (2012). Predicting Responses to Microblog Posts. In E. Fosler-Lussier, E. Riloff, & S. Bangalore (Ed.), *Proceedings of the 2012 Human Language Technologies Conference of the North American Chapter of the Association of Computational Linguistics (HLT-NAACL 2012) - Montréal, Canada, June 3-8, 2012* (pp. 602-606). Pittsburgh, PA, USA: NAACL.

Aula, P. (2010). Social media, reputation risk and ambient publicity management. *Strategy and Leadership*, *38*(6), 43–49. doi:10.1108/10878571011088069

Backstrom, L., Huttenlocher, D. P., Kleinberg, J. M., & Lan, X. (2006). Group formation in large social networks: membership, growth, and evolution. In T. Eliassi-Rad, L. H. Ungar, M. Craven, & D. Gunopulos (Ed.), *Proceedings of the 12th ACM SIGKDD International Conference on Knowledge Discovery and Data Mining (KDD 2006)* (pp. 44-54). New York, NY, USA: ACM Press.

Backstrom, L., & Leskovec, J. (2011). Supervised random walks: predicting and recommending links in social networks. In I. King, W. Nejdl, & H. Li (Ed.), *Proceedings of the 4th International Conference on Web Search and Web Data Mining (WSDM 2011)* (pp. 635-644). New York, NY, USA: ACM Press. doi:10.1145/1935826.1935914

Baltrunas, L., & Amatriain, X. (2009). Towards Time-Dependant Recommendation based on Implicit Feedback. In G. Adomavicius, & F. Ricci (Ed.), *Proceedings of the Workshop on Context-Aware Recommender Systems (CARS 2009), 3rd ACM Conference on Recommender Systems (RecSys 2009) - New York, NY, USA, October 23-25, 2009.* New York, NY, USA: ACM Press. Retrieved from http://ids.csom.umn.edu/faculty/gedas/cars2009/

Barabási, A. L., Jeong, H., Néda, Z., Ravasz, E., Schubert, A., & Vicsek, T. (2002). Evolution of the social network of scientific collaborations. *Physica A: Statistical Mechanics and its Applications, 31*(3-4), 590-6114.

Barbieri, D., Braga, D., Ceri, S., Valle, E. D., Huang, Y., & Tresp, V. et al. (2010). Deductive and Inductive Stream Reasoning for Semantic Social Media Analytics. *IEEE Intelligent Systems, 25*(6), 32–41. doi:10.1109/MIS.2010.142

Becker, H., Naaman, M., & Gravano, L. (2010). Learning similarity metrics for event identification in social media. In B. D. Davison, T. Suel, N. Craswell, & B. Liu (Ed.), *Proceedings of the 3rd International Conference on Web Search and Web Data Mining (WSDM 2010) - New York, NY, USA, February 4-6, 2010* (pp. 291-300). New York, NY, USA: ACM Press. doi:10.1145/1718487.1718524

Berendt, B., Hotho, A., Mladenič, D., Someren, M. v., Spiliopoulou, M., & Stumme, G. (2003). A Roadmap for Web Mining: From Web to Semantic Web. In B. Berendt, A. Hotho, D. Mladenič, M. v. Someren, M. Spiliopoulou, & G. Stumme (Ed.), *Proceedings of the 1st European Web Mining Forum (EWMF 2003) - Cavtat-Dubrovnik, Croatia, September 22, 2003. Lecture Notes in Computer Science (LNCS) 3209*, pp. 1-22. New York, NY, USA: Springer.

Berkman, L. F., & Syme, S. L. (1978). Social networks, host resistance, and mortality: a nine-year follow-up study of. *American Journal of Epidemiology, 109*(2), 186–204. PMID:425958

Berkovsky, S., Freyne, J., Kimani, S., & Smith, G. (2011). Selecting Items of Relevance in Social Network Feeds. In J. A. Konstan, R. Conejo, J.-L. Marzo, & N. Oliver (Ed.), *Proceedings of the 19th International Conference on User Modeling, Adaption, and Personalization (UMAP 2011) - Girona, Spain, July 11-15, 2011. Lecture Notes in Computer Science (LNCS) 6787*, pp. 329-334. New York, NY, USA: Springer.

Berkovsky, S., Freyne, J., & Smith, G. (2012). Personalized Network Updates: Increasing Social Interactions and Contributions in Social Networks. In J. Masthoff, B. Mobasher, M. C. Desmarais, & R. Nkambou (Ed.), *Proceedings of the 20th International Conference on User Modeling, Adaption, and Personalization (UMAP 2012) - Montreal, Canada, July 16-20, 2012. Lecture Notes in Computer Science (LNCS) 7379*, pp. 1-13. New York, NY, USA: Springer. doi:10.1007/978-3-642-31454-4_1

Bilgic, M., Mihalkova, L., & Getoor, L. (2010). Active Learning for Networked Data. In J. Fürnkranz, & T. Joachims (Ed.), *Proceedings of the 27th International Conference on Machine Learning (ICML 2010) - Haifa, Israel, June 21-24, 2010* (pp. 79-86). Madison, WI, USA: Omnipress.

Bollacker, K. D., Lawrence, S., & Giles, C. L. (1998). CiteSeer: An Autonous Web Agent for Automatic Retrieval and Identification of Interesting Publications. In K. P. Sycara, & M. Wooldridge (Ed.), *Proceedings of the 2nd International Conference on Autonomous Agents (Agents 1998)* (pp. 116-123). New York, NY, USA: ACM Press.

Bollacker, K. D., Lawrence, S., & Giles, C. L. (2000). Discovering relevant scientific literature on the Web. *IEEE Intelligent Systems and Their Applications, 15*(2), 42–47. doi:10.1109/5254.850826

Boman, M. (2011). On Understanding Catastrophe: The case of highly severe influenza-like illness (Position Paper). In W. H. Hsu, S. Kallumadi, & J. Han (Ed.), *Working notes of Workshop W-16, 22nd International Joint Conference on Artificial Intelligence (IJCAI 2011): Heterogeneous Information Network Analysis (HINA 2011) - Barcelona, Spain, July 16, 2011*. Retrieved March 9, 2014, from http://www.kddresearch.org/KDD/Workshops/IJCAI-2011-HINA/Papers/

Borgatti, S. P., Mehra, A., Brass, D. J., & Labianca, G. (2009). Network Analysis in the Social Sciences. *Science, 323*(5916), 892–895. doi:10.1126/science.1165821 PMID:19213908

Boulos, M. N., Sanfilippo, A. P., Corley, C. D., & Wheeler, S. (2010). Social Web mining and exploitation for serious applications: Technosocial Predictive Analytics and related technologies for public health, environmental and national security surveillance. *Computer Methods and Programs in Biomedicine, 100*(1), 16–23. doi:10.1016/j.cmpb.2010.02.007 PMID:20236725

Box, G. E., Jenkins, G. M., & Reinsel, G. C. (2008). *Time Series Analysis: Forecasting and Control* (4th ed.). Hoboken, NJ, USA: John Wiley & Sons. doi:10.1002/9781118619193

boyd, d. m., & Ellison, N. B. (2007). Social Network Sites: Definition, History, and Scholarship. *Journal of Computer-Mediated Communication, 13*(1), 210-230. doi:10.1111/j.1083-6101.2007.00393.x

Brown, C., Nicosia, V., Scellato, S., Noulas, A., & Mascolo, C. (2012). Where Online Friends Meet: Social Communities in Location-Based Networks. In J. G. Breslin, N. B. Ellison, J. G. Shanahan, & Z. Tufekci (Ed.), *Proceedings of the 6th International Conference on Weblogs and Social Media (ICWSM 2012)*. Menlo Park, CA, USA: AAAI Press.

Cacheda, F., Carneiro, V., Fernández, D., & Formoso, V. (2011). Comparison of collaborative filtering algorithms: Limitations of current techniques and proposals for scalable, high-performance recommender systems. *ACM Transactions on the Web (TWEB), 5*(1), 2:1-2:33. doi:10.1145/1921591.1921593

Cao, B., Liu, N. N., & Yang, Q. (2010). Transfer Learning for Collective Link Prediction in Multiple Heterogenous Domains. In J. Fürnkranz, & T. Joachims (Ed.), *Proceedings of the 27th International Conference on Machine Learning (ICML 2010) - Haifa, Israel, June 21-24, 2010* (pp. 159-166). Madison, WI, USA: Omnipress.

Cao, M. D., & Gao, X. (2005). Combining Contents and Citations for Scientific Document Classification. In S. Zhang, & R. Jarvis (Ed.), *Advances in Artificial Intelligence: Proceedings of the 18th Australian Joint Conference on Artificial Intelligence (AI 2005), Sydney, Australia, December 5-9, 2005. Lecture Notes in Computer Science (LNCS) 3809*, pp. 143-152. New York, NY, USA: Springer.

Caragea, D., Bahirwani, V., Aljandal, W., & Hsu, W. H. (2009). Ontology-based link prediction in the LiveJournal social network. In V. Bulitko, & J. C. Beck (Ed.), *Proceedings of the 8th Symposium on Abstraction, Reformulation and Approximation (SARA 2009)*. Lake Arrowhead, CA, USA.

Catanese, S., De Meo, P., Ferrara, E., Fiumara, G., & Provetti, A. (2011). Crawling Facebook for social network analysis purposes. In R. Akerkar (Ed.), *Proceedings of the 1st International Conference on Web Intelligence, Mining and Semantics (WIMS 2011) - Sogndal, Norway, May 25-27, 2011* (p. 52). New York, NY, USA: ACM Press. doi:10.1145/1988688.1988749

Chae, J., Thom, D., Bosch, H., Jang, Y., Maciejewski, R., Ebert, D., & Ertl, T. (2012). Spatiotemporal social media analytics for abnormal event detection and examination using seasonal-trend decomposition. *Proceedings of the 7th IEEE Conference on Visual Analytics Science and Technology (VAST 2012) - Seattle, WA, USA, October 14-19, 2012* (pp. 143-152). Los Alamitos, CA, USA: IEEE Computer Society. doi:10.1109/VAST.2012.6400557

Chang, J., Boyd-Graber, J., & Blei, D. M. (2009). Connections between the lines: augmenting social networks with text. In J. F. Elder IV, F. Fogelman-Soulié, P. A. Flach, & M. J. Zaki (Ed.), *Proceedings of the 15th ACM SIGKDD International Conference on Knowledge Discovery and Data Mining (KDD 2009) - Paris, France, June 28 - July 1, 2009* (pp. 169-178). New York, NY, USA: ACM Press. doi:10.1145/1557019.1557044

Chatfield, C. (2004). *The Analysis of Time Series: An Introduction* (6th ed.). Boca Raton, FL, USA: CRC Press.

Chen, H., Chiang, R. H., & Storey, V. C. (2012). Business Intelligence and Analytics: From Big Data to Big Impact. *Management Information Systems Quarterly, 36*(4), 1165–1188.

Chen, T., Tang, L., Liu, Q., Yang, D., Xie, S., Cao, X., & Wu, C. (2012). *Combining Factorization Model and Additive Forest for Collaborative Followee Recommendation. KDD Cup 2012.* New York, NY, USA: ACM Press.

Chen, Y., Liu, Z., Ji, D., Xin, Y., Wang, W., Yao, L., & Zou, Y. (2012). Context-aware Ensemble of Multifaceted Factorization Models for Recommendation Prediction in Social Networks. *Proceedings of the KDD Cup 2012 Workshop, 18th ACM SIGKDD International Conference on Knowledge Discovery and Data Mining (KDD 2012) - Beijing, China, August 12-16, 2012.* San Francisco, USA: Kaggle.

Christley, R. M., Pinchbeck, G. L., Bowers, R. G., Clancy, D., French, N. P., Bennett, R., & Turner, J. (2005). Infection in Social Networks: Using Network Analysis to Identify High-Risk Individuals. *American Journal of Epidemiology, 162*(10), 1024–1031. doi:10.1093/aje/kwi308 PMID:16177140

Clauset, A., Moore, C., & Newman, M. E. (2008). Hierarchical structure and the prediction of missing links in networks. *Nature, 453*, 98–101. doi:10.1038/nature06830 PMID:18451861

Clauset, A., Shalizi, C. R., & Newman, M. E. (2009). Power-Law Distributions in Empirical Data. *SIAM Review, 51*(4), 661–703. doi:10.1137/070710111

Cooley, R., Mobasher, B., & Srivastava, J. (1997). Web mining: information and pattern discovery on the World Wide Web. *Proceedings of the 9th International Conference on Tools with Artificial Intelligence (ICTAI 1997) - Newport Beach, CA, USA, November 3-8, 1997* (pp. 558-567). Los Alamitos, CA, USA: IEEE Computer Society. doi:10.1109/TAI.1997.632303

Corley, C. D., Cook, D. J., Mikler, A. R., & Singh, K. P. (2009). Monitoring Influenza Trends through Mining Social Media. In H. R. Arbnia, & M. Q. Yang (Ed.), *Proceedings of the 4th International Conference on Bioinformatics & Computational Biology (BIOCOMP 2009) - Las Vegas Nevada, USA, July 13-16, 2009* (pp. 340-346). Atlanta, GA, USA: CSREA Press.

Corley, C. D., Cook, D. J., Mikler, A. R., & Singh, K. P. (2010). Text and Structural Data Mining of Influenza Mentions in Web and Social Media. *International Journal of Environmental Research and Public Health, 7*(2), 596–615. doi:10.3390/ijerph7020596 PMID:20616993

Cruz, J. M., Nagurney, A., & Wakolbinger, T. (2006). Financial engineering of the integration of global supply chain networks and social networks with risk management. *Naval Research Logistics, 53*(7), 674–696. doi:10.1002/nav.20179

Culotta, A., Bekkerman, R., & McCallum, A. (2004). Extracting social networks and contact information from email and the Web. *Proceedings of the 1st Conference on Email and Anti-Spam (CEAS 2004) - Mountain View, CA, USA, July 30-31, 2004.* Retrieved March 9, 2014, from http://scholarworks.umass.edu/cs_faculty_pubs/33/

Danowski, J. A., & Cepela, N. (2010). Automatic Mapping of Social Networks of Actors from Text Corpora: Time Series Analysis. In N. Memon, J. J. Xu, D. L. Hicks, & H. Chen, *Data Mining for Social Network Data.* [New York, NY, USA: Springer.]. *Annals of Information Systems, 12*, 31–46. doi:10.1007/978-1-4419-6287-4_3

Davenport, T. H., Barth, P., & Bean, R. (2012). How `Big Data' is Different. *MIT Sloan Management Review, 54*(1), 22–24.

Davenport, T. H., & Patil, D. J. (2012, October). Data Scientist: The Sexiest Job of the 21st Century. *Harvard Business Review*, 70–76. PMID:23074866

Davitz, J., Yu, J., Basu, S., Gutelius, D., & Harris, A. (2007). iLink: search and routing in social networks. In P. Berkhin, R. Caruana, & X. Wu (Ed.), *Proceedings of the 13th ACM SIGKDD International Conference on Knowledge Discovery and Data Mining (KDD 2007) - San Jose, CA, USA, August 12-15, 2007* (pp. 931-940). New York, NY, USA: ACM Press. doi:10.1145/1281192.1281292

De Liddo, A., Shum, S. B., Quinto, I., Bachler, M., & Cannavacciuolo, L. (2011). Discourse-centric learning analytics. In P. Long, G. Siemens, G. Conole, & D. Gasevic (Ed.), *Proceedings of the 1st International Conference on Learning Analytics and Knowledge (LAK 2011) - Banff, AB, Canada, February 27 - March 1, 2011* (pp. 23-33). New York, NY, USA: ACM Press. doi:10.1145/2090116.2090120

Deerwester, S., Dumais, S. T., Furnas, G. W., Landauer, T. K., & Harshman, R. (1990). Indexing by latent semantic analysis. *Journal of the American Society for Information Science and Technology, 41*(6), 391–407. doi:10.1002/(SICI)1097-4571(199009)41:6<391::AID-ASI1>3.0.CO;2-9

Deng, H., Han, J., Zhao, B., Yu, Y., & Lin, C. X. (2011).: Probabilistic topic models with biased propagation on heterogeneous information networks. In C. Apté, J. Ghosh, & P. Smyth (Ed.), *Proceedings of the 17th ACM SIGKDD International Conference on Knowledge Discovery and Data Mining (KDD 2011)* (pp. 1271-1279). New York, NY, USA: ACM Press. doi:10.1145/2020408.2020600

Dietterich, T. G., Domingos, P., Getoor, L., Muggleton, S., & Tadepalli, P. (2008). Structured machine learning: the next ten years. (H. Blockeel, & J. Shavlik, Eds.) Machine Learning, 73(1), 3-23.

Do, T. M., & Gatica-Perez, D. (2011). GroupUs: Smartphone Proximity Data and Human Interaction Type Mining. *Proceedings of the 15th Annual International Symposium on Wearable Computers (ISWC 2011) - San Francisco, CA, USA, June 12-15, 2011* (pp. 21-28). Piscataway, NJ. USA: IEEE Press. doi:10.1109/ISWC.2011.28

Do, T. M., & Gatica-Perez, D. (2013). Human interaction discovery in smartphone proximity networks. *Personal and Ubiquitous Computing, 13*(7), 413–431. doi:10.1007/s00779-011-0489-7

Driskill, R., & Riedl, J. (1999). Recommender Systems for E-Commerce: Challenges and Opportunities. *Working Notes of the Workshop on Artificial Intelligence for Electronic Commerce (AAAI Technical Report WS-99-01)* (pp. 73-76). Menlo Park, CA, USA: AAAI Press.

Du, N., Wu, B., Xu, L., Wang, B., & Pei, X. (2006). A Parallel Algorithm for Enumerating All Maximal Cliques in Complex Network. *Workshops Proceedings of the 6th IEEE International Conference on Data Mining (ICDM 2006)* (pp. 320-324). Los Alamitos, CA, USA: IEEE Computer Society.

Erdős, P., & Rényi, A. (1960). On the Evolution of Random Graphs. [Bulletins of the Mathematical Research Institute of the Hungarian Academy of Sciences]. *Magyar Tudományos Akadémia Matematikai Kutató Intézete Közlemények, 5*, 17–61.

Ferguson, N. M., Donnelly, C. A., & Anderson, R. M. (2001). The Foot-and-Mouth Epidemic in Great Britain: Pattern of Spread and Impact of Interventions. *Science, 292*(5519), 1155–1160. doi:10.1126/science.1061020 PMID:11303090

Fire, M., Tenenboim, L., Lesser, O., Puzis, R., Rokach, L., & Elovici, Y. (2011). Link Prediction in Social Networks Using Computationally Efficient Topological Features. *Proceedings of the 2011 IEEE International Conference on Privacy, Security, Risk and Trust and 3rd IEEE International Conference on Social Computing (PASSAT/SocialCom 2011) - Boston, MA, USA, October 9-11, 2011* (pp. 73-80). Piscataway, NJ, USA: IEEE Press. doi:10.1109/PASSAT/SocialCom.2011.20

Gao, J. (2012). *Exploring the power of heterogeneous information sources (Doctoral dissertation).* Computer Science. Urbana, IL, USA: University of Illinois at Urbana-Champaign. Retrieved March 9, 2014, from http://hdl.handle.net/2142/29822

Gehrke, J., Ginsparg, P., & Kleinberg, J. (2003). Overview of the 2003 KDD Cup. *ACM SIGKDD Explorations Newsletter, 5*(2), 149–151. doi:10.1145/980972.980992

Gershenfeld, N. A., & Weigend, A. S. (1994). The Future of Time Series. In N. A. Gershenfeld & A. S. Weigend (Eds.), *Time Series Prediction: Forecasting the Future and Understanding the Past (Santa Fe Institute Series, Book 15)* (pp. 1–70). Boulder, CO, USA: Westview Press.

Getoor, L. (2003). Link Mining: A New Data Mining Challenge. *ACM SIGKDD Explorations Newsletter, 5*(1), 84–89. doi:10.1145/959242.959253

Getoor, L., & Diehl, C. P. (2005). Link Mining: A Survey. *ACM SIGKDD Explorations Newsletter, 7*(2), 3–12. doi:10.1145/1117454.1117456

Getoor, L., Rhee, J. T., Koller, D., & Small, P. (2004). Understanding tuberculosis epidemiology using structured statistical models. *Artificial Intelligence in Medicine, 30*(3), 233–256. doi:10.1016/j.artmed.2003.11.003 PMID:15081074

Giles, C. L., Bollacker, K. D., & Lawrence, S. (1998). CiteSeer: An Automatic Citation Indexing System. *Proceedings of the 3rd ACM International Conference on Digital Libraries (DL 1998)* (pp. 89-98). New York, NY, USA: ACM Press.

Glance, N. S., Hurst, M., Nigam, K., Siegler, M., Stockton, R., & Tomokiyo, T. (2005). Deriving marketing intelligence from online discussion. In R. Grossman, R. J. Bayardo, & K. P. Bennett (Ed.), *Proceedings of the 11th ACM SIGKDD International Conference on Knowledge Discovery and Data Mining (KDD 2005) - Chicago, IL, USA, August 21-24, 2005* (pp. 419-428). New York, NY, USA: ACM Press. doi:10.1145/1081870.1081919

Goldberg, L., Lide, B., Lowry, S., Massett, H. A., O'Connell, T., Preece, J., . . . Shneiderman, B. (2011). Usability and Accessibility in Consumer Health Informatics: Current Trends and Future Challenges. *American Journal of Preventive Medicine - Supplement on Cyberinfrastructure for Consumer Health, 40*(5), S187–S197. doi:10.1016/j.amepre.2011.01.009

Goyal, A., Bonchi, F., & Lakshmanan, L. V. (2010). Learning influence probabilities in social networks. In B. D. Davison, T. Suel, N. Craswell, & B. Liu (Ed.), *Proceedings of the 3rd International Conference on Web Search and Web Data Mining (WSDM 2010) - New York, NY, USA, February 4-6, 2010* (pp. 241-250). New York, NY, USA: ACM Press. doi:10.1145/1718487.1718518

Gregersen, H., & Sailer, L. (1993). Chaos Theory and Its Implications for Social Science Research. *Human Relations, 46*(7), 777–802. doi:10.1177/001872679304600701

Guerra, P. H., Veloso, A., Meira, W., Jr., & Almeida, V. (2011). From bias to opinion: a transfer-learning approach to real-time sentiment analysis. In C. Apté, J. Ghosh, & P. Smyth (Ed.), *Proceedings of the 17th ACM SIGKDD International Conference on Knowledge Discovery and Data Mining (KDD 2011)* (pp. 150-158). New York, NY, USA: ACM Press. doi:10.1145/2020408.2020438

Gupta, M., Gao, J., Sun, Y., & Han, J. (2012). Integrating meta-path selection with user-guided object clustering in heterogeneous information networks. In Q. Yang, D. Agarwal, & J. Pei (Ed.), *Proceedings of the 18th ACM SIGKDD International Conference on Knowledge Discovery and Data Mining (KDD 2012) - Beijing, China, August 12-16, 2012* (pp. 859-867). New York, NY, USA: ACM Press. doi:10.1145/2339530.2339738

Hair, J. F. Jr. (2007). Knowledge creation in marketing: the role of predictive analytics. *European Business Review, 9*(4), 303–315. doi:10.1108/09555340710760134

Han, J. (2009). Mining Heterogeneous Information Networks by Exploring the Power of Links. In J. Gama, V. S. Costa, A. M. Jorge, & P. Brazdil (Ed.), *Proceedings of the 12th International Conference on Discovery Science (DS 2009) - Porto, Portugal, October 3-5, 2009. Lecture Notes in Computer Science (LNCS) 5808*, pp. 13-30. New York, NY, USA: Springer.

He, Y., Lin, C., Gao, W., & Wong, K.-F. (2013). Dynamic joint sentiment-topic model. *ACM Transactions on Intelligent Systems and Technology (TIST) - Special Section on Intelligent Mobile Knowledge Discovery and Management Systems and Special Issue on Social Web Mining, 5*(1), 6:1-6:21. doi:10.1145/2542182.2542188

Henderson, K., Gallagher, B., Eliassi-Rad, T., Tong, H., Basu, S., & Leman Akoglu, D. K. (2012). RolX: Structural Role Extraction & Mining in Large Graphs. In Q. Yang, D. Agarwal, & J. Pei (Ed.), *Proceedings of the 18th ACM SIGKDD International Conference on Knowledge Discovery and Data Mining (KDD 2012) - Beijing, China, August 12-16, 2012* (pp. 1231-1239). New York, NY, USA: ACM Press.

Horn, J. K. (2005). Parameters for sustained orderly growth in learning organizations. In K. Richardson (Ed.), *Managing Organizational Complexity: Philosophy, Theory and Application* (pp. 473–492). Charlotte, NC, USA: Information Age Publishing.

Hsu, W. H., King, A. L., Paradesi, M. S., Pydimarri, T., & Weninger, T. (2006). Collaborative and Structural Recommendation of Friends using Weblog-based Social Network Analysis. In N. Nicolov, F. Salvetti, M. Liberman, & J. H. Martin (Ed.), *Computational Approaches to Analyzing Weblogs, Papers from the 2006 AAAI Spring Symposium, Technical Report SS-06-03 - Stanford, CA, USA, March 27-29, 2006* (pp. 55-60). Menlo Park, CA, USA: AAAI Press.

Hsu, W. H., Koduru, P., & Zhai, C. (2013). Heterogeneous Information Networks for Text-Based Link Mining: A Position Paper on Visualization and Structure Learning Methods. In W. H. Hsu, S. Kallumadi, & Y. Sun (Ed.), *Working notes of the 2nd International Workshop on Heterogeneous Information Network Analysis (HINA 2013). Workshop W36, 23rd International Joint Conference on Artificial Intelligence (IJCAI 2013) - Beijing, China, August 5, 2013*.

Hsu, W. H., Lancaster, J. P., Paradesi, M. S., & Weninger, T. (2007). Structural Link Analysis from User Profiles and Friends Networks: A Feature Construction Approach. In N. S. Glance, N. Nicolov, E. Adar, M. Hurst, M. Liberman, & F. Salvetti (Ed.), *Proceedings of the 1st International Conference on Weblogs and Social Media (ICWSM 2007)*, (pp. 75-80). Boulder, CO, USA.

Hsu, W. H., Roy Chowdhury, S., & Scoglio, C. (2011). Mitigation Strategies for Foot and Mouth Disease: A Learning-Based Approach. *International Journal of Artificial Life Research, 2*(2), 42–76. doi:10.4018/jalr.2011040103

Hsu, W. H., Weninger, T., & Paradesi, M. S. (2008). Predicting links and link change in friends networks: supervised time series learning with imbalanced data. In C. H. Dagli, D. L. Enke, K. M. Bryden, H. Ceylan, & M. Gen (Ed.), *Intelligent Engineering Systems Through Artificial Neural Networks: Proceedings of the 18th International Conference on Artificial Neural Networks in Engineering (ANNIE 2008) - St. Louis, MO, USA, November 9-12, 2008. 18*. New York, NY, USA: ASME Press. doi:10.1115/1.802823.paper68

Hu, X., & Liu, H. (2012). Text Analytics in Social Media. In C. C. Aggarwal & C. Zhai (Eds.), *Mining Text Data* (pp. 385–414). New York, NY, USA: Springer. doi:10.1007/978-1-4614-3223-4_12

Hu, Y., John, A., Wang, F., & Kambhampati, S. (2012). ET-LDA: Joint Topic Modeling for Aligning Events and Their Twitter Feedback. In J. Hoffmann, & B. Selman (Ed.), *Proceedings of the 26th AAAI Conference on Artificial Intelligence (AAAI 2012) - July 22-26, 2012, Toronto, Ontario, Canada*. Menlo Park, CA, USA: AAAI Press.

Hu, Y., Wang, F., & Kambhampati, S. (2013). Listening to the crowd: automated analysis of events via aggregated twitter sentiment. *Proceedings of the 23rd International Joint Conference on Artificial Intelligence (IJCAI 2013) - Beijing, China, August 3-9, 2013*. Menlo Park, CA, USA: AAAI Press / International Joint Conferences on Artificial Intelligence.

Huang, Z. (2006). Link Prediction Based on Graph Topology: The Predictive Value of Generalized Clustering Coefficient. In M. Grobelnik, J. Adibi, N. Milic-Frayling, D. Mladenic, & P. Pantel (Ed.), *Working Notes of the Workshop on Link Analysis, 12th ACM SIGKDD International Conference on Knowledge Discovery and Data Mining (LinkKDD 2006) - Philadelphia, PA, USA, August 20–23, 2006*. New York, NY, USA: ACM Press. Retrieved March 9, 2014, from http://citeseerx.ist.psu.edu/viewdoc/summary?doi=10.1.1.67.2613

Jamali, M., & Ester, M. (2010). A matrix factorization technique with trust propagation for recommendation in social networks. In X. Amatriain, M. Torrens, P. Resnick, & M. Zanker (Ed.), *Proceedings of the 2010 ACM Conference on Recommender Systems (RecSys 2010) - Barcelona, Spain, September 26-30, 2010* (pp. 135-142). New York, NY, USA: ACM Press. doi:10.1145/1864708.1864736

Jansen, R., Yu, H., Greenbaum, D., Kluger, Y., Krogan, N. J., & Chung, S. et al. (2003). A Bayesian Networks Approach for Predicting Protein-Protein Interactions from Genomic Data. *Science, 302*(5644), 449–453. doi:10.1126/science.1087361 PMID:14564010

Ji, M., Han, J., & Danilevsky, M. (2011). Ranking-based classification of heterogeneous information networks. *Proceedings of the 17th ACM SIGKDD International Conference on Knowledge Discovery and Data Mining (KDD 2011)* (pp. 1298-1306). New York, NY, USA: ACM Press.

Ji, M., Sun, Y., Danilevsky, M., Han, J., & Gao, J. (2010). Graph Regularized Transductive Classification on Heterogeneous Information Networks. In J. L. Balcázar, F. Bonchi, A. Gionis, & M. Sebag (Ed.), *Machine Learning and Knowledge Discovery in Databases: European Conference (ECML PKDD 2010) - Barcelona, Spain, September 20-24, 2010, Proceedings, Part I* (pp. 570-586). New York, NY, USA: Springer.

Kannan, P. V., & Vijayaraghavan, R. (2013). *Patent No. US 20130282430*. USA. Retrieved March 9, 2014, from www.google.com/patents/US20130282430

Kashima, H., Kato, T., Yamanishi, Y., Sugiyama, M., & Tsuda, K. (2009). Link Propagation: A Fast Semi-supervised Learning Algorithm for Link Prediction. *Proceedings of the 9th SIAM International Conference on Data Mining (SDM 2009) - Sparks, NV, USA, April 30 - May 2, 2009* (pp. 1100-1111). Philadelphia, PA, USA: SIAM Press.

Kendrena, K. R., Donchetz, J. G., & Istre, R. R. (2012). *Patent No. US 20130246339*. USA. Retrieved March 9, 2014, from http://www.google.com/patents/US20130246339

Ketkar, N. S., Holder, L. B., & Cook, D. J. (2005). Comparison of graph-based and logic-based multi-relational data mining. *ACM SIGKDD Explorations Newsletter, 7*(2), 64–71. doi:10.1145/1117454.1117463

King, I., Li, J., & Chan:, K. T. (2009). A brief survey of computational approaches in Social Computing. *Proceedings of the 2009 International Joint Conference on Neural Networks (IJCNN 2009) - Atlanta, Georgia, USA, 14-19 June 2009* (pp. 1625-1632). Piscataway, NJ, USA: IEEE Press.

Koenigstein, N., Dror, G., & Koren, Y. (2011). Yahoo! music recommendations: modeling music ratings with temporal dynamics and item taxonomy. In B. Mobasher, R. D. Burke, D. Jannach, & G. Adomavicius (Ed.), *Proceedings of the 5th ACM Conference on Recommender Systems (RecSys 2011) - Chicago, IL, USA, October 23-27, 2011* (pp. 165-172). New York, NY, USA: ACM Press. doi:10.1145/2043932.2043964

Konstas, I., Stathopoulos, V., & Jose, J. M. (2009). On social networks and collaborative recommendation. In J. Allan, J. A. Aslam, M. Sanderson, C. Zhai, & J. Zobel (Ed.), *Proceedings of the 32nd Annual International ACM SIGIR Conference on Research and Development in Information Retrieval (SIGIR 2009) - Boston, MA, USA, July 19-23, 2009* (pp. 195-202). New York, NY, USA: ACM Press. doi:10.1145/1571941.1571977

Koren, Y. (2009). Collaborative Filtering with Temporal Dynamics. In J. F. Elder IV, F. Fogelman-Soulié, P. A. Flach, & M. J. Zaki (Ed.), *Proceedings of the 15th ACM SIGKDD International Conference on Knowledge Discovery and Data Mining (KDD 2009) - Paris, France, June 28 - July 1, 2009* (pp. 447-456). New York, NY, USA: ACM Press.

Krackhardt, D. (1988). Predicting with networks: Nonparametric multiple regression analysis of dyadic data. *Social Networks, 10*(4), 359–381. doi:10.1016/0378-8733(88)90004-4

Kunegis, J., & Lommatzsch, A. (2009). Learning Spectral Graph Transformations for Link Prediction. In A. P. Danyluk, L. Bottou, & M. L. Littman (Ed.), *Proceedings of the 26th Annual International Conference on Machine Learning (ICML 2009)* (p. 71). New York, NY, USA: ACM Press.

Lathia, N., Hailes, S., Capra, L., & Amatriain, X. (2010). Temporal diversity in recommender systems. In F. Crestani, S. Marchand-Maillet, H.-H. Chen, E. N. Efthimiadis, & J. Savoy (Ed.), *Proceedings of the 33rd Annual International ACM SIGIR Conference on Research and Development in Information Retrieval (SIGIR 2010) - Geneva, Switzerland, July 19-23, 2010* (pp. 210-217). New York, NY, USA: ACM Press. doi:10.1145/1835449.1835486

Lau, R. Y. (2013). A Probabilistic Generative Model for Mining Collaborative Cybercriminal Networks. In W. H. Hsu, S. Kallumadi, & Y. Sun (Ed.), *Working notes of the 2nd International Workshop on Heterogeneous Information Network Analysis (HINA 2013). Workshop W36, 23rd International Joint Conference on Artificial Intelligence (IJCAI 2013) - Beijing, China, August 5, 2013.*

Lauw, H. W., Lim, E.-P., Pang, H., & Tan, T.-T. (2011). Social Network Discovery by Mining Spatio-Temporal Events. *Computational & Mathematical Organization Theory, 11*(2), 97–118. doi:10.1007/s10588-005-3939-9

LaValle, S., Lesser, E., Shockley, R., Hopkins, M. S., & Kruschwitz, N. (2011). Big Data, Analytics and the Path From Insights to Value. *MIT Sloan Management Review, 52*(2), 21–31.

Lawrence, S., Giles, C. L., & Bollacker, K. D. (1999). Digital Libraries and Autonomous Citation Indexing. *IEEE Computer, 32*(6), 67–71. doi:10.1109/2.769447

Leskovec, J., Huttenlocher, D. P., & Kleinberg, J. M. (2010). Predicting positive and negative links in online social networks. In M. Rappa, P. Jones, J. Freire, & S. Chakrabarti (Ed.), *Proceedings of the 19th International World Wide Web Conference (WWW 2010) - Raleigh, NC, USA, April 26-30, 2010* (pp. 641-650). New York, NY, USA: ACM Press. doi:10.1145/1772690.1772756

Levin, D. Z., & Cross, R. (2004). The Strength of Weak Ties You Can Trust: The Mediating Role of Trust in Effective Knowledge Transfer. *Management Science, 50*(11), 1477–1490. doi:10.1287/mnsc.1030.0136

Li, H., Fang, D., Mahatma, S., & Hampapur, A. (2011). Usage analysis for smart meter management. *Proceedings of the 8th International Conference & Expo on Emerging Technologies for a Smarter World (CEWIT 2011) - Long Island, NY, USA, November 2-3, 2011* (pp. 1-6). Stony Brook, NY, USA: CEWIT. doi:10.1109/CEWIT.2011.6135871

Liben-Nowell, D., & Kleinberg, J. (2007). The Link-Prediction Problem for Social Networks. *Journal of the American Society for Information Science and Technology, 58*(7), 1019–1031. doi:10.1002/asi.20591

Liu, J., & Han, J. (2013). HINMF: A Matrix Factorization Method for Clustering in Heterogeneous Information Networks. In W. H. Hsu, S. Kallumadi, & Y. Sun (Ed.), *Working notes of the 2nd International Workshop on Heterogeneous Information Network Analysis (HINA 2013). Workshop W36, 23rd International Joint Conference on Artificial Intelligence (IJCAI 2013) - Beijing, China, August 5, 2013.*

Ma, H., Zhou, D., Liu, C., Lyu, M. R., & King, I. (2011). Recommender systems with social regularization. In I. King, W. Nejdl, & H. Li (Ed.), *Proceedings of the 4th International Conference on Web Search and Web Data Mining (WSDM 2011)* (pp. 287-296). New York, NY, USA: ACM Press.

Ma, T., Yang, Y., Wang, L., & Yuan, B. (2014). Recommending People to Follow Using Asymmetric Factor Models with Social Graphs. In V. Snášel, P. Krömer, M. Köppen, & G. Schaefer (Eds.), *Soft Computing in Industrial Applications: Proceedings of the 17th Online World Conference on Soft Computing in Industrial Applications. Advances in Intelligent Systems and Computing 223* (pp. 265-276). New York, NY, USA: Springer.

Macskassy, S. A. (2009). Using graph-based metrics with empirical risk minimization to speed up active learning on networked data. In J. F. Elder IV, F. Fogelman-Soulié, P. A. Flach, & M. J. Zaki (Ed.), *Proceedings of the 15th ACM SIGKDD International Conference on Knowledge Discovery and Data Mining (KDD 2009) - Paris, France, June 28 - July 1, 2009* (pp. 597-606). New York, NY, USA: ACM Press. doi:10.1145/1557019.1557087

Manjunatha, J. N., Sivaramakrishnan, K. R., Pandey, R. K., & Murthy, M. N. (2003). *Citation Prediction Using Time Series Approach: KDD Cup 2003 (Task 1)* (pp. 152–153). New York, NY, USA: ACM Press.

Mathioudakis, M., & Koudas, N. (2010). TwitterMonitor: trend detection over the twitter stream. In A. K. Elmagarmid, & D. Agrawal (Ed.), *Proceedings of the ACM SIGMOD International Conference on Management of Data (SIGMOD 2010) - Indianapolis, IN, USA, June 6-10, 2010* (pp. 1155-1158). New York, NY, USA: ACM Press. doi:10.1145/1807167.1807306

Matsuo, Y., & Yamamoto, H. (2009). Community gravity: measuring bidirectional effects by trust and rating on online social networks. In J. Quemada, G. León, Y. S. Maarek, & W. Nejdl (Ed.), *Proceedings of the 18th International World Wide Web Conference (WWW 2009) - Madrid, Spain, April 20-24, 2009* (pp. 751-760). New York, NY, USA: ACM Press.

May, R. M., Levin, S. A., & Sugihara, G. (2008). Complex systems: Ecology for bankers. *Nature, 451,* 893–895. doi:10.1038/451893a PMID:18288170

McCallum, A., Corrada-Emmanuel, A., & Wang, X. (2005). *The Author-Recipient-Topic Model for Topic and Role Discovery in Social Networks: Experiments with Enron and Academic Email (Computer Science Department Faculty Publication Series, Paper 44).* University of Massachusetts - Amherst, Department of Computer Science. Amherst, MA, USA: ScholarWorks@UMass Amherst. Retrieved March 9, 2014, from http://scholarworks.umass.edu/cs_faculty_pubs/44/

McCallum, A., Wang, X., & Corrada-Emmanuel, A. (2007). Topic and Role Discovery in Social Networks with Experiments on Enron and Academic Email. *Journal of Artificial Intelligence Research, 30,* 249–272.

McCue, C. (2005). Data Mining and Predictive Analytics: Battlespace Awareness for the War on Terrorism. *Defense Intelligence Journal, 13*(1-2), 47–63.

McPherson, M., Smith-Lovin, L., & Cook, J. M. (2001). Birds of a Feather: Homophily in Social Networks. *Annual Review of Sociology, 27*, 415–444. doi:10.1146/annurev.soc.27.1.415

Meyers, L. A., Pourbohloul, B., Newman, M. E., Skowronski, D. M., & Brunham, R. C. (2005). Network theory and SARS: predicting outbreak diversity. *Journal of Theoretical Biology, 232*(1), 71–81. doi:10.1016/j.jtbi.2004.07.026 PMID:15498594

Min, J.-K., Wiese, J., Hong, J. I., & Zimmerman, J. (2013). Mining smartphone data to classify life-facets of social relationships. In A. Bruckman, S. Counts, C. Lampe, & L. G. Terveen (Ed.), *Proceedings of the 2013 ACM Conference on Computer Supported Cooperative Work (CSCW 2013) - San Antonio, TX, USA, February 23-27, 2013* (pp. 285-294). New York, NY, USA: ACM press. doi:10.1145/2441776.2441810

Mladenic, D. (1999). Text-Learning and Related Intelligent Agents: A Survey. *IEEE Intelligent Systems & Their Applications, 14*(4), 44–54. doi:10.1109/5254.784084

Mobasher, B., Burke, R., Bhaumik, R., & Sandvig, J. (2007). Attacks and Remedies in Collaborative Recommendation. *IEEE Intelligent Systems, 22*(3), 56–63. doi:10.1109/MIS.2007.45

Mobasher, B., Cooley, R., & Srivastava, J. (2000). Automatic personalization based on Web usage mining. *Communications of the ACM, 43*(8), 142–151. doi:10.1145/345124.345169

Murata, T. (2011). Detecting Communities from Social Tagging Networks Based on Tripartite Modularity. In W. H. Hsu, S. Kallumadi, & J. Han (Ed.), *Working notes of Workshop W-16, 22nd International Joint Conference on Artificial Intelligence (IJCAI 2011): Heterogeneous Information Network Analysis (HINA 2011) - Barcelona, Spain, July 16, 2011*. Retrieved March 9, 2014, from http://www.kddresearch. org/KDD/Workshops/IJCAI-2011-HINA/Papers/

Myers, S. A., & Leskovec, J. (2010). On the Convexity of Latent Social Network Inference. In J. D. Lafferty, C. K. Williams, J. Shawe-Taylor, R. S. Zemel, & A. Culotta (Ed.), *Advances in Neural Information Processing Systems 23: Proceedings of the 24th Annual Conference on Neural Information Processing Systems (NIPS 2010) - Vancouver, BC, Canada, December 6-9, 2010* (pp. 1741-1749). Red Hook, NY, USA: Curran & Associates.

National Research Council. (S. L. Magsino, Rapporteur). (2009). Social Network Analysis for Improved Disaster Preparedness and Intervention Planning. In S. L. Magsino, Applications of Social Network Analysis for Building Community Disaster Resilience: Workshop Summary (pp. 33-42). Washington, DC, USA: The National Academies.

Newman, M. E. (2003). The Structure and Function of Complex Networks. *SIAM Review, 45*(2), 167–256. doi:10.1137/S003614450342480

Nguyen, T., Phung, D. Q., Adams, B., & Venkatesh, S. (2012). A Sentiment-Aware Approach to Community Formation in Social Media. In J. G. Breslin, N. B. Ellison, J. G. Shanahan, & Z. Tufekci (Ed.), *Proceedings of the 6th International Conference on Weblogs and Social Media (ICWSM 2012)*. Menlo Park, CA, USA: AAAI Press.

Nov, O., Naaman, M., & Ye, C. (2009). Motivational, Structural and Tenure Factors that Impact Online Community Photo Sharing. In E. Adar, M. Hurs, T. Finin, N. S. Glance, N. Nicolov, & B. L. Tseng (Ed.), *Proceedings of the 3rd International Conference on Weblogs and Social Media (ICWSM 2009).* Menlo Park, CA, USA: AAAI Press.

Nov, O., Naaman, M., & Ye, C. (2010). Analysis of participation in an online photo-sharing community: A multidimensional perspective. *Journal of the American Society for Information Science and Technology, 61*(3), 555–566.

O'Donovan, J., & Smyth, B. (2005). Trust in recommender systems. In R. St. Amant, J. Riedl, & A. Jameson (Ed.), *Proceedings of the 10th International Conference on Intelligent User Interfaces (IUI 2005)* (pp. 167-174). New York, NY, USA: ACM Press.

O'Madadhain, J., Hutchins, J., & Smyth, P. (2005). Prediction and ranking algorithms for event-based network data. *ACM SIGKDD Explorations Newsletter, 7*(2), 23–30. doi:10.1145/1117454.1117458

Ohara, K., Saito, K., Kimura, M., & Motoda, H. (2011). Efficient Detection of Hot Span in Information Diffusion from Observation. In W. H. Hsu, S. Kallumadi, & J. Han (Ed.), *Working notes of Workshop W-16, 22nd International Joint Conference on Artificial Intelligence (IJCAI 2011): Heterogeneous Information Network Analysis (HINA 2011) - Barcelona, Spain, July 16, 2011.* Retrieved March 9, 2014, from http://www.kddresearch.org/KDD/Workshops/IJCAI-2011-HINA/Papers/

Olsman, K., Roxendal, O., & Åkerblom, V. (2013). *Designing for Collaboration Using Social Network Analysis - Towards a Conceptual Method to Understand Organisational Interaction. Lund University, Department of Informatics.* Lund, Sweden: Lund University School of Economics and Management.

Pan, S. J., & Yang, Q. (2010). A Survey on Transfer Learning. [TKDE]. *IEEE Transactions on Knowledge and Data Engineering, 22*(10), 1345–1359. doi:10.1109/TKDE.2009.191

Parimi, R., & Caragea, D. (2011). Predicting Friendship Links in Social Networks Using a Topic Modeling Approach. In J. Z. Huang, L. Cao, & J. Srivastava (Ed.), *Advances in Knowledge Discovery and Data Mining - 15th Pacific-Asia Conference, PAKDD 2011, Shenzhen, China, May 24-27, 2011, Proceedings, Part II. Lecture Notes in Computer Science (LNCS) 6635*, pp. 75-86. New York, NY, USA: Springer.

Pennock, D. M., Flake, G. W., Lawrence, S., Glover, E. J., & Giles, C. L. (2002). Winners don't take all: Characterizing the competition for links on the web. [PNAS]. *Proceedings of the National Academy of Sciences of the United States of America, 99*(8), 5207–5211. doi:10.1073/pnas.032085699 PMID:16578867

Pennock, D. M., Horvitz, E., Lawrence, S., & Giles, C. L. (2000). Collaborative filtering by personality diagnosis: a hybrid memory- and model-based approach. In C. Boutilier, & M. Goldszmidt (Ed.), *Proceedings of the 16th Conference on Uncertainty in Artificial Intelligence (UAI 2000) - Stanford, California, USA, June 30 - July 3, 2000* (pp. 473-480). San Francisco, CA, USA: Morgan Kaufmann.

Piatetsky-Shapiro, G., Djeraba, C., Getoor, L., Grossman, R., Feldman, R., & Zaki, M. J. (2006). What are the grand challenges for data mining?: KDD-2006 panel report. *ACM SIGKDD Explorations Newsletter, 8*(2), 70–77. doi:10.1145/1233321.1233330

Pizzato, L., Rej, T., Akehurst, J., Koprinska, I., Yacef, K., & Kay, J. (2013). Recommending people to people: the nature of reciprocal recommenders with a case study in online dating. *User Modeling and User-Adapted Interaction, 23*(5), 447–488. doi:10.1007/s11257-012-9125-0

Popescul, A., Ungar, L. H., Pennock, D. M., & Lawrence, S. (2001). Probabilistic models for unified collaborative and content-based recommendation in sparse-data environments. In J. S. Breese, & D. Koller (Ed.), *Proceedings of the 17th Conference on Uncertainty in Artificial Intelligence (UAI 2001) - Seattle, Washington, USA, August 2-5, 2001* (pp. 437-444). San Francisco, CA, USA: Morgan Kaufmann.

Pryymak, O., Rogers, A., & Jennings, N. R. (2011). Efficient Sharing of Conflicting Opinions with Minimal Communication in Large Decentralised Teams. In W. H. Hsu, S. Kallumadi, & J. Han (Ed.), *Working notes of Workshop W-16, 22nd International Joint Conference on Artificial Intelligence (IJCAI 2011): Heterogeneous Information Network Analysis (HINA 2011) - Barcelona, Spain, July 16, 2011.* Retrieved March 9, 2014, from http://www.kddresearch.org/Workshops/IJCAI-2011-HINA/Papers/

Pujol, A., Mosca, R., Farrés, J., & Aloy, P. (2010). Unveiling the role of network and systems biology in drug discovery. *Trends in Pharmacological Sciences, 31*(3), 115–123. doi:10.1016/j.tips.2009.11.006 PMID:20117850

Qian, R., Zhang, W., & Yang, B. (2006). Detect community structure from the Enron Email Corpus Based on Link Mining. *Proceedings of the 6th International Conference on Intelligent Systems Design and Applications (ISDA 2006). 2,* pp. 850-855. Los Alamitos, CA, USA: IEEE Computer Society.

Raymond, R., & Kashima, H. (2010). Fast and Scalable Algorithms for Semi-supervised Link Prediction on Static and Dynamic Graphs. In J. L. Balcázar, F. Bonchi, A. Gionis, & M. Sebag (Ed.), *Machine Learning and Knowledge Discovery in Databases: European Conference (ECML PKDD 2010) - Barcelona, Spain, September 20-24, 2010, Proceedings, Part III. Lecture Notes in Computer Science (LNCS) 6323,* pp. 131-147. New York, NY, USA: Springer.

Romero, D. M., & Kleinberg, J. M. (2010). The Directed Closure Process in Hybrid Social-Information Networks. In S. G. William W. Cohen (Ed.), *Proceedings of the 4th International Conference on Weblogs and Social Media (ICWSM 2010).* Menlo Park, CA, USA: AAAI Press.

Rowe, M., Stankovic, M., & Alani, H. (2012). Who Will Follow Whom? Exploiting Semantics for Link Prediction in Attention-Information Networks. In P. Cudré-Mauroux, J. Heflin, E. Sirin, T. Tudorache, J. Euzenat, M. Hauswirth, . . . E. Blomqvist (Ed.), *The Semantic Web: Proceedings of the 11th International Semantic Web Conference (ISWC 2012) - Boston, MA, USA, November 11-15, 2012, Proceedings, Part II. Lecture Notes in Computer Science (LNCS) 7649.* New York, NY, USA: Springer.

Rual, J.-F., Venkatesan, K., Hao, T., Hirozane-Kishikawa, T., Dricot, A., & Li, N. et al. (2005). Towards a proteome-scale map of the human protein–protein interaction network. *Nature, 437,* 1173–1178. doi:10.1038/nature04209 PMID:16189514

Russom, P. (2011). *Big Data Analytics: TDWI Best Practices Report, 4th Quarter 2011.* The Data Warehousing Institute (TWDI). Renton, WA, USA: TDWI Research. Retrieved March 9, 2014, from http://public.dhe.ibm.com/common/ssi/ecm/en/iml14293usen/IML14293USEN.PDF

Rutherford, A., Cebrian, M., Dsouza, S., Moro, E., Pentland, A., & Rahwan, I. (2013). Limits of social mobilization. [PNAS]. *Proceedings of the National Academy of Sciences of the United States of America, 110*(16), 6281–6286. doi:10.1073/pnas.1216338110 PMID:23576719

Salem, N. J. (2009). *Link Prediction in Static and Dynamic Graphs*. Retrieved March 9, 2014, from Graph Mining: Washington State University AI Lab: http://ailab.wsu.edu/graphmining/node/14

Sarawagi, S., & Bhamidipaty, A. (2002). Interactive deduplication using active learning. *Proceedings of the 8th ACM SIGKDD International Conference on Knowledge Discovery and Data Mining (KDD 2002) - Edmonton, AB, Canada, July 23-26, 2002* (pp. 269-278). New York, NY, USA: ACM Press.

Scellato, S., Noulas, A., & Mascolo, C. (2011). Exploiting place features in link prediction on location-based social networks. In C. Apté, J. Ghosh, & P. Smyth (Ed.), *Proceedings of the 17th ACM SIGKDD International Conference on Knowledge Discovery and Data Mining (KDD 2011)* (pp. 1046-1054). New York, NY, USA: ACM Press.

Schulte, O., & Qian, Z. (2013). Learning Bayes Nets for Relational Data With Link Uncertainty. In W. H. Hsu, S. Kallumadi, & Y. Sun (Ed.), *Working notes of the 2nd International Workshop on Heterogeneous Information Network Analysis (HINA 2013). Workshop W36, 23rd International Joint Conference on Artificial Intelligence (IJCAI 2013) - Beijing, China, August 5, 2013.*

Schulte, O., Riahi, F., & Li, Q. (2013). Identifying Important Nodes in Heterogenous Networks. In W. H. Hsu, S. Kallumadi, & Y. Sun (Ed.), *Working notes of the 2nd International Workshop on Heterogeneous Information Network Analysis (HINA 2013). Workshop W36, 23rd International Joint Conference on Artificial Intelligence (IJCAI 2013) - Beijing, China, August 5, 2013.*

Semertzidis, K., Pitoura, E., & Tsaparas, P. (2013). How people describe themselves on Twitter. In K. LeFevre, A. Machanavajjhala, & A. Silberstein (Ed.), *Proceedings of the 3rd ACM SIGMOD Workshop on Databases and Social Networks (DBSocial 2013) - New York, NY, USA, June, 23, 2013* (pp. 25-30). New York, NY, USA: ACM Press.

Sen, P., Namata, G., Bilgic, M., Getoor, L., Galligher, B., & Eliassi-Rad, T. (2008). Collective Classification in Network Data. *AI Magazine, 29*(3), 93–106. doi:10.1609/aimag.v29i3.2157

Shen, Z., Ma, K.-L., & Eliassi-Rad, T. (2006). Visual Analysis of Large Heterogeneous Social Networks by Semantic and Structural Abstraction. *IEEE Transactions on Visualization and Computer Graphics. Special Issue on Visual Analytics, 12*(6), 1427–1439.

Shmueli, G., & Koppius, O. R. (2011). Predictive Analytics in Information Systems Research. *Management Information Systems Quarterly, 35*(3), 553–572.

Silow-Carroll, S., Edwards, J. N., & Rodin, D. (2012). *Using Electronic Health Records to Improve Quality and Efficiency: The Experiences of Leading Hospitals (Publication 1608)*. New York, NY, USA: The Commonwealth Fund.

Singh, B., & Singh, H. K. (2010). Web Data Mining Research: A Survey. In N. Krishnan, & M. Karthikeyan (Ed.), *Proceedings of the 1st IEEE International Conference on Computational Intelligence and Computing Research (ICCIC 2010) - Coimbatore, India, December 28-29, 2010* (pp. 1-10). Piscataway, NJ, USA: IEEE Press. doi:10.1109/ICCIC.2010.5705856

Soler-López, M., Zanzoni, A., Lluís, R., Stelzl, U., & Aloy, P. (2011). Interactome mapping suggests new mechanistic details underlying Alzheimer's disease. *Genome Research, 21*, 364–376. doi:10.1101/gr.114280.110 PMID:21163940

Stodder, D. (2012). *Customer Analytics in The Age of Social Media: TDWI Best Practices Report, 3rd Quarter 2012.* The Data Warehousing Institute (TWDI). Renton, WA, USA: TDWI Research. Retrieved March 9, 2014, from http://www.businesstimes.com.sg/archive/monday/sites/businesstimes.com.sg/files/Customer%20Analytics%20in%20the%20Age%20of%20Social%20Media.pdf

Sun, C., Lin, L., Chen, Y., & Liu, B. (2013). Expanding User Features with Social Relationships in Social Recommender Systems. In G. Zhou, J. Li, D. Zhao, & Y. Feng (Ed.), *Natural Language Processing and Chinese Computing: Proceedings of the 2nd CCF Conference (NLPCC 2013) - Chongqing, China, November 15-19, 2013. Communications in Computer and Information Science (CCIS) 400*, pp. 247-254. New York: Springer.

Sun, Y., Aggarwal, C. C., & Han, J. (2012). Relation strength-aware clustering of heterogeneous information networks with incomplete attributes. (Z. M. Ozsoyoglu, Ed.) *Proceedings of the VLDB Endowment, 5*(5), 394-405.

Sun, Y., & Han, J. (2012). Mining heterogeneous information networks: a structural analysis approach. *ACM SIGKDD Explorations Newsletter, 14*(2), 20–28. doi:10.1145/2481244.2481248

Sun, Y., Han, J., Aggarwal, C. C., & Chawla, N. V. (2012). When will it happen?: relationship prediction in heterogeneous information networks. In E. Adar, J. Teevan, E. Agichtein, & Y. Maarek (Ed.), *Proceedings of the 5th International Conference on Web Search and Web Data Mining (WSDM 2012) - Seattle, WA, USA, February 8-12, 2012* (pp. 663-672). New York, NY, USA: ACM Press. doi:10.1145/2124295.2124373

Sun, Y., Han, J., Yan, X., Yu, P. S., & Wu, T. (2011). Yizhou Sun, Jiawei Han, Xifeng Yan, Philip S. Yu, Tianyi Wu: PathSim: Meta Path-Based Top-K Similarity Search in Heterogeneous Information Networks. (H. V. Jagadish, Ed.) *Proceedings of the VLDB Endowment, 4*(11), 992-1003.

Sun, Y., Norick, B., Han, J., Yan, X., Yu, P. S., & Yu, X. (2013). PathSelClus: Integrating Meta-Path Selection with User-Guided Object Clustering in Heterogeneous Information Networks. *ACM Transactions on Knowledge Discovery from Data (TKDD) - Special Issue on ACM SIGKDD 2012, 7*(3), 11:1-11:23. doi:10.1145/2500492

Sun, Y., Yu, Y., & Han, J. (2009). Ranking-based clustering of heterogeneous information networks with star network schema. *Proceedings of the 15th ACM SIGKDD International Conference on Knowledge Discovery and Data Mining (KDD 2009) - Paris, France, June 28 - July 1, 2009* (pp. 797-806). New York, NY, USA: ACM Press. doi:10.1145/1557019.1557107

Sycara, K. (2012). Dynamics of Information Propagation in Large Heterogeneous Networks. In F. M. Brazier, K. Nieuwenhuis, G. Pavlin, M. Warnier, & C. Badica (Ed.), *Intelligent Distributed Computing V: Proceedings of the 5th International Symposium on Intelligent Distributed Computing (IDC 2011) - Delft, The Netherlands, October 2011. Studies in Computational Intelligence 382*, p. 3. New York, NY, USA: Springer.

Szell, M., Lambiotte, R., & Thurner, S. (2010). Multirelational organization of large-scale social networks in an online world. [PNAS]. *Proceedings of the National Academy of Sciences of the United States of America, 107*(31), 13636–13641. doi:10.1073/pnas.1004008107 PMID:20643965

Tang, J., Lou, T., & Kleinberg, J. M. (2012). Inferring social ties across heterogenous networks. In E. Adar, J. Teevan, E. Agichtein, & Y. Maarek (Ed.), *Proceedings of the 5th International Conference on Web Search and Web Data Mining (WSDM 2012) - Seattle, WA, USA, February 8-12, 2012* (pp. 743-752). New York, NY, USA: ACM Press. doi:10.1145/2124295.2124382

Taskar, B., Wong, M.-F., Abbeel, P., & Koller, D. (2004). Link Prediction in Relational Data. In S. Thrun, L. K. Saul, & B. Schölkopf (Ed.), *Advances in Neural Information Processing Systems 16: Proceedings of the 17th Annual Conference on Neural Information Processing Systems (NIPS 2003) - Vancouver and Whistler, BC, Canada, December 8-13, 2003*. Cambridge, MA, USA: MIT Press.

Taylor, J. (2011). *Decision Management Systems: A Practical Guide to Using Business Rules and Predictive*. Upper Saddle River, NJ, USA: Pearson Education.

Thelwall, M. (2008). Social networks, gender, and friending: An analysis of MySpace member profiles. *Journal of the American Society for Information Science and Technology, 59*(8), 1321–1330. doi:10.1002/asi.20835

Thom, D., Bosch, H., Koch, S., Worner, M., & Ertl, T. (2012). Spatiotemporal anomaly detection through visual analysis of geolocated Twitter messages. In H. Hauser, S. G. Kobourov, & H. Qu (Ed.), *Proceedings of the 2012 IEEE Pacific Visualization Symposium (PacificVis 2012) - Songdo, South Korea, February 28 - March 2, 2012* (pp. 41-48). Piscataway, NJ. USA: IEEE Press. doi:10.1109/PacificVis.2012.6183572

Thomas, J., & Kielman, J. (2009). Challenges for Visual Analytics. *Information Visualization, 8*(4), 309–314. doi:10.1057/ivs.2009.26

Tsai, W. (2002). Social Structure of "Coopetition" Within a Multiunit Organization: Coordination, Competition, and Intraorganizational Knowledge Sharing. *Organization Science, 13*(2), 179–190. doi:10.1287/orsc.13.2.179.536

Tumasjan, A., Sprenger, T. O., Sandner, P. G., & Welpe, I. M. (2010). Predicting Elections with Twitter: What 140 Characters Reveal about Political Sentiment. In W. W. Cohen, & S. Gosling (Ed.), *Proceedings of the 4th International Conference on Weblogs and Social Media (ICWSM 2010)* (pp. 178-185). Menlo Park, CA, USA: AAAI Press.

Tylenda, T., Angelova, R., & Bedathur, S. J. (2009). Towards time-aware link prediction in evolving social networks. In C. L. Giles, P. Mitra, I. Perisic, J. Yen, & H. Zhang (Ed.), *Proceedings of the 3rd Workshop on Social Network Mining and Analysis (SNAKDD 2009), 15th ACM SIGKDD International Conference on Knowledge Discovery and Data Mining (KDD 2009) - Paris, France, June 28, 2009* (p. 9). New York, NY, USA: ACM Press. doi:10.1145/1731011.1731020

Van Hentenryck, P. (2013). Computational Disaster Management. In F. Rossi (Ed.), *Proceedings of the 23rd International Joint Conference on Artificial Intelligence (IJCAI 2013) - Beijing, China, August 3-9, 2013*. Menlo Park, CA, USA: AAAI Press / International Joint Conferences on Artificial Intelligence.

Wakita, K., & Tsurumi, T. (2007). Finding community structure in mega-scale social networks: [extended abstract]. In C. L. Williamson, M. E. Zurko, P. F. Patel-Schneider, & P. J. Shenoy (Ed.), *Proceedings of the 16th International World Wide Web Conference (WWW 2007) - Banff, AB, Canada, May 8-12, 2007* (pp. 1275-1276). New York, NY, USA: ACM Press. doi:10.1145/1242572.1242805

Wang, X., & Sukthankar, G. (2013). Multi-label classification by mining label and instance correlations from heterogeneous information networks. In I. S. Dhillon, Y. Koren, R. Ghani, T. E. Senator, P. Bradley, R. Parekh, . . . R. Uthurusamy (Ed.), *Proceedings of the 19th ACM SIGKDD International Conference on Knowledge Discovery and Data Mining (KDD 2013) - Chicago, IL, USA, August 11-14, 2013* (pp. 464-472). New York, NY, USA: ACM Press. doi:10.1145/2487575.2487577

Wang, Y., & Vassileva, J. (2007). A Review on Trust and Reputation for Web Service Selection. *Proceedings of the 27th International Conference on Distributed Computing Systems Workshops (ICDCSW 2007) - Toronto, Ontario, Canada, June 25-29, 2007* (p. 25). Los Alamitos, CA, USA: IEEE Computer Society. doi:10.1109/ICDCSW.2007.16

Washio, T., & Motoda, H. (2003). State of the art of graph-based data mining. *ACM SIGKDD Explorations Newsletter, 5*(1), 59–68. doi:10.1145/959242.959249

Wenger, G. C. (1997). Social networks and the prediction of elderly people at risk. *Aging & Mental Health, 1*(4), 311–320. doi:10.1080/13607869757001

Weninger, T., Bisk, Y., & Han, J. (2012). Document-topic hierarchies from document graphs. In X.-W. Chen, G. Lebanon, H. Wang, & M. J. Zaki (Ed.), *Proceedings of the 21st ACM International Conference on Information and Knowledge Management (CIKM 2012)* (pp. 635-644). New York, NY, USA: ACM Press.

Wex, F. (2013). *Coordination Strategies and Predictive Analytics in Crisis Management. Albert-Ludwigs-Universität Freiburg im Breisgau, Department of Economic Behavior and Sciences (Wirtschafts- und Verhaltenswissenschaftlichen Fakultät)*. Breisgau, Germany: University of Freiburg.

Woods, W. A. (1975). What's in a Link: Foundations for Semantic Networks. In D. G. Bobrow, & A. Collins (Eds.), *Representation and Understanding: Studies in Cognitive Science (Language, Thought & Culture)* (pp. 35-82). New York, NY, USA: Academic Press. Retrieved March 9, 2009, from http://oai.dtic.mil/oai/oai?verb=getRecord&metadataPrefix=html&identifier=ADA022584

Wu, H., Sorathia, V., & Prasanna, V. (2012). Predict Whom One Will Follow: Followee Recommendation in Microblogs. In K. Aberer, A. Flache, W. Jager, L. Liu, J. Tang, & C. Guéret (Ed.), *Proceedings of the 4th International Conference on Social Informatics (SocInfo 2012) - Lausanne, Switzerland, December 5-7, 2012* (pp. 260-264). New York, NY, USA: Springer. doi:10.1109/SocialInformatics.2012.74

Wu, S., Hofman, J. M., Mason, W. A., & Watts, D. J. (2011). Who says what to whom on twitter. In S. Srinivasan, K. Ramamritham, A. Kumar, M. P. Ravindra, E. Bertino, & R. Kumar (Ed.), *Proceedings of the 20th International World Wide Web Conference (WWW 2011) - Hyderabad, India, March 28 - April 1, 2011* (pp. 705-714). New York, NY, USA: ACM Press. doi:10.1145/1963405.1963504

Yan, X., & Han, J. (2002). gSpan: Graph-Based Substructure Pattern Mining. *Proceedings of the 2nd IEEE International Conference on Data Mining (ICDM 2002)* (pp. 721-724). Los Alamitos, CA, USA: IEEE Computer Society.

Yan, X., & Han, J. (2003). CloseGraph: Mining Closed Frequent Graph Patterns. In L. Getoor, T. E. Senator, P. Domingos, & C. Faloutsos (Ed.), *Proceedings of the 9th ACM SIGKDD International Conference on Knowledge Discovery and Data Mining (KDD 2003)* (pp. 286-295). New York, NY, USA: ACM Press.

Yang, Q., & Wu, X. (2006). 10 challenging problems in data mining. *International Journal of Information Technology & Decision Making, 5*(4), 597–604. doi:10.1142/S0219622006002258

Yu, P. S., Han, J., & Faloutsos, C. (2010). *Link Mining: Models, Algorithms, and Applications*. New York, NY, USA: Springer. doi:10.1007/978-1-4419-6515-8

Yu, X., Gu, Q., Zhou, M., & Han, J. (2012). Citation Prediction in Heterogeneous Bibliographic Networks. *Proceedings of the 12th SIAM International Conference on Data Mining (SDM 2012) - Anaheim, California, USA, April 26-28, 2012* (pp. 1119-1130). Philadelphia, PA, USA: SIAM Press.

Yu, X., Ren, X., Gu, Q., Sun, Y., & Han, J. (2013). Collaborative Filtering with Entity Similarity Regularization in Heterogeneous Information Networks. In W. H. Hsu, S. Kallumadi, & Y. Sun (Ed.), *Working notes of the 2nd International Workshop on Heterogeneous Information Network Analysis (HINA 2013). Workshop W36, 23rd International Joint Conference on Artificial Intelligence (IJCAI 2013) - Beijing, China, August 5, 2013.*

Zaraté, P. (2012). *Integrated and Strategic Advancements in Decision Making Support Systems*. Hershey, PA, USA: IGI Global. doi:10.4018/978-1-4666-1746-9

Zhang, J. HI, W. C., Lee, B. S., Lee, K. K., Vassileva, J., & Looi, C. K. (2010). A Framework of User-Driven Data Analytics in the Cloud for Course Management. In S. L. Wong, S. C. Kong, & F. -Y. Yu (Ed.), *Proceedings of the 18th International Conference on Computers in Education (ICCE 2010): Enhancing and Sustaining New Knowledge through the Use of Digital Technology in Education - Putrajaya, Malaysia, November 29 - December 3, 2010* (pp. 698-702). Jhongli City, Taiwan: Asia-Pacific Society For Computers in Education.

Zhao, X. (2012). Scorecard with Latent Factor Models for User Follow Prediction Problem. In B. Dalessandro, C. Perlich, G. Sun, & A. Yue (Ed.), *Proceedings of the KDD Cup 2012 Workshop, 18th ACM SIGKDD International Conference on Knowledge Discovery and Data Mining (KDD 2012) - Beijing, China, August 12-16, 2012. Track 1, 3rd Place.* San Francisco, CA, USA: Kaggle. Retrieved March 9, 2014, from https://kaggle2.blob.core.windows.net/competitions/kddcup2012/2748/media/FICO.pdf

Zheng, T., Salganik, M. J., & Gelman, A. (2006). How Many People Do You Know in Prison? Using Overdispersion in Count Data to Estimate Social Structure in Networks. *Journal of the American Statistical Association, 101*(474), 409–423. doi:10.1198/016214505000001168

Zhou, D., Councill, I. G., Zha, H., & Giles, C. L. (2007). Discovering Temporal Communities from Social Network Documents. *Proceedings of the 7th IEEE International Conference on Data Mining (ICDM 2007) - Omaha, NE, USA, October 28-31, 2007* (pp. 745-750). Los Alamitos, CA, USA: IEEE Computer Society.

Žliobaitė, I. (2009). *Learning under Concept Drift: an Overview.* Vilnius University, Faculty of Mathematics and Informatics. Ithaca, NY, USA: Cornell University Library. Retrieved March 9, 2014, from http://arxiv.org/abs/1010.4784

Zolfaghar, K., & Aghaie, A. (2011). Evolution of trust networks in social web applications using supervised learning. (A. Karahoca, & S. Kanbul, Eds.) *Procedia Computer Science: World Conference on Information Technology - Istanbul, Turkey, October 6–10, 2010, 3,* 833-839.

This research was previously published in Emerging Methods in Predictive Analytics edited by William H. Hsu, pages 297-333, copyright year 2014 by Information Science Reference (an imprint of IGI Global).

Chapter 43
The Effectiveness of Big Data in Social Networks

Khine Khine Nyunt
University of Wollongong, Singapore

Noor Zaman
King Faisal University, Saudi Arabia

ABSTRACT

In this chapter, we will discuss how "big data" is effective in "Social Networks" which will bring huge opportunities but difficulties though challenges yet ahead to the communities. Firstly, Social Media is a strategy for broadcasting, while Social Networking is a tool and a utility for connecting with others. For this perspective, we will introduce the characteristic and fundamental models of social networks and discuss the existing security & privacy for the user awareness of social networks in part I. Secondly, the technological built web based internet application of social media with Web2.0 application have transformed users to allow creation and exchange of user-generated content which play a role in big data of unstructured contents as well as structured contents. Subsequently, we will introduce the characteristic and landscaping of the big data in part II. Finally, we will discuss the algorithms for marketing and social media mining which play a role how big data fit into the social media data.

PART I: SOCIAL NETWORKS ANALYSIS

Social Networks

Social Networks is a social structure which involves different subjects of any interested topics internationally whereby at least a group of two people interactively exchange. It is in an open space where it gives to post like a common forum for representatives of anthropology, sociology, history, social psychology, political science, human geography, biology, economics, communications science and other disciplines who are share with an interest in the study of the empirical structure of social relations and associations that may be expressed in network form.

DOI: 10.4018/978-1-5225-5637-4.ch043

The behind abstract concept was based on discrete mathematics using graph theory to construct the pairwise structure relation model between them comprising nodes which is starting point in social networks. Most social network services are web-based internet applications and provide users to interact over the Internet with exchanging interested information, such as including e-mail and instant messaging, chatting, mobile connectivity, photo & video sharing and blogging. Social networks allow to users to post unstructured social contents to share ideas, pictures, posts, activities, events, and interests with people in their network. In this session, we will discuss the issues of characteristic, model, security & privacy, demographic and analysis on social networks.

1.1 Characterization

Online social networks are based on users while web pages are based on contents. Users of social networking sites form a social network, which provides a powerful means of sharing, organizing, and finding content and contacts. The researchers found three main points (Mislove, Marcon, Gummadi, Druschel, & Bhattacharjee, 2007) – 1) the degree of distributions in social networks follow a power-law and the coefficients for both in-degree and out-degree are similar so that nodes with high in-degree also tend to have high out-degree. 2) Social networks appear to be composed of a large number of highly connected clusters consisting of relatively low degree nodes so that the clustering coefficient is inversely proportional to node degree. 3) The networks each contain a large, densely connected core. As a result, path lengths are short, but almost all shortest paths of sufficient length traverse the highly connected core.

Based on the research, we conclude that the "nodes" or the relation between members of the network are those users who established the number of "friends" within the online network, establishing themselves as many as friendship and as close to the "core" of that social network as possible. This means that the closer to the core of a social network that you are, the faster you're able to propagate information out to a wider segment of the network. This is exactly the kind of opportunity that most marketers look for. Furthermore, we will discuss the some core characteristics of social networks:

1. **Interactive User Based:** Unlike the websites which based on content that was updated by one user and read by Internet visitors, social networks like Facebook, Twitter, LinkedIn etc. are so interactive timely. User can create the account themselves, populate the network with conversations and content and fill with network-based online gaming application. Moreover, social media services have openness for feedback and participation. They encourage voting, comments and the sharing of information. This is what make social networks so much more exciting and dynamic for Internet users.

2. **Community:** Social media allows communities to form quickly and communicate effectively. Communities share common interests, beliefs or hobbies such as a love of photography, a political issue. Social Media allow not only to discover new friends within these within these interest based communities, but you can also reconnect with old friends that you lost contact with many years ago.

3. **Emotion:** The social networks provide not only the information but also allow the users with emotional sense that no matter what happens, can easily reach to their friends so that friends can instantly communicate over any of crises or issue and give support or suggestion on the current situation. Beyond the characteristics, Social Networks can generate social influence among the users by changing thought and actions by actions of others. There can be the companionship by

sharing information or other activities among the user. Another function is Social Support as aid and assistant exchanged through social relationship and interpersonal transactions.

1.2 Social Networks Modeling

Nowadays, there are many applications for social network analysis or graph theory comes out from many academic department like mathematics, computer science and physics for studies of online social networks such as Facebook, Twitter or Google+. By definition a network is a structure of nodes which are connected by edges. In Social Networks, the nodes as representing people and edges as representing relationships and the nodes can be assigned attributes which could be demographic information about the individual.

In this section we will discuss very fundamental networks model which are applied in Social Networks. Modeling social networks serves at least two purposes. First, it helps us understand how social networks form and evolve. Secondly, in studying network-dependent social processes by simulation, such as diffusion or retrieval of information, successful network models can be used for specifying the structure of interaction. (Toivonena, et al., 2009)

a. Erdos-Renyi Model or Bernoulli Random Graph

Erdos-Renyi model is the simplest underlying distribution model and also known as a Bernoulli Random Graph or Bernoulli Network. By Definition, the model G(n,p) assumes that it is a random graph which have n nodes and for every pair of nodes (i,j), with probability p ($0 \leq p \leq 1$) an edge exists between the two nodes.

This random graph model can find the application of Analysis of Social Network of all kinds. For example, one person who is a Facebook user u can form a graph of network of friends $N(u)$, where nodes are people and two people are connected by an edge if they are mutual friends, call this particular user's friendship neighborhood. It resembles a random graph which is the structure of small networks of friends. This says that most people in the average user's immediate friendship neighborhood are essentially the same and essentially random in their friendships among the friends of u.

b. Clustering

Even though the Erdos-Renyi model is the very fundamental of modeling network formation, there is some lacking characteristics in social and economic networks. The main issue is that the presence of link tends to be correlated. For example, we consider the triple of nodes and two of them are each connected to the third one. So the consideration is those two nodes (first and second) are linked to each other. This concept lead to be much larger in social network. For instance, social networks tend to exhibit significant clustering which is a collection of individuals with dense friendship patterns internally and sparse friendships externally. This has led to a series of richer random graph-based models of networks.

- **Markov Graphs:** (Frank & Strauss, 1986) generalized the Bernoulli random graphs and identified a class of random graphs which they called Markov graphs. Their finding was a link forms to be dependent on whether neighboring link are formed or not. It means making one link dependent on a second, and the second on the third, can imply some interdependencies between the first and third. These sorts of dependencies are difficult to analyze but statistical estimation of networks.

- **Small World Network:** Another variation on a Bernoulli network was explored by (Watts & Strogatz, 1998). The model demonstrates how to construct a tractable family of toy networks that can simultaneously have significant clustering and small geodesic distances. The famous feature of this model is possession of large range of P (0<=P<=1) that produces small-world graphs with significant clustering (Scholarpedia.org, 2012). They started with a very structured network that exhibits a high degree of clustering. Then by randomly rewiring enough links, one ends up with a network that has a small average distance between links but still has substantial clustering. This rewiring process widely used in Social Networks.
- **Exponential Random Graph Models:** Exponential random graph models (ERGMs), also called p∗ models, constitute a family of statistical models for social networks. These models take the form of a probability distribution of graphs:

$$\Pr\left(X = x\right) = (1 / k)\exp\left\{\eta'g\right\}$$

for a set of tie indicator valuables X on a network of fixed note size n, where x is a realization, with a parameter vector η and a vector of network statistics g. Each value of the parameter vector corresponds to a probability distribution on the set of all graphs with n nodes. (Robins, 2009)

There are some basic theoretical assumptions about social networks which are main reason for using ERGM. (Lusher, Koskinen & Robins, 2013)

1. Social networks are locally emergent which permits instant transmission of messages direct to followers.
2. Network ties not only self-organize but they are also influenced by actor attributes and other exogenous factors.
3. The patterns within networks can be seen as evidence for ongoing structural processes.
4. Multiple processes can operate simultaneously.
5. Social networks are structured, yet stochastic.

1.3 Security and Privacy

Popularity of social networking sites such as Facebook and Twitter have gained large user base, and large amount of information in recent year. On the other hand, many attackers exploit different way of attack on social networking sites. Many social networking sites try to prevent those exploitations, but still not overcome yet. In this section, we will discuss the more issues on Privacy, Identity theft, spam and malware which are the threats that social network users may not be aware.

a. Privacy Issues

Privacy issue is one of the main concerns, since many social network user are not careful about what they expose on their social network space. Social networking sites are a powerful and fun way to communicate with the world and they are vary in the level of security and privacy offered. The basic contents of security information is called profile which is provided by users however the large volume and accessibility of profile information are available on social networking sites which is attracted to whom are seeking to exploit the information. This becomes profile information security concern. There can be stealing the profile credentials information using some technologies that invite users to persuade malicious programs with the intention of malware activities. Social networking sites are fundamentally providing privacy concern however most of social networking site guideline are not enough for any intruders. The potential privacy breach is actually real concerned into the systematic framework of social media sites. Unfortunately, the flaws render social media system to almost indefensible. Privacy concern has been alerted over a number of profile incidents which has considered embarrassing for users. It has created a wide range of online interpersonal victimization. Sources of users' profile and personal information leakage are as below;

- **Poor Privacy Settings:** Most social network users are not aware about their privacy settings who can access online which their profile is public. Also, many social networking sites default privacy setting is still not safe, even the safest privacy setting, there are still flaws that allow attackers to access user's information.
- **Leakage of Information to Third Party Application:** These third party applications are very popular among social network users. Once users add and allow third party applications to access their information, these applications can access user's data automatically. It is also capable of posting on users' space or user's friend's space, or may access other user's information without user's knowledge (Krishnamurthy & Will, 2008).
- **Leakage of Information to Third Party Domain:** The use of third party domain in many social networking websites to track social network user's activities, or allows advertisement partner to access and aggregate social network user's data for their commercial benefit (Krishnamurthy & Will, 2008).

b. Identity Theft

The second issue is identity theft, attackers make use of social networks account to steal victim's identities. Profile cloning is one of the most famous identity theft and there are couple of different method to be clone the profile. The first method is that the attackers create a profile and sending a friend request to those who targeted. Social network user are not careful when accept friend request. This is one of the method that attackers take advantage of trust among friends. The second method is eyeing on the profile those are public online. So attackers can easily duplicate the information of the user. The third method is that attackers steal user's profile from one social networking site and use that information to register an account in another social network site. The last method is social phishing. The attackers provide a fake website which is very authentic and users are providing personal information.

c. Spam Issues

The third is the spam issue which attackers make use of social networks to increase spam click through rate, which is more effective than the traditional email spam. According to Nexgate, social media brand protection and compliance, social media spam has risen 355% on a typical social media account in the first half of 2013 (Nexgate, 2013). There are two types of spam in social network which are "Link Spam" and "Text Spam".

- **Link Spam:** It will appear as a single link with no surrounding text. If user click on the link, it route to the spammer's website which contain ads. This spamdexing process helps to increase the website rank in search result. Other method is to put a short phrase accompanying the link to attract the user that promises easy money, pills, porn, etc. Another method of remaining mysterious or vague is to shorten the link altogether without revealing where the link is pointing. This links can also automatically send similarly spammy links to all of the user's contacts.
- **Text Spam:** Spammers try to engage text through private message box or chat box to the user for telling fake story which is to distribute the message to as many people as possible or something horrible will happen. Some message can be like donation such as cancer or other needy issues to share a link. There may be the request to send money to the original sender. Some message are promise easy money like "work from home" schemes. The spammer typically extorts money from the victim by charging a fee to join the program. Text spam is more on phishing attack which allow the perpetrator to gather identification information from the victim, which may then be used to gain access to other accounts, such as bank accounts.

d. Malware Issue

The forth is the malware issue which is widely used by attackers use to spread malware very speedy through connectivity among users. Social networking sites are always facing new kind of malware and cannot determine whether URLs or embedded links are malicious or not.

There are many possible ways that attackers can spread malware among the social networks. Fake Account is one of the method for attacker to easily connect with social network users to view their profile. For example, attacker can create fake profile as a celebrity that attracts victims to contact them. Second method is using APT (Application Programming Interface) third party application for leakage of user's personal information. This application seems to be good but some malicious link hide inside and takes users to malicious domain and spread malware to users. Third method is that attacker uses advertisement as a medium to spread malware across social networks. When users click on ads, it will be redirected to the malicious websites and ask user to download malicious cod such as Java or Active X content to their browser. This is the way malware will be infected user's computer. The fourth method is "Clickjacking". When user click on the item such as video, link or photo, the hidden code will be triggered to perform malicious action. Some of the worst case is, user has asked to input their particular when user click on the video or link or page. The last method to discuss here is Cross-site scripting (XSS) attacks which are type of injection. Attackers can use XSS to send a malicious script to user which can access cookies, session tokens or other sensitive information.

For example, *Koobface* is a worm that can spread social networking websites and email websites. Upon successful infection, it can gather login information for sites like Facebook, Myspace, Skype and so on. For example in Facebook, the message with video link can be spread to user who are friend of a Facebook user whose computer had already been infected. Upon receipt, it can be routed to a third party website and ask user to download the Adobe Flash player. If user download and execute the file, Koobface can easily infect user's system and attacker can easily steal the user's information.

Social networking media should aware of new age spammers and attackers in this technology age. Social networking media should truly investigate the new age spammers and their technique and empower the media security with automated detection, classification and removal of spam, malicious and inappropriate content across all major social media platforms.

1.4 Analysis

Based on the research data between 2012 and 2013 from Pew research center, 42% of online adults use multiple social networking sites, but Facebook remains the platform of choice. 71% of online user are in Facebook so that Facebook remains the dominant social networking platform. (Pewinternet, 2013) Currently, Pinterest and Instagram get popular among younger adults. Pinterest is a social bookmarking site where users collect and share photos of their favorite events, interests and hobbies. Instagram is an online mobile photo and video sharing social networking sites and allow to share digital media to other social networking sites like Facebook and Twitter. LinkedIn is business oriented social networking service and mainly use for professional networking.

In our analysis, we are indicating comparison chart for Facebook vs Twitter based on the distinct differences which gather from the variety of internet sources.

Facebook and Twitter, both are basically Social Networking Services lunched in February, 2004 and July, 2006 respectively. Currently, Facebook has 1.28 billion as of March 2014 and Twitter has over 500 million users. *We can say that Facebook still remains the dominant social networking platform. Here we have couple of analysis based on the both services.*

- **Features:** Facebook features include Friends, Fans, Wall, News Feed, Fan Pages, Groups, Apps, Live Chat, Likes, Photos, Videos, Text, Polls, Links, Status, Pokes, Gifts, Games, Messaging, Classified section, upload and download options etc. while Twitter has Tweet, Retweet, Direct Messaging, Follow People & Trending Topics, Links, Photos and Videos. Based on the features,

Table 1. The comparison chart for Facebook vs Twitter

Description	Facebook	Twitter
Launch date	February 4, 2004	July 6, 2006
Number of users	1.28 billion (monthly active, March 2014)	Over 500 million
Languages	Available in 70 languages	Available in 29 languages
Users express approval of content by	"Like" or "Share"	"Retweet" or "Favorite"
Privacy settings	Can use different settings for various groups	Either public or private
Post length	Unlimited	140 characters
Users express opinions of content by	"Comment" or "Reply"	"Reply"
Edit posts	Yes	No
Add friends	Yes	No
Instant messaging	Yes	No
Follow trending topics	No	Yes

we can say that Facebook has more features to attract users. Some of the features can do both services like post updates, share links, private messages, upload photos and follow people. Some differences like language availability which is 70 languages available in Facebook and only 29 languages in Twitter. Moreover, Facebook allow unlimited length for post while twitter allow to tweet with 140 characters. Facebook allow friends to comment on the post and edit after post but twitter doesn't allow either. Facebook has a good feature to add friends but Twitter doesn't have "add friend" feature as well as no instant messaging allow.

- **Privacy:** When comes to this privacy point, Facebook has various privacy setting for user choices which allows users to set privacy settings independently. Users can be able to select their profile as public (visible everyone) or not even searchable except by acknowledged friends. Additionally, users can set any privacy setting on individual post or upload photos and other sharing link as public, friends or custom. Furthermore, users can control their timeline and tagging as individual can view whether hide or allow the post before public. Twitter has two privacy settings which are public and private. Private messages is only for the people who follow the user. User are also allow to select "Protect my Tweets" feature. And Twitter also have option to choose for photo tagging but there is no review feature like Facebook.

- **Communication:** All connection must be mutual in Facebook. Facebook allow individuals to share their interest to friends such as posting messages on the wall, upload photos and video as instant messages, share link, write long notes, send private message to friends, instant chat and even playing game together as well as friends are allow give comment on posting of their view. So from communication point of view, if many people interact with your post via likes, comments and share, it's possible for your post to have a longer news feed shelf life and if your community share your post, there's a higher probability by seeing people who aren't not in your friend list. In contrast, connection can be one way or two way in Twitter. You can make friend as much as you can by using follow features without knowing each other. It seems more active in the way of social communication. You should choose Twitter, if you have a lot of content to share and plan to be proactive in your interaction with other accounts. But the limitation is that Twitter allows users to tweet with 140 character messages and other users can follow these messages on their twitter feed. It is main feature to communicate with other individual who has similar interest. Moreover, depending on how many people you follow, a tweet can literally stay in your feed for mere seconds unless you retweets your post.Twitter is basically centered on real-time conversation, while Facebook is more of an ongoing conversation that people get to eventually.

- **Advertising:** Based on research report by resolution (Resolution, 2014), advertiser spend much more with Facebook but Twitter perform better. Of course, most advertiser would eyeing on the number of users so that Face book is the great place of social networking to advertise. But Facebook ads is much more complex than Twitter. In the Facebook ads, you have to identify your marketing objective first. Facebook will guide you to the most appropriate type. Then you have to decide target people by location, age, gender, interest, language, education, etc. You can also target the friends of people who already like page or app. lastly, there is a budget which will allow you to space out your ads over a broader timeframe. You can either pay for specific action or per thousand impressions. Price can be varied due to the competition in the demographic you are targeting. Then you can see which ads and images are performing the best through Facebook's analytics dashboard and it is final stage to advertise.

Twitter is simple. There is two categories: Promoted tweets which you want to advertise a specific message of product. Another one is Promoted Account which is suitable who goal is new followers. You need to pay only when you add new followers. You have two kinds of targeting. The first one is by keyword which will allow you to target who search or tweet with a specific term. The second one is by interest and followers who follow the specific accounts. For example, a skin care band might want to target users who follow accounts that tweet about anti-aging advice. There is a budget too. But it is different with Facebook that you can set lifetime and daily maximum budgets for your campaign. If you set promoted tweets, you set the amount you are willing to pay every time someone retweets, replies, favorites, follows or clicks on your tweet. If you set promoted account, you pay per follower.

PART II: BIG DATA

Big Data

"Big data is the term increasingly used to describe the process of applying serious computing power – the latest in machine learning and artificial intelligence – to seriously massive and often highly complex sets of information." (Microsoft enterprise insight, 2013). Big data is accepted both the structured and the unstructured data which go beyond relational database and traditional data warehousing platforms to incorporate technologies that are suited to processing and storing non transactional forms of data.

The fundamental challenge of Big Data is not collecting data. It is about - what is the starting point; what are the computation paths to discover; what are the appropriate algorithms; and How to visualize the findings. According to statistics published by IBM in 2011, the massive adoption of Facebook, Twitter and other social media services has resulted in the generation of about 2.5 quintillion bytes each day. (International Business Machine, 2011) Conducting big data analysis has a significant role in maximizing the utility of social media.

2.1 Characteristics

In recent year, we have heard of the 3Vs' of big data characteristic, Volume, Variety and Velocity. Now IBM scientists break big data into four dimension: 4V's of big data which getting attention on most notably of Veracity. (IBM, 2014).

- **Volume:** the scale of data which determines the value and whether it can actually be considered as big data or not. Social Media has many factors to increase the data volume such as unstructured data streaming or increase of sensor and machine to machine data being collected. Referring IBM, It is estimated that 2.5 quintillion bytes (2.3 Trillion gigabyte) of data are created each day and in coming 2020 it would be 40 Zettabytes (40Trillion gigabyte), an increase of 300 times from 2005
- **Velocity:** It is the speed of generation of data or how fast the data is generated and processed to meet the demands and challenges. It is all about data streaming in social media at exceptional speed.
- **Variety:** Variety refers to the many sources and types of data both structured and unstructured. Data in social media come in all types of formats. Having reference from IBM, as of 2011, the global size of data in healthcare was estimated to be 150 Exabyte (161 billion gigabytes). By 2014,

there will be 420 million wearable wireless health monitors, estimated four billions videos per hour on YouTube, 400 million tweets are sent per day and 30 billion pieces of content are shared on Facebook every month.

- **Veracity:** It is uncertainty of data. Social Media data flows can be highly unpredictable with periodic peaks. According to IBM analysis, one in three business leaders don't trust the information to make decision.

2.2 Infrastructure

Infrastructural technologies are the core of the Big Data. The main purpose is the process and store both structure and unstructured data. For many decades, enterprises relied on relational databases which are the collections of data in a form of rows and column in a table for structured data. In this technology aged, new form of unstructured data which comes from sensors, devices, video/audio, networks, log files, transactional applications, web, and social media - much of it generated in real time and in a very large scale which is meant that data capture had to move beyond merely rows and columns in tables. As a result, new infrastructural technologies emerged, capable of wrangling a vast variety of data, and making it possible to run applications on systems with thousands of nodes, potentially involving thousands of terabytes of data.

By literature review, here we are presenting some key infrastructural technology:

- **Hadoop:** Hadoop is one of the popular java open-source programming framework that support the processing of large data sets in a distributed computing environment. Hadoop implements a data-crawling strategy over massively scaled-out, share-nothing data partitions where various nodes in the system are able to perform different parts of a query on different parts of the data simultaneously (Maltby, 2011). This works very well for big data and it can run applications on systems with thousands of nodes involving thousands of terabytes. Hadoop's distributed file system facilitates rapid data transfer rates among nodes and allows the system to continue operating uninterrupted in case of a node failure. This approach lowers the risk of catastrophic system failure, even if a significant number of nodes become inoperative (Kakade & Chavan, 2014). Hadoop is used by Google, Yahoo and IBM for search engines and advertising. The preferred operating systems for Hadoop are Windows, Linux, BSD (Berkeley Software Distribution) and OS X which is Unix- based graphical interface operating systems developed and marketed by Apple Inc.
- **NoSQL Databases:** It stands for Not Only SQL, represents the new class of data management technologies which involved in processing large volume of structured, semi-structured and unstructured data. They scale very well as agile sprints, quick iteration and frequent code pushes. Moreover, NoSQL databases are flexible and easy to use object-oriented programming. And they use efficient scale-out architecture instead of expensive monolithic architecture. But Most of the early NoSQL systems did not attempt to provide ACID which is atomicity, consistency, isolation and durability guarantees, contrary to the prevailing practice among relational database systems. NoSQL databases are typically used in big data and real time web application. Some NoSQL databases, like HBase, can work concurrently with Hadoop.
- **Massively Parallel Processing (MPP) Databases:** Data is partitioned across multiple servers or nodes and queries are processed via network interconnect on central server and running parallel. MPP databases provide ACID (Atomicity, Consistency, Isolation and Durability) compliance as

well as include cost based optimizers and monitor the distribution of data within the system. In general, MPP is more efficient than Hadoop. Based on the literature review, we conclude some comparison between Hadoop and MPP. 1) Hadoop expand existing programming technology into large scale processing while MPP expand existing database technology into large scale processing. 2) Hadoop is designed to run on any hardware, cheaper cluster of commodity server while MPP run on expensive specialize software. 3) Hadoop is open source community while MPP is invented by Teradata, Netezza, GreenPlum, Vertica, ParAccel, etc. 4) Hadoop uses Java while MPP use SQL.

2.3 Analytics

Big data analytics is the process of examining large amount of data (big data), in an effort to uncover hidden patterns, unknown correlations and other useful information (Shang et.al, 2013). Major goal of big data analytics is to help data scientists and others who analyse huge volumes of transaction data and other source of data that conventional analytics and business intelligence solutions can't touch. High performance of analytics is necessary to process that much data and the result analysis can provide competitive advantages in business benefit for more effective marketing strategy and increased revenue for organization.

Big data accepted both structured and unstructured data which comes from sensors, devices, video/audio, networks, log files, transactional applications, web, and social media - much of it generated in real time and in a very large scale. Big data analytic can be done by software which commonly used an advanced analytic disciplines such as predictive analytics, data mining, text mining, forecasting and optimization. But unstructured data may not be fit in traditional data warehouses. As a result, a new paradigm shift of big data technology has emerged with traditional one in big data analytics environments. The new technology such as NoSQL database, Hadoop and Hadoop MapReduce which are the open source software framework that can process large data sets.

By literature review, there are variety of techniques has been developed and adapted to visualize, analyse, manipulate and aggregate big data. Here we are presenting some techniques for big data analytic:

- **Data Mining:** is an analytic process designed to explore data (usually large amounts of data - typically business or market related - also known as "big data") in search of consistent patterns and/or systematic relationships between variables, and then to validate the findings by applying the detected patterns to new subsets of data. The ultimate goal of data mining is prediction and predictive data mining is the most common type of data mining and one that has the most direct business applications. (Kaur & Paul, 2014)
- **Cluster Analysis:** Cluster analysis is used for classifying objects that splits a diverse group into smaller groups of similar objects.
- **Crowdsourcing:** A technique for collecting data submitted by a large group of people or community (i.e., the "crowd") through an open call, usually through networked media such as the Web. This is a type of mass collaboration and an instance of using Web 2.0.
- **Association Rule Learning:** A way of finding relationships among variables. It is often used in data mining and these techniques consists of a variety of algorithms to generate and test possible rules.

- **Machine Learning:** A subspecialty of computer science (within a field historically called "artificial intelligence") concerned with the design and development of algorithms that allow computers to evolve behaviors based on empirical data. A major focus of machine learning research is to automatically learn to recognize complex patterns and make intelligent decisions based on data. Natural language processing is an example of machine learning.
- **Visualization:** It is used for creating images, diagrams, or animations to communicate, understand, and improve the results of big data analyses.
- **Time Series Analysis:** A collection of observations of well-defined data items obtained through repeated measurements over time. Examples of time series analysis include the hourly value of a stock market index or the number of patients diagnosed with a given condition every day.

2.4 Application

Nowadays, many applications come up with big data technology in many industries. Enterprises can save money, grow revenue and achieve many other business objectives by using big data technology. Big Data allow company to build new applications, improve the effectiveness and lower cost of existing applications. Here we presented the some key type of applications and their characteristics and some example of commercial software in niche market.

- **Vertical Applications:** This type of application can define and built based on the user's specific requirements to achieve their business process and goal. Example: AutoGrid, ellucian, Knewton and etc.
- **Consumers:** This type of application uses central data warehouse for reporting, planning, trend-tracking, analysis and accounting for specific user needs. Example: Facebook, twitter, Google, Amazon, ebay, Linkedin and etc.
- **Operational Intelligence:** It is a form of real-time dynamic, business analytics that delivers visibility and insight into business operations. Example: AppDynamics, New Relic, Splunk, Sumo Logic and etc.
- **Data as a Service:** It is a cloud strategy used to facilitate the accessibility of business-critical data in a well-timed, protected and affordable manner. Example: DataSift, Factual, FICO, Gnip and etc.
- **Ad / Media Applications:** This type of application build in the digital media and fully integrated with marketing solutions. Example: DataXu, LuckySort, Media Science, MetaMarkets and etc.
- **Business Intelligence:** BI is a transformation software that from raw data to meaningful and useful information for business analysis purpose. Example: IBM Cognos, MicroStrategy, Oracle Hyperion, SAP Business Objects, and etc.
- **Analytics and Visualization:** This type of application is ability to derive actionable information to help business competition and growth. It provides data driven strategies to share, innovate and deliver very quickly and easily real-time information. Example: 1010Data, Opera, SAS, Teradata Aster, TIBCO Spotfire and etc.

PART III: ALGORITHMS AROUND SOCIAL NETWORKS

Algorithms around Social Networks

Nowadays, popular sites like Facebook, Instagram, Twitter, and Pinterest create massive quantities of data and they need a very large scale applications to process the customer's perspective in a fastest way. And the data in Social Media are both structured and unstructured. So the task of capturing, processing and managing data is beyond the traditional scale of most common software. Now, Big Data fits into this picture to manage unstructured data. It is in a trends that many Big Data applications have been introduced algorithms specifically to make sense of social media data. So we need to look into the important of social media algorithms. Among the algorithms we are presented in this paper for Marketing and Social Media Mining.

3.1 Social Media Algorithm for Marketing

As marketing becomes increasingly digitized, it is important for businesses to remain in competitive edge. So enterprise are finding new way to retain their customers. Social Media is a good platform to advertise in technology age by leveraging big data, social media sites and mobile experiences with marketing algorithms which are playing a big role in these trends.

Here we will discuss with example of giant media Facebook and Twitter.

In Facebook, the content which shows up in a user's News Feed is dictated by an algorithm which determine on post-by-post basis whether a post is qualified to pass into a user's News Feed. Facebook used an algorithm – named EdgeRank. There are three ways to measure EdgeRank: Affinity Score, Edge Weight and Time decay. (EdgeRank, 2014)

- **Affinity Score:** Means how "connected" a particular user is to the Edge. For example, if I write frequently on my friend's wall and we have 100 mutual friends. So my affinity score with my friend is very high. So Facebook knows I will probably want to see his status updates.
- **Edge Weight:** Each category of edges has a different default weight. In plain English, this means that comments are worth more than likes.
- **Time Decay:** How old the story is, it loses points because it consider old news. Every time, when you log into Facebook, you will see the stories with the highest EdgeRank in your News Feed.

For marketing, how a marketer can increase EdgeRank. First, you encourage user to visit your page frequently, "like" your page and write on your page wall so that user's friends can see your brand information and your band will be promoting among the user's friends. Second, you encourage user for sharing and commenting on your post so that your brand affinity score will be high. Third, keep your post on regular schedule so that users can see your brand information whenever they log into Facebook at any time.

In Twitter, the service that enables users to send and read short 140 character text messages, called "tweets". Another feature is "Trending topics" on Twitter, it shows the most popular conversation topics to user. Trends are determined by an algorithm that looks through all tweets on Twitter. This algorithm identifies topics that are immediately popular, rather than topics that have been popular for a while or on a daily basis, to help you discover the hottest emerging topics of discussion on Twitter that matter most to you. You can see "trends" whenever you go to your stream. You can see location based trends those are trending in the same geographic region or you can activate tailored trends for those who you follow.

Form marketing point of view, this is the point that how can we create trending topics. First method is that your post should require action. Based on how many people you follow or how many follower you have, your post will get more interactions and that will become a trending topics for your post. Second method is encourage retweets. It is a strong action because it is kind of a personal endorsement who retweeting your post. If the more people retweet, the more likely it to get trend.

Based on this two example, Facebook and Twitter, each platform is different. So we can conclude that understand the basic social media algorithms will help you to develop your online marketing and attracting the right audience.

3.2 Social Media Mining

Social Media Mining is the process of representing, analyzing, and extracting actionable patterns from social media data (Zafarani, Abbasi, & Liu, 2014). Social Media Mining introduces basic concepts and principal algorithms suitable for investigating massive social media data which is different from the traditional data.

Social Media Data is unstructured and large amount of volume in real time data. So new trend of computational data analysis approaches in social media combines social theories with statistical and data mining methods. In social media mining, we collect information about individuals and entities, measure their interactions, and discover patterns to understand human behavior (Zafarani et al., 2014). The task of mining in social media data is mining content with social relation which is generated by user. In this challenges in social media data, big data is playing the role to exploit the characteristics of social media and use its multidimensional, multisource, and multisite data to aggregate information with sufficient statistics for effective mining. Social Media Mining is a new interdisciplinary field in Social Media.

a. Data Mining in Social Media

Data Mining is the search for valuable information in large volumes of data. The process of discovering useful information from a collection of raw data is Knowledge Discovery in Databases (KDD). KDD process takes raw data as input and knowledge as output. In social media mining, the raw data is the content generated by individuals, and the knowledge encompasses the interesting patterns observed in this data (Zafarani et al., 2014). The standard KDD process is based on generic 5-steps model which developed by Fayyad et al. (Fayyad, Piatetsky-Shapiro, and Smyth, 1996).

Step 1: Data Selection and Extraction. Firstly, we have to decide what raw data is needed for the project goal and extract it from the data source to create a target data set. In social media mining, the raw data is the content generated by individuals, and the knowledge encompasses the interesting patterns observed in this data. We can collect this raw data from social media sits by using

APIs (Application Programming Interfaces). Data instances are represented in tabular format using features. These instances can be labeled or unlabeled. Data representation for text data can be performed using the vector space model.

Step 2: Data Preprocessing. Quality measures need to be completed before processing the data. Quality measures include removing redundancies or noisy data, detecting sources of errors and substituting missing values. Preprocessing techniques commonly performed are aggregation, discretization, feature selection, feature extraction and sampling.

Step 3: Transformation. It is about data reduction and projection. First, we have to fine useful features to represent the data depending on the goal of the task. Second, the effective number of variables under consideration can be reduced by dimensionality reduction or transformation methods.

Step 4: Data Mining. This process is to select the appropriate data mining algorithms for searching patterns. Based on our literature review, here we are presenting some data mining algorithms which are suit to social media mining which involve both structured and unstructured data. These are decision tree learning, naïve Bayes classifier (NBC), nearest neighbor classifier, classification with network information, regression and clustering algorithms.

Step 5: Evaluation or Interpretation. This step can also involve visualization of the extracted patterns and models or visualization of the data given the extracted models. After visualization, it is ready to act on the discovered knowledge and incorporate the discovered knowledge into another system for further action.

b. Community Detection

Community is formed by individuals such that those within a group interact with each other more frequently than with those outside the group (Tang & Liu, 2010). Community detection is discovering groups in a network where individuals' group memberships are not explicitly given (Tang & Liu, 2010).

In the social networking community, the issue of community detection in social media has been widely studied in the context of the structure of the underlying graphs. In community detection, data points represent actors in social media and similarity between these actors is often defined based on the interests these users share (Zafarani et al., 2014). The major difference between clustering and community detection is that in community detection, individuals are connected to others via a network of links, whereas in clustering, data points are not embedded in a network (Zafarani et al., 2014). In particular, graph based community detection techniques are used and many important extensions that handle dynamic, heterogeneous networks in social media.

Communities in social media are either explicit (groups) or implicit (individuals). The researcher introduced community detection algorithms which are member based community detection and group based detection algorithms (Zafarani et al., 2014).

- **Member Based Community Detection Method:** It is based on three general nodes characteristic: node degree (familiarity), node reachability and node similarity.
  - ○ **Node Degree:** The most common subgraph searched for in networks based on node degrees is a clique. Clique is a maximum complete subgraph in which all nodes are adjacent to each other. When using node degree, cliques are considered as communities. To find communities, we have to search for the maximum clique. To find maximum clique, Brute-force clique identification algorithm can be used theoretically. In practical, due to the computa-

tional complexity of clique identification, they added some constraints such that "Relaxing cliques" which comes from sociology with k-plex concept or "using cliques as a seed of a community" which is used by a well-known algorithm, Clique Percollation Method (CPM).

- **Node Reachability:** The subgraphs where nodes are reachable from other nodes via a path. There are two concern, the first concern is in theoretical way that there is a path between them (regardless of the distance). In this case any graph traversal algorithm such as **Breadth-First Search** (**BFS**) and **Depth-First Search** (**DFS**) can be used to identify connected components (communities). But researcher found that this is not a very useful in large social media networks. The second concern is practical way that they are so closed as to be immediate neighbors. In this case, finding cliques is very challenging process. Well-known method with roots in social science are three subgraphs: k-clique, k-club, and k-clan.
- **Node Similarity:** It is to determine the similarity between two nodes and similar nodes are assumed to be in same community. To compute node similarity, various normalization procedures such as the Jaccard similarity or the cosine similarity can be used.
- **Group-Based Community Detection:** In this section, researchers discussed communities that are balanced, robust, modular, dense or hierarchical based on their findings.
  - **Balanced Communities:** Is that one can employ spectral clustering which provides a relaxed solution to the normalized cut and ratio cut in graphs.
  - **Robust Communities:** Is search for subgraphs (example: K-edge, k-vertes) that are hard to disconnect.
  - **Modular Communities:** Is that modularity is a measure the community structure which is created at random. Modularity maximization method can be used to find modular communities.
  - **Dense Communities:** Which is particular interest in social media where we would like to have enough interactions for analysis to make statistical sense. Quasi-cliques method can be used for finding cliques in this communities.
  - **Hierarchical Communities:** Previous communities are consider a single level. In practical, it is common to have hierarchies of communities mean that each community can have sub/super communities. Hierarchical clustering is a solution to find hierarchical communities. The Girvan-Newman algorithm is specifically designed for finding communities using divisive hierarchical clustering.

4. CONCLUSION

Big Data and Social Networks have been a hot topic for research in the last few years and continues to attract attention and significant research funding around the world. With social media, Data is flowing from daily life which generates from collection of collections data that includes different format of unstructured data. Social media becomes a one unique source of Big Data. Big Data lies real-time that can only manage by Big Data Applications. In fact, Big Data revolutionary is competition by Social Media organizations that how best they can improve complexity of dynamic contents which indeed is now exploring to improved computational methods in Social Networking. Therefore, Big Data with new computational method is definitely to remain foreseeable future in computational world.

Apart from Social Network and Big Data, we introduce the new field Social media mining which is a rapidly growing interdisciplinary field deeply rooted in computer science and social sciences. Any social media, there requires active community that communicates community detection to be interactive. The interest of social media is fast growing new arena & research technologies that needs greater intensifying to harness social media data and be developing a standardized frame work for utilizing big social media data.

This paper is one of the efforts to introduce the understanding of Big Data and Social Networks. It is designed to enable students, researchers, and practitioners to acquire fundamental concepts and algorithms for social network, big data and social media mining.

REFERENCES

Big Data at the Speed of Business. (n.d.). Retrieved Apr 10, from http://www-01.ibm.com/software/data/bigdata/what-is-big-data.html

Big Data for Enterprise. (n.d.). Retrieved Aug 01, from http://www.mongodb.com/big-data-explained#big-data-enterprise

Characteristics of Social Networks. (n.d.). Retrieved Mar 03, from http://socialnetworking.lovetoknow.com/Characteristics_of_Social_Networks

Chen, H., Chiang, R. H. L., & Storey, V. C. (2012). Business Intelligence and Analytics: From Big Data to Big Impact. *Management Information Systems Quarterly*, *36*(4), 1165–1188.

Cios, K., Pedrycz, W., & Swiniarski, R. (1998). *Data Mining Methods for Knowledge Discovery*. Boston: Kluwer Academic Publishers. doi:10.1007/978-1-4615-5589-6

Definition of Big Data. (n.d.). Retrieved Apr 20, from http://www.opentracker.net/article/definitions-big-data

Easley, D., & Kleinberg, J. (2010). *Networks, Crowds, and Markets: Reasoning about a Highly Connected World*. Cambridge: Cambridge University Press. doi:10.1017/CBO9780511761942

EdgeRank. (n.d.). Retrieved Aug 04, from http://edgerank.net/

Fayyad, U. (1996). Data Mining and Knowledge Discovery: Making Sense Out of Data. *IEEE Expert*, *11*(5), 20–25. doi:10.1109/64.539013

Fayyad, U., Piatetsky-Shapiro, G., & Smyth, P. (1996). From Data Mining to Knowledge Discovery in Databases. *AI Magazine*, 37–54.

Frank, O., & Strauss, D. (1986). Markov Graphs. *Journal of the American Statistical Association*, *81*(395), 832–842. doi:10.1080/01621459.1986.10478342

How the Big Data Explosion Is Changing the World. (n.d.). Retrieved Apr 20, from http://blogs.msdn. com/b/microsoftenterpriseinsight/archive/2013/04/15/the-big-bang-how-the-big-data-explosion-is-changing-the-world.aspx

Intel Corporation. (2013). *Big Data in the Cloud: Converging Technologies*. Retrieved Mar 01, from http://www.intel.com/content/www/us/en/big-data/big-data-cloud-technologies-brief.html

Kakade, K. N., & Chavan, T. A. (2014). Improving Efficiency of GEO-Distributed Data Sets using Pact. *International Journal of Current Engineering and Technology*, *4*(3), 1284–1287.

Kaur, D., & Paul, A. (2014). Performance Analysis of Different Data mining Techniques over Heart Disease dataset. *International Journal of Current Engineering and Technology*, *4*(1), 220–224.

Koobface. (n.d.). Retrieved May, 10 from http://en.wikipedia.org/wiki/Koobface

Krishnamurthy, B., & Wills, C. E. (2008), *Characterizing Privacy in Online Social Networks*. WOSN '08 Proceedings of the first workshop on Online social networks. Retrieved from http://www2.research. att.com/~bala/papers/posn.pdf

Learn the Latest Social Advertising Trend. (n.d.). Retrieved July 20, from http://resolutionmedia.com/ us/white-papers/resolution-media-social-trends-report

Lusher, D., Koskinen, J., & Robins, G. (2013). *Exponential Random Graphs Models for Social Networks: Theory, Methods and Application*. Cambridge: Cambridge University press.

Maltby, D. (2011). Big Data Analytics. *ASIST Conference*, New Orleans, LA.

Manyika, J., Chui, M., Brown, B., Bughin, J., Dobbs, R., Roxburgh, C., & Byers, A. H. (2011). *Big data: The next frontier for innovation, competition, and productivity*. The McKinsey Global Institute.

Map Reduce. (n.d.). Retrieved Aug 01, from http://docs.mongodb.org/manual/core/map-reduce/

McAfee, A., & Erik Brynjolfsson, E. (2012). Big Data: The Management revolution. *Harvard Business Review*, 59–68. PMID:23074865

Mislove, A., Marcon, M., Gummadi, K. P., Druschel, P., & Bhattacharjee, B. (2007). Measurement and Analysis of Online Social Networks. *5th ACM/USENIX Internet Measurement Conference, IMC'07*, San Diego, CA. doi:10.1145/1298306.1298311

Porter, M. A. (2012). *Small World Network*. Retrieved Apr 12, from http://www.scholarpedia.org/article/ Small-world_network

Research Report. (2013). *State of Social Media Span*. Retrieved July 12, from www.nexgate.com

Robins, G. (2009). Social Networks, Exponential Random Graph (P*) Models for Computational Complexity: Theory, Techniques, and Applications. New York: Springer.

Robins, G., Pattison, P., Kalish, Y., & Lusher, D. (2007). An introduction to exponential random graph (p*) models for social networks. *Social Networks*, *29*(2), 173–191. doi:10.1016/j.socnet.2006.08.002

Russom, P. (2011). *Big Data Analytic, The Data Warehouse Institute (TDWI), Best Practices Report.* Fourth Quarter.

Shang, W., Jiang, Z. M., Hemmati, H., Adams, B., Hassan, A. E., & Martin, P. (2013). Assisting Developers of Big Data Analytics Applications When Deploying on Hadoop Clouds. *35th International Conference on Software Engineering (ICSE 2013).* doi:10.1109/ICSE.2013.6606586

Social Media Update. (2013). Retrieved July 20, from http://www.pewinternet.org/2013/12/30/social-media-update-2013

Social Networks Modeling. (n.d.). Retrieved July 07, from http://columbiadatascience.com/2012/11/02/brief-introduction-to-social-network-modeling

Tang, L., & Liu, H. (2010). *Communication Detection in Mining in Social Media for Data Mining and Knowledge Discovery.* Morgan & Claypool Publishers.

The 4V's of Big Data. (n.d.). Retrieved Apr 20, from http://www.ibmbigdatahub.com/infographic/four-vs-big-data

The Big Data Landscape for Type of Application & Examples. (n.d.). Retrieved Apr, 15, from http://www.bigdatalandscape.com

Toivonena, R., Kovanena, L., Kiveläa, M., Onnelab, J., Saramäkia, J., & Kaskia, K. (2009). A comparative study of social network models: Network evolution models and nodal attribute models. *Social Networks*, *31*(4), 240–254. doi:10.1016/j.socnet.2009.06.004

Trending Topics. (2010). Retrieved Aug 13, from https://blog.twitter.com/2010/trend-or-not-trend

Watts, D. J., & Strogatz, S. H. (1998). Collective dynamics of 'small-world' networks. *Nature*, *393*(6684), 440–442. doi:10.1038/30918 PMID:9623998

Zafarani, R., Abbasi, M., & Liu, H. (2014). *Social Media Mining: An Introduction.* Cambridge: Cambridge University Press. doi:10.1017/CBO9781139088510

KEY TERMS AND DEFINITIONS

Big Data: Extremely large and highly complex data sets that can be analyzed computationally contextually which describes approximately contemporary to human interaction based on oneself emotion.

Big Data Analytics: The process of examining very large and diverse of data which can be used of advanced analytic techniques in an effort to uncover hidden patterns, unknown correlations and other useful information.

Big Data Infrastructure: The main purpose is the process and store both structure and unstructured data.

Community Detection: Discovering groups in a network where surveillance is implicitly to each individual membership.

Knowledge Discovery in Databases (KDD): The process of discovering useful information from a collection of raw data.

Social Media Mining: The computationally process of social media data which patterns can be compute analytically.

Social Networks: Social structure which involves different subjects of any interested topics internationally whereby at least a group of two people interactively exchange.

This research was previously published in the Handbook of Research on Trends and Future Directions in Big Data and Web Intelligence edited by Noor Zaman, Mohamed Elhassan Seliaman, Mohd Fadzil Hassan, and Fausto Pedro Garcia Marquez, pages 362-381, copyright year 2015 by Information Science Reference (an imprint of IGI Global).

Chapter 44
Social Media Tools for Quality Business Information

Sérgio Maravilhas
Porto University, Portugal & Aveiro University, Portugal

ABSTRACT

Information, as a tool to reduce uncertainty and to develop knowledge in organizations, is an important aid in the decision-making process and must be of quality to improve its value. We are living in an information society where organizational and personal life are mediated by information and knowledge, with the help of technologies that gather, disseminate, and deliver that raw material to support our decisions. There are several characteristics that describe the quality of information that will allow the analysis of the value of the information used. In the globalized world we are living in, quality information warrants best results when competing with other organizations. Its value is related to the results that it will allow to be obtained and the dependability on its context. Marketing trends and competitive information is needed for clear decision making about what products to develop, for what customers, at what cost, through which distribution channels, reducing the uncertainty that a new product/service development always brings with it. Social Media tools allow the knowledge of competitor's moves and the analysis of trends from the communications exchanged in the networks of individual consumers, making it easy for companies to develop solutions according to their clients and prospects desires. Learning how to extract quality information, unbiased, valuable for business, from these social tools is the aim of this work, sharing with the interested parties some ways of using it for their profit and competitive sustainability.

INTRODUCTION

We are living in an information society (IS) (Webster, 2000) where organizational and personal life are mediated by information and knowledge (Castells, 2000; Negroponte, 1995), with the help of technologies that gather, disseminate and deliver that raw material to support our decisions (McGee & Prusak, 1995; Penzias, 1995; Tapscott, 1995; Tapscott & Williams, 2008; Ward & Peppard, 2002).

DOI: 10.4018/978-1-5225-5637-4.ch044

After World War II, in 1948, Claude Shannon formulated "The Mathematical Theory of Communication", better known by "Theory of Information" (Gleick, 2011). At the same time two almost simultaneous inventions, the transistor and the digital computer came to reveal themselves with an enormous revolutionary potential when the social effects of their application, producing new goods and services were discovered, especially in the production and distribution of a new immaterial good and service: the information (Castells, 2000). Information, opposite to material goods, is infinitely expandable, doesn't waste itself (meaning that we can give an information without losing it, which may allow us to give it to several people, something we can't do with a material good), and once created difficult to vanish (although its economical value may decrease). It's easy to transport and distribute and the costs of keeping it in data warehouses is lesser every day. The speed and easiness in processing and transporting information electronically, it's almost instantaneous ability in feed itself, start to subvert the traditional ways of labour division, fragmentation, expertise and centralization of the human experience and its sociological configuration (Cleveland, 1983, 1985).

Some authors (Brown & Duguid, 2000; Castells, 2000, 2004; Webster, 2000) observed that a huge transformation is taking place; that we are moving towards a society that is no longer dependant in a massive industrialization or agriculture. They often talk about the knowledge and information based transformation of the world economy we are living in, with flux and flows of information gaining advantage to the exchange of goods. This notion is interconnected with the birth of the information technology, characterized by computers and electronic means of producing and transmitting information at the speed of light through a network of other technological apparatus (Godeluck, 2000).

Nowadays, we tend to call information society to the constraints we move in, sociologically interpreted. An IS, tend to describe a society no longer based in the production of materials, goods, production means, but in the production of knowledge.

Information, as a tool to reduce uncertainty and to develop knowledge in organizations (Best, 1996b; Kahaner, 1997; Porter & Millar, 1985), is an important aid in the decision making process and must be of quality to improve its value (Best, 1996b; Beuren, 1998; Choo, 2003; Davenport, Marchand, & Dickson, 2004; Marchand & Horton Jr., 1986; Tapscott, 1999; Wilson, 1985, 1987).

There are several characteristics that describe the quality of information that will allow the analysis of the value of the information used. In the globalized world we are living in, quality information warrants best results when competing with other organizations (Brophy & Coulling, 1996; Redman, 1996; Wormell, 1990). Its value is related to the results that it will allow obtaining and it's dependable on its context (Best, 1996b; Davenport, 1997; Lattès, 1992; Marchand & Horton Jr., 1986; Orna, 1999; Penzias, 1989; Tapscott, 1995; Tapscott, Ticoll, & Lowy, 2000).

Quality information is needed to clear decision-making about what products develop, for what customers, at what cost, through which distribution channels, reducing the uncertainty that a new product/service development always brings with it (Garber, 2001; Kotler, Armstrong, Saunders, & Wong, 1999; Mohr, Sengupta, & Slater, 2010; Scott, 2008; Trott, 2008).

Competitive Intelligence (CI) aims to monitor a firm's external environment for information relevant to its decision-making process (Choo, 2003).

Intelligence activities are based on the intelligence cycle. The intelligence cycle involves accurately identifying your information needs, collecting relevant information, analysing it, communicating the results to the people who need it, and taking rapid and appropriate action (Besson & Possin, 1996; Martinet & Marti, 1995; Taborda & Ferreira, 2002).

As an excellent information source, the Internet provides significant opportunities for CI (Sage, 2013).

Internet search engines have been widely used to facilitate information search on the Internet (Gomes & Braga, 2001; Taborda & Ferreira, 2002). However, many problems minimize their effective use in CI research (Bedell, 2011; Kahaner, 1997).

Many major companies, such as Ernst & Young, Motorola, Xerox, and almost all the pharmaceutical companies, have formal and well-organized CI units that enable managers to make informed decisions about critical business matters such as investment, marketing, and strategic planning (Prescott & Miller, 2002).

Traditionally, CI relied upon published company reports and other kinds of printed information. In recent years, Internet has rapidly become an extremely good source of information about the competitive environment of companies (Hawthorne & Cromity, 2012; Ojala, 2012; Revelli, 2000; Sage, 2013).

Although the Internet represents significant CI opportunities, it has also many technical, cognitive, and organizational challenges. The amount of information available on the Internet is gigantic, so, CI professionals are constantly facing the problem of information overload (Barbosa & O'Reilly, 2011; Dearlove, 1998). "Information overload is a real phenomenon, but progress is being made in tapping into social media to increase marketing intelligence" (Hawthorne & Cromity, 2012, p.38).

Much time and effort is required for CI professionals to search for relevant information on the Internet and then analyze the information collected in the correct context.

Internet search engines have been useful in helping people search for information on the Internet. Nevertheless, the exponential growth of information sources on the Internet and the unregulated and dynamic nature of many Web sites are making it increasingly difficult to locate useful information using these search engines (Scott, 2008).

Social Media tools allow the knowledge of competitor's moves and the analysis of trends from the communications exchanged in the networks of individual consumers (Russell, 2011; Tsvetovat & Kouznetsov, 2011), making it easy for companies to develop solutions according to their clients and prospects desires (Berthon, Pitt, Plangger, & Shapiro, 2012; Bramston, 2009; Burgelman, Christensen, & Wheelwright, 2009; Canhoto, 2013; Christensen, Anthony, & Roth, 2004; Kotze, 2013).

Web 2.0 and Social Media are more than tools where you can keep track of your old school and college friends (Bedell, 2011). Due to the amount of information exchanged in these platforms, companies can look at Web 2.0 tools like Wikis, Blogs, Social Networking sites and so forth, to check for some pieces of information that come in first hand to these communication tools (Berkman, 2008; Brown, 2012; Canhoto, 2013). We have to trust in the human nature that makes us want to be appreciated by our peers and wait to see if someone discloses his research results and applications to the world, in a medium faster than company reports and research articles (Kotze, 2013). If we have enough patience, it will pay off the time spent in this activity because it will be possible to identify micro-trends that have not yet gained momentum (Sage, 2013).

Companies can use this information, from these social tools, for competitor surveillance, consumer satisfaction monitoring, trend development and technology watch.

There are not, yet, many bibliographic resources dealing with this subject, because it's still a new medium that needs to be proved and tested, that is being currently used to perform competitive strategies so companies can excel in their areas of business (Berthon, Pitt, Plangger, & Shapiro, 2012).

Learning how to extract quality information, unbiased, valuable for business, from these social tools is the aim of this work, sharing with the interested parties some ways of using it for their profit and competitive sustainability.

If properly done, this monitoring activity even allows a company to measure the level of satisfaction of its own employees by the analysis of the content of what they post online about their employer (Ojala, 2012).

That gives you clues about improvements and changes to be made.

We will start with a brief explanation of the importance of information quality and its value for decision making and business governance, describing CI and Social Networking, identifying some tools that will ease monitoring requirements, and conclude with a few ideas for analyzing Blogs, Wikis and Tag Clouds to identify consumer signals and trends (Barbosa & O'Reilly, 2011; Canhoto, 2013; Higham, 2010; Kotze, 2013; Rasquilha, 2010; Scott, 2008).

We will survey the applications of Web 2.0 relative to CI and consumer trends, and explore approaches of gathering information for CI through Web 2.0. Some applications of Web 2.0 (Blog, Wiki, RSS and Tag Clouding) are discussed for CI and business intelligence use.

QUALITY INFORMATION FOR BUSINESS GOVERNANCE

Wagner asserts that "the term 'quality of information' is scarce in the literature" (1990, p. 69).

Quality is a difficult concept to define because what is quality for one person may be different for another.

Some managers state that they will recognize quality when they see it. That may be possible if we are evaluating a tangible product but applying this to immaterial and intangible goods, like data, information and knowledge makes it more difficult.

For Ginman there is no "generally accepted definition of quality information. (…) Both quality and information are in themselves difficult concepts to grasp and to evaluate, and the whole process is further coloured by the subjective views of the person making the evaluation" (1990, p. 18). For that reason, several different definitions of quality arise "however, they all accept the notion that quality is defined by the customer" (Cortada, 1996, p. 6) and Redman suggests the need to "understand what customers want in their terms" (1996, p. 141). Other authors state that "quality is achieved when customer needs are met; quality is central to all organizations, not an optional extra; quality is not dependent on high price or high levels of resourcing" (Brophy & Coulling, 1996, p. 7).

Companies "must define, measure, analyze, and improve the quality of information, treating information as a product" because "creating quality information and organizational knowledge is the prerequisite for any firm to gain competitive advantage" (Huang, Lee, & Wang, 1998, p. 5, 6).

Relating the subject of information quality with business management and the need of quality information for good decision making, Marchand describes the differences and common points that connect the information quality and the product quality. His information quality list comprises eight dimensions:

1. The actual value an information product or service may have for the information user;
2. The 'features' associated with an information product or service;
3. The reliability of the information product or service;
4. Its meaning over time;
5. Relevance;
6. Validity;
7. 'Aesthetics';

8.   Perceived value (1990, pp. 11, 12).

He concludes that "understanding the interrelationships among the dimensions of information quality is what is critical to strategic information management" (1990, p. 10).

For most of the evolution of the business management function, information quality has not been a major strategic asset, but "has been perceived and thought about as simply one aspect of decision-making (…) only one of the many dimensions of decision-making and often not a very important one" (1990, p. 8). Thinking about the business value of information quality and its relation with profitability, some authors (Brophy & Coulling, 1996; Cortada, 1996; Garvin, 1988) mention that quality, in general, increases profits by gaining the consumers preference and obtaining a bigger market share. In information, the same occurs because quality lowers the costs of production and the adequacy of the information product or service to the user's needs makes it preferable to the ones who need and use it (Marchand, 1990, pp. 15, 16). Therefore cost plays a significant role to lower the price charged to the user of that information.

Criteria for Quality Information

To be considered of quality, information must meet several criteria such as: completeness, accessibility, accuracy, precision, objectivity, consistency, relevancy, timeliness, and understandability (Brünger-Weilandt, Geiß, Herlan, & Stuike-Prill, 2011).

Burk and Horton state that the quality of information itself includes attributes and examples, such as "Accuracy – Precision; Comprehensiveness – Relevance; Credibility – Reliability; Currency – Simplicity; Pertinence – Validity" (Burk Jr. & Horton Jr., 1988, p. 93).

Other authors mention that information, to have quality, must be:

1.   **Precise:** Correct and true;
2.   **Timely:** Available when and where needed;
3.   **Complete:** Ensuring the presence of its several elements;
4.   **Concise:** Easy to handle;
5.   **Authoritative:** Quality depends on the provider (Brown & Duguid, 2000; Cleveland, 1985; Cooke, 2001; Davenport, 1997; Davenport et al., 2004; Hinton, 2006; Marchand & Horton Jr., 1986; McGee & Prusak, 1995; Penzias, 1989, 1995; Shapiro & Varian, 1999).

For Marchand the quality of information products depends on their attributes such as coverage, reliability and validity, which makes it highly measurable and quantifiable. Also, when looking at the production level, the quality of information is associated with "meeting requirements and with doing the job right the first time within budget, and on time" (1990, p. 9).

Huang, Lee and Wang divide information quality (IQ) in four categories, each one with several dimensions, as follows:

1.   **Intrinsic IQ:** Accuracy, objectivity, believability, reputation;
2.   **Contextual IQ:** Relevancy, value-added, timeliness, completeness, amount of information;
3.   **Representational IQ:** Interpretability, ease of understanding, concise representation, consistent representation;
4.   **Accessibility IQ:** Access, security.

These authors consider that, defined by the perspective of the consumer, information quality "can be used by researchers and practitioners to direct their efforts for information consumers instead of the IS professionals" (Huang, Lee, & Wang, 1998, p. 42, 43).

If information is not delivered with the right quality, proportion and measure it can originate "information overload" (Dearlove, 1998), which occurs when excess of information suffocates businesses and causes employees to suffer mental anguish and physical illness, exacerbated nowadays by the huge amount of information from Web 2.0 and Social Media (Tapscott & Williams, 2008).

Information overload causes high levels of stress that can result in illness and the breakdown of individuals' personal relationships.

The effects of the "information glut are procrastination and time wasting, leading to the delaying of important decisions, distraction from main job responsibilities, tension between colleagues and loss of job satisfaction" (Dearlove, 1998, p. 111).

Remember that "information is a bit like money: the more you've got, the more headaches it causes — but you still can't get enough" (Suhr, 2004, p. 41).

So, it's important to understand that customers will evaluate the quality of information according to its adequacy to the satisfaction of their needs. After all, that's the reason why information is stored and disseminated, to satisfy someone's information needs. That is why it has to be of high quality in order to be used and aggregate value to the users' tasks being performed.

THE VALUE OF ACCURATE INFORMATION FOR BUSINESSES

According to Best it's not easy to assign a value to information and there is no "commonly accepted and universally applicable way of valuing the information resource" (1996a, p. 14).

Burk and Horton define information value as "the value attributed to information produced or acquired by organizations, entities and persons, and delivered in the form of an information product or service". For them, this value can be perceived immediately but, sometimes, this valuation occurs only several years later like in the case of "the values attached to information created by scientific research" that "are often realized long after it is created" (Burk Jr. & Horton Jr., 1988, p. 79).

Orna also points out the fact that information has no implicit value in itself since it depends on its use, purpose and context (1996, p. 20).

Wagner states that the "terms value and quality share a common meaning: the degree of excellence, but the former also denotes an economic exchange worth" (1990, p. 69), being the value of information and not the quality of information the preferred concept.

For Orna, the functional part of valuing can be defined as "the process of determining and applying appropriate criteria for estimating the value of things" (1996, p. 19).

An indirect valuation occurs, and the measures used are the value of the investment in information technologies used to hold the information, the costs associated with staff that collects and maintains the information resources, or the value the information has when it's put to a specific use.

To explain why the process of valuing is so difficult, we must remember that "fixing a value is always an indirect process that involves finding appropriate equivalents and standards, not necessarily or always in money terms, and the estimation of those who use it has to be taken into account as well" (Orna, 1996, p. 19).

McPherson (1994, pp. 207, 208) proposes three models for information valuing. The first one is related with the cognition process, in which the value is dependent on the contribution of information to the achievement of organizational goals. The second relates to the value of information when it enhances the knowledge not only in the user's brain but also in external, operational and recognizable actions that are observable. The third deals with traditional accounting, highly cost oriented that does not recognize the value of information unless it can be sold externally as a good or product.

Orna, to make this clearer, says that "to have value, information has to be transformed by human minds into knowledge, without which no products of tangible value can be created or exchanged" (1999, p. 141). That occurs because the valuation has three parts, the value triangle:

1. Object;
2. Human judgement;
3. Use to which person judging puts the object.

It's a three way relationship, involving human judgment, based on the relationship between the object valued and the person that judges and evaluates, and the relationship between that object and the uses that the human will put the object into. It also involves criteria, which imply thinking and feeling (1999, pp. 143, 144).

What we can observe is that it's not easy to apply to information the traditional economic and accounting measures applied to tangible products, the cost benefit analysis. Nevertheless, it's important to do so in order to avoid "failure to spot potential threats in time because of lack of intelligence gathering and correlations; failure in attempts to innovate; (…) and failure to recognize opportunities for using information resources more productively" (Orna, 1996, p. 25).

Information is called the 'glue' that holds the organizational structure together, and there are four ways of using information to create value for a business:

1. Minimize risks;
2. Reduce costs;
3. Add value, orienting the output to the market and customers;
4. Innovation, through the creation of new realities (Davenport, 1997; Davenport et al., 2004).

Characteristics of Valuable Information

Information has some characteristics that differentiate it from tangible products, such as: "If information is exchanged and traded, the value from using it can increase for all parties to the transaction. The value of information is not diminished by being used; it can be (…) used many times by many users for adding value to many activities and outputs" (Orna, 1999, p. 141).

Cleveland (1985, pp. 29-33) highlights the value of information and its characteristics, saying that information is:

1. **Expandable:** The more we have, the more we use and more valuable it gets;
2. **Compressible:** Can be concentrated, integrated, summarized, miniaturized for easier handling;
3. **Substitutable:** Replaces land, labour and capital;

4. **Transportable:** At the speed of light, using e-mail or video-conference we can be anywhere like if we were there;
5. **Diffusive:** It tends to leak and the more it leaks the more we have and the more of us have it, making it available to a growing number of people;
6. **Shareable:** Allows exchange and sharing transactions because giving or selling a information lets the seller to keep it anyway, unlike physical goods.

For Grant (2002, pp. 242; 245, 246; 516), information is the medium through which an organization relates to its environment and allows the individuals to know how to react and adapt to external changes. For him, the value of information is related to what he designates "imperfect availability of information" and "imperfection of information". If, in a given market, not all the players have access to all the information available, or it's difficult to identify all the information needed to decide effectively in accordance to other competitor's moves, then the ones who possess or know the sources where the information needed exists, have a competitive advantage in that market.

This is going to be very important because even if all the players have access to the same information, again it will be the use that they make of it that is going to distinguish the success that they can obtain. It's only after the information gets inside someone's mind and is applied and put to use in something useful, like a product or a process that has the preference of the consumers in that market, that it becomes valuable and originates a big return on investment to his owner, the "value for money" valuation (Best, 1996a; Grant, 2002; Kotler et al., 1999; Mohr et al., 2010; Orna, 1996, 1999).

Even if everybody can access quality patent information, not everyone will innovate thanks to that. Furthermore, not everyone that does innovate will be successful because the results will be dependent on the output obtained and the accession of the consumers to the solution found, that is to say, it will depend on the product's characteristics, on its adequacy to the market and its consumers' needs, and on consumer satisfaction.

Again, a method to value information can be "through seeking indirect evidence of its value to businesses in promoting competitiveness, productivity, or innovation and successful marketing of the results" (Orna, 1996, p. 26), "and in avoiding risk and reducing uncertainty" (Orna, 1999, p. 142).

Although an information can be valuable for a long period of time, certain types of information are only valuable within a given time frame limit (Huang, Lee, & Wang, 1998). Information may lose its value because its timing has passed, like if you could knew the lottery numbers in advance for a certain week, after that week those numbers would be useless, or "a tip on the fourth race at Belmont might be valuable at lunchtime and valueless by dinnertime. Yesterday's weather forecast is of merely historical interest tomorrow" (Cleveland, 1985, p. 29). Nevertheless, some information retains its value and can be applied in the same field or in complementary fields, enhancing the final result obtained with this strategy.

COMPETITIVE INTELLIGENCE AND BUSINESS MANAGEMENT

CI is the use of public sources to develop information about the competition, consumers, and market environment (J. Miller & Business Intelligence Braintrust, 2002).

CI is different from espionage (Bergier, 1970; Fialka, 1997; Guisnel, 1997; Rustmann Jr., 2002; Winkler, 1997), which implies illegal means of information gathering. CI is restrained to the gathering of public information (Kahaner, 1997; Mordecai, 2013c).

One of the main differences between CI and general business information, such as business growth rate and operating ratios, is that CI is of strategic importance on the organization. It is not only the collection of information from a variety of sources, but also the analysis and synthesis of such information, which could help the company decide the course of action to improve its position (Choo, 2003).

Because of the broad reach and potential of CI, involvement in intelligence activities can provide first-class training for managers and marketers. In fact, an increasing number of leading companies insist that their best people spend some time in intelligence operations prior to promotion to the highest ranks (J. Miller & Business Intelligence Braintrust, 2002; Prescott & Miller, 2002; Taborda & Ferreira, 2002).

Intelligence must be passed to decision makers in a timely manner, and in a style and format that will encourage them to take appropriate measures and decisions. Intelligence reports and briefings should aim, above all, for clarity and brevity, and should provide the decision maker with suggestions or recommendations for action (Besson & Possin, 1996; Choo, 2003; Garber, 2001; Martinet & Marti, 1995).

Executives have a major part to play in ensuring the success of your intelligence activities. Among other things, they must offer commitment, involvement, and support (Johnson, 2005; Prescott & Miller, 2002). Managers have a part to play in making intelligence activities successful because they already spend lots of time talking with others and that enables them to collect information. However, it is essential that they keep their intelligence manager informed of any significant change in the business environment (J. Miller & Business Intelligence Braintrust, 2002; Prescott & Miller, 2002).

A typical CI process consists of a series of business activities that involve identifying, gathering, developing, analyzing and disseminating information (Besson & Possin, 1996; Martinet & Marti, 1995; Taborda & Ferreira, 2002).

"Every competitor broadcasts a large amount of data to you in their advertising and their product itself. Every feature that they have in their products and every special technique that's part of their service is data you can use" (Mordecai, 2013c).

The following list shows a typical sequence in which these activities take place: i) identify competitors, markets, customers, suppliers, or other variables in the environment to be monitored. Identify what information is to be collected; ii) specifically identify possible sources of information and collect the information from these sources; iii) evaluate the validity, reliability, and usefulness of the information collected; iv) gather information collected from different sources and integrate them; v) interpret and analyze the information for strategic or tactical significance. Draw conclusions and recommend actions; vi) disseminate and present analyzed findings to management; vii) respond to ad hoc inquiries for decision support (Ribault, Martinet, & Lebidois, 1995).

Information gathering and information analysis are the key areas of the CI process.

Competitive Intelligence and the Internet

The Internet is currently the most popular medium for gathering information and it has enormous advantages for that function (Russell, 2011; Tsvetovat & Kouznetsov, 2011). At the same time, it calls for a minimum level of expertise if it is to be effective. For instance, you need to be able to find specific information (Berkman, 2008), and that calls for familiarity with search engines and sophisticated retrieval techniques (Prior, 2006, 2007).

Nevertheless, "search engines are severely lacking in the realm of exploratory search. (...) If you want to find new things with which you're unfamiliar, the online world has a market gap" (Hawthorne & Cromity, 2012, p. 36). Social Media can reduce that gap.

With very few exceptions, standards for citing and classifying information are poor, unenforceable or non-existent, and there is a distinct absence of identifying information (metadata) (Chen, Chau, & Zeng, 2002). "Content often lacks depth and substance, and it is almost impossible to distinguish between fact, editorial, advertising and news. But, many of these disadvantages will be overcome with time" (Prior, 2007).

Commercial online databases, such as Dialog (http://www.dialog.com) and Lexis-Nexis (http://www.lexisnexis.com), contain a large amount of well-organized information on a variety of subjects, storing information ranging from company annual reports to US patent documents, and from history journals to chemistry periodicals (Chen et al., 2002; Taborda & Ferreira, 2002). These commercial databases are among the major sources used by CI professionals (Herring, 2002).

"Recent years have seen the tremendous growth of the Internet. Many commercial online databases are now accessible through the Internet. The Internet also enables organizations to monitor and search the websites of their competitors, alliances, and possible collaborators" (Chen et al., 2002). Internet-based information sources are becoming increasingly important in the CI process (Guisnel, 1997). "In the old days, corporate intelligence gathering meant painstakingly gleaning information from experts and competitors' reports, subscribing to expensive online data aggregators such as Factiva or Dialog, and scanning unstructured documents from the media" (Kotze, 2013).

Corporate Web sites usually contain useful information, including company history, corporate overviews, business visions and missions, product overviews, financial data, sales figures, annual reports, press releases, biographies of top executives, locations of offices, hiring ads, among others (Godeluck, 2000; Weiss, 2008).

The data is "valuable in providing direct or indirect contextual information and enable the CI professionals to analyze corporate strategies. Another reason attracting CI professionals to use the Internet is that most of the contents available on the Internet are free of charge" (Chen et al., 2002). In fact, Internet is now one of the most important resources for CI information collection (Deng & Luo, 2007; Kirsch, Gregory, Brown, & Charley, 2006).

Corporate or employees Wikis and Blogs also contain a vast amount of useable information because everybody likes to tell in what they are working, what are they good at, the results that they were capable of reaching with their work, the goals and objectives they provided and so on.

As Kotze (2013) declares "none of the employee's actions were 'leaks' and taken alone they are all innocuous. But taken together they may reveal more than the company wants. For the competitive intelligence professional at the competitor they are a vital stream of information."

Managers tend to think that more information is better. In today's business environment, however, it is not necessarily true. CI professionals could be spending too much time and effort on data collection rather than data analysis. For CI professionals to manually access the Internet, extract and analyse the information on every single Web page at a company Web site to locate the useful information, and to synthesize information is very exhausting and time consuming.

"To address this information and cognitive overload problem, research has been conducted in developing techniques and tools to analyze, categorize, and visualize large collections of Web pages, among other text documents" (Chen et al., 2002).

In turn, a variety of tools have been developed to assist searching, gathering, monitoring and analyzing information on the internet (Guisnel, 1997; Prescott & Miller, 2002; Revelli, 2000)[1].

SOCIAL MEDIA NETWORKING

Social Networks, made possible by Web 2.0, are one of several next generation communications and collaboration tools that include Blogs, Wikis and Social Bookmarking.

Participants worldwide contribute to and collaborate in readily available online discussions, creating new knowledge bases that can become recognized as information sources.

"Web 2.0 technologies transform broadcast media monologues (one too many) into social media dialogues (many to many). Social media is the product of internet-based applications that build on the technological foundations of Web 2.0" (Berthon, Pitt, Plangger, & Shapiro, 2012, p. 263).

Social networks are free to join, to search for a vast amount of reference questions, and to find experts for all kinds of requirements and research projects (Qualman, 2010).

The concept of a social network, meaning a social structure made of nodes (which are generally individuals or organizations) that are tied by one or more specific types of interdependency, is as valuable as the number of nodes that constitute it (Castells, 2004; Tapscott & Williams, 2008).

This means that, the bigger the number of nodes, the more valuable that network becomes (Godeluck, 2000).

With this in mind, it's easy to perceive that this trend in modern communication and interaction among humans will be very important to achieve results that it will be very difficult with other non-interactive means (Tapscott, 1995, 1999; Tapscott et al., 2000; Tapscott & Williams, 2008).

The relation of confidence among each node will open a number of possibilities that a traditional media, like TV or Newspapers, couldn't impose simply because we don't know who those people are or, if we do, we know that they are trying to earn something at our expenses (Tapscott et al., 2000).

With this new possibility, either we know the person communicating with us, or we know someone who knows him. That condition gives us the confidence and trust that will induce the preference on a certain product or service and makes us discard others. That's basic consumer behaviour (Scott, 2008).

For companies, this new possibility can be the most important decision of all times. It will allow to transform our brand in a major player among the preferences of customers (Carrera, 2012b; Hortinha, 2002; Mohr et al., 2010).

With Social Media companies can gain a better knowledge of their business environment, using visual tools that can enhance the analysis of the huge amount of posts, comments, and shares (Mordecai, 2013b).

Also for employees, that can be a major source of information and knowledge, because we can now access the information we need among a network of thousands of specialists in a certain subject that can answer us almost immediately saving us precious time in the searching process (Libert & Spector, 2009; Surowiecki, 2007).

If someone thought that social networking was only for the youngsters, like with MySpace (http://www.myspace.com), or with Facebook (https://www.facebook.com), that is a huge mistake. Web 2.0 introduced many new types of applications for users to express their thoughts, concerns, needs, desires and level of satisfaction with what they buy (Berthon, Pitt, Plangger, & Shapiro, 2012; Hawthorne & Cromity, 2012).

This allows, in a very fast and inexpensive manner, to scan the trends of a market, understand consumer motivation and the actual preferences in the business area where companies act and compete (Rasquilha, 2010)[2].

New applications of Web 2.0 provide new opportunities for CI, such as Web Blogs (Blogs) which are created by thousands of individuals (Blood, 2004; Deng & Luo, 2007), Wikis (ex. Wikipedia) which allow public group creation, RSS (Rich Site Summary or Really Simple Syndication) using XML (Extensible Markup Language) to classify and organize the information (Tsvetovat & Kouznetsov, 2011) making it more transparent and open (Carrera, 2012b; Hortinha, 2002; Scott, 2008).

All of them bring convenience for CI especially in collecting information. "In the view of CI, Web 2.0 paved new ways and channels for gathering information" (Deng & Luo, 2007).

All these tools, like Blogs and Wikis, provide intelligence for consumer trend monitoring (Barbosa & O'Reilly, 2011; Higham, 2010; Rasquilha, 2010; Sage, 2013).

In conjunction with existing consumer intelligence and CI resources, Social Networks can highlight significant issues that affect your brands, identify competitor weaknesses, opportunities in the marketplace and those specific to a brand (Qualman, 2010).

Monitoring Blogs and Podcasts can help develop actionable solutions to fuel organizations (Carrera, 2009, 2012a, 2012b; Hortinha, 2002).

When looking at Blogs and Wikis, we must also look at some of the networking sites, like LinkedIn. com, Xing.com, Facebook.com, Myspace.com, and search tools for people such as Zoominfo.com for company and competitor employees. Sites like these will mention what people are doing, their interests and past achievements. This information is very valuable because contacts can be found easily. "Sites such as LinkedIn.com and Xing.com allow you to see where people used to work as well as where they are now. The networking sites can also be searched using tools such as yoname.com and wink.com" (Weiss, 2008).

Also, creative consumers help companies developing new and better products by their feedback on using them and what to improve for better results (Berthon, Pitt, Plangger, & Shapiro, 2012).

Although Social Media includes Blogs, Podcasts, Wikis and more, we will just explore some of them, and will demonstrate how monitoring and analyzing what consumers create on Blogs and Wikis can enrich our understanding of their needs and desires (Higham, 2010; Hortinha, 2002; Kotler et al., 1999; Rasquilha, 2010; Scott, 2008), and thus support our CI efforts.

Online Social Networking for Business Intelligence

Online Social Networking enables us to find people who may not be familiar with our organisation, becoming quality prospects and then effective clients, creating an opportunity to connect with them and sell them our products and services.

Social Networking offers a high level of integration, and focuses on the sharing elements of the various applications. Sharing resources can increase the possibility of finding relevant information, like sharing our favourite bookmarks or photos and in return having access to the favourite resources of others who share our interests. It can mean being able to read comments and chat with people on topics of shared interest and being able to tap into collective knowledge (Russell, 2011)[3].

If we already know someone in that network, we can feel more comfortable that they can become quality prospects. And, because of that mutual connection, we can overcome difficulties and begin a business relationship with more trust.

These "new tools, based on social networking and deployed on mobile devices, are enabling companies to streamline operations, enhance customer satisfaction and improve financial performance across their entire businesses" (Bedell, 2011), allowing to accurately perform a SWOT (Strengths, Weaknesses; Opportunities and Threats) analysis to scan the macro-environment where the company develops its activity (Mordecai, 2013a).

Some advantages are that you can contact people or companies in your network to:

1. Regenerate old connections;
2. Maximise value in your weak connections;
3. Build business relationships with clients or hiring managers;
4. Find and meet prospective jobseekers;
5. Grow a referral network;
6. Enlarge your corporate and personal brand;
7. Make new connections and grow your sphere of influence;
8. Open doors to future career opportunities, increased salary or promotions;
9. Increase visibility, which improves influence and effectiveness internally with your organisation as well as externally;
10. Educate yourself and ask questions about other organisations;
11. Conduct competitive intelligence on companies, industries or individuals;
12. Make fewer cold calls and better prepare for them;
13. Leverage contacts you already have (Steckerl, 2007).

Although a major opportunity for business, companies with brands in the luxury market are failing to take advantage of these tools (Dickins, 2013).

As some authors declare, "better social searching tools will enable information professionals to find reliable sources for sentiment or common knowledge for word-of-mouth coverage" (Hawthorne & Cromity, 2012, p. 36), what is already being performed by some companies that analyze attitudes, emotions, brand evangelism, and its sponsor correlation present in the Social Media conversation share (Focalytic, 2013).

Social Interactions and Communities of Practice

The advantage of Blogs is that they facilitate the growth of Social Networks into true communities of practice (Blood, 2004). Much of the value of these networks is in their advantage for the "social capital required for effective decision support to grow based on relationships between analytically opinionated minds" (Johnson, 2005).

This defies the control hierarchies that still define most businesses where top-down decision making is still the rule of the day (Scott, 2008). Here, the reputations of writers are built on the value of their ideas, their ability to convince others that their ideas are valid and therefore develop the most respect and authority (Curtis, 2006; Kassel, 2008; A. Miller, 2007).

Collaboration applications that build such communities of practice socialize critical business decisions in an open forum based on the social capital of merit.

CONCERNS WITH NETWORKING SITES

"There's a tension between the audience participation model of Web 2.0 and business need for confidentiality and verification" (A. Miller, 2007). Some questions must be addressed like:

1. If an employee is blogging, what are they saying about the firm?
2. In a world where Wikis or Social bookmarks and tags are popular research tools, who is responsible for the accuracy and quality of information?
3. If you create an online community, how will you moderate what should be an open and free forum?
4. If you let your employees access Facebook at work, how can you be sure that they will remain alert to whether it's a work or social conversation they're having? (Steckerl, 2007).

According to some authors (A. Miller, 2007; Steckerl, 2007), other issues that raise some questions are:

1. **Privacy:** The more we share the more we are exposed. But, we will increase our benefit from the network with more exposure. This concept involves a little trust. For the network to be most useful to us there needs to be a little reciprocity. People very secretive about their privacy may not get great results from using these tools;
2. **Barriers to entry:** Getting started means investing time to put your information into the application. This can take a few minutes or a few hours, it depends on how much we want to disclose to the network. The more we share about us the easier it will be to make new connections. If we only upload a few contacts we get little benefit since these systems only search for connections through people we already know;
3. **Maintenance:** If we have a large network we can get to a point where we are receiving lots of requests. We can turn off e-mails about our connections, and with some networks we can even change our settings to accept requests from specific levels. We may get requests from people we don't know or don't remember. We shouldn't add everyone because we are a reflection of our networks;
4. **Cost:** Many of these services may begin to charge membership fees.

Sage (2013) warns that the "speed and volume of information that is published on social media can cause significant damage. (...) *A misleading comment* can damage a company's reputation in seconds". He also points out to the problem of hackers and cyber security because Social Media can be used by hackers to acquire "personal information about employees, then use it to befriend them. Having built a relationship, the criminal may be able to deceive the employee into revealing how to access to their company's *systems, and so opening the door to cyber attacks*". [4]

Ojala warns that "in minding our own business, we need to know what information about our employer can be gathered from social media **and whether it is what should be publicly available**" (2012, p. 53). [5]

The weakness in this new Social Networking sites is that "if users do not trust the system to protect their relationships, then they will not use the application effectively and gain very little incremental advantage from their connections" (Steckerl, 2007) [6].

In the end, the quality and value of this information will be dependent on the user and related to the results that it will allow obtaining, always integrated on its context.

SOCIAL TOOLS FOR THE WORKPLACE

The high number of social tools indicates an enthusiastic acceptance of this new media by individuals and companies (Steckerl, 2007).

Organisations cannot afford to ignore Social tools. If they don't know how they can use these tools, maybe they have already lost opportunities to faster competitors. For example, a business can help its staff save time searching if it encourages them to bookmark useful sites and share them with their co-workers.

We must remember that participation drives traffic. "Wikipedia is far more popular than Encarta, and Flikr is used more than Kodak Gallery. If you want people to use a tool, letting them contribute to it will engage their interest" (A. Miller, 2007).

For individuals, the benefits of using social tools often feel obvious but difficult or even impossible to measure. But, for most organisations, there's a need to demonstrate return on investment. "Those responsible for proving value have a dilemma: on the one hand, hard targets such as page hits or number of posts are easier to collect but have relatively little meaning" (A. Miller, 2007). On the other hand, measurements such as the ability of an organisation to innovate are hard to measure or directly attribute but are of fundamental importance to its financial health[7].

The idea that social tools are of interest to companies is unquestionable. As long as collaborators have basic Internet knowledge, the problem is the time needed to be actively involved. The more you use these new tools the more obvious the advantages become. To ignore these new tools is to ignore the unique benefits that they can offer (Zarrella, 2013).

Those companies who have opened their organisation to social tools had more positive results than they expected. The strategy is to treat your networked individuals as intelligent adults and minimize the need to be in control. Open and honest support is more constructive and usually works. However, we must stay involved and assume that the community can't grow without some time and attention (Curtis, 2006; Kassel, 2008; Steckerl, 2007).

SOME OF THE BIGGEST TOOLS AND HOW THEY OPERATE

For most of the services, the initial sign up is free. Users begin by filling out a form with personal data and then inviting friends. Some networks allow uploading current contacts, but others ask users to invite contacts directly through the application's interface. The connections then invite their own contacts, and that's how the network grows (Steckerl, 2007).

There are several Social Networking sites. Most of the applications competing for your attention offer a combination of professional and personal networking. Some of them are seriously oriented to business. From the top 20 players, three of them stand out:

1. **LinkedIn.com** (http://www.linkedin.com): Profiles look very much like a CV, excellent mix of people from different levels in the organisation, and many industries (Schaffer, 2011). Used mostly as a business research tool without the noise and redundant information that occurs in other social media platforms (Ojala, 2012). A fast growing business network with more than 200 million members worldwide. The most concrete application of LinkedIn is developing a network of associates, an excellent way to stay connected with current and past friends and clients (Kawasaki,

2007). Search for: industry experts, potential employees, hiring managers, deal-makers, people from specific geographies, or people with particular keywords in their profiles;

2. **Plaxo.com** (http://www.plaxo.com): Keeps all of your current contacts' information updated automatically thus is extremely useful in repair old relationships and staying in touch. Not a tool to build your network yet, though it does have a very useful 'mini Blog' feature to help you keep friends informed. More than 40 million people use Plaxo;

3. **Spoke.com** (http://spoke.com): Focused on providing sales prospects. Deeply integrated, extracts contact data from enterprise applications (Outlook, Notes, etc.) to establish and leverage connections. Provides more than 30 million contacts.

There are so many Social Networks that they are too numerous to list here. Most of them, like friendster. com, flickr.com, orkut.com, among hundreds of others tend to serve only social categories like dating, common interests, finding friends, photo sharing and others not directly related to business. Nevertheless they might contain important information about their users like brands they wear, satisfaction, or not, with the products they own, special needs and interest in solve their problems with new technologies, products or services, among others (Mordecai, 2013a).

Some web sites can also be networking sites, like MySpace.com, Windows Live Spaces, LiveJournal. com, and Blogger.com.

Other networks with a decidedly business or professional purpose, ranked by number of users, are:

1. **Hi5.com** (http://www.hi5.com/): More than 330 million users. General social networking and business;

2. **Passado.com** (http://passado.com): More than 4 million users (already had more than 7 million);

3. **Europe's largest business network, now called Wasabi** (http://www.wasabi.com/signup): More than 13 million users, about 6 million of whom are based in German-speaking countries. Business networking;

4. **Ryze.com** (http://www.ryze.com/): More than 500,000 users. Business networking;

5. **Ecademy.com** (http://www.sunzu.com/): Became Sunzu in January 2013. More than 100,000 users before the name change. Business networking.

Two other networks reflect some specialty in social networking:

1. **BiomedExperts** (http://www.biomedexperts.com): "The first literature-based scientific social network - brings the right researchers together and allows them to collaborate online. Collexis provides the BiomedExperts social network free of charge to researchers worldwide in an effort to increase collaborative biomedical research for the common good." More than 434.000 experts;

2. **globalEDGE** (http://globaledge.msu.edu/): "Sponsored and developed by the International Business Center at Michigan State University includes more than 350.000 registered users from across the globe and connects users to prospective collaboration partners and industry experts."

Social Networks for Business Use

Social Networks are one source, among many others, to consider in everyday reference and research work. There are tools like SlideShare (http://www.slideshare.net) that makes possible to share slide presentations, and includes the text of the slides in a format called a transcript. We can use the search box to find relevant topics, watch the presentation slides at the SlideShare site, or download them for future use. Some require registration based on the poster's preference before downloading is permitted, and Vidipedia (http://www.vidipedia.org) which is a selection of a multimedia picture social networking. Similarly to Wikipedia, Vidipedia is a free encyclopaedia that anyone can edit, search for key terms or browse by category. The results are encyclopaedic answers that link to relevant videos. When only one result is available, the video is automatically launched and all videos can be downloaded. Running a search on a given term produces an extensive description with definitions and videos.

A great advantage of Social Networking is connecting anyone who needs with those who have direct experience with companies, products, or services and are experts in some field (Kassel, 2008).

Businesses can use social tools to improve creativity, productivity, collaboration and visibility in certain markets, as well as engaging clients and partners in more fruitful collaboration (Berkman, 2008; Brown, 2012; Holloman, 2012).

There are a huge range of tools and sites (Russell, 2011; Tsvetovat & Kouznetsov, 2011), including:

1. Wikis;
2. Blogs;
3. Mash-ups[8];
4. Social Tagging;
5. Instant Messaging;
6. Video;
7. Social Bookmarking;
8. Podcasts; and
9. Services, like Facebook, Twitter, NetVibes, Flock and others (A. Miller, 2007).

There are practical examples of how geographically dispersed organisations could improve networking, knowledge sharing and collaboration using these tools (Tapscott & Williams, 2008).

The biggest benefit of such social tools for business is that this ongoing social contact with a colleague or client can mean that face-to-face meetings start with a deeper personal trust and understanding (Berkman, 2008; Brown, 2012; Zarrella, 2009).

If a person posts in his or her Social Networking community something like "I'm walking my dog to the dog park and his leash just broke. It was brand new. I'm so frustrated" (Leonard, 2013), we get to know several important things that can be used on the behalf of our company. This person has a need, the need to purchase a new leash for the dog. We also know that there is frustration with a new leash that just got broke leaving a bad evaluation and opinion about the manufacturer of that product. That person shows a real love and care for its animal friend so he must want the best for it. A dog needs food, toys, veterinarian care, among other things and we may know where that person lives, which dog park uses and the stores where he passes to reach the park[9].

For a company in the pet business this is gold because we have a behavioural segmentation (Kotler et al., 1999; Scott, 2008) that allows contacting the owner with a full range of services and products adapted to the animal, the climate where it lives and other specific needs. Perhaps the dog breed, name and birth date of the animal are posted also in the network and the offers can be personalized to target the prospect with some empathy.

Leonard (2013) calls this "the Anatomy of an Expression of Intent" and this can be used in a large sort of situations like animals, children, jobs, marriages and other businesses if we pay attention and learn how to read between the lines.

Blogs

According to Blog search engine Technorati (http://www.technorati.com), more than 180 million Blogs are being written in the public cyberspace known as the Blogosphere, up from just 100,000 in late 2002. Technorati's '2013 Digital Influence Report' shows that "consumers are turning to blogs when looking to make a purchase. In fact, blogs rank favorably with consumers for trust, popularity and even influence" (Leonard, 2013).

The report states that blogs are now the third-most influential digital resource (31%) when making overall purchases, behind retail sites (56%) and brand sites (34%), making it a useful resource to watch for consumer behavior and needs.

Ojala states that "blogs – or at least some blogs – gained the status of reputable sources for reporting and informed commentary. Curated blog content of interest to business researchers is part of online services such as ProQuest (in its Entrepreneurship product), LexisNexis, and Factiva." (2012, p.53).

Some Blogs with interest in CI like Traction (http://traction.tractionsoftware.com), MovableType (http://www.movabletype.org), and Manila (http://manila.userland.com) are used to streamline dissemination and collection[10] (Johnson, 2005). Now, enterprises in every industry are learning the power and risks of unleashing their employees' ideas on both their colleagues and the marketplace (Blood, 2004; Qualman, 2010).

Blogs have also taken on a greater role in CI practice within the enterprise, alongside Blogs in product, R&D, information technology, legal and financial teams, sales and marketing and even executive management (Johnson, 2005). Today, blogging is helping to create real communities of practice within organizations large and small (Curtis, 2006).

To obtain information about "which Blogs are reliable and worthy, the content aggregator and distributor Newstex (http://newstex.com/)" (Ojala, 2012, p.53) is the right place to start.

Wikis

The Wiki is a new collaboration tool in the corporate environment and is gaining significance in organizational information sharing. Borrowed from the Hawaiian word for quick, the first Wiki was originally developed by Ward Cunningham in 1995. Today they take the form of dozens of software applications that have Wiki-like capabilities (Johnson, 2005). Like Blogs, Wikis allow for very easy publishing and commenting on topics of collective interest to the community. Its unique social dynamics, allowing all contributors to change anything on any or all of the documents available, subjects the entire community to consensus-building (Carrera, 2012b).

Many of these tools are open-source and available free of charge, such as OpenWiki, Kwiki and Twiki. The best example of a Wiki is the Wikipedia. It begun in 2001 to build a free, multi-lingual encyclopaedia of knowledge on every subject in the human knowledge (Johnson, 2005). It has now more than 4.000.000 individual articles and serves as the laboratory for what Wikis can ultimately become given time and attention in the enterprise (Libert & Spector, 2009; Qualman, 2010; Surowiecki, 2007).

Wikis are just like Blogs. With Wikis, the same social interaction happens, but much faster and with far more intense collaboration (Tapscott & Williams, 2008). "They are based on the notion that the best results come from allowing decision-making to emerge from the bottom up with minimal editorial control from the top down (Johnson, 2005).

Wikis are great tools because of their editing and contribution characteristics. Wikis are made of hypertext documents linked together and edited collectively by the community in a web browser interface (Qualman, 2010). It is a very open medium where all authors can add to, change, or delete other people's work. "To prevent the damaging effects of creative destruction this can obviously lead to, Wikis have a means of comparing two states of a page, known as a *diff*, so that revisions can be viewed and rolled back and mistakes can be corrected" (Johnson, 2005).

The only way anyone can write something that will survive is if it's written with such quality that even its opponents can agree that it has value (Carrera, 2009, 2012a; Tapscott & Williams, 2008).

In CI, focus must be on the analysis of options available and the arguments that make one course stand apart from its alternatives as superior. This ascertains the quality of the information retrieved, allowing for a sustainable business decision making in organisations.

RSS

The technology that made all this possible is RSS (Rich Site Summary or Real Simple Syndication). It is an XML specification for distributing published media files to a web address that can be read by a RSS feed reader[11].

RSS has become the modern example for what XML can do for the user. It is also the most wide-spread form of XML in use today. RSS could very well become the principal mean by which all data, structured or unstructured, is broadcasted and applied (Johnson, 2005). This includes applications such as change-detection in Weblogs, retrieving spam-free email, or passing transactional data through a complex workflow environment (Carrera, 2009, 2012a).

"In addition to receiving posts from news sites and other Weblogs, RSS feeds can contain data from corporate systems: sales information, financial data, inventory or vendor information, data from partner or distribution systems, competitor events, and all manner of real-time data relevant to the enterprise" (Johnson, 2005).

The challenge now is to disseminate examples where collaborative social community applications have an impact on competitive intelligence efficiency or effectiveness (Carrera, 2012b; Hortinha, 2002).

Tag Clouding

Analysis of Blogs, Wikis and Web pages is an excellent way to gain an understanding of the individuals who use those particular tools of Social Media, and thus put the information into context.

Social Media search engines provide important data through Tag Clouds and through lists, such as the week's top ten tags and/or Blogs. Tags are words that content creators use to describe their works (http://en.wikipedia.org/wiki/Tag_cloud). In effect, they are keywords, guides that lead content users to the posts of content creators. Analyzing Tag Clouds, groups of tags within content, provides powerful insights into what Blog and other Social Media content creators and users are interested in (Curtis, 2006).

Tag Clouds can be used to build up a picture of the demographics of particular sites as a Wordle[12]. If we look at a Tag Cloud and we see a big number of technology-related words, such as: Ajax, Apple, CSS, Linux and Web 2.0, this helps us to analyze what type of consumer uses that site, segmenting them in psychographic means, and correlate it to the site's popular tags.

To begin monitoring, we must match keywords with the tags created by active consumers. Content creators are active consumers that rely on tags to help other consumers find them. Tags connect content creators with the readers, and are an important tool for monitoring consumer trends.

Over time, the use of tags results in a folksonomy, "a user-defined, keyword system in which tags are defined by users rather than by a provided vocabulary. Unfortunately, folksonomies often diverge from keywords that researchers might use" (Curtis, 2006).

Tag Clouds provide an excellent way to identify the most popular trends and can be used in reverse. "Rather than matching keywords you choose in advance, let them lead you to toward what seems popular" (Curtis, 2006).

Squidoo (http://www.squidoo.com/browse/top_lenses) allows users to set up a web page where they control the content. Squidoo has a number of tags that will help you. Each web page (Squidoo calls them lenses) has the tags prominently displayed. In addition, the site has a number of tags compiled based on popularity, and category. After some examination we will have a better understanding of tags and consumer interests and needs disclosed in Social Media.

By watching tags carefully you can monitor and correlate product category, brands, uses, interests and needs. Tag Clouds will show consumer interests integrated in the social media space (Kassel, 2008; A. Miller, 2007; Steckerl, 2007).

This way, consumer trends can be revealed.

CONCLUSION

In the globalized world quality information warrants best results when competing with other organizations, enabling a competitive advantage.

After describing what CI is and what is it good for, we have mentioned the advantages of being involved in CI projects. How to receive information for competitive decisions and the benefits of continually scan the business environment are some issues also analysed.

We have described several web tools available for information retrieval purposes and some features of each one, after showing the relations and benefits of the Internet for CI.

Social Networking is getting involved and getting your brand name being discussed every time you can. With the Internet we have the ability to reach more people and make more money in a highly personalized manner, knowing their needs and desires and the trends that are getting more attention (Kassel, 2008; A. Miller, 2007). Nevertheless, Ethics and good practice still play a major part.

Companies look at Social Media as a way of attracting and retaining customers (Brown, 2012; Ojala, 2012; Schaffer, 2011; Zarrella, 2009, 2013) but are not taking benefit (Dickins, 2013) of its major advantage in obtaining feedback from the market and be aware of competitors moves and market trends discussed by the clients (Berkman, 2008; Holloman, 2012). Customer and employee satisfaction is another invaluable information scanning that social tools allow to perform (Hawthorne & Cromity, 2012; Ojala, 2012; Sage, 2013).

Being connected is an incredible leverage, invaluable in your business development (Steckerl, 2007). Connections can have many unexpected positive results (Carrera, 2009; Kawasaki, 2007).

Also, creative consumers help companies developing new and better products by their feedback on using them and what to improve for better results (Berthon, Pitt, Plangger, & Shapiro, 2012).

We've concluded with a short description of some of the social network tools that can be adopted to gain current awareness about all the unexpected events in the macro environment of the companies, allowing the anticipation of what's going on with trends among specific market segments (Higham, 2010; Sage, 2013).

Web 2.0 tools are impacting the definition, collection and dissemination of CI but there is still much more untapped potential (Canhoto, 2013; Ojala, 2012).

CI professionals must redefine their roles in terms of strategic analysis (Kotze, 2013). Regardless of whether you show enthusiasm or scepticism in the face of this new Internet collaborative and communication tools, there is no excuse to be uninformed.

Consumers have always wanted to be heard, have always wanted their desires to be taken into account in the creation of new products and services. Consumer trends begin life through a series of small or big signals (Rasquilha, 2010). Through monitoring and analyzing the Social Media space, information professionals can provide a valuable analysis within consumer trend monitoring, knowing the consumer's interests and needs directly from the consumer posts and commentaries (Curtis, 2006), building the adequate solution to those clients' problems[13].

Like much of the web, corporate Blogs of Social Network web sites can be a good place to keep track of what the company is exploring for future products and services (Ojala, 2012). Blogs also provide excellent flags in response to consumer needs (Blood, 2004; Carrera, 2012a; Hortinha, 2002). BlogPulse point us toward the direction of trends we might otherwise let go (Curtis, 2006)[14].

In a fast moving business world, like the one we are living in, it should be a competitive edge having the chance of monitoring the market trends, the competition moves and still improve internal communication to flat the channels and downsize the hierarchy inside companies.

We must watch closely what the competitor employees are posting online and also keep an eye on what our employees are posting and check if they are, unconsciously, giving away valuable information to the competitors. We are not the only ones looking at the competition; they are doing the same thing with us and our company. Be aware.

Sage (2013) explains that social intelligence is better than traditional market research because it provides answers that companies consider critical to business strategy.

Only future research will tell if this is effectively true and the real value obtained by companies that perform this task accurately.

It's our expectation to contribute to take this relevant subject further in ulterior research to disseminate all the advantages in adopting Web 2.0 tools in companies.

Let's hope CEO's learn how to leverage all this advantages and know how to make a good use for them all.

ACKNOWLEDGMENT

I wish to thank the Portuguese Science and Technology Foundation (FCT) and the support from the following programs: POPH - Programa Operacional Potencial Humano, QREN - Quadro de Referência Estratégica Nacional, and UE-FSE – União Europeia-Fundo Social Europeu.

REFERENCES

Barbosa, P., & O'Reilly, A. (2011). *Harvard trends: Tendências de gestão*. Porto, Portugal: Vida Económica.

Bedell, D. (2011, March). Business intelligence. *Global Finance,* 46-47.

Bergier, J. (1970). *A espionagem industrial*. Porto, Portugal: Editorial Inova.

Berkman, R. (2008). *The art of strategic listening: Finding market intelligence in blogs and social media*. Paramount Market Pub.

Berthon, P., Pitt, L., Plangger, K., & Shapiro, D. (2012). Marketing meets web 2.0, social media, and creative consumers: Implications for international marketing strategy. *Business Horizons,* (55): 261–271. doi:10.1016/j.bushor.2012.01.007

Besson, B., & Possin, J. (1996). *Do serviço de informação à inteligência económica: Detectar as ameaças e oportunidades da empresa*. Instituto Piaget.

Best, D. (1996a). Business process and information management. In D. Best (Ed.), *The fourth resource: Information and its management*. Hampshire, UK: Aslib/Gower.

Best, D. (1996b). *The fourth resource: Information and its management*. Hampshire, UK: Aslib/Gower.

Beuren, I. M. (1998). *Gerenciamento da informação: Um recurso estratégico no processo de gestão empresarial*. São Paulo, Brazil: Atlas.

Blood, R. (2004). *O livro de bolso do weblogue: Conselhos práticos para criar e manter o seu blogue*. Porto, Portugal: Campo das Letras.

Bramston, D. (2009). *Basics product design: Idea searching*. Lausanne: Ava Publishing.

Brophy, P., & Coulling, K. (1996). *Quality management for information and library managers*. Guildford: Aslib/Gower.

Brown, E. (2012). Working the crowd: Social media marketing for business (2ª ed.). London: British Informatics Society.

Brown, J., & Duguid, P. (2000). *The social life of information*. Boston: Harvard Business School Press.

Brünger-Weilandt, S., Geiß, D., Herlan, G., & Stuike-Prill, R. (2011). Quality: Key factor for high value in professional patent, technical and scientific information. *World Patent Information, 33*(3), 230–234. doi:10.1016/j.wpi.2011.04.007

Burgelman, R., Christensen, C., & Wheelwright, S. (2009). Strategic management of technology and innovation (5ª ed.). Singapore: McGraw-Hill.

Burk, C. Jr, & Horton, F. Jr. (1988). *InfoMap: A complete guide to discovering corporate information resources*. Hoboken, NJ: Prentice Hall.

Canhoto, A. (2013). *Social media as a source of competitive intelligence*. Retrieved 28-02-2013, from http://anacanhoto.com/2013/01/18/social-media-as-a-source-of-competitive-intelligence/

Carrera, F. (2009). *Networking: Guia de sobrevivência profissional*. Lisboa, Portugal: Sílabo.

Carrera, F. (2012a). *Comunicar 2.0: A arte de bem comunicar no século XXI*. Lisboa, Portugal: Sílabo.

Carrera, F. (2012b). Marketing digital na versão 2.0: O que não pode ignorar (2ª ed.). Lisboa, Portugal: Sílabo.

Castells, M. (2000). *The information age: The rise of the network society* (2nd ed.). London: Blackwell.

Castells, M. (2004). *A galáxia internet: Reflexões sobre internet, negócios e sociedade*. Lisboa, Portugal: Fundação Calouste Gulbenkian.

Chen, H., Chau, M., & Zeng, D. (2002). CI spider: A tool for competitive intelligence on the web. *Decision Support Systems*, (34): 1–17. doi:10.1016/S0167-9236(02)00002-7

Choo, C. W. (2003). *Gestão de informação para a organização inteligente: A arte de explorar o meio ambiente*. Lisboa, Portugal: Editorial Caminho.

Christensen, C., Anthony, S., & Roth, E. (2004). *Seeing what's next: Using the theories of innovation to predict industry change*. Cambridge, MA: Harvard Business School Press.

Cleveland, H. (1983). A informação como um recurso. *Diálogo*, (16), 7-11.

Cleveland, H. (1985). *The knowledge executive: Leadership in an information society*. New York: Dutton.

Cooke, A. (2001). A guide to finding quality information on the internet: Selection and evaluation strategies (2ª ed.). Cornwall, UK: Library Association Publishing.

Cortada, J. (1996). *TQM for information systems management: Quality practices for continuous improvement*. Singapore: McGraw-Hill.

Curtis, P. (2006). *Gleaning consumer intelligence from blogs and podcasts*. Retrieved 02-12-2012, from http://www.freepint.com/issues/040506.htm#tips

Davenport, T. (1997). *Information ecology: Mastering the information and knowledge environment*. New York: Oxford University Press.

Davenport, T., Marchand, D., & Dickson, T. (2004). *Dominando a gestão da informação*. Porto Alegre, Portugal: Bookmann.

Dearlove, D. (1998). *Key management decisions: Tools and techniques of the executive decision-maker*. Wiltshire, UK: Financial Times/Pitman.

Deng, Z., & Luo, L. (2007). An exploratory discuss of new ways for competitive intelligence on web 2.0. In Wang (Ed.), Integration and innovation orient to e-society (pp. 597-604). Boston: Springer.

Dickins, J. (2013). Social media is an underused opportunity for luxury brands. *Digital Marketing Hub: The Guardian*. Retrieved 14-06-2013, from http://www.guardian.co.uk/media-network/media-network-blog/2013/jun/14/social-media-opportunity-luxury-brands

Fialka, J. (1997). *War by other means: Economic espionage in America*. Norton.

Focalytic. (2013). Social media content analysis of the 2013 masters golf tournament. *Focal Point*. Retrieved 16-06-2013, from http://www.focalytic.com/Portals/182440/docs/themastersgolfebook.pdf

Garber, R. (2001). Inteligência competitiva de mercado: Como capturar, armazenar, analisar informações de marketing e tomar decisões num mercado competitivo. São Paulo, Brazil: Madras.

Garvin, D. (1988). *Managing quality*. New York: Free Press.

Ginman, M. (1990). Quality information, and information for quality. In Wormell (Ed.), Information quality: Definitions and dimensions. London: Taylor Graham.

Gleick, J. (2011). *The information: A history, a theory, a flood*. St. Ives: 4th Estate.

Godeluck, S. (2000). *A explosão da economia na internet*. Lisboa: Livros do Brasil.

Gomes, E., & Braga, F. (2001). *Inteligência competitiva: Como transformar informação em um negócio lucrativo*. Rio de Janeiro, Brazil: Campus.

Grant, R. M. (2002). *Contemporary strategy analysis: Concepts, techniques, applications*. Oxford, UK: Wiley-Blackwell.

Guisnel, J. (1997). *Espionagem na internet: As guerras no ciberespaço*. Lisboa: Difusão Cultural.

Guynn, J. (2013). Facebook releases information on NSA requests for user data. *Los Angeles Times*. Retrieved 14-06-2013, from http://www.latimes.com/business/technology/la-fi-tn-facebook-releases-first-information-on-fisa-requests-20130614,0,3315731.story

Hawthorne, K., & Cromity, J. (2012, March/April). Social search for market intelligence. *Exploring Technology & Resources for Information Professionals, 36*-38.

Herring, J. P. (2002). Tópicos fundamentais de inteligência: Processo para identificação e definição de necessidades de inteligência. In Prescott & Miller (Eds.), Inteligência competitiva na prática. Rio de Janeiro, Brazil: Campus.

Higham, W. (2010). *The next big thing: Spotting and forecasting consumer trends for profit*. Bodmin: Kogan Page.

Hinton, M. (2006). *Introducing information management: The business approach*. Burlington, UK: Elsevier Butterworth-Heinemann.

Holloman, C. (2012). *The social media MBA: Your competitive edge in social media strategy development and delivery*. Hoboken, NJ: John Wiley & Sons.

Hortinha, J. (2002). *X-marketing*. Lisboa: Sílabo.

Huang, K., Lee, Y., & Wang, R. (1998). *Quality information and knowledge*. Upper Saddle River, NJ: Prentice Hall.

Johnson, A. (2005). Blogs, wikis & RSS: Colaborative social communities and the value of distributed CI. *Competitive Intelligence Magazine*. Retrieved 10-02-2013, from http://www.aurorawdc.com/blog-swikisrss_scipcimag_20050102.pdf

Kahaner, L. (1997). *Competitive intelligence: How to gather, analyze, and use information to move your business to the top*. New York: Simon & Schuster.

Kassel, A. (2008). *Social networking: A research tool*. Retrieved 15/12/2012, from http://web.fumsi.com/go/article/find/3196

Kawasaki, G. (2007). *Ten ways to use linkedin*. Retrieved 05-01-2007, from http://blog.guykawasaki.com

Kirsch, G., Brown, J., & Charley, F. (2006). Using patents in competitive intelligence. *Competitive Intelligence Magazine*, *9*(1), 17–21.

Kotler, P., Armstrong, G., Saunders, J., & Wong, V. (1999). Principles of marketing (2ª ed.). Cambridge, UK: Prentice Hall.

Kotze, L. (2013). *Social media increasingly important in competitive intelligence*. Retrieved 08-03-2013, from http://www.ibis.co.za/Competitive-Intelligence-Blog/social-media-increasingly-important-in-competitive-intelligence.html

Lattès, R. (1992). *O risco e a fortuna: A grande aventura da inovação*. Lisboa: Difusão Cultural.

Leonard, H. (2013). *Blogs outrank social networks in influence*. Retrieved 09-03-2013, from http://www.businessinsider.com/blog-influence-outranks-social-networks-2013-3

Libert, B., & Spector, J. (2009). *Muitas cabeças pensam melhor: Como mobilizar o poder das multidões para o seu negócio*. Porto: Lua de Papel.

Marchand, D. (1990). Managing information quality. In Wormell (Ed.), Information quality: Definitions and dimensions. London: Taylor Graham.

Marchand, D., & Horton, F. Jr. (1986). *Infotrends: Profiting from your information resources*. Hoboken, NJ: Wiley.

Martinet, B., & Marti, Y. (1995). *A inteligência económica: Os olhos e os ouvidos da empresa*. Instituto Piaget.

McGee, J. V., & Prusak, L. (1995). *Gerenciamento estratégico da informação: Aumente a competitividade e a eficiência de sua empresa utilizando a informação como uma ferramenta estratégica*. Rio de Janeiro, Brazil: Campus.

McPherson, P. (1994). Accounting for the value of information. *Aslib Proceedings*, *46*(9), 203–215. doi:10.1108/eb051366

Miller, A. (2007). *Social tools for business use: Messages from a web 2.0 conference*. Retrieved 12-12-2012, from http://web.fumsi.com/go/article/find/3916

Miller, J., & Business Intelligence Braintrust. (2002). *O milênio da inteligência competitiva*. Porto Alegre. *The Bookman*.

Mohr, J., Sengupta, S., & Slater, S. (2010). Marketing of high-technology products and innovations (3ª ed.). Upper Saddle River, NJ: Pearson.

Mordecai, V. (2013a). 4 things social media analysis can tell you about your business. *Focal Point: Focalytic*. Retrieved 23-05-2013, from http://www.focalytic.com/focal-point/bid/291330/4-Things-Social-Media-Analysis-Can-Tell-You-About-Your-Business

Mordecai, V. (2013b). What businesses can gain from a custom social media listening tool. *Focal Point: Focalytic*. Retrieved 20-05-2013, from http://www.focalytic.com/focal-point/bid/291331/What-Businesses-Can-Gain-from-a-Custom-Social-Media-Listening-Tool

Mordecai, V. (2013c). What is competitive intelligence? *Focal Point: Focalytic*. Retrieved 14-06-2013, from http://www.focalytic.com/focal-point/bid/297577/What-Is-Competitive-Intelligence

Negroponte, N. (1995). *Being digital*. New York: Knopf.

Ojala, M. (2012, July/August). Minding your own business: Social media invades business research. *Exploring Technology & Resources for Information Professionals*, 51-53.

Orna, E. (1996). Valuing information: Problems and opportunities. In D. Best (Ed.), *The fourth resource: Information and its management*. Hampshire, UK: Aslib/Gower.

Orna, E. (1999). Practical information policies (2ª ed.). Cambridge, UK: Gower.

Penzias, A. (1989). *Ideas and information: Managing in a high-tech world*. New York: W. W. Norton.

Penzias, A. (1995). *Harmony: Business, technology & life after paperwork*. New York: Harper Collins.

Porter, M. E., & Millar, V. E. (1985). How information gives you competitive advantage. *Harvard Business Review*, *63*(4), 149–160.

Prescott, J. E., & Miller, S. H. (2002). *Inteligência competitiva na prática: Técnicas e práticas bem sucedidas para conquistar mercados*. Rio de Janeiro: Campus.

Prior, V. (2006). *Competitive intelligence: An introduction*. Retrieved 06-10-2008 from http://www.freepint.com/issues/050106.htm#feature

Prior, V. (2007). *DIY detection: Competitive intelligence for SMEs*. Retrieved from http://web.freepint.com/go/features/2483

Qualman, E. (2010). *Socialnomics: Como os media sociais estão a transformar o modo como vivemos e como fazemos negócios*. Lisboa: Presença.

Rasquilha, L. (2010). *Tendências e gestão da inovação: Como aplicar as tendências na estratégia de inovação empresarial*. Lousã: Verlag Dashöfer.

Redman, T. (1996). *Data quality for the information age*. Norwood, MA: Artech House.

Revelli, C. (2000). *Inteligência estratégica na Internet: Como desenvolver eficazmente actividades de monitorização e de pesquisa nas redes*. Instituto Piaget.

Ribault, J.-M., Martinet, B., & Lebidois, D. (1995). *A gestão das tecnologias*. Lisboa: D. Quixote.

Russell, M. (2011). *Mining the social web: Analyzing data from Facebook, Twitter, LinkedIn, and other social media sites*. Sebastopol, CA: O'Reilly Media.

Rustmann, F., Jr. (2002). *CIA, Inc.: Espionage and the craft of business intelligence*. Dulles: Brassey's.

Sage, N. (2013). *How to create business value from social intelligence*. Retrieved 30-05-2013, from http://www.computerweekly.com/opinion/How-to-create-business-value-from-social-intelligence

Schaffer, N. (2011). *Maximizing LinkedIn for sales and social media marketing: An unofficial, practical guide to selling & developing B2B business on LinkedIn*. CreateSpace Independent Publishing Platform.

Scott, D. (2008). *As novas regras de marketing e relações públicas: Como usar os blogues, o podcasting, os media online e as notas informativas para chegar directamente aos consumidores*. Porto: Ideias de Ler.

Shapiro, C., & Varian, H. (1999). *Information rules: A strategic guide to the network economy*. Boston: Harvard Business School Press.

Steckerl, S. (2007). *Survival guide: Online social networking*. Retrieved 12/12/2012, from http://web.fumsi.com/go/article/use/2346

Suhr, C. (2004). A change of paradigms: looking back to the pioneer years of patent information management (1960-1990). *World Patent Information, 26*(1), 41–43. doi:10.1016/j.wpi.2003.10.017

Surowiecki, J. (2007). *A sabedoria das multidões: Como a inteligência colectiva transforma a economia e a sociedade*. Porto: Lua de Papel.

Taborda, J. P., & Ferreira, M. D. (2002). *Competitive intelligence: Conceitos, práticas e benefícios*. Pergaminho.

Tapscott, D. (1995). *The digital economy: Promise and peril in the age of networked intelligence*. New York: McGraw-Hill.

Tapscott, D. (1999). *Creating value in the network economy*. Boston: Harvard Business School Press.

Tapscott, D., Ticoll, D., & Lowy, A. (2000). *Digital capital: Harnessing the power of business webs*. Boston: Harvard Business School Press. doi:10.1145/341836.336231

Tapscott, D., & Williams, A. (2008). *Wikinomics: A nova economia das multidões inteligentes*. Matosinhos: Quidnovi.

Trott, P. (2008). *Innovation management and new product development* (4ª ed.). Essex, UK: Prentice Hall | Financial Times.

Tsvetovat, M., & Kouznetsov, A. (2011). *Social network analysis for startups: Finding connections on the social web*. Sebastopol, CA: O'Reilly Media.

Wagner, G. (1990). The value and the quality of information: The need for a theoretical synthesis. In Wormell (Ed.), Information quality: Definitions and dimensions. London: Taylor Graham.

Ward, J., & Peppard, J. (2002). Strategic planning for information systems (3ª ed.). Chichester, UK: Wiley.

Webster, F. (2000). *Theories of the information society*. Cornwall, UK: Routledge.

Weiss, A. (2008). *If they only knew: Finding competitive intelligence from the web sites of your competitors*. Retrieved 21/01/2013, from http://web.fumsi.com/go/article/find/3355

Wilson, T. (1985). Information management. *The Electronic Library*, *3*(1), 62–66. doi:10.1108/eb044644

Wilson, T. (1987). Information for business: The business of information. *Aslib Proceedings*, *39*, 275–279. doi:10.1108/eb051066

Winkler, I. (1997). *Corporate espionage: What it is, why it's happening in your company, what you must do about it. Rocklin*. Prima Publishing.

Wormell, I. (1990). *Information quality: Definitions and dimensions*. London: Taylor Graham.

Zarrella, D. (2009). *The social media marketing book*. Sebastopol, CA: O'Reilly Media.

Zarrella, D. (2013). *The science of marketing: When to Tweet, what to post, how to blog, and other proven strategies*. Hoboken, NJ: John Wiley & Sons.

KEY TERMS AND DEFINITIONS

Business Information: Information needed by all kinds of organizations about their competitive environment to allow sound decision making, such as business growth rate and operating ratios. Some tools to gather this information can be used, like PEST analysis (information about the Political, Economical, Sociological and Technological factors that can affect the organization), and SWOT analysis (information about the Strengths, Weaknesses, Opportunities and Threats), amongst others.

Business Management: The activity of conducting all the necessary operations in order to make the organization grow, benefiting all the shareholders and stakeholders and the society in general. It involves several specialized functions like Finance, Marketing, Operations, Human Resources, Production, etc.

Competitive Intelligence: CI is the use of public sources to develop information about the competition, consumers, and market environment. It aims to monitor a firm's external environment for information relevant to its decision-making process. It involves accurately identifying your information needs, collecting relevant information, analysing it, communicating the results to the people who need it, and taking rapid and appropriate action. Traditionally, CI relied upon published company reports and other kinds of printed information. In recent years, Internet has rapidly become an extremely good source of information about the competitive environment of companies.

Information Quality: Quality information is needed to clear decision-making about what products develop, for what customers, at what cost, through which distribution channels, reducing the uncertainty that a new product/service development always brings with it. It warrants best results when competing with other organizations. To be considered of quality, information must meet several criteria such as: completeness, accessibility, accuracy, precision, objectivity, consistency, relevancy, timeliness, and understandability.

Information Value: The value attributed to information produced or acquired by organizations, entities and persons, and delivered in the form of an information product or service. Information has no implicit value in itself since it depends on its use, purpose and context. Its value is related to the results that it will allow obtaining and it's dependable on its context.

Market Trends: Trends begin by knowing the consumer's interests and needs. What's new and differentiates who wears it. In a fast moving business world it should be a competitive edge having the chance of monitoring the market trends. Market trends inform organizations about what products develop, for what customers, at what cost, through which distribution channels, reducing the uncertainty that a new product/service development always brings with it. To scan the trends of a market, understand consumer motivation and the actual preferences in the business area where companies act and compete may induce a competitive advantage.

Social Media: Online Web 2.0 tools like Wikis, Blogs, and Social Networking with a two way communication channel, allowing receiving and sharing information. Also allow the knowledge of competitor's moves and the analysis of trends from the communications exchanged in the networks of individual consumers, making it easy for companies to develop solutions according to their clients and prospects desires.

ENDNOTES

[1]   For a list of CI software, Cf. (http://www.thecisource.com/resources/software).

[2]   Cf., also, (http://trendwatching.com/).

[3]   Cf. Flock (http://www.flock.com/) and StumbleUpon (http://www.stumbleupon.com/).

[4]   In **Bold** in the original text.

[5]   In **Bold** and *Italic* in the original text.

[6]   Facebook releases information on NSA requests for user data (Guynn, 2013).

[7]   For information in Marketing metrics and analytics, Cf. (http://blog.eloqua.com/marketing-analytics/?utm_source=feedburner&utm_medium=email&utm_campaign=Feed%3A+ItsAllAb outRevenue+%28It%27s+All+About+Revenue%29). For calculating Return on Investment, Cf. (http://businesscenter.eloqua.com/roi-calculator/).

[8]   For good examples of Mash-ups, Cf. (Tapscott & Williams, 2008).

[9]   "Julie Doe posts (…): "I love this particular brand of soda, though I really wish they had a diet option!" Social media analysis can then add this (…) to the group of opportunities that your business can pursue" (Mordecai, 2013a).

[10] See, for example: IceRocket (http://www.icerocket.com), Technorati (http://www.technorati.com), Google (http://blogsearch.google.com/blogsearch), NM Incite (http://nmincite.com), Blogger (Google-owned) (http://www.blogger.com/start), Bloglines (http://www.Bloglines.com), Feedster (http://www.feedster.com), del.icio.us (http://del.icio.us/), and Podcast Alley (http://www.podcastalley.com).

11   For a list of several news readers for Mac and Windows, Cf. RSS Info (http://blogspace.com/rss/readers). You can subscribe to an RSS feed for each individual term, simplifying your monitoring.

12   "Wordle is a toy for generating 'word clouds' from text that you provide. The clouds give greater prominence to words that appear more frequently in the source text. You can tweak your clouds with different fonts, layouts, and color schemes. The images you create with Wordle are yours to use however you like. You can print them out, or save them to the Wordle gallery to share with your friends". Retrieved 03-11-2008 from (http://www.dailyack.com/2008/06/worlde.html).

13   Retrieved 02-11-2012 from http://www.buzzlogic.com/press/news.html?postdate=1225203064 now Twelvefold Media (http://www.twelvefold.com/splash/?postdate=1225203064).

14   Cf. (http://blog.blogpulse.com/).

This research was previously published in Information Quality and Governance for Business Intelligence edited by William Yeoh, John R. Talburt, and Yinle Zhou, pages 167-193, copyright year 2014 by Business Science Reference (an imprint of IGI Global).

Chapter 45
A Review of Tools for Overcoming the Challenge of Monitoring of Social Media

Carlos Figueroa
University of Turabo, Puerto Rico

Abraham Otero
University San Pablo, Spain

ABSTRACT

Until recently, a company's communications with the public were unidirectional and mostly limited to advertisements in mass media. This gave companies almost complete control over their brand and image. Nowadays, a new set of media, in which the public has similar capabilities for creating content as companies has emerged: social media. The growth of this medium has been exponential, endowing it with a reach that can dwarf traditional mass media. Having or not having a presence in such media is not just a choice of the company. The company's customers and the general public can generate content related to a company without the company's consent. There is no way for the company to avoid it. All they can do is listen to the conversations, engage in them, and try to dampen negative feelings while steering the overall conversation in positive directions. Given the size of social networks and the large number of conversations that they support on a daily basis, manual monitoring is impossible. In this chapter, the authors review and evaluate various tools to support the tasks of monitoring and managing the content of social media that is relevant for a company, a brand, or a product.

INTRODUCTION

Part of Web 2.0 is comprised of social networks, blogs, wikis, and other collaborative applications where end users are no longer mere spectators, but participants that generate content continuously and guide the direction of the conversation. In the past, business communications with the public were unidirectional and mostly limited to advertisements in mass media. Therefore, companies had strong control over their brand and image. Now the public has new ways to spread messages about companies through

DOI: 10.4018/978-1-5225-5637-4.ch045

social media. These messages sometimes have a reach equal to or even superior to the reach of mass media messages. Heinlein and Kaplan (2010) found that at least in one medium (Internet) companies have lost complete control of the messages related to their own brand and products, since the public can guide the conversation and respond to the company on equal terms. The lack of full control over this new media forces companies to monitor and react to what happens in these new avenues of communication. (O'Reilly, 2007; Gallaugher, 2010; Constantinides, et al., 2008; Dösinger, et al., 2007)

To monitor social media, large amounts of heterogeneous information such as text, images, audio, videos and other unstructured data need to be analyzed. Sometimes these contents are negative, requiring prompt intervention to reduce or prevent damage to the reputation, products and/or services of the business or organization (Heinlein, Kaplan, 2010; Constantinides, et al., 2008; Bhattacharya, Du, & Sen, 2010). When no adequate and prompt action is taken, the image of the company may be affected negatively (Constantinides, et al., 2008; Social Media Report, 2010; Sterne, 2010; Leganza, 2010; Hutley, 2009).

All social networks provide user interfaces, usually via the Web browser or mobile applications, for creating and accessing user-created content. But these interfaces are intended for personal use, and for accessing only the content created by users who have some relationship between them such as friends, followers, etc. They are not intended for use by several people working within the same account (a very common scenario in a company). They do not provide effective mechanisms for discovering or monitoring discussions on a certain topic throughout the entire network. In addition, they only allow the user to manage content within the social network itself, while a company must maintain a presence in multiple social networks simultaneously.

Currently, there are various monitoring tools that provide assistance in the overwhelming task of social media content monitoring. These tools can monitor the generation of new content relevant to a certain area (a company, a brand, a product...), analyze the scope of the conversation, provide a sentiment analysis classifying the discussions in categories such as "Positive," "Neutral," and "Negative" trigger alerts or actions whenever a conversation on a certain topic is started, etc. (Constantinides, et al., 2008; Sterne 2010; Leganza, 2010; FreshMinds Research, 2010; Koch & Richter, 2008). There are over a hundred monitoring solutions of this nature (A Wiki of Social media Monitoring Solutions, 2011), making it difficult to select the most appropriate tool/tools for the particular context and needs of each company (FreshMinds Research, 2010).

Well exploited, social media monitoring can not only be used to respond to negative content related to a company, but it can also be integrated into business processes in the areas of marketing, market research, customer service, public relations, and sales among others. With the adequate support of monitoring tools, these functions can be carried out in a more effective manner and at a lower cost than with traditional solutions (Gleanster, 2010). However, before such tools can be used effectively in a company, both the staff who is going to participate in the social media monitoring task and the management must understand the potential of social media and how it can make a difference in their company (Harvard Business Review Analytic Services, 2010).

In this chapter we will analyze the capabilities of the most popular tools currently available for monitoring and reacting to social media content. We will examine their ability to track, analyze, obtain metrics, manage, and respond to what is said about a given topic (in our case, a company, its products and its business) in social media. In the next section, we briefly present several case studies that demonstrate how the social media can provide considerable value if the business knows how to properly take advantage of it. However, when it is ignored or misused the social media can cause considerable damage to the brand and reputation of a business. The following section reviews the main tools that can provide support in the management of the social media presence of a company. Finally, we discuss the results of our review and provide some conclusions.

BACKGROUND

Well exploited, social media channels can be used for market research, and public relations. Starbucks is a poster child on how to use social media for this purpose. On their Website, MyStarbucksIdea (My Starbucks Idea, 2011) the company allows customers to suggest ideas to improve services, products, stores and the brand itself. These ideas can be voted and discussed by users. The ideas that receive the most votes not only tend to be good ideas from the point of view of increasing the quality of services or products, but the voting process itself is a prospective market study showing the support these ideas receive from the customers. And the company not only gets these ideas for free, but it increases the perception that it values and considers customers' opinions.

Starbucks also stands out for the speed and effectiveness with which they issue corrective replies to negative comments about the brand. For example, there is an urban legend that the firm does not send coffee to the U.S. military because of a corporate position against "the war" (whatever "the war" is at that moment). Users of the popular microblogging network Twitter often echo this legend in their messages, which are usually followed by a fast response from Starbucks stating that it is not true, and providing a link to a Web page that sets the record straight (Starbucks Newsroom, 2011). The company also maintains a presence in all the major social networks: Facebook (Starbucks-In Facebook, 2011), Youtube (Starbucks Producer, 2011), LinkedIn (Starbucks-In LinkedIn, 2011) and Twitter (Starbucks Coffee, 2011) among others. The pages of the company are updated regularly, show a high level of activity, and have fans numbering in the millions.

The computer maker Dell is a good example of using social media for promotional purposes. The company was an early adopter in the social media space and has mastered how to leverage blogs and community outreach. For example, it maintains multiple Twitter accounts tailored for content that may be of interest to different customer profiles. Through one of these accounts, Dell Outlet, which is being followed by more than a million and a half users, Dell offers promotions and discount coupons. According to the company, this account alone produces tens of millions of dollars in sales a year. The company also maintains Twitter accounts designed to provide technical support to customers, and accounts for keeping customers up to date with the latest news about Dell. In the latter case, the company has two different accounts, one for consumers and another for corporate clients, to target content to each of these two profiles.

These two case studies could lead the reader to think about social media as just another marketing channel. As is the case of any marketing channel, each company should evaluate whether it should maintain a presence in it or not, but there is no requirement for participation in the channel. This assumption is wrong. Social media is different from any other channel. Having or not having a presence in the channel is not a decision that depends entirely on the company, but it also depends on the customers. Customers can choose to talk about the company in the channel, both in positive or negative terms. There is nothing that the company can do to prevent this. The only thing it can do is engage in conversation. Failure to do this in time can have significant negative consequences.

Dell itself learnt this lesson the hard way. In June 2005, before Dell had a social media communication strategy, it began to receive major complaints concerning their customer support services; especially from the popular blogger Jeff Jarvis (Williams 2009). Recently he had bought a Dell laptop, as well as a four year in home warranty service plan. Just after he received the machine, it malfunctioned. Jarvis contacted Dell's customer support and learnt that he would need to send the machine back to the company because the technician wouldn't be able to get the parts needed to fix the laptop to his home. On June 21, 2005 he posted his first blog related to this matter in BuzzMachine.com (Jarvis 2005). This blog post, entitled "Dell lies. Dell sucks", was commented by 253 bloggers, who also had been receiving a poor customer service from Dell. In June 23, 2005 he wrote another blog post entitled, "Dell hell, continued" where he stated, "But that's what bothers me most: I bought that warranty, the top-of-the-line, most expensive warranty that warrant (Dell 2012) to send someone to my home to repair my machine. Except that's a big fat Dell lie. The person they would send to my home would not have the parts (or, according to some of my commenters, the expertise, training, and intelligence) to repair that machine". He kept on blogging for almost a month about Dell's poor customer service and also sending emails to Dell representatives at the same time; but he never received a reply from them. Jarvis blog Website caught the attention from many other bloggers that have had negative experiences with the Dell's technical support, triggering criticism and bad publicity through the net, and it finally was reported by Business Week Online. It is possible that the 5 points dropped on the score of the American Customer Satisfaction Index on August 2005 was related to the bad campaign generate by the blogosphere. If Dell had pay attention to claims and negative comments adequately, rather than remain in silent; the damage caused to the reputation of the company would have been minimal.

The songwriter and singer Dave Carroll (Rotman, 2010) after having a bad experience with his baggage, specifically with an expensive guitar that was damaged by United Airlines employees during a flight, uploaded a video entitled "United Breaks Guitars" to YouTube on July 6, 2009. This video was viewed by 150,000 people by the end of the first day, and had been seen by over five million people by August 15, 2009. It is possible that the 2009 reduction in passengers of 12.67% compared to 2008, and the decline in profits of 19.19% compared to the previous year bore some relationship to the negative promotion created by this video (Kaplan, 2010; Rotman, 2010; Soule, 2010). Currently, the video continues to accumulate views on YouTube and Dave Carroll has registered the domain http://www.UnitedBreaksGuitars.com to continue to focus attention on his case. The original video has been watched by more than 11 million people, and Dave Caroll has uploaded two more videos in which he criticizes different departments of the company for failing to satisfactorily address the problem. The damage to the image of the airline has been and is still considerable. An appropriate and prompt response by United would have completely avoided this situation.

Sometimes, these types of problems do not originate outside the firm. In 2009, employees of a Domino's Pizza outlet created what they thought would be a funny gross-out video for their friends and they posted on YouTube. The video showed the firm's brand alongside gross mishandling of the brand's food products. The video was seen by over 1 million viewers before it was removed from YouTube. The two employees who made the video were arrested and fired. The Domino's store where the incident occurred was closed, and the firm's president had to make a painful apology.

Companies cannot avoid conversations about their brands, their products or their services on the social media. All they can do is listen to the conversations and engage in them. Given the size of the social networks and the large number of conversations that occur in them every day, monitoring these conversations can only be done in an efficient manner with monitoring tools that help identify and manage the relevant content.

TOOLS TO MONITOR SOCIAL MEDIA AND GENERATE ENGAGEMENT

Materials and Methods

The authors of this paper have been early adopters of social networks, with six years of experience participating both at a personal level and in the role of "social media manager" of communities (mainly the javaHispano.org community [JavaHispano, 2011]). In the latter case, the social presence of the organization in Twitter, Facebook, Youtube, Google+, Vimeo, and the organization's own Website is not managed by a single person, but by a team geographically distributed among Spain, Mexico, Chile, Colombia and Peru. From the early days of social media, this led us to search for tools that enable collaboration among several persons to manage an organization's online presence, assigning tasks among the team members and monitoring activity relevant to the organization.

To this experience in the field of social media, we add a personal interest and curiosity about the whole ecosystem. This has led us to always keep track of the latest developments in the social media ecosystem, beyond the search for tools to support our own use of social networks. Therefore, even before starting the more formal and methodical study presented in this chapter we already had good knowledge of the social media field, the tools that can be used to maintain a presence more sophisticated than personal use requires, and the main players which develop tools to support building an online presence.

Building on this experience, we developed a draft list of tools to include in this study. We completed the list by querying Google for terms like "tool for monitoring social media," "support tools for social media managers", "online reputation" and so on. Based on our previous experience and the initial information we found regarding the different tools, more than 100 existing solutions were reduced to a total of 11 tools, which were finally included in this study. The main criteria used in selecting the tools were the size of the tool's user base, the functionality it provides, and its suitability for use in a business environment. Inevitably, some readers will feel that some other tool should also have been included in this study. Unfortunately, time and space constraints forced us to limit the scope of the study to a manageable number of tools.

Again, relying on our previous experience, we defined a list of features that would be checked when evaluating all the tools. When evaluating a tool for functionality relevant to a business context, we sometimes found some feature that was not included in our initial feature list. In this case, we extended the list with the new functionality. The tools that had already been studied without evaluating this functionality were reviewed again to recheck whether or not they had a similar feature.

The list of features analyzed in each tool is:

- **The Social Networks Supported by the Tool:** Facebook and/or Twitter support is considered essential for inclusion in the study, given the prevalence and magnitude of these social networks (over 800 million in the case of Facebook [2011] and over 200 million in the case of Twitter, Shiels, [2011]). Support for other networks such as LinkedIn, Youtube, Vimeo, Google + or blogging sites was considered a plus. We also evaluated the tool for its capability of maintaining multiple identities in each of these social networks. As we have seen in the background section with the firm Dell, it is sometimes recommended that a company maintains more than one identity/user account on a given social network.

- **Support for Searching for Key Terms in Social Networks:** We also evaluated whether these searches were in real time ("live searches" that update themselves automatically), and the functionality that the tool provided to store search results.
- **Alarm Triggering:** We assessed the functionality that the tools had to generate warnings (sending e-mail, SMS or similar) to warn of certain events (such as a user with considerable influence in a social network that is talking negatively about a company's product).
- **Support for Sentiment Analysis of the Content:** It is often the case that a prompt reaction to negative content limits the damage it can cause to an organization, and stop its spread through a social network. Often the positive content does not require a response from the organization. Hence there is an interest in being able to identify content associated with an organization and classify it as positive, negative or neutral, and to be able to effectively prioritize content management.
- **Analysis of Influence of Social Network Users:** The content, either positive or negative, will have more impact and diffusion the more influence the user who created it has. Negative content from influential users must be addressed immediately. Positive comments by influential users may be encouraged with some kind of reward, for example, by sending him/her free evaluation units of their products. Sometimes, companies also contact these users for advertising purposes. In any case, knowing who the influential users are that speak of a company's products, services or brand is useful information.
- **Support for Teamwork:** The social presence of a medium or large company will often not be managed by a single person. The availability of tools to assign tasks to different team members, prioritize tasks, provide real-time collaboration between various team members, and support for multiple user profiles in the tool are useful features when more than one person will be responsible for managing the social presence.
- Internationalization of the user interface, and geo-targeting of the users who engage in conversations with our organization.
- Possibility of integration of the tool with internal information systems of the company, such as ERP, CMR, a marketing data base, etc.
- **Reporting Functionality:** Ideally, the tools should generate reports that summarize the organization's online activity, the activity of influential users who talk about the products, reports about discussions regarding a topic of interest for the company and other relevant information. They should also provide metrics such as number of clicks on links, or number of responses/comments generated by the content we create.
- **Price of the Tools:** Price is important, and can determine if, for example, a small business cannot afford to use a certain tool.
- **Clients Available for the Tool:** In almost all cases there are Web clients who can be accessed from any Web browser. The availability of mobile clients for smart phones or tablet devices is desirable.

To evaluate each of the tools, we started by reading the user guide of the tool. In most cases, videos showing diverse functionality of the tools were available. Whenever possible, we requested a demo of the product from a company representative who developed the tool. In this way we could see the tool being used by an expert user. We also used the tool ourselves. When necessary, we requested trial accounts for the testing. The tools were tested using social media profiles created specifically for the purpose of evaluating the tools. This permitted certain tests (such as the creation of negative content) to be carried out freely. The tools also were tested with real users' profiles that had a long time presence in social networks and a considerable number of followers (several thousands).

Results

There are some similarities and differences that should be pointed out in order to categorize the different tools according to their capabilities and functionalities. On one hand, we have those tools that are mainly used to monitor the social media, and on the other hand, those that also can generate content, promote engagement, and launch advertising or public relations campaigns. Trackur, Klout, Viralheat, StepRep, and Brandwatch are tools that are essentially used to perform monitoring activities. Radian6, SocialFlow, SproutSocial, Sysomos, Hootsuite, and TweetDeck are mainly used to monitor and generate engagement.

All the tools use some kind of dashboard from which monitoring, searching, engagement and other activities are launched. From the dashboard the operator or social media manager may perform different actions such as view user generated content from blogs, forums, YouTube, news and other traditional and non-traditional social media networks. Figure 1 shows how two different dashboards may present almost the same information, but in a different manner. The functionality and capabilities of each dashboard may differ in terms of user interface, arrangement, components, icons, links, tabs and other features that may comprise it. There are three common functionalities across all dashboards: to monitor or listen to what is said; search or query key terms, topics and other kind of information such as competitors; and generate engagement in a real time basis with fans (Facebook), followers (Twitter), or users from other social media content sites.

Most of the tools may monitor or listen to what has been said about a brand, product, or company. This ongoing process generates facts to which analytic techniques are applied to obtain statistics of mentions, reputation, reach, sentiment, posts' tone, influence, competitors, demographics, and even the number of clicks that users make to specific URL's links. StepRep, Brandwatch, Trackur, and ViralHeat have common grounds when it comes to monitoring the reputation of a brand, product or company; they all search different social media content for mentions and keywords to determine if what has been published affects the enterprises' reputation in a positive or negative manner; giving more emphasis to the negative content. This does not mean that other tools do not pay attention to the reputation dimension as part of their whole monitoring tasks. Sometimes, it is seen as a derived functionality of the monitoring process itself and it might be incorporated within the sentiment analysis functionality or even by means of other functions.

The ability to search social media for keywords, persons, competitors or topics in order to get a better picture of what is happening around a specific brand, product, or company is an invaluable feature. All the tools have searching capabilities, but they may differ in terms of how, what, where, and when a search is done.

- How the search is performed determines to some extent the results that will be obtained; some tools may search using some kind of query structure, but others may only search individual keywords, brands, or users.
- What can be searched refers to: keywords, topics, brands, user accounts or user identifier, businesses, places, videos, competitors, people, mentions, and Facebook wall content.
- Where the search is performed is about specific social media where user generated content is available: Twitter, Facebook, Linkedin, Google Buzz, YouTube, Blogs, WordPress, Flickr, Foursquare,

Figure 1. SproutSocial dashboard (top) and Sysomos Twitter dashboard (bottom)

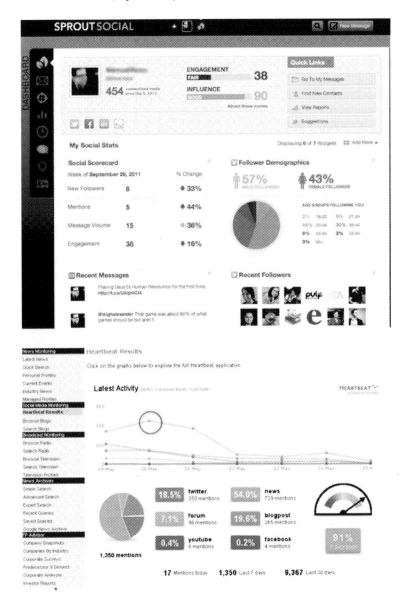

Go Walla, Yelp, Trip advisor, Tumblr, Instagram, last.fm, Yelp, Citysearch, Urbaspoon, Metacafe, bliptv, MySpace, Typepad, LiveJournal, Ping.fm, mixi, news sites, and forums. Some tools can be configured so the scope of the search can be limited to a specific region(s), country, city, or area in order to obtain results that are meaningful to an enterprise whose activities are limited to that region.

- When the search is going to be executed or in what interval of time will new results be obtained for a specific search. Some tools may provide options to save searches for future reference and execution. Most of the tools execute searches in a real time basis, which is an ideal situation for businesses that want to be aware of conversations in real time, especially of those that require a rapid response to mitigate negative publicity.

Searches are usually based on queries that are defined using a simple user interface that in many cases is part of the main dashboard. Constraints on the search can sometimes be imposed by means of combo boxes to constrain the media in which the search is performed (videos, images, news, Twitter, Facebook, etcetera) to city, country or any other predetermined constraints or filters. In some cases, the user may select or even write some logical or binary operators to combine several search terms and build the search query. Searches may be performed manually or automatically in time intervals (minutes, hours, days or even on a virtually continuously basis). Searches generate results that can be analyzed, graphed and displayed to obtain a better picture of who, what, when, where, and how (format used: text, image or video) something was said. Almost all tools have the capability of saving a searchable query for future references, modifications or for future use.

The counterpart of monitoring and searching is being able to generate engagement using real time conversations, posts or results from the executed searches. The solution used to reply to posts or conversations does not differ much between the tools, and it is influenced by the mechanism that each social network provides to perform this task. Almost all tools provide means to reply to posts or conversations by sending a direct message or writing into the user's Facebook wall; by adding a comment to a post or conversation, or by sending an email to the social media user account. Replying to posts or conversations is only part of the picture. The real power of the engagement functionality relies in the capability to launch or schedule advertising or public relations campaigns, as well as to publish messages in different social media networks at the same time. In many cases these messages may be composed of text, attachments, images, videos and even location information. Furthermore, some tools have mechanisms to track and assign posts or comments to other team members of the enterprise (for example, the sales force, customer service or any other member of the organization). Engaging with customers benefits business because each customer might influence a potential customer who, in turn, is connected to other users who influence others, consequently generating a domino effect.

Predominantly all dashboards are Web based client applications that are executed on the server side and the interface is provided by a Web server. The user only needs a Web browser to access the application. The only exception is the TweetDeck dashboard, whose interface runs as a standalone desktop application. Twitter and Facebook are the main social networks supported by the tools. Although Twitter is the main social network used by Trackur, SocialFlow and TweetDeck, most of these tools can collect information of what has been published from different social media networks, like: Linkedin, Google Buzz, YouTube, Blogs, Wordpress, Flickr, Foursquare, GoWalla, Yelp, Trip advisor, news sites, forums, and many other media that are not necessarily composed of text, links, and images.

The capability that some tools have to trigger alarms when some potentially damaging content is created by a user is a very useful feature. Many businesses are already well aware of the damage that a bad comment or post can do to their reputation. Almost all the tools have some kind of alarm function, but only a few can produce real alerts when a truly bad post, comment, image, video or news is published. An alarm should be triggered immediately by the monitoring tool as soon a harmful publication is identified, especially if the content has been originated by a user with well-known reputation that is highly influential. This alert can take the form of an email, an audible sound, a visible object on the screen, RSS feed or a combination of these.

Many of the tools generate some type of warning every time a comment or post is made regarding our company, or a new fan or follower signs in, or there is an update to the content of some social media and for many other reasons that do not require any prompt action (sometimes no action at all). In this study we have not considered these types of warnings as "alarms".

We shall now describe each of the tools included in this study, emphasizing the points which differentiate each tool from the others. Table 1 summarizes the results of our study.

Radian6

Radian6 is a high budget, real-time, multi-language monitoring tool which also has capabilities for engagement and workflow management. It allows a business to view, analyze and display in real time any relevant conversations by searching through more than 150 million public sites, including the open Facebook, API and the Twitter Firehose. Radian6 has a powerful dashboard that can be quickly setup using the Quick Start topic profile set-up tool. The dashboard can be customized with the Widget Gallery to only show items that are meaningful for a certain social media team. The workflow management tool is used to assign posts or comments to team members, add internal notes, flag priority, categorize, and classify conversations that are taking place.

The integration of CRM and Web analytics with the "river of news" created by Radian 6 generates a database that can be used by the sales force to create leads and by customer support. The engagement console can be used on the Web or as an iPhone application that filters conversations and enables engagement in real-time with collaboration throughout the entire enterprise improving effectiveness and efficiency without duplicating effort. The social profile of a person can be seen in detail in each social media network where it was created along with the entire history of conversations that the business has had with him/her including the replies. Reporting and measuring tied to analytics and social metrics are seamless capabilities that can be integrated with business functions like marketing, public relations, sales, customer support and other administrative activities.

We may contract four plans with Radian6. All of them are paid monthly and the rate is based on the number of results returned by each topic. The basic plan, called: "Getting Started" has a price tag of $600 for 1 topic and up to 10,000 mentions. The "Advance" plan costs $4,000 and provides up to 6 topics and up to 200,000 mentions; it also includes Web analytics integration, using: Omniture, Webtrends, and Google Analytics. The "Enterprise" solution has a custom price and is intended for businesses that have more than 6 topics and a large number of members on the social media team. A plan called: "Agency" is designed for agencies that build and execute social media strategies for others and its price is $600 for 1 topic and up to 10,000 mentions. They offer a 50% discount for registered and qualified charitable organizations, but the organization must be validated by an account representative. This software runs as a Web client in any Web browser. There is also a smartphone application called, Radian6 Mobile for iPhone, which has most of the functionality of the Web client version.

Trackur

This is an online reputation tool used to search and keep track of mentions of keywords or topics in the Web; it is somehow similar to Google Alerts. Its searches can be saved and executed every 30 minutes generating graphs with the new mentions, velocity of the creation of mentions, and sources in the past 24 hours. Trackur has four different monthly plans that can be purchased; each plan has a specific number of searches that can be saved; from 5 searches in the Basic plan up to unlimited searches in the Ultimate plan. Trackur scours the Web using a tagging system to determine the mentions of a specific keyword, phrase or topic. It mostly searches in social media like Technorati, Flickr, Youtube, Reddit, Digg, Delicious, Twitter, and Facebook. It may be configured to update RSS feeds or send emails each time new mentions are detected for a specific search.

Trackur has four plans which differ in the permitted quantity of saved searches. All plans have RSS/Email alerts, manual sentiment tagging, CSV export, Twitter, Facebook & Google+ and other social media monitoring and influence metrics. Other features are only available on certain plans. These features are: Trackur Insights, Upload RSS Feeds, branding of the company in Trackur dashboard, and unlimited client logins. The only plan that includes all features is the Ultimate plan, which has a price of $377 per month and unlimited saved searches. The Premium plan costs $197 and provides 250 saved searches. The Plus plan costs $88 and provides 50 saved searches with one extra feature (Trackur Insights) than the Basic plan. The Basic plan costs $8 and provides 5 saved searches. Trackur offers a free plan limited to 1 save search and no Facebook, Google+ or Forums, slower updates, and no analytics. This tool can only be used as a Web application.

Klout

This is a free tool that uses a scoring system on a scale of 1 to 100 points, which is calculated using over 35 different variables to determine the social media reach of a business or person. The scores are grouped into three metrics: True Reach, Amplification Probability and Network Influence. Klout focuses on how influence and messages are spread within the social networks, mainly from Twitter and Facebook. Upon registration a business has to subscribe their Twitter and Facebook accounts through Klout, so it may have access to comments and messages generated by users within these networks. Klout classifies a person or business using a matrix of what they call "style", which describes how different people interact with one another in an online social media. Plot line charts display metrics for the three different scores and for an overall score that's related to clicks, comments, or retweets, depending on the social media site. True Reach uses engagement in terms of followers and friends that are listening and reacting to the posts. Amplification Probability measures how tweets are received, replied or retweeted in Twitter and how many comments or likes are received in Facebook. Network Influence or Impact is used to determine how much influence the business network has with the audience. Klout has neither sentiment analysis metrics nor other features like demographics, multi-language support, team tasks assignment, or other similar capabilities. The company aspires to be the online gold standard for measuring reputation.

SocialFlow

This is an engagement tool that uses Twitter accounts to determine the precise moment to post messages of certain topics or to start conversations that are more relevant for the best accessible audience at certain time frame. It may be used for optimizing outbound communications and to launch marketing and public relations campaigns. It uses bit.ly (bitly, 2011) to shrink domain names of the companies or brands and analyzes the number of clicks given to a certain link. Using the "Twitter Firehose", it can follow up to 400 keywords, 5,000 user identifiers, links that contain http, and https, "retweets", and other parameters enabling queries to get statistics of an IP's location and other filtered data. It may publish content in Twitter, Facebook and Google Buzz. The goal of the tool is to say the right thing at the right moment when conversations are shifting in any specific direction. It provides reports in real time about what is being said, and what the brand followers like and dislike. This tool is not actually used for monitoring purposes, but it may be used as an analytical tool.

SocialFlow prices are not public. According to an interview given by Frank Speiser, the founder of the company, prices start at $2000 per month, with the average price being about $ 5,000 per month (This WeekIn Startups-Producer, 2011) A free version of the product may be solicited, but it is limited to Reddit, Digg, delicious, Twitter and news sites and it has several other limitations. SocialFlow does not have a mobile application client; it only runs as a Web application.

SproutSocial

This is an all-in-one tool that monitors social media. It enables engagement and has reporting and analytics capabilities. Its dashboard can be customized to show several different widgets, which may provide a summary for engagement and influence scores, number of clicks, follower's demographics by age and gender, new followers, mentions, volume or tone of the messages, Twitter statistics, recent followers and messages. It has a "Social Inbox" where all the messages that come from different media are received, as if it were a personal email account. Within the Social Inbox a user can be followed back, his profile may be seen, messages can be replied to or flagged to get back to them later, and mentions can be looked for so a specific action can be taken.

Alerts may occur every time that a mention or a direct message is received in the Social Inbox. The user can see summary reports either daily or weekly of these mentions or the messages received. Messages from a particular contact can be stored if he has been added to the contacts list. Discovery is an option that enables searching for keywords that people write in their profiles such as "President" or "CEO". Using this option we can also search for competitors to compare ourselves to them in terms of engagement, influence, followers and demographics. All searches may be restricted to a geographical area. It has a variety of reports that include: a report of followers or friends, new followers or friends, clicks, messages sent, messages received and "retweets", summary of messages or mentions, demographic reports and others. Reports and analytics are executed automatically, or they can be restricted to specific dates.

SproutSocial offers four monthly plans: "Pro" for $9, "Small Biz" for $39, "Deluxe" for $59, and "Premium" for $899. All plans have access to Twitter, Facebook, LinkedIn and Google Reader. They all allow publishing to multiple accounts, scheduling messages, and posting from any Website. All plans share the same features for engagement: "Smart Inbox," contact management with conversation history, identification of influential users, RSS reader, and task creation from messages. But they differ in the analytics and reporting features, branding, monitoring, team support, and local business tools. The Pro plan only adds to the base features support for team work. The "Deluxe" and "Premium" plans have Foursquare, Gowalla, and Google Analytics support, flexible account grouping, report exporting, local search and targeting, check-in monitoring and reporting, and team collaboration features such as tasks and assignments. The "Premium" plan adds branded reports, and branded portal. SproutSocial can be used as a Web application or as an iPhone application.

Sysomos: Heartbeat

Heartbeat is a real-time monitoring tool, which is also used for engagement and to compare your business with competitors. It has a customizable user-friendly dashboard to display a snapshot of social media activity. The dashboard can display the most active keywords and graph the mentions of a brand or product in comparison with other competitor's mentions. A panel called; "Your Heartbeat", permits the managing of unlimited social media profiles and the monitoring of conversations that happen in real-time, enabling engagement with "fans" or followers.

Heartbeat uses a powerful search function based on queries filtered by one or more keywords, social media network, tags, sentiment, demography, country and many other options. A query may combine more than one filter using boolean operators. Although the user does not need to know anything about the syntax, the queries can be built as SQL-like statements. The results of queries can be tagged. These tags function as user-defined rules which are related to a product, brand, service, competitor, or any other topic that can be used to validate, classify or store query results for later analysis and graphic presentation. Searches can be stored and scheduled on a regular basis; monthly, weekly, daily. A list of keywords can be created and used to automatically delete messages or posts that contain one or more of these keywords. Alarms can be configured using a list of keywords defined by the user or from a list of terms predefined by Sysomos for a specific industry or business. The alerts generated by these alarms may be configured in a variety of forms.

This tool has the ability to classify the sentiment as negative, neutral or positive. To perform this classification previous conversations and top influencers are considered. Terms can be defined to support the classification of the conversations into one of the three categories, although a set of rules created by Sysomos are used. The other users' influence is measure and plotted automatically. The Social media Manager can drill-down into the chart, make comments and translate it into 20 different languages.

The workflow feature can assign one or more comments or tweets to be managed by a person or team within the organization, such as the "sales force team". Sysomos provides multiple metrics and graphs related to the demographics of the population (sex, age, language...), reports about the different geographical world regions where content is created or where emerging conversations have more influence, and reports comparing the business with competitors by different demographics and/or geographic world regions, by number of mentions, and by several other dimensions.

This tool has a monthly price of $500. Sysomos also offers an academic version for $250 with the same capabilities and functions, and which may also be used at the same time on multiple computers for educational purposes. This application runs as a Web client and doesn't have a mobile client yet.

ViralHeat

ViralHeat is designed for listening or monitoring social media; it does not have many engagement functionalities, except that it may identify the top influencers. The tool uses "profiles" to monitor content and perform advanced analysis on it. Each profile can be created with a user-friendly wizard or an advanced configuration interface. In both cases the profile will have its own name and it will be composed of one or more of the following: keywords or phrases to track for mentions; keywords or phrases that are going to be used to remove any mention when they are detected; location (e.g., Madrid, Spain) that will limit mentions to a specific city or within a specified radius; and an email reporting method to be used when a mention for the profile keyword(s) or phrase(s) is detected. ViralHeat enables producers of content to monitor the profiles in multiple social media networks in order to identify key trends and understand the participation of the community. This information is used to generate competitive analysis.

To monitor the social media in real-time, it uses over 200 video sharing sites, including YouTube, blogs, Twitter, Facebook, and other social networks. It can monitor tweets to realize a competitive analysis, discover new tracks and optimize marketing campaigns. It can discover new Fan Pages in Facebook which mention the brand, topic or product. It has built-in intelligence to analyze the ROI on Facebook campaigns.

Alerts can be defined as emails that can be sent (to more than one person) on a daily basis or each time a mention is detected for a specific profile. If the option called: "Daily Digest" is enabled, a summary of all profiles will be sent daily. ViralHeat adds comment stats for the sentiment of each post in Facebook, showing percentages for positive, neutral and negative sentiment.

ViralHeat has three monthly plans with prices of $9.99 (Basic), $29.99 (Professional), and $89.99 (Business). The Basic Plan permits 5 profiles, 7 days of previous data to analyze, and Twitter, Real-time Web, Facebook Fan Pages, and Viral Video analytics. The Professional Plan permits 20 profiles and adds viral content and sentiment analysis. It also has influencer analytics. The Business Plan permits 40 profiles, 30 days of previous data to analyze and 6 months of data archiving. It also adds Facebook link analytics (Real-time Web), the entire social graph of influencers (Twitter), Klout analytics (Twitter), and Twitalyzer analytics (Twitter). The Business plan also provides custom branding.

The cost of this plan is $199.99 per month which includes search for three of the following: competitors, key people, and terms that will create searches on Twitter. This tool runs as a Web application, but there is also a version of the Website optimized for mobile clients.

StepRep

StepRep started with a company called MyFrontSteps which was intended to connect service providers with their customers through social networks. This product was withdrawn from the market in 2009 and in 2010 StepRep took its place as a tool for corporate reputation management. The tool was created for small and medium-sized businesses. It uses a spider search engine to constantly search through comments, blogs, articles, links and any Website that might refer to a product, brand or company. It uses searches in the major search engines and some minor ones, plus searches that are executed within social media networks, such as Twitter, Flickr, YouTube, and Facebook. All searches are performed on an ongoing basis and the results may be seen in the dashboard as soon as they arise, or may be received via email anytime something new is found. Each search result might be composed of text, images, videos, articles or any other format. These results are displayed on a single page where they can be sorted, inspected and assigned a sentiment (negative, neutral or positive). If any of the results are classified as "Positive", they can be added to the StepRep widget and posted in the company blog, social media page or any other online Website where the company has presence. Duplicated results will be deleted and not shown more than once. Using a component called: "Visibility" a comprehensive search to determine if the company is listed in any search engines, line of business or social networking directories can be can performed.

The tool doesn't use social media accounts because it focuses on mentions rather than Twitter or Facebook pages. Mentions are places where a business appears; these might include a detailed article or a comment in Twitter. The tool graphs mentions by different sentiment type. The sentiment report shows those positive or negative mentions that obtained the highest relevance scores. Sentiment analysis uses various methods to analyze the sentiment, which are constantly evolving. These methods are: weighted scores based on normative emotional skills of commonly used English words; processing of natural language which includes techniques for determining sentiment based on context of the post, and a Bayesian statistical analysis of the sentiments assigned over time by the users.

Brandwatch

This is a social media monitoring tool used to constantly track reputation based on queries and workspaces. A query is composed of a set of parameters and criteria that are used to monitor or search the Web for mentions that meet such query. Each time a new query is created the tool generates a new workspace using a basic template which in turn is composed of several pages. Each query may be composed of one or more main terms, context terms, terms to be excluded, and Boolean operators: AND, OR and NOT. In addition one or more languages may be selected from where the mentions may arise. An industry filter may be chosen for the query from a list of predetermined industries; for example: learning, jewelry, loyalty, media, and retail among others. Once a query is created it might be tested to determine if the resulting mentions are related to the topic or if the theme is specified in the criteria. If the query brings spam results it can be modified until the desired results are obtained. Once the setup of a query has been finished, it will take between 25 to 30 minutes to check the 24 databases that the tool uses for this task; but in the meantime intermediate outcomes may be seen in the workspace. Once the process is completed an email will be sent by the tool indicating that the query results are available.

Each query can generate various graphs in real-time that may be drilled-down by the user clicking in any part of the plot lines and opening the comments. The common summary reports are: number of mentions, positive, negative and neutral sentiment, graphs indicating the origin of the mentions (news, blogs, etc.), history of entries by date, in addition to a summary by site (e.g. www, facebook.com, twitter.com, answers.yahoo.com, etc.). The "Share of Voice" functionality shows how a business is doing against the competition. The tool also has individual tabs for volume reports, graphics, feelings, site and recurring phrases, and honorable mentions. More details on each of these aspects can be obtained from the corresponding tab. Individual posts can be assigned to specific business areas, such as: customer service, support, or other areas. Posts are classified as open, answered or closed, and a priority (high or low) is assigned to them.

Brandwatch offers two monthly plans: "Pro" for $640 and "Enterprise" for $2,325. Both plans include unlimited users, sentiment analysis in 16 languages, free initial training, full API access, and multilingual coverage. The Pro plan is limited to 10 thousand mentions, which may seem at first glance as a good deal, but a single query may generate more than 10 thousand mentions. Brandwatch provides two upgrades for the Pro plan that includes 20 thousand mentions for $1,125 or 50 thousand mentions for $1,525 per month. The Enterprise plan includes unlimited mentions and only 15 queries; if more queries are needed they are offered for an additional cost of $110 each. This tool can only be used as a Web application.

HootSuite

This is an affordable social media managing tool used to launch marketing campaigns, track conversations, make the audience grow, and distribute or schedule messages through multiple channels at the same time. Using the social media dashboard, teams can collaborate and schedule posts to Twitter, Facebook, LinkedIn, Word Press and other social media over the Web. The dashboard is composed of tabs and within each tab there are columns that can be associated with one or more accounts of Twitter, Facebook, LinkedIn, Ping.fm, WordPress, MySpace, Foursquare and Mixi. Each column is associated with a type of feedback, such as: home feed, mentions, direct messages, favorites, or others. Every time a stream or column is defined within a tab, key terms used to search can be defined. It is possible to search for multiple terms using multiple columns within the same tab associated with a social environment.

Each tab is stored as part of the dashboard when it is configured initially. A user or group of users may be defined for a specific tab or column.

The number of simultaneous profiles in a single session depends on the plan we have bought; the Pro and Enterprise version have no limits of social profiles, the free version allows up to 5 social identities that may be used within any tab. Sentiment analysis is done automatically using an analyzer called Lymbix (Lymbix, 2011) which analyzes the text using four areas: emotional context (language learning), measurement of subjectivity (human emotions), construction of lexicons (data analysis) and delivery in real-time (sentiment black boxes). This tool measures the sentiment in several aspects, such as: condition, joy, excitement, happiness, sadness, anger, fear and humiliation. In general terms, any text may be analyzed, but the tool tends to analyze all tweets to determine the sentiment. The tool may be used in several languages: English, French, Italian, Spanish, Japanese, Arabic, Chinese, Czech, German, Greek, Indonesian, Korean, Norwegian, Persian, Polish, Portuguese, Romanian, Russian, Turkish, Dutch and Wales.

The graphics may reflect demographics of users that generate content relevant for a business by gender, age and others. Results from a query can be filtered by a specific geographical area. The tool permits the assignment of tasks to others within the work team with ease, but they may only become editors of one or more social media accounts already defined. At any time messages or comments can be assigned to someone on the team, but only the enterprise plan allows an unlimited number of contributors. If a particular stream wants to be included in a Blog or CRM site, the embedded code can be generated from the stream column top right hand menu; this feature is not available on the free plan. This tool has an impressive amount of customizable reports and graphs which can be saved and reused. Figure 2 shows one of the readymade analytic reports that may be used to display various results over a period of time; usually HootSuite uses the last 7 days from the current date.

HootSuite offers two monthly plans: "Pro" for $5.99 and "Enterprise" for $210. The Pro plan provides social analytics, unlimited Facebook or Twitter profiles, one team collaborator, and one report. It also includes integration with Google Analytics and several Facebook analytics. The Enterprise plan includes unlimited social network profiles, up to 10 reports, unlimited team members, unlimited RSS/Atom, enhanced analytics, priority technical support, VIP setup, free advertisement and 10 seats for the HootSuite certification program. There is a free plan called; "Basic", which includes: social analytics, 5 free profiles on either Facebook or Twitter and 2 RSS/Atom for blogs or news. The dashboard runs as Web based client, but there also are clients for iPhone, iPad, Android and BlackBerry.

TweetDeck

This is a free desktop application based on Adobe Air for a single-user. Its main purpose is to keep in touch with conversations and messages in various social media like, Twitter, Facebook, LinkedIn, Google Buzz and Foursquare, in addition to replying to (generate engagement) conversations or messages. It permits the use of multiple Twitter accounts at the same time; however it only allows one account from Facebook, LinkedIn, Google Buzz, MySpace and Foursquare. The dashboard is composed of columns to present information from the social media accounts, such as messages or comments. By clicking on a given user, we obtain a new column with the "posts" of that user. If the mouse pointer is dragged over the top of a user image, several small buttons will pop out. Depending on the account type, these buttons enable different tasks. If it is a Facebook account, the user may make comments on posts published by that user, click "Like", write into the users' wall, send a message to the user, send an e-mail, translate the

Figure 2. Click analytics in HootSuite

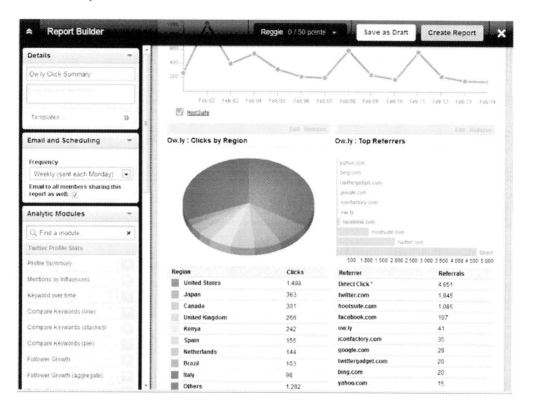

message, or comment in the language selected in the configuration panel and perform the translation of the text automatically. If the column is associated with a Twitter account, the options are: send a tweet, replicate a tweet, follow the user, unfollow the user, see the profile, find the user in all tweets, retweets, mentions or posts generated, block a user or block the user and report him/her as spammer.

The search option for key terms is not available, but a keyword may be used to filter the content of a column. Real-time searches are limited to users' ids or lists of Twitter users. Once the user or list is found a column will be added where you can see the "posts" from that user or list. Audible alerts are generated when an incoming message is received, or a comment or image is added. Although it lacks the ability to identify the top influencers, each time a new message or comment is received from the user a red circle with a number in it indicates the total number of messages sent by the user. With this information we may determine whether or not the user is an influencer. TweetDeck has clients for iPhone and Android mobile devices.

DISCUSSION AND CONCLUSION

Social media is still a relatively recent phenomenon. Many companies still do not understand and do not know how to take advantage of it. Gradually, more managers are starting to grasp the potential of social media and how it can make a difference in their organization. The companies that embraced social media earlier on were often Information Technology (IT) related, especially large companies. Having

Table 1. Summary of the features of each tool

	Radian6	Trackur	Klout	Socialflow	SproutSocial	Sysomos (Heartbeat)	ViralHeat	StepRep	Brandwatch	HootSuite	TweetDeck
Monitoring*	Strong	Average	Not supported	Average	Strong	Strong	Average	Average	Strong	Strong	Average
Engagement*	Strong	Weak	Not supported	Strong	Strong	Strong	Average	Average	Weak	Strong	Strong
Reputation*	Strong	Average	Not Supported	Weak	Average	Average	Strong	Strong	Strong	Average	Weak
Influence*	Strong	Average	Strong	Not Supported	Strong	Strong	Strong	Weak	Weak	Average	Weak
Preferred Network	Facebook & Twitter	Twitter	Facebook & Twitter	Twitter	Facebook & Twitter	Facebook & Twitter	Facebook & Twitter	Facebook & Twitter	Facebook & Twitter	Facebook & Twitter	Twitter
Social Network Support	Strong	Strong	Strong	Weak	Average	Strong	Strong	Strong	Strong	Average	Average
Multiple Profiles Support	Strong	Weak	Strong	Weak	Strong	Strong	Strong	Not Supported	Not Supported	Average	Strong
Search	Strong	Average	Not Supported	Average	Strong	Strong	Strong	Strong	Strong	Strong	Strong
Store searches	Strong	Strong	Not Supported	Not Supported	Strong	Strong	Strong	Average	Strong	Average	Strong
Alerts/Alarms	Strong	Average	Weak	Strong	Average	Strong	Average	Average	Average	Average	Average
Sentiment analysis	Strong	Weak	Not Supported	Not Supported	Average	Strong	Strong	Strong	Strong	Average	Not Supported
Influence Analysis	Strong	Average	Average	Not Supported	Strong	Strong	Strong	Weak	Strong	Average	Weak
Internationalization	Strong	Average	Weak	Weak	Weak	Strong	Weak	Weak	Average	Strong	Average
Geotargeting	Strong	Average	Weak	Weak	Strong	Strong	Strong	Weak	Average	Strong	Weak
Team collaboration	Strong	Average	Weak	Weak	Strong	Strong	Average	Weak	Strong	Strong	Weak
CRM Integration	Strong	Weak	Weak	Weak	Weak	Strong	Average	Weak	Average	Average	Weak
Min and Max Price (monthly payment)	$600 -$2,000	$8 - $377	Free	Starts at $2,000	$9 - $899	$500	$9.99 - $89.99	$199	$640 - $2,325	$5.99 - $210	Free
Available Clients	Web & iPhone	Web	Web	Web	Web & iPhone	Web & iPhone	Web	Web & iPhone	Web	Web, iOs Android & Blackberry	Desktop, iPhone, Android

*Based on the top plan that each company can offer

an IT-related business increases the likelihood that the customers of the company are technology savvy. Consequently, they are often early adopters of social media. Because of the large size of the company, they are likely to generate a large volume of conversations. Therefore, these companies have seen the need for having full-time staff dedicated to monitoring and engaging in social media within their marketing departments. This is one of the main reasons why many of the tools reviewed in this article are oriented to the high end portion of the market, having prohibitively expensive prices for small businesses. Four of the 11 companies in our study have a minimum monthly fee over $ 500. The highest plan for eight of the 11 companies has a monthly cost over $ 200, with three of them being over $ 2000 per month.

For large businesses, having a strategy to manage their presence in social networks is of paramount importance. Given the volume of conversations they have to monitor and manage, the use of tools to support this task is mandatory. In these cases, where possibly more than one person will be managing the company's online presence, Radian6, Socialflow and Heartbeat are integral solutions to be considered. Brandwatch and Trackur also are interesting solutions which focus more on monitoring and comparison with the competition.

As the use of social media spreads further, more small business will understand its utility and the need to have a presence in social networks. As a consequence, we expect to see more tools tailored to their needs in the future. Nowadays having a presence in social networks is very desirable for a small business if it is related to technology. Otherwise having a good social media strategy can still be a competitive advantage and an excellent marketing tool. Of the tools studied here, we consider that HootSuite and ViralHeat offer a reasonable feature set for small and medium businesses at an affordable price. TweetDeck is also a good option if only a casual use of social media is intended.

One trend that will undoubtedly help to increase the use of social media by small businesses is "local". All the main social networks have local strategies that aim to connect users with other users living in the same city or neighborhood and that frequent the same locations. They also want to connect users with local businesses. This permits, for example, displaying advertising on the social network Website only to users who live in the same neighborhood where the small mom and pop store is located. The wide availability of smart phones, which often have GPS capabilities, also enable social networks to know exactly where the user is at every moment. This permits, for example, sending an SMS with a discount coupon or an offer just as the user enters the mall where the store is.

The goal of the local trend is to serve the long tail (Anderson, 2008) of small businesses that are only interested in reaching a geographically targeted and relatively small audience. These businesses can only make small investments to reach potential new customers. These investments will only pay off if the advertising is very well targeted. There are tens of millions of such businesses in the world; i.e., they can be a significant revenue source. The local features of social networks will make the presence of the small business in social media more appealing. Thus, they will increasingly need to use tools to manage their online presence. In the near future, we expect more development of tools to serve this purpose. In this scenario there will be no staff dedicated full time to manage the business presence in social networks. Features such as internationalization, team collaboration, and integration with the company information systems are irrelevant. Geolocation is crucial, but should be automatic and transparent to the user. On the contrary, having a highly intuitive user interface that has a very low learning curve will be very important given that it is not realistic to require from these users a long training process. Providing mechanisms for scheduling content creation will also be an important feature to maintain the online presence of the business when the person responsible for maintaining it is not on duty.

Many of the small and medium businesses will likely enter the social media world supported by a social media manager (Wollan, Smith, & Zhou, 2011). The role of these people will be crucial in defining the social media strategy of mom and pop stores, which are often run by non-tech savvy people. Social media managers will need tools designed specifically for them, which can manage the online presence of multiple businesses from a single integrated dashboard. Right now only Radian6 has plans specifically designed for social media managers, but we expect that in the future there will be more tools for this purpose.

Finally, we expect that eventually there will be some consolidation in the market of tools to support the management of the social media presence of a business. As usual in the IT field, when a new business opportunity appears many players jump into the new market. Ultimately, there is a consolidation in which some of them disappear and others are absorbed by the strongest leaving only a small number of players. It happened to the PC market, with the operating systems market and with Internet search engines, among others. Currently, there are over a hundred tools with a purpose similar to the 11 tools studied in this chapter. The 11 tools addressed in this chapter are among the strongest in the market (we believe they are the strongest), and thus have a good chance of survival, either independently or integrated into a larger company that acquires them. Whatever the case may be, we expect significant market consolidation in the near future.

REFERENCES

A Wiki of Social Media Monitoring Solutions. (2011). *Monitoring solutions master list*. Retrieved from http://wiki.kenburbary.com

Anderson, E. (2008). *The long tail: Why the future of business is selling less of more*. New York: Hyperion.

Bhattacharya, C. B., Du, S., & Sen, S. (2010). Maximizing business returns to corporate social responsibility (CSR): The role of CSR communication. *International Journal of Management Reviews, 12*(1), 6–19.

Bitly. (2011). *Bitly: Shorten, share and track your links*. Retrieved November 15, 2011, from https://bitly.com/

Coffee, S. (2011, November). *Freshly brewed tweets from Brad and Lee at Starbucks in Seattle, WA.* Retrieved from http://twitter.com/#!/starbucks

Constantinides, E., Gómez, M., & Lorenzo, C. (2008). Social media: A new frontier for retailers? *Europea Retail Research, 22*, 1–28.

Dell. (2012). *Peace of mind! We've got covered!* Retrieved from http://www.dell.com/content/learnmore/learnmore.aspx?c=us&l=en&s=dhs&~id=serv_inspn&~line=notebooks&~lt=popup&~series=inspn&ref=CFG#tn2

Dösinger, G., Stocker, A., Us, A., & Wagner, C. (2007). The three pillars of 'corporate web 2.0': A model for definition. In *Proceedings of I-MEDIA '07 and I-SEMANTICS '07*. Graz, Austria: IEEE.

Facebook. (2011). *Statistics*. Retrieved November 15, 2011, from http://www.facebook.com/press/info.php?statistics

FreshMinds Research. (2010). *Turning conversations into insights: A comparison of social media monitoring tools*. Retrieved from http://shared.freshminds.co.uk/smm10/whitepaper.pdf

Gallaugher, J. (2010). Get S.M.A.R.T. – Social media awareness & response team. In *Information Systems: A Manager's Guide to Harnessing Technology* (pp. 125–134). Flat World Knowledge.

Gleanster. (2010). *Gleansight: Social media monitoring*. Gleanster, LLC

Haeniein, M., & Kaplan, A. (2010). Users of the world, unite! The challenges and opportunities of social media. *Business Horizons, 53*(1), 59–68. doi:10.1016/j.bushor.2009.09.003

Harvard Business Review Analytic Services. (2010). *The new conversation: Taking social media from talk to action*. Boston: Harvard Business School Publishing.

Hutley, R. (2009). *Social networking as a business tool*. Cisco Internet Business Solutions Group.

JarvisJ. (2012). *BuzzMachine*. Retrieved from http://buzzmachine.com/archives/cat_dell.html

JavaHispano. (2011, November 15). *Tu lenguaje, tu comunidad*. Retrieved from http://javaHispano.org

Koch, M., & Richter, A. (2008). Functions of social networking services. In *Proceedings of COOP '08: the 8th International Conference on the Design of Cooperative Systems*. COOP.

Leganza, G. (2010). *The top 15 technology trends EA should watch: 2011 To 2013*. Forrester Research, Inc.

Lymbix. (2011). *Add sentiment intelligence to your applications*. Retrieved from http://www.lymbix.com/

My Starbucks Idea. (2011, November). *Share. Vote. Discuss. See. Share your ideas, tell us what you think of other people's ideas and join discussion*. Retrieved from http://mystarbucksidea.force.com/

Newsroom, S. (2011, January). *Starbucks support of the troops/military*. Retrieved from http://news.starbucks.com/about+starbucks/myths+facts/militarydonations.htm

O'Reilly, T. (2007). What is web 2.0: Design patterns and business models for the next generation of software. *International Journal of Digital Economics, 65*, 17–37.

Report, S. M. (2010). *Lightspeed research and the internet advertising bureau UK*. Retrieved from http://www.iabuk.net/en/1/socialmedialanding.html

Rotman, J. (2010). *Unite breaks guitars – Case study*. Toronto, Canada: School of Management, University of Toronto.

Shiels, M. (2011). Twitter co-founder Jack Dorsey rejoins company. *BBC News*. Retrieved from http://www.bbc.co.uk/news/business-12889048

Soule, A. (2010). *Fighting the social media wildfire: How crisis communication must adapt to prevent from fanning the flames*. (Thesis). University of North Carolina at Chapel Hill, Chapel Hill, NC.

Starbucks. (2011a). *LinkedIn*. Retrieved November 15, 2011, from http://www.linkedin.com/company/starbucks

Starbucks. (2011b). *Facebook*. Retrieved November 15, 2011, from http://www.facebook.com/Starbucks

Starbucks (Producer). (2011, October 28). *The create jobs for USA fund* [informative video]. Retrieved November 15, 2011, from http://www.youtube.com/user/Starbucks

Sterne, J. (2010). *Social media metrics: How to measure and optimize your marketing investment*. New York: John Wiley & Sons, Inc.

This WeekIn Startups (Producer). (2011, January 4). *This week in startups - Frank Speiser, founder of SocialFlow.com* [informative video]. Retrieved November 15, 2011, from http://thisweekin.com/thisweekin-startups/this-week-in-startups-105-frank-speiser-founder-of-socialflow-com/

Williams, K. T. (2009). Case study: Dell hell: The impact of social media on corporate communication. Hoboken, NJ: CorpCommCollab.

Wollan, R., Smith, N., & Zhou, C. (2011). *The social media management handbook: Everything you need to know to get social media working in your business.* New York: John Wiley & Sons, Inc.

ADDITIONAL READING

Asur, S., & Huberman, B. (2010). *Predicting the future with social media.* Retrieved from http://www. hpl.hp.com/research/scl/papers/socialmedia/socialmedia.pdf

Balasubramanyan, R. O'Connor, Routledge, B., & Smith, N. (2010). From tweets to polls: Linking text sentiment to public opinion time series. In *Proceedings of the International AAAI Conference on Weblogs and Social Media.* Washington, DC: AAAI. Retrieved from http://www.cs.cmu.edu/~nasmith/papers/oc onnor+balasubramanyan+routledge+smith.icwsm10.pdf

Bale, K., & Lasica, J. (2011). *Top 20 social media monitoring vendors for business.* Retrieved from http:// www.socialmedia.biz/2011/01/12/top-20-social-media-monitoring-vendors-for-business/

Balegno, S. (2010). *Social marketing ROAD map handbook: A method for mapping an effective social strategy.* Retrieved from http://www.marketingsherpa.com/heap/SocialMediaHandbookExcerpt.pdf

Bhattacharjee, B., Druschel, P., Gummadi, K., Marcon, M., & Mislove, A. (2007). Measurement and analysis of online social networks. In *Proceedings of the IMC'07,* (pp. 29-42). San Diego, CA: IMC.

Blackshaw, P., & Nazzaro, M. (2006). *Consumer-generated media (CGM) 101 word-of-mouth in the age of the web-fortified consumer.* Retrieved from http://www.nielsen-online.com/downloads/us/buzz/ nbzm_wp_CGM101.pdf

Boyd, M., & Ellison, N. (2008). Social network sites: Definition, history, and scholarship. *Journal of Computer-Mediated Communication, 13,* 210–230. doi:10.1111/j.1083-6101.2007.00393.x

Brandwatch Social media Monitoring. (2011). *Guest post: The fox news twitter hack.* Retrieved from http://www.brandwatch.com/2011/07/guest-post-the-fox-news-twitter-hack/

Bright, L., Daugherty, T., & Eastin, M. (2008). Exploring consumer motivations for creating user-generated content. *Journal of Interactive Advertising, 8*(2), 16–25.

Chou, D., Fink, C., Llorens, A., & Kopecky, J. (2011). Coarse- and fine-grained sentiment analysis of social media text. *Johns Hopkins APL Technical Digest, 30*(1). Retrieved from http://www.jhuapl.edu/ techdigest/TD/td3001/Fink.pdf

Corporate Executive Board. (2008). *Leveraging social networking sites in marketing communications.* Retrieved from http://www.ittoolbox.com/advertising/pdf/Leveraging-Social-Media-Networking-Sites-in-Marketing-Communications.pdf

Godbole, N., Skiena, S., & Srinivasaiah, M. (2008). *Large-scale sentiment analysis for news and blogs.* Retrieved from http://icwsm.org/papers/3--Godbole-Srinivasaiah-Skiena.pdf

Hackford, C., Morris, H., & Palomba, M. (2010). *Social media marketing – Protecting your brand online*. Retrieved from http://www.advertisingcompliancelaw.com/uploads/file/Social%20Media%20Marketing%20-%20Protecting%20your%20brand%20online.pdf

Han, J., Liu, L., Tang, J., & Yang, S. (2010). Mining topic-level influence in heterogeneous networks. In *Proceedings of the 19th ACM International Conference on Information and Knowledge Management (CIKM '10)*, (pp. 199-208). New York, NY: ACM Press. Retrieved from http://keg.cs.tsinghua.edu.cn/jietang/publications/KDD09-Tang-et-al-Social-Influence-Analysis.pdf

Hernández, S., & Sallis, P. (2011). *Sentiment-preserving reduction for social media analysis*. Paper presented at the XVI Iberoamerican Congress on Pattern Recognition CIARP. Pucon, Chile.

Huhtamaki, J., Poschko, J., Rubens, N., Rusell, M., Still, K., & Yu, J. (2011). *Social media: Reputation and branding of innovation hubs: A periscope using content analysis of twitter*. Retrieved from http://www.leydesdorff.net/th9/Social%20media,%20reputation%20and%20branding%20of%20innovation%20hubs.pdf

Lee, E. (2008). Warming up to user-generated content. *University of Illinois Law Review, 5*, Retrieved from http://ssrn.com/abstract=1116671

Lee, L., & Pang, B. (2008). Opinion mining and sentiment analysis. *Foundations and Trends in Information Retrieval, 2*(1-2), 1-135. Retrieved from http://www.cs.cornell.edu/home/llee/omsa/omsa.pdf

Michael, M. (2010). *The real questions about social media monitoring/web listening*. Retrieved from http://www.digital-mr.com/UserFiles/File/Social-Media-Monitoring-wp.pdf

Orcutt, M. (2011). *How occupy wall street occupied twitter, too: Software reveals how the occupy wall street idea spread across to the social web as protesters took to the streets*. Retrieved from http://www.technologyreview.com/blog/editors/27324/

Seiple, P. (2008). *How to leverage social media for public relations success: Using social media to generate media coverage and improve brand sentiment*. Retrieved from http://www.hubspot.com/Portals/53/docs/hubspot_social_media_pr_ebook.pdf

Steinert-Threlkeld, T. (2011). *How to deal with the brave new world of social network policies*. Retrieved from http://www.socialware.com/about/news-events/how-to-deal-with-the-brave-new-world-of-social-network-policies/

Sun, J., Tang, J., Wang, C., & Yang, Z. (2009). *Social influence analysis in large-scale networks*. Retrieved from http://keg.cs.tsinghua.edu.cn/jietang/publications/KDD09-Tang-et-al-Social-Influence-Analysis.pdf

Sysomos a Marketwire Company. (2011). *The 24/7 customer experience: Automating and improving customer service through the social web*. Retrieved from http://info.marketwire.com/rs/marketwire/images/Sysomos-Automate-Customer-Service.pdf

Tromp, E. (2011). *Multilingual sentiment analysis on social media*. (Master's Thesis). Eindhoven University of Technology, Eindhoven, The Netherlands. Retrieved from http://www.win.tue.nl/~mpechen/projects/pdfs/Tromp2011.pdf

KEY TERMS AND DEFINITIONS

Alert/Alarm: Action that is taken automatically in response to a mention, post, comment, image, video or news has been published. It might take form of an email, an audible sound, a visible object on the screen, an RSS feed or a combination of them.

Engagement: Interest and participation that the followers or fans demonstrate to the brand, product or company through concrete actions such as commenting content, sharing content, clicking a like button, retweeting, etc.

Influence Analysis: Metric to quantify the influence that certain social network users (influencers) have over other social network users because of their knowledge and reputation on a certain topic.

Monitoring: Action of identifying the creation of new content that can take the form of text, audio, video, images or any other kind of user generated content that can be posted or upload in any social media. The ultimate goal of this task is to identify what is being said about a company, competitor, product or brand.

Online Community: Group of people with common interests who use Internet-based applications to interact with each other and share information.

Reputation Analysis: Capability to automatically determine how different keywords, terms, topics or user generated content within the mentions may harm a brand name, product or company.

Search or Query: Consult looking for mentions of brands, companies, products, topics, keywords or key terms, persons, Twitter or Facebook account users, businesses, URL's, places, and other types of information on social media sites, news streams, and other Websites.

Sentiment Analysis: Capability to automatically classify user sentiment when performing a certain engagement action as, for example, negative, neutral or positive.

Social Media: Group of Internet-based applications where users can engage with other users and share ideas, messages, information, videos, images, and other content.

Social Profile: Account registered in some social media site that can be used to participate in the social media site, or to listen for user generated content or to launch marketing or public relations campaigns for a brand name, product, or company.

User Generated Content (UGC): Includes videos, images, audio files, messages in Facebook, posts in Twitter and other forms of media that can be created by social media users in any online community, and that is visible to others users in that online community, or to any Web user.

This research was previously published in the Handbook of Research on Enterprise 2.0 edited by Maria Manuela Cruz-Cunha, Fernando Moreira, and João Varajão, pages 49-71, copyright year 2014 by Business Science Reference (an imprint of IGI Global).

Chapter 46
Exploring the Hidden Pattern From Tweets:
Investigation into Volkswagen Emissions Scandal

Ying Kei Tse
University of York, UK

Minhao Zhang
University of York, UK

Bob Doherty
University of York, UK

Paul Chappell
University of York, UK

Susan R. Moore
University of York, UK

Tom Keefe
University of York, UK

ABSTRACT

Social media has recently emerged as a key tool to manage customer relations in industry. This chapter aims to contribute a step-by-step Twitter Analytic framework for analysing the tweets in a fiscal crisis. The proposed framework includes three major sections – demographic analytic, content analytic and integrated method analytic. This chapter provides useful insights to develop this framework through the lens of the recent Volkswagen emission scandal. A sizable dataset of #volkswagescandal tweets (8,274) was extracted as the research sample. Research findings based upon this sample include the following:

DOI: 10.4018/978-1-5225-5637-4.ch046

Consumer sentiments are overall negative toward the scandal; some clustered groups are identified; male users expressed more interest on social media in the topic than female users; the popularity of tweets was closely related with the timing of news coverage, which indicates the traditional media is still playing a critical role in public opinion formation. The limitations and practical contribution of the current study are also discussed.

INTRODUCTION

The Volkswagen (VW) scandal broke when the United States Environment Protection Agency (USEPA) declared that over 482,000 cars in the US had been fitted with a so-called "defeat device" to guarantee the passing of Government conditions emission tests (Hotten, 2015). The "defeat device" allows a diesel car to turn on the "safety mode" to pass emission tests. Under the "safety mode", the engine of the car will run below normal power and performance (Hotten, 2015) so as to guarantee low emissions but once customers drove the car on the road, the car will automatically switch out of "safety mode" into "road mode", thus improving the performance of the car, but increasing emissions. This means that a VW car with "road mode" enabled produces significantly more air pollution than would be suggested by calculations based upon "safety mode" emissions[1]. On 23 September 2015, VW admitted that there are around 11 million diesel cars worldwide that have the relevant "defeat device" fitted (Winston, 2015).

The VW emission scandal is a new form of automobile reputational crisis, which is not related to automobile quality or safety issues (such as the Aston Martin recall in 2014). Instead, it is characterized as a form of deliberate fraud and/or criminal intent, rather than stemming from negligence or corporate wrongdoing (Hartman, 2015). According to Hartman (2015), the VW scandal has therefore *"set the bar at a whole new level"*. The consequences of the VW emission scandal are threefold. Firstly, the VW scandal might raise industrial concerns regarding related diesel car supply chains. VW also supplies diesel engines to both Audi and Porsche (as subsidiary firms) and therefore these firms may also be suspected to have sold cars containing the affected engines (Rucker and Gardner, 2015; Saarinen, 2015).

Secondly, the emission fraud threatens the health of millions in Europe, because of the high levels of nitrogen oxide pollutants. The World Health Organization (WHO) estimates there are around 7 million premature deaths are associated with air pollution (Winston, 2015). Therefore, the emission scandal might make the public more concerned about the issues of air pollution and the need for sustainable development. Thirdly, the VW incident potentially increases the public mistrust of the diesel car industry as a whole, as VW plays a central role in this market sector (Bach, 2015). In fact, it could even be argued that the scandal is risking the reputation of the entire automobile industry as a whole, and its efforts in using technology to achieve environmental sustainability (Winston, 2015; Bach, 2015). Currently, sustainability is of growing importance in business strategy and firm credibility (Elkington, 1994). In short, VW's reporting of sustainability performance data to enhance 'green' positioning and the nature of the VW scandal demonstrates highly unethical conduct (Szekely, 2015) and could harm VW's brand reputation and result in financial losses to the company (such as the government's fines and sales loss), as well as harm public health, and have knock-on reputational effects for the whole of the car industry.

For the automobile industry stakeholders (not only the company, but also the industry and governments), rebuilding public confidence is key to recovering from the emissions scandal. In the immediate post-crisis phase, communicating with consumers should be a priority in order to rebuild public trust.

In this case, understanding the demands and attitudes of consumers is an essential step in designing an effective communication strategy. Due to the importance of consumer opinion, exploring data from social media could provide important insights to aid those designing such communication strategies.

Social media is an emerging tool that can be used to assess and manage relationships with customers (Agnihotri et al., 2012). According to Blackshaw and Nazzaro (2004), social media is a variety of information sources that are created, initiated, circulated and applied by consumers' intent on educating each other about products, brands, services, personalities, and issues. There are various social media platforms, such as Twitter, Facebook, LinkedIn and Instagram, where companies can keep in touch with their customers and also promote products. Accordingly, the adoption of social media could contribute to a company's long-term profitability (Hoffman & Fodor, 2010; Kaplan & Haenlein, 2010). Moreover, customer ideas and feedback generated from social media could assist company innovation as well (Piller et al., 2012). In recent years, a wide range of academic studies have investigated and explored the application of social media. For example, through analysing tweets, Bollen et al. (2011) attempt to predict changes in the stock market. Also, Veil et al. (2011a) regard social media as a particular channel for risk communication with the public. In the field of marketing research, Ngai et al. (2015) stress that social media has become a critical component in current business strategy setting. However, dealing with a company's reputational risks when faced with a crisis is still largely uncovered by academic social media research (Tse et al., 2016).

To fill this gap in academic social media research and to contribute to insights of the VW scandal for practitioners, this study aims to propose a comprehensive analytic framework for analysing the massive social media data set based on the Text Mining (TM) techniques, combined with demographic and integrated analytics to complete the rounded picture. As a tool for data mining, there are many examples of application of TM in social media, ranging from identifying customers' satisfaction levels (Liau and Tan, 2014), predicting stock market changes (Nguyen et al., 2015; Wong et al., 2008), and monitoring political preferences of the public (Ceron et al., 2014). According to Feldman and Sanger (2007), TM refers to a research method that overcomes the challenges of analysing loaded, unstructured texts by adopting different, but complimentary, approaches, including machine learning, natural language processing (NLP), information retrieval, and knowledge management. In this study, our analytic framework combines two TM techniques, which are sentiment analysis (SA) and clustering analysis (CA) in order to reveal the strength of feeling about the scandal within the sample of consumer tweets tested.

Within TM studies, sentiment analysis (SA) is widely adopted (Ghiassi et al., 2013; Kontopoulos et al., 2013; Liau & Tan, 2014; Mostafa, 2013; Paltoglou & Thelwall, 2012). SA refers to the automatic analysis approach of classifying the sentiment scores from large numbers of texts, which includes three categories – positive, neutral and negative. This technique is helpful to determine opinions of consumers towards their products or service promptly. For example, Zhang et al. (2012) apply the sentence-based SA to identify product weaknesses through exploring the sentiment from online customer reviews. Customers' attitudes towards particular product features could also be extracted by the SA approach (Zhang et al., 2012). According to Jansen et al. (2009), tweeting or microblogging is regarded as 'electronic word of mouth' (WOM), which can play a critical role in customer's buying decisions. This is because consumers tend to believe the information transfer in their social network (i.e. family or friends) rather than those from outside sources (such as online reviews) (Duan et al., 2008; Jansen et al., 2009). When managing a crisis, such as the VW emissions scandal, timely SA can help companies understand customers' opinions from their social network activity. This can be a critical first step to rebuilding corporate reputation, minimising brand damage and toxicity and regaining public trust (Tse et al., 2016).

This chapter provides a Tweets Analysis framework, which combines three types of research approach – demographic analytics, text analytics and integrated analytics. The scope of the observation period (i.e. tweets data collection time frame) is from September 22, 2015, to October 1, 2015, which is the first week after the VW emission scandal broke. A total of 8,274 tweets and associated metadata form the data sample of this chapter, which was collected using the hashtag #volkswagenscandal. The application of the proposed framework strives to examine the following research questions:

1. What is consumers' sentiment toward Volkswagen in the emission scandal?
2. What are the most common concerns and interests of consumers regarding the emission scandal?
3. How can the analysis framework provide practitioners with better decision making in PR crisis management in the future?

The next section reviews the relevant literature regarding social media, then the tweets analysis framework detail is presented. This is followed with the results of the application of the analysis framework, the findings of which are discussed and practical implications outlined for industry. Finally, alongside conclusions, limitations of this study are addressed, together with suggestions for future research.

BACKGROUND: SOCIAL MEDIA REASEARCH

With the growing tide of big data, the topic of social media has attracted extensive research from different disciplines, such as sociology (Jin et al., 2014; Veil et al., 2011b), marketing (de Vries et al., 2012; Hoffman and Fodor, 2010; Michaelidou et al., 2011), supply chain management (Chae, 2015; O'Leary, 2011), educational research (Tess, 2013), political and government research (Bertot et al., 2010; Loader and Mercea, 2011; Shirky, 2011), and financial prediction (Bollen et al., 2011; Zhang et al., 2011).

Social media has been regarded as a supplement to the traditional communication approaches, such as telephone or mail (Mcafee, 2006). With the increasing public demand for social media, individuals are currently responsible for the generation of larger quantities of publicly accessible, shared information than ever before (Oeary, 2011). According to Malita (2011), social media is defined as a set of "tools that facilitate the socialisation of content and encourage collaboration, interaction, and communication through discussion, feedback, voting, comments, and sharing of information from all interested parties". Currently, Facebook, Twitter and Linkedin are the most frequently used social media by businesses (eCoonsultancy, 2010). All of these platforms are regarded as social network sites (SNS), which is a common form of social media. According to Ellison (2007), there are three characteristics of this kind of social media, in which users:

1. Construct a public or semi-public profile within a bounded system.
2. Articulate a list of other users with whom they share a connection.
3. View and traverse their list of connections and those made by others within the system.

Due to the strengths of instant response and direct communication, practitioners and professionals have extensively studied customer relationship management and explored consumer attitudes in social media (Hajli, 2014; Jin & Phua, 2014; Liau & Tan, 2014; Pentina et al., 2013; Tsai & Men, 2013). The opinions expressed by customers in their social networks play a significant role in influencing public opinion and behaviour (Mostafa, 2013). Although previous researchers have widely analysed data from social media in various contexts, the fields of commercial crisis management and supply chain risk management are still under-researched, although Tse et al (2016) provide a good example of this type of analysis, through an analysis of the horse meat adulteration scandal in the UK in 2013.

In this chapter, we only focus on one particular social media platform - Twitter. According to ALEXA (2015), Twitter is the ninth most visited website in the world, so provides an excellent place for us to explore the opinions from customers. Moreover, the growth of Twitter is much faster than its other two major competitors – Facebook and Google+ (Bennett, 2013). Recently, the number of monthly active users of Twitters has achieved 320 million (Twitter, n.d.). The information from microblogging (i.e. Tweeting) has become a valuable resource to extract the opinion and the sentiment from customers (Zhang et al., 2012). Twitter provides a friendly environment for the client to read and create the posts quickly, as it requires users to control the length of a post in a concise manner (Jansen et al., 2009). A tweet post is a message of 140 characters, which includes three categories: original tweets, replies, and retweets. Additionally, compared with other social media platforms, the data from Twitter is more "open" (Chae, 2015). Specifically, researchers can access Twitter data through Twitter's Application Programming Interface (API) (Twitter, 2013), providing a considerable sample of data for in-depth research (Chae, 2015). However, it is not possible for us to extract valuable information from a significant amount of tweet data without the help of text mining (TM) techniques (Liau & Tan, 2014).

TWEETS ANALYSIS FRAMEWORK

According to Chae (2015), collecting tweet data (which includes both the text of the tweet and accompanying metadata [2]) begins with identifying the topic of interest using a keyword(s) or hashtag(s), and requires the use of Application Programming Interface (APIs). There are two possible data collection methods adopted, which are individual API collection and the use of data providers (such as GNIP, DataSift). Both of these data collection methods have their advantages and disadvantages. For the individual API collection, it is totally free and more flexible. However, this method can only collect 1% of publicly available Twitter data (Chae, 2015). On the other hand, through the help of commercial data providers, 100% of tweets can be accessible to the researchers. At the same time, it is a very costly option (Chae, 2015). With a variety of information in every tweet, a comprehensive framework is needed to be developed in order to peel the "onion" of the tweet. In this chapter, three main sections are covered: Demographic analytics, content analytics and integrated analytics.

Demographic Analytics

In the first step of the framework, the metadata of the tweets is scrutinised. The demographic analytics include two subsections: the tweet statistics (i.e. descriptive analysis) and the user information analysis. First, the descriptive analysis focuses on the basic statistics of the tweet data, such as the number of tweets, distribution of different types of tweets, and the number of hashtags etc. (Chae, 2015). The user information analysis focuses on a more advanced basis, for instance, the gender distribution and the geographic information of the tweet source.

Generating the simplistic but essential data (such as the basic statistics of the tweets – number of tweets, retweets, word counts, the number of hashtags and URL information) should be the purpose of this descriptive Tweet analysis (Bruns and Stieglitz, 2013; Chae, 2015), because the descriptive statistics of the tweets provide the basis for many other metrics (Chae, 2015). For instance, we can identify the most influential account/people through counting the "numbers of retweets". Moreover, a number of tweets include a URL (such as news and business report, etc.), which would be a valuable resource for examining the popular topics, and their source, used in the online discussion. According to Waller et al. (2011), "Analyses may focus on the types of resources that are referenced in URLs". On the other hand, customer information like gender and geographic information could offer the gateway for our subsequent analysis – content analysis. Although the gender information is not available in Twitter, we can predict the gender through analysing the username. Accurate prediction of a demographic attribute like gender from social media could be valuable for marketing, personalisation and legal investigation (Burger et al., 2011).

Content Analytics (or Text Mining)

Compared with the Demographic Analytics, which focuses mostly upon the data accompanying the tweet, the Content Analytics portion of the analysis focus entirely on the text of the tweets. Initially, the social media text data is "unstructured" or "raw", and is not suitable to directly be used for analysis. Hence, in the first step of the content analysis, data preparation is necessary. In this chapter, a structured text pre-processing is applied as the tool to manage the "raw texts", usingtechniques like tokenization and stemming (Delen et al., 2012; Liau & Tan, 2014).

After this, the structured text is used for the word frequency analysis to identify hot topics in the sample. Hot topics identified from the term frequency analysis then guide the way to the clustering analysis. Clustering is an important tool to automatically organise and explore information (such as unanticipated trends or correlations) from text-based data (Agnihotri et al., 2012; Liau & Tan, 2014). According to Jansen et al. (2011), clustering analysis enables companies to identify different groups of customers by extracting their similarities quickly. To explore the individual information, we also need to conduct sentiment analysis (SA), which is also known as opinion mining (Feldman, 2013). Positive and negative opinion words normally have a sentiment score of "+1" to "-1" respectively (Liau & Tan, 2014). Likewise, the tweet with sentiment score 0 represents the neutral expression. Through examining the polarity, which ranges from negative to positive, sentiment can be interpreted and understood through analysis (Chae, 2015).

Integrated Analytics

The aim of this final stage of the analysis is to combine the Demographic Analytics and Content Analytics stages. For instance, through combining the results from sentiment analysis and clustering, some interesting findings could be obtained. In this case, the general sentiment level of a particular theme could be identified. Moreover, another possible combination would be demographic information and clustering analysis. This analysis could answer the question of "what is the sentiment difference between US and UK customers?". Furthermore, the integrated analytics could also explore the particular topics with a focus upon gender, answering questions such as "is there a gender difference to opinions concerning the VW emission scandal?"

DATA ANALYSIS

The ideal method of collecting the insights from the tweets related to the VW scandal would be collecting the whole Twitter sample including the directly related tweets (i.e. tweets that explicitly mention the scandal) and indirectly related tweets (i.e. tweets that concern the scandal but do not explicitly mention it) (Chae, 2015). It is not realistic or practical to collect the entire dataset, due to the vast amount of information and the cost of obtaining it. Therefore, this chapter applies a sampling process to collect the directly related tweets data. In the pilot research, several search terms and Hashtags were tested, such as "VW" "Volkswagen" "Emission Scandal". Through reviewing the results of the key terms, the hashtag "#VolkswagenScandal" is the most relevant search term to identify our dataset. The data collection period is between 22 September and 1 October 2015, which is just ten days after the scandal exposed. In this chapter, the tweets dataset includes 8,274 tweets with the hashtag #VolkswagenScandal and their metadata. The data used in this study was collected through the NVIVO add-on software - NCapture.

Demographic Analytics

Several statistical techniques were used to conduct the descriptive analysis (Bruns and Stieglitz, 2013; Chae, 2015), such as the tweet statistics and URL analysis. Regarding the user information analysis, identifying geographic data and gender information are the focus. Python software was utilised to try to identify the gender of Twitter users.

- **Tweets Statistics:** Regarding the dataset, we first apply the basic statistical analysis for the tweets by categorising the types of tweets and hashtags. Among 8,274 original tweets, retweets, and @Volkswagen group account for 4083 (49.35%), 3365 (40.67%), 826 (9.98%). To analyse the Hashtags statistics, we applied the software called QDAminer. This chapter identifies 1434 unique Hashtags in the tweets dataset. 3506 tweets include more than two hashtags in a single tweet. According to Chae (2015), this indicates that a large amount of tweets are intersecting multiple areas of interest. For example, tweets contain two or more hashtags: #Volkswagescandal, #reputational risk and #emissions. The URL information regarded as an indirect reference from the users. In the dataset, the URLs are vital: 59.26% (4902) of the total tweets (8,274) include at least one URL. Most of these URLs are related to news websites reporting on the VW emission scandal.
- **Users' Meta-Analysis:** In the whole dataset there are 3689 unique users involved. In this case, each user posts 2.4288 tweets: 1.1068 original tweets, 0.9121 retweets, and 0.9121 @Volkswagen group. The result implies that the tweets are not particularly focused and that many users share their individual opinions. The top four significant (i.e. visibility) accounts are heat_io (243 retweets received[3]), 247Fame (198 retweets received), Greenpeace (133 retweets received) and jen2seely (94 retweets received). To identify the gender from the username, we applied the US Census Bureau library[4] to estimate the gender through Python 2.7. However, due to a large amount of public accounts that have no gender information and non-English names, there are 2286 tweets that can be identified as hailing from people of a specific gender. Among these tweets, 1628 tweets (71.21%) were posted by male users and 658 tweets (28.79%) posted by female users.

Table 1. The most visible users

Account	Types of Accounts	Retweets Received	Number of Followers
heat_io	News Media	243	5051
247Fame	News Media	198	1027
Greenpeace	Independent Organisation	133	1461511
J***seely	Individual	94	491

Content Analytics

The aim of the content analytics stage of the analysis is to scrutinise the actual text content of the tweets. Before conducting the step-by-step analysis, the process of data preparation needs to be applied to transform the "unstructured text" into "structured data". After this, three types of text mining approaches were conducted, including 1) word count analysis, 2) clustering analysis and 3) sentiment analysis. The word count analysis is based on the keywords frequency analysis and the hashtag frequency analysis. Also, using multidimensional scaling methods, several topic groups were clustered. Regarding the sentiment analysis, the lexicon-based method was adopted to capture the sentiment score from the customers.

- **Data Preparation:** To transform the unstructured text to analysable data, it is necessary to first conduct the data pre-processing. Tokenization is the first step of this process, which can be defined as the process of identifying the meaningful words through breaking up the text into discrete words (Liau and Tan, 2014). Additionally, the stopping words were removed in the second stage. For example, personal pronouns, demonstrative pronouns and prepositions were eliminated. As Twitter is a kind of informal blogging, the problem of misspelling is common. In this case, the spelling of each word within the tweets was carefully checked. Then, the stemming approach was applied to further process the text by deducting the prefixes and suffixes to normalised words (Delen et al., 2012). For instance, the words "points", "pointing" and "pointed" were all transformed to "point". To import all the data into our text analysis software – QDA Miner, all the lower case words were changed to upper cases words. At the end of the data pre-processing, the word frequency analysis can be used to reflect the quality of the data preparation. For example, those meaningless words with high frequency, which were not considered as stopping words or stemming, such as HTTP; HTTPS and RT, were excluded. Moreover, the phrases or words with duplicated meaning were transferred into a single word, for instance, "HAHA", "HAHAHA" as "lol".

- **Word Count Analysis:** The most popular key terms in tweets were emission (found in 1217[5]), CEO (620), Car (1019), German (481), Test (256), Hell (250), Software (224), Crisis (162), Cheating (295), Pollution (274), Trust (118). The themes toward the keywords in tweets were generally focused on the aspect of customer trust, and on the resignation of the VW group CEO. Moreover, 1,435 unique hashtags were found in the tweets and they appear 17,757 times. The most popular hashtags include #Volkswagenscandal, #Volkswagen, #VW, #VWGATE, #DISELGATE, #TDI, #CARTOON, #DASPROBLEM, #AUDI, #CORPGOV, #CLMATECHANGE, #ICYMI, #BMW, #HUDDERSFIELD, #MECCA, #TESLA, #FIFA, #GREEN, #SAYINGTRUTH, #FOSSILFUELS, among others. Similar to the prior research of Chae (2015), two hashtags were most common in the tweets. There were average 2.15 hashtags per tweet. In this case, it is important to investigate associations among the hashtags. In the next section, we will adopt the clustering analysis to observe the association among the hashtags and key terms.

- **Clustering Analysis:** To check the relevant hashtags of the research focus, the proximity plot was used to overview the association. As shown in Figure 1, on a single axis, the distance from a particular object to all other objects represents the strength of the association (Mostafa, 2013). Hashtags such as #DIESELGATE, #EMISSIONS, #CARMAGEDDON, #AIRPOLLUTION, #TDI, #CARTOON, #DASPROBLEM, #AUDI are most associated with the research focus - #VolkswagenScandal. Interesting, two other brands of the automobile manufacturers also appeared in the proximity analysis, which are BMW and AUDI.

The multidimensional scaling (MDS) method allows the holistic analysis of the co-occurrence of keywords within a dataset. Co-occurrence is defined as happening every time two words appear in the same case (WordStat, 2014). Figures 2 and 3 illustrate the co-occurrence concept map based on the MDS method. The concept maps are graphic representations of the proximity values computed on all included keywords using MDS. In this case, the Jaccard's coefficient[6] was the index used to measure the co-occurrence. As shown in Figure 3, the triangle represents the high frequency terms (the size of triangle is representative of to the word's frequency) in the dataset and the distance between the concepts indicates the strength of correlation.

Below are some clustered concepts identified:

1. **Responsibility Group:** "RESPONSIBLITY" (68) [7] "SOCIAL" (65) "DANAGEROUS" (57): *Corporate Social Responsibility has become a racket - and a dangerous one* #Volkswagenscandal
2. **Recall Group:** "RECALL" (142) "FIX" (103) "WORKING" (111): #VolkswagenScandal: *No recall but Volkswagen says it's working on a fix*

Figure 1. Proximity plot of hashtags

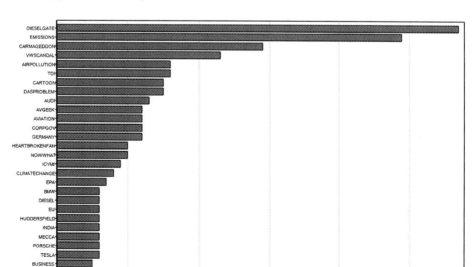

3. **Spread over Risk Group:** "AUDI" (187) "SKODA" (41) "AFFECTED" (121): *Damn! The scandal spreads to Porsche and Audi #Volkswagenscanal*

4. **Focal Group:** "VOLKSWAGEN" (2891) "DIESELGATE" (465) "EMISSIONS" (1040) "CEO" (631): *Think it's great @Volkswagen tried to screw Big #government on auto emissions. CEO should get raise. Might buy one now. #VolkswagenScandal*

5. **Air Pollution Group:** "AIRPOLLUTION"; "DEATHS"; "VIOLATIONS" *How many extra deaths from #airpollution from Volkswagen violations? #Volkswagenscanal*

- **Sentiment Analysis:** Although we can explore the key tweets or hot topics through MDS, it is difficult to systematically understand the meaning behind the tweets. Therefore, the sentiment analysis can assist the researcher to identify the opinions of the customers. Here we adopted the

Figure 2. 2D maps of clustering analysis

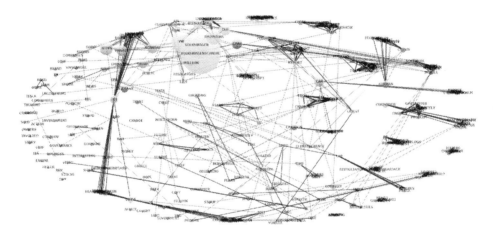

Figure 3. 3D maps of clustering analysis

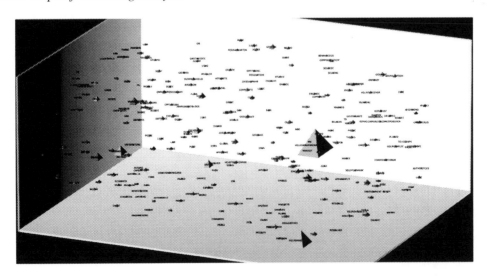

lexicon-based approach to annotate the tweets for determining customer's polarity through a particular dictionary of the words. We applied the dictionary of Hu and Liu (2004), due to its successful adoption in a series of research projects (Miner et al., 2012; Mostafa, 2013; Tse et al., 2016). 2006 positive words and 4783 negative words are in this library. Typically, the average sentiment score for the entire dataset is -0.21347. To clarify how the software rates the sentiment scores of individual tweets, we picked some examples from our tweets (Table 2).

Integrated Analytics

- **Gender Group Analytics:** Compared with the male group, the topics of female users are more focused. As shown in Figures 4 and 5, the clustered topics in the male group are more than the clustered topics in the female group. Compared with the male users, female users are more likely to focus on topics such as "Cheating" and "Trust". The total aggregate female sentiment score was -0.09285, which compared to the male sentiment score of -0.1763299. Towards the VW emission scandal, the attitudes of male customers are worse than the female clients. Also, using the scale of necessary Tweets statistics, the tweeting behaviour differences were also investigated. For the identified female users, 19.6% of posts were retweets, 76.1% of posts were original tweets, and 4.3% mentioned (@Volkswagen) the involved company in their tweets. On the other hand, regarding the male users, 27.9% of posts were retweets, 53% of posts were original tweets, and 19.1% mentioned the Volkswagen group.

- **Time Series Analysis:** Other than the gender group discussion, this chapter also breaks down the entire dataset to separate dates and times to investigate the changes in customer opinions following the development of the scandal. The time series analysis includes two sections, which are the geographic popularity changes and the sentiment changes along the time frame. First, this study breaks down the entire dataset into a 8 day - period (in a half day manner, AM/PM, see table 3 and 4) to investigate the changes in tweets frequency. The popularity of the tweets related to the VW emission scandal was the top on 24th of September afternoon. The average sentiment of the tweets is negative along the observation period. The worst sentiment score appears on the first few days after the scandal broke. Second, this analysis illustrates three days that have highest tweets frequency on the Google map (i.e. 24 Sep, 25 Sep and 26 Sep). As shown in Figure 6, the UK and US are the centres of discussing the emissions scandal on Twitter. Interestingly, on the 25 September, Dubai and India have both become the discussion centres in the world.

Table 2. Examples of tweets with sentiment analysis

Example	Sentiment
One more brand highlighted for wrong reasons. #Curious on how it controls the damage caused. #VolkswagenScandal	-3 (negative)
Dishonesty cn get u outta mess today bt in the future it'll haunt & cost u dearly. #volkswagenscandal	-3 (negative)
#VolkswagenScandal is sickening. pple who bought BS car aren't only effected but those who have to breathe the dirty air too.#dicks	-3 (negative)

Figure 4. Clustering analysis of male users

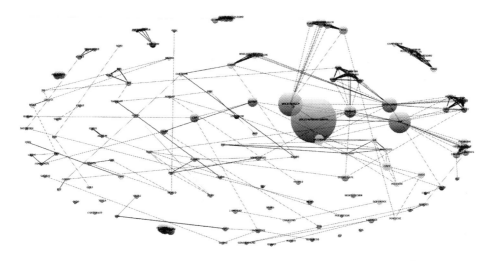

Figure 5. Clustering analysis of female

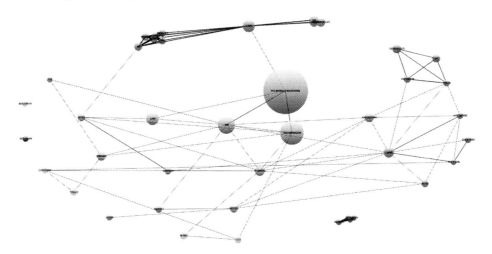

Table 3. Time series Tweets frequency

Date	24-Sep	25-Sep	26-Sep	27-Sep	28-Sep	29-Sep	30-Sep	01-Oct
AM	233	756	356	217	247	244	209	196
PM	1768	1117	624	387	642	503	655	59
Total	**2001**	**1873**	**980**	**604**	**889**	**747**	**864**	**255**

Table 4. Time series sentiment changes

Date	24-Sep	25-Sep	26-Sep	27-Sep	28-Sep	29-Sep	30-Sep	01-Oct
AM	-0.412	-0.306	-0.053	-0.046	-0.235	-0.291	-0.167	-0.281
PM	-0.183	-0.219	0.207	-0.271	-0.298	-0.207	-0.473	-0.254
Total	**-0.210**	**-0.254**	**0.112**	**-0.190**	**-0.280**	**-0.234**	**-0.399**	**-0.275**

Figure 6. Geographic illustration of tweets: A. September 24, 2015, B. September 25, 2015, C. September 26, 2015

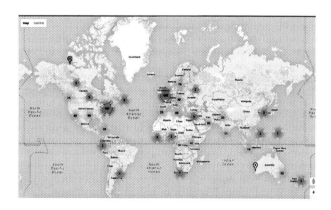

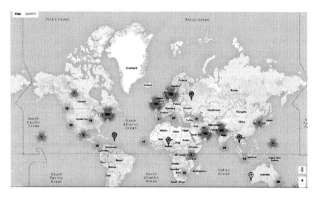

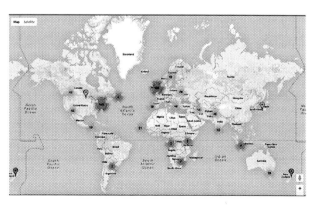

DISCUSSION

There are three major information dissemination patterns in Twitter, posting original tweets, using URL and Hashtag, retweeting and mentioning other people or parties (@other users). In the dataset of this chapter, over half of the tweets (i.e. 5926) include at least one URL. Compared with a random sample of tweets, the use of URL in VW tweets is very popular - only 22% of the random tweets have URL information. Java et al. (2007) state that sharing URLs information to report news is common in Twitter. In the VW emission scandal, the result of URL information sharing indicates that news and professional blogging are widely shared by customers via the uses of URLs in Tweets. The highly visible users (i.e. those that receive most retweets) are the press media and the environmental protection agencies. Additionally, among the #volkswagenscandal tweets, around 10% of them (over 800 tweets) have mentioned the Volkswagen group accounts (including @Volkswagen; @VW; @UKvolkswagen; @VWcanada). This indicates that the customers demonstrate a high demand to communicate with the company involved in this emission scandal. Nevertheless, although the involved companies (such as Volkswagen and Audi) have their twitter accounts, they are almost invisible in our dataset, which means that the companies received few retweets.

The findings from the tweets hashtag are consistent with the statement of Chae (2015) that tweets related to timely or 'breaking' issues are widely diffused by the use of hashtags. On average, there are two hashtags in a single tweet related to the VW scandal. The results show that the Twitter users who are interested in the VW emission scandal are more willing to diffuse the tweets by using the hashtags function. The heavy use of hashtags could also explain the high proportion of retweets. According to Suh et al. (2010), the use of hashtags has a strong relationship with "retweetability". In the tweets of the VW scandal, over 40% of the tweets are retweets. Based on our further investigation, the tweet with highest retweet rate includes five hashtags in a single tweet. The main purpose of using a hashtag for Twitter users is to indicate the topic of the tweets and raise the interest of a wider audience (Chae, 2015). Among the topics of VW scandal tweets, users express concern about environmental issues such as; #climatechange and the influence of other automobile brands like #BMW and #AUDI. Also, a large proportion of users regarded the VW scandal as an extremely important topic as they are using #ICYMI[8].

Based on the data from the US Census Bureau, this chapter identifies the gender information of the tweets. Overall 2,000 tweets could be identified in terms of gender according to the usernames. Those tweets without gender information are due to two major reasons: language and public account. Because the username library is based on the data of English names, the username of other languages, such as Indian, Arabic, German and Chinese, etc., could not match the data from the gender library. Moreover, a large proportion of tweets were posted by public accounts, such as the press media and commercial accounts. Hence, this portion of the accounts could not be classified either. Although the rate of identification is relatively low, the absolute amount of identified tweets is still sizeable. Among the identified tweets, 658 and 1628 were posted by women and men respectively. This result implies that the topic of the emission scandal is more important to the men than the women. It seems contrary with previous research that women have higher environmental concern and stronger willingness to contribute (Hunter et al., 2004; L.C. et al., 2000). A possible implication of the gender difference is that practitioners can contribute a more effective strategy to communicate with the customers based on the gender information.

The topic of the VW emissions scandal has undoubtedly raised broad interest across the world. According to the geographic information within the tweets, we illustrated three global maps to indicate the popularity of the topic in different parts of the world. There is no doubt the US and UK are two key discussion centres, as these two countries were profoundly influenced by the scandal. Surprisingly, people of two Asian countries, the United Arab Emirates and India, also widely discussed the topic. The results could also explain why the gender information cannot be identified in some tweets, as a big proportion of them were posted in the Asian countries. The analysis shows that the emission scandal has already made a global impact, which is consistent with a brand of global reach.

The subjects of the VW tweets are diverse. Five groups of topics were identified by the clustering analysis. The analysis is based on the co-occurrence index of the elements within an individual group. One noticeable group concerns Air Pollution. Customers are more concerned with the consequences of air pollution, because of the emission scandal. According to Lave and Seskin (2013), air pollution has been a public problem with growing national and international interest. Moreover, the group showing supply chain concern has revealed that customers are also concerned with other companies in the VW Group, such as AUDI and Porsche. The clustering method could be a new approach for practitioners to identify different topic areas of customer importance, hence market segments and issues related to trading and business improvement strategy. It allows companies to segment marketing messages and communication strategies based on the customer reflections in the post-crisis period.

Additionally, understanding the sentiment of tweets could help the company to rebuild the consumer confidence and monitor market reaction. Opinions expressed by the consumers could be benchmarked against financial metrics (such as sales and stock prices) (Mostafa, 2013; Nguyen et al., 2015). In the VW emission scandal, the average sentiment of the tweets is negative (-0.21347). Nevertheless, the tweets of the emission scandal contain relatively low sentiment, as around 50% of them are zero. This can be explained by the tweets statistics that a considerable part of tweets are retweeted tweets of business news. The texts of these tweets are the title of the news. Exemplar tweets are "*RT @CNNMoney: Here's what you need to know about the #VolkswagenScandal*" and "*RT @avgerinosx: #VolkswagenScandal #Volkswagen (#BMW diesels also shown to be 11 TIMES over emissions limit)*". However, there are many tweets found to contain extremely negative sentiment toward the scandal, from the perspective of air pollution and trust (e.g. "how many have died because of #Volkswagen emission?? #fraud #corruption #VolkswagenScandal Lying bastards fuck their customers for money" and "VW lied on emission testing. Germany uses gas for evil once shame on U, use gas for evil twice...shame on U again actually #VolkswagenScandal").

In the integrated analytics, we combined the demographic and content analytics to investigate the important information regarding the gender differences and changes in customers' opinions. The word frequency and the sentiment analysis were broken down in a half-day manner to observe the changes in customers' sentiment during the outbreak of VW emission scandal. Except for the last day of the observation, the results show that users are more likely to post tweets in the afternoon. Also, the sentiment of the customers is also generally lower in the afternoon. At the very beginning of the scandal (i.e. the first day of the scandal), the sentiment score was the worst of the sample and thereafter improved. The findings from the time series analysis are consistent with the research of Franca et al. (2015), which indicates the difference of tweets usage in New York across 24 hours. A possible implication is that the company needs to prioritise and enhance the social media monitoring and communication in the afternoon time-period. Second, as shown in Figure 4 and Figure 5, more clustered groups were identified in the male users than female users. This indicates that the tweet topics of men are more diverse than that of women. Although the result is surprising initially, the frequency of tweets could help explain why. The identified male users are more than twice the number of female users. Moreover, the sentiment of men was worse than that of women. The result of the gender sentiment analysis might be contrary to previous studies which argue that women are more concerned with environmental issues (such as Stern et al., 1993). The tweets statistics of both gender groups could also confirm our argument; compared with the female users, male users are more likely to mention VW in their tweets, to express directly their opinions to the company. Women therefore can be seen to express their opinions more indirectly in our findings.

CONCLUSION

The VW emission scandal has revealed a significant challenge in managing the supply chain network. Moreover, with increased vulnerability of the global environment, topics related to environmental sustainability are of interest globally. The corporate fraud scandal is extremely important to customers, with the recent UK horsemeat scandal acting as a good example (Tse et al., 2016). Therefore, it is crucial for practitioners to learn the lessons of the VW emissions scandal through scrutinising public attitudes, particularly in businesses with global brands where the risk to the business can be perceived to be greater. 8,274 #volkswagenscandal tweets were analysed by a comprehensive tweets analysis framework. Using the demographic analytics, the user information and relative tweeting behaviour could be quickly generalised. Based on the username, our analysis identified the gender information from part of tweets and showed that male users of Twitter showed more interest than female users of Twitter in this scandal.

The frequent use of hashtags in tweets should also draw the attention of practitioners. Regarding the content analytics, this chapter adopts a mixed text mining method, including clustering analysis and sentiment analysis. Based on the MDS clustering approach, five clustered groups were identified. According to the identified groups, this chapter suggests that practitioners should explore new potential customer segments of importance. Also, the sentiment analysis indicates the general sentiment of customers in the VW emission scandal is negative. The integrated analytics indicate the gender difference and sentiment changes along the outbreak of emission scandal.

Certainly, this chapter is not without limitations. The gender data library is restricted to English names. Therefore, future research could extend the database of gender to identify more information, such as including more names from other languages. The duration of data collection is relatively short, as this chapter only focuses on the related tweets in the ten days after the scandal happened. A more longitudinal approach may provide further insights. Also, because this chapter collects the tweets by using only one search term (i.e. #volkswagenscandal), more related search terms could be used in the future research to get a more comprehensive sample. In spite of these few limitations, this chapter offers practitioners and policy makers useful insights.

REFERENCES

Agnihotri, R., Kothandaraman, P., Kashyap, R., & Singh, R. (2012). Bringing "Social" Into Sales: The Impact of Salespeople'S Social Media Use on Service Behaviors and Value Creation. *Journal of Personal Selling & Sales Management, 32*(3), 333–348. doi:10.2753/PSS0885-3134320304

ALEXA. (2015). *The top 500 sites on the web.* Alexa. Available: http://www.alexa.com/topsites

Bach, D. (2015). *Seven Reasons Volkswagen Is Worse than Enron.* Yale Insights. Available: http://insights. som.yale.edu/insights/seven-reasons-volkswagen-worse-enron

Bennett, S. (2013). *Twitter Was The Fastest-Growing Social Network In 2013, Says Study [STATS]*. SocialTimes. Available: http://www.adweek.com/socialtimes/social-networks-growth-2012/476560?red=at

Bertot, J. C., Jaeger, P. T., & Grimes, J. M. (2010). Using ICTs to create a culture of transparency: E-government and social media as openness and anti-corruption tools for societies. *Government Information Quarterly, 27*(3), 264–271. doi:10.1016/j.giq.2010.03.001

Blackshaw, P., & Nazzaro, M. (2004). *Consumer-Generated Media (CGM) 101: Word-of-mouth in the age of the Web- fortified consumer.* Available: http://www.nielsenbuzzmetrics.com/whitepapers

Bollen, J., Mao, H. N., & Zeng, X. J. (2011). Twitter mood predicts the stock market. *Journal of Computational Science, 2*(1), 1–8. doi:10.1016/j.jocs.2010.12.007

Bruns, A., & Stieglitz, S. (2013). Towards more systematic Twitter analysis: Metrics for tweeting activities. *International Journal of Social Research Methodology, 16*(2), 91–108. doi:10.1080/13645579.2012.756095

Burger, J. D., Henderson, J., Kim, G., & Zarrella, G. (2011). Discriminant gender on Twitter. *Conference on Empirical Methods in Natural Language Processing*. Association for Computational Linguistics.

Ceron, A., Luigi, C., Iacus, S. M., & Porro, G. (2014). Every tweet counts? How sentiment analysis of social media can improve our knowledge of citizens' political preferences with an application to Italy and France. *New Media & Society, 16*(2), 340–358. doi:10.1177/1461444813480466

Chae, B. (2015). Insights from hashtag #supplychain and Twitter Analytics: Considering Twitter and Twitter data for supply chain practice and research. *International Journal of Production Economics, 165*, 247–259. doi:10.1016/j.ijpe.2014.12.037

De Vries, L., Gensler, S., & Leeflang, P. S. H. (2012). Popularity of Brand Posts on Brand Fan Pages: An Investigation of the Effects of Social Media Marketing. *Journal of Interactive Marketing, 26*(2), 83–91. doi:10.1016/j.intmar.2012.01.003

Delen, D., Fast, A., Hill, T., Elder, J., Miner, G., & Nisbet, B. (2012). *Practical Text Mining and Statisitical Analysis for Non-structured Text Data Applications*. Elsevier.

Duan, W. J., Gu, G., & Whinston, A. B. (2008). Do online reviews matter? - An empirical investigation of panel data. *Decision Support Systems, 45*(4), 1007–1016. doi:10.1016/j.dss.2008.04.001

ECOONSULTANCY. (2010). *Value of social media report (sample version)*. Author.

Elkington, J. (1994). Towards the Sustainable Corporation - Win-Win-Win Business Strategies for Sustainable Development. *California Management Review, 36*(2), 90–100. doi:10.2307/41165746

Ellison, N. B. (2007). Social network site: Definition, history, and scholarship. *Journal of Computer-Mediated Communication, 13*(1), 210–230. doi:10.1111/j.1083-6101.2007.00393.x

Feldman, R. (2013). Techniques and Applications for Sentiment Analysis. *Communications of the ACM, 56*(4), 82–89. doi:10.1145/2436256.2436274

Feldman, R., & Sanger, J. (2007). *The text mining handbook advanced approaches in analyzing unstructured data*. Cambridge, UK: Cambridge University Press.

Ghiassi, M., Skinner, J., & Zimbra, D. (2013). Twitter brand sentiment analysis: A hybrid system using n-gram analysis and dynamic artificial neural network. *Expert Systems with Applications*, *40*(16), 6266–6282. doi:10.1016/j.eswa.2013.05.057

Hajli, M. N. (2014). A study of the impact of social media on consumers. *International Journal of Market Research*, *56*(3), 387–404. doi:10.2501/IJMR-2014-025

Hartman, N. (2015). *VW needs massive marketing campaign to regain consumer trust and survive*. MIT Sloan Management. Available: http://mitsloanexperts.mit.edu/tag/vw-scandal/

Hoffman, D. L., & Fodor, M. (2010). Can You Measure the ROI of Your Social Media Marketing? *Sloan Management Review*, *52*, 41.

Hotten, R. (2015). *Volkswagen: The scandal explained - BBC News*. BBCNews. Available: http://www.bbc.co.uk/news/business-34324772

Hunter, L. M., Hatch, A., & Johnson, A. (2004). Cross-national gender variation in environmental behaviors. *Social Science Quarterly*, *85*(3), 677–694. doi:10.1111/j.0038-4941.2004.00239.x

Jansen, B. J., Sobel, K., & Cook, G. (2011). Classifying ecommerce information sharing behaviour by youths on social networking sites. *Journal of Information Science*, *37*(2), 120–136. doi:10.1177/0165551510396975

Jansen, B. J., Zhang, M. M., Sobel, K., & Chowdury, A. (2009). Twitter Power: Tweets as Electronic Word of Mouth. *Journal of the American Society for Information Science and Technology*, *60*(11), 2169–2188. doi:10.1002/asi.21149

Java, A., Song, X., Finin, T., & Tseng, B. (2007). Why we twitter: understanding microblogging usage and communities. *9th WebKDD and 1st SNAKDD 2007 Workshop on Web Mining and Social Network Analysis*.

Jin, S. A. A., & Phua, J. (2014). Following Celebrities' Tweets About Brands: The Impact of Twitter-Based Electronic Word-of-Mouth on Consumers' Source Credibility Perception, Buying Intention, and Social Identification With Celebrities. *Journal of Advertising*, *43*(2), 181–195. doi:10.1080/00913367.2013.827606

Jin, Y., Liu, B. F., & Austing, L. L. (2014). Examining the role of social media in effective crisis management: The effects of crisis origin, information form, and source on publics' crisis responses. *Communication Research*, *41*(1), 74–94. doi:10.1177/0093650211423918

Kaplan, A. M., & Haenlein, M. (2010). Users of the world, unite! The challenges and opportunities of Social Media. *Business Horizons*, *53*(1), 59–68. doi:10.1016/j.bushor.2009.09.003

Kontopoulos, E., Berberidis, C., Dergiades, T., & Bassiliades, N. (2013). Ontology-based sentiment analysis of twitter posts. *Expert Systems with Applications*, *40*(10), 4065–4074. doi:10.1016/j.eswa.2013.01.001

Lave, L. B., & Seskin, E. P. (2013). *Air Pollution and Human Health*. Taylor & Francis.

Liau, B. Y., & Tan, P. P. (2014). Gaining customer knowledge in low cost airlines through text mining. *Industrial Management & Data Systems*, *114*(9), 1344–1359. doi:10.1108/IMDS-07-2014-0225

Loader, B. D., & Mercea, D. (2011). Networking democracy? Social media innovations and participatory politics introduction. *Information Communication and Society, 14,* 757–769. doi:10.1080/136911 8X.2011.592648

Malita, L. 2011. Social media time management tools and tips. *World Conference on Information Technology (Wcit-2010).* doi:10.1016/j.procs.2010.12.123

Mcafee, A. P. (2006). Enterprise 2.0: The dawn of emergent collaboration. *Sloan Management Review, 47,* 21.

Michaelidou, N., Siamagka, N. T., & Christodoulides, G. (2011). Usage, barriers and measurement of social media marketing: An exploratory investigation of small and medium B2B brands. *Industrial Marketing Management, 40*(7), 1153–1159. doi:10.1016/j.indmarman.2011.09.009

Mostafa, M. M. (2013). More than words: Social networks' text mining for consumer brand sentiments. *Expert Systems with Applications, 40*(10), 4241–4251. doi:10.1016/j.eswa.2013.01.019

Ngai, E. W. T., Moon, K. L. K., Lam, S. S., Chin, E. S. K., & Tao, S. S. C. (2015). Social media models, technologies, and applications An academic review and case study. *Industrial Management & Data Systems, 115*(5), 769–802. doi:10.1108/IMDS-03-2015-0075

Nguyen, T. H., Shirai, K., & Velcin, J. (2015). Sentiment analysis on social media for stock movement prediction. *Expert Systems with Applications, 42*(24), 9603–9611. doi:10.1016/j.eswa.2015.07.052

O'Leary, D. E. (2011). The use of social media in the supply chain: Survey and extensions. *Intelligent Systems in Accounting, Finance & Management, 18*(2-3), 121–144. doi:10.1002/isaf.327

Paltoglou, G., & Thelwall, M. (2012). Twitter, MySpace, Digg: Unsupervised Sentiment Analysis in Social Media. *ACM Transactions on Intelligent Systems and Technology, 3*(4), 66. doi:10.1145/2337542.2337551

Pentina, I., Zhang, L., & Basmanova, O. (2013). Antecedents and consequences of trust in a social media brand: A cross-cultural study of Twitter. *Computers in Human Behavior, 29*(4), 1546–1555. doi:10.1016/j.chb.2013.01.045

Piller, F. T., Vossen, A. & Ihl, C. (2012). From social media to social product development: the impact of social media on co-creation of innovation. *Die Unternehmung, 65.*

Rucker, P., & Gardner, T. (2015). *Porsche, more Audi models pulled into VW emissions scandal.* Available: http://www.reuters.com/article/us-volkswagen-usa-epa-idUSKCN0SR22L20151102

Saarinen, M. (2015). *VW emissions scandal: everything you need to know.* Available: http://www.autoexpress.co.uk/volkswagen/92893/vw-emissions-scandal-recalls-compensation-is-your-car-affected-latest-news

Shirky, C. (2011). The Political Power of Social Media Technology, the Public Sphere, and Political Change. *Foreign Affairs, 90,* 28.

Stern, P. C., Dietz, T., & Kalof, L. (1993). Value orientations, gender, and environmental concern. *Environment and Behavior, 25*(5), 322–348. doi:10.1177/0013916593255002

Suh, B., Hong, L., Pirolli, P., & Chi, E. H. (2010). Want to be retweeted? Large scale analytics on factors impacting retweet in Twitter network. In *Proceeding of the 2010 IEEE Second International Conference on Social Computing*. IEEE Computer Society. doi:10.1109/SocialCom.2010.33

Szekely, F. (2015). *Sustainable leadership means engaging honestly with your stakeholders: VW failed the test*. International Institute for Management Development. Available: http://www.imd.org/news/VW-scandal.cfm?mrk_cmpg_source=SM_TW_FI&utm_source=Twitter&utm_medium=Social&utm_campaign=SM_TW_FI

Tess, P. A. (2013). The role of social media in higher education classes (real and virtual) – A literature review. *Computers in Human Behavior*, 29(5), A60–A68. doi:10.1016/j.chb.2012.12.032

Tsai, W. H. S., & Men, L. R. (2013). Motivations and antecedents of consumer engagement with brand pages on social networking sites. *Journal of Interactive Advertising*, 13(2), 76–87. doi:10.1080/15252019.2013.826549

Tse, Y. K., Tan, K. H. & Zhang, M. H. (2014). *Exploring Quality Risk in the Food Supply Chain: Strategic Insights from Horsmeat Scandals*. Charter Institute of Logistics and Transport.

Tse, Y. K., Zhang, M., Doherty, B., Chappell, P. J., & Garnett, P. (2016). Insight from the horsemeat scandal: Exploring the consumers' opinion of tweets toward Tesco. *Industrial Management & Data Systems*, 116(6), 1178–1200. doi:10.1108/IMDS-10-2015-0417

Twitter. (2013). *Twitter Developer Documentation*. Author.

Twitter. (n.d.). *About*. Retrieved from; https://about.twitter.com/company

Veil, S. R., Buehner, T., & Palenchar, M. J. (2011). A Work-In-Process Literature Review: Incorporating Social Media in Risk and Crisis Communication. *Journal of Contingencies and Crisis Management*, 19(2), 110–122. doi:10.1111/j.1468-5973.2011.00639.x

Waller, K., Droge, E., & Puschmann, C. (2011). Citation Analysis in Twitter: Approaches for Defining and Measuring Information Flows within Tweets during Scientific Conference. *1st Workshop on Making Sense of Microposts*.

Winston, A. (2015). *What VW Didn't Understand About Trust*. Harvard Business Review. Available: https://hbr.org/2015/09/what-vw-didnt-understand-about-trust?utm_source=Socialflow&utm_medium=Tweet&utm_campaign=Socialflow

Wong, K. F., Xia, Y., Xu, R., Wu, M., & Li, W. (2008). Pattern-based opinion mining for stock market trend prediction. *International Journal of Computer Processing of Languages, 21*, 347-361.

Zelezny, L. C., Chua, P.-P., & Aldrich, C. (2000). Elaborating on gender differences in environmentalism. *The Journal of Social Issues*, 56(3), 443–457. doi:10.1111/0022-4537.00177

Zhang, W. H., Xu, H., & Wan, W. (2012). Weakness Finder: Find product weakness from Chinese reviews by using aspects based sentiment analysis. *Expert Systems with Applications*, 39(11), 10283–10291. doi:10.1016/j.eswa.2012.02.166

Zhang, X., Fuehres, H., & Gloor, P. A. (2011). Predicting Stock Market Indicators Through Twitter "I hope it is not as bad as I fear". *2nd Collaborative Innovation Networks Conference (Coins2010).*

ENDNOTES

[1] The engines emitted nitrogen oxide pollutants up to 40 time above what is allowed in the US (Hotten, 2015).

[2] Including geographic information, username, user's profile etc.

[3] Note that the number of retweets received are the tweets already in the dataset.

[4] Library – "gender-from-name" - https://github.com/Bemmu/gender-from-name.

[5] Frequency of words.

[6] A / (A+B+C), where A represents cases where both item occur, and B and C represent cases where one item is found but not the other. In this coefficient equal weight is given to matches and non matches.

[7] Number in bracket represents the word count frequency of the words.

[8] Initialism of "in case you missed it".

This research was previously published in Supply Chain Management in the Big Data Era edited by Hing Kai Chan, Nachiappan Subramanian, and Muhammad Dan-Asabe Abdulrahman, pages 172-198, copyright year 2017 by Business Science Reference (an imprint of IGI Global).

Chapter 47

A Netnographic Analysis of Facebook Content Strategy of World's Top 10 Management Institutes

Anandan Pillai
Management Development Institute, India

Kalpana Chauhan
Delhi University, India

ABSTRACT

This research paper analyzes the content strategy of World's top 10 management institutes that they followed on Facebook to understand the importance of content strategy in building brand communities. It uses the Netnographic approach to analyse the content strategy and establishes that the content context i.e. its relevance to the community matters the most in building strong community. This research would fill the gap that existed in the brand community literature where researchers hardly discussed about relevance of content strategy in brand's social media strategy.

INTRODUCTION

Since Muniz and O'Guinn (2001) introduced the concept of Brand Community (BC) it has drawn substantial attention in the marketing literature by academicians. They conceptualized BC as, *"specialized, non-geographically bound community, based on structured set of social relations among admirers of a brand"* (Muniz and O'Guinn, 2001) and proposed that BCs would exhibit three traditional community characteristics– *shared consciousness, rituals and traditions, moral responsibility* (Muniz and O'Guinn, 2001, p. 413). In the pre-Internet era, brands connected with their community members in offline World, the most commonly referred example being Harley Davidson community (McAlexander *et al.*, 2002). However, with the penetration of Internet, virtual communities (Armstrong and Hagel III, 1996) came into existence. In the post 2000 period, with the proliferation of social media (Kaplan and

DOI: 10.4018/978-1-5225-5637-4.ch047

Haenlein, 2010; Mangold and Faulds, 2009), brands realized the incremental benefit of establishing their communities on these social media websites (Laroche *et al.*, 2012). The value additional features on social media websites (SMWs) have further strengthened brands to have real-time customer engagement (Van Doorn *et al.*, 2010) at a much accelerated pace than it was possible in any of the traditional media channels. It has been observed that BCs created on SMWs have positive impact on customer/product, customer/brand, customer/company and customer/other customers relationships (Laroche *et al.*, 2013, Papagiannidis et al 2013). On the other hand, customers and stakeholders of a brand also find it convenient and effective to converse with brands through these SMWs (Kietzmann *et al.*, 2011; Baird and Parasnis, 2011; Fisher, 2009).

In order to ensure effective customer engagement which has a strong probability to build brand loyalty among community members (Brodie *et al.*, 2013; Goldsmith, 2011; Hollebeek, 2011; *Malhotra et al.*, 2013) brands need to follow a well-planned content strategy. However, it isn't an easy task for brands to create effective content on a regular basis. Hence, some brands become successful on social media while others don't. It is a huge challenge for brands to formulate their content strategy for building and sustaining high customer engagement on these BCs created on SMWs (Malhotra *et al.*, 2013; Drury, 2008). As part of their content strategy, BCs share necessary information about and around the brand to community members, and help organization build a strong brand (Fournier and Lee, 2009).

In this research paper we have analyzed the content strategy that World's top 10 management institutes are following on Facebook. Facebook happens to be the world's leading SMWs with over 1 billion users (Fowler, 2012). The focus was on to understand the influence of content strategy on customer engagement. We analyzed the content strategy of World's top 10 management institutes on Facebook, for the period of six months. A General Linear Model (GLM) was run between metric dependent variable *customer engagement*, measured in terms of - *no. of likes, no. of comments* and *no. of shares*; and non-metric dependent variables – *content type, posting day, posting agility* and *content context*. It was found that *content context* was the significant variable for *customer engagement*. Thus, relevance of content mattered the most, i.e. more relevant the content with respect to community's expectations, more are the chances of customer engagement. This might seem to be an obvious phenomenon. However if it was so obvious, almost every other brand on social media would have gained popularity, unlike few as of now. Hence, we have tried to establish the importance of content strategy in BC phenomenon through this research paper which would be of importance to both academicians and practicing brand managers.

The paper is organized as follows: in the next section of literature review, the literature on the major topics of study namely Brand Communities, Content Strategy and Customer engagement has been discussed and their association is identifies to reach to the conceptual model (Figure 1) and the research question. The following sections describe the research context and operational definition of the variables. Next section pertains to the research methodology adopted followed by the results, discussion and implications. Lastly, the paper ends with the limitations and the future research avenues.

LITERATURE REVIEW

Brand Communities and Its Theoretical Foundation

Brand equity has been an important phenomenon in marketing for quite some time now (Aaker and Biel, 1992; Leuthesser, 1988; Maltz, 1991). It is defined in terms of the marketing effects uniquely attributable to the brand-for example, when certain outcomes result from the marketing of a product or service because of its brand name.

Customer-based brand equity is defined as the differential effect of brand knowledge on consumer response to the marketing of the brand (Keller, 2013). Given higher costs, greater competition, and flattening demand in many markets, firms seek to increase the efficiency of their marketing expenses and Perhaps a firm's most valuable asset for improving marketing productivity is the knowledge that has been created about the brand in consumers' minds from the firm's investment in previous marketing programs. Marketers realize that the long-term success of all future marketing programs for a brand is greatly affected by the knowledge about the brand in memory that has been established by the firm's short-term marketing efforts. Since the content and structure of memory for the brand will influence the effectiveness of future brand strategies, marketers understand how their marketing programs affect consumer learning and thus subsequent recall for brand-related information (Keller, 1993). The brand-communities on social media are also a marketing program to connect with the customers and enhance the brand equity. Brand communities, which are fundamentally social relationships, directly affect brand equity and are consistent with the trend toward broadening definitions of consumer brand loyalty in general (Fournier, 1998; Fournier and Yao, 1997; Lutz, 1987; McAlexander and Schouten, 1998; Olsen, 1993; Sherry, 1998). The customer engagement on brand communities, that draws its theoretical roots in relationship marketing (Vivek et al 2012), is shaped by various factors including the functional drivers like benefits, information quality, monetary and other explicit incentives; brand community factors like its size, how it is managed and social & brand related drivers (Wirtz et al 2013) and this engagement leads to higher commitment, loyalty and sales.

Consumers psychologically engage with brands based on their needs, motives and goals. Schmitt (2012) proposed an informative taxonomy where he suggested that the customers' engagement with the brand occurs at three levels - *object-centered*, *self-centered* and *social* (p. 8). Brand communities are part of the *social* level where community members share a common goal and in the process of attaining that goal they help, support and recommend each other. Hence, brand communities are increasingly emerging prominent means to generate "buzz" around a brand and help customers in their pre and post-purchase situations (Adjei, Noble and Noble, 2012). A positive brand community trust and affect have been observed to influence the brand community commitment, which further could have a positive impact on brand loyalty (Hur*et al.*, 2011, O'Reilly & Lancendorfer 2013). The recent conceptualizations of BC have emphasized that it is not sufficient to just get a community of people around a brand, but for the phenomenon to be comprehensive and rewarding, social interactions amongst the community members (Dholakia and Algesheimer, 2009; Godes *et al.*, 2005) is essential. In order to facilitate and sustain social interactions amongst the brand community members, brands need to engage them with the help of relevant and interesting content. The extant marketing literature indicates that the communities that do not facilitate interaction and engagement tend to lose their audience (Barnes and Lescault, 2011). However, the focus on content strategy has been rarely addressed in the brand community literature, which seems to be very essential in an asynchronous social networking phenomenon.

Customer Engagement

Customer engagement has been defined in literature from various perspectives:

The level of a customer's physical, cognitive and emotional presence in their relationship with a service organization. (Patterson et al., 2006)

Customer's behavioral manifestations that have a brand or firm focus, beyond purchase, resulting from motivational drivers. (Van Doornet al., 2010)

The level of a customer's motivational, brand-related and context dependent state of mind characterized by specific levels of cognitive, emotional and behavioral activity in brand interactions. (Hollebeek, 2011)

The intensity of an individual's participation and connection with the organization's offerings and activities initiated by either the customer or the organization. (Vivek et al., 2012)

Though customer engagement has been often referred and defined by various academicians in the past in the context of brand communities, the term has been rarely theorized to the core (Brodie *et al.*, 2013). The latest conceptualization available in marketing literature about customer engagement is:

It involves specific interactive experiences between consumers and the brand, and/or other members of the community. Consumer engagement' is a context-dependent, psychological state; characterized by fluctuating intensity levels that occur within dynamic, iterative engagement process. (Brodie et al., 2013)

Vargo (2009) proposed this conceptualization in the realms of 'service dominant logic' (S-D) proposed by Vargo (2009) which contrasts with the traditional 'goods dominant logic' (G-D) perspective.

However, in the online context, the behavioral manifestations of customer engagement occur through word-of-mouth activities, blogging, customer ratings, comments that customers make on the content (Verhoef *et al.*, 2010). In order to break the competition clutter and differentiate themselves, brands are getting involved in non-transactional behavior and hence engaging with the customers (Verhoef *et al.*, 2010).

The customer engagement in the social media would differ from one social media channel to other as the features on each channel differ to a great extent. In this study we have considered Facebook as context and the behavioral manifestations on this social networking website were measured from "Likes. "Comments" and "Shares" features.

As this phenomenon is very dynamic and requires continuous engagement, the responsibility always remains on the firm that the right kind of messages is shared. The content shared could be organizational / promotional / relational (Ahuja and Medury, 2010) by which they can keep the community members interested and engaged with the BC. If the activity is not regularly conducted or if the content shared is not relevant with the community members, then community members might lose interest in the BC (Barnes and Lescault, 2011). The loss of community member's interest would defeat the purpose of the brand to be on social media. The content shared by the brands follows a sequential process of a perception creation, which further builds positive attitudes and finally results into favorable behavior (Peng *et al.*, 2004).

Content Strategy

Halvorson (2010) defined the content strategy for BC as, *"diligent practice of planning for the creation, delivery and governance of useful, usable content"* on brand communities. A well-defined content strategy:

- Consists of producing the kind of content their target audiences really need;
- Allows organizations to develop realistic, sustainable, and measurable publishing plans that keep their content on track in the long term.

Kissane (2011) has further identified the characteristics of content strategy and identified following as what constitutes good content:

1. It should be right for user and also for business;
2. It should be clear and well-presented such that target users are able to understand it well; and
3. It should be consistent.

Content Strategy and Customer Engagement

The concept of Content strategy finds its roots in message strategy that a brand wants to convey to its target audience. Advertising message strategy is a well-researched topic in both the academic as well as practitioners community. It is the first step in creating an effective advertising message and provides the foundation for the rest of the advertising campaign. An effective message strategy helps capture the attention of target audience. Marketing communication consists of various message points to be communicated to the audience. An important aspect of message strategy is, knowing the best way to communicate these points. Extensive research has been carried out to know how the structure of persuasive message can influence its effectiveness in terms of attention it is able to gather, including the order of presentation, verbal vs. visual message characteristics (Belch and Belch, 2003). The Yale approach (Hovland *et al.*, 1953) to persuasion suggests that the message has a great impact on attention of and persuasion to the target audience. Attention, defined as the general distribution of mental activity to the tasks being performed by the individuals (Moates and Schumacher, 1980). In the case of brand communities on social media, this attention may be reflected in the form the engagement the users show by liking, commenting on or sharing the post.

The empirical study by Roth (2003) established that there was a direct impact of message content on the awareness spread by that message. The importance of content strategy is well emphasized in the extant marketing literature (Van den Putte, 2009; Beckmann and Gjerloff, 2007; Gregory, 2006; Arora and Arora, 2004). However, no empirical work is available in the literature to establish a relationship in the context of online brand communities. Therefore, the major research question we address in this study is:

How does the content strategy influence the customer engagement on brand communities created on Facebook?

The messages can be divided into two basic parts: the content and its organization. In brand communities on Facebook, the message (content) organization can be seen in the form of content type and context content. Also, since people cannot be persuaded by message they ignore, so after the message is presented to the audience, the next step in the persuasion process is to receive the users' "attention." The brands can control the day and time of posting the content (message) to affect the attention of the target users. Therefore, the major elements of content strategy on brand community are:

1. Content context;
2. Content type;
3. Day of posting; and
4. Posting agility the content.

OPERATIONAL DEFINITION OF VARIABLES

Dependent Variable

Customer engagement, unlike in traditional times, is measured now by customer's behavioural manifestations on online platforms. These behavioural manifestations would differ from one platform to another with respect to the features of the respective SMW. As the scope of this research paper was restricted to Facebook, the behavioural manifestations of customers on brand's BC were measured in terms of three variables – no. of like, no. of comments and no. of shares. For every update made by brand on its BC, customers had an option to show their reaction by any of the three manifestations – 1) click the *like* button which showed that the customers liked the content displayed; 2) *Comment* in the space provided just below the content about the content; customers usually shared their views in the space provided, commonly referred to as 'comment box'; 3) the third manifestation that customer could do was *share* the content with their own network members. This last type of manifestation earned the brand most viral effect as the content was shared across lot of people.

Figure 1. Conceptual model

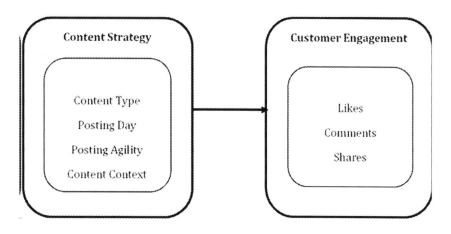

Independent Variables

The major characteristics of a content shared on a SMW are:

1. **Content Type:** Whether it is just a text; or a combination of text and image; or a combination of text and weblink; or a combination of text and video and so on;
2. **Posting Day:** On what day of a week the content is shared on the SMW. Customers do not remain active on all days of a week, hence it is necessary for a brand to understand and judge days of a week when their target audience would be active on SMW;
3. **Posting Agility:** On what time of the day, the content should be shared. Due to the inherent characteristic of a SMW, not all content shared by a brand would reach every user who has subscribed to the brand's updates. Hence, brands need to identify the best time of the day when their target audience would be using the SMW and there are high chances for the content to be consumed by the user;
4. **Content Context:** The theme of the content – whether it would be about the brand or the parent company or about a recent offer to be promoted or tips for customers etc.

Hypotheses

As we have followed the content strategy definition proposed by Kissane (2011), we have tested the three characteristics of content strategy in the context of Facebook – *content context, content type* and *agility*. Also, we have added another characteristic that is *posting day* which reflect on which day of the week the content is made available to users for consumption:

H1: There is significant impact of content type on customer engagement.
H2: There is significant impact of posting day on customer engagement.
H3: There is significant impact of posting agility on customer engagement.
H4: There is significant impact of content context on customer engagement.

RESEARCH DESIGN

This section details about research context, scope and sampling strategy & research methodology.

Research Context

The higher education institutes have been noticed to be using social media extensively for communicating with their target audience (Zailskaite-Jakste and Kuvykaite, 2010; Wankel, 2009). The higher education (H-E) institutions have been exercising diligent brand management efforts (Bunzel, 2007; Curtis *et al.*, 2009). The branding of H-E institutions helps them in building their identity and positive image amongst their key stakeholders – prospects, students, parents, recruiters, institution partners and society at large (Harvey, 1996). The importance of branding H-E institutions was felt in emerging Asian markets too (Gray *et al.*, 2003). The uprising competition for students and program recognition as well as demand for financial support tools prompt the higher education institutes to use strategic and planned PR and to allocate more efforts for communication in the Internet (Zailskaitė-Jakštė and Kuvykaitė, 2010).

The higher education institutes attract and connect to their various stakeholders: students-current and prospective, alumni, recruiters, Industry collaborators, International collaborators etc. through their brand communities on various social networking sites like Facebook, YouTube, Twitter, Blogging and Podcasting.

Scope and Sampling Strategy

The scope of our study was limited from two perspectives – 1) Type of brands sampled and 2) Type of social media website. As academicians in the past have focused on understanding the branding of higher education institutions, we followed the same path. However, the higher education institutes segment would be very diverse which would include various disciplines like science, engineering, management education, art, literature, etc. Hence, we scoped our study to *management education institutes*. This study attempts to understand the role of content strategy followed by top 10 management institutions in the World (as ranked by Financial Times[1]) which have created their BC on SMWs to initiate and enhance customer engagement. Every year Financial Times, the renowned publication publishes a list of top 100 MBA colleges across the world based on parameters like placement, employment, weighted salary, recommendations etc. We referred to that list and chose top ten colleges.

Secondly, there are hundreds of SMWs on the Internet. However, brands choose the relevant ones to create their presence with reference to their target audience and try to engage with their customers. Hence, we restricted our scope to one popular SMW – Facebook, which is not only popular among individual users but also among brands, as this website as of 2012 had more than 1 billion active users (Fowler, 2012).

Research Methodology

The study follows Netnography methodology. Netnography as a methodology is considered suitable for understanding phenomena pertaining to online communities and has been defined as:

A written account resulting from fieldwork studying the cultures and communities that emerge from online, computer mediated, or Internet-based communications, where both the field work and the textual account are methodologically informed by the traditions and techniques of cultural anthropology. (Kozinets, 1997, 1998)

Netnography follows a pragmatic interactionist approach, which treats online environment as a social world and online data as a social act exhibited by users (Kozinets, 2010). Netnography has been found to be non-obtrusive, less costly and less time-consuming a methodology to understand social act of online users (Langer and Beckman, 2005).

The Netnography data was collected from BCs on social networking site (Facebook) and was coded into various categories and then subjected to MANOVA. MANOVA is suitable when two or more groups are compared on a set of two or more dependent (outcome) variable (Dimitrov & Rumrill, 2005). This study establishes the significant difference that various types of *content type, posting agility, posting day* and *content context* have on *customer engagement*. The variables *content type, posting agility, post-*

ing day and *content strategy,* are categorical in nature. The *customer engagement* has been measured in terms of three continuous variables – *no. of likes, no. of comments,* and *no. of shares.*

The unit of analysis was 'a Facebook post' made by brand on its Page for its community members. This post could be a simple text message, an image, video, website URL or a combination of these. The Facebook pages of the top ten management institutes were tracked for a period of six months. As and when the Facebook pages were updated with posts by the brands, researchers recorded them in a document. The total number of Facebook posts analyzed in the study was 1,939.

Later, both the researchers individually read each Facebook post, comprehended them and coded them into various categories of the *content type, posting day, posting agility,* and *content context.* In the second step researchers followed 'investigator triangulation', the iterative process of triangulated suggested by Bryman and Bell (2007), (Brodie *et al.,* 2013). A consensus was attained after successive readings, discussions and interpretations between both researchers.

RESULTS

Descriptive

The descriptive results about the four variables – *Content Type, Posting Day, Posting Agility* and *Content Context* are as follows.

Content Type

The data was classified into nine different types of content as shown in Table 1. The most popularly (73.5%) used type of content was *Text + Weblink,* i.e. wherein a website link shared along with a brief introductory text describing about the content that was present in that link. The second distant (10.2%) type of content was *Text + Video,* i.e. wherein a video was shared along with an introductory text. It is evident that *image only* and *video only* content were not preferred mode of content for brands.

Table 1. Content type distribution

Content Type	Percentage
Text	2.9%
Text + Link	73.5%
Text + Video	10.2%
Text+ Image	6.5%
Image only	1.2%
Link only	3.0%
Video only	1.3%
Text + Weblink +Image	1.0%
Text + Weblink + Video	3.0%
Total	**100%**

Posting Day

The content posted during a week was classified into three categories – *beginning of the week*, *mid-week* & *weekends*. Initially we analysed data for each day, however we couldn't find any significant statistical differences. Hence, we decided to combine few days and reduce the number of categories to gain significant statistical differences. The labelling of categories as beginning, mid-week and weekends is assumed for the purpose of the study. It may or may not be the reality with respect to the local countries. As shown in Table 2 about 56.2% of content was shared during the *mid-week*, followed by 38.3% during *beginning of the week*. It could be interpreted that brands expected their fans to be active on Facebook during the *mid-week*.

Posting Agility

The content during a particular day was further classified into six slots each of four hours (Table 3) to understand the most popular timing for sharing the content on Facebook page. The posting time was captured without logging into the Facebook platform. If we login to the Facebook, it would consider the local time zone. In order to maintain uniformity across countries, we captured the timing by not logging into the platform. The most popular timing (38.5%) was 0800-1200 hours local time. The second most prominent timing (26.4%) was 0400-0800 hours local time. This pattern was interesting to note and deserves a detailed attention in the discussion section.

Table 2. Posting day distribution

Posting Day	Percentage
Monday-Tuesday	38.3%
Wednesday-Thursday-Friday	56.2%
Saturday-Sunday	5.5%
Total	**100.0%**

Table 3. Posting agility distribution

Posting Agility	Percentage
0000-0400 hours	14.0%
0400-0800 hours	26.4%
0800-1200 hours	38.5%
1200-1600 hours	16.0%
1600-2000 hours	3.4%
2000-2400 hours	1.8%
Total	**100.0%**

Content Context

The content shared on Facebook pages were reviewed and coded into categories based on the content theme as shown in Table 4. It was interesting to observe that most popular (32.2%) content theme was about the *faculty news* and the second most popular (17.0%) was content *about college*, followed (14.1%) by content about *events*. It was surprising to see that very less content on *industry related news* was shared on these pages, counterintuitive to authors' thought that these could be informative content for the community members.

Inferential

MANOVA

The data was further subjected to MANOVA analysis. The data analysis was conducted in two iterations. In the first iteration the statistic for Box's Test of Equality of Covariance was 5158.83 with F-value of 7.916 (534, 20653.0). This statistic was significant and hence it violated the basic required assumption that covariances of dependent variables should be equal across groups. Subsequently, Levene's Test of Equality of Error Variances was conducted and they were also found to be significant for all three dependent variables. Hence, the conclusion was that the model wasn't satisfying the basic assumption.

In the second iteration, the dependent variables were transformed into log format and then subjected to MANOVA analysis. The statistic for Box's Test was 166 with F-value of 1.114 (108, 3008.5) and was insignificant. Thus, the assumption of equal covariance of dependent variables across groups was met. The Pillai's trace statistic of multivariate tests indicated that *content context* contributed the most to the model and *content type* was significant at 10% confidence interval. Hence, H4 was supported, while H1 was supported at 10% confidence interval (Table 5). However, H2 and H3 were not supported.

Table 4. Content context distribution

Content Context	Percentage
About College	17.0%
Alumni News	6.4%
Existing Students' News	9.5%
Business and Management News	6.3%
Industry News	1.9%
General Engagement	7.4%
Faculty News	32.2%
College Events	14.1%
Industry Interaction	5.1%
Total	**100.0%**

Table 5. MANOVA results

Effect	Value	F	Hypothesis df	Error df	Sig.
Intercept	**0.845**	**331.13**	**3.00**	**182.00**	**0.000**
Content Type	0.164	1.52	21.00	552.00	0.064
Posting Day	0.024	0.74	6.00	366.00	0.615
Posting Agility	0.100	1.26	15.00	552.00	0.221
Content Context	**0.214**	**1.77**	**24.00**	**552.00**	**0.014**
Content Type * Posting Day	0.028	0.44	12.00	552.00	0.948
Content Type * Posting Agility	**0.239**	**1.77**	**27.00**	**552.00**	**0.010**
Content Type * Content Context	**0.314**	**1.43**	**45.00**	**552.00**	**0.037**
Posting Day * Posting Agility	0.131	1.19	21.00	552.00	0.245
Posting Day * Content Context	0.195	1.07	36.00	552.00	0.364
Posting Agility * Content Context	0.402	1.24	69.00	552.00	0.105
Content Type * Posting Day * Posting Agility	0.028	0.58	9.00	552.00	0.811
Content Type * Posting Day * Content Context	0.032	0.67	9.00	552.00	0.735
Content Type * Posting Agility * Content Context	**0.339**	**2.13**	**33.00**	**552.00**	**0.000**
Posting Day * Posting Agility * Content Context	0.166	0.770	42.00	552.00	0.852
Content Type * Posting Day * Posting Agility * Content Context	0.000	-	0.00	0.00	-

Discriminant Analysis (Content Context)

Discriminant analysis is advised to be followed up with MANOVA to have better understanding about differences between groups of variables (Green *et al.*, 2008, Huberty, 1975). It helps in:

1. The establishment of significant group-differences;
2. The study and explanation of these differences; and
3. The utilization of multivariate information from the samples studied in classifying a future individual known to belong to one of the groups represented" (Tatsuoka and Tiede-man, 1954 - p. 414).

Discriminant analysis was applied to investigate the differences between the groups of *content context* on the basis of attributes of cases, indicating which attributes contribute most to the separation of groups. Hence, in this analysis *content context* was inserted as dependent variable and *no. of likes, no. of comments* and *no. of shares* were entered as independent variables. Significant differences between groups were observed for all three independent variables as shown in Table 6.

The Box's M test result was significant. Box's M was 1940.17 with F = 40.003, significant at p<0.000. The details of canonical discriminant function coefficients are in Table 7.

The classification results indicated that about 32.5% of original grouped cases were correctly classified and 32.4% of cross-validated grouped cases were correctly classified.

Table 6. Wilk's lambda

	Wilk's Lambda	**F**	**Df1**	**Df2**	**Sig.**
Likes	0.971	7.277	8	1930	0.000
Comments	0.976	5.946	8	1930	0.000
Shares	0.991	2.177	8	1930	0.027

Table 7. Function

	Function		
	1	**2**	**3**
Likes	0.044	-0.015	-0.048
Comments	0.124	0.099	0.492
Shares	-0.150	0.278	-0.002
(Constant)	-0.545	-0.239	0.201

DISCUSSION

There has been a considerable amount of research in the area of brand communities, but most of the studies have focused from the user perspective. This study aimed to focus on brand community from the brand's perspective. The major objective was to understand the impact of various content strategy factors on the dependent variable, i.e. customer engagement. This understanding could be of help for practitioners in knowing, how they can manage their brand communities in an effective manner and achieve better customer engagement. Unlike traditional media, social media gives immense opportunity to the brands to interact and engage with users, but it also makes brands susceptible to downfall if the smallest of the factors are overlooked. Therefore, it becomes essential for the brands to pay attention even to seemingly insignificant factors. In a hyper competitive environment, where various competing brands are trying hard to grab the attention of the same customer group it becomes inevitable for brands to focus on the smallest of the factors related to content posted by them to achieve desired customer engagement levels. This would help brands in managing and sustaining the interest of community members in community.

There are various popular SMWs; however they all have specific orientation. For e.g. LinkedIn is a professional SMW, where the users interact on professional aspects, Twitter is a microblogging site, where people tend to share their interests, in a formal or an informal manner and interact with like-minded people. Facebook is mostly used for social interaction and to connect with friends and family. It is one of the most used SMWs with large number of active users spending time on it. In Unites States, 66% of adult online users have active Facebook profile and 58% of Fortune 500 companies have also established their presence on this platform (Becker, 2013). The figures are similar for other parts of world also, as Facebook is the most popular and most visited social network site across nations (Facebook Statistics). Therefore the study focused on the brand communities at Facebook. We took the top 10 management institutes of the world (Global MBA Rankings, FT 2012) which exist across the globe. These institutes not only attract students but also recruiters from across the globe. Therefore, theoretically they have similar target customer group whom they want to participate and engage with on their communities.

However, it restricts the generalization of results across industries. Also, it has been seen that brands do not behave similar throughout the year on their communities but come up with different strategies during different periods like festivals and some major events like Olympics etc.; and therefore, it may result into misrepresentation of the community members' engagement pattern.

The study analyzed the impact of the strategy followed by brand on the customer engagement generated on its brand community. A brand may decide upon the 'context of content' it posts, the type of content (e.g. text, image etc.), the day and time of posting; and a community member may engage with the brand by liking, commenting and/or by sharing the posts depending upon their level of interest in the post. Therefore all these factors were taken into consideration.

The results established that the *'content context'* and *'content type'* contributed to the model and were found to have significant impact on the customer engagement. This signifies that the message of the brand is of prime importance to the community members and different contexts generate different level of engagement. The discriminant analysis on *'content context'* recognized that there is a significant difference in groups within *'content context'* affecting engagement. Furthermore, the form in which the message is presented to the community members also has significant impact on customer engagement. The appeal of a message rests in the creativity with which it is presented to garner more attention and influence the community members. Therefore, brands may experiment with the *content context* and *content type* to influence the customer engagement. Well, this was in contrast to a similar study conducted by researchers in the Indian context Chauhan and Pillai (2013). In their study, Chauhan and Pillai (2013) observed that *content type* and *posting agility* were the prime factors that influenced the customer engagement. This calls for a need to conduct similar studies on a larger scale and analyze the differences between the community members' expectations and how brands should adapt their content strategy accordingly.

The results also revealed that the *posting day* and *content agility* were not significant enough to contribute to the model and were not found to have impact on the customer engagement. This may be due to the reason that youth are more internet savvy and due to higher connectivity through laptops, tablets and mobile devices, the community members have access to brand community updates on an ongoing basis, thereby eliminating the significance of posting day or time. An interesting point that emerged through the data analysis was, that a bigger percentage of posts (26.4%) was made during early morning i.e. 4:00 to 8:00 AM local time slot. This indicates that these brand communities would have been managed by group of students, who work late at night and find it convenient to post messages at this hour slot. However, since the posting agility (timing of the posting) wasn't found to have significant impact on the engagement level, it may be concluded that community members are not engaged more on brand community during this time slot. The validity of these results restricts only on the focused industry (management institutes) and might not be valid for other kind of brand communities in which the major proportion of community members are not student groups.

IMPLICATIONS

The research establishes the relationship between the content strategy of the brand and the customer engagement on BC on social media. It also makes it evident that in order to enhance the customer engagement on BC on social media; the brands need to focus on their own *content context* that their target audience deem relevant. Also, *content type* matters when it comes to drive customer engagement. This research would fill the gap that existed in the BC literature where academicians hardly discussed about relevance of content strategy in brand's social media strategy. This research would also help practicing brand managers, brand community managers and content strategists/managers to understand and develop effective content strategy which would lead to desired level of customer engagement on their BC.

LIMITATIONS AND FUTURE RECOMMENDATIONS FOR RESEARCH

1. The data collection period was for six months. Hence, the interpretations are subjected to the sensitivities involved for that period. Data collection for longer periods of time may help academicians to validate the findings of this research with much more confidence;
2. We considered only management institutions in this research. A research on wider scale with sample of other higher education institutions from other disciplines like medicine, science, arts, sociology etc. would help academicians generalize the findings for the larger context of higher education institutions;
3. This research can be extended to understand if the powerfulness of a content strategy helps brands in generating offline brand loyalty and improvement in sales;
4. In this research all community members of a BC have been treated as equal. However, in a brand's community, members would be with diverse intentions like existing students, alumni, recruiters, faculty members, staff etc. So, understanding the influence of content strategy on each strata of community member could be attempted;
5. In this study the impact of frequency of posts and the tone of the posts on customer engagement was not studied and that also may be attempted to understand the impact of brands' content strategy on customer engagement in a better manner;
6. We have ignored the C2C communications that often occur on brand communities. Future research could study how brands allow and facilitate the C2C communications on their social media platforms;
7. A research could be attempted to understand how brands monitored the C2C communications and used the insights from those conversations for brand's benefit.

REFERENCES

Aaker, D., & Biel, A. (1992). *Building Strong Brands*. Hillsdale, NJ: Lawrence Erlbaum Associates.

Adjei, M. T., Noble, C. H., & Noble, S. M. (2012). Enhancing relationships with customers through online brand communities. *MIT Sloan Management Review*, *53*(4), 22–24.

Ahuja, V., & Medury, Y. (2010). Corporate blogs as e-CRM tools – Building customer engagement through content management. *Database Marketing & Customer Strategy Management*, *17*(22), 91–105. doi:10.1057/dbm.2010.8

Armstrong, A., & Hagel, J. III. (1996). The real value of online communities. *Harvard Business Review*, *74*(3), 134–141.

Arora, R., & Arora, A. (2004). The impact of message framing and credibility: Findings for nutritional guidelines. *Services Marketing Quarterly*, *26*(1), 35–53. doi:10.1300/J396v26n01_03

Baird, C. H., & Parasnis, G. (2011). From social media to social customer relationship management. *Strategy and Leadership*, *39*(5), 30–37. doi:10.1108/10878571111161507

Barnes, N. G., & Lescault, A. M. (n.d.). Social media adoption soars as higher-ed experiments and reevaluates its use of new communications tools. available at http://www.umassd.edu/cmr/studiesandresearch/socialmediaadoptionsoars/ (accessed 15 August 2011).

Becker, P. (2013). Brands are still failing to engage with Customers in social media. Available at http://wallblog.co.uk/2013/01/09/brands-are-still-failing-to-engage-with-customers-in-social-media-infographic/#ixzz2K94ofEZk (accessed 11 January 2013).

Beckmann, S. C., & Gjerloff, M. (2007). A framework for communicating with brand communities. in Proceedings of paper presented at Australian and New Zealand Marketing Academy (ANZMAC) Conference, pp. 1710-1716.

Belch, G. E., & Belch, M. A. (2003). *Advertising And Promotion*. Tata McGrawhill.

Brodie, R. J., Ilic, A., Juric, B., & Hollebeek, L. (2013). Consumer engagement in a virtual brand community: An exploratory analysis. *Journal of Business Research*, *66*(1), 105–114. doi:10.1016/j.jbusres.2011.07.029

Bunzel, D. L. (2007). Universities sell their brands. *Journal of Product and Brand Management*, *16*(2), 152–153. doi:10.1108/10610420710740034

Chauhan, K., & Pillai, A. (2013). Role of content strategy in social media brand communities: A case of higher education institutes in India. *Journal of Product and Brand Management*, *22*(1), 40–51. doi:10.1108/10610421311298687

Curtis, T., Abratt, R., & Minor, W. (2009). Corporate brand management in higher education: The case of ERAU. *Journal of Product and Brand Management*, *18*(6), 404–413. doi:10.1108/10610420910989721

Dholakia, U. M., & Algesheimer, R. (2009). Brand Community. Available at: http://papers.ssrn.com/sol3/papers.cfm?abstract_id=1444833 (accessed 15 December 2010).

Dimitrov, D.M. and Rumrill, Phillip D. (2005). Multivariate methods in rehabilitation. *Work (Reading, Mass.)*, *24*(2), 205–212. PMID:15860910

Drury, G. (2008). Social media: Should marketers engage and how can it be done effectively?" Journal of Direct. *Data and Digital Marketing Practice.*, *9*, 274–277. doi:10.1057/palgrave.dddmp.4350096

Facebook statistics. (n.d.). Available at: www.socialbakers.com/facebook-statistics/ (accessed 1 February 2013).

Fisher, T. (2009). ROI in social media: A look at the arguments. *Journal of Database Marketing & Customer Strategy Management*, *16*(3), 189–195. doi:10.1057/dbm.2009.16

Fournier, S. (1998). Customers and Their Brands: Developing Relationship Theory in Consumer Research. *The Journal of Consumer Research*, *24*(March), 343–373. doi:10.1086/209515

Fournier, S., & Lee, L. (2009). *Getting brand communities right* (pp. 105–111). Harvard Business Review, Vol. April.

Fournier and Yao J.L. (1997). Reviving Brand Loyalty: A Reconceptualization within the Framework of Consumer-Brand Relationships. *International Journal of Research in Marketing, 14*(December), 451–472.

Fowler, G. (2012). Facebook Tops Billion-User Mark. Available at: http://online.wsj.com/news/articles/SB30000872396390044363540457803616402738112 (accessed 4 October 2012).

Godes, D., Mayzlin, D., Chen, Y., Das, S., Dellarocas, C., & Pfeiffer, B. (2005). The firm's management of social interactions. *Marketing Letters, 16*(3/4), 415–428.

Goldsmith, R. E. (2011). Brand engagement and brand loyalty. In A. Kapoor & C. Kulshrestha (Eds.), *Branding and sustainable competitive advantage: Building virtual presence* (pp. 1–294). IGI Global.

Gray, B. J., Fam, K. S., & Llanes, V. A. (2003). Branding universities in Asian markets. *Journal of Product and Brand Management, 12*(2), 108–120. doi:10.1108/10610420310469797

Green, S. B., Salkind, N. J., & Akey, T. M. (2008). *Using SPSS for Windows and Macintosh: Analyzing and Understanding Data*. New Jersey, NJ: Prentice Hall.

Gregory, J. (2006). Using message strategy to capture audience attention: Readers' reactions to health education publications. *Journal of Nonprofit & Public Sector Marketing, 15*(1/2), 1–23. doi:10.1300/J054v15n01_01

Halvorson, K. (2010). *Content Strategy for the Web*. Berkeley, California: New Riders.

Harvey, J. A. (1996). Marketing schools and consumer choice. *International Journal of Educational Management, 10*(4), 26–38. doi:10.1108/09513549610122165

Hollebeek, L. D. (2011). Demystifying customer brand engagement: Exploring the loyalty nexus. *Journal of Marketing Management, 27*(7-8), 785–807. doi:10.1080/0267257X.2010.500132

Hovland, C. I., Janis, I. L., & Kelley, H. H. (1953). *Communication and persuasion: Psychological studies of opinion change*. New Haven, CT: Yale University Press.

Huberty, C. J. (1975). Discriminant analysis. *Review of Educational Research, 45*(4), 543–598. doi:10.3102/00346543045004543

Hur, W.-M., Ahn, K.-H., & Kim, M. (2011). Building brand loyalty through managing brand community commitment. *Management Decision, 49*(7), 1194–1213. doi:10.1108/00251741111151217

Kaplan, A. M., & Haenlein, M. (2010). Users of the world, unite! The challenges and opportunities of social media. *Business Horizons, 53*(1), 59–68. doi:10.1016/j.bushor.2009.09.003

Keller, K. L. (1993). Conceptualizing, Measuring, and Managing Customer-Based Brand Equity. *Journal of Marketing, 57*(1), 1–22. doi:10.2307/1252054

Kietzmann, J. H., Hermkens, K., McCarthy, I. P., & Silvestre, B. S. (2011). Social media? Get serious! Understanding the functional building blocks of social media. *Business Horizons, 54*(3), 241–251. doi:10.1016/j.bushor.2011.01.005

Kissane, E. (2011). Elements of content strategy. A Book Apart. New York, New York

Kozinets, R. V. (1997). "I want to believe":A netnography of the X-Philes' subculture of consumption. *Advances in Consumer Research. Association for Consumer Research (U. S.)*, *24*, 470–475.

Kozinets, R. V. (1998). On netnography: Initial reflections on consumer research investigations of cyberculture. *Advances in Consumer Research. Association for Consumer Research (U. S.)*, *25*, 366–371.

Kozinets, R. V. (2010). *Netnography: Doing Ethnographic Research Online*. London: Sage Publications Inc.

Langer, R., & Beckman, S. C. (2005). Sensitive research topics: Netnography revisited. *Qualitative Market Research: An International Journal*, *8*(2), 189–203. doi:10.1108/13522750510592454

Laroche, M., Habibi, M. R., & Richard, M. (2013). To be or not to be in social media: How brand loyalty is affected by social media? *International Journal of Information Management*, *33*(1), 76–82. doi:10.1016/j.ijinfomgt.2012.07.003

Laroche, M., Habibi, M. R., Richard, M., & Sankaranarayanan, R. (2012). The effects of social media based brand communities on brand community markers, value creation practices, brand trust and brand loyalty. *Computers in Human Behavior*, *28*(5), 1755–1767. doi:10.1016/j.chb.2012.04.016

Leuthesser, L. E. (1988). Defining, Measuring and Managing Brand Equity: A Conference Summary. Report #88-104. Cambridge, MA: Marketing Science Institute.

Lutz, R. (1987). Multidisciplinary Perspectives of Brand Loyalty. Paper presented at the Association for Consumer Research Conference, Boston

Malhotra, A., Malhotra, C. K., & See, A. (2013). How to Create Brand Engagement on Facebook. *Sloan Management Review*, *54*(2), 17–21.

Maltz, E. (1991). Managing Brand Equity: A Conference Summary," Report #91-110. Cambridge, MA: Marketing Science Institute.

Mangold, W. G., & Faulds, D. J. (2009). Social media: The new hybrid element of the promotion mix. *Business Horizons*, *52*(4), 357–365. doi:10.1016/j.bushor.2009.03.002

McAlexander, J. H., & Schouten, J. W. (1998). Brandfests: Servicescapes for the Cultivation of Brand Equity. In J. F. Sherry Jr., (Ed.), *Servicescapes: The Concept of Place in Contemporary Markets* (pp. 377–402). Chicago: NTC Business Books.

McAlexander, J. H., Schouten, J. W., & Koenig, H. F. (2002). Building Brand Community. *Journal of Marketing*, *66*(1), 38–54. doi:10.1509/jmkg.66.1.38.18451

Moates, D. R., & Schumacher, G. M. (1980). *An Introduction to Cognitive Psychology*. Belmont, CA: Wadsworth Publishing.

Muniz, A. M. Jr, & O'Guinn, T. C. (2001). Brand Community. *The Journal of Consumer Research*, *27*(4), 412–432. doi:10.1086/319618

O'Reilly, K., & Lancendorfer, K. M. (2013). Consumers as "Integrators" of Marketing Communications: When "Like" is as Good as "Buy". *International Journal of E-Business Research*, *9*(4), 1–15. doi:10.4018/ijebr.2013100101

Olsen, B. (1993). In L. McAlister & M. Rothschild (Eds.), *Brand Loyalty and Lineage: Exploring New Dimensions for Research," in Advances in Consumer Research* (Vol. 20, pp. 574–579). Provo, UT: Association for Consumer Research.

Papagiannidis, S., Stamati, T., & Behr, H. (2013). Online Engagement and Impact: The Case of Greek Politicians during the Financial Crisis. *International Journal of E-Business Research*, *9*(4), 47–66. doi:10.4018/ijebr.2013100104

Patterson, P., Yu, T., & de Ruyter, K. (2006). Understanding customer engagement in services, Advancing theory, maintaining relevance. in *Proceedings of ANZMAC 2006 conference*, Brisbane, 2006.

Peng, K. F., Fan, Y. W., & Hsu, T. A. (2004). Proposing the content perception theory for the online content industry – A structural equation modeling. *Industrial Management & Data Systems*, *104*(6), 469–489. doi:10.1108/02635570410543780

Roth, M. S. (2003). Media and message effects on DTC prescription drug print advertising awareness. *Journal of Advertising Research*, *43*(2), 180–193.

Schmitt, B. (2012). The consumer psychology of brands. *Journal of Consumer Psychology*, *22*(1), 7–17. doi:10.1016/j.jcps.2011.09.005

Sherry, J. F. (1998). *The Soul of the Company Store: Niketown Chicago and the Explored Brandscape," in Servicescapes: The Concept of Place in Contemporary Markets* (J. F. Sherry Jr., Ed.). Chicago: NTC Business Books.

Tatsuoka, M. M., & Tiedeman, D. V. (1954). Discriminant analysis. *Review of Educational Research*, *24*, 402–420.

Van de Putte, B. (2009). What matters most in advertising campaigns? *International Journal of Advertising*, *28*(4), 669–690. doi:10.2501/S0265048709200813

Van Doorn, J., Lemon, K. N., Mittal, V., Nass, S., Pick, D., Pirner, P., & Verhoef, P. C. (2010). Customer engagement behavior: Theoretical foundations and research directions. *Journal of Service Research*, *13*(3), 253–266. doi:10.1177/1094670510375599

Verhoef, P. C., Reinartz, W. J., & Krafft, M. (2010). Customer engagement as a new perspective in customer management. *Journal of Service Research*, *13*(3), 247–252. doi:10.1177/1094670510375461

Vivek, S. D., Beatty, S. E., & Morgan, R. M. (2012). Customer Engagement: Exploring Customer Relationships Beyond Purchase. *Journal of Marketing Theory and Practice*, *20*(2), 122–146. doi:10.2753/MTP1069-6679200201

Wankel, C. (2009). Management education using social media. *Organizational Management Journal*, *6*(4), 251–262. doi:10.1057/omj.2009.34

Wirtz J, Ambtman A., Bloemer J., Horváth C., Ramaseshan B, van de Klundert J, & Kandampully J, (2013). Managing brands and customer engagement in online brand communities." Journal of Service Management 24.3 223-244.

Zailskaite-Jakste, L., & Kuvykaite, R. (2010). Internet based communication with target audiences: Case study of higher education institutions. *Economics and Management, 15*, 849–856.

ENDNOTES

[1]   "Global MBA Rankings, 2012" http://rankings.ft.com/businessschoolrankings/global-mba-rankings-2012, last accessed on 10th September, 2012

This research was previously published in the International Journal of E-Business Research (IJEBR), 11(3); edited by Payam Hanafizadeh and Jeffrey Hsu, pages 1-17, copyright year 2015 by IGI Publishing (an imprint of IGI Global).

Chapter 48

Towards a Unified Semantic Model for Online Social Networks to Ensure Interoperability and Aggregation for Analysis

Asmae El Kassiri
Mohammed V University, Morocco

Fatima-Zahra Belouadha
Mohammed V University, Morocco

ABSTRACT

The Online Social Networks (OSN) have a positive evolution due to the diversity of social media and the increase in the number of users. The revenue of the social media organizations is generated from the analysis of users' profiles and behaviors, knowing that surfers maintain several accounts on different OSNs. To satisfy its users, the social media organizations have initiated projects for ensuring interoperability to allow for users creating other accounts on other OSN using an initial account, and sharing content from one media to others. Believing that the future generations of Internet will be based on the semantic web technologies, multiple academic and industrial projects have emerged with the objective of modeling semantically the OSNs to ensure interoperability or data aggregation and analysis. In this chapter, we present related works and argue the necessity of a unified semantic model (USM) for OSNs; we introduce a kernel of a USM using standard social ontologies to support the principal social media and it can be extended to support other future social media.

DOI: 10.4018/978-1-5225-5637-4.ch048

INTRODUCTION

In this chapter, we argue the advantages of the OSN semantic modeling, the advantages of Unified Semantic Model, and we investigate related works.

The idea is to use a Unified Semantic Model USM to present different social media for aggregating data from these media. The model reuses the existent social ontologies, more precisely FOAF, SCOT, MOAT, AMO, SKOS and SIOC. To respond to needs not covered by these ontologies, it uses three other ontologies ActOnto, InterestOnto and AclOnto extending the SIOC ontology.

The USM is not only an aggregation model from OSN, it is also an interoperability model supposed allowing to a user migrating from a media to another with his profile, his relations and his posts. It will facilitate comprehension between social media to cooperate for a better management of users' data. It can be used as a storage model for social networks data what allow simplifying the social mining process.

Many factors motivate us to think that the idea of adopting a unified semantic model seems relevant:

- The evolutionary success of OSN;
- The phenomenon of purchasing the small actors of OSN by the giants, such as the purchase of Tumbler by Yahoo in Mai 2013, and Facebook who bought Instagram, Whatsapp and Oculus in 2014. The USM could allow having the same model for these different social medias and simplifying their data aggregation and analysis;
- The academic attempts to federate and unify some existent ontologies like MUTO (Lohmann, 2011) (Kim, Scerri, Passant, Breslin, & Kim, 2011);
- The necessity of ensuring the interoperability between OSN proved by the OGP;
- The adoption of the W3C of the FOAF, SKOS and SIOC as standards;

BACKGROUND

Mika was the first to thought to a semantic model for OSN (Mika, 2005), and then Chen and al. studied a method based on social network ontology to annotate nodes and edges (Chen., Wei., & Qingpu, 2010). Others proposed their proper ontologies; we cite for example the SNO (Social Network Ontology) (Masoumzadeh & Joshi, 2011), the SNS (Social Network Sites) Ontology (Kumar & Kumar, 2013) and the TPO (Tours Plan Ontology) limited to tourism social medias (Luz, 2010). These models are suited to analyze some kinds of OSN and for some cases but not to ensure their interoperability. While the unified semantic model USM must model the pertinent existent OSN and be easily extended to support other OSN.

The social web has raised lot of attention from the semantic community, so several ontologies are used to represent OSN. We class them into four principle categories: User description, online activities, tagging and access management.

User Description

The *FOAF (Friend Of A Friend)* (Brickley & Miller, 2014) is the ontology proposed to describe users' profiles. The FOAF project was launched in 2000 with the objective of creating web documents network. The documents must be understandable by machines and describe persons and their relationships; then

FOAF was considered by the W3C as a good ontology (Golbeck et Rothstein 2008) (Brickley et Miller 2010). The ontology give concepts that can be classed according four axes:

- **The Identity:** Elementary properties are proposed to identify a user like foaf:title, foaf:name, foaf:firstName, foaf:familyName, foaf:nick, foaf:birthday, foaf:depiction, etc.
- **The Contact Information:** Information concerning users' accounts like foaf:account, foaf:mbox, foaf:homepage, foaf:jabbered, etc.
- **The Web Activities:** A reduced number of activities like foaf:publication, foaf:interest, etc.
- **The Relationships:** A specific module (RELATIONSHIP) was conceived to specialize the "knows" property of FOAF, so it characterizes users relationships (rel:friendOf, rel:acquaintanceOf, rel:parentOf, rel:siblingOf, rel:childOf, rel:grandchildOf, rel:spouseOf, rel:enemyOf, rel:antagonistOf, rel:ambivalentOf) (Vitiello, 2002).

Online Activities

SIOC (Semantically-Interlinked Online Communities) is a standard ontology describing user's activities to allow the interoperability between social media activities. However, it constitutes the core ontology for online interaction description, it focuses on the activities forums (Breslin, Passant, & Decker, 2009). So, it was extended to support other OSN.

Figure 1. FOAF Concepts (Brickley et Miller 2010)

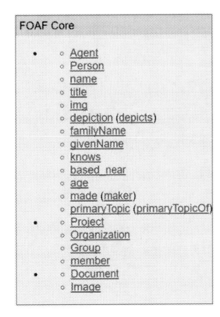

1. Core SIOC Ontology

SIOC (Breslin, Passant, & Vrandečić, 2011) is a standard ontology with the goal to extend FOAF for a specific description of user's activities. Harth and al. created it in 2004 (Harth, Breslin, I., & Decker, 2004); later in 2007 W3C consortium adopted it (Bojārs, Breslin, Passant, & Polleres, 2007) The initial goal of this ontology was to describe the content publishing activities in forums and the interactions with these contents. It defines respectively the Item and Container classes; Post is an Item that can answer another and have as a scope a given topic; Forum is a Container hosted in a Site. SIOC also defines the UserGroup, UserAccount and Role classes. A user account represents a member of a UserGroup, which plays a role (e.g. administrator or simple user) in the forum and can create posts.

The SIOC ontology defines respectively the classes Post, Forum, Site as subclasses of Item, Container and Space; and also defines the relationships between these classes. A post can answer another and have as a scope a given topic. It is contained in a forum that can be parent of another forum hosted in a given site. SIOC also defines the UserGroup, UserAccount and Role classes. A user account represents a member of a UserGroup, which plays a role (e.g. administrator or simple user) in the forum and can create posts.

The example shown in Figure 3 illustrates two users in a forum. The User WATI BG created a post on diabetes forum of the Health forum located in the forum of doctissimo Site, and the user Colley5 replied by another post.

The SIOC ontology has been the subject of extensions to meet new needs. So, multiple modules were proposed, some are maintained and other were abandoned like the SIOC Chat Module and the SIOC Mining Module.

2. SIOC Types Module (SIOCT)

As we mentioned above, the initial SIOC ontology focused on the description of the activities especially in the forums. Many extensions were directed by W3C consortium and academic researchers to make it able to describe other elements and cover new needs.

Figure 2. Core SIOC Ontology classes (Berrueta, et al., 2010)

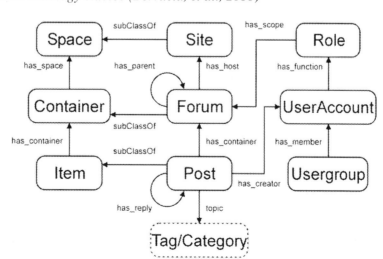

Figure 3. Example of forum activities described using SIOC

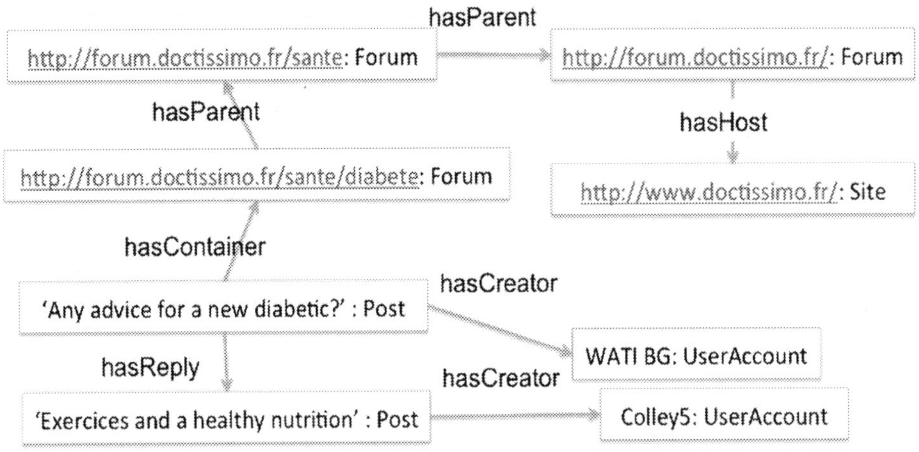

The SIOC Types module (Passant, 2009) extends the SIOC ontology by subclasses that specify the types of contents and containers (Breslin, Passant, & Vrandečić, 2011). As shown in Table 1, it defines new subclasses of containers and published contents such as Weblogs, chat channels, video channels, galleries, images and blog posts elements. It also introduces new concepts such as sioct:Answer, sioct:BestAnswer and sioct:Question to support sites like Yahoo!Answers.

The Figure 4 illustrates an example of interactions between two persons using SIOCT. The user Belouadha sent a message to the mailling list siweb and the user EL Kassiri replied by another message. In this case, SIOCT allows explicitly expressing the notions of message and mailing list against SIOC that describes them respectively as post and forum.

3. SIOC Services (SIOCS) Module

module allows describing a service available on a given site and binding it to its interface, a service can be in the WSDL format (Web Services Description Language) (Kopecký & Innsbruck, 2007). For this purpose, it defines the siocs:Service class and the siocs:Service_definition property.

4. SIOC Orlandi Module

In 2008, under the supervision of Passant, Orlandi has proposed an extension of SIOC (Orlandi, 2008) to improve the representation of wikis. He proposed to use the class sioct:Category and the property

Table 1. Examples of sioct sub-classes

SIOC Classes	SIOC Types Sub-Classes
sioc:Container	sioct:AddressBook, sioct:AnnotationSet, sioct:AudioChannel, sioct:BookmarkFolder, sioct:Briefcase, sioct:EventCalendar
sioc:Forum	sioct:ChatChannel, sioct:MessageBoard, sioct:Weblog, sioct:MailingList, sioct:VideoCannel, sioct:ImageGalery
sioc:Post	sioct:InstantMessage, sioct:MailMessage, sioct:WikiArticle, sioct:Comment, sioct:BlogPost, sioct:BoardPost,

Figure 4. Example of mailing activities described by SIOCT

has_discussion to express the type of wiki articles and the discussions associated with them, as well as the properties earlier_version, later_version, next_version and previous_version to identify its different versions.

5. SIOC Argumentation Module

The aim is to model argumentative discussions. The SIOC Argumentation module (Lange, Bojārs, Groza, Breslin, & Handschuh, 2008) enrich SIOCT module by a new type "sioct:ArgumentativeDiscussion" as a sub-class to sioc:Forum, a post specialization by the statement notion "sioc_arg:Statement" that can express an "Issue", an "Idea" based on an issue, or a an "Elaboration" using an idea to solve a problem; and the "Decision" concept is supported by a "Position". The "Position" can approve, disapprove or neutralize a "Statement". The "Argument" notion is not formalized explicitly by the ontology.

Figure 5. The SIOC Argumentation module (Lange, Bojārs, Groza, Breslin, & Handschuh, 2008)

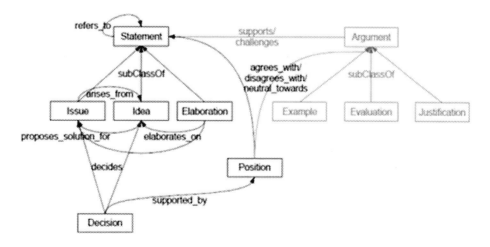

6. SIOC Actions Module

Collaborating with Passant, in 2010, Champin proposed the SIOC Argumentation Ontology to present the dynamics of online communities. This module was based on the existent ontology EVENT to present how users interact with the digital artefacts supported by the media (Champin & Passant, 2010).

7. SIOC Quotes Module

Passant and al. have collaborated to develop an ontology supporting quoting in online conversations; the objective was modeling conversations permitting identifying posts, its responses and responses concerning a sub-part of a post. It was engineered as a SIOC Module because ontologies are suited to give a common scheme and SIOC is widely used in the Web and gives the basic classes and properties that can be reused by the Quotes ontology (Passant, Zimmermann, Schneider, & Breslin, 2010).

8. SemSNI Ontology

Another extension of the SIOC ontology has been proposed as part of a research project (Erétéo, Buffa, Gandon, & Corby, 2009). In this work, Erétéo and al. propose the SemSNI ontology (Semantic Social Network Interaction) that introduces new elements to express interactions such visits and private messages as shown in Figure 8.

The SemSNI ontology also introduces the notion of the user profile page used in social media such as Facebook or Google+, but it considers it as an item and not container. A major advantage of this ontology is that it allows to gather the visits made by a user to a resource and the private messages exchanged between two users in a social media.

Tagging

There are two main objectives of Tagging Ontologies: the first one is to have a unified representation of tagging activity to facilitate the tags sharing and reuse. The aim is to respond to these questions: which tag used? Which user? Which resource? And when? the second one is to present the semantic of the used tag.

Concerning the first objective, Mika proposed a tripartite graph to model the tagging activity: three kinds of nodes A = {a1,...,ak}, C = {c1,...,cl}, I = {i1,...,im}. A represent Actors, C for tags and I for tagged items (Mika, 2005), then Newman and al. translate it to an ontology named Tag Ontology (Newman, Ayers, & Russell, 2005). And Knerr proposed Tagging Ontology based on tag Ontology by adding

Figure 6. Equivalency between the SIOC Action Module and the EVENT Ontology (Champin & Passant, 2010)

Figure 7. The SIOC Quotes Module with an example of Modeling Quotes in a Conversation (Passant, Zimmermann, Schneider, & Breslin, 2010)

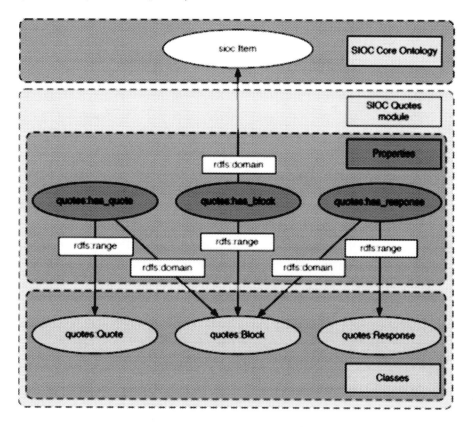

Figure 8. SemSNI Ontology (Erétéo, Buffa, Gandon, & Corby, 2009)

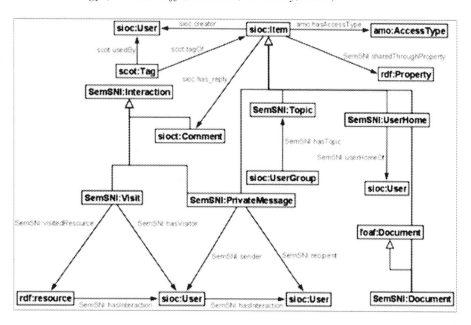

the concept of tagging (domain, type and a visibility) (Knerr, 2007). when the Gruber's model (Gruber, 2007) added the source concept; it means the space where the tagging action has been performed (Flickr, Facebook, etc.).

Concerning the formal representation of tags semantics allowing understanding the semantic relations between tags. We cite four pertinent ontologies:

- **The SKOS (Simple Knowledge Organization System):** (Alistair & Sean, 2013) (Brickley & Miller, 2014) describes concepts and their relations (matching, mapping, semantics, transitive, etc.) and their alternatives in different languages. Using SKOS, we can specify the meaning of tags and posts topics.
- **The SCOT (Social Semantic Cloud of Tags):** (Kim, Breslin, Yang, & Kim, 2008) gives a semantic structure of tagging data for a social interoperability among the different social medias. It uses concepts and properties of Tag Ontology, SIOC and SKOS with the main objective to aggregate tags used by the same persons in clouds.
- **The MOAT (Meaning Of A Tag):** (Passant & Laublet, 2008) describes a tagging by (tag, resource, user, meaning) to specify the local meaning of a tag because there are several terms with a multitude of global meanings. For example, if we use the tag « Washington » it can mean the US city or the American president « George Washington ».
- **The MUTO (Modular Unified Tagging Ontology):** (Lohmann, 2011) is an extensible ontology of tagging and folksonomies unifying existing ontologies. It supports different forms of tagging, such as common, semantic, group, private, and automatic tagging.

Figure 9. Comparison between tagging ontologies (Lohmann, 2011)

Name	Release	Main purpose	Newly introduced concepts	OWL sublanguage	RDF/XML URI reference
Tag Ontology	23/03/2005	First formal tagging ontology	Fundamental concepts and structure, restricted tagging	OWL Full	http://www.holygoat.co.uk/owl/redwood/0.1/tags/
Tagging Ontology	2006	Comprehensive domain description	Tagging source and note, private and group tagging	OWL Full	http://bubb.ghb.fh-furtwangen.de/TagOnt/tagont.owl
Ontology of Folksonomy	2007	Comprehensive domain description	Aggregated tag, tag position, polarity, and type	OWL DL	http://www.eslomas.com/tagontology-1.owl
Social Semantic Cloud of Tags	23/03/2007	TAGS extension for tag clouds	Tag clouds, frequencies, coccurrences, and spelling variants	OWL Full	http://scot-project.org/scot/ns#
Meaning of a Tag	15/01/2008	TAGS extension for semantic tagging	Tag meaning, automatic tagging	OWL Full	http://moat-project.org/ns#
Upper Tag Ontology	2008	Upper ontology	Voting via tags	OWL Lite	http://info.slis.indiana.edu/~dingying/uto.owl
Common Tag	08/06/2009	Minimal ontology (optimized for RDFa)	Author vs. reader tags	OWL Full	http://commontag.org/ns#
TAGora Tagging Ontology	2009	Automatic tag sense disambiguation	--	OWL Lite	http://tagora.ecs.soton.ac.uk/schemas/tagging
NiceTag Ontology	09/01/2009	Taggings as speech acts (intention of tags)	Named graphs, tag intensions	OWL Full	http://ns.inria.fr/nicetag/2010/09/09/voc
Modular Unified Tagging Ontology	02/09/2011	Unification, modularization	--	OWL Lite	http://purl.org/muto/core#

Access Management

The access management ontologies aim is giving a semantic description of users' roles and permissions on resources. They are used to manage and protect privacy on OSN by inferring permissions (Carminati, Ferrari, Heatherly, Kantarcioglu, & Thuraisingham, 2009) (Pwint Oo, 2013) (Kumar & Kumar, 2013), and to predict trust propagation (Barbian, 2011).

The issue of defining access control semantically has been addressed by multiples ontologies:

- **The WAC (Web Access Control Vocabulary):** (Villata, Delaforge, Gandon, & Gyrard, 2011) made for specifying ACL (Access Control List) concerning the permissions Read, Write, Control and Append;
- **The S4AC (Social Semantic SPARQL Security for Access Control Ontology):** (Villata, Delaforge, Gandon, & Gyrard, 2011) based on WAC, allows expressing the Access Condition concept to have a privilege with a temporal validity;
- **The AMO (Access Management Ontology):** (Buffa & Faron-Zucker, 2012) allows annotating the resources and modelling the access control policy.

Besides, the SIOC Access (SIOCA) module is another extension of SIOC ontology (Breslin, Passant, & Vrandečić, 2011) developed to describe access rights for containers and content items and the user role. This module defines the sioca:Status property which can be assigned to content items to indicate their publication status (e.g. public, private, draft, etc.), and the sioca:Permission property to describe the type of action that can be performed on a container such as a forum or a site.

Figure 10. AMO classes and properties (Buffa & Faron-Zucker, 2012)

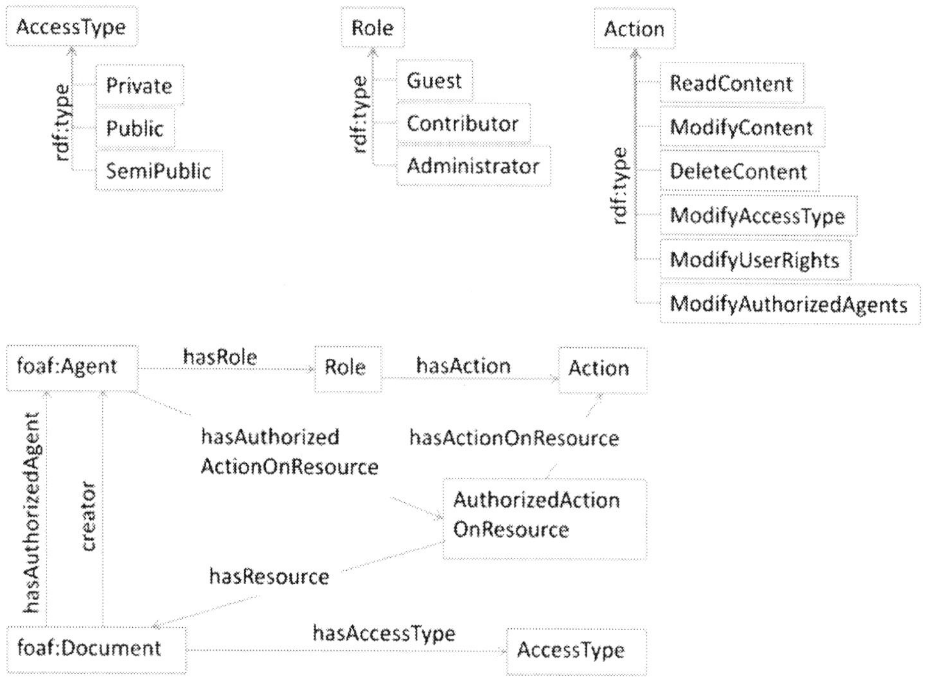

WHY A UNIFIED SEMANTIC MODEL

Social networks enable users to communicate and offer possibilities to share user-generated content like photos and videos and features such as social games. Social advertising and social gaming are two major points of revenue for social networks (Number of social media users worldwide from 2010 to 2020 (in billions), 2017).

The unified model seems benefit to ensure interoperability between social media and to aggregate data from the different OSN for a pertinent analysis.

Aggregation

Recent statistics prove that approximately 74% of adults use OSN, and the average of accounts by user reach 5,54 including 2,82 active accounts (Lim, Lu, Chen, & Kan, 2015), and more than 56% of online adults uses more than one social media platform (Lister, 2017). In parallel, analyzing users' behavior online earns interests of both scientific and industrial communities. Kosinkia and al. have demonstrated that from public behavior like "likes/dislikes" it's possible to predict personal properties like religious, politic and sexual orientations, age, emotions and other personality traits (Kosinskia, Stillwella, & Graepel, 2013).

Otherwise, analyzing users' data from different accounts allows better comprehension of their behavior on the different OSN. In this context, Kong and al. have introduced the Anchor Link notion, that means a link maintained between two users over the different OSN, they use it to predict links for a new user on an OSN using his relations from author OSN (Kong, Zhang, & Yu, 2013). In parallel, Lu and al. use several OSN as sources to calculate topographic properties for a supervised link prediction (Lu, Savas, Tang, & Dhillon, 2010). While Gilbert and Karahalios analyze users' interactions over different OSN to predict the link straight (Gilbert & Karahalios, 2009).

Other researches were oriented to analyze behavioral variation over OSN. Lim and al. have conclued that users describe themselves differenttly according the networking site and reproduct posts from a network source towards destination networks (Lim, Lu, Chen, & Kan, 2015). Zafarani and Liu have demostrated that reputation is influenced and friends' distribution of users change from an OSN to another (Zafarani & Liu, 2016). Even Buccafurri and al. have compared behavior of the same users on Facebook and Twitter, and they have deduced that 87% of users prefer keeping their Facebook accounts private on Twitter, they are rather inactive on Twitter, while users having just a Twitter account are more active, and they led to the same result concerning the difference of friends' distribution on the both OSN (Buccafurri, Lax, Nicolazzo, & Nocera, 2015).

And recently, UnifyID (a Startup company in San Francisco) decided to develop an implicit authentication based on an automatic detection of the user identity by analyzing his behavior and interactions on his proper devices. The idea is based on two modules a users' devices app and a cloud service; the app collect sensor data from users' devices, process it and send features to the cloud server to discover what make a user unique; it generates specific data, send it to the concerned devices that encrypt and anonymize and store in local to be used online and offline (UnifyID's ingenious user authentication platform wins Innovation Sandbox Contest, 2017).

Interoperability

Social media organizations are conscious that surfers maintain multiple accounts on other OSN. And it's evident that social media create business value by analyzing users profile and they try to obtain more information about users from others social media (Looy, 2016), per example Instagram earns $595 million in mobile ad revenue per year, 50 million businesses use Facebook Business Pages whose 2 million use it for advertising (Lister, 2017). So, having at least, a partial interoperability is benefic for social media organizations.

In this context, the social graph API and the open graph protocol were proposed in order to insure this interoperability. In 2007, Facebook has proposed the social graph API and Google initialized the open social API. Both uses the FOAF ontology and XFN micro-formats (XHTML Friends Network) (Breslin, Passant, & Vrandečić, 2011). Those two API were developed to allow a user using its account created in a given networking site, to authenticate in other OSN implementing this API, without having to create a new profile, and to recuperate his data and his old relations. The user can select among his profile data and friendship relations those that he wishes to share.

Then, Facebook decided to pass to the Open Graph (OGP), the OGP is managed by the Open Web Foundation. It allows different sites such as twitter, google+ and Facebook to interact via an interpretable information exchange. It uses in addition to FOAF and XFN, a name space OG that defines a controlled vocabulary based on RDF metadata to describe the web page data. A web page with annotated content by the OGP allows an automatic interpretation of its semantics. Using the open graph protocol, a user can share a content via a site like YouTube on another site like Facebook, and Facebook could identify the elements of the shared content (video title, associated description, etc.).

Based on the use of FOAF and XFN and/or a name space describing the web page content, the social graph API and the open graph protocol allow respectively to social media sharing the users' profiles and their friendship relations, and exchanging objects with normalized representation. Otherwise, they allow interoperability between social media at the level of users' profile and objects composing the web pages' content.

OSN Analysis Challenges

By the analysis of OSN data, the researchers were confronted to three categories of challenges (Gundecha et Liu 2012):

- **Unstructured and Dynamic Data:** Each social platform use its proper structuration method for data storage, and data is permanently updated by users;
- **Large and Distributed Data:** There are multiple social media on line, and each one has a fragment of source data needed to OSN Analysis. Recent statistics estimate that Snapchat hits 10 billion daily video views and its revenue were close to 1 billion dollars in 2016, and Instagram reached 600 Million users (Roberts, 2016); 100 million hours of video content are watched on Facebook daily, and 22% of the world's total population uses Facebook; and LinkedIn boasts more than 450 million user profiles (Lister, 2017); On Facebook, the number of active users has reached 1.871 billion (Chaffey, 2017);
- **Noised Data:** Spammers generate more data than legitim users (Yardi, et al. 2010) (Chu, et al. 2010).

Other issues were raised like the online accounts duplicated, the inactive nodes (unused and undeleted accounts), the malicious users, the diversity of sources, the privacy and the size of the OSN making the identification and analysis of implicit relationships between users more difficult (Bonchi, et al. 2011).

Tang and Liu have studied the OSN characteristics, and they have identified three main properties (Tang et Liu 2010): the *scale-free distributions* reporting an heterogenous distribution of friends proved by an analysis done on YouTube and Flicker (Mislove, et al. 2007); the *small-world effect property* deduced from an applied study on a network with more than 180 million users, it proved that the average path between each pair of users is 6.6 nodes (Leskovec et Horvitz 2008); and the *strong community structure* property raised from the clustering coefficient, it estimate that those networks can be partitioned into communities.

Tang and Liu have identified three other challenges (Tang et Liu 2010):

- **The Dynamic Nature of the OSN:** It's a natural result of the services kind deserved by the social media allowing users changing their relationships and expressing new interests over time;
- **The OSN Size:** It makes unused the traditional algorithms of Social Network Analysis SNA, because those algorithms were adapted to networks of few thousand of nodes;
- **The OSN Heterogeneity:** The type nodes diversity in the OSN is another challenge making the tradition SNA algorithms inadequate for its analysis.

In brief, the OSN analysis challenges are: the modeling, the data cleaning; and the adaptation of SNA algorithms to support the size, the heterogeneity and the dynamism of OSN.

In the present chapter, we are interested in the modeling of OSN data to ensure interoperability and aggregation using existent ontologies cited above.

SOLUTIONS AND RECOMMENDATIONS

Works and efforts cited above prove that interoperability and aggregating data from the different OSN is a serious need and issue, so we thought about a unique model to ensure the both needs. Convinced that semantic web will be a part of the future version of the web, and knowing its benefits for normalizing data presentation, and its capacities for reusing data and inferring latent information, we have opted for a unified model based on ontologies.

Based on the successful attempts of using the well-known ontologies to represent OSN for aggregating users data, EL KASSIRI & BELOUADHA have decided to participate in improving existent ontologies to produce a USM allowing a unique representation for the OSN ensuring their interoperability, a semantic description of users profile (name, city, birth date, etc.) and online activities (posting, sharing, liking, tagging, etc.) allowing inferring behaviors thanks at ontologies (EL KASSIRI & Belouadha, 2015).

Furthermore, the combination between the two good ontologies recommended by the W3C: FOAF and SIOC with the standard SKOS is possible and allow presenting users and most of their behavior. So, EL KASSIRI & BELOUDHA decide to start out with these three ontologies to develop the USM and try covering detected lacks by three other ontologies, with the open possibility to improve it to ensure potential future needs.

The three proposed ontologies are:

- **ActOnto:** Ontology is an extension of SIOC used to describe OSN resources and interactions not supported by SIOC (EL KASSIRI & BELOUADHA, 2014);
- **InterestOnto:** Is an ontology designed to detail the local meaning of a tag for simplifying the SNA and enhance the process inferring of equivalent tags (EL KASSIRI & Belouadha, 2015);
- **AclOnto:** To meet the security and privacy needs in OSN by defining roles and permissions (authorizations and restrictions) concepts (EL KASSIRI & Belouadha, 2015).

ActOnto Ontology

The ActOnto ontology (EL KASSIRI & BELOUADHA, 2014) is another extension of SIOC structured on two modules: the SiocCont module specifying containers (UserHome and SocialPage <page/group>) and the SiocInt module that describing the interactions with posted contents (visits, evaluations <like, dislike, note> and modifications). ActOnto allows presenting the creator of a Social Resource (Item or container) and the date of creation to accompany the OSN evolution over time.

Although the SIOC Types module extended SIOC to support the representation of several types of containers such as wikis, blogs, image galleries and video channels, this ontology doesn't represent information related to other types of containers used by several social networking sites such as profile pages, pages and groups. As shown in Figure 11, the SiocCont module specializes the SIOC:Container class by two subclasses UserHome describing a profile page and SocialPage generalizing two other subclasses Page and Group. Page and Group have respectively the properties hasFun and hasMember to describe pages and groups created on Facebook or LinkedIn and their funs/members (they have more access privileges compared to simple Subscribers) and administrators. We note that the SIOC:User class is equivalent to the SIOC:UserAccount class.

Given that every container has a creator, creation date and subject, we defined the class SocialResource that generalizes both the Item and Container classes, and we add the properties hasCreator, CreatedAt and isAbout. The page properties hasFun and isAbout can be used to infer the user's interest for a given

Figure 11. SiocCont module of the ontology ActOnto

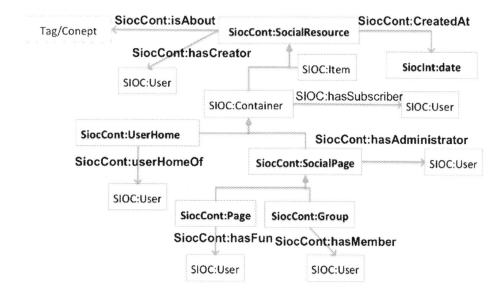

topic. While the group property hasMember allows us to deduce a possible relationship between two members of a given group. Similarly, the property CreatedAt would permit to deduce, when analyzing social networks, the fact that a user was interested in a topic during a given time period and that it is no longer the case now.

Moreover, the ActOnto permits describing the scenario on Facebook when a user X wants to share a photo P on his friend Y profile page. However, SIOC can describe the fact that the user X published the item P on the container Page_Y found on the Facebook website, without being able to express the fact that Page_Y is the profile page of the user Y. The SemSNI ontology also can't fill this need because it represents a profile page (SemSNI:UserHome) as an Item and not as a container where it is possible to publish items. However, being able to identify the owner of a profile page on which an item has been shared, can guide the social network analysis to deduce that he should be interested in the topic of the shared item.

Besides, as shown in Figure 12, the SiocInt module defines the SiocInt:Interaction class generalizing three subclasses SiocInt:Visit, SiocInt:Evaluation and SiocInt:Modification. We note that we keep the SIOC properties modified_at and has_modifier for specifying the user who modified the Item, a container can also be modified (e.g. it is possible to change the subject of a page). So, we have associated the class SiocInt:Modification with the class SiocInt:Resource. The subclass SiocInt:Evaluation is specialized by three subclasses SiocInt:Like, SiocInt:Dislike and SiocInt:Note. These classes allow integrating the concept of content evaluation by users. So, it become possible describing user activities related to the use of "like" and "dislike" buttons in Facebook and Youtube, the "+1" button in Google+ and a numerical value to evaluate an item. The ActOnto ontology defines also the SiocInt:madeBy and SiocInt:madeAt properties to specify the maker and the date of the interaction. The classes and properties defined allow: firstly, gathering the feelings and opinions of users about the published contents, and secondly, detecting or predicting their potential interesting through the resources (containers or content) visits and modifications, per example, regular visits to a given page or a given profile page can be interpreted by a special interest for the page topic or a friend. The property madeAt permits to identify new and old user interactions, and the changes of page topic done by a given user over time, can therefore be used to analyze his trends and predict his interest for some subjects in the future.

Figure 12. SiocInt module of the ontology ActOnto

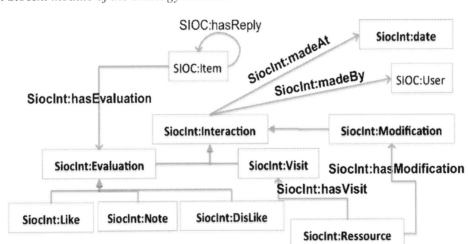

Figure 13. Example of activities described by ActOnto

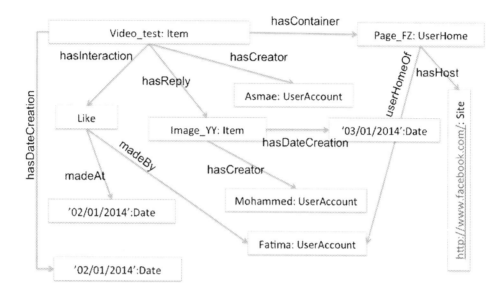

The example given in Figure 13, written according to the ontology ActOnto, represents a scenario where a user has shared a video on the Facebook profile page of his friend who liked this publication that another user who commented it by an image.

InetrestOnto Ontology

The tagging ontologies allow specifying tags used by actors for resources. An inferring process based on tags and SKOS can deduce posts with the same topics, or identify users with the same interests. But, the informal language contains multiple homonyms, and only the MOAT allows specifying the meaning of the tag by the user but it doesn't give a precise semantic context, so the user can use other terms more ambiguous. The objective of InetrestOnto is to define specific sub-classes of the Tag class.

The aim of Interest Ontology (InetrestOnto) is to meet the following requirements:

- InterestOnto concepts have to respond to the main SNA (Social Networks Analysis) needs. A tag can reference a person (user, famous person), a subject, a product or a location (city, country, etc.) (See Figure 14);
- InetrestOnto must be extensible and combinable with FOAF, MUTO, SKOS, SIOC and their extension to ensure the interoperability.

AclOnto Ontology

We note some limits concerning the existent Access Control Ontologies:

993

Figure 14. InterestOnto Classes

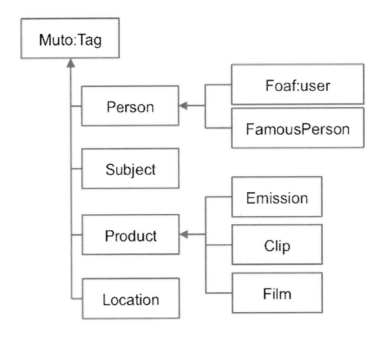

Figure 15. On the channel Hit Radio on Youtube, the admin has shared a Video about an emission « *Test Machmoum », and the subscriber Asmae has tagged it with the 'Momo', a famous person. Another subscriber Amine has published a video about the clip « Inta Maallam » and tagged it with a name of a famous person « Saad Lamjarred ».*

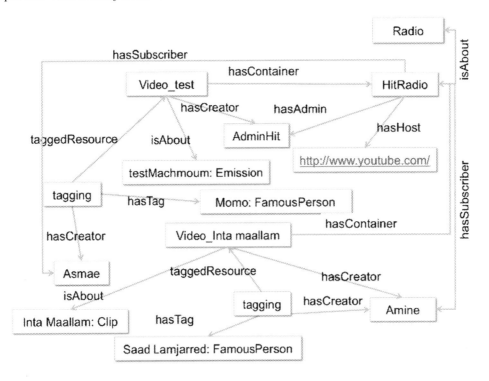

Figure 16. AclOnto Classess and properties

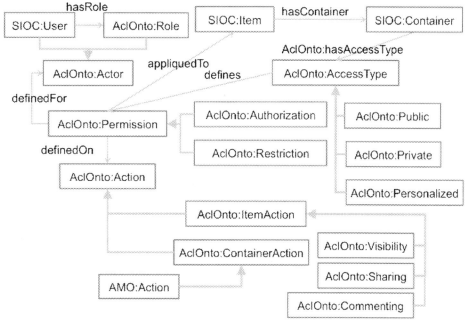

- Lack of compatibility with the existent ontologies that we have choice for our unified sematic model;
- SIOC Access allows defining permissions only by users;
- AMO allows authorizing permissions only by roles;
- There is no restriction of permissions.

Our AclOnto ontology is based on AMO. It applies roles and AccessType on SoicalResources (item or container), it defines the Actor concept that can be a role or a user to receive authorizations or restrictions.

The class AclOnto:Role allows to a user to create groups of permissions. The Container Access Type defines the default permissions to applying on all its items, and the different actions (AMO:Action) concerning the container.

Based on this ontology, we can represent the case when, on Facebook for example, a user wants allow to a group of his friends with a specific role to see a post but forbid it to a user having this role. Generally, restriction is higher priority than authorization, and user direct permissions are higher than permissions inherited from roles. For examples:

A user on facebook has a default role defined on his profile (ActOnto:UserHome) named "Friends". For a user X having a profile with a private access type (all permissions are granted for friends only ("Friends" role)), has defined the "Family" role. Y is an X's Friend:

- X limits Sharing and Commenting permissions on an Item I to "Family" and revoke it from "Friends". If Y belongs or not to "Friends", he has only the Visibility permission (restriction is high priority). But if X gives the Commenting permission to Y, he will have the Visibility and Commenting permission on I.

Figure 17. X shares an Item I on his profile, so Y has all permissions because he belongs to "Friends"

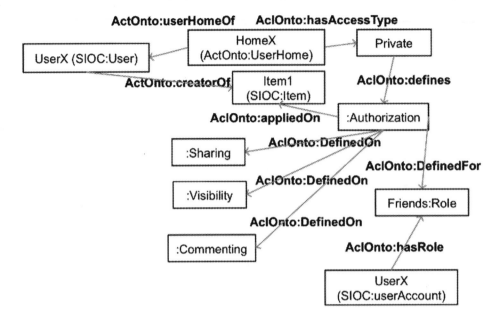

- If X changes his profile access type to public; by defaults, all users will have all permissions on all Items to be sharing after.
- A profile with Personalized access type is a home page with different permissions granted to different users and roles.
- For a social page (ActOnto:SocialPage) or group (ActOnto:Group) with private access type, there are two default roles "Administrators" and "Members". The first ones are authorized to modify the page's contents and properties (AMO:Action), to share, comment and see (AclOnto:ItemAction); while the "Members" have only authorization for the AclOnto:ItemAction permissions.

An Example of Implementation and Experimentation

To illustrate the easy possibility to use the ActOnto ontology for aggregating data from social media, EL KASSIRI & BELOUADHA developed in Eclipse environment an application in Java and we tested it through an example collected from Facebook (EL KASSIRI & BELOUADHA, ActOnto: An extension of the SIOC standard for social media analysis and interoperability, 2014). This application allows generating the RDF file that represents, according to ActOnto ontology, data extracted from social media. To first extract the data that form the input of the application, we used the Graph API Explorer tool to extract data from Facebook. This tool allows, through a graphical interface, specifying data access permissions that will be granted to the graph explorer by the user. According to these permissions, an access token is provided by Facebook to the social graph explorer that will be able to return relevant data, annotated according to the vocabulary of the open graph protocol, in JSON (JavaScript Object Definition) format. The JSON format is a simple text data format which is generic, derivative from objects notation JavaScript and used to represent structured information in Web applications.

Figure 18. Graph API Explorer Interface

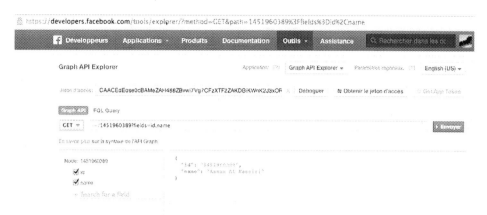

We used Protégé OWL, an open source ontology editor distributed by the University of Stanford Medical Informatics, to create our ActOnto ontology. Protégé is not a tool especially dedicated to OWL, but a highly extensible editor, able to handle a wide variety of formats.

As illustrated in Figure 19, the implemented application allows generating a RDF file from both a JSON file of social media data and ActOnto ontology. It consists of two components: Processing Component and Instantiation Component. The mission of the Processing Component is to analyze the JSON file in order to identify the different pairs (attribute, value) from the data it contains. For this purpose, it uses JSON Processing API (Java API for JSON Processing (JSON-P)). The Instantiation Component is designed to instantiate the ActOnto ontology. Using the Jena API recommended for semantic applications development, it is able to read and reuse ActOnto pairs (attribute, value) which are obtained through the Processing Component, to instantiate RDF triplets and generate the corresponding RDF file.

Figure 19. Architecture of the experimentation tool

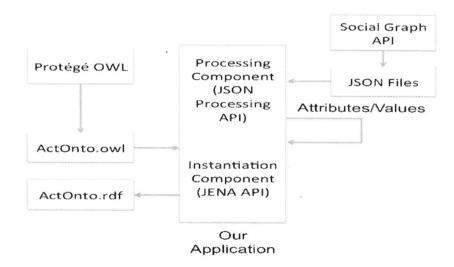

For experimenting the developed application, we extracted from Facebook, the data concerning the user El Kassiri (personal data, list of friends, group list, pages and publications she likes). Figure 20 shows a mapping of an extract of the content of the obtained JSON file, and concepts from ActOnto ontology. This extract interprets the fact that the user El Kassiri (id 1451960389) published a post (id 1451960389_10202266540812228) about the topic (161 signatures are still needed!) on its profile page in the date (2013 - 11-13). Figure 20 illustrates, as a graph, a part of the RDF file content, relating to this extract. This part further indicates that the user (id 509268650) evaluated the post published on the profile page (https://www.facebook.com/asmae.kass) using 'LIKE' at the same day of its publication. We can remark that the generated file specifies a profile page as container, dates of activities and an interaction of evaluation type, which are details not provided by SIOC.

FUTURE RESEARCH DIRECTIONS

As cited above, the OSN are business organizations aiming engaging a business value from users data by analyzing their profile and their online behavior for publicity recommendation, product or service or person reputation analysis, etc., so the USM will offer an interoperability permitting accessing to data from other OSN, and by consequence the leader organizations (Facebook, Google, Twitter, etc.) should refuse sharing its data because it maintain the giant volume of data and the share will increase the concurrency. By the way those organizations can use the USM to aggregate data from all its social media for a complete analysis.

Figure 20. A mapping example from JSON to ActOnto RDF triplets

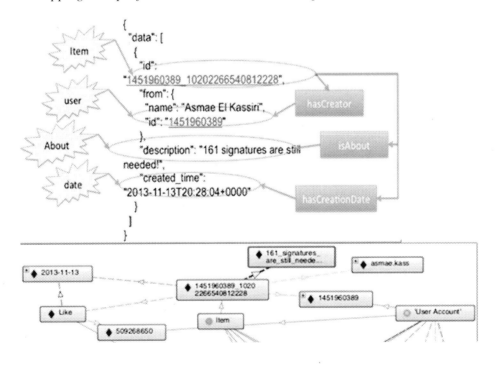

We have demonstrated that is possible to model Facebook data by the proposed model (El Kassiri & Belouadha, 2014), but we let to OSN administrators the choice to implement their own solutions to immigrate their data to the USM and select data to disclose and data to keep in dark according to their business plan and their strategy.

The advantage of using ontologies for representation of OSN data is the *modularity* allowing extending model to support other OSN not supported by the actual model; and the data *reusability* thanks to the standardization ensured by ontologies.

The *USM* must offer *interoperability* to permit, if used as platform of structuring data by the social media, users moving between social media with a unique account; and *aggregation* for a complete and efficient *analysis*, in next papers, we intend to explain how use it to analyze data from heterogeneous sources and for diverse needs.

Our idea consists on an ontological approach aiming offering a platform for *generic analysis* covering the different aspects of OSN analysis needs (influence propagation, trust analysis, recommendation, privacy and confidence, similarity analysis, expert detection, community detection and link prediction), and supporting the *most popular social media*. The objective of the USM is preparing the platform to support the most popular social media.

CONCLUSION

OSN are a rich source of information that can be exploited in different domains such as marketing and politics, for product recommendation, reputation management, electoral prediction, detecting terrorist communities, protecting privacy, trust mining, etc. The OSN analysis has attracting a lot of interests from business and academic communities, motiving by the web evolution towards a semantic web, several ontologies were proposed to model OSN.

To engineer a unified semantic model for OSN to describe the social medias content, we proposed the ActOnto (El Kassiri & Belouadha, 2014) extending SIOC, and the InterestOnto and the AclOnto (El Kassiri & Belouadha, 2015) to enrich, respectively, the tagging ontologies and the access control ontologies. Those ontologies are aligned with the standard ontologies of semantic social Web.

The unified model will allow collecting and aggregating knowledge from different OSN, to lead to efficient results of social analysis. For example, federating relationships of a user from Facebook, YouTube and Twitter can reveal interesting patterns. But, it remains a basic framework of a semantic analysis approach that can be extended.

REFERENCES

Alistair, M., & Sean, B. (2013, June 4). *SKOS Simple Knowledge Organization System Reference*. Retrieved from W3C Recommendation: http://www.w3.org/TR/skos-reference/

Barbian, G. (2011, 09 12-14). Trust Centrality in Online Social Networks. *Proceedings of Intelligence and Security Informatics Conference (EISIC'11)*, 372 - 377.

Berrueta, D., Brickley, D., Decker, S., Fernández, S., Görn, C., Harth, A., . . . Polo, L. (2010, March 25). *SIOC Core Ontology Specification*. Retrieved from RDFS: http://rdfs.org/sioc/spec/

Bojārs, U., Breslin, J. G., Passant, A., & Polleres, A. (2007, June 12). *SIOC Ontology: Related Ontologies and RDF Vocabularies.* Retrieved from W3C Member Submission.

Bonchi, F., Castillo, C., Gionis, A., & Jaimes, A. (2011). 04). Social Network Analysis and Mining for Business Applications. *ACM Transactions on Intelligent Systems and Technology, 2*(3). doi:10.1145/1961189.1961194

Breslin, J., Passant, A., & Decker, S. (2009). *The Social Semantic Web.* Springer-Verlag Berlin Heidelberg. doi:10.1007/978-3-642-01172-6

Breslin, J., Passant, A., & Vrandečić, D. (2011). Social Semantic Web. In J. Domingue, & D. Fensel (Eds.), Handbook of Semantic Web Technologies (pp. 467-506). Springer Berlin Heidelberg. doi:10.1007/978-3-540-92913-0_12

Brickley, D., & Miller, L. (2010, Août 9). *FOAF Vocabulary Specification 0.98.* Retrieved June 4, 2013, from http://xmlns.com/foaf/spec/

Brickley, D., & Miller, L. (2014, Janvier 14). *FOAF Vocabulary Specification 0.99. Namespace Document.* Retrieved from xmlns.com: http://xmlns.com/foaf/spec/

Buccafurri, F., Lax, G., Nicolazzo, S., & Nocera, A. (2015). 11). Comparing Twitter and Facebook user behavior. *Journal Computers in Human Behavior, 52*(C), 87–95. doi:10.1016/j.chb.2015.05.045

Buffa, M., & Faron-Zucker, C. (2012). Ontology-Based Access Rights Management. In F. Guillet, G. Ritschard, & D. A. Zighed (Eds.), Advances in Knowledge Discovery and Management (pp. 49-61). Springer Berlin Heidelberg. doi:10.1007/978-3-642-25838-1_3

Carminati, B., Ferrari, E., Heatherly, R., Kantarcioglu, M., & Thuraisingham, B. (2009). A semantic web based framework for social network access control. *Proceedings of the 14th ACM symposium on Access control models and technologies SACMAT'09,* 177-186. doi:10.1145/1542207.1542237

Chaffey, D. (2017, February 27). *Global social media research summary 2017.* Retrieved from Smart Insights: http://www.smartinsights.com/social-media-marketing/social-media-strategy/new-global-social-media-research/

Champin, P. A., & Passant, A. (2010). SIOC in Action – Representing the Dynamics of Online Communities. *Proceedings the 6th International Conference on Semantic Systems, I-SEMANTICS 2010* (pp. 12:1-12.7). Graz, Austria: ACM.

Chen, L., Wei, S., & Qingpu, Z. (2010). Semantic Description of Social Network Based on Ontology. *International Conference on E-Business and E-Government* (pp. 1936 - 1939). IEEE. doi:10.1109/ICEE.2010.489

Chu, Z., Gianvecchio, S., Wang, H., & Jajodia, S. (2010). Who is tweeting on Twitter: Human, bot, or cyborg? *Computer Security Applications Conference ACSAC, 10*(26), 21–30.

El Kassiri, A., & Belouadha, F.-Z. (2014). ActOnto: An extension of the SIOC standard for social media analysis and interoperability. *Third IEEE International Colloquium in Information Science and Technology (CIST'14),* 62-67.

El Kassiri, A., & Belouadha, F.-Z. (2015). Towards a Unified Semantic Model for Online Social Networks Analysis and Interoperability. *10th International Conference on Intelligent Systems: Theories and Applications (SITA)*, 62-67.

Erétéo, G., Buffa, M., Gandon, F., & Corby, O. (2009). Analysis of a Real Online Social Network Using Semantic Web Frameworks. *8th International Semantic Web Conference, ISWC 2009* (pp. 180-195). Chantilly, VA: Springer Berlin Heidelberg. doi:10.1007/978-3-642-04930-9_12

Gilbert, E., & Karahalios, K. (2009). Predicting tie strength with social media. *Proceedings of the SIGCHI Conference on Human Factors in Computing Systems CHI '09*, 211-220.

Golbeck, J., & Rothstein, M. M. (2008). Linking social networks on the web with FOAF: a semantic web case study. *Proceeding AAAI'08 Proceedings of the 23rd national conference on Artificial intelligence, 2*, 1138-1143.

Gruber, T. (2007). Ontology of folksonomy: A mashup of apples and oranges. *International Journal on Semantic Web and Information Systems, 3*(2).

Gundecha, P., & Liu, H. (2012). *Mining Social Media: A Brief Introduction.* The Institute for Operations Research and the Management Sciences (INFORMS), TutORials in Operations Research. Retrieved from http://www.public.asu.edu/~pgundech/book_chapter/smm.pdf

Harth, A., Breslin, J. G., & Decker, S. (2004). Linking Semantically Enabled Online Community Sites. *1st Workshop on Friend of a Friend, Social Networking and the Semantic Web.* W3C.

Java API for JSON Processing (JSON-P). (n.d.). Retrieved April 03, 2017, from Java.net: https://json-processing-spec.java.net/

Kim, H.-L., Breslin, J., Yang, S.-K., & Kim, H.-G. (2008). *Social Semantic Cloud of Tag: Semantic Model for Social Tagging. In Agent and Multi-Agent Systems: Technologies and Applications.* Springer Berlin Heidelberg.

Kim, H.-L., Scerri, S., Passant, A., Breslin, J. G., & Kim, H.-G. (2011). Integrating Tagging into the Web of Data: Overview and Combination of Existing Tag Ontologies. *Journal of Internet Technology, 12*(4), 561–572.

Knerr, T. (2007, Jan 15). *tagont.* Retrieved from code.google.com/archive: https://code.google.com/archive/p/tagont/downloads

Kong, X., Zhang, J., & Yu, P. S. (2013). Inferring anchor links across multiple heterogeneous social networks. *Proceedings of the 22nd ACM international conference on Conference on information & knowledge management*, 179-188. doi:10.1145/2505515.2505531

Kopecký, J., & Innsbruck, D. (2007, June 26). *Web Services Description Language (WSDL) Version 2.0: RDF Mapping.* Retrieved from WSDL: http://www.w3.org/TR/wsdl20-rdf/

Kosinskia, M., Stillwella, D., & Graepel, T. (2013). Private traits and attributes are predictable from digital records of human behavior. *Proceedings of the National Academy of Sciences of the United States of America, 110*(15), 5802–5805. doi:10.1073/pnas.1218772110 PMID:23479631

Kumar, V., & Kumar, S. (2013). Access Control Framework for Social Network System using Ontology. *International Journal of Computers and Applications, 79*(4), 10–18. doi:10.5120/13728-1524

Kumar, V., & Kumar, S. (2013). Access Control Framework for Social Network System using Ontology. *International Journal of Computer Applications, 7*(4).

Lange, C., Bojārs, U., Groza, T., Breslin, J., & Handschuh, S. (2008). Expressing Argumentative Discussions in Social Media Sites. *First Workshop on Social Data on the Web (SDoW2008)*.

Leskovec, J., & Horvitz, E. (2008). Planetary-scale views on a large instant-messaging network. *WWW '08: Proceeding of the 17th international conference on World Wide Web*, 915–924. doi:10.1145/1367497.1367620

Lim, B. H., Lu, D., Chen, T., & Kan, M.-Y. (2015, 08 25-28). #mytweet via Instagram: Exploring User Behaviour across Multiple Social Networks. *Proceedings of the 2015 IEEE/ACM International Conference on Advances in Social Networks Analysis and Mining ASONAM '15*, 113-120. doi:10.1145/2808797.2808820

Lister, M. (2017, Jan 20). *40 Essential Social Media Marketing Statistics for 2017*. Retrieved from Word Stream: http://www.wordstream.com/blog/ws/2017/01/05/social-media-marketing-statistics

Lohmann, S. (2011, November 16). *Modular Unified Tagging Ontology (MUTO)*. Retrieved from muto socialtagging: http://muto.socialtagging.org/core/v1.html

Looy, A. V. (2016). *Social Media Management*. Springer International Publishing. doi:10.1007/978-3-319-21990-5

Lu, Z., Savas, B., Tang, W., & Dhillon, I. S. (2010). Supervised Link Prediction Using Multiple Sources. *Proceedings of the 2010 IEEE International Conference on Data Mining ICDM '10*, 923-928. doi:10.1109/ICDM.2010.112

Luz, N. (2010). *Semantic Social Network Analysis* (PhD Thesis). Instituto Politécnico do Porto, Instituto Superior de Engenharia do Porto.

Masoumzadeh, A., & Joshi, J. (2011). Ontology-based access control for social network systems. *International Journal of Information Privacy, Security and Integrity*, 59 - 78.

Mika, P. (2005). Ontologies are us: A unified model of social networks and semantics. *International Semantic Web Conference LNCS* (pp. 522–536). Springer. doi:10.1007/11574620_38

Mislove, A., Marcon, M., Gummadi, K. P., Druschel, P., & Bhattacharjee, B. (2007). Measurement and analysis of online social networks. *IMC '07: Proceedings of the 7th ACM SIGCOMM conference on Internet measurement, 7*, 29–42. doi:10.1145/1298306.1298311

Newman, R., Ayers, D., & Russell, S. (2005, December 21). *Tag ontology design*. Retrieved from holygoat. co.uk: http://www.holygoat.co.uk/projects/tags/

Number of social media users worldwide from 2010 to 2020 (in billions). (2017, April 3). Retrieved from The Statistics Portal: http://www.statista.com/statistics/278414/number-of-worldwide-social-network-users/

Orlandi, F. (2008). *Using and extending the sioc ontology for a fine-grained wiki modeling* (Master's Thesis). Università degli Studi di Modena e Reggio Emilia.

Passant, A. (2009, Octobre 20). *SIOC Types and Health Care and Life Sciences.* Retrieved from W3C Submission: http://www.w3.org/TR/hcls-sioc/

Passant, A., & Laublet, P. (2008). Meaning of a tag: A collaborative approach to bridge the gap between tagging and linked data. *Proceedings of the WWW 2008 Workshop Linked Data on the Web (LDOW2008).*

Passant, A., Zimmermann, A., Schneider, J., & Breslin, J. G. (2010). A semantic framework for modelling quotes in email conversations. *Proceedings of the 1st International Conference on Intelligent Semantic Web-Services and Applications (ISWSA '10)* (pp. 11:1-11:8). Amman, Jordan: ACM. doi:10.1145/1874590.1874601

Pwint Oo, S. H. (2013). Intelligent access control policies for social network site. *International Journal of Computer Science & Information Technology*, 183-190.

Roberts, P. (2016). *Social Media Statistics for 2017.* Retrieved from Our Social Times: http://oursocial-times.com/7-social-media-statistics-for-2017/

Tang, L., & Liu, H. (2010). *Community Detection and Mining in Social Media* (Vol. 1). Morgan & Claypool.

UnifyID's ingenious user authentication platform wins Innovation Sandbox Contest. (2017, Febrary 15). Retrieved from Help Net Security: https://www.helpnetsecurity.com/2017/02/15/unifyid-user-authentication-platform/

Villata, S., Delaforge, N., Gandon, F., & Gyrard, A. (2011). An Access Control Model for Linked Data. On the Move to Meaningful Internet Systems: OTM 2011 Workshops, 454-463.

Vitiello, E. J. (2002, July 19). *Relationship: A module for defining relationships in FOAF.* Retrieved April 03, 2017, from http://www.perceive.net: http://www.perceive.net/schemas/20021119/relationship/

Yardi, S., Romero, D., Schoenebeck, G., & boyd, d. (2010, Janvier 4). Detecting spam in a Twitter network. *First Monday, 15*(1).

Zafarani, R., & Liu, H. (2016). Users joining multiple sites: Friendship and popularity variations across sites. *Journal Information Fusion, 28*(C), 83–89. doi:10.1016/j.inffus.2015.07.002

This research was previously published in Graph Theoretic Approaches for Analyzing Large-Scale Social Networks edited by Natarajan Meghanathan, pages 267-292, copyright year 2018 by Information Science Reference (an imprint of IGI Global).

Chapter 49
Irritating Factors While Navigating on Websites and Facebook and Its Reactions Using Different Devices

Sana El Mouldi
IAE Université Bordeaux IV, France & ISG Tunisia, Tunisia

Norchene Ben Dahmane Mouelhi
Université de Carthage, Tunisia

ABSTRACT

The research presented in this chapter identifies sources of the irritation felt by internet users while browsing websites and Facebook. A qualitative approach was taken, including 40 individual interviews, enabled the authors to determine the irritating factors and user reactions when using different devices such as smartphones, computers and tablets to navigate websites and Facebook. The implications of this research will help marketers and web developers to reduce internet user irritation and better understand their behavior to better meet their expectations.

INTRODUCTION

The internet is considered as the biggest invention of 21th century. Indeed, the internet has permitted individuals to evolve from a simple information receptor status to an active searcher status. According to Belk (2013, p.477), the internet is "a cornucopia of information, entertainment, images, films, and music mostly all free for accessing, downloading, and sharing with others". Nowadays, "information and communication technology (ICT) has a large impact on the society in which we live and on the development and interactions of individuals, communities, corporations" (Vošner & al., 2016, p.230). Today, there are 3.7 billion internet users – roughly half of the world's 7.4 billion population.[1] Besides, more than 60 percent of internet users are drawn to social networks every month. Sakas & al. (2015)

DOI: 10.4018/978-1-5225-5637-4.ch049

stipulate that customers are co-creators of a company's marketing approaches and communication strategies through social networks.

Consumers have access to all kinds of information on the internet especially with the development of mobile devices, which reduces the use of other media. The growth in the prominence of digital, social media and mobile marketing has conducted to several technological innovations such as the increasing penetration of home internet and affordable high-speed broadband connections, the development of social media platforms such as Facebook, and widespread consumer adoption to "smart" mobile devices (Lamberton & al., 2016). Through "the advent of smartphones and social media, accessibility of information is higher than it ever has been before" (Agnihotri, 2016, p.173). The use of mobile devices is increasing exponentially threw different devices such as tablets and smartphones. Global Net Index study in 2015 revealed that the most used devices are laptops, smartphones and tablets but there are other new devices that are taking important places in consumer's internet use habits such as smart TVs, Smart Watches and smart wristband. Since the digitalization of our lifestyle, internet became a world a world in itself and like the real world it has its own irritating factors. Indeed, the internet users is frequently facing irritating factors as he's surfing on websites and mobile applications, and it leads generally to a negative emotion.

This chapter aims to identify the sources of irritation experienced by internet users while navigating on websites and social media, depending on the device used (i.e., smartphone, tablet, or laptop). Moreover, this study will reveal the reactions to the identified irritation sources.

BACKGROUND

Evolution of Internet User's Behavior

In the era of web 1.0, the internet user was passive, had access to static web pages, and could only do research with simple words, until the advent of the web 2.0 which provided the opportunity to become active with access to various tools such as blogs, wikis, and social networks. Individuals can research with tags and participate to the diffusion and creation of the information. According to Byrne & al. (2016, p. 456), "internet facilitates work, social connections, and education". Social networks, which are an essential tool of Web 2.0, allowed users to take power. The social networking phenomenon appeared in 1997 with the launch of the website "Six Degrees.com" (Boyd and Elisson, 2007). During the 90's, many social networks emerged, such as Asian Avenue, Blackplanet, and MoveOn (Edosomwan & al., 2011). Since the 2000s, social networks have increased in number, taking an important place in consumers' lives. Today, social networks have become an essential communication platform for many companies. Boyd and Ellison (2009) define the social networks as web services that allow individuals to create a public or semi-public profile, articulate a list of users with whom they are in contact, and view and scroll through the list of their contacts and those of other users. Lenhart and Madden (2007) see social networks as an effective and powerful channel through which consumers create a personal profile, build a personal network and display interpersonal comments publicly. Koh & al. (2007) introduce social networks as virtual community websites where people who are separated by time and space, can share interests, build relationships, exchange information and conduct transactions. Mayol (2011, p. 35) defines social networks as "tools that allow a connection of users with their friends, relationships to create a private relationship and / or professional network." These tools allow exchange of content (audio, video, photo ...), exchange of applications, monitoring of activities and especially the ability to create and integrate groups based on common interests, common cultures, joint opinion or common lifestyles. Wellhoff (2012) has also identified social networks as "a virtual space where people of the same affinity can meet and interact. Social networks allow the exchange between members, by e-mail or instant messaging and sharing their personal information". According to Vošner and al. (2016), "online social networks can be used to connect with people regardless of time or place". According to these definitions, it is possible to note that social networks bring people together regardless of where they are. Felix (2016, p. 2) stipulate that social networks help "stimulating sales, increasing brand awareness, improving brand image, generating traffic to online platforms, reducing marketing costs, and creating user interactivity on platforms by stimulating users to post or share content". Caseway (2016, p. 759) affirms "companies viewed social media as an opportunity to cultivate customer engagement and to strengthen their relationships with the other businesses who were their customers". Dahnil (2014, p. 120) confirms that social media is a unique marketing communication tool as it "allow the production of information and being collaborate among users and leverage mobile and web-based technologies to create interactive medium where users and groups member sharing, co-creating, discussing, and modifying known as user-generated content". An experiment conducted by Stanley Milgram in 1969 demonstrated that to connect two people it takes an average of six intermediaries. This experiment was called the rule of "six degrees" or the hypothesis of the "small world". Forsé (2012) reproduced this experience on Facebook, he found that the average distance between two users is 4.7 intermediaries. Today Facebook is the first social network in the world with over one billion, seven million users[2].

The advent of technology also impacted the consumer behavior while surfing the internet. Indeed, consumers are using numerous devices to access internet such as computers, mobiles, and tablets. With the evolution of the web and infrastructure, individual can use internet wherever he is through mobile networks and using mobile devices. For example, in France over 50 percent of internet users are connected via mobile devices (Figure 1).

Figure 1.

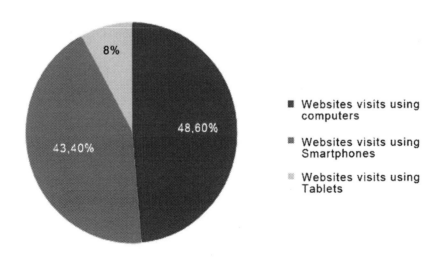

Table 1. Web1.0 VS 2.0

WEB 1.0	WEB 2.0
Passive internet user	Active internet user
Individual web pages	Blogs, Wikis and social networks on internet
Diffusion and information	Participation in the diffusion of information
Research by key words	Apparition of tags which facilitate the research
Broadcast news releases by email	Using RSS Feeds and feed aggregators
Bookmarks via the browser	Social bookmarks (exp: de.li.cio.us)
Content created by the service	Content created by the users
Read only and copyright	Add, edit, delete: some rights protected, open source
Some API's	Tool box (Jquerry or CMS), Open source API (Ajax)
Page views	Cost by clic
DoubleClick	Google Adsense
Ofoto	Flicker

Source: Fayon D., Web 2.0 et au-delà, Economica 2010

Store Atmosphere and Website Atmosphere

It is possible to induce the atmospheric elements of a physical store the virtual store, although Eroglu and al. (2001) emphasize the lack of some atmospheric variables on the internet such as smell, touch, temperature (Volle, 2000), to better understand the impact of the atmosphere on consumer behavior, researchers are interested in the variables that make up that environment by providing different classifications (Turley & Milliman, 2000). As for the physical store atmosphere, several researchers (Eroglu and al., 2001; Childers and al., 2001; Chang and al., 2002) have developed taxonomies for the atmosphere's elements on the internet. Table 2 presents an overview of various classifications related to environmental factors on the internet.

Table 2. Classifications of environmental factors on internet

Author (Year)	Categories	Observations
Eroglu and al. (2001)	2 categories: • High task relevant cues • Low task relevant cues	Eroglu and al. (2001) are the first to suggest a typology of environmental factors on internet.
Childers and al. (2001)	2 categories: • Utilitarian elements • Hedonic elements	This classification was based on internet user motivation
Chang and al. (2002)	2 categories: • Functionnal elements • Symbolic elements	Chang and al. (2002) based their study on the typology of Childers and al. (2001). The functional elements correspond to utilitarian elements and symbolic elements to hedonic elements.

Importance of Irritation Sources in the Study of the Consumer Behavior

Irritation is a derived emotion from anger but which is more moderated (Shaver and al., 1987). Pelet and al (2016) demonstrated that emotions have a positive influence on purchase intent and website recommendation. D'Astous (2000, p. 150) defines irritation as "Elements of the shopping environment that create negative feelings among customers". Touzani & al. (2007) suggest that negative feelings such as discontent or excitement are studied by simple opposition (pleasure/displeasure). The study of the negative influence related to environmental factors on consumer behavior account for a reversal of perspective, according to Helme-Guizon (2002). Many researchers were interested in studying the influence of environment on internet user's behavior, but their research only focused on its positive effects (Jacob, 2005). It is important to explore the dark side of the experience, because negative information plays a larger role in judgment formation than does positive information due to a superior cognitive treatment (Mizerski, 1982).

There are relatively few studies on the influence of the environment on consumer behavior. The works of d'Astous (2000) and Touzani & al. (2007) on sources of irritation felt by consumers in points of sale are notable, as are those of Helme-Guizon (2002) concerning the sources of irritation felt by the user while browsing on merchant sites, and finally, Ben Dahmane Mouelhi & al. (2009), with their research on sources of irritation in hotels.

METHODOLOGY

Given the exploratory nature of this research, a qualitative study seems most appropriate. Thus, semi-structured individual interviews, lasting between 30 and 45 minutes, were conducted among 40 people. These interviews were completed by the critical incident method involves asking the interviewee to talk about a situation already experienced. The 40 interviews were recorded and transcribed. The interviews were conducted using an interview guide previously established. The sample is characterized by the diversity in terms of their professional situations, family, and ages (between 15 and 35 years old). The choice of this age group is justified by the Facebook usage statistics, provided by Facebook stats 2016. Indeed, according to recent research, the 18 to 29 are the most important segment of Facebook users, with 87 percent of users registered in this age bracket[3]. According to Vošner and al. (2016, p. 236), "social networks such as Facebook, Twitter, LinkedIn, etc." are mostly used by youth.

CONTENT ANALYSIS

Thematic analysis was conducted on the transcribed data. Each interview was cut into recording units that were subject to a calculation to know their frequency of occurrence. Then, these recording units were grouped into units of meaning to finally be classified into thematic units to facilitate the understanding and interpretation of results (Bardin, 1996).

Analysis of Sources of Irritation Felt by Users on Websites

Thematic analysis performed for the sources of irritation experienced by users during their navigation on websites helped detecting six major themes that have been classified according to the typology of Childers and al. (2001), hedonic and utilitarian elements (Table 2).

1. **Utilitarian Elements:** In this research, utilitarian elements concerns advertising, the information content and website functionalities.

    a. **Advertising:** Through interviews, advertising proves to be a very irritating element for users. In fact, different forms of advertising were mentioned by respondents. They have cited banner ads, pop-ups, commercials and "spam". Note that pop-ups and advertising were also mentioned by Helme-Guizon (2002).

        i. **Advertising Banners:** For some respondents, the mere presence of banner ads on a website is a source of irritation. Indeed, they found that companies are desperate to make themselves known and to manipulate consumers. One respondent explained that "if I need something I would do a search and I would find it myself". Another clarified: "why showing me ads 10 times while I have no interest?" The number of banner ads on the same website is also an "inconvenient" element for users, they found that "there is more advertising than information. It should be noted that 13 respondents are irritated by banners with sound and one respondent explained that "these are banners like the others, but if you pass it with the cursor they make a weird sound." Faced with the presence of those banners on websites, respondents adopt different reactions. Seven of them try to avoid the banner, for example, one said: "I did not even look at them in order to avoid irritation", while others have a much stronger reaction "it annoys me so much that when I need that stuff I would not go to this brand." The presence of banners is not a source of irritation for some respondents, but when dealing with too large banners 14 respondents say they are very angry. For example, the one respondent explained: "I can only see that giant banner in the middle and nothing else".

        ii. **Pop-Ups:** Through interviews, pop-up were shown to be the most irritating form of advertising for respondents. In fact, 24 respondents do not support the presence of pop-ups on websites and found this form of advertising "very irritating". One respondent noted that "ads that open by themselves and appear in the middle of the page are very annoying". Respondents also insist on the lack of solution to remove these pop-ups which increases irritation. As well, the respondent who stated: "[...] and the worst part, there is no a red button so that I can close those windows." It seems that pop-ups are a very strong source of irritation for respondents as they were cited by more than half of respondents. This result was also confirmed by Helme-Guizon (2002) which found that pop-ups are a very irritating element. Windows that appears on their own and follow the user throughout its navigation were also cited by respondents as the pages of advertisements that open alone. Facing these various forms of pop-up, respondents have almost the same reaction. In fact, three respondents gave answers similar to that of one particular who noted: "I'm too pissed I leave the website immediately", while another respondent said: "I'm already pretty stressed by my work I will not also endure those advertisements that move". In conclusion, when faced with this kind of advertisements users adopt escape behavior to avoid irritation.

iii. **Video Advertising:** When discussing advertising spots on websites, respondents mention two types of irritating situations. The first is the presence of advertising spot without the possibility for the user to stop or mute the ad. This was mentioned by four respondents and it causes two types of reaction either the person leaves the site or she deactivates the mute button on his computer. The second situation is forcing the user to watch an advertising spot so he can access the site or watch a video. This was mentioned by 5 respondents and their reaction is unanimous "I leave the website. By what right it makes me look a spot? That's blackmail."

iv. **Advertising Mail:** According to the interviews, "spam emails" are a source of irritation for respondents. Indeed, nine respondents are bothered by emails sent by companies while they have not asked for anything. For example, the respondent 14 states that "companies are bombarding me with emails while it does not interest me".

b. **The Informational Content:** The informational content is a very important variable because during navigation on internet, users are primarily looking for information whatever their motivation (utilitarian or hedonic). Indeed, Helme-Guizon (2002) have shown that the informational content was the most irritating factor for the user. When respondents evoke the information found on the websites, they insist on five negatives aspects:

i. The lack of information on websites was mentioned by 16 respondents who do not find the information sought. This lack of information damages the reputation of the website given that respondents say they are disappointed and leave the website.

ii. The reliability of the information provided by some websites: This issue was raised by 4 respondents who find that certain websites are not reliable and they take information from social networks without checking if it is true or false.

iii. Websites that are not updated respondents are irritated by browsing a website and not finding any change compared to the course of events. For example, the respondent 22 states "I am surprised that some sites of certain brands of clothes are still in the winter collection when we are in the summer".

iv. Sites suggested by Google are not in accordance to the research initiated: Three of the respondents found that the Google results are the websites with the words they used, but when they click on these websites are that they don't find what they wanted.

v. Paying for information on respondent noted: "I am shocked, we are students and in order to access to a course I have to pay 10 euros, this is intolerable." Facing this irritating condition two respondents felt the same "no way to pay I'm sure I can find the same thing for free on another website."

c. **Navigability:** Through interviews and responses of informants, navigability concerns mainly the time of transfer of web pages. According to the study of Helme-Guizon (2002), the transfer time of web pages is not very irritating for users.

In this research, the transfer time seems to be quite irritating since it was mentioned by 18 respondents. It is a very irritating factor for respondents. Indeed, 18 of the respondents struggled with websites that are very slow to open and one explained that "To read an article or watch a video you have to wait an hour." Browsing the internet, users expect to find what they want quickly and this situation is not very appreciated by them. Evoking the transfer time, respondents also talked about videos that are buffering all the time in the streaming websites but in this situation the respondents have patience and wait until the video works. Respondent 37 says "I have no choice I have to wait, it is only on this website that I can see the lastest episodes from the USA."

2. **Hedonic Elements:** Hedonic elements correspond to website design, sound factors and functionality of the website.

    a. **Website Design:** The website design seems to be quite important for users who find nice to navigate on and pleasant websites with a minimum of decoration. During interviews, two factors about web design were mentioned by respondents. These are colors of the website and its architecture.

        i. **Colors:** Through interviews, respondents identified two situations where color provoked in them irritation. The first situation "*too flashy colors that hurt the eyes*" and this was considered very irritating to 4 respondents. The second situation concerns very dull colors that make the text illegible and it was perceived as irritating from seven respondents.

        ii. **Website Architecture:** When respondents talk about the architecture of the website, they insist on four negatives factors. The first aspect is related to congested websites; 10 respondents felt that the "congested" or "loaded" websites are very irritating, the respondent 23 states that "very cluttered websites where there is so much information, images and advertisements make me even forget the purpose of my visit..." The second negative aspect concerns the sections of the websites that are not very "clear" or are "put no matter how" or "poorly organized". This aspect has been considered very irritating to the respondents and the issue was raised by 16 of them. Indeed, while browsing a website, users want to find the right information in the right place. One respondent said "I'm sorry, but I don't have time to waste trying to guess where the information sought is". The third aspect concerns too "sophisticated" websites. Indeed, four respondents say they are upset by websites very "complicated" to handle. Thus, one respondent explained that "they believe it is innovation, whereas for me it's a true Chinese puzzle." The last negative aspect is the architecture of the website that is perceived by seven respondents as "ugly" or not very "original". The lack of originality was addressed especially to websites that two respondents claimed are "too basic and lacking in originality compared to websites that are much more original and organized."

    b. **Audible Factors:** Respondents expressed primarily on the presence of music on websites. In recalling music on websites, respondents highlighted three irritating or annoying situations. The first situation concerns the presence of music on websites, 7 respondents find it irritating. For example, a respondent explained that "if I need to listen to music, I would put on my computer". The second situation concerns the presence of music with the absence of the "mute" button. Confronted with this situation, the seven respondents say they are very upset and the respondent 29 says "I'm going crazy it stresses me, I look for the button, but there is none, I bangs for it to stop and ultimately I close the website". The third situation is related to the presence of rhythmic music.

c.   **Functionality:** The first type of irritation about Web sites with a single language and respondent 2 says "I'm not fluent in English and websites where I can't translate the text into French annoys me". The second type of irritation is related to the "copy / paste" on the website. Indeed, respondents often find interesting information they would like to copy but the site does not allow it.

Analysis of Irritation Sources Felt by Users on Websites Via Smartphone or Tablet

During this research, the interviewees were asked if they encountered sources of irritation during their navigation on websites using a smartphone or tablet. Once the analysis performed, it was possible to note that respondents encountered the same sources of irritation on the computer but there are also others that we will be classified in the category functionality. The first kind of irritation is related to web sites that are not adaptable with smartphones or tablets (non-responsive). One respondent said "websites that are not adapted to phones annoys me, I have to stretch or shrink, I cannot manipulate it". A different type of irritation was taken by our respondents, these websites that do not open and force them to download the application for access. One of our respondent states "it is not normal I do not want to download the application, why forcing me to do it I just need the site".

By connecting via their smartphone or tablet, users are using certain applications. They explained that the applications accounted also sometimes some sources of irritation such as updates, bugs or too heavy to downloaded applications.

Analysis of Irritating Sources Felt by Facebook Users Connected by Computers

During the content analysis on the sources of irritation on Facebook, 4 thematic units were identified. These four themes were then grouped into two broad categories namely "social factors" and "factors related to the use of the site".

1.   **Social Factors:** Respondents insist on interaction within groups and pages firstly and relationships with their friends and people they do not know secondly.
     a.   **Groups and Pages:** Groups and pages on Facebook are very important as they allow subscribers to talk about topics that interest them and meet new people who have the same interests. However, through interviews, it turned out that there is a lot of irritation caused by certain groups or pages.
          i.   **Group's Manipulation:** Through the interviews, respondents mentioned several irritating situations they experienced in Facebook groups. The first situation is related to fake groups. Indeed, 11 respondents were very irritated by fake groups who claim to be something but share and publish other things. Confronted with this situation, respondents left the group and even report it. One respondent stated "I feel betrayed, I left the group and I am disappointed by the dishonesty of the group in question". The second situation

concerns irritating videos or photos modified with Photoshop software, respondents find that some groups are having fun mounting photos and videos just to sow discord in the country or harm the reputation of people. A respondent said that "some groups have fun photoshoping images and it is obvious that this is not real but people believe and continue to criticize." The third irritating situation corresponds to groups that do not stop making publications. Being a fan of certain business pages, "Facebook fans" expect to find news of these companies and not to be bombarded with the same information throughout the day. For example, one respondent stated "I'm a fan of a brand and it turns out that this brand does not stop sharing every two minutes the same promotions it offers for one week, in the end it becomes heavy". The fourth situation concerns adding a person to a group without his permission. Confronted with this situation, respondents say they are very upset because they have the feeling to endure an obstacle to their freedom. For example, one respondent said that "sometimes they add me to a group without my permission, but by what authority? They can suggest me before adding me like that, "besides it happens with groups that are against my principles and my ideological positions". The latest situation concerns the videos of some groups that oblige respondents put "like" to other pages so they can view videos. Confronted with this situation, respondents give up watching the video because they feel manipulated by groups "Why should I like the pages that I do not like?"

b. **Violence in Groups:** Speaking of violence in groups, respondents mention two types of irritation. The first kind of irritation concerns "personal attacks on respectable people". Respondents find that on Facebook it is very easy to damage the reputation of people and spread out rumors about their families while they are "respectable" and "trustworthy". The second type of irritation is related to vulgarity and verbal violence in groups, seven respondents thought that people are frustrated because that they take advantage of not being able to see them and drop on Facebook "free insult".

c. **Friends or People:** Facebook is a social network that allows each subscriber to keep in touch with friends, family or even to meet new people. Through interviews, it seems evident that friends and people on Facebook can cause irritation to the user.

    i. **Friend's Behavior:** In recalling the behavior of their friend, respondents insist on seven irritant factors. The first factor irritating is related to friends who "reveal their lives on Facebook". Indeed, respondents find that Facebook is a way to stay in touch with with friends and exchange ideas and not to "share the lastest thing I've done" and one respondent added that "some people have no modesty even when they go to shower they publish it but this is madness!!!" The second negative aspect relates to the friends who share without verifying the reliability of information. Respondents describe these people as being "too naive" or "unconscious". The third aspect concerns the friends who spend their time on Facebook instead of working. In fact, two respondents say they are very irritated by people who spend their time on Facebook. For example, one respondent specified "[...] but it is amazing every time I log they are there if I did not know I would say they are unemployed while they have a work and family". The fourth aspect is the "mentality" of friends since 20 percent of respondents felt that with Facebook they discovered some faces of the personality of their friend they did not know before and this was a true "disappointment". Respondents describe the behaviors of their friends by using the terms "macho", "extremist", "uneducated", and "rude". The fifth aspect concerns the "curiosity of people", three respondents felt that Facebook has made people too curious. This can be seen in one response that noted: "they want to know everything as soon as I put a picture everybody wants to know when, where and with whom". The last negative point mentioned by respondents concerns the spelling level of their friends; some respondents say they are disappointed with the language level of some people.

d. **Invitations and Options:** Among the sources of irritation on Facebook, it is possible to mention invitations and options that Facebook offers. First of all, invitations to events and games are a real irritation for nine respondents who have yet to find a solution to avoid it "[...] there is not even an option to block it this is very troublesome". Then the people who send friend requests to strangers are also a source of irritation for 6 respondents who do not understand "why someone who does not know me want to become my friend". Finally, one respondent said that he was shocked by the option "delete a friend" that Facebook offers because for him it is an incitement to hatred "[...] but what is this option? Someone bothers me, I delete her, so if I reason by analogy in real life I conclude that if someone bothers me to kill her?".

2. **Factors Related to the Use of Facebook:** Through interviews, respondents identified two sources of irritation which are related to the use of Facebook; informational content and updates.

a. **Informational Content:** On Facebook, informational content is presented in different forms. Indeed, there are articles, videos, photos and discussions between subscribers. Respondents insist on two sources of irritation, the first type of irritation concerns the rumors and misinformation. Indeed, 23 respondents felt that Facebook is a source of information "very dangerous" and "not reliable". Thus, one respondent spoke of misinformation and another noted that "seeing the same information in three versions in less than 5 minutes, we do not know which information should be taken". The second type of irritation is related to the excessive presence of political information. Respondents feel that this has become "boring" and "irritating". In fact, for 7 respondents Facebook is basically a means of entertainment and reunion between friends who, over time, turned into "TV news".

b. **Version and Security:** Facebook versions correspond to the updates made by the leaders of this social network. Indeed, at every update subscriber is facing a new version and through interviews, it appears that the updates irritate some respondents. Safety on Facebook can be controlled by the subscriber through the privacy settings.

i. **Updates:** Through interviews, Respondents highlighted the irritation caused by the updates made by Facebook. The first one concerns the frequent changes of versions and this was mentioned by 25 respondents who felt that Facebook is changing too often versions and one respondent said that "every two weeks there is a new version, but it is not possible I barely managed to adapt to the previous that Mr. Zuckerberg puts us another". The second is related to the complexity of the new versions. Indeed, another respondent felt that new versions that Facebook offers are "very complicated" and that "I should have a degree in computer science in order to understand them". The third irritating factor concerns the fact of being obliged to adhere to the new version. Indeed, as for "adding to a group without permission" and "Becoming a fan of a group to watch a video", internet users do not like to be forced to do anything because they feel "controlled" and "manipulated". Confronted with this situation, respondents fit although they prefer to have the choice. The latest irritating factor is concerning options of the new version because with the latest "as soon as a person I know doing something I get a notification and vice versa". Respondents find that this option is very irritating and that it "hurts their privacy" because they do not necessarily want others to see what they do.

c. **Confidentiality:** Throughout the interviews, respondents talked of 4 sources of irritation caused by confidentiality. Eighteen respondents are irritated by the change in privacy settings every time Facebook changes version and one respondent stated: "[...] if Facebook modify version and I do not open my account during this time will my data be accessible to everyone given that each change of version of Facebook puts privacy parameters to zero." The second irritating factor on confidentiality on Facebook concerns piracy. Indeed, 12 respondents said they had been hacked at least once and in this situation, respondents blame Facebook privacy settings they describe as "not very reliable". The third situation involves the fact that Facebook has the right to retain all subscriber data. One respondent explained that "from the beginning I am aware that by signing up to Facebook I allow it to have all my data but it annoys me anyway". The latest irritating factor is related to finding pictures "private" on Google images and one respondent explained that "recently I realized that most of my Facebook photos that are normally accessible only my friends are displayed on Google !!! I'm just shocked."

Analysis of Irritation Sources Felt by Facebook Users Via Smartphone / Tablet

During this research, interviewees were asked if they encounter irritating factors during their navigation on Facebook using a smartphone or tablet. Once the analysis performed, it was possible to note that respondents encountered not only the sources of irritation felt using a computer but also other sources of irritation that we will rank in the "factors related to the use of the Facebook". The first irritating factor on Facebook application is that it stops occasionally or blocks on "tablet or smartphone". The respondent 37 says "I prefer to use Facebook on my pc at least there is no bug as with the tablet". The second source of irritating factor is the fact to make a "copy / paste". According to respondents, on some mobile devices it is difficult or sometimes impossible to copy information on Facebook using a smartphone or tablet. Among the encountered irritating factor on the Facebook application, 12 of the respondents mentioned that on tablet or smartphone, the loupe that exists in groups to make a search does not exist. It must be connected by computer to use this loupe. Finally, some interviewees expressed their irritation due to the fact that Messenger (private messages on Facebook) is a separate application which must be downloaded to access to message.

1. Reactions of Internet Users Face of Irritation on Websites

Confronting irritation encountered during their navigation on internet using different devices (computer, tablet, smartphone), respondents adopt different behaviors. Through the analysis of the content, three kinds of reactions occurred.

There are reactions depending on the importance of the website. If the website or application are really important to them, respondents remain despite the irritation. For example, a respondent stated: "I do not have a choice, if I know that I can't not find the information somewhere else, I have to stay". However, if the site is not very important and they know they can find the information somewhere else respondents leave the website directly. These two reactions were also cited in Helme-Guizon (2002). Some respondents reported reacting to irritation depending on their degree. Indeed, if the irritation is

Table 3. Summary of irritants factors on websites and Facebook using different devices (Computer, tablet, Smartphone)

	Irritating Factors on Websites	
Irritating utilitarian elements	**Advertising:** Concerns various types of ads, there are banner ads, pop-ups, ad spots and spams.	
	Informational Content: Refers to the information and its reliability.	
	Navigability: Corresponds to the heaviness of the website and mobile applications and the slowness of download.	
Irritating functional elements	**Design:** Regards colors and architecture of the website.	
	Audible Factors: Corresponds to the music found on the websites.	
	Functionalities: Concern the "featured" options that can suggest a website to be distinguished from others, They also concerns the websites that are not adapted to different devices.	
	Irritating Factors on Facebook	
Irritating social factors	**Groups/Pages:** Concerns manipulating groups and violence within these groups.	
	People/Friends: Refers to the irritating behavior of some people and unwanted invitations.	
Irritating factors related to the use	**Informational Content:** Corresponds to distorted news and rumors.	
	Updates and Confidentiality: Includes updates made by Facebook for versions and privacy settings that, in principle, ensure account security.	
	Irritation of the Facebook Application: Concerns the absence of the loupe in tablet and smartphone, download the messenger apart, no copy / paste, the heaviness of the application.	

not very strong 10 respondents declared continuing navigation without any problems. However, if the irritation is too strong respondents adopt avoidance behavior by leaving the website. It should be noted that by leaving the website, some respondents declared they will never come back in the future (this reaction is the most probable it was mentioned by 25 respondents) others declared they will come back to check if there have been changes. Through content analysis, other reactions occurred. Among these reactions, ask for help to a friend. In fact, two respondents seek help to a close person "I'm so upset that I asked for help because in my state I know I would not be able to continue navigating although it is very important for me". The second type of behavior is very rare and it was mentioned by one respondent.

2. Reactions of Internet Users Face of Irritation on Facebook

When analyzing the reactions of internet users facing irritation on Facebook (website or application), it turned out that they have different reactions.

Dealing with manipulating groups and violence that takes place there, respondents adopt two types of reactions. The first reaction is very common, it is to leave the group by deleting it and respondent 5 says that "I am disappointed and feel betrayed so I delete the group". The second reaction is stronger than the first, it is to leave the group and report it, and the respondent 14 states that "there are Facebook groups so dangerous that I do not hesitate to report them". Confronting irritating behaviors of their friends and unwanted invitations, respondents adopt five types of reactions. The first reaction is to delete the person who has an unpleasant behavior. The second reaction is related to hiding the latest news of the person. The third reaction is the fact of blocking unwanted invitations and the fourth one is related to disabling Facebook, and the last reaction is to block out invitations to games.

Confronting frequent changes of versions and privacy settings that are not very reliable according to some respondents, two types of behavior emerged through interviews, the first reaction concerns security settings it is materialized by constant checking these parameters. Respondent 26 explains that "I become paranoid I did not stop checking the security settings for fear a sick person having access to my information". The second reaction is related to the changes in versions, in this situation the majority of respondents say they have no particular reaction, they adapt. Respondent 8 says, "I have no choice even if it pisses me off I try to familiarize myself with it I cannot do otherwise".

Confronting multiple rumors and information, respondents have become very distrustful of the information they find on Facebook, for this reason, they adopt two different types of behaviors. Some respondents said they check all the information before sharing it and others prefer not to look at the information on Facebook, For example, the respondent 9 states "Facebook is not a reliable source of information if I need information I will read a newspaper". Finally, regarding the irritation felt by using the Facebook application, respondents say they have no particular reaction because they do not really have a choice and there is not a substitute solution.

MANAGERIAL RECOMMENDATIONS

Through interviews, irritation on websites and Facebook seems to be very present. In this section, some recommendations that will help designers of websites and community managers will be suggested.

Sources of Irritation on Websites Using a Computer, Smartphone, or Tablet

Respondents evoked advertising, information, navigability, the website design, music and functionalities as sources of irritation on a website. People are exposed to advertising every day on the radio, on TV, in the streets, in the malls, in their mailboxes and on the internet. Suddenly, they feel stifled and manipulated by companies. So it would be better for websites managers to avoid large banners, to set the option to mute commercials, to not oblige the user to look at advert to access the websites. Information is very important for users, therefore websites managers need to update their website, check the reliability of the information they provide on the website, be sure to reference their site on engines research and provide

Table 4. Summary of results for reactions to irritation on the Facebook website and application

Reactions	Themes
Reactions to irritation on websites	Depending on the importance of the website
	Depending on the degree of irritation
	Other types of reactions
Reactions to irritation on Facebook	Reactions related to irritation in groups
	Reactions related to the irritation caused by friends
	Reactions to Information
	Reactions to confidentiality and updates
	Reactions to the Facebook application

information to users for free or for a reasonable price. internet users are impatient and want everything immediately so it would be better for websites not charge too much their site with text, images and videos so their website becomes less slow. The website design is important to respondents. For this reason, websites designers should not neglect it and it would be appropriate to use warm colors but not very flashy, do not put the information in "bulk", well organized topics put all information in the adequate category and adopt innovative architecture but simple and easy to understand. Music is also a source of irritation for some respondents. We advise web designers to not use rhythmic music and provide a mute button in case the user does not want to listen. Finally, it would be better for websites designers to make their website available in several languages. Thus, it could be visited by several targets (different languages and/or countries) and enable the "copy/paste" if they accept that people have their information. Companies should also make a mobile version of their site that can adapt to all types of devices.

Sources of Irritation on Facebook Using a Computer, Tablet, or Smartphone

By joining a group or becoming a fan of a page, respondents expect to find information concerning the group or _ page in a good mood in an atmosphere of mutual exchange. For these reasons, it would be interesting for directors of groups and pages Indicate the purpose of the group from the beginning, avoid publishing the same thing all the time, check the comments judged "violent", "displaced" from some people, avoid forcing people to join a group or to watch a video and check the reliability of some photos or videos before sharing. According to the interviewees, the Facebook application on tablet or smartphone causes some irritation as the absence of loupe, the application is stopped or the "messenger" which is a program in itself. It would be preferable to find some solutions to avoid any inconvenience to the user.

CONCLUSION

By examining the different results, we conclude that the irritation is quite present on websites and on Facebook using different devices. Today we talk about the customer as a "king" (or "queen") because they are spoiled and know they can have what they want, when they want – especially on the internet. Besides, individuals are surfing the internet, using various devices such as smartphones, computers, tablets, and other smart objects like Smart-TVs and game consoles. So, at the slightest irritating factor they know they can find happiness elsewhere. As explained above, irritating factors can lead to leave the website or app and never use it again, that's why identifying them is crucial. It is somewhat nonsensical to spend money on advertising to attract individuals to use an app or to visit a website, and they permanently leave it because they will find those irritating factors. This chapter highlighted the different irritating factors and their impact on internet users throughout a qualitative research, aiming to enhance the user experience.

The managerial interest from this study is helping managers of websites and apps and community managers to reduce sources of irritation and to better understand the behavior of internet users to try to better meet their needs. The results found can help professionals to better understand the sources of irritation that provoke in the visitor reactions that can harm their site. The theoretical value of this study is to address a problem that, until now to our knowledge, has not been treated before. On the other hand, exploring irritating factors on mobile devices will help marketers to design efficient mobile advertising campaigns.

However, it should be noted that this research holds a certain number of limitations, such as the lack of literature on sources of irritation. Indeed, apart from the work of Helme Guizon (2002) on the sources of irritation on internet there are no other references. The second limitation is related to the age range of interviewees, only youth (15-35 years old).

FUTURE RESEARCH DIRECTIONS

The limitations of this study allow suggestion of some future directions. Indeed, it would be appropriate to verify whether the sources of irritation are the same to over 35 years. Furthermore, a comparison between Irritating factors felt by the 15-35 years old and the over 35 years old might be useful. It will be also interesting to verify and compare the irritating factors felt on other social networks and medias such as Youtube and Twitter using different devices. Finally, developing a measurement scale that would quantify the negative emotions experienced by consumers on the internet would give both practitioners ant researchers a solid tool for their future Market-studies and researches.

REFERENCES

Agnihotri, R., Dingus, R., Hu, M. Y., & Krush, M. T. (2016). Social media: Influencing customer satisfaction in B2B sales. *Industrial Marketing Management*, *53*, 172–180. doi:10.1016/j.indmarman.2015.09.003

Balagué, C., & Fayon, D. (2010). *Facebook, Twitter and the others: integrate social networks into a business strategy*. Pearson Editions.

Bardin, L. (1996). Content analysis. Paris: SAGE Publications Ltd.

Belk, W. (2013). Extended Self in a Digital World. *The Journal of Consumer Research*, *40*(3), 477–500. doi:10.1086/671052

Ben Dahmane Mouelhi, N., Hassen, S., & Souissi, N. (2009). An exploratory approach to sources of irritation felt by the French customer in hotels in Tunisia. *Revue Marocaine de Recherche en Management et Marketing*, (2-3), 137 – 156.

boyd, d., & Ellison, N. B. (2007). Social Network Sites: Definition, History, and Scholarship. *Journal of Computer-Mediated Communication*, *13*(2), 210–230.

Byrne, Z. S., Dvorak, K. J., Peters, J. M., Ray, I., Howe, A., & Sanchez, D. (2016). From the users perspective: Perceptions of risk relative to benefit associated with using the internet. *Computers in Human Behavior*, *59*, 456–468. doi:10.1016/j.chb.2016.02.024

Cawsey, T., & Rowley, J. (2016). Social media brand building strategies in B2B companies. *Marketing Intelligence & Planning*, *34*(Iss: 6), 754–776. doi:10.1108/MIP-04-2015-0079

Chang, J. E., Simpson, T. W., Rangaswamy, A., & Tekchadaney, J. R. (2002). *A good website can convey the wrong brand image! A preliminary report*. Working paper. E-Business Research Center (EBRC), University of Pennsylvania.

Childers, T. L., Carr, C. L., Peck, J., & Carson, S. (2001). Hedonic and Utilitarian Motivations for Online Retail Shopping Behavior. *Journal of Retailing, 77*(4), 511–535. doi:10.1016/S0022-4359(01)00056-2

Dahnil, M. I., Marzuki, K. M., Langgat, J., & Fabeil, N. F. (2014). Factors influencing SMEs adoption of social media marketing. *Procedia: Social and Behavioral Sciences, 148*, 119–126. doi:10.1016/j.sbspro.2014.07.025

DAstous, A. (2000). Irritating aspects of the shopping environment. *Journal of Business Research, 49*(2), 149–156. doi:10.1016/S0148-2963(99)00002-8

Edosomwan, S., Prakasan, S. K., Kouame, D., Watson, J., & Seymour, T. (2011). The history of social media and its impact on business. *Journal of Applied Management and Entrepreneurship, 16*(3), 79–91.

Eroglu, S. A., Machleit, K. A., & Davis, L. M. (2001). Atmospheric Qualities of Online Retailing: A Conceptual Model and Implications. *Journal of Business Research, 54*(2), 177–184. doi:10.1016/S0148-2963(99)00087-9

Felix, R., Rauschnabel, P. A., & Hinsch, C. (2016). Elements of Strategic Social Media Marketing: A Holistic Framework. *Journal of Business Research.*

Forsé, M. (2012). Today's Social Networks. *OFCE Revue, 7*, 155–169.

Helme-Guizon, A. (2002). *Sources and consequences of the irritation felt during navigation on a retail website. An exploratory study.* 18th AFM International Symposium, Lille, France.

Jacob, C. (2005). *The influence of the music of a business website on consumer responses* (PhD Thesis). Rennes1 University.

Koh, J., Kim, Y. G., Butler, B., & Bock, G. W. (2007). Encouraging participation in virtual communities. *Communications of the ACM, 50*(2), 68–73. doi:10.1145/1216016.1216023

Lamberton, C., & Stephen, A. T. (2016). A thematic exploration of digital, social media, and mobile marketing researches evolution from 2000 to 2015 and an agenda for future research. *Journal of Marketing, 27*(6), 146–172. doi:10.1509/jm.15.0415

Lenhart, A., & Madden, M. (2007). Social networking websites and teens: An overview. Pew Research Center/Internet.

Mayol, S. (2011). *Marketing 3.0.* Dunod Editions.

Milgram, S. (1969). Interdisciplinary thinking and the small world problem. *Interdisciplinary Relationships in the Social Sciences*, 103-20.

Miserski, R. (1982). An attribution explanation of the disproportionate influence of unfavorable information. *The Journal of Consumer Research, 9*(3), 301–310. doi:10.1086/208925

Pelet, J. E., Taieb, B., & Ben Dahmane Mouelhi, N. (2016). From m-commerce website's design to behavioral intentions. *Information and Management Association Symposium.*

Sakas, D. P., Dimitrios, N. K., & Kavoura, A. (2015). The Development of Facebooks Competitive Advantage for Brand Awareness. *Procedia Economics and Finance, 24*, 589–597. doi:10.1016/S2212-5671(15)00642-5

Shaver, P., Schwarz, J., Kirson, D., & OConnor, C. (1987). Emotion Knowledge: Further exploration of a prototype approach. *Journal of Personality and Social Psychology, 52*(2), 1061–1086. doi:10.1037/0022-3514.52.6.1061 PMID:3598857

Touzani, M., Khedri, M., & Ben Dahmane Mouelhi, N. (2007), An exploratory approach to sources of irritation felt during a shopping activity: case of food predominantly malls. *6th Marketing Trends International Symposium.*

Turley, L. W., & Milliman, R. E. (2000). Atmospheric effects on shopping behavior: A review of the experimental evidence. *Journal of Business Research, 49*(2), 193–211. doi:10.1016/S0148-2963(99)00010-7

Volle, P. (2000). From marketing of points of sale to the merchant websites: Specificities, opportunities and research questions. *Revue Française du Marketing, 177 /178*(2/3), 83–101.

Vošner, H. B., Bobek, S., Kokol, P., & Krečič, M. J. (2016). Attitudes of active older internet users towards online social networking. *Computers in Human Behavior, 55*, 230–241. doi:10.1016/j.chb.2015.09.014

ENDNOTES

[1] http://www.blogdumoderateur.com/50-chiffres-medias-sociaux-2016/

[2] http://www.blogdumoderateur.com/50-chiffres-medias-sociaux-2016/

[3] http://www.leptidigital.fr/reseaux-sociaux/profil-demographique-utilisateurs-reseaux-sociaux-4924/

This research was previously published in Mobile Platforms, Design, and Apps for Social Commerce edited by Jean-Éric Pelet, pages 135-152, copyright year 2017 by Business Science Reference (an imprint of IGI Global).

Chapter 50
Analyzing Blending Social and Mass Media Audiences Through the Lens of Computer–Mediated Discourse

Asta Zelenkauskaite[1]
Drexel University, USA

ABSTRACT

In recent years, mass media content has undergone a blending process with social media. Large amounts of text-based social media content have not only shaped mass media products, but also provided new opportunities to access audience behaviors through these large-scale datasets. Yet, evaluating a plethora of audience contents strikes one as methodologically challenging endeavor. This study illustrates advantages and applications of a mixed-method approach that includes quantitative computer-mediated discourse analysis (CMDA) and automated analysis of content frequency. To evaluate these methodologies, audience comments consisting of Facebook comments and SMS mobile texting to Italian radio-TV station RTL 102.5 were analyzed. Blended media contents through computer-mediated discourse analysis expand horizons for theoretical and methodological audience analysis research in parallel to established audience analysis metrics.

INTRODUCTION

Social media have transformed not only media consumption and production, but also the audiences (Livingstone, 2004). Increased non-professional audience content integration in mass media settings thus is an observed trend, rather than an exception (Karlsen, Sundet, Syvertsen, & Ytreberg, 2009). User contributions through social media in the past years constitute a large variety of online content exchanges (Doyle, 2010). In addition to call-in participation, mass media companies have expanded audience contributions through text-based communication, known as "backchannels" (Herring, 2004). Audiences contribute to the mass media programs – ranging from entertainment to political debates, and

DOI: 10.4018/978-1-5225-5637-4.ch050

news – with tweets, Facebook messages, and mobile texting. Currently, text-based participation expanded through social networking sites. Increased user contributions, particularly in online environments, have been ascribed to "prosumer culture" (Jenkins, 2006). Bruns (2010) discussed professional and amateur content blurring in terms of "produsage" where users not only read contents but also share, rate, and exchange comments on social media outlets. In light of increased social media, audience research is presented with new challenges to meaningfully analyzing audiences' contents.

While challenging, text-based contributions opened opportunities to study audience behaviors where user-based programming has been particularly popular, especially in European, Latin American contexts with growing popularity in Asia. Audience contribution through text messaging formats was analyzed in Norwegian contexts (Beyer, Enli, Maasø, & Ytreberg, 2007; Enli, 2007). User interactions through text were studied in Italian settings (Zelenkauskaite & Herring, 2008a). Texting as a form of personal ads were analyzed in a Lithuanian (Zelenkauskaite & Herring, 2008b), Spanish and Colombian cases were compared by Mafé, Blas, and Tavera-Mesías (2010), to name a few. In these text-based, mediated environments, user interaction with the program was predominantly based via text-based technologies such as mobile phone texting. Subsequently, audience contributions were extended to social networking sites such as Facebook (Beyer et al., 2007; Enli, 2007; Enli & Syvertsen, 2007; Mafé et al., 2010; Zelenkauskaite & Herring, 2008a; Zelenkauskaite & Herring, 2008b).

With growing popularity of social media and increasing amount of user-based contents, methodological challenges are still lingering. Challenges include the large-scale dataset management, time sensitivity of user-generated content (UGC), the dynamic nature of the content, and no predefined consistency in content flows. These challenges, related to audience contributions, highlight the need to re-evaluated audiences' analysis methodologically. The need to re-configure methodological trajectories in studying audiences becomes especially pronounced in the recent decade when media are becoming more multiplatform (Blythe & Cairns, 2009; Livingstone, 1999; 2004) in the context of "convergence culture" (Jenkins, 2006). Despite new opportunities that social media and interpersonal media bring to the study of mass media audiences, little research has been devoted to the analysis of text-based audience interactions through social media.

To address methodological issues, computer-mediated discourse analysis has proven to be a useful tool to analyze user communicative practices and behaviors in online settings (Herring, 2001; 2004; 2007). CMDA has been further extended to account for convergent media settings that combine mass media and social media (Herring, 2009; 2013). The goal here is to examine advantages and shortcomings of automated tools comparing them with manually coded CMDA and to evaluate the utility of CMDA as an approach to large-scale datasets.

The article is structured as follows. The article first explicates the CMDA. Next, it discusses the intertwined nature of audience research is presented in light of social media and mass media paradigms. Computer-mediated discourse analysis is illustrated as a bridging tool that analyses audience in the era of multimodal mass communication. Then, CMDA approach is applied to a case study analysis of Italian multimodal Radio-TV-Web station RTL 102.5. Finally, it provides theoretical, methodological, and practical implications of this approach and looks at various pitfalls that can plague audience analysis by using quantitative discourse analysis approach.

BACKGROUND

Computer-Mediated Discourse Analysis Explicated

To analyze audiences' behaviors in blended media environments, computer-mediated discourse analysis was applied in this study. Herring (2004) defines computer-mediated discourse in the following way:

CMDA as an approach to researching online behavior provides a methodological toolkit and a set of theoretical lenses through which to make observations and interpret the results of empirical analysis. (p. 4)

The CMDA approach resides in a linguistic discourse analysis tradition and involves the micro-linguistic, context-independent level of structure, and the macro hierarchical level, as well as, the participation level of a given social phenomenon (Herring, 2011). Micro-linguistic and structure-based analyses have been extensively applied in various online media contexts that range from interpersonal media to social media. Micro-linguistic and structure-based computer-mediated discourse analysis is predominantly based on manual coding and frequency of the categories. It is a useful framework for various units of analyses that range from structure, meaning, interaction, and social behavior (Herring, 2004).

Computer-mediated discourse analysis was proven to be a valuable tool to analyze online linguistic behaviors not only on a micro-level but also on a content-independent structural level. Examples of the latter include a comprehensive analysis of instant message exchanges in a dyadic setting that was performed on around 2,000 utterances (Baron, 2010). Structure and discourse strategies such as sequential organization of messages in dyadic exchanges were analyzed through CMDA. Individual communicative styles were compared in two different contexts: short text messages communication and IM communication (Ling & Baron, 2007). The analysis provided insights about the differences between communicative practices in these two modes. Text messages were found to be longer, contained more contractions compared to IM messages. Short-message service exchanges have presented rich data revealing turn-taking and interactional coherence strategies as ways to assess social presence (Spagnolli & Gamberini, 2007). The meaning of small talk on users' online wall posts on social networking site Orkut revealed politeness strategies among its participants (Das, 2010). Micro-level computer-mediated language analysis of mobile texting in Swedish contexts revealed disambiguation communicative strategies in mediated environments (Hård af Segerstad, 2005). Text-based comments left to Spanish Youtube videos were used to analyze users' linguistic expression (Bou-Franch, Lorenzo-Dus, & Blitvich, 2012). Twitter tweet posts were analyzed to study emergent practices of user interaction by using the @ sign (Honeycutt & Herring, 2009).

CMDA approach has been thus further theorized to account for communication in multimodal environments (Androutsopoulos & Beißwenger, 2008; Herring, 2009). Herring (2009) defines multimodal interactive environments as convergent media computer-mediated communication or CMCMC as environments, distinct due to interactive component which is often secondary by design and accompanies the main information or entertainment-related activities such as television. Examples of CMCMC include interactive television where mass media content is primary by design, while user social interaction broadcast concurrently is secondary. CMDA has been thus a valuable approach to study micro-level meanings that underlie audience exchanges in CMCMC. A fine-grained manual coding of text message exchanges in interactive television revealed the lack of coherence in television-mediated interactions (Zelenkauskaite & Herring, 2008a).

Analyzing Changing Audiences

Active audience participation has been studied since the inception of mass media. Talk radio programs in particular provided a solid ground to research active audiences. Audience call-in participation and the manner in which host interacts with audiences was analyzed by employing qualitative discourse analysis (Hutchby, 1996). In digital contexts, MacGregor (2007) proposed to study feedback traffic as an instant quantitative measurement of audience behavior, given that online environments provide the possibilities to attend to such behaviors. Similarly, mass media outlets started to devote attention to audience behaviors through social media. Audiences' comments are increasingly brought for the editorial considerations in newsroom meetings (Lowrey & Woo, 2010). In light of increasing readers' comments, blogger comments were also taken into account as a source in the newsrooms (Howe, 2007; Klein, 2009; Lowrey & Mackay, 2008; Lowrey & Woo, 2010). Thus, in previous mass media contexts, according to contribution level, audiences' voices have been placed along a continuum from passive viewers to fan cultures (Abercrombie & Longhurst, 1998; Jenkins, 2006).

As a result, audience participation challenges classical perception of audience analysis not only theoretically, but also methodologically (Carpentier, 2007; Doyle, 2010). Livingstone (1999) underlines the need to reconceptualize mass audiences:

Mediated communication is no longer simply or even mainly mass communication (from one to many) but rather the media now facilitate communication among peers (one to one and many to many). (p. 4)

Livingstone (1999), thus, emphasizes the changing nature of the audiences, where audiences' communicative needs go beyond interaction with mass media outlets. The need to study audiences in a context of social media is related to the shift from a media-centric view to an audience-centric view. Audience-centric view entails that audiences' needs are regarded as a key aspect. Digital media use and increased ways of audience feedback have drawn attention to media companies. In the news contexts, feedback monitoring has emerged as an increasingly popular phenomenon due to an audience's comment availability (McKenzie, Lowrey, Hays, Chung, & Woo, 2012).

Audience analysis in the digital era reconfigures the notions of audience analysis in various ways, thus providing new challenges and opportunities to audience analysis. The first challenge of audience analysis is based on the premise audience fragmentation. In a cross-platform realm, audiences are more mobile, thus they tune-in the programming whenever they are on thus questioning the concept of a solidified mass audience (Livingstone, 2004). Fragmentation also provides new opportunities to get multifaceted insights about audiences.

The second challenge reflects the spatial dimension. Conceptualized as audience spatial dispersion, it was proposed as a contributing factor to audiences' invisibility (McQuail, 1997). Mass audiences do not belong to any given space. Social media concentrate mass audiences around a given mass media outlet. Through contributions or engagement with audience text-based contributions, mass audiences are physically present through their texts in a social media stream.

Finally, audiences' invisibility (McQuail, 1997) is considered as another challenge of audience analysis. Mass media audiences have been categorized as "outside of the range of direct observation and record" (McQuail, 1997, p. 6). Yet, this study shows that audiences become visible through social media and mobile phone contributions to the programming. Thus, by studying audiences through the lens of social media it is possible to account for two challenges that were pointed out by McQuail (1997) in mass media contexts – the visibility of audiences or the direct access to the audiences and the juxtaposition of the audiences in a given space.

Blended Audience in Multiplatform Settings

The changing aspect of audiences is based on the blending nature between mass audience and online users. Blended audiences are particularly pronounced in multiplatform settings. Through the process of contributions to online and mass media, audiences blend with no clear distinction between mass media audiences and online users. Through the blending process, media platforms no longer compartmentalize audiences – the same audiences are present in multiple platforms. Blending audiences is operationalized as audiences that extend the notion of mass media audiences to social media. Specifically, blending mass media audiences comprise mass media audiences as well as social media users who engage with mass media products through social media. Thus, audiences' contributions are becoming increasingly integral part of mass media contexts (Bolin, 2010; Livingstone, 1999).

The blending process of the audiences intersects social and mass media, once the Internet was attributed to function as a mass medium (Moris & Ogan, 1996). The active side of user contribution constitutes a shared component between the Internet and mass media. Users' experiences in online environments have been theorized as early as 1990, when the interactive nature of online environments had been first observed (Rafaeli, 1988) and compared to mass media contexts (Rafaeli, 1989). Interactive applications in the last decade became ubiquitous in the social media scene, and then moved to the mass media realm. Thus, with the increased social media feedback, users become co-producers of the content and become visible not only to the broadcasters, but also to the other audience members (Bruns, 2010).

In the social media paradigm, users' behaviors started to be explored based on their contribution frequency, as well as linguistic expression. User contributions have been analyzed not only to study the contents but as a proxy to classify online users and their behaviors. For example, in Wikipedia contexts, users have been analyzed through their contribution quantity and nature of contributions (Ortega, Gonzalez-Barahona, & Robles, 2008; Viégas, Wattenberg, Kriss, & Ham, 2007); users were classified by the longevity – the time spent and contribution frequency in various Wikipedia namespaces (Zelenkauskaite & Massa, 2011); user-editor interrelation with text-based article contents were analyzed through content contributions (Iba, Nemoto, Peters, & Gloor, 2010). Linguistic expression was used to classify Youtube users through interaction types through content tagging (Paolillo, 2008).

The present study is based on an overarching question which asks: How to account for the blended audiences that involve social media mass media? In particular, this study aims to answer the following questions: What are recurrent content topics discussed through social media and to whom are the contents addressed in an automatically extracted large-scale corpus compared to manually-coded corpus? How does the nature of contents evolve over time?

METHOD

To analyze the nature of audiences' interactions and addressees to whom contents are directed through social media outlets, a leading interactive Italian radiovision[2] RTL 102.5 was studied. RTL 102.5 started out as radio and expanded to TV, and the Web radio. With the rise of social media, the station started integrating text-based audience contributions. In addition to listening to the radio and call-ins, audience members can send a text message (SMS) from their phone or comment on the station's Facebook wall whenever, just as they do in their interpersonal networks. RTL 102.5 case serves as an example of the technologically forward-looking radio station. It pioneered integrating social media outlets starting with mobile texting in 2001 and audience contribution via Facebook in 2009.

RTL 102.5 uses a radio talk show format for part of its programming, which is heavily dependent on the audience. Viewers and listeners therefore may function as co-producers of the programming content (Enli & Syvertsen, 2007). There are no specific guidelines given to the audiences with regards to the acceptable content types. Audiences are simply given a phone number to which they can send a message which is advertised during the program on the bottom of the screen, as well as announced by the speakers in a given program. In addition, once messages from Facebook are integrated, RTL 102.5's Facebook wall URL is provided as well on the bottom of the screen of the televised version of the program. SMS messages were first integrated by RTL 102.5 in 2003 as a result of an agreement between the Acotel group and the station. Even now, RTL 102.5 listener calls are only broadcast twice during a two-hour program on average, while the incorporation of SMS and Facebook messages is much higher, especially in the radiovision part of the program where messages are displayed on TV screens.

RTL 102.5 station is available on at least three types of platforms: radio, television (satellite and digital terrestrial television, channel 750), and internet with live streaming of both radio and television. It is also possible to download applications that allow for connections to radio via cell phones (smartphones). The station broadcasts on all the platforms simultaneously. Programming runs 7 days a week, 24 hours a day. Most of the programs are divided into two-hour time slots. During all these programs, audience members can send messages to the programs, either via SMS or by posting on the program's Facebook wall. The station decides which messages to include in the program to be broadcast. This radio-TV station has on average five million listeners a day and is one of the top radio stations' in Italy according to average listeners per day (Audiradio, 2009).

Figure 1 displays a screen shot how messages appear on televised version of the radio which can be accessed via tradition television and also digital terrestrial TV on channel 750. The same screen can also be viewed on RTL's website by choosing online streaming via audiovision.

The bottom of the screen is graphically divided by a horizontal line. In Figure 1 the space below the line contains an SMS message with text in Italian: *Sorellina ti voglio tanto bene! Daniela* ['My little sister, I love you so much! Daniela']. This is one of the messages sent by the spectators and listeners of RTL that was selected to be broadcast during the program. At the top-left corner of the screen is RTL 102.5 's logo and the clock indicating time. The top-right corner contains the name of the singer in the music video being played and the title of the song that is being sung at the moment.

Audience contribution via mobile texting (SMS) is stored on the RTL 102.5 website, "community" section. It contains a complete list of the 200 most recent SMS messages that were sent to the program by their audiences. Messages are displayed as they are posted in real time in reverse chronological order, with the newest messages replacing the oldest ones. Archived messages includes the date, the time (hour, minute, second), and the text of the message (that contains up to 160 characters with spaces – the regular length of a typical SMS message).

RTL 102.5 also encourages audience contributions via the RTL 102.5 Facebook group profile. Audience members who are Facebook subscribers are encouraged to leave comments on the group's wall. Comments left on a subsection of the group's wall titled *youONair* are sometimes selected for broadcasting. Anyone willing to post on or read the RTL 102.5 Facebook wall's *youONair* section must first confirm it by clicking the "like" button. A list of Facebook users who "liked" this section's Facebook group can

*Figure 1. RTL 102.5 television screenshot: televised version with SMS message (March 22, 2011). (©
2012, RTL 102.5. Used with permission.)*

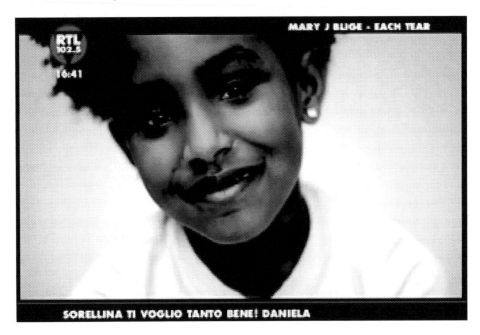

be seen in the left corner below the RTL logo. By December 12, 2010, 300,745 people had "liked" it.
Messages for potential broadcast have to be placed in the *youONair* section, which states the following
at the top: *Scrivi il tuo messaggio che potrebbe essere visualizzato in "Radiovisione" sul canale 750
di Sky e tv digitale* ['Write your message; it could be shown in *Radiovision* on the Sky 750 channel or
digital terrestrial.'] There were 15,794 "likes" below this post, indicating that many audience members
are eager to have their messages aired. The "like" button is followed by a button for "Audiovision"
which links directly to the RTL website's live streaming of the program. Messages posted by audience
members are displayed in reverse chronological order. Similar to other Facebook pages, each message
is accompanied by the user's profile picture, first name, last name, the text of the message, and the time
when the message was posted (date, hour, minutes). Messages do not bear additional costs from RTL
102.5, except for the mobile provider fees for SMS.

Data

Data for RTL 102.5 case study were collected from 1st January 2011 to 30th April 2011: sample comprised
a total of 370,491 messages that combine SMS (*N*=308,339); and Facebook messages (*N*=62,152). All
these messages were sent by the audience members, reflecting a high audience contribution level to this
station. From the total sample, the following stratified samples were used to perform further analyses.
To contextualize the frequency of the messages over time, a composite week was constructed. Composite week sampling comprises a random sample of seven days of the week randomly selected from the
entire sample. It accounts for variability of the contents, thus giving a representative dataset that can be
generalizible for the entire sample.

To identify the most salient keywords, a ten-day stratified sample was analyzed (January 18th-28th, 2011). It included 27,064 messages equal to 411,062 words. While subsamples for one-day analysis, January 18th comprised 2.146 messages or 33,081 words. For this analysis a word-frequency was performed and visualized through frequency graphs. To illustrate semantic relatedness of the words in a given message, a cluster-based dendrogram was performed using automated software (Provalis, 2012).

A randomly selected subsample of 2,000 messages was coded manually to account for addressee analysis by using a composite day sampling procedure which includes randomly selected hour-based time slots. To analyze the addressee of messages, computer-mediated discourse analysis techniques were used that take account of medium-based and situational factors (Herring, 2004; 2007). Messages were coded based on a coding scheme established by Zelenkauskaite & Herring (2008a) to study the addressees to whom messages were directed. Analyses were applied to SMS and Facebook messages.

Coding

To employ a macro-level computer-mediated discourse analysis, word frequency, and dendrogram were used as techniques that quantitatively identifies the range of content themes. A dendrogram was used as a technique that subsequently organized data through hierarchical content structure (Provalis, 2012).

To validate the data analysis, randomly selected sample was manually coded for the addressee. Based on the assumptions that underlie CMCMC, this study applied the CMDA approach to study audience addressee to analyze messages that are sent by the audience members through SMS and Facebook to RTL 102.5 programming and broadcast on its televised version. Unit of analysis was an utterance of a message. A single message could have more than one utterance and addressee. The following example shows two-utterance message with two addressees:

[1] Vi ascolto tutte le mattine un saluto dal bar me exita... Barbara ti amo

[I listen to you all the mornings and send you greetings from bar me exita... Barbara, I love you]

The example [1] was coded for addressee as program for the first part of the message, while the second part of the message was coded as directed to one person. A complete addressee codebook with examples is presented in Table 1.

Interrater Reliability

An additional 100 SMS messages and 100 Facebook wall "youONair" section wall messages were randomly collected to conduct interrater reliability tests. Two coders coded 10% of the messages to test the reliability of the established coding categories. The code values assigned were compared using Krippendorff's alpha (2004) as a reliability measurement. Krippendorff's alpha is considered one of the most rigorous and conservative interrater reliability tests for content analysis; it controls for the types of content as well as the number of coders (Krippendorff, 2004). A level of .60-.70 agreement between the coders was considered the threshold of reliability (Lombard, Snyder-Duch, & Bracken, 2002).

Table 1. Addressee codebook

Code	Description	Example (original)	Example (translation)
To program	Coded as present when the utterances were addressed to RTL 102.5 or to specific announcers.	RTL siete grandi!	RTL you are great!
To one person	Coded as present when the utterances were addressed to a specific audience member.	mi manchi da morire fragolina. TI AMO	I miss you to death, little strawberry. I LOVE YOU
To all public	Coded as present when the utterances were addressed to audience members as a whole (referring as to "all of you").	Ciao a tt da teresa da Cerignola. 1 bacione....	Hello to everyone from Teresa from Cerignola. A kiss...
No addressee	Coded as present when the utterances did not contain an explicit addressee.	Aiuto...mi sto innamorando...anna	Help...I am falling in love...anna

RESULTS

Message Flows

To provide contextual background about the frequency of message posting, messages were plotted over the period of a composite week to assess the intensity of message flow over the weekdays compared to weekends. In addition, messages flows were analyzed over a course of a given day. Thus, in addition to message content, and structure such as length, large-scale datasets from social media can provide access to content flows over time.

Table 2 shows that on average, messages flows differ. As expected, Friday and Saturday are the most active days in relation to audience contributions, while Wednesday is the least active day. To account for generalizability for this sample, a grand-average of audience participation was calculated by averaging out messages by hour in a composite-week sample.

Figure 2 displays that messages' flows differed based on a given hour with peaks at 6am, 10-11am, increases around 6pm-7pm and the highest peak at 9pm-10pm.

Table 2. Message distribution over a composite week

Month	Day	Weekday	Messages (total N)
March	14	Mo	2.712
April	26	Tue	3.072
January	26	We	1.987
February	3	Thur	2.537
February	25	Fri	3.569
March	19	Sat	3.890
April	10	Sun	2.897
Average			2.952

Figure 2. Grand average of message distribution by hour over a composite week

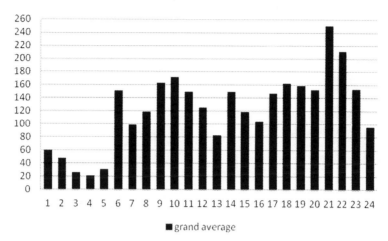

Word Frequency

To answer the first research question *What are recurrent content topics discussed through social media by their users in an automatically extracted large-scale corpus compared to manually-coded corpus?* The following steps were taken: First, automated message analysis was performed to assess the salience of the contents. Word frequency was counted for a 10-day week period of time and compared with the subsample of a single day. A single-day data was further divided into three phases of the day–morning, afternoon, and evening–to identify the most salient content changes over the course of a day.

A ten-day sample comprised messages with the average of 15 words or 86 characters. A one-day sample from January 18th presents with similar results where messages were equal to 15 words and message length by characters equaled 89 characters including spaces.

Word distribution of the 10-day worth of sample comprising 411,062 words showed the following word-frequency lists.

Word frequency distribution in Figure 3 shows the top list consisted of the following words: hi, love, kisses, great, greetings, woman, many, long live, awesome, I wanted, we have, luca, family, fantastic, Stefano, knows, TV.

Word Frequency over Time

To test if content differs within a given time-frame. Contents were divided through the arch of one day (January 18th, 2011) into three arbitrarily assigned groups: morning (ranging from 3am-9am); afternoon (ranging from 9am-7pm); and night (ranging from 7pm-3am).

Morning (3am-9am) programming comprised the word frequency list featured the greeting word *ciao* as the most frequent item, followed by this sequence: women, for, RTL, no, Alberto, children, it is necessary, bruno, fulvio, good, people, mother, I would like, family, work, equality, radio, kisses, make, wives, Bisi, good morning, things, Marco. These keywords refect the essence of the two programs that are displayed at night directed by Alberto Bisi and Fulvio Giuliani as well as they transition into the subsequent program called *The Family*.

Figure 3. Word frequency distribution for a ten-day sample

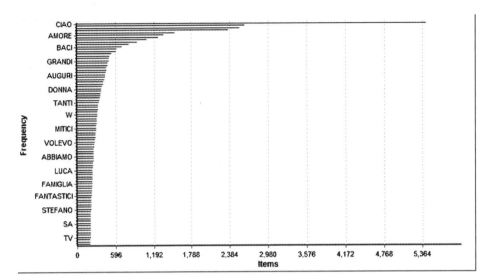

Afternoon programming included the word frequency list such as hello, RTL, you, all, I am, you are, with, my, greet, my, I love, always, kiss, thank you, love, kisses, no, great, I want, good morning, women, a lot, years, to do, all, when, life, good, hour, song, day, Proce, friends, work, heart, fantastic, great, today, I would like, Angelo, company, marco, man, thing, love, then, radio, only, berlusconi, family, greetings. This word-cloud speaks to the fan-based positive audience feedback that is based on greetings, kisses, love, appreciation of the radio's company. It addresses messages to the program announcers Proce and Angelo, mentions a program *The Family*. It also covers place such as work, issues such as Berlusconi.

In the evening, the most prominent keyword was found to be hello (*'ciao'*) followed by I love, RTL, for, love, that, no, greeting, I want, kiss, night, antonio, anna, greetings, guys, I love you, I would like, good, greetings, kisses, company, woman, laura, mother, sara,waste, miss you, I think, money, you make, good, friends, listening, beautiful, father, also, fog, I can, soon, awesome, music, person, night, I hope, stefano, a lot, and wants.

These keywords comprise the positive fandom messages that express love, greetings and descriptives such as awesome and great. However, it reflects that messages are directed to individuals through references such as 'I love you', 'mother', and 'I miss you.' It also refers to community mentioning the word 'friends.' It emphasised weather condition descriptives of the day such as 'fog', referred to issues 'money', made temporal refernece 'night.'

Content Clusters over Time

A more detailed analysis was obtained through word similarity dendogram that clusters keywords into themes based on similarity and proximity on a message level.

From 9am to 7pm the most prominent cluster in dendrogram comprised the segment displayed in Figure 4. It centers around three big themes: appraisals to RTL; greetings to friends of RTL; love sentiments expressed to the loved one through this radio station.

Figure 4. Dendrogram the most prominent cluster in a 9am-7pm similarity cluster

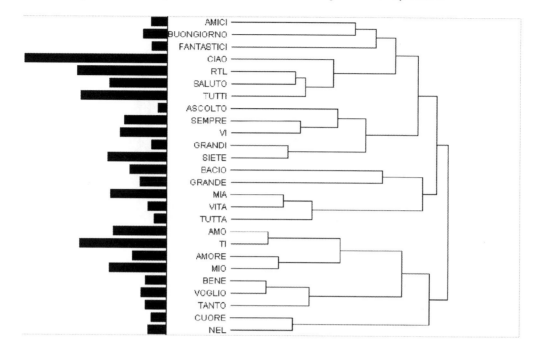

Dendrogram of the most prominent cluster of the 7pm-3am and 3am-9am segments (with highest peaks of used content) comprises the thematic segments illustrated in Figure 5.

Dendrogram's cluster from 7pm-3am (the above cluster of Figure 5) was surrounded by the words ciao ['hello'], RTL, and saluto ['greeting'] constitutes one nucleo of communication referring to the radio program itself. While the other correlary contains words such as I love ['amo'], a friend ['amica'], and special ['speciale'] referring to a single user. The presence of word clusters referring to the fact that audience members talk with the program as well as they express emotions to a single person throughI miss you ['manchi'] or love ['amore']. The most prominent cluster was composed by two main co-occuring items produced by dendrogram. Dendrogram analysis infers that users actualy engage into conversations that go beyond conversation to the radio station.

The dendrogram's segment for 3am-9am (corresponding to the lower cluster of Figure 5) is centered on words such as: need, women which is further related to hi, woman, family. The other larger cluster comprises the following words: hello, that Marco, things, children, parity, child, man, mother, to work, I would like.

Message Addressee

Given that quantitative word similarity dendrogram shows that contents refer to single person as well as to the radio station, messages were further analyzed to assess the addressee. This analysis was performed to answer the second part of the research question that aimed to compare automated and manually-assessed findings. Utterance analysis per message shows that majority of messages contained only one addressee comprising $n=1,471$ messages (73.6%) followed by two addressees comprising $n=478$ messages (23.9%). Three addressees were found in $n=50$ cases (2.5% of the sample); 4 addressees were found 1 time (.1%).

Figure 5. Dendrogram the most prominent cluster in a 7pm-3am (the cluster above) and 3am-9am (the cluster below) similarity cluster

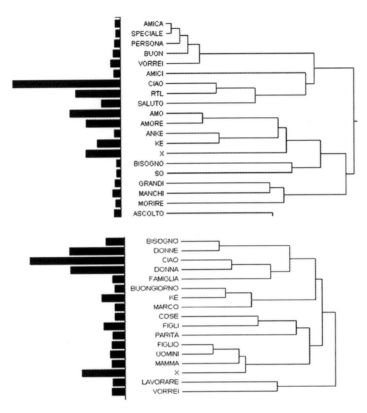

Addressee analysis is summarized in the Table 3.

Relative to addressee, Table 3 shows that majority of the contents were addressed to a single person or to audience members as a whole (user-to-user and user-to-all audience members combined) resulting in $n=1,090$ utterances. User-to-program comprised $n=912$ cases. Messages directed to unspecified addressee resulted in $n=582$ utterances (user-to-no addressee category).

DISCUSSION

This study analyzed audiences through the lens of text-based audience contributions via a unified broadcast stream of Facebook and mobile texting to the radio-TV program. Automated analysis tools were proven to be useful to identify most salient themes that were found to cluster around greetings, interaction with

Table 3. Addressee analysis for 2,000 messages

Addressee	To program	To one person	To all public	No addressee	Total
Total	912	563	527	582	2,584

the program and centered on specific themes that were related to the specific topics discussed in the program. Moreover, topics pertinent to interpersonal communication were also present. Word frequency reflected the most salient content discussed in the program. However, for a ten-day subsample, the multiplicity of identified theme-clusters made it challenging to identify clear-cut themes. Word-cluster data representation was more manageable with message counts at approximately 3,000 messages per day, providing the binary nature of radio-centered interaction and interpersonal interaction. Data segmented into three periods of a given day revealed specific topics and addressees of a given interaction.

Period-based analyses' results led to manually-coded CMDA, showing that overall, messages were addressed not only to the program, but also messages between the users. In fact, addressee analysis showed that indeed messages contained multiple addressees that included not only radio station and its personnel but also to other users. Moreover, there were slightly fewer messages directed to the program ($n=912$) compared to the combined number of user-to-user and user-to-audience messages that comprised 1,090 messages. Moreover, there were quite a large number of messages with no clear addressee. This finding indicates that audiences contribute contents to the audience overall, emulating traditional broadcaster's role. As for contents, while the majority of messages consisted of one utterance, yet about 23% messages contained two utterances showing that audience members engaged into messages that were directed to several addressees which can comprise more than one audience member, or the radio-tv station itself.

Quantitative computer-mediated discourse analysis based on frequency counts aims mostly towards the most salient content and leaves out less prominent content themes. Methodologically, this can be considered as a limiting factor. To account for such limitations, advancements on quantitative automated tools based on word frequency open new research opportunities for discourse analysis (Pennebaker & Graybeal, 2001). In particular, frequency-based word count provides insights about discourses that have conversational topics, while are less informative about interpersonal topics that are aimed towards small talk rather than topic discussion. Dendrogram-based content hierarchies provide a more fine-grained analysis of conversation. These automated tools thus can be successfully applied as diagnostic tools that identify a terrain of conversations. More fine-grained analyses could be performed in a micro-scale based on specific research questions.

One caveat of automated analysis is that word frequency analysis and cluster-based data can be meaningful only if the researcher is familiar with the context of a given dataset. Otherwise, the valence of the emerged themes can be misinterpreted. For example, words can be used in positive or negative contexts. In contexts, where there are multiple addressees, content keywords can be attributed to any given addressee. In addition, only the most salient contents emerge in dominant positions, while less prominent topics get lower hierarchical prominence in the analysis. Also, automated coding can not reveal the absence of certain categories. For example, no addressee was found relatively frequent in manual coding, while in automated coding would not be able to reveal this aspect. However, the shortcoming related to not capturing the absent categories is related to content analysis overall, yet not specific to automated word frequency analysis (Krippendorff, 2004).

Solutions and Recommendations

Audience analysis through CMDA bears practical implications. In addition to social science research that advances the understanding of audiences' behaviors, audience analysis through CMDA can serve as tools for media organizations, being especially relevant for media organizations that incorporate UGC into their programming through backchannels such as social media. Audience analysis can be applied to access contribution flows and contextualization of the contents to overcome design-based challenges.

Large-scale datasets of audience contributions can serve as tools to study incoming audience's content and its development over time. Message flows can provide insights about audience engagement levels during specific time-frames ranging from monthly analysis to week analysis, days of the week analysis, and hour-by-hour analysis. Such analyses can provide insights about audience behaviors during a given time-frame, as well as focus on particular issues. Such content flow analysis can be used as a proxy to understand audience activity for a given time-frame or a program. It could be used as a diagnostic tool to assess the level of audience involvement levels. By knowing when audiences are mostly involved, editorial logics of content integration could be matched accordingly.

Specific recommendations in light of the findings of this study include the need to evaluate the interpersonal nature of audience members' communication, given that results of this study indicate that audiences actively engaged in interpersonal communication, in addition to communicating with the program. Media organizations could highlight the most prominent content by providing a constantly-changing word cloud. This prominent content could be displayed and updated to their audience members to enhance levels of audience contributions thus further engage audience members. Media producers could provide audiences a summary of communicative contents by constantly changing word cloud on their website or Facebook wall. Content synthesis through automated CMDA of audiences' contributions and constant update on content change reflect inclusivity of diverse topics of interests by the radio station.

The other practical recommendation to the radio stations would be to diversify the contents that audiences send to the program, based on content and addressee types. Specifically, if content is dedicated to the audience members, they can be broadcast during specific time slots, dedicated to a specific addressee. For example, "audience time" could be defined as time specifically dedicated to audience interaction, in a one-hour programming; while reactive content could be aired during the time when the speakers pose their questions or trigger prompts to them.

Finally, audience contents that are unified in a single stream and simultaneously broadcast on at least four platforms – radio programming, televised radiovision, web-based programming, and portable devices such as iPad or smarphone – could be diversified and streamed in more prominent ways. There could be possible to access the aggregator of all contents with each platform; as well as subscribe to the aggregated messages, as well as subscribe only for a certain number of filtered contents based on identified criteria such as program time, addressee or another. Such content aggregator approach would provide users with a perception of increased agency of content selection control that would be tailored to their personal needs rather than ongoing stream of content that loses its relevance to the generic audience.

FUTURE RESEARCH DIRECTIONS

This study analyzed audience exchanges through computer-mediated discourse analysis through social media backchannels such as Facebook and SMS of traditional media to extend ways to analyze mass media audiences. However, this approach can be subject to several limitations. The approach treating audiences through their textual expression poses some limitations. Given that not all the audience members actively engage into content contribution, the active audience is limited in numbers. However, active audiences define the core audience behaviors on a given channel, station, or program. In other words, audiences' messages through Facebook and mobile texting provide ways to assess what really matters to the audiences, the way they want to exchange if they are given such a possibility. However, the results obtained in CMDA have to be interpreted contextually – taking into a close consideration the extent to which contents are moderated.

The case of a national radio-TV station represents a small fraction of audience members' contributions compared to the total number of listeners per day (which was estimated to be five million). Thus a 3,000 of active users compared to five million listeners is a small proportion of the audience. However, compared to a number of aired call-ins by audience members, that comprises about two calls from a listener per a given hour, or 48 per 24 hours, 3,000 messages per day is a much higher number. Also, this finding is compliant with the research in mass media context, showing that the expectation for all audience members to be active is overrated (Abercrombie & Longhurst, 1998). In fact, active participation expectation has been dismissed as well as in online contexts, where the presence of passive users – the lurkers – was argued to constitute a great part, sometimes a majority of online forums' users (Rafaeli, Ravid, & Soroka, 2004). However, these active audience members are given much prominence with the programming. Despite the limited percentage of activity, these audience members are given an exceptional prominence compared to the passive listeners because their contents get actually broadcast on TV, web, and also shape the program's content. Finally, a case study methodology, as other methodologies suffer from its limitations, yet provide benefits such as rich data analysis that other methodologies cannot offer (Flyvbjerg, 2006).

Future studies could employ computer-mediated discourse analysis to study content selection process and associated implications in addition to studying the types of addresses and exchanged contents. Future studies could address the analysis of reciprocal exchanges that would allow the frequency of such exchanges, despite the fact that the number of responses was not very low, consistent with the previous research on audience exchanges in *Allmusic* channel *Inbox* program (Zelenkauskaite & Herring, 2008a). Future studies could provide a better understanding of audience contributions types in other contexts – such as moderated interactive programming where specific criteria are established for the content inclusion. Also, other contextual variables that influence audiences could be considered such as guidelines of best practices. However, in the case of RTL 102.5 given that there are no restrictions, this analysis shows how it is important for the audiences to incorporate interpersonal messages while maintaining radio-based communication.

Despite the fact that the studied contents are publicly available on the television screen as well as audience members are aware that their content will be publicly posted, audience research is subject to ethical considerations. Addressee analysis coding provides only information regarding overall data while leaving out the specifics of it. Similarly, the contents have been coded as larger categories "personal content" without defining specifics of that content. Such messages might include greetings. The others provide quite specific information about audience members' location. From this perspective CMDA as a method to study any type of contents should ensure audience members' privacy while still expanding scholarly and practical knowledge that is associated with the content exchange in which audiences engage.

In this study, CMDA was contextualized with content traffic analysis. Future studies would couple CMDA with content traffic analysis or with other methodological approaches, such as focus groups, questionnaires, in-depth interviews to provide a richer understanding of blending mass media and social media audiences. More cases studies should be conducted to account for various culture-specific aspects of mass audience and social media blending. Future studies could provide a better understanding of these audience contribution patterns by comparing controlled contexts with the ones what are pre-defined. Also, audience gratifications could be studied to understand the underlying forces for such participation, as well as content selection process could be studied, how messages are handled, selected, and integrated into the programming to provide a more complete understanding of this blending audience phenomenon.

CONCLUSION

CMDA has been employed to study user behaviors through their linguistic expression as ways to analyze user behaviors exemplified by Italian convergent Radio-TV-Web station RTL 102.5. This case study exemplified how computer-mediated discourse analysis provides new opportunities to analyze audiences in complex multimedia environments.

The study found that automated word-frequency was a useful diagnostic tool to identify the most salient terms that emerge from the large dataset. Word cluster analysis was found to be useful for a more context-sensitive analytical tool for salient theme and its context such as addressee extraction. Addressee analysis was cross-validated through manually-coded computer-discourse analysis on a randomly selected dataset and found support for the automated data cluster extraction. The findings of RTL 102.5 audience analysis behavior through text suggest that audience members in addition to the radio-based content, triggers, and responses to the programming also send messages to each other. The conclusion of this study is that CMDA revealed audience-based contents that were sent to the program. This result shows that communication occurred not only with the radio station, but audiences were involved in interpersonal communication. This study presents CMDA as methodological approach established in computer-mediated communication paradigm to study online users who are also mass audiences aiming at contributing to audience analysis studies and studies of changing media landscapes.

Broader implications of automated computer-mediated discourse are that existing modes of audience inquiry can be coupled with the text-based audience discourse. The availability of the plethora of audiences' online user data gives access to audiences' through their contents thus increasing mass media audiences' visibility through their text-based contents, as well as address issues regarding the difficulty of studying fragmented audiences. Thus, audiences are studied through the backchannels such as social media building on previous research proposing the idea that active audiences serve as a proxy to understanding to audience behaviors (Abercrombie & Longhurst, 1998).

The benefit of computer-mediated discourse analysis resides in its power to study user interaction, which occurs through the text through social media outlets. User contributions through the texts become a valuable source to understand language-based interaction of the users in online environments (see Herring, 2001) which could potentially be coupled with other audience methodologies. This study proposes computer-mediated discourse analysis as a methodological tool that serves to capture fragmented audiences' behaviors on various platforms through their contributions.

CMDA thus is proposed as an integral framework that was applied to a micro-level, combined with more macro-levels quantitative analyses such as audience participation patterns to account for changing media landscapes. Analysis of interactive audiences through CMDA provides an additional perspective to account for increasing complexity of audience studies that in interactive contexts that blend audiences. Facebook users, SMS users and radio and TV audiences blend traditional mass media audiences with online users. RTL 102.5 suggests that CMDA as methodological approach can provide an additional lens to audience analysis to account for audience as the most salient exchanged content types as ways to deal to what McQuail identifies as "alternative models" as audience-sender relationship that emerges in a mass media contexts (McQuail, 1997). Given that CMDA and audience analysis share overlapping areas of inquiry, an integrative approach could enrich the changing concept of audiences. Based on RTL 102.5 analysis this study suggests an integrative approach to study blended audiences that combines automated and manual coding categories extracting macro and micro levels of quantitative computer-mediated discourse coupled with another metrics established in audience analysis paradigm.

There are several implications to study audiences' participation and interaction through social media within mass media contexts. First, theoretically, such analysis contributes to audience analysis research by providing insights about the most active, core members of their audiences as well as an extension to general understanding of audiences (Abercrombie & Longhurst, 1998). Practical implications include contributions to multiplatform mass media design that would fulfill communicative needs of the audiences. In addition, mixed methodological approaches to study online data are proposed considering not only publicly available data points increase in quantity, but also in light of emergent trends in data aggregation through such paradigms as Internet of Things and Big Data (Amer-Yahia, Doan, Kleinberg, Koudas, & Franklin, 2010) where data have to be meaningfully analyzed and interpreted.

Finally, despite the fact that media contexts are changing, audience participation and contribution via social media and mobile texting serve as a powerful tool to reveal audience participation patterns, structure, and nature of these conversations. Given this increasing number of text-based UGC expressed through social media and interpersonal media in mass media contexts, audiences behaviors enacted through texts, provide new opportunities to study audiences.

REFERENCES

Abercrombie, N., & Longhurst, B. (1998). *Audiences: A sociological theory of performance and imagination*. London: Sage.

Amer-Yahia, S., Doan, A., Kleinberg, J., Koudas, N., & Franklin, M. (2010). Crowds, clouds, and algorithms: Exploring the human side of "big data" applications. In A. K. Elmagarmid & D. Agrawal (Eds.), *Proceedings of SIGMOD International Conference on Management of data* (pp. 1259-1260). Indianapolis, IN, USA.

Androutsopoulos, A., & Beißwenger, M. (2008). Introduction: Data and methods in computer-mediated discourse analysis. *Language@Internet, 5*. Retrieved December 10, 2012, from http://www.languageatinternet.org/articles/2008/1609

Audiradio. (2009). *Dati Audiradio annuale 2009*. Retrieved October 10, 2010, from http://www.audiradio.it/upload/File/Dati%20Audiradio%20annuale%202009.pdf

Baron, N. S. (2010). Discourse structures in Instant Messaging: The case of utterance breaks *Language@Internet, 7*. Retrieved October 11, 2012, from http://www.languageatinternet.org/articles/2010/2651

Beyer, Y., Enli, G. S., Maasø, A. J., & Ytreberg, E. (2007). Small talk makes a big difference: Recent developments in interactive, SMS-based television. *Television & New Media, 8*(3), 213–234. doi:10.1177/1527476407301642

Blythe, M., & Cairns, P. (2009). Critical methods and user generated content: The iPhone on YouTube. In *Proceedings of the 27th international conference on Human factors in computing systems*. Boston, MA, USA.

Bolin, G. (2010). Digitalization, multiplatform texts, and audience reception. *Popular Communication*, *8*(1), 72–83. doi:10.1080/15405700903502353

Bou-Franch, P., Lorenzo-Dus, N., & Blitvich, P. G.-C. (2012). Social interaction in YouTube text-based polylogues: A study of coherence. *Journal of Computer-Mediated Communication*, *17*(4), 501–521. doi:10.1111/j.1083-6101.2012.01579.x

Bruns, A. (2010). *Blogs, Wikipedia, Second life, and beyond: From production to produsage*. New York: Peter Lang Publishing.

Carpentier, N. (2007). Participation, access, and interaction: Changing perspectives. In V. Nightingale & T. Dwyer (Eds.), New media worlds: Challenges for convergence (pp. 214-231). New York: Oxford.

Das, A. (2010). Social interaction process analysis of Bengalis' on Orkut. In R. Taiwo (Ed.), *Handbook of research on discourse behavior and digital communication: Language structures and social interaction* (pp. 66–87). Hershey, PA: Information Science Reference. doi:10.4018/978-1-61520-773-2.ch004

Doyle, G. (2010). From television to multi-platform. *Convergence: The International Journal of Research into New Media Technologies*, *16*(4), 431–449. doi:10.1177/1354856510375145

Enli, G. S. (2007). Gate-keeping in the new media age: A case study of the selection of text-messages in a current affairs programme. *Javnost - The public*, *14*(2), 47-62.

Enli, G. S., & Syvertsen, T. (2007). Participation, play and socializing in new media environments. In T. Dwyer & V. Nightingale (Eds.), *New media worlds: Challenges for convergence* (pp. 147–162). South Melbourne: Oxford University Press.

Flyvbjerg, B. (2006). Five misunderstandings about case-study research. *Qualitative Inquiry*, *12*, 219–245. doi:10.1177/1077800405284363

Hård af Segerstad, Y. (2005). Language use in Swedish mobile text messaging. *Mobile Communications* (Vol. 31, pp. 313-333). Springer: London.

Herring, S. C. (2001). Computer-mediated discourse. In D. Schiffrin, D. Tannen, & H. Hamilton (Eds.), *The Handbook of discourse analysis* (pp. 612–634). Oxford: Blackwell Publishers.

Herring, S. C. (2004). Computer-mediated discourse analysis: An approach to researching online behavior. In S. A. Barab, R. Kling, & J. H. Gray (Eds.), *Designing for virtual communities in the service of learning* (pp. 338–376). New York: Cambridge University Press. doi:10.1017/CBO9780511805080.016

Herring, S. C. (2007). A faceted classification scheme for computer-mediated discourse. *Language@ Internet*, *4*. Retrieved December 24, 2012, from http://www.languageatinternet.org/articles/2007/761

Herring, S. C. (2009). *Convergent media computer-mediated communication: Introduction and theory. Panel on Convergent Media Computer-Mediated Communication*. Paper presented at the Internet Research 10.0, Milwaukee, WI.

Herring, S. C. (2011). Computer-mediated conversation, Part II. Special issue. *Language@Internet*, *8*. Retrieved December 24, 2012, from http://www.languageatinternet.org/articles/2011

Herring, S. C. (2013). Discourse in Web 2.0: Familiar, reconfigured, and emergent. In D. Tannen & A. M. Tester (Eds.), *Georgetown University round table on languages and linguistics 2011: Discourse 2.0: Language and new media* (pp. 1–25). Washington, DC: Georgetown University Press.

Honeycutt, C., & Herring, S. C. (2009). Beyond microblogging: Convesation and collaboration via Twitter. In *Proceedings of the Forty-Second Hawai'I International Conference on System Sciences* (pp. 1-10). Los Alamitos, CA: IEEE Press.

Howe, J. (2007). *To save themselves, US newspapers put readers to work*. Retrieved August 17, 2012, from http://www.wired.com/techbiz/media/magazine/15-08/ff_gannett?currentPage=all

Hutchby, I. (1996). Power in discourse: The case of arguments on a British talk radio show. *Discourse & Society*, *7*(4), 481–497. doi:10.1177/0957926596007004003

Iba, T., Nemoto, K., Peters, B., & Gloor, P. A. (2010). Analyzing the creative editing behavior of Wikipedia editors: Through dynamic social network analysis. Social and Behavioral Sciences, 2(4), 6441-6456.

Jenkins, H. (2006). *Convergence culture: Where old and new media collide*. New York: University Press.

Karlsen, F., Sundet, V. S., Syvertsen, T., & Ytreberg, E. (2009). Non-professional activity on television in a time of digitalization: More fun for elite or new opportunities for ordinary people. *Nordicom Review*, *30*(1), 19–36.

Klein, B. (2009). Contrasting interactivities: BBC radio message boards and listener participation. *The Radio Journal: International Studies in Broadcast and Audio Media*, *7*(1), 11–26. doi:10.1386/rajo.7.1.11/1

Krippendorff, K. (2004). *Content analysis: An introduction to its methodology*. Thousand Oaks: Sage.

Ling, R., & Baron, N. S. (2007). Text messaging and IM: Linguistic comparison of American college data. *Journal of Language and Social Psychology*, *26*(3), 291–298. doi:10.1177/0261927X06303480

Livingstone, S. (1999). New media, new audiences? *New Media & Society*, *1*(1), 59–66. doi:10.1177/1461444899001001010

Livingstone, S. (2004). The challenge of changing audiences: Or, what is the audience researcher to do in the age of the internet? *European Journal of Communication*, *19*(1), 75–86. doi:10.1177/0267323104040695

Lombard, M., Snyder-Duch, J., & Bracken, C. C. (2002). Content analysis in mass communication: Assessment and reporting of intercoder reliability. *Human Communication Research*, *28*(4), 587–604. doi:10.1111/j.1468-2958.2002.tb00826.x

Lowrey, W., & Mackay, J. (2008). Journalism and blogging: A test of a model of occupational competition. *Journalism Practice*, *2*, 64–81. doi:10.1080/17512780701768527

Lowrey, W., & Woo, C. W. (2010). The news organization in uncertain times: Business or institution? *Journalism & Mass Communication Quarterly*, *87*(1), 41–61. doi:10.1177/107769901008700103

MacGregor, P. (2007). Tracking the online audience: Metric data start a subtle revolution. *Journalism Studies*, *8*, 280–298. doi:10.1080/14616700601148879

Mafé, C. R., Blas, S. S., & Tavera-Mesías, J. F. (2010). A comparative study of mobile messaging services acceptance to participate in television programmes. *Journal of Service Management, 21*(1), 69–102. doi:10.1108/09564231011025128

McKenzie, C. T., Lowrey, W., Hays, H., Chung, J. Y., & Woo, C. W. (2012). Listening to news audiences: The impact of community structure and economic factors. *Mass Communication & Society, 14*(3), 375–395. doi:10.1080/15205436.2010.491934

McQuail, D. (1997). *Audience analysis.* Thousand Oaks, London, New Delhi: Sage Publications.

Morris, M., & Ogan, C. (1996). The Internet as mass medium. *Journal of Computer-Mediated Communication, 1*(4). Retrieved May 10, 2012, from http://jcmc.indiana.edu/vol1/issue4/morris.html

Ortega, F., Gonzalez-Barahona, J. M., & Robles, G. (2008). On the inequality of contributions to Wikipedia. In *Proceedings of the 41st Annual Hawaii International Conference on System Sciences.* Waikoloa, HI, USA.

Paolillo, J. C. (2008). Structure and network in the YouTube core. In *Proceedings of the 41st Annual Hawaii International Conference on System Sciences.* Waikoloa, HI, USA.

Pennebaker, J. W., & Graybeal, A. (2001). Patterns of natural language use: Disclosure, personality, and social integration. *Current Directions in Psychological Science, 10*(3), 90–93. doi:10.1111/1467-8721.00123

Provalis. (2012). *Provalis research.* Retrieved November 5, 2012, from http://provalisresearch.com/products/content-analysis-software/

Rafaeli, S. (1988). Interactivity: From new media to communication. In R. P. Hawkins, J. M. Wiemann, & S. Pingree (Eds.), *Sage annual review of communication research: Advancing communication science* (Vol. 16, pp. 110–134). Beverly Hills, CA: Sage.

Rafaeli, S. (1989). Interacting with media: Para-social interaction and real interaction. In B. D. Ruben & L. A. Lievrouw (Eds.), *Mediation, information, and communication* (Vol. 3, pp. 125–184). New Brunswick, NJ: Transaction Publishers.

Rafaeli, S., Ravid, G., & Soroka, V. (2004). De-lurking in virtual communities: A social communication network approach to measuring the effects of social and cultural capital. In *Proceedings of the 37th Hawaii International Conference on System Sciences.* Los Alamitos, CA: IEEE Press. Retrieved December 24, 2012, from http://www.languageatinternet.org/articles/2011

Spagnolli, A., & Gamberini, L. (2007). Interacting via SMS: Practices of social closeness and reciprocation. *The British Journal of Social Psychology, 46*(2), 343–364. doi:10.1348/014466606X120482 PMID:17565786

Viégas, F., Wattenberg, M., Kriss, J., & Ham, F. V. (2007). Talk before you type: Coordination in Wikipedia. In *Proceeedings of the 40th Annual Hawaii International Conference on System Sciences.* Los Alamitos, CA: IEEE Press.

Zelenkauskaite, A., & Herring, S. C. (2008a). Television-mediated conversation: Coherence in Italian iTV SMS chat. In *Proceedings of the Forty-First Hawai'i International Conference on System Sciences*. Los Alamitos, CA: IEEE Press.

Zelenkauskaite, A., & Herring, S. C. (2008b). Gender differences in personal advertisements in Lithuanian iTV SMS. In F. Sudweeks, H. Hrachovec, & C. Ess (Eds.), *Proceedings of Cultural Attitudes Towards Technology and Communication 2008* (pp. 462–476). Murdoch, Australia: School of Information Technology, Murdoch University.

Zelenkauskaite, A., & Massa, P. (2011). Digital libraries and social web: Insights from Wikipedia users' activities. In *IADIS Multiconference on Computer Science and Information Systems* (pp. 39-47). Rome, Italy.

ADDITIONAL READING

Androutsopoulos, J. (2006). Introduction: Sociolinguistics and computer-mediated communication. *Journal of Sociolinguistics*, *10*(4), 419–438. doi:10.1111/j.1467-9841.2006.00286.x

Armstrong, C. B., & Rubin, A. M. (1989). Talk radio as interpersional communication. *The Journal of Communication*, *39*(2), 84–94. doi:10.1111/j.1460-2466.1989.tb01031.x

Avery, R. K., Ellis, D. G., & Glover, T. W. (1978). Patterns of communication on talk radio. *Journal of Broadcasting*, *22*(1), 5–17. doi:10.1080/08838157809363862

Colombo, F. (2004). Interactivity and digitalization of the television system: An introduction. In F. Colombo (Ed.), TV and interactivity in Europe: Mythologies, theoretical perspectives, real experiences (pp. 7-14). Milano: V&P Strumenti.

Dahlgren, P. (1995). *Televisoin and the public sphere*. London: Sage.

Enli, G. S. (2009). Mass communication tapping into participatory culture: Exploring strictly come dancing and Britain's Got Talent. *European Journal of Communication*, *24*(4), 481–493. doi:10.1177/0267323109345609

Erjavec, K., & Kovačič, M. P. (2009). A discursive approach to genre: Mobi news. *European Journal of Communication*, *24*(2), 147–164. doi:10.1177/0267323108101829

Georgakopoulou, A., & Goutsos, D. (2004). *Discourse analysis: An introduction* (2nd ed.). Edinburgh: Edinburgh University Press. doi:10.3366/edinburgh/9780748620456.001.0001

Herring, S. C. (2010). Web content analysis: Expanding the paradigm. In J. Hunsinger, M. Allen, & L. Klastrup (Eds.), *The International Handbook of Internet Research* (pp. 233–249). Berlin: Springer Verlag.

Kensing, F., Simonse, J., & Bødker, K. (1998). Participatory design at a radio station. *Computer Supported Cooperative Work*, *7*(3-4), 243–271. doi:10.1023/A:1008683004336

Kjus, Y. (2009). Impact of prestige programs on production practices: The case of crossmedia and audience participation in public service organization. *Journal of Media Practice, 10*(2&3), 167–184. doi:10.1386/jmpr.10.2-3.167_1

Ling, R. (2005). *The sociolinguistics of SMS: An analysis of SMS use by a random sample of Norwegians. Mobile Communications* (Vol. 31, pp. 335–349). London: Springer.

Nastri, J., Peña, J., & Hancock, J. T. (2006). The construction of away messages: A speech act analysis. *Journal of Computer-Mediated Communication, 11*(4), 1025–1045. doi:10.1111/j.1083-6101.2006.00306.x

Page, B. I., & Tannenbaum, J. (1996). Populistic deliberation and talk radio. *The Journal of Communication, 46*(2), 33–54. doi:10.1111/j.1460-2466.1996.tb01473.x

Rafaeli, S., & Sudweeks, F. (1997). Networked interactivity. *Journal of Computer-Mediated Communication, 2*(4). Retrieved December 21, 2012, from http://jcmc.indiana.edu/vol2/issue4/rafaeli.sudweeks.html

Rettie, R. (2009). SMS: Exploiting the interactional characteristics of near-synchrony. *Information Communication and Society, 12*(8), 1131–1148. doi:10.1080/13691180902786943

Roscoe, J. (2004). Multi-plaform event television: Reconceptualising our relationship with television. *Communication Review, 7*, 363–369. doi:10.1080/10714420490886961

Rubin, A. M., & Step, M. M. (2000). Impact of motivation, attraction, and parasocial interaction on talk radio listening. *Journal of Broadcasting & Electronic Media, 44*(4), 635–654. doi:10.1207/s15506878jobem4404_7

Ruddock, A. (2007). *Investigating audiences*. London: Sage.

Sanger, C., Taylor, A., & Vincent, J. (2005). An SMS history. In L. Hamill, A. Lasen, & D. Diaper (Eds.), *Mobile world* (pp. 75–91). London: Springer.

Sihvonen, T. (2003). TV chat communities. In M. Tarkka (Ed.), *Digital television and the consumer perspective: National Consumer Research Centre discussion papers* (pp. 30–33). Torshavn, Faroe Islands.

Skjerdal, T. S. (2008). New media and new editorial challenges: Lessons from Norway. *Informacijos Mokslai, 47*, 66–77.

Squires, L. (2011). Voicing "sexy text": Heteroglossia and erasure in TV news broadcast representations of Detroit's text message scandal. In C. Thurlow & K. Mozcrek (Eds.), *Digital discourse: Language in the new media* (pp. 3–26). New York, London: Oxford University Press. doi:10.1093/acprof:oso/9780199795437.003.0001

Svoen, B. (2007). Consumers, participants, and creators: Young people's diverse use of television and new media. *ACM Computer in Entertainment, 5*(2). Retrieved December 20, 2012, from http://cie.acm.org/articles/consumers-participants-and-creators/

Tuomi, P., & Bachmayer, S. (2011). The convergence of TV and Web (2.0) in Austria and Finland. [Lisbon, Portugal.]. *Proceedings of EuroITV, 11*, 55–64. doi:10.1145/2000119.2000131

Turow, J. (1973). Talk show radio as interpersonal communication. *Journal of Broadcasting & Electronic Media, 18*(2), 171–179.

Van Dijck, J. (2009). User like you? Theorizing agency in user-generated content. *Media Culture & Society, 31*(1), 41–58. doi:10.1177/0163443708098245

Van Dijk, J. (2004). Digital media. In J. D. H. Downing, D. McQuail, P. Schlesinger, & E. Wartella (Eds.), *The Sage handbook of media studies* (pp. 145–164). Thousand Oaks, CA: Sage Publications. doi:10.4135/9781412976077.n8

Vorderer, P. (2000). Interactive entertainment and beyond. In D. Z. P. Vorderer (Ed.), *Media entertainment: The psychology of its appeal* (pp. 21–36). Mahwah: Lawrence Erlbaum Associates.

Walther, J. B., Carr, C. T., Choi, S. S. W., Deandrea, D. C., Kim, J., Tom Tong, S., & Van der Heide, B. (2010). Interaction of interpersonal, peer, and media influence sources online: A research agenda for technology convergence. In Z. Papacharissi (Ed.), *Networked self: Identity, community, and culture on social network sites* (pp. 17–38). New York, London: Routlege.

Ytreberg, E. (2004). Formatting participation within broadcast media production. *Media Culture & Society, 26*(5), 677–692. doi:10.1177/0163443704045506

Ytreberg, E. (2009). Extended liveness and eventfulness in multi-platform reality formats. *New Media & Society, 11*, 467–485. doi:10.1177/1461444809102955

KEY TERMS AND DEFINITIONS

Audiences: Refers to mass media audiences.

Blending Audiences: Audiences that comprise or constitute a part of social media users and mass media audiences.

Computer-Mediated Communication: When humans interact with each other via computer networks.

Computer-Mediated Discourse Analysis (CMDA): Herring (2004) defines CMDA as "an approach to the analysis of computer-mediated communication (CMC) focused on language and language use; it is also a set of methods (a "toolkit") grounded in linguistic discourse analysis for mining networked communication for patterns of structure and meaning, broadly construed."

Interpersonal Media: Applications that allow for interpersonal user exchange.

Mass Media: Refers to traditional media outlets, traditionally viewed by mass media audiences, examples of which comprise but are not limited to television, radio, newspapers.

Short Message Service (SMS): Mobile texting that occurs through mobile devices or mobile device supported platforms. It comprises users-to-user interaction through message exchange, as well as text-message services that are established through tertiary parties, including commercial services such as text-based messages to banks, as well as entertainment services such as SMS messages to the TV and radio programming.

Social Media: Comprise web applications that allow user interaction and content distribution and exchange. Examples of which include but are not limited to social networking sites such as Facebook, microblogging such as Twitter, as well as online chat.

Users: Refers to web users, online users, social media users.

ENDNOTES

[1]   The author thanks Ernest Hakanen for revisions of this manuscript and thanks anonymous reviewers for suggestions that improved this manuscript.

[2]   Radiovision refers to the term used by RTL 102.5 that refers to the radio and the visual component of the radio programming broadcast via TV.

This research was previously published in Innovative Methods and Technologies for Electronic Discourse Analysis edited by Hwee Ling Lim and Fay Sudweeks, pages 304-326, copyright year 2014 by Information Science Reference (an imprint of IGI Global).

Chapter 51
Generation Y and Internet Privacy:
Implication for Commercialization of Social Networking Services

Zdenek Smutny
University of Economics, Czech Republic

Vaclav Janoscik
Academy of Fine Arts in Prague, Czech Republic

Radim Cermak
University of Economics, Czech Republic

ABSTRACT

This chapter addresses the issue of privacy settings with a focus on Generation Y from a technological, social, generational, cultural and philosophical point of view. After introducing the issue of Internet privacy and other relevant areas—generational and cultural differences, the philosophical framework, the postinternet condition, the possibilities of processing and (mis)using personal data, and privacy policy—the authors present their perspective on the issue, drawing implications for individuals and organizations based on their own research and other relevant studies. The authors discuss the possible implications in terms of a prospective use of personal data by companies (e.g. for marketing and management) and possibility of processing user data. Such perspective will allow them to formulate a critical basis for further assessment of social networking and Generation Y's attitudes to privacy. The chapter concludes by outlining several recommendations concerning the commercialization of social networking services with respect to the constantly changing conception of privacy.

DOI: 10.4018/978-1-5225-5637-4.ch051

INTRODUCTION

This chapter provides an interdisciplinary perspective on the attitude of today's young people from Generation Y towards self-disclosure and on the impact of such behaviour on the individual, as well as on the challenges for commercial exploitation of social networking services. A definition of Generation Y is given in the part *Cultural and generational difference*s. From a firm's perspective, there are two reasons why it is important to focus on Generation Y:

- Generation Y has a positive attitude to information and communication technologies (ICT) (Valentine & Powers, 2013), which are already a common element in their lives (Benckendorff, Moscardo & Pendergast, 2010, p. 20; Lahtinen, 2012). This part of their life is reflected in social networking services and thus shared with other people. These (personal) data from various Internet-based services can be used in commercial and professional activity.
- Members of Generation Y are economically active. From a firm's perspective, this means that they can act as customers or as employees.

Internet privacy is viewed as the right of a subject (human) for the protection of their personal data and the way they are handled (Puddephatt et al., 2012) – i.e. stored, processed, used (including changes in their use), provided to third parties and displayed on the Internet. The information collected during an individual's interaction in a particular social networking service can be divided into personally identifying information (e.g. information that relates to a particular person or identifies them) and non-personally identifying information (e.g. anonymous information about an individual's behaviour on a web portal). (Cermak, Smutny & Janoscik, 2014)

A long-term trend in companies' activity is the collection of such data and its subsequent evaluation for various purposes of the companies (e.g. marketing). The sources of these data are the information and front-end systems of an organization (e.g. the collection of consumer data) (Roberts & Zahay, 2012, pp. 101-105), as well as freely accessible data on the Internet (e.g. the discussion of people on a particular web) (Sperkova & Skola, 2015). This also affects common users, who interact within various Internet-based services and thus create a large amount of personal data – this concerns mainly social networking services. The reason for such behaviour is today's information society, which unobtrusively prompts users to share their personal information on the Internet (e.g. people are positively motivated to share their personal information). This can also be described by the term self-disclosure (Benson, Saridakis & Tennakoon, 2015). Personal information accessible on the Internet can thus, on the one hand, help companies and their customers, from whom they can receive feedback or achieve personalisation to their customers based on individual data processing. On the other hand, it is a temptation for third parties to exploit these data.

A dual perspective (individual and firm) will be considered in this chapter. Companies should be aware of the challenges connected with individuals' Internet privacy, because those individuals may comprise customers and also their employees. Their personal information could be used for bullying or manipulating them to reveal a company secret or to become a serious security risk (Benson et al., 2015). This chapter focuses on the use of individual information disclosed on social networking services, primarily for marketing and management. Such systemic view on Internet privacy may be beneficial for organizations.

This chapter is organized as follows: Firstly, it introduces the theoretical foundations of technological, social, generational, cultural and philosophical issues of Internet privacy. It then discusses Generation Y's approach to self-disclosure on social networking services of users from France and the Czech Republic. The final two sections suggest future directions of research and highlight implications for policy and practice. This means particularly the possibilities of commercialization of available personal data.

BACKGROUND

In this section authors address various issues of privacy in the social web. After stressing the cultural and generational differences, the authors raise some questions stemming from the work of various thinkers in order to frame the problem of privacy in the postinternet condition. Postinternet is described as the 'moment in which the Internet is no longer a fascination or taboo, but rather a banal fact of daily living' (Arche, 2013). The postinternet condition is typical for the daily lives of Generation Y. The aim of the thematic sections is to expose essential standpoint in respect to Internet privacy connected with the needs of firms and other commercial activities online.

Cultural and Generational Differences

This chapter is focused on the representatives of the so-called Generation Y. The term Generation Y is nowadays assigned to young people who are newly economically active or will become economically active in the near future. Another important aspect is that this is the first generation that could in their childhood use ICT, especially computers and mobile devices. Its specificity can be defined using the time chronology.

Each generation overlaps, but we can, nevertheless, introduce at least an approximate chronological division: Baby Boomers (from the mid-1940s up to the early 1960s), Generation X (from the early 1960s to the early 1980s), Generation Y (from the early 1980s to the early 2000s), Generation Z (from the mid-1990s up to the early 2010s), Generation Alpha (after 2010). Representatives of Generation Y are the descendants of a significant generation called the baby boomers, who were born in the post-war period, and the oldest representatives of Generation X (Savage, 2011). Generation Y is also called the Next Generation, Millennials or the Net Generation and it is divided into three generation sub-units (Pendergast, 2010): Generation Why (born 1982-1985), Millennials (born 1985-1999) and iGeneration (born in 1999 -2002). In this chapter we focus on the first two sub-units. The reason for the focus on a selected group is the already mentioned fact that its members are gradually becoming fully economically active and are able to intuitively use modern Internet-based technologies (Benckendorff, Moscardo & Pendergast, 2010, p. 20; Valentine, Powers, 2013).

Along with the differences in generations, cultural differences should also be taken into account when discussing the differences in the approach to privacy. The term glocalization has been frequently discussed since the 1980s. It refers to the localization of a global product or service to a particular country or region. Web services are inherently ideal for global action and thus the issue of website localization for different cultures began to be researched intensively at the beginning of the millennium. The society of each country has its national traits, qualities, recognized values, habits, history and so on. All of this together creates a complex mix that forms the culture. It is therefore a complex concept that must be grasped somehow.

In this context, Hofstede's cultural dimensions are the most widely used tool. We can describe culture of each state by these dimensions. There are many studies showing a higher efficiency of culturally localized websites or Internet-based services – e.g. (Vyncke & Bergman, 2010; Cermak, 2015). This fact suggests that people from different countries have different expectations and behaviour, even when it concerns so global a medium as the Internet. For instance Li *et al.* (2009) supports this influence of cultural values on the approach to the use of ICT with a focus on online services. The results show that time orientation plays a significant role in the willingness to use new technology. Long-term oriented cultures are more compliant to use new technologies, because the features of long-term oriented users fit the nature of technology use. An important problem presents the dimension of individualism/collectivism. Users with higher values of individualism are more confident when working with technology in general and would find it less difficult.

Culture (as well as age, as mentioned above) is an important factor also in terms of the approach to the use of personal data. Miltgen and Peyrat-Guillard (2014), for example, provide interesting results within Europe. There is a difference in the north and the south of Europe concerning the importance of responsibility as opposed to trust. Another difference regards disclosure as a choice in Southern and as forced in Eastern Europe. Concerning the age, more positive attitudes toward data management, greater responsibility and greater confidence in the ability to prevent possible misuse of data can be found within the Generation Y.

Moreover, culture is stated as an important factor in a field of privacy also in the today's reflection about privacy in the information age (Dinev, 2014). The importance of culture show also previous articles of the author. Dinev *et al.* (2006) refer to the connection of cultural dimensions (especially Individualism-collectivism and Uncertainty Avoidance) and the concepts of trust and Internet privacy concerns and perceived risk, as the main variables for the use of services requiring personal data. Dinev *et al.* (2009) examined cross-cultural differences between South Korea and the United States in user behaviour towards protective information technologies and found that cultural factors are significant within the context of user attitudes and behaviour towards this type of technologies.

PHILOSOPHICAL ANCHORING OF SUBJECT PRIVACY

It is necessary not to lose sight of the theoretical and indeed the philosophical level. The reason is obvious: proceeding with the research of the issues concerning company growth or marketing would lead to a complete abandonment of the ethical or, more precisely, the normative and critical level, as illustrated by the relationship of ethical and economic behaviour of companies in (Sigmund, 2015). It is not possible only to propose how to target people within marketing; it is necessary to know what for and what social relations it affects or creates. It is impossible to simply describe what is being shared or kept in secret; it is necessary to know what concept of privacy it articulates. This attitude can prevent us from simply adhering to instrumental concepts of social media and privacy, for instance. More than ever before, it is important to realize that media, namely online social networks, are not mere means for our readymade identities and goals but that they involve their intrinsic rules of conduct deeply affecting our notions of identity, privacy or marketing communication. Therefore, the conclusion of this chapter is not simply deduced from research or the collected data itself, it rather springs from a deeper interest that is fuelled by critical thinking and philosophy.

These are inherently linked to art and its social imagination. Let us therefore begin with one artistic example – *Balconism* by Constant Dullaart (2014). It presents a text that is a kind of postinternet manifesto but also a gallery installation. On a general level, the balcony presents us with a spatial metaphor of the Internet itself. The basic, underlying condition of any conduct we take online is, that we are both in private and public. As on the balcony, we consider the space to be part of our private sphere. We excercize quite personal type of conduct here and that is why we actually talk about Internet privacy. But, on the other hand, we are visible. It does not matter whether someone actually watches us or uses our personal data; the important thing is that, potentially, we are being watched all the time, as if we were on a balcony. This brings us to the basic assumption concerning Internet privacy and its impact on our idea of the private sphere. Due to its inextricable connection with the public, we need on the one hand, to reflect its danger of abusing our private data (publically available), but on the other hand, we may address its mediatory potential, whether it is in political (the impact of social media in the Arab spring, for instance) or economic terms (tubers and bloggers).

On a theoretical level, we can summarize the historical development with Hannah Arendt's influential book *Human Condition* (*Vita Activa*) (Arendt, 1998). She argues that (1) in the ancient polis, the private sphere of a household (*oikos*) was strictly disengaged from and subordinate to the public sphere of the agora; everybody (except for slaves and women, of course) was equal within the public sphere, no matter what their private interests were. Nonetheless, this hierarchy is overturned in (2) the modern times, with individuals being determined by their profession, class or social position – i.e. by their private realm, which invades the public sphere. We seem to be entering yet another stage (3), in which it is increasingly difficult to disentangle these two spheres. Our privacy is constantly redefined and used within the public realm (of the Internet). Let us now connect this brief remark to our issue. Unlike common inquiries into the problem of Internet privacy, we tend not to take the very concept of privacy as predetermined, unequivocal or universal; it simply cannot be identified as a set of personal data (e.g. email address, pictures, consumption preference). Contrary to such implicit preconceptions, we believe that privacy is a deeply multifactorial and flexible concept that is being redefined along with its cultural, historical and even technological context.

As such, it cannot be separated from other underlying philosophical conditions, such as social order, economic system or media channelling. It is precisely (but of course not exclusively) through the notion of privacy that the phenomena of the Internet and social networking in particular transform our social communication and culture. And from the opposite direction, Internet environment not only poses new challenges for our privacy and its protection (Young & Quan-Haase, 2013), but our very notion of privacy is fundamentally transformed in an entirely new perspective. In a sense, the hypermedia reality is brought to its pinnacle. This means that the Internet environment as a medium absorbs all other media that are directed towards plurality and heterotopia of content and forms, thus creating a new logic of transparency of media content (Bolter & Grusin, 1999), along with setting a new dynamic of accessing one's private domain. Let us set the problem of privacy within a philosophical context with respect to its practices and human activities on three critical levels; namely in the context of (1) consumption, (2) freedom and (3) power.

Consumption

One of these lines is a critique of consumer culture. Perhaps the most radical formulation is provided by the so-called Frankfurt School and specifically Theodor Adorno. In his book *Minima Moralia* he states in the fragment *Asylum for the Homeless*: 'The predicament of private life today is shown by its arena. Dwelling, in proper sense, is now impossible. (...) It is part of morality not to be at home in one's home.' (Adorno, 2005, pp. 38-39) Throughout the entire book Adorno aims at an analysis of alienation, particularly in terms of consumerist culture. He concludes that, due to mass reproduction penetrating into all spheres of life, even our privacy is not the domain of individual freedom.

In 1951, when the book was first released, he provided an insight into the prospective development of reproductive technologies and their impact on privacy. Adorno is preoccupied mainly with radio and television. Nonetheless, it points again to the lack of division between private and public. For Adorno, it stems from the false identity of individual and general implied by modern media, including the Internet. Our identity and privacy falls prey to the public sphere ruled by uniformity and commercial exploitation. Uniformity of the private sphere is thus enforced as a means of identification with the community. Privacy in terms of mass media and especially social networking is not a sphere that would be only opposed to the threat of misuse, and thus driven by the dynamics of protection against the logic of the media. It also works in reverse dynamic through the pressure to publish the private content by the user himself. As users, we are motivated by a desire to identify ourselves with others on the basis of common or uniform private contents (holiday or celebration pictures, as well as information about school or hobbies).

Freedom and Its Media Logic

While on the first level we addressed the uniformity enforced within the medium, in the next stage we need to address the problem of new possibilities which the media provide us with. For it is true that new means create new forms of communication and action. In this respect we may turn to Michel de Certeau, who provides us with critique of these possibilities of media as they do not enlarge our freedom but on the contrary they entangle our action within their own logic. Media strive for a deeper penetration of their mechanisms into our lives and specifically our privacy.

In the words of De Certeau, as he writes in the chapter 'Reading as Poaching' in his book *The Practice of Everyday Life*: 'In any event, reader's increased autonomy does not protect him, for the media extend power over his imagination, that is, everything he lets emerge from himself into the nets of the text – his fears, his dreams, his fantasized and lacking authorities. This is what the powers work on that make out of "facts" and "figures" a rhetoric whose target is precisely this surrendered intimacy.' (De Certeau, 1984, p. 176) Though the text of 1980 was directed towards the medium of text and reading, we see its topicality in the perspective of social networking services. De Certeau shows here that the new options, such as the possibility to dispose of one's own personal data, may not be an increase of privacy protection. Because our will to limit this access to our personal data is based on the idea ('imagination') we have about our privacy, which is already incorporated in the logic of the social networking services. In addition, this phantasm of 'surrendered intimacy' allures through the promise of authentic human presence within otherwise highly impersonal communication in the Internet environment. Nonetheless, we can be cautious or even ironical; we can play along the lines of the medium and still keep our position safe. In one word, we can poach. This also resonates in the *Balconism* of Constant Dullaart who calls for self-awareness, coding and encryption that spring from the very nature of the (Internet) environment we entered.

Power

Both the preceding levels of critique of media direct our attention to the issues of power, surveillance or influence in shaping our personality. At this level, it is almost indispensable to take recourse in the analysis of Michel Foucault. In his work he dealt with the particular techniques of discipline in modern societies and institutions. He analysed the rise of modern hospitals (Foucault, 1963), psychopathology (Foucault, 1972), prisons (Foucault, 1975) or the history of sexuality (Foucault, 1976). Throughout his entire oeuvre Foucault warns against the reification or objectification of power as such. It cannot be simply seen as mere repression or a particular institution. Power is not only an invasion into the freedom of individuals. It is interplay of forces that have already shaped our concept of freedom. They are ubiquitous and inescapable. Not because they always surround us, but because power itself helps to shape our individuality, which seeks to resist the power (Foucault, 1976).

Foucault's analysis is even more appropriate in the perspective of Internet environment and the issue of privacy. He invites us not to define abuse on one side and, on the other, the protection of privacy on the Internet as two opposites. Undoubtedly, we enter a play of intersecting forces, which themselves constitute the entire sphere of privacy in the Internet environment. There is not only a counterweight or the result of our actions in the Internet environment, but rather its condition and constantly changing basis.

Summary of the Section

To conclude our philosophical exposition of the concept of privacy, we can note that (1) it naturally springs from our consumerist culture which defies any unproblematic notion of privacy ('to feel at home'), driving us constantly forward to look for means of identification with others or, more precisely, with their commoditized representations. (2) Nonetheless, this does not prevent us from developing our identity and Internet privacy. We just need to be self-aware and instead of relying on these commoditized forms we should critically appropriate them (therefore the concept of poaching). (3) Our privacy, just as our very subjectivity online (the condition of being an Internet user), is subjected to power and disciplination (of the medium). Therefore, we cannot disengage the protection and violation of one's privacy. We cannot divide our freedom and determination in the Internet environment; and last but not least, we do not have a shared preconception of privacy as it is constantly reshaped by our actual activities online. Like being on our balcony in slippers and housecoat – while being (potentially) visible to anybody.

Just as a person's cognitive abilities influence how he or she perceives and approaches the world, so the possibilities of processing personal data of (potential) customers create a broader view of firms on the environment in which they conduct their business and in which their activities take place. It is only at this basis that organizations can make decisions about their future activities, as is discussed in the following part.

THE POSSIBILITIES OF PROCESSING AND USING PERSONAL DATA ACCESSIBLE ON THE INTERNET

Personal data that can be accessed through various Internet-based services (blogs, forums, Facebook, Twitter) can be further processed and evaluated according to the objectives of a company. Personal data in particular are of a great help when analysing a large dataset and segmenting it. For example, the messages posted in discussion on forum are automatically processed and can be categorized by the sex or the hobbies of the users on the basis of acquired personal data. This way we can see the difference between opinions of women and men or categorize the posts by topic. In relation to the privacy of a subject on the Internet, it is appropriate to mention the basics of the acquisition, processing and evaluation of freely accessible personal data on the Internet, and the fundamental analytic approaches used in company and marketing management. Data can be acquired:

- Manually.
- **Automatically:** Data can be put in a database directly or by an artificial actor (softbot) programmed to acquire data on selected web pages or via selected Application Programming Interfaces (API).

In the case of manual data acquisition, an employee goes through each Internet-based service and creates his or her own database (e.g. in a spreadsheet application), which will be later interpreted and used for decision-making. For example, a marketing specialist can register data about the progression of marketing activities (e.g. the numbers of positive and negative feedbacks) which they will use later for the evaluation of marketing activities arranged through various tools (e.g. social media, forums, specialized web portals).

In the case of automatic data acquisition, it is necessary to select data sources and the way of acquiring data. With external data sources, it could be structured data acquired via API interface of a particular service, data acquired by front-end systems (e-shops), or non-structured data from web pages or documents – see the paper (Pavlicek & Novak, 2015) focused on external data sources. The application of a particular method of data acquisition relies on (besides the financial and technological state of a company) a specialist's conclusion – the resources and time needed to create a program for data acquisition vs. data volume, data processing, the extent of a campaign, future utilization of the data acquired, etc.

Data acquisition is followed by data processing – e.g. data conversion that enables their evaluation by methods used in knowledge discovery in databases (Witten, Frank & Hall, 2011; Rauch, 2013). Pre-processed data are further evaluated – e.g. by a reporting or analytic application (Kliegr et al., 2011), in most of cases with an objective to detect hidden correlations between variables (Pour, Maryska & Novotny, 2012). The results acquired this way must be put into context with other results and further interpreted. It should be considered that even in the case of automatically processed and evaluated data, the results are assessed by a specialist. When non-structured data (e.g. text on a web page without semantics for machine analysis) are processed, the pre-processing of these data is necessary to ensure a fundamental level of understanding of the content by a machine. Recently, the development of Web 3.0 technologies has started. These technologies are designated not only for human, but also for artificial actors, to whom they provide semantical information about the content of web pages. Possibilities of data processing and evaluation:

- **Manual:** An employee may use the tools of a selected office suite and put the acquired data into a table
- **Automatic:** Processing using selected technologies and approaches
  - **Structured Data:** Data available in the databases of particular systems, e.g. Customer Relationship Management (CRM) systems, e-shops or Enterprise Resource Planning (ERP) systems

- ◦ **Non-Structured Data:** Data available mostly on the web or in documents, which need to be pre-processed by Natural Language Processing (NLP) approaches to ensure a fundamental level of understanding of the content by a machine

Among the necessary and the applied techniques for data acquisition and processing for companies are 'intelligence' approaches (particularly reporting and analytical applications). In the lead is business intelligence which is 'a set of processes, know-how, applications and technologies, which are targeted to support effectively and functionally the management activities in a company' (Pour, Maryska & Novotny, 2012, p. 16). These intelligence approaches amplify the ability of a company to use knowledge assets in action. Similar approaches were developed in other specific areas which affect management on a strategical and tactical level and related activities (e.g. competitive intelligence, marketing intelligence, customer intelligence, media intelligence). The term business intelligence has been used since the 1980s (Bartes, 2010), but similar intelligence systems used by big companies have been in use since the 1970s. As ICT was being developed, including the Internet, an emphasis was put on the acquisition and evaluation of internal and external data related not only to a company, but also to competitive subjects. Thus, Pranjic (2011) considers the two dimensions needed to make the right business decisions: business intelligence (to know yourself) and competitive intelligence (to know your environment, competitive subjects). It is competitive intelligence that allows companies and their brands to be integrated in a specific market environment and a socio-cultural context of particular phases of a company's or a product's life cycle. For example, it is very difficult to enter a new foreign market without a deeper understanding of the social, cultural and political environment. Thus, it is necessary to conduct a market survey on the level of competitive intelligence to understand its specifics and to use these pieces of knowledge for the strategic management of marketing activities (Tej Adidam, Gajre & Kejriwal, 2009).

Recent approaches have focused on the analysis of structured and non-structured data; non-structured data are pre-processed and converged to structured data using NPL dictionaries and are further analyzed (Baars & Kemper, 2008). Since we were evaluating non-structured data, we were not able to converge them to structured data absolutely correctly. Nevertheless, the available options are in most cases sufficient for the subsequent data processing. For example, in sentiment analysis (Liu, 2012) we are able to focus on the categories of sentiment, i.e. positive or negative feedback (Sperkova & Skola, 2015).

Some approaches and techniques used in business intelligence and other segments related to knowledge discovery in databases belong to the field of Data science, which is based on data-analytic thinking and data-managed decision-making across the organization (Provost & Fawcett, 2013). The roots of this scientific discipline go back to the 1960s. It is not a system or set of practices as in the case of business intelligence, but there are particular and generally applicable ways of knowledge discovery from acquired data which must be further integrated into specific models. One such example is data processing for predictive analysis. Data science also involves approaches dealing with datasets which are too large to be processed by common methods or systems – so-called big data (Provost & Fawcett, 2013). The processing and evaluation of big data is a current trend in many interdisciplinary informatics fields (e.g. community, humanistic, social or historical informatics) and also in the fields of the medial-communication cycle of science or marketing in relation to the evaluation of online communication or marketing activities.

Processing data available on the Internet is no longer just a challenge, but a reality. Both personal (consumer intelligence, marketing intelligence) and company (competitive intelligence) data is processed for commercial purposes. Apart from that, these data can be used in e-research and other activities which are in the public interest (e.g. security intelligence). We are witnessing a new dynamics and continuous changes in individuals' views on their privacy, which are influenced by the possibilities brought by ICT. Similarly, this dynamics affects the organizational context of firms (mainly security and communication) and their ability to process enormous sets of data, which has an impact mainly on their marketing and management.

The Limitations of Handling Private Data in Internet-Based Services

Information technology and the possibilities of Internet-based services constantly evolve. Almost every online service requires users' personal data for the possibility of its use. The safety and the handling of these data is a very important issue these days, both for the users and providers of online services – see also *Guide to data protection for public and organization* available at (ICO, 2015). Within the European Union – see (DLA Piper, 2014) – the default privacy principles are primarily governed by the European Directive 95/46/EC from 24 October 1995 on the protection of individuals with regard to the processing of personal data and on the free movement of such data. The year of its inception suggests that this directive is already quite old and therefore does not reflect the current situation. This directive needs to refine and thereby at least partially reflect current development.

Currently we can mention for example the act from 15 June 2015 when the EU Council approved a general approach to the general data protection regulation. It establishes rules adapted to the digital era and according to that cookies should be included in personal data. The current EU Directive 2002/58/EC on Privacy and Electronic Communications (known as the E-Privacy Directive) obliges member states to adopt legislation requiring a prior approval of the use of cookies. In practice, this means that when you use cookies, which are designed to collect users' personal data, you need to obtain the users' consent with the use of cookies on your website.

Besides the refinement and fragmentation of laws within the EU, there is a number of clarifications on the level of national laws – see (European Commission, 2015). This leads to each state having slightly different laws. When doing business in a foreign country, it is necessary to become familiar with the specific legislation of a particular state. The fragmentation of legislation worldwide is even greater. For example, the US laws vary across the individual states, but also with regard to the type of sector and media. In addition, there are often various exceptions.

If we are to summarize the basic principles, the following recommendations for practice can be drawn. User's consent must be obtained when collecting personal data (i.e. the opt-in principle) for a specific purpose. This purpose should be stated, for example in business conditions. Using personal data for subsequent marketing purposes makes it obligatory to give users the option of cancelling their agreement with the use of their personal data, and thus to 'unsubscribe' from a database of respondents. The user has the right to request a statement of his personal data stored by the data manager. He or she can also ask for their personal data to be deleted. The data manager must comply with the user's request.

THE NEGATIVE CONSEQUENCES RELATED TO THE ACCESSIBILITY OF PERSONAL DATA ON THE INTERNET

An important issue is the use and the possible misuse of the freely available personal data that can be manually or automatically harvested by bots (data-harvesting softbot) and further processed by third parties. As an example, It is presented information that can be obtained from the Facebook service, which can be used for human resource management (Bohmova & Malinova, 2013; Benson, Morgan & Filippaios, 2014), marketing (Jasek, 2015), or abused for various forms of (cyber)bullying in a workplace or used by malicious data miners to threaten the privacy of users (Al-Saggaf & Islam, 2015):

- **Personal Information:** Belief, orientation, references to family, political opinions, contact information, what the user likes, employment/school, partially also pictures and multimedia content.
- **Information on Location:** Address, current position.
- **Data on Interaction:** A post on the wall, partially pictures and multimedia content, comments.

These data can be (mis)used mainly for unfair marketing practices. On the one hand, these data are used by Facebook itself for targeted advertising. On the other hand, the publicly available data are misused by harvesting and subsequently selling them to third parties. These include e-mail, phone and instant messaging, which can be supplemented with additional information (e.g. physical location) of the subject that owns it and used for targeting in an unfair commercial communications campaign.

Equally important are the social consequences when these data are used by any person for the purpose of discrediting or damaging the reputation of a particular individual. It could be personal data, available posts, comments and pictures, which are a gate into his or her private activities. In the work environment the information can be used for cyberbullying a worker in a particular group. An example: an innocent photo from Facebook can be simply modified and send anonymously to group members. This conduct can have serious implications for team communication and working environment, which is negatively projected into the business activities of the organization. The following types of bullying are specific for a working team:

- **Mobbing:** Bullying by colleagues in a team.
- **Bossing:** Bullying by superiors.
- **Staffing:** Bullying by the subordinates of a superior, with the aim of unseating him or her.

The misuse of selected data (beliefs, political opinions, etc.) along with other forms of pressure – underestimation of work performance, constant criticism, assigning meaningless actions that have nothing to do with the working position or a person's real character – may amplify the negative effects. These are only some of the problems arising from the use of private information available about a person in the context of an organization and it is only one side of the coin. Concerning our topic, it is appropriate to refer to other resources where authors deal with the consequences associated with data available via social media – (Lashkari et al., 2010; Young & Quan-Haase, 2013; Ibrahim, Blandford & Bianchi-Berthouze, 2012).

Despite these potential dangers and possible negative consequences, today's young people leave in the Internet environment reflections of their daily activities, which together with other personal data present new possibilities for individual or personal online address. It is not only companies offering services to their customers, which can carry out a better segmentation of their customers and individually address them thanks to this information (Sperkova & Skola, 2015; Jasek, 2015). It is also for those who want to exploit a person – gaining control over their e-mails or identities and their potential future misuse, for example for botnet attacks (Boshmaf et al., 2013), gaining the trust and then manipulating a person in order to carry out certain actions, obtain certain information (e.g. credit card numbers) and disclose their secrets (Hadnagy, 2010). On the one hand, this provides greater comfort and thus better meets people's needs (connected with a better segmentation of customers), and on the other hand, there are risks that cannot be underestimated on the personal (gaining control over online identities, manipulation, etc.), organizational (disclosure of company secrets, cyberbullying in workplace) or societal level (ethics, different approach to privacy).

GENERATION Y'S PRIVACY SETTINGS IN SOCIAL NETWORKING SERVICES

After an overview of topics related to Internet privacy and the possibilities of the acquisition and processing of the data of the users of Internet-based services, we focus on the results of relevant research studies. We start with own research (Cermak, Smutny & Janoscik, 2014), in which we compare the approaches of young people (age 15-30) from France and the Czech Republic. In this survey, such differences in behaviour are accented that originate in the cultural specifics of each country. This section also includes other interesting results from relevant surveys focused on Internet privacy. The conclusions following from these studies will enable companies to create their own strategy for obtaining information about customers and their interactions – e.g. for the purposes of marketing and management. This concerns mainly the different tendencies of young people in different countries to publish certain types of personal data, which can then be automatically processed; and the elements that motivate a person to give away personal data of their own free will.

The survey (Cermak, Smutny & Janoscik, 2014) presents two perspectives on privacy in the social networking services, both from a theoretical and a philosophical point of view, as well as from the perspective of practical research on the social network Facebook. The aim is to synthesize those views and discuss the positives and negatives of the actual phenomena occurring in this environment during social interaction.

In total, we analysed 531 Facebook profiles of people aged 15-30 years. For each profile was gathered visible data in two cases. The first was the visibility of data from the perspective of a friend (i.e. we explored the account from a profile which was in the friends list). The second was the visibility from the perspective of a random user of Facebook, i.e. the user who was not included in the circle of friends in the monitored Facebook account. At first, we introduce the answers to the three main research questions of this study, which will be followed by a discussion:

- *What kind of information is most frequently freely available?* The most freely published data are name, gender, friends, liked pages, current location, school/university and posts on the wall related to personal experiences, posts containing entertaining content and comments on current events – i.e. the data of general character. In contrast, data containing contact information, such as address, phone number or e-mail and data relating to personal beliefs (religion, political beliefs) are published with the least frequency.

Interestingly, users from France do not publish their true name in more than a quarter of cases. They use a profile under a different name or nickname. But (unlike Czechs) the French frequently publish their e-mail address, date of birth and information about their current location and hometown. Czech users disclose more information about their current school/university, as well as about their friends and the pages they like.

- *What information is most often available to friends but hidden to other users?* When comparing the differences among public and private data available in each country, the most significant differences were found out in posts on the wall, date of birth and photos presented on Facebook. In the Czech Republic, there is a difference of about 70% (for example 96% of users from the Czech Republic make posts from personal life available to their friends, but only 23% to general public), in France it is about 50%. Approximately a 40% difference was found in data relating to family, employment position, e-mail, school and the pages that the user likes. For these data the differences are more or less the same for users from the Czech Republic and France. The most significant differences in data availability between France and the Czech Republic relate to the current employment position (33%), funny posts on the wall (28%), information about the user (25%) and published pictures (25%).

- *What is the most frequently shared information on the wall of Facebook in each country and is the information only visible to friends or to other users as well?* In the case of public posts, the French frequently publish posts about their personal life, work and past events. Czech people make more often available to public only the posts with funny character, compared to the French. In the case of posts published for a circle of friends, majority of Czechs and the French write on the wall posts from their personal life. The differences can be found in other types of posts. Czech people more often than the French publish on their wall posts commenting current events (news) and posts that are funny. On contrary, the French publish more posts associated with their employment. Overall, Czechs publish their posts frequently only in their circle of friends, while the French often leave their posts freely available.

Results from the evaluation of publishing pictures and information about friends and favourite websites show that in the case of friends, the information is more often published by Czech users in all cases. It is the same when publishing for the general public, except for pictures, which are more frequently published by the French.

With regard to the philosophical basis outlined in the background section, we can continue with a particular archaeology of subjectivity in the environment of social networks on the Internet. Based on our data collection, there is an obvious difference not only in the actual administration of users' personal data, but also in their relationship to the network as a whole. While French Facebook users show more effort to protect their information in general, in the case of the key items in relation to the profile on the network and their real lives, the opposite is true. Despite a greater tendency to publish a large number of surveyed items, Czech users very strictly protect information that makes them identifiable at other levels (phone number, email, location). For most of these items, the publishing rate by Czech users is around 1%, some items such as telephone number or zip code are not published at all. As opposed to a premature conclusion that could only quantitatively evaluate French privacy, we provide a more accurate insight. Differences in the data indicate rather a different role that the social networking services plays. In France, the network is more tightly linked to other layers of identity of the users. This naturally puts pressure on a better control of the published data. In the Czech Republic, social networks follow first the logic of remediation – rather than create a supplement to real identities, so they act as an alternative to real identities: social networking services is a space in which the users do not follow their identification data but rather generate new relationships on media basis. This can explain the lesser pressure on protecting the remaining items of personal data that are involved in the creation of an alternate reality (e.g. status, friends, favourite pages).

The survey results are therefore consistent with the philosophical basis. (1) At the level of criticism of consumer culture, we can use Adorno's conceptualization of the attack on privacy in data analysis. This happens not only through the threat of misuse, but from the opposite side by putting pressure on the publishing of personal information by a user. (2) At the level of media reflection along with De Certeau, we see that the media (in our case the social networks) extend the possibilities of user behaviour in relation to their data, but do not add autonomy of their users. Media logic penetrates the user's imagination, forms 'his fears, his dreams, his fantasized and lacking authorities' (De Certeau, 1984, p. 176) and thus also his or her idea of privacy. (3) We can expand together with Foucault these media penetration mechanisms into individual ideas. He tries to conceptualize the phenomenon of power not as a substance or a centre, which attacks our individuality, but as the fabric of the network which helps to create it, including our ideas about privacy and its protection. In the study of outlined power we cannot only monitor cases of penetration of privacy. It is necessary to describe and assess the acts of users themselves, who are always already shaped by that power relation.

In general, we can summarize that the social networks on the Internet are at a very specific level at which the individuality of the user interferes with the invasion of transpersonal structures, which are characterized here:

1. Their mass,
2. Media logic, and
3. Nature of power.

Naturally, this issue calls for a specialized interdisciplinary elaboration. It can not only provide the analysis, description and evaluation of the dangers that are hidden in the accessibility of personal data published by users, but it also develops some considerations (based on Adorno and Foucault) about the development of the human personality in today's dynamic environment. Although the survey is relatively limited and the comparison is only bilateral, the authors consolidated the general perspective on how to approach the issue of privacy on social networking services.

The afore-mentioned research will now be supplemented with the results of other relevant inquiries. Let us begin with (Syn & Oh, 2015), who confirm the diverse motivations for sharing private information within social networking services. These depend on demographic characteristics, experience with these services and Internet usage, as well as the characteristics and features of the services themselves. Users could be highly motivated by the learning and social engagement aspects of social networks.

Different attitudes can be found even among men and women. The latter are prone to a proactive privacy protection behaviour on social networking services and generally in a Web 2.0 environment than it was reported around the year 2000. Almost a half of both genders are not aware of how personal information is being used (Hoy & Milne, 2010). However, results from the research study (Benson, Saridakis & Tennakoon, 2015) show that control over personal information published in social networking services is negatively and statistically associated with information disclosure. Both user awareness and security notices have a positive statistical effect on information disclosure.

Another research (Cecere, Le Guel & Soulie, 2015) conducted in 26 European countries verifies that the conception and awareness of privacy is positively affected by national policies concerning personal data protection, which differs in individual countries. Similarly, it asserts that cultural and socio-demographical variables affect the level of concerns one has about his or her privacy online.

Although privacy is valued for many reasons, as was mentioned about Generation Y, who take the Internet as an integral part of their lives, this issue is still not taken seriously (Al-Saggaf & Islam, 2012). The educational programs currently implemented point towards information and security risks (Kolin, 2011), but this process started relatively late and it affects rather the Generations Z and Alpha, not the Generation Y, which currently becomes economically active. Another problem presents the relatively weak and fragmented support in the legislation of particular countries concerning possible misuse of personal data (Al-Saggaf & Islam, 2015). Nonetheless, we can consider the efforts taken by the social network providers themselves, in order to maintain the anonymity of their users using their particular services, as positive initiative (Wang et al., 2015; Rajaei, Haghjoo & Miyaneh, 2015). Despite that, the technological possibilities of misuse of available data has technologically advanced further than the options of both direct (technological) and indirect (awareness, proactive attitude of individuals) protection of user privacy.

On the other hand, social networking services make possible a leak of private information as observed by another study (Li et al., 2015) focused on Facebook, Google+ and Twitter services. This stems from the conflicts between privacy control and social networking services functionalities. Besides online social networking services themselves, we can observe the games played via social networking services. According to existing research (Chae & Lee, 2015), the attitude of users towards privacy in specific social networking service does affect their perception of advertisements within the games. Primarily, these games use the identity of a user to address his or her friends. Despite the fact that social networking services have been successful in limiting the risks of direct access to personal data, the danger resides in communication through the profile of a player, which can be seen as unfair marketing communication. These findings confirm our philosophical exposition of the problem of privacy in which we have argued against the extrapolated scheme (privacy versus intrusion) in favour of a more holistic view in which the privacy is not intruded but rather formed by the online social networks.

There is significant group of users who are aware of the potential dangers of personal data being accessible through various social media. Nonetheless, these negative aspects are in many cases outweighed by certain benefits. Existing research (Min & Kim, 2015) introduces three enticements: the motivation of relationship management through social networking services, the perceived usefulness of social networking services for self-presentation, and the subjective social norms of using social networking services. 'The results regarding the positive and negative effects of suggested benefit and cost factors on information disclosure show that only the combined positive effects of all three behaviour enticements exceed the negative effect of privacy concerns, suggesting that privacy concerns can be offset only by multiple benefit factors.' (Min & Kim, 2015) Possible threats connected to social networking services affecting users, including the means of their prevention, are listed here, for instance (Fogues et al., 2015).

SELECTED FUTURE RESEARCH DIRECTIONS AND ISSUES

Within the reflection on future paths of research and development approaches to Internet privacy it is necessary to offer once again the perspective of two levels – personal and organizational. If we begin with the personal level, we have to highlight the increasing global information and security literacy even among the representatives of Generation X and Y. On the other hand, new technologies still emerge. Consequently, these technologies bring new perspectives on privacy and also remake old approaches. We should mention mainly the services based on Web 3.0 and ubiquitous technologies.

In the case of Internet-based services built on the Web 3.0 technology, which focus mainly on the semantization of content on the Internet for artificial actors, there are new ways of influencing the subjectivity of the human user by the behaviour of artificial actors. Because of the fact that Internet-based services are not user-tailored only to people, but will also be readable for softbots, it can be expected that even the artificial actors will enter into relationships with human actors and will influence their subjectivity[1]. Artificial actors and their actions will thus affect human subjectivity more than now – see also the marketing concept of the management of subjectivity (Firat, 2014; Tadajewski & Jones, 2014).

For example, an artificial actor can seek and reach a human (at a similar level of communication as another human) who has a specific mix of interests, establish a relationship with him or her and influence them by its contributions. In the context of Internet privacy, this is an issue of the selective approach of artificial actors to personal information, primarily within a field of social networking services. In other words, we can distinguish between good softbots (e.g. indexing Googlebot) which increase attendance and bad softbots which abuse the personal data for the needs of their maker.

Ubiquitous technologies develop at the level of both physical and virtual environments (e.g. the terms as the Internet of Things, Internet of Services) as well as on the level of mixed reality. In the area of social networking, future development is associated with the development of ubiquitous social networking that will support the social wellbeing of people in their everyday lives. This means a diversion from the centralized web-based social networks and the transition to ad hoc social networks that are limited by certain physical areas, where they promote social interaction. Although there are not many real applications, an important aspect of these technologies is privacy – controlling the access to personal data (Sapuppo & Seet, 2015). A current trend is the development of general models that deal with specific problems associated with ubiquitous technologies – e.g. (Chikhaouia et al., 2014; Lopes et al., 2014; Pesout & Matustik, 2012).

From the perspective of organizations and the usefulness of freely available data on the Internet, mainly for marketing activities, current development focuses on the identification of customers through various Internet-based services. The aim is to identify the different identities (e.g. profiles on Facebook or Twitter) as one customer, which will contribute to a better monitoring of customer behavior (their web traffic), the individualization of services and enhancing marketing models working with customer data such as customer lifetime value or electronic word-of-mouth analytical models (Jasek, 2015; Sperkova & Skola, 2015; Cheunga & Thadani, 2012). First studies concerning this identification are currently available – see (Long & Jung, 2015) – which for this purpose process available (personal) data. Let us add that this task may become easier in the future if Web 3.0 technologies are fully enforced.

Although companies focus their attention mainly on the processing of internal and external data (of their customers), they are at the same time caught in a trap created by their problems (inability) with processing large amounts of data from a wide variety of structured and unstructured sources. For instance, according to a survey among Czech small and medium-sized companies (Smutny, 2015) the results show that the fundamental problems perceived in connection with the processing of data from the Internet for marketing purposes are in particular:

1. Increasing time demands associated with the use of a large number of tools and services (e.g. social media, advertising systems).
2. The inability to create a holistic view of the success of their marketing activities. Currently, they rely only on partial instruments providing individual statistics.

On the other hand, it should be noted that only a small proportion of companies from Central and Eastern Europe (contrary to Western Europe and the USA) is pressed by competition to increase their use of potential data sources, or rather to a synergistic use of online marketing tools (Janoscik, Smutny & Cermak, 2015; Smutny, 2015).

The issue of Internet privacy is closely associated with technological development as well as with information literacy of the users of Internet-based services – i.e. the awareness of the risks associated with the availability of personal data, especially within the group of users of social networking services. As stated above, there is a large number of empirical studies dealing with the approach of Generation Y to self-disclosure, including the phenomena supporting this sometimes risky behaviour. From the perspective of firms, there is a trend to increase economic efficiency by supplying current marketing, data-driven and others models with qualitatively new data (Pavlou, 2011). However, this trend, in our opinion, is slowed down by a related problem, which is the lack of technological and expert resources within companies (Maryska & Doucek, 2012) that would enable carrying out the gathering and processing of available data at the required level.

CONCLUSION

This chapter brought up an array of topics directly attached to Internet privacy both from the perspective of a regular user and from that of commercial organizations. This view from both sides can provide companies with better understanding of various aspects of Internet privacy. Our main concerns with generational and cultural differentiations, philosophical scrutiny, possibilities of data acquisition and analysis, legal framework, and negative consequences of personal data availability, all these aspects do intersect and form a basis, on which we can articulate other ideas focused for instance on prospective usage of personal data available on the Internet with the emphasis on the needs of firms. On the other hand, it was addressed even the issues of their misuse in personal and organizational context (manipulation of users, security risks etc.).

In order to understand the contemporary behaviour of Generation Y and their attitudes towards self-disclosure through social networking services we have discussed our preceding comparative research[2] in its wider system-oriented framework and based on selected set of other studies. In concluding parts we have provided not only important findings of recent research concerned with young users of social networking services and their treatment of their personal data.

We discuss even some prospective technological trends, but also some problems involved in economic interests of companies. In this respect the chapter outlines basic directions for companies to set and realize their activities connected with usage of freely available (personal) data. These might be outlined as consolidating available means of data sources, using analytical approaches (e.g. business intelligence) and models (e.g. customer lifetime value, electronic word-of-mouth) and secondly clear set of ethical principles of work with personal data including legal integrity. These courses of action are essentially dependent on technically educated employees and technical possibilities of particular company.

The most important implication for company practice can be summarized in the following points:

1. In companies' effort to acquire data for their marketing and management activities through Internet-based services, it is necessary to motivate people to provide personal data of their own free will (e.g. special commercial offers, discounts, presents, promo actions, individual approach). Different

generations (and target groups) have a different understanding of privacy and tendencies to self-disclosure. Privacy is not intruded but rather formed by social networking services. This way of acquiring personal data seems to be more fair, as opposed to e.g. harvesting personal data from selected websites without involving their owners.

2. Cultural and generational differences are reflected in social interactions via social networking services, but also in a preference for certain products or services and thus a demand for them. Every culture or country has a different set of values, which are reflected in the feedback or reactions of people on media and marketing communication activities. Connected with that is the *Agenda-Setting Theory*, i.e. the ability of mass media to influence the audience and suggest topics which are then further dealt with via social networking services.

3. The *Glocalization* principle needs to be applied in the current Internet-mediated environment mainly for cultural and geographical reasons. This means adapting globally offered services and products on a defined local level (e.g. continent, country, language group), and their specific conditions (see *Hofstede's cultural dimensions theory*).

4. In the same spirit it is necessary to consider different aspects when targeting marketing activities (market segmentation). Those include generational (every generation has different needs, priorities, the ability to use modern technologies) and the above-mentioned cultural (the tradition of an established brand, established schemes and product types) specification of a particular group.

5. A problem connected with privacy is that of security and decreasing the danger of a leak of sensitive company data, which happens mainly via company employees. The basic solution is to limit access to individual data sources of potential information according to objective information requirements of a certain position.

6. When using social networking services on individual or company level, it is necessary to consider possible (mis)use of the published information, for example by business rivals (e.g. as part of competitive intelligence, targeted damage by unfair communication campaigns). Data can be automatically processed by softbots, which will increase further with the gradual supplication of Web 3.0 technologies.

Let us also mention two current technological trends with a great social impact that are connected with the continuous development of ICT and mainly social networking services, which will in the near future affect the majority of companies doing business over the Internet:

1. The development of Web 3.0 technologies and mainly the semantization of webs will lead to more effective use of artificial actors (softbots), which will no longer process only unstructured data, but more often rather structured data freely available on the Internet. Other artificial actors with their profiles on social networking services will then be able to affect human subjectivity – even now it is very difficult e.g. on Twitter to determine whether a profile belongs to a human, a softbot, or a human acting like a softbot. It can therefore be expected that there will be a massive use of various forms of artificial actors, for instance for marketing, communication or competitive activities of firms. This issue concerns not only collecting and processing available personal data, but mainly the direct effect on a person's subjectivity and thus also on their perception and understanding of certain topics (including their attitude to privacy).

2. The expected development of ubiquitous technologies brings also the so-called ubiquitous social networks. Ad hoc social connections will be established within a certain area, which again concerns the issue of privacy. This technology will affect mainly retailers in stores, who will have new possibilities for propagation thanks to localized social interaction. For a better idea, let us give an example: A person walking in a street will be notified via his or her mobile device (on the basis of their interests, age, recent social activity) about a relevant shop located nearby. If interested, this person will be able to see their current offer (e.g. he or she is motivated by some discount if he or she makes a purchase there during the following hour).

Nonetheless our excursus into the problem of Internet privacy has not been limited to exposing and discussing basic issues, risks and prospectives. Mainly due to our philosophical grounding we have critically reassessed the very notion of privacy after our massive experience with social networking services. We need to think about their impact on our private sphere neither in terms of intrusion nor with some preconceived understanding of what privacy actually is. By no doubts it is being rearticulated and not only distorted by new technological means. Moreover there is no unequivocal private sphere since the publicity on social networking services capitalizes precisely on exposing our personal data. Like being on our balcony; on one hand confined to our private household, and on the other hand being completely exposed (Arendt). Nonetheless even this irritating situation has its prospective courses of action. Firstly we need to be aware of this exposure (Adorno). But this does not prevent of from reaching into this metaphorical space of social networks. We just need to appropriate its consumerist background and turn it into more critical "alterconsumerist" approach (De Certeau) admitting our very privacy to be informed by the networking (Foucault).

REFERENCES

Adorno, T. W. (2005). *Minima Moralia: Reflections on a Damaged Life*. London: Verso.

Al-Saggaf, Y., & Islam, M. Z. (2012). Privacy in Social Network Sites (SNS): The threats from data mining. *Ethical Space: The International Journal of Communication Ethics*, 9(4), 32–40.

Al-Saggaf, Y., & Islam, M. Z. (2015). Data Mining and Privacy of Social Network Sites' Users: Implications of the Data Mining Problem. *Science and Engineering Ethics*, 21(4), 941–966. doi:10.1007/s11948-014-9564-6 PMID:24916538

Arche, K. (2013). *Postinternet Observations*. Retrieved November 20, 2015, from https://artaftertheinternet.files.wordpress.com/2013/10/eeadf-postinternetessay.pdf

Arendt, H. (1998). *The Human Condition*. Chicago: University of Chicago Press. doi:10.7208/chicago/9780226924571.001.0001

Baars, H., & Kemper, H.-G. (2008). Management Support with Structured and Unstructured Data — An Integrated Business Intelligence Framework. *Information Systems Management*, 25(2), 132–148. doi:10.1080/10580530801941058

Bartes, F. (2010). Competitive Intelligence. *Acta Universitatis Agriculturae et Silviculturae Mendelianae Brunensis*, *58*(6), 43–50. doi:10.11118/actaun201058060043

Benckendorff, P., Moscardo, G., & Pendergast, D. (2010). *Tourism and Generation Y*. Cambridge: CAB International.

Benson, V., Morgan, S., & Filippaios, F. (2014). Social career management: Social media and employability skills gap. *Computers in Human Behavior*, *30*, 519–525. doi:10.1016/j.chb.2013.06.015

Benson, V., Saridakis, G., & Tennakoon, H. (2015). Information disclosure of social media users: Does control over personal information, user awareness and security notices matter? *Information Technology & People*, *28*(3), 426–441. doi:10.1108/ITP-10-2014-0232

Benson, V., Saridakisa, G., Tennakoonb, H., & Ezingeard, J. N. (2015). The role of security notices and online consumer behaviour: An empirical study of social networking users. *International Journal of Human-Computer Studies*, *80*, 36–44. doi:10.1016/j.ijhcs.2015.03.004

Bohmova, L., & Malinova, L. (2013). Facebook User's Privacy in Recruitment Process. In P. Doucek, G. Chroust, V. Oskrdal (Eds.), *Proceedings of the 21st Interdisciplinary Information Management Talks* (pp 159-168). Linz: Trauner Verlag.

Bolter, J. D., & Grusin, R. (1999). *Remediation: Understanding New Media*. Cambridge, MA: MIT Press.

Boshmaf, Y., Muslukhov, I., Beznosov, K., & Ripeanu, M. (2013). Design and analysis of a social botnet. *International Journal of Computer and Telecommunications Networking*, *57*(2), 556–578.

Cecere, G., Le Guel, F., & Soulie, N. (2015). Perceived Internet privacy concerns on social networks in Europe. *Technological Forecasting and Social Change*, *96*, 277–287. doi:10.1016/j.techfore.2015.01.021

Cermak, R. (2015). Multicultural Web Design: A Review. In P. Doucek, G. Chroust, V. Oskrdal (Eds.), *Proceedings of the 23nd Interdisciplinary Information Management Talks* (pp. 303–310), Linz: Trauner Verlag.

Cermak, R., Smutny, Z., & Janoscik, V. (2014). Analysis of the Facebook Privacy Settings of Young People with an Emphasis on the Czech Republic and France. In A. Rospigliosi & S. Greener (Eds.), *The Proceedings of the European Conference on Social Media ECSM 2014* (pp. 613-621). Reading: ACPI.

Chae, J. H., & Lee, Y. J. (2015). A Study on the Impact of Apprehension for Privacy concern and Attitude for Social Network Game Advertisement on the Use of Promotion Advertisement of SNG. *Journal of the Korean Society for Computer Game*, *28*(2), 151–157.

Cheunga, C. M. K., & Thadani, D. R. (2012). The impact of electronic word-of-mouth communication: A literature analysis and integrative model. *Decision Support Systems*, *54*(1), 461–470. doi:10.1016/j.dss.2012.06.008

Chikhaouia, B., Wanga, S., Xionga, T., & Pigot, H. (2014). Pattern-based causal relationships discovery from event sequences for modeling behavioral user profile in ubiquitous environments. *Information Sciences*, *285*, 204–222. doi:10.1016/j.ins.2014.06.026

De Certeau, M. (1984). *Practice of everyday life*. Berkeley: University of California Press.

Dinev, T. (2014). Why would we care about privacy? *European Journal of Information Systems, 23*(2), 97–102. doi:10.1057/ejis.2014.1

Dinev, T., Bellotto, M., Hart, P., Russo, V., Serra, I., & Colautti, C. (2006). Privacy calculus model in e-commerce – A study of Italy and the United states. *European Journal of Information Systems, 15*(4), 389–402. doi:10.1057/palgrave.ejis.3000590

Dinev, T., Goo, J., Hu, Q., & Nam, K. (2009). User behaviour towards protective information technologies: The role of national cultural differences. *Information Systems Journal, 19*(4), 391–412. doi:10.1111/j.1365-2575.2007.00289.x

Dullaart, C. (2014). Balconism. *Art Papers*. Retrieved September 15, 2015, from http://artpapers.org/feature_articles/feature3_2014_0304.html

European Commission. (2015). *Fifteenth annual report of the Article 29 Working Party on Data Protection*. Luxembourg: Publications Office of the European Union.

Firat, A. F. (2014). Marketing challenges: A personal history. *Journal of Historical Research in Marketing, 6*(3), 414–429. doi:10.1108/JHRM-11-2013-0062

Fogues, R., Such, J. M., Espinosa, A., & Garcia-Fornes, A. (2015). Open Challenges in Relationship-Based Privacy Mechanisms for Social Network Services. *International Journal of Human-Computer Interaction, 31*(5), 350–370. doi:10.1080/10447318.2014.1001300

Foucault, M. (1963). *Naissance de la clinique*. Paris: Presses Universitaires de France.

Foucault, M. (1972). *L'histoire de la folie à l'âge classique*. Paris: Gallimard.

Foucault, M. (1975). *Surveiller et punir*. Paris: Gallimard.

Foucault, M. (1976). Histoire de la sexualité, 3 volumes: La volonté de savoir, L'usage des plaisirs, and Le souici de soi. Paris: Gallimard.

Hadnagy, C. (2010). *Social Engineering: The Art of Human Hacking*. New York: Wiley.

Hoy, G. M., & Milne, G. (2010). Gender Differences in Privacy-Related Measures for Young Adult Facebook Users. *Journal of Interactive Advertising, 10*(2), 28–45. doi:10.1080/15252019.2010.10722168

Ibrahim, S. Z., Blandford, A., & Bianchi-Berthouze, N. (2012). Privacy Settings on Facebook: Their Roles and Importance. In *IEEE/ACM International Conference on Green Computing and Communications* (pp. 426-433). IEEE. doi:10.1109/GreenCom.2012.67

ICO. (2015). *Guide to data protection*. Information Commissioner's Office. Retrieved November 20, 2015, from https://ico.org.uk/for-organisations/

Janoscik, V., Smutny, Z., & Cermak, R. (2015). Integrated Online Marketing Communication of Companies: Survey in Central and Eastern Europe. In A. Kocourek (Ed.), *The Proceedings of the 12th International Conference Liberec Economic Forum* (pp. 376–383). Liberec: Technical University of Liberec.

Jasek, P. (2015). Impact of Customer Networks on Customer Lifetime Value Models. In R. P. Dameri, & L. Beltrametti (Eds.), *Proceedings of the 10th European Conference on Innovation and Entrepreneurship* (pp. 759-764), Reading: ACPI.

Kliegr, T., Svatek, V., Ralbovsky, M., & Simunek, M. (2011). SEWEBAR-CMS: Semantic analytical report authoring for data mining results. *Journal of Intelligent Information Systems*, *37*(3), 371–395. doi:10.1007/s10844-010-0137-0

Kolin, K. K. (2011). Social informatics today and tomorrow: Status, problems and prospects of development of complex lines in the field of science and education. *TripleC: Communication. Capitalism & Critique*, *9*(2), 460–465.

Lahtinen, H. J. (2012). Young people's ICT role at home – A descriptive study of young Finnish people's ICT views in the home context. *Quality & Quantity*, *46*(2), 581–597. doi:10.1007/s11135-010-9409-6

Lashkari, A. H., Parhizkar, B., Ramachandran, A., & Navaratnam, S. (2010). Privacy and Vulnerability Issues of Social Networks (Facebook). In H. Xie (Ed.), *Proceedings of the International Conference on Internet Technology and Security* (pp. 157-163). New York: ASME. doi:10.1115/1.859681.paper31

Li, X., Hess, T. J., McNab, A. L., & Yu, Y. (2009). Culture and Acceptance of Global Web Sites: A Cross-Country Study of the Effects of National Cultural Values on Acceptance of a Personal Web Portal. *ACM SIGMIS Database*, *40*(4), 62–87. doi:10.1145/1644953.1644959

Li, Y., Li, Y. J., Yan, Q., & Deng, R. H. (2015). Privacy leakage analysis in online social networks. *Computers & Security*, *49*, 239–254. doi:10.1016/j.cose.2014.10.012

Liu, B. (2012). *Sentiment analysis and opinion mining*. San Rafael: Morgan.

Long, N. H., & Jung, J. J. (2015). Privacy-Aware Framework for Matching Online Social Identities in Multiple Social Networking Services. *Cybernetics and Systems*, *46*(1-2), 69–83. doi:10.1080/0196972 2.2015.1007737

Lopes, J. L., Souza, R. S., Gadotti, G. I., Pernas, A. M., Yamin, A. C., & Geyer, C. F. (2014). An Architectural Model for Situation Awareness in Ubiquitous Computing. *IEEE Latin America Transactions*, *12*(6), 1113–1119. doi:10.1109/TLA.2014.6894008

Maryska, M., & Doucek, P. (2012). ICT Specialists Skills and Knowledge – Business Requirements and Education. *Journal on Efficiency and Responsibility in Education and Science*, *5*(3), 157–172. doi:10.7160/eriesj.2012.050305

Miltgen, C. L., & Peyrat-guillard, D. (2014). Cultural and generational influences on privacy concerns: A qualitative study in seven european countries. *European Journal of Information Systems*, *23*(2), 103–125. doi:10.1057/ejis.2013.17

Min, J., & Kim, B. (2015). How Are People Enticed to Disclose Personal Information Despite Privacy Concerns in Social Network Sites? The Calculus Between Benefit and Cost. *Journal of the Association for Information Science and Technology*, *66*(4), 839–857. doi:10.1002/asi.23206

Pavlicek, A., & Novak, R. (2015). Big data from the perspective of data sources. In R. Nemec, F. Zapletal (Eds.), *Proceedings of the 11th international conference on Strategic Management and its Support by Information Systems* (pp. 454–462). Ostrava: VSB-TU FE.

Pavlou, P. A. (2011). State of the information privacy literature: Where are we now and where should we go? *Management Information Systems Quarterly, 35*(4), 977–988.

Pendergast, D. (2010). Getting to know the Generation Y. In P. Benckendorff, G. Moscar, & D. Pendergast (Eds.), *Tourism and Generation Y* (pp. 1–15). Wallingford: CABI.

Pesout, P., & Matustik, O. (2012). On a Modeling of Online User Behavior Using Function Representation. *Mathematical Problems in Engineering, 784164*. doi:10.1155/2012/784164

Piper, D. L. A. (2014). *Laws of the World Handbook: Third Edition*. Retrieved September 15, 2015, from http://dlapiperdataprotection.com/#handbook/

Pour, J., Maryska, M., & Novotny, O. (2012). *Business intelligence v podnikové praxi*. Praha: Professional Publishing.

Pranjic, G. (2011). Influence of Business and Competitive Intelligence on Makong Right Business Decisions. *Economic Thought and Practice, 20*(1), 271–288.

Provost, F., & Fawcett, T. (2013). *Data science for business: What you need to know about data mining and data-analytic thinking*. Sebastopol, CA: O'Reilly.

Puddephatt, A., Mendel, T., Wagner, B., Hawtin, D., & Torres, N. (2012). *Global survey on Internet privacy and freedom of expression*. Paris: United Nations Educational, Scientific, and Cultural Organization.

Rajaei, M., Haghjoo, M. S., & Miyaneh, E. K. (2015). Ambiguity in Social Network Data for Presence, Sensitive – Attribute, Degree and Relationship Privacy Protection. *PLoS ONE, 10*(6), e0130693. doi:10.1371/journal.pone.0130693 PMID:26110762

Rauch, J. (2013). *Observational Calculi and Association Rules*. Berlin: Springer-Verlag. doi:10.1007/978-3-642-11737-4

Roberts, M. L., Zahay, D. L. (2012). *Internet Marketing: Integrating Online and Offline Strategies*. Mason, OH: South-Western Cengage Learning.

Sapuppo, A., & Seet, B. C. (2015). Privacy and technology challenges for ubiquitous social networking. *International Journal of Ad Hoc and Ubiquitous Computing, 18*(3), 121–138. doi:10.1504/IJA-HUC.2015.068127

Savage, S. (2011). Making sense of Generation Y: The world view of 15-25 year olds. London: Church House Publishing.

Sigmund, T. (2015). The Relationship of Ethical and Economic Behaviour. *Politicka Ekonomie, 63*(2), 223–243. doi:10.18267/j.polek.998

Smutny, Z. (2015). Analysis of Online Marketing Management in Czech Republic. *Organizacija – Journal of Management. Informatics and Human Resources, 48*(2), 99–111. doi:10.1515/orga-2015-0010

Sperkova, L., & Skola, P. (2015). E-WoM Integration to the Decision-Making Process in Bank Based on Business Intelligence. In P. Doucek, G. Chroust, V. Oskrdal (Eds.), *Proceedings of the 23nd Interdisciplinary Information Management Talks* (pp. 207–216). Linz: Trauner Verlag.

Syn, S. Y., & Oh, S. (2015). Why do social network site users share information on Facebook and Twitter? *Journal of Information Science, 41*(5), 553–569. doi:10.1177/0165551515585717

Tadajewski, M., & Jones, D. G. (2014). Historical research in marketing theory and practice: A review essay. *Journal of Marketing Management, 30*(11-12), 1239–1291. doi:10.1080/0267257X.2014.929166

Tej Adidam, P., Gajre, S., & Kejriwal, S. (2009). Cross-cultural competitive intelligence strategies. *Marketing Intelligence, 27*(5), 666–680. doi:10.1108/02634500910977881

Valentine, D. B., & Powers, T. L. (2013). Generation Y values and lifestyle segments. *Journal of Consumer Marketing, 30*(7), 597–606. doi:10.1108/JCM-07-2013-0650

Vyncke, F., & Bergman, M. (2010). Are culturally congruent websites more effective?: An overview of a decade of empirical evidence. *Journal of Electronic Commerce Research, 11*(1), 14–29.

Wang, Y., Hou, J., Xia, Y., & Li, H. Z. (2015). Efficient privacy preserving matchmaking for mobile social networking. *Concurrency and Computation, 27*(12), 2924–2937. doi:10.1002/cpe.3284

Witten, I. H., Frank, E., & Hall, M. A. (2011). *Data Mining: Practical Machine Learning Tools and Techniques*. Burlington, MA: Morgan Kaufmann.

Young, A. L., & Quan-Haase, A. (2013). Privacy protection strategies on Facebook: The Internet privacy paradox revisited. *Information Communication and Society, 16*(4), 479–500. doi:10.1080/1369118X.2013.777757

ADDITIONAL READING

Adorno, T. W. (2007). *Dialectics of Enlightenment*. Stanford: Stanford University Press.

Fromm, J., & Garton, C. (2013). *Marketing to Millennials: Reach the Largest and Most Influential Generation of Consumers Ever*. New York: AMACOM.

González-Fuster, G. (2014). *The emergence of personal data protection as a fundamental right of the EU*. New York: Springer. doi:10.1007/978-3-319-05023-2

Havens, J. (2015). *Hacking h(app)iness: Why your personal data counts and how tracking it can change the world*. New York: Penguin Group.

Luppicini, R. (2010). *Technoethics and the Evolving Knowledge Society: Ethical Issues in Technological Design, Research, Development, and Innovation*. PA: IGI Global. doi:10.4018/978-1-60566-952-6

Nissenbaum, H. (2010). *Privacy in Context: Technology, Policy, and the Integrity of Social Life*. Stanford: Stanford Law Books.

Patil, D. J., & Hilary Mason, H. (2015). *Data Driven: Creating a Data Culture*. Sebastopol: O'Reilly Media.

Quinn, M. J. (2014). *Ethics for the Information Age*. Boston: Pearson.

Sladek, S. (2014). *Knowing Y: Engage the Next Generation Now*. Lawrence: Association Management Press.

Sumner, S., & Rispoli, M. (2015). *You: For sale – Protecting your personal data and privacy online*. Waltham, Massachusetts: Elsevier.

Tanner, A. (2014). *What stays in Vegas: The world of personal data – lifeblood of big business – and the end of privacy as we know it*. New York: Public Affaires.

Ward, B. (2014). *Online Privacy: How to Remain Anonymous & Protect Yourself While Enjoying a Private Digital Life on The Internet*. Grand Reveur Publications.

Xu, Q., & Mocarski, R. (2014). A cross-cultural comparison of domestic american and international chinese students' social media usage. *Journal of International Students, 4*(4), 374–388.

Yang, K. C. C., & Kang, Y. (2015). Exploring big data and privacy in strategic communication campaigns: A cross-cultural study of mobile social media users' daily experiences. *International Journal of Strategic Communication, 9*(2), 87–101. doi:10.1080/1553118X.2015.1008635

Ziegeldorf, J. H., Morchon, O. G., & Wehrle, K. (2014). Privacy in the Internet of Things: Threats and challenges. *Security and Communication Networks, 7*(12), 2728–2742. doi:10.1002/sec.795

ENDNOTES

[1]   Subjectivity can be understood as the condition of being an Internet user. Human subjectivity is individual experience, which is always unique and influenced by the environment and the actors in the environment (in the Internet environment, these could be human but also artificial actors) in which the subject resides.

[2]   This chapter was prepared thanks to the same research project VSE IGS F4/18/2014 at the University of Economics, Prague.

This research was previously published in Analyzing the Strategic Role of Social Networking in Firm Growth and Productivity edited by Vladlena Benson, Ronald Tuninga, and George Saridakis, pages 95-119, copyright year 2017 by Business Science Reference (an imprint of IGI Global).

Chapter 52

Multimodal Mapping of a University's Formal and Informal Online Brand:
Using NodeXL to Extract Social Network Data in Tweets, Digital Contents, and Relational Ties

Shalin Hai-Jew
Kansas State University, USA

ABSTRACT

With the popularization of the Social Web (or Read-Write Web) and millions of participants in these interactive spaces, institutions of higher education have found it necessary to create online presences to promote their university brands, presence, and reputation. An important aspect of that engagement involves being aware of how their brand is represented informally (and formally) on social media platforms. Universities have traditionally maintained thin channels of formalized communications through official media channels, but in this participatory new media age, the user-generated contents and communications are created independent of the formal public relations offices. The university brand is evolving independently of official controls. Ex-post interventions to protect university reputation and brand may be too little, too late, and much of the contents are beyond the purview of the formal university. Various offices and clubs have institutional accounts on Facebook as well as wide representation of their faculty, staff, administrators, and students online. There are various microblogging accounts on Twitter. Various photo and video contents related to the institution may be found on photo- and video-sharing sites, like Flickr, and there are video channels on YouTube. All this digital content is widely available and may serve as points-of-contact for the close-in to more distal stakeholders and publics related to the institution. A recently available open-source tool enhances the capability for crawling (extracting data) these

DOI: 10.4018/978-1-5225-5637-4.ch052

various social media platforms (through their Application Programming Interfaces or "APIs") and enables the capture, analysis, and social network visualization of broadly available public information. Further, this tool enables the analysis of previously hidden information. This chapter introduces the application of Network Overview, Discovery and Exploration for Excel (NodeXL) to the empirical and multimodal analysis of a university's electronic presence on various social media platforms and offers some initial ideas for the analytical value of such an approach.

INTRODUCTION

Web 2.0, the so-called Read-Write Web, has been lauded as a major vector for human connectivity. This social Web has enabled mediated connections between people regardless of distance, nationality, social backgrounds, or languages. Social media platforms are online spaces designed for human social interactions, and many of them attract different user bases. These include social networks, multimedia (photo -, video-, slideshow- and other) sharing sites, blogging sites, microblogging sites, wikis, discussion forums, virtual worlds, and mash-ups of various functionalities of the above. The sites all have different functionalities, vetting of human identities, interface designs, and terms of agreement (end user license agreement or EULAs). Currently, sites like Facebook and Twitter are some of the most trafficked Websites in the world, accessible on a range of mobile and other computing devices.

Ideally, socio-technical systems, which are designed for human interactions and engagement, should be designed to enhance human actualization and social support for others (Lanier, 2010). For all the efforts at proper management of such sites, there are examples of anti-social behavior: content pollution, self-promotion, malicious content, copyright infringements, pornography, and spam. There are attempts to game the system or compromise information. Further, not all accounts are humans; rather, there are accounts set up for robots ('bots), cyborgs (people and robots posting contents together), and humans.

The social connections that arise through social media platforms have been described in various ways. For many, these are "loose ties," with light connections between people who are essentially strangers. There are instances of "weak cooperation" between individuals who express themselves through videos and photos, often without direct awareness of each other until certain digital artifacts are published and shared. Others are sparked by social media to participate in mass events like flash mobs. Strangers play augmented reality games on their mobile devices and interact with each other within the rules of the game. The movement of peoples en masse to social media platforms has been a distinct phenomenon among youth, many of whom are university students. This means that universities that want to engage their students in electronic spaces would benefit from being aware of where their students are engaging and knowing how to teach them.

Data extractions (or crawls) from social media sites may shed light on these various online communities, their structures, and their functions. This knowledge may support university outreach and (formal and informal) branding endeavors.

A REVIEW OF THE LITERATURE

To offer a brief overview: research into social networks started in the early 20th century within sociology. Researchers started to create quantitative measures of network relationships in the 1930s with sociometry. Psychologists contributed to this work in the 1940s by formally defining cliques (or subnetworks). In the 1950s and 1960s, anthropologists started applying social network analysis to their work. Some researchers integrated elements of game theory and economics into their social network analyses—for a highly multi-disciplinary approach. Various researchers have since contributed rich research and theorizing about social networks. In the 2000s, the computing sciences offered ways to analyze and visualize social networks.

To contextualize, there are some basic governing logics and underlying assumptions. One central concept is that much of human endeavor occurs in social groupings and fairly stable human relationships (defined by social roles, bureaucratic structures, social practices, and others). Human groups tend to be fairly hierarchical, and those with power accrue much more than others in terms of decision-making, power, information, and resources. They are theorized to have a clearer sense of a social network than others who are relatively less privileged in terms of positions. Human connections matter. People do not connect randomly, but they tend to build relationships in homophilous ways, with similarity being attracted to similarity (or "preferential attachment"). On some work teams, heterophily (the like of differences) is preferred to ensure a diverse skill set and variant perspectives. Social network analysis involves the analysis of the structural aspects of such connections. The proximity of an individual's nodes suggests a direct influence; network analysis shows that an influential node may have distal influence as well (influence at a distance). The structure of a network may shed light on its capabilities.

Other canonical concepts examine how resources, practices, and ideas "diffuse" or flow through a network along certain human channels. A flow may be stopped at a particular node based on particular threshold effects (a signal not reaching a particular threshold for that node to respond). That said, information may also flow around a non-responsive node through lines of acquaintance, trust, and familiarity.

People are said to be separated from each other by "degrees of separation" or certain hops from node-to-node to connect with another. "Power laws" are at play in many scale-free social networks in which a small percentage of nodes are the most powerful, popular, influential, and rewarded, with a "long tail" of others who are not. "Small world" networks are described as having small clusters of people who are close to each other (with dense ties or edges), and then a few degrees of separation among even stranger nodes.

Figure 1 provides a sense of a simple node-link depiction. At the near-center is the focal node, or the ego around which there is an ego neighborhood. This neighborhood of direct ties consists of so-called "alters". A one-degree trawl of the network includes a listing of all those with direct ties to the focal node. A 1.5 degree crawl involves transitivity or the connections between the alters themselves. (If a -> b, and b-> c, then a-> c.) A two-degree capture of the focal node's network involves not only the ego neighborhood but all the ego neighborhoods of the alters for that focal node.

Figure 1. Degrees or levels in social networks

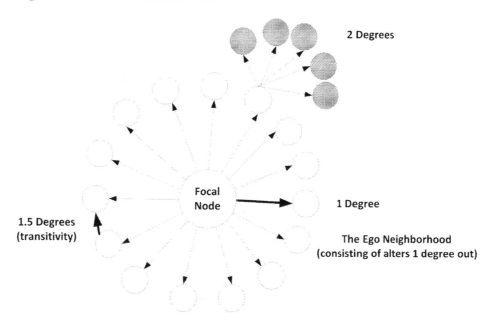

Degrees or Levels in Social Networks

Social network analysis is supported by the so-called Two-Step Flow of Information model (also known as the Multistep Flow Model), which suggests that most people rely on "opinion leaders" whom they know and trust to vet their intake of news—in order to have a sense-making frame for that information. The forwarding of links and news headlines is one way that this intermediation occurs.

In terms of graph visualizations, social networks are depicted as node-link diagrams. On a two-dimensional graph, nodes represent entities or egos; links represent relationships (of varying types, intensities, and frequencies). Here, a core-periphery dynamic is in play. Layout algorithms place the most powerful nodes ("fat nodes") at the center of the two-dimensional space, and the least connected or engaged nodes ("thin nodes") are in the periphery. A node may be influential in one community but peripheral in another. Peripheral nodes should not be seen as "marginal" simply because they are not central in one grouping; many such nodes serve as critical bridging (boundary-spanning) nodes between communities and provide powerful value that way. Social networks that are densely connected are theoretically considered positive for democratization, with a more egalitarian flow of information and resources. These networks are considered to have interaction effects, and differing degrees of mutual influence. However, many densely tied networks tend to be quite homogeneous. Weak-tie networks are thought to be more outward looking, welcoming, and diverse.

Also, nodes change positions in a network over time, so there is a temporal element. Depending on the salience of an event, a particular peripheral node may gain centrality...but lose it over time, when it is no longer the focus of a particular event or activity. (Sometimes, node influence is depicted by the physical size of the node in the graph). A graph visualization is only one tool among many to understand social networks. These are inevitably used in connection with graph metrics, contextual information, and other research-based data.

In social network analysis, there are varying levels of analysis. Traditionally, these may be understood as the individual node (or entity); dyads (pairs of two nodes), triads (groups of three nodes), and motifs (various sub-structures in various combinations of nodes); the clique (or sub-network), and the entire social network. While this may sound straightforward, there are challenges to defining the boundaries of social networks. Table 1 provides an overview of these levels of analysis and some measures that are applied.

To elaborate, cognitive social networks focus on perceptions of the network at the ego node, motif, clique, and network levels. Here, the point-of-view matters and will affect what is able to be seen of the network from the particular location of a node, entity, or group in the structure. The more active and powerful nodes have the most accurate perspectives of the network and often show themselves to be the most effective informants. Kaplan (2012) writes of geography and human culture: "A good place to understand the present, and to ask questions about the future, is on the ground, traveling as slowly as possible" (p. xiii). In a sense, understanding a human geographical network may involve working at very local levels with particular informants or groups of informants.

Researchers have begun to analyze the "sociology of online knowledge" by using electronic research (Meyer & Schroeder, 2009). Such research may be done with artificial as well as real-world data. Real-world data extractions from microblogging sites, for example, are tied to "naturalistic interactions" and are similar to information seeking in more traditional environments (Efron & Winget, 2010, n.p.). In the past few years, social network analysts have started studying social media platforms and extrapolating social network structures (network topologies) from "crawled" data extractions. This is seen as providing empirical bases for particular observations of public communities, their communications, their shared multimedia objects, and other elements. Electronic communications may enhance the efficiencies in the movements of information, and they may even alter the structures of networks. Online Social Networks (OSNs) are seen to display small world and scale-free properties, with power law applications (highly privileged few nodes).

SOCIAL MEDIA PLATFORMS

To understand online social network analysis, it is important to consider the various types of social media platforms that are in wide use today. These various types have been presented on a continuum from most static (least-often updated by users) to the most dynamic (most-often updated by users). At the most static are digital content sharing platforms; then Web logs and video logs (and the more old-school forums); wikis; open-source collaborative work sites; email networks; social networking sites, and microblogging / Short Message Service (SMS) sites. These are conceptualized as general communications vehicles and not particular dedicated ones. This is a generality, so there will certainly be exceptions in different platforms and their levels of activity.

Figure 2 provides a generalized view of social media, writ large. Semi-static networks may be crawled occasionally for a particular slice-in-time view. The more often digital contents and messages are updated, the more critical it is to conduct more frequent data crawls of the site to update the information. For critical events, data crawls are continuous with real-time captures of information.

An abstraction of the process of data extraction from social media platforms and the ensuing analysis is depicted in Figure 3. The visual is to be read left-to-right. At the far left is the contextual analysis to set the baseline for the university's presence on social media sites and the outreach, branding, and marketing needs. Here, it is important to identify university-related accounts and search terms as leads for

Table 1. Four general levels of structural analysis in social network analysis and analytical factors

Local Node-Level Measure				
	Individual Node (Agent, Ego, or Entity)	**Dyads, Triads, and other Motifs**	**Clique (Including Sub-Cliques, Sub- Networks, or Islands)**	**Social Network**
Degree centrality	In-degree / out-degree	Frequency counts	In-degree / out-degree	In-degree / out-degree
Bias	Tendencies or propensities of the node particularly in relation to decision-making (and thresholds before actions may be sparked); nodes are depicted as "multiplex" or multi-faceted		Cultural or behavioral tendencies of the respective cliques and sub-cliques	Cultural or behavioral tendencies of the respective social network
Type of node	Types of nodes		Multimodal analysis	Multimodal analysis
Global Network Structure Measures				
	Individual Node (Agent, Ego, or Entity)	**Dyads, Triads, and other Motifs**	**Clique (Including Sub-Cliques, Sub- networks, or Islands)**	**Social Network**
Betweenness centrality				The total number of shortest paths for each pair of dyadic nodes (with the understanding that information and resources move between the shortest paths in a social network); the importance of a node as a recipient of information
Closeness centrality				The geodesic path distance between a node and every other node
Eigenvector centrality (diversity)				The distance between a node and every other node, with those connected to higher-value or popular nodes equated with a greater value; the importance of a node in a network
Clustering coefficient				The aggregating for multiple nodes based around definitions of similarity or proximity or other closeness factor among an ego neighborhood's proximate nodes; transitivity
Geodesic distance of the network (diameter)				The farthest distance between the furthermost nodes in a social network
Motif (censuses)		Various types of identified structures of relationships among different numbers of vertices (nodes)	Internal structures and patterns	Internal structures and patterns

Figure 2. Semi-static to dynamic continuum of social media platforms

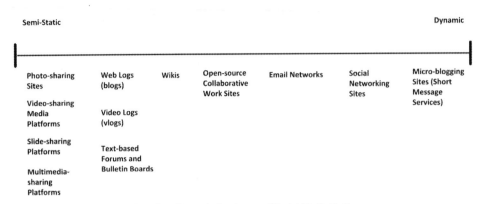

Semi-Static-to-Dynamic Continuum of Social Media Platforms

Figure 3. Extracting data from social media platforms for formal and informal branding analysis

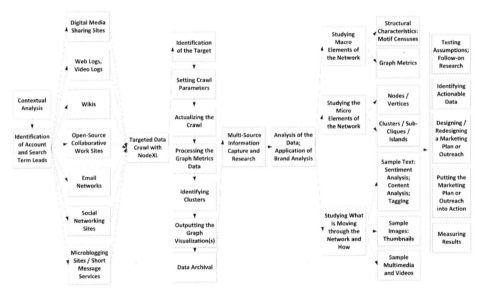

Extracting Data from Social Media Platforms for Formal and Informal Branding Analysis

various data crawls. (In some written accounts, this is called the "crawl frontier" for social media sites.) Separate strategies are applied for each of the social media platforms because of how the platforms collect data, how the Application Programming Interfaces (APIs) work, how the data extraction software functions, and what the layout algorithms mean in terms of the encapsulated calculations. The actual data extractions are then actualized. These take from under an hour to many days depending on the size of the network being acquired. The data is processed, and social network visualizations are created. The data is analyzed in conjunction with other related information. The analysts then apply their specialty to the data in order to design outreaches. Those plans are actualized, their results are measured, and the process may repeat.

There are wide ranges of variations in how this research may be conducted. There may be pre-processing of data before visualizaitons are run; there may be post-processing as well. Further, there may be a wide range of research questions that may be asked.

NODEXL OPEN-SOURCE SOFTWARE TOOL

A popular open-source tool that enables the crawling of some current social media platforms is Network Overview, Discovery and Exploration for Excel (NodeXL) (formerly .NetMap), created under the auspices of the Social Media Research Foundation (http://www.smrfoundation.org/), with a tagline of "Open Tools, Open Data, Open Scholarship for Social Media," and released through the CodePlex site (http://nodexl.codeplex.com/). The makers of this tool have worked with developers to access the APIs of major social media platforms, who make such public data more widely accessible because it helps drive traffic to the social media platform (Jung & Lee, 2010). The tools that may currently be accessed are Facebook (limited), Twitter, Flickr, and YouTube. Additional Web crawls may be possible with the addition of a plugin from Uberlink's The Virtual Observatory for the Study of Online Networks (VO-SON) (http://www.uberlink.com/), which makes its servers available for Web crawling and the social network depictions of http networks (only if the seed URLs are approved by their team). Wikis, blogs, and email accounts may be crawled as well but entail further complexities (Hansen, Smith, & Schneiderman, 2011). This software tool provides a range of options for social network analysis and visualizations. (Other "helper applications" may add value to social media by enabling other types of data extractions.)

The type of data capture here is known as Representational State Transfers (REST). These are slice-in-time captures, not streaming or dynamic captures.

To maintain the privacy protections promised by various social media platforms, crawlers that download information from social media sites are privacy-compliant (Catanese, DeMeo, Ferrara, Fiumara, & Provetti, 2011). This is so for NodeXL as well. Research into privacy on social media platforms shows that users tend to be ambivalent about privacy. Even so, privacy concerns have not been found to restrain people from participating in social networking platforms, in part, because there are misconceptions about people's privacy rights and powers in online sites. Many have an outsized sense of their amount of control over their private information. Researchers found "evidence of members' misconceptions about the online community's actual size and composition, and about the visibility of members' profiles" (Acquisti & Gross, 2006, p. 1).

Figure 4 shows NodeXL on pause per the requirements of the social media platform's download limitations during a data crawl. This NodeXL template is built over the Excel tool, and all Excel functionalities may be applied to any dataset created from the NodeXL add-in (plug-in).

Effectively conducting a data crawl involves a depth of knowledge and various dependencies on multiple computer systems. New researchers would do well to put the tool through its paces by conducting many dozens of data crawls on the respective social media platforms before striving to make initial exploratory observations. Further, it helps to have a real-world expectation for how long a crawl may take. Those that are too large will result in no usable information capture. Those that are too small will be too limited to draw any semi-valid conclusion. It may help to have a dedicated machine to conduct the crawls, so the crawl is not interrupted. To get a sense of the complexity of this, a quote from one of the NodeXL's programmer's back-of-the-envelope rough calculations was quoted from the NodeXL community site. Wangela wrote in May 10, 2012:

Figure 4. A screenshot of the NodeXL® add-in to Microsoft Excel®

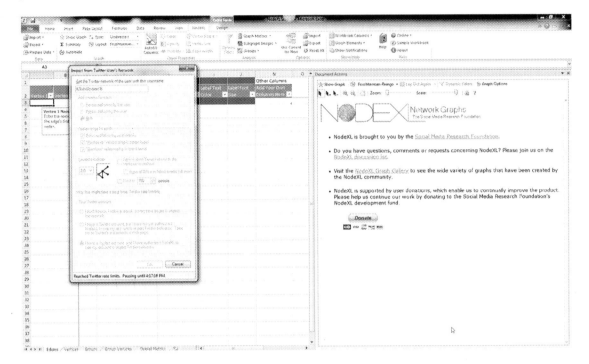

Can you estimate how long it will take to "import from Twitter user's network" if I choose the following options:

- User has 15,000 followers, is following 7,000.
- Add a vertex for both followers and following.
- Add an edge for each followed/following relationship.
- 1.5 levels.
- I have a Twitter account and have authorized it.

(Note: I tried this with much more rigorous options (2 levels, replies and mentions relationships, include latest tweet column) and it kept having to retry each hour, but only got a partial network after about 15 hours and is taking a long time to show the graph for a sheet with 196K edges, so I gave up. The file so far is 82 MB. I want to try this again with the proposed lesser options but don't want to start the task if I'm not going to be able to finish it tomorrow.) ("Size Limits on Twitter Import," 2012)

tcap479, identified as a Coordinator, writes on May 10, 2012:

- For 1.0 starting point, the IDs of the user's followers and followings are obtained 5,000 at a time, so 22,000 followers and followings for user take 5 requests.
- Follower and friend names are obtained 100 at a time, so 22,000 follower and following names take 220 additional requests.

- For the 1.5 connections, must get follower and following IDs for each of the 22,000 followers and followings. Assuming each of the followers and followings has no more than 5,000 followers and followings, this requires 22,000 additional requests.
- Total requests: At least 22,225.
- Maximum requests allows before a one-hour pause: 350.
- Minimum number of one-hour pauses: 64.

Answer: It will take at least 3 days. And that assumes that Twitter won't arbitrarily kick you out in the middle of getting the network, which it has been known to do at times of high traffic. ("Size Limits on Twitter Import," 2012)

Some of the social media platforms offer faster data crawls if individuals have an account on their system. Some not only require an account but also application for "whitelisting," so the machines may prioritize which crawls should go faster (in trade for the user's identity through email-verified accounts or other types of authentication.).

The NodeXL tool, as of this publication, does not have an initial indicator of the size of a network crawl. A dataset may be re-run to collect new information using the old or new parameters (Smith, Schneiderman, Milic-Frayling, Rodrigues, Barash, Dunne, Capone, Perer, & Gleave, 2009). All crawls are necessarily somewhat constrained because of various limitations of the software tools, social media platforms, and commonplace computers.

Academic Scholarship and Social Media

In some ways, the social media platforms have been a support for academic culture. The media platforms are used for widespread research in terms of e-governance and public policymaking (Kolcz, 2012). Social media platforms enable collaborations between political elites and users of social media (Auer, 2011, p. 709). Various communities of learning coalesce around persistent social media, through which their collaborations are shared and archived.

Microblogging sites are used for Massively Open Online Courses (MOOCs), stand-alone courses, and as augmentation to online and blended courses. Scholars use Twitter to cite scholarly works, particularly in fast-moving discourses (Priem & Costello, 2010). Academics use microblogging sites like Twitter to promote their careers:

Findings indicate that scholars participating on Twitter (1) shared information, resources, and media relating to their professional practice; (2) shared information about their classroom and their students; (3) requested assistance from and offered suggestions to others; (4) engaged in social commentary; (5) engaged in digital identity and impression management; (6) sought to network and make connections with others; and (7) highlighted their participation in online networks other than Twitter. These findings assist the field in understanding the emerging practice of scholarly participation in online networks (Veletsianos, 2012, p. 336).

The researcher identified a number of themes in scholars' Twitter practices: "information, resource, and media sharing; expanding learning opportunities beyond the confines of the classroom; requesting assistance and offering suggestions; living social public lives; digital identity and impression management; connecting and networking; presence across multiple online social networks" (Veletsianos, 2012,

p. 342). Social networking sites are used to create learning communities with individuals with shared interests. Student work, both individual and group, is showcases on wikis, blogs, and content-sharing sites (both video- and photo-sharing). Plenty of academic contents are shared on multimedia-sharing sites. Academic conferences encourage the uses of microblogging sites as a public and unofficial back-channel for communications, with a resulting electronic "event graph" from the interactions. Microblogged messages are collated using particular hashtags (indicated by a # and a keyword) often linked to the event or sponsoring organization. Some researchers are studying some of the different structural patterns from such events (Hansen, Smith, & Schneiuderman, 2011). Other researchers have suggested that the electronic residuals from conferences have limited usefulness post-event, particularly for those who were not part of the direct event (Ebner, Mühlburger, Schaffert, Schiefner, Reinhardt, & Wheeler, 2010).

For learners, social media platforms may mitigate "friendsickness," which may occur with the "loss of connection to old friends when a young person moves away to college" (Paul & Brier, 2001, as cited in Ellison, Steinfield, & Lampe, 2007, p. 1148). Using social media, college students may maintain their friend ties from high school. They may find emotional resilience and support online. Another researcher found Facebook at the center of the "identity politics" of being a student, which plays a critical role in the addressing of role conflicts that students experience "in their relationships with university work, teaching staff, academic conventions" (Selwyn, 2009, p. 157). In a survey of undergraduate students, social networking sites were found to support student formation and maintenance of social capital, friendship bonding, and bridging social circles; Facebook use was linked to "measures of psychological well-being" (Ellison, Steinfield, & Lampe, 2007, p. 1143). Social networking sites have been particularly helpful for those college students with lower self-esteem bridge social capital through heterogeneous social networks created online (Steinfield, Ellison, & Lampe, 2008).

Individual satisfaction with the level of social support that they attain in social networks varies. It is not necessarily density or sparseness of ties that lead to satisfaction (both have been shown to be related to satisfaction, depending on the type of network and the membership and the members' respective needs). Stokes (1983) identified the importance of having a trusted confidant in the network.

KANSAS STATE UNIVERSITY IN SOCIAL MEDIA

To apply social network analysis in an academic setting, to understand a university's social presence on multiple platforms, data extractions will be conducted on a range of accounts and multimedia contents from social media platforms.

Kansas State University (K-State) was founded in 1863. It has 1,275 academic staff. This year, 19,385 undergraduates and 3,885 post-graduates are attending this land grant institution. A slightly different number is offered by the Registrar's Office, which suggests that K-State has 24,378 students enrolled in the most recent term. It has a $374 million endowment. Its official color is royal purple, and its members are known as Wildcats. Its mascot is Willie the Wildcat. Kansas State University's mission statement reads:

The mission of Kansas State University is to foster excellent teaching, research, and service that develop a highly skilled and educated citizenry necessary to advancing the well-being of Kansas, the nation, and the international community. The university embraces diversity, encourages engagement and is committed to the discovery of knowledge, the education of undergraduate and graduate students, and improvement in the quality of life and standard of living of those we serve.

To map some of the formal and informal social media presences linked to Kansas State University, the researcher identified various accounts directly and indirectly related to K-State. The research does not claim to capture all accounts in all venues. As a matter of fact, this was only a convenience sample or selection of the available social media contents related to this university.

Microblogging Relationships and Messaging

Twitter, which was founded in 2006, is the most popular microblogging service on Earth, with emulator sites in other countries. Its approach is simple. It offers a 140-character short message service (SMS) to distribute Tweets to all those who follow particular Tweetstreams. On Twitter, there is the full spectrum of communications: personal and private messages, so-called "mass personal" messages (mediated personal messages), and highly public messages to curate networks of people around shared interests.

The lifespan of most contents is ephemeral and transient. The most long-lived re-tweeted URLs last for 200 days (Wu, Hofman, Mason, & Watts, 2011). The authors point out that ".05% of the population accounts for half of all posted URLs in Twitter (another sign of the power law); elite users of Twitter tend to be homophilous and to follow each other. That said, the Library of Congress is also archiving all the 170 billion Tweets created so far for posterity, for research, and for analysis—into perpetuity.

K-State Search Network on Twitter

First, a search for "K-State" was made on Twitter in early 2013. This would capture any mention of K-State. What resulted was a social network with 1,115 vertices, with 5,018 edges (high connectivity) of following / followed, re-tweets, and mentions (see Table 2).

The data from the crawl is depicted using the Fruchterman-Reingold force-based algorithm. In Figure 5 there is a clear center-periphery dynamic with the most deeply connected nodes in the center. This network is predominantly single-centered but has 383 clusters or groups, for a highly diversified group of clusters in the network.

The same data is also portrayed using a Harel-Koren Multi-Scale layout algorithm in Figure 6. This also shows high density in the center but offers clearer senses of which nodes are clustered based on the spatial placement of the various nodes, along with their colors and shapes.

Hashtag #KState Search Network on Twitter

An unlimited #KState (hashtag KState) search was conducted on Twitter in early 2013 to see what sort of microblogging chatter might be occurring on Twitter. (The researcher was aware that "kstate" could also be used to indicate Kennesaw State University, but there was not a simple way—even using Boolean operators—to disambiguate the term further.) An informal perusal of some of the messages did seem to show a majority of the microblogging messages were in relation to Kansas State University though. The messages dealt with a friendly collegiate sports rivalry (see Table 3).

Table 2. K-State search on Twitter (graph metrics)

Graph Metric	Value
Graph Type	Directed
Vertices	1115
Unique Edges	5018
Edges With Duplicates	760
Total Edges	5778
Self-Loops	1290
Reciprocated Vertex Pair Ratio	0.240310078
Reciprocated Edge Ratio	0.3875
Connected Components	366
Single-Vertex Connected Components	319
Maximum Vertices in a Connected Component	689
Maximum Edges in a Connected Component	5178
Maximum Geodesic Distance (Diameter)	11
Average Geodesic Distance	3.335514
Graph Density	0.003477953
Modularity	Not Applicable
NodeXL Version	1.0.1.229

The hashtag #KState search network on Twitter crawl found 62 clusters of communicators using the #kstate to label the message. Indeed, the transience of the messages and moods flowing around a particular hashtagged term is common and often influenced by real-world events spilling into electronic spaces. Figure 7 shows a Harel-Koren Fast Multiscale algorithm depiction in graph form.

K-State President (kstate_pres) User Network on Twitter

Another strategy in mapping a university's social media presence involves identifying key people and mapping their networks. For example, a university president not only has a critical leadership role but also symbolic importance. Kansas State University's president models a progressive use of social network connectivity (see Table 4).

During a relatively quiet period, 12,228 vertices with 13,502 edges were captured. (An earlier crawl had found 80,000 vertices—but that was at the height of enthusiasm about a college sports event. The researcher decided to go with one that is a more typical data extraction.) Figure 8 is a visualization from the Fruchterman-Reingold force-based visualization algorithm. Ten clusters were extracted, suggesting a fairly homogeneous network.

The same data was used for a different visualization, expressed in Figure 9 as a vertical sine wave. There are varying levels of effectiveness for using particular visualizations for particular data sets and crawls on various social media platforms.

Figure 5. K-State search on Twitter (graph)

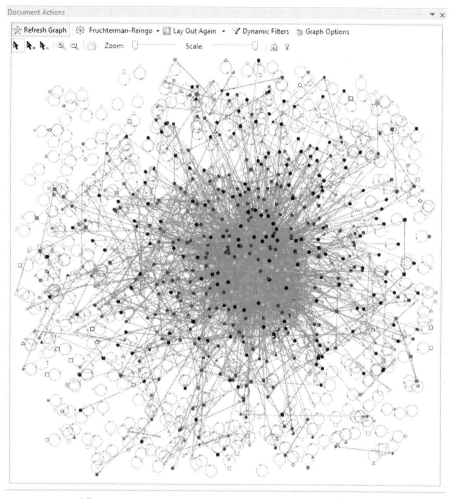

For a more accurate representation see the electronic version.

K-State News (k_state_news) User Network on Twitter

A two-degree unlimited-person crawl of the KStateNews user network on Twitter (https://twitter.com/KStateNews) showed 10,551 vertices with 12,992 edges. The official account has 1,838 Tweets, 53 following, and 7,271 followers (see Table 5).

This K-State News user network data resulted in Figure 10 visualization using the Fruchterman-Reingold force-based layout algorithm. This visualization is especially revealing because there are such disparate clusters (8 in total), some connected in a thin way with critical bridging connectors. There does not seem to be much in the way of overlaps in this network. This could suggest some structural risks in the loss of particular nodes.

The NodeXL Graph Gallery enables a public version of the graph that is interactive. When a cursor is placed on a particular node, the name of that communicator on Twitter is highlighted. In the actual data set, hovering over a node brings up not only the name of the Tweeter but the contents of their most recent message (recorded in the .xlsx file in a separate column).

Figure 6. K-State search on Twitter (graph 2)

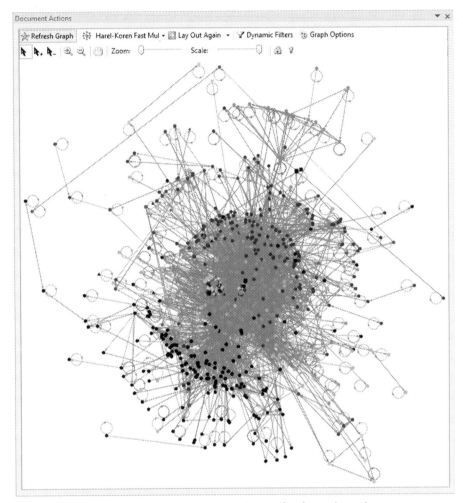

For a more accurate representation see the electronic version.

In Figure 11 scrolling into the graph above will reveal the proximity of the relationships between the various vertices. There is a zoom feature which enables a close-in view of the various nodes and their interconnectivity. See Figure 12 for a close-in view.

K-State on Facebook

The author would be remiss in not mentioning Facebook, which is a major force in social media today. Currently, the Social Network Importer for NodeXL does not enable crawling Facebook networks except for the user's own account's ego network. According to the official NodeXL site, though, just such a tool is forthcoming for the crawling of fan pages.

Table 3. Hashtag #KState search network on Twitter (graph metrics)

Graph Metric	Value
Graph Type	Directed
Vertices	1037
Unique Edges	9368
Edges With Duplicates	855
Total Edges	10223
Self-Loops	1140
Reciprocated Vertex Pair Ratio	0.306401766
Reciprocated Edge Ratio	0.469077391
Connected Components	52
Single-Vertex Connected Components	47
Maximum Vertices in a Connected Component	981
Maximum Edges in a Connected Component	10153
Maximum Geodesic Distance (Diameter)	9
Average Geodesic Distance	2.663492
Graph Density	0.008262809
Modularity	Not Applicable
NodeXL Version	1.0.1.229

K-State Sports (kstatesports) User Network on Twitter

Kansas State Athletics is a source of pride (and funding) for Kansas State University. Its formal account (https://twitter.com/kstatesports) has 9,011 Tweets, 234 following, and 28,728 followers. It is a highly active account with Tweets going out multiple times a day during intense moments of the respective sports seasons. A two-degree data crawl was captured, with no limits on the numbers of persons in the capture, but the software only captured a partial directional graph. The social network for kstatesports involved 37,581 vertices, with 40,944 unique edges (see Table 6).

There were 7 clusters or groups identified by the software. This social network is expressed as a horizontal sine wave in Figure 13.

KSREsupport User Network on Twitter

The K-State Research & Extension Support (https://twitter.com/ksresupport) site is an apparently semi-public work group that rides on an open-source microblogging platform. At the time of the data crawl, the account only had 213 Tweets, 67 followers, and 18 following (followed by the account). The most recent message had been Tweeted that day. The graph metrics are summarized in the NodeXL table (Table 7). This crawl found 19,894 nodes or vertices in a 2.0 degree data extraction.

When related groups were extracted, 14 clusters were found. These are depicted on a grid below. Some of the clusters are more insular (fewer overlapping dots of different colors) while others are more integrated with diverse members of other clusters, according to the grid visualization in Figure 14.

Figure 7. #KState search network on Twitter (graph)

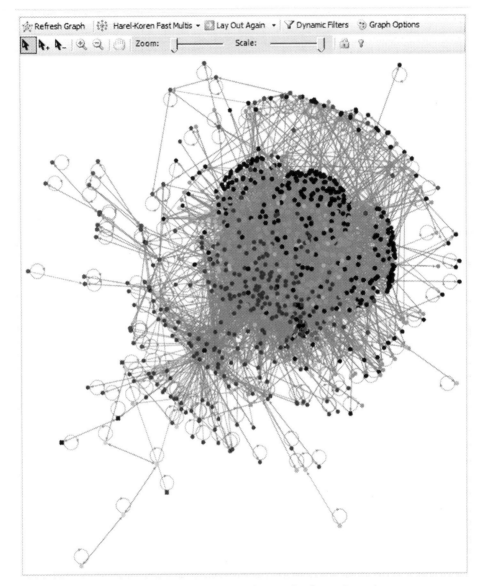

*For a more accurate representation see the electronic version.

Grids are a type of graph that resembles treemaps to a degree, where the amount of space covered reflects the size of a particular cluster.

K-State Collegian (kstatecollegian) User Network on Twitter

The Kansas State Collegian is the university's student newspaper. As such, it is a critical learning tool for journalism students. Further, it is a critical voice for students' points-of-view. This two-degree unlimited-persons crawl of the network highlighted 12,732 vertices, with 13,733 unique edges. The official account (https://twitter.com/kstatecollegian) shows that it has 2,734 Tweets, 216 following,

Table 4. K-State president user network on Twitter (graph metrics)

Graph Type	Directed
Vertices	12620
Unique Edges	13502
Edges With Duplicates	16
Total Edges	13518
Self-Loops	0
Reciprocated Vertex Pair Ratio	0.022091088
Reciprocated Edge Ratio	0.043227239
Connected Components	1
Single-Vertex Connected Components	0
Maximum Vertices in a Connected Component	12620
Maximum Edges in a Connected Component	13518
Maximum Geodesic Distance (Diameter)	4
Average Geodesic Distance	2.30551
Graph Density	8.48342E-05
Modularity	Not Applicable
NodeXL Version	1.0.1.229

and 2,826 followers. The most recent posting was the day before the crawl, which shows quite a bit of activity. The topics of this Twitter feed generally consisted of retweets of shortened URLs to published stories, requests for social media responses for forthcoming stories, student-related campus events, and comments about impending weather, at the time of this crawl. Only five clusters were found, suggesting a fairly heterogeneous network (see Table 8).

Figure 15 is a visual depiction of this social network using the Harel-Koren Fast Multiscale algorithm in NodeXL.

Figure 15 shows a network with some possible fragility, such as bridging nodes that are chokepoints for possible information or connectivity to larger communities in this social network. A higher rate of connectivity instead of single linkages or edges to various nodes would possibly enhance the social integration of those engaging the K-State Collegian.

K-State Football Feedr (KstateFBFeedr) on Twitter

Other Twitter accounts seem to be automated robots that collect data and distribute it to subscribers. One such account is the K-State Football Feeder account (https://twitter.com/KstateFBfeedr). Such accounts capitalize on public information. The URL for this site (http://fanfeedr.com/ncaa-football/kansas-st-wildcats) was a "dead link." A data crawl may be achieved on a 'bot account as it is with those that are led by people or even cyborgs (people and 'bots together) (Chu, Gianvecchio, Wang, & Jajodia, 2010). Such accounts are not uncommon to collect news and information in an automated way to keep people in the loop (see Table 9).

Figure 8. K-State president user network on Twitter (graph)

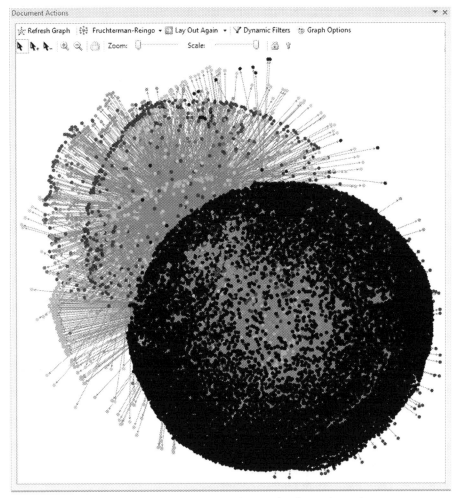

For a more accurate representation see the electronic version.

A crawl of this account in early February, 2013, shows 10,742 vertices, with 13,470 edges. The social network is expressed as a graph using the Fruchterman-Reingold force-based layout algorithm, which shows 10 clusters or groups. With only 10 unique groups, this is not a highly diversified network. (However, there is more diversity in this group than for the K-State basketball statistics social network.) Figure 16 shows this social network depicted using a Fruchterman-Reingold force-based layout algorithm.

Real people may still maintain conversations and interactivity around a robot-driven account, in this case, because of a shared appreciation of college football.

K-State Wildcats Basketball (@KStateUpdateBB) User Network on Twitter

The KStateUpdateBB (https://twitter.com/KStateUpdateBB) account also seems to be a commercial account consisting of statistics collected by a 'bot and distributed to those who follow the account. The logo consists of a robot wearing a shirt with a Wildcat logo. This microblogging account consists of 2,861 Tweets, with 13 following, and 693 followers. An unlimited-persons crawl was conducted with a

Figure 9. K-State president user network on Twitter (a vertical sine wave)

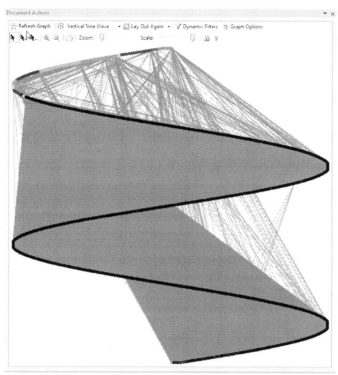

*For a more accurate representation see the electronic version.

Table 5. K-State news user network on Twitter (graph metrics)

Graph Metric	Value
Graph Type	Directed
Vertices	10551
Unique Edges	12992
Edges With Duplicates	40
Total Edges	13032
Self-Loops	0
Reciprocated Vertex Pair Ratio	0.009386394
Reciprocated Edge Ratio	0.018598217
Connected Components	1
Single-Vertex Connected Components	0
Maximum Vertices in a Connected Component	10551
Maximum Edges in a Connected Component	13032
Maximum Geodesic Distance (Diameter)	4
Average Geodesic Distance	2.559059
Graph Density	0.000116896
Modularity	Not Applicable
NodeXL Version	1.0.1.229

Figure 10. K-State news user network on Twitter (graph)

*For a more accurate representation see the electronic version.

Figure 11. K-State news user network on Twitter (interactive graph)

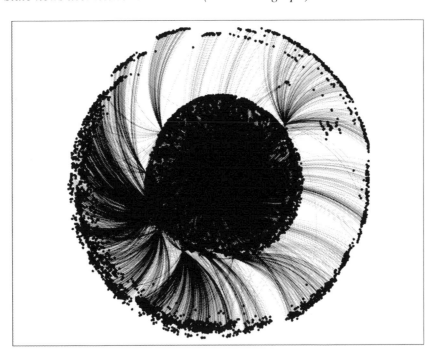

k_state_news User Network on Twitter (experimental version)

Figure 12. A close-up of the K-State news user network on Twitter

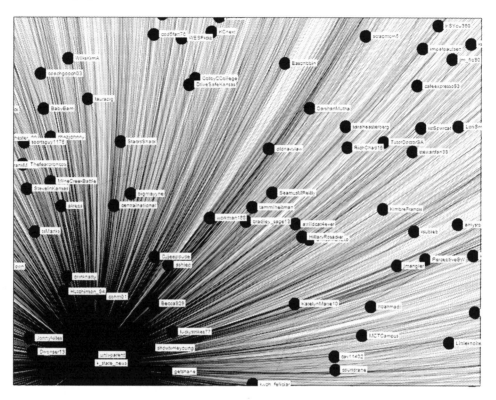

Table 6. K-State athletics (kstatesports) user account on Twitter (graph metrics)

Graph Metric	Value
Graph Type	Directed
Vertices	37581
Unique Edges	40944
Edges With Duplicates	16
Total Edges	40960
Self-Loops	0
Reciprocated Vertex Pair Ratio	0.002227062
Reciprocated Edge Ratio	0.004444227
Connected Components	1
Single-Vertex Connected Components	0
Maximum Vertices in a Connected Component	37581
Maximum Edges in a Connected Component	40960
Maximum Geodesic Distance (Diameter)	4
Average Geodesic Distance	2.393323
Graph Density	2.89968E-05
Modularity	Not Applicable
NodeXL Version	1.0.1.229

Figure 13. K-State athletics (kstatesports) user account on Twitter in a horizontal sine wave

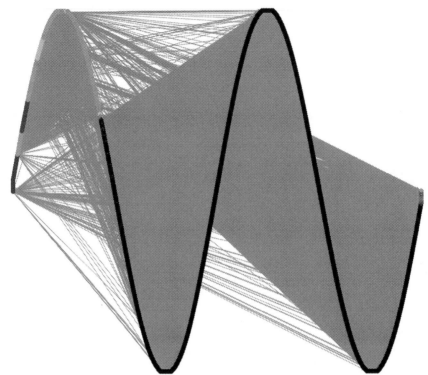

For a more accurate representation see the electronic version.

Table 7. KSREsupport user network on Twitter (graph metrics)

Graph Metric	Value
Graph Type	Directed
Vertices	19894
Unique Edges	30647
Edges With Duplicates	1286
Total Edges	31933
Self-Loops	0
Reciprocated Vertex Pair Ratio	0.222719598
Reciprocated Edge Ratio	0.364302001
Connected Components	1
Single-Vertex Connected Components	0
Maximum Vertices in a Connected Component	19894
Maximum Edges in a Connected Component	31933
Maximum Geodesic Distance (Diameter)	4
Average Geodesic Distance	3.753718
Graph Density	7.86832E-05
Modularity	Not Applicable
NodeXL Version	1.0.1.229

Figure 14. KSREsupport user network on Twitter in a grid

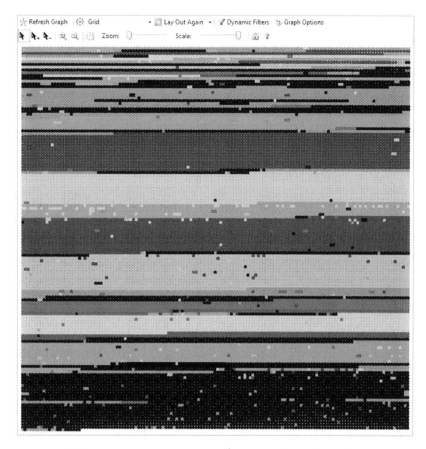

For a more accurate representation see the electronic version.

two-degree capture and resulted in the following graph metrics: 884 nodes and 984 unique edges (see Table 10).

There were ten clusters identified in the analysis, which does not indicate a very heterogeneous network. Of these, there seem to be two major groupings only. This K-State Wildcats Basketball user network is depicted using a Harel-Koren Fast Multiscale network graph (see Figure 17).

K-State Proud (K-State-Proud) User Network on Twitter

K-State Proud is described as a student organization of students helping each other. This organization funds a range of scholarships ("student opportunity awards") for learners. This organization's Twitter site (https://twitter.com/KStateProud) has 221 Tweets, 97 following, and 1,686 followers. The formal site for this student-led organization is http://www.found.ksu.edu/k-stateproud/. An unlimited-persons two-degree crawl of the user network for this organization found 13,258 nodes or vertices, connected by 13,746 links or edges (see Table 11).

Table 8. K-State collegian user network on Twitter (graph metrics)

Graph Type	Directed
Vertices	12732
Unique Edges	13733
Edges With Duplicates	12
Total Edges	13745
Self-Loops	0
Reciprocated Vertex Pair Ratio	0.007553535
Reciprocated Edge Ratio	0.014993813
Connected Components	1
Single-Vertex Connected Components	0
Maximum Vertices in a Connected Component	12732
Maximum Edges in a Connected Component	13745
Maximum Geodesic Distance (Diameter)	4
Average Geodesic Distance	**3.000885**
Graph Density	**8.4761E-05**
Modularity	Not Applicable
NodeXL Version	1.0.1.229

Figure 15. K-State collegian user network on Twitter (graph)

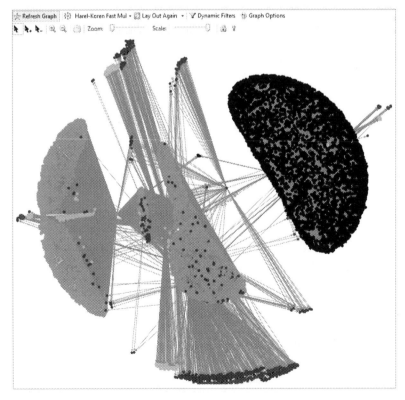

*For a more accurate representation see the electronic version.

Table 9. KstateFBFeedr user network on Twitter (graph metrics)

Graph Metric	Value
Graph Type	Directed
Vertices	10742
Unique Edges	13470
Edges With Duplicates	0
Total Edges	13470
Self-Loops	0
Reciprocated Vertex Pair Ratio	0.014765707
Reciprocated Edge Ratio	0.029101707
Connected Components	1
Single-Vertex Connected Components	0
Maximum Vertices in a Connected Component	10742
Maximum Edges in a Connected Component	13470
Maximum Geodesic Distance (Diameter)	4
Average Geodesic Distance	3.184187
Graph Density	0.000116745
Modularity	Not Applicable
NodeXL Version	1.0.1.229

The resulting data visualization is fairly simple. Figure 18 shows three main colors: dark blue (navy) at the top, green at the middle layer, and blue with speckles of green at the bottom. This grid shows the three extracted clusters for this social network, which suggests a fairly homogeneous network.

Women of K-State (WomenofKState) User Network on Twitter

Started in January 2012, the Women-of-K-State (https://twitter.com/WomenofKState) user network is an endeavor of the university's First Lady (and member of the engineering faculty), Dr. Noel Schulz. This endeavor not only offers mentoring for female administrators, faculty, and staff, but there are recreational activities and fun events. This user account has 82 Tweets, 48 following, and 89 followers. The account has approximately 2-5 messages a month. An unlimited-person two-degree crawl of this network found the following, in a partial extraction: a network of 35,141 vertices, with 48,385 unique edges (see Table 12).

The network is fairly intimate, with the two nodes at the farthest points of path-distance from each other at four hops. Both the university's first lady (@kstate_1stlady) and president (@kstate_pres) are active on this network (that would be Drs. Noel Schulz and Kirk H. Schulz). This social network is depicted using a Fruchterman-Reingold force-based layout algorithm in Figure 19.

Figure 19 shows a visualization of the 21 related clusters in this social network. The differing clusters may be understood as representational of various interest groups.

Figure 16. KstateFBFeedr user network on Twitter (graph)

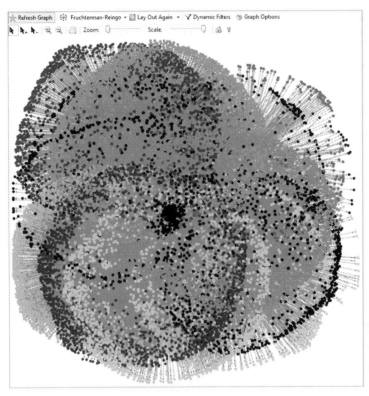

*For a more accurate representation see the electronic version.

Table 10. K-State Wildcats basketball (KStateUpdateBB) user network on Twitter (graph metrics)

Graph Metric	Value
Graph Type	Directed
Vertices	884
Unique Edges	984
Edges With Duplicates	0
Total Edges	984
Self-Loops	0
Reciprocated Vertex Pair Ratio	0.041269841
Reciprocated Edge Ratio	0.079268293
Connected Components	1
Single-Vertex Connected Components	0
Maximum Vertices in a Connected Component	884
Maximum Edges in a Connected Component	984
Maximum Geodesic Distance (Diameter)	3
Average Geodesic Distance	2.330358
Graph Density	0.001260614
Modularity	Not Applicable
NodeXL Version	1.0.1.229

Figure 17. K-State Wildcats basketball (KStateUpdateBB) user network on Twitter (graph)

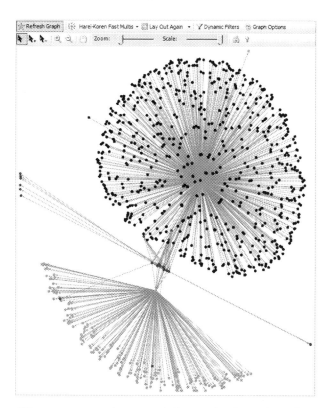

For a more accurate representation see the electronic version.

Table 11. K-State proud user network on Twitter (graph metrics)

Graph Metric	Value
Graph Type	Directed
Vertices	13258
Unique Edges	13746
Edges With Duplicates	0
Total Edges	13746
Self-Loops	0
Reciprocated Vertex Pair Ratio	0.005486065
Reciprocated Edge Ratio	0.010912265
Connected Components	1
Single-Vertex Connected Components	0
Maximum Vertices in a Connected Component	13258
Maximum Edges in a Connected Component	13746
Maximum Geodesic Distance (Diameter)	4
Average Geodesic Distance	2.406957
Graph Density	7.82083E-05
Modularity	Not Applicable
NodeXL Version	1.0.1.229

Figure 18. K-State proud user network on Twitter (graph)

For a more accurate representation see the electronic version.

Table 12. "Women of K-State" user network on Twitter (graph metrics)

Graph Metric	Value
Graph Type	Directed
Vertices	35141
Unique Edges	48385
Edges With Duplicates	116
Total Edges	48501
Self-Loops	0
Reciprocated Vertex Pair Ratio	0.01273153
Reciprocated Edge Ratio	0.025142952
Connected Components	1
Single-Vertex Connected Components	0
Maximum Vertices in a Connected Component	35141
Maximum Edges in a Connected Component	48501
Maximum Geodesic Distance (Diameter)	4
Average Geodesic Distance	3.362832
Graph Density	3.92297E-05
Modularity	Not Applicable
NodeXL Version	1.0.1.229

Figure 19. "Women of K-State" user network on Twitter (graph)

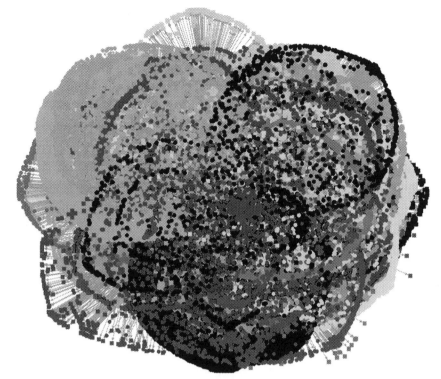

*For a more accurate representation see the electronic version.

K-State Student Union Program Council (kstateUPC) User Network on Twitter

The K-State Student Union Program Council (UPC) schedules a range of entertaining, educational, and cultural activities and events for students and the larger Manhattan, Kansas, community. The events are substance-free ones, so they are inclusive of those of college age who do not drink. The formal Website for the K-State Union Program Council is http://www.k-state.edu/upc.

The official Twitter page for the kstateUPC user account is https://twitter.com/kstateUPC. At the time of the data crawl in early February 2013, the account had 840 Tweets. There were 1,071 following and 854 followers. The social network had 18 clusters or groups. The crawl resulted in 9,169 vertices or related accounts, and these were connected by 13,608 links (edges). The diameter of the network was 4, which suggested short paths connected the two farthest-most nodes in the network (see Table 13).

The kstateUPC user network extraction showed that there were 18 clusters in this network. This is dramatically illustrated in the Harel-Koren Fast Multiscale layout algorithm in Figure 20.

Kansas State University Salina (kstatesalina) User Network on Twitter

The K-State Salina branch campus (http://salina.k-state.edu/) focuses on arts, sciences, and business; aviation; engineering technology; family studies and human services; social work; a professional masters of technology, and continuing education. Its official Twitter account "kstatesalina" (https://twitter.com/kstatesalina) features 365 Tweets, 131 following, and 707 followers. The most recent posting was

Table 13. K-State union program council (kstateUPC) network on Twitter (graph metrics)

Graph Metric	Value
Graph Type	Directed
Vertices	9169
Unique Edges	13608
Edges With Duplicates	0
Total Edges	13608
Self-Loops	0
Reciprocated Vertex Pair Ratio	0.030284676
Reciprocated Edge Ratio	0.058788948
Connected Components	2
Single-Vertex Connected Components	0
Maximum Vertices in a Connected Component	9167
Maximum Edges in a Connected Component	13607
Maximum Geodesic Distance (Diameter)	4
Average Geodesic Distance	3.395783
Graph Density	0.000161882
Modularity	Not Applicable
NodeXL Version	1.0.1.229

Figure 20. K-State union program council (kstateUPC) network on Twitter (graph)

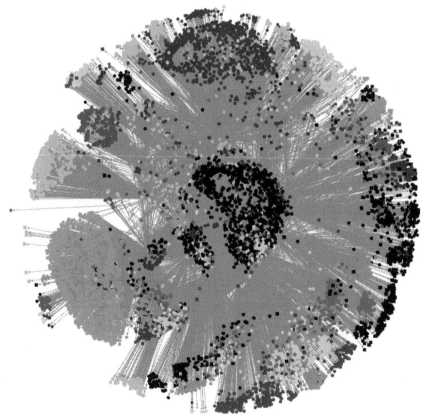

*For a more accurate representation see the electronic version.

within a week and a half of the data crawl. A two-degree 400-persons (limited) data extraction found 62,216 vertices and 89,942 unique edges (The limitation was put into place after multiple unlimited crawls resulted in crashed computer systems and lost data.) (see Table 14).

This social network had 66 clusters, which indicates relatively high diversity in the social network. The K-State Salina user network on Twitter is depicted in Figure 21, using the Fruchterman-Reingold layout algorithm.

K-State Olathe (KStateOlathe) User Network on Twitter (Crawl 1)

The Olathe Innovation Campus opened in Olathe, Kansas, in April 2011. It features a curriculum with a focus on a range of distance master's programs; it also features special learning on animal health and food safety. Its official Twitter account (located at https://twitter.com/KStateOlathe) only has 10 Tweets, with 30 following, and 49 followers. A partial crawl of its network was achieved in mid-February and was limited to 1,000 persons because of the failure of several attempts at an unlimited two-degree (level) crawl. The partial crawl resulted in the identification of 36,366 node, with 59,269 edges. The diameter of this social network is 4. With so few followers and yet so many vertices and ties, this suggests that some of the alters in the social network are highly connected individuals (or entities) with many connections (links) (see Table 15).

A visualization of this social network found 17 clusters. These are depicted below as a horizontal sine wave in Figure 22. Each of the different color and shape groupings indicate a different cluster. The gray vertices show the ties between the various clusters.

Table 14. K-State salina (kstatesalina) user network on Twitter (graph metrics)

Graph Type	Directed
Vertices	62216
Unique Edges	89942
Edges With Duplicates	392
Total Edges	90334
Self-Loops	0
Reciprocated Vertex Pair Ratio	0.006285236
Reciprocated Edge Ratio	0.012491957
Connected Components	1
Single-Vertex Connected Components	0
Maximum Vertices in a Connected Component	62216
Maximum Edges in a Connected Component	90334
Maximum Geodesic Distance (Diameter)	4
Average Geodesic Distance	3.858298
Graph Density	2.32868E-05
Modularity	Not Applicable
NodeXL Version	1.0.1.229

Figure 21. K-State salina (kstatesalina) user network on Twitter (graph)

For a more accurate representation see the electronic version.

Table 15. K-State olathe user network on Twitter (lim. 1000) (graph metrics)

Graph Metric	Value
Graph Type	Directed
Vertices	36366
Unique Edges	59269
Edges With Duplicates	3873
Total Edges	63142
Self-Loops	0
Reciprocated Vertex Pair Ratio	0.091432698
Reciprocated Edge Ratio	0.167546196
Connected Components	1
Single-Vertex Connected Components	0
Maximum Vertices in a Connected Component	36366
Maximum Edges in a Connected Component	63142
Maximum Geodesic Distance (Diameter)	4
Average Geodesic Distance	3.619615
Graph Density	4.57099E-05
Modularity	Not Applicable
NodeXL Version	1.0.1.229

Figure 22. K-State olathe user network on Twitter (lim. 1000) (graph)

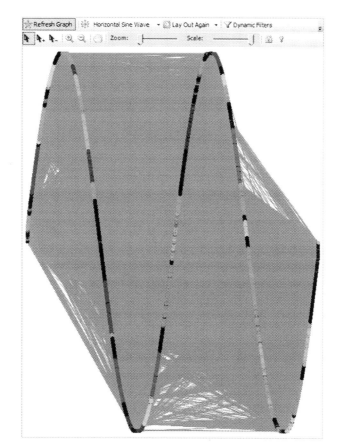

For a more accurate representation see the electronic version.

K-State Olathe (KStateOlathe) User Network on Twitter (Crawl 2)

A second simultaneous run on the KStateOlathe user network on Twitter was run at 2.0 degrees and with no limits—to see what differences there may be with the 1,000-persons limited crawl. Again, the account at the time (a day later from the first crawl) still had 10 Tweets, 30 following, and 49 followers—which are deceptively low numbers. The degree of the crawl (2.0) adds much complexity because these pull in all the networks of the ego node's neighborhood or "alters." A no-limit crawl means that there is no artificial stop on the number of persons (nodes) represented in the crawl (see Table 16).

Eight clusters were identified as contrasted to the 17 found of the social network with a more limited crawl. It may be that with a larger data set, what appeared to be variances were less pronounced, and there were some consolidations of prior groupings. In Figure 23, this data was represented as a horizontal sine wave to echo the original social network visualization with the limited crawl.

K-State Cancer Research (KStateCancerRes) on Twitter

The K-State Cancer Research (KStateCancerRes) user account on Twitter has 410 Tweets, 67 following, and 144 followers at the time of the data crawl in February 2013. This account was crawled three

Table 16. K-State olathe user network on Twitter (no limits crawl) (graph metrics)

Graph Metric	Value
Graph Type	Directed
Vertices	45569
Unique Edges	53291
Edges With Duplicates	84
Total Edges	53375
Self-Loops	0
Reciprocated Vertex Pair Ratio	0.01295322
Reciprocated Edge Ratio	0.02557516
Connected Components	1
Single-Vertex Connected Components	0
Maximum Vertices in a Connected Component	45569
Maximum Edges in a Connected Component	53375
Maximum Geodesic Distance (Diameter)	4
Average Geodesic Distance	2.934201
Graph Density	2.56842E-05
Modularity	Not Applicable
NodeXL Version	1.0.1.229

Figure 23. K-State olathe user network on Twitter (no limits crawl) (graph)

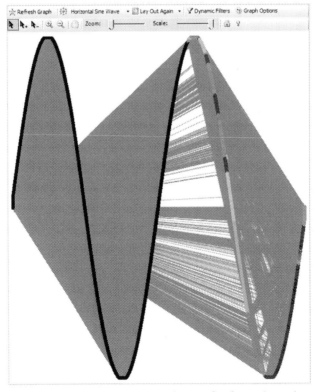

*For a more accurate representation see the electronic version.

different times in February 2013. It was crawled in an unlimited-persons way for 1 degree, 1.5 degree, and 2.0 degree, and the differences in the findings are presented in Figure 24. The URL for the official Twitter site is https://twitter.com/KStateCancerRes.

In ring lattices, or circles, the vertices are placed in a circle. The edges are the lines connecting elements of the circle. Visually, these provide a quick snapshot of the density of both the vertices and the ties (edges or arcs). A data extraction was done to analyze the KStateCancerRes (K-State Cancer Research) user network on Twitter, based on the three levels of degrees enabled by NodeXL. A one-degree crawl only identifies all the ties directly connected to the account. A 1.5 degree crawl includes both the alters in an ego neighborhood as well as the ties between the alters (for a measure of transitivity). A 2.0 degree crawl includes the ego neighborhood of the focal node, the ties between alters in the neighborhood, and the direct ties of the alters, which adds exponential complexity.

At the far left, the 1-degree unlimited-persons data crawl shows 180 vertices, with 218 unique edges. A 1-degree or 1-level crawl only captures the focal ego node (KStateCancerRes) and its alters (directly connected ego neighborhood). The maximum geodesic distance (diameter) of this network is only 2, with a graph density of 0.006828057. The 1-degree crawl had 4 clusters; the 1.5-degree crawl had 3 clusters; the 2-degree crawl had 3 clusters.

At the center ring lattice is a 1.5 degree unlimited-persons data crawl of the same network in the same time frame. This is a multi-directional network which shows transitivity or the connectivity between the alters in the ego neighborhood (how well connected the ego neighborhood alters are to each other). The graph metrics are very similar on some variables: 180 vertices and 117 unique edges. However, the edges with duplicates have jumped from 4 to 5,906, and the total edges from 222 to 6,023.

Finally, at the far right ring lattice is a 2.0 degree crawl, with involves the ego node's direct neighborhood, the connections between the alters, and then the ego neighborhoods of the alters, two levels out from the center. This capture increases the numbers of the vertices or nodes exponentially, from 180 (1 degree) to 180 (1.5 degrees) to 28,514. There are 28,899 unique edges, with no edges with duplicates, for a total of 28,899 edges or links. The diameter or maximum geodesic distance has gone to 4, with 2.17 as the average geodesic distance. The graph has a density of 3.56. There are three main clusters, so there

Figure 24. Three ring lattices of the KStateCancerRes user network on Twitter (in varying degrees)

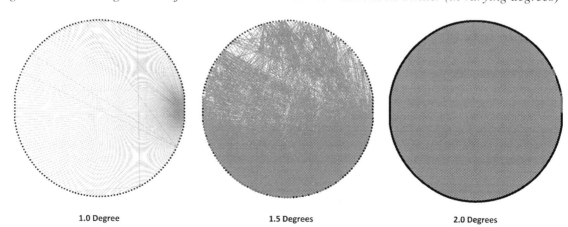

1.0 Degree   1.5 Degrees   2.0 Degrees

Three Ring Lattices of the KStateCancerRes User Network on Twitter (in Varying Degrees)

is not a wide diversity of types within this cultivated network. Even visually, the changes in the capture parameters result in a wide range of variation in the captured data, with fast-expanding complexities.

K-State Soccer Club (k_stateSoccer) User Network on Twitter

The K-State Soccer (k_stateSoccer) user network on Twitter represents both female and male teams at K-State, according to their official site on Twitter (https://twitter.com/k_stateSoccer). This account has 110 Tweets, with 369 following, and 93 followers. (This was the only account analyzed that had more following than followers.) At the formal page, the account represents K-State Club soccer teams and came with the hash tags: #KState #soccer #EMAW ("Every Man a Wildcat"). A perusal of the messages show announcements of events, kudos, and well wishing. The K-State Soccer Club has an official presence on Facebook as well, at https://www.facebook.com/#!/KStateClubSoccer.

The data crawl was achieved in mid-February and set at a 1,000-persons crawl and a two-degree (levels) of capture. (Multiple initial unlimited-persons crawls were attempted with multiple system crashes, so a limited crawl was created.) This crawl found 9,895 vertices, with 13,076 unique edges (links) (see Table 17).

A visualization of this network using the Fruchterman-Reingold force-based layout algorithm is available in Figure 25. Twenty-one clusters were found in this K_stateSoccer user network, which is quite diverse for a student club's Twitter network.

Table 17. K-State soccer user network on Twitter (graph metrics)

Graph Metric	Value
Graph Type	Directed
Vertices	9895
Unique Edges	13076
Edges With Duplicates	0
Total Edges	13076
Self-Loops	0
Reciprocated Vertex Pair Ratio	0.008250443
Reciprocated Edge Ratio	0.016365861
Connected Components	1
Single-Vertex Connected Components	0
Maximum Vertices in a Connected Component	9895
Maximum Edges in a Connected Component	13076
Maximum Geodesic Distance (Diameter)	4
Average Geodesic Distance	3.694039
Graph Density	0.000133563
Modularity	Not Applicable
NodeXL Version	1.0.1.229

Figure 25. K-State soccer user network on Twitter (graph)

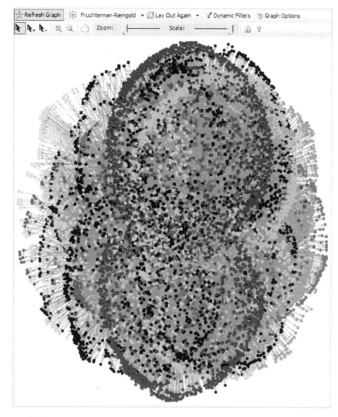

For a more accurate representation see the electronic version.

SOCIAL SHARING CONTENT ANALYSIS

The phenomenon of "social sharing" of user-generated contents has emerged as another facet of Web 2.0. In these social media platforms, images, videos, and other digital contents are uploaded and tagged with metadata based on "bottom-up user-proposed tagging convention" (Chang, 2010). The contributors are often independent-minded and individually motivated and working individually to share information, in what has been termed "weak cooperation" in collective production. In other cases, whole groups collaborate around shared projects and publish their contents for others. There are acts of co-creation of digital works. The social aspects of this content sharing involve a co-experience (such as viewing videos together in virtual film festivals). There are shared communications around digital contents. There are response photos or videos to others' works in a kind of public mass media discourse. Social media interactions involve a range of relationships: object-to-object, objects-to-people, people-to-objects, and people-to-people. Data crawls may be obtained in each of these directions. Based on digital contents, people organize actions, socialize, and create understandings.

The corpus of information may be depicted as content networks. User accounts may be mapped along with those with whom they are connected in terms of co-commenting or video linking. In photo- or video-sharing sites, contents may be analyzed based on metadata tags and how related they are to others (in semantic clusters) to identify content clusters (see Table 18).

Table 18. K-State video search on YouTube (graph metrics)

Graph Metric	Value
Graph Type	Undirected
Vertices	733
Unique Edges	61656
Edges With Duplicates	2731
Total Edges	64387
Self-Loops	0
Reciprocated Vertex Pair Ratio	Not Applicable
Reciprocated Edge Ratio	Not Applicable
Connected Components	4
Single-Vertex Connected Components	0
Maximum Vertices in a Connected Component	694
Maximum Edges in a Connected Component	63930
Maximum Geodesic Distance (Diameter)	7
Average Geodesic Distance	2.573515
Graph Density	0.23417127
Modularity	Not Applicable
NodeXL Version	1.0.1.229

K-State Videos on YouTube (Google)

In Figure 26 this content network is depicted using the Harel-Koren Fast Multiscale layout algorithm.

K-State Libraries' Photostream on Flickr

Multi-media content sharing sites enable the creation of collections of digital contents. The K-State Libraries photostream (user account) on Flickr (http://www.flickr.com/photos/kstatelibraries/) was mapped to examine the social network (see Table 19).

The unlimited data crawl at two-degrees found that the K-State Libraries photostream on Flickr had a social network consisting of 5,766 nodes or vertices, and 7,848 unique edges. A perusal of the main page showed various collections of information, some focused around the financial contributors to the library and others around particular data collections. In Figure 27 this social network is depicted in a grid format.

This crawl resulted in the identification of 7 clusters based on the semantic relatedness of the metadata tags. This same information is shown as a Harel-Koren Fast Multiscale graph in Figure 28.

Figure 26. K-State video search on YouTube (graph)

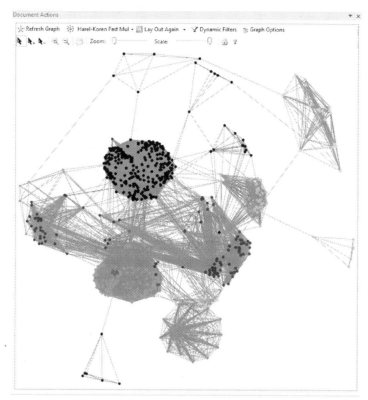

*For a more accurate representation see the electronic version.

Table 19. K-State libraries photostream on Flickr (graph metrics)

Graph Metric	Value
Graph Type	Directed
Vertices	5766
Unique Edges	7848
Edges With Duplicates	36
Total Edges	7884
Self-Loops	11
Reciprocated Vertex Pair Ratio	0.007307692
Reciprocated Edge Ratio	0.014509355
Connected Components	1
Single-Vertex Connected Components	0
Maximum Vertices in a Connected Component	5766
Maximum Edges in a Connected Component	7884
Maximum Geodesic Distance (Diameter)	4
Average Geodesic Distance	2.861327
Graph Density	0.000236365
Modularity	Not Applicable
NodeXL Version	1.0.1.229

Figure 27. K-State libraries photostream on Flickr (grid visualization)

For a more accurate representation see the electronic version.

K-State Search Network on Flickr

A search for "K-State" on the Flickr multimedia content site shows a fairly stable network of 561 nodes, with 1,507 edges. Two unlimited runs were done, and both resulted in similar data crawls and similar numbers, even though two months had passed between the data crawls (see Table 20).

The contents were mostly photos as Flickr had only recently introduced the video feature. The information clustering shows semantic clusters around reading, nature, weather, sports, Kansas State University, and activities. There is also some clear semantic drift in terms of moving to distal ideas such as sports in S. America. (This Harel-Koren Fast Multiscale algorithm used to lay out the data in Figure 29 shows a range of associations with "K-State" as understood by mostly amateur photographers and metadata taggers.

Established relational paths are critical for the delivery of new contents. One research study about Flickr looked at its growth data. The researchers found the following:

Over 50% of the observed new links in Flickr are between users that have, a priori, some network path between them (the remainder of the observed new links are between users which are, a priori, disconnected). For these new links among already connected users, Figure 5 shows the cumulative distribution of shortest-path hop distances between source and destination users. It reveals a striking trend: over 80% of such new links connect users that were only two hops apart, meaning that the destination user was

Figure 28. K-State libraries photostream on Flickr (graph)

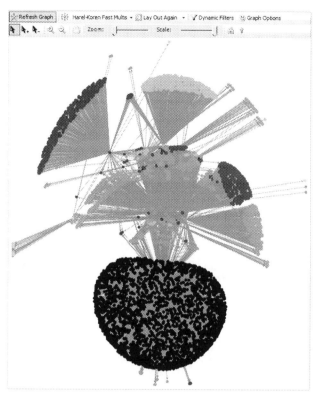

For a more accurate representation see the electronic version.

Table 20. K-State search network on Flickr (graph metrics)

Graph Metric	Value
Graph Type	Directed
Vertices	561
Unique Edges	1507
Edges With Duplicates	0
Total Edges	1507
Self-Loops	0
Reciprocated Vertex Pair Ratio	0.02726653
Reciprocated Edge Ratio	0.053085601
Connected Components	1
Single-Vertex Connected Components	0
Maximum Vertices in a Connected Component	561
Maximum Edges in a Connected Component	1507
Maximum Geodesic Distance (Diameter)	4
Average Geodesic Distance	3.072054
Graph Density	0.004796919
Modularity	Not Applicable
NodeXL Version	1.0.1.229

Figure 29. K-State related tag search network on Flickr (graph)

For a more accurate representation see the electronic version.

a friend-of-a-friend of the source user before the new link was created (Mislove, Koppula, Gummadi, Druschel, & Bhattacharjee, 2008, p. 5).

Prior links matter. Social proximity matters. Like roads, relational social network paths may involve some long-standing connectivity.

Delimitations

The essential work of data extractions from social media platforms is the mapping of the human terrain, with humans acting as unwitting sensors in the network. Certainly, there are limitations to crawling social media platforms to understand a formal brand presence as well as an informal one. Comprehending these limitations will enhance the understandings that may be drawn from this empirical network analysis approach.

The nature of social media: One limitation stems from the nature of social media and human presences. Not all people choose to go online. Those who opt-in tend to be less cynical (mistrustful of others' motives) and more optimistic dispositionally and tend to be more pro-social and supportive of others; they tend to be more generous with social and emotional support (Kaplan, Bradley, & Ruscher, 2004). Those who engage in social sharing in mediated environments may be a powerful resource in times of social stress. People self-select into sharing online. Of that group, a subset makes their presences semi-public or public (with a segment who engage totally privately). The data crawls are unable to access private networks; only public information is available. Of the public group, only a small percentage is participatory. Many follow others' accounts as lurkers without ever interacting in a mediated way. This means that the few who actually share in microblogging or digital content sharing have an outsized effect in social networks. This means that those who are private or silent will not register on a social media data crawl. What is intangible or invisible must be quantifiable to some degree as uncertainty. The views of those who are offline or who are inactive online will have to be elicited in other ways. Also, there have been signs of social media fatigue. Sufficiently popular social network platforms that attract a high number of users will likely vary over time, if history is any indication.

How well does the electronic world map to the larger external one? Do social media platforms really strengthen the role of identity and self-concept and self-exploration? In some cases, fairly closely; in others, not so much. A study was done to test how accurate online profiles were in the nonymous Facebook space to the individual in terms of expressions of personality. The authors were testing the "idealized virtual-identity hypothesis." Were online presences mirrors to the real world with personal information "found in personal environments, private thoughts, facial images, and social behavior, all of which are known to contain valid information about personality"? The researchers found that online Facebook presences, with reputational data and information from individuals' acquaintances, mapped fairly closely to peoples identities in Facebook profiles on the dimensions of extraversion, agreeableness, conscientiousness, neuroticism, and openness. The authors came to their conclusion after comparing observer ratings of Facebook profiles and correlations of their observations with the actual personality and the idealized self. This group affirmed the extended real-life hypothesis by identifying the electronic space as an extension of the real world, with people's depictions of themselves on Facebook reflecting "no evidence of self-idealization." The profile owner's ideal self-ratings "did not predict observer impressions above and beyond actual personality." The authors write:

In contrast, even when controlling for ideal-self ratings, the effect of actual personality on OSN (online social network) impressions remained significant for nearly all analyses. Accuracy was strongest for extraversion (paralleling results from face-to-face encounters) and openness (similar to research on personal environments).

Accuracy was lowest for neuroticism, which is consistent with previous research showing that neuroticism is difficult to detect in all zero-acquaintance contexts (Funder, 1999; Kenny, 1994). These results suggest that people are not using their OSN profiles to promote an idealized virtual identity. Instead, OSNs might be an efficient medium for expressing and communicating real personality, which may help explain their popularity. (Back, Stopfer, Vazire, Gaddis, Schmukle, Egloff, & Gosling, 2009, n.p.)

Other researchers show that consumers of social media information may apply a healthy skepticism about others networks when there is an overabundance of connections, which may be seen as raising doubts about the focal individual's actual "popularity and desirability" (Tong, Van Der Heide, Langwell, & Walther, 2008). That said, people are interpreted by the company they keep. While social media spaces are places for identity performances, these performances contain some checks and double-checks for the validation of identity.

What occurs electronically may reveal something of what is happening in the real world, but there is not a one-to-one correlation between what is seen electronically and what is happening in the real and the actual. Researchers show how there is even a wide discrepancy between professed or declared friends and acquaintances in electronic social networks vs. the actual interconnections (intercommunications and reciprocated ties) between individuals (Huberman, Romero, & Wu, 2008). The authors point to what they call "the networks that matter" as those who act as friends than those who merely claim to be. Links between people alone do not mean actual interactions.

Technological limitations: Another limitation comes from the available technologies. Whether open-source or proprietary, publicly-available software programs for such data crawls all have their limits. One limit involves the size of the crawl. Capturing a social network at two-degrees means that the capture inly involves the direct ego neighborhood of a focal node, and then the ego neighborhoods of the alters. Anything beyond that circle is outside the bounds of the data capture (Those who have more high-powered machines may capture and analyze more and to a higher level of rigor.).

Their performance depends on the computer's Random Access Memory (RAM) and Central Processing Unit (CPU). Further, there are limits in Excel, depending on the version, which also adds constraints. One of the NodeXL coordinators wrote on the NodeXL Discussion Forum: "For very large data sets we recommend that users consider the more powerful tools like Python/NetworkX or RSNA or iGraph. If you need a much more powerful machine for a short period of time I suggest exploring the Amazon EC2 service (aws.amazon.com)" (Smith, Jan. 1, 2013). Such software requires high computational processing, which is often beyond the limits of even the most high-end desktop and laptop computers. (In most universities, high performance computing is set aside for better-paid science research.) The "big data" extractions and analyses require much in the way of computational resources and time; there are challenges of scale. There are other dependencies for full data extractions. The software acquires and downloads information through APIs which enable access to social media platforms, which have to limit access to their resources in order to meet needs.

Partial data extractions: Because of the computational expense of social media crawls, most samples of networks are only partial. A partial crawl could be generalizable if social networks were expressible as patterned fractals, but currently, they are not. Each network is a unique case because so little is known of the various types of networks and their patterns (expressed as motif censuses or machine counts of these structures). This means that pattern mining can only inform researchers of so much. In terms of Large-Scale Network Analysis (LSNA), it is important then to crawl the whole network and collect as much information as possible for generalizability about the network topology (structure of entities and relationships). In this early stage, there are a handful of theories about pattern mining social networks, and many of these theories are as-yet untested. Suffice it to say that the concept here is that a social network topology is to human interactions as geography has been to human civilizations; the topology provides a context and constraints, and it is an influencing factor for human interactions but does not wholly determine human outcomes. The storing of large online social network datasets also incurs computational load or cost.

These strategies for data crawls of social media platforms may be applied to email repositories (albeit only with the permission of the email account holder), public wikis, public blogs, threaded discussions (from learning management systems and other types of forums) and http networks. This information may have value for a variety of internal and external uses, even if not all of that data may be publishable.

High learning curves: Social Network Analysis (SNA) entails some 80 – 100 years of research to understand thoroughly. The theories in use are complex, and there are no fully consensus-accepted theories. For example, the methods for the identification of an influential node in a network—a fundamental or canonical assumption—are not widely accepted; these standards vary depending on the type of social network. There has been research that has shown that even with saturation coverage of a product, with millions of Tweets, it may not necessarily result in any direct sales (Schaefer, 2012). Another example involves the analysis of "cold spots" or tie absences in networks. Researchers need to distinguish between a lack of data and data confirming the absence of a tie. The quantification of influence is still in debate. Engaging in social network analysis is cognitively demanding of researchers.

Various social network analysis and visualization tools are complex to use. They are computationally intensive. That said, they do enable the capturing of various "motif censuses." They enable the pruning of node sets and the analysis of smaller branches of the social network. Dynamic filters may be employed to highlight particular aspects of a social network in relation to the network itself or to other branches of the network. Nodes may be removed from a network to see what would happen as the network reconfigures around the absence. Social analysis software tools enable closer analysis of particular focal nodes and ego-node neighborhoods. Various algorithms for drawing graphs from a dataset differ greatly, and differing interpretations may be made based on the visualizations.

What this all means is that researchers need to hone their skills for the most effective data crawls. Just extracting a social network structure may be insufficient, for example; capturing the actual microblogging messages and thumbnails would be helpful in gleaning more information for qualitative, quantitative, and mixed methods research. Researchers have to apply creative and validated methodologies to elicit information (from multiple information streams, including trace data, survey data, and others) and then to analyze the data. In a so-called "data hungry" approach, they need to be able to triangulate data for insights. They need to be able to define the social context and cultural elements to understand social networks. They need to be able to test and validate or invalidate understandings.

Another next step is to develop more sophisticated analysis of what is knowable. What assertions may be made about particular nodes in the network and their relative influences? What may be asserted about the interrelationships between nodes? What may be asserted about a social network's capabilities based on its structure and the resources moving through it (and the paths that the resources are taking)? How may a professional social network be strengthened?

Validation and invalidation of theories: The work of validating or invaliding social network analysis insights vary. There does not seem to be any accepted percentage of a network captured that would be considered a valid sampling.

The research so far has begun with grounded theory (what is observable) and moved to abstractions (moving from specific to general). It has also worked the other way, with theorists proposing hypotheses, conducting research, and drawing conclusions. Others use the triangulation of data method, by collecting copious amounts of information and testing theories against various data sets. There have also been theorists who have offered theories that have not yet been tested. This may well be expected in a fairly nascent field (particularly in the analysis of online social networks).

Some practitioners in this field have asserted that a social network analysis is not truly validated until an intervention is conducted on the in-world population to see how the network behaves postvention. For example, the sending out of a "lever" (a friendly agent) to influence an unfriendly one directly or indirectly, proxemically or distally, may be one such test—assuming measureable and observable reactions may be seen. Another example of this is in the attempts by law enforcement to disrupt or fragment terror networks. Some believe that removal of an influential node may fragment or break apart a network; others suggest that the network will generally only readjust around the absence of an influential leader and may even become stronger. Such ideas are applied to the creation of societal resilience in the face of natural or human-made disasters. How may a social network or community be made more resilient? There is research on the structuring of innovation teams (less connected is better) to create new approaches, and then there is research on structuring company compliance trainings (highly connected is better).

Actionable information: Network effects occur when people move en masse to particular behaviors and spaces, and in that act, add value. The network effects of people going to social media platforms to interact means that universities have to move there, too, to engage and to understand the effects of their outreach endeavors. They need to track the effects of their faculty's research, their funding campaigns, their launching of new academic programs, and other endeavors. Too often, there are outreach endeavors made without any "closing the loop" to understand effects on their stakeholders.

Then, too, the new awareness from SNA may lead to ideas for other engagements or actionable information. This is where branding and marketing understandings need to be delved into with more depth. How may universities start positive trends or spark social cascades? Which influential nodes should universities reach out to to promote research or public good will or access to resources? How may university fund-raisers be made more effective by tapping into social networks? How may universities support their students and other stakeholders better using social media? Where should universities put resources in terms of digital content development for content sharing sites? What should universities do with the awareness of what is out on social media even if they do not have direct control? ["Freedom of the Internet" is a core value for "online expression, assembly and association" (Fontaine & Rogers, 2011, p. 5). Further, the archival properties of the Internet ensure that "long-tail content" may be accessible on dedicated sites into perpetuity.]

Information updates: Even though this approach is highly data-intensive, this work involves information that is transient and often fast-moving. This would suggest that information would need to be constantly updated for it to be valid. A slice-in-time view is only applicable for a particular period before the power of current relationships fades (through tie entropy and dissolution).

A sequence of data captures for a particular account may result in some insights from "autocorrelation" methods, where cross-correlations are made of a signal with itself. At various time intervals, what are the differences between various measures of an account?

Finally, there are endeavors towards actualizing real-time monitoring of electronic social networks and the information flowing through them. This would theoretically enable not only an understanding of social network structures but the dynamism within in terms of both structure and content flows. Such analysis includes temporal patterning of communications around various news, weather, and human-made events, from a head period to a trend peak to the ending of an event (Naaman, Becker, & Gravano, 2011).

There have been studies on the analysis of how trends heat up, popularize through word-of-mouth and forwarded messages, and then dissipate or transmute into something else. There are moves to enhance geosocial analysis, which links social networks to both dynamic space and dynamic time, for deeper understandings. There are endeavors towards predictive analysis—such as focusing on a particular node as a possible future leader or understanding social network trajectories (rarely simply linear progressions) or predicting the probabilistic future for particular social networks (such as political groups). There are also analyses of tie antecedents or precursors to network position or the creation of certain edges (relationships).

FUTURE RESEARCH DIRECTIONS

With the exponential popularization of a range of social media platforms and the capturing of so much electronic data (public as well as trace), there is plenty of latent information from social media to exploit in ways that are beneficial to the conduct of a university in reaching out to its many constituencies.

This chapter focuses on extractive social (and content) network analysis to enhance branding efforts by a university. This is by no means representative of the limits of what is knowable. Rather, this offers a brief look at what is easily accessible currently. A simple value-added research approach could involve downloading the communicated texts and running them through a text analysis tool. The data sets could be run through other social network graphing tools for different kinds of statistical analysis.

One example of the integration of locative information is cartoblography, which combines microblogging information overlaid over a map (with words depicted as larger in size based on text frequency found in the data crawl) (Field & O'Brien, 2010). Tweet maps are combinations of textual data (ranked by frequency) with geolocation data. The introduction of spatial elements in network analysis suggests the ability to analyze for proximity or adjacency influences. Locative events may be analyzed.

There are tools that enable multi-nodal Dynamic Network Analysis (DNA) through live data feeds (with people as sensors) to detect and capture emergent or real-time events (for situational awareness through "social awareness streams" as termed by Naaman, Becker, & Gravano, 2011); independent cascades or word-of-mouth riffs; activity peaks and declines. With sufficient vigilance, entire events may be detected from originating spark to the final quiet. Some researchers are mapping conversations around particular topics and analyzing who is engaging with those topics—whether individuals who are parts of formal networks, clustered nodes, or those from unrelated nodes—to label structural, coordinated, or uncoordinated trends. Researchers are looking to create publicly available tools for real-time analysis of data moving through evolving networks. Much progress has been made in the machine analysis of sentiment as expressed in "opinion lexicon" text and symbols (and other psycholinguistic phenomena). Other software programs strive to read human intent based on their textual language contents and frequency of posts. There have been remote reads of individuals' learning styles preferences, personality dispositions (based on the Five Factor Model, including neuroticism, extraversion, openness to experience, agreeableness, and conscientiousness) emotional states, and organizational roles and responsibilities based on their positions in social media networks. Various computer programs have been created to read information moving through social networks to identify "confirmed truths" vs. "false rumors" (Mendoza, Poblete, & Castillo, 2010, p. 77).

Not only have there been innovations in computing research, but as more researchers are read into the capabilities of this approach, it's possible that currently unforeseen questions may arise that may further push innovations. Online social network analysis will certainly evolve as new insights are achieved and new theories proposed and technologies evolve. It may be possible to provide electronic doppelgangers of whole digital communities from origination to sunset.

CONCLUSION

The application of social network analysis to data extracted from social media sites is a promising approach to understanding a university's formal and informal branding in electronic spaces. This chapter brings together some of the latest knowledge in the field in terms of computational social network analysis and social media research. However, it is critical to knowledge that this approach entails a high learning curve. As such, this is not an easy-to-integrate approach. Any decision-makers who would be read into this approach would have to be introduced to some pretty complex theory and statistical analysis.

The potential benefits of this approach outweigh the known costs, however, given the richness of the data and the impossibility of acquiring this information in other ways. This approach of mapping online social networks enables a more comprehensive branding approach; it enables the generating and developing of leads.

ACKNOWLEDGMENT

I am grateful to my university's social networks that make this a very joyful place to work. Thanks to the NodeXL team for a fantastic tool that simplifies the work of researchers. Thanks to the various social media platforms for their generous and open approach to the world in making Application Programming Interfaces (API) available. Let no one say that social network analysis is easy or simple. It took me more than a year of reading in-depth and experimenting with a range of social network analysis software tools before being able to apply this approach to a very simple application.

REFERENCES

Acquisti, A., & Gross, R. (2006). *Imagined communities: Awareness, information sharing, and privacy on the Facebook*. Retrieved from http://link.springer.com/chapter/10.1007%2F11957454_3?LI=true

Auer, M. R. (2011). The policy sciences of social media. *Policy Studies Journal: the Journal of the Policy Studies Organization*, *39*(4), 709–736. doi:10.1111/j.1541-0072.2011.00428.x

Back, M. D., Stopfer, J. M., Vazire, S., Gaddis, S., Schmukle, S. C., Egloff, B., & Gosling, S. D. (2010). *Facebook profiles reflect actual personality, not self-idealization*. Psychological Science Online First. doi:10.1177/0956797609360756

Catanese, S. A., De Meo, P., Ferrara, E., Fiumara, G., & Provetti, A. (2011). Crawling Facebook for social network analysis purposes. In *Proceedings of WIMS '11*. Sogndal, Norway: WIMS.

Chang, H.-C. (2010). A new perspective on Twitter hashtag use: Diffusion of innovation theory. In *Proceedings of ASIST 2010*. Pittsburgh, PA: ASIST.

Chu, Z., Gianvecchio, S., Wang, H., & Jajodia, S. (2010). Who is tweeting on Twitter: Human, bot, or cyborg. In *Proceedings of ACSAC '10*. Austin, TX: ACSAC.

Ebner, M., Mühlburger, H., Schaffert, S., Schiefner, M., Reinhardt, W., & Wheeler, S. (2010). Getting granular on Twitter: Tweets from a conference and their limited usefulness for non-participants. In N. Reynolds & M. Turcsányi-Szabó (Eds.), *KCKS 2010, IFIP AICT 324* (pp. 102–113). IFIP International Federation for Information Processing. doi:10.1007/978-3-642-15378-5_10

Efron, M., & Winget, M. (2010). Questions are content: A taxonomy of questions in a microblogging environment. In *Proceedings of ASIST 2010*. Pittsburgh, PA: ASIST.

Ellison, N. B., Steinfield, C., & Lampe, C. (2007). The benefits of Facebook 'friends': Social capital and college students' use of online social network sites. *Journal of Computer-Mediated Communication*, *12*, 1143–1168. doi:10.1111/j.1083-6101.2007.00367.x

Field, K., & O'Brien, J. (2010). Cartoblography: Experiments in using and organizing the spatial context of micro-blogging. *Transactions in GIS*, *14*(s1), 5–23. doi:10.1111/j.1467-9671.2010.01210.x

Fontaine, R., & Rogers, W. (2011). Internet freedom: A foreign policy imperative in the digital age. Washington, DC: Center for a New American Security.

Hansen, D., Smith, M. A., & Schneiderman, B. (2011). EventGraphs: Charting collections of conference connections. In *Proceedings of the 44th Hawaii International Conference on System Sciences*. IEEE.

Hansen, D. L., Schneiderman, B., & Smith, M. A. (2011). *Analyzing social media networks with NodeXL: Insights from a connected world*. Amsterdam: Elsevier.

Huberman, B. A., Romero, D. M., & Wu, F. (2008). Social networks that matter: Twitter under the microscope. *Social Computing Laboratory, HP Labs*. Retrieved on Feb. 9, 2013, from http://www.hpl.hp.com/research/scl/papers/twitter/

Jung, G., & Lee, B. (2010). Analysis on social network adoption according to the change of network topology: The impact of 'Open API' to adoption of Facebook. In *Proceedings of the 12th International Conference on Electronic Commerce (ICEC), Roadmap for the Future of Electronic Business* (pp. 23 – 32). ICEC.

Kaplan, R. D. (2012). *The revenge of geography: What the map tells us about coming conflicts and the battle against fate*. New York: Random House.

Kaplan, S. A., Bradley, J. C., & Ruscher, J. B. (2004). The inhibitory role of cynical disposition in the provision and receipt of social support: The case of the September 11th terrorist attacks. *Personality and Individual Differences*, *37*, 1221–1232. doi:10.1016/j.paid.2003.12.006

Kolcz, A. (2012). Large scale learning at Twitter. In E. Simperl et al. (Eds.), *ECWC 2012 (LNCS)* (Vol. 7295). Berlin: Springer.

Lanier, J. (2010). *You are not a gadget*. New York: First Vintage Books.

Mendoza, M., Poblete, B., & Castillo, C. (2010). Twitter under crisis: Can we trust what we RT? In *Proceedings of the Workshop on Social Media Analytics (SOMA '10)*, (pp. 71-79). Washington, DC: SOMA.

Meyer, E. T., & Schroeder, R. (2009). Untangling the web of e-research: Towards a sociology of online knowledge. *Journal of Informetrics*, *3*, 246–260. doi:10.1016/j.joi.2009.03.006

Mislove, A., Koppula, H. S., Gummadi, K. P., Druschel, P., & Bhattacharjee, B. (2008). Growth of the Flickr social network. In *Proceedings of WOSN '08*. Seattle, WA: ACM.

Naaman, M., Becker, H., & Gravano, L. (2011). Hip and trendy: Characterizing emerging trends on Twitter. *Journal of the American Society for Information Science and Technology*, *62*(5), 902–918. doi:10.1002/asi.21489

Priem, J., & Costello, K. L. (2010). How and why scholars cite on Twitter. In *Proceedings of ASIST 2010*. Pittsburgh, PA: ASIST.

Schaefer, M. (2012). *Return on influence: The revolutionary power of Klout, social scoring, and influence marketing*. New York: McGraw Hill.

Selwyn, N. (2009). Faceworking: Exploring students' education-related use of Facebook. *Learning, Media and Technology*, *34*(2), 157–174. doi:10.1080/17439880902923622

Size Limits on Twitter Import. (2012). Retrieved from http://nodexl.codeplex.com/discussions/348565

Smith, M. (2013). *A cloud large-data processing function? NodeXL discussion board*. Retrieved Feb. 12, 2013, from http://nodexl.codeplex.com/discussions/428064

Smith, M. A., Schneiderman, B., Milic-Frayling, N., Rodrigues, E. M., Barash, V., & Dunne, C. … Gleave, E. (2009). Analyzing (social media) networks with NodeXL. In *Proceedings of C&T '09*, (pp. 255-263). University Park, PA: C&T.

Steinfield, C., Ellison, N. B., & Lampe, C. (2008). Social capital, self-esteem, and use of online social network sites: A longitudinal analysis. *Journal of Applied Developmental Psychology*, *29*, 434–445. doi:10.1016/j.appdev.2008.07.002

Stokes, J. P. (1983). Predicting satisfaction with social support from social network structure. *American Journal of Community Psychology*, *11*(2), 141–182. doi:10.1007/BF00894363

Tong, S. T., Van Der Heide, B., Langwell, L., & Walther, J. B. (2008). Too much of a good thing? The relationship between number of friends and interpersonal impressions on Facebook. *Journal of Computer-Mediated Communication*, *13*, 531–549. doi:10.1111/j.1083-6101.2008.00409.x

Veletsianos, G. (2012). Higher education scholars' participation and practices on Twitter. *Journal of Computer Assisted Learning*, *28*, 336–349. doi:10.1111/j.1365-2729.2011.00449.x

Wu, S., Hofman, J. M., Mason, W. A., & Watts, D. J. (2011). Who says what to whom on Twitter. In *Proceedings of the World Wide Web 2011*. Hyderabad, India: IEEE.

ADDITIONAL READING

Hansen, D. L., Schneiderman, B., & Smith, M. A. (2011). *Analyzing social media networks with NodeXL: Insights from a connected world*. Amsterdam: Elsevier.

NodeXL Graph Gallery. (n.d.). Retrieved from http://nodexlgraphgallery.org/Pages/Default.aspx

NodeXL: Network Overview, Discovery, and Exploration for Excel. (n.d.). Retrieved from http://nodexl.codeplex.com/

KEY TERMS AND DEFINITIONS

Add-In: A set of software components that may be added to a software application to add functionality; plug-in.

Application Programming Interface (API): A protocol used as an interface by software to communicate with each other (for interactions, such as the exchange of services or information).

Arc: An undirected link between two vertices or nodes.

Cluster: A unique grouping of nodes or entities based on shared interests or similarities.

Data Crawl: Automated (but usually human directed) data extraction, such as from a social media site.

Data Extraction: The downloading of data from a social media platform; a data crawl.

Data Harvesting: The culling and exploitation of data from a socio-technical system for assessment.

Directed: Links with arrowed ends to show the directionality of a relationship between two nodes.

Diameter: The farthest path distance between extreme-most nodes in a network.

Edge: A link that may be directed (with arrows on the ends) or undirected (without arrows on the end).

Edge (Betweenness) Centrality: The number of shortest paths through an edge in a graph or network (as an indicator of how traveled that edge is in terms of resources or information moving through the network); a value indicating edge betweenness centrality.

Eigenvector Centrality: Various measures which analyze the value of a node's ties to other nodes, with popular node connections seen as more valuable.

Equivalence: Similarity in structure (such as in-degree and out-degree); similarity in some other dimension.

Geodesic Distance: The shortest paths (in terms of numbers of edges or links) between two vertices or nodes.

Graph: A two-dimensional space on which entities and relationships are depicted, usually in node-link diagrams.

Hashtag: A tag consisting of the hash sign # and alphanumeric characters included in a microblogging message to help organize the contents.

Heterophily: The preference or "like" of differences in others; the phenomenon of finding others likeable who are different from oneself.

Homophily: The preference or "like" of similarity in others; the phenomenon of finding others likeable who are similar to oneself.

Lever: A friendly agent who might influence unfriendly ones directly or indirectly.

Link: A tie, edge, or arc that represents a relationship.

Mass-Personal: A public and mediated personal form of interconnectivity.

Multimodal: Involving multiple types of vertices or nodes.

Node: A vertice, representing an individual, group, or entity.

Node-Link Diagram: A 2D diagram that consists of nodes (entities, egos, or agents) and links (lines, edges, or arcs), which represent entities and relationships.

Nonymous: Having an acknowledged name, named (the opposite of anonymous).

Path: A "walk" through a social network or between vertices (or nodes).

Predictive Analytics: Various techniques used to make predictions of the future.

Random walk: A chance-based movement through a social network along paths with all paths having an equal chance of being used; an unpatterned movement of information through a network.

Social Network: A human grouping expressed as an abstracted network.

Social Network Analysis (SNA): The science of studying social structures and human interrelationships to achieve various aims.

Topology (of Networks): The structure of a network; the arrangement of nodes and links representing the structure of a network.

Undirected: Links (without arrowed ends) between nodes which indicate symmetric binary relations.

Walk: The movement of resources or information through a social network along particular paths (whether random or determined or other).

This research was previously published in Packaging Digital Information for Enhanced Learning and Analysis edited by Shalin Hai-Jew, pages 120-162, copyright year 2014 by Information Science Reference (an imprint of IGI Global).

Section 4
Industry–Specific

Chapter 53

The Use of Social Media in College Recruiting and the Student Job Search

Amy Diepenbrock
St. Mary's University, USA

Wanda Gibson
Pomona College, USA

ABSTRACT

This chapter addresses the gap in the literature regarding employer recruitment of college students, and more specifically, the use of social media in the recruitment and hiring processes by both students and employers. Background information on traditional recruiting strategies is briefly discussed as well as how employers are using social media. Additionally, how millennial college students typically communicate and how they should be using social media in the job search process are addressed. This chapter also includes data from a survey, administered by the authors, of U.S.-based employers who recruit college students with anecdotal information about how they utilize, or do not utilize, social media in their recruiting and hiring practices.

INTRODUCTION

For over a decade, the popularity of connecting with others through social media has been steadily increasing. Friends following friends - or even following others not connected through friendship - to see what they are doing, where they are, who they know, or just to explore one's personal interests is a normal daily activity supported through Facebook, Twitter, LinkedIn and similar outlets. Also becoming more common place is the use of social media in the job search and hiring process. Candidates and employers are using social media as a new way of interacting and finding out about each other.

Candidates are creating profiles, following organizations, researching opportunities, and finding job leads through various social media outlets. In the Class of 2012 Student Survey Report conducted by the National Association of College and Employers (NACE) about 41 percent of graduating students

DOI: 10.4018/978-1-5225-5637-4.ch053

used social media in their job search (NACE 2012). In the coming years, this number should be on the rise. So what are some of the best social media sources presently used for this purpose and how should they be used?

For those candidates who are using or planning to use social media in their employment searches, it is necessary to be aware of their online presence and how that may affect their ability to be hired. Creating a "'brand" that speaks to who they are as candidates, highlights their positive attributes, enables them to interact with others in a professional manner, and does not shed any negative light on their candidacy is essential. Candidates should be mindful that with the prevalence of employers' access to such platforms, something they did not wish a potential employer to know about them could be discovered.

As for the other side of the employment perspective, ever-changing technology has altered methods employers use for recruiting new talent. While traditional avenues for recruiting may still exist, the cliché that it is not what you know, but who you know is even more present through social media. In the *2012-2013 Recruiting Trends* study created and published by the Collegiate Employment Research Institute at Michigan State University, 29 percent of employers surveyed indicated that "social media is becoming well established as an important strategy for engaging students" (p. 23). This report lists travel costs, time away from the office, and efficiency in recruitment as top reasons for leaning on social media and other technologies within hiring practices. Employers are utilizing social media for a variety of purposes. Some recruiters effectively utilize these online outlets to connect with candidates and advertise opportunities. Others utilize such networks to conduct informal screenings or unofficial background checks on candidates.

Further, social media is a rapidly changing environment, and which outlets hiring managers are choosing to utilize continues to evolve at warp speed. Is Facebook the 2013 version of MySpace from 2005? Will recruiters be able to continue the same methods used today in one, two, or five years? As candidates are online earlier and earlier, will employers expect candidates to be where they are online or will employers continue to adapt and change to keep up with the younger workplace generation? Should we expect to find images of job postings on Instagram in the near future? For candidates, are there other social media sources that will yield more opportunities for them in the coming years? Will Foursquare, and Pinterest help in the job search?

This chapter will address the use of social media in the employment realm from the hiring agents' point of view and from the perspective of candidates, specifically the students. The chapter will highlight how hiring agents are utilizing social media through use of anecdotal evidence and survey data collected from U.S. based college recruiting staff by the authors. Questions of how and why candidates' employment searches should include using social media as one of the tools in their job search kit will be explored. How candidates should create a brand worth showcasing to potential employers will be discussed. Additionally, this chapter will address how to protect the personal brand to minimize unintended access of information that would contribute negatively to that image. Current trends in what social media outlets are most used by candidates and recruiting professionals will be addressed in this chapter. Finally, the chapter will provide recommendations on how to move forward in the 21st century with recruiting millennial students through the use of social media and questions for further research will be posed.

BACKGROUND

Definitions of Terms

For the purpose of this chapter, it is necessary to define several key terms as they may be confusing to those outside of the realm of the employment recruiting process of students on college or university campuses. Throughout this chapter, when "college" is mentioned as an entity, it will also refer to those institutions that identify themselves as a college or a university. "College students" or "students" may also refer to both undergraduate and graduate students alike unless stated otherwise. The words "employer" and "recruiter" will be used interchangeably to indicate the companies who hire and the individuals who represent those companies. "College recruiting," a term which can often be used in the college admission process, will be used to describe those activities that recruiters employ to interact with students in an effort to gain future employees; and additionally, "(on) campus recruiting" will have the same meaning as "college recruiting". Finally, "social media" and "social networking (sites)" will be used interchangeably.

Mobile Technology Generation

We live in a technology era. According to the Pew Research Center's Internet and American Life Project, in 2012, 88 percent of all US adults owned a mobile phone, an increase from 65 percent in 2004. Moreover, 45 percent owned a "smart phone", often referred to as a mini computer that is also able to make calls. Such phones are constantly connected to the Internet, allowing for ongoing connection to information and individuals. Younger adults, often college aged individuals, are most likely to own a smart phone. Of all mobile phone users, 66 percent who are between the ages of 18 and 29 use a smart phone (M. Brinton, personal communication, 2013).

How connected are college students and what do they use these phones for? According to hackcollege. com (2011), "one quarter of all college students whip out their phone every single class period". Most students surveyed indicated that their phones never left their side (75%) and that it made their lives easier (93%). Additionally, during those class periods, students use their phones to connect with friends based upon a survey by Hanson, Drumheller, Mallard, McKee, and Schlegel (2010). They took daily pictures and videos with these devices and uploaded them to share with friends. Many reported that they cannot go more than ten minutes without checking their phone. College students reported leaning away from email use and towards texting. Further, access to social media has heightened with the ease of utilizing smart phones. Ninety-seven percent of college student smart phone users reported utilizing their phone to access social media. In order to keep up with the trends, most social media sites offer applications, also known as "apps", allowing 95 percent of reported smart phone users to access Facebook, and 47 percent to access Twitter (M. Brinton, personal communication, 2013).

Students use their mobile devices for academic purposes as well as for social reasons. According to the ECAR Study of Undergraduate Students and Information Technology produced by the EDUCAUSE Center for Applied Research (Dahlstrom, 2012), 62 percent of the students had a smart phone and of that 62 percent, 67 percent said they used their phone for academic reasons. Students also reported that they used tablets and e-readers for academics, too. Fifteen percent of the students had tablets and 12 percent had e-readers with 67 percent of the tablet users and 47 percent of the e-reader users utilizing them for academic reasons.

Additional research conducted by the Pew Center's Internet and American Life Project focused on social media use, reporting the most frequent usage by Internet users under the age of 50. Specifically, their study found that 83 percent of all users, those between ages 18 and 29 were most likely to engage in social media. Women were also found to be more likely to utilize social media than men. Further, individuals with some college (69%) and a household income under $30,000 per year (72%) were found to be most frequent social media users. Facebook, which was most popular, was followed by Twitter, Pinterest, Instagram, and Tumblr (Duggan & Brenner, 2013).

Social Media and Employer Use

Social media use by employers is also increasing. Hunt (2010) discussed a Career Builder survey that found an increase in employer usage of social media for recruitment purposes. Within these results, 35 percent of employers reported using social media to promote their organization, 21 percent to recruit or research potential employees, and 18 percent to increase their company brand. Hunt pointed out that candidates in today's market expected their employers of choice to be online. Additionally, McGrath (2012) pointed out that human resources agents have been utilizing online information to conduct background checks for some time. She referenced a Microsoft sponsored study that reported 79 percent of hiring managers used online information to make a decision about a candidate and 70 percent had rejected a candidate because of that information.

Online information about candidates varies and recruiters should be careful to use judgment to determine if the information is valid. "The challenge presented by the use of these sites is related to how well they provide reliable and valid, job-relevant information. Little is also known about the accuracy of the information provided within social networking profiles or about the prevalence of different types of faking on web pages" (Davison, Mariast, & Bing, 2011, p. 155). Despite such skepticism or warning, recruiters reported numerous reasons for rejecting a candidate based on information found via social media profiles. Provocative or inappropriate pictures or information, evidence of poor communication skills, discussion of illegal activity related to drugs or alcohol, revealing falsified information, or speaking negatively of previous employers have caused recruiting professionals to reject a candidate otherwise of interest (Brown & Vaughn, 2011).

At this point in time, social media neither can, nor should replace traditional recruiting methods; however, it is necessary for organizations to supplement their efforts online. "Fueling traditional recruiting strategies with social media requires understanding how the different sites operate" (Hunt, 2010, p. 38). Having a virtual strategy is critical in times of reduced human resources staff and ability to travel for recruitment purposes. Simply creating the account is not enough, but allowing social media to take on the persona of the organization and keeping a high level of activity are keys to success (Hunt, 2010; Russo, 2011).

Pinnington (2011) pointed out that with 120 million users in 200 countries; LinkedIn is equivalent to the 13th most visited site on the planet. Grant (2011) further discussed the difference between Facebook and Twitter. He argued that Facebook allows users to connect to those they may already know while Twitter offers the access to showcase expertise and connect to those the user wants to know. Twitter gives a person or organization the chance to build credibility. With such diversity, hiring organizations not only need to be involved in social media, but the site(s) selected are important. Russo (2011) discussed the Jobvite annual survey of recruiters who planned to hire through social media. Recruiters who indicated a plan to hire through these sites rose from 83 percent in 2010 to 89 percent in 2011. LinkedIn appears to be the most widely used (87%), followed by Facebook (55%) and Twitter (49%).

The available literature focuses on trends for social media use in recruiting. The information gathered gives an overview across all industries and position levels. There is a gap in the literature related to the specific recruitment and hiring of college students and recent graduates into entry-level positions. Given the communication patterns and social media use of today's college and university students, the way in which recruiters interact via social media with these future and potential employees should rely heavily on social media interactions. In addition to the dearth of literature related to college student recruitment, there is a lack of scholarly research on social media and its effects on recruiting and hiring in general (Herbold & Douma, 2013) as social media is a relatively new practice in the job search, recruiting, and hiring process. This chapter begins to address this gap and focus on patterns utilized by college recruiters and how this affects recruitment of college students.

EMPLOYER RECRUITMENT (CAMPUS RECRUITMENT) ON COLLEGE CAMPUSES

Employer recruiting, more commonly known as "campus recruiting," on college campuses in the U.S. has been a staple for decades. Campus recruiting would be classified as those activities by an employer in which the company engages, in some way, with a college in an effort to hire students for positions. These activities traditionally have included such things as information sessions (employers sharing company related information with students such as opportunities, company structure, and culture), resume referrals (student resumes are gathered by the career services office and forwarded to the employer), faculty contacts, on-campus interviews, career fairs, job postings, print ads in campus newspapers, presentations/participation with student organizations or in classrooms, and having a robust internship program as a pipeline for conversions to full-time hires (Barton, 2007; Wheeler, 2004). Campus recruiting provides employers with access to a captive audience of interested students who are ready to move into the world of work. This is the intersection of where employers, trying to fill a need, meet those students whose end goal for college is to find a job.

According to the Cooperative Institutional Research Program's (CIRP) Freshman Survey report from fall 2012, of the 192,912 first year students, 87.9 percent of them said that they were attending college to get a better job (HERI, 2013). This is an important factor for employers to capitalize on for the foreseeable future as 85.9 percent of the first year students who responded to the same survey in 2011 said getting a better job was a priority of going to college. However, for this generation of students, the millennials, will traditional campus recruiting methods continue to work and for how long?

There seems to be some varying opinions on whether on-campus recruiting activities will die out or if they will remain strong. In a Wall Street Journal article from 2011, several of those interviewed believed that for large companies, on campus recruiting will still be a major source for new college hires for the years to come. A reason given for continued on-campus hiring from one person interviewed for the article was that, "During a tighter job market, employers feel that recruiting through a college campus will be a safer bet, given company ties with colleges" while another said that "Face-to-face relationships are critically important" (Weigley, 2001).

Of the previously mentioned campus recruiting activities, there are some that employers rely heavily on in their recruiting process. In the *Recruiting Trends* report, the number one campus based recruiting strategy reported by employers was their internship/coop program. Sixty-two percent of employers said they used this strategy. The second most popular strategy by employers was career fairs (61%) followed by information sessions (47%) – which they often sent employees who were alumni of that particular school to conduct, resume referrals (46%), faculty connections (41%), and on campus interviewing (37%). While these strategies were the main ones employed by recruiters, and the report does give average hires for each strategy, one would wonder if greater success might be had if employers were willing to adjust their strategies to the ways that college students communicate today.

COLLEGE STUDENTS' PREFERENCES FOR INFORMATION AND COMMUNICATION

On many college campuses, students are on their smart phones either looking for information or communicating with others. They are on a laptop doing one task while using their smart phone to do something else. They are digital learners who want information at their fingertips and they often want it instantly. Gone are the days of getting information (outside of textbooks) from a print resource. That has been replaced with the internet. In a research report by the Platt Retail Institute based out of the Chicago School of Professional Psychology entitled, "Communication Effectiveness in Higher Education," the report found that students prefer to receive information digitally – through such mediums as the internet, e-mail, and text messages (Platt, King, & Dommer, 2010). While the conventional way of face-to-face communication is still the preferred method of communicating for school and social interactions (Robinson & Stubberud, 2012), the anecdote of students sitting in their rooms and texting or instant messaging their roommates who are in the same room have been heard on countless occasions. In a study of undergraduate students by Hanson et al. (2010), they reported that the students spent a significant amount of time, 14.35 hours per week on texting. Therefore, communicating via the use of technology is of no surprise either.

Students have spoken about how they prefer to receive information or to communicate, and overwhelmingly it is through digital forms. The convergence of information and communication in a single digital format would be an ideal platform to ensure that students are reached. The use of various social media outlets merges these preferences for communication and information gathering. Facebook, YouTube, and Twitter are some of the most popular social media sites (Abdelraheem, 2013; Capano, Deris, & Desjardins, n.d.; Ratliff, 2011). According to Ratliff (2011), "Social media, in the beginning, was used as a means for individuals to communicate on personal interest and stay connected with friends, family, and co-horts. Now information is disseminated through these avenues to educate, inform, survey…" (p.66). Armed with this knowledge, colleges and universities need to adjust their methods of communication to ensure that whatever message they are trying to convey is received by its students.

Colleges have realized that to interact with students, they need to use the same technology resources that students regularly use. For this reason, many schools have ventured into the world of social media for communication purposes. E-mail is typically the college authorized communication method for official information, but schools are also using Facebook, YouTube, Twitter, and Pinterest for communicating with students (Mangan, 2012). Through these digital mediums, information can be delivered and likely, seen, that might otherwise have been missed in an e-mail because a student chose not check his or her school issued e-mail or purposely ignored the e-mail after seeing that it came from the school. Furthermore, some learning management platforms, such as Blackboard, used on college campuses are now allowing the integration of social media tools, Facebook for example, for seamless interaction between the academic and social lives of students (Kolowich, 2011). According to Kolowich (2011), students can get course information through an application for Facebook that is linked to Blackboard.

Knowing the preferred methods by which students communicate is critical; however, that is only part of the equation. What devices are they picking up to carry out this communication? It was previously discussed that this is the mobile technology generation and that is true. From the ECAR Study (2012), 86 percent of the students owned a laptop. Of the 62 percent of the students who had a smart phone, 46 percent preferred the Android while 44 percent preferred the iPhone device. This study also showed that a growing number of students utilized tablets and e-readers, 15 percent and 12 percent respectively. They preferred iPads over Androids and Kindles over Nooks.

It is necessary to know what devices students are using because colleges need to make their information mobile device accessible. Otherwise, the gap in communication between student and institution will only increase, because more and more students are coming to school equipped with the latest mobile devices. Students who use mobile technology want to have access to the same type of information as those using traditional technology. Colleges need to support many different mobile platforms as tech savvy students continue to embark on their campuses with the expectation that their school will provide the necessary technological support. Some colleges are beginning to develop strategies to meet the needs of these mobile users by implementing mobile web-only strategies (device-neutral applications), native application-only strategies (mobile specific platform applications), or hybrid strategies (ECAR, 2012).

If the constant use of technology is so critical to students' livelihood at college, then why not use that technology to get them to the next phase of their lives – the world of work? As colleges are adjusting communications methods with students, employers are encouraged to do the same.

2013 SOCIAL MEDIA RECRUITING AND HIRING PRACTICES SURVEY

Given the trends discussed above, the traditional methods that recruiters have used time and again to recruit and hire graduating college students must change. Whether employers like it or not, the ways that today's college students connect with each other is affecting how they search for jobs and communicate with potential employers. Employers are recognizing these communication trends and therefore they are looking to capitalize on potential candidate use of social media in a variety of manners.

Use of Social Media

An April 2013 survey conducted by the authors of approximately 1,200 U.S. based college recruiters, receiving a 15 percent return rate (n = 179), indicated that 70.4 percent of responding college recruiters stated that their organization utilizes social media within the recruiting and hiring processes. Given the *Recruiting Trends* finding stated previously, that 29 percent of all recruiters utilize social media, this study shows that U.S. based recruiters focused solely on filling entry-level positions with graduating college students are finding ways to meet their candidates in the manner in which they respond. This number should continue to grow as today's college graduates, comfortable and savvy with social media, move up in ranks within the workplace and in turn become hiring managers. Additionally, as social media sites add job listing, searching, and other related features, the ease of utilizing such resources in recruiting and hiring will increase.

It is interesting to note the rationale stated by the 29.6 percent of survey respondents who explained why their organization does not utilize social media. There is not simply one reason offered to illustrate the why for those who have not jumped onto this bandwagon yet. Of those who currently do not utilize social media in their practices, 30.3 percent noted that they have had discussions or are presently in the process of building a plan to incorporate such technologies into their recruitment and hiring of college students. Another 7.5 percent of those who stated no use indicated that their response is a result of a lack of resources or a lack of manpower to effectively and efficiently oversee such responsibilities. Such response indicates that future studies will find an increased number of organizations will have moved in this direction.

Further, 46.8 percent of responses indicated additional and negative rationale in relation to why they do not utilize social media in recruitment and hiring practices. Twelve percent of no use responders said that use of social media for such tasks would violate corporate or executive level policies. On top of this set of responses, 16.7 percent of no use respondents indicated that they simply do not need to use social media to receive the number of applications necessary to fill their positions. And finally, 18.1 percent of no use respondents stated that they do not approve or agree with such practices for reasons that include venues such as Facebook or Twitter are for friendship, not business purposes and that they do not want to see what college students post nor do they want their information seen by potential candidates.

Previously, a search on any company website or in an employee handbook would find no information related to use of social media. Some organizations have added to existing internet use policies the inclusion of social media or they have developed a freestanding social media policy. Such policies typically include information that discourages fraternization between employees or social use of the internet during work hours. Twelve percent of the survey respondents who do not use social media in recruiting and hiring have a policy against it at some level. It is imperative that organizations who wish to hire college graduates engage via social media. Similarly, it is 18.1 percent of no use respondents steer clear of social media because they cannot see the business relevance and consider such tools to be for personal use only. As will be discussed later in this chapter, some sites lend themselves to easier business use than others, yet when focused, multiple social media sites can be productive resources for college recruiters.

With a large percent of college recruiters utilizing social media in their recruiting and hiring processes, the question of how an organization can use these online tools needs to be answered. Of the survey respondents who reported utilizing social media, 48.1 percent stated that the primary reason they engage in this online activity is to promote their company and its opportunities. An additional 42.5 percent of social media user respondents indicated that the primary reason they utilize these sites is to outreach to potential candidates in order to actively increase applicant pools. This total of 90.6 percent of reported social media users who are engaged through Facebook, LinkedIn, Twitter, and other sites to increase candidate numbers and promote opportunities shows that significant time and energy is spent here. While it is not clear how many organizations employ a social media specialist, one can assume that college recruiters are being tasked with such duties. Finally, for 9.4 percent of user respondents, the primary reason for using social media is to search user profiles for candidate information.

Interacting With Potential Candidates

How do U.S. based college recruiters want to interact in the online environment with up and coming graduates who are potential candidates? What is considered to be professional or appropriate by human resource officers who are tasked with recruiting and hiring today's college students? When does the line become blurred or crossed? These questions and more are often posed by students to their career counselors and career services staff members on campus. When questioned, college recruiters offer a variety of responses to what is acceptable, appropriate, or even appreciated and desired online communication and interaction with candidates, particularly those in or graduating from college.

When asked, "during the recruiting and hiring process, what are your thoughts on a potential candidate attempting to connect to or friend you as their college recruiter?" responses ranged from statements of appreciate and support (28.2%) to those who find it unprofessional, inappropriate, or an otherwise unhelpful move by the candidate (21.7%). Positive responses included statements such as "I'm comfortable with that approach. The world and information move at very quick speeds so it helps to understand information that may be relevant through social. It also shows a level of interest and innovation in the candidate" or "I welcome the invitation and think it's the person who is eager for employment that goes the extra step in knowing not only the company, but the people he or she is interviewing with." Other responses indicated that requesting to connect is "a smart move," "a good networking opportunity," and "a chance for the recruiter to access the candidate's profile to gather more information." Some approve with caution though, indicating that they have no problem with candidates connecting to them "as long as they use proper language and grammar" and "are professional in nature." Responses also indicated a preference for the candidate to connect to a recruiter's professional page, not personal pages.

Respondents who indicated that their organization will not connect to or friend potential candidates also stated a variety of reasons. Many included rationale that explained the awkward or uncomfortable position they would be in if they connected with a candidate who was then not offered a position. One respondent stated that "It's very unprofessional. Especially if we do not hire that potential candidate, it can feel awkward. It's fine if a potential candidate looks up our employees on LinkedIn, as that's normal, but asking to make a connection before the hiring process is over seems ambitious and premature." Another college recruiter described that even if they post positions via social media, their instructions for applications state to apply online. Therefore, the respondent stated that they "recognize that social media users often blur the unstated boundaries that are implied in job postings that provide explicit steps to apply for an available position. We do not accept friend requests from job applicants and submission of such requests are considered a negative indicator for compliance with company policies when our job application instructions specify the required steps that do not include social media connections."

While the question regarding connection to candidates did not include specific site information, 17.3 percent of recruiter respondents indicated that if the contact was made via LinkedIn it would be deemed appropriate. On the other hand, 2.1 percent of respondents listed Facebook as a personal means to communicate, not professional. One recruiter explained that they are "okay with it on LinkedIn, as they may connect with those who may not only be viable candidates now, but also with those who may be candidates in the future. They also may likely be connected with people with similar backgrounds, educations or interests that could prove to be candidates in the future." Another stated that "on LinkedIn it is not a problem. It shows they want to do research on your background." Other responses indicated that although there is acceptance of connections on LinkedIn, it doesn't actually help a candidate move forward in the process over another who is not connected online. Facebook on the other hand, appears to be considered as personal over professional for many college recruiters. Liking an organization's page is desired but not connecting to the actual recruiter. More than one respondent indicated that they "would be suspect of a friend request to the personal Facebook account."

Regardless of site, 10.8 percent of respondents stated that requests to connect to their personal page or account would not be accepted but that their organization has a page or account that would be the ideal place for a candidate to become a fan or follower. Consensus amongst these respondents is that mixing personal pages with business is not appropriate, but that organizations have pages on various sites in order to disseminate information to candidates in a more fair and objective manner. Simply put as one recruiter stated, "Contacting the organization through social media is fine. Contacting the recruiter personally is not."

In the end, some college recruiters are still conflicted on their thoughts regarding a connection or friend request by a candidate. Explained by one respondent, "It makes me feel uncomfortable to actually connect to them. Though, it shows some business savvy for them to seek you out." Another respondent said that they "sees the intent as positive, but prefer to keep the boundaries and not accept the request."

College Recruiter Use of Student/Candidate Profiles

More and more, anecdotal stories tell us that recruiters, particularly those who are seeking to fill positions with college students or graduates are utilizing social media to conduct an unofficial background check on their candidates. Is this the norm? What exactly are they looking for? How do college recruiters utilize such information? Interestingly, in the survey conducted by the authors, 49 percent of respondents stated that their organization reviews and gathers information from candidate social media profiles during the recruiting and hiring process. Further, 46.9 percent of those respondents admitted that their organization had at least once rejected a candidate due to information gathered via his or her social media profile.

When probed deeper, those organizations who had rejected at least one candidate due to their profile findings stated a variety of reasons for the rejection. The top three reasons offered were that 1) the candidate displayed poor communication skills, 2) provocative pictures were found on the candidate's profile, and 3) the candidate conveyed information associated with alcohol or illegal drug use. Additionally, college recruiters listed negative comments about current or past employers and/or colleagues, candidate seemed immature, candidate is a member of questionable groups or organizations, or skills were not highlighted enough as other common reasons for deciding on rejection. One respondent stated that, "one example of a rejection was a candidate who claimed to be a Ruby expert, yet had no endorsements on their LinkedIn profile and worked for no companies that utilize a Ruby platform."

Such rejection and potential for negative response to a candidate's profile may make college students wonder if they should have a social media presence at all. Career center staff members are often asked if it is better to be findable, or to have no online presence in order to protect one's image. When asked if their organization perceives it to be a negative factor if a student or candidate does not have a social media presence, 83.7 percent of college recruiters did not think so.

Because of the recent discussion over recruiters asking candidates for passwords to their social networking sites, the authors surveyed the recruiters on the question of if they thought it was ethical to ask for passwords. 13.5 percent of college recruiters surveyed believe that it is ethical for an organization to request a candidate's social media passwords during the recruiting and hiring processes. Presently, more and more states are putting forth legislation that would prohibit employers from requesting such information. NACE's position on this is that should an employer request this kind of information, the password or username, it would be a violation of NACE principles. "NACE's 'Principles for Professional Practice' provides for a recruitment process that is consistent with EEO and privacy laws and a process in which students are free from undue pressure." (NACE, 2012).

Social Media Use by Site

Social media trends are constantly changing and with that, it can be difficult to keep up with all existing sites. Is Facebook really more for personal use and LinkedIn for business purposes only? Is there a place in the workplace and the recruiting and hiring processes for Instagram, Pinterest, or other online arenas? Where does Twitter, YouTube, or Tumbler lie in the priority list for college recruiters? To start, 79.4 percent of surveyed college recruiters stated that their organizations used both Facebook and LinkedIn within their recruiting and hiring processes, far surpassing reported use of other sites. Specifically, LinkedIn was found by 77.8 percent of the recruiters to be either most effective or effective, and Facebook was rated similarly with 69.2 percent. Not surprising, Twitter followed with 52.6 percent of respondents admitting to tweeting within the scope of their work. Yet, only 41.6 percent of respondents found that Twitter was either most effective or effective in their work. YouTube users were found in 28.9 percent of responses, with a 34.1 percent stating that this medium is either most effective or effective in recruiting and hiring practices. And, while not used by a significant number of college recruiters, Instagram, Pinterest, Tumblr, FourSquare, and Google+ were each listed as additional social media sites sometimes utilized in recruiting and hiring.

Upon additional investigation, it is clear that each social media site serves a different purpose for college recruiters. Facebook for example, was reported to be most commonly used to post job announcements (70.2%). Other popular uses of Facebook included promoting an employment brand and increasing interest in working at the organization (66.7%), posting photos of what it looks like to work at the organization (57.1%), connecting with potential employees (53.6%), and posting video clips that show the work culture (42.9%). Less common, but still viable options for how college recruiters utilize Facebook for recruiting and hiring included mini blogs by staff, searching user profiles for candidate information, or polling or survey fans of the organization. One can see from this data that Facebook's role for college recruiters focuses more on the promotion of the organization and opportunities within it, and less about building relationships with potential candidates.

LinkedIn on the other hand appears to be used more frequently by college recruiters in hopes of making individual connections with potential hires. While the most commonly reported use of LinkedIn was the same as that of Facebook - to post job announcements (78.1%), searching for candidates (72.6%) and establishing relationships with potential candidates (67.1%) served as frequent uses as well. Searching user profiles for candidate information is significantly more popular on LinkedIn (50.7%) than Facebook (20.2%). Just under half of all surveyed recruiters admitted using LinkedIn to send private messages to potential candidates and to solicit introductions through connections for potential candidates. Clearly, LinkedIn's use by college recruiters takes on a heavier relationship focus than Facebook.

While used somewhat less frequently by organizations for recruiting and hiring, Twitter has a place in the social media arena as well. For example, 71.4% of college recruiters surveyed use this venue to post job announcements. Announcements of company news (89.3%) and the sharing of industry information (66.1%) were also high use tasks on Twitter by recruiters.

Not utilized frequently enough by college recruiters to collect reliable data on how they were used were YouTube, Instagram, Pinterest, and Tumblr. Less conventional in the ways of which an organization might choose to use these mediums, the authors believe that growth in the use of such sites will occur in the near future. Work culture or recruitment videos, photos of work events or the organization's headquarters, or blogs by interns or full time employees are examples of ways such social media will be expanded.

STUDENT USE OF SOCIAL MEDIA IN THE JOB SEARCH

Earlier, it was mentioned that overall, approximately 41% of graduating seniors in the NACE Class of 2012 Student Survey Report utilized social media in their job search. This survey included 15, 715 seniors from across the nation. Twenty-six percent of the students used social media to network with employers and 26 percent used it to research employers. Nineteen percent used social media platforms to discuss job openings. Of those students who reported using social media, 90 percent used Facebook, 76 percent used LinkedIn, and 51 percent used Twitter (NACE, 2012). This indicates that students are using social media for professional purposes and interacting with employers. They, however, are not using it at the pace that employers, based upon the authors' survey, are utilizing it to interact with them.

Reasons to Use Social Media in the Job Search

Today's college students were born using technology. According to Hartman and McCambridge (2011), "All their lives millennials have been with cell phones, pagers, computers, personal electronic entertainment, and most recently are constantly connected to social media outlets. They have more technology exposure than any previous generation" (p. 24). Based upon this assumption, because it has been readily available to them, students should use social media in their job search. In the Hanson et al. (2010) study, students spent an average of 5.43 hours per week on social networking sites. Therefore, they are already familiar with the technology it takes to engage in this type of job search strategy. They use social media with various constituents ranging from family members to their academic institutions, so to employ the use of social media in the job search is not a stretch.

The primary reason students should use social media in their job search is because that is where employers are (Recruiting Trends, 2012; Sewell, Martin, Barnett, & Jenter, 2011). Recruiters expect that students are using social media, so increasingly more and more companies are using social networking outlets as a tool for recruitment. Understanding that the original intent of social networking sites was not to search for jobs, times are changing. As Ratliff (2011) stated, social networking originally was created as a way to communicate with others on a personal level and stay connected. However, now that employers are on these sites, students should reframe their thoughts about using them for professional purposes in addition to personal interactions. Just as colleges know they must reach students where they are, employers are thinking in the same manner. Recruiters need potential employees and students are on social networking sites; recruiters need to be on those sites, too. In the survey conducted by the authors, 70.4 percent of the college recruiting respondents said they utilize social media in their recruiting and hiring process. The conclusion drawn here is that college recruiters and students meeting through social media should be mutually beneficial strategy for both parties.

Another reason students should consider using social media in their job search is that it can help to showcase communication skills. The typical process in hiring for positions includes the submission of resumes and cover letters and then interviews – more formal types of communication. If done appropriately, social media platforms allow students to add an additional dimension to their candidacy. A potential employer can see how the student interacts and communicates with others, can see other activities the student is interested in, and can get a sense of fit for the organization in a less traditional manner. Sacks and Graves (2012) believe that students who can exhibit both formal and informal communication skills are highly desirable by companies. Social media enables students to exhibit both sets of communication skills, with an emphasis on the informal.

A fourth reason for using social media in the job search process is the ability to show other soft skills. Along with communication skills, in the NACE Job Outlook 2013 report, it was stated that some of the top soft skills recruiters looked for were obtaining and processing information and computer software programs competency (NACE, 2013). A student's appropriate presence and use of social media outlets can show these skills. Students reported that they used social media to research employers, exhibiting the ability to obtain information. The very presence on a social networking site requires some degree of computer competency as many of the sites necessitate various technical skill levels to navigate them.

Creating a Personal Brand

Although showcasing one's communication and other soft skills through the use of social media can have positive effects in the job search process, caution needs to be taken to ensure that a student's full presence on social media outlets is positive and that it does not detract from the persona the student attempts to portray. Students need to recognize that if they plan to use social networking sites in their job search, whether intentionally or not, whatever is projected on these sites is a reflection of who they are. It is their personal brand and they should create something that they are comfortable having others view. Sewell et al. (2011) stated that creating a personal brand "conveys their professionalism, strengths, and talents and they will attract potential employers" (p. 8). Beal and Strauss as cited in Roberts and Roach (2009) had a four part process of how to create a personal brand for online purposes. Steps one and two are to identify the constituents who will be targeted by the social media outlet and to decide on how the person creating the brand wants to be perceived by those constituents. The third step is to identify career goals and the fourth step is to decide how much information to disclose online (p. 113).

Creating an online personal brand for the job search should be intentional. It should be a well thought out picture of who the student is which includes what the student wants a prospective employer to know. Additionally, this could be an opportunity for the student to show interests and, perhaps, accolades that may not be able to be seen otherwise through traditional job search measures. A student's online brand can include a virtual résumé posted on a social media site, the other social media sites the student can be found on, posts to a group the students is a member of, or a blog the student writes. Something to keep in mind is consistency. If using social media for the job search, students should represent themselves in the same manner throughout all social networking outlets. Also, students should remember that what is on the internet is difficult to erase, so they must be sure that they will be satisfied with what is out there because it will exist indefinitely.

Protecting the Professional Brand

Most students have begun interaction on social networking sites before they start to think about them as potential job search tools. For those students, depending on how active they were and what has been communicated via social media, they may need to make adjustments to their image. While no solution is absolute, there are several ways students can, at least, minimize the likelihood of someone obtaining unwanted information about them.

The first mechanism for protection is to see what is out there and make adjustments. Students should do an internet search on themselves to see what they can find. If they can find something, then employers can, too. Ding and Ding (2013) constructed a rhetorical exercise for students to see what they could find on themselves. "Through Google searches they begin to realize the need to either adjust their privacy and access settings or to change the way they portray themselves in Facebook to avoid jeopardizing their job searches" (Ding & Ding, 2013, p. 244). Students need to ensure that the profiles they do not want employers to have easy access to, are private.

Profiles are not the only sources that can affect one's brand. Words in the blogosphere can have the same effect. Students need to be careful that what they have said on blogs, if they have them, or in online groups they might have joined does not negatively overshadow what they are trying to project for potential employers. What a student has said can deter a prospective employer from pursuing the student's candidacy.

Another consideration about protecting one's personal brand is to think about those people with whom the person is connected. Students should consider their Facebook friends and realize that perhaps their friends do not plan to use Facebook or other social media outlets for their job search. Therefore, they may have unprofessional information about the student within their profile. An example of this would be if the student's friend "tagged" him or her in a picture that was inappropriate for a potential employer to see. Students should ensure that they know about all pictures their friends post of them in order to deem them suitable for public viewing.

Appropriately Using Social Media

From the results of the NACE Class of 2012 Survey, students are using social networking sites to network with employers, research employers, and to discuss job opportunities (NACE, 2012). They are using the three main sites that employers use, Facebook, LinkedIn, and Twitter. The good news is that a large number of students who reported using social media are using LinkedIn. Nearly eighty percent of the employers from the authors' survey use LinkedIn and the NACE Survey stated that seventy-six percent of the students who actually use social media in their job hunt use LinkedIn (NACE 2012). This is promising because students are on the social media site that was created as professional network to connect people with common professional interests.

How should students, who use social media in the job search, use it appropriately and most effectively? Students should be aware that each of the three main social networking sites can have a very different function in their job search. Therefore, it is beneficial to participate, in some way, in all three as well as to use other appropriate social media platforms.

For Facebook, the site that is typically most associated with being more for personal use, students must decide first, if Facebook will be used for professional purposes. If so, assuming students have already made any necessary adjustments to their account like cleaning up their profile and changing privacy settings, they can connect to an organization's Facebook page by "liking" it. Additionally, just as in face-to-face networking, students should let others know they are looking for opportunities and keep those in their networks apprised of their search. Students can do that through their status updates. They should be specific in what they are looking for as someone else they are connected to might be able to assist them. As for connecting with specific recruiters as students do with their friend, there are mixed feelings from recruiters on this subject who responded to the authors' survey, so it would be advised to use caution if a student wants to connect directly to the recruiter. Not knowing how a recruiter feels about the subject could be risky, so the safest route to take would be to connect to the organization's Facebook page.

LinkedIn is typically the site most people think of when asked what professional networking site should one use when they are in the midst of a job search. Here, students can connect with individuals who are in their industry interest, look for positions using the feature that allows a search for entry level jobs, and because employers are on the site looking as well, perhaps be contacted for opportunities. Although connecting with like-minded professionals is a goal of this site, connecting with potential recruiters comes, again, with mixed feelings from the respondents to the survey. While students may want to connect in order to obtain additional information on the person who may be their recruiter, there may be other methods to collect this information. They may be able to see parts of the profile without actually connecting to the recruiter or they may be able to find information on other social media sites like Twitter. Finally, utilizing LinkedIn for the search, one thing to keep in mind is that students need to ensure that their profiles are completely filled out as this is the best way to get noticed by a potential employer.

Twitter only allows for 140 characters, so students will have to be brief and explicit when letting their followers know they are looking for a position. They should also follow others, particularly leaders in their industry of interest. Employers often post links to jobs on Twitter, so students should be looking for those opportunities as well. Students can join chats that are related to their industry of interest. In joining these chats, students can use Twitter as their platform to show their expertise on a particular subject, intriguing others about their skills.

Additional social media sites that might be helpful in the job search are blogs, industry specific online groups, and specific social networking sites such as Pinterest and Google+. Other sites that may be helpful in the job search and networking realm are Meetup, which is a social networking site used to bring local people together who share interests and Classmates, where students can find high school classmates with whom to reconnect. For the most part, students can join groups, submitting posts and discussing their expertise on many of the major social networking sites. They can upload information to these sites that will give recruiters a more rounded view of who they are and, perhaps, what they may be able to do for an employer. Ultimately, these social media sites can be internet advertisements for students and their abilities.

SOLUTIONS AND RECOMMENDATIONS

Based upon the survey by the authors, while social media use within the recruiting and hiring processes appears to be significantly higher for recruiters specifically focused on attracting college students compared to recruiters overall, there is still room for growth. Today's college students have iPods, iPads, iPhones, MacBooks and numerous other technologies. Their world is at their fingertips, and they expect their job search to be the same. For those who focus on recruiting entry level employees, social media is a must. Organizations that believe they do not need such tools will soon be outpaced by competitors who appear more high tech and high touch to these young candidates. It is critical not only for organizations to have a social media presence, but organizations must begin to fund positions responsible for the upkeep of accounts and communications on these sites as the information is continually changing. Until social media focused positions can be created, recruiters should look to put responsibility on each individual to manage a specific social media site in order for the organization to have multiple presences. Employers should also, just as colleges are making the adjustment, ensure that the social media platforms they are using to reach these students are mobile friendly.

Furthermore, those employers who do not use social media in the workplace must change their mindset in order to effectively recruit today's generation of college graduates. As discussed above, social media has multiple uses within the recruiting and hiring processes. Hiring organizations need a social media plan. Given the different nature and potential purpose of each site, organizations must first determine which social media sites they will invest in, and what activity will be the focus of each account. Should photos of headquarters or company events go on a Facebook page or should an Instagram account be created? Which site offers the best venue for discussion? Moreover, is discussion desirable or does it make sense to lock accounts so that candidates can view but not interact? Determining the answers to these questions in order to create a social media plan is recommended to all recruiters, especially those focused on recruiting college and university students or recent graduates.

Social media continues to expand and change. While not long ago, MySpace would have dominated this chapter, today it is not mentioned in discussion of current trends for social media and the job search. What will be the next site to explore? College recruiters must stay on top of social media. Willingness to try a new venue and connect with students where they are will increase the candidate pool and enable the recruiter to develop a unique understanding of candidates through such interaction.

The job market is tough these days and students need to take advantage of every strategy they can to secure their post graduation position. Nearly 55 percent of the seniors who responded to the NACE Class of 2012 Student Survey Report did not actively use social media in their job search (NACE, 2012). This is a resource that needs to be added to their job search arsenal if they want to be confident they are utilizing as many avenues as possible for the search.

Students should not just have a presence on social media outlets, they should be active participants. Having a Twitter handle but not using it is does very little in the job search. Creating a LinkedIn profile with very little information on it is not enough and could be detrimental to a student's brand. Employers are searching for candidates on these sites, so students should give them a reason to be interested in them. Students should think of their presence as one big resume. Just as career center staff members tell students they should tailor their résumés to the employer, they should think similarly when presenting themselves online in the job search.

Finally, as integral connectors of students and employers, career center staff members need to embrace social media to be an example for students. Not only is it important for them to tell students about the use of social networking sites in their job search, but they need to be models of utilizing social media themselves. Their offices need to use social media to reach out to students, use it in workshops, and be active users to stay current on the various outlets. They should educate students on the appropriate use of social networking sites for employment purposes, being partners in the process. Career centers can assist students with personal branding (e.g. creating a thorough LinkedIn profile), with discovering sites that would be most beneficial to them, and with helping students protect their online persona.

FUTURE RESEARCH DIRECTIONS

While the limited current literature offers an overview of social media use by employers in the recruiting and hiring process, this chapter serves to fill a gap relating specifically to college student recruitment. Together, the variety of such tools and how they are utilized illustrates today's landscape. Replication of studies is necessary due to the continuous growth and change of all realms of technology and communication. In five years, data captured today will be outdated and social media sites will have expanded in variety and use. New sites will have an active presence and relevance in the recruiting and hiring processes.

Additionally, future research is needed to fully understand the effectiveness of these efforts. As organizations increase use of social media in recruiting and hiring, questions such as how many candidates are communicated with, what questions are asked, are candidates more informed and knowledgeable in their application and interviews, or are the candidate pools more diverse must all be answered. Data must be captured to highlight which sites are best used for which purposes and to determine which social media venues are more effective than others. Added to the effectiveness, specific research should be done to see how many hires actually result directly from the use of social networking sites in general and which sites yield the most hires.

Although college recruiters are becoming more savvy users of social media, college students will always be college students. The ethical debate surrounding recruiters requesting the passwords of candidate accounts must be further investigated. What are the trends surrounding this activity, and is there an increase in related requests or will legislation be enough to quiet those requests? It is important for recruiters to know the laws surrounding privacy and how password requests may or may not violate such law.

For students, future research around their use of social networking sites in the job search should include such questions as how this affects their communication skills, or if they become so adept at using these sites, will their personal online brand be an accurate portrayal of who they are once on the job. Additional consideration for research could center on the amount of social networking activity it might take to land a position and which means is most effective – i.e. is following the Twitter feeds of multiple organizations more beneficial than connections on LinkedIn or being a part of a specific industry group and participating in group conversations through posts? There is much room for research on this relatively new topic of social media and employment.

CONCLUSION

This chapter's intent was to add to the sparse body of scholarly research on college student recruiting and the use of social media. The authors' investigation into the topic proved to substantiate what has been suspected – that social media use should be and is an integral component in the recruiting and hiring process for employers to attract millennial students. From the perspective of the students, they should include social media in their job searches, while being mindful of their personal brand. Social media will continue to increase popularity in all facets of life in the 21st century. Therefore, its inclusion in the job search, recruiting, and hiring process will continue to both amplify and evolve.

REFERENCES

Abdelraheem, A. Y. (2013). University students' use of social networks sites and their relation with some variables. In *Proceedings of the West East Institute International Academic Conference*. Academic Press.

Barton, K. (2007). *Rethinking college recruiting*. Retrieved from http://www.adlerconcepts.com/resources/column/newsletter/rethinking_college_recruiting.php

Brinton, M. (2013, March). *Tech on the go: Meeting the needs of the mobile generation*. Paper presented at the annual meeting of the National Association of Student Personnel Administrators. Orlando, FL.

Brown, V. R., & Vaughn, E. D. (2011). The writing on the (Facebook) wall: The use of social networking sites in hiring decisions. *Journal of Business and Psychology, 26*, 219–225. doi:10.1007/s10869-011-9221-x

Capano, N., Deris, J., & Desjardins, E. (n.d.). *Social networking usage and grades among college students*. Whittemore School of Business & Economics/University of New Hampshire.

Dahlstrom, E. (2012) *ECAR student of undergraduate students and information technology, 2012* (Research Report). Retrieved from http://www.educause.edu/ecar

Davison, K. H., Maraist, C., & Bing, M. N. (2011). Friend or foe? The promise and pitfalls of using social networking sites for HR decisions. *Journal of Business and Psychology, 26*, 153–159. doi:10.1007/s10869-011-9215-8

Ding, H., & Ding, X. (2013). 360-degree rhetorical analysis of job hunting: A four-part, multimodal project. *Business Communication Quarterly, 76*(2), 239–248. doi:10.1177/1080569912475207

Duggan, M., & Brenner, J. (2013). *The demographics of social media users – 2012*. Retrieved from http://pewinternet.org/Reports/2013/Social-media-users/The-State-of-Social-Media-Users.aspx

Grant, A. (2011). How to use Twitter to change careers. *U.S. News Digital Weekly, 3*(26), 15–15.

Hackcollege.com. (2011). *Infographic: Generation mobile*. Retrieved from http://www.hackcollege.com/blog/2011/10/31/generation-mobile.html

Hanson, T. L., Drumheller, K., Mallard, J., McKee, C., & Schlegel, P. (2010). Cell phones, text messages and Facebook: Competing time demands of today's college students. *College Teaching, 59*(1), 23–30. doi:10.1080/87567555.2010.489078

Hartman, J. L., & McCambridge, J. (2011). Optimizing millennials' communication styles. *Business Communication Quarterly, 74*(1), 22–44. doi:10.1177/1080569910395564

Herbold, J., & Douma, B. (2013). Students' use of social media for job searching. *The CPA Journal, 83*(4), 68–71.

Higher Education Research Institute. (2013). *The American freshman: National norms Fall 2012*. Retrieved from http://www.heri.ucla.edu/briefs/TheAmericanFreshman2012-Brief.pdf

Hunt, K. G. (2010, November/December). Finders keepers: Social media strategies help find top talent. *Journal of Property Management,* 36-40.

Kolowich, S. (2011, January 6). *How will students communicate?* Retrieved from http://www.insidehighered.com/news/2011/01/06/college_technology_officers_consider_changing_norms_in_student_communications

Mangan, K. (2012, September 10). *As students scatter online, colleges try to keep up.* Retrieved from http://chronicle.com/article/Digitally-Savvy-Students-Play/134224/

McGrath, L. C. (2012). Social media and employment: Is there a Limit? Interdisciplinary. *Journal of Contemporary Research in Business, 4*(1), 17–24.

National Association of Colleges and Employers. (2012). *Requiring logins/passwords violates NACE principles.* Retrieved from: http://naceweb.org/s04112012/interview-passwords-social-media/

National Association of Colleges and Employers. (2012). *The class of 2012 student survey report (executive summary).* Retrieved from http://www.naceweb.org/Research/Student/Student_Survey.aspx

National Association of Colleges and Employers. (2013). *Job outlook 2013: Spring update.* Retrieved from http://www.naceweb.org/Research/Job_Outlook/Job_Outlook.aspx?referal=research&menuID=69

Pinnington, D. (2011). Essential do's and don'ts for LinkedIn users. *Law Practice: The Business of Practicing Law, 37*(6), 22–24.

Platt, S. K., King, K., & Dommer, M. R. (2010). *Communication effectiveness in higher education.* Retrieved from http://go.blackbox.com/forms/EduComm-Study

Ratliff, A. F. (2011). Are they listening? Social media on campuses of higher education. *Journal of Australia and New Zealand Student Services Association, 38,* 65–69.

Recruiting Trends 2012-2013. (2012). Retrieved from http://www.ceri.msu.edu/recruiting-trends/recruiting-trends-2012-2013/

Roberts, S. J., & Roach, T. (2009). Social networking websites and human resource personnel: Suggestions for job searches. *Business Communication Quarterly, 72*(1), 110–114. doi:10.1177/1080569908330380

Robinson, S., & Stubberud, H. A. (2012). Communication preferences among university students. *Academy of Leadership Journal, 16*(2), 105–113.

Russo, F. (2011). The new online job hunt. *Time, 178*(13), B14–B16.

Sacks, M. A., & Graves, N. (2012). How many friends do you need? Teaching students how to network using social media. *Business Communication Quarterly, 75*(1), 80–88. doi:10.1177/1080569911433326

Sewell, R. C., Martin, M., Barnett, S., & Jenter, C. (2011). *Graduating to success in employment: How social media can aid college students in the job search.* Retrieved from http://www.heldrich.rutgers.edu/sites/default/files/content/Graduating_to_Success_Brief.pdf

Weigley, S. (2011, August 4). *Employers recruiting off campus.* Retrieved from http://online.wsj.com/article/SB10001424053111904800304576476552817595120.html

Wheeler, K. (2004, June 9). *8 essentials for effective college recruiting.* Retrieved from http://www.ere.net/2004/06/09/8-essentials-for-effective-college-recruiting/

ADDITIONAL READING

Benson, V., Filippaios, F., & Morgan, S. (2010). Applications of social networking in students' life cycle. In C. Wankel (Ed.), *Social media approaches to business education: teaching with Linkedin, Facebook, Twitter, Second Life, and Blogs (PB)* (pp. 73–93). Greenwich, U.K.: Information Age Publishing.

Benson, V., Morgan, S., & Tennakoon, H. (2012). A framework for knowledge management in higher education using social networking. *International Journal of Knowledge Society Research, 3*(2), 44-54. ISSN (print) 1947-8429

Benson, V., Morgan, S., & Tennakoon, H. (2012). Social networking in higher education: a knowledge convergence platform. *World Summit on the Knowledge Society (WSKS) 2011* [CCIS]. *Communications in Computer and Information Science, 278,* 416–425. doi:10.1007/978-3-642-35879-1_50

Cain, J., Scott, D. R., & Smith, K. (2010). Use of social media by residency program directors for resident selection. *American Journal of Health-System Pharmacy, 67,* 1635–1639. doi:10.2146/ajhp090658 PMID:20852165

Chen, C. C., Jones, K. T., & Xu, S. (2012). The communication methods of today's students. *The CPA Journal, 82*(11), 66–71.

Clark, A. S. (2006). *Employers look at Facebook, too: Companies turn to online profiles to see what applicants are really like.* CBS Evening News, Retrieved from http://www.cbsnews.com/stories/2006/06/20/eveningnews/main1734920.shtml

Decarie, C. (2010). Facebook: Challenges and opportunities for business communication students. *Business Communication Quarterly, 73*(4), 449–454. doi:10.1177/1080569910385383

Dutta, S. (2010). Managing yourself: what's your personal social media strategy? *Harvard Business Review.* Retrieved from http://hbr.org/2010/11/managing-yourself-whats-your-personal-social-media-strategy

Gourniak, A. L. (2010). Navigating the 21st century job search. *Strategic Finance, 91*(7), 49–53.

Luse, D. W. (2009). An examination of college students' awareness of social web site usage and employability. *The Journal of Academic Administration in Higher Education, 5*(1), 21–26.

Miller, R., Parsons, K., & Lifer, D. (2010). Students and social networking sites: the posting paradox. *Behaviour & Information Technology, 29*(4), 377–382. doi:10.1080/01449290903042491

Peluchette, J., & Karl, K. (2010). Examining students' intended image on Facebook: 'What were they thinking?!'. *Journal of Education for Business, 85,* 30–37. doi:10.1080/08832320903217606

Rishi, R. (2007). Always connected, but hard to reach. *EDUCAUSE Quarterly, 20*(2), 7–9.

Smith, A. (2012). The best (and worst) of mobile connectivity. Retrieved from Pew Research Center website: http://pewinternet.org/Press-Releases/2012/The-Best-%28and-Worst%29-of-Mobile-Connectivity.aspx

Van Rooy, D. L., Alonso, A., & Fairchild, Z. (2003). In with the new, out with the old: Has the technology revolution eliminated the traditional job search process? *International Journal of Selection and Assessment, 11*(2/3), 170–174. doi:10.1111/1468-2389.00240

KEY TERMS AND DEFINITIONS

College Recruiting: Activities that organizations employ to interact with college students in order to develop a relationship with potential employees.

Entry Level: A lower, but professional level classification for positions, typically obtained by recent college graduates.

Hiring: The process of engaging someone for employment.

Millennial Generation: Individuals born between 1982 and the early 2000's – the generation following "X".

On-Campus Recruiting: Similar to college recruiting, refers to activities that organizations employ to interact with students on the college campus such as career fairs, information sessions, and resume reviews.

Social Media: Online sites through which users create online profiles and develop communities in order to share information, ideas, personal messages, or photos.

Social Networking: Through the use of social media, the act of interacting with others online through such sites.

This research was previously published in Cutting-Edge Technologies and Social Media Use in Higher Education edited by Vladlena Benson and Stephanie Morgan, pages 274-293, copyright year 2014 by Information Science Reference (an imprint of IGI Global).

Chapter 54

The Role of Social Media in Creating and Maintaining Social Networks Including Its Impact on Enhancing Competitive Positioning Within the Education Sector

Adam Raman
Kingston University, UK

ABSTRACT

Social media is being increasingly utilised within society as an interactive communication platform. It has revolutionised the manner in which organisations communicate with their stakeholders, from the old way of simply designing messages and transmitting them across a desired medium, described as a static, one-way communication channel. Communications are the means by which organisations achieve their strategic goals through influencing their stakeholders. Social media allows stakeholders to connect to one another in relational, interactional networks. This means that stakeholders can now interact with organisations and each other and have a greater influence on the outcomes of communication strategies, which was impossible with traditional media. Organisations have less power dictating communications to stakeholders who in turn have more power in co-creating communication with each other. Social media is likely to have a major competitive impact on higher education institutions and these institutions should be accounting for these changes in their future strategy development. This chapter explores how social media is being utilized in organisations.

DOI: 10.4018/978-1-5225-5637-4.ch054

INTRODUCTION

Social media is being extensively utilised by organisations including those in higher education to raise awareness, build and maintain their reputation, as well as create demand for their courses. It is also being used to effectively communicate and engage with other stakeholders such as motivating and retaining current as well as attracting prospective students and employees. It can also be used to raise the profile of a university amongst its board of governors, research & funding bodies and local community. Social Media can be seen as a communication and promotional platform but a major question arises as to the extent to which this new platform is similar or different to previous platforms utilised in the past. For example is it the same as advertising or public relations (PR) or is it significantly different? This question is pertinent in the sense that the traditional methods utilised in strategic communications planning (developing and transmitting messages) tend to rely on single transactional communications between a supplier (education provider) and a consumer (student) where interaction between the two is not seen as being important. Therefore, students are subject to static on-line and off-line brochures including advertorials and third party publications endorsing the institutions or the academic staff working for them. The only interactions that any potential new student may have with an academic institution are dyadic communications between themselves and course directors, administrators, recruitment staff and current students when they either phone, email or visit the institution. Social media on the other hand is different as it allows interactions between multiple stakeholders who are embedded in social network communities. This calls for a different sort of strategic communication planning and Higher Education establishments who are not considering this factor could be inappropriately developing their social media strategies, leading to a detrimental situation of being ineffective and possibly losing their competitive position to other establishments who are planning more appropriately and effectively.

ISSUES RELATING TO THE STRATEGIC PLANNING OF SOCIAL MEDIA WITH HIGHER EDUCATION INSTITUTIONS

Parallel to the changes occurring in the fields of strategic management and marketing strategy, there has been a shift from a reliance on traditional media (print and television for example) to the widespread inclusion of social media (Hanna, Rohm, and Crittenden, 2011; Andrew and Galak, 2012) within integrated marketing communication strategies. Classical approaches to strategy are believed to be driving the planning of newer digital and social media strategies within organisations. Executives are believed to be explicitly or subconsciously using older, outmoded strategy frameworks for planning their social media or worse still, they are not using any strategy techniques at all and are simply being tactical. Several executives are also likely to be outsourcing their strategy development to external communication agencies who themselves are likely to be implementing outmoded approaches.

Although there are some theoretical suggestions regarding social media strategy (Kaplan and Haenlein, 2010; Weinberg and Pehlivan, 2011; Hanna, Rohm, Crittenden, 2011; Kietzmann et al., 2011), at present there appears to be no research into the appropriateness of the social media strategies that firms are actually creating and implementing.

This chapter will evaluate the applicability of newer emergent strategy perspectives to social media strategy development with theories being linked from the relational and interactional network theoretical marketing literature (Håkansson, 1982; Håkansson & Johanson, 1992; Håkansson & Snehota, 1995) as well as the customer – supplier value co-creation literature (Vargo & Lusch, 2004; 2008). These perspectives will then be used to explore how some firms operating within the Pet Industry in the United States are planning and implementing their social media strategies. In particular we will explore whether firms are incorporating social media as simply one element of a traditional Integrated Marketing Communications (IMC) promotional mix, therefore employing social media as a tactic aimed at increasing purchase behavior (Weinberg and Pehlivan, 2011; Mintzberg and Waters, 1985; Kumar and Mirchandani, 2012), or conversely whether firms are creating more appropriate strategies, based on the principles of marketing's interactional, relational and co-creation of value (Håkansson, 1982; Håkansson & Johanson, 1992; Håkansson & Snehota, 1995; Vargo and Lusch, 2004).

THE IMPORTANCE AND RELEVANCE OF SOCIAL MEDIA IN HIGHER EDUCATION

Social media can no longer be ignored and not using it will deny an institution access to its potential source of students and employees as well as adversely affect its corporate reputation and future performance. Students and other stakeholders should no longer be viewed as single unconnected individuals not influencing each other who can be influenced using mass communications. Historically when this was the case the source of competitive advantage of a university would be its historic reputation, the current reputation of its academics achieved through publication, the perceived relevance of its courses and the resources that it deployed to its media budget communicating its reputation. Today the first three are still relevant but a university will need to build their competitive advantage by building social capital, which is defined as the relational links between communities (networks) of students and stakeholders interacting with each other. Social media is a highly effective tool in developing social capital. Higher Education institutions should think of social media in two ways, the first being that using social media is only the entry ticket for institutions to access the new competitive game and the second is working more appropriately and effectively with the new media. It is not simply the technology but the application of the technology with the appropriate resources, mind set and processes.

The purpose of this chapter will be the conceptual evaluation of reviewing and applying established network theories to developing and implementing more appropriate and effective social media strategies within the context of Higher Education, in order to improve the longer competitive positioning of the institutions embedded within this sector.

DEFINING COMPETITIVE ADVANTAGE WITHIN THE CONTEXT OF HIGHER EDUCATION

The competitive advantage of a higher education academic institution can be described using theories from the strategic management literature. Several theories exist from the classical to the contemporary perspectives of business strategy. These theories were originally developed within the context of profit making organisations but it is important to note that they are adaptable and applicable to non for profit organisations such as universities. There exists a tendency to reject theory developed in the profit making sector that could potentially be applied in the non for profit sector with the result of reinventing theory and frameworks that already exist. However, it is important that one considers the specific context in which the theory was originally developed including the new context in which it is being applied. Extending theoretical applications without extending the theory so that it is appropriate and applicable can be fraught with errors which can increase risk and uncertainty, severely impacting strategic decision making. Appropriate measures will be taken to ensure that any theory that is extended from a different context is modified to match its new environment.

The fact that strategic business concepts such as competitive advantage are only applicable to profit making organisations is a misnomer, as non for profit organisations still need to generate an incremental economic value or deliver their products or services within an agreed externally funded budget. The only major difference between the different types of organisations is that the ultimate existence and strategic goal for a non for profit organisation is not simply to make a profit for profit's sake, which is the case for profit making organisations. Non for profits make a profit in order to be used to achieve other non–financial goals. Therefore non for profit organisations still need to have very efficient business operational processes to raise money, as inefficient processes will tend to consume cash in order to run the operations required to raise funds and leave very little funding to achieve the non-financial aims of the organisation.

One perspective of competitive advantage is that it can be thought of as consisting of the primary and secondary operational activities supporting the primary activities that a higher education institution must undertake, in order to deliver value to its students and other stakeholders (Porter, 1985). If a university can deliver the same offering, as perceived by the students and other stakeholders, as competing institutions using fewer activities, it will incur less cost generating greater profits and therefore have a greater source of competitive advantage relative to the competition. Therefore competitive advantage can be thought of as achieving an efficient, optimal operational configuration, described as its value chain, that matches its value proposition (Porter, 1980) offered to students and funding institutions. This is the reason why some institutions can still make a profit by charging less for their courses, but their value chain processes will be designed to incur less costs. Other institutions charging higher fees will need to justify to potential students why this is the case and usually this will be justified by a strong reputation. Stronger reputed institutions can have fewer students and more inefficient value chains as their excessive costs are likely to be covered by the higher fees.

In addition to operational processes (the value chain – Porter, 1985) universities can develop their sources of competitive advantage by being distinctive. By developing distinctive capabilities (Kay, 1993) for an institution that are considered valuable, rare, non-substitutable and inimitable relative to competing institutions (Barney 1991), these institutions can therefore be described as possessing a greater source of competitive advantage relative to the competition. Specifically distinctiveness can be achieved through having developed a better reputation, a unique regulatory or legal position, being continuously innovative and regularly reinventing oneself and finally through developing unique relationships between yourself and your suppliers. Institutions can be thought of as competing on distinctiveness through either one or more of the attributes described.

Strategic activities occur within institutions to build or exploit distinctive competitive positioning. To understand how social media can enhance the competitive positioning of higher education institutions one needs to consider the likely different models of strategic decision making within universities.

DELIBERATE AND EMERGENT STRATEGY FORMULATION WITHIN HIGHER EDUCATION INSTITUTIONS

Strategic decision making within organisations tends to occur as a deliberate planning process (Mintzberg, 1985) where higher education institutions will plan their strategic objectives and identify the initiatives required to achieve their goals. The initiatives will be carried out as planned and the results obtained will also occur as expected. This model follows a hierarchical chain of command approach, where senior managers plan the strategies and middle to lower managers implement them without question. Senior management will identify whether strategies have been through implementing financial and operational control measures. There is no opportunity for lower management to adapt the strategy through a learning process. Alternatively management can follow an emergent strategy process (Mintzberg, 1985), where plans are initially developed but are continuously adapted during the implementation process as management learn from changes occurring within the environment. Strategic decision making is therefore an emergent process requiring flexible resources to continuously adapt to the environment.

Deliberate strategic planning processes tend to occur in organisations operating in stable environments whereas emergent strategies are more suitable for organisations operating in turbulent and changeable environments. Conventionally, communication strategies within organisations including higher education institutions have tended to be planned using traditional, deliberate approaches of strategy.

TRADITIONAL MODELS OF COMMUNICATION PLANNING

Integrated communication strategies involve the complete development and implementation of an organisation's communication strategies across a number of media platforms designed to meet the needs of different stakeholders being targeted (Fill, 2002). Strategic communication goals are developed in line with the overall corporate goals of the institution and aligned to the goals of different units or faculties within the HE institution such as Medicine, Business, Science and Law. These goals are also aligned to the overall goals of the individual courses being run within each faculty. Overall strategic goals can be considered as either financial, environmental, or social as well as goals relating to increasing awareness, interest, desire or call for action, including handling post adoption stress caused through post cognitive dissonance surrounding whether the right course or the right institution has been selected by the student.

Having identified the overall corporate, faculty and individual course objectives specific communication goals are identified relating to the desired change required of the stakeholders. It could be that stakeholders simply need to be informed, or be made aware of the differentiated offerings, or remind stakeholders of attributes and offerings or finally to persuade them to take action. Different communication tools such as advertising, sales promotion, personal selling and public relations are then utilised to achieve desired objectives with market research being used to assess strategic goals and verify whether communication goals have been achieved.

Traditional communication strategic frameworks are linear and static frameworks with the exception of personal selling which is dyadic and interactional. All other communication tools tend to be one-sided transactional communications which involve identifying the message required to achieve specific communication goals with the specific stakeholders. This is followed with transmitting the message using a specific communication medium which is finally received by the stakeholder along with numerous other messages from competing sources. The institution needs to ensure that it achieves "the greatest share of the voice" to beat the competition. The traditional communication strategies have been the mainstay of communication within HE and the most appropriate way of deploying communications was to out-promote the competition by having a bigger promotional budget. Traditional communications linked with word of mouth and attracting good academics were sufficient to attract funds and build an effective competitive positioning.

THE CURRENT WEAKNESSES OF TRADITIONAL COMMUNICATION MEDIA IN HIGHER EDUCATION

Traditional models of strategic planning tend to be used in traditional communication planning. Traditional communication media rely on strategy processes which are considered transactional and developed and implemented according to the traditional classical methods of strategic planning. Current communication strategies are developed using what Mintzberg (1994, 1998) describes as the planning school frameworks of strategy. Mintzberg (1994, 1998) describes the development and evolution of strategy within the literature as composing of ten different schools consisting of the design, planning, positioning, entrepreneurial, cognitive, learning, and power, cultural, environmental and the configuration schools representing the different ways that strategies are believed to be being developed within organisations. These frameworks can be described as one-sided transactional strategy, "closed system" frameworks where organisations develop strategy based on scanning the needs of their external and internal environments followed by developing and implementing strategies at a distance of their customers. The strategies that are developed are based on what senior academics feel are appropriate and important to their stakeholders and not what the stakeholders themselves feel are important. Limited opportunities exist for students and organisations to interact with HE institutions in order to co-develop value offerings and communications. Organisations using these rational classical frameworks tend not to wish to develop direct relationships with their customers and stakeholders. Organisations prefer for their stakeholders to develop relationships with the reputation of their brand rather than establishing long term relationships with the organisations themselves. Finally, performance measurements as to whether strategies have been successful or not are once again measured at a distance where organisations will monitor sales from customers through internal records or through market research using outsourced external agencies. Strategy is therefore a one way directional process from the corporate centre directed throughout the organisation with limited interaction between external and internal stakeholders. Communication strategies within marketing departments of organisations including communication agencies have adopted these strategic planning approaches.

The process is circular with thinking, learning and adapting strategy being the privilege of only the senior management team with them being the only ones allowed to make strategic decisions regarding positioning and promotional initiatives. Strategy in this type of organisation is described as a "top down" (Earl, 1989) or "outside in" (Dewit & Meyer, 1994) process where senior management think and decide whilst junior staff simply do as they are told. Alternative strategies include what the same author describes as "bottom up" (Earl, 1989) approaches where strategy is developed at the "coal face" by the staff and the role of senior management is ensuring that their staff are appropriately resourced to carry out their duties. Finally "inside out" (Earl, 1989) approaches involve the strategizing process resulting in a complete transformation of the existing organisation. It should be noted that Dewit & Meyer (1994) also refer to "inside out" strategy development but they use it to describe the "bottom up" strategic approach instead whereas Earl (1989) uses the term to describe transformational strategy development. It is very common in the strategy literature for similar terms to have different meanings, hence the importance to define or explain all the terms being used. Although Fill (1995) states that his Integrated Communications framework is supposed to be used in an "open systems" interactive approach, considered as a more contemporary perspective of strategy development, its actual usage, in terms of practice as well as how the framework has been taught in numerous communication courses, has been more of a stepwise classical planning approach. Classical strategy perspectives are believed to be redundant with newer more modern theoretical processes involving experiential, learning, flexibility and adaptability emergent rather than command and control (Mintzberg, 1985).

LIMITATION OF CLASSICAL STRATEGY AND COMMUNICATIONS FRAMEWORKS

The traditional models of strategy and communications development rely on the assumptions originally developed in classical economics. Under these assumptions purchasers and suppliers were seen as independent entities where no relational or cooperation was thought to exist between different customers and competing suppliers as well as between customers and suppliers. Customers were thought to act independently from each other and competed against each other by wanting the best (cheapest) prices. Suppliers on the other hand wanted to gain the highest possible price and assumed limited communications with customers amongst themselves comparing prices. Transactions between suppliers and customers were deemed to be the most useful unit of analysis in strategic purchasing behaviour research and all activities during transactions were evaluated and any activities occurring prior and after the transactions were considered irrelevant. These frameworks were not seen as appropriate for businesses doing business with each other as it failed to provide an appropriate explanation of actual business behaviour which relied on interactions and relationships between suppliers and customers. These Business to Business (B2B) transactions were seen as being different to Business to end consumer transactions (B2C) because B2B transactions were affected by historical relationships between supplier and customer and future transactions were also likely to be affected by historic and current interactions during the transactions. Relationships were seen as the most appropriate unit of analysis in business research and transaction approaches were confined to B2C environments. It is important to note that service businesses also showed a lack of conformity to transactional frameworks with relationships being seen as more important than the transactions. Additionally, relationship approaches were initially developed and adopted by the Europeans, particularly the Nordic countries. The North Americans initially resisted relational aspects of strategy development as being the predominant strategy perspective a number of times, but are now appreciating its value. Within B2B and Service industries, purchasing is influenced by interactions between parties who have previous experience through historic relationships between the relevant parties as well as being influenced by third parties embedded in an interactional relational network. In recent times with the increasing use of social media where stakeholders are forming relational ties in large networks over the internet, the differential gap between B2C and B2B is narrowing with both fields being described as converging (Vargo & Lusch, 2011; Ellis, 2010). Higher Education involves end consumers - students as well as a number of business customers; public funding bodies as well as other stakeholders. These classical approaches to strategy are believed to be a major driver for planning the newer digital and social media strategies. Executives within organisations are either explicitly using these frameworks or are subconsciously driven towards these approaches in their social media strategy planning. These planning frameworks are suitable for use in stable and predictable business environments but are poor at predicting outcomes in complex, turbulent and unpredictable environments where newer strategy perspectives are recommended. The weakness of classical promotional strategies in social media strategizing is emphasised by Kaplan & Haenlein (2010:P60) who state that "historically, companies were able to control the information available about them through strategically placed press announcements and good public relations managers. Today, however, firms have been increasingly relegated to the sidelines as mere observers, having neither the knowledge nor the chance - or, sometimes, even the right - to alter publicly posted comments provided by their customers." Social media is believed to be disruptive to existing business environments therefore creating increased complexity therefore rendering traditional frameworks useless. Therefore executives are believed to be either adopting outdated modes of strategizing their social media, or worse that they are not using any strategy techniques and simply being tactical. Finally some executives are likely to be outsourcing their strategizing to external agencies who are themselves implementing outmoded approaches.

The HE institutions are also service based, therefore considering the B2B and service elements traditional communications which have been used extensively historically are not appropriate. With the introduction and increased usage of social media, students are creating social networks meaning that newer interactional/relational network perspectives of strategy behaviour are required to model influencers and adoption behaviour within HE.

SOCIAL MEDIA AND SOCIAL CAPITAL IN HIGHER EDUCATION

Social media can be considered as all the current web technologies which allow end stakeholders to interact with organisations and institutions by adding content. Social media allows different stakeholders (actors), including other customers and third parties, as well as staff from an organisation, to interact with one another and form interactional social networks. Social media can be thought of as consisting of bespoke organisational sites which consist of stakeholders being recruited and exposed to content, for which said stakeholders are invited to comment as well as add their own content. Specific social media sites such as Facebook and LinkedIn differ from bespoke sites as they allow different organisations and individuals to connect. Content sites such as Youtube allow students and academics to create and upload content relating to academia as well as share content uploaded from other academics and students relating to academic topics and events. To date social media has been used in HE as a platform to enhance the teaching experience in lectures as well as allowing students access to material outside of lectures. Until recently HE institutions had considerable power over their students, who were attracted to the reputation of a university made known to them through advertising or word of mouth through friends, family and links with former students. Social media over the internet has provided students and other stakeholders with considerable power to interact with a large number of other students and stakeholders in a relational network, providing them with the power of co-creating reputational value of the HE in a short space of time.

THE UTILISATION OF SOCIAL CAPITAL IN HIGHER EDUCATION

Capital can be defined as the investment of resources with the expected return of an economic profit (Lin, 2002). With regards to HE capital can be seen as producing resources such as knowledge, materials and reputation followed by utilising that knowledge, material and reputation to secure grants and generate profits from selling courses. HE institutions had used social capital historically; capital derived from the unique relational ties with their academics and students through ties with schools and other organisations. Nowadays social media offers the opportunity to create unique relational network ties globally at great speeds and can enhance or damage the reputation of HE institutions in a matter of hours. Social media through social capital through accessing networks can affect long term competitive advantage. Historically theories of competitive advantage focussing on B2C marketing did not recognise the importance of networks which are now being recognised as being vital, through the rise of social media which involves the creation of networks.

DEVELOPING A NETWORK THEORY OF THE FIRM

Network approaches are increasingly being used to gain a better understanding of business behaviour (Johanisson, 1995). They have been described as being the fabric of human interactions (Jackson, 2006). They are relationally based affecting the way people regularly relate to one another through sharing information and favours in varied settings, including influencing decisions taken inside organisations across the world. Networks affect how and with whom organisations conduct business (Jackson, 2006). The regularities regarding network structures across many disciplines make the "scientific study" of networks a possibility (Jackson, 2006: P1) and the depth and impact that networks have on human behaviour make such studies "a necessity" (Jackson, 2006: P1). Network analysis has been described as a "fundamental intellectual tool for the study of social structures (as) social structures can be represented as networks" (Wellman and Berkowitz 1988: 4). Within the social sciences network theory has been a goldmine and has provided explanations for social phenomena in a wide variety of disciplines ranging from psychology to economics (Borgatti et al, 2009). Networks have also proved to be useful in exploring complex organizational phenomena such as power and influence, organising efforts, strategic alliances, multinational corporations and inter-firm competition (Borch & Arthur, 1995).

Network theory in the form of Social Network Analysis (SNA) has a long and complex history (Durland & Fredericks, 2005). The origins of Network theory in the social sciences occurred during the 1930s where it stayed as a social science tool until the 1950s when it was linked with graph theory and mathematics by Cartwright and Harary (1956). Networks as a scientific pursuit were originally developed in sociology over a hundred years ago and became established as a central field within the same subject area over the last fifty years (Jackson, 2006). The mathematical research into networks has progressed over the same period with regards to the structure of random graphs with intermittent links to sociology (Jackson, 2006) and resulted in the array of contemporary and conventional network models. Network theory includes "small worlds" models, also known as "six degrees of separation" since, in the social network of the world, any person turns out to be linked to any other person by roughly six connections. Small world networks are founded on fairly complex mathematics even though the principles are straightforward to understand. Despite the complexity of the subject it is very popular, and has established itself in many different fields ranging from computer networks, to biological ecosystems, to business management.

Network theory can be described as still being in a period of rapid development even though a significant literature has accumulated in the field and new articles are appearing on regular basis. Borgatti et al (2009) express the increasing interest in network research as "an explosion of interest" in the subject within the physical and social sciences (P892).

Over the years, networks have been independently researched by a diverse group of scientists, including mathematicians, physicists, computer scientists, sociologists, and biologists who have been building the new field of network theory or the "science of networks" (Barabási 2002; Buchanan 2002; Watts 2004). Economists have shown little interest in the field but over the last decade the amount of research relating to the game theoretic and economic perspectives has mushroomed (Jackson, 2006). The rise of network research in physics and computer science has only occurred recently. They are distinct in their approaches and methods and have a different literature and are beginning to become more aware of each other, including acknowledging and sharing experiences with each other. There has been a significant amount of "reinventing the wheel" between network theory developed in the physical and social sciences, with the physical sciences not acknowledging or taking into account the original findings from social sciences.

Network theory originated in mathematics and was adopted in sociology. Graph theory over the decades has spread beyond the domain of pure mathematics to applications in engineering (Ahuja et al. 2014), operations research (Nagurney 1993), and computer science (Lynch 1996). However it has found a welcome home in sociology, where it has been extensively present for a number of years, with sociology also being the first of the social sciences to adopt it.

Network analyses have been used in management to develop understandings of job performance, innovation, promotion, creativity and unethical behaviour and are also ever increasingly being utilised in management consultancy as diagnostics and prescriptive tools (Borgatti and Halgin, 2011). In the field of marketing, business networks have been used to research internationalisation, technological development, purchasing, services, new product development and marketing strategy (McCloughlin & Horan, 2000; Welch, 2000).

Networks involve the interaction of actors. Actors can be people but can also consist of groups, organisations and societies with links occurring at the macro social-structural level as well as the micro level (Ritzer, 2011).

Network approaches, according to Burt (1982) and Granovetter (1985), are different to "atomistic" and "normative" approaches to sociology. Modern day organisations should no longer be viewed by a firm existing within a distinctive boundary enclosing its internal environment and separating it from the external environment. Instead organisations should be viewed as a collection of intra-organisational and inter-organisational relational networks all interacting with one another (Achrol, 1997). These intra and inter organisational networks can also be linked to additional network structures to form nets (Mintzberg & Van Der Heyden, 1999), or if these networks link different levels of analysis across society, organisations, groups and individuals, as they are most likely to do, these will result in "nested networks" (Moliterno & Mahony, 2011:P444).

Networks of organisations by themselves do not create superior competitive advantages for focal firms located within them, but it is the manners in which they are developed and effectively managed as well as utilised that potentially yield competitive benefits and value (Huston & Sakkab, 2006)

Networks are the means by which new ventures are mainly created in so-called "voluntaristic settings" (Johannison, 1995:P215). Networks have the potential of being both restrictive, potentially hampering innovative ideas on the one hand, as an enabler for creating new ventures depending on whether they are being used in deterministic paradigmatic context or in "voluntaristic settings" (Johannisson, 1995).

DEFINING NETWORK CONCEPTS AND NETWORK THEORY IN MARKETING

Strategic networks are defined as firms investing in co-operative relationships between themselves in order to exchange or share information and/or resources (Borch & Arthur, 1995). Economic exchanges between firms are seen by the authors Borch & Arthur (1995) as a central part of network research where social bonds are believed to create a basis for trust, reciprocity and commitment among network firms.

Although social network analysis is not a new area, its application to marketing particularly the practitioner applications can be regarded as novel (Doyle, 2007). The introduction of network theory into the understanding of markets and marketing can be said to have occurred in 1982, in Sweden with the publication of two books; Hagg and Johanson, 1982; and Hammarkvist et al., 1982. These publications were perceived as being distinctive as they were a departure from current perspectives as they viewed markets as networks (Mattsson & Johanson, 2004). The first publication; "Firms in Networks: A New View on Competitiveness", contributed to the contemporary discussions regarding what constituted international competitiveness of Sweden's industry. The authors rejected the "micro economic perspective on markets with its focus on relative production costs, the market price as the coordinating mechanism, disregard of marketing and negative attitude to relationships in the market. They argued for a network perspective on industrial markets with focus on relationships between firms in a market as the mechanism for coordination and development and as a valid base for discussions about competitiveness of Swedish industry" (P259). The second publication "Marketing for Competitiveness", contributed to the discussion of the role of marketing and market orientation relating to the success of Swedish industrial firms in international markets. It presented a network perspective on markets and argued against the marketing mix perspective which was seen to have a focus on sellers' "means of competition" and had a disregard for interactions between sellers and buyers and its role in inter-firm cooperation (Mattsson & Johanson, 2004: P260). These publications according to the authors were simply "a small step" in the development of network theory in marketing, but they have great significance in the fact that they were first publications that "explicitly argued for a network view" (P260).

NETWORKS AS AN ADDITIONAL CONTRIBUTION TO THE MACRO/MICRO PERSPECTIVES IN SOCIAL SCIENCES

Research within social sciences have traditionally tended to focus either on studying individuals at the micro level being affected by attributes, or at the macro level where all individual behaviours are combined and measured as a single aggregate where the impacts of attributes on aggregate behaviour is studied. Whether research is focussing on the attribute effects on aggregate or individual behaviour, there exists an underlying assumption that all individuals are acting independently of each other and there are no relational interactions linking them. Networks provide a suitable alternative to view and study social science settings as they allow the study of combined relational units interacting with each other and embedded within a relational network structure. The network environment is different to the macro and micro environments usually used to describe social science setting, as it describes a new environment perspective that consists of relational links between specific actors in networks that cuts across both the macro and micro settings.

RELEVANT NETWORK THEORIES

There are several articles relating to social and business networks available across a wide spectrum of different disciplines. Two network theoretical approaches in particular, the Industrial Marketing (IMP) Group (http://www.impgroup.org/about.php - accessed April 2013) approach developed within the B2B marketing arena and the Service Dominant Logic approach (Vargo & Lusch, 2004; 2008) could provide insights as to how competitive advantages of HE institutions can be achieved using social media. The IMP approach identified that most business transactions were affected by interactions (Håkansson, 1982; Turnbull & Valla, 1986) between suppliers and customers, where customers were co-creators of value in the interaction. Transactions only tended to occur if there were pre-existing relationships between customer and supplier groups. Interactions involved the formation of actor bonds between different parties within the different organisations as well as the sharing of activity links and resource ties. This is called the Actor, Resources and Activity (ARA) IMP model. In later IMP studies (Håkansson & Johanson, 1992; Håkansson & Snehota, 1995) it was shown that the specific dyadic interactions were also affected by further dyads interactions within a wider network.

Individuals within HE organisations consisting of existing and historic students can form relationships and share informational resources and activities over social media sites, with the specific interactions contributing to specific relational ties which can therefore create distinctive capabilities which lead to a sustainable competitive advantages.

SERVICE DOMINANT LOGIC: STRATEGY AS "OPERANT AND OPERAND" RESOURCES AND CUSTOMERS AND SUPPLIERS BEING CONSIDERED AS EQUAL PARTNERS IN CO-CREATING VALUE

Although developed within marketing, a newer controversial strategy perspective can be considered as being introduced in 2004 focussing on the area of service rather than services marketing. This new theoretical perspective called Service Dominant Logic - SDL (Vargo & Lusch, 2004; 2008) has contributed to the marketing and strategic management debate by linking the ideas of services marketing, relationship marketing, market orientation, network perspectives, integrated marketing communications (IMC) and the resource based view of the firm (Lusch & Vargo, 2006) in a novel approach that has created a holistic "service logic" for marketing practice. Vargo & Lusch (2004 & 2008) claim that SDL represents a paradigm shift in the way that we should think about marketing. According to the authors we should move away from a paradigm that emphasises goods (Goods Dominant Logic - GDL) to one that considers service (Service Dominant Logic - SDL) as all goods are bought for their service application. Value in the SDL paradigm is co-created through using the product or service (value in use) rather than value in exchange and embedded value through manufacturing which are concepts from GDL (sdlogic.net homepage - http://www.sdlogic.net/ - accessed April 2013).

SDL is based on ten foundational premises (FPs), 8 of which were proposed in the 2004 Vargo & Lusch Journal of Marketing article and an additional two which were introduced in their 2008 article in the Academy of Marketing Science. The FPs consists of:

1. Service is the fundamental basis of exchange;
2. Indirect exchange masks the fundamental basis of exchange;
3. Goods are a distribution mechanism for service provision;
4. Operant resources are the fundamental source of competitive advantage;
5. All economies are service economies;
6. The customer is always a co-creator of value;
7. The enterprise cannot deliver value, but only offer value propositions;
8. A service-centred view is inherently customer oriented and relational;
9. All social and economic actors are resource integrators; and
10. Value is always uniquely and phenomenologically determined by the beneficiary.

SDL's major contribution to strategy involves the conceptualisation and actions of two types of organisational resources that potentially yield competitive advantage. Organisations consist of tangible operand resources which include tangible buildings, people and cash and they are acted upon by intangible operant resources which include skills, competences and capabilities, values, attitudes and beliefs. The manner in which organisations leverage the combined effects of their operand and operant resources often characterises their strategizing approaches. Intangible resources can be considered to add value to achieving a sustainable differential competitive advantage within organisations and often it is the intangible resources that give to the heterogeneity, inimitability, rare and valuable resources (Barney 1991) described in the RBV perspectives of strategy that are difficult to copy and substitute.

SDL and the RBV of strategy can be said to share similar perspectives with SDL providing additional detail of what constitutes valuable, rare, inimitable, non-substitutable (VRIN) resources. The view that intangible assets or resources add value to organisations has been considered a controversial issue, particularly in financial accounting where intangibles such as brands are often not included as a specific asset on the balance sheet and are at best only represented as goodwill. Doyle (2009) suggests that with the exception of patents, developing strong relationships and brand reputations through promotional efforts are the best ways of securing a sustainable differential competitive advantage. Finally Hunt & Madhavaram (2006) discuss that the Resource Advantage (RA) theory would be an ideal integrative theory across the different areas of strategic management and strategic marketing. SDL according to authors (ibid) is perfectly accounted for in RA theory. Therefore SDL can be thought of as an appropriate theory to evaluate issues regarding strategic marketing and management, which includes how social media strategies are developed and implemented within organisations.

An additional important area of contribution of SDL to strategic marketing and management, particularly in relation to social media strategizing, is the fact that "the customer is always a co-creator of value" (FP6 Vargo & Lusch, 2004) and "all social and economic actors are resource integrators" (FP9 Vargo & Lusch, 2008). Value co-creation and all actors being resource integrators in SDL are similar and related concepts to the interaction of actors in the IMP B2B business networks literature. These two foundational premises clearly demonstrate that value co-creation and resource integration leading to a sustainable differential competitive advantage is reliant on the fact that organisations allow customers and other stakeholders to freely interact and build networked relationships. Social media can be considered as an enabler to creating interactional, relational dynamic networks. Therefore classical transactional marketing communication frameworks are unlikely to be appropriate. This sentiment is shared by Kaplan & Haenlein (2010:P65); "Yet, whatever the ultimate decision—to buy, make, or both— it is vital that there is an understanding of the basic idea behind Social Media. It's all about participation, sharing, and collaboration, rather than straightforward advertising and selling."

In relation to HE institutions SDL provides the perfect theoretical platform in explaining how social media can develop competitive advantage. The interaction and co-creation of value using operand and operant resources provides a suitable explanation for B2B interactions (HE institution and funding body), B2C interactions (HE institution and students) and finally C2C (students interacting with other students).

MANAGERIAL IMPLICATIONS FOR SOCIAL MEDIA STRATEGIZING IN HE

The traditional approaches to strategic and promotional planning provided managers with greater control over the strategy process and ultimately the strategic outcome. Managers within HE will often have little or no control over the outcomes with emergent perspectives of strategy, particularly those involving the co-creation of communications with end customers and stakeholders, as it is with using social media. Managers should realise that customers are affected by the quality, credibility and legitimacy of communication messages (Fill, 2002), with promotional messages created by organisations and their agencies being considered the least credible and having the lowest legitimacy. As evidenced through word of mouth research studies, legitimacy and credibility of communications are highest amongst peer group members, therefore allowing these groups to freely communicate on the social media sites is very important. Within social media end customers and stakeholders are unlikely to want organisations to communicate with them using one way communication approaches as they do with traditional advertising. Organisations will need to be excluded or considered as being equal partners (actors) in the dialogue embedded in an interactional, relational network. "Wikipedia, for example, expressly forbids the participation of firms in its online community" (Kaplan & Haenlein, 2010:P60). Howard Schultz, the chairman of Starbuck's who's confidential memo about the current situation of the organisation at the time was leaked and widely discussed on social media sites and rapidly diffused to mainstream news sites, remarked that everyone outside the company had an opinion about the intention of the Starbucks memo as well as Schultz as an effective leader. He also remarked that nothing was confidential relating to the internet and noted that Starbuck's voice was nowhere to be found in these discussions; they had been excluded (Gray & Vander Val, 2012). This has major implications for HE institutions.

Several managers will not be accustomed to democratic styles of management that rely on relinquishing control of communications to their end customers and stakeholders, as described in the following sentence; "Yet, not overly many firms seem to act comfortably in a world where consumers can speak so freely with each other and businesses have increasingly less control over the information available about them in cyberspace" (Kaplan & Haenlein, 2010:P59). Managers should also not be tempted to interfere with negative comments by trying to delete messages on social network sites managed by their organisations as this can have disastrous effects. Actors linked together and interacting within networked systems can amplify effects. Small disturbances such as a decision to delete a dialogue within a site is likely to cause greater disturbances through amplification as it travels through the system using a process of positive feedback. This is commonly known as the "Butterfly effect" (Lorenz, 2000) where a butterfly flapping its wings on one continent can cause tornadoes on another continent due to interconnected weather systems.

This effect in social media is described in the following sentence from an interview with Muhtar Kent, CEO of Coca Cola; "[Question]: That's the challenge: To what extent do you control the message? Coke has had to deal with things like those viral videos that show people putting Mentos in Diet Cokes and creating giant fountains. Do these things cause concern? Or do you try to embrace them? [Answer]: It's not just that you can't control it—when you try, it backfires. You have to understand consumers: They would like to be heard. It's a question of co-creating content. Five years ago social media was 3% of our total media spend. Today it's more than 20% and growing fast" (Ignatius, 2011:P96).

CONCLUSION AND RECOMMENDATIONS

Social media is not like any other media that has previously existed as it allows interactions across B2B, B2C and C2C and networked relationships to be formed across different stakeholders. It is a revolutionary form of communication as it does not use technology simply to improve the efficiency of processes that were previously undertaken, but uses technology to revolutionise how communication takes place between an organisation and its stakeholders. This means that it is a disruptive medium which enhances the power of end customers and stakeholders to enter a dialogue regarding organisations and their offerings. A different emergent strategy approach is required in planning social media strategies and the theoretical foundations from network theory and Service Dominant Logic can offer significant insight and should be adopted by managers to develop and implement their social media strategies. Managers within HE institutions need to think very carefully about how they engage and plan HE's future social media strategies, as these can affect both social capital and competitive advantage.

FUTURE RESEARCH AGENDA

This is a conceptual article and empirical research is required to verify the propositions developed from this critical review of social media strategizing in HE institutions. These propositions include:

- Traditional static models of strategic planning and communications planning are inappropriate for planning an HE's organisation's social media strategies.
- The realised strategies relating to social media planning within HE are likely to be emergent rather than deliberate.
- Dynamic, relational, interactional and networked perspectives are considered more appropriate to evaluating how social media strategies are formulated and implemented within HE.
- Service Dominant Logic and the Resource Based View (RBV) also provide a better perspective on understanding how social media strategies should be planned and implemented within HE.
- Managers within HE are either planning and implementing their social media strategies on inadequate traditional communication planning mind-sets, or outsourcing their SM strategies to communication agencies who are using outdated thinking, or finally they may be simply being tactical in developing their SM initiatives.
- Social media is an environment which primarily allows organisations to build and manage relationships and establish their reputation amongst their customers and other stakeholders.

- Organisations should audit and maximise and align their technological, design & managerial capabilities to enhance their relational, reputational, interactional capabilities with their end customers and stakeholders.
- A different managerial style is required with social media strategizing and managers need to apply a democratic style rather than an autocratic command and control style.
- The impact of social media on selling goods and services is a secondary effect of having established appropriate relationships and reputation.
- End customers and stakeholders do not wish for organisations to communicate with them on social media sites using a traditional one way mechanism as they do with advertising; customers want organisations to participate in a dialogue as an equal actor interacting in a relational social network.
- Due to amplification effects caused in network systems caused by positive feedback mechanisms, organisations should refrain from the temptation of deleting and stopping chats amongst interacting stakeholders as this is likely to cause a backlash which is likely to severely impact upon an organisation's reputation.
- Organisations that are establishing successful social media strategies are consciously or subconsciously applying emergent, relational, interactional strategies.

REFERENCES

Achrol, R. S. (1997). Changes in the theory of interorganizational relations in marketing: Toward a network paradigm. *Journal of the Academy of Marketing Science, 25*(1), 56–71. doi:10.1007/BF02894509

Ahuja, R. K., Magnanti, T. L., & Orlin, J. B. (2014). *Network flows: Theory, algorithms, and applications*. Harlow, UK: Pearson Education Limited.

Andrew, S., & Galak, J. (2012). The effects of traditional and social earned media on sales: A study of a microlending marketplace. *JMR, Journal of Marketing Research, 49*(5), 624–639. doi:10.1509/jmr.09.0401

Barabasi, A. L. (2002). *Linked: The new science of networks*. Cambridge, MA: Perseus.

Barney, J. (1991). Firm resources and sustained competitive advantage. *Journal of Management, 17*(1), 99–120. doi:10.1177/014920639101700108

Borch, O. J., & Arthur, M. B. (1995). Strategic networks among small firms: Implications for strategy research methodology. *Journal of Management Studies, 32*(4), 419–441. doi:10.1111/j.1467-6486.1995.tb00783.x

Borgatti, S. P., & Halgin, D. S. (2011). On network theory. *Organization Science, 22*(5), 1168–1181. doi:10.1287/orsc.1100.0641

Borgatti, S. P., Mehra, A., Brass, D. J., & Labianca, G. (2009). Network analysis in the social sciences. *Science, 323*(5916), 892-895.

Buchanan, M. (2003). *Nexus: Small worlds and the groundbreaking theory of networks*. New York, NY: WW Norton & Company.

Burt, R. S. (2001). Structural holes versus network closure as social capital. *Social Capital: Theory and Research*, 31-56.

Cartwright, D., & Harary, F. (1956). Structural balance: A generalization of Heider's theory. *Psychological Review, 63*(5), 277–293. doi:10.1037/h0046049 PMID:13359597

Dewitt, B., & Meyer, R. (1994). *Strategy: Process, content, context*. St Paul, MN: West Publishing.

Doyle, P. (2009). *Value-based marketing: Marketing strategies for corporate growth and shareholder value*. Chichester, UK: Wiley.

Doyle, S. (2007). The role of social networks in marketing. *Journal of Database Marketing & Customer Strategy Management, 15*(1), 60–64. doi:10.1057/palgrave.dbm.3250070

Durland, M. M., & Fredericks, K. A. (2005). An introduction to social network analysis. *New Directions for Evaluation, 2005*(107), 5–13. doi:10.1002/ev.157

Earl, M. J. (1989). *Management strategies for information technology*. Upper Saddle River, NJ: Prentice-Hall, Inc.

Ellis, N. (2010). *Business to business marketing: Relationships, networks and strategies*. Oxford, UK: OUP.

Fill, C. (1995). *Marketing communications*. Harlow, UK: Prentice-Hall.

Fill, C. (2002). *Marketing communications: Contexts, strategies, and applications* (3rd ed.). Harlow, UK: Financial Times Prentice Hall.

Granovetter, M. (1985). Economic action and social structure: The problem of embeddedness. *American Journal of Sociology, 91*(3), 481–510. doi:10.1086/228311

Gray, D., & Vander Wal, T. (2012). *The connected company*. North Sebastopol, CA: O'Reilly Media, Inc.

Hägg, I., & Johanson, J. (1982). *Företag i nätverk-ny syn på konkurrenskraft. Stockolm*. Academic Press.

Håkansson, H. (1982). *International marketing & purchasing of industrial goods: An interaction approach*. Chichester, UK: John Wiley & Sons.

Håkansson, H., & Johanson, J. (1992). A model of industrial networks. In B. Axelson & G. Easton (Eds.), *Industrial networks a new view of reality*. London, UK: Routledge.

Håkansson, H., & Snehota, I. (1995). *Developing relationships in business networks*. London, UK: Routledge.

Hammarkvist, K. O., Håkansson, H., & Mattsson, L. G. (1982). Marknadsföring för konkurrenskraft. Liber Ekonomi.

Hanna, R., Rohm, A., & Crittenden, V. (2011). We're all connected: The power of the social media ecosystem. *Business Horizons, 54*(3), 265–273. doi:10.1016/j.bushor.2011.01.007

Hunt, S. D., & Madhavaram, S. (2006). The service – dominant logic of marketing – Theoretical foundations, pedagogy, and resource-advantage theory. In *The service-dominant logic of marketing: Dialog, debate, and directions*. Armonk, NY: ME Sharpe Inc.

Huston, L., & Sakkab, N. (2006). Connect & develop. *Harvard Business Review*, *84*(3), 58–66.

Ignatius, A. (2011). Shaking things up at Coca-Cola - An interview with Muhtar Kent by Adi Ignatius. *Harvard Business Review*, (October), 94–99.

Jackson, M. O. (2006) The economics of social networks. In Advances in economics and econometrics: Volume 1: Theory and applications. Cambridge University Press.

Johannisson, B. (1995). Paradigms and entrepreneurial networks–Some methodological challenges. *Entrepreneurship & Regional Development*, *7*(3), 215-232.

Johanson, J., & Mattsson, L. G. (1994). *The markets-as-networks tradition in Sweden*. Springer.

Kaplan, A. M., & Haenlein, M. (2010). Users of the world, unite! The challenges and opportunities of social media. *Business Horizons*, *53*(1), 59–68. doi:10.1016/j.bushor.2009.09.003

Kay, J. (1993). *Foundation of corporate success: How business strategies add value*. Oxford, UK: Oxford University Press.

Kietzmann, J., Hermkens, K., McCarthy, I., & Silvestre, B. (2011). Social media? Get serious! Understanding the functional building blocks of social media. *Business Horizons*, *54*(3), 241–251. doi:10.1016/j.bushor.2011.01.005

Kumar, V., & Mirchandani, R. (2012). Increasing the ROI of social media marketing. *Sloan Management Review*, *54*(1), 55–61.

Lin, N. (2002). *Social capital: A theory of social structure and action* (Vol. 19). New York: Cambridge University Press.

Lorenz, E. (2000). *The butterfly effect: The chaos avant-garde: Memories of the early days of chaos theory*. Singapore: World Scientific Publishing.

Lynch, N. A. (1996). *Distributed algorithms*. San Francisco, CA: Morgan Kaufmann.

Mcloughlin, D., & Horan, C. (2000). The production and distribution of knowledge in the markets-as-networks tradition. *Journal of Strategic Marketing*, *8*(2), 89–103. doi:10.1080/096525400346196

Mintzberg, H. (1994). *Rise and fall of strategic planning*. New York: Free Press.

Mintzberg, H., Ahlstrand, B. W., & Lampel, J. (1998). *Strategy safari: The complete guide trough the wilds of strategic management*. London, UK: Financial Times Prentice Hall.

Mintzberg, H., & Van der Heyden, L. (1999). Organigraphs: Drawing how companies really work. *Harvard Business Review*, *77*, 87–95. PMID:10621269

Mintzberg, H., & Waters, J. A. (1985). Of strategies, deliberate and emergent. *Strategic Management Journal*, *6*(3), 257–272. doi:10.1002/smj.4250060306

Moliterno, T. P., & Mahony, D. M. (2011). Network theory of organization: A multilevel approach. *Journal of Management*, *37*(2), 443–467. doi:10.1177/0149206310371692

Nagurney. (1993). *Network economics: A variational inequality approach.* Boston: Kluwer Academic Publishers.

Porter, M. E. (1980). *Competitive strategy.* New York: Free Press.

Porter, M. E. (1985). *Competitive advantage.* New York: Free Press.

Ritzer, G. (2011). *Sociological theory* (7th ed.). New York: McGraw Hill, International.

Turnbull, P. W., & Valla, J. P. (1986). Strategic planning in industrial marketing: An interaction approach. *European Journal of Marketing, 20*(7), 5–20. doi:10.1108/EUM0000000004652

Vargo, S. L., & Lusch, R. F. (2004). Evolving to a new dominant logic for marketing. *Journal of Marketing, 68*(1), 1–17. doi:10.1509/jmkg.68.1.1.24036

Vargo, S. L., & Lusch, R. F. (2008). Service-dominant logic: Continuing the evolution. *Journal of the Academy of Marketing Science, 36*(1), 1–10. doi:10.1007/s11747-007-0069-6

Vargo, S. L., & Lusch, R. F. (2011). It's all B2B… and beyond: Toward a systems perspective of the market. *Industrial Marketing Management, 40*(2), 181–187. doi:10.1016/j.indmarman.2010.06.026

Watts, D. J. (2004). *Six degrees: The science of a connected age.* New York: WW Norton & Company.

Weinberg, B., & Pehlivan, E. (2011). Social spending: Managing the social media mix. *Business Horizons, 54*(3), 275–282. doi:10.1016/j.bushor.2011.01.008

Welch, C. (2000). The archaeology of business networks: The use of archival records in case study research. *Journal of Strategic Marketing, 8*(2), 197–208. doi:10.1080/0965254X.2000.10815560

Wellman, B., & Berkowitz, S. D. (Eds.). (1988). *Social structures: A network approach.* Cambridge, UK: Cambridge University Press.

KEY TERMS AND DEFINITIONS

Actor: A term specifically used in network theory which is synonymous with stakeholder but can also include organisations, resources and activities that can be linked to create value for HE institutions.

Industrial Marketing and Purchasing (IMP) Group: A group of academics who subscribe to the belief that economic and social outcomes of organisations are a result of their interactions with other organisations linked together in relational networks. Positive outcomes can only occur by the sharing of resources and activities between individuals in different organisations located within and between networks. Their theory provides the means to explain why social media can affect the competitive position of HE institutions through the multiple communication interactions of students with each other regarding the quality of an HE institution's offering.

Integrated Marketing Communications: Planned communication strategies developed by HE institutions ensuring that their advertising, public relations, professional selling, sales promotional, digital marketing strategies are fully integrated and aligned with the institutions overall marketing and corporate strategies.

Network: A collection of interacting stakeholders connected to each other through social media and having influence over educational institutions and potentially impacting upon their reputation and competitiveness.

Network Theory: A group of theories developed independently in mathematics, social and natural sciences that focus on evaluating phenomena based on the relational interactions between variables rather than considering them as being simply dependent and independent.

Network: A collection of interacting stakeholders connected to each other through social media and having influence over educational institutions and potentially impacting upon their reputation and competitiveness.

Operant and Operand Resources: The tangible and intangible resources possessed by an HE institution that drives competitiveness. The competitive positioning of HE institutions is based on the way that they develop and exploit their unique and rare intangible processes, skills, leadership styles and systems on their tangible asset resources. It is the interaction between these tangible and tangible resources which give rise to competitive advantage.

Service Dominant Logic (SDL): A theory that explains that students are important integrators of value with suppliers of higher education and that HE institutions need to co-create the manner in which they promote their offerings with the direct involvement of students using social media.

Social Media: External global independent electronic platform allowing stakeholders to connect as well communicate to one another.

Strategy Formulation and Implementation: Concerns how strategy is developed and implemented within HE. Strategy within HE institutions should be viewed as identifying and implementing activities to exploit opportunities to increase student satisfaction and eliminate threats that could reduce it relative to the competition. It is imperative that competition should be viewed as collaborative to raise the profile for the whole sector and competitive to differentiate the merits of different institutions at dealing with HE issues.

This research was previously published in Implications of Social Media Use in Personal and Professional Settings edited by Vladlena Benson and Stephanie Morgan, pages 212-230, copyright year 2015 by Information Science Reference (an imprint of IGI Global).

Chapter 55
Measuring the Social Impact:
How Social Media Affects Higher Education Institutions

Vladlena Benson
Kingston Business School, Kingston University, UK

Stephanie Morgan
Kingston Business School, Kingston University, UK

ABSTRACT

Effective social media usage has particular challenges for HE institutions. The many opportunities afforded by social media, increasingly demanded by students, have negative potential. Social technology requires substantial investment to do well, and in particular, it can be very hard to measure its performance. In this chapter, the authors focus on how aligning with strategic objectives can reduce the risk and enhance the effectiveness of social media use throughout the student lifecycle. They also consider the risks which social media investment entails in HE. Using a case study of a UK university, the authors identify common themes for social media adoption in educational settings. They offer practical recommendations and key areas to consider before launching or enhancing a social media strategy in the field of HE.

1. INTRODUCTION[1]

The significance of social networking is no longer contested; it is viewed by many as a game-changing innovation set to transform the face of higher education. Social media is on its way to earning a distinctive position amongst educational technologies, attracting the attention of academic and industry researchers. The adoption of social media for academic purposes became inevitable with the wide acceptance of the tool by end-users. Social media in higher education took on a multi-faceted role: serving as networking enabler, marketing and recruitment tool, collaboration, teaching and learning tool as well as a medium presenting career management and entrepreneurship opportunities (Benson & Morgan, 2014). Extant literature offers rich accounts of the integration of social media in educational settings; the positive impact of this technology outweighs the negative potential. However, this area requires further exploration.

DOI: 10.4018/978-1-5225-5637-4.ch055

We hope that this chapter will provide a balanced view which will be helpful for the use of social media within university strategy while raising the awareness of the challenges presented by this technology.

Earlier research (see for review Benson, Morgan & Tennakoon, 2012) opened up a discussion of how universities adopt social media, not only for marketing but for relationship building, career management and learning and teaching purposes. Conole and Alevizou (2010) systematically reviewed literature on the benefits and challenges presented by the integration of web 2.0 technologies into higher education. They emphasise the widely accepted benefit of enabling new communication channels and media sharing with a specific emphasis on content generation (in the case of video sharing through YouTube, and virtual interaction e.g. on SecondLife). The rich picture of the uses of social technologies emerges as a means for content production, collaboration and communications. Serving not only as a new communication mechanism, social technologies also changed the mode of communication, - as well as synchronous communication new forms of asynchronous connections delivered by blogging and micro-blogging sites and various social networking services have been developed. Perhaps one of the earliest applications of social media - community enablement, has found its potential in the HE context. Support for existing communities and facilitating the formation of new ones through social media reflects the earlier ideas of the Community of enquiry framework (Garrison et al, 2000) and offers opportunities for instructors to move away from the didactic to student-led, constructivist approaches in their practice (Garrison & Arbaugh, 2007). However, the opportunities presented by social media have significant challenges associated with them in the HE context. For example, the shift of control in a social networking environment towards students who are more accustomed to leading communication virtually and the impact of user generated content and its validity present only some of the emerging challenges (Conole & Alevizou, 2010). This chapter focuses on the implications of social media channels for universities, not only from the measurement of success, but also from the challenges presented by the 'dark side' of social technology which are yet to be fully understood. Multiple stakeholders are involved in the integration of social media by universities: students, instructors, alumni, support staff, marketers, industry, etc. By employing social media universities may find themselves charting the unknown waters of technology with yet to be defined principles for data handling, privacy and information protection, cognitive and behavioural implications, and more. We provide insights into the dual-edged sword of the social technology: enable Higher Education Institutions (HEIs) to get a step closer to being able to define their goals for social media effectiveness and at the same time keep the challenges of social media in sight, for example privacy, information security, psychological implications and other challenges. This will enable HEIs to establish a successful, as well as efficient, social media communication strategy and to be in a position to measure the effectiveness of the new technology investment, enabling effective decision making regarding investment and approach. Further, it will help HE institutions in identifying the 'pain points' of social media and addressing the needs of internal and external stakeholders.

We discuss a case of an established multi channel social media strategy at a UK university and offer insights from academic staff into the benefits and challenges presented by the social technology in learning and teaching. We also present the dimensions of social media uses in an HE context and open the discussion on the set of metrics necessary for measuring the effectiveness of social media adopted in line with the goals of HEIs. Literature on business marketing provides plenty of metrics for social media analysis (Fodor & Hoffman, 2010), however the HE context is rather different. To address these differences we suggest a framework for aligning strategic objectives of HEIs along with possible social media strategies to achieve them. These strategies are applicable in various stages of the student lifecycle, which differs markedly in terms of university goals, students' expectations and the objectives /involvement of a wide variety of external stakeholders. This case is of a successful application of a mature social media strategy at a UK university, which is located in the London metropolitan area and has a network of international links. The social media strategy has been facilitating internal and external communication of the HEI with a wide range of stakeholders. The paper proposes a framework for aligning social media practices with university goals, taking into account the characteristics of individual higher education institutions. It is argued that student recruitment, engagement, achievement and employability can be improved through the integration of social media in higher education. We hope that the article will help in bringing HEIs closer to solving the dilemma of being able to justify investment into social media and to measure effectiveness (or the lack of thereof) of the technology, which is itself continually changing. The article concludes with a practical social media strategy matrix for the adoption of social media, based on strategic objectives which can be tailored to individual HEIs.

2. SOCIAL NETWORKING AND HIGHER EDUCATION

We live in a digital world where social media touches every aspect of the whole student lifecycle, from initial search, pre-entry, the education itself, job search and as alumnus. HE organizations have incorporated social media into the education process as well as its marketing communication channels, often without fully understanding the impact this may have on their operation or their students. The nature of students is changing (and perhaps, being changed) by technology and the increasingly large, always-on community which is enabled through social media. Today's Digital Natives are used to 'bite-sized, on-demand' learning, but also are increasingly collaborative and experienced in global communications. Many years have passed from the time Prensky (2001) originally came up with the term 'digital natives', the technology is ubiquitous and continually changing, impacting on the learning landscape on a global scale.

There has been substantial academic research on the application of social media technology to learning and teaching. Online social media allows learners to communicate and collaborate across national and cultural boundaries, generate academic content, and become active participants in the learning process. The use of social media has increased across a range of disciplines, as wide ranging as medical, architecture, marketing, and business as well as communications studies. With the proliferation of mobile devices social networking in higher education is likely to continue its successful adoption (Benson & Morgan 2012, Morgan & Benson 2014). However the implications of such devices for student learning are still unclear.

Employability is increasingly important in education and as businesses increase their own use of social media it becomes even more important to encourage students to make appropriate use of these. Employers are increasingly expecting such skills and will discuss these capabilities in job interviews. However Tuten & Marks (2012) suggest that even in marketing education these tools are not yet much used. Barriers cited by staff include lack of time and issues with adjusting to the quantity of tools available. HE institutions need to invest in staff time and support to enable them to make effective use of tools, however this can be hard to justify without a clear strategy linked to the specific HEI employability objectives.

The concept of fully integrating social media into coursework and teaching is increasingly gaining attention. George & Dellasega (2011) discuss this in the specialist area of medical education. They argue that this integration helps students to acquire the skills needed for problem solving and collaboration using technology required in the 21st century. Student feedback has been excellent supporting the value of this approach. Staff will need support however in understanding how this integration can be achieved.

A range of studies suggest that this integration into teaching and learning does have many benefits, and is worth the investment in training and time that faculty will require to achieve true integration. Okoro (2012) suggests that social media improves the quality of student learning outcomes however also emphasises the importance of selective use of the medium. Blaschke (2012) shows that social media can encourage self determined learning to develop autonomy and capability to learn. Although aimed at distance learning, these aspects can be applied to more traditional learning environments. McCarthy (2010) used Facebook within a blended delivery model and found that today's digital natives engage readily with this approach. The first year experience of students was considerably enhanced in this case. In a Taiwanese study, Hung & Yuen (2010) found that the use of social media enhanced student's sense of community, giving a strong feeling of social connectedness which improved their learning experience. Okoro, Hausman & Washington (2012) found use of social media encourages active engagement, collaboration, and participation in class activities. Whilst they agree that social media can be a distraction for students, effective use was shown to sustain quality instruction and skills development. A number of studies support the view that the use of social media increases student independence and autonomy, enabling them to learn methods of assimilating information, and suiting the learning styles of today's 'digital natives'.

However, there are many other potential negatives with distraction being only one of the minor considerations. Hrastinski & Aghaee (2012) found evidence of 'digital dissonance' (the divide between personal and educational use, see Clark et al. 2009) although the majority of students in this small study did use Facebook to initiate contact with peers and found social media useful to facilitate groupwork. They rightly emphasise the importance of ensuring there is a teaching strategy in place. Friesen & Lowe (2012) argue against the claim that social media places the learner at the centre of a network of knowledge and expertise. They argue for the questionable promise of the use of this in learning as in their view social media constrains debate, and therefore learning. Kurkela (2011) emphasised the potential for unintended, usually negative, consequences of this technique and argued for the need for a systematic understanding of the purpose of the use of social media. There have been suggestions that digital natives have reduced empathy or emotional intelligence due to the over-focus on communicating online (Kuss et al., 2013), although this is controversial and requires further research it could have a major impact on social media use in education. Issues with privacy, data security and trust have been highlighted in a number of studies (see this book chapters 1, 4, 5 and 7) and the impact on well-being, including increases in loneliness and depression and the potential to normalise the use of alcohol and drugs, has been demonstrated (see chapters 2 and 3). There has been some research focusing on the impact on those required to teach online, with issues of time and concerns about over-use of technology being prominent (e.g. this book chapter 9). Some studies suggest that young people are particularly prone to over-use of social media to the stage of addiction, where it begins to impact on their private and educational lives (Beard & Wolf, 2001, see also Kuss et al, 2013). It is possible that by encouraging social media use within the learning environment educators could make this more likely. Finally there is still insufficient understanding of the actual impact on learning, with some suggesting that the use of social media will encourage superficial approaches to learning (Cifuentes, 2011).

Many positives have been found, suggesting that as long as there is a clear strategic use of social media it can have benefits. For example, Laire, Castelyn & Mottart (2012) demonstrated that using social media such as Storify (which collects content from multiple social networks, and creates the possibility for students to write their own memorable story by adding text) increased student engagement and improving student performance in EFL writing instructions. Ravenscroft et. al. (2012) give an overview of the issues involved and strategies that may be needed to integrate informal and formal learning, and these are taken up in their special issue on social media in learning (Journal of Computer Assisted Learning, Volume 28, issue 3, 2012).

Nyangau & Bado (2012) offer a full review of the literature on marketing through social media in HE and found many HE organizations are using this increasingly for student recruitment, although it was still unclear whether social media actually influences student decision making. Benson et al. (2012) outline the advantages of integrating the strategy for marketing and educational use of social media throughout the student lifecycle. We suggest that the use of social media for marketing, if strategically integrated with use in the curriculum, may increase student awareness of social media and use within coursework, and thereby reduce digital dissonance. It is clear from the above, that social media in HE has a number of positive and negative possibilities. We will argue that taking a strategic approach to the use of social media will reduce risk and enhance effectiveness, however to develop a strategy does require an understanding of the different types of social media that may be used, as they have different issues. We offer below some categorisations that should prove helpful.

3. CATEGORIES OF SOCIAL MEDIA APPLICATIONS

From the early days of social networking research attempts were made to classify social networks. Curiously early typologies recognised the informal nature of social networks and suggested a dichotomous classification of social networking services into personal and professional (Dutta & Fraser, 2009; Benson, Morgan & Fillipaious, 2010). Social networking sites providing a way to connect, communicate, and share content with friends and family, e.g. Bebo, MySpace, vContacte and others have been considered personal social networks. On the other hand, networks enabling business connections or set up to offer commercial services have been coined as professional. LinkedIn has been a de rigueur example of professional social networks set up solely for business activity. However, with the proliferation of social media into every area of life the delineation between personal and professional social platforms began to blur. A prominent example of this process is the innovation of the Facebook platform. Started as a network for leisure use only, it eventually encompassed professional networking, as well as enabled business and commercial interactions and opportunities. Similar trends are characteristic of other social media. Both YouTube and Instagram started off as multimedia self publishing and sharing networks, but eventually turned into effective media communication channels serving varied purposes from marketing to career portfolio management tools. Therefore we argue that the classification into personal and professional social networks is now obsolete, as many social platforms effectively serve dual purposes and new entrants into the social media arena continue to appear.

Another stream of attempts to categorise social networks was based on their functionality. While the research studies were conducted in a variety of settings, from tourism to marketing, their findings tend to cluster around a finite number of categories. Xiang & Gretzel (2010) analysed Google search queries on social media and classified the types of social media included in the search results by their frequency. According to the researchers, the majority of the social media landscape is used as virtual community enablers (40%), followed by the review platforms (27%), bloggs (15%), social networking (9%), media sharing sites (7%) and other category. Kaplan & Haenlein (2010) offer another functional classification of social platforms including: Blogs, Collaborative Projects (e.g. Wikipedia), Social Networking Sites (e.g. Facebook), Content Communities (e.g. YouTube), Virtual Social Worlds (e.g. Second Life) and

Virtual Game Worlds (e.g. WarCraft). This classification also introduces self-Presentation/self-Disclosure and Media - richness/Social presence. According to this classification blogs and collaborative projects have a low media-richness and social presence factor, as they are text-based and enable relatively simple exchange, unlike technically sophisticated Virtual worlds, for example. On the other hand Content Communities score low on self disclosure, while social networks (e.g. Facebook) naturally offer a higher level of self-presentation opportunities. The functional perspective on social media provides the rationale for the categorisation presented by Fodor & Hoffman (2010). They discern the following types: Blogs and microblogging (e.g. Twitter), Cocreation (e.g. NikeiD), Social Bookmarking (e.g. StumbleUpon), Forums and Discussion Boards (e.g. Google Groups), Product Reviews (e.g. Amazon), Social Networks (e.g. LinkedIn) and Media Sharing sites (e.g. Flickr, YouTube). Depending on the purpose of the social media channel, the measurement of its performance changes accordingly.

4. MEASURING THE EFFECTIVENESS OF SOCIAL MEDIA

Commercial presence on social media has facilitated the rise of social technologies over the last few years. Projections for the growth of social marketing are extremely positive, facilitated by the expansion of applications, rise of mobile device capabilities and diversification of mobile networks (Woodhouse, 2012). Woodhouse also cites statistics of the top most popular internet sites, which include Facebook, Twitter and LinkedIn amongst the top 12 most visited in the world. The organic growth of social media marketing and convergence of social networking sites offers opportunities for consolidated marketing. Assessing the success of a social media investment has always presented difficulties in the business world. Coming into the next stage of maturity, social technology is moving away from the phase of inflated expectations and is now expected to deliver real return on investment (Blanchard 2011). Holistic evolutions of social media ROI on the basis of "We have members, so we think it works..." are no longer sufficient to answer management level questions, such as "Social marketing is everywhere, but how can we justify the ROI?" Social return on investment is notoriously difficult to calculate (Anderson 2012). Recent statistics suggest that only a small proportion of companies can measure their social media channel effectiveness; 80% of those investing in social media marketing have no idea of how to measure their ROI. The same study reports that nearly half of marketing managers, for whom social marketing is a priority, are under pressure to report on the ROI of their corporate social channel and quantify the outcomes (Lenskold 2012). These findings indicate the developing trend of social media channel turning from a 'nice-have' into a 'must-have', while proven quantifiable KPIs appear unavailable. Work by Fodor & Hoffman (2010) presents three dimensions of social media evaluation objectives, including brand awareness, brand engagement and word of mouth. They base their evaluation metrics on easily accessible statistics, such as unique visits, number of retweets, number of likes and references. While the list offered by Fodor & Hoffman (op cit) is very extensive, not all of them are applicable in the context of applications other than marketing.

Sales focused firms integrate social engagement into their sales processes. This type of social activity is centred round the metrics of 'social conversation' rate in the context of the sales cycle (Anderson 2012). Social conversation rate, measurable through virtually any social networking site, is obtained from the number of replies and comments per post. This helps to measure whether what the firm is saying to customers translates into business value. Those firms who set brand awareness as their business goal for social media investment, cultivate trust as the basis of their customer relationships and loyalty building, and employ social engagement metrics for community building. For example the number of members or followers and the community growth rate could serve as indicators of increasing brand awareness and expansion of reach on social media. Responses to posts, likes and retweets are treated as social effects which reflect brand influence and therefore have measurable business value (Shaefer 2012). Finally, amplification rate, so called 'spreading the word' through the network in the form of retweets and shares per post, and applause rate, knowing what your audience 'likes', are another set of measurements which are argued to measure ROI of a social media channel.

Organizations are not focused on achieving just a single business objective through their social media channels. Very often a combination of objectives drives the choice of social media strategy, necessitating a mix of effective metrics for social media channels (Gallaugher & Ransbotham 2010). The business rate on marketing investment has historically been calculated through econometric analysis of spending and sales, as well as competitor comparison. As higher education would have different objectives for social media strategies, it is difficult to extend commercial firms' approaches to measuring HE marketing effectiveness. Aligning a firm's business goals and social media objectives, as well as estimation of available resources are paramount for identifying the right mix of metrics for social investment evaluation. Having a clear view of user/customer journey through the firms' or HEI's social channels will help increase understanding of customer expectations and ways to meet them through social engagement.

Earlier technology had an incremental influence on learning and teaching innovation. The advent of blogs, electronic assessment, wikis, gamification, etc. has had a significant impact on higher education as new tools became available to instructors (Pimmer, Linxen, & Grohien, 2012). New ways of doing traditional things meant that technology represented incremental innovation. Since the emergence of the Internet social media is the key technology which now has a pervasive influence on the educational sector (see Benson et al., 2010).

Social media is a cross-disciplinary field. A substantial body of research on social networking research has been accumulated in the areas of psychology and sociology (Wilson, Gosling, & Graham, 2012), criminology (Conger, Pratt, & Loch, 2013) and marketing (Fodor & Hoffman, 2010), social capital theory (Valenzuela, Park, & Kee, 2009) and information systems research (Smith, Dinev, & Xu, 2011). Social media includes Facebook, LinkedIn, Twitter, blogs, virtual worlds such as Second Life, YouTube, vlogs, etc. These various media are increasingly used by students throughout their time in Higher Education and beyond, while academics including from the fields not directly related to technology are beginning to embrace social media adoption.

We now turn to our case study of social media integration to further the discussion of potential ways of measuring effectiveness.

5. THE CASE OF A UK UNIVERSITY: SOCIAL MEDIA CHANNEL INTEGRATION[2]

Kingston University established its presence on social media over seven years ago, and has been using a range of social applications to interact with various stakeholders. Twitter and Facebook are key, with LinkedIn being used particularly with the Business School. Since 2010 specific pages were set up on Facebook to target students considering joining the University. This aspect has been developed in scope over time and now covers a full range of support and communication at every stage of the selection, admission and induction process. The main Facebook page has over 25,500 'likes', now, increasing by 10,000 in the last 12 months and demonstrating a strong acceptance of the social networking site in this area. Twitter has been used for five years and the main 'tweet' hashtag has just over 22,300 followers, up by 4,000 in the last six months. Many of the 'followers' on twitter are journalists, alumni and indeed other Universities. As HE becomes more competitive globally, it is increasingly important to track activities of others in the sector and understand the competitive environment.

The central communications team started to integrate the use of social media channels into the communication strategy in a formal way about two years ago, and at first this was slow to take-off. This is fairly typical of early entrants to new media. Careful consideration had to be given to balance the conflicting needs to make the channel meaningful to the student (e.g. by having an area dedicated to a specific course) whilst having sufficient activity to make the area appealing and give the feel that the site is worth regular return visits.

In the past eighteen months a much more strategic approach has been taken, with a new member of staff employed centrally, along with additional support in faculties, with a main part of the role to work on the schedule of campaigns linked to pre-application, post application, joining and then during their time at the University. Important links are also being made with alumni. Clearly this has taken commitment (and resources) but it is starting to succeed in Kingston's aims of encouraging relationship development.

Adding multimedia seems to enhance social engagement; graduation pictures for example are always popular. Videos are also increasingly used on social networking sites and are the most popular aspects of the course pages. Being able to see and hear other students and the teaching staff talking about the experience of studying at Kingston appears to be very important to potential students. It is vital to tie in to the recruitment cycle and student life-cycle and ensure a coherent and integrated approach. The use of social media cannot just be passive, setting up initial pages is just the first step in a long process, and the integration of the different media needs careful thought throughout.

Not all of the work has to be done by University staff. One of the most successful social media sites we run was started on Facebook (with staff blessing) by Kingston students to enable students to easily raise issues and offer ideas to their course representatives, who can then feed this back to the relevant staff. The group has over 450 members, with hundreds of posts and the course teams have learnt a great deal about student views from this. Furthermore they can respond immediately if necessary rather than have to wait for the more formal student committees or feedback forms. However this does require a good relationship with the students who set up the space, as twice so far inaccurate statements have been made and we have requested that these statements be deleted or modified and responded to 'offline'. Without a level of trust and engagement with the students, this could cause difficulties.

Social media is being used increasingly in teaching and coursework. The use of Facebook, blogs, wikis and indeed twitter has enabled staff and students to collaborate and develop communities of practice. Staff in all faculties have set up blogs, wikis and Facebook pages, and many are now encouraging students to use their mobiles in class to access these pages, in an attempt to increase usage. As always, these staff tend to be the 'early adopters', who are comfortable with technology and are willing to invest time in developing a clear strategy for the use of social media, ensuring this is meaningful to the students. Analysis so far indicates that the benefits proposed in the literature cited above are being found, with students engaging fully in the tasks and commenting that they feel more confident regarding the use of social media for their discipline.

Blogs are also being used to increase collaboration between students and staff outside the standard learning situation. For example the University Student Academic Development Research Associate Scheme (SADRAS) brings together staff and students to research in areas that will improve the student experience, and all create blogs to record their collaboration as part of the process. This is helping to ensure that staff and students reflect on their work together, and facilitates evaluation of the scheme.

Social technologies have successfully proven themselves as pedagogical tools. However as the innovation and changes to communication medium brought around by social media are spreading through society, these sweeping changes force HE institutions to embrace social innovation in more areas than learning and teaching. A qualitative pilot study of the technology adoption by business instructors helped shed some light on the perceptions of social technologies by academic staff at the research site[3]. The general view of instructors is that pedagogy drives technology adoption, not vice versa. The quote from one of the study participants summarises the role of technology in their practices follows:

One of the things that is quite interesting is how sometimes you don't actually have to think about technology; it sort of emerges in because it's just the way of the world.

Indeed social technologies weaved themselves into the fabric of everyday life, then proliferated into professional areas and applications, such as learning and teaching, alumni and recruitment, student support and many other HE areas. While examples of the integration of social media in teaching were reported by all participants, the range of techniques varied. They included the extensive use of interactive discussion capabilities on various social networks - e.g. to escape the 'four walls' confinement of the classroom in Twitter; rich use of blogs - from project management to e-commerce implementation; study social presence of organization, on Second Life or other networks; explore how business leverage and operate on social media. The objective of keeping teaching interesting and engaging, immersing students into the environment they are comfortable with emerged as a leading driver for social technology adoption among interviewed academic staff. Strategies of social technologies have been mentioned by all participants and instructors measured how effective the strategy was by its effect on students. For example, empowerment of individual learners was achieved in the following setting:

....I tried to start a trending discussion where people in the classroom were responding to a blog comment from a lecturer at Oxford about recruitment. So that really encouraged them and made them think that their opinions are valuable.

Releasing the control of the classroom to students was reported to have a positive impact on student participation in self organising environment as the following example illustrates:

We have a student Facebook group which is intended just for student feedback amongst themselves so it's student led, student run, student populated group. I quite often participate in that just to clarify issues.

While alumni relationship were one of the earliest manifestations of social media applications in HE, student networking and career management opportunities have since been extended to benefit current students as well as the following quote illustrates:

I set up an alumni group on LinkedIn for graduates of our specialist degrees both the undergraduates and the postgraduates and now we have extended it so we allow the current students to join the group as well[...] using social media to help network and help them find jobs for each other, research opportunities and so on.

Social technologies have also been reported as a trouble-shooting mechanism in case of unforeseen circumstances, for instance:

We had a wonderful example of using a discussion board when we had to cancel a class, so we ran the lecture on a discussion board so we had this sort of the community spirit[...] it's a good fall back.

While the benefits of social technologies for student learning have been widely acknowledged in the University, drawbacks have been also voiced. For example staff were concerned about the reliability of technology or lack thereof, especially in the case of third party social networking sites or learning management systems plugins. Some mentioned that 'three out of four times' something goes terribly wrong when teaching with technology. Others voiced students' expectations for immediate feedback and lecturer's availability 24/7, as the following quote illustrates:

I'm sure there's quite an expectation that if students put something on the discussion board at 2 o'clock in the morning, there's almost an expectations that they will get a reply very soon.

Finally, fluency with social media seemed to be the determinant factor towards its adoption in the class room. As one of the interviewees, a younger member of academic staff, said:

...I am generation Y. I don't really remember life before mobile phones and so on.

Technical skill acquisition for staff also surfaced as self-taught rather than owing to formal staff development activities. Some of technically savvy instructors mentioned that there are academics who ' would not touch technology with a barge pole, while others are very much into it'.

The social dimension of media seemed to have had in impact on the diffusion of teaching innovation as instructors genuinely interested in technology formed interest groups where they 'self-support each other'. Interestingly enough this presented a challenge for 'traditionalists' venturing out into the social technologies field:

The only difficulties there are if you're forced to do it [using social technology] and you are out of your comfort zone. I think frankly if people are happy with technology then they can see a great role for it and it works for students, go for it every time. This Twitter idea from one of my colleagues is fantastic. But I don't think we all should do the same thing anyway. I really do believe that we should have a whole portfolio of innovations that we own.

Ultimately, it was the effect of social media foot print on students which raised instructors' concerns:

It's something that we talk to students a lot about, because we're all passionate about employability and telling students to be terribly careful about what they put about themselves online and on social media, maintaining the integrity of their Facebook sites and not divulging too much [information]...

Aiming to meet student expectations and include a popular communication channel into their communication strategy, universities have incorporated social networking into the marketing of their courses, learning and teaching strategy, maintaining alumni connections, and other areas. However, universities remain unclear about the effectiveness of their social media channels, and are even less aware about the resources which social media management requires. HEIs are making ad hoc attempts to employ social media without the appropriate tools or metrics for measuring the effectiveness of their social media communication channels.

Through the exploratory study of social media adoption at this UK University we identified five areas of social media influence in HE. These dimensions of the social platform are: learning and teaching objectives, development of social capital and career management skills among students, social creativity and innovation space for students, university social marketing and student recruitment strategy, and finally areas of privacy in information handling compliance. The challenge of measuring effectiveness in each of these domains remains, however below we give some pointers:

- **Learning and Teaching:** Measuring effectiveness here is complex, and clearly more research is needed. However analysis of the quantity and quality of student uptake of social media linked directly to their learning should be undertaken, along with more qualitative evaluation of student engagement and approaches to social media, and assessment of links to and achievement of learning outcomes. If staff have been alerted to potential negative aspects of using social media there is potential to reduce these, and again many of these can be measured (for example, student self-esteem, reported feelings of isolation etc.).

- **Social Capital and Career Management:** Analysis could be undertaken of the number of students using social media to initiate and maintain contacts related to their chosen careers, and the extent of their interactions with their network. The number of alumni members, their levels of activity, and their links to students and other alumni, as well as monitoring of success (e.g. promotions, salary etc.) can also be analysed. However, students need to be aware that their social activity may become public due to inadvertent or intentional actions of themselves and others. Their skills in managing their social profiles for professional vs personal purposes need to be developed at the university level or earlier.

- **Space for Creativity and Innovation:** The quantity of items uploaded or discussed linked to new ideas, creativity and innovation could be counted, and the number of items successfully launched (e.g. as a business or submissions for copyright, patents etc.). However we would argue for a more qualitative approach as well, assessing student and staff evaluations of the levels of creativity and innovation generated.

- **Marketing and Recruitment:** Here more typical measurements such as number of visits, 'likes', re-tweets and so on could be used, in a similar way to many other organizations assess social media ROI as highlighted above. Ideally longitudinal analysis should be made of which students engage before joining, how they progress through their time in the HEI, and their engagement as alumni, to assess patterns over time. While social media can significantly enhance recruitment and marketing campaigns, universities must have crisis management strategies in place. Social media has served as a fruitful platform for spreading information damaging reputation of many organizations. Universities should think about putting reputation management plans in place and their online profile monitoring.

- **Privacy and Compliance Considerations:** Here we are often looking for absence rather than presence. We would hope that educating students and staff successfully about privacy and good practice would lead to an absence of negative press stories, students not losing jobs due to social media exposure, and low levels of complaints or non-compliance.

Social media has created a paradigm shift in the way universities interact with students and a variety of stakeholders, from industry to government. The communication between the university and its students is no longer one way, but is transforming into a mutual and powerful dialogue empowering the voice of stakeholders in shaping up the future of higher education.

6. DISCUSSION

Starting a new social media strategy for an HEI is not an easy task and many factors need to be taken into account, including allocation of resources and an in depth analysis of external and internal needs and drivers. Taking a more strategic approach will enable HEIs to increase their understanding of the return they receive for their investment, and reduce the potential negative consequences of social media use. Below we give some suggestions based on the literature and our own research.

6.1 Key Areas to Consider Before Launching Your Social Media Strategy

1. **Focus on Relationship Building Rather than Sales:** Whilst the position of social marketing has recently gained a lot more clarity and understanding, it has yet to deliver the expected benefits as a sales channel, while delivering effectively as a relationship realisation tool.

2. **Multi Social Networking Site Presence:** Marketing strategists make assumptions that with the growth and diversification of the social media landscape and intensification of use over time, presence in social media becomes vital to any organization. The social media landscape changes rapidly; therefore the choice of the social platform may be a short term decision rather than a long-term strategy.

3. **Aligning Resources to Stakeholder Needs:** Starting a social media strategy is often associated with initiating multiple profiles on as many social networks as possible. Social media presence should be driven by business objectives and alignment of resources according to the strategy, including the choice of social platform(s).

4. **Single Channel Social Marketing:** Choosing one social marketing platform, e.g. LinkedIn or Facebook, offers some advantages, while limiting marketing opportunities. The popularity of social sites tends to vary geographically. While Facebook, Google, etc. have originated in the West and retain popularity in English speaking countries, the emerging markets, e.g. Russia and China, give preference in popularity to other social networking sites, virtually unknown to the rest, such as China's Renren (Vincos 2012). Also, stable social networking sites have become a platform for fierce competition of developed brands as well as emerging ones. Investigating competitors' presence on social marketing channels should be the initial point for assessment of new social marketing initiatives and identifying whether you can measure up and/or compete with the existing successful brands.

5. **Short Term vs. Long Term Campaigns:** Social media facilitates relationship building, when deciding on the social strategy marketers need to be aware that a social channel as a successful conversation-based engagement tool for all stakeholders is difficult to realise, and requires persistence and appropriate resources. However, this ambitious, resource intensive endeavour has the promise to deliver long term strategic objectives, unlike short term campaigns that help test feasibility and determine effectiveness of social channels. Integrating the student lifecycle will also

offer benefits; students who interact on social media during their courses are more likely to remain active as alumni.

6. **The Promise of Social Mobile:** The long term plans of many social networking sites, including Facebook and LinkedIn, emphasise the future development of the mobile dimension of social networking. The evolution of social marketing onto the mobile platform is on the mind of marketers worldwide. The outlook for mobile social marketing presents a logical progression from web based to a more convenient on-the-go platform, and is anticipated to go mainstream in the next year or so, further strengthening the current standing of social mobile applications (Benson & Morgan 2012).

6.2 Strategic Alignment

Assessment of the effectiveness of the social media investment has been notoriously problematic for organizations in public and private sectors alike. Social media has been widely adopted by higher education institutions looking for innovative communication channels with their stakeholders. However, social media management requires continuous investment, persistent engagement and monitoring of its effectiveness. Strategic business goals commonly sought through the introduction of social media which are emerging in private sector companies fall into the categories of brand management and sales. KPIs emerging in social media marketing comprise social traffic, social engagement, amplification rate, applause rate and social response rate. However, metrics for social media effectiveness differ markedly in the higher education area. While quantifiable monetary outcomes are a high priority in the private sector, higher education draws largely intangible benefits from social media presence. The strategic objectives of social media investment in HE may include benefits such as life-long learning, alumni engagement, wider community stakeholder management, research interest group community formation and growth, as well as relationship building with and between learners. In order to help universities establish and prioritise their strategic objectives within social media we attempted to summarise key benefits which social media may deliver in the HE sector. These include marketing as well as learning and teaching goals, some of which may serve dual roles in the HE context.

Those HEIs who are looking to 'test the waters' of social media must conduct an in-depth analysis of stakeholders, any party that is likely to play a role or be impacted by social media channels, and establish metrics for social effectiveness. It is important to establish KPI monitoring strategy against which the effectiveness of the social media channel for the specific HEI is continually assessed. When the goals of the social media investment for a university focus on stakeholder engagement, for example student, business and research community interactions are a priority, then stakeholder analysis needs to drive the HEI communication plan, supported by the diffusion of innovation strategy engaging not only innovators, but also cautious adopters, into the social dialogue. Formation of special interest groups, as in the case described earlier, promotes growth of the conversation rate and serves as a natural platform for community building. Alumni management is a specific example of relationship management. Well established or professionally oriented social networking sites tend to provide a common platform connecting individuals for professional and leisure purposes, while fostering a sense of belonging to their 'alma mater'.

A common driver for social media investment becomes a necessity to keep up with competitors, i.e. 'they have it, so it should work for us too' approach. This goal is the most risky and may see a university plunge into the social media waters with presence on multiple social networking sites but either lacking resources or a clear strategy. The risk of negative posts overwhelming the marketing team is also possible if the resources are not there to monitor and deflect negatives (a good social media approach will include 'service recovery' strategies that can turn negative chatter into positives). Allocating a social media manager and monitoring of the social channel performance are key actions in this case to avoid this risk. In the study of the views of academic staff towards adoption of social technologies we found that personal interest in technology itself and having supportive colleagues play an important role in the successful integration of social media tools into practice. The main driver behind the decision to adopt social technology is student engagement and development of the rapport with learners using social technology they can't do without. In the evaluation of effectiveness of technology intervention such indicators as student motivation, attendance, learner (and lecturer) satisfaction played a significant part.

In a similar way to commercial firms, universities are concerned about building stronger brand awareness amongst their current and prospective students, as well as for maintaining their business image and research reputation with external stakeholders, including employers, alumni and other Universities. Brand awareness as a result of social media integration helps build trust as the basis of customer relationships and loyalty building; therefore it is paramount to employ social engagement metrics for community building. This includes the number of members or followers, and the community growth rate. Responses to posts, likes and retweets are considered to have social impact which demonstrates brand influence and therefore have measurable business value.

7. CONCLUSION

Over the past few years organizations in the public and private sectors have turned to social media in the hope of establishing an effective communication channel with their customers, suppliers and other stakeholders. Following this trend, Higher Education Institutions (HEI) have adopted social media channels for a variety of purposes. Accounts about HEIs' use of social media are plentiful in academic literature (see for a review Conole & Alevizou, 2010). Aiming to meet student expectations and include a popular channel into their communication strategy, universities have incorporated social networking into the marketing of their courses, learning and teaching strategy, maintaining alumni connections, and other areas. However, universities remain unclear about the effectiveness of their social media channels, and are even less aware about the resources which social media management requires. HEIs are making ad hoc attempts to employ social media without the appropriate tools or metrics for measuring its value.

In this chapter we discussed a case of a multichannel social strategy applied at a UK HEI for the past seven years. The metrics used for the analysis of the channel effectiveness comprises of marketing, and learning and teaching goals. Through the exploratory study of the university efforts around social media adoption, five dimensions critical to the implementation of social strategy have been identified. They are learning and teaching objectives, development of social capital and career management skills among students, social creativity and innovation space for students, university social marketing and student recruitment strategy, and finally areas of privacy in information handling compliance. We also listened to the voice of the academic staff on social media adoption in learning and teaching, community building and alumni relationship management. While student motivation, engagement and interest in the subject surfaced as the key metrics of successful social media integration into pedagogy, instructors were concerned about students' privacy and personal information handled through social sites - a third party in the instructor-learner information exchange. An overall view of the inevitability of social technology entering the learning and teaching process has emerged as younger generation of lecturers represent generation Y.

Whether the primary objective of an HEI social media strategy becomes alumni engagement or marketing of its courses, it is important to consider key issues in the specific context before launching or during re-assessment of the effectiveness of a social media strategy. The choice between a single social networking service and multi-channel marketing strategy is down to the specific institution and its objectives and resources available. Consequently, a specific set of KPIs must be established by HEIs reflecting their individual needs and strategic goals. We argue that student recruitment, engagement, achievement and employability can be improved by higher education institutions opening a strategic social media communication channel. In a similar way, the potential risks involved with the increased use of social media can be reduced.

REFERENCES

Anderson, B. (2012). Cracking the social ROI code: Social media performance indicators demystified. *Cambridge Marketing Review*, (4), 12-15.

Beard, K. W., & Wolf, E. M. (2001). Modification in the proposed diagnostic criteria for Internet addiction. *Cyberpsychology & Behavior*, 4(3), 377–383. doi:10.1089/109493101300210286 PMID:11710263

Benson, V., Filippaios, F., & Morgan, S. (2010). Online social networks: Changing the face of business education and career planning. *International Journal of Business and Management*, 4(1), 20–33.

Benson, V., & Morgan, S. (2012). Student experience and learning management systems: Issues of wireless access and cloud deployment. In *Proceedings of the International Conference on Wireless Information Networks and Systems (WINSYS)*. Rome, Italy: Academic Press.

Benson, V., Morgan, S., & Tennakoon, H. (2012). A framework for knowledge management in higher education using social networking. *International Journal of Knowledge Society Research*, 3(2), 44–54. doi:10.4018/jksr.2012040104

Blanchard, O. (2011). *Social media ROI: Managing and measuring social media efforts in your organization*. Indianapolis, IN: QUE Publishing.

Blaschke, L. M. (2012). Heutagogy and lifelong learning: A review of heutagogical practice and self-determined learning. *International Review of Research in Open and Distance Learning*, 13(1), 56–71.

Cifuentes, L., Xochihua, O. A., & Edwards, J. (2011). Learning in web 2.0 environments: Surface learning and chaos or deep learning and self-regulation? *Quarterly Review of Distance Education*, 12(1).

Clarke, T., & Clarke, E. (2009). Born digital? Pedagogy and computer-assisted learning. *Education + Training*, 51(5–6), 395–407. doi:10.1108/00400910910987200

Conole, G., & Alevizou, P. (2010). *A literature review on the use of web 2.0 tools in higher education*. York, UK: Higher Education Academy.

Dutta, S., & Fraser, M. (2009). When job-seekers invade Faceebok. *The McKinsey Quarterly, 2009*(March). Available online at http://www.mckinsey.com/insights/high_tech_telecoms_internet/when_job_seekers_invade_facebook

Fodor, M., & Hoffman, D. (2010). Can you measure the ROI of your social marketing? *MIT Sloan Review, 52*(11), 40–50.

Friesen, N., & Lowe, S. (2011). The questionable promise of social media for education: Connective learning and the commercial imperative. *Journal of Computer Assisted Learning, 28*(3), 183–194. doi:10.1111/j.1365-2729.2011.00426.x

Gallaugher, J., & Ransbotham, S. (2010). Social media and customer dialog management at Starbucks. *Management Information Systems Quarterly Executive Journal, 9*(4), 197–211.

Hrastinski, S., & Aghaee, N. (2012). How are campus students using social media to support their studies? An explorative interview study. *Education and Information Technologies, 17*(4), 451–464. doi:10.1007/s10639-011-9169-5

Hung, H. T., & Yuen, S. C. (2010). Educational use of social networking technology in higher education. *Teaching in Higher Education, 15*(6), 703–714. doi:10.1080/13562517.2010.507307

Kaplan, A., & Haenlein, M. (2010). Users of the world, unite! The challenges and opportunities of social media. *Business Horizons, 53*(1), 59–68. doi:10.1016/j.bushor.2009.09.003

Kurkela, L. (2011). Systemic approach to learning paradigms and the use of social media in higher education. *International Journal of Emerging Technologies in Learning, 6*(1), 14–20.

Kuss, D. J., van Rooij, A. J., Shorter, G. W., Griffiths, M. D., & van de Mheen, D. (2013). Internet addiction in adolescents: Prevalence and risk factors. *Computers in Human Behavior, 29*(5), 1987-1996.

Laire, D., Casteleyn, J., & Mottart, A. (2012). Social media's learning outcomes within writing instruction in the EFL classroom: Exploring, implementing and analyzing storify. *Procedia: Social and Behavioral Sciences, 69*, 442–448. doi:10.1016/j.sbspro.2012.11.432

Lenskold, J., & Qaqish, D. (2012). *Lead generation marketing effectiveness study*. LenskoldGroup. Retrieved from http://www.lenskold.com/content/LeadGenROI_2012.html

McCarthy, J. (2010). Blended learning environments: Using social networking sites to enhance the first year experience. *Australasian Journal of Educational Technology, 26*(6), 729–740.

Nyangau, J.Z., & Bado, N. (2012). Social media and marketing of higher education: A review of the literature. *Journal of the Research Center for Educational Technology, 8*(1), 38-51.

Ofcom. (2012). *Adults media use and attitudes report 2012*. Retrieved from http://stakeholders.ofcom.org.uk/

Okoro, E. (2012). Social networking and pedagogical variations: An integrated approach for effective interpersonal and group communications skills development. *American Journal of Business Education., 5*(2), 219–224.

Okoro, E. A., Hausman, A., & Washington, M. C. (2012). Social media and networking technologies: An analysis of collaborative work and team communication. *Contemporary Issues in Education Research.*, *5*(4), 295–299.

Onlinemba.com. (2012). *Social demographics: Who's using today's biggest networks*. Retrieved from http://mashable.com/2012/03/09/social-media-demographics/

Ravenscroft, A., Warburton, S., Hatzipanagos, S., & Conole, G. (2012). Designing and evaluating social media for learning: Shaping social networking into social learning? *Journal of Computer Assisted Learning*, *28*(3), 177–182. doi:10.1111/j.1365-2729.2012.00484.x

Shaefer, M. W. (2012). *ROI (return on influence): The revolutionary power of Klout, social scoring, and influence marketing*. McGrawHill.

Tuten, T., & Marks, M. (2012). The adoption of social media as educational technology among marketing educators. *Marketing Education Review*, *22*(3), 201–214. doi:10.2753/MER1052-8008220301

Vincos. (2012). *World map of social networks*. Retrieved from http://vincos.it/world-map-of-social-networks/

Woodhouse, P. (2012). Global social networking version 2.0. *Cambridge Marketing Review*, (4).

Xiang, Z., & Gretzel, U. (2010). Role of social media in online travel information search. *Tourism Management*, *31*(2), 179–188. doi:10.1016/j.tourman.2009.02.016

KEY TERMS AND DEFINITIONS

Categorisation of Social Networking Services: Types of social media services according to various characteristics, such as purpose (e.g. personal/professional), functionality (e.g. microblogging or virtual communities).

Social Engagement: A special metrics applicable to social media which measures the level of active involvement of user with the brand/network/community. It is suggested that likes, comments and shares on social media sites are indicators of social engagement of users with the social media site.

Social KPI: A set of metrics which help monitor and evaluate performance of a social media channel. For example, number of members, registration rate or even salary level in a University LinkedIn alumni group.

Social Return on Investment (ROI): The economic principle of calculating the extra value in relation to the original invested resources; based on the cost-benefit analysis, in the context of social media it measures the value provided to the organization through the employment of social media channels. These costs and benefits may be tangible (e.g. savings/costs) or intangible (e.g. satisfying stakeholder expectations).

Social Strategy: A set of formulated strategic objectives towards social media use and social tools to implement organizational goals.

Student Experience: Measurement of how universities cater to students based on various criteria, ranging from campus environment and student welfare to helpfulness of staff and class sizes.

Student Lifecycle: Process of becoming, being a student and entering the alumnus stage. Includes aspirations rising, pre-application and application support, university entry, learning, assessment and support, alumni relations and life-long learning stages.

ENDNOTES

1   This is an updated and extended version of a chapter that appeared in the 2014 book *Cutting Edge Technologies and Social Media Use in Higher Education* also published by IGI Global.

2   This case has been presented earlier at the ICEL 2013 conference and has been further developed for this chapter.

3   The study was conducted internally as a part of a wider research into the longitudinal insights into technology adoption by business academics conducted as a part of an MA dissertation. We would like to thank Bernadette Delaney for her valuable contribution to this research.

This research was previously published in Implications of Social Media Use in Personal and Professional Settings edited by Vladlena Benson and Stephanie Morgan, pages 174-191, copyright year 2015 by Information Science Reference (an imprint of IGI Global).

Chapter 56
Retail and Social Media Marketing:
Innovation in the Relationship Between Retailers and Consumers

Francesca Negri
University of Parma, Italy

ABSTRACT

The Internet has revolutionized almost every facet of business and personal life. We are facing a far-reaching revolution, driven by Social Networking Sites (SNSs) where people talk about their life, purchases, and experiences. Mobile devices and tablets are replacing computers as the main access point to the Internet. Customer expectations are rising constantly with the development of new technologies. Social Media comes in many forms: blogs, media sharing sites, forums, review sites, virtual worlds, social networking sites, etc. Social Networking Sites (SNSs), the focus of this chapter, are the most disruptive social media and a key opportunity for business. Most industries recognized in that shift the potential for a more intimate and productive relationship with customers. Nowadays, retailers have no choice in whether they do social media: they only have the choice of how well they do it. Retailers need to convert browsers to buyers, and one-time customers to loyal sharing fans, so that they become advocates in the real and virtual worlds. The shift is deep: from one-way communication to conversation, and from advertising as an interruption to the interactivity in all locations. The originality of the chapter consists on its introduction of the concept of Social Networking Sites (SNSs) as an integration of the retailing marketing mix, defining its role in a marketing strategy, and providing some managerial implications for practitioners. After an introductive overview of the trend adopting a retailer point of view, four are the chapter's cornerstones: opportunities belonging from geolocation; how to plan a social media strategy; a new channel of interaction between customers and retailers: the social customer service; how to face a crisis in a Web 2.0 context. These are four brand new ways to engage consumers. This topic is relatively new and in continuous becoming, and much of interest remains to be said about it. The chapter's approach is to present what the authors believe to be the most relevant for a retailer facing a social networking challenge.

DOI: 10.4018/978-1-5225-5637-4.ch056

INTRODUCTION

The purpose of the Chapter is to highlight the innovation in the relationship between shoppers and retailers: Web 2.0 permits the retailers to engage customers on Social Networking Sites (SNSs). The new contest determines new rules, opportunities and threats in engaging customers.

Something has changed. Web 2.0 is a set of economic, social, and technology trends that collectively form the basis for the next generation of the Internet, a more mature, distinctive medium characterized by user participation, openness, and network effects. Qualman (2013) defines Socialnomics as "the value created and shared via Social Media and its efficient influence on outcomes economic, political, relational, etc.). Or, more simply put, it's word of mouth on digital steroids."

There is need to investigate the managerial and organizational implications of engaging with consumers in various ways through SNSs. This Chapter therefore makes an exploratory investigation into the new interactions between retailers, shoppers, and consumers.

The interactive capabilities of SNSs can be used to engage the shopper as customer in many ways, and it is imperative for retailers and academics to learn about the role of Social Media in this new context.

Providing detailed description and a general overview of the trend, the chapter identifies the role of social networks in retailer marketing strategy through a review of existing literature, recent data provided by eminent Research Institutes (MGI, Nielsen, eMarketer, et al.) and empirical research findings from the Author's research process.

BACKGROUND

The trend toward networked applications is accelerating, and Social Media Marketing is at the moment an important topic of conversation amongst academics and researchers.

Kozinets (2010) states that our social worlds are going digital. Everyday 2.23 billion people around the world go online (cmo.com), and many express their feelings and experiences about products and services through Social Media. Internet users spend 23% time online social networking. Many contributions (McKinsey Global Institute, 2012; Nielsen, 2012; Hinchcliffe & Kim, 2012) underline the far-reaching opportunities belonging from social challenge. So businesses and social researchers are finding that to understand society they must follow people's social activities and encounters on the Internet and Social Networking Sites. Andzulis, Panagopoulos and Rapp (2012) state that "companies today are wrestling with how to adopt Social Media into their business models and strategy" (p. 306).

But in spite of the expansion of Social Media, there is a paucity of research and academic literature on the role Social Media play in the retailing mix. From a business perspective, the lack of a strategic approach represents a significant barrier to effective engagement with Social Media.

"Web 2.0," the Web constructed by users themselves through blogs, communities and file sharing was first referred to in 2004 by Tim O'Reilly (Doherty et al., 2010). It is a context based on sharing platforms (blogs, YouTube, Flickr, ...) and platforms hosting Social Networking Sites (Facebook, Myspace, Ning, ...). In the words of Tim O'Reilly (2006 "Web 2.0 is much more than just pasting a new user interface onto an old application. It's a way of thinking, a new perspective on the entire business of software - from concept through delivery, from marketing through support. Web 2.0 thrives on network effects: databases that get richer the more people interact with them, applications that are smarter the more people use them, marketing that is driven by user stories and experiences, and applications that interact with each other to form a broader computing platform." Blogs, social networks like Facebook, and microblogging platforms like Twitter are simply technologies that foster communication, sharing, and collaboration (Barefoot et al. 2010). Or more precisely, Facebook, Linkedin, Twitter, Myspace and so on are not Social Networks themselves, but the tools and the platforms that allow people to manage and to expand their Social Network online. "With millions of people around the world, from an ever widening age profile, spending ever more time communicating with their "friends" via sites, such as Facebook, it is very likely that the power of social networking will continue to expand, and have a far greater affect on the modern consumers' online shopping behaviour" (Doherty et al., 2010).

In order to describe the context of the new relationship between businesses and customers, it is useful to refer to the POEM Model proposed by Forrester Research (Corcoran, 2009). POEM stands for Paid, Owned and Earned Media and shows the different ways a brand can reach its audience. Shown below, the POEM Model adapted to retailing companies.

Paid Media: All advertising bought by retailers on digital or traditional media, e.g. TV and radio campaigns, display ads and paid search, or the house organ and flyers diffusion. Content is entirely controlled by the retailer and communication flows only in one direction, from retailer to audience, with no opportunity for interaction. This type of advertising is very expensive, and is showing a progressive loss of effectiveness. Paid media is a channel that can be controlled, but response rates and credibility are declining very fast. On the other hand, no other type of media can guarantee the same immediacy and scale.

Owned Media: All points of contacts and exposures owned and controlled by the retailer. In a digital context, the most important owned medium is often the Website. In a Social Media panorama, owned media can be official Facebook and Twitter accounts and brand blogs. Retailers' mobile APPs and games are owned media too. Owned media create brand portability: retailers can extend brand presence beyond their own Website online through Social Media sites and communities. These new contexts are built for longer-term relationships with customers, in a bid for two-way conversation. The retailer writes a post on the Facebook page, and the fans can reply, share and comment, positively or negatively. Many customers enjoy engaging with their brand through long-term relationships through Social Media sites (Harris & Dennis, 2011; Gummerus et al., 2012). Owned media consists essentially of social content strategy.

Earned Media: Gives visibility through people and customer comments, shares and recommendations. In this case, the customers become the channel. Earned media consist essentially of consumer comments and reviews, viral video views, etc. A retailer's tweet is owned media, but if the tweet is retweeted by a loyal customer it becomes earned media. This is the most credible form of media, but from the retailer point of view it also represents the biggest opportunity and threat. Social Media has also created a new currency, "social currency," referring to the concept of influence. This is the era of "value to many," where the customers is the real king. "Social Media is the mechanism that allows users to avoid information indigestion" (Qualman, 2013): people want to know what peers think about products and services, and it doesn't matter if they are friends or unknown people "met" on Social Networking Sites. The "Like" button allows users to share things/brands/places they like, and seek approval from others within their network (Walker Naylor et al., 2012). Influencing the buyer in no longer sufficient: retailers need to influence the potential buyer's network, through this kind of advocate customer. Zarrella found (2010) that many rating and review sites initially allowed users to post anonymously. But over time, many, such as TripAdvisor and Amazon, have incorporated a reputation system where users or their individual reviews can be rated on a scale of usefulness or accuracy. Recently, a new kind of review site has emerged that combines local ratings with social networking features, like the popular site Yelp.com.

Exists also the possibility to pay or sell with a tweet (paywithatweet.com): people sell and buy products through the value of their social networks. Every time people pay with a tweet, their social friends see information about the product. And the product soon becomes known.

Earned media are free for retailers. Customer word of mouth (WOM) is spontaneous and voluntary, as well as being the most reliable (Harvey et al, 2011). Earned media are a gift.

On the other hand, WOM can sometimes be negative, and difficult or impossible to control. Retailers need to learn to respond, and consider carefully when it is appropriate or useful to stimulate earned media through WOM marketing. Measuring the ROI of earned media is difficult and requires continuous monitoring.

Paid, Owned and Earned media work best when used together, but retailers need to make the hard choice of what to include and what not to include, especially when budgets are tight. They are in any case a supplement to more traditional trade and in store marketing, and not a substitute.

Table 1 shows how retailers are committed in Social Networking Sites: between the top ten companies most talked about on Facebook, as of August 19, 2013 (Richter, 2013), Walmart is the third.

The table shows clearly that people are talking about Walmart, a FMCG retailer. And although Walmart is the biggest retailer in the world, it would be hard to define it as a "lovebrand." So Social Networking Sites now represent a big opportunity, as well as a threat, for other retailers and chains, because customers are yet talking about them online, and an increasing numbers of customers are accessing retail information on-the-go, using mobile phones, and looking for a more personal and relevant experience.

ENGAGING CUSTOMERS ON SOCIAL NETWORKING SITES: CHALLENGES FOR RETAILERS

How Social Networking Sites are contributing to innovate in retailing? The answer is shown in the Table 2 that highlights the disruptive elements as well as the opportunities and threats.

The most important components and elements of the table will be analyzed in depth in the further pages.

Table 1. Top ten companies most talked about on Facebook

Brand	People Talking About Them on Facebook
Coca-Cola	1.04 m
Avon	929k
Walmart	757k
Disney	737k
Samsung Mobile	634k
Intel	588k
Bud Light	504k
Guarana Antarctica	494k
NBA	477k
Visa	470k

Source, Richter (2013)

Table 2. Challenges and innovation in retailing

Traditional Relationship	Challenges for Retailers	Innovation in Retailing
Touch point: store, Website.	Touch point: store, Website and **Social Media**.	New opportunities of engagement trough integration online/in store marketing (geolocation). Retailers need to be where customers are, setting a Social Networking plan. Threat: a low-cost but high-energy strategy.
From Communication *Top down* (one to many)	**To** Conversation *Top down* (one to many) *Peer to peer* (many to many) *Bottom up* (many to one)	The conversation is personal, bidirectional, very fast. User Generated Contents become Social Currency. Retailers need to plan a Social Customer Care (social caring) to match the interactive and real time conversations.
Focused on Company.	Focused on **People**.	Retailers must listen and monitor conversations. Contents must be engaging, not spamming.
Retailers owned media and contents.	Retailers **share** contents. Contents are **created** by customers. Customers are media.	Threat: loss of control. Retailers need a Crisis Management planning.
Relationship not mediated by technology.	**Portable devices** are very important in the customer shopping experience.	Retailers need to consider mobile and tablet as part oh their retailing mix: the new relationship is mediated by mobile devices.

Social Networking Sites (SNSs)

Boyd and Ellison (2007) define "social network sites as Web-based services that allow individuals to (1) construct a public or semi-public profile within a bounded system, (2) articulate a list of other users with whom they share a connection, and (3) view and traverse their list of connections and those made by others within the system."

Social networking is one element of the "Web 2.0" environment, and adapting it to retail, retailers will face increasingly intense pressure from consumers to deliver a more authentic dialogue and provide opportunities to both customize the interface and allow consumers to generate their own content (Wirtz et al., 2010). In an increasingly competitive retail environment, successful retailers are finding new ways to connect with their customers in order to drive sales, loyalty and customer awareness (Negri, 2011).

The dozens of practitioner articles on SNSs agree on several points (Andzulis et al., 2012): first, they are important. Second, "the balance of power has moved, inexorably, and forever, from the company to the customer" (Baer, 2010). And last, but not least, they require resources in terms of money and people, integration and deep commitment. Practitioner articles do not point out that a Social Media strategy is not a medley of disjointed tactics and promotional operations.

Many retailers, such as Walmart, Inditex Zara, Amazon, Best Buy, and Abercrombie & Fitch are now managing Social Media Marketing through Facebook or Twitter. This section describes some of the most important Social Networking Sites, and discusses how to create a Social Media Marketing Plan, with the use of key performance indicators.

The social network Website *Facebook* was launched in 2004 at Harvard University by Mark Elliot Zuckerberg and now has more than 1 billion members worldwide. Facebook's mission is "to give people the power to share and make the world more open and connected." Millions of people around the world use Facebook everyday to keep up with friends, upload photos, share links and videos, and learn more about the people they meet and the products/services they buy. Facebook Inc. began selling stock to the public and trading on the NASDAQ on May 18, 2012. Most of Facebook's revenue comes from advertising.

Twitter is a Website owned and operated by Twitter Inc., which offers a social networking and micro-blogging service, enabling its users to send and read messages called tweets. These are text-based posts of up to 140 characters: the creators of Twitter chose this length because the number was close to the 160 characters typical of an SMS, with the extra 20 characters used for a username. By default, tweets are publicly visible, but senders can restrict message delivery to their followers. Users may subscribe to other users' tweets, which is known as following, and subscribers are known as followers. Since its creation in March 2006 and launch in July 2006, by Jack Dorsey, Twitter has gained popularity worldwide, with over 500 million registered users as of 2012, generating over 340 million tweets daily and handling over 1,6 billion search queries per day. Twitter official (verified) corporate accounts enjoy greater acceptance.

Pinterest is a pinboard-style photo-sharing Website that allows users to create and manage theme-based image collections such as events, interests, and hobbies. Users can browse other pinboards for images, "re-pin" images to their own pinboards, or they can "like" photos. Pinterest was founded by Ben Silbermann, Paul Sciarra, and Evan Sharp; development began in December 2009, and the site launched as a closed beta in March 2010. In December 2011, the site became one of the top 10 largest social network services, according to Hitwise data, with 11 million total visits per week. Pinterest also allows businesses to create pages aimed at promoting their businesses online: business pages can include prices of products, ratings and reviews. In February 2013, Reuters and ComScore stated that Pinterest had 48,7 million users globally.

Google+ (pronounced and sometimes written as Google Plus) is a social networking site and identity service owned and operated by Google Inc. It is the second-largest SNS in the world, and is said to have overtaken Twitter in January 2013 with approximately 359 million users, although these figures are contested.

Retailing is increasingly a high-tech industry with retailers using communications and information systems technologies to increase operating efficiencies and improve customer service (Levy & Weitz, 2012). These new applications and virtual presences include the use of Websites to sell products and services to customers, providing a seamless multichannel interface, activating co-creation processes, building a more rewarding shopping experience in store and out of store and creating a new interactive and real time relationship through Social networking Sites (Burton et al., 2011). The result is that customers can interact with retailers anytime, anywhere.

Despite rapid growth in marketing use of SNSs, there is a little theoretical or empirical research examining how retailers, belonging to different sectors, use those popular sites. Andzulis, Panagopoulos and Rapp (2012) proposed a review of Social Media and their implications for the sale process and in the sales force, but with a producers point of view.

Catching the Social Media networking wave is neither as easy nor as straightforward as might seem at first. It is a low-cost but high-energy strategy. Many companies have built up experience in managing it, but as yet there are few retailers among them.

Retailers today however are starting to use Social networking Sites for several reasons:

- Social networking presence gives retailers a more personal identity, which can differentiate it from competitors. As customers grow tired of one-sided marketing messages, Social Media provides a new way for retailers to engage customers in conversations. On April 27, 2011, IKEA in Hong Kong ran their "Happy Inside" campaign through a "Bedroom Makeover" Facebook contest, offering a 90-second shopping spree to the person who submitted the best photos to show how IKEA helped "turn his/her bedroom nightmare around." The IKEA Website shows a video of the three lucky IKEA fans sweeping up $10,000 in products in seconds;

- Social networking accounts can be used to promote new products and services or new stores, and to publicize promotions. Retailers are using Pinterest to display grouped and curated selections of their products in a visual and creative way (Sevitt & Samuel, 2013).

- The new relationship means firms can gather customer insight and incorporate it into strategy. SNSs also allow retailers to engage honest feedback, both solicited and unsolicited. SNSs allow retailers to monitor comments, understand how messages are perceived, what information customers want, highlight purchasing and buying preferences (Casteleyn et al., 2009; Patino et al., 2012). Trough surveys and pools retailer can test new services or assortments. It was pressure from online responses that forced fashion retailer Gap to withdraw its planned logo redesign in October 2010;

- Retailers can also sell on Social networking Sites (social commerce, or f-commerce). New functions on Facebook allow retailers to launch secure, transactional stores as APPs, so that customers can buy from within the site. Transactional Facebook stores give a purpose and measurability to f-commerce, although the market is still relatively small. There are however companies such as Blooming which offer social-focused capabilities to firms aiming to sell through these sites.

Geolocation

Customers are increasingly armed with mobile devices, such as smartphones and tablets. Inside the store, in an instant, they can thus find out everything they want to know about what is on the shelves, and whether any friends are in the store or have been there. They can read, and rate, reviews of the products and assortments, opinions about employees courtesy, and they can make price comparisons with the nearest shop.

Singh (2012) identifies in geo-socialisation one of the mega-mega trends of today. "The next platform of social networking will rely on geographic services and capabilities such as geocoding and geotagging to allow social network to connect and co-ordinate users with local people or events that match their interest" (p. 81).

Retailers need to take advantage of this sharing. Quoting Salt (2011), "Social location sharing is happening to your product, service, venue, and location whether you are active or not."

"Social location marketing" is the process of utilizing social location sharing tools as a marketing channel, while "social location sharing" defines the platforms and applications used for sharing the information about locations. What differentiates social location sharing from much of the rest of SNSs is that it is specific to a location. And retailers well know that is all about "Location Location Location." When a customer "checks in" in a specific location, a supermarket or a clothes shop, s/he is telling the network where s/he is. This is a public declaration of approval or affinity for the place. This is earned media. A customer checking in at an Apple Store is stating a preference for that brand, and advocating it as a social location sharer. From a user perspective, social location sharing sites are often a sort of game, including rewards and prizes. Foursquare, for example, awards check-in badges and points.

Retailers are thus able to promote check-in into a store, or a single department of the store. Segmented offers also allows rewards to be tied to in-store promotions - especially those offered in partnership with third party suppliers.

At the time of writing, *Foursquare* is the most important social location mobile site (SoLoMo). It is a free APP that helps people make the most of where they are and share and save the places they visit. People use it to find the best place to go based on what their friends and experts recommend. They check in at store in the real world and leave tips to tell others what they like, or dislike. People can also receive personalized recommendations and deals based on where they are, or where their friends are, or where people with the same tastes have been. Foursquare co-founders Dennis Crowley and Naveen Selvadurai met in 2007 in New York City: they began building the first version of Foursquare in fall 2008, and launched it at South by Southwest Interactive in Austin, Texas in March 2009. Today (January, 2013) the community consists of over 30 million people worldwide, with over 3 billion check-ins, one million every day. Over a million businesses use the Merchant Platform. Retailers may promote news, events, and discounts with Foursquare Local Updates, or set up a Foursquare Special to attract and reward visitors. Foursquare free analytics informs retailers about customers checking in to their business – they can see who customers are, when they come, how much they're talking about the brand across other SNSs, and more.

Social location marketing is an activity very close to gaming. Many retailers organize treasure hunts into the shop, inviting customers to interact with, rate and snap pictures in various shop areas.

Finally, some social location APPs are being rolled out to integrate with retailers loyalty programs.

Social Networking Strategy and Plans

This section examines the components of a Social Networking Plan. Social networking sites have the potential to effect many strategy, in different ways. Listening is the primary step in engaging a customer.

1. Listen first! Monitoring

One of the most exciting aspect of SNSs for retailers is the opportunity 1) to identify consumer preferences and use this information to shape business strategy through customer endorsement and 2) to monitor what people is thinking of them and have the chance to effectively manage brand reputation.

Those opportunities have already given certain retailers a significant and long-lasting competitive advantage. Rick Bendel, Global Chief Marketing Officer of Walmart, said: "Social Media is a free, massive focus group, taking place in real time. And it is taking place with or without your permission."

Retailers need to monitor conversations and respond to them, especially if the commentary is negative. The three steps of Social Media Monitoring, which underpin Social CRM are: listening (first!), understanding, and reporting.

Listening gives retailers the appropriate baseline and credibility to join the conversation. Before a retailer can face the social networking arena, needs to identify and understand the value proposition for the customer. In a context in which "Markets are conversations" (first thesis of the The Cluetrain Manifesto, Levine et al, 1999), hearing is not enough: listening is a technique used in conversations, which requires a person to pay attention to the speaker and provide feedback.

Quoting Qualman (2013, p. 36), "Negative comments and posts are easier for companies to find with Social Media. Hence, those companies have more time to focus on the solution rather than spending time finding the problem. (…) Ineffective companies spend time attempting to obfuscate or manipulate negative comments within Social Media." Once a retailer starts to monitor what is being said about its brand/products/services, they should get to know their audience. They need to know who they are, where they hang out online, how they use the Web and their expectations as well as which competitors' page/ accounts they follow.

Zarrella's advice (2010) is to "Lurk, lurk, and lurk some more; get to know the community before you start posting."

A very interesting new qualitative marketing research technique for providing consumer insight has been developed by Kozinets: the "Netnography," a market-oriented ethnography conducted on online communities dedicated to marketing-relevant topics. It uses the information publicly available in online forums and communities to identify, and understand, the needs and decision influences of relevant online consumer groups. (Kozinets, 2010)

2.   Know the global marketing strategy of the company, aiming for total integration

Retailer Social Media strategy should fit with the retailers established identity and core values. Selective retailers, for example, need to offer the same level of service and conversational tone on Social Networking Sites as they do offline.

3.   Identify the right strategy

Strategy and tactics are inseparable, but strategy must come before tactics. Before opening a page on Facebook, retailers need to identify their goals and strategy. The majority of Social Media Marketing handbooks today describe tactics and Facebook micro-marketing tools, which, however, are changing day by day. Strategic thinking, according to Drucker (1999), is knowing the right questions to ask. Before learning how to manage a Facebook page or a Twitter account, a retailer should answer a few basic questions: What is the purpose of using SNSs? What resources do we have? Where are customers talking about their preferences, commenting on shops and services? Where are our competitors? Which are expected threats, and our weaknesses in Web 2.0?

To answer these questions, it is helpful to make a SWOT analysis, highlighting retailers' strengths and weaknesses in approaching Web 2.0 and the opportunities and threats of facing Social Networking Sites.

4.   Set the goal of the strategy and Key Performance Indicators (KPI)

Using free Social Media tools and placements is more time- and cost-effective than traditional advertising, but retailers must remember that Social Media marketing is a low-cost, high-energy type of strategy. Opening an official page on Facebook is free, although it can be costly in terms of time and money to create appropriate content and respond rapidly to customer queries and so on.

It is difficult to measure the return on investment (ROI) of Social Media (Hoffman, 2010). Some companies even state, "We aren't doing Social Media because there isn't any ROI." But this leads to the more urgent question of the cost of doing nothing. As Qualman (2013) states, "The ROI of Social Media is that in five years your company will still exist."

There are some aspects of advertising campaigns that can be measured (Avinash, 2009) through key performance indicators (KPI). Paid media and Owned media are traceable, like more traditional forms of media. But Earned media, the most effective form, is not. To calculate the ROI of Social Media, retailers deduct the cost of their financial and time investment from the income generated. But not all the fans who visit the retailer's Facebook page turn into customers or leads. The open question is how to measure effective engagement rates. Simply counting the number of fans or followers does not work: first of all, not all fans are active and, secondly, at the time of writing, it is possible to buy targeted fans for few cents on eBay. The numbers of customer posts, retweets, sharing and reviews are on the other hand useful metrics.

A further aspect not covered by traditional KPI is the cultural change brought about by social networking marketing. Catching the Social Media wave, retailers abandon one-way communication and embrace a new conversational paradigm where communication between retailers and customers flows in two directions.

Most SNSs makes control dashboards available to retailers in freemium: basic insights are offered free while fees are charged for more sophisticated marketing instruments.

5. Build up the team, and invest in training. Create and share the social media policy

Retailers must synchronize their strategic and tactical activities to create, deliver, and communicate customer value trough SNSs. One of the most common error is to delegate to the last incoming stagers the Social Media marketing activities, only because "they're young." Social Media marketing requires high level of planning, commitment and competence. Retailers need to pay attention selecting the Social Media marketing team, and an ongoing training is required. Moreover, SNSs also make it possible to search for new human resources, in line with the mood of the brand. As well as more traditional sites such as Linkedin, Facebook can also be used, as in the Jobs APP from Zara on their official Facebook page.

The Social Media Policy (SMP) of a company is a corporate code of conduct (Negri, 2013). An internal SMP provides guidelines for employees who post online either as part of their job or as a private person. An external SMP regulates the relationship between company/fans-followers and fans-followers/fans-followers in the social networking context. The main goal of an SMP is to set standards for appropriate behavior and ensure that an employee posts will not expose the company to legal problems or public embarrassment. The SMP is one of the most important parts of a social network plan. The Walmart SMP is very interesting and covers employees, customers and associates. The main points are shown Box 1 (source: Walmart).

6. Select the Social Networking Sites where you want operate, and choose the right tools.

Retailers need to know their target and their audience, and select SNSs where these can be found. They should understand the special features offered by each SNSs and use them. Social Networking Sites vary greatly based on their feature sets, but there are some common elements across most of them.

Accounts: Pinterest, YouTube, Linkedin, Facebook and Twitter offer special accounts and tools for businesses. For example, it is not possible for retailers or other businesses to have a profile on Facebook, but they can manage a page showing information about the company, its history, contact information, and so on.

Social networking sites allow retailers to operate multiple accounts that can target specific groups of shoppers, for example by location, store or private labels.

Some retailers are targeting local customers. In the UK, Waterstones has Twitter accounts for individual stores, and can notify customers of book signing and other local events. Other retailers are tailoring communications to user interests. Amazon, for example, manages various different Twitter accounts and various Facebook pages including Amazon Student, Amazon Mom, Amazon Fashion, Amazon Kindle

Box 1. Walmart's social media guidelines

We engage with our customers and stakeholders beyond the walls of our stores: you can find us on Facebook, Twitter, YouTube, Flickr and Foursquare. This page will give you a better idea on how to engage with us in social media, what you can expect from us, and where to find more information.

Walmart's Twitter Engagement Guidelines

Twitter asks a very basic question of its users: "What's happening?" And we know the answer to that question – we're working every day to help people save money so they can live better.

Through our Twitter account we aim to provide you with information on Walmart's major activities and initiatives - from sustainability to diversity, from healthier foods to charitable giving. We welcome your thoughts on any and all of those topics.

Please note that we won't be able to reply to store or service issues through Twitter. If you would like to comment about customer service or other issues please visit our Walmart Facebook feedback app, leave a comment through our Contact Us page or call 1-800-WALMART.

Here are a couple of things you should know about our Twitter engagement:

All official Walmart Twitter users are identified at walmart.com/twitter.

We are committed to having a dialogue with our followers. We count on you to use @ messages in a way that contributes to the dialogue. Please support any claims with links to information sources whenever possible. We love opinions; we love them even more when you back them up with facts.

We strive to respond to as many relevant questions and comments as possible, but we reserve the right to use our judgment in selecting the messages we respond to.

Following a Twitter account or including an account in a Twitter list does not constitute an endorsement; the same applies to re-tweeting messages posted on accounts that Walmart does not own, or marking them as "favorites."

The posting and presence of content on Twitter and on this site does not necessarily mean that Walmart agrees with the content, ensures its accuracy or otherwise approves of it. Nothing in any Twitter page constitutes a binding representation, agreement or an endorsement on the part of Walmart. Please review Twitter's terms of use carefully when engaging on the site.

Walmart's Facebook Engagement Guidelines

We're excited that you've joined us on our Facebook Fan page, and we know you've got plenty to say. At Walmart, our mission is our purpose: we save people money so they can live better.

While you're with us, we hope you'll take a moment to read the following guidelines we ask you to follow when contributing to our Facebook Fan page:

Don't do anything that breaks the law.

Be polite and courteous, even if you disagree. Excessive name calling, profanity, fighting words, discriminatory epithets, sexual harassment, bullying, gruesome language or the like, will not be tolerated.

Stay on topic. Keep the conversation relevant to the community and contribute to the dialogue. We reserve the right to remove off-topic, out of context, spam or promotional postings.

Keep it real. All wall postings should come from a real person and Facebook profile. Postings from fake or anonymous profiles will be deleted when discovered.

There is a place for customer service-related questions, complaints, concerns or ideas from customers. If you are a customer and have a customer service comment, complaint, concern or idea, we encourage you to post it on Walmart's Facebook Feedback tab, to ensure that we can respond in a timely manner. Please note that any customer service posts published on a Walmart page by customers will be removed when discovered. As always, if you would like to comment about customer service or any other issue you can visit our Contact Us page or call 1-800-WALMART.

We reserve the right to remove content posted to Facebook that violates these guidelines.

If you are a Walmart associate, please follow these additional guidelines:

Know the rules. Before engaging on Facebook, or on any other social media property, make sure you read and understand Walmart's Social Media Policy and Walmart Information Policy. In any and all interactions make sure that you don't share confidential or private information about the Company's business operations, products, services, or customers; respect financial disclosure laws; and do not say you speak for the Company without express written authorization from the Company to do so.

Remember that we have a dedicated FB team tasked with responding to customer inquiries or criticism. Our Official Walmart Facebook team is responsible for engaging customers through our page. To avoid confusion, we ask that you not attempt to respond to customer inquiries or comments directed specifically to the Company or asking for an official Company response on this site.

Consider using company established channels for job-specific issues. While we encourage associates to join our Facebook community and participate in conversations with our customers and other users, we encourage you to direct your complaints or concerns about your job or working environment to your store management team using the established Open Door Process or MyWalmart.com.

For Walmart managers: If you are a manager, please make sure you are familiar with our Social Media Management Guidelines, available on the Walmart Wire.

Guidelines for Associates' Use of Walmart-Sponsored Location Based Promotions

Walmart is currently experimenting with in-store promotional campaigns for users of location-based services like Foursquare and Facebook Places. If you are an associate using these services, you may have the opportunity to check in at your store's location every day, which could give you an unfair advantage over our customers. That's why we ask you not to participate in location based-promotions for your own store. Please feel free to take advantage of location-based promotions when you check in at other Walmart stores offering these promotions.

and Amazon Tech Deals. In 2011, with the launch of Facebook.com/SearsLatino and its Twitter handle @SearsLatino, Sears added a Sears Latino Social Media channel so that it could engage culturally and strengthen relationships with Hispanic customers. In order to make online shopping more accessible and convenient, these customers are encouraged to share stories and ideas, provide feedback and learn more about Sears' Latino initiatives.

If the retailer has a recognizable spokesperson, a profile for him/her, or for the Social Media team, can be created, endowed with photo and signage.

Connecting: The most important action on a SNS is the act of two people connecting. Facebook reserves the term "friending" for individuals, and uses the term "fanning" when people connect with a brand. Twitter term is "following." Retailers must conduct active efforts to drive prospects and customers to their Social Media pages, starting from their Websites, flyers or store. In the search for a two-way relationship, retailers would be well-advised to follow everyone who follows their brand on Twitter.

7. Set the style of your presence, and the editorial plan. Create interesting contents, promotions, events, and share.

Retailers must invest in a good editorial plan, looking for interesting content and good design, and establish a regular activity of pasting and sharing. Different types of content can be combined on SNSs, and multimedia, such as APPs and videos can be added. Retailers need to regularly update their status, pin on their board and tweet. Every SNS requires particular content. There should be content that is exclusive to Social Media, not only the replica of Website/flyers. Fans/followers should be motivated to create content on SNSs themselves: organic content is much more convincing.

To make a content more viral, it should be posted to media-sharing sites using effective tags. Media-sharing sites make it easy to distribute multimedia content to thousands or millions of viewers. It is important to use open licensing and embedding features to encourage viewers to share media. Where possible, voting badges should be used to make it easy to vote so content can be rated. Social media make it easier to launch seasonal and promotional campaigns in conjunction with external events in the real world, for example Thanksgiving or Father's Day.

Events: The majority of SNSs allows retailers to create an event and invite their fans/followers to attend it. These events most commonly occur in the real world/store, but some are online-only events. RSVP function is included, as are commenting and photo uploads.

Pricing Strategy and Promotion: Literature presented Social Media as the new hybrid element of the promotion mix (Glynn Mangold & Faulds, 2009). SNSs are a good context to test pricing policies and promotions, as shown by the experiences of Marks and Spencer (M&S) and Tesco. M&S in May 2009 backed down from charging extra for larger bra sizes (£2 more for bras with a cup size above DD) after a consumer-led Facebook protest against the so called "tit-tax." More than 14,000 consumers joined a Facebook group calling for an end to differential pricing. Under the headline "We boobed" M&S's adverts on Facebook page say: "We were wrong, so as of Saturday 9th May the storm in a D cup is over."

In November 2011 Tesco allowed Facebook fans to vote on items they wanted to see as part of its Big Price Drop promotion, converting fans into brand advocates through customer involvement and endorsement. As part of the promotion, Tesco introduced the Big Price Drop Vote on its Facebook page, giving fans the option to vote for the items they wanted to see reduced in the next stage of the offer. In addition, customers could enter a photo competition based on spotting Tesco's promotional lorry and playing the Price Drop Challenge.

This is coherent with Planet Retail intuition (2012) about one of the biggest changes to have occurred in the FMCG sector in recent times: the rise of customer endorsement, as retailers increasingly involve shoppers in the decision-making process. Social Networking Sites are particularly suitable for this. Walmart, again, has used CrowdSaver since November 2010 to trial price reductions based on a voting system. If the required number of fans "like" an offer on Facebook, it goes live, driving participation and increasing loyalty. The first item, a plasma television, required 5,000 "likes" for a reduction from USD488 to USD398 – this was achieved in around 12 hours, generating great brand loyalty and publicity for the company (Planet Retail).

Price promotions are used by retailers to educate customers in new shopping process. The e-commerce site Yoox, for example, offered an extra 15% off on its collection when customers shop via a smartphone or tablet.

SNSs learn about customer' preferences and their buying habits, so they can plan advertising (Facebook paid media) and suggest other products or brands. This recorded history permits to provide real time pricing offers on selected items coherently with customers' preferences. Dell successfully implemented promotional offers and discounts trough Twitter.

And, maybe in a later future, SNSs could intersect data belonging from fidelity cards with social networking' data set. At the time of this writing, Facebook said that is considering the possibility.

Applications (APPs): Social networking sites have increased their functions through Application Programming Interfaces (APIs) which allow them to create new Apps to plug into their site. As noted above, Facebook now offers an App by which a complete purchasing transaction can take place on Facebook.

Calls to Action (CTAs): A call to action (CTA) is "an invitation you make to your Website visitors to engage in some type of action that benefits your business aims—and hopefully theirs, too" (Zarrella, 2010, p. 201). There are two kinds of CTAs: sticky and conversion. Sticky CTAs turn ephemeral waves of traffic into return visitors, for example, asking them to fill in a form or a newsletter. Whereas conversion-based CTAs lead a visitor into the sales funnel: these are more intrusive and useful for promotion.

8. Responding to fans (See also the section on social customer care).

Retailers must always answer online greetings and criticisms. Their answers will stay on the Internet forever, having an amplifying effect. When responding to a post, tweet or a review, the protocols of the SMP and/or crisis management guidelines must always be followed, even if the user has posted incorrect or grossly misleading information. The retailer should ask the customer if there is anything specific that can be done to remedy the situation, and perhaps offer a discount.

9. Monitor continuously and make the necessary fine tuning. Plan crisis management (See also the section on crisis management).

"Set-it-and-forget-it" is not a good social network marketing strategy. Retailers should be active with updates and interaction. Real time marketing is required on Web 2.0. Monitoring Social Networking Sites, and Social Media in general, is an ongoing process. Retailers can use dedicated software and programs like Google Alerts, or spiders. It is important to remember that although data collection can be managed by programs, analysis needs to be performed by a person. Spiders and analytical software cannot in fact read sarcasm, very informal/urban slang, plays on words, mistyped words and emoticons.

Monitoring can be initially based on keywords related to the retailer's brand, products, sector, competitor and key employees' names.

Retailers today are mostly trying out different strategies, ranging from using SNSs for marketing and promotions, to localization, customer endorsement and full integration.

Coming to the conclusion, strongly emerges that this social strategy requires substantial commitment and continuous monitoring activity. Social strategy must be managed as an explicit strategic activity, and requires a unique strategy and a coherent framework for implementations.

Social Customer Care

Social sites like Facebook and Twitter are key sources of information about customers, and can provide insight into what customers are saying about private label products, competitors and employees. Customers often appear keen to share their experiences and opinions on their social network accounts, and the penetration and diffusion of Social Networking Sites have led to big changes and opportunities for customer service. Retailers and consumers no longer have to rely on a busy call center agent to solve a problem, check the status of an order or get advice on choosing the right store address (Fraticelli & Negri, 2013). Today there is an array of digital customer service tools at their disposal, including live chat, Social Networking Sites and smartphones. Alongside traditional customer care services, such as dedicated phone numbers, call centres, email and online contact forms or in store desk, retailers now can plan a social customer service: the so called social caring. Customers often demand an immediate and sympathetic response to their complaints, and the online social network context is perfect for that. Twitter is the most suitable Social Media. Responsiveness, the ability to help customers and provide prompt service, is one of the benefits it offers: the microblogging service is a simple and efficient way of sending messages far and wide, offering the added value of the human touch. Customer experience is enhanced by the use of informal friendly tones, and signing-off with the employee's name, putting a name to a voice, provides reassurance.

Best Buy, the American multinational consumer electronics corporation, is one of the many firms today to manage effective customer care on Twitter. It offers the verified account "Best Buy Support" - @BestBuySupport

"Have questions about @BestBuy? Need Support? Let us know! We're here to help 24x7." is the promise. The account currently has a tweet count of over 46,882.

Conversocial (2012) highlights that many businesses - an estimated 71% - claim to use Social Media for customer service, but many do not appear to be using it to its full potential, with only a small percentage fulfilling customer expectations for having their issues solved online.

Social customer service brings two main benefits:

- Off line customer care becomes lighter, involving fewer queues, calls and emails to manage;
- Visibility is gained through helping customers. All the followers/friends of the customer see the prompt solutions offered. Simply letting customers know that Social Media is a channel they can turn to for help and queries makes a great impression. It offers an opportunity to please even the unhappiest of customers.

Companies often turn customers to a dedicated Facebook App as an alternative to collecting customer queries. Walmart has a Feedback APP where all questions are responded to and its invitation on

Facebook reads: "For all of us here at Walmart, there's only one boss, the customer. So let us know if you've got a question, concern or idea. I look forward to hearing your feedback."

Other companies have found the maximum of 140 characters to be a limitation in responding to complicated customer questions. Responses to individual customer queries can thus be recorded on video, uploaded to YouTube, and tweets replied to with a link to the video. These videos have received favorable response, and have been retweeted (becoming earned media), creating a positive word of mouth and a "sense of community" around the brand.

Leveraging Social Media for customer service gives daily opportunities to make a highly visible impact which can be positive or negative. Research by eMarketer (2013) underlines that delivering good customer service does not necessarily come cheap, but it is one of the few remaining ways retailers can hold on to customers without cutting deeply into margins. It finds that consumers are willing to pay more if a retailer appears to act in their best interest, helps them to get more value out of the products they purchase, creates convenient new ways to shop, and lets them know when to expect delivery of an order.

Crisis Management

Retailer mistakes are clearly identifiable. And partly because retailers are part of the everyday experience for consumers, the retail landscape is invariably rich in failures and near failures, increasingly so in the current global economic downturn – (Palmer et al., 2009). The retail sector receives a large amount of media coverage, particularly where there are accusations of wrongdoing, and this can provide a reputation decline. When a retailer finds, or creates, an unhappy customer, this should be used as a customer service opportunity; the consumer should be engaged and efforts made to remedy the situation. By proactively engaging with its customers, a retailer can build stronger relationships (Levy & Weitz, 2012).

But the speed and depth of Social Media means a crisis can explode and spread like wildfire. There are several examples of companies whose involvement in social networks and online communities has done them more harm than good. And there is nothing that bloggers and efolks love more than a story of a company that has screwed up its "social capital" by misusing the Social Media tools available to it.

One of the most recent cases showing how social marketing can be a positive force for crisis management was Tesco's management of the frozen beef burger outrage: a crisis born on the shelves, but immediately arrived on the net. Tesco private label burgers, like many other similar products from numerous manufacturers, were involved in a scandal when government scientists in Ireland, where many burgers are produced, found traces of horse DNA. Tesco and other retail chains were widely blamed for the contamination.

Tesco immediately cleared its shelves in store, and on line, on its Facebook fanpage, laid out the facts. Fans' reaction was not slow. On 16 January 2013 Tesco posted "We Apologise":

We apologise.

You have probably read or heard that we have had a serious problem with three frozen beef burger products that we sell in stores in the UK and Ireland.

The Food Safety Authority of Ireland (FSAI) has told us that a number of products they have recently tested from one of our suppliers contained horsemeat.

While the FSAI has said that the products pose no risk to public health, we appreciate that, like us, our customers will find this absolutely unacceptable.

The products in our stores were Tesco Everyday Value 8 x Frozen Beef Burgers (397g), Tesco 4 x Frozen Beef Quarter Pounders (454g) and a branded product, Flamehouse Frozen Chargrilled Quarter Pounders.

We have immediately withdrawn from sale all products from the supplier in question, from all our stores and online.

If you have any of these products at home, you can take them back to any of our stores at any time and get a full refund. You will not need a receipt and you can just bring back the packaging.

We and our supplier have let you down and we apologise.

If you have any concerns, you can find out how to contact us at the bottom of this page, or go to any of our customer service desks in-store, or ask to speak to your local Store Manager.

So here's our promise. We will find out exactly what happened and, when we do, we'll come back and tell you.

And we will work harder than ever with all our suppliers to make sure this never happens again.

This post is part of a complete and careful Social Media strategy (https://www.ourtesco.com).

Tesco replied to customer complaints on an individual basis, even posts which were tasteless and offensive. Customer care employees were tactful, down-to-earth and apologetic. All Tesco posts were signed by a single employee, as "Matt from Customer Care." On the fanpage there was a conversation rather than one-way communication. As the weeks passed, Tesco brought fans up to date, posted news and reassured people. Finally, Tesco declared the end of the emergency with a post.

The first 6,649 posts were analyzed using netnography (Negri, 2013). The findings show a range of fans' reactions: from the joking to the blaming. The majority of them are positive in tone. The data shows there was overall positive reaction to the apology post. Tesco was able to use Social Media monitoring to stay on top of what people and fans were saying. It apologized publicly and engaged people with a simple apologetic message which was perceived as authentic and honest. Fans and clients served as Tesco's advocates, actually helping to contain and manage the crisis. Tesco received more visibility and trust than any traditional paid-for advertising could have achieved.

Tesco's experience, as well as relative literature, allows us to formulate the following guidelines for 2.0 crisis management by retail firms.

- Monitor Social Networking Sites to unveil potential crises. It is important to realize that the warning signs of a potential crisis probably do not usually show up as a spike in the volume of conversation, but as a shift in sentiment.
- Prepare a Social Media Policy, a Crisis Management Plan and organize a crisis team: the more prepared you are, the more active you can be.
- Take action to remove contaminated products from store shelves as soon as possible.

- Do not under- or over-react, and keep your tone appropriate to every situation, personal, simple, and authentic. Humor can be used lightly in response to satirical comments.
- Act quickly and decisively: apologize before being discovered and attacked. The real-time Web requires real time marketing.
- Make sure to apologize for and solve any customer service problems as soon as possible. Reply to customer complaints on an individual basis.
- Pay attention to what followers/fans are saying and show that you are listening and considering their opinions.
- Communicate continually with customers and contact media to advise them about what is going on.
- Document your actions.
- Evaluate material/immaterial compensations.
- Declare the end of the crisis.

Unlike the past, crises today move at speed, and follow the rules of Social Media. Retailer reputation depends among other things on responses made to those who highlight mistakes.

SOLUTIONS AND RECOMMENDATIONS

Recommendations for Retailers

The most common mistakes in Social Media Marketing are listed below, along with suggestions on how they can be avoided.

1. Not setting realistic goals or knowing how to measure results. Results are not immediate: building networks, getting credibility and becoming trustworthy takes time, resources and patience.
2. Misunderstanding or, worse, ignoring the peculiarities of Social Networking Sites and their marketing tools. Retailers must research and understand the platforms they are interested in using, and choose the tools that work best for the goals and the audience they are trying to reach. Retailers need to follow the rules of the context, communities and Social Networking Sites.
3. Don't be inconstant: using a Social Media platform once then never again makes it seem that you are ignoring your customers. Interact appropriately, positively and frequently. The real-time Web requires real time marketing. If you only intend to reserve your brand name to avoid fakes, keep your profile/page/account hidden. Create a venue on Foursquare, a page on Facebook, a channel on YouTube or a group on Linkedin is the same of being listed in the Yellow Pages. Customers can find you, but to engage a relationship with them, retailers need to interact and create consistent contents.
4. Be transparent and personal, and not (only) promotional. People become fans on Facebook or follow firms on Twitter because they love your work and want to connect with you as a person. Automated responses and impersonal messages are counter-productive. Post and share original, relevant and interesting contents. Contribute, rather than pitch.

5. Rewards and special offers. Literature has shown (Palmatier et al, 2009) that relationship marketing investments generate short-term feelings of gratitude that drive long-lasting performance benefits based on gratitude. As the conversation is bi-directional, the benefits cannot be unidirectional: customers need to receive value from their Social Media efforts. And customers expectations are increasing. They also desidered to be rewarded for their loyalty to the store, and for fanning and following the retailer presence on SNSs. They also start to find couponing sales (Auchan in Italy, and WholeFoods in UK trough Groupon) in a deal-of-the-day Websites. Retailer need to plan special offers not available to the general customers, dedicated to fans and followers, in the forms of reductions that customers can request on line and use in store. For example, Carrefour is offering a discount to customers that made a "chek-in" on Foursquare, Lidl offered a special bonus to its fans on Facebook once reaching the 500.000 fans. Other retailers are giving virtual badges (made of an HTML code), a social proof of their loyalty.

6. Basic errors in spelling or grammar are the best way to alienate fans in Social Media Marketing communications. This type of mistake harms opinion of a brand. Double check your spelling and grammar. Once you publish a post in your wall, it's out there forever.

7. Posting too often (over-exposure), or trying too hard to be funny. Before rushing in to an aggressive Social Media push, retailers should bear in mind that social networks have been set up to be just that – social. Keep the post short, and remember that fans prefer infographics, video, gaming APPs and image.

8. Censorship or redirection might be a temptation for those focused on brand image. A mistake often made by companies on Facebook is disabling the ability for fans to post on their official page. Although at first this may sound like a good idea to preserve the "good name" of the retailer and to prevent negative comments being displayed for the world to see, in the medium term it can cause more damage to your brand reputation. Customers, fans, competitors and employees will not be discouraged from speaking about your company if they have something to say, and they will go in another page, or blog, that you're not able to monitor and manage.

And of course, retailers, like anyone else using the Internet and Social Networking Sites, need to remember that it has downsides relating to issues like privacy and security management, scamming, cookies policy, and fake identities or trolls.

FUTURE RESEARCH DIRECTIONS

The following lines try to highlight the next Social Media trends.

Changing of Social Networking Sites: SNSs are constantly changing, and appear to follow a sort of lifecycle: Facebook usage is currently stable, and it is still the largest social networking site, but there are many more local sites as well. Google+ is struggling to take off. Visual social networks, such as Pinterest and YouTube are expanding rapidly. The only thing that is constant is change.

Peer review sites can determine your reputation and business. Yelp is today becoming more widely established, while TripAdvisor is declining slightly. Retailers need to check and revise Social Media plans and budgets considering these rapid shifts.

Mobile: The fastest growing marketplace on the planet is unfolding in the palms of our hands on smartphones. "M-commerce" has arrived. With the proliferation of mobile devices and tablets, retailers are facing increasingly new ways of shopping. There is an urgent need to develop APPs and sites optimized for mobiles. Retailers can yet use QR codes and new shopping Apps that deliver customized coupons based on past spending habits when the shopper is in the store, or permit to create a shopping list.

Big data: Digital information is exploding in the form of information, tweets, posts, reviews pictures, and video. The site http://onesecond.designly.com/ reveals new developments on internet. Retailers have the possibility to collect and use big data to fine tune services for their customers, linking loyalty card data with other sources. But it will be an expensive investment.

F-commerce is at present a niche. British online fashion retailer ASOS operates a transactional f-commerce APP, allowing customers to buy from within Facebook. However, the majority of retailers, including Gap, recently removed their transactional Facebook stores, indicating that it is a niche market with limited ROI. Most retailers are opting to add "Like," "Pin" and "Tweet" social buttons to their existing e-commerce and m-commerce sites. On the other hand, digital and virtual goods such as music and streamed or downloaded content can be purchased more simply using Facebook Credits. The Spotify Facebook APP allows users to play music from within the social site and share it with their friends.

There are also numerous area and trends for further research that were uncovered in this Chapter, including the role of devices in the purchasing behaviour, privacy and security management, augmented reality, co-creation opportunities, and fakes management. The additional reading section offers some follow-up materials.

CONCLUSION

With the rise of mobile devices and an increasing number of Internet users worldwide, retailers are beginning to experiment with their presence on Social Networking Sites such as Facebook, Pinterest and Twitter. Best Buy, for example, is managing a fully-transactional store on Facebook. Costly television advertising and traditional communicational channels are no longer the best way to reach and retain shoppers. Customers themselves, referring and reviewing products, shops and services via Social Media tools, are the new retail marketing frontier. They can do all of this from the sofa through tablets (while TV is broadcasting advertisements), or directly inside stores with smartphones.

The difference between online and offline experience is fading: customers standing into the store are at the same time on line through their tablets, mobiles and, will soon be using new devices like augmented reality glasses. So business models based on the distinction between online/off line marketing need to shift, and simply digitizing old business models and marketing plans is not sufficient.

In-store integration is already happening as retailers introduce click and collect services (E.g. Mango), kiosks and mobile devices (E.g. Burberry) and build offers around check-in rewards (E.g. Carrefour through Foursquare). There will be an increased blurring of channels between brick and mortar and online stores. Increasing mobile usage will continue to drive this transition.

Retailers will soon need to be equipped with new ICT and infrastructure to take advantage of geo-socialisation opportunities, and create touch points for digitally equipped customers.

Retailers need an integrated approach to the new media, and recognize and respect the specific characteristics of each type. Entire retail organizations, including the most senior levels, need to be involved, not only the digital marketing office or PR: the "Talking Shop" blog was recently launched by Philip Clark, the chief executive of Tesco.

Social Networking sites are a retail marketing channel, a customer service instrument, an engagement opportunity and a crisis management tool – and retailers need to bear all of these aspects in mind to engage customers through an exciting and high-value experience.

REFERENCES

Andzulis, J., Panagopoulos, N. G., & Rapp, A. (2012). A review of Social Media and implications for the sale process. *Journal of Personal Selling & Sales Management*, *3*, 305–316. doi:10.2753/PSS0885-3134320302

Avinash, K. (2009). *Web Analytics 2.0: The Art of Online Accountability and Science of Customer Centricity*. Indianapolis, IN: Wiley Publishing, Inc.

Baer, J. (2010). Operationalizing in 2010. *Marketing in 2010: Social Media Becomes Operational*. Retrieved August 2013, from http://conversationagent.typepad.com/Marketingin2010.pdf

Barefoot, D., & Szabo, J. (2010). *Friends with Benefits: A Social Media Marketing Handbook*. San Francisco, CA: No Starch Press, Inc.

Boyd, D. M., & Ellison, N. B. (2007). Social network sites: Definition, history, and scholarship. *Journal of Computer-Mediated Communication*, *13*(1), 11. doi:10.1111/j.1083-6101.2007.00393.x

Burton, S., & Soboleva, A. (2011). Interactive or reactive? Marketing with Twitter. *Journal of Consumer Marketing*, *28*(7), 491–499. doi:10.1108/07363761111181473

Byfield-Green, L. (2012). *Retail & Social Media: How and why are successful retailers tapping into social networking channels?* Planet Retail.

Casteleyn, J., Mottart, A., & Rutten, K. (2009). How to use Facebook in your market research. *International Journal of Market Research*, *51*(4), 439–447. doi:10.2501/S1470785309200669

Conversocial. (2012). *Evolving Social Customer Service*. Retrieved May, 2013, from http://www.conversocial.com/resources/whitepapers

Corcoran, S. (2009). Defining Earned, Owned and Paid Media. *Forrester Research Blogs*. Retrieved November 2011, from http://blogs.forrester.com/interactive_marketing/2009/12/defining-earned-owned-and-paid-media.html

Divol, R., Edelman, D., & Sarrazin, U. (2012). Demystifying social media. *McKinsey Quarterly*. Retrieved August, 2012, from http://www.mckinsey.com/insights/marketing_sales/demystifying_social_media

Doherty, N. F., & Ellis-Chadwick, F. (2010). Internet retailing: the past, the present and the future. *International Journal of Retail & Distribution Management*, *38*(11/12), 943–965. doi:10.1108/09590551011086000

Drucker, P. (1999). *Management Challenges for 21st Century*. New York, NY: Harper Business.

eMarketer. (2013). *Multichannel Customer Service*. Retrieved July, 2013, from https://www.emarketer.com/go/multichannelcustomerservice

Fraticelli, F., & Negri, F. (2013). Twittering organizations' customer service: evidences from top 100 companies. In *Proceedings of 10th SIM Conference*. SIM.

Glynn Mangold, W., & Faulds, D. J. (2009). Social media: The new hybrid element of the promotion mix. *Business Horizons, 52*, 357–365. doi:10.1016/j.bushor.2009.03.002

Gummerus, J., Liljander, V., Weman, E., & Pihlstrom, M. (2012). Customer engagement in a Facebook brand community. *Management Research Review, 35*(9), 857–877. doi:10.1108/01409171211256578

Harris, L., & Dennis, C. (2011). Engaging customers on Facebook: Challenges for e-retailers. *Journal of Consumer Behaviour, 10*, 338–346. doi:10.1002/cb.375

Harvey, C. G., Stewart, D. B., & Ewing, M. T. (2011). Forward or delete: What drives peer-to-peer message propagation across social networks? *Journal of Consumer Behaviour, 10*, 365–372. doi:10.1002/cb.383

Hinchcliffe, D., & Kim, P. (2012). *Social Business by Design*. San Francisco, CA: Jossey-Bass, a Wiley Imprint.

Hoffman, D. L., & Fodor, M. (2010). Can You Measure the ROI of Your Social Media Marketing? *MIT Sloan Management Review, 52*(1), 41–49.

Kozinets, R. V. (2010). *Netnography. Doing ethnographic research online*. Thousand Oaks, CA: Sage.

Levine, R., Locke, C., Searls, D., & Weinberger, D. (1999). *The Cluetrain Manifesto*. Retrieved November, 2013, from http://www.cluetrain.com/

Levy, M., & Weitz, B. A. (2012). *Retailing Management* (8th ed.). New York, NY: McGraw-Hill Companies, Inc.

McKinsey Global Institute. (2012). *The social economy: Unlocking value and productivity through social technologies*. Retrieved September, 2012, from http://www.mckinsey.com/insights/high_tech_telecoms_internet/the_social_economy

Negri, F. (2013). NetworkCracy. Giappichelli Ed.

Nielsen. (2012). *State of the Media: The Social Media Report*. Nielsen.

O'Reilly, T. (2006). *Web 2.0 Principles and Best Practices*. Retrieved June 2011, from http://oreilly.com/catalog/web2report/chapter/web20_report_excerpt.pdf

Palmatier, R. W., Burke Jarvis, C., Bechkoff, J. R., & Kardes, F. R. (2009). The Role of Customer Gratitude in Relationship Marketing. *Journal of Marketing, 73*, 1–18. doi:10.1509/jmkg.73.5.1

Palmer, M., Simmons, G., & de Kervenoael, R. (2009). Brilliant mistake! Essays on incidents of management mistakes and mea culpa. *International Journal of Retail & Distribution Management, 38*(4), 234–257. doi:10.1108/09590551011032072

Patino, A., Pitta, D. A., & Quinones, R. (2012). Social media's emerging importance in market research. *Journal of Consumer Marketing, 29*(3), 233–237. doi:10.1108/07363761211221800

Qualman, E. (2013). *Socialnomics* (2nd ed.). Hoboken, NJ: John Wiley & Sons, Inc.

Richter, F. (2013). *Coca-Cola is the No. 1 Brand on Facebook.* Retrieved August 2013, from http://www.statista.com/markets/14/media-advertising/chart/1377/most-talked-about-brands-on-facebook/

Salt, S. (2011). Social Location Marketing. Indianapolis, IN: Que.

Sevitt, D., & Samuel, A. (2013, July-August). How Pinterest Puts People In Stores. *Harvard Business Review*, 26–27.

Singh, S. (2012). *New Mega Trends*. New York, NY: Palgrave MacMillan. doi:10.1057/9781137008091

Walker Naylor, R., Poynor Lamberton, C., & West, P. M. (2012). Beyond the Like Button: The Impact of Mere Virtual Presence on Brand Evaluations and Purchase Intentions in Social Media Settings. *Journal of Marketing*, *76*, 105–120. doi:10.1509/jm.11.0105

Wirtz, B. W., Schilke, O., & Ullrich, S. (2010). Strategic development of business models: implications of the web 2.0 for creating value on the Internet. *Long Range Planning*, *43*(2/3), 272–290. doi:10.1016/j.lrp.2010.01.005

Zarrella, D. (2010). *The social media marketing book*. Sebastopol, CA: O'Reilly Media, Inc.

ADDITIONAL READING

Ailawadi, K. L., Beauchamp, J. P., Donthu, N., Gauri, D. K., & Shankar, V. (2009). Communication and Promotion Decisions in Retailing: A Review and Directions for Future Research. *Journal of Retailing*, *85*(1), 42–55. doi:10.1016/j.jretai.2008.11.002

Anderson, C. (2006). *The Long Tail: Why the Future of Business is Selling Less of More.* New York, NY: Hyperion.

Anderson, C. (2009). *Free: How Today's Smartest Businesses Profit by Giving Something for Nothing.* New York, NY: Hyperion.

Anderson, C. (2012). *Makers: The New Industrial Revolution.* New York, NY: Hyperion.

Anderson, E. (2010). *Social Media Marketing. Game Theory and the Emergence of Collaboration.* Heidelberg: Springer.

BCG, The Boston Consulting Group (2011). *The Digital Manifesto. How Companies and Countries Can win in the Digital Economy.*

Benkler, Y. (2006). *The Wealth of Networks*. CT: Yale University Press.

Blanchard, O. (2011). *Social Media ROI*. Boston, MA: Pearson Education, Inc.

Capozzi, L., & Berlin Zipfel, L. (2012). The conversation age: the opportunity for public relations. *Corporate Communications: An International Journal*, *17*(3), 336–349. doi:10.1108/13563281211253566

Chatfield, T. (2013). Netymology. UK: Quercus Ed.s Ltd.

Cross, R., Liedtka, J., & Weiss, L. (2005). A Practical Guide to Social Networks. *Harvard Business Review*, (march): 124–132. PMID:15768681

Fiorito, S., Gable, M., & Conseur, A. (2010). Technology: advancing retail buyer performance in the twenty-first century. *International Journal of Retail & Distribution Management, 38*(11/12), 879–893. doi:10.1108/09590551011085966

Furht, B. (Ed.). (2010). *Handbook of Social Network Technologies and Applications.* New York, NY: Springer. doi:10.1007/978-1-4419-7142-5

Heinonen, K. (2011). Consumer activity in social media: Managerial approaches to consumers' social media behavior. *Journal of Consumer Behaviour, 10*, 356–364. doi:10.1002/cb.376

Kaplan, A., & Haenlein, M. (2010). Users of the World, Unite! The Challenges and Opportunities of Social Media. *Business Horizons, 53*(1), 59–68. doi:10.1016/j.bushor.2009.09.003

Kozinets, R. V. (2002). The Field Behind the Screen: Using Netnography for Marketing Research in On-line Communities. *JMR, Journal of Marketing Research, 39*(1), 61–72. doi:10.1509/jmkr.39.1.61.18935

Kozinets, R. V., de Valck, K., Wojinicki, A. C., & Wilner, S. J. S. (2010). Networked Narratives: Understanding Word-of-Mouth marketing in Online Communities. *Journal of Marketing, 74*, 71–89. doi:10.1509/jmkg.74.2.71

Kumar, V., & Rajan, B. (2012). Social coupons as a marketing strategy: a multifaceted perspective. *Journal of the Academy of Marketing Science, 40*, 120–136. doi:10.1007/s11747-011-0283-0

Lovink, G. (2008). *Zero Comments: Blogging and Critical Internet Culture.* London, UK: Routledge.

Lovink, G. (2011). *Networks Without a Cause: A Critique of Social Media.* Cambridge, UK: Polity Press.

Ludwig, S., de Ruyter, K., Friedman, M., Bruggen, E. C., Wetzels, M., & Pfann, G. (2013). More Than Words: The Influence of Affective Content and Linguistic Style Matches in Online Reviews on Conversion Rates. *Journal of Marketing, 77*(January), 87–103. doi:10.1509/jm.11.0560

Masum, H., & Tovey, M. (Eds.). (2011). *The Reputation Society.* MA: The MIT Press.

Negri, F. (2011). Retail 2.0, or not? *Proceedings of 16th International EAERCD Conference on Research in the Distributive Trades, Parma.*

Piskorski, M. J. (2013). *Networks as Covers: Evidence from an On-Line Social Network.* Working paper 13-083, Harvard Business School.

Sennet, F. (2012). *Groupon's Biggest Deal Ever: The Inside Story of How One Insane Gamble, Tons of Unbelievable Hype.* New York, NY: St. Martin's Press.

Smith, T. (2009). The Social Media Revolution. *International Journal of Market Research, 51*(4), 559–561. doi:10.2501/S1470785309200773

Sridhar, S., & Srinivasan, R. (2012). Social Influence Effects in Online Product Ratings. *Journal of Marketing, 76*(September), 70–88. doi:10.1509/jm.10.0377

Thai, M. T., & Pardalos, P. M. (Eds.). (2012). *Handbook of Optimization in Complex Networks. Communication and Social Networks.* New York, NY: Springer.

Trusov, M., Bucklin, R. E., & Pauwels, K. (2009). Effects of Word-of-Mouth Versus Traditional Marketing: Findings from an Internet Social Networking Site. *Journal of Marketing, 73,* 90–102. doi:10.1509/jmkg.73.5.90

Van Dijk, J. (2006). *The Network Society* (2nd ed.). London: SAGE.

Venkatesan, R., & Farris, P. W. (2012). Measuring and Managing Returns from Retailer-Customized Coupon Campaigns. *Journal of Marketing, 76*(January), 76–94. doi:10.1509/jm.10.0162

Walker Naylor, R., Poynor Lamberton, C., & West, P. M. (2012). Beyond the Like Button: The Impact of Mere Virtual Presence on Brand Evaluations and Purchase Intentions in Social Media Settings. *Journal of Marketing, 76*(November), 105–120. doi:10.1509/jm.11.0105

Weinschenk, S. M. (2009). *Neuro Web Design: What Makes Them Click?* Berkeley, CA: New Riders.

KEY TERMS AND DEFINITIONS

Check-In: The process whereby a person announces their arrival to a physical place trough a mobile application and the phone's GPS to find the current location. At the same time, users share their locations with their friends.

Mobile Application (APP): A software application designed to run on smartphones, tablet computers and other mobile devices.

Paid, Owned and Earned Media (POEM): Refers to the different means for a brand to gain visibility on the Internet.

Social Currency: Is information shared which encourages further social encounters, in a viral loop.

Social Gamification: The process of using Social Media features and behaviors to amplify gamification effects and experience of Social Media.

Social Networking Sites: Platforms that allow people to manage and to expand online their social network.

SoLoMo: Integration of social, local and mobile platforms.

Tag: A non-hierarchical keyword or term assigned to a piece of information that helps to describe an item and allows it to be found again by browsing or searching.

Web 2.0: A Web 2.0 site may allow users to interact and collaborate with each other in a Social Media dialogue as creators of user-generated content in a virtual community.

This research was previously published in the Handbook of Research on Retailer-Consumer Relationship Development edited by Fabio Musso and Elena Druica, pages 426-448, copyright year 2014 by Business Science Reference (an imprint of IGI Global).

Chapter 57
The Strategic Use of Social Media in the Fashion Industry

Hanna Kontu
London College of Fashion, UK

Alessandra Vecchi
London College of Fashion, UK & University of Bologna, Italy

ABSTRACT

The importance of social media is evident as millions of people use it to connect with others, share content, and discuss different topics (Kaplan & Haenlein, 2010; Kim & Ko, 2010). Although it is clear that social media is powerful and ubiquitous, many fashion brands have been reluctant or unable to develop strategies and allocate resources to effectively engage with the new media. The goal of this chapter is to critically review the literature that explicitly addresses the adoption, application, and impact of social media by fashion brands. In particular, the purpose of this chapter is to provide a critical assessment of the adoption of social media amongst three well-established fashion brands in order to identify the importance of social media as a strategic marketing tool and to propose a number of alternative social media strategies for fashion brands. Such a critical assessment is necessary since, as demonstrated by the research findings, implementing these strategies will allow brands not only to survive, but also to create new competitive advantages and thrive in the new global fashion business environment.

INTRODUCTION

Fashion can be related to any object or phenomenon that changes over time and is based upon individuals' collective preferences (Barnard, 1996). In our work, the word "fashion" mostly refers to the production and the fruition of garment and accessories, or as Luigi Maramotti, CEO of Max Mara Fashion Group describes, "I must emphasize that I consider a designed garment "fashion" only when it is marketed and worn by someone" (Maramotti, 2000, p. 96).

As a business sector, these distinctive features of changeability, likeability, and wearability signify the presence of major challenges in the integration of fashion within social media and the broader digital environment and the requirement of complex strategies to overcome them. However, the question of the

DOI: 10.4018/978-1-5225-5637-4.ch057

state of fashion in the digital context remains largely unexplored, particularly with regards to the particularities of fashion management, which have posed a challenge in adopting digital technologies in the sector over the past two decades (Okonkwo, 2010; Tungate, 2009; Vecchi & Kontu, 2012). Until recently, the fashion industry has shown low commitment towards integrating advanced Internet technologies and its associated interactive and digital tools in the sector's marketing and overall business strategies (Okonkwo, 2010). The fashion industry seems to be present and conduct business on the Internet as a result of ever evolving consumer needs and expectations. For instance, notable international fashion brands such as Versace and Prada did not have corporate websites until 2005 and 2007, respectively. The slowness of the fashion industry in establishing an online presence in comparison to other sectors visibly clashes with the common idea of an industry that is known for innovation, avant-gardism and creativity (Michault, 2009).

Coupled by the growing demand for a stronger online presence, the rise of social media in recent years brings forth new challenges to fashion brands. The importance of social media is evident as millions of people utilize it to connect with others, share content and discuss different topics (Hanna, Rohm, & Crittenden, 2011; Kaplan & Haenlein, 2010, 2011; Kietzmann, Hermkens, McCarthy & Silvestre, 2011). Although it is clear that social media is powerful and ubiquitous, many fashion brands have been reluctant or unable to develop strategies and allocate resources to effectively engage with social media (Michault, 2009; Okonkwo, 2010; Tungate, 2009). This attitude has changed in the last few years; social media such as YouTube, Facebook, Twitter, Tumblr, Instagram, Pinterest, Vimeo, and Vine have become an integral part of how fashion brands connect with their consumers, providing immense opportunities for innovative marketing communication (Arthur, 2013; Bautista, 2013a; Kim & Ko, 2010; Nguyen, 2011; Wasserman, 2012). Furthermore, it has been suggested that the digital and social media are changing the entire "fashion system" as it was previously understood; the new media often includes the consumer in the creation, delivery, and dissemination of the brand message (Bautista, 2013a; Kim & Ko, 2010). As a result, social media are exacerbating the on-going process of democratization of fashion – today, consumers can view collections live on the Internet, make buying decisions and subsequently give instant feedback on various social media outlets. These recent changes have only been a glimpse of what the old elitist fashion world could quickly become: a business in which designers take their collections directly to customers, no longer filtered through editors at the major fashion magazines and buyers at the leading fashion stores (Michault, 2009; Okonkwo, 2009, 2010). These developments and consumer demands situate fashion brands at crossroads. As suggested by fashion editor Suzy Menkes (2010), "fashion brands have to decide which way to go: back to the comfort zone of craftsmanship and quality, as Gucci has done; fast forward into the world of live screening and e-commerce; or a delicate balance between the two?"

Our chapter provides a critical assessment of the adoption of social media amongst three well established fashion brands in order to identify the importance of social media as a strategic marketing tool, and to propose a number of alternative social media strategies for fashion brands. As demonstrated by our findings, implementing such strategies will allow fashion brands not only to survive, but also create new competitive advantages and thrive in the new global business environment.

The chapter is divided into eight sections. After the Introduction, the second section provides an overview of the existing social media literature highlighting the gap in the current knowledge and presenting the rationale of the study. The three subsequent sections broaden the theoretical discussion across three key areas: the evolution of the social media environment (section three), the changing nature of brand relationships (section four), and the role of social media in marketing (section five). After the theoretical foundations have been established, the sixth section provides an overview of the methods adopted and the seventh section discusses the findings. The final section presents conclusions, addressing the original contribution of the work, the managerial implications of the findings, their limitations as well as the directions for future research.

THEORETICAL OVERVIEW

The academic literature on social media is still in the early stages and there is limited evidence of its potential as a strategic marketing tool. Furthermore, the connections between social media and fashion remain largely unexplored with little academic research on the applications of social media in the fashion context. Table 1 summarizes the scholarly literature currently existing on the topic and identifies the different aspects that have been studied in relation to social media.

Deriving from the previous discussion, the rationale for this research is threefold.

First, despite an increased interest in the relationship between social media and the final consumer, little scholarly knowledge exists on the subject (Kim & Ko, 2012). As discussed previously, the emergence of social media has not only transformed the media environment and businesses, but it also has altered the relationship between organizations and the consumer (Edelman, 2010; Singh et al., 2008). Companies are starting to acknowledge the potential of social media: today, 39% of companies use social media channels as their primary digital tool to reach customers, and that percentage is arguably expected to rise to 47% within the next four years (Divol, Edelman, & Sarrazin, 2012). More research is needed to better understand how social media has altered the brand relationships, in particular how it influences consumers to make choices and recommend products to their social networks.

Second, there is a demand for more quantitative and qualitative research to understand how social media has already changed marketing strategies. Despite the existence of some early contributions in terms of both academic and grey literature on the relevance of social media, little consensus exists on its potential as a strategic marketing tool. Overall there is insufficient research on social media from the strategic perspective, leaving room for new inquiries in the area (Kim & Ko, 2010). Without knowing

Table 1. Overview of the existing social media literature

Author	Social Media Landscape	New Brand Relationships	Marketing Strategy	Social Media and Fashion
Constantinides et al. (2008)			✓	
Edelman et al. (2010)	✓	✓	✓	
Divol et al. (2012)	✓	✓	✓	
Hanna et al. (2012)	✓			
Kim & Ko (2010)	✓		✓	✓
Kim & Ko (2012)			✓	✓
Kaplan & Haenlein (2010)	✓			
Kaplan & Haenlein (2011)	✓		✓	
Kietzmann et al. (2011)	✓			
Okonkwo (2010)	✓			✓
✓ *The topic has been investigated by the author(s)*				

how social media impacts marketing strategies, companies run the risk of focusing on the wrong targets, wasting time and money on ineffective efforts, and generally failing to harness its potential (Divol et al., 2012).

Finally, the relationships between social media and fashion require further interrogation. The early literature that exists is often focused on other industries and refers to fashion sector as the "laggards", those that were reluctant or slow to embrace social media (e.g., Okonkwo, 2010; Tungate, 2009). Additional research can propose how fashion brands can capitalize on social media, and how these companies can successfully incorporate social media into their overall branding and marketing strategies towards the achievement of new forms of sustainable competitive advantage in the global market place. As new channels of communication emerge through digital and social media, an increased number of designers are questioning traditional marketing formats (Michault, 2009). To maintain a competitive edge, many fashion companies have sought new digital strategies to reach consumers. For example, exclusive runways shows are arguably no longer the most practical way of promoting labels, and some companies elect to live stream catwalk shows straight to audiences at home (Michault, 2009; Nguyen, 2011). This study aims to provide novel insights that are of practical relevance to industry professionals, as companies struggle to understand how social media can contribute to brand building and marketing by involving consumers in the creation, delivery, and dissemination of brand messages.

EVOLVING SOCIAL MEDIA ENVIRONMENT

There currently exists a rich and diverse ecology of social media sites, which vary in scope and functionality (Kietzmann et al., 2011). Despite the increasing interest in and usage of social media, the establishment of systematic categorization schemes for different social media applications is in its infancy. Furthermore, as new sites appear daily and are replacing some of the existing platforms, it is important that any classification or framework is flexible and takes this ongoing growth into account, such as new applications that may be forthcoming.

For the purpose of our research, we define social media as a group of Internet-based applications that build on the ideological and technological foundations of Web 2.0, and that allow the creation and sharing of user-generated content (Kaplan & Haenlein, 2010, 2011; Kietzmann et al., 2011). Moreover, the focus of this classification is on the integration across the distinct social media channels. Within this general definition, there are various types of social media that need further differentiation.

One of the more established taxonomy of social media is the one provided by Kaplan and Haenlein (2010). In order to introduce their taxonomy, they rely on a set of theories within the field of media research (social presence, media richness) and social processes (self-presentation, self-disclosure), and present six different types of social media: collaborative projects (e.g., Wikipedia), blogs and microblogs (e.g., Twitter), content communities (e.g., YouTube), social networking sites (e.g., Facebook), virtual game worlds (e.g., World of Warcraft), and virtual social worlds (e.g., Second Life). Applications within these platforms include blogs, picture sharing, wall-postings, email, instant messaging, music sharing, crowdsourcing and others (Kaplan & Haenlein, 2010).

Through the numerous social media applications and technologies available, the rise of visual content sharing sites in recent years has introduced further changes to the social media landscape across industries (Pew Research Center, 2013). The explosive growth of the latest visual content sites such as Pinterest, Instagram, and Vine illustrates how visual content is becoming increasingly important in social media – especially in an industry like fashion which is heavily focused on aesthetics and visual representations (Workman & Caldwell, 2007). In the current social media landscape, fashion brands are experimenting with the power of visual content, using images and videos to build awareness and encourage consumer engagement (Arthur, 2013; Bautista, 2013a; Wasserman, 2012). In parallel with this trend toward the visual, Pinterest is currently growing faster than any other website (Bautista, 2013b; Reuters, 2013). While Facebook still reigns supreme in the social media landscape engaging 67% of all users, the latest study by Pew Research Center (2013) shows that consumers today are pinning just as much as they are tweeting. In 2012, Twitter attracted 16% of social media users followed by 15% on Pinterest (Pew Research Center, 2013).

For the purposes of this chapter, we use a subset of the classification scheme derived from the taxonomy introduced by Kaplan and Haenlein (2010), by focusing on three major groups: social networking sites (Facebook), blogs and microblogs (Twitter) and content sharing sites. The latter particularly focuses on the visual content sharing sites such as Pinterest, Instagram, Tumblr, Vimeo and Vine, which are extensively used by fashion companies and that are widespread amongst consumers within the fashion industry (Arthur, 2013; Bautista, 2013a; Wasserman, 2012).

TOWARDS NEW BRAND RELATIONSHIPS

Two decades after its commercial launch, the Internet has become a significant distribution channel and a leading source of consumer information and empowerment (Constantinides, Lorenzo, & Gómez, 2008; Doherty & Ellis-Chadwick, 2010; Goldsmith & Goldsmith, 2002). Moreover, through the rise of digital and social media in recent years, the online environment is in the middle of the greatest revolution in its history so far (Papathanassopoulos, 2011). New applications of social communication technologies are replacing the previous dependence that brands traditionally had on mass print media.

The emergence and proliferation of the Internet and social media have not only transformed the media environment, but have also altered the relationship between brands and consumers (Hanna et al., 2011). Today, subsets of consumers are strongly engaged with brands, publicly promoting or assailing their products, thus collaborating in brand building and challenging and shaping their meanings (Divol et al., 2012). Edelman (2010) notes that as a result of these changes, traditional ways of doing business have become unsustainable for many organizations that have previously primarily relied on print marketing campaigns. Therefore, new marketing models must be explored, developed and tested.

Traditionally, marketing's primary goal has been to reach consumers at the moments, or "touch points", which influence their purchasing behavior (Singh et al., 2008). Before the digital revolution, the general conception among marketers was that consumers started with a wide selection of brands in mind and stepwise narrowed their choices to arrive at a final selection and subsequently make purchase decisions. Companies typically used paid-media and push marketing at a few specific touch points along the decision process to increase awareness and ultimately encourage purchase (Edelman, 2010; Singh et al., 2008). Today, this linear "funnel metaphor" fails to capture the shifting nature of consumer engagement; new research by Edelman (2010) and Divol et al. (2012) shows that rather than systematically narrowing their choices, consumers add and subtract brands from a group under consideration during an extended evaluation stage.

Edelman (2010) proposes an alternative model, the new "consumer decision journey", for understanding how consumers interact with brands during purchase decisions. Describing consumer behavior as a winding journey with multiple feedback loops (Edelman, 2010), Edelman defines social media as a unique component during the extended decision process. After a purchase, consumers enter into an open-ended relationship with the brand, evaluating a shifting range of options and sharing their experiences online. Social media is arguably a prominent marketing channel to reach consumers at every step of this journey; from the beginning when consumers are assessing brands and products right through the period after the purchase, as their experience influences the brands and their advocacy inspires other consumers (Edelman, 2010; Singh et al., 2008).

Despite the suggested changes in the decision-making journey, consumers still desire a clear brand promise and brand offerings they value. Hence, the base role of marketing remains unchanged: as suggested by Edelman (2010) "what has changed is when – at what touch points – they are most open to influence, and how you can interact with them at those points" (p. 64). In the past, companies invested extensive resources into building brand awareness through traditional paid media. Today it is evident that touch points have evolved and traditional marketing methods no longer reach consumers in an optimal way. As a result, marketing strategies and budgets require a major revision and realignment with customers' purchase behavior and engagement patterns.

These recent developments have altered the way fashion brands communicate with consumers and market and sell their products (Bautista, 2013a; Kim & Ko, 2010; Wright, 2011). Social media have given consumers more control of content development and opened up direct channels for conversation and collaboration. Moreover, the rise of visual social media platforms in recent years has helped to make this dialogue more appealing, inviting millions of new consumers to engage with branded content (Pew Research Center, 2013). The recent advances in social media coupled with consumer indifference to traditional marketing tools force fashion brands to seek new opportunities; the desire is that marketing messages not only capture consumers' attention, but also engage them with the company (Singh et al., 2008). Social media is arguably an effective channel to achieve this aim, yet it requires careful management and integration not only across the different platforms, but also with the brands' overall marketing strategy.

SOCIAL MEDIA AND MARKETING STRATEGIES

Recent contributions have raised the issues of the compatibility of fashion and the Internet, the suitability of fashion products in the virtual environment and strategic approaches to maximizing a fashion brand's presence online (Atwal & Williams, 2009). Others have indicated that the Internet presents a "dilemma" that fashion firms require to overcome through avoiding e-Commerce (Tungate, 2009), whereas various literature have suggested that the Internet is purely a channel of communications for fashion brands (Okonkwo, 2009, 2010).

In addition to the instability brought by the digital era, during the last two decades the fashion industry is finding itself in a state of constant evolution and transformation. Globalization, mergers and acquisitions, and technological developments have drastically changed its retailing landscape (Doherty & Ellis-Chadwick, 2010; Okonkwo, 2010; Tungate, 2009). In this context, the explosive growth of the Internet and social media has been one of the main catalysts in this process. The effects of digital and social media have been mostly felt in retail sectors dealing mainly with intangibles or information products. However, these are not likely to be limited to these sectors; increasingly retailers of physical products such as the ones in the fashion sector realize that the empowered, sophisticated, critical and well-informed consumer of today is essentially different to the consumer they have always known. The web, and particularly social media, have given consumers much more control, information and power, posing fashion brands with a number of important dilemmas and challenges.

One of the main advantages of relying on social media is that consumers can access richer information, due not only to the fact that this information can be of higher quality or more trustworthy (e.g., other users' opinions from a virtual community), but also due to fact that the information can be easily processed (e.g., using different applications for comparing prices or product features) and edited (Edelman, 2010; Divol et al., 2012). Information accessibility, availability, quality, and comparability are clearly reinforced. Simultaneously, brands have additional tools and resources in place for delivering a better shopping experience, improving their originality, and enhancing consumer experiences on the web. Moreover, more products are bought online due to the additional option of customization. In addition, social media can reduce risks and uncertainty of shopping online. Their main advantage is the new interactive and social dimension. This interaction both with the brands and other consumers can enhance consumer confidence and trust (e.g., live agents, virtual communities) and improve consumer service (e.g., chat or live agents, Internet-based telephony applications). At the same time, the shopping experience is improved both by richer stimuli and by different tools that allow a more enjoyable and easier interaction with the web site (Doherty & Ellis-Chadwick, 2010; Okonkwo, 2010).

The process of adopting social media as part of the company's marketing program requires new thinking and new tactics; traditional push marketing methods are incompatible with social networking (Li, Bernoff, & Feffer, 2007; Singh et al., 2008). Lack of experience in engaging social media as marketing communication tools means that for many pioneers this is still a trial-and-error process. In this respect, there is a considerable knowledge gap in the real nature and importance of Web 2.0 and its added value for marketing strategy. Most knowledge of the role of Web 2.0 applications as marketing tools is primarily based on anecdotal evidence. Paradoxically, this evidence also suggests the majority of firms pioneering in engaging social media as a marketing tool are large corporations. Based on field experience, this chapter outlines three digital strategies that fashion brands can follow in order to extract value from the strategic use of social media.

Constantinides et al., (2008) identify three ways in which brands can capitalize on the use of social media, in particular this might occur when:

1. **Engaging Social Media as Public Relations (PR) and Direct Marketing Tools:** Several businesses are actively engaged in dialogue with the customer by launching their own corporate blogs and discussion forums. Business executives post daily on their corporate blogs, encouraging customers to interact and freely express their feelings, ideas, suggestions or remarks about their postings, the company or its products. A widely applied variant of this strategy (initiated by Microsoft in 2003) is to encourage company employees to become publishers of content themselves in corporate blogs and forums. An alternative and more simple way to engage social media as a PR tool is to use content communities like the video sharing sites YouTube, Vimeo and others as broadcasting media for distributing advertising material. Commercials uploaded to these sites have the potential to be viewed by thousands or even millions of viewers or virally distributed among users at marginal or no cost.

2. **Engaging Social Media Personalities for Customer Influence:** This approach is based on proactively engaging the online sources of customer influence (blogs, podcasts, online forums etc.) as customer influence tools. This requires identifying, reaching and informing the trendsetters or the

"new influencers" (Gillin, 2007) about the firm, its brands or its new product offers. The objective is to attract the attention of leading blogs or users' forums so that they review, discuss, comment on or recommend the firm's products. Besides obtaining and engaging these sources as company advocates, brands can also reach very specific consumers' segments by advertising in well-selected blogs and special interest networks or communities. This enables immediate access to target markets, even to very specific market segments at a fraction of the costs required by traditional media.

3. **Engaging Social Media for Personalizing the Customer's Online Experience:** This approach could lead to closer ties between the customer and the brand by offering customers the opportunity to personalize their online experiences in an environment created and controlled by the firm itself. Many brick-and-mortar firms are already experimenting with such tactics as part of their direct marketing: seeking communication, interaction, and customer feedback. They do this by introducing web sites based on user-generated content, encouraging customers to customize them to their needs, and often create their own social networks. There are two ways in which this mainly occurs. One way is tapping and disseminating customer creativity in the form of advertising concepts or product reviews which is likely to increase customer goodwill and advocacy. A growing number of corporations are partnering with talented amateurs who review their products, generate advertising concepts or even create TV commercials for them. The idea behind such partnerships is that advertisements created by peers are perceived as being more credible and, therefore, more effective than those created by advertising experts. Another way is making the customer a co-producer. The latter variant of utilizing customer creativity is capitalizing on growing customer individualism by making online tools available that allow partial or full customization of the company's products.

The three strategies are further explored through case studies of three different fashion companies by critically assessing their social media strategy. The next section illustrates the methods that were adopted for the research.

METHODS

In line with the exploratory nature of the study, the current research relied on comparative case study research to critically assess the social media campaigns of three fashion companies. "Case studies represent a methodology that is ideally suited to creating managerially relevant knowledge" (Gibbert & Ruigrok, 2010) and they are considered the most appropriate as tools in the critical, early phases of a new management theory, when key variables and their relationships are being explored (Eisenhardt, 1989; Yin, 2008). Therefore, case study research is particularly useful at the early stages of theory development, in which key themes and categories have yet to be empirically isolated (Eisenhardt, 1989; Elg & Johansson, 1997; Yin, 2008). Although we acknowledge the richness of adopting a single case study, multiple case studies provide a more solid basis for generalization and can provide substantial opportunities for theory-building (Dyer & Wilkins, 1991).

As illustrated in Table 2, we purposefully selected three case studies of fashion companies (Donna Karan, Calvin Klein, and Burberry) to illustrate the strategic use of social media in the fashion industry.

These fashion companies were chosen as they all offer a very diversified product range. Donna Karan and Calvin Klein are from the USA and Burberry is from the UK. In particular, while Burberry and Calvin Klein can be considered heritage brands for the UK and the USA respectively, Donna Karan is

Table 2. Overview of case companies

Company	Founded	Country	Short Description
Donna Karan	1984	USA	An international New York-based fashion house designing and marketing men's and women's clothing, sportswear, accessories and shoes through its own retail stores, department stores and specialty stores worldwide. Donna Karan International is part of the publicly traded LVMH Group since 2001.
Calvin Klein	1968	USA	A New York-based fashion house designing and marketing women's and men's collections from apparel, accessories, underwear and fragrances, to home furnishings through an extensive network of licensing agreements and other retail formats worldwide. The company is publicly listed.
Burberry	1856	UK	An international UK-based fashion house designing, manufacturing and marketing men's, women's and children's clothing and non-apparel accessories globally through a diversified network of retail (including digital), wholesale and franchise channels worldwide. The firm is publicly listed.

of more recent establishment. Owning to the diversity of their retail operations ranging from a very narrow retail format such as own stores and flagship stores to a very diversified network of retail platforms they represent three emblematic examples of fashion brands and they all implement substantially very different digital strategies. In the light of both the exploratory nature of the study and the wide variety of the fashion brands' features, three case-studies was deemed as adequate to provide rich insights over the use of social media in the fashion industry.

The fashion industry was deemed as the ideal industry setting for the study since it is by definition a very creative industry (Vecchi, 2008) which is consumer-driven (Mosca, 2008), and where establishing empathy with the final consumers is of paramount importance (Venturi, 2011). Additionally, the choice of the sector was driven by the acknowledgment that in the creative industries, technology adoption is considered to be more extensive than in any other sector (Florida & Gates, 2001).

Data collection for each case study relied on the adoption of the following research protocol as outlined in the Table 3 below.

In order to produce three robust case studies, we relied on a wide variety of sources ranging from secondary sources such as newspapers, industry reports, and grey literature through primary sources by the means of online observations and content analysis.

First, in order to contextualize the brand within the broader development of the company we collected information about the *company background*. Second, in order to contextualize the social media strategy within the broader marketing strategy adopted, we collected information about the *company history*. While these two case study dimensions were investigated by mostly consulting secondary sources such as industry reports and grey literature, the brand's *social media strategy* was critically assessed by relying on primary data collection. More precisely, as previously completed by Ross (2010) and Nguyen

Table 3. Research protocol

Case Study Dimension	Research Objective	Sources of Evidence
Company background	To contextualize the brand within the broader development of the company	Secondary literature Grey literature
Company history	To contextualize the social media strategy within the broader marketing strategy adopted	Secondary literature Grey literature
Social media strategy	To contextualize the social media strategy adopted in relation to the specific brand	Online observations and content analysis

(2011), the investigation of the social media strategy relied on a qualitative online observations of the aforementioned three fashion brands whose social media activities across several social media were observed. For the purpose of the study, these were deliberately restricted to Youtube, Facebook, Twitter, Tumblr, and Pinterest. Social media activity was then observed from January to June, 2013. More specifically, as part of the qualitative observations of the brands' social media activities, these were assessed in relation to their content and according to the theoretical framework previously described in the literature review (Constantinides et al., 2008).

Amongst the five most common qualitative research methods used are structured observation and content analysis (Silverman, 2003). "Content analysis is an accepted method of textual investigation, particularly in the field of mass communications" (Silverman, 2003, p. 123), and as content analysis was also used for either text-based or image-based analysis from visual material such as web-sites and social media platforms this was considered the most viable methodology. The method of content analysis either text-based or image-based combined with structured observations makes for an analysis "that will not be considered woolly but rigorous, reliable and objective" (Rose, 2003, p. 55).

FINDINGS

We analyzed the social media campaigns of the three purposefully selected fashion companies to illustrate their use of social media: Donna Karan, Calvin Klein, and Burberry. In the case of Donna Karan, the social media strategy is mainly driven by its DKNY brand as explained in the following sections.

Donna Karan

Company Background

Launched in 1984, Donna Karan International is a wholly-owned subsidiary of LVMH with approximately 2,000 employees (LVMH Annual Report, 2012). The company's second line DKNY was introduced in 1989, and it is considered to be one of the most successful launches in the fashion sector (Moore, Fernie, & Burt, 2000). The development of the company's marketing strategy can be summarized in the following key milestones as depicted in Table 4.

Company History

Donna Karan International was created by the designer and entrepreneur Donna Karan and her sculptor husband Stephan Weiss in 1984. The two teamed up as co-chief executives of the new design company, and Karan showed her first collection in 1985 (Sischy, 2004). Her clothing line offered women an elegant, classic alternative to the often uncomfortable designs of the day (Moore et al., 2000). Karan was a risk-taker; she broke new ground by designing practical, comfortable, refined garments that were well received by women. For her efforts, Karan was awarded the Council of Fashion Designers of America's (CFDA) Designer of the Year Award in 1985. Throughout the middle and late 1980s Karan relied primarily on her Donna Karan New York collection of upscale clothing that was originally launched in 1985 (Sischy, 2004).

Table 4. Donna Karan's marketing strategy development and its milestones

Year	Milestone
1984	Donna Karan, with the help of husband Stephan Weiss, forms Donna Karan New York.
1985	The first Donna Karan New York collection is introduced; Karan is named Designer of the Year by the Council of Fashion Designers of America (CFDA).
1989	DKNY is launched.
1990	DKNY Jeans hit stores; Karan's wins the second CFDA Designer of the Year award.
1992	Karan's first menswear collection, signature fragrance, and DKNY Kids are introduced.
1993	DKNY Men, a more casual line of menswear, is introduced.
1994	The first DKNY store opens in London.
1996	Donna Karan International goes public on the New York Stock Exchange; a DKNY store opens in Manchester, England.
1998	DKNY stores open in Beverly Hills, Las Vegas, Manhasset (New York), and Short Hills (New Jersey).
1999	Two DKNY fragrances are launched through Estée Lauder; five more stores open across US.
2000	Four more DKNY stores open, and several new products are rolled out including DKNY jeans for juniors, DKNY watches through Swatch and Fossil, and scarves through Mantero.
2001	Luxury group LVMH acquires the company.
2002	DKNY Kids is re-launched through a deal with CWF.
2009	The fictional social media persona, DKNY PR Girl, is launched on Twitter and Tumblr.
2009	DKNY PR Girl wins the Best Twitter Award in Fashion 2.0 Awards for the first time.
2012	DKNY enters China and open its first store in Russia.
2013	DKNY PR Girl wins the Best Twitter in Fashion 2.0 Awards for the fourth year in a row.

In 1987, Karan jumped into the very competitive hosiery business, convinced women would be willing to spend more money for better quality hosiery. In 1989, Karan launched her second line dubbed "DKNY". The DKNY line was designed to provide stylish, casual, and affordable clothing for a less elite market segment. The apparel was still expensive, but it brought an entirely new and much broader range of customers to Karan's designs. The introduction of the DKNY line is considered one of the most successful launches in fashion industry generating approximately US$115 million in sales in 1989 (Moore et al., 2000).

Encouraged by the remarkable gains, Karan pushed ahead with her plans for new products ranging from fragrance and accessories to children's clothing. The company started selling clothes in Germany and Japan as early as 1986, and opened a store in London in 1989 (Fernie, Moore, Lawrie, & Hallsworth, 1997; Moore et al., 2000). To help make the transition from a family-owned business to a more formal corporate entity, Karan hired an apparel industry consultant Stephen Ruzow, who was mainly hired to eliminate production problems and to improve quality control.

In 1992, Karan extended the design house's reach further with the introduction of men's clothing under the DKNY label. DKI began licensing its name for products ranging from intimate apparel and furs to shoes and eyewear. The company also launched a more aggressive overseas strategy, started Donna Karan Beauty Company, and tried to market its own fragrance rather than hire an outside marketing firm (Fernie et. al., 1997). Early results from the sales campaign were disappointing, and problems started in the form of financial losses, late deliveries and insufficient cash flows (Sischy, 2004). The additions of the men's line and beauty business were both expensive efforts, which combined with other large investments loaded the company with debt. By 1993, DKI was making heavy losses and struggled under its debt load. The company started to restructure its debt, cut the unnecessary costs and restructure its management team.

As the company's finances stabilized, sales growth continued at a rampant pace, helped by the opening of a new London flagship store and the launch of the first in-house magazine (Moore et al., 2000). Substantial gains came from several DKI operations, including the DKNY lines and the once-lagging beauty business. Internationalization also started to develop with the establishment of distribution centers in Hong Kong, Amsterdam, and Japan, as well as 15 freestanding stores in Europe, Asia, and the Middle East (Fernie et. al., 1997). In 1996, Donna Karan International went public on the New York Stock Exchange. The opening of new stores in London and Manchester occurred over the following three years; Las Vegas and Beverly Hills; Short Hills and New Jersey; the sale of Donna Karan Beauty to Estée Lauder; the introduction of DKNY jeans, DKNY underwear, coat collections and a home furnishings line. Two scents, DKNY Men and DKNY Women, debuted in 1999.

After a slew of losses, DKI ended the new century with an upswing in sales, and in 2000, rumors began to circulate that the French luxury group LVMH Moët Hennessey – Louis Vuitton, was interested in DKI. The acquisition for US$500 million was completed in early 2001 (Carr, 2013). Karan's husband Weiss died in June 2001, and while Karan was devastated by this loss, she went on designing for her next New York show scheduled for September 11 in 2001. Due to the World Trade Center tragedy, the show was cancelled. In November, 2001, Karan sold DKI's manufacturing and distribution units to LVMH for US$243 million while she remained as the Chief Designer and Chief Creative Officer of the company (Sischy, 2004). Although Donna Karan was still considered one of the most important designers in New York, the first decade of the 21st century was difficult both for DKI and for Donna Karan.

According to the LHMV Annual Report in 2009, Donna Karan started recovering by moving forward with its marketing strategy. The key focus was on the qualitative expansion of the brand's distribution network combined with efforts to intensify the spirit of its designs, always reflecting the pulse of New York, so central to brand's values. According to the report, this was coupled by implementing a strong and convincing social media strategy to further promote the DKNY brand (LHMV Annual Report, 2012).

Social Media Strategy

A major turning point in DKNY's social media strategy can be traced to 2009 when a new anonymous Twitter persona, *DKNY PR Girl,* was created. The Twitter account was launched in April, 2009 followed by the creation of a DKNY PR Girl Tumblr blog a few months later. At the time of the launch, DKNY had an existing YouTube channel, a mobile application and a Facebook account, which were further strengthened through the new DKNY PR girl strategy.

As stated by the PR Girl's Twitter bio, she is the "well-placed fashion source bringing the consumer behind-the-scenes scoop from inside Donna Karan New York and DKNY and her life as a PR girl living in NY" (https://twitter.com/dkny). Her filter-less, insider, and funny tweets have successfully appealed to consumers' emotions and accumulated more than 450,000 Twitter followers to date. After maintaining her anonymity for two years, DKNY PR Girl revealed herself on February, 2012 as Aliza Licht, the Senior Vice President (SVP) for Global Communications at Donna Karan International (Chang, 2012). In March, 2013, DKNY PR Girl won the Best Twitter Award for the fourth year in a row at the Fashion 2.0 Awards.

DKNY's fictional Twitter persona DKNY PR Girl set and still holds the standard for what fashion brands can accomplish on Twitter (and Tumblr) (Chang, 2012). The brand's innovative use of Twitter is an emblematic example of how fashion brands can use social media as a PR and direct marketing tool (Constantinides et al., 2008) by interacting with consumers' emotions on a very personal level.

According to an interview given in occasion of the Luxury Roundtable: State of Luxury 2013 Conference in New York, Aliza Licht discussed how the brand leverage social media to drive evangelism and brand loyalty (Fiorletta on "Donna Karan Exec Shares Social Media Best Practices, 8 May 2013). "*It's called social media for a reason,*" explained Aliza Licht "*It's not called "push media" or "message board media". You're meant to engage. In the luxury industry, the whole concept of engaging can be scary. Brands think that in doing so, they're giving away their "secret sauce" or what makes them coveted, but that's not the case*". Rather than sharing promotional information with consumers at their leisure, fashion brands should use social media to respond to inquiries and generate genuine conversations with their customers, Licht explained (Fiorletta, 2013).

Since the inception of the DKNY PR Girl Twitter account in 2009, the company has expanded its social presence tremendously. The SVP of Global Communications, Aliza Licht, has transformed DKNY's marketing efforts with her implementation of the new social media strategy. Not only has she elevated Donna Karan's rank in L2's, "The Digital IQ Index: Fashion Study", but has also set the bar extremely high for other competing fashion brands to follow (Carr, 2013). By having a PR representative openly control all social media platforms, DKNY was able to establish a transparent, consistent social media strategy that enables authentic conversations with the customers. By providing interesting and relatable material surrounding the brand, the DKNY PR Girl approach is personable, hilarious and strategic.

Calvin Klein

Company Background

Calvin Klein Inc. is a fashion company founded in 1968 by Calvin Klein. The company is headquartered in Manhattan, New York City and currently owned by Phillips-Van Heusen. The company was incorporated in 1967 as Calvin Klein, Ltd. The development of the Calvin Klein's marketing strategy can be summarized in several milestones as depicted in Table 5.

Company History

Calvin Klein, Inc. designs, licenses, and, in some cases, produces clothing, accessories, fragrances, and home furnishings bearing the name of the designer Calvin Klein. Born and raised in New York City, Calvin Klein graduated from the Fashion Institute of Technology in 1963. He worked for women's coat and suit manufacturers in the Manhattan's garment district before starting his own firm in 1968. One of his childhood friends, Barry Schwartz, loaned him $10,000 in start-up money and joined the firm a month later (ME, 2013).

Klein initially rented a dingy showroom to exhibit a very small line of samples. His success came when a vice-president at Bonwit Teller stopped with the lift on the wrong floor, liked the collection, and invited Klein to bring his samples to the president's office. Klein wheeled the rack of clothes personally and won an order of US$50,000 immediately. Teller gave the merchandise impressive exposure, and soon after, Calvin Klein was besieged by orders.

Table 5. Calvin Klein's marketing strategy development and its key milestones

Year	Milestone
1968	Calvin Klein Ltd. is incorporated.
1973	Klein wins his first Coty American Fashion Critics Award.
1979	Calvin Klein controls one-fifth of the designer jeans market.
1982	Calvin Klein enters the underwear business.
1985	A new perfume called Obsession is launched with a $17 million advertising campaign.
1989	A Unilever Co. subsidiary purchases the Calvin Klein cosmetics and fragrance line.
1994	A unisex fragrance, CK One, is introduced; the company's underwear business is licensed to Warnaco Group Inc.
2000	Klein files a lawsuit against Warnaco Group and its CEO Linda Wachner.
2003	Phillips-Van Heusen Corporation acquires Calvin Klein.
2007	Mobile applications and social media are introduced to Calvin Klein's marketing strategy.
2012	Tumblr collaboration with Hanneli Mustaparta is launched.

Klein mainly designed women's coats and two-piece suits until 1972 when he started expanding to sporty sweaters, skirts, dresses, shirts, and pants that could be mixed and matched for a complete wardrobe. In 1875, the firm shipped US$12 million worth of merchandise, and earned another US$2 – 6 million from licensing. Klein not only designed every item but also closely watched every step of the production process (ME, 2013). Since the prices were generally below those of its major competitors, the firm was able to gain the loyalty of young working women as well as wealthier buyers.

In 1978, Klein introduced his first menswear collection followed by his own line of fragrances and a complete makeup collection. Moreover, Calvin Klein jeans were quickly becoming the company's greatest hit due to high profile advertising campaigns (Schroeder, 2000). The biggest lift to the jeans line was a television campaign directed by Richard Avedon that featured 15-year-old actress Brooke Shields provocatively posed in a skin-tight pair of CK jeans (Schroeder, 2000; Tucker, 1998). In 1982, Calvin Klein entered the underwear business, once again exploiting the allure of youth in provocative poses to push the brand. Klein continued to design and promote women's underwear, later adding hosiery and sleepwear lines.

The fragrance Obsession was launched in 1985. Again, Calvin Klein created a heavy-breathing print and TV campaign, followed by another big campaign for the Obsession Men's fragrance. Obsession soon became one of the best selling fragrances in the world (Schroeder, 2000). In 1988, Calvin Klein introduced a new floral scent, Eternity. This time, Klein, who had recently married, devised a softer promotional campaign based on the themes of spirituality, love, marriage, and commitment (Tucker, 1998).

In 1991, Calvin Klein introduced a new scarf collection. Later that year, the company resumed its menswear line and licensed it, along with the eyewear and sunglasses bearing the designer's name. Despite significant royalty payments and own sales operations, the company started falling into financial troubles in the new decade (ME, 2013).

Calvin Klein, Inc. was restored to financial health in 1994 through the efforts of David Geffen, an entertainment tycoon who was a long-time friend of the designer. Geffen bought Calvin Klein's fading jeans business for about US$50 million. Calvin Klein introduced a khaki collection in 1996 and licensed it, along with CK Calvin Klein Jeans Kids and CK Calvin Klein Kids Underwear, also introduced that year.

Advertisements for Calvin Klein jeans continued to provoke controversy (Schroeder, 2000; Tucker, 1998). Posters featuring a notably skinny Kate Moss were festooned with stickers reading "Feed this woman". In 1996, an anti-drug group called for a boycott of Calvin Klein products to protest against a new advertisement campaign featuring skinny and glassy-eyed models, as they claimed the campaign mostly glamorized heroin addiction. The magazine and television advertisements in question provoked substantial losses, and in 2000 the company was put on sale.

After three years of seeking a suitable buyer, Klein and Schwartz stroke a deal with Phillips-Van Heusen Corporation, the largest shirt maker in the USA. The US$430 million transaction was completed in February 2003 (ME, 2013). Under the terms of the deal, Klein remained a design consultant for Calvin Klein while the acquisition marked a new era for the brand. For the first time, Klein did not have complete control over the products sold under his name, and his partner Schwartz retired.

Social Media Strategy

Since the early 1990s, Calvin Klein's image has suffered. This can be attributed to the controversial advertising which was extensively employed as a part of the brand's marketing strategy (Schroeder, 2000; Tucker, 1998). After the acquisition in 2003, the company started to introduce social media to its marketing strategy with the attempt to re-launch the brand. Taking full advantage of one of its most successful campaigns from the 1990s, Calvin Klein began to revamp its approach to consumers. *CK One*, the name of its most popular unisex fragrance, became one of Calvin Klein's first global digital campaigns.

Aiming to appeal to a wider audience and to regain its popularity, Calvin Klein took further steps with its social media strategy in 2007. This time, the company approached social media with a younger generation in mind, investing in mobile applications and novel advertising concepts. These initiatives opened the brand to a new digital savvy audience, allowing customers to interact and engage with the brand at a whole new level, for example posting videos of themselves and talking about the brand on the *CK One* website. The new social media strategy was further supported by the company's Facebook page and Twitter account.

A successful example of engaging social media personalities for customer influence (Constantinides et al., 2008) is Calvin Klein's latest blogger collaboration. In May, 2012, the company expanded its social media reach through the launch of a Tumblr blog with the photographer, blogger and model, Hanneli Mustaparta serving as contributor (Davis, 2012). This official Calvin Klein Tumblr® blog, located at calvinklein.tumblr.com, provides readers a more editorial point of view of the brand, allowing them to browse through the company's current and archival advertising campaigns, and to explore inspiring visuals from the brands intersection with the worlds of art, architecture, style and music. Hanneli Mustaparta is providing content for her own designated category, #Hanneli, of the Calvin Klein Tumblr® blog. The blog is supported by the Calvin Klein's official Facebook page and Twitter account, which regularly promote her latest blog posts. The blogger first collaborated with Calvin Klein in February 2012 for the Fall 2012 runway show, providing behind the scenes photos that were posted on the brand's Twitter account. Calvin Klein's celebrity collaboration illustrates how the company has successfully identified a current trendsetter and social media personality and engaged her as an influential brand advocate.

Burberry

Company Background

Listed on the London Stock Exchange, Burberry Group plc is a British luxury fashion house designing and manufacturing clothing, fragrance, and fashion accessories. Established in 1891, it currently operates branded stores and franchises around the world. Burberry's trademark products are trench coats, handbags, and fragrances, and its distinctive check pattern has become one of the most widely copied trademarks in the fashion sector. Through a variety of pioneering digital initiatives, the current Chief Creative Officer, Christopher Bailey, has led the company into the digital era, shaping some of the old industry practices. The development of the company's marketing strategy can be summarized in the following milestones as shown in Table 6 (Moore & Britwistle, 2004; Kapferer, 2012):

Company History

Burberry Ltd. is a manufacturer and marketer of men's, women's, and children's apparel, as well as accessories and fragrances. The homonymous brand was established in 1891 by Thomas Burberry. He undertook an internship in the drapery trade and later established his own drapery business in Basingstoke in 1856. A sportsman, Burberry was dissatisfied with the then-popular mackintosh raincoat, which was heavy, restricting, stifling, and thus unsuitable for extended outings. Burberry designed a tightly woven fabric made from water-repellent linen or cotton yarn. Although sturdy and tear-resistant, this cloth

Table 6. Burberry's marketing strategy development and its key milestones

Year	Milestone
1856	Thomas Burberry establishes his first shop.
1891	Burberry is launched and the company starts selling clothing under the Burberry name in London's Haymarket section.
1909	The firm registers the "Equestrian Knight" trademark.
1915	Burberry ships its first raincoats to Japan.
1966	The firm becomes a wholly owned subsidiary of Great Universal Stores.
1994	The company begins using the well-known model Christy Turlington in its ad campaigns.
1996	Burberry has received a total of six Queen's Awards for Export Achievement and ranks among Great Britain's leading clothing exporters.
1997	Rose Marie Bravo is hired as CEO.
1998	The Asian economic crisis causes financial problems for the firm.
1999	Burberry Prorsum designer collection is launched.
2000	Burberry breaks ground on a new flagship store in London.
2001	Christopher Bailey joins Burberry as a Creative Director.
2002	Burberry Group plc is floated on the London Stock Exchange.
2006	Chief Executive Rose Marie Bravo, who as has led Burberry to mass market success, retires. Angela Ahrendts is appointed as the new CEO.
2009	Christopher Bailey becomes the Chief Creative Officer.
2010	The first live broadcast 3D of Burberry's fashion show.

was lightweight and allowed air to circulate, making it considerably more comfortable than the heavy mackintosh. The tailor trademarked this cloth as "Gabardine" (Moore & Britwistle, 2004).

Having used a variety of labels to distinguish its garments from imitations, the Burberry first registered the "Equestrian Knight" trademark in 1909, a logo used continuously through 19th century (Kapferer, 2012; Moore & Britwistle, 2004). By 1910, Burberry offered a broad line of outerwear. The company designed hats, jackets, pants, and gaiters especially for hunting, fishing, golf, tennis, skiing, archery and mountaineering. The garments' tested reputation for durability helped make them to become the gear of choice for adventurers (Moore & Britwistle, 2004). Burberry opened its first foreign outlet in Paris in 1910, and it soon had retail establishments in the USA and South America. The company exported its first shipment of raincoats to Japan in 1915. However, it was World War I which brought widespread acclamation and fame to Burberry. First worn by high-ranking generals during the turn-of-the-century Boer War, the Burberry coat was quickly adopted as standard issue for all British officers. With the addition of some military trappings, the garments came to be known as the "Trench Coat," so named for its ubiquity and its durability through trench warfare (Kapferer, 2012).

Burberry's export business increased dramatically during the 1980s, fuelled primarily by Japanese and American consumers craving for prestigious designer goods. Realizing that "a fine tradition is not in itself sufficient today," Burberry sought to broaden its appeal to a younger, more fashion-conscious female clientele. As a result, the Thomas Burberry collection, first introduced in Great Britain in 1988, was subsequently expanded to the USA two years later. The collection emphasized more casual sportswear, as opposed to career wear. At the upper end of the scale, the company launched a personal tailoring service for the ladies (Kapferer, 2012). Burberry garments enjoyed a loyal following among royalty and celebrities around the world and ranked among Great Britain's leading clothing exporters, receiving several Export Achievement Awards from Her Majesty Queen Elizabeth II and H.R.H. The Prince of Wales (Kapferer, 2012).

Although it continued to manufacture 90 percent of its merchandise in British factories, Burberry also started licensing its name, plaid, and knight logo to other manufacturers. By the mid-1990s, the Burberry name appeared on handbags and belts, throw pillows and boxer shorts, cookies and crackers, and fragrances and liquor. Childrenswear, stuffed toys, watches, handbags, golf bags, and even a co-branded VISA credit card displayed the Burberry logo. This was a turning point in the company's merchandising scheme nonetheless rainwear remained Burberry's single largest line into the late 1970s and early 1980s (Kapferer, 2012). Burberry's efforts at product and geographic diversification started to pay off in the mid-1990s (Moore & Britwistle, 2004).

Despite the diversification efforts, the company management recognized that the Burberry brand had lost the spark it once claimed. In 1997, Rose Marie Bravo was elected the new CEO. Her expertise in brand management fit in with company plans to strengthen the Burberry brand throughout the USA and Europe. While the company focused on positioning itself among the leaders in the fashion industry, it started facing problems caused by its over-dependence on Asian customers during the Asian economic crisis. As a major exporter, Burberry was also hurt by the strength of the British pound. The company began to slow down its shipments to the Asian market and shut down three production facilities in the United Kingdom. In 1999, the company profits continued to falter (Moore & Britwistle, 2004). Amidst its financial struggles, however, the company continued to focus on brand development and strong marketing. Under the leadership of Bravo, Burberry was once again re-emerging as an international luxury brand.

In 1999, the firm launched the Prorsum designer collection as part of its efforts to reinvent Burberry's luxury brand status. In 2000, Burberry operated 58 company-owned stores, and its products were also sold in department and specialty stores around the world (Moore & Britwistle, 2004). As Burberry entered the new millennium, its financial results improved dramatically (Kapferer, 2012). The Asian market recovered, its European and American markets grew, and the new marketing strategy was successful. The company opened new stores in Las Vegas, Nevada and Tokyo, Japan, and launched a new three-floor flagship store in London. In 2001, Burberry management continued to push the aggressive brand strategy and focused heavily on the USA and on European markets such as France and Italy. Burberry Group plc was initially floated on the London Stock Exchange in July, 2002.

By 2009, fashion house Burberry was feeling the pressure of the new economic downturn, even though its financials had been strong over the past decade. In this harsh reality of the retail environment, the company recognized the potential value of social media. Building a social media presence seemed critical, but the question was, "how"?

Social Media Strategy

In November, 2009, Christopher Bailey who had joined Burberry as a Creative Director in 2001 became the Chief Creative Officer. With some 175 million users on Facebook and 600,000 more joining it each day, Burberry made a strategic decision to allocate marketing and public relations spend and dedicated personnel to pursue new tech-age marketing. Burberry was the first luxury fashion brand to invest whole-heartedly in social media. Burberry's Facebook page now has more than 15 billion fans and its Twitter account has nearly 2 billion followers, way ahead of Louis Vuitton, Gucci and other luxury brands.

The so-called "digital revolution", led by Christopher Bailey was initially implemented with twofold aims to rejuvenate the brand and to streamline the organization. According to Phan, Thomas and Heine (2011), Burberry was the first fashion brand to broadcast its catwalk show live and in 3D from London to five international cities simultaneously in 2010. In April, 2011, Burberry staged a catwalk show in Beijing where live models were mixed with holograms, creating a groundbreaking unique experience for its audience. Videos from the show were immediately posted on YouTube resulting in massive numbers of views. The results were encouraging and Burberry was ranked the Best Luxury Brand in the Top Social Network ranking by Famecount in 2011, ahead of big brand names such as BMW and Chanel. In the overall brand category, Burberry spotted the 22nd position behind major consumer brands like Coca-Cola and Starbucks (www.famecount.com). Overall, the new digital strategy helped Burberry to rejuvenate and reposition the brand to attract younger consumers. The level of consumer engagement across the company's digital initiatives is extraordinary – Burberry's live shows are not merely a gim-mick but truly drive consumers to interact and push the purchase button. Burberry is often considered to be the "pioneer of all things digital in fashion", shaking and reshaping some of the old practices and structures in the somewhat conservative industry.

A pioneering example of engaging social media for personalizing the customer's online experience is Burberry's online project, "The Art of the Trench", winning prizes for digital innovation as the brand celebrates its heritage though social networking. "The Art of the Trench" is a social networking site that encourages visitors to upload pictures of themselves wearing a Burberry trench coat (Design Council, 2010). The site disseminates customer creativity by making customers' pictures part of Burberry's brand communication and thus distributing them to a wider audience. Moreover, "The Art of the Trench" is an innovative example of tapping into customer creativity and encouraging user-generated content. The concept builds on one specific element of the brand heritage, the trench coat, which is tangible and easy for consumers to relate to, regardless of their age. The campaign has been very well received from its outset: it attracted over 200,000 unique users and 3 million page views during only the first week after its launch (Design Council, 2010).

This example illustrates how fashion brands can utilize social media to allow customization, gauge the impact of a product and appeal to individual consumers' emotions (Constantinides et al., 2008). Moreover, the user involvement and social networking aspects of the site have helped the brand to change consumer perceptions and positioned Burberry firmly in the Web 2.0 world. Today it is considered a brand that – while representing tradition and vintage British styling – is also relevant to the modern consumer. Overall, the strategic use of social media has helped to bring a younger audience to the brand, building a new generation of Burberry wearers and enthusiasts along with remarkable sales (Design Council, 2010; Moore & Birtwistle, 2004; Wasserman, 2012).

CONCLUSION

Table 7 below outlines the effectiveness of the social media strategies implemented by the three fashion brands as measured by number of likes on Facebook, number of followers on Twitter, number of subscribers on their YouTube channel and number of followers on Pinterest.

While the value of these numbers is surely questionable, they need to be contextualized within the brands' respective digital strategies as they provide a useful indication of the different social media platforms on which these brands tend to rely the most. Quite interestingly, while the two heritage brands Calvin Klein and Burberry more extensively engage across all the distinct social media platforms (Calvin Klein does not focus on Pinterest but instead uses Tumblr for visual material as previously discussed), DKNY tends to rely more extensively on Twitter.

Arising from the discussion in the findings, Table 8 summarizes the different digital strategies implemented by the three fashion brands considered. Referring to the taxonomy previously introduced by Constantinides et al. (2008), DKNY seems to use social media as a PR and direct marketing tool, while Calvin Klein mostly engages with social media personalities and Burberry uses social media to allow customization.

Table 7. Overview of the case brands' social media presence on 30 June 2013

Brand	Facebook (Likes)	Twitter (Followers)	YouTube (Subscribers)	Pinterest (Followers)
DKNY	1,229,091	456, 181	2,212	13,275
Calvin Klein	7,252,805	722,415	17,384	n/a
Burberry	15,437,483	1,948,686	71,993	49,616

Table 8. Overview of the brands' digital strategies

Brand	Digital strategy
DKNY	Engaging social media as a PR and direct marketing tools
Calvin Klein	Engaging social media personalities for customer influence
Burberry	Engaging social media for personalizing the customer's online experience

Original Contribution of the Research

The importance of social media is evident as millions of people utilize it to connect with others, share content and discuss different topics. Despite its significant marketing potential, the literature review highlights how many fashion brands have been initially reluctant or unable to develop digital strategies and allocate resources to effectively engage with social media (Okonkwo, 2010; Tungate, 2009). As it emerges from our three case studies, this attitude has been changing in recent years, and social media such as YouTube, Facebook, Twitter, Tumblr, Instagram, Pinterest, Vimeo, and Vine have become an integral part of how fashion brands communicate with their consumers (Arthur, 2013; Bautista, 2013a; Kim & Ko, 2010; Nguyen, 2011; Wasserman, 2012), often providing new opportunities to enhance fashion firm's identity and brand equity (Vecchi & Kontu, 2012; Kim & Ko, 2012). In particular, by considering the three fashion brands we have seen how DKNY was able to use social media as a PR and direct marketing tool (as shown in the case of DKNY PR Girl), while Calvin Klein successfully engaged with social media personalities for customer influence as seen in the collaboration with Hanneli Mustaparta. Burberry has taken a step further by using social media to allow customization, gauge the impact of a product and appeal to individual consumers' emotions (as demonstrated by "The Art of the Trench"). By implementing social media strategies, despite a hesitant start, fashion brands seem to start capitalizing on them (Constantinides et al., 2008). This shift raises the question of whether these brands from being the laggards are actually becoming the new leaders of the digital revolution.

Although fashion brands were cautious to embrace digital marketing, most brands are finding that e-commerce, mobile applications, and social media are some of the most efficient ways to engage with affluent consumers and to drive sales. Often viewed as slow-to-the-game or too hesitant as compared to mainstream brands, fashion marketers are slowly but surely fighting their way into the digital medium. Differently from previous studies (e.g., Okonkwo, 2010; Tungate, 2009), our findings tend to suggest that fashion brands are now well ahead of the game by starting to capitalize on the strategic use of social media. In particular, our findings illustrate how fashion brands are now finding new and unique tactics to share their own voices that connect to consumers in a manner that has not been done before.

By contrast, as found by Ross (2010) our findings support the idea that the extensive use of technology underwrites the literature on fashion marketing and that social media platforms are radically changing the fashion industry, its supply chain practices along with its consumer practices (Nguyen, 2011; Ross, 2010). We endorse the view that the digital revolution, led by pervasive approach of creativity and marketing, despite showing remarkable developments in recent times is still at the very early stage to accurately forecast what these fashion brands are going to be able to deliver.

Managerial Implications

Our findings illustrate how there is a perceptible shift in fashion marketing. Newer tools in marketing such as social media are giving fashion brands the option to not only address their audience but also to interact with them in real-time. Indeed, social media is single-handedly changing the face of fashion marketing. Accordingly, the rapid adoption of social media requires marketers to have a 360-degree strategy to deal with more discerning consumers. Our findings demonstrate that fashion marketing is evolving into two-way communication and social media play a pivotal role in this process. While initially considered digital late-comers (e.g., Okonkwo, 2010; Tungate, 2009), the findings from our three illustrative case studies outline how fashion brands have often found novel and creative ways to implement digital strategies aimed at PR and direct marketing (as in the case of DKNY), new ways to engage celebrities to endorse their products (as in the case of Calvin Klein), new solutions to tap into consumer's creativity in the form of advertising concepts and to make the customer a co-producer (as discussed in relation to Burberry).

In particular, our findings highlight some peculiarities in their use of social media and can surely provide useful lessons and valuable guidelines for companies in other creative sectors such as the design, the music, the film and the luxury industries. Social media were identified as a substantive method of promoting the fashion brands' identity by leveraging on consumers' emotions. Similarly, social media are increasingly employed to change consumers' perceptions of a fashion brand or a product. A very few fashion firms tend to use social media as a distribution channel – those pioneers who do appears to have fully understood the broader implications that social media utilization might have for traditional fashion retail and implement a digital strategy that can successfully capitalize on their complementarities and synergies. This could be seen as the biggest innovation and change in practice in recent times. From a marketing perspective, the valuable experience of the three fashion brands provides novel insights into fully reaping the benefits associated with social media capitalization.

Limitations and Directions for Future Research

Several limitations need to be acknowledged. In line with the exploratory ethos of the research, despite providing in-depth insights over some exemplary digital strategies implemented by fashion brands, our case studies mostly provide anecdotal evidence which is scarcely generalizable. We thus endorse the idea that a project involving a larger number of fashion brands as case studies could provide a fuller understanding on how social media has altered the brand relationships, in particular how it influences consumers to make purchase decisions and recommend products to their social networks. Despite relying on primary data collection such as observations and content analysis the study relies on qualitative data and on secondary data. In order to gain a fuller understanding of digital strategy implantation from the companies' perspective, employing primary data in the form of in-depth interviews with relevant managers would have been beneficial.

Similarly, conducting a large survey with consumers could have provided valuable insights over social media strategy implications in terms of purchase intentions and product recommendations. This led us to conclude that overall there is room for further quantitative and qualitative research to better identify the extent to which social media has already altered fashion marketing strategies and to assess the implications for fashion consumers. As such, there is a valuable opportunity to further undertake multi-disciplinary research to more closely investigate the broader impact that the implementation of an effective social media strategy might have on the firm supply chain practices and whether it can ultimately lead to the adoption of innovative business models that are, more congruent with the ever changing consumers needs both environmentally and ethically sustainable.

REFERENCES

Arthur, R. (2013). *Vine, Google+ take center stage at London fashion week*. Retrieved 12 March 2013 from http://mashable.com/2013/02/16/london-fashion-week-vine-video/

Atwal, G., & Williams, A. (2009). Luxury brand marketing – The experience is everything! *Journal of Brand Management, 16*(5–6), 338–346. doi:10.1057/bm.2008.48

Barnard, M. (1996). *Fashion as communication*. London: Routledge.

Bautista, C. (2013a). *How social media is making over the fashion industry*. Retrieved 16 March 2013 from: http://mashable.com/2013/02/15/fashion-social-media/

Bautista, C. (2013b). *Social media users say pinterest is as popular as Twitter*. Retrieved 16 March 2013 from http://mashable.com/2013/02/15/social-media-pew-study/

Carr, T. (2013). *Donna Karan: No one else can tell your brand story*. Retrieved 12 May 2013 from: http://www.luxurydaily.com/donna-karan-no-one-else-can-tell-your-brand-story/

Chang, B.-S. (2012). *P.R. girl revealed as P.R. executive*. Retrieved 15 November 2012 from http://www.nytimes.com/2012/02/16/fashion/aliza-licht-unnamed-twitter-fashion-star-comes-out-on-youtube.html?pagewanted=print

Constantinides, E., Lorenzo, C., & Gómez, M. A. (2008). Social media: A new frontier for retailers? *European Retail Research, 22,* 1–28.

Davis, M. (2012). *Hanneli Mustaparta for Calvin Klein Tumblr*. Retrieved 14 November 2012 from: http://fashionreporters.com/9663/hanneli-mustaparta-for-calvin-klein-tumblr/

Design Council. (2010). *Christopher Bailey: The art of the trench*. Retrieved 10 December 2012 from http://www.designcouncil.org.uk/about-design/Types-of-design/Fashion-and-textile-design/Burberry/

Divol, R., Edelman, D., & Sarrazin, H. (2012). *Demystifying social media*. Retrieved 15 May 2012 from: https://www.mckinseyquarterly.com/Demystifying_social_media_2958

Doherty, N., & Ellis-Chadwick, F. (2010). Internet retailing: The past, the present and the future. *International Journal of Retail & Distribution Management, 38*(11–12), 943–965. doi:10.1108/09590551011086000

Dyer, W. G., & Wilkins, A. L. (1991). Better stories, not better constructs, to generate better theory: A rejoinder to Eisenhardt. *Academy of Management Review, 16*(3), 613–619.

Edelman, D. C. (2007). From the periphery to the core: As online strategy becomes overall strategy, marketing organisations and agencies will never be the same. *Journal of Advertising Research, 47*(2), 130–134. doi:10.2501/S0021849907070146

Edelman, D. C. (2010). Branding in the digital age: You're spending your money in all the wrong places. *Harvard Business Review, 88,* 62–69.

Eisenhardt, K. M. (1989). Building theories from case study research. *Academy of Management Review, 14*(4), 532–550.

Elg, U., & Johansson, U. (1997). Decision making in inter-firm networks as a political process. *Organization Studies*, *18*, 361–384. doi:10.1177/017084069701800302

Fernie, J., Moore, C. M., Lawrie, A., & Hallsworth, A. (1997). The internationalization of the high fashion brand: The case of central London. *Journal of Product and Brand Management*, *6*(3), 151–162. doi:10.1108/10610429710175673

Fiorletta, A. (2013). *Donna Karan exec shares social media best practices*. Retrieved 11 May 2013 from: http://www.retailtouchpoints.com/shopper-engagement/2534-donna-karan-exec-shares-social-media-best-practices

Florida, R., & Gates, G. (2001). *Technology and tolerance: The importance of diversity to high-technology growth*. The Brookings Institution, Center on Urban and Metropolitan Policy.

Gibbert, M., & Ruigrok, W. (2010). The what and how of case study rigor: Three strategies based on published work. *Organizational Research Methods*, *13*(4), 710–737. doi:10.1177/1094428109351319

Gillin, P. (2007). *The new influencers, a marketer's guide to the new social media*. Sanger.

Goldsmith, R., & Goldsmith, E. (2002). Buying apparel over the Internet. *Journal of Product and Brand Management*, *11*(2), 89–102. doi:10.1108/10610420210423464

Hanna, R., Rohm, A., & Crittenden, V. L. (2011). We're all connected: The power of the social media ecosystem. *Business Horizons*, *54*(3), 265–273. doi:10.1016/j.bushor.2011.01.007

Kapferer, J.-N., & Bastien, V. (2012). *The luxury strategy: Break the rules of marketing to build luxury brands*. Philadelphia, PA: Kogan Page.

Kaplan, A. M., & Haenlein, M. (2010). Users of the world, unite! The challenges and opportunities of social media. *Business Horizons*, *53*(1), 59–68. doi:10.1016/j.bushor.2009.09.003

Kaplan, A. M., & Haenlein, M. (2011). Two hearts in three-quarter time: How to waltz the social media/viral marketing dance. *Business Horizons*, *54*(3), 253–263. doi:10.1016/j.bushor.2011.01.006

Kietzmann, J. H., Hermkens, K., McCarthy, I. P., & Silvestre, B. S. (2011). Social media? Get serious! Understanding the functional building blocks of social media. *Business Horizons*, *54*(3), 241–251. doi:10.1016/j.bushor.2011.01.005

Kim, A. J., & Ko, E. (2010). Impacts of luxury fashion brand's social media marketing on customer relationship and purchase intention. *Journal of Global Fashion Marketing*, *1*(3), 164–171. doi:10.1080/20932685.2010.10593068

Kim, A. J., & Ko, E. (2012). Do social media marketing activities enhance customer equity? An empirical study of luxury fashion brand. *Journal of Business Research*, *65*(10), 1480–1486. doi:10.1016/j.jbusres.2011.10.014

Li, C., Bernoff, J., Feffer, K. A., & Pflaum, C. N. (2007). Marketing on social networking sites. *Forrester Research*. Retrieved 14 September 2012 from http://www.forrester.com/Marketing+On+Social+Networking+Sites/fulltext/-/E-RES41662?docid=41662

LVMH. (2013). *Annual report 2012*. Retrieved 3 June 2013 from http://www.lvmh.com/uploads/assets/Com-fi/Documents/en/RA_LVMH_Complet_GB_2012.pdf

Maramotti, L. (2000). Connecting creativity. In S. Bruzzi & P. C. Gibson (Eds.), *Fashion cultures: Theories,explorations and analysis*. London: Routledge.

ME. (2013). *Calvin Klein's marketing strategy*. Retrieved 10 April 2013 from http://giantkillers13.wordpress.com/2013/03/27/calvin-klein-marketing-strategy/

Menkes, S. (2010). *Heritage luxury: Past becomes the future*. Retrieved 20 February 2013 from: http://www.nytimes.com/2010/11/09/fashion/09iht-rsuzy.html?pagewanted=all

Michault, J. (2009). *From couture to conversation*. Retrieved 14 October 2012 from http://www.nytimes.com/2009/11/17/fashion/17iht-rsocial.html

Moore, C. M., & Birtwistle, G. (2004). The Burberry business model: creating an international luxury fashion brand. *International Journal of Retail & Distribution Management, 32*(8), 412–422. doi:10.1108/09590550410546232

Moore, C. M., Fernie, J., & Burt, S. (2000). Brands without boundaries – The internationalisation of the designer retailer's brand. *European Journal of Marketing, 34*(8), 919–937. doi:10.1108/03090560010331414

Mosca, F. (2008). Market-driven management in fashion and luxury industries. *Symphonya Emerging Issues in Management, 1*(1).

Nguyen, H. (2011). *Facebook marketing in the fashion industry*. Retrieved 20 November 2012 from http://publications.theseus.fi/bitstream/handle/10024/26391/Nguyen_Han.pdf.pdf?sequence=1

Okonkwo, U. (2009). Sustaining the luxury brand on the Internet. *Journal of Brand Management, 16*(5–6), 302–310. doi:10.1057/bm.2009.2

Okonkwo, U. (2010). *Luxury online: Styles, systems, strategies*. New York: Palgrave Macmillan. doi:10.1057/9780230248335

Papathanassopoulos, S. (2011). *Media perspectives for the 21st century*. London: Routledge.

Pew Research Center. (2013). *Photos and videos have social currency online*. Retrieved 12 March 2013 from http://pewinternet.org/~/media//Files/Reports/2012/PIP_OnlineLifeinPictures_PDF.pdf

Phan, M., Thomas, R., & Heine, K. (2011). Social media and luxury brand management: The case of Burberry. *Journal of Global Fashion Marketing, 2*(4), 213–222. doi:10.1080/20932685.2011.10593099

Reuters. (2013). *Start-up Pinterest wins new funding, $2.5 billion valuation*. Retrieved 15 March 2013 from http://www.reuters.com/article/2013/02/21/net-us-funding-pinterest-idUSBRE91K01R20130221

Rose, G. (2003). *Visual methodologies*. London: Sage Publications.

Ross, F. (2010). Leveraging niche fashion markets through mass-customisation, co-design, style advice and new technology: A study of gay aesthetics and website design. *Fashion Practice The Journal of Design Creative Process & The Fashion Industry, 2*(2), 175–198. doi:10.2752/175693810X12774625387431

Schroeder, J. (2000). Édouard Manet, Calvin Klein and the strategic use of scandal. In S. Brown & A. Patterson (Eds.), *Imagining Marketing: Art, Aesthetics, and the Avant-Garde*. London: Routledge.

Silverman, D. (2001). *Interpreting qualitative data*. London: Sage Publications.

Singh, T., Veron-Jackson, L., & Cullinane, J. (2008). Blogging: A new play in your marketing game plan. *Business Horizons*, *51*(4), 281–292. doi:10.1016/j.bushor.2008.02.002

Sischy, I. (2004). The journey of a woman: 20 years of Donna Karan. Ed.s Assouline.

Tucker, L. R. (1998). The framing of Calvin Klein: A frame analysis of media discourse about the August 1995 Calvin Klein jeans advertising campaign. *Critical Studies in Media Communication*, *15*(2), 141–157. doi:10.1080/15295039809367039

Tungate, M. (2009). *Luxury world: the past, present and future of luxury brands*. London: Kogan Page.

Vecchi, A. (2008). *Globalisation and the viability of industrial districts*. Saarbrucken, Germany: Verlag Dr Muller.

Vecchi, A., & Kontu, H. (2012). Social media and their impact on organizational emotional intelligence: Some illustrative evidence from the fashion industry. In *Proceedings of the Joint International Conference on Advances in Management (ICAM) and Social Intelligence* (SI). Nassau, The Bahamas: ICAM.

Venturi, D. (2011). *Luxury hackers*. Turin, Italy: Linday.

Wasserman, T. (2012). *Burberry tops fashion brands in social media this week*. Retrieved 20 February 2013 from http://mashable.com/2012/09/29/burberry-top-10-fashion-brands/

Workman, J. E., & Caldwell, L. F. (2007). Centrality of visual product aesthetics, tactile and uniqueness needs of fashion consumers. *International Journal of Consumer Studies*, *31*, 589–596. doi:10.1111/j.1470-6431.2007.00613.x

Wright, M. (2011). *How premium fashion brands are maximizing their social media ROI*. Retrieved 10 January 2013 from http://mashable.com/2011/02/11/fashion-brands-social-media-roi/

Yin, R. K. (2008). *Applications of case study research*. Thousand Oaks, CA: Sage.

This research was previously published in Transcultural Marketing for Incremental and Radical Innovation edited by Bryan Christiansen, Salih Yıldız, and Emel Yıldız, pages 209-233, copyright year 2014 by Business Science Reference (an imprint of IGI Global).

Chapter 58

The Intersection of Social Media and Customer Retention in the Luxury Beauty Industry

Ellen Stokinger
London Metropolitan University, UK

Wilson Ozuem
Regents University, London UK

ABSTRACT

Debates regarding the ontological relationship between Social Media and customer retention have attracted considerable attention, particularly in the luxury beauty industry. The use of Social Media in the luxury beauty industry has caused many heated debates as it is seen as a form of interference in the exclusivity of luxury brands by limiting the physical and sensual contact between brand and customer. The purpose of this chapter is to provide some insights into how social media impacts on the cosmetics industry. Further, we provide evidence that the effective application of social media in the luxury beauty industry could lead to wider market share, and customer retention. The chapter concludes with some strategies that practitioners and researchers can adopt to develop effective marketing communication strategies, using social media platforms.

INTRODUCTION

The concept of social media and its relevance to effective marketing communications has gained much attention (Bolton et al., 2013; Brennan & Croft, 2012; Hamid, Akhir & Cheng, 2013; Hanna, Rohm & Crittenden, 2011; Hoffman & Fodor, 2010; Mangold & Faulds, 2009; Ozuem & Tan, 2014). The evolution of Social Media has led to the democratisation of corporate communications, with power shifting from advertising departments towards the opinions of individuals and communities, who like or dislike, comment upon and share content (Kietzmann, Hermkens, McCarthy & Silvestre, 2011; Dann & Dann, 2011). The online social landscape has converted the standard one-to-many media monologue into many-to-many dialogue. Social Media has increasingly become a product of consumers (Berthon, Pitt,

DOI: 10.4018/978-1-5225-5637-4.ch058

Plangger & Shapiro, 2012). Online conversations have become the new fuel and forefront of customer-firm relationships. Practitioners of the Cluetrain Manifesto (Levine, Locke, Searle &Weinberger, 2011) even describe conversations as "new products" that are part of a marketplace of organisations that permanently pitch to each other. As the rise of Social Media offers great opportunities to connect with consumers, Mangold and Faulds (2009) have made a case for the long-term incorporation of Social Media in a company's integral Marketing Communications strategy.

Bain and Company (2013), the leading strategy consultancy in the global luxury goods industry, expects the worldwide market of luxury goods to continue its double-digit growth, accounting for a total of £208 billion sales by 2015. In the UK specifically, the Walpole (2013), a non-profit association representing more than 180 British luxury brands such as Harrods, the Royal Opera House and Selfridges, reports an estimated growth of 12 per cent in the UK luxury industry, reaching an estimated record of £11.5 billion in the year 2017. With regard to beauty in particular, the global luxury beauty market outpaced mass-market beauty growth by 1.6 per cent in 2012 (BW Confidential). The luxury beauty industry in the UK is especially unique, as the nation's beauty market grew by 5 per cent to £2.2bn in 2012, propelling the UK to the third biggest luxury beauty market in Europe after France and Italy (Euromonitor International, 2013). The luxury beauty market in the UK is forecasted to be the fastest growing developed market in Western Europe with a growth rate of 6 per cent over the next five years, compared with an average growth of 2 per cent in the region (Euromonitor International, 2013).

The rise in the standard of living and consumer education about products has led to a democratisation of what were originally considered the most exclusive products (Garland, 2008). Globalisation has furthermore contributed to an increased level of competition, leading companies to create more exclusive products in order to differentiate from each other (Vickers & Renand, 2003). Many companies seek to add value to their brand by simply adding the term "luxury" or by extending their product portfolio with a luxury range, whilst others have created a truly luxury-oriented brand as their core business proposition. This study focuses on the last group, luxury brands that authentically carry the original meaning of luxury. We differentiate our approach by highlighting the principal theoretical starting points of this rapidly burgeoning literature related to social media and customer retention in the luxury beauty industry.

THEORETICAL CONTEXT AND FOUNDATIONS

The growing desire of consumers for exclusivity and personalisation motivates luxury retailers to strongly invest in beauty. Evidence for this can be seen in for example the new "Beauty Workshop" area in Selfridges, the recently opened "Beauty Mart" section in Harvey Nichols in London or the new Luxury Beauty store on Amazon. Nowadays luxury beauty brands increasingly use Social Media to give consumers a more actively engaging brand experience. Despite the growing popularity of online shopping, so far only one in five women purchases beauty products via the Internet and many consumers are still uncomfortable about buying beauty products online, as the preference to explore, assess and test the products prior to purchase still holds true (YouGov, 2012). Some scholars, for example, Kane, Alavi, Labianca & Borgatti (2014) suggested that social media provide users and companies with capabilities that they do not possess in traditional offline social networks, such as visualising network structure and searching for content in a network without using relational ties. Others have cautioned that social media's impressive rise comes with meaningful challenges in the social media world. One of the challenges is that whereas good information travels quickly, bad information can even more quickly (Goldenberg, 2015; Holloman, 2013)

Social Media has become an integrated part of everyday life, but its entry into the luxury goods industry has been far from easy. The use of Social Media in the luxury beauty industry has caused many heated debates as it is seen as interference to the exclusivity of a luxury brand by limiting the physical and sensual contact between the customer and the luxury brand (Choo,Moon, Kim & Yoon,2012; Dall'Olmo Riley & Lacroix, 2003; Dubois & Paternault, 1995; Khang, Ki & Ye, 2012;Okonkwo, 2010; Seung-A, 2013; Smith, 2009). However, as the number of affluent customers purchasing online increases, luxury brands face the challenge of retaining their customer base in order to create more sustainable revenue streams (Bolton, 1998; Buttle, 2009). Companies have reacted to this recent evolution in the marketing landscape and almost every luxury brand has adopted Social Media to connect with customers (Kim & Ko, 2010). A survey by the Luxury Interactive Conference's research team reported that 78 per cent of digital marketing executives for luxury brands increased their spend on Social Media in 2012, with 73 per cent of those surveyed planning to further increase their Social Media spend in 2013 (Alston, 2012).

The last decade has seen the production of a vast range of literature about Social Media. Topics of preference have so far included communication (Ozuem, Howell & Lancaster, 2008; Quinton & Harridge-March, 2010; Powers, Advincula, Austin, Graiko & Snyder,2012), the impact of word of mouth (Kozinets, Valck, Wojnicki & Wilner, 2010; Hennig-Thurau, Gwinner, Walsk & Gremler, 2004, Prendergast & Yuen, 2010), purchase intentions (Naylor, Walker, Cait & West, 2012) and service creation (Jarvenpaa & Tuunainen, 2013; Onook, Manish & Raghave, 2013; Trainor, 2012). Some of the literature focuses on how Social Media influences customer relations (Katsioloudes, Grant & McKechnie, 2007; Kim & Ko, 2010; Clark & Melancon, 2013; Laroche, Habibi, & Richard, 2013; Hennig-Thurau et al., 2010).

Most of these studies have focused on customer loyalty (Clark & Melancon, 2013; Gummerus, Liljander, Weman & Pihlström, 2012; Hawkins & Vel, 2013; Laroche et al., 2013; Ozuem & Lancaster 2014) yet Hennig-Thurau et al. (2010) considered customer retention as the outcome of engagement with new media. Their observations, however, were out-with the context of the UK luxury beauty industry. Blattberg, Getz and Thomas (2001) emphasised the need to clearly distinguish between customer loyalty and customer retention. Just because a customer is retained does not automatically imply that the individual is also loyal to a brand. Whereas customer loyalty is a customer reward that occurs once customers have changed their hearts and minds in favour of a particular product or service, customer retention is an organisational reward and focuses on how to keep customers without first having to change their hearts or minds (The Customer Institute, 2010).

Furthermore, Kim and Ko (2010) identified the impact of Social Media on customer equity, thereby emphasising the correlation between purchase intention and customer equity. Referring to the financially driven customer equity model as described by Blattberg et al. (2001), customer equity consists of three steps – customer acquisition, customer retention and add-on selling. It can thus be argued that evaluating the impact of Social Media marketing on customer equity jumps to the end without considering important hurdles in between such as customer retention. Therefore, instead of directly measuring customer equity or focusing on customer loyalty, this study recommends first analysing the extent to which Social Media impacts on customer retention. Whilst Social Media is often viewed as a positive lever in the customer-firm relationship, few studies refer to the luxury industry and fewer yet speak to the context of the UK luxury beauty industry.

Kim and Ko (2010; 2012) have made a substantial contribution to the literature on Social Media in the luxury market. However, as with many other studies, the researchers primarily focus on the luxury fashion industry (Choo et al., 2012; Kim & Ko, 2010; Kim & Ko, 2012; Jin, 2012; Moore & Doyle, 2010; Phan, Thomas & Heine, 2011). In contrast to the consumption of luxury fashion, buying luxury beauty products involves a high level of pre-purchase testing, which raises the question of whether or not Social Media provides an adequate tool to retain customers, as product testing is difficult and complex to implement online. This study therefore aims to identify the extent to which Social Media is a convenient tool to support the retention of luxury beauty customers and in which ways a brand's communication via Social Media can impact on customer retention.

The proliferation of Social Media is closely related to and facilitated by the development of Web 2.0 technologies (Berthon et al., 2012; Brennan & Croft, 2012; Fieseler & Fleck, 2013; Kaplan & Haenlein, 2010; Laroche et al., 2013; Tuten, 2008; Ozuem, Borrelli & Lancaster, 2015). The term "Web 2.0" was first introduced by the American media company O'Reilly and can be thought of as a set of technological innovations including hardware and software, which have the aim of empowering the user instead of the firm by allowing for content creation and increased interaction (Berthon et al., 2012; O'Reilly, 2005). While its predecessor, Web 1.0, had already laid the foundation for connecting people online via email and chat, Web 2.0 takes connectivity to another level by providing a variety of tools which enable the user to create, publish and share content and give recommendations to online friends and followers (Atta & Mahmoud, 2012; Evans & McKee, 2010).

This development has allowed for a new and disruptive marketing platform: Social Media and this was quickly identified as a revolution of the online generation and it has thus attracted the interest of researchers whose definitions bring Social Media into contact with different aspects such as the power of "social sharing" behaviour (Kaplan & Haenlein, 2010, Jevons & Gabbott, 2000; Nair, 2011; Safko & Brake, 2009; Stokes, 2008), interconnectivity (Dann & Dann, 2011; Hoffman & Novak, 2012; Laroche et al., 2013), influence (Brown & Fiorella, 2013), education (Blackshaw & Nazzarro 2004, Mangold & Faulds, 2009) and comparisons with traditional marketing (Mangold & Faulds, 2009; Zarella, 2010; Ozuem, O'Keeffe & Lancaster, 2015).

The most widespread definition of Social Media was originated by Kaplan and Haenlein (2010), who suggested that Social Media refers to a range of internet-based applications that build on the foundation of Web 2.0 and enable users to create and exchange User Generated Content (UGC). UGC is the engine of today's participative web and to "count" as UGC it must be published, creative and produced outside the professional context (Daugherty, Eastin &Bright, 2008; OECD, 2007). Many researchers emphasise the importance of exchanging and sharing UGC (Jevons & Gabbott, 2000; Nair, 2011; Safko & Brake, 2009; Stokes, 2008), after all the "social" in Social Media already promises a high degree of contact and exchange with other people.

Stokes (2008) sees the sense of Social Media in its ability to make users share content. Safko and Brake (2009) develop this further and define Social Media as a tool that allows users to share information, knowledge and opinions by engaging in online dialogues. On Social Media platforms, users have the opportunity to create a specific image of themselves, which is maintained through the sharing of posts, pictures, videos, liking certain posts and groups and extending the network of online friends. However, one might have the impression that some users pursue purely narcissistic interests (Nair, 2011), which can then quickly evoke negative attitudes towards users, brands or companies. In addition, the opportunity for self-expression might not be available to such an extent offline (Hoffman & Novak, 2012) and can thus result in some exaggeration of the personal self.

It is undisputed that Social Media can bring together like-minded people and businesses (Hagel & Armstrong, 1997; Wellman & Gulia, 1999) and hence it satisfies a need rooted deeply in human nature for a sense of belonging, (Maslow, 1943; Gangadharbhatla, 2008). Hoffman and Novak (2012) describe this as another revolutionising aspect of Social Media, as it is a tool that enables users to connect and re-connect even over long distances. Social Media allows for interconnectivity between users and between content and communication technologies (Dann & Dann, 2011). In the context of interconnectivity Tuten (2008) describes Social Media as an online community categorised as either social networks or virtual worlds that are participatory, conversational and fluid. Significantly, an online community "promotes the individual while also emphasizing an individual's relationship to the community" (Tuten, 2008, p.20). The motivation to engage in an online community derives from the need for contact comfort, also referred to as a need for affiliation, and a need for entertainment (Tuten, 2008). A brand community in particular is defined as a "specialised, non-geographically bound community, based on a structured set of relations among admirers of a brand" (Muniz & O'Guinn, 2001, p.412). Brands are referred to fundamentally as social entities (Muniz & O'Guinn, 2001) created through the inter-play of consumers and marketers (Firat & Venkatesh, 1995), which can thus be leveraged through the utilisation of Social Media.

Enabling users to talk to each other can be considered as an extension to traditional word-of-mouth communication (Divol, Edelman & Sarrazin, 2012; Mangold & Faulds, 2009). Amongst online users, some establish a more dominant position than others by sharing more information and opinions and thus procuring more buzz around them. Marketers have quickly discovered the power of targeting Social Media communities and they recognise that such groups gave rise to a new form of "influence market-ing" (Williams & Cothrell, 2000; Brown & Fiorella, 2013). As well as exerting influence, Social Media also impacts upon persuasive acts, as persuasion is based on social connections and cultural assumptions (Noor Al-Deen & Hendricks, 2012).

Furthermore, the emergence of Social Media has led to a shift in power asymmetry from the marketer to the consumer, who now has a greater mandate over media consumption than ever before (Vollmer & Precourt, 2008). Social Media can spur consumer education about brands, products and services (Blackshaw & Nazzaro, 2004; Mangold & Faulds, 2009, Hoffman & Novak, 2012). Since Social Media is about sharing, consumers can use the web as a way to educate themselves and to contribute to the education of others within their network. In addition to collecting information from Social Media sources, users also see Social Media as a service channel that enables them to remain in easy touch with organisations (Leggat, 2010).

Whereas Social Media has all the hallmarks of the traditional paths of communication between company and consumer, it has also evolved as a new communication channel between consumer and consumer and it can thus be considered as a hybrid addition to the promotional mix (Mangold & Faulds, 2009). Mangold and Faulds (2009) therefore stress the permanent incorporation of Social Media in every company's Integral Marketing Communication's strategy. However, only implementing Social Media in the promotional mix does not guarantee success, as it is also crucial that public relations practitioners adapt their strategies to newly evolving media (Pavlik, 2007). Kietzmann et al. (2011) furthermore suggest that a firm's performance on Social Media (if done passionately and appropriately) can significantly impact upon reputations, turnover and even survival but it can cause damage if done half-heartedly (Kietzmann et al., 2011).

Dimensions of Social Media

The variety of Social Media allows for many different kinds of users and marketers have to distinguish between these different Social Media users if they want to target them effectively (Hanna et al., 2011). Sukoco and Wu (2010) have identified two kinds of interests groups in Social Media communities. One group seeks to fulfil a self-related interest including knowledge and enjoyment and another follows socially-related interests which refer to their search for affiliation and social status. Humans generally want to create a specific image of themselves and want to control how other people perceive this image (Goffmann, 1959) by disclosing selected pieces of their daily lives to the public.

Cavazza (2013) suggests another model to categorise the motivations of online consumers according to four categories (sharing, discussing, networking and publishing). Whereas these categories adequately describe the most common online behaviour of today's user, it is doubtful if users already know the exact action they undertake during a browsing session. This study argues that users are more likely to know only the general purpose of what they want from their Social Media visit instead of planning the exact action beforehand. Rather than already knowing what exactly to discuss with other users prior to browsing, customers are more likely to first seek to satisfy general needs such as entertainment once only and find an inspiring article which they spontaneously decide to share. In examining Social Media platforms, the current paper identifies four different kinds of Social Media users and allocates the most appropriate Social Media tools aligned to each of these users.

The trefoil model (figure 1) distinguishes between four purposes of the users' online activity, their desire for status, entertainment, knowledge or business. In most cases the users' online activity has at least one and at maximum all four identified purposes. During browsing on Social Media the user might spontaneously switch between the purposes.

- *Status-seekers* generally use social networking sites and visual Social Media, which allows them to construct a certain image through tweeting, sharing pictures with sophisticated filters and following particular brands. Examples include Facebook, twitter, Instagram, Pinterest and Flickr.
- *Entertainment-seekers* visit Social Media in order to have a good experience, to feel better through browsing. They seek platforms, which cover a certain topic of interest, such as music-focused Social Media platforms including YouTube, my space and Soundcloud, or, according to hobby and interest through organised blogs like Tumblr.
- *Knowledge-seekers* have the goal of extending their knowledge whilst using Social Media and so they target science-based learning platforms such as Wikipedia, TED or the Khan Academy.
- *Business-seekers* generally use Social Media because they want to leverage their career perspectives, either indirectly, through extending their professional network and updating their online CV, or even directly by applying for positions using, for example, their LinkedIn profiles.

Social Media is growing at a phenomenal speed and the increasing number of platforms provides challenges for companies to decide which newly developed media are sustainable and which are not (Kaplan & Haenlein, 2010). Possibly the most successful example of a sustainable medium is Facebook. Founded in 2004 by Harvard student Mark Zuckerberg Facebook has become the world's number one social medium in just under 10 years with 1 billion active users (Kirckpatrick, 2010; Socialmediatoday, 2013). Another example of a Social Medium that successfully re-shaped the communication landscape of today is Twitter. This micro-blog was launched as a secondary project in 2006 by a San-Francisco-based podcasting company but it quickly turned into a major project when it reached 215 million monthly active users and 500 million tweets a day in 2013 (Geron, 2013; O'Reilly & Milstein, 2012). However, not every Social Medium is qualified to survive in the long-term and even Apple's music sharing platform Ping has not managed to find success (Hof, 2012).

With such a rich amount of Social Media types it is useful to categorise these in order to afford an overview. Kaplan and Haenlein (2010) divide Social Media into six types comprising of collaborative projects, blogs, content communities, social networking sites, virtual game worlds, and virtual social worlds. However, new Social Media tools frequently emerge and in this context Kaplan and Haenlein's (2010) categorisation seems to offer only a limited perspective of the vast array of Social Media types. Mangold and Faulds (2009) provide a more detailed understanding of different Social Media types and tools, and their list is broken down and allocated to the appropriate user in the previously identified trefoil model of Social Media users and tools (Table 1).

For now the trefoil model of Social Media users and tools in combination with Mangold and Faulds' (2009) adjusted categorisation of Social Media tools and types provides a comprehensive overview about today's Social Media landscape. However, Social Media tools evolve quickly and the model therefore requires regular updates.

Critics have already raised the argument that text-based Social Media such as posts on Facebook and Twitter are outdated and are being replaced by visual-based Social Media (Walpole, 2013; Moritz, 2012).

Figure 1. The trefoil model of Social Media users and tools
Source: Researcher

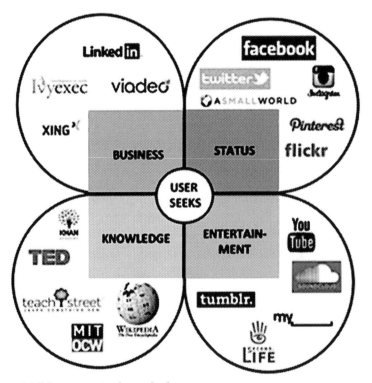

*All logos are trademarked.

Table 1. Examples of Social Media types and tools

Status-seekers   • Social networking sites (Myspace, Facebook)   • Invitation only social networks (ASmallWorld.net)   • Photo sharing sites (Flickr)

Entertainment-seekers
 • Creative work sharing sites:
     - Video sharing sites (YouTube)
     - Music sharing sites (Soundcloud)
     - Content sharing combined with assistance (Piczo)
     - General intellectual property sharing sites (Creative Commons)
 • Virtual worlds (Second Life)
 • Commerce communities (EBay, Amazon)
 • Social bookmarking sites allowing users to recommend music, videos (Digg)
 • Open Source Software communities (Linux)

Knowledge-seekers   • User-sponsored blogs (The Unofficial Apple Weblog, Cnet.com)   • Company-sponsored websites/blogs (Apple)   • Company-sponsored cause/help sites (click2quit)   • Collaborative websites (Wikipedia)   • Podcasts   • News delivers sites   • Educational materials sharing (MIT OpenCourseWare)
Business-seekers   • Business networking sites (LinkedIn)

Source: Mangold and Faulds, 2009, p.358.

The latest development in Social Media supports this critique. Instagram, the photo-sharing networking service, has garnered 7,302,000 users and overtook Twitter with 6,868,000 users in August 2012. Pinterest, another content sharing service, has emerged as the 4th largest driver of traffic worldwide (Moritz, 2012).

Mapping of Social Media for Marketing

The first predecessor of today's Social Media was introduced in 1979, when Tom Truscott and Jim Ellis from Duke University created "Usenet" (Kaplan & Haenlein, 2010). By allowing its users to post public messages this platform served as a Bulletin Board System (BBS) similar to today's forums (Kaplan & Haenlein, 2010). In addition to Usenet, the Internet ran a variety of protocols such as email, the chat system IRC and Gopher, a system to browse files (Rettberg, 2008). Towards the end of 1990 Tim Berners-Lee, a CERN scientist, implemented the first graphical web browser, which allowed for text with embedded images at the same time (Rettberg, 2008). This gave rise to the construction of the first webpages, both private and corporate, which (retrospectively considered) were the precursors of today's blogs (Rettberg, 2008). In 1998 Bruce and Susan Abelson launched the first social networking site "Open Diary", which connected online diary writers together in one community and gave them the opportunity to comment on other bloggers' opinions (Kaplan & Haenlein, 2010; Safko, 2012).

The development of high-speed Internet was the break-through of the constantly changing and evolving Social Media environment. Critics formulated doubts as to whether Social Media could survive in today's fast-paced media environment and labelled it as short-term trend. However, in 2012 there were 1.43 billion social network users worldwide (Arno, 2012) and many additional email and search engine users deliver sufficient proof that Social Media is a permanent, integrated part of life for young and old users. The serious advancement of Social Media leads to a shift in marketing thinking. Transactional marketing, which was identified by McCarthy's (1960) 4P model of Product, Price, Promotion and Place is now being replaced by the more relevant notion of relational marketing, which aims to satisfy the unique needs of each individual customer (Bhatnagar, 2012). To understand the different desires of every consumer, marketers need to involve them from early on in product development (Hoffman, Kopalle & Novak, 2010). Taking this into consideration, Lauterborn (1990) complements the concept of the 4Ps with the 4Cs including Consumer wants and needs, Cost to satisfy, Convenience to buy and Communication (Lauterborn, 1990). While the 4C concept provides a better fit with today's marketing environment, both the concepts were introduced before the take-off of Social Media.

In the meantime, the development of new technologies has challenged traditional ways of communication between companies and consumers (Ozuem et al., 2008). Instead of one-way communication directed by the company and with a passively receptive customer, consumers are now actively involved in a dialogue with companies. Brown and Fiorella (2013) acknowledge that the Internet and Social Media have disrupted direct communication between brands, its influencers and their followers. Nowadays, companies can no longer rely on the bandwagon effect of appealing directly to the influencers of a marketplace to win more consumers. The researchers conclude that the facilitation of word-of-mouth and the enormous amount of noise have proven to be critical to consumer trust in brands, which is the basis for a successful online marketing campaign. Brown and Fiorella (2013) thus suggest the 4As model, a concept specifically suitable for an increasingly word-of-mouth-based marketing environment (figure 2).

Regardless of which kind of Social Media a company chooses it must ensure that the audience receives the message. Google's Pay Per Click and Facebook's Insight algorithm help to ensure that the right audience is targeted. In order to accept the message, the user must trust the chosen medium. This can be achieved by social influencer endorsements and a seamless application of the brand's message by planning every step. Amplification is a further success factor for Social Media marketing, as people thrive on the sharing and multiplication of messages. Brown and Fiorella (2013, p.43) furthermore state that Social Media have completely changed the "ballgame" of marketing to consumers. An important aspect thereof is the impact of Social Media on customer service. Companies can no longer afford to ignore criticism and customer apathy. The conversation-enabling nature of Social Media spreads negative word-of-mouth very rapidly, which, in the worst case, can lead to complete consumer detachment from a company with accompanying loss of revenue (Khammash & Griffiths, 2010; Sandes & Urdan, 2013).

Figure 2. Paradigm shifts in technologically-induced environments
Source: McCarthy, 1960; Lauterborn, 1990; Brown and Fiorella, 2013.

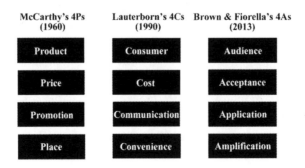

For marketers the emergence of Social Media implies one dominant benefit: the forming of close relationships with the consumer. Information exchange with a brand's followers and amongst followers themselves on Social Media uncovers the way consumers think and feel about a product. Gunelius (2011) remarks that online conversations between users are beneficial for companies in the sense that they build brand awareness, brand recognition and brand loyalty. Literature increasingly recognises the importance of co-creation and collaboration with customers online (Vargo & Lusch, 2004). Sharing details about the brand's history, lifestyle, product range and events keeps the consumer close and allows for the creation of emotional bonds (Quinton & Harridge-March, 2010). The researchers suggest that social bonding with the customer results in a sense of loyalty and the more participative the nature of these social bonds, the less the consumer is stimulated to look elsewhere. Trainor (2012) thus remarks that the utilisation of Social Media represents a competitive advantage for companies as it helps to generate superior customer value and increased profitability for the firm. Tuten (2008) identifies further advantages of a brand's presence on Social Media, including strengthening its personality and extending its ethos as well as providing a positive contribution to brand equity through internationalisation.

Many advocates of Social Media are convinced that the recent development has completely replaced traditional media. Whereas this can be confirmed to some extent, the 2012 CMO survey provides evidence of some contradiction (The CMO survey, 2013). Even though marketers can increase their Social Media spend in the next five years to around three times the current level, Social Media spend will only account for 20% of the Marketing budget with the remaining 80% still being spent on traditional media advertising (The CMO survey, 2013).

SOCIAL MEDIA AND CUSTOMER RETENTION INTERPLAY

Studies on the emergence of Social Media and its impact on customer retention are scarce. In analysing the effects of ten different kinds of new media, Hennig-Thurau et al. (2010) conclude that new media releases a higher level of brand engagement and thus positively impacts on customer retention. Liang, Chen and Wang (2008) focus on online, instead of offline, customer relationships and predict that online relationship marketing contributes to customer loyalty through perceived relationship investment and relationship quality. The researchers see customer loyalty as the precursor of customer retention and cross-buying. Blattberg et al. (2001) suggest that customer retention and customer loyalty are not the same, as a customer can be retained but does not necessarily need to be loyal. This contradicts the conception of Liang et al. (2008) and motivates this research to further elaborate on the impact of Social Media on customer retention.

In order to analyse the extent to which Social Media influences customer retention, it is crucial to understand the key drivers of customer retention. Buttle (2009) suggests measuring customer retention by tangible and intangible means. Tangible measures include key performance indicators such as raw customer retention rates, sales-adjusted retention rates, profit-adjusted retention rates or cost of customer retention (Buttle, 2009). Furthermore, he identifies four intangible drivers of customer retention as customer delight, customer perceived value, social and structural customer bonds and customer engagement. To create customer delight companies need to introduce detailed customer knowledge systems, which address and exceed the desire of each individual customer (Buttle, 2009). The emergence of Social Media provides an additional channel of communication and if integrated with other channels, marketers can more easily spread the word of value adding benefits like loyalty schemes and customer clubs. Social bonds are personal ties that are created during the interaction with others and the virtual world can be considered as distant at first, so companies need to consider their online interfaces with customers in order to transmit vividly what the brand stands for (Srinivasan, Anderson&Ponnavolu.2002; Wilson, 1995). Structural bonds exist when the company and the customer dedicate resources to the relationship (Buttle, 2009). Moreover, customer engagement involves commitment and experience and significantly contributes towards the formation of competitive advantage (Buttle, 2009).

Referring to the tangible and intangible measures of customer retention, Hoffman and Fodor (2010) remark that many marketers still focus solely on return numbers, such as Buttle's (2009) tangible customer retention KPIs, which the researchers consider to be short-term oriented and only suitable for traditional media. The emergence of Social Media comes with a set of unconventional and more intangible character-istics and marketers need to adjust their measurement schemes to this. Hoffman and Fodor (2010) provide four strategic options to measure Social Media effectiveness and these are presented below (figure 3).

The aim for every company should be to move away from fuzzy measurement attempts to more quantifiable metrics in the direction of the upper right quadrant. At first sight, many intangible factors might seem immeasurable, but Hoffmann and Fodor (2010) stress that marketers need to implement metrics for intangible factors as well, such as brand awareness, brand engagement and word-of-mouth in order to create successful campaigns.

Literature on customer retention cannot be considered complete without citing further intangible drivers such as customer satisfaction and customer loyalty (Crosby, 1990; Ozuem, Thomas & Lancaster, 2015). Satisfaction has been identified as one of the key influencing factors of customer retention (Gus-tafsson, Johnson& Roos2005; Liang et al., 2008; Sashi, 2012; Buttle, 2009) due to the long-term impact on customer behaviour (Oliver, 1980; Yi, 1990). Customer satisfaction generally refers to a customer's impression of product quality, service quality and price equity (Bolton & Lemon, 1999; Fornell, 1992). The more satisfied a customer is with a brand experience, the greater the retention rate (Anderson & Sullivan, 1993; Ranaweera & Prabhu, 2003).

Figure 3. Strategic options for Social Media measurement
Source: Hofmann and Fodor, 2010, p.47.

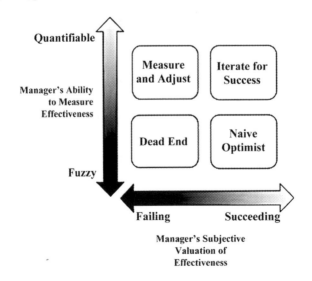

The quality of a product can be divided into three levels; basic quality, which the customer routinely expects, linear quality, which the customer more or less wants and attractive quality, which surprises, delights and excites the customer (Kano, 1995). Delight, which can be traced back to satisfaction, therefore is another key driver of customer retention (Buttle, 2009). The advance of Social Media has found appeal in the literature of satisfaction as it gives customers the opportunity to communicate faster with a company, and likewise it allows companies to respond faster to customer complaints and thus enhances the level of customer service (Krishna, Dangayach & Jain, 2011; Clark & Melancon, 2013).

Morgan and Hunt (1994) define trust as one party's confidence in another party's reliability and integrity. Chaudhuri and Holbrook (2001) refer to trust as the willingness of consumers to rely on the brand to perform its intended function. Satisfaction alone is not enough to retain customers (Danesh, Nasab & Kwek, 2012), and it has been widely discussed in literature that satisfaction goes hand in hand with customer trust in a company (Crosby, Ewans & Cowles, 1990; Dwyer, Schurr & Oh, 1987; Hart & Johnson, 1999; Liang et al., 2008). According to Betrand (2013), the emergence of Social Media has had a strong impact on customer trust.

The level of online word-of-mouth is multiplied and as consumers generally trust personal sources to a higher extent than they trust non-personal sources (Weber, 2007), companies have an additional opportunity to influence their customers (Brown & Fiorella, 2013). Trust in online environments was found to reduce the cognitive uncertainty related to online purchasing (Dash & Saji, 2007) and instead increased customer retention (Abhamid, Akhir& Cheng, 2013). However, the uncertainty of the Internet in terms of e-commerce (Pavlou, 2003) and personal information (Flavian & Guinaliu, 2006; Kelly & Erickson, 2004) provides challenges to the long-term preservation of customer trust.

Social Media and Customer Engagement

Customer engagement seems to occupy the centre stage of Social Media literature and is often referred to as impacting customer loyalty (Brodie, Hollebeek, Biljana & Ilic, 2011; Clark & Melancon, 2013; Hoffman & Fodor, 2010; Quinton & Harridge-March, 2010). In addition, various studies have shed light on the positive impact of customer engagement on commitment and trust (Agnihotri, Kothandaraman, Kashyap & Singh, 2012; Bowden, 2009; Verhoef, 2003). Bowden (2009) suggests that customer engagement results from calculative commitment, which then leads to emotional commitment forming the foundation for customer loyalty and finally, increases trust through constant involvement. Gummerus et al. (2012, p.857) provide a simple definition of customer engagement as a "set of behavioural activities towards a firm", whereas Agnihotri et al. (2012, p.335) consider customer engagement in the new light of Social Media and base its existence on repeated buyer-seller interactions on Social Media, "in which positive (negative) feedback strengthens (weakens) buyer-seller relationships". Referring to the emergence of new media, Libai (2011) states that this not only gives customers the possibility to engage with a company through purchase, but also via non-purchase behaviour. Although all these definitions of customer engagement agree that it contributes to the customer-firm relationship to some extent, the extent to which it impacts on customer retention has so far not been extensively elaborated upon in literature (Hennig-Thurau et al., 2010).

In addition, Gummerus et al.'s (2012) research on consumer engagement behaviour suggests that by engaging in different ways in online communities, users accordingly harvest relationship benefits such as entertainment. Dholakia, Bagozzi, & Pearo (2004) and Nonnecke, Andrews & Preece (2006) credit the entertainment of customers to relaxation, fun, community participation and online services. Adding to customer engagement impact on entertainment, Prahalad and Ramaswamy (2004) and Brodie et al. (2011) consider customer engagement as something formed by interactive customer experiences and as an important step in the co-creation of value, which is especially promoted through the participative nature of Social Media (Atwal & Williams, 2009; Kumar et al., 2010).

MANAGERIAL IMPLICATIONS AND RECOMMENDATIONS

The current paper proposes a number of managerial implications. Before beginning with a Social Media presence, luxury beauty brands need to first reflect upon their core values and their vision and mission. They must develop a clear and succinct Social Media strategy based on these factors. This strategy needs to include not only obvious objectives such as sales, cost efficiencies and product development, but also needs to consider objectives such as brand awareness, customer engagement and word-of-mouth. It is important that all the objectives are assessable. In the future, retailing will increasingly follow an Omni-channel approach, focusing on a seamless provision of experiences through whichever channel, digital or offline, the brand participates in. In order to make this work, the Social Media strategy needs to be integrated within the corporate strategy. Every department and every employee has to be aligned with it in order to convey authentic experiences through every single touch point.

For a Social Media strategy to be successful, a continuous budget needs to be ensured. It is therefore crucial to equip every objective of the Social Media strategy with measurable key performance indicators. Every campaign on Social Media is different and in order to continuously improve their activities, luxury beauty brands need to measure the effect of each campaign on customer retention by looking at conversion rates, positive sentiment analysis and successful customer complaints rates amongst others. Picking up the Omni-channel trend cited above, luxury beauty brands would greatly benefit from integrating online and offline data about customers. Customers nowadays expect companies to know when they have previously purchased from them and combining these two databases does not only open up an entirely new dimension to customer experiences but also enables a more complete measurement of customer retention, which ultimately allows for a more personalised communication with customers.

Without investing in traditional media a luxury beauty brand cannot expect any form of engagement from its customers. Prior to a participating in Social Media, customers have to be made aware of the brand's existence. Therefore luxury beauty brands need to continue investing in advertising, whilst at the same time balancing this with content creation. Whereas under-investment in advertising and over-creation of content lead to a brand's unknown exposure in the market place, vice versa, over-investment in advertising and under-creation of content can provoke a customer expectation gap, ultimately leading to customer disappointment and rejection of the brand. Luxury beauty brands have to find the right balance between advertising and content creation to achieve maximum brand exposure.

Customers aspire to luxury beauty brands. The products are highly coveted for their exclusivity and this is influenced by the brand's story and price point. Therefore, luxury beauty brands should not engage their customers via promotions, as this removes part of the exclusivity from the brand and can even lead to customer disappointment, realising that the brand is not as luxurious as expected when the same promotion tools as in the mass market are applied. The luxury beauty customer is not a value-for-money customer and their involvement starts with the brand's roots, the story. Therefore, luxury beauty brands should engage customers via value-adding content, such as previews, 'How to'- videos, beauty expert interviews - giving customers exclusive content they cannot get anywhere else, delighting them by going the unexpected extra mile. Beauty is fun and so is Social Media, now the brands need to leverage this by being innovative and having the courage to try things out. Luxury beauty brands should not be afraid to fail; mistakes contribute to the learning curve and prevent becoming rooted in a comfort zone.

Luxury beauty brands participating on Social Media should be aware that growth is incredibly fast-paced. Some already consider the Facebook social network, founded in 2004, as out-dated. An array of new, visual-based Social Media tools is on the rise. Whereas text-based Social Media are convenient for customer service purposes, and therefore have to remain a part of the strategy, visual Social Media allow for a more vivid and luxurious presentation of the brand. A healthy mix of text and visual-based Social Media is necessary. Text-based Social Media communications should have the aim of leveraging customer dialogue via reviews and posts, whereas communication through visual Social Media should increase emotional engagement by encouraging customers to share photos of important and meaningful moments. To further humanise the image of luxury beauty brands it is important to relax the communication and to not always share perfectly retouched pictures but to allow for natural and more imperfect looks. The aim of every luxury beauty company should be to become truly customer-centred. The participative nature of Social Media implies that word-of-mouth, and especially negative word-of-mouth, can spread very fast. Therefore luxury beauty companies need to have sufficient resources at hand to follow what their customers say about the brand in each channel and to immediately react to issues in an authentic and transparent manner. Only when the company proves to be reactive and honest will customers feel valued and able to establish a feeling of trust towards the brand. A customer that trusts a brand will ultimately come back.

REFERENCES

5 Surprising Social Media Statistics for 2013. (2013, October 12). *Social Media Today*. Retrieved from http://socialmediatoday.com/docmarkting/1818611/five-surprising-social-media-statistics-2013

Abhamid, N. R., Akhir, R. M., & Cheng, A. Y. (2013). Social media: An emerging dimension of marketing communication. *Journal of Management and Marketing Research*, *12*, 4–11.

Agnihotri, R., Kothandaraman, P., Kashyap, R., & Singh, R. (2012). Bringing 'Social' into Sales: The Impact of Salespeople's Social Media Use on Service Behaviours and Value Co-creation. *Journal of Personal Selling & Sales Management*, *XXXII*(3), 333–348. doi:10.2753/PSS0885-3134320304

Alston, M. (2012, October 5). 78% of Luxury Marketers Spent More on Social Media in 2012 Than 2011, Luxury Interactive. Retrieved from http://finance.yahoo.com/news/78-luxury-marketers-spent-more-141500809.html

Anderson, E. W., & Sullivan, M. W. (1993). The antecedents and consequences of customer satisfaction for firms. *Marketing Science*, *12*(2), 125–143. doi:10.1287/mksc.12.2.125

Annie Jin, S.-A. (2012). The potential of social media for luxury brand management. *Marketing Intelligence & Planning*, *30*(7), 687–699. doi:10.1108/02634501211273805

Arno, C. (2012, December 26).Worldwide Social Media Usage Trends in 2012, Search Engine Watch. Retrieved from http://searchenginewatch.com/article/2167518/Worldwide-Social-Media-Usage-Trends-in-2012

Atta, A., & Mahmoud, A. (2012). Web 2.0: A Movement within the Learning Community. *Information Management and Business Review, 4*(12), 625–631.

Atwal, G., & Williams, A. (2009). Luxury brand marketing – The experience is everything! *Brand Management, 16*(5-6), 338–346. doi:10.1057/bm.2008.48

Worldwide luxury goods continues double-digit annual growth; global market now tops €200 billion, finds Bain & Company. (2013, March 16). *Bain & Company*. Retrieved from http://www.bain.com/about/press/press-releases/worldwide-luxury-goods-continues-double-digit-annual-growth.aspx

Beauty Customer Journey. (2012). *YouGov*. Retrieved from http://d25d2506sfb94s.cloudfront.net/cumulus_uploads/document/wa32oxme7c/Beauty%20Customer%20Journey.pdf

Berthon, P. R., Pitt, L. F., Plangger, K., & Shapiro, D. (2012). Marketing meets Web 2.0, social media, and creative consumers: Implications for international marketing strategy. *Business Horizons, 55*(3), 261–271. doi:10.1016/j.bushor.2012.01.007

Bertrand, G. (2013). Socialmedia research: Developing a trust metric in the social age. *International Journal of Market Research, 55*(3), 333–335. doi:10.2501/IJMR-2013-032

Bhatnagar, N. (2012). Customer Relationship Marketing: Customer-Centric Processes for Engendering Customer- Firm Bonds and Optimizing Long-Term Customer Value. *Intechopen*. Retrieved from http://cdn.intechopen.com/pdfs/35309/InTech-Customer_relationship_marketing_customer_centric_processes_for_engendering_customer_firm_bonds_and_optimizing_long_term_customer_value.pdf

Blackshaw, P., & Nazzaro, M. (2004). Consumer-Generated Media (CGM) 101: Word-of-mouth in the age of the Webfortified consumer. *Intelliseek*. Retrieved from http://www.brandchannel.com/images/papers/222_cgm.pdf

Blattberg, R., Getz, G., & Thomas, J. S. (2001). *Customer Equity: Building and Managing Relationships as Valuable Assets*. Boston: Harvard Business School Press.

Bolton, R. N. (1998). A Dynamic Model of the Duration of the Customer's Relationship with a Continuous Service Provider: The Role of Satisfaction. *Marketing Science, 17*(1), 45–65. doi:10.1287/mksc.17.1.45

Bolton, R. N., & Lemon, K. N. (1999). Dynamic Model of Customers' Usage of Services: Usage as an Antecedent and Consequence of Satisfaction. *The Journal of Consumer Research, 36*(2), 171–186.

Bolton, R. N., Parasuraman, A., Hoefnagels, A., Migchels, N., Kabadayi, S., Gruber, T., & Solnet, D. et al. (2013). Understanding Generation Y and their use of social media: A review and research agenda. *Journal of Service Management, 24*(3), 245–267. doi:10.1108/09564231311326987

Bowden, J. L. H. (2009). The process of customer engagement: A conceptual framework. *Journal of Marketing Theory and Practice, 17*(1), 63–74. doi:10.2753/MTP1069-6679170105

Brennan, R., & Croft, R. (2012). The use of social media in B2B marketing and branding: An exploratory study. *Journal of Consumer Behaviour, 11*(2), 101–115. doi:10.1362/147539212X13420906144552

Brodie, R. J., Hollebeek, L. D., Juric, B., & Ilic, A. (2011). Customer engagement: Conceptual domain, fundamental propositions, and implications for research. *Journal of Service Research, 14*(3), 252–271. doi:10.1177/1094670511411703

Brown, D., & Fiorella, S. (2013). Influence Marketing, US: Que Publishing.

Buttle, F. (2009). *Customer relationship management – concepts and technologies* (2nd ed.). Oxford: Elsevier.

Chaudhuri, A., & Holbrook, M. B. (2001). The chain of effects from brand trust and brand affect to brand performance: The role of brand loyalty. *Journal of Marketing, 65*(2), 81–93. doi:10.1509/jmkg.65.2.81.18255

Choo, H., Moon, H., Kim, H., & Yoon, N. (2012). Luxury customer value. *Journal of Fashion Marketing and Management, 16*(1), 81–101. doi:10.1108/13612021211203041

Clark, M., & Melancon, J. (2013). The Influence of Social Media Investment on Relational Outcomes: A Relationship Marketing Perspective. *International Journal of Marketing Studies, 5*(4), 132–142. doi:10.5539/ijms.v5n4p132

Crosby, L. A., Evans, K. R., & Cowles, D. (1990). Relationship quality in services selling: An interpersonal influence perspective. *Journal of Marketing, 54*(3), 68–81. doi:10.2307/1251817

Dall'Olmo Riley, F., & Lacroix, C. (2003). Luxury branding on the internet: Lost opportunity or impossibility? *Marketing Intelligence & Planning, 21*(2), 96–104. doi:10.1108/02634500310465407

Danesh, S. N., Nasab, S. A., & Kwek, C. L. (2012). The Study of Customer Satisfaction, Customer Trust and Switching Barriers on Customer Retention in Malaysia Hypermarkets. *International Journal of Business and Management, 7*(7), 141–150.

Dann, S., & Dann, S. (2011). *E-marketing: theory and application.* Basingstoke, England: Palgrave Macmillan.

Dash, S., & Saji, K. B. (2008). The role of consumer self-efficacy and website social presence in customers' adoption of B2C online shopping: An empirical study in the Indian context. *Journal of International Consumer Marketing, 20*(2), 33–48. doi:10.1300/J046v20n02_04

Daugherty, T., Eastin, M., & Bright, L. (2008). Exploring Consumer Motivations for creating User-Generated Content. *Journal of Interactive Advertising, 8*(2), 16–25. doi:10.1080/15252019.2008.10722139

Dholakia, U. M., Bagozzi, R. P., & Pearo, L. K. (2004). A social influence model of consumer participation in network- and small-group-based virtual communities. *International Journal of Research in Marketing, 21*(3), 241–263. doi:10.1016/j.ijresmar.2003.12.004

Divol, R., Edelman, D., & Sarrazin, H. (2012). Demystifying social media. *The McKinsey Quarterly, 2*, 66–77.

Dubois, B., & Paternault, C. (1995). Observations: Understanding the world of international luxury brands. *Journal of Advertising Research, 35*(4), 69–76.

Dwyer, F. R., Schurr, P. H., & Oh, S. (1987). Developing buyer–seller relationships. *Journal of Marketing*, *51*(2), 11–27. doi:10.2307/1251126

Europe's Prestige Beauty Market 2012. *BW Confidential*. (2013). Retrieved from http://www.bwconfidential.com/en/europe-s-prestige-beauty-market-2012,article-1875.html

Evans, D., & McKee, J. (2010). *Social Media Marketing – The Next Generation of Business Engagement*. Indianapolis: Wiley Publishing Inc.

Fieseler, C., & Fleck, M. (2013). The Pursuit of Empowerment through Social Media: Structural Social Capital Dynamics in CSR-Blogging. *Journal of Business Ethics*, *118*(4), 759–775. doi:10.1007/s10551-013-1959-9

Firat, A. F., & Venkatesh, A. (1995). Liberatory Postmodernism and the Reenchantment of Consumption. *The Journal of Consumer Research*, *22*(3), 239–267. doi:10.1086/209448

Flavian, C. & Guinaliu, M. (2006). Consumer trust, perceived security and privacy policy: Three basic elements of loyalty to a web site. *Industrial Management + Data Systems, 106(5)*, 601-620.

Fornell, C. (1992). A National Customer Satisfaction Barometer: The Swedish Experience. *Journal of Marketing*, *56*(1), 6–21. doi:10.2307/1252129

Gangadharbhatla, H. (2008). Facebook me: Collective self esteem, need to belong and Internet self efficacy as predictors of the I-generations attitudes toward social networking sites. *Journal of Interactive Advertising*, *8*(2), 5–15. doi:10.1080/15252019.2008.10722138

Garland, E. (2008). The experience economy: The high life of tomorrow. *The Futurist*. Retrieved from http://mestovetra.files.wordpress.com/2008/06/experience-economy.pdf

Geron, T. (2013, March 10). Twitter Reveals Long-Awaited IPO Plans With 215 Million Users. *Forbes*. Retrieved from http://www.forbes.com/sites/tomiogeron/2013/10/03/twitter-reveals-long-awaited-ipo-plans-253m-revenue-in-first-half-of-2013/

Goffman, E. (1959). *The presentation of self in everyday life*. New York: Doubleday Anchor Books.

Goldenberg, B. (2015). *The Definitive Guide to Social CRM: maximizing customer relationships with Social Media to gain market insights, customers, and profits*. Harlow: Pearson.

Gummerus, J., Liljander, V., Weman, E., & Pihlström, M. (2012). Customer engagement in a Facebook brand community. *Management Research Review*, *35*(9), 857–877. doi:10.1108/01409171211256578

Gunelius, S. (2011). *30 minute Social Media Marketing: Step by Step Techniques to Spread the Words about your Business*. USA: McGraw-Hill.

Gustafsson, A., Johnson, M. D., & Roos, I. (2005). The Effects of Customer Satisfaction, Relationship Commitment Dimensions, and Triggers on Customer Retention. *Journal of Marketing*, *69*(10), 210–218. doi:10.1509/jmkg.2005.69.4.210

Hagel, J., & Armstrong, A. G. (1997). *Net gain: Expanding markets through virtual Communities*. Boston: Harvard Business School Press.

Hanna, R., Rohm, A., & Crittenden, V. L. (2011). We're all connected: The power of the social media ecosystem. *Business Horizons, 54*(3), 265–273. doi:10.1016/j.bushor.2011.01.007

Hart, C. W., & Johnson, M. D. (1999). Growing the trust relationship. *Marketing Management, 8*(1), 8–19.

Hawkins, K., & Vel, P. (2013). Attitudinal loyalty, behavioural loyalty and social media: An Introspection. *Marketing Review, 13*(2), 125–141. doi:10.1362/146934713X13699019904605

Hennig-Thurau, T., Gwinner, K., Walsh, G., & Gremler, D. (2004). Electronic word of-mouth via consumer-opinion platforms: What motivates consumers to articulate themselves on the Internet? *Journal of Interactive Marketing, 18*(1), 38–52. doi:10.1002/dir.10073

Hennig-Thurau, T., Malthouse, E., Friege, C., Gensler, S., Lobschat, L., Rangaswamy, A., & Skiera, B. (2010). The Impact of New Media on Customer Relationships. *Journal of Service Research, 13*(3), 311–330. doi:10.1177/1094670510375460

Hof, R. (2012, September 2). Google+'s Success and Failure, in Two Images. *Forbes.* http://www.forbes.com/sites/roberthof/2012/02/09/googles-success-and-failure-in-two-images/

Hoffman, D. L., & Fodor, M. (2010). Can you measure the ROI of your social media marketing? *MIT Sloan Management Review, 52*(1), 41–49.

Hoffman, D. L., Kopalle, P. K., & Novak, T. P. (2010). A New Marketing Paradigm for Electronic Commerce. *JMR, Journal of Marketing Research, XLVII*, 854–865. doi:10.1509/jmkr.47.5.854

Hoffman, D. L., & Novak, T. P. (2012, January 17). Why Do People Use Social Media? Empirical Findings and a New Theoretical Framework for Social Media Goal Pursuit. *Social Science Research Network.* Retrieved from http://ssrn.com/abstract=1989586

Holloman, C. (2013). *The Social Media MBA in practice.* Chichester: Wiley.

Jarvenpaa, S., & Tuunainen, V. K. (2013). How Finnair Socialized Customers for Service Co-Creation with SocialMedia. *MIS Quarterley Executive, 12*(3), 125–136.

Jevons, C., & Gabbott, M. (2000). Trust, Brand Equity and Brand Reality in Internet Business Relationships: An Interdisciplinary Approach. *Journal of Marketing Management, 16*(6), 619–634. doi:10.1362/026725700785045967

Kane, G, & Alavi, M, Labianca &Borgatti. (2014). What's different about Social Media Networks? A Framework and Research Agenda. *Management Information Systems Quarterly, 38*(1), 275–304.

Kano, N. (1995). Upsizing the organization by attractive quality creation. In G.K. Kanji (Ed.), Total Quality Management: Proceedings of the First World Congress. London: Chapman & Hall. doi:10.1007/978-94-011-0539-2_6

Kaplan, A., & Haenlein, M. (2010). Users of the world, unite! The challenges and opportunities of Social Media. *Business Horizons, 53*(1), 59–68. doi:10.1016/j.bushor.2009.09.003

Katsioloudes, M., Grant, J., & McKechnie, D. S. (2007). Social marketing: Strengthening company-customer bonds. *The Journal of Business Strategy, 28*(3), 56–64. doi:10.1108/02756660710746283

Kelly, E. P., & Erickson, G. S. (2004). Legal and privacy issues surrounding customer databases and e-merchant bankruptcies: Reflections on Toysmart.com. *Industrial Management & Data Systems*, *104*(3), 209–217. doi:10.1108/02635570410525762

Khammash, M., & Griffiths, G. H. (2011). Arrivederci CIAO.com, Buongiorno Bing. Com - electronic word-of-mouth (eWOM), antecedences and consequences. *International Journal of Information Management*, *31*(1), 82–87. doi:10.1016/j.ijinfomgt.2010.10.005

Khang, H., Ki, E., & Ye, L. (2012). Social Media Research in Advertising, Communication, Marketing, and Public Relations. *Journalism & Mass Communication Quarterly*, *89*(2), 279–298. doi:10.1177/1077699012439853

Kietzmann, J. H., Hermkens, K., McCarthy, I. P., & Silvestre, B. S. (2011). Social media? Get serious! Understanding the functional building blocks of social media. *Business Horizons*, *54*(3), 241–251. doi:10.1016/j.bushor.2011.01.005

Kim, A. J., & Ko, E. (2010). Impacts of Luxury Fashion Brand's Social Media Marketing on Customer Relationship and Purchase Intention. *Journal of Global Fashion Marketing*, *1*(3), 164–171. doi:10.1080/20932685.2010.10593068

Kim, A. J., & Ko, E. (2012). Do Social Media marketing activities enhance customer equity? An empirical study of luxury fashion brand. *Journal of Business Research*, *65*(10), 1480–1486. doi:10.1016/j.jbusres.2011.10.014

Kirkpatrick, D. (2010). *The Facebook effect: The inside story of the company that is connecting the world*. New York: Simon & Schuster.

Kozinets, R., deValck, K., Wojnicki, A., & Wilner, S. (2010). Networked Narratives: Understanding Word-of-Mouth Marketing in Online Communities. *Journal of Marketing*, *74*(2), 71–89. doi:10.1509/jmkg.74.2.71

Krishna, A., Dangayach, G., & Jain, R. (2011). A Conceptual Framework for the Service Recovery Paradox. *The Marketing Review*, *11*(1), 41–56. doi:10.1362/146934711X565288

Kumar, V., Aksoy, L., Donkers, B., Venkatesan, R., Wiesel, T., & Tillmanns, S. (2010). Undervalued or Overvalued Customers: Capturing Total Customer Engagement Value. *Journal of Service Research*, *13*(3), 297–310. doi:10.1177/1094670510375602

Laroche, M., Habibi, M. R., & Richard, M. O. (2013). To be or not to be in social media: How brand loyalty is affected by social media? *International Journal of Information Management*, *33*(1), 76–82. doi:10.1016/j.ijinfomgt.2012.07.003

Lauterborn, B. (1990). New Marketing Litany: Four P's Passe: C-Words Take Over. *Advertising Age*, *61*(41), 26.

Leggatt, H. (2010, October 19). Rebuild Brand Loyalty with Social Media. Bizreport. Retrieved from http://www.bizreport.com/2010/08/price-sensitiveshoppers-still-seeking-out-deals.html

Levine, R., Locke, C., Searle, D., & Weinberger, D. (2001). *The Cluetrain Manifesto: The end of business as usual*. New York: Basic Books.

Liang, C. L., Chen, H. J., & Wang, W. H. (2008). Does online relationship marketing enhance customer retention and cross-buying? *Service Industries Journal*, *28*(6), 769–787. doi:10.1080/02642060801988910

Libai, B. (2011). Comment: The perils of focusing on highly engaged customers. *Journal of Service Research*, *14*(3), 275–276. doi:10.1177/1094670511414583

Loyalty Versus Retention - Is There a Difference? (2010, April 9). The Customer Institute. Retrieved from http://thecustomerinstitute.blogspot.co.uk/2010/04/loyalty-versus-retention-is-there.html

Luxury Beauty Having a Love Affair with the UK. (2013). *Euromonitor International*. Retrieved from http://www.euromonitor.com/

Mangold, W. G., & Faulds, D. J. (2009). Social media: The new hybrid element of the promotion mix. *Business Horizons*, *52*(4), 357–365. doi:10.1016/j.bushor.2009.03.002

Maslow, A. H. (1943). A theory of human motivation. *Psychological Review*, *50*(4), 370–396. doi:10.1037/h0054346

McCarthy, E. J. (1960). *Basic Marketing - A Managerial Approach*. Homewood: Richard D. Irwin.

Moore, C. M., & Doyle, S. A. (2010). The evolution of a luxury brand: The case of Prada. *International Journal of Retail & Distribution Management*, *38*(11), 915–927.

Morgan, R. M., & Hunt, S. (1994). The commitment-trust theory of relationship marketing. *Journal of Marketing*, *58*(3), 20–38. doi:10.2307/1252308

Moritz, D. (2012, December 15).The Shift to Visual Social Media – 6 Tips for Business, Socially Sorted. Retrieved from http://sociallysorted.com.au/shift-to-visual-social-media-6-tips-for-business-infographic/

Muniz, M. A. Jr, & O'Guinn, C. T. (2001). Brand community. *The Journal of Consumer Research*, *27*(4), 412–432. doi:10.1086/319618

Nair, M. (2011). Understanding and Measuring the Value of Social Media. *Journal of Corporate Accounting & Finance*, *22*(3), 45–51. doi:10.1002/jcaf.20674

Naylor, R., Walker, L., Cait, P., & West, P. M. (2012). Beyond the 'Like' Button: The impact of Mere Virtual Presence on Brand Evaluations and Purchase Intentions in Social Media Settings. *Journal of Marketing*, *76*(6), 105–120. doi:10.1509/jm.11.0105

Nonnecke, B., Andrews, D., & Preece, J. (2006). Non-public and public online community participation: Needs, attitudes and behaviour. *Electronic Commerce Research*, *6*(1), 7–20. doi:10.1007/s10660-006-5985-x

Noor Al-Deen, H. S., & Hendricks, J. A. (2012). *Social Media – usage and impact*. Plymouth: Lexington Books.

O'Reilly, T. (2005, September 30). What is Web 2.0? Design Patterns and Business Models for the Next generation of Software. *O'Reilly*. Retrieved from http://www.im.ethz.ch/education/HS08/OReilly_What_is_Web2_0.pdf

O'Reilly, T., & Milstein, S. (2012). *The Twitter Book*. Sebastopol: O'Reilly Media Inc.

Working Party on the Information Economy – Participative Web: User-created content. (2007, April 12). OECD, Organisation for Economic Co-operation and Development. Retrieved from http://www.oecd.org/sti/38393115.pdf

Okonkwo, U. (2010). *Luxury Online*. New York: Palgrave Macmillan.

Oliver, R. L. (1980). A Cognitive Model of the Antecedents and Consequences of Satisfaction Decisions. *JMR, Journal of Marketing Research*, *17*(4), 460–469. doi:10.2307/3150499

Onook, O., Manish, A., & Raghave, R. H. (2013). Community intelligence and social media services: A rumor theoretic analysis of tweets during social crisis. *Management Information Systems Quarterly*, *37*(2), 407–A7.

Ozuem, W., Borrelli, M., & Lancaster, G. (2015). Leveraging the co-evolution of offline and online video games: An empirical study. *Journal of Strategic Marketing*, 1–23. doi:10.1080/0965254X.2015.1076883

Ozuem, W., Howell, K. E., & Lancaster, G. (2008). Communicating in the new interactive marketspace. *European Journal of Marketing*, *42*(9/10), 1059–1083. doi:10.1108/03090560810891145

Ozuem, W., & Lancaster, G. (2014). Recovery strategies in on-line service failure. In A. Ghorbani (Ed.), *Marketing in the cyber era: strategies and emerging trends* (pp. 143–159). Hershey, PA, USA: IGI Global. doi:10.4018/978-1-4666-4864-7.ch010

Ozuem, W., O'Keeffe, A., & Lancaster, G. (2015). Leadership Marketing: An exploratory study. *Journal of Strategic Marketing*, 1–25. doi:10.1080/0965254X.2014.1001867

Ozuem, W., Thomas, T., & Lancaster, G. (2015). The Influence of customer loyalty on small island economies: An empirical and exploratory study. *Journal of Strategic Marketing*, 1–23. doi:10.1080/0965254X.2015.1011205

Pavlik, J. V. (2007, June 4). Mapping the consequences of technology of public relations, Institute for public relations. Institute for Public Relations. Retrieved from http://www.instituteforpr.org/topics/mapping-technology-consequences/

Pavlou, P. A. (2003). Consumer acceptance of electronic commerce: Integrating trust and risk with the technology acceptance model. *International Journal of Electronic Commerce*, *7*(3), 101–134.

Phan, M., Thomas, R., & Heine, K. (2011). Social Media and Luxury Brand Management: The Case of Burberry. *Journal of Global Fashion Marketing*, *2*(4), 213–222. doi:10.1080/20932685.2011.10593099

Powers, T., Advincula, D., Austin, M., Graiko, S., & Snyder, J. (2013). Digital and Social Media in the Purchase Decision Process. *Journal of Advertising Research*, *52*(4), 479–489. doi:10.2501/JAR-52-4-479-489

Prahalad, C. K., & Ramaswamy, V. (2004). Co-creation experiences: The next practice in value creation. *Journal of Interactive Marketing*, *18*(3), 5–14. doi:10.1002/dir.20015

Prendergast, G., Ko, D., & Yuen, S. Y. V. (2010). Online word of mouth and consumer purchase intentions. *International Journal of Advertising*, *29*(5), 687–708. doi:10.2501/S0265048710201427

Quinton, S., & Harridge-March, S. (2010). Relationships in online communities: The potential for marketers. *Journal of Research in Interactive Marketing, 4*(1), 59–73. doi:10.1108/17505931011033560

Ranaweera, C., & Prabhu, J. (2003). The influence of satisfaction, trust and switching barriers on customer retention in a continuous purchasing setting. *International Journal of Service Industry Management, 14*(4), 374–395. doi:10.1108/09564230310489231

Rettberg, J. W. (2008). *Blogging – Digital Media and Society Series*. Malden: Polity.

Safko, L. (2012). *The Social Media Bible– Tools, Tactics and Strategies for Business Success* (3rd ed.). New Jersey: John Wiley & Sons Inc.

Safko, L., & Brake, D. K. (2009). *The Social Media Bible*. New Jersey: John Wiley & Sons, Inc.

Sandes, F. S., & Urdan, A. T. (2013). Electronic Word-of-Mouth Impacts on Consumer Behaviour: Exploratory and Experimental Studies. *Journal of International Consumer Marketing, 25*(3), 181–197. doi:10.1080/08961530.2013.780850

Sashi, C. M. (2012). Customer engagement, buyer-seller relationships and Social Media. *Management Decision, 50*(2), 253–272. doi:10.1108/00251741211203551

Smith, T. (2009). The Social Media Revolution. *International Journal of Market Research, 51*(4), 559–561. doi:10.2501/S1470785309200773

Social Media Landscape 2013. (2013, April 17). *Fred Cavazza*. Retrieved from http://www.fredcavazza.net/2013/04/17/social-media-landscape-2013/

Srinivasan, S. S., Anderson, R., & Ponnavolu, K. (2002). Customer loyalty in e-commerce: An exploration of its antecedents and consequences. *Journal of Retailing, 78*(1), 41–50. doi:10.1016/S0022-4359(01)00065-3

Stokes, R. (2008).E-marketing: The essential guide to online marketing, South Africa: Quirk eMarketing (Pty) Ltd.

Sukoco, B. & Wu, W. (2010). The personal and social motivation of customers' participation in brand community. *African journal of business management, 4(5)*, 614-622.

Highlights and Insights February 2013. (2013, February). The CMO Survey. Retrieved from http://cmosurvey.org/files/2013/02/The_CMO_Survey_Highlights_and_Insights_Feb-2013-Final2.pdf

Annie Jin, S.-A. (2012). The potential of Social Media for luxury brand management. *Marketing Intelligence & Planning, 30*(7), 687–699. doi:10.1108/02634501211273805

Trainor, K. (2012). Relating Social Media Technologies to Performance: A Capabilities-Based Perspective. *Journal of Personal Selling & Sales Management, 32*(3), 317–331. doi:10.2753/PSS0885-3134320303

Tuten, T. L. (2008). *Advertising 2.0 – Social Media Marketing in a Web 2.0 World*. Westport: Praeger Publishers.

Vargo, S. L., & Lusch, R. F. (2004). Evolving to a new Dominant Logic for Marketing. *Journal of Marketing, 68*(1), 1–17. doi:10.1509/jmkg.68.1.1.24036

Verhoef, P. C. (2003). Understanding the Effect of Customer Relationship Management Efforts on Customer Retention and Customer Share Development. *Journal of Marketing*, *67*(4), 30–45. doi:10.1509/jmkg.67.4.30.18685

Vickers, J. S., & Renand, F. (2003). The Marketing of Luxury Goods: An exploratory study – three conceptual dimensions. *The Marketing Review*, *3*(4), 459–478. doi:10.1362/146934703771910071

Vollmer, C., & Precourt, G. (2008). *Always on: Advertising, marketing, and media in an era of consumer control*. New York: McGraw-Hill.

Walpole (2013). British Luxury Showcase.

Weber, L. (2007). *Marketing to the Social Web: How Digital Customer Communities Build Your Business*. New Jersey: John Wiley & Sons Inc.

Wellman, B., & Gulia, M. (1999). Net-surfers don't ride alone: Virtual communities as communities. In B. Wellman (Ed.), Networks in the global village (pp. 331-366). Boulder: Westview.

Williams, L., & Cothrell, J. (2000). Four smart ways to run online communities. *Sloan Management Review*, *41*(4), 81–91.

Wilson, D. T. (1995). An integrated model of buyer–seller relationships. *Journal of the Academy of Marketing Science*, *23*(4), 335–345. doi:10.1177/009207039502300414

Yi, Y. (1990). A critical review of consumer satisfaction, In V.A. Zeithaml (Ed.), Review of Marketing (pp. 68-123). Chicago: American Marketing Association.

Zarella, D. (2010). *The social media marketing book*. California: O'Reilly Media Inc.

ADDITIONAL READING

Baer, J. (2013). *Youtility*. New York: Penguin Group.

Brown, D., & Fiorella, S. (2013). Influence Marketing. US: Que Publishing.

Clark, M., & Melancon, J. (2013). The Influence of Social Media Investment on Relational Outcomes: A Relationship Marketing Perspective. *International Journal of Marketing Studies*, *5*(4), 132–142. doi:10.5539/ijms.v5n4p132

Hoffman, D. L., & Fodor, M. (2010). Can you measure the ROI of your social media marketing? *MIT Sloan Management Review*, *52*(1), 41–49.

Sandes, F. S., & Urdan, A. T. (2013). Electronic Word-of-Mouth Impacts on Consumer Behaviour: Exploratory and Experimental Studies. *Journal of International Consumer Marketing*, *25*(3), 181–197. doi:10.1080/08961530.2013.780850

KEY TERMS AND DEFINITIONS

Cosmetics: A cosmetic product is applied on the human body with the purpose of cleaning, protecting, maintaining or perfuming it.

Customer Retention: Customer retention describes a company's activities in order to ensure that the customer repeatedly comes back to repurchase from the company and does not move on to the competition.

Loyalty: Customer loyalty is expressed through an attitudinal and behavioural preference for one brand.

Luxury Beauty Industry: The luxury beauty industry belongs to the consumer products industry. It provides premium products in a set of different subcategories such as colour cosmetics, skin care, fragrances, sun care, hair care and men's grooming.

Marketing Communications: Marketing communications are coordinated messages through which a company reaches out to its target audience.

Social Media: Social media is the totality of different online channels and platforms, which enable online users not only to receive but also to create and share content.

Word of Mouth: Word-of-mouth is a powerful form of advertising based on peer-to-peer recommendations.

This research was previously published in Competitive Social Media Marketing Strategies edited by Wilson Ozuem and Gordon Bowen, pages 235-258, copyright year 2016 by Business Science Reference (an imprint of IGI Global).

Chapter 59
The Role of Social Media Strategies in Competitive Banking Operations Worldwide

Nurdan Oncel Taskiran
Kocaeli University, Turkey

Recep Yilmaz
Beykent University, Turkey

Nursel Bolat
Istanbul Arel University, Turkey

ABSTRACT

Social media has rapidly taken its place among the important phenomenons of today. It has an important role in institutionalization and companies' financial effectivness in many fields. This chapter discusses concept, development of social media, investigations about social media in different continents, its relation with institutionalization, and its role in the banking sector in the process of globalisation. In this study, social media strategies of a global bank on different continents are empirically analysed. Obtained data sheds light on the relationship between the social and economic capital in today's world in an interdisciplinary platform.

INTRODUCTION

A study conducted in USA puts forward various findings indicating a positive relationship between brain health of the elderly and social interaction. According to the same study, on- line social networks also support brain health of the elderly although it is realized in virtual environment (Ristau, 2011). What are the institutional and financial influences of these virtual formations which we define as new media? Can differences be seen between countries or continents? This study is based on such a problematique.

Being one of the social media accountant is very favourable nowadays and is a sign of being updated and instancy in the digital age. It is a must and vital for enterprenuers, who are rivals in the age of digi-

DOI: 10.4018/978-1-5225-5637-4.ch059

tal speedity on the social media. We have already known that the world is nothing than a small village anymore thanks to digital social media. The first popular social media is Facebook, where a news or a photo or an opinion or a suggession for action is shared once, then almost hundres or more see it, like it or hate it instantly. By the time, people, in pursuit of earning more, discovered how fruitful social media is and how earnings would be duplicated via advertisements on the social media pages. Many enterpreneurs in various fields have already attempted to take their places on the social media. However, banking business was not the first to involve with the social media. ING Bank is one of the assertive Banks, with its registered quality in the field of global banking.

ING Bank has many offices around the world; four of them are Australia, Canada, India and Turkey. The objective of the research is to investigate how ING Global Banking manages social media affairs and how it gets into contact with its customers and what kind of strategies it developed on Facebook. This is an emprical study in which discourse and semiological analyses and the significance of the subject matter is that ING Bank was awarded as "the most successful effective banking management" in Eastern Europe in 2012, with the products and services it provided to global customers. This investigation relates to the ways it deals with its global customers on social media and from that point it worths investigation. The research is limited to three months December 2012, January 2013, and February 2013.

Through a quick investigation on the social media, it can simply be recognised that ING banking is one of those whose global banking affairs expanded from America to Australia; Asia to Europe in the world. ING Banking seems well updated itself with Facebook and has taken its place among Facebook accountants, which is very popular for instant communication among people and private organizations for public announcements or civil public institutions especially governmental or political propagandas all around the world just like an epidemic. Beforehand, it would be beneficiary to learn more about some terms or concepts like globalism, social media, Facebook and the relationship among them.

VIRTUAL STRUCTURES OF COMPANIES AND CORPORATE COMMUNICATIONS

This part of the study investigates virtual structure types of companies. Virtual structures will be evaluated in the context of corporate communications. As known, internet has arisen with computer network constituted by Pentagon in 1969 for sharing data of Advanced Research Projects Agency (ARPA). Excghanging messages have also been enabled beside data through this network and expanded towards community and became World Wide Web (www) today. The concept of syber space formed as the result of this structure defines the interaction space in which global computer network which constitutes internet is formed (Giddens, 2000:418-420). Today, syber space not only forms a part of our reality but also has become a place which significantly reforms it. However there is no doubt about the presence of this place but also it becomes impossible to mention about its presence. So the concept 'virtual' is used to define that type of a reality. Virtual means something that is not actually present but seems as present. Virtual reality emphasizes the virtuality of reality by referring to a similar definition. This reality also reflects to corporate communication field and activities done by companies in syber space are integrated in the structure of reality (Koçel, 2001:361).

This new extent which is effective in formation of reality has begun to pull the business enterprises towards itself. It emerges as a quite effective tool particularly in public relations studies beside all activities of enterprises. Public relations activity which follows a way from institutionalization to nationalization constitutes an institution image through institutionalization and works on a plane which targets to control the institution perception of the target group (Yılmaz and Ertike, 2011:132-134). The concept of corporate communication is used in order to refer to communication field within this system. Concept is used to discriminate marketing-based public relations and esteem-based public relations. The concept of corporate communication may be defined as " a social process which enables continuous data and idea exchange between both varius departments and elements of the enterprise and, enterprise and environment or constitution of required relationships between departments" (Akat, Budak and Budak, 1994:272). Corporate communication transfers the effectiveness of corporate behaviours to all marketing fields and stakeholders (Steidl and Emery,1999:77). It refers to the communication between various target groups with this aspect. Communication channels gradually gain importance when communication is taken into consideration. Communication in virtual environment extremely gains importance as social media is one of the most important communication channels today.

Emergence of communication in virtual environment is possible through formers of communication. This formation requires a team work. Virtual team at that point is defined as "a group of people which works independently from time, place and group borders using technology in order to reach a common goal" (Akdoğan and Oflazer, 2002:827). Conducting this team work is enabled by virtual offices. Virtual work and workplace is used to determine "offices which are supported by information and communication technologies and which do not need dependence to a certain physical environment, and work trough a web site used commonly by a group of virtual workers" (Tutar, 2002).

Virtuality may be tool which is used to communicate and also sometimes the enterprise itself is seen to become virtual. Virtul companies which are defined as " independent company groups boud to each other with information technology in order to share skills, costs and market access" (Li and Xiao, 2006). Products or services may also become virtual as virtual companies. Virtual products or services mean " the products or services which are produced, distributed and sold in computer networks" and we usually see them today (Skyrme, 2012).

Companies which become completely virtual or use virtual environment as a tool are obliged to some type of network place. These formations which are named as virtual web are defined as "the open-ended clusters in which the companies are included which can contribute to any projects before the establishment of virtual organizations and of which properties are accepted by others as a result of a preliminary assessment," (Franke, 2012). Organizations constituted with these webs are named as virtual organizations and defined as " a group of companies which behave as a temporal and a single enterprise through joining to each other" (Wang, 2000). Maintainability of that type of enterprises depends on the continuity of supply and demand relationship.

A final concept is the concept of telework which refers to work from home. Telework is an expanded form of telecommunicating which is used to enable to work from home in order to reduce the time to go between home and workplace. The concept telework emphasizes the telecommunicating's converting the work to holism (Ölçer, 2004).

Working structure which is tried to describe under the light of basic concepts refers to the companies which maintain some part of their presence in virtual environment beside the companies which completely work with a virtual structure. These formations may reach houses of people through computer hardwares and enable an intense mind contact. Mind contact manifests in in-house and external dimensions.Corporate culture and institutional commitment may develop and it also contributes to relationships with media which are indirect public relations tools. Virtual reality forms a significant domain of corporate communication also during crisis (Sayımer, 2008; Uzunoğlu et al., 2009).

Social network which is out of the enterprise and thereby not controlled by the enterprise but also enables access may be used as market based and for corporate communication purposes. Especially the messages in facebook and twitter may be used for promotion and announcement of corporate activities. The present study is focused on announement types in different continents. Although data will be discussed in 'Results' part, usage of social networking site must also be discussed. The following part mentions about this issue.

AN OVERVIEW OF SOCIAL MEDIA STUDIES IN DIFFERENT CONTINENTS

While value is focused in America, it is seen that on- line networks and influences of them on social life are focued in other parts of the world. However, while it is tried to analyse whether on-line life has a negative effect on off-line social life in Europe, it is questioned whether social media has a positive effect in Asia. The research has indicated that only a trend difference is present in studies investigating the same research object however the principle of the universality of science is preserved. The main factor which determines the trends is the closed gaps by level of knowledges produced by countries. Mental concerns become specific as information gaps are closed. Another factor which determines trends is the traditional cultures in which scientists grew and the effect of presence of sub-cultures composed of academies as a group. So, while value is in the foreground in USA which is a more individualist and cosmopolitan community, destructive aspect of social media on daily relationships is the deterministic factor of the examination plane in European countries in which traditional culture is strong and positive aspects of social media on socialization is emphasized in Asian countries in which community culture is dominant. However we must state that specific characteristcs of the studies are at leve of nuance. Particularly, if we may state that social structures become similar in globalisation process and the world which gradually becomes a global village produces individuals who have similar conscious structure, it may also be possible to mention about the similarity of conscious structures and awaraness levels of scientists. Universality of science becomes closer to its real meaning. It may be useful to emphasize that the abovementioned differences would not localize them.Given that there is only a trend difference between studies, it would be possible to state that scientific studies are global in fact and each trend gives a different color and dimension to common global efforts (Stefanone, Lackaff and Rosen, 2011; Gosling et al., 2011; Gonzales and Hancock, 2011; Junghyun and Lee, 2011; Kalpidou, Costin and Morris, 2011; Thomas, Robert and Dunbar, 2011; Hsu, Wang and Tai, 2011).

GLOBALISM, SOCIAL MEDIA AND BANKING SECTOR

Ino Rossi points out the increasing and deepening interaction among different cultures and traditional conflicts. To him, globalism is a process manifested within the social layers of a society itself. These conflicts are motivated by social interest in a society. Gradually, it is accompanied by multi cultural affairs and information technology as well (Ceylan, 2011: 37).What bears a major significance here is its strict observation over intercultural behaviours of people. Countries are in hard rivalry to acquire the capital, which is a principal element of production, on their side. Thanks to ICT developments and globalism, economical and social substratum have to face a radical change (Soros, 2003: 2).

One of the crucial points with the globalization is some critical thoughts about its eliminating of traditional values. It is an inevitable process which can be denied conversely. Globalism establishes a threat against cultural values and identities (Stiglitz, 2006: 273). Functionally, globalism is established upon hard competing which enables setting its own values separately. It means that traditional culture substantially might get injured.

Some researchers evaluate globalism prior to its political cultural and ideological aspects (Ertürk, 2010: 25). One of the factors of its fast expansion lies in the developments of Information Communication Technologies (ICT). Data improvements and ICT developments especially on the internet phenomena affected financial markets directly and inevitably (Ceylan, 2011: 52). The undeniable impact of ICT during 1980's, almost extinguished the concept of "distance" on earth. Within its ideological respect, globalism exists on a dialectical base (Ertürk, 2010: 26-27). Expansion of globalism is not estimated as limited only with the developments of technology and ideology, but also economically. Globalism has an active role on the global integration of expansion and improvement of economical, political, and social systems of countries (Ertürk, 2010: 28).

The internet has become an ubiquitous tool for users ranging from professional careers to casual housewives and being online has prompted curiosity and speculation about the interaction between this technology and individual person variables (Mitchell et al., 2011). Therefore, the equilibrium between the counterparts are highly considerable. On Facebook, there is a heterogenious population on each social level, some are disguised, some fake, some not. Institutions with a good image and profound vision for the future have to be on good terms with online social media users.

According to Marshall, social media means one or more people connected each other with social activities (Marshall, 1999: 4).Thanks to ICT and globalisation, today we have a different sort of media which is called "networking society". Today individuals are surrounded with nets which provide them immense facilities. On the other side, users, doomed to computer screen only, lead an unsocial life. Social net works can be defined as individual web pages that enable people sharing some fruitful information around and making socialization possible for those who would like to have interactive relationships (Özmen et al., 2011). Contents are bound to people and can be determined independently. In other words, social media eliminates time and space boundaries and develops a kind of communicational system in which mobile sharing based on "discussion". Social media platforms are mainly established on the basis of "communication and "sharing" (Erkul, 2009: 8).

Facebook is a networking system which provides people interactions and sharings, join other groups, write about a subject and express his opinion on open access platforms online (Gonzales, 2010). Facebook was created by a Havardian student Mark Zuckerberg to keep in touch with other Havard students over the Internet and get to know each other better. By the time, Facebook became so popular that is was soon opened to other colleges. By the end of the following year it was also open to high schools. The year after that, it was opened to the general Internet public. According to the statistics, Facebook has reached 1 bilion users in the world and day by day it is getting incresed. At present, most instutions, companies have Facebook accounts and make their business via online transactions. As a conclusion, explosive innovation thanks to the growth of ICT, particularly the provision of welfare services, largely unchanged. Where socialising, commerce, information finding, entertainment and travel have all undergone profound structural transformations (Shah, 2012).

Another aspect of this new world set on a technological basis emerges in the increase of cross- border activities of financial sector. Global ownership and global activities have already come into prominence and the expansion of ICT at top speed also caused the increase of cross- border capital flows. Besides the removal of exchange questioning, major reasons of globalism are easy accessibility of foreign securities thanks to technological revolutions and the rapid increasing importance of institutional investors in addition to the diversification of the portfolio (Şener, 2012). Along with the technology, financial sector has been expandad all around and brougt facilities to some daily business. People have alreday achieved the facilities of banking transactions online at desk, which exposed globalisation of banking systems as well.

Internet users are now broadly representative of large swathes of the population, with far fewer groups remaining unconnected to the Internet – the elderly, low-educated and disabled being the main examples. From the point of view of public service delivery, it is of course highly important to encourage these groups to get online, to ensure equality of access to the opportunities available there (Shah, 2012).

People, as a must of information society, should be provided technological conveniences by govenmental subsidaries as a need of cross-border relations.

Establishing groups in the social media are closely related with social capital idea which is defined as people's social networks and mutual trust that they can draw upon in order to solve common problems. Social capital is very important for improving group social participation (e.g. perceived membership and influence (Tsai et al., 2012).

Social media consists of tools that enable open online exchange of information through conversation and interaction. Unlike traditional Internet and communication technologies (ICTs), social media manage the content of the conversation or interaction as an information artifact in the online environment (Yates & Paquette, 2011).

Banking hosts seem quite beneficiary part here as costumers are ready to interact online from social capital point of view.

What social media online system exposed on banking institutions generally is integration of some new units. Additionally, it also provided standardization of information flow system, improvement of efficiency, recurrence of the same transactions and more work in less time.

Moreover, it provided a decrease in manager employment, less cost and distribution of management responsibilties and globalization, as well (Işın, 2006).

These days' computers, mobile phones and the Internet serve as central means of communication, social interaction and entertainment, and the popularity of new technology has played a prominent role in the rise of different online networks (Näsi et al., 2011) Among the social media sites, Facebook is the first and the most prevalent one. On networking, people have the opportunity of expressing themselves in louder voices. Therefore being instant and have an account on the social media is one of the musts of information society. Social networks gained much respect for many institutions as a source of information and feedback for social networksa re environments where most people react negatively or positively but independently. Similarly, Facebook users actively use and follow online banking occasions or ask questions, like or dislikes about transactions or bank officials, in the trendy way of the digital age.

Investigations demonstrate 44% of global customers use social networks in order to get individual banking information. Türkiye is categorized one of the leading countries. Generally, 78% of customers use social media with the purpose of banking products and services and 53% as feedback they experienced (Elhadef & Hatipoglu, 2012: 7). Facebook, as the most preferred social site in Türkiye provides an environment on which users evaluate products, experiences, feedbacks, services, opinions or actions, etc. as likes or dislikes independently. As a conclusion of globalisation, Facebook gained a huge number of banking hosts as new accountants and their customers as well. ING Bank is one of them participated and establised a remarkable position among counterparts.

On examining four web pages of ING Bank Global Offices on Facebook, an apparent similarity about the visual frame is remarkable. The orange colour at the background and the lion image on it toghether are the components of official ING Bank logo. Each Facebook Time Tunnel page of ING Bank includes many themes under different titles within Time tunnel windows. According to their contents these windows can be classified into seven sections;

- Contents relating to ING Bank advertisements, announcements and campaigns and videos relating to products and services.
- Customers' Questions &ING Bank Answers; Customers' feedbacks (positive and negative.)
- Contents relating to ING social (responsibility) activities.
- Surveys and contests relating to product and services.

It can be submitted that contents are mosty focused on advertisements, announcements, campaigns and feedbacks.

AMPRICAL ANALYSIS

ING Bank Australia on Facebook

ING AUSTRALIA began operating in Australia in 1999 and joined Facebok in 2010. By doing business online, over the phone and through intermediaries, they keep overheads low and pass the savings onto customers in the form of competitive rates. Today, ING DIRECT has $23 billion in deposits, more than $37 billion in loans and around 1.4 million customers. The page has 4872 likes. (March 9th, 2013, GMT 16.15)

FACEBOOK TIME TUNNEL CONTENTS 2012 DEC. ING BANK AUSTRALIA

Contents Relating to Advertisements, Announcements, Videos and Campaigns, Services and Products

1. Make a list, check it twice (and more tips to make your money go further this Christmas). http://bit.ly/INGxmasSavingTips.
2. Only a few hours to go! What are your resolutions for the new year?
3. We've just announced that we'll be decreasing interest rates on ING DIRECT variable residential home loans by 0.25% per annum, effective Monday 24 December. ING IRECT's Mortgage Simplifier will be 5.72% per annum.
4. Are you Super savvy?
5. All sorted for gift buying, or are you a last-minute shopper?

6. Do you splash out, or save over the holidays? BBQ or Banquet?
7. Please look what Ing Direct do for italian market:http://www.youtube.com/watch?v=vB6cFsAgkbw
8. They stole the dream of many generation, why they do that?
9. Is terrible realy no soul, no respect.

Customer's Questions, Answers and Feedbacks

1. Thank you, but why is it it taking so long to pass on the rates cuts?
2. Hi. Is it possible to add my fiancee to my current everyday account so she can get a card and access it? Or would we have to open a new joint account together?
3. Hi, I just wanted to find out that whether your fixed rate for home loan will reduce sooner or not? Thank you.
4. Hey! I was just looking up everyday accounts and came across your Orange Everyday account... I want to know how ATM withdrawal fees work. Do we pay them first, then get reimbursed for them once I withdraw $200?
5. I have a savings maximiser account and I was wondering how I can go about requesting a statement for a specific time period which I need for an application. It needs to be a standard bank statement so the export function available isn't going to help. Thanks! P.s. a 1300 or 1800 number would be great! I can't call the 133 number without getting charged on either my landline or mobile.
6. Yay. The Reserve Bank have lowered interest rates by 25%. Come on ING. Pass on the WHOLE cut! (u sure raise it by the full amount when interest rates go up)
7. Come on ING Direct the RBA just cut rates by 0.25% it's time to pass that cut on in FULL to your customers
8. Well Done guys, the big 4 need someone here to create some competition... I'm Glad I'm with ING - Leading the way once again...
9. Thanks for passing on the full rate cut, love your work! Show the big 4 up ING!
10. Why three weeks to get a rate cut? Surely it doesn't take that long to change a number on a computer? An increase is almost instantaneous on our loans. I don't understand. I am happy or the cut, but it seems like you are taking what you can for three weeks.
11. Bravo ING Direct on passing on the full rate cut! Thank you for leading the way!
12. Well done ING! The full 25 points. Corporate creed set aside!
13. yay for passing on the rate cut!
14. ING Without a doubt best bank, but considering you are purely Online based only, you would think your Android App would be semi usable. Huge let down in that department. Other than that, I am Happy.
15. Thanks for passing on the full interest rate cut ING - You guys Rock!
16. Hi, New ING Direct customer here, signed up a few days ago and my accounts were activated this morning; just waiting for my debit card to arrive:) Just a suggestion, maybe you could point your improvements team to have a look at the mobile banking apps from ANZ and Commonwealth. I just switched from anz and the login process on their app is much easier, a once off registration of your mobile device... then just a 4 digit pin next time you log on- which saves time. ING's current app is okay. But trying to find your client number to log on takes up time, Also aesthetically. if ING Directs new app looks like these or compared quality wise, everything would be perfect. http://www.gomoney.anz.com/ http://www.commbank.com.au/mobile/commbank-kaching/what-is-kaching.html

17. After years of international travel, which unfortunately yet rather inevitably results in occasional fraudulent bank account activity while abroad, I haven't had an Australian banking instituation to sort it out so consumately, quickly and quietly as ING! Thanks team for restoring some faith!
18. Best. Everyday. Account. Ever. ♥ u ING Direct.
19. I had a really bad customer service experience today & decided to close down all my accounts from ING (although started to a build my little savings for future home). No matter how good they offer to attract the potential clients. One of the customer service officers unable to explain & provide the written form of the policy that she asked me for a simple enquire and they call it SECURITY purpose! Finally I would like to score them below 5 out of 10 & I quit. Thanks to social networking so that we can express our satisfaction.
20. Will you consider matching your interest rate in saving maximiser with what others are at, such as Rabo? Im a long time customer but I partly moved towards rabo due to the better rates, every little cent counts!
21. I am really unhappy with the online banking system. It constantly times out and I am having to log in multiple times in the space of a few minutes!
22. LOVE your customer service! Painless, friendly and efficient. TOPS!:D
23. Hey! Absolutely love you guys!! My one year old sons have accounts with Commonwealth and I'm already horribly dissatisfied. Do you have any accounts that are more directed to children? Or any benefits to a child joining? Also, can a child join?? If so, I'd really love to sign them up with you guys and make my life easier! Thanks, Amanda
24. I know not many people can say this but - I love my bank!

Surveys and Contests

1. Are you spent up already, or do you manage your pay-cycle budget with your savings?
2. Got any sneaky savings secrets?
3. How will you be spending Boxing Day?

Social (Responsibility) Activities

(None for this month)

FACEBOOK TIME TUNNEL CONTENTS 2013 JAN. ING BANK AUSTRALIA

Contents Relating to Advertising, Announcements, Videos and Campaigns, Services and Products

1. Happy New Year, everyone! If you're back in the office today like us, ease in to it, and spend your first 2013 working day well.
2. We're happy to announce this week's winners of our Year of the Saver prize draw. They have won $2013 by opening a Savings Maximiser. You could too! Find out more at ingdirect.com.au/2013. Promoter ING Bank (Australia) Limited. Authorised under NSW Permit No. LTPS/12/11332, Victorian Permit No. 12/3404, ACT TP12/05079, SA Licence No. T12/2636.

Customer's Questions, Answers and Feedbacks

1. ING you disappoint me! Your customer service if by far the worst I have ever had to deal with. You were absolutely no help at all when my account was drained overseas and with the 'glitch' that you admitted to has brought my account into overdraw. Your customer service people don't seem to know how to perform simple tasks when asked a question. I can't wait to close my account with you. It has been nothing but problems. I am now in debt over $150 out of my own pocket just in phone calls because not one of you can give me a straight answer!

Survey and Contests

1. Are you plugged-in to the news? Do you need to know what's happening in the world 24/7? We're wondering; where do you get your news from?

Social (Responsibility) Activities

(None for this month)

FACEBOOK TIME TUNNEL CONTENTS 2013 FEB. ING BANK AUSTRALIA

Contents Relating to Advertisements, Announcements, Videos and Campaigns, Services and Products

1. 2013 is the Year of the Saver! To celebrate we are rewarding 10,000 of our existing Savings Maximiser customers. Terms and conditions apply.Visit http://ingdirect.com.au/saverrewards, check if you are eligible and tell us what you're saving for.
2. Want cash back? Here's how video!

Customer's Customer's Questions, Answers and Feedbacks

1. Hi, is it possible to have a secondary orange everyday visa debit card for my partner to use overseas?
2. Hi Alain, we have 2 cards on my account and my husband used his overseas. Just let ING know he's travelling so they don't think overseas transactions are suspicious / potentially fraudulent!
3. Thanks Jo. do both cards have the same number and security digits on the back Jo?
4. **ING DIRECT Australia** Hi Alain, is your partner an Australian resident? To open a new account with ING DIRECT you must be an Australian resident. If they meet these criteria they can certainly apply and have a card issued in their name. There are some fees associated with using the VISA Debit Card internationally, you can view the information on our website under 'Everyday' - 'Where are the fees?' Cheers, Tash
5. If not am I able to change my solo account to a joint account for a secondary card?
6. **ING DIRECT Australia** Hi Alain, a single account will only be issued with one card for the account holder. If you wish to apply for a second joint account you certainly can and each account holder is issued with a card, but you must meet the criteria to open an account. Thanks, Tash

7. Hi, how long does it take to transfer Funds from Commonwealth to ING Direct orange everyday account?

8. Does ING offer any sort of savings accounts for children?

9. how do i stop all this annoying crap coming up on my page?

10. My husband and I recently took out our first home loan with ING Direct. As expected we were very excited to be joint home owners for the first time. When I arrived home there was a parcel waiting for him at the post office. I went and picked it up and left it for him to open. However I was extremely disappointed to discover the parcel my husband received was in fact a house warming pack from ING direct which had excluded me completely. I was not referred to in the whole welcome letter......disgraceful ING to discriminate against the joint home owner. I'm equally involved in this home loan, I share the debt & the home loan repayment responsibilities yet you send the welcome pack to only one of us - how can you justify that? I'm offended. I called the support line & nothing. The least you could do is apologize and send the other home owner their welcome pack. I'll be waiting for mine in the mail. We are planning to refinance in a year and if I am not equally acknowledged we'll be finding other lenders.

11. **ING DIRECT Australia** Hi Michelle, we are sorry to hear that the experience of receiving your welcome pack has left you with a feeling of disappointment. As I am sure you are aware you have not been excluded on purpose. The pack itself is sent only with the intention of congratulations. Our apologises again. Cilla

12. **ING DIRECT Australia** Hi Michelle, I have investigated your enquiry and have attempted to call you today. Are you able to confirm a good time to call back and have a chat over the phone? Looking forward to your reply. Regards Kayla.

13. Thanks Kayla, I much appreciated your call this afternoon. Thank you for your response to my concern. I'm glad to hear you are changing your procedures going forward & I thank you in advance for my house warming gift. Well done ING!

14. **ING DIRECT Australia** Hi Michelle, I'm so happy to hear this has been resolved and you're happy with the outcome. It was lovley speaking with you. Congratulations again of your new home and hope you and your partner are enjoying all the little treats in your housewarming gift. Cheers, Kayla

15. Time to update your iphone app I think. Use the ANZ app as inspiration:)

16. I received this email today:

Hi Peter,

This is just a short note to say thanks for banking with ING DIRECT and being a loyal customer. We value your business and we want tothank you for banking with us. If there's anything you need, or if you have some feedback you'd like to share, we always want to hear from you so call us anytime, 24/7 on 133 464.

Thanks again, Brett Morgan, Executive Director, Customers ING DIRECT. Feedback is always welcomed in my business (good or bad) and on this occassion I'm happy to say its all GOOD for your bank. I spruke ING everywhere. Banks rarely receive feedback of that nature. The only issue I have is attempting to forward my feedback, might I suggest an email requesting feedback with a reply email address. I tried the 133464 number but refuse to go through the whole prompt system, other than that congratulations on a job well done to date... Regards Peter

1. I wish the interest rates would go up my investments arnt growing very fast.

Surveys and Contests

1. How do you plan to spend your Valentine's Day well?
2. Got a favourite to win? What's your pick for the Best Picture?Oscars night!
3. How would you caption these pictures of Guy Sebastian? Caption one today and you could win a VIP Backstage Double Pass to one of his Get Along 2013 Tour concerts. More info on how to enter here:http://bit.ly/GetAlongWithGuy
4. We've got over 200 tickets to Guy Sebastian's next tour to give away, including VIP Backstage Double Passes. Enter to win:http://bit.ly/GetAlongWithGuy
5. Guy Sebastian fans, this is your last chance to win tickets to his upcoming tour. We've got over 200 tickets including VIP Backstage Double Passes to give away. Don't miss out. Enter before the competition closes:http://bit.ly/GetAlongWithGuy!

Social (Responsibility) Activities

1. Do some good Australia – rain or shine! Today is clean up australia day! So get outside and lend a hand!

ING Direct Canada on Facebook

ING DIRECT is Canada's leading direct bank with over 1.8 million Clients and close to $40 billion in total assets. ING DIRECT has been operating in Canada since 1997, and paid more than $5 billion in interest to clients. ING DIRECT is open for banking 24 hours a day, 7 days a week, at ingdirect.ca, on mobile devices at m.ingdirect.ca The mission is to help Canadians live better lives through changing the conversation about money. Welcome to Forward Banking. ING Bank Canada joined Facebook in 2009. 23.030 people liked the page (9th March, GMT 16.14).

FACEBOOK TIME TUNNEL CONTENTS 2012 DEC. ING DIRECT CANADA

Contents Relating to Advertising, Announcements, Videos and Campaigns, Services and Products

1. Happy Holidays from everyone at ING DIRECT Canada!
2. Time to double the rewards! We've doubled our Refer A Friend Bonus to $50 and you have until December 31st 2012 to participate. Refer friends with your Orange Key and you are both rewarded with $50! Rules and restrictions here:http://www.ingdirect.ca/referafriend/To help you spread the word we've created these handy Orange Key cards. Print them out, cut them and start referring all your friends.

Customer's Questions, Answers and Feedbacks

(None for this month)

Surveys and Contests

(None for this month)

Social (Responsibility) Activities

1. The month of "Movember" is officially in the books. To do our part in helping change the face of men's health, we assembled a team of ING DIRECT's finest Mo Bros and Mo Sistas to raise money and awareness for prostate cancer and male mental health initiatives. Our team, The MOward Bankers, raised $6,500 for this worthy cause – which ranked us #685 out of 23,664 teams in Canada. To learn more about our team and the Movember initiative, visit our official Movember page:http://ca.movember.com/team/581653

FACEBOOK TIME TUNNEL CONTENTS 2013 JAN ING DIRECT CANADA

Contents Relating to Advertisements, Announcements, Videos and Campaigns, Services and Products

1. Millions of Canadians suffer from TFSA everyday... Get fast acting TFSA (Tax-Free Savings Account)relief now. Treat TFSA with great rates, no fees and no minimums. Get fast- acting TFSA relief now. http://www.ingdirect.ca/en/landingpage/tfsarelief/index.html
2. Start 2013 on the right fiscal foot:http://ow.ly/guvGO
3. Suffering from TFSA confusion? Here's a great source from the Canada Revenue Agency to help clear the fog! http://ow.ly/gxygB
4. Regardless of what side of the fence you sit on with the return of pro hockey, it's nice to read that the players wanted to improve the structure of their pension. Now, it has become a defined benefit and players are also able to contribute some of their own money to improve their pension package. Yes, we're talking about the 1%, but it's nice to see that they're planning for their futures, too.http://ow.ly/gCovy
5. T.F.S... A? Have you given any thought to your Tax Free Saving Account? This year the contribution limit is $5,500 - sweet!
6. Get fast-acting TFSA relief.
7. No minimums, no service charges. It's tax-free and the rate is great. In just one dose you'll be feeling better. http://ow.ly/gI9Fy
8. Ideally, we prefer more economical modes of transportation (public transit, two feet and a heartbeat), but the ongoing discussion of whether it's best fix-up, buy, or lease a new vehicle continues to challenge many drivers. Included in this article is the idea that '$4K in annual repairs is about the break-even point financially'.For those that drive, which side of the argument do you fall on? http://ow.ly/gO2iK
9. The ability to send money via text is apparently headed to Britain by Spring 2014. Would you feel comfortable sending your money by sharing only a phone number? http://ow.ly/gQjK5
10. For some of us, an #RSP account can seem like a blur, @Moneyville has got 10 facts that can get you focused:http://ow.ly/h6sRv
11. Confused & disoriented about the difference between an RSP and a TFSA? The Globe and Mail helps shed some light:http://ow.ly/h6ro5

12. Spending problem? Blame it on your brain. The Financial Post has got some great tips on how your mind can work for you:http://ow.ly/h6sTl

13. Think you're too young for RSPs? Think again! The Globe and Mail has got pointers for every generation. http://ow.ly/h6sSy

14. Need relief from RSP Season? Moneyville's got some quick pointers when it comes to your yearly contributions:http://ow.ly/h6sUO

15. What better time to check on your financial health than a Thursday morning? http://ow.ly/hijwI

16. Happy New Year Savers! May all your savings goals be achieved in 2013!

17. "I will only spend money on what I need". We've learned our lesson after the holidays!

18. It's RSP season and which means it's the perfect time to check your financial health. Hop on over to our RSP Check-up app and see how you're doing: http://ow.ly/h41N0 How do you feel about saving during RSP season?

19. It's RSP season again. Time to get out your tissues, aroma therapy candles, and RSP remedies. http://ow.ly/h4FqX

20. It's cold, flu, and RSP season. Time to make sure your financial health is just as strong as your physical: http://ow.ly/h7PL9

21. Does size matter? If you're feeling overwhelmed about how big your #RSP contribution should be Globe and Mail can help:http://ow.ly/h6qV0

22. Think you're too young for RSPs? Think again! The Globe and Mail has got pointers for every generation. http://ow.ly/h6sSy

23. One of our Orange Ambassadors - Chris Vollick (aka @Canadian88 on Twitter) - has shared the '52 Week Money Challenge' chart that has been making its rounds online, and has plegged to save north of $1,300 this year. Who's going to join Chris? Have you set a savings goal for 2013? To read more about the challenge itself, read Chris' blog post here: http://ow.ly/gRw0q

Customer's Questions, Answers and Feedbacks

(None for this month)

Surveys and Contests

1. Let's talk about budgets! How much do you usually spend on a night out with friends?

2. Who has been the most influential person in helping you take care of your personal finances?

3. Let's pretend your magic money tree grew a new $100 bill for the weekend. What fun would you plan to make the most of it? Spend it wisely...

4. We're looking for some good reads this lazy Sunday. Who has a good book or article suggestion for us?

5. It's TFSA season! Let's start the week off with a little quiz. What year did the Government of Canada introduce the Tax Free Savings Account (TFSA) as a savings vehicle for Canadians?

6. Our TFSA quiz week continues! The NEW annual contribution limit for 2013 has increased to....

7. Happy Wednesday, let's keep this #TFSA quiz week rolling. TRUE or FALSE: Having a TFSA has an impact on federal benefits and credits?

8. Need a cure to the mid-week blues? Maclean's Magazine shared a list of '99 stupid things the government did with your money'.http://www2.macleans.ca/2013/01/07/99-stupid-things-the-government-did-with-your-money-part-i/

9. Sunday mornings are best for which of the following? a) Brunch b) RSP planning c) Sleeping in
10. Interesting idea from the Financial Post today - would you rather pay down debt or make contributions to your RRSP? http://business.financialpost.com/2013/01/16/have-we-given-up-on-retirement-saving/
11. Following yesterday's RSP question, how much do you plan on contributing to your RSP this year?
12. When someone mentions 'money', the first thing that comes to mind is _____?
13. We'd like to thank all of our Clients and followers for their feedback. While it was never our intention to make light of any health concerns related to mental illness, we have heard you loud and clear. We have decided to remove our RSP (Retirement Savings Plan)) commercial from TV. It may take a few days for it to come off air, but the process is in motion. Please accept our apologies if you were offended by our commercial.
14. We're in the heart of RSP (Retirement Savings Plan) season, and we thought there is no better way to keep the momentum going than to start an RSP quiz week. Besides saving for your retirement, one of the main advantages of contributing to an RSP is that it helps to reduce your taxable income for the year. Question 1: what is the deadline to contribute to your RSP for 2013?
15. RSP Quiz time! True or false. Can you borrow money to contribute to your RSP?
16. Happiness is _____.
17. True or False: Canadians who plan their finances are happier. http://ow.ly/he1c3
18. What's the best retirement advice you've heard?

Social (Responsibility) Activities

(None for this month)

FACEBOOK TIME TUNNEL CONTENTS 2013 FEB. ING DIRECT CANADA

Contents Relating to Advertising, Announcements, Videos and Campaigns, Services and Products

1. There's just a month till the 2012 #RSP deadline! Are you a procrastinator? Money Sense Mag has some tips for you:http://ow.ly/hiN1i
2. Are you in your 20s and trying to figure out how to start saving up for your RSP? Money Sense has some advice for you:http://ow.ly/hiSoU
3. The past two days we've posted Retirement advice for people in their 20s and 30s. Don't worry, we've got tips for those of you in your 40s too! Have a look.
4. This Valentine's Day, I'm being a smart saver by.
5. With Valentine's Day around the corner, here are 6 ways to save money! http://ow.ly/hEVMU
6. If a relative gives me American money, do I deposit it in the same way as I would deposit an American cheque? By sending it to ING Direct via snail mail in Toronto? I don't get USD very often, but it would be nice to know what I have to do to deposit it. Can I put it in one of the Exchange Network ABM's?
7. The Psychology of Smart Savings via savings.com
8. Thinking about applying for a mortgage soon? Here are some pointers from The Star that could help you clean up any errors on your credit score first. http://ow.ly/hRrgk

9. Don't you think you deserve a vacation? Financial Post has got some great ideas to help you start saving up for a trip, plus they've got some tips on how to travel on a budget.http://ow.ly/hTjrY

10. Think you know everything about mortgages? Here are 5 things you most likely didn't know about the Canadian mortgage market via Rate Hub. Link to image:http://www.ratehub.ca/images/info-graphics/mortgage-market-statistics.jpg

11. Your future self wants to thank your present self for stashing away some of those hard-earned dollars

12. "The person who doesn't know where his next dollar is coming from usually doesn't know where his last dollar went." Anonymous

13. In a few days we say goodbye to pennies! How do you feel about that? Hoard all the pennies!

14. Different generations have different needs and priorities, we get that! So to help you guys out, next week we'll be posting some Money Sense articles that will help shed some light on how each age group can invest in their Retirement. Check in everyday at 9am ET starting tomorrow!

15. Did you know that today is the day that our Canadian pennies are phased out?! So now what? Check out Royal Canadian Mint's website for some answers on what happens next.http://ow.ly/hj6Ek

16. For those of you in your 30s, we know things can be tough financially as you try to balance family, debts, and savings. Need a bit of help when it comes to retirement savings? Here's some RSP advice for you from Money Sense: http://ow.ly/hiT3y

17. THRILLED & honoured to be teaching a series of by donation yoga classes at ING DIRECT Canada's Orange Cafe in Toronto all March long, in support of Power of Movement! (also excited to be volunteering at the event March 3rd w/ YogaFit Canada)http://www.powerofmovement.ca/

18. Hey Savers! The price of gas has gone up yet again. Here are a few tips to help you save in these kinds of circumstances:

    a. Try to keep your car as light as possible by removing excess weight. With less to pull, your car will use less fuel!

    b. Consider commuting. You will be doing your wallet and the environment a big favor!

    c. Keep your tires properly inflated. Believe it or not, this will make a big difference in your gas mileage!

    d. Turn off your car if you are idling. It costs less fuel to restart your car than to keep it on when you're not moving.

    e. Drive at the speed limit! Constantly accelerating only wastes gas. Besides, a speeding ticket is much more expensive.

19. If you're in your 50s and 60s, you're most likely thinking pretty seriously about your retirement plans.Read this Money Sense article for some insight on how to use your RSPs to reach your goals: http://ow.ly/hiVcy

20. Ever wish you could deposit a cheque just by snapping a picture of it? Well, it's on the way. http://ow.ly/hC87i

21. Do you know the top 10 financial mistakes made by Generation Y, according to the Financial Post? Take a look at this article which also gives some great tips on how to avoid these mistakes in the future! http://ow.ly/hQVgP

22. Get Rich Slowly shares 10 tips on how to make extra cash. Turning a hobby into a business sounds good to us! Some of these you can do while having a full-time job as well! Can you think of more ways that aren't mentioned?http://ow.ly/hvQ10

23. On March 1st, don't forget to RSP. Everybody's (hopefully) doing it. If you want to join the cool kids, RSP here: http://www.ingdirect.ca/en/save-invest/rsps/index.html

24. Here's a fun little infographic from mint.ca on the History of the Penny. Since it was removed from circulation just over a week ago, we're wondering - do you miss the Penny? http://www.mint.ca/store/mint/learn/infographic-history-of-the-penny-7200012

Customer's Questions, Answers and Feedbacks

1. Does ING do RESP's? I need to move the one for my toddler, and since I'm moving all other accounts to ING, I'd like to bring the RESP over too.

2. Do you have locations with tellers? or just sign up locations?

3. So did the Capital One buyout only impact ING Direct in the USA?

4. Hello, how do I delete my account with ING and remove my details from your system? Please let me know what is the procedure for that. Thanks!

5. From a recent mail I got from you, under the "stuff your lawyers make you say" (cute), I saw that you've been acquired by The Bank of Nova Scotia. Can you please let me know what changes will happen and how it will affect your customers? Thank you.

6. I am wondering what the fees are to transfer RSPs from ING to another institution... (don't panic!! i am not saying i will do it, but curious to know anyway)

7. **ING DIRECT Canada** Hi Kyle and Dogger, While we know that credit cards are a hot topic, we don't have an update as to when an ING DIRECT credit card will be offered. Keep your eyes open for updates here and on our website!

8. ING used to have the best USD exchange rates, now it is not!

9. How long until our 2012 RRSP and TFSA receipts are available online?

10. **ING DIRECT Canada** Hi Rae, 2012 RSP Receipts were mailed out starting the week of January 9, 2013 and e-Receipts were made available at the same time. Receipts are not issued for your TFSA as that account is just that - tax-free! No need to claim interest earned on Tax-Free accounts. Be sure to check your tax receipt preferences online to see if you're set for "Electronic" e-Receipts. If you are and don't see your RSP receipts, call us at 1-888-464-3232. We're here 24/7

11. Dear ING, please come back to America. It was a poor choice to sell out to Capital One, but I know your fans will easily forgive you. Just come back and we will come back as loyal customers.

12. C'est la fin de ING pour ma famille. Le fait que ING ne permette pas les paiement de factures à la SAAQ vient de nous couter un beau $35.00 de frais de chèque sans fond. Erreur d'institution.

13. In your ads, you shouldn't make fun of people with illnesses and diseases.

14. I was offended to see the ING ad pop on my screen today while surfing......I thought they had pulled the ad or was that just pulled from CTV.

15. After outcry, you pulled your TV ads but I see your pop up ads on websites continue with the same mocking tone. Are you just not getting it? Forward banking??? How about forward THINKING??? The shame continues...ridiculous.

16. Please, please, PLEASE roll this out for all clients quickly. This would instantly become the single most convenient feature of my chequing account. No more trudging to the ATM in -20 just to make a deposit. Seriously, please make this available for all of us very, very soon.

17. David Green How secure is this with programs like photoshop etc???

18. **ING DIRECT Canada**. Great comments, keep them coming. It's good to keep in mind this feature is still a pilot-project and we're testing it out to see what works. While our goal is to go paperless, for now, we still require the original cheque be mailed or dropped off to us. There isn't actual legislation in place just yet for features like this and until that happens, we're unable to be rid of the paper portion .

19. Buying with credit online and paying $25 for delivery.

20. Forgetting the chocolate and gifts and going to dinner at a restaurant; instead going to a local "wild game night" dinner with venison and other game for the low price of $15pp.

21. Me and my significant other wait until the 15th or 16th to buy each other chocolate. It always gets marked way down after Valentine's Day has passed by. Still the same chocolate, and the day isn't significant to us.

22. Credit cards? How much longer do we have to wait!

23. I asked the same question a few weeks ago and did not get a direct answer. Perhaps now that they are part of BNS those plans are being scrapped.

24. But you would think the opposite. they should offer a mastercard or visa at 9.99%

25. What happened the Apple Gift Cards for switching our payroll to ING? It was promised to be sent 30 days after - my payroll was transfered in October 2012. We're going on 100+ days late...

26. my roommate switched payroll on jan3 and got his a week ago.

27. February 26, 2013 and still nothing.

28. yours - 0.988, interchangefinancial - 0.998 !

29. You're complaining about 0.010%? Dont get me wrong I'd want my money as well but when you look at how "off" Ing directs TFSA compared to other online banks measuring in full percentages is, you'd have more of a shoebox to stand on.

30. i joined ths banking 1 thing thy dont tell ya you will not get ur pin number untill u have urselves idea notorized whch comes out of ur pockets.first u join then send a cheque they deposit in ur account u have set up on line.u awit for ur banking

31. **ING DIRECT Canada** Hi Vwd Garcia, While we aim to make your banking experience as easy as possible, sometimes we require extra identification. Normally, by cashing your cheque and doing a soft credit check, we have everything we need to get you started. In some cases, there isn't enough credit history, and we ask for your help. This is where the form and your ID come in. Once verified, you have full access to your account and you'll have your new bank card before you know it! If you'd like some help completing the form, call 1-888-464-3232 anytime! If you live close to a Café, we can even help ID you instead. Check here for a location near you: http://www.ingdirect. ca/en/aboutus/contactus/index.html

32. No family day HERE!

33. Cool! Actually felt good after reading this yay Canada

34. some good news here.

35. This graph is only true if your house already is n great shape. If I am buying a home and I will need to remodel it after I buy, I will take 5 - 15% off what the house would be worth after remodeling (depending how much work i will have to put in). If the seller did a really good job with remodeling I and I don't want to do the work myself of course I would pay a premium because remodeling can be a huge headache and i just saved on a headache!

36. Well I must say this is a heated topic. No wonder, the banks have been telling us for years to invest in rrsp But if you go into a bank and ask a teller to explain how it works, most can't. It has never

been in the banks interest to teach people how their money works. They make money from people who trust them. If you have your investments with a bank you are not richer than you think. It is time people woke up and realized there is a better way. Ask me..

37. If there were a branch here I would. I have an autoimmune disorder and would like to see an answer more than your immune system attacked you but we don't know why. Good luck!!

38. **ING DIRECT Canada** Thanks for your support, Debra! There are teams all over Canada not just in the Cafe cities. You can still participate at a location closer to you. Here's a list of locations:http://powerofmovement.ca/Register.aspx. Bring friends and start your own team!

39. I heard from the news, once you retire/withdraw your money, your tax will be 70% in total.. my goodness.. RSP is good for now, but they will bite you at the end...

40. Unhappy cat is unhappy about the low 1.35% savings account rate.

41. Sometimes People don't like when savings account fee is $5 plus and the bank pays interests less than 2%.

42. **ING DIRECT Canada** Prosperity Good thing we don't charge fees on our Savings Account

43. Unhappy that you could at least match Canadian Tire Financial at 1.5%!

44. Here's one 20 year old planning for retirement.

45. Paid off my credit cards with my tax refund. Now my payments that I would have made to them are going to my savings account!

46. Paying myself first and not buying junk I don't need!

Survey and Contests

1. RSP Quiz time! To regulate your RSP contribution, there is a limit to how much you can contribute. What is that limit?

2. How are you finding ways to save this week?

Social (Responsibility)Activities

1. Happy Valentine's Day! Let's all join together and share some love for the Penny.

2. It's time to start hating debt again.

3. http://www.youtube.com/watch?v=XMo1dRiezaA&feature=youtu.be

4. Happy Family Day! For those that are enjoying a long weekend today, how are you making the most of your Monday?

5. If you're thinking about starting a family, or have a baby on the way, Money Sense has an article that can help you prepare financially for that little bundle of joy. http://ow.ly/hVaHp

6. Admit it - there are many who eat out regularly and this winds up costing more than if you prepared our own meals. Luckily, US News has an article that can help us save some money when we dine out. http://ow.ly/hVlUX

7. "The question isn't at what age I want to retire, it's at what income." - George Foreman

8. Now's the time to contribute to your RSP as the deadline is literally just around the corner (*cough* tomorrow *cough*). Don't be late!

9. Your future self thanks you for saving your green, to get you on the green.

ING Direct India (VysyaBank) On Facebook

ING Vysya Bank Ltd is a premier private sector bank with retail, private and wholesale banking platforms that serve over two million customers. With 80 years of history in India and leveraging ING's global financial expertise, the bank offers a broad range of innovative and established products and services, across its 526 branches. ING Vysya Bank was ranked among top 5 Most Trusted Brands among private sector banks in India in the Economic Times Brand Equity – Neilsen Survey 2011.

The ING bank was incorporated at Banglore city of India in 1930 and has been a Facebook accountant since 2012. People liking the page: 7.031 (9th March 2013GMT:16.16)

FACEBOOK TIME TUNNEL CONTENTS 2012 DEC. ING (VYSABANK) INDIA

Contents Relating to Advertisements, Announcements, Videos and Campaigns, Services and Products

1. First day, first shows burning a hole in your pocket? Not anymore! Get great discounts while you book your movie tickets online with ING edeals. Visit www.ingvysyabank.com/edeals We would love to hear your take on the movies you watch. Post them here.
2. Only time when $12+12+12 = 62$ is right! Wishing Super star Rajinikanth a happy 62nd birthday!
3. May this Christmas bring you all the love and luck in the World. Merry Christmas!
4. Wishing you a Happy New Year! 2013!
5. Dr Priya Sequeira from Mumbai is all set to go places; Europe to be precise!3 more tickets up for grabs. Would you want to be next? Drop in @ www.ingvysyabank.com/europe
6. ING Swipe and Win a Trip to Europe. Our third winner is Jeebak Dasgupta. Jeebak has won a 'Trip to Europe' for the fortnight 16th – 30th Nov. There are 2 more 'Trips to Europe' up for grabs. Visit www.ingvysyabank.com/europe to know more. Winners of the Gift Vouchers will be informed separately by mail.

Customer's Questions, Answers and Feedbacks

(None for this month)

Surveys and Contests

1. "In our endeavor to learn from you – innovate and improve our services, we request you to spare a few minutes and participate in ING's Annual 'Money and your child' survey by clicking the link below" www.surveymonkey.com/s/MoneyAndYourChildSurvey
2. Do you budget for your festive spending?
3. Share your New Year resolution with us. Come back after a week and tell us how it is going.
4. All of us know the best combination to unleash on the field. Give us your pick from India's finest. The 1st correct answer will win a special gift. Send your entries before 7am, December 5. Calling all the Super-Selectors!

Social (Responsibility)Activities

1. Christmas is around the corner and Santa is making his list. Was your child Naughty or Nice? Share photos of your child, tell us how they've been nice and if Santa is impressed, he might just come over with a gift The nicest kids watch out, Santa is gonna come home with a gift. Remember due to Santa's busy schedule, he'll only visit a selected few.
2. NAUGHTY or NICE? (159 pics) Here is a glimpse at all the kids who are NAUGHTY or NICE! Think your kid fits in here? Upload HIS or HER photo on the page!
3. It's time to deliver the presents! Santa is already preparing his list of the nicest kids to visit on Christmas. So hurry, send in your entries latest by 2 PM tomorrow (19th Dec). Remember, Santa has a long list and would only be visiting a selected few.
4. Santa visited some very nice kids this Sunday.

FACEBOOK TIME TUNNEL CONTENTS 2013 JAN. ING(VYSABANK) INDIA

Contents Relating to Advertisements, Announcements, Videos and Campaigns, Services and Products

1. Great Savings while you shop online with ING e-deals. Find out more @ http://bit.ly/11DK1tJ Maximum shopping, Maximum savings.
2. Traveling this weekend? Check out exclusive travel deals at ING e-deals. Find out more: http://bit.ly/11DK1tJ Exotic holidays, exciting Discounts. Get great Discounts on Travel. Book online with ING edeals.
3. Non-CTS cheques will not be valid after 31st March, so order your CTS cheque now! More info: http://bit.ly/YFJ3gd
4. Wishing everyone happiness and prosperity on the occasion of Milad un Nabi.
5. Let's pledge to take our country to new heights! Happy Republic day!
6. ING Swipe and Win a Trip to Europe. Our Fourth winner is Akshay Wagh. Akshay has won a 'Trip to Europe' for the fortnight 1st – 15th Dec.
7. Get exciting offers on Shoes & Clothing. Read more: http://bit.ly/11DK1tJ Jabong.com. Get 20% off . Offer valid till 31 th March 2013.
8. We have the final winner for the "Swipe and Win" Contest. Congratulations Rajesh Rathi ! Find all winners @ http://bit.ly/XHbe7E

Customer's Questions, Answers and Feedbacks

1. **ING Vysya Bank** Dear Aesha Gupta Kapoor, as per your discussion with Ms Simrat from our Delhi Team, we are processing your request for the Foreclosure and the List of Documents. A copy of the same will be couriered as well.
2. **ING Vysya Bank** Hello Ankit, We are quite sorry to hear about your disappointment. Our Team would be getting in touch with you soon.

3. I have a similar fate.. I have been following up for a month to get the Foreclosure letter and each time I get a response that it will be provided in 15 days. Can you please let me know who to escalate and how to take it forward.

4. how to purchase rail tickets through net banking ? (irctc.co.in > net banking option)

5. **ING Vysya Bank** Hello, We are already working on this and ING Vysya bank would be listed in IRCTC shortly. We will keep you updated.

6. Wat will u do ??? By giving adds on media u spend so much.. But u have free space for display board.. Its been wasted....

7. **ING Vysya Bank** Hello Prabhjot, Thanks for brining this to our notice. We will surely look into this.

8. **ING Vysya Bank** Hello Vamshi, This is the Debit Card Annual Maintenance Fee that is levied on the 14th day from Account Activation for ING Orange Savings Accounts.

9. **ING Vysya Bank** Hello Rajkumar, Apologies for the inconvenience. please PM us your contact number and also the branch with which you have your OD account.

10. **ING Vysya Bank** Hello Santhi, We are already working on this and ING Vysya bank would be listed in IRCTC shortly. We will keep you updated and thank you for choosing ING Vysy

11. **ING Vysya Bank** Hello Ankit, Hope the issue is resolved and you have received the courier.

12. Is there a cut in Floating interest rate because of the recent RBI announcement?

13. 13. **ING Vysya Bank** Hello Dharmik, please find the winners list at the following url: http://bit. ly/XHbe7E

14. I have account at Ahmedabad and now I am in London. I was able login to my account but now it is not working and I have written them a letter but nobody is worried I think. Please help.

15. Yes, this is right way to expose them, how they serve the customer. Good idea.

16. **ING Vysya Bank** Hello Ajit Parekh, please use the message option available in the page to send us your contact number.

17. **ING Vysya Bank** Apologies for the inconvenience. Please PM your contact number.

18. **ING Vysya Bank** Hello CA Yogeshwar Bajaj, Could you please confirm the receipt?

19. **ING Vysya Bank** Hello Matlapudi Seshu Prabhakar, we are sorry for the inconvenience. Please PM your contact number.

20. I want a credit card... pls. guide me

21. Good bank.

22. Phew...got my offer letter after a long long time... today I can say m employed. ...thank u each and everyone for ur support and special thanx to ING Vysya Bank.....

23. Nice Bank with encouraging features....Friendly staff.....quick service..lot many attractive features.

24. I feel very Good Performance .....

25. I found it is very easy & Comfortable to work with ING Vysya Bank Net Banking. They are faster to send the report/stmnt as compare to other bank. There customer care executive are also good to resolve the problem instantly. In a single line i can say Jiyo easy.(Good Banking System)

26. I am also acustomer of ing..... its true........

27. i ng bank very good to anther bank .

28. I am salary account holder, staff in this bank are very friendly & helpful.

29. Worst Bank .. frustrating experience .. have no work ethics... make customer suffer till death. Home loan division is pathetic. In today's world I am paying 14% as ROI and the bank ensures that I cannot foreclose my account.

30. (Ankit Lakhera) Why complaints are getting closed even that are not addressed by ING redressalf-grievances?? and No response on the query after that??????????? Now I have no choice left but to go to RBI and file a complaint against ING.

31. And the frustration continues! Finally after so much of escalations and follow ups I got the documents which I believe are the simplest kind of documents for a International standard Bank can provide! Those are merely List of documents and the Foreclosure letter! Now inspite of the delay from the bank, ING has charged me with the late fees and the broken period interest! what is that? The bank delays on such small things and is charging customers for that! Such things is certainly not acceptable.. I suggest the customers of the bank to make a note of the sufferings which the bank offers to their loyal customers! BIG DISAPPOINTMENT !- I have decided not to have any kind of association with the bank even I am making a loss!

32. Horrible service with no care attitude for its customers.

33. Absolutely ridiculous customer satisfaction...it jst seems they want customers but dnt care about after services.

34. I think the Bank would surely take an action on this & close it your satisfaction and avoid any social media viral image & rbi ombudsmen action.

35. I think u should refer this mattter to Bnaking Ombuds man......u will get the information abt that from RBI site.

36. first go to ING ombudsman if they are of no help approach RBI ombudsman.

37. Very Bad experience with ING Vysya bank...certainly not acceptable.

38. Thats truly disappointing! They're going to lose huge amount of customer base if this kind of service continues.

39. Hi Aesha.. Hard to see one more bearer of the same pain. Well in addition to the social networking site I have escalated to Ing ombudsman. But I must tell you that the bank will charge you for the delays from their side and you will get this response.'This is a system generated report and we cannot do anything' so be ready for the same however I will not let it go like this after all this is about the hard money that we earn.

40. Guys be careful in opening ING -ORANGE account. ING welcomes you by debiting 225 Rs.

41. My account is 745044032948 .I have OD account and i was charged O D renew charges some 11000+ and when i issued a cheque of Rs. 1,53,189 it bounced, on 11 aug 2012 and when i asked the bank about this, i got a reply that my O.D account is not renewed. When i told its already renewed and the account has been debited too, I was asked to contact to consult Mr Krishna Kishore. He said sorry and promised to pay me by cash the chq. returned charges. Later on i went to the bank, new manager promised me that the money will be returned to you if the account was not renewed. Kindly do the needful. I had other very serious problems too and that was a police case but as the bank employees are good, i did not inform to the police.

42. i am new customer to the bank and when i tried to use the Internet banking platform for booking my train ticket through IRCTC, ING was not there. It has almost all the Banks where there in IRCTC except ING VYSYA. what is the use of ING Online Bnaking then even if we cannot use it for a smal transaction like booking a train Ticket.

43. Worst ever experience with the bank services.Even after charging highest interest rates the services that the bank provide is pathetic. Its hard to say but INGVYSYA is not upto the mark to meet at least the basic standards.

44. Extremely regret to write that in spite of all good about the bank the bank have not able to deliver my ATM card in 9 months. My account was debited in April 2012 and couriered the card to my residence address and since we were travelling the card went back to the bank and after that i have requested to send it again and till now i yet to receive the card. pathetic people in call center, no responsibility on anybody to address the issue. Thanks to the system and procedures bank follow to run the operation where a customer grievances not addressed for such a long time. In case it reaches to ING my account no. is 550010002377. Thanks and best regards.

45. How r u Vinay. Tired of their call center no response and hence posted this. The bank is having relationship of 15 years and i m astonished by the service standard. You know in their TV commercial they r showing a man running behind the customer to hand over ATM card before expiry and here its just opposite i m running behind them to get my card. The spending on tv commercial is not justified by the service standard.

46. I am Good. Thanks! Good one. their tiger is sitting since inception-lazy (logo).Hahaha.

47. I agree with CA Yogeshwar Bajaj. I had similar experience since 2007 and gave up. I've few accounts in the bank but did not had Internet Login (Mi-B@nk). When asked at the branch, I was asked to contact call center for the password to be mailed to me. I contacted the call center and the lady verified my details and told me that the login id and password would be mailed. I contacted the call center again only to be given the EMS speedpost number. However, it never came. Now, I want close my accounts and open a new one since past few months but nothing moved. Their accounts dept come with bizzaire questions while opening a new account even for an existing customer. Still trying the worst bank to bank with in India! bunch of thugs and thieves looting the regular customer! I have closed by accounts with you'll and will encourage everyone to do so! CHOR CHOR.

48. I am really feeling very bad while writing this post on facebook about my very bad and awkward experience with ing vysya indore branch and team - Abhishek kukreti - BM. He is very unprofessional guy and not respond to customer. at the time of account opening he committed a lot and now the condition is he is not picking phone. He has made the branch local kirana shop. He is not committed for the word vikas jain – 93003887911.

49. Robert Varda. SONIA GANDHI daughter Prinanka's Gandhi husband he is the most corrupted man in India he has became one ofthe most richest man and business icon of India.he has earned millions and billions of dollars in very short period.RAHUL GANDHI...he has been arrested by US police once.Because he was carrying suitcase full of $ 2million dollars with his girl friend who is a daughter of Columbian drug dealer.Police and media is not doing any thing against them because they have got power, they will kill people who will say any word against them and they have already done this before.

50. This is what I received from ING Vysya: Dear Customer This is in response to your mail/letter dated: 16-12-2012 with regard to updation of Mobile no and refund of policy amount posted in Blog. In reply we inform as under: As per the request your Mobile no is already updated in the account. The reversal of your policy amount will be credited into your SB a/c with in friday as confirmed to you by our concerned officer from the branch dated 08/01/2012. Hence treating your complaint as resolved and closed. MY ANSWER: Dear ####, From what you mention in your email, it appears that the matter is closed. You fail to mention in your email that it took me 2 visits to the bank branch and even then the cell no. never got updated. Then I had to raise the issue with the customer care and thereafter the no. was updated. What was done to ensure that it does not repeat in future?

You just mention that the no. has been updated. Was it updated in time? Was it update in a manner that should have been? Also, my policy has been freelooked and I have received money in my account today. However ~200 Rs have been deducted from the 25000 Rs. Why were these deducted? Its not a matter of 200 Rs. But, first I am fradulently sold a policy by Aparna Kumar. And then I have to wait, visit the branch 3 times and then get money deducted and for what? My question is if it should have been freelooked or some other action had to be taken?`Was there any action taken against Aparna Kumar? Does the bank authorities know of this case? Or was it reported to be a case of simple freelook? Please note that I need an answer to my queries within 72 hours. I will then lodge a complaint with IRDA and Banking Ombudusman. Also, I am posting this conversation on the ING FB page so that others can read it and be cautioned. Abhiram Mishra.

Survey and Contests

1. Have you set a Financial Resolution for 2013?

Social (Responsibility) Activities

(None for this month)

FACEBOOK TIME TUNNEL CONTENTS 2013 FEB. ING (VYSYABANK) INDIA

Contents Relating to Advertisements, Announcements, Videos and Campaigns, Services and Products

1. **Zovi.com:** Get Flat 15% discount on all products with ING Net Banking. More info: http://bit.ly/11DK1tJ Flat %15 discount on Zovi.com. Offer valid till 30 th June 2013.
2. Get 10% off next time you book bus tickets online with redBus. More about this deal @ http://bit.ly/XHbe7E
3. **Valentines Day Exclusive:** Get flat 18% off on flowers only at Ferns N Petals with ING Debit Card and ING Net Banking. More info: http://bit.ly/11DK1tJ
4. **Valentines Day Exclusive:** Shop from Jewelskart.com and get Rs 500 off*. More info: http://bit.ly/11DK1tJ
5. **ING eDeals:** Get 20% off on shoes, accessories and much more only at Bestylish.com. More info: http://bit.ly/11DK1tJ
6. **ING edeals:** Get 6% off on over 10 million products at eBay India with ING Net-banking, Debit and Credit Cards. More info: http://bit.ly/11DK1tJ
7. **ING edeals:** Get 15% off on exciting range of apparel, accessories and footwear at inkfruit.com with ING debit cards and ING Net banking. More info: http://bit.ly/11DK1tJ
8. **ING edeals:** Get Rs. 200 to Rs. 500 off across categories on Tradus.com with ING Debit Card and ING Net Banking. More info: http://bit.ly/11DK1tJ
9. **ING edeals:** Get Get 8% off on mobiles, laptops and much more at shopping.indiatimes.com with ING Net Banking and ING Debit cards. More info: http://bit.ly/11DK1tJ

10. **ING edeals:** Get up to Rs 5000 off on international and domestic air tickets and up to 10% off on Hotel at VIA.com with ING Net Banking. More info: http://bit.ly/11DK1tJ

11. Wishing everyone a Happy rose day! Buy flowers from Ferns N Petals and get flat 18% off. More info: http://bit.ly/11DK1tJ

12. **Today is Propose Day:** Gift your loved one jewellery from Jewelskart and get Rs 500 off* with ING Net banking and Debit card. More info: http://bit.ly/11DK1tJ

13. **Valentines Day Special ING edeal:** Get up to 50% off on photo books, photo mugs and calendars at Zoomin.com with ING Debit cards. More info: http://bit.ly/11DK1tJ

14. With ING FD+ get the best rates and enjoy freedom to withdraw your money when you need it with No Penalty!. Find out more: http://bit.ly/WDNrtF Earn higest interest on your savings! 9.25% no penalties!

15. **ING edeals:** Get 6% cash back on your recharge at mobikwik.com. Offer valid for ING Net-Banking and ING Debit Card customers only. More info: http://bit.ly/11DK1tJ

16. This Valentines Day, let your gifts speak. Shop Online with ING eDeals and enjoy special deals & discounts. More info: http://bit.ly/11DK1tJ

17. With ING FD+ earn higher interest rates on your savings and enjoy freedom to withdraw your money when you need it with No Penalty!. Find out more: http://bit.ly/WDNrtF

18. No Pre-payment penalties with ING FD+. Now withdraw your fixed deposit anytime without any penalties. Find out more: http://bit.ly/WDNrtF

19. **ING e-deals:** redBus - 10% off. http://bit.ly/XHbe7E. Get 10% off next time you book bus tickets online with redBus.

20. **Indiatimes Shopping @ ING edeals:** Get 8% off on mobiles, laptops and much more with ING Net Banking and ING Debit cards. More info: http://bit.ly/11DK1tJ

21. Now get up to 9.25% on your FD with ING. Find out more: http://bit.ly/WDNrtF

22. **ING e-Deals:** Get Rs. 200 off on minimum purchase of Rs. 1000 @ Hoopos.com with ING Debit Card and Net-banking. More info: http://bit.ly/11DK1tJ

23. Get more from your savings with ING FD+. Try the Calculator to find out. More info: http://bit.ly/WDNrtF

24. **ING eDeals for your KID:** Get Rs. 100 off on minimum billing of Rs. 500 at SkoolShop.com. More info: http://bit.ly/11DK1tJ Let everyday be Children's Day! SkoolShop.com

25. **ING eDeals:** Get 5% discount on your bookings for a minimum transaction value of Rs. 1000 at Savaari.com. Offer applicable for ING Net Banking customers only. More info: http://bit.ly/11DK1tJ SAVAARI car Rentals.

26. **ING FD+:** Enjoy zero pre-closure charges with ING FD+. Now withdraw your fixed deposit anytime without any penalties. More info: http://bit.ly/WDNrtF . Withdraw your Money when you need it with no penalty.

27. **Introducing ING Dining Deals:** Get up to 25% discount when you eat out and pay using ING Debit Card. Know more: http://bit.ly/WkTUff .

28. **ING Dining Deals:** Save more when u dine in Bangalore using ING Debit card. Know more: http://bit.ly/WkTUff

29. Non-CTS cheques will not be valid after 31st March, so order your CTS cheque now!. More info: http://bit.ly/YFJ3gd The OLD has to make way for the NEW!

30. The Best thing to hold onto in life is Each other. Happy Valentines Day! Check out the exclusive Valentines Day Offers: http://bit.ly/XDu17V

31. Wishing everyone a Happy rose day! Buy flowers from Ferns N Petals and get flat 18% off. More info: http://bit.ly/11DK1tJ

32. **VIDEO:** The Oscar for best chase sequence goes to......The chaser becomes the chased. A fantastic chase sequence on foot with a twist in the tale in the end. - ING Vysya Bank. Quick replacement of lost Debit Card

Customer's Questions, Answers and Feedbacks

1. ING Vysya offered a forex rate of INR 54.01 on Jan 03, 2013 . The IBR rate on the day is INR 54.34 . The executive promised 5 paisa less than IBR rate. With rate of INR 54.29 (5 paisa less), the total amount of money will be INR 81,43,500 while it is just INR 81,00,960 . A total loss of around INR 43k . Is this right ? Please comment.

2. With regard your bad experience, you can drag them to consumer court!

3. Citibank did the same. The difference was Rs 1.65/Euro

4. This is for the current account. Its for an amount $150k . Their executive already promised 5 paisa less than the IBR rate. So guess this is not right.

5. They gave 50 paisa less. So we loss 43k INR.

6. If 5paisa less then for 150k dollars se u will be losing 7.5k Indian rupees!

7. Damn these bank. Somebody need to do the dirty job of dragging them to consumer forum.

8. Surely bhaiya...this is not right...you should write back to them first...and plan for the next step after their revert...because once you get the clarifications/justifications from their end, you can then base your case on that as well as on the email confirmation sent by them earlier...

9. Yes Shilpa. They have agreed to revert the money. There are couple of other complaints for which I have written to them. Also engaged www.akosha.com to give it more formal process.

10. ing.no.1

11. (Victor Samson) A VERY VERY FRIENDLY AND FEEL FREE BANK FOR A COMMON MAN.

12. (Ankit Lakhera) Worst ever experience with the bank services..Even after charging highest interest rates the services that the bank provide is pathetic. Its hard to say but INGVYSYA is not upto the mark to meet at least the basic standards.

13. **ING Vysya Bank** Hello Ankit, we are really sorry for the experience you had. Please private message your mobile number and the brief of your problem. ((ING Vysya Bank) Hello Ankit, Hope the issue is resolved and you have received the courier.

14. (Santhi Krishna) i am new customer to the bank and when i tried to use the Internet banking platform for booking my train ticket through IRCTC, ING was not there. It has almost all the Banks where there in IRCTC except ING VYSYA. what is the use of ING Online Bnaking then even if we cannot use it for a smal transaction like booking a train Ticket.

15. **ING Vysya Bank** Hello Santhi, We are already working on this and ING Vysya bank would be listed in IRCTC shortly. We will keep you updated and thank you for choosing ING Vysya.

Survey and Contests

1. What do you think was the most striking announcement of Budget 2013?

Social (Responsibility)Activities

(None for this month)

ING Bank Türkiye on Facebook

Ing Bank Türkiye was established in 2008. ING is one of the leading financial service institutions that provides people in the fields of banking business, assurance, assesment and loyality managementand expanded services and products in individual and institutional areas for almost five years in Türkiye. It has been expanded from Asia to America, Europe to Australia, having 85 million customers with 125.000 officers over 50 countries. ING Bank, originated from Holland, is awarded on the 81 st grade among Interbrand's the best 100 brands of 2007. ING Bank is successfully placed on the 7th grade among the biggest 500 company list of Fortune Global. ING Bank Türkiye has joined the Facebook in 2009 and 98.328 people liked this (9th March 2013 GMT 16.16).

FACEBOOK TIME TUNNEL CONTENTS 2012 DEC. ING BANK TÜRKİYE

Contents Relating to Advertisements, Announcements, Videos and Campaigns, Services and Products

1. Big support to minors! Savings seminars! We cordially thank our "volunteer personnel" who gave "Savings Seminars" at schools within our Project.
2. "Access notifications on time" and click "Show it" buttons and chase after ING Bank campaigns and occasions for you!

Customer's Questions, Answers and Feedbacks

1. I was also one of the vounteers, it was a real experience and a matter of pride.
2. First you sent a platinum card then cancelled it; then I investigated you asked for name and surname with the promise of calling back but its all silence! When will you be calling back me, I really wonder!
3. Aha ah..very good picture!

Survey and Contests

1. Secondhand selling and buying are highly favourable in smart phones and motor cars. Have you ever tried this kind of business when your budget is insufficient?

Social (Responsibility)Activities

1. General Manager of ING Türkiye Pınar Abay has been awarded as "The best woman leader" by Bosphorus University, Engineering Club.(6 photos)
2. We wish you an endless happiness and many realizations of your dreams in the new year!

FACEBOOK TIME TUNNEL CONTENTS 2013 JAN. ING BANK TÜRKİYE

Contents Relating to Advertisements, Announcements, Videos and Campaigns, Services and Products

1. Credit for land (within 2/B project) property for %0,94 interest! Submission to http://bit.ly/WeckYf-
2. Access your bank via online banking (mobile or ipad) and get your e reader from reeder.com.tr % 35 less. Last day January the 31th. For details; http://bit.ly/UmfHfK
3. All your expectations is here! Open a savings account with provision and get the advantage of tax reduce! For details and submission: http://bit.ly/UDbaYh
4. This offer is a real occasion! Access your bank via online banking, mobile or ipad till Feb.15 th, and try your chance for packing up for London, Arsenal- Manchester United home match! http://bit.ly/VIgGdM
5. Everybody Save!! No expiry date! In order to start saving with % 8 welcome interest; http://bit.ly/VMwlsE
6. Pay Tax on Motor Vehicles with your Bonus Card in 6 installments!! Grab the opportunity! Deadline; January 31th!! click for the details ;http://bit.ly/UUli2K
7. ING Bank purpose loan for 10,000 YTL, without cost, special to Şehrikeyif', for submission refer to http://bit.ly/ZOaIqh
8. According to the "Financial resolutions Survey", 2013 will be the "Year of Savings". In the survey, among the new year wishes are mostly "more saving" and " less spending". %49 of Turkish people wished to start the new year with the previlege of better investments http://bit.ly/XeSu5w
9. "ING International Savings Investigations 2013 Survey" showed that last year most cut down was on entertainment and recreation. People who claim no cutting down on expenses rated %28 in Türkiye.Details of the investigation ;http://bit.ly/V73kbe
10. Send an SMS to 2205 "mobile" and access your bank on your mobile! Log in instantly with your user code; for details; http://bit.ly/ViAWji
11. ING Bank Bills and Bonds are being offered to the public! Demand for lucrative investment opportunity in this collection! Final date January 9th! For more information;http://bit.ly/11f6eOF
12. ING Bank is supporting entrepreneurship in Turkey now! The European Investment Bank (EIB) provides employment and financial growth to Turkish SMEs with 100 million Euro credit via ING Bank in Türkiye! http://bit.ly/Wmzihq
13. In the "Case Management Achivement List" organised by Şikayetvar.com, we had the most successful Bank rate in the field of "Private Banks and Banking"in 2012!
14. Your ID Card is your Credit! For Public Officials Only!! Do not miss the credit without cost, with %1,09 interest;http://bit.ly/V6l6Rt
15. Do you need motivation for saving? ING's Senior Economist Ian Bright advises you to set a goal achievible by the end of the year and suggests to put aside a small amount on a monthly basis: http://bit.ly/XeSu5w
16. "Future is mine" Practica Camp submissions! the ultimate day!! Join with the Camp to give a direction to your career; http://bit.ly/V6nj7p
17. Searching for branch office managers of the future! Candidates for Retail, SME, Commercial Banking or sales executive positions!! come on! Applications must be submitted; http://bit.ly/14qrjol

Survey and Contests

1. According to a one-year data analysis "Saving Trends Survey in Türkiye" prepared by ING Bank Türkiye shows that Working Women tend to save more than men; but men tend to save less, in case she is a housewife.
2. On the very early days of the new year what's your major reason for savings?
3. In the ING Group Survey, the most popular answer to the question "What's your major reason for saving at the moment" is "my children and family". For whom or what are you saving ?http://bit.ly/Ztm3kL

Customers' Questions /Customers' Feedback

1. Will you need more personnel?
2. I wish I could....
3. Why don't you have a housing loan configuration?
4. **ING Bank Türkiye** Hi Mr. Hüseyin, in order to contact with you, could you kindly send your communication information to our address at http://on.fb.me/QHkA1K Thank you.
5. We are not satisfied with your dealing with credit system; may be the problem is with the personnel. Early deposited installments are not paid in due time. Are we allowed to move our credit to another bank?
6. I have tried all cahnnels of communication to configure my housing loan but all are in vain! No reply for 15 days! Having customers follow the bank personnel is not pleasant! In case I were obliged to pay an high interest rate again, I would give a petition to Consumer's Court!
7. **ING Bank Türkiye** Hi, in order to contact with you, could you kindly send your communication information to our address at http://on.fb.me/QHkA1K . Thank you.
8. What's the afterwards interest rate of welcome campaign,and what is the net interest does 1000 YTL bear?
9. **ING Bank Türkiye** Hello Mr. Yiğit, in order to get detailed information about Orange Account and interest calculations please visit our page at http://www.ingbank.com.tr/turuncuhesap/vadeli-yekarsi.asp Thank you for your interest.
10. How can I close my flexible account?
11. My retiring pension is deposited in your bank, shall I have the Orange Account as well or should I apply for it?
12. **ING Bank Türkiye** Hello, Mr. Mustafa you could submit your application online at http://www.ingbank.com.tr/turuncuhesap/ozellikler.asp or via telephone banking 0850 222 0 600.Thank you for your interest.
13. Wanna 5000 YTL consumer loan.
14. How much is the interest rate, what are the required docs?
15. I applied 3 days ago for the credit, but nobody called me back negatively or positively! It seems quite utopic!
16. Are we supposed to pay any filing fee?
17. Hi, I made four installments on Nov 11th, 2012 with my credit card and the refund was made by the company to concerned bank on Dec 31st, 2012, but the bank reflected this process as nine installments on my extract. Customer service seems unable to find a solution for my problem.

What kind of banking you are dealing with?? You keep my money for five months more and there is no collocutor and no explanation! I am the victim here!ING Bank should compensate this error immediately!.

18. I love ING Bank!

19. Very good campaign! Congratulations!

20. When we arrive at the bank, you wont speak like that!

21. I applied for a "without cost loan" and had to pay 60 YTL for filing fee and had no reply yet!! Quit such tricks ING Bank!!

22. Here is Banking, I call

23. Hi here! I am a student. Can I get a consumer's loan for 2500 YTL? Thank you!

24. **ING Bank Türkiye** Hello Mr. Ozgur.We are sorry to tell you that we are unable to give you more details about the evaluating criteria. You are kindly asked to visit our offices. Nearest Office addresses and phone nubers are available at http://www.ingbank.com.tr/subeler.asp Thanks for your interest.

25. **ING Bank Türkiye** Hello Mr.Orhan, you can fill in the job application form at https://ik.ingbank.com.tr/ You will be contacted when a positionis vacant, appropiate with your qualifications.Thank you for your interest.

26. I went to ING Bank Antalya Office, Manavgat Branch, which I have an account beforehand. I would tend to change it an Orange Account but I was almost scolded on my question, and couldn't even get a reply to my question! I am through with ING Bank!!

27. **ING Bank Türkiye** Hello Mr. Ali, Hi, in order to contact with you, could you please send your communication information to our address at http://on.fb.me/QHkA1K . Thank you.

28. I failed to get any contact by telephone to your Ankara, Cankaya Office. So many times I have tried to call Cankaya Office, which is a vain struggle! Right now your number 0 312 441 84 27 is inaccessable! Could Mr. Ozturk examine his e post address and reply me back soon, please? Note: As a conclusion of my victimization, I will be changing my bank as soon as I land onTürkiye.

29. In addition to my vain efforts, International Fax Service Staples has already failed to send any docs to fax number given by ING Bank. I also failed to transmit my credit card debit interaction, therefore please do regard the petition I signed and scanned to you. I have been struggling with it for a week. For the information of authorities concerned, best regards.

30. **ING Bank Türkiye** Hello Mrs Pınar, in order to investigate the issue you happened to meet, could you please share your phone number with us at https://www.facebook.com/messages/ingbankturkiye. Thank you.

31. I am an ING customer who has a stable salary but they refuse to loan me some credit! What's the problem?

32. We are the followers! I love INGBank! Thanks!

33. Great Bank!

34. Congratulations! You are very good at the business!

35. Congratualtions! By the way, I would like to take your attention to customer's service to reply faster.

36. Congratulations! Good job!

37. I am surprised! In fact, it is not!

38. I am beyond being surprised!

39. At the bottom of being surprised I am!

40. **ING Bank Türkiye** Hello,Mr. Kemal, we would like to inform you that your opinions are highly appreciated for us and they will absolutely be evaluated on the way to upgrade our service quality. Thank you for your concern.

41. When I called up your customer's service for a transaction, he asked my ID number; I refused and ask for an another way to do the transaction. He was so rude and priggish! It is not surprising your rank in the list! You must have plenty of complaints at şikayetvar.com!

42. I am also shocked that you're awarded on the first rank!

FACEBOOK TIME TUNNEL CONTENTS 2013 FEB. ING BANK TÜRKİYE

Contents Relating to Advertising, Announcements, Videos and Campaigns, Services and Products

1. Save 300 YTL a year!! Account management or Daily Banking transactions for free!; http://bit.ly/Y7mmBl

2. Private Credit from ING to Facebook accountants!! Apply fort he credit without cost up to 10.000 YTL!! Submit http://bit.ly/SplpBa

3. With ING Orange Account, Now saving is much more possible! For further details; http://bit.ly/XX6zyH

4. Now St Valentine Day's about to come ! Do your interactions online branches and get a 100 YTL off at Modagram.com, Trendyol's fashion site for her unique gift. Get discounts on your purchases over 100 YTL! http://bit.ly/14HLVZq

5. Feel the experience of "Premier League" on the stands! Try your chance for one of the three couples!; http://bit.ly/VIgGdM

6. Meet ING Bank Orange Account today and start saving!! For further details and submission: http://bit.ly/VKdgrr

7. VIDEO:When applying for Available Credit, you won't need any recognisance at ING Bank! http://bit.ly/YBq3d3

8. If you think you wont need any recognisance when applying for Available Credit please click http://bit.ly/YBq3d3

9. Hi there, I do not like to save Turkish Lira but gold. Is it ok? We are not supposed to save only cash?

10. They had online interactions and had their ipad 2! here is the name list; http://bit.ly/VzyytW

11. Lucky three couple to watch the Arsenal- M.U match will have the pleasures of five o'clock tea at Ritz Carlton and "Panthom of the Opera" on the stage (8 pics).Just take the opportunity of this gorgeous weekend!! Get the opportunity and be one of the three couples!! Use internet banking, mobile banking and ipad banking.:http://bit.ly/VIgGdM

12. Have you revised your expenses before you started savings? According to ING Group Survey we mostly cut off from entertainment and clothing expenses.

13. Installments from 99 YTL, total 7.000 YTL consumer's loan click for submission; http://bit.ly/YBq3d3

Customer's Questions, Answers and Feedbacks

1. **ING Bank Türkiye,** Hello Mr. Emir ING Orange Account is a TL checking account, (demand deposit),therefore you can withdraw or invest your Money any time without prior notice . Thanks for your concern.

2. As far as I am informed, most fruitful interest is here. I dont wanna credit card. How much interest does 5000 YTL make for 4 month? I will save 200 YTL every week; How much is the welcome rate? I wont withdraw for 4 months.

3. **ING Bank Türkiye** Hello Mr.Tolga, you can evaluate your savings in Orange Account.Welcome interest rate is 8.25% and you can calculate it at https://www.ingbank.com.tr/turuncuhesap/vadeli-yekarsi.asp.Thanks for your concern.

4. Good evening, could you please tell me about the calculation of overdraft deposit account interest?

5. **ING Bank Türkiye** Hello, Mr.Halil. ING Bank Holland and ING Bank Türkiye have different banking systems that's why you should apply to ING Bank Türkiye in order to have an account in Türkiye. Thanks for your concern.

6. When do the job applications start?

7. You can train people when they're younger. One should teach his children about money management. Do ING Bank have such a Project?

8. **ING Bank Türkiye**, Mrs Bahar, unfortunately we havent such kind of Project yet. your opinions are highly appreciated for us and absolutely be evaluated on the way to upgrade our service quality. Thank you for your concern.

9. Do we have to have a credit card in advance before we apply for a loan to ING Bank?

10. We are unable to join your contest "The Time comes", because somethin wrong with the system and refuses applications. For your infomation, sincerely Author Journalist Muharrem Akduman

11. I am a customer of another ban and I am in need of 18.000 YTL. Am I supposed to lend credit from your bank?

12. **ING Bank Türkiye,** Hello Mr. Berat, there is no obligation of having a credit card to get a loan. You could apply for loan at https://www.ingbank.com.tr/sizinicin-kredibasvuru2.asp.Thanks for your concern.

13. **ING Bank Türkiye**, Hi Mr. Can, unfortunately we are unable to give information about the terms of credit card ownership.You could have a meeting at your nearest ING Bank Office.Here is the list of nearest offices and telephone numbers: http://www.ingbank.com.tr/subeler.asp. Thanks.

14. 14. **ING Bank Türkiye** Hi Muharrem Bey, in order to contact with you about the problem you faced, could you please send your communication information to our address at http://on.fb.me/QHkA1K

15. What are the terms of credit card ownership?

16. I loaned vehicle credit on 60 months installations from this bank but they didnot provide me any convenience. I will never deal my business with this bank at all!!

17. ING Bank Türkiye; Hi Mr. Ercan, You could have a meeting with the office to configure of your credit. Please kindly find addresses and phone numbers of the nearest ING Offices at http://www.ingbank.com.tr/subeler.aspThanks for your concern.

18. I am so satisfied with the credits I loaned from ING Bank. I would like to loan again.

19. Let him die who hates you!

20. Great Bank for me!

21. Better than Finance Bank!

22. I will, If had the chance of meeting Ronoy!

23. I think you'd better to train your personnel be on time first! Give up searching "the manager for the future"! Employ more personnel who are punctual and respectful as well!

24. (Zehra) You are great ING Bank!! There is no any other alikeeeee!! I sincerely celebrate St Valentine's Day of all ING personnell, primarily administartive board and the rest and wishing never ending success and smiling faces .. with loveee, thanks a lot for your kindnessss

25. (Rafi Tuere) Zehra works for ING Bank! Gee!

26. They are liars! They wont give you any credits!

27. We live abroad, we applied for housing loan, but you refused! you externalized us, you didnot hold us esteemed! We are Turkish citizens, as well!

28. Can anybody help me? Tell me how can I get into contact with this bank! I sent a message but nobody's back!

29. Bravo!

30. Congratualtions! We wish you establish one in Erzincan, too.

31. YOUR MONEY IS PRECIOUS HERE!

32. Thank you very much indeed! We have to g oto Türkiye to open an account! Good job! That's very kind of you!

33. ING Bank! In November I faxed the doc related with the filing fees. Last week, you WOULD FAX TO ESKİŞEHİR BRANCH, BUT STILL YOU DIDN'T! WE HAD FEEDBACKS FROM ALL BANKS EXCEPT YOU!!

34. Smart boys! Managers of the future! May God save you all!

35. Dear sirs; since yesterday I have had some unpleasant situations with ING Bank İzmir Karşıyaka Office. I withdraw some Money from ATM at Karşıyaka and the machine payment was missing . ATM was broken therefore other people and me were in a helpless situation, we had payments but we couldnt get the rest of the amount in the machine!! We gave a petition to the Office related but nothing changed! I really wonder, If I were obliged to overpay because of this situation, would ING Bank compensate my penalty? Yesterday was the expiry date of my credit card. The problem is clear, total amount is clear why all these process take so much time? Be reasonable!

36. **ING Bank Türkiye**, Hi Mrs. Nevbahar, in order to contact with you, could you please send your communication information to our address at http://on.fb.me/QHkA1K . Thank you.

37. The Bank whose number-0850 222 0 600- has always been inaccessable! Since last night I couldnot have a contact, so funny the situation!

38. **ING Bank Türkiye**,Hi Mr.Murat, in order to contact with you about the problem you faced, could you please send your communication information to our address at http://on.fb.me/QHkA1K . Thank you.

Survey and Contests

1. Guess, who wins, Arsenal or Manchester United ? Get chance of Premier League experience in London and be one of the lucky three couples! The opportunity is on your mobile, iPad or the internet!; http://bit.ly/VIgGdM

2. As a matter of buying a house, we very often take loans from "parent's bank". According to a survey of ING Group, Türkiye is on the second rank among twelve European countries where people

mostly barrowed loans from their families or friends when they are about to buy a house. http://www.ingbank.com.tr/ingbank-basinbultenleri_25_10_2012.asp

3. Personal Finance Professionals recommends some accumulation of 3-6 months income for emergencies. In Türkiye, in case of a fall people who have a 3 month's subsistence is 52%. How much can you save from your income? http://bit.ly/V73kbe

4. Would you like to learn your probablity of saving ?; http://bit.ly/Z5j6a7

5. Special to birliktealalim.com users !! Customer's credit for %0,99 interest, without cost! http://bit.ly/WZ39z5

6. We are searching for the "manager of the future"!;http://bit.ly/14qrjol

7. Happy Valantine's Day! It could be a good idea for a unique gift and making your partner happy by writing notes, cooking some special food or forming a collage work of your pics! What do you think?

8. When applying for Available Credit, you won't need any recognisance at ING Bank! Installments starting from 99 YTL, totally 7.000 YTL consumer's credit: http://bit.ly/YBq3d3

9. ING Bank was awarded as "the most successful effective banking management" in Eastern Europe in 2012, with the products and services it provided to global customers.

10. What's your most important savings goal right now? Accoprding toING Group Survey we save mosty for "children and families": http://bit.ly/Ztm3kL

Social (Responsibility)Activities

1. By June 2013, we will have built an "Operation Centre"which will be employing 500 people in Kahramanmaraş. We will both contribute to employment business and carry the quality of our service one step further at the same time:http://bit.ly/XOJWMS

EVALUATION AND CONCLUSION

On a three month's observation, pages seem to include vernacular events as well as banking business affairs in accompaniment with pictures in attractive colours. Administators of pages seem supporting the famous PR approach. "think globally, act locally" for pages include various kind of announcements, photos, advertisements relating to credit card campaigns, local and universal activities, news, videos, customers' feedbacks, surveys or contests, etc. Before the argument, it would be fruitful for customers categorized into two: really involved with finance affairs or probably have plans for the future visit the page just for fun. A recent research shows kinds of using social media for functional benefits, social benefits, psychological and hedonic benfits and it also reveals that the *use of social media is both pleasing and fun for them; Individuals who participate in collaborative environments by expressing opinions and sharing tourist experiences are proud of doing so* (E. Parra-López et al..2010)

Finally, four offices on four different continents seem applying the same strategies for the social media Facebook users. Let's have a look how they manage to realise this.

Contents of advertising videos or written announcements are naturally composed of the advertisements everyday watched or met on the media. They are nothing but just repetitions; sometimes there are temporary ones like Valentine's Day Celebration or Austraian Cleaning up Day. Facebook pages can be assumed as the smartest way to keep such archives at hand. On the other side, most people who have enough time, are affected readily by means of some enticing tricks such as surveys, contests or awards. These are highly attractive means for social media accountants. The bank could easily attract people and they read or watch almost evething on the page including complaints, appraisals or any news they would like to hear or read or see. There are also people really involved with the banking business, as well. Major target here is to attract people to the events as much as possible and persuade them to submit a credit card or housing loan application form and reach the customer via Facebook events or emphatic pictures or cute images of lion "the logo".There are also nice pictures from real life, working or saluting personnel or contest winners. Today, where advertising has had a major impact on consumers, companies do their best to go ahead. One of the advertising starategies in this way is employing a celebrity in the advertising film. ING Bank Global seems to neglect about it; there is only a Turkish celebrity, Acun Ilıcalı performs with the puppet lion in ING Bank Türkiye advertising films and videos on Facebook page. There is no any other celebrity performing in the Bank's videos or films during these three months.

As come to feedbacks, Banking personnel charged with finding solutions for the problems written by the customers on Facebook page are almost rightful. If they had reviewed the page once, they would have got all the answers and wouldnt be in need of asking the same question again and again On the page sufficient information is given mostly. Sometimes people complain of getting no reply soon. What most complaints revealed here is related with primarily Customer's service's rudeness or being late for the replies. Secondly comes about the banking processes and interactions and procedures. When people write up with a rightful tone, ING personnel replies in a "copy –paste" structure, only the names change! They kindly direct them to another link on which the customer could give his ID or problem details, which they seem as if they could provide a solution. A few of them seem to achieve the happy ending.

Some customers are not satisfied enough with the service they have so that they get so much surprised at ING Bank's being awarded a prize of "the most successful effective banking management" in Eastern Europe in 2012. They even supported each other online. *Online social support plays a critical role in a virtual group, which is inherently regarded as an innovative form of a social network linking people, organizations, and knowledge* (Yuan-Hui Tsai,et al. 2012)

Another strategy ING Bank applies to online customers especially who are aggresive and rude aginst the banking proceedings is no replying at all. Especially messages including accuses or insults they do not reply. Sometimes customers are right and the Bank is not fair all the time. They often have errors during interactions or transactions or they are late in doing some transactins or replying or compensating soon; so this causes some financial penaties by the INGBank. However, they might not know what the missing thing is or they are too confused and overloaded the whle day. On the other hand, the Bank employs many young people for the future and provides employment resources. However, this situation might have been caused by lack of experience. Replying customers' questions on a fixed format might sometimes cause misinformation and change the course of dialogue in a wrong way, as well. Customers should be treated as do gooders.

Treating an organization's publics well goes far beyond the tactical and behavioral decisions made when incorporating reciprocity, responsibility, and reporting into the public relations programming. The final stewardship strategy– relationship nurturing – requires that organizations engage in extra efforts to ensure that these relationships are nurtured carefully and consistently. It is vital that practitioners let stakeholders know on a regular basis that they are important to organizations, that organizations respect and care about them, and they appreciate their involvement (Richard D. Waters,2011).

On the other side, there are many people supporting and following the events or activities taken over by ING Bank. Besides, there are ING personnel who cordially support their employer.

Surveys are striking points for customers, but not all the time. That's why percentage of participation is lower than others. ING Bank should search for or create more attractive contests, concerts or events appealing different classes of society. Major reason of this low participation must be correlated with the products of the Bank. Unless having a credit card or having an online interaction via smart media, such as mobiles or ipads, nobody seems to acquire the opportunity of joining a contest, which is not fair on one hand, whereas pure commercial on the other.

This reaseach also reveals how far interested a global Bank in social activities. It is clear that they pay much attention to social event s like Mother's Day, New Year, Republic Days, Celebrity Birthdays beyond themselves. Turkish, Indian, Canadian and Australian ING Facebook pages are good examples for this phenomenon. They provide not only their services and products but involve with local and universal events as well. On ING Direct Australia Facebook page "Australian Clean up Day" is induced with a nice scenery of people cleaning up around, which recalls "Think global, act local" approach again which is one of the most successively applied approaches in Public Relations Field. India is an hetereogenious country from religion point of view but prevalent belief is Islam. By this respect ING VysaBank celebrates the sacred day of Islam on its Facebopok page, whereas the other ING Bank Facebook pages do not. ING VysaBank Facebook page directly appeals to Islamic customers in order to make them feel at home, as his own Islamic Bank.Other pages also celebrate and participate universal events like New Year and X-mas but, it is inexcusable for ING VysaBank neglecting to celebrate a universal day like Christmas!

As a conclusion, it can be assumed that ING Bank social media management strategies are almost the same with each other in different continents. It also implies institutional identity and institutional unity of ING Bank wordwide. Here it deserves being voted for the most successful Bank rate in the field of "Private Banks and Banking"in 2012.

In the age of digital convergency, social media will lead societies for further steps to learn and teach each other gradually on the way to all kind of literacies via commercial enterprises like banking business, which has been vital for everyone, anytime, anywhere in the world. Consequently, as a whole, ING Bank is a good candidate for social media global leadership and could be the best anytime, in case it recovers the deficiencies pointed out on Facebook pages by its customers.

REFERENCES

Akat, İ., Budak, G., & Budak, G. (1994). *İşletme yönetimi*. İstanbul: Beta.

Akdoğan, A., & Oflazer, S. (2002). *Bilgi çağında fark yaratacak bir örgütsel araç: Sanal ekipler*. İzmit: I. Ulusal Bilgi, Ekonomi ve Yönetim Kongresi.

Bavli, U. (2011). Sosyal medyanın dayanılmaz cazibesi. *Zorlu Dergisi, 33*, 4–5.

Ceylan, C. (2011). *Küreselleşmenin sektörel etkileri*. Istanbul: Istanbul Ticaret Odası Publication.

Elhadef, S., & Hatipoğlu, M. (2012). Kontrol artık müşteride. *Global Bireysel Bankacılık Araştırması 2012 Türkiye Raporu*.

Erkul, R. E. (2009). Sosyal medya araçlarının (web 2.0) kamu hizmetleri ve uygulamalarında kullanılabilirliği. *Türkiye Bilişim Derneği, 116*, 96–101.

Ertürk, K. Ö. (2010). *Küreselleşme ekseninde halkla ilişkiler*. Ankara: Birleşik Publication.

Facebook. (2013a). Ingdirectusa. Retrieved from https://www.facebook.com/INGDIRECTAUS?fref=ts

Facebook. (2013b). *Superstarsaver*. Retrieved from https://www.facebook.com/SuperStarSaver?fref=ts

Facebook. (2013c). Banklimiter. Retrieved from https://www.facebook.com/INGVysyaBankLimited/info

Facebook. (2014d). Ingbankturkiye. Retrieved from ttps://www.facebook.com/ingbankturkiye?fref=ts

Franke, U. J. (2012). *The concept of web organizations and its implications on changing market conditions*. Retrieved from www.virtual-organizations.net

Gerson, I. (2011). Un-friend my heart: Facebook, promiscuity, and heartbreak in a neoliberal age. *Anthropological Quarterly, 84*(4), 865–894. doi:10.1353/anq.2011.0048

Giddens, A. (2000). *Sosyoloji*. Ankara: Ayraç.

Gonzales, A. L., & Hancock, J. T. (2011). Mirror, mirror on my Facebook wall: Effects of exposure to Facebook on self-esteem. *Cyberpsychology, Behavior, and Social Networking, 14*(1-2), 79–83. doi:10.1089/cyber.2009.0411

Gonzales, L., & Vodicka, D. (2010). Top ten internet resources for educators. *Leadership*, 32–37.

Gosling, S. D., Augustine, A. A., Vazire, S., Holtzman, N., & Gaddis, S. (2011). Manifestations of personality in online social networks: Self-reported Facebook-related behaviors and observable profile information. *Cyberpsychology, Behavior, and Social Networking, 14*(9), 488–493. doi:10.1089/cyber.2010.0087

Hsu, C. W., Wang, C. C., & Tai, Y. T. (2011). The closer the relationship, the more the interaction on Facebook? Investigating the case of Taiwan users. *Cyberpsychology, Behavior, and Social Networking, 14*(7-8), 473–476. doi:10.1089/cyber.2010.0267

ING. (2013a). *History*. Retrieved from https://www.ing.com/Our.../History-of-ING.htm

ING. (2013b). *Tarihçemiz*. Retrieved from https://www.ingbank.com.tr/ingbank-tarihcemiz.asp

Isın, F. B. (2006). Teknoloji araçlarının bankacılık sektöründe uygulanabilirliği ve Türkiye'deki bu doğrultudaki bankacılık uygulamalarının değerlendirilmesi. *İktisadi ve İdari Bilimler Dergisi, 20*(2), 107-120.

Jacobsen, W. C., & Forste, R. (2011). The wired generation: Academic and social outcomes of electronic media use among university students. *Cyberpsychology, Behavior, and Social Networking, 14*(5), 275–280. doi:10.1089/cyber.2010.0135

Kalpidou, M., Costin, D., & Morris, J. (2011). The relationship between facebook and the well-being of undergraduate college students. *Cyberpsychology, Behavior, and Social Networking, 14*(4), 183–189. doi:10.1089/cyber.2010.0061

Kim, J., & Lee, J. E. R. (2011). The Facebook paths to happiness: Effects of the number of Facebook friends and self presentation on subjective well-being. *Cyberpsychology, Behavior, and Social Networking, 14*(6), 359–364. doi:10.1089/cyber.2010.0374

Koçel, T. (2001). *İşletme yöneticiliği.* İstanbul: Beta.

Li, H., & Xiao, R. (2006). A multi-agent virtual enterprise model and its simulation with swarm. *International Journal of Production Research, 44*(9), 1715–1732. doi:10.1080/00207540500445289

Marshall, G. (1999). *Sosyoloji sözlüğü.* Istanbul: Bilim ve Sanat Publication.

Mitchell, M. E., Lebow, J. R., Uribe, R., Grathouse, H., & Shoger, W. (2011). Internet use, happiness, social support and introversion: A more fine grained analysis of person variables and internet activity. *Computers in Human Behavior, 27,* 1857–1861. doi:10.1016/j.chb.2011.04.008

Näsi, M., Räsänen, P., & Lehdonvirta, V. (2011). Identification with online and offline communities: Understanding ICT disparities in Finland. *Technology in Society, 33,* 4–11. doi:10.1016/j.techsoc.2011.03.003

Ölçer, F. (2004). Telework: 21 yüzyılın çalışma biçimi. *Öneri Dergisi, 6*(22), 144-153.

Özmen, F., Aküzüm, C., Sünkür, M., & Baysal, N. (2011). Sosyal ağ sitelerinin eğitsel ortamlardaki işlevselliği. In *Proceedings of 6th International Advanced Technologies Symposium (IATS'11).* Elazığ, Turkey: IATS.

Parra-López, E., Bulchand-Gidumal, J., Gutiérrez-Taño, D., & Díaz-Armas, R. (2011). Intentions to use social media in organizing and taking vacation trips. *Computers in Human Behavior, 27,* 640–654. doi:10.1016/j.chb.2010.05.022

Pollet, T. V., Robert, S. G. B., & Dunbar, R. I. M. (2011). Use of social network sites and ınstand messaging does not lead to ıncreased offline social network size, or to emotionally closer retationships with offline network members. *Cyberpsychology, Behavior, and Social Networking, 14*(4), 253–258. doi:10.1089/cyber.2010.0161

Ristau, S. (2011). People do need people: Social ınteraction boosts brain health in older age. *Journal of American Society and Aging, 35*(2), 70–76.

Sayımer, İ. (2008). *Sanal ortamda halkla ilişkiler.* İstanbul: Beta.

Şener, A. (2012). Finansal piyasalarda kurumsal regülasyon. *Sosyo Ekonomi Dergisi, 8*(18), 173–194.

Shah, N. (2012). Welfare and technology in the network society - Concerns for the future of welfare. *Futures, 44,* 659–665. doi:10.1016/j.futures.2012.04.004

Skyrme, D. (2012). *Networking to a beter future.* Retrieved from http://dev.skyrme.com/insight.html

Soros, G. (2003). *Küreselleşme üzerine.* Istanbul: İstanbul Bilgi Üniversitesi Publication.

Stefanone, M. A., Lackaff, D., & Rosen, D. (2011). Contingencies of self-worth and social-networking-site behavior. *Cyberpsychology, Behavior, and Social Networking, 14*(1-2), 41–49. doi:10.1089/cyber.2010.0049

Steidl, P., & Emery, G. (1999). *Corporate image an identity strategies and professional.* Australia: Business & Professional.

Stiglitz, J. E. (2006). *Küreselleşme büyük hayal kırıklığı.* Istanbul: Plan B Publication.

Tsai, Y. H., Joe, S. W., Lin, C. P., Wang, R. T., & Chang, Y. H. (2012). Modeling the relationship between IT-mediated social capital and social support: Key mediating mechanisms of sense of group. *Technological Forecasting and Social Change, 79,* 1592–1604. doi:10.1016/j.techfore.2012.05.013

Tutar, H. (2002). *Sanal ofislerde koordinasyon ve iletişim: Teorik bir çerçeve.* Retrieved from http://www.ttef.gazi.edu.tr/dergi/dergi2002-2.html (in 01.02.2013)

Uzunoğlu, E., Onat, F., Alikılıç, Ö. A., & Çakır, S. Y. (2009). *İnternet çağında kurumsal iletişim.* İstanbul: Say.

Wang, S. (2000). Meta-management of virtual organizations: Toward information technology support. *Internet Research, 10*(5), 436–462. doi:10.1108/10662240010349462

Waters, R. D. (2011). Redefining sewardship: Examining how fortune 100 organizations use stewardship with virtual stakeholders. *Public Relations Review, 37,* 129–136. doi:10.1016/j.pubrev.2011.02.002

Yates, D., & Paquette, S. (2011). Emergency knowledge management and social media technologies: A case study of the 2010 Haitian earthquake. *International Journal of Information Management, 31,* 6–13. doi:10.1016/j.ijinfomgt.2010.10.001

Yılmaz, R., & Ertike, A. S. (2011). *Reklâmcılığın anahtar kavramları.* İstanbul: Kitabevi.

This research was previously published in Global Strategies in Banking and Finance edited by Hasan Dinçer and Ümit Hacioğlu, pages 304-340, copyright year 2014 by Business Science Reference (an imprint of IGI Global).

Chapter 60
The Role of Social Media in Shaping Marketing Strategies in the Airline Industry

Deniz Akçay
İstanbul Gelişim University, Turkey

ABSTRACT

Tourism is one of the leading sectors based on other people's views and comments found on the Internet. Prior to deciding where they would like to go, individuals obtain information about the travel agencies they will use, the hotels they will stay at and the regions they would like to visit, plus the views and experiences of others in terms of these issues, which are largely shared via social media environments. Accordingly, it has become a necessity for establishments to follow the main social media platforms, such as Facebook, Twitter, Instagram and so on, and develop their goods and services in line with the comments shared on these platforms. In this study, how national and international airline companies implement the 4Ps of marketing (product, price, place, promotion) in social media environments is investigated through examples and analysed through data obtained via interviews.

INTRODUCTION

With the adaptation of the Internet to mobile devices, social media applications have become a part of smart phones and tablets. Today, social media has come to be positioned as a separate marketing tool from the Internet. Blackshaw and Nazzaro (2004) stated that social media is consumer-gererated and that various online information sources, which are created, are employed by users to educate one another on other brands, services and various issues (as cited in Mangold & Faulds, 2009)

Kane, Alavi, Labianca and Borgatti (2004) stated that although social media has adapted to the majority of users, social media applications have organizational purposes that take priority, such as marketing and information management.

Leonardi and Et al. define social media as external parties that enable communication with customers, salespeople and the public through various platforms, such as Facebook, Twitter and MySpace (Leon-

DOI: 10.4018/978-1-5225-5637-4.ch060

ardi, Huysman, & Steinfeld, 2013). In the digital world, users follow brands they like and are interested in, and that the groups formed by these brands come together on a common platform in support of the brands. For instance, there are groups that are interested in certain brands and brand communities, such as Harley Davidson or Volkswagen, which have been created on the Internet environment. Kucuk (2009) stated that these new customer groups, defined as brand communities, put pressure on the brand to re-evaluate brand management, which has been grounded in basic disciplines for years (as cited in Quinton, 2013). Jevons et al. (2005) stated that brands are no longer passive agents, and that through consumers who provide input via online brand communities, in particular, brands exist as a partially independent from the market (as cited in Quinton, 2013).

According to a study conducted by Tomoson Research Institute (2015), consumers are increasingly using the Internet and social media to inform their preferences and purchases because of the influencers. In light of these results, it can be stated that the importance of social media in the service sector will gradually increase. Establishments within the service sector are able to reach more people through social media. Customers make great use of the Internet and social media in order to conduct research, evaluate alternatives, select/purchase products and broadcast behaviours displayed after purchasing in the area of airline transportation, which constitutes an important part in the service sector.

In this study, social media will be investigated through the lens of the historical development of marketing, and then evaluated in its use in airline marketing. In the section entitled Main Focus of the Chapter, we will evaluate how Turkish Airlines and Emirates use social media; their social media accounts and websites will be analysed and compared to the interviews conducted with the social media managers of both airline companies. Based on our analysis, we will evaluate how Emirates and Turkish Airlines use the 4P elements of marketing (*product, price, place, promotion*) in their social media marketing. According to our analysis, both airline firms use all product elements in order to improve their services. In addition, they use the *place* element to make sales through the Internet and the *price* element to give information about ticket prices. These airline firms also use another 4P component, *promotion*, to effectively advertise and promote products on social media platforms.

BACKGROUND

For establishments in competitive environments, which are shaped by information communication technologies, marketing is as important as the quality of goods and services. Today, with developments in the areas of industry, science and technology, the competition environment has increased even more. It has become a necessity to analyse the target groups and understand rivals in this competition environment. This entails the planning of marketing that uses new scientific methods. McCarthy created the concept of the 4Ps in order to show how to begin marketing during this process of change and within the overbearing competition environment; and through which stages it should move and be promoted (as cited in Anderson & Taylor, 1995:5) McCarthy defined the 4Ps as price, product, place and promotion.

Constantinides (2006) stated that the original marketing mix is based on the 12 controllable marketing elements (goods, pricing, branding, distribution channels, individual sales, advertising, promotion, packaging, exhibition, service, physical distribution, data collection and analysis), which have been defined by Neil Borden as result of "profitable business operation." Constantinides (2006) stated that McCarthy later on condensed these factors developed by Borden into four elements (product, price, promotion, place) and conceptualized these four elements into a marketing model (Constantinides, 2006: 408)

"Philip Kotler (1986) suggested an expansion of 4Ps to include 'power' and 'public relations', so he emphasized the growing importance of the exercise of 'power' and 'public relations', with traditional targets (i.e., consumer and the trade) and others with whom the typical marketer might have less experience (i.e., labor unions, government agencies, special interest groups, etc.)" (as cited in Anderson & Taylor, 1995, p. 5). Anderson and Taylor stated that Kotler's power and public relations argument is particularly important in the international market. Kotler (1994) defined his marketing management as analysis, planning, implementation and control and emphasized how important public relations is in marketing management (as cited in Anderson & Taylor, 1995, p. 5). Kotler argued, "[a] more basic criticism has been that the 4Ps represent the seller's mind-set, not the buyer's mind-set" (2003, p. 109). "The inclusion of product policy and channel policy, as well as market research, as part of the 'plan behind the campaign' was essential in the 4Ps type of idea and distinguished it from sales management or sales force management" (Usui, 2008, p. 16). Dann (2011) argued, "4P represents those elements of marketing that are controllable and can be manipulated by marketing managers to ensure the maximum appeal of their campaign" (as cited in Wasan & Tripathi, 2014, p. 128).

The purpose in the *goods* part is to develop goods or services that are marketable. Within this framework, the elements that should be considered in terms of goods or services are branding, functionality, shape, variety, name, packaging, guarantee, quality and reliability. Within the scope of *pricing*, aspects include how the goods are to be marketed with suitable prices (e.g., pricing strategies, price reductions, loans). In the *promotion* section, activities include brand positioning, advertising and public relations in order to encourage the target group to purchase the goods or services. In the area of *distribution*, companies need to decide through which channels goods or services will be transported to the target groups.

In the Internet environment, it is possible for target groups to perceive or feel the characteristics of goods or services as if in real life. Companies are able to share quality visuals of their goods or services with their customers through technology. Talpau (2014) stated that the Internet environment presents opportunities for establishments to sell their goods or services, and separated these goods and services into three basic categories:

1. Physical or tangible products, such as clothing, books, electronics, and furniture.
2. Intangible products/services, such as tickets, travel insurance, and holidays.
3. Digitized products, such as electronic books and software products.

AIRLINE MARKETING AND SOCIAL MEDIA

Today, creating technical solutions to the problems faced by customers and achieving superiority in terms of competition are not sufficient for establishments to increase their market share and achieve continuity. In order to be competitive and increase customer loyalty, establishments must provide the service during the process and afterwards. Within this framework, service marketing plays a significant role for establishments to prove themselves on the international platform. There are certain criterion that are used in defining services, as outlined below (Murdick, Render, & Russell, 1990):

- Services are intangible and provide benefits to those who purchase them.
- Customers also participate in the production of services.
- Services provide variable benefits that are not standard.

- There is a great amount of communication between the producer and customers during the service process.
- Services cannot be stored; they are consumed the moment they are produced.
- Pricing options are more detailed.
- The measuring of service quality is subjective.
- Service production is labour intensive.
- Mass production cannot be performed for services.
- Quality control is basically limited with process control.
- Service production and consumption take place at the same time.
- Services cannot be protected with patents.

Marketing plans are generally constructed around the traditional 4Ps (price, product, place, promotion). However, when services begin to position themselves as a marketing tool, an additional 3Ps (personnel, physical facilities, process management) are added to the process (Magrath, 1986). *Personnel* is about the external appearance of the people providing the service; for instance, whether they are cheerful. *Process management* is how the service is provided (i.e., its speed, quality, cleanliness) and *physical facilities* is everything about the physical place, such as the ambiance of the decoration, and the premises' cleanliness and lighting. "The sub-discipline of service(s) marketing is recognized as having a mid–late-20th-century origin" (Baron,and et al. 2014, p. 150).Service marketing cannot be seen, tasted or touched, unlike other tangible goods and other types of marketing. "The rationale for a separate treatment of services marketing centers on the existence of a number of characteristics of services which are consistently cited in the literature: intangibility, inseparability of production and consumption, heterogeneity, and perishability" (Zeithaml, et al. 1985, p. 33).

According to the *process* aspect of the 3P characteristics of service marketing, the quality, layover and cleanliness of airlines, food, beverages, accommodation, finance, health, etc., which are services that can benefit from service marketing, influence the perception of target groups about them. For instance, the 90-second service time at McDonald's for all its customers in cars is a determining factor of its service performance (Lund & Marinova, 2014).

The main purpose of airline services, as mentioned earlier, is to provide passengers with safe and comfortable flights and allow them to reach their desired destination on time. Additionally, passengers expect to receive quality service, be greeted by cheerful personnel and travel in a safe and comfortable manner, in return for the price they pay. Regarding airline services, passengers assess the quality of the service in accordance with how the service is provided. Therefore, airline companies can obtain information about the quality of the services they provide through feedback from passengers. Airline companies that give priority to service quality make changes to their service in line with the expectations of customers. Sickert (2010) stated that airline marketing teams' primary strategy is the immediate operational readiness in their relationship with customers and that service facilities, such as check-in counters, ticket offices, lounge spaces and back offices, are all assessed by customers. Therefore, airline customers will give certain advantages to airline companies that meet their expectations. Shaw (2007) stated that the segmentation of the airline passenger market is based on three traditional variables, and defined these as the purpose of the passenger's journey, the length of their journey and their country or culture of origin. More specifically, Shaw stated the following:

- The purpose of airline passengers' journey can be classified as business or leisure, where the ticket fees of those who go on business journeys are paid by the companies they work for, whereas those who go on leisure journeys either work in smaller companies or freelance.
- Journeys that take place within continents and those that are intercontinental differ. While services, such as the comfort of the seats or quality of the food, are more important in airline experiences within continents, flight experience is more important for intercontinental flights. The number of international passengers must be taken into consideration when assessing the quality of intercontinental flights. As Petrevska stated, "international tourist arrivals reached 1,138 million in 2014 (a 4.7% increase over 2013), while the number of overnight visitors reached 1,138 million in 2014 (51 million more than in 2013)" (Petrevska, 2015, p. 263).
- Passengers from different cultures have different needs. For example, most people in northwest Europe or North America would recognize a stereotypical 'business traveller' as someone who is middle-aged, soberly dressed and carrying only a small amount of baggage.

Lovelock and Wright (1999) stated that although services involve elements such as seats, food or repair of damaged equipment, service performance is essentially intangible, and the perceived value is derived from the performance. For instance, Lovelock and Wright (1999) stated that Southwest Airlines follows a low-priced airline ticket strategy and has established a culture in which employees try to perform their roles at as low cost to the airline as possible. According to Southwest Airlines' Annual Reports from 1996–1999, the airline company has used only Boeing 737 and 350 vehicle fleets, thus simplifying their operations and reducing costs (as cited in Lovelock and Wright, 1999). The reports also revealed that Southwest Airlines provides transportation for the basic needs of passengers. The reports stated that the passengers had not encountered any surprises concerning unreserved seats, flights not having menus, and a lack of baggage transfer service to other airlines. It is also stated that Southwest is characterised by safe flights and cheerful employees, and creates value in this manner.

Today, many companies determine and implement strategies through social media, in terms of public relations, customer relationship management, customer loyalty, marketing, and so on. While social media environments, which play an important role in increasing brand recognition and allowing brands to connect with large audiences, they also allow brands to connect with the correct target group. Social media platforms, which are among the most important marketing strategies of brands today, are important in creating a quality brand perception. When brands are joined with the contexts they create, social media and other communication channels become more effective in connecting with the target groups. "Social media should be serving a company's previously established strategic marketing plan as a successful channel integrated among other communications channels ranging from radio and print advertising to the customer service person answering the phone" (Reid, 2015, p. 27). In terms of how companies use social media, Deutsch stated that the problem with the use of social media is that companies treat it as a marketing tool; what is important in social media is understanding what people are saying, and instead of selling them something, communicating with them should be the main purpose (as cited in Reid, 2015). Brands that interact with target groups and answer their questions and views create a positive perception among those groups. Social media environments play an effective role in transmitting the voice of brands to the correct target groups in the most efficient manner. Therefore, it is important for brands to analyse their social media performance and determine their strategies in line with certain criteria by evaluating the results they achieve. Schlinke and Crain (2013) listed the following priorities of companies in their use of social media:

- To establish a reputation as thought leaders in their subject area,
- To be the source of current, relevant news around a topic,
- To make the members of the organization more accessible and create more robust relationships with existing clients, and/or
- To extend the current brand as one serving a specific demographic.

The greatest advantage social media provides, in terms of brand recognition, is that it allows for word-of-mouth (wom) communication. "The brands have realized that, by establishing a close and long-term relationship between their brands and consumers, and by converting the latter into brand ambassadors willing to support the brand in obtaining new clients through WOM, they would be able to achieve economical advantages" (Blackstone, 2000; Dowling, 2002; Reichheld, 1996; Winer, 2001, as cited in Barreto, 2013, p. 632).

Kates (2004) and Muñiz-O'Guinn (2001) argued that social media communities of which consumers are a part of during the postmodern process of production can be seen as tribes; through the sharing views, organizations and promotions by these tribes, the value of communities increases and a contribution is made to their existence (as cited in Csordas & Gati, 2014). Piskorski (2011) posited that a social media strategy differs largely from a digital marketing communications strategy (as cited in Csordas & Gati, 2014). The use of social media is increasing throughout the world. For instance, according to the Pew Research Center, 71% of adults used Facebook and 23% used Twitter in 2014. It is stated that "[c]hances are, your potential customers are on one or both of these sites" (as cited in Reid, 2015, p. 28).

Due to the rapid access to information afforded by the Internet, consumers can shape their travel plans using social media. In this aspect, the Internet and, in particular, social media have become platforms from which users obtain references on tourism. "Generally, travelers place a high degree of trust in their social media networks – information is gathered and synthesized from other travelers" (Popesku, 2014, p. 717). Toh and Raven (2003) stated that as the Internet has begun to be used in the airline sector passengers have been able to purchase flight tickets on the Internet, and that customers who purchase their tickets using the Internet are usually cost-conscious and non-business passengers.

Social media plays a special role in the activities of destination marketing organizations. Destinations marketers can use social media before (e.g., to inspire, inform, engage), during (e.g., to facilitate at the destination) and after travel (e.g., to remember, share and engage) (Popesku, 2014). Nick Smith, investment director at Scottish Widows Investment Partnership woe deals with logistics warehouses at major UK airports, including London Heathrow, has stated that he can only see social media use – such as Facebook, Twitter and LinkedIn – growing in the airfreight industry (Solomon, 2014). However, VanAuken (2015) stated that social media is not extensive or supplementary in marketing strategies and that it is an effective tool in the recognition of airline companies' brands and promotion of key services. With the expansion of information communication technologies, airline companies have begun using these technologies in an effective manner. Peterson stated that "[w]hile many airports still use cameras solely for security purposes, video analytics and other technologies, e.g., bar coded boarding pass tracking, Bluetooth, thermal sensors, and Wi-Fi are being introduced in airports across the globe to monitor customer habits and use that data to improve their overall experience" (2012, p. 1).

According to the 12th annual SITA/Airline Business IT Trends Survey (2015), 129 airline companies stated that 25.8% of 40.8% of tickets they sold were purchased on the Internet, 10.7% were bought through call centres and 4.3% were sold interlining tickets (Eye for Travel, 2015). Additionally, the SITA/Airline Business IT Trend Survey announced that 86% of airline companies provide service through social media and, by the end of 2017, 86% will be using social media for their promotions. The report also stated that as of 2017, 80% of airline companies will make their announcements via social media and 73% will provide customer service in the same manner, while 61% of airline companies will provide the opportunity for their passengers to check in over Facebook and 65% will be providing ticket sales and services over social media (SITA, 2015).

MAIN FOCUS OF THE CHAPTER

Airline companies currently, and will continue, to use social media effectively. A general look at the use of social media by airline companies reveals that they communicate with customers by answering the latter's questions and suggestions via social media. In addition, airline companies have reservation buttons on their social media accounts with the purpose of facilitating their customers' purchase activities via social media environments, in particular through their Facebook pages. It is also observed that airline companies follow the positive or negative comments made via social media and develop their goods or services accordingly, using the *product* characteristic of the 4Ps. In addition, while using the *place* characteristic of the 4Ps to sell tickets on the Internet and using the Internet as a distribution channel of their services, they use the *price* characteristic to broadcast information via social media about the prices of flight tickets. The other aspect of the 4Ps, *promotion*, which is the activity of advertising and public relations for the promotion of goods/services, is used actively on social media by airline companies. Additionally, as mentioned earlier, the 3Ps (personnel, physical facilities and process management) were developed as a complement to the 4Ps for the service sector and is added to this chaos as well. The *personnel* characteristic is about the external appearance of the people providing the service, such as whether they are cheerful; *process management* is about how the service is presented (e.g. its speed, quality, cleanliness); and *physical facilities* is everything about the physical place, such as its decoration, ambiance, cleanliness and lighting. Within the 3Ps, it is observed that airline companies reflect in particular the characteristics of *process management* and *personnel* through the videos and photographs they share on social media regarding the quality and speed of service and photographs that display the cheerfulness of their personnel.

In this study, the social media representatives of international airline companies such as Air France, Qatar, Virgin Atlantic, Swiss Airlines, Aeroflot Russia, Emirates and Turkish Airlines were sent questions regarding how they use social media. John Saydam, the social media representative of Emirates Airlines, and İnanç Emre Albayrak, the social media representative of Turkish Airlines, Turkey's national airline company, answered the questions.

The questions sent to the airline company representatives included whether they follow the comments posted on social media, share all of the comments they see regarding their organisation, and communicate with their customers over social media, and whether they have developed any goods or services within the framework of the comments on social media. In this study, we analysed the Facebook, Twitter and Instagram accounts of Emirates and Turkish Airlines to determine how they use social media. In addition, we analysed the official websites of both airline companies and evaluated the policies they implemented over social media in terms of service marketing.

Emirates Airlines, which is based in Dubai, UAE (United Arab Emirates), was founded in 1985. It assets include 229 planes, and it offers two service types, First Class and Business Class. It flies to over 140 points in six continents, informs its customers of discount flights through a "special offers" button on its website, and rewards customers with flight points through its Emirates Skyward and Business Rewards cards.

Emirates operates an exclusively wide-bodied aircraft fleet, consisting of three aircraft families: A330/340, A380 and Boeing 777. Reflecting the nature of Emirates operations with no real short haul network, it is one of only nine airlines to operate an all wide-body aircraft fleet, and it is now the largest in the World in terms of scheduled international passenger-kilometres flown (http://www.airreview.com/Emirates/Fleet.htm). Emirates keeps its customers informed through special buttons such as *online check-in, baggage status, check flight status, planning and reservation* and *special offers* on its corporate website. The airline uses Facebook, Twitter and Instagram, as well as other social media environments.

While Emirates provides information about its flight routes and planes in general on Facebook, it also informs customers about activities using this medium. Emirates, which has received 4,828,170 likes on Facebook, shares videos and photographs about its planes, flight schedules, activities and countries with users. Using its *book a flight* button on its Facebook page, users are able to make a reservation with the click of a button without having to go to the Emirates website. The company has 560,000 followers on its Twitter account, through which it again shares information, videos and photographs about its sponsored activities, flight schedules, planes and countries, similar to its Facebook page. Emirate's Instagram account has 645,000 followers. Through Instagram, Emirates shares various visuals about its planes, flight schedules, activities and countries, similar to its Facebook and Twitter accounts.

In general, Emirates' social media shows that the airline company provides information about its A380 and Boeing 777 planes and cabin crew; through sharing context about its investments, it shows its customers that it is one of the leading international airline companies. Emirates approaches consumers candidly, as can be seen from its social media promotion activities. Similar to how social media users share their experiences in the form of videos and photographs, Emirates allows its customers to get to know its brand through a fictionalized story presented through videos and photographs (http://bethere.emirates.com/globalista/jeremy-christine). In the fictional story, titled Culture & Vultures, as seen in Figure 2, two members of the cabin crew named Jeremy and Christine share their cultural experiences regarding the destinations they have been to through videos and photographs on Emirates' social media pages (see Figure 1). Jeremy and Christine's sharing of images in the Culture&Vultures applications is similar to the Periscope and Swarm applications. In the Periscope application, users share videos recorded from their own point of view with other users around the world. Swarm is a mobile app which allow to users share their locations in social media platforms. People who watch these videos can share them in other social media environments. In a similar manner, Jeremy and Christine share videos of countries they go to with users via social media. The Foursquare application allows users to check in at places they go to and are awarded with titles, such as "mayor" or "being adventurous", in line with the number of check-ins.

For the last 19 years, Emirates has shared with its customers information about its investments in the Boeing 777 programme; it supports business and innovation in the USA, as illustrated through the information it provides over Facebook and Twitter (see Figure 3). Similarly, the airline company gives information on the A380, thus informing its customers about the safety of its planes, as seen in Figures 4, 5, 6.

Emirates sponsors sports events and announces these sponsorships via social media. Its most important sponsorship has been the Rugby World Cup, which it has continually sponsored since 2007. The purpose of the Rugby World Cup sponsorship, which Emirates first sponsored in 2007 in France, is to preserve the basic values of the sport; the airline company expends efforts to enrich the experiences

Figure 1. Jeremy and Christine adventures on Emirates Facebook page

Figure 2. Emirates website

Figure 3. Information about Boeing 777 on Emirates Facebook page

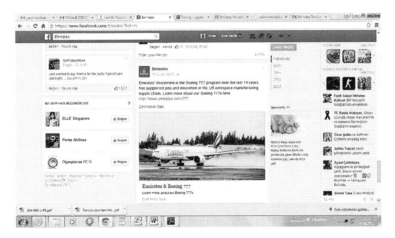

Figure 4. Information about A380 on Emirates Facebook page

Figure 5. Information about A380 on Emirates Twitter page

of rugby fans throughout the world (http://www.emirates.com/ae/english/about/emirates-sponsorships/rugby/rugby.aspx).

Emirates aims to increase the experiences of fans by interacting with them on social media through various activities, as seen Figure 7; the company has shared clues with its users on social media outlets, such as Facebook, Twitter and Instagram, in order for the flag of Cardiff, a city in Wales, to be included in the Rugby World Cup organization with the rugby star James Hook (Griffiths, 2015).

Emirates announced through the #BringingRugbyHome hashtag, created on its Facebook page for the Rugby World Cup organization, that it would be giving away various prizes to users through a competition; users were able to participate by posting photographs taken during the organization (2015).

Through the activity "Share Your Passion", Emirates asked its followers on Instagram to take selfies with the Cardiff flag, which the company placed in various parts of the world, similar to how James Hook had done with his own flag, as seen Figure 8, and send these to the company between the 9:00AM–9:00 PM timeframe. The person with the best photograph won the opportunity to be the team captain in the Rugby World Cup.

Figure 6. Information about A380 on Emirates Instagram account

Figure 7. #emiratesflag hashtag search on Twitter

Figure 8. Cardiff flag selfies on Instagram

In the interview with John Saydam, Emirates Group's Social Media Department official, he stated that Emirates actively uses both its own websites and social media accounts. Saydam, who stated that Emirates actively communicates with its customers on social media platforms, said the company follows all comments made about Emirates on social media and tries to develop its services accordingly. For instance, he stated that the company has developed services such as *delay notification, exact notifications for customers about ticket reservation, selling, cancellation and refund, lost and damaged baggage, customer relationship management, special day offers and discounts (e.g., honeymoon, birthday, festival, the New Year)* and *VIP service on the plane,* in accordance with comments made on social media. Saydam also stated that the company obtains the views of its customers about Emirates through social media. Saydam stated that Emirates interacts with customers on its website through initiatives such as *games, special day offers, contact forms,* etc. and that the website is updated every 15 days.

As a result, Emirates develops its own services in the *product* 4P area using comments shared on social media. In addition, its customers' purchasing of tickets and making reservations via its website shows that the airline company uses the Internet, the 4P characteristic area, *place,* for the distribution of goods and services and that its customers save time in such processes as purchasing tickets and following up on baggage. Emirates also underlines how high quality its *goods* are through the videos and photographs it shares about its planes' characteristics.

Turkish Airlines, which is the first national airline company of Turkey, was founded in 1933. Turkish Airlines has 267 planes. With its Miles & Smiles card, customers can gain flight points, and the airline presents three types of flights: Economy, Comfort and Business Class. Turkish Airlines shares its flight information and menu information with customers prior to, during and after flights. Through the online services menu of its website, Turkish Airlines' passengers can manage and view missing luggage, flight reservations, online check-ins, take-off and landing hours, the reservations; additionally, they can learn about the reward points they have earned with their Miles & Smiles cards. Through the Turkish Airlines corporate menu, customers can retrieve information on the company's vision and mission, history, business partners and investor relationships.

On its corporate website, Turkish Airlines defines the strategy it follows in terms of being a global brand as a worldwide sponsorship activity and states that it sponsors sports, which attract the most attention, in order to increase its brand recognition Turkish Airlines generally sponsors world-famous football teams, such as Barcelona and Manchester United. According to a news article published on September 22, 2015 in the Economy section of *Milliyet*, one Turkey's national newspapers, Turkish Airlines will be sponsoring Rome at a cost of 7 million euros annually (*Milliyet*, 22.09.2015).

Turkish Airlines has received 7,103,888 likes on its Facebook page. The airline generally provides information about ticket prices of flight destinations (as seen in Figures 9 and 10), various social activities (Figure 11), countries, favourite cities in Turkey (as seen in Figure 12) and various foods that belong to the Turkish culture (as seen in Figures 13 and 14). The Turkish Airlines Facebook page has a *make a reservation* button; however, there is no reservation button on the airline's English Facebook page.

Turkish Airlines has 894,000 followers on its official Twitter account. On this account, the airline provides information about ticket prices of flight destinations, various social activities, countries, favourite cities in Turkey and various foods that belong to Turkish culture, similar to its Facebook page. However,

Figure 9. Information about ticket prices on Turkish Airlines Facebook page

Figure 10. Information about ticket prices on Turkish Airlines Twitter page

Figure 11. Information about Venice Film Festival on Turkish Airlines Facebook page

Figure 12. Information about Cappadocia on Turkish Airlines Facebook page

Figure 13. Information about mooncake on Turkish Airlines Twitter page

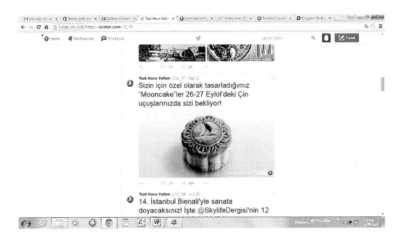

Figure 14. Information about cheese stuffed pastry on Turkish Airlines Facebook page

the use of its Twitter account in English, as well, will allow Turkish Airlines to reach more users. Additionally, the airline has a total of 10,800 followers on its "TK Help Support" twitter account. Turkish Airlines generally provides information about cancelled flights to its customers via this Twitter account.

Turkish Airlines does not have an Instagram account that is actively used. However, in 2014, Turkish Airlines sponsored five foreign Instagram photographers with the purpose of sharing their Istanbul-themed photographs on social media to increase recognition of Istanbul worldwide. Within the #InstaMeetTK0001 project, photographers took photographs of Istanbul from 11 different points.

In the interview carried out with Turkish Airlines social media manager, İnanç Emre Albayrak, he stated that the company constantly interacts with its customers regarding different topics, such as games or offers about special days, via social media.

Albayrak stated that the company has an official who answers the comments made on social media, and that it shares all positive/negative comments regarding interactions with the Turkish Airlines personnel on social media. He stated that the company constantly interacts with its customers through its corporate website in different contexts (e.g., games, offers on special days, communication forms) and that it also communicates with customers through e-mail. Albayrak also explained that Turkish Airlines obtains the views of its customers through telephone calls, surveys, observation and social media.

Thus, Turkish Airlines, in general, *places* importance on its sponsorship and promotional activities with leading sports teams throughout the world. Additionally, the airline does not use social media to develop its good or services, as Emirates does. Turkish Airlines uses the 4P *price* aspect through the information it provides on flight prices. In addition, Turkish Airlines does not actively use social media to reach target groups/customers, as it does not have an active Instagram account and its twitter accounts are only in Turkish.

SOLUTIONS AND RECOMMENDATIONS

Companies in the service sector, particularly airline companies, can earn more in the future by following developing technology trends and especially using these as a marketing tool, which lowers information communication technology costs. However, there are certain points that airline companies need to take into consideration, in terms of being more productive in their use of the Internet and social media.

Firstly, airline companies should make social media icons visible on their websites and allow these icons to give users direct access to their social media accounts. In addition, messages transmitted through social media should be translated into English, which will create an opportunity to interact with tourists. Incentivising airline companies' customers with various prizes for sharing photographs, videos or information from their social media accounts will allow companies to reach other customers as well. Additionally, airline companies should make the necessary updates to keep their social media accounts active at all times. Providing options, such as allowing customers to purchase flight tickets, make reservations via social media accounts and carry out other processes without accessing the airline companies' official sites, will positively affect the companies' sales. Lastly, airline companies can increase their number of followers through special offers announced via social media.

FUTURE RESEARCH DIRECTIONS

In order for customers to benefit from social media and mobile applications, in terms of airline service marketing, customers need to use both their mobile applications and social media in a much simpler manner. Within this framework, creation of related applications in accordance with users' perceptions of users will allow service marketing to benefit much more effectively from the Internet. Accordingly, future research should evaluate how airline companies use their websites, social media platforms and mobile applications through experimental observation of a selected focus group. The data obtained can be evaluated in line with the ISO 9241 principles, which are international standards developed with the purpose of facilitating the use of computers. According to Bevan (2006), these standards, especially parts 10 through 17, include requirements and recommendations for creating the most ergonomic features for users. (as cited in Akçay, 2013:51-52). Below are examples of such ISO 9241 principles:

- **Part 10 - ISO 9241-10 (1996) Dialogue Principles:** This part deals with general ergonomic principles, which apply to the design of dialogues between humans and information systems: suitability for the task, suitability for learning, suitability for individualization, conformity with the user expectations, self-descriptiveness, controllability, and error tolerance.

- **Part 12 - ISO 9241-12 (1998) Presentation of Information:** This part contains specific recommendations for presenting and representing information on visual displays. It includes guidance on ways of representing complex information by using alphanumeric and graphical/symbolic codes, screen layout, and design, as well as windows.
- **Part 13 - ISO 9241-13 (1998) User Guidance:** This part provides recommendations for the design and evaluation of user guidance attributes of software user interfaces, including prompts, feedback, status, on-line help and error management.
- **Part 14 - ISO 9241-14 (1997) Menu Dialogues:** This part provides recommendations for the ergonomic design of menus used in user–computer dialogues. The recommendations cover menu structure, navigation, option selection and execution, as well as menu presentation (e.g., by various techniques including windowing, panels, buttons, fields).
- **Part 15 - ISO 9241-15 (1997) Command Dialogues:** This part provides recommendations for the ergonomic design of command languages used in user–computer dialogues. The recommendations cover command language structure and syntax, command representations, input and output considerations, as well as feedback and help.
- **Part 16 - ISO 9241-16 (1999) Direct Manipulation Dialogues:** This part provides recommendations for the ergonomic design of direct manipulation dialogues and includes manipulation of objects, and design of metaphors, objects and attributes. It covers those aspects of graphical user interfaces that are directly manipulated and not covered by other parts of ISO 9241.

CONCLUSION

Today, the Internet and, in particular, social media has become an inevitable part of marketing. Some aspects that make social media the strongest in marketing include: its low cost, the speed at which information is expanded and updated, its honest environment, the ability to understand target groups and the reliability of information provided by references.

The development of Web 2.0 technology and users being able to comment on all types of news has allowed companies to follow comments on social media; thus, listening to and analysing the target groups/users is quite important for establishments, in terms of creating their strategies and implementing them. As mentioned earlier, consumers decide how to shape their travel plans over social media using the Internet. The Internet and, in particular, social media have become platforms through which users can obtain information in the area of tourism. Among the most basic reasons for this are that online communities have an efficient role in the lives of their members and give an important "reference group" service for the participants of these communities. In addition, the numerous personal spaces and profiles created by users in the Internet environment constitute a large database and establishments can measure and evaluate their marketing strategies in this manner. As a result, companies, in terms of the airlines' marketing, can easily collect information on customers through the Internet and social media and can evaluate their expectations, satisfaction and dissatisfaction. Thus, they get a chance to create their marketing strategies in a much more effective manner.

REFERENCES

Akçay, D. (2013). *The effects of interaction design in mobile publishing: Research on newspaper web pages compatibility to mobile devices.* (Unpublished doctoral dissertation). Yeditepe University's Graduate Institute Of Social Sciences, Istanbul.

Anderson, L., & Taylor, R. (1995). McCarthy's 4PS: Timeworn or time-tested? *Journal of Marketing Theory and Practice, 3*(3), 1–9. doi:10.1080/10696679.1995.11501691

Baron, S., Warnaby, G., & Hunter-Jones, P. (2014). Service(s) marketing research: Developments and directions. *International Journal of Management Reviews, 16*(2), 150–171. doi:10.1111/ijmr.12014

Barreto, A. (2013). The word-of-mouth phenomenon in the social media era. *International Journal of Market Research, 56*(5), 632.

Constantinides, K. (2006). The marketing mix revisited: Towards the 21st century marketing. *Journal of Marketing Management, 22*(3-4), 407–438. doi:10.1362/026725706776861190

Cornelissen, J. (2004). *Corporate communications: Theory and practice.* London: Sage Publications.

Csordas, T., & Gati, M. (2014). The new (marketing) role of firms as media content providers: The case of SME's strategic social media presence. *Budapest Management Review, 45*(2), 22–32.

Emirates Fleet & Seats. (n.d.). Retrieved from http://www.airreview.com/Emirates/Fleet.htm,15.09.2015

Eye for Travel. (2015, September 12). *Airlines to sell the majority of tickets direct to passengers by 2013: Survey.* Retrieved from http://www.eyefortravel.com/mobile-and-technology/airlines-sell-majority-tickets-direct-passengers-2013-survey

Fauld, D., & Mangold, W. (2014). Developing a Social Media and Marketing Course. *Marketing Education Review, 24*(2), 127–144. doi:10.2753/MER1052-8008240204

Griffiths, G. (2015, June 19). *Rugby World Cup 2015: James Hook launches Emirates hunt to find official tournament flag bearers.* Retrieved from http://www.walesonline.co.uk/sport/rugby/rugby-news/rugby-world-cup-2015-james-9482006

Gundclach, G., & Wilkie, W. (2009). The American Marketing Association's new definition of marketing: Perspective and commentary on the 2007 revision. *Journal of Public Policy & Marketing, 28*(2), 259–264. doi:10.1509/jppm.28.2.259

Kane, G. C., Alavi, M., Lacianca, G., & Borgatti, S. P. (2014). What's different about social media networks? A framework and research agenda. *Management Information Systems Quarterly, 38*(1), 275–304.

Kotler, P. (2003). *Marketing mix.* Hoboken, NJ: John Wiley & Sons, Inc.

Leonardi, P. M., Huysman, M., & Steinfeld, C. (2013). Enterprise social media: Definition, history, and prospects for the study of social technologies in organizations. *Journal of Computer-Mediated Communication, 19*(1), 1–19. doi:10.1111/jcc4.12029

Lovelock, C., & Wright, L. (1999). *Principles of Service Marketing and Management* (2nd ed.). Prentice Hall.

Lund, D., & Marinova, D. (2014). Managing revenue across retail channels: The interplay of service performance and direct marketing. *Journal of Marketing*, *78*(5), 99–118. doi:10.1509/jm.13.0220

Magrath, A. (1986). When marketing services, 4Ps are not enough. *Business Horizons*, *29*(3), 44–50. doi:10.1016/0007-6813(86)90007-8

Milliyet. (2015, September 22). *Thy which fly to Roma*, Retrieved from http://www.milliyet.com.tr/roma-ya-ucan-thy-/ekonomi/detay/2105730/default.htm

Murdick, R. G., Render, B., & Russell, R. S. (1990). *Service operations management*. Allyn and Bacon.

Peterson, K. (2012). How social media and emerging technologies influence passenger flow. *Airport Business*. Retrieved from. http://www.aviationpros.com/article/10815625/how-social-media-and-emerging-technologies-influence-passenger-flow,29.08.2015

Petrevska, B. (2015). Assessing tourism development: The case of Krusevo, Macedonia. *Economic Development*, *17*(1–2), 261–275.

Popesku, S. (2014). *Social media as a tool of destination marketing organizations*. E-Business in Tourism and Hospitality Industry.

Quinton, K. (2013). The community brand paradigm: A response to brand management's dilemma in the digital era. *Journal of Marketing Management*, *29*(7–8), 912–932. doi:10.1080/0267257X.2012.729072

Reid, K. (2015). *Social media and your business: How to approach this marketing channel with balance and control*. Retrieved from https://www.highbeam.com/doc/1G1-413779851.html, 02.09.2015

Schlinke, J., & Crain, S. (2013). Social media from an integrated marketing and compliance perspective. *Journal of Financial Service Professionals*, *67*(2), 85–92.

Shaw, S. (2007). *Airline Marketing and Management*. Ashgate Publishing Limited.

Sickert, A. (2011). Airline marketing and service quality: Foundations for growing nonaeronautical revenue — An Indian perspective. *Journal of Airport Management*, *5*(3), 213–225.

SITA. (2015, September 10). *The social journey*. Retrieved from http://www.sita.aero/resources/air-transport-it-review/air-transport-it-review,issue-3-2014/the-social-journeya-bigger-role-for-social-media

Solomon, A. (2014). *The question of social media and air cargo*. Retrieved from http://aircargoworld.com/the-question-of-social-media-and-air-cargo-9822/

Talpau, A. (2014). The marketing mix in the online environment. *Bulletin of the Transylvania University of Braşov. Series V. Economic Sciences*, *7*(56), 53–58.

Toh, R., & Raven, P. (2003). Perishable asset revenue management: Integrated internet marketing strategies for the airlines. *Transportation Journal Press*, *42*(4), 30–43.

Tomoson Research Institute. (2015). *Influencer marketing study*. Retrieved from http://blog.tomoson.com/influencer-marketing-study/,02.12.2015

Turkish Airlines. (2010, September 15). *Turkish Airlines annual report 2010.* Retrieved from http://investor.turkishairlines.com/documents/ThyInvestorRelations/kurumsal/faaliyet-raporu/2010/tr/m-6-8-1.html

Usui, K. (2008). *The development of marketing management: The case of U.S.A 1910–1940.* Ashgate Publishing Limited.

VanAuken, K. (2015). Using social media to improve customer engagement and promote products and services. *Journal of Airport Management, 9*(2), 109–117.

Wasan, P., & Tripathi, G. (2014). Revisiting social marketing mix: A socio-cultural perspective. *Journal of Service Research, 14*(2), 128.

Zeithaml, V. A., Parasuraman, A., & Berry, L. L. (1985). Problems and strategies in services marketing. *Journal of Marketing, 49*, 33–46.

KEY TERMS AND DEFINITIONS

3P: Personnel, physical facilities and process management.
4P: Price, product, place, promotion.
CRM: Customer Relation Management.
Periscope: An application that allows users to do live broadcasts on Twitter on the Internet.
Swarm: An application that allows users to share their place, city and other kinds of locations with their friends.
Web 2.0: Both writeable and readable web.
WOM: Word-of-Mouth.

This research was previously published in Analyzing the Strategic Role of Social Networking in Firm Growth and Productivity edited by Vladlena Benson, Ronald Tuninga, and George Saridakis, pages 214-233, copyright year 2017 by Business Science Reference (an imprint of IGI Global).

Chapter 61
Role of Social Media in Tourism

Vipin K Nadda
University of Sunderland – London, UK

Sumesh Singh Dadwal
Glyndwr University, UK

Dirisa Mulindwa
University of Sunderland, UK

Rubina Vieira
University of Sunderland – London, UK

ABSTRACT

Revolutionary development in field of communication and information technology have globally opened new avenue of marketing tourism and hospitality products. Major shift in web usage happened when Napster in 1999 released peer-to-peer share media and then with pioneer social networking websites named 'Six Degrees'. This kind of interactive social web was named as 'Web 2.0'. It would create openness, community and interaction. Web2. is also known as Social media base. Social media is incudes "all the different kinds of content that form social networks: posts on blogs or forums, photos, audio, videos, links, profiles on social networking web sites, status updates and more". It allows people to create; upload post and share content easily and share globally. Social media allows the creation and exchange of user-generated content and experiences online. Thus, social media is any kind of information we share with our social network, using social networking web sites and services.

INTRODUCTION

In the tourism industry, websites and social media provide a wealth of information with regards to experiences and review of the destination, property, facilities and restaurants (Manap KhairulHilmi A., 2013). Social media has added new channels of communication to tourists. Most tourists always use the Internet for destination information seeking to decision-making .The tourism industry value chain starting from countries Tourism boards, tourism agents, tour operators, transportations and airline companies, hotel

DOI: 10.4018/978-1-5225-5637-4.ch061

and restaurant operators, destination management companies and local tourism management organisation all use social media tools to reach potential customers (Ernestad V., 2010).

The social media marketing generates more business exposure, increased traffic and improved search, generating leads and improved sales at lower cost (Stelzner, 2011).Social media or web 2.0 is changing the methods by which tourists search, find, evaluate, trust and collaboratively produce information about tourism suppliers and other members of the value chain. Consequently tourists are becoming consumers who not only participate in production but also marketing of tourist's products. Using social media, travellers become co-producers, co-marketiers, co-consumers by creating user generated content (UGC) and social intelligence. (Manap KhairulHilmi A., 2013).This user generated contents of the online comments, profiles, and photographs a mixture of facts and opinions shared by tourists is trustworthy for new users .UGC have AIDA effect on travellers by creating attention, interest, desire and action (Sigala M.,Christou E.,Gretzel U.,2012),),sources of information and its evaluation, channels used for booking and buying travel products including travel itineraries and reservations and also disseminating experiences through word of mouth after the trip. The UGC content it can be in the form of any comments on Amazon, Facebook or YouTube. Nielsen (2009) argues that Internet is the mass medium used for social media marketing. However, Kessler et al. (2007) argue that social media is still in competition with traditional marketing techniques. User generated content value chain of Internet is shown below.

Consumer behaviour in tourism has always been influenced by information and communication technologies.

THEORETICAL MODELS OF SOCIAL MEDIA

Research indicates that there can be multiple reasons of why people want to share online content using offline or online medias. These motivations may be narcissism, social and hedonistic reasons, pursuit of personal identity as a gratifications,, status seeking self-concept, social support, selflessness, fame, having fun and passing time etc. on the other hand reasons for not sharing information may be a desire to remain anonymous due to issues of privacy, security time constraints, and anxiety, laziness, and shyness, vengeance, and anxiety (Manap KhairulHilmi A., 2013). Various theories (Pan B., 2011) have been discussed as basis of this such as discussed below :

Figure 1. UGC Value Chain of Internet
Source: (The Equity Kicker, 2012)

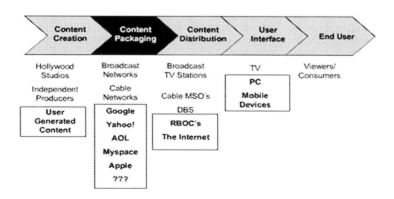

Micro Theories

Word of mouth and psychological ownership theory: This theory postulates that loyal customers would express their loyalty and sense of ownership by expressing their views to others. Psychological ownership theory explains why tourists are motivated to talk through word of mouth due to the fact that tourist start identifying with company or destination and start feeling it as their own. Another reasons may be that they feel in control and get feelings of efficacy, intrinsic pleasure, and extrinsic satisfaction in providing such an advice. The information communicated by friends is considered as more credible, honest, and trustworthy than that generated by marketers (Pan B., 2011).

Social exchange theory: this theory uses a cost-benefit framework and comparison of alternatives to explain how and why tourists wish to share information. They will engage of benefit such as such as opportunity, prestige, conformity, approval, or acceptance are more than costs of sharing and reciprocity (Pan B., 2011).

Social penetration theory: states that as the relationship progresses, a person would start to with public, visible, and superficial information, such as gender, clothing preferences, and ethnicity; and then will penetrated deeper layers of self and slowly start sharing feelings; at the deepest level,, goals, ambitions, and beliefs (Pan B., 2011).

Macro-Theories

Social network analysis: Social network theory views the community of individuals as connected actors or nodes that are connected by commination edged at multiple levels of hierarchy from individual people, to families, communities, and nations . This theory uses mathematical models to study its structure, development, inter-prelateship and evolution (Pan B., 2011).

McLuhan's Media Theory: theory postulated media is message and the media itself, rather than its actual content, will transform people and society. Theoretically one can perform all the Twitter functions through a blog service. However, limited 140 words itself made Twitter more successful.

SOCIAL MEDIA MARKETING

Marketers can create and implement marketing campaigns through use of social media that is an inexpensive way of marketing. Marketers' major focus during use of social media is to create such content that can generate attention. Moreover, the marketers focus on creation of such content that can offer motivational incentive to individuals. Mahnomen and Runnel (2008) argue that user motivations, user loyalty and user participation are the keys to success of social media. Establishment of social networks, collaborative content creation, and user centred content and flexible design facilitation is the major factors that can make social media attractive to the users.

Eely and Tilley (2009) argue that social media enables the individuals to share their experiences with others even if they have no knowledge of web development or coding. It can be done through status updates, profiles on social networking websites, links, videos, audio, photos, posts on blogs or forums.. Weber (2009) points out numerous opportunities provided by social media that help the organisations in expanding and strengthening the relationships with the customers. Some of the opportunities highlighted by him include targeted brand building that can be done through microsites, executive blogs and podcasts.

In spite of many opportunities provided by social media, there are certain challenges for marketers as well. As reported by Weber (2009), marketers using social media have to adopt many techniques that they do not need to adapt while using traditional marketing techniques. A clear understanding of opportunities and challenges arising due to social media marketing is extremely important to stay competitive. Moreover, marketers should be fully aware of the potential gains and risks and it should be done through comparisons with traditional marketing channels as hinted by Hearn et al. (2009).

In business context, engaging people is the major purpose of social media marketing. People can be engaged using four different ways. These ways include communication, collaboration, education and entertainment. All these attributes can change over time and this result in desired action or outcome.

SOCIAL MEDIA IN DECISION MAKING PROCESS

Decision making process include stages such as need identification, information search, evaluation of alternatives and selection, purchasing, and post purchase behaviour. Social media is useful for tourists during each stage and also for businesses at corresponding value chain of tourism and hospitality industry; tourist product planning and development, product production and consumption, tourist product marketing and logistics, post purchase support to the consumers. The consumer decision-making models guide that, buying behaviour results from consumer involvement and engagement in multistage problem solving tasks. The stages are: need recognition, information search, evaluation of alternatives (evoked set), evaluation result and when buying, post-purchase evaluation (Schiffman & Kanuk, 2009). Marketing communication using social platforms provides consumers information, so they become able to support the learning process by which they acquire the purchase and consumption knowledge. Consumers' learning, attitude and motivation can change due to any newly acquired knowledge gained from reading, observation, discussions and virtual or actual experience. Social platform can effect consumer perception about evaluating the desired and actual state, and can drive active or latent 'problem recognition' and also offer solution to the problem. During second stage of 'the information search', social platform can aid in learning process by helping to search either internal or external memory sources. The evaluation of alternative stage is conditioned by the type of consumer's choice and discussion on social platform can aid by influencing consumers' learning, motivation and attitudes with help of augmented reality experiences. In last stage of consumer decision-making process-post-purchase evaluation, the consumer compares the product real performance with his expectations, and right discussions and word of mouth on platforms is useful in setting right levels expectations at well above consumers' minimum noticeable threshold levels and by reducing any uncertainty in offerings or services. Right evaluation not only sets evokes set and helps in making choice of brand offerings or destination but also, can create positive word of mouth, customer loyalty, feedback and cross product buying.

The social platforms can provide conditions for high level of customer involvement and engagements with the product or the services. Level of customer involvement in buying process means amount of psychophysical energy spent by consumer in the buying process. Higher levels of involvement are associated with greater use of affective and cognitive decision making strategies across different cultures (Edgett & Cullen, 1993). During buying or consuming highly involved individuals compared to lower involved individuals will use more criteria search for more information, accept fewer alternative, process relevant information in detail, and will form attitudes that are more resistant to change. Involvement levels, therefore, can have an impact on the information processing decision-making and responses to

Figure 2. Purchasing process
Source: (Turner and Shah, 2011)

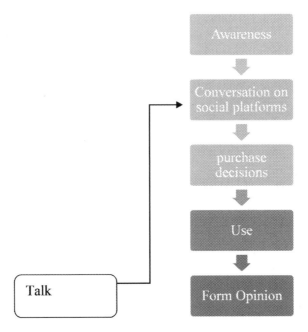

advertising. Lack of proper management of touch points / customer encounters can cause a churn among the firm's existing customers. Social platform not only increases customer relations but also enhances loyalty, satisfactions through customer's involvement and encounter management, socially, emotionally, visually, auditory and kinaesthetically. The social media marketing platforms are useful for businesses to spread a positive word of mouth through which they could influence them and exchange information. These platforms also provide an opportunity to clear any mis- understanding that could have become the hindrance in the purchasing decisions of customers. Singh et al (2008) states that because of the sharing of instant information the developed societies have got in the habit of creating awareness, sharing it on the Internet on social platforms and then making purchasing decisions.

The above diagram clearly shows that when people use a product, they then share their experiences on the internet with others on the conversation on social media platforms and this makes others to revise their purchasing decisions. A business can effectively take the advantage of such a platform and interact with its customers in order to help them satisfy their needs through addressing their issues promptly. (Turner and Shah, 2011)

It has also been noticed that social media also plays a pivotal role in the launching of the product. A wealth of word of mouth information regarding the brands and products, on social platforms leads to its use as a new channel that has features of search engines, review sites, and price comparison. It directly act as least two marketing mix place and promotion and aids in other 2 Ps Price and product strategies (Bolotaeva, 2011).

Like any other media, social platform also offers challenges to the business. Challenges such as invasion of user privacy, aggressive advertising, lack of e-commerce abilities, lack of brand controls, and certain legal pitfalls, can be major disruptions to social platforms. The consumers don't like intrusive advertisements and communications and they are not ready to share their privacy that can be pervaded in an online platform.

SOCIAL MEDIA IN TOURISM INDUSTRY

Social Media is a group of Internet-based applications that contribute towards building of ideological and technological foundations of Web 2.0. Marketing via Social Media is trendy method market communication using different tools of Social Media; Facebook, LinkedIn, YouTube, Twitter, Blogs. YouTube, social bookmarking, forums, group on etc. (Stelzner, 2011) . Other type of tools include; email marking, search engine optimisation, event marketing, press releases, online adds St. Google ad word, direct mail, print display ads, sponsorships, webinars and other ads. .There are many tools or platforms of social media marketing (Ernestad V., 2010).

Social networking platforms develop virtual communities, or social networks, for individuals, who have similar Attitude, interests, education, opinion and lifestyles, thus creating communities of practices. Bolotaeva, (2011) defines social networking platform as: "… a loose affiliation of people who interact, communicate and share contents through the platforms building relationships among communities. The companies have to mange a social platform management in order to development, deployment, use it for customer services. A social platform' empowers customers in, posting, editing, sorting, co-creating and sharing a variety of contents. Thus it enables in communication implicitly or explicitly with specific person or broadcast to all. More features are used in adding friends into the network, setting privacy controls etc (Leonardi, 2013). In technological dimension, a social platform consists of dimensions of social mark-up language for creating native applications, an application programming interface (API) for third party application integration and a back-end admin console for managing the entire user base and preferences, etc. It provides continuous visibility and persistence to people and content.

INFORMATION TECHNOLOGY AND TOURISM

Tourism as a global industry is one of the biggest job providers and technology has seen a development that brought fundamental changes in the industry. Besides improving communications, ICTs are increasing the competitiveness of tourism organisations and destinations.

Travellers use technologies to plan their journeys, access reliable information and to make reservations, while tourism organisations have become more efficient and effective. Buhalis and Law (2008) believe that ICTs have benefited the new tourist who is sophisticated and more demanding. This means that package tours are losing their appeal as tourists prefer to organise independently organised trips to explore their personal and professional interests.

Technological progress and tourism have been going hand in hand for years. Developments in ICTs have changed business practices as well as strategies and the structure of the industry. In the 1970s, Computer Reservation Systems were establishment and in the late 80's was the time for Global Distribution Systems, followed by the development of the Internet in the 1990's.

Technology has been the focus of the last 20 years and since 2000 communication technologies have brought new developments and tools that facilitate international interactions between the different stakeholders.

Travellers have now more access to information provided by the different tourism organisations, can book flights and accommodation and as a results most tourism organisations have embraced internet technologies as part of their marketing strategy (Buhalis and Law, 2008).

As a consequence, consumers have an active role in co-creating the product design as well as promotional messages. Consumers use digital media not only to research products but also to engage with the companies and other consumers.

In a new social media-driven business model which is dominated by customers' connectivity and interactivity, content goes hand in hand with technology in the form of social networks and blogs that enable individuals to create, share and recommend a product (Hanna, Rohm and Crittenden, 2011).

Mobile devices will be used to access these platforms but it is not easy to classify the different types of social media. Facebook, YouTube, Blogger, Twitter, MySpace and Flickr are characterised as social networks, social networking and social media.

Marketers are using several of the major platforms and interactive digital marketing platforms are changing the marketing landscape by empowering consumers to connect, share and collaborate and to create spheres of influence (Hanna, Rohm and Crittenden, 2011).

This means that traditional media cannot be the solely tool to capture the attention of consumers. The focus cannot be in reaching the customers but on continuing attention via engagement that involves traditional and social media.

Social media is seen as a development of digital media where communities share and discuss information. It has been defined as the evolution of digital media based on the notion of discussing and sharing information between the social community's online users (Serlen, 2013). The word refers to the development of audio, videos, pictures and words by integrating social interactions, telecommunications and technology (Corstjens and Umblijs, 2012).

On one hand, social media connects individuals of different nationalities, religion and cultural background and messages are spread internationally very easily (Bertrand, 2013). On the other hand, social media is an effective tool for marketers to develop brand awareness and loyalty, increase sales and to improve customer service. It is a tool which can be used by large corporations as well as small businesses (Schlinke and Crain, 2013).

Although the benefits and impacts of social media have yet to be understood, social media turns passive consumers into active consumers through what people share in networks (Corstjens and Umblijs, 2012). Clients feel they are valuable and have more control and responsibility, while tourism companies end up spending less time and money on promotion (Seth, 2012).

Historically, companies could control the information available about them by placing press announcements and using public relations managers. Thus, today firms have been relegated as mere observers having neither the knowledge, chance or the right to change publicly posted comments that customers provide. The current trend toward social media can be seen as an evolution, making the internet a platform to facilitate information exchange between users (Kaplan and Haenlein, 2010).

User Generated Content is the sum of all ways in which people use social media. The terms is applied to describe content that is publicly available and created by end-users. According to Kaplan and Haenlein, social media is *«a group of Internet-based applications that build on the ideological and technological foundations of Web 2.0, and that allow the creation and exchange of User Generated Content, pp. 61»*

In terms of types of social media and the opportunities they bring, there are the 'Collaborative projects' that enable the creation of content by end-users. The main goal is the joint effort of different people to a better outcome and the fact that they are becoming the main source of information for many consumers. An example would be Wikipedia.

Blogs represent one of the earliest forms of Social Media. They are personal web pages and are normally managed by one person but provide the possibility of interaction with others through the addition of comments.

Content communities are another social media that share media content between users including text, photos, videos, PowerPoint presentations, etc.

Social networking sites are applications that enable users to connect by creating personal information profiles and the information can include photos, videos, audio files, etc. Facebook and Myspace are examples of social networking sites.

Creating customer awareness about a product is one of the main reasons tourism companies may use social media. Thus, the company business strategy should contemplate a strategy for the use of social media (Manap, 2013/Schlinke and Crain, 2013) and these can help the company to find out what customers want and how do they behave and what do they purchase.

Dewey (2013) wrote in the 'Business Journal' that as mobile device users increase, traveller's reliance on app and online resources for tourism and travel planning is also increasing. The use of online resources has grown, with more consumers reading travel blogs and destination reviews, as well as photos and videos.

In relation to mobile phones, 53% of travellers are using apps and 29% of travellers have used mobile apps to search for flight deals and 30% to find hotel deals.

Because of the increased use of the Internet and apps, social media are more important than ever to travellers' purchase decision, even if 'word of mouth' is of online strangers. Companies are trying to establish relationships with consumers and some managers respond to comments and complaints. Some large corporations even have a full-time social media person who read and respond to reviews (Dewey, 2013).

ELECTRONIC WORD-OF-MOUTH

Consumers have the ability to develop powerful influences upon each other and virtual interactions have spread with electronic technologies. A good example is the website tripadvisor.com where consumers share their hospitality and tourism opinions.

With more than 2 million reviews and being updated every minute, hospitality and tourism marketers realised its importance do to the intangibility of the goods they sell. Tourism products are cannot be evaluated before consumption and are seen as high-risk purchases. Therefore, more studies should be developed to understand what kind of information consumers seek online and how they actually use information acquired online from other consumers to make their travel and hospitality decisions (Litvin, Goldsmith, Pan, 2007).

Interpersonal experiences and influences flows from opinion leaders to followers and among followers. Thus, favourable word-of-mouth (WOM) increases the probability of purchase while negative WOM has the opposite effect. The low-cost access to information exchange can create new dynamics in the market and greater control over format and communication types.

Travellers are using search engines to locate travel information and as a consequence this brings changes to the structure of travel information, to travellers knowledge and perception of travel products.

e-WOW strategies will be informal and revenue generating. Marketers will use the online feedback left by customers to enhance visitors satisfaction, improve the product, solving visitor problems and monitor companies reputation and image (Litvin, Goldsmith, Pan, 2007).

Social media constitute part of the online tourism domain and play an important role. However, they do not consume all places on search result pages and leave room open for marketers to compete with social media for customers attention (Xiang, Gretzel, 2010).

DIGITAL DIVIDE AND ITS IMPACTS

Innovation technologies are critical for the management and marketing of tourism organisations and destinations. Consumer behaviour is affected from product search to consumption and memories and the web allows users to compare products and prices and to build personalised itineraries (Minghetti and Buhalis, 2010).

Thus, disparities exist in access, skills, use of ICTs and services. Not everybody has the opportunity to benefit from internet opportunities and digital divide can lead to digital and social exclusion. For tourists and destinations, this means being unable to participate in the emerging electronic market and benefit from its opportunities.

The global digital divide is caused but differences in GDP and income, human capital and digital skills, telecommunications infrastructure and connectivity, policy and regulatory mechanisms.

The geographical evolution of tourism is followed by a similar development of the digital divide. More than 50% of the international tourism flows and receipts are concentrated in the developed areas of the world where (with the exception of China) are also included within the high-opportunity digital access economies. Not all ICT users will use technology wisely or effectively. Some people lack the knowledge, trust, literacy or language skills.

As for destinations, ICT-Skilled tourism companies and destination marketing organisations will increase their visibility on the marked and to strengthen their competitiveness. On the contrary, tourism companies with low ICT use are often cut off from electronic distribution channels and e-commerce and may risk in becoming invisible for a share of the market (Minghetti and Buhalis, 2010). Tourists and destinations suffer from a multiplicity of technological divides which lead to different levels of digital exclusion.

SOCIAL MEDIA TOOLS/PLATFORMS AND USER BEHAVIOURS

Thus a social platform enables in creating social media websites and services with complete social media network along with technical, user specific and social functionality. These are second generation (Web 2.) websites/ platforms that provide users the ability and tools to create and publish their own mini web sites or web pages using the "bottom up" — using a many-to-many model. Such platforms provide features such as; user created contents, high degree of user participation in communities of practice and ability to integrate with multiple sites or networks (Campbell, 2010). Thus a social platform include things like social networking (Facebook, Google+ MySpace, twitter, LinkedIn); photo and video sharing sites (Flickr, Vimio and YouTube); blogs (such as Blogger, WordPress, Typepad), social bookmarking

(Delicious, Stumble Upon) news sharing (Digg, Yahoo! Buzz) (Campbell, 2010). The social networked platforms can attract traffic by managing touches of 4Ps; Personal, Participatory, Physical, Plausible (Clemons, 2009. cited in Bolotaeva, 2011).

The companies have used social platforms for internal and external communication and marketing . Its increasing use can be attributed to demand side factors (the fact that social media give us that we can't get offline and let us meet our social needs) and supply side factors (websites such as Facebook, Twitter, and LinkedIn have more than 1.2 billion users and account for almost 25 per cent of Internet use). To get full advantaged of social media, companies need to develop and harness their social strategy (Piskorski, 2014).

Over 1.7 billion people use social platforms on the Internet. Different platforms have certain distinctive features or USP. For instant platforms, such as Twitter, MeetUp and eHarmony, enable "strangers" to connect. eHarmony let meet people to meet up for marriages. LinkedIn helps one expand business relationships. Other platforms, like Facebook or Renren in China, creates more relationships with other "known" peoples. In fact, Facebook boasts staggering 750 million users, and valuation in excess of $100 billion (Piskorski, 2014). Different platforms have different levels of restrictions to users' choices and uses . Platforms like e-Harmoney (dating site), Whatsup (social one to one texting on phone), headhunting (recruitment) etc., are successful even with restrictive access and a user fee. On the other hand platforms like Facebook (social networking), Monster (job hunting), Lastminute.com (travel and tourism), YouTube etc. that offers unlimited free access are also successful. The understanding becomes more complex when even platforms with middle grounds on access like twitter (limited in words with unlimited in access to network) and LinkedIn etc. are also growing. Thus, It can be argued that the value of participating in a social platform often depends on the number of choices offered, and a platform offering unrestricted access (yet in user's control) could quickly displace a platform that restricts choice or provides restricted access.

SOCIAL MEDIA SEGMENTS

Social platforms has been ranked by comprehensively average of integrating rankings from others ranking evaluators (Alexa Global Traffic, compete and Quantcast) (EbizMBA, 2014). In 2013, the studies have found that users segments of different platforms are distinct and sometime duplicate. Facebook is preferred by diverse mix of demographic segments and who also visit site daily many times. Pinterest has four times high appeal to female users, LinkedIn has more college graduates with higher income households. On the other hands the segments of Twitter and Instagram are overlapping with younger adults, urban dwellers, and non-whites (Duggan, 2013). Further 90% of Twitter users, 93% of instagram and 83% of linkedin users also use users also use Facebook. A small number of users use only one type of plateform; 8% use only LinkedIn, 4% use only Pinterest, and 2% Instagram or Twitter only (Duggan, 2013). This pattern shows high level of similarities between user needs to visit social platforms on one hand and also put forward a question that why people visit many platform if one platform can meet their social needs! Do people have different motives at each platform or do they have different network of connections at each of the platform or they want to exhibit different personalities and roles at different platforms. Marketers can also target users as Word of Mouth marketer, according to their characteristics or social media preferences there can be seven kinds of social media users. The 'Deal Seekers' are always hunting for bargain or value deals from the marketers, so companies should always offer them deals along with a request to refer more friends to the brand; the 'Unhappy Customer' can cause harm to a company by creating stream of negative words of mouth (-WOM), so company should solve their problems immediately; the 'Loyal Fans' are useful to spread positive word of mouth (+WOM) and even defends their brand, so the company should reward their behaviour; a 'Quiet Follower' is neutral and is just there because his friends are there, so the company should put effort them to engage them as active users; the 'Cheerleaders' are top-class fans of the brand and likes everything a company does, hence the company should keep them updated and inspiring; and lastly the 'Ranters' can fight virtually due to their strong opinions about everything, so the company should react cautiously and very selectively to their opinioins (SEOPressor, 2012). Hence in overall the company should have a customised social platform strategy and the contents of the messages should be engaging with a sense of community, inclusive in action, newsworthy, and contents from all followers be allowed and recognised.

SOCIAL MEDIA STRATEGIES

Piskorski, (2012) argued that companies that simply ported their digital strategies onto the social environments, 'maximising number of followers', and merely trying to broadcast their commercial information to customers, do not succeed on social platforms. Social strategies should be gradually unfolded in stages. At stage one, advises business to build better relationships between people and provide incentives if people undertake corporate tasks for free. At second stage the company should make non-intrusive attempt to build relationship between companies and consumers. A social strategist will create social presences of 'many to many interaction'. For example the Nike Plus platform, that allows its 5 million customers of Nike's digital products to interact with their friends; has contributed up to the 30% increase in sales. Similarly Cisco's social platform is not only protecting the company from aggressive moves of Chinese giant Huawei but also it has enabled engineers to interact with each other, achieve a number of certifications and become more effective on their jobs (Olensky, 2014).

Piskorski, (2014) supports three kinds of social stargic pardigms The first pardigm is, 'the pipes view', it conciders social networks are conduits which transfer trustworthy information about exchange opportunities between interested prties. The second vparadigm is 'prisms view' and posits that a platform offers a network tie between two parties, it has implications not only for the parties but also for third-parties not involved in the exchange. A third pardigm is 'networks as cover', that assumes that interactions with friends and acquaintances give actors an excuse to engage in other kind of prying activities, while still maintaining plausible deniability that they are not engaging in such behaviors. For instant, LinkedIn allows users who are currently employed to go on the job market without apearing that they are on the job hunt, and facebook networks can allow people to look for new parteners without others realising this explicitely. Similaraly on social networking sites people can peek into privace areas that social norms may not allow in physical world. The study found that, only 50 per cent of profile and picture views are of friends, the remaining 50 per cent is of strangers (Piskorski, 2012).

A well thought out social strategy is usefull in toursim sector. following section sections details main social startgic actions using different social media tools .

VARIETY OF SOCIAL MEDIA TOOLS

1. Social Networking

Social networking sites- Facebook, Google Plus, Cafe Mom, Gather, Fitsugaretc allows users to connect and share with people who have similar interests and backgrounds. The most famous example of social networking is Facebook, Twitter, and LinkedIn etc. That enables the tourists to efficiently communicate and interact with other members of social network like friends, family and co-workers and world at large. For using Facebook as a tool The business need to develop their brand profile through creating a Facebook page and share interesting, and newsworthy information with consumers. The company needs to help consumer meet their social needs and let them fulfil each other needs. Do not intrude or be pushy like salesman, and act as facilitator for creating social presence. Depending upon kind of users they can offer customised communications. Foe example does offer incentives or recognitions for new needs for deal seekers. Do respond to comments from complainers or fans and weave into your comments and posts to continually extend this. They can also create discussion forums to have feedback about their products and services. (Treadway and Smith, 2010). Another social platform is Linkedin. LinkedIn has 225 million registered users and on the average 110 million unique monthly visitors. Remember to follow effective communication principle of AIDA – attention- interest- desire and action. Request cheerleaders and opinion leaders for testimonials. Promote company through 'follow' button and remember to link your other social media accounts to your LinkedIn Company Page. Make the information engaging and varied but also remember pictures speak more than words.

2. Micro-Blogging Sites

Twitter, Tumblr, Posterous etc allow the users to submit short written entries, which can include links to product and service sites, as well as links to other social media sites. Twitter is very popular micro blogging site amongst the celebrities and Politicians, due to which it attracts a wide variety of fans of such personalities from around the globe. It provides an excellent opportunity to businesses to market there offerings through celebrates or by themselves. The message or tweet can be personal thoughts, quotes, news and picture links, brand, and product and service links, thus creating interest and buzz. Invite friends or brand cheer leaders and follow opinion leaders or media channels that are of interest to your customers & followers. Your followers are following you as role models or reference groups or your brand leadership due to power, authority, rank, expertise, referrals, coercive etc. ensure that you continuously perform your role. Tweet yourself and retweet from higher ups in industry, media, consumer groups, government reports and news channels etc.

3. Blog

Web log, is a web page that serves as a publically accessible personal journal for an tourists (Blood 2002 in (Ernestad V., 2010)). A blog is powerful and inexpensive tool to can convey different types activities, interests and opinions such as political, commercial, public and personal word of mouth. They are also known as Publishing tools; like WordPress, Blogger, Squarespace etc. allows users engage in conversations by posting and responding to community message. Blogs can be updated on a frequent basis. Blogs can also be regularly developed for a variety of different marketing and branding campaigns. They are an active source of promoting products and services and spreading information (Khare, 2012). There are many different blogs that cover and attract people from specific industry. Marketers generally develop their profile and carry on updating them so that the fans and connected users are kept well informed.

4. Multimedia or Video Sharing

It enables sharing of multimedia content, for example Flickr (photographs) and YouTube (videos) are used by Millions of people exchange information and interests. Video sharing sites- YouTube, Vimeo, Viddler; etc.allow users to share different types of media, such as pictures and video. YouTube has more than 1 billion registered users at which videos are viewed 4 billion times per day is largest media sharing site in the world. Once registered a business can upgrade with a fee to get YouTube's 'branded channel' option. The business can increase traffic by using SEO keys and tags that are in line with interests of your consumer segment and your brand. Business should stay current and follow the rules of movie making and education. People like seeing more than reading but it must be something for them (SEOPressor, 2012).

5. Collaboration Tools

Wikipedia, WikiTravel, WikiBooks; etc are Apps or software based social platforms where users can work together (synchronously or asynchronously) to create, modify and manage content (Decidedlysocial, 2012; SEOPressor, 2012; About.com 2014).

6. Rating/Review Sites

Amazon ratings, Angie's List; Kind of platforms allow reviews to be posted about people, businesses, products, or services. It is a social strategy tool professionally designed and written to maximize conversions sales. (Decidedlysocial, 2012; SEOPressor, 2012; About.com 2014)

7. Photo Sharing Sites

Flickr, Instagram, Pinterest; etc. enable users to upload, transform edit, publish and share pictures and videos etc (Decidedlysocial, 2012; SEOPressor, 2012; About.com 2014). Instagram is very popular photos and videos sharing platform and recently purchased by Facebook. It has 130 million active monthly users. The business can upload photos or videos of brands or other issues of interests and can link with other social platforms and invite people to click for favourite ones. To keep always in the trend continuously upload new actions photos about your actions that would be of interest to users. That addresses their social, rational, emotional and epistemic needs. (SEOPressor, 2012).

8. Personal Broadcasting Tools

Blog Talk radio, Ustream, Livestream, tumbler are platforms that offers a way of participatory journalism and synonyms to personal publishing.

9. Platforms Like Virtual Worlds

Second Life, World of Warcraft, and Farmville Are 3D computer based online community environment in which users are represented on screen as themselves or as made-up characters and interact in real time with other users using texts, or 2D or 3D models, knows as Avatars (Decidedlysocial, 2012; SEOPressor, 2012; About.com 2014).

10. Location Based Services

Check-ins, Facebook Places, Foursquare, and Yelp etc are Apps on gadgets and mobiles that uses geographical position (GPS) and link it with information, entertainment, or social media service that is available nearby location. E.g. gas prices and services or restaurants near your location (Decidedlysocial, 2012; SEOPressor, 2012; About.com 2014).

11. Widgets

Profile badges, Like buttons etc are sets of small helpful software program or Apps, which gives extra power an control to the user when embedded directly into a web page. These can be used to add features like, weather, clock, local news, Twitter widget, Mailing list, gossips and joke of the day etc (Decidedlysocial, 2012; SEOPressor, 2012; About.com 2014).

12. Group Buying Sites

Groupon, Living Social, Wowcer, Crowdsavings etc are latest trend in money saving, with the power to pull in big discounts(Decidedlysocial, 2012; SEOPressor, 2012; About.com 2014).

13. Social Bookmarking and News Aggregation

Digg, Delicious, StumbleUpon and son on allow users to save and organize links to any number of online resources and websites (Decidedlysocial, 2012; SEOPressor, 2012; About.com 2014). Social bookmarking such as StumbleUpon discovery engine has 25 million registered users. It searches and recommends web pages to its users and can also be shared by others to 'like it'. This also recommends users other related sites or sites that your network has liked or submit industry related sites and blogs or create a stumble upon channel (SEOPressor, 2012).

14. Email Marketing

Sending emails to exiting or potential tourists is one of the most effective Internet marketing.

15. Search Engine

Like Google, bing, yahoo etc are used by tourist to find the company or destination information and search engine optimisation can bring a particular site at top search position (Ernestad V., 2010).

MEASURING SOCIAL MEDIA PERFORMANCE AND EFFECTIVENESS IN TOURISM

Social media marketing has become a critical success factor that is driving the success of many businesses today. However as more and more tourism organisations investing money into their social media strategy questions are now emerging on whether this spending on social media result in better performance for the whole business. Unfortunately there is no clear answer to this question at the moment. Social media marketing is still in its infancy stages for many tourism businesses, this makes it difficult to measure its performance. Managers and marketers responsible for promoting the use of social media continue to find it challenging to demonstrate the value of their investment on Facebook, Twitter and other bring to their business. Hoffman and Fodor (2010) noted that business in general and their marketing departments in particular are still searching for the right way to measure the impacts of their social media strategy because most of the models used are primarily by 'reach and frequency'.

Business Metrics provide a feedback mechanism that is critical to the organisation's continuous improvement. Organisations just like working with metrics, the CEO and department managers need a number to measure the performance of their investment; this is because orient people towards a goal, help them to focus and measure success. It is believed that activities that are not measured they often do not get done. However, much as the numbers have their advantages if they are note well managed they may bring problematic behaviour and ultimately detract from broader organisational goals. Therefore, without a reliable measurement it may be difficult to judge whether goals have been successfully achieved (Demopolous, Futch and Pisello 2008). Thus measuring the impacts of social media on the organisations is likely to guide investment on the right networks to use, though this poses other questions 'what is to measure?'; what key metrics can help the organisation to understand the influence of social media in the context of their own industries, size, and geographies? And lastly how should the organisation interpret these metrics?

One would wonder if organisations can realistically specify bottom line benefits that result directly from the use of social media as a marketing strategy. Much as Social media starts with ideation and creativity, differs from any other marketing tool, because it is a science that revolves around big data, statistics and numbers. It is also much more than just posting or sharing or number of likes or followers. Tourism organisations need to measure not only its influence on the overall performance of the business but also to justify the time and money invested in social media. Organisations that fail to scrutinise the deep data generated by social networks they use data are doomed to fail in their social media marketing. Tourism organisation should note that social media bears many of the core principles of measuring other marketing tools and also apply them to social media. For instance, marketers and managers are still interested in understanding how big is their audience on the social media? The rate at which the business is growing on the social media, as well as, the extent of the traffic generated to their business from the social media networks.

When measuring the influence of social media to the business performance, there are two main aspects to consider: impacts and Return on Investment (ROI). Regarding impacts of social media, the business has to find answers to the following questions:-

The impact of social media on a business performance can vary significantly from one organisation to another, and between industries and sectors, the size of the organisation as well as the geographical region. Thus making it difficult to measure and determine whether the investment on social media provide the desired effect to the business. However, it is now accepted by many business managers and marketers that a well-designed social media strategy can provide a competitive advantage. Measuring a business social media influence has become important as more and more people use these networks to seek for advice from their peers on the products and services about what they think, say and by (Elderman 2007). Online social networks produce information every minute, whenever, someone posts something on Facebook, Twitter or Pinterest, they create a digital footprint. Similarly, every time someone reads the post on any of the social networks or watch a video on Vimeo or YouTube they add to their digital trail. But how does a business identify these opportunities and justify its investment on social media channels that will deliver the best return?

Social media measurement is not straight forward process as it has various areas numbers may not provide the real insights on its impacts to the business. One of the problem of measuring social media's ROI is that the organisation is trying to convert non quantifiable elements such as people's interactions and conversations into numeric quantities. Organisation that try to measure the impact of social media on the business often rely on the number of followers but, it is difficult to measure the number of tweets a day or to determine the worth of 1000 followers on Facebook.

Some commentators have argued that much as it may not be easy to measure social media, there are ways this can be done but the managers have decide what could be regarded as 'return' (Bitzer, 2012). This is so because the social media metrics such as the number of likes or followers cannot be relied on when measuring the revenue generated to the tourism business from social media though other social metrics such as customers' sentiments of the business and feedback can provide valuable insights that can help the business to improve.

On the other hand without a proper framework for measuring, there is no way of knowing how an activity is performing. Therefore the number of tweets a day or followers provides the initial basis it is not enough to give the true picture of social media strategy success. Organisations need to be able to identify and develop a criteria as well as metrics that can enable them not only to understand the landscape of their social media strategy but also its impact on it operations and audiences. Tourism managers and marketers using social media need to understand that it is not the destination; it is just a vehicle. They need to ask themselves question such as 'what is the ROI of social media?'; what is the ROI of the particular activities that the organisation engage in using the social media?. Answering these question will help organisation to focus on measuring only the right things instead of wasting resources measuring each and every activity

The market as well as the internet is full of tools to measure social media as well as numerous metrics, measurement gurus making it extremely difficult for tourism managers and marketers to wade through this maze of options to choose the right one that will help them. However, there are models that can help the managers to understand the value of their efforts on social media, for example Etlinger (2011) developed a the Altimeter's social measurement compass framework and identified six main organisa-

Table 1. Impact on social media

Impacts	ROI
	Did sales, revenue and profit increase due to the business' activities on the social media
How the messages were communicated?	Did the business get the right type of customers
Did the relationship improve?	Did the relationship with the customers and other businesses change
Did the business get the exposure it was looking for?	Did the customers' behaviour change

Figure 3. The seven steps to social media measurement
Source: Paine (2011)

1.	Define the "R" — Define the expected results?
2.	Understand your audiences and what motivates them
3.	Define the "I" -- What's the investment?
4.	Determine what you are benchmarking against
5.	Define the metrics (what you want to become)
6.	Pick a tool and undertake research
7.	Analyze results and glean insight, take action, measure again

tion goals that social media can help influence including *brand health, marketing optimisation, revenue generation, operational savings, customer experience,* and *innovation.*

Paine (2011) argued that measurement of social media should always be linked to the business objectives and goals and provides the following framework that can also be used by tourism and hospitality managers.

As Table 1 above indicates this framework is made up of seven steps that can be summarised as business objectives, audience, and cost of social media management, benchmarking, KPIs, data collection tools, and action. In this chapter we will outline these steps because they are not exclusive to social media but instead provide a basis for measuring the other business strategies. Moreover these steps are familiar to most managers and marketers as they are not knew instead Paine used the same steps marketers have been using for a long a time. The purpose of Paine's framework is to provide a models that can help managers prove that social media is working and be able to use the results to plan for future performances.

Firstly, social media should be treated like any investment a tourism organisation undertake to achieve its business objectives. For example a hotel may have one of its objective as 'increase occupancy by X% by the end of December 2014. By having such a specific objective it helps the business to focus their social media campaigns. This way the business can claim that the time spent on updating their Facebook page and competitions they hosted there in the past 2 months have helped to drive the business to achieving its objective. Focussing the social media strategy on the business objectives may also lead to creating sub-objectives or tasks that social media should meet in order to achieve the business objectives. For instance, if the business objective is to increase hotel occupancy b X% by the end of the year then what should be the social media strategy? In this case the strategy may use short term campaigns such as time-limited offers lasting a fortnight, a month or two and then measure their impact on the main business objective. On the other hand the strategy may be to increase brand awareness, in this case viral campaigns targeting potential customers may be initiated by using general awareness messages. The bottom line is that when a business link its objectives to their social media strategy it is able to measure the success of individual tasks and determine its impacts on how the business achieved its objective or objectives.

The second step on Paine (2011) model is the identification of the audience. That is who is the business talking to? This question will help the tourism business identify the people associated with their brand and then the next questions are 'how will the business know that thy have reached their audience?' When identified and reached, 'what is it that they business want them to do?' and lastly, how will this help the business to achieve its objectives? For a tourism business such as a hotel or restaurant the target audience is most likely to be varied. For instance for a hotel the audience could be business or leisure customers of varied age, geographical locations and cultures. All these groups may be on different social media channels, therefore, whilst the hotel message may be seen by all the people on that channel, the hotel has to make it clear as to which message is intended for business or leisure customers and the actions expected from them intended audience. Note that the messages for each audience group is different as each group has different needs and requirements.

The next step for the hotel would be to attach a value to each of these audience groups, this will to determine if the business audience group picking up on the message is more valuable than the leisure audience. Just like in the 1st step the business need to relate its social media activities to its objectives such as 'increase leisure customer engagement, because the recent analysis of the business showed that games and competitions on Facebook led to more leisure guests bookings in the past'. In this case, the business measure of social media could be to count the number of leisure customers following the hotel brand and to monitor the number of reviews they produce about the brand.

Thirdly the business has to determine the cost of running the social media campaign in terms of the money invested and the number of hours put in the campaign to be able not only to put a monetary value to the cost but also to be able to determine the opportunity cost. This is Delahaye Paines model is referred to as the 'I' in ROI (Paine, 2011).

The fourth step is to determine some benchmark to help the business to compare against something, this could be the business past performance and/or a competitor. The business need to set up baseline numbers to compare to in order to measure change. This is just like if a hotel's objective is to increase occupancy by X% by the end of the year, what was the occupancy last year? Then how has the use of social media led to his increase. Benchmarking can also be based on the other marketing campaigns to measure its influence or effectiveness compared to the other ways the business is promoting itself. For instance in terms of the Facebook what could be the worth of a 'page view' as compared to for example the cost of a click in pay per view campaign. Comparing with other marketing campaigns or past performance can help the business to measure the success or social media campaign in achieving its business objectives.

Following determination of the business objectives and identification of the audience, as well as establishing benchmarks the fifth step of measurement detail is to determine the criterial for success or the Key Performance Indicators [KPIs] (Lovett, 2011). These are the outcome metrics that focus on the different objectives of the business social media strategy which may be for example increase leisure customer followers on Twitter. In this case the audience is leisure customers while the benchmark is the current number of followers, therefore the KPI would be how many follower have been signed up among leisure and business customers, this could be classifying the customers in their audience groups and carry out a head count.

Analysis of KPIs may be an important tool for determining the effectiveness of the social media marketing strategy. KPIs can be measured by deterring both the pre and post- campaign periods, this will allow the business to have a clear understanding of the success or failure of the social media strategy. KPIs analysis also help the business to be able to produce quantified metrics that may lead to making informed decision as well as producing qualitative data that may provide the analysis for future social media trends. Qualitative data such as feedback expressed by the customers on social media platforms can help organisations to improve the product or service.

The sixth step involves selecting tool to measure data gathered. On the social media such as Facebook the business may put their main focus on three key areas likes, shares and links and comment on post, this is because when someone likes the business' page it will know that its audience is listening. While a comment made by a follower on the business post means a two way conversation is taking place and the customer is engaged; and when the customer share the hotel's post with their friends on Facebook, it is a sign that the audience has expanded. Likewise the process of gathering data and analysing it for social media may differ depending on the type of data the business gather. Today, there is a great number of data collection tools available each of them produce a different kind of data. What is to be noted is that there is not a single tool that can measure all the nuances of social media by itself, though each tool may be used to gather data on a particular aspect and the sum of all the data gather by each tool may provide a better understanding of the effectiveness of social media strategy. For data involving sentiments, messaging or conversations content analysis is the best tool to use, whereas measuring perceptions, awareness or relationships survey research would the tool to use. However, when the data to be measured involves making predictions or correlations then web analytic tool such as google analytics would provide better outcomes

Lastly, Paine (2011) noted that measuring social media is an iteration process that involves doing something, measure the results and act or make changes where necessary, which will eventually lead to new results. At this point the business may ask questions such did we meet our business objectives? Then based on the results go through the process may be with some changes for improved results. The whole process is ongoing aimed at optimisation or continuous improvement.

As has been noted in this discussion social media is the way of marketing a tourism related business. Paine's seven steps are of measuring social media performance are grounded in the fundamentals, they are not different from the way other business performances are measured. Failure to relate social media to the underlying business fundamentals chances of understanding the business performance from the social media may be futile.

REFERENCES

Anjum, A. (2011). *Social Media Marketing*. GRIN.

Barefoot, D., & Szabo, J. (2010). *Friends with Benefits: A Social Media Marketing*. Handbook, California: No Starch Press Inc.

Bitzer, M. (2012). *Social Media ROI and Why Your Hotel May Be Focussing on the Wrong Turn*. Available at http://www.bluemagnetinteractive.com/blog/117-social-media-roi-and-why-your-hotel-may-be-focusing-on-the-wrong-return.html

Bolotaeva, V. A. (2011). Marketing Opportunities with Social Networks. *Journal of Internet Social Networking and Virtual Communities*.

Borgan, C. (2010). *Social Media 101*. New Jersey: John Wiley and Sons. doi:10.1002/9781118256138

Bryan, D. (2013). *Small business advertising and brand promotion using Facebook Ads*. Retrieved June 20, 2014 from OpaceWeb: http://www.opace.co.uk/blog/social-media-ppc-facebook-ads-vs-linkedin-ads-vs-google-adwords-which-would-you-choose

Buhalis, D., & Law, R. (2008). Progress in information technology and tourism management: 20 years on and 10 years after the Internet – The state of e-Tourism research. *Tourism Management*, 29(4), 609–623. doi:10.1016/j.tourman.2008.01.005

Campbell, A. (2010, Jan 21). *Social Media — A Definition*. Retrieved June 16, 2014 from Amy Cambell's Web log: https://blogs.law.harvard.edu/amy/2010/01/21/social-media-a-definition/

Conrad, J. (2010). *Guerrilla Social Media Marketing*. Entrepreneur Media Inc.

Corstjens, M, & Umblijs, A. (2012). The Power of Evil: The Damage of Negative Social Media Strongly Outweigh Positive Contributions. *Journal of Advertising Research, 52*(4), 433-449.

Decidedlysocial. (2012). *13 Types of Social Media Platforms and Counting*. Retrieved June 20, 2014 from Decidedlysocial: http://decidedlysocial.com/13-types-of-social-media-platforms-and-counting/

Deighton, J. K. (2007, Sept 26). *Digital Interactivity: Unanticipated Consequences for Markets, Marketing, and Consumers*. Retrieved June 20, 2014 from HBS.edu: http://www.hbs.edu/faculty/Publication%20 Files/08-017_1903b556-786c-49fb-8e95-ab9976da8b4b.pdf

Demopoulos, P., Futch, J., & Pisello, T. (2008). *The Importance of measuring ROI: the Indicators of Business and IT performance*. An Alinean White Paper.

Dewey, C. (2013). Tourism goes mobile and social. The Business Newspaper, 31(18).

Duggan, M. S. (2013, Dec 30). *Social Media Update 2013*. Retrieved June 25, 2014 from Pew Internet Reserch: http://www.pewinternet.org/2013/12/30/social-media-update-2013/

EbizMBA. (2014, June). *Top 15 Most Popular Social Networking Sites | June 2014*. Retrieved June 25, 2014 from EbizMBA: http://www.ebizmba.com/articles/social-networking-websites

Edelman, J. B. (2007). *Distributed Influence: Quantifying the Impacts of Social Media*. Available at http://technobabble2dot0.files.wordpress.com/2008/01/edelman-white-paper-distributed-influence-quantifying-the-impact-of-social-media.pdf

Ernestad V., H. R. (2010). *Social media marketing from a bottom-up perspective - the social media transition*. Retrieved March 28, 2014 from http://www.carphonewarehouse.com

Etlinger, S. (2011). *A Framework for Social Analytics: Six Use Cases for Social media Measurement*. Altimeter Group Publication.

Evans, D. (2012). *Social Media Marketing* (2nd ed.). Indiana: Wiley Publshing.

Evans, D., & McKee, J. (2010). *Social Media Marketing*. Indiana: Wiley Publishing.

Gunelius, S. (2011). *30 Minute Social Media Marketing*. Ontario: McGraw Hill.

Hajir, K. (2012). *Your Social Media Marketing Plan*. Available at: http://yoursocialmediamarketingplan.com/

Halligan, B., & Shah, D. (2010). Inbound Marketing. New Jersey: Wiley Publishing.

Hanna, R., Rohm, A., & Crittenden, V. L. (2011). *We're all connected: The power of the social media ecosystem Kelley School of Business, 54* (pp. 265–273). Elsevier.

Hendricks, J. (2010). *The 21ˢᵗ Century Media Industry*. Lexington Books.

Hoffman, D. L., & Fodor, M. (2010). Can you measure the ROI of your social media marketing? *MIT Sloan Management Review, 52*(1), 41–49.

Jaoker, A., Jacobs, B., & Moore, A. (2009). *Social Media Marketing*. Future Text.

Kabani, S., & Brogan, C. (2010). *The Zen of Social Media Marketing*. Dallas, TX: Barbell Books.

Kaplan, A. M., & Haenlein, M. (2010). *'Users of the world, unite! The challenges and opportunities of Social Media', Kelley School of Business, 53* (pp. 59–68). Elsevier.

Khare, P. (2012). *Social Media Marketing Elearing Kit for Dummies*. New Jersey: John Wiley and Sons.

Kimbarovsky, R. (2009). *10 Small Business Social Media Marketing Tips*. Available at: http://mashable.com/2009/10/28/small-business-marketing/

Leonardi, M. H., Huysman, M., & Steinfield, C. (2013). Enterprise Social Media: Definition, History, and Prospects for the Study of Social Technologies in Organizations. *Journal of Computer-Mediated Communication, 19*(1), 1–19. doi:10.1111/jcc4.12029

Litvin, S. W., Goldsmith, R. E., & Pan, B. (2008). Electronic word-of-mouth in hospitality and tourism management. *Tourism Management, 29*(3), 458–468. doi:10.1016/j.tourman.2007.05.011

Lovett, J. (2011). *Social Media Metrics Secrets*. Indianapolis: John Wiley and Sons.

Manap, K. A. (2013). The Role of User Generated Content (UGC) in Social Media for Tourism Sector. *International Academic Conference Proceedings*, 11-78.

Manap KhairulHilmi, A. A. N. (2013). *The Role of User Generated Content (UGC) in Social Media for Tourism Sector*. Retrieved March 28, 2014 from http://www.westeastinstitute.com/wp-content/uploads/2013/07/Khairul-Hilmi-A-Manap.pdf

Minghetti, V., & Buhalis, D. (2010). Digital divide in Tourism. *Journal of Travel Research, 49*(3), 267–281.

Olensky, S. (2014, March 3). *Social Media And Branding: A One On One With A Harvard Business Professor*. Retrieved June 24, 2014 from Forbes: http://www.forbes.com/sites/steveolenski/2014/03/17/social-media-and-branding-a-one-on-one-with-a-harvard-business-professor/

Paine, K. D. (2011). *Measuring What matters: online Tools for Understanding Customers, Social Media, Engagement and Key Relationships*. Indianapolis: John Wiley and Sons.

Pan, B. C. J. (2011). *Theoretical Models of Social Media, Marketing Implications, and Future Research Directions*. Retrieved March 25, 2014 from Theoretical Models of Social Media, Marketing Implications, and Future Research Directions: https://www.google.co.uk/search?q=Theoretical+Models+of+Social+Media%2C+Marketing+Implications%2C+and+Future+Research+Directions&rlz=1C5CHFA_enGB513GB513&oq=Theoretical+Models+of+Social+Media%2C+Marketing+Implications%2C+and+Future+Research+Directions&aqs=chrome.69i57j0.1765j0j4&sourceid=chrome&espv=2&es_sm=91&ie=UTF-8

Piskorski, M. (2012). *Networks as covers: Evidence from business and social on-line networks*. Retrieved June 20, 2014 from HBS. Edu: http://www.people.hbs.edu/mpiskorski/papers/FA-Platforms.pdf

Piskorski, M. (2014). *A Social Strategy: How We Profit from Social Media*. http://www.amazon.com/Social-Strategy-How-Profit-Media/dp/0691153396

Safko, L. (2010). *The Social Media Bible*. New Jersey: John Wiley and Sons.

Schlinke, J., & Crain, S. (2013). Social Media from an Integrated Marketing and Compliance Perspective. *Journal of Financial Service Professionals, 67*(2), 85-92.

SEOPressor. (2012). *Social Media Marketing*. Retrieved June 20, 2014 from Seopressor: http://seopressor.com/social-media-marketing/

Singh, S. (2008). *Social Media Marketing for Dummies*. John Wiley and Sons.

Stelzner, M. (2011). *2011 Social Media Marketing Industry Report How Marketers Are Using Social Media To Grow Their Businesses*. Retrieved March 16, 2014 From 2011 Social Media Marketing Industry Report: http://www.socialmediaexaminer.com/SocialMediaMarketingReport2011.pdf

Sterne, J. (2010). Social Media Metrics. New Jersey: John Wiley and Sons

Taylor, E., & Riklan, D. (2009). *Mastering the world of Marketing*. New Jersey: Wiley and Sons.

The Equity Kicker. (2012). *More on the future of TV*. Retrieved March 20, 2014 from http://www.carphonewarehouse.com

Thomases, H. (2010). *Twitter Marketing: An Hour a Day*. Indiana: Wiley Publishing Inc.

Treadway, C., & Smith, M. (2010). *Facebook Marketing: An hour a Day*. Indiana: Wiley Publishing.

Turner, J., & Shah, R. (2011). *How to Make Money with Social Media*. New Jersey: FT Press.

Tuten, T. (2008). *Advertising 2.0: Social Media Marketing*. Westport: Greenwood Publishing.

Xiang, Z., & Gretzel, U. (2010). *'Role of social media in online travel information search', Tourism Management, 31* (pp. 179–188). Elsevier.

Zarrella, D. (2009). *The Social Media Marketing Book*. Sebastopol, CA: O`Reilly Books.

Zimmerman, J., & Sahlin, D. (2010). *Social Media Marketing for Dummies*. New Jersey: Wiley Publishing. doi:10.1002/9781118257661

This research was previously published in the Handbook of Research on Global Hospitality and Tourism Management edited by Angelo A. Camillo, pages 142-162, copyright year 2015 by Business Science Reference (an imprint of IGI Global).

Chapter 62
Using Social Networks to Create and Share Experiences in Creative Tourism

Róbert Štefko
University of Prešov in Prešov, Slovakia

Martin Mudrík
University of Prešov in Prešov, Slovakia

ABSTRACT

The presented chapter deals with creative tourismwhich is often considered marginal, however is a form of tourism with the great potential for future growth. The Slovak Republic has, thanks to the historical context, all necessary preconditions to exploit this potential. There is a large number of customs and traditions, which can be attractive to visitors by their nature, historical or cultural-religious value. There is also a big potential to create new experiences, spirituality, singing, dancing in customs and traditions. Religious and pilgrimage sites are also sites where visitors can experience strong emotions. Sharing these experiences on social networks is quite frequent during the last decades. This chapter therefore deals with the legal possibilities of sharing these experiences by using social networks that represent a powerful marketing communication tool.

INTRODUCTION

The desire to travel, explore, discover and experience something new has always belonged to basic human qualities (Pizam & Mansfeld, 2012). Travel and tourism are currently important parts of economic sector in almost every state and it is one of the sectors with the fastest growth. It makes up over a quarter of services in the world (Matias, Nijkamp, & Sarmento, 2011). Before reaching this level of significance, travel and tourism sector went through gradual development. Since the end of the World War II, its importance has been constantly increasing and its impact has been observable in almost every area of human society (Walton, 2005).

DOI: 10.4018/978-1-5225-5637-4.ch062

Travel and tourism have grown in importance to such an extent that they currently account for an essential part not only at the level of national economies, but they also form a significant component of the economy at the European Union level (El-Agraa, 2011). Their development is influenced by several policies, such as foreign affairs policy, environmental policy and likewise. One of the important objectives of the European Union in the context of regional policy is the effort to gradualy decrease differences among individual regions within the EU. To meet this objective, various programmes supporting the development of travel and tourism in the countries with less developed economies have been introduced (Milovčíková, 2008).

The development of travel and tourism is encouraged by many factors related to gradual increase in population, overall improvement of human health (thus prolonging life expectancy), as well as improvement of education (Rickly-Boyd, Knudsen, & Braverman, 2016). Improved education gradually helps to overcome language barriers and stimulates the desire for getting to know new places and cultures as well as for extraordinary experiences (Indrová et al., 2008).

Travel and tourism are nowadays global issues. Besides, it is a sector which has been developing in a quick and positive pace (Costa, Panyik, & Buhalis, 2013). At the present time, there are thousands of travel agencies in the world offering holidays, and stays and constantly making an effort to improve and innovate their offers (Ślusarczyk, Smoląg, & Kot, 2016; Singh, 2008). Since tourism has been growing at a fast pace, possibilities of offers are increasing respectively, which consequently contributes significantly to the growth of economy. In addition to that, early detection of new trends seems to be a unique opportunity for potential investors interested in this sector to assert themselves in the market (Mariani, Czakon, Buhalis, & Vitouladiti, 2016).

BACKGROUND

Creative Tourism

Creative tourism could be ranked among the latest innovations of tourism itself. As the name suggests, it refers to something creative. That is exactly something that people have started to look for (Fernandes, 2011). A creative tourist differs from a common tourist by directly searching for and/or expecting a new experience. Moreover, they are willing to pay much more money for such a holiday (Wurzburger, Aageson, Pattakos, & Pratt, 2010). Since the mojority of the hotels are insufficiently occupied, the question arises here why not to use their potential (Harssel, Jackson, & Hudman, 2014). There is a number of ideas and inspirations how to use this new trend in the sector. Schools, workshops and numerous crafts courses represent interesting factors with the potential for growth and an important role in the selection of destinations for shor-term holidays, or stays, chosen by the tourists themselves (Walsh, 2011).

According to the Toursim Portal (2013), every tourist is welcome, especially the creative one. Although, this type of tourists is still in minority in terms of figures, according to the survey carried out by the Commission for Travel and Tourism of the European Union, it is the tourist with the highest potential for future growth (Nelson, 2013). The number of those who are not attracted to standard sightseeing or experiential tourism products any more is increasing (Gburová, Matušíková, & Benková, 2015). The creative tourist looks for interesting opportunities allowing them to learn something new and inspiring, for example, how various useful and nice things were created in the past as well as how to handmake them today. They are attracted by tradititional crafts and goods and this applies to representatives of both younger and older generations as well as domestic and foreign visitors (Richards & Wilson, 2007).

Considering reasons that motivate visitors to opt for this type of a creative journey, one cannot help but notice the changes that have recently occurred (Conrady & Buck, 2011). Approximately five years ago, creative tourists were mainly creative people that went in for some kind of artistic activity in their home country and they were interested in perfecting and improving it especially during the summer holidays (e.g. painting courses, dance, quitar, etc.) (Tan, Kung, & Luh, 2013). However, at present, a new trend is emerging and tourists normally add to their traditional programme of visits more creactive and participatory activities with the aim of living culturally and exchanging experience in the given area (Creative Tourism Network, 2016). At the same time, they are willing to leave their home country and travel abroad. This trend is caused by the need and (or) desire to explore and get to know some new particularities of other nations and other cultures (Smith & Richards, 2013).

According to the portal dromedar.sk (2014), the Slovak Republic has not been able to exploit its tourism potential at a sufficient level yet. Creative tourism can help tourism sector in all regions, regardless of the fact whether they boast of major tourist attractions or not (Dallen, 2015). It implies something more than just searching for ways how to fill vacancies. It encompasses cooperation of entrepreneurs in the area of services within the region.

One of the most popular forms of cultural tourism practised today is religious heritage tourism, which is interesting especially for modern tourists who like to experiment and seek cultural enrichment. (Lois-González, Santos-Solla, & Taboada-de-Zuñiga, 2014).

Religious and Pilgrimage Tourism

Human desire to understand the meaning of life and give one's existence certain direction led to the origins of religions. Religious and pilgrimage tourism represents one of the oldest forms of tourism (Whalen, 2011). In the past, it was actually the second most common reason for travel. Practising faith through religious symbols, such as ceremonies, prayers or music led to creation of places of worship. At the time of ancient Greece, many pilgrimage sites were registered, among the most significant ones, Dodona and Delphi. With gradual growth and spread of Christianity, in the first centuries of this era, more and more adventurers went on pilgrimages to the Holy Land and later to Rome and other parts of Europe (Šoporová, 2013). In medieval times, people travelled mainly to visit places with reports of apparitions of the Virgin Mary.

At first glance it might seem that the religious and pilgrimage tourism currently accounts for only a relatively marginal sector. According to surveys, it is, however, this sector that has great potential (Shahshahani, 2009). It is necessary to take into account that it occurs in all religions and cultures. Religious and pilgrimage tourism is currently becoming one of the fastest developing and growing tourism sectors (Badone & Roseman, 2004). More than for religious reasons, people travel only for adventure. The World Tourism Organization ranks religious tourism at the fifth place in their classification of reasons for travelling:

1. Leisure, recreation and holidays;
2. Visiting friends and relatives;
3. Business and professional interests;

4.   Health tourism;
5.   Religious and pilgrimage tourism;
6.   Others (UNWTO, 2014).

In the world today, there is a great number of religions and almost each of them has its own mystical places that are sacred to the believers. These places have been frequently visited (Douglas, 2006). Of the world's best known, authors mention Lourdes, Santiago de Compostela, Bethlehem and Jerusalem for Christians; Mecca, Al-Aqsa Mosque and the Kaaba, for Muslims; or Varanasi, Mathura and Ayodhya for Hinduists. These places are known worldwide and almost all inhabitants of the planet have at least heard about them (Olsen, 2010).

There are still many places that are local and known only by the people living in a certain region. These sites, however, have considerable spiritual significance for the locals. At the same time, they have significant potential to attract the attention of visitors, if not for religious reasons, then for reasons related to history, architecture, artistic value or desire to have a spiritual experience that would enrich one's inner life (Beaver, 2005).

Religious tourism is becoming a greater source of business. As the portal Tourist and More (2009) shows, according to estimates, approximately 25% of travellers practice this form of tourism in the United States. It is also necessary to add the relatively high number of people travelling to events related to their faith, such as weddings, bar mitzvahs or funerals. A resulting final number is much higher. The enormous importance of religious tourism is proven by measurable indicators based on which it is known that 330 million tourists from around the world participate in it, with this number increasing every year. As the Portal Tourist and More (2009) also shows, the annual turnover from these activities amounts to over $ 18 billion.

Travelling for religious motives is often less prone to economic fluctuations in the market than other forms of tourism. As believers are engaged travellers, they have a tendency to save for these trips in advance and travel regardless of the current economic situation. Travellers travelling because of their faith consider their travel to be a part of their religious obligations, or a fulfilment of their religious mission (Raj & Griffin, 2015). For this reason, this form of travel can account for regular and steady income in the local economy.

A modern religious tourism does not have a long tradition in the Slovak Republic. This is due to the fact that the conditions for its implementation were interrupted during the totalitarian regime (Černá, 2014). The change occurred after the fall of the former regime, after November 1989, when the persecution of the churchgoers stopped and the borders to Western Europe were open (Sucháček, 2013). According to Maštrla (as stated in Jancura, 2010), an increased interest in pilgrimage tours to the holy places in the world began to emerge in 1990 after the fall of communism, when they were no longer forbidden, and it culminated around the year 1995.

SPIRITUALITY AS ONE OF THE MAIN REASONS IN CREATIVE TOURISM

One of the first tasks in efforts to discuss spiritual tourism is to define what it exactly is and which tourists belong to this category (Timothy & Olsen, 2006). For the believers, who attend significant religious pilgrimages (such as Muslims when visiting the sacred places of Mekka and Medina, or the supporters of Budhism, who visit four sacred places in India and Nepal), it is not a problem to be labeled as so-called spiritual tourists (Baranowski & Furlough, 2001). It is also not a problem to include in this group other approximately 500,000 people who are part of various religions and every year they pass Camino de Santiago (the road of St. Jacob).

The problem arises only when one starts to consider where to include the large number of tourists who visit, for example, the Notre Dame cathedral, only to admire its architecture and history. Are these tourists really spiritual tourists? If someone visits the Australian army memorial in Somme, where their great grandfather fought during the First World War, is it possible to include them in the group of true spiritual tourists? Opinions on this matter continue to vary (Bowler, 2013).

In efforts to discuss spirituality as a reason for travelling, it is important to understand firstly the significance of spirituality as such. Philosophers argue that because spirit is the essence of being human, and one's spirituality is incorporeal, essentially spirituality concerns a human being's individual search for meaning in life, which inevitably will be undertaken by all humans (Bahm, 1974). Author Kelly Jr, (1995) in his publication defines spirituality as a deep sense of belonging, of wholeness, of connectedness, and of openness to the infinite. Basically, it may be claimed that spirituality is closely linked to the discussions about the sense of life and self-reflection and is generally perceived as more than just a temporary experience (Filep, 2016).

Spirituality, or expanding the spiritual perspective, may bring quite a large number of various stimuli to many people. Essentially, it does not matter if it means creating various objects or things, singing, visiting different places, talking to interesting people or dancing. After all, there were quite a number of studies conducted in this area and in one of them it was found out that passing a flamenco course at a dance school had a significantly strong spiritual impact on its participants (Matteucci, 2013). In the current materialistic world more and more people have a tendency to develop their spirituality. From the history it is clear that the greatest role in development of spirituality has been played by religion (Lennon & Foley, 2000).

One of the simplest definitions of a spiritual tourist was proposed by Norman (2013), who in his work claims that a spiritual tourist is a person who travels for the purpose of improving their spirituality. Based on the aforementioned it should be concluded that there exist significant differences between a tourist, who visits sacred or spiritual monuments only to admire them, and a tourist, who visits these places out of his or her own spiritual beliefs. Also from the religious viewpoint, the former group of tourists seems to be less important (Stausberg, 2013).

In any case, spirituality in the area of tourism becomes more and more the center of attention of experts in this field (Maciocco & Serreli, 2009). Findings acquired from the studies of spiritual experiences in the area of tourism bring one closer to the theoretical understanding of complex meanings within the decision-making process of groups and individuals in travelling (Lois-González, Santos-Solla, & Taboada-De-Zuñiga, 2014). Spiritual experiences related to religion can attract a large number of visitors annually. At the first sight it may seem that a spiritual tourist is placed somewhere between a pilgrim and a standard tourist. This assumption is correct in principle but Norman (2004) states that in this case it is important to regard this category as an individual one connecting certain elements of both mentioned groups.

Religion and tourism have quite a long mutual history. Currently it is necessary to understand that it is spirituality that can provide the religious tourism with a new dimension as well as partially change the understanding of the term religion from the dogmatic to a more flexible one (Lew, Hall, & Williams,

2014). Visiting a religious place, talking to other believers or participating at some religious event do not inevitably create a believer out of a non-believer. However, they may influence this person spiritually and thus secure meeting their expectations as a tourist (Aramberri, 2010).

SHARING EXPERIENCES

Experiencing spirituality can enrich a person but many people have a natural need to share their experience with their peers (Gray, Jeffery, & Shao, 2008). Reasons for this need have been discussed by many psychologists for a long time, but from the perspective of marketing, it is crucial to keep it that way (Gort, Vroom, Fernhout, & Wessels, 1992). Existence of this phenomenon represents an interesting opportunity from the viewpoint of marketing, as the positive references from acquaintances represent a significant stimulus in decision-making (Middleton & Clarke, 2012). The objective of this chapter is to describe the options of sharing various experiences and thus simultaneously promote activities offered by particular destinations.

Social Networks as a Tool for Sharing Experiences

Sharing experiences has a long history among people. First, it was about the experiences that were necessary for survival. With a gradual development also less important aspects started to be shared, things which made life more pleasant (Ihamaki, 2010). Globally, people are sociable and therefore it is not surprising that they have a need to share their happy moments with someone close (Zhao, Lin, & Liu, 2011). Options of fulfilling this were limited in the past; basically, it used to be all about verbal or written reproduction of the experienced moment (Adair, Filene, & Koloski, 2012). This state lasted several millennia and has changed only recently. An indubitable turning point was the invention of photography which could capture interesting moments and preserve them (Brennen & Hardt, 1999). Another very significant step was the development of audiovisual technology and a possibility of capturing events in the form of a video, which contributed to a better, more precise reproduction of the experienced (Williams, 2004).

It is important to mention also another aspect which played a key role in sharing experiences. It is the distance and outreach to people a regular person had in the past and has now. In the past, this outreach was significantly limited and basically also limited to people who lived nearby and with whom the given person usually came in contact with (Moran, 2010). Ways of overcoming the distance gradually destroyed this barrier. It does not concern only the development of transportation means but, primarily, the development of technological machinery which enabled a long-distance communication (Suchacek, Seda, Friedrich, & Koutsky, 2014). One of the most significant was clearly the discovery of telegraph, followed by telephone, radio and television (Donsbach, 2015). In the last decades, however, the most significant role in overcoming the distance has been played by the Internet (Curran, Fenton, & Freedman, 2015).

Development of the Internet caused a significant change in possibilities of communication among people. This relatively big change has in the last ten years been supported also by the expansion of social networks which basically enable a constant contact with anyone almost anywhere in the world (Iosifidis & Wheeler, 2016). Reaching this state was significantly aided by the development of mobile technology and smartphones. In the well-developed parts of the world it is absolutely natural that people own smartphones and are non-stop online. It is thus very easy to connect with them and share their news (Wang & Wu, 2014).

Development of social networks and various applications designed for communication or sharing photos or videos is very swift. According to the portal refresher, in the course of 2015 there were approximately 1.59 billion of users per month who signed in on Facebook. WhatsApp was used by approximately 900 million of users, Messenger by 800 million of users and Instagram by about 400 million of users. These numbers clearly prove that social networks represent an important tool in experience sharing (Kobilke, 2016).

The importance of social networks to promote tourism is possible to be confirmed by The Report on New Challenges and Strategies to Promote Tourism in Europe. A separate section is dedicated to options how civil society can contribute to the promotion of new forms of tourism through social networks, voluntary organizations, cultural and sports associations, citizen action groups and organizations representing young people, women, and communities of foreigners.

At the same time, another aspect joins this game. People do not share their experiences only among their acquaintances. The social networks include various groups which are administered for the purpose of sharing various photographs or videos (Bačík, Fedorko, Kakalejčík, & Pudło, 2016). These groups are thematically aimed at various areas of life and many of them focus primarily on the spiritual experiences. Any user can find this shared content and have it at their disposal (Lytras, Ordóñez de Pablos, Damiani, & Diaz, 2010).

For easier finding of the searched material, many social networks have recently started to use hashtags. A hashtag may be a word or a phrase marked with the prefix "#". Nowadays, hashtag has become an inseparable part of many social networks. It is used as a sign for a key term by more than twenty global social networks (Jeffares, 2014). Among the most famous are Facebook, Flickr, Google+, Identi.ca, Instagram, Kickstarter, LinkedIn, Orkut, Pinterest, Tumblr, Twitter, Vkontakte.ru or YouTube. Using adequate hashtags in "tweets" helps other users on Twitter to find the particular "tweets" more easily (Laniado & Mike, 2010).

Sharing or searching for the content on social networks is a phenomenon because of which a number of people live in a so-called virtual reality, in which they are quite happy (Minazzi, 2014). On the other hand, due to an excessive use of these networks, there is a more and more frequent threat of an identity crisis (Noor Al-Deen & Hendricks, 2012). Social networks, such as Facebook, Twitter or Google+, have created a generation of young people who are very self-oriented. When using this type of contact excessively, these people tend to behave like children who constantly need to hear reactions of their peers to what they did during the day (Zheleva, Terzi, & Getoor, 2013). Some social network users feel the need to be mini-celebrities. They want others to watch and admire them permanently. They do only those things which are Facebook-worthy. It is the only way they are able to define themselves. They gain their identity through people who know about them (De Souza, 2016).

Several authors point out the possibility of links between the use of social networking and spiritual experience for the people. There are some examples in the following text. By all means, in the correct use of social networks, sharing events and experience has its indisputable significance (Richards, De Brito, & Wilks, 2013). It could inspire many people to desire similar experiences and besides, watching certain content as such can provide people with some form of spiritual experience (Scott, Laws, & Boksberger, 2013). Another aspect may be a decision to give some of these experiences as a gift to others. Scientific studies prove that it is better to spend money on experiences than, for example, the newest iPhone (Killingsworth & Gilbert, 2010). This claim works also for gifts (Rodriguez, 2012). There are several reasons why experiences make people happier regardless of whether these experiences are bought or given/obtained (Prebensen, Chen, & Uysal, 2014). In case a person gets a material thing, the joy of it will last more than a few weeks. This phenomenon is called adaptation (Morgan, Lugosi, & Ritchie, 2010). It is based on the fact that if someone obtains, for example, some piece of technology, it can always be compared with other colors, with other models of other brands. A better model comes and suddenly ours is not good enough (Bohunický, 2015).

In contrast, the experiences are unique and can not be so easily compared. Experiences also bring very often the social aspect. If one decided to buy someone, for example, a trip to a location associated with spiritual experiences, one often goes there with this person. These are the gifts the donee does not forget and which lead to happiness (Taylor, Varley, & Johnston, 2013). People are social beings, and social interactions have a major impact on their happiness (Goodman & Lim, 2015). It should be noted that even social interactions through the social networks can at least partially invoke this feeling of happiness in people.

MATERIALS AND METHODS

Data collection on the basis of the questionnaire survey was conducted for more than a month via a social network Facebook, through email communication, as well as by personal collection. After creation and subsequent encoding of individual questionnaire entries, it was publicized on April 2nd 2016. In the following weeks, it was published and resent several times. Data collection was finally finished on May 7th 2016, when the process of classification, coding and subsequent evaluation started. In the given time period, the data from from 586 respondents were collected. While this work focuses on social networks, only data from such respondents, which were active in this field were used, what was one of the questions in the questionnaire. There were 433 such respondents.

All the collected data were subsequently classified, processed, coded and evaluated. Spreadsheet Excel 2007 by Microsoft Office was used for their primary analysis. All the necessary calculations were done with the help of two statistical programs © StatisticaCz 12 and © Minitab Statistical Software 16.

While this chapter deals with an influence of social networks on the decision to travel and experience something creative or spiritual, the focus of the analysis was whether and to what extent the social networks influence was present. The fact that social networks were predominantely used by younger generation was taken into account. Based on this, the following hypothesis was formulated:

H1: It is supposed that the age of respondents statistically significantly affects the measure of perceived influence of social networks information on deciding to travel to experience something creative.

SOLUTIONS AND RECOMMENDATIONS

For the verification of the hypothesis H1, two variables of each analysed item, i.e. the age of the respondents and the measure of perceived influence of social networks information on deciding to travel to experience something creative were observed (scale from 1 to 5, while 1 = do not affect at all, 5 = affect absolutely). Correlation analysis was used for testing. Both variables were quantitative, so Pearson´s correlation coefficient was used for verification of their statistical correlation. At the beginning of verification, the analysed data will be displayed with the help of scatter plot:

Given Figure 1 shows negative correlation between the age of respondents and the measure of the influence of social networks information on deciding to travel. Graphic representation of the relationship between observed variables will be confirmed by calculating the correlation coefficient (r).

Table 1 presents the calculation of the correlation coefficient for the observed variables.

As it is shown by the calculated value of Pearson´s correlation coefficient r $\doteq$ -0,233, the correlation between the age and the perceived influence is negative. The verification of statistical significance of the calculated coefficient, similarly as the calculation of Pearson´s correlation coefficient, was realized in the program © StatisticaCz 12. P-value of the test of statistical significance was calculated at the

Figure 1. Correlation between the measure of the influence of social networks information on deciding to travel and the age
Source: Mudrík & Štefko, 2016

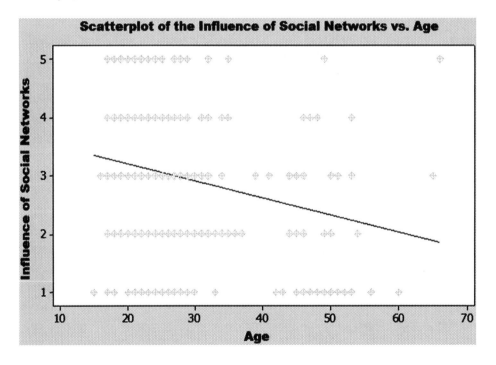

Table 1. Calculation of correlation coefficient

Variables	Correlation (Questionnaire – Evaluation) Correlations Are Sifnificant at the Level of p < .05000						
	Average	Standard Deviation	r(X,Y)	r²	t	p	N
Measure of Interest	3.03002	1.059142					
Age	25.94226	8.304611	-0.232711	0.054155	-4.96759	0.000001	433

Source: Mudrík & Štefko, 2016

lower level as the set level of significance, which means that the correlation is statistically significant. Nevertheless, the relationship can be characterized as a relationship with a zero level of correlation (i.e. a correlation that is present between the observed variables is too weak).

Hypothesis H1 was confirmed. It can be concluded that the age of respondents statistically significantly influences the measure of perceived influence of social networks information when deciding to travel to experience something creative. With increasing age, the measure of influence of this information on deciding decreases.

FUTURE RESEARCH DIRECTIONS

Social networks, on which people spend a substantial part of their free time, represent at present increasingly important phenomenon. After all, more and more web sites are entered by users via links at social networks after recommendations or sharing by their friends. It is highly probable that when something is liked or interesting for people that someone gets on well with, because they share similar views, then it will be liked by or interesting also for that person. Based on this it is necessary to constantly update and fill in the Internet content. Only this way, it can provide all the necessary information for that part of the public which is interested in it.

In presented research, the attention was also paid to the impact of social networks on deciding to travel to experience something creative. Based on the well-known power and effectiveness of referral marketing, the existence of such impact is considered higly probable and that is why the level of this power was measured. It was shown that the measure of this influence is higher for younger respondents and decreases with increasing age, what was confirmed also by statistical testing. This conclusion represents a fairly significant finding which proves legitimacy and importance of analyzing the given problem.

CONCLUSION

Each period brings with it new approaches. Tenacious persistence in usual stereotypes is a guaranteed way leading to failure. On the contrary, following current trends and the ability of flexible and timely adaptation to them represent, in today´s rapidly changing and highly competitive society, one of the main conditions of distinguishing itself and achieving success. This claim is basically possible to generalize about any area of human activities and thus, of course, it also covers the possibilities of creative tourism promotion, either in at home or abroad. Using various tools of marketing communication is a continuous process, in which it is necessary to follow new trends and be prepared to respond flexibly to any changes. While using the Internet and social networks, the changes in these trends are often very fast and what was useful yesterday, does not need to bring satisfactory results today. Correct and timely reaction can bring a competitive advantage, while ignoring these new trends in the long term results in decreasing interest in the offer, which in this case means decline in a number of tourists.

REFERENCES

About the Creative Tourism. (2016, March 7). Retrieved from http://www.creativetourismnetwork.org/about/

Adair, B., Filene, B., & Koloski, L. (2012). *Letting Go? Sharing Historical Authority in a User-Generated World*. Philadelphia: The Pew Center for Arts & Heritage.

Ako na tom boli Facebook, Messenger, Instagram či iné sociálne siete v roku 2015? (2016, January 29). Retrieved from http://refresher.sk/31038-Ako-na-tom-boli-Facebook-Messenger-Instagram-ci-ine-socialne-siete-v-roku-2015

Aramberri, J. (2010). *Modern Mass Tourism*. Bingley: Emerald Group Publishing Limited.

Bačík, R., Fedorko, R., Kakalejčík, L., & Pudło, P. (2016). The Importance of Facebook Ads in Terms of Online Promotion. *Journal of Applied Economic Sciences, 10*(5), 677–684.

Badone, E., & Roseman, S. R. (2004). *Intersecting Journeys: The Anthropology of Pilgrimage and Tourism*. Chicago: University of Illinois Press.

Bahm, A. (1974). *Metaphysics: An introduction*. New York: Barnes & Noble Books.

Beaver, A. (2005). *A Dictionary of Travel and Tourism Terminology*. Cromwell Press.

Bohunický, M. (2015, December 21). *Prečo by si mal radšej darovať zážitky, nie veci*. Retrieved from http://www.startitup.sk/daruj-zazitky/

Bowler, B. (2014, January 31). *How Spiritual Tourism Might Change the World*. Retrieved from http://www.huffingtonpost.co.uk/ben-bowler/can-the-changing-face-of-_b_4363378.html

Brennen, B., & Hardt, H. (1999). *Picturing the Past: Media, History, and Photography*. Chicago: University of Illinois Press.

Černá, J. (2014). Religiousness and Religious Tourism in Slovakia. *European Journal of Science and Theology, 10*(1), 29–37.

Conrady, R., & Buck, M. (2011). *Trends and Issues in Global Tourism 2011*. New York: Springer. doi:10.1007/978-3-642-17767-5

Costa, C., Panyik, E., & Buhalis, D. (2013). *Trends in European Tourism Planning and Organisation*. Bristol: Short Run Press Ltd.

Curran, J., Fenton, N., & Freedman, D. (2015). *Misunderstanding the Internet*. Oxon: Routledge.

Dallen, J. T. (2015). *Heritage Cuisines: Traditions, identities and tourism*. New York: Routledge.

De Souza, M. (2016). *Spirituality in Education in a Global, Pluralised World*. London: Routledge.

Donsbach, W. (2015). *The Concise Encyclopedia of Communication*. Chichester: John Wiley & Sons, Inc. doi:10.1002/9781118789353

Douglas, D. (2006). *Atlas of Sacred and Spiritual Sites: Discover Places of Mystical Power from Around the World.* Ottawa: Octopus Books.

El-Aggra, A. M. (2011). *The European Union: Economics and Policies.* Cambridge: Cambridge University Press. doi:10.1017/CBO9780511844041

Fernandes, C. (2011). Cultural Planning and Creative Tourism in an Emerging Tourist Destination. *International Journal of Management Cases,* 629-636.

Filep, S. (2016, March 11). *Tourism and spirituality.* Retrieved from https://www.elsevier.com/social-sciences/business-and-management/hospitality-sport-and tourism-management/tourism-and-spirituality

Gburová, J., Matušíková, D., & Benková, E. (2015). Perception of tourist destination brand. *Economic Annals, 5-6,* 20-23.

Global Code of Ethics for Tourism. (2014, April 20). Retrieved from http://dtxtq4w60xqpw.cloudfront.net/sites/all/files/docpdf/gcetbrochureglobalcodeen.pdf

Goodman, J. K., & Lim, S. (2015, May 15). *Giving Happiness: Consumers Should Give More Experiences but Choose Material Gifts Instead.* Retrieved, from http://apps.olin.wustl.edu/faculty/goodman/Giving%20Happiness.pdf

Gord, J. D., Vroom, H. M., Fernhout, R., & Wessels, A. (1992). *On Sharing Religious Experience: Possibilities of Interfaith Mutuality.* Amsterdam: Wm. B. Eerdmans Publishing Co.

Grabara, J., Starostka-Patyk, M., & Kot, S. (2011). *Urban transport system in Czestochowa City. 4th International Conference on Logistics, LOGISTIQUA'2011, Hammamet,* Tunisia. doi:10.1109/LOGISTIQUA.2011.5939295

Gray, A., Jeffery, K., & Shao, J. (2008). Sharing Data, Information and Knowledge: *25th British National Conference on Databases.* New York: Springer.

Harssel, J. V., Jackson, R., & Hudman, L. (2014). *National Geographic Learning's Visual Geography of Travel and Tourism.* Stamford: Cengage Learning.

Ihamaki, P. (2010). Geocachers: The creative tourism experience. *Journal of Hospitality and Tourism Technology, 3*(3), 152–175. doi:10.1108/17579881211264468

Indrová, J., et al. (2008). *Cestovní ruch pro všechny.* Praha: Ministerstvo pro místní rozvoj ČR.

Iosifidis, P., & Wheeler, M. (2016). *Public Spheres and Mediated Social Networks in the Western Context and Beyond.* London: Palgrave Macmillan. doi:10.1057/978-1-137-41030-6

Kelly, E. W. Jr. (1995). *Spirituality and religion in counseling and psychotherapy.* Alexandria: American Counseling Association.

Killingsworth, M. A., & Gilbert, D. T. (2010). A Wandering Mind Is an Unhappy Mind. *Science, 330*(6006), 932. doi:10.1126/science.1192439 PMID:21071660

Kobilke, K. (2016). *Erfolgreich mit Instagram: Mehr Aufmerksamkeit mit Fotos & Videos.* Wachtendonk: MITP-Verlags GmbH & Co.

Laniado, D., & Mike, P. (2010). *Making Sense of Twitter.* The Semantic Web – ISWC 2010: 9th International Semantic Web Conference, ISWC 2010, Shanghai, China.

Lennon, J., & Foley, M. (2000). *Dark Tourism: The Attraction of Death and Disaster.* Padstow: TJI Digital.

Lew, A. A., Hall, C. M., & Williams, A. M. (2014). *The Wiley Blackwell Companion to Tourism.* Wiley-Blackwell.

Lois-González, R. C., Santos-Solla, X. M., & Taboada-De-Zuñiga, P. (2014). *New Tourism in the 21st Century: Culture, the City, Nature and Spirituality.* Cambridge: Cambridge Scholar Publishing.

Lystas, M., Ordóñez de Pablos, P., Damiani, E., & Diaz, L. (2010). *Digital Culture and E-Tourism: Technologies, Applications and Management Approaches.* Hershey, PA: IGI Global.

Maciocco, G., & Serreli, S. (2009). *Enhancing the City.: New Perspectives for Tourism and Leisure.* London: Springer. doi:10.1007/978-90-481-2419-0

Mariani, M. M., Czakon, W., Buhalis, D., & Vitouladiti, O. (2016). *Tourism Management, Marketing, and Development: Performance, Strategies, and Sustainability.* New York: Palgrave Macmillan. doi:10.1057/9781137401854

Maštrla, V. (2010). *Dovolenka? Niekto radšej cestuje na sväté miesta.* Retrieved from http://cestovanie. pravda.sk/cestovny-ruch/clanok/4416-dovolenka-niekto-radsej-cestuje-na-svaete-miesta/

Matias, Á., Nijkamp, P., & Sarmento, M. (2011). *Tourism Economics: Impact Analysis.* Berlin: Springer-Verlag. doi:10.1007/978-3-7908-2725-5

Matteucci, X. (2013). Experiencing flamenco: an examination of a spiritual journey. In S. Filep & P. Pearce (Eds.), *Tourist Experience and Fulfilment: Insights from Positive Psychology* (pp. 110–126). London: Routledge.

Middleton, V., & Clarke, J. R. (2012). *Marketing in Travel and Tourism.* Oxford: Reed Educational and Professional Publishing Ltd.

Milovčíková, Ľ. (2008). *Komparácia financovania cestovného ruchu zo štrukturálnych fondov krajín V4.* Brno: Ekonomicko správní fakulta.

Minazzi, R. (2014). *Social Media Marketing in Tourism and Hospitality.* Heidelberg: Springer.

Moran, T. P. (2010). *Introduction to the History of Communication: Evolutions & Revolutions.* New York: Peter Lang Publishing. doi:10.3726/978-1-4539-0002-4

Morgan, M., Lugosi, P., & Ritchie, J. R. B. (2010). *The Tourism and Leisure Experience: Consumer and Managerial Perspectives.* Bristol: MPG Books Group Ltd.

Nelson, V. (2013). *An Introduction to the Geography of Tourism.* Plymouth: Rowman & Littlefield Publishers, Inc.

Noor Al-Deen, H. S., & Hendricks, J. A. (2012). *Social Media: Usage and Impact.* Lanham: The Rowman & Littlefielfd Publishing Group Inc.

Norman, A. (2004). *Spiritual Tourism: Religion and Spirituality in Contemporary Travel.* Sydney: University of Sydney.

Norman, A. (2013, April 15). *Alex Norman on Spiritual Tourism.* Retrieved from http://www.religiousstudiesproject.com/podcast/podcast-alex-norman-on-spiritual-tourism/

Olsen, B. C. (2000). *Sacred Places: 101 Spiritual Sites Around the World.* San Francisco: Consortium of Collective Consciousness.

Pizam, A., & Mansfeld, Y. (2012). *Consumer Behavior in Travel and Tourism.* Routledge.

Prebensen, N. K., Chen, J. S., & Uysal, M. S. (2014). *Creating Experience Value in Tourism.* Reading: CPI Group Ltd. doi:10.1079/9781780643489.0000

Raj, R., & Griffin, K. (2015). *Religious Tourism and Pilgrimage Management* (2nd ed.). London: CABI Publishing. doi:10.1079/9781780645230.0000

Religious and Pilgrimage Tourism. (2009, December 15). Retrieved from http://www.tourismandmore.com/tidbits/religious-and-pilgrimage-tourism/

Richards, G., De Brito, M. P., & Wilks, L. (2013). *Exploring the Social Impacts of Events.* New York: Routledge.

Richards, G., & Wilson, J. (2007). The Creative Turn in Regeneration: Creative Spaces, Spectacles and Tourism in Cities. In M. K. Smith (Ed.), Tourism, Culture and Regeneration (pp. 12-24). Trowbridge: Cromwell Press.

Rickly-Boyd, J. M., Knudsen, D. C., & Braverman, L. C. (2016). *Tourism, Performance, and Place: A Geographic Perspective.* Oxon: Routledge.

Rodriguez, C. (2012). *Gifts of the Soul: Experience the Mystical in Everyday Life.* Woodbury: Llewellyn Worldwide.

Scott, N., Laws, E., & Boksberger, P. (2013). *Marketing of Tourism Experiences.* New York: Routledge.

Shahshahani, S. (2009). *Cities of Pilgrimage.* Münster: LIT Verlag.

Singh, L. K. (2008). *Fundamental Of Tourism And Travel.* Delhi: Isha Books.

Slovenský turizmus upadá – Slovensko je na chvoste celej Európy. (2014, December 12). Retrieved from http://dromedar.zoznam.sk/cl/11161/1442175/Slovensky-turizmus-upada---Slovensko-je-na-chvoste-celej-Europy

Ślusarczyk, B., Smoląg, K., & Kot, S. (2016). The supply chain of a tourism product. *Actual Problems of Economics., 179*(5), 197–207.

Smith, M., & Richards, G. (2013). *The Routledge Handbook of Cultural Tourism.* New York: Routledge.

Šoporová, D. (2013, March 10). *Viete, ako sa vyvíjal cestovný ruch v Európe?* Retrieved from http://webmagazin.teraz.sk/cestovanie/cestovny-ruch-vyvoj-europa-rim/504-clanok.html

Stausberg, M. (2013, April 17). *Some Questions about Spiritual Tourism*. Retrieved from http://www.religiousstudiesproject.com/2013/04/17/some-questions-about-spiritual-tourism/

Sucháček, J. (2013). Transition in the Czech Republic from Institutional Point of View. *International Journal of Mathematical Models and Methods in Applied Sciences.*, *7*(3), 320–332.

Sucháček, J., Seda, P., Friedrich, V., & Koutsky, J. (2014). Media Portrayals of Regions in the Czech Republic: Selected Issues. *E+M Ekonomie a management, 17*(4), 125-140.

Tan, S. K., Kung, S. F., & Luh, D. B. (2013). A Model of Creatice Experiemce in Creative Tourism. *Annals of Tourism Research, 41*, 153–174. doi:10.1016/j.annals.2012.12.002

Taylor, S., Varley, P., & Johnston, T. (2013). *Adventure Tourism: Meaning, Experience and Learning*. New York: Routledge.

Timothy, D. J., & Olsen, D. H. (2006). *Tourism, Religion and Spiritual Journeys*. New York: Routledge.

Walsh, T. (2011). *Creative Tourism*. New Delhi: Discovery Publishing House.

Walton, J. K. (2005). *Histories of Tourism: Representation, Identity and Conflict*. Clevedon: MPG Books Ltd.

Wang, J., & Wu, Y. (2014). *Opportunistic Mobile Social Networks*. Boca Raton: Taylor & Francis Group.

Whalen, B. E. (2011). *Pilgrimage in the Middle Ages: A Reader*. Toronto: University of Toronto Press Incorporated.

Williams, S. (2004). *Tourism: The experience of tourism*. New York: Rotledge.

Wurzburger, R., Aageson, T., Pattakos, A., & Pratt, S. (2010). *Creative Tourism, a Global Conversation*. Santa Fe: Sunstone Press.

Zhao, H. V., Lin, W. S., & Liu, K. J. R. (2011). *Behavior Dynamics in Media-Sharing Social Networks*. Cambridge: Cambridge University Press. doi:10.1017/CBO9780511973369

Zheleva, E., Terzi, E., & Getoor, L. (2013). *Privacy in Social Networks*. San Rafael: Morgan & Claypool.

ADDITIONAL READING

Anderson, D. (2015). *World Gone Mobile Apps*. North Charleston: CreateSpace Independent Publishing Platform.

Annand, A. (1997). *Advance dictionary of tourism*. New Delhi: Sarup & Sons.

Baranowski, S., & Furlough, E. (2001). *Being Elsewhere: Tourism, Consumer Culture, and Identity in Modern Europe and north America*. Michigan: The University of Michigan Press. doi:10.3998/mpub.16478

Barker, D. A. (2014). *Identity and Intercultural Exchange in Travel and Tourism*. Bristol: Short Run Press Ltd.

Brown, M. (1999). *The Spiritual Tourist: A Personal Odyssey Through the Outer Reaches of Belief.* London: Bloomsbury Publishing.

Burkard, A. J., & Medlik, S. (1974). *Tourism, past, present and the future.* London: Butterworth Heinemann.

Campelj, M. (2015, September 12). Creative Tourism: From sightseeing to life experiencing. Retrieved from http://www.majacampelj.com/creative-tourism

Chang, L., Backman, K. F., & Huang, Y. C. (2014). Creative tourism: A preliminary examination of creative tourists' motivation, experience, perceived value and revisit intention. *International Journal of Culture. Tourism and Hospitality Research, 8*(4), 401–419.

Coats, C. D., & Emerich, M. M. (2015). *Practical Spiritualities in a Media Age.* London: Bloomsbury Publishing.

Cooper, C. et al.. (2005). *Tourism: Principles and Practice.* London: Pearson Education.

Fullagar, S., Markwell, K., & Wilson, E. (2012). *Slow Tourism: Experiences and Mobilities.* Bristol: Short Run Press, Ltd.

Gibson, C., & Connell, J. (2005). *Music and Tourism: On the Road Again.* Clevedon: Cromwell Press.

Haq, F., & Wong, H. Y. (2010). Is spiritual tourism a new strategy for marketing Islam? *Journal of Islamic Marketing, 1*(2), 136–148. doi:10.1108/17590831011055879

Hinterholzer, T. (2013). Facebook, Twitter und Co. In *Hotellerie und Gastronomie: Ein Handbuch für Praktiker.* Berlin: Springer. doi:10.1007/978-3-642-37954-3

Hyndman - Rizk. N. (2012). Pilgrimage in the Age of Globalisation: Constructions of the Sacred and Secular in Late Modernity. Cambridge: Cambringe Scholars Publishing.

Ivanovic, M. (2008). *Cultural Tourism.* Cape Town: Juta & Compady, Ltd.

Jeffares, S. (2014). *Interpreting Hashtag Politics: Policy Ideas in an Era of Social Media.* London: Palgrave Macmillan. doi:10.1057/9781137357748

Jennings, G., & Nickerson, N. P. (2012). *Quality Tourism Experiences.* Burlington: Routledge.

Kaplan, A. M., & Haenlein, M. (2010). Users of the World, Unite! The Challenges and Opportunities of Social Media. *Business Horizons, 53*(1), 59–68. doi:10.1016/j.bushor.2009.09.003

Knudsen, B. T., & Waade, A. M. (2010). *Re-Investing Authenticity: Tourism, Place and Emotions* (3rd ed.). Bristol: Short Run Press Ltd.

Kotler, P. T., Bowen, J. R., & Makens, J. (2013). *Marketing for Hospitality and Tourism.* London: Pearson Education.

Kotler, P. T., & Keller, K. L. (2015). *Marketing Management.* London: Pearson Education.

Lester, J. A., & Scarles, C. (2016). *Mediating the Tourist Experience: From Brochures to Virtual Encounters.* New York: Routledge.

Lloyd, D. W. (2014). *Battlefield Tourism: Pilgrimage and the Commemoration of the Great War in Britain, Australia and Canada, 1919-1939*. New York: Bloomsbury Publishing Plc.

Lussier, R. N. (2015). *Management Fundamentals: Concepts, Applications, and Skill Development*. Thousand Oaks: SAGE Publications.

Miles, J. (2013). *Instagram Power: Build Your Brand and Reach More Customers with the Power of Pictures*. Blacklick: McGraw Hill Professional.

Minazzi, R. (2014). *Social Media Marketing in Tourism and Hospitality*. New York: Springer Science.

Munar, A. M., & Jacobsen, J. K. S. (2014). Motivations for sharing tourism experiences through social media. *Tourism Management*, *41*(1), 46–54. doi:10.1016/j.tourman.2014.01.012

Norman, A. (2011). *Spiritual Tourism: Travel and Religious Practice in Western Society*. London: Continuum International Publishing Group.

Partridge, K. (2011). *Social Networking*. New York: Hw Wilson Co.

Pazos, A. M. (2014). *Redefining Pilgrimage: New Perspectives on Historical and Contemporary Pilgrimages*. Farnham: Ashgate Publishing Limited.

Power, D., & Scott, A. (2004). Working Through Knowledge Pools: Labour Market Dynamics, the Transfer of Knowledge and Ideas, and Industrial Clusters. *Urban Studies (Edinburgh, Scotland)*, *41*(5/6), 1025–1044. doi:10.1080/00420980410001675850

Rakić, T., & Lester, J. A. (2014). *Travel, Tourism and Art*. London: Ashgate Publishing, Ltd.

Reader, I. (2013). *Pilgrimage in the Marketplace*. New York: Routledge.

Richards, G., & Wilson, J. (2006). Developing creativity in tourist experiences: A solution to the serial reproduction of culture? *Tourism Management*, *27*(6), 1209–1223. doi:10.1016/j.tourman.2005.06.002

Roesch, S. (2009). *The Experiences of Film Location Tourists*. Bristol: Cromwell Press Group.

Sharpley, R., & Jepson, D. (2010). Rural Tourism: A Spiritual Experience? *Annals of Tourism Research*, *38*(1), 52–71. doi:10.1016/j.annals.2010.05.002

Sharpley, R., & Stone, P. R. (2014). *Contemporary Tourist Experience: Concepts and Consequences*. New Yourk: Rotledge.

Sigala, M., Christou, E., & Gretzel, U. (2016). *Social Media in Travel, Tourism and Hospitality: Theory, Practice and Cases*. New York: Routledge.

ST. (2013). Kreatívny turizmus - pole takmer neorané. (2013, April 7). Retrieved from http://www.slovenskyturizmus.sk/kreativne/c-126/slovensky-kreativny-turizmus-pole-takmer-neorane/#.V0ctBb5gDcs

Swatos, W. H., & Tomasi, L. (2002). *From Medieval Pilgrimage to Religious Tourism: The Social and Cultural Economics of Piety*. London: Praeger.

Timothy, D. J. (1997). Tourism and the personal heritage experience. *Annals of Tourism Research*, *24*(3), 751–754. doi:10.1016/S0160-7383(97)00006-6

Tsiotsou, R. H., & Goldsmith, R. E. (2012). *Strategic Marketing in Tourism Services*. Bingley: Emerald Group Publishing Limited.

Tuten, T. L., & Solomon, M. R. (2014). *Social Media Marketing*. Thousand Oaks: SAGE Publications.

Wang, Y., & Pizam, A. (2011). *Destination Marketing and Management: Theories and Applications*. London: CABI Publishing. doi:10.1079/9781845937621.0000

Wearing, S. (2001). *Volunteer Tourism: Experiences That Make a Difference*. London: CABI Publishing. doi:10.1079/9780851995335.0000

Yeoman, I. (2012). *2050 - Tomorrow's Tourism*. Salisbury: Short Run Press Ltd.

KEY TERMS AND DEFINITIONS

Creative Tourism: Tourism which offers visitors the opportunity to develop their creative potential through active participation in courses and learning experiences, which are characteristic of the holiday destination where they are taken.

Emotions: An affective state of consciousness in which joy, sorrow, fear, hate, or the like, is experienced, as distinguished from cognitive and volitional states of consciousness.

Experiences: The totality of the cognitions given by perception; all that is perceived, understood, and remembered.

Pilgrimage: A journey or search of moral or spiritual significance. Typically, it is a journey to a shrine or other location of importance to a person's beliefs and faith, although sometimes it can be a metaphorical journey into someone's own beliefs.

Religion: A specific fundamental set of beliefs and practices generally agreed upon by a number of persons or sects.

Social Networks: An online service or site through which people create and maintain interpersonal relationships.

Spirituality: Subjective experience incorporating personal growth or transformation, usually in a context separate from organized religious institutions.

Travel: The movement of people between relatively distant geographical locations, and can involve travel by foot, bicycle, automobile, train, boat, airplane, or other means, with or without luggage, and can be one way or round trip.

This research was previously published in Driving Tourism through Creative Destinations and Activities edited by Alžbeta Királová, pages 260-277, copyright year 2017 by Business Science Reference (an imprint of IGI Global).

Chapter 63
Gamification and Social Media as Tools for Tourism Promotion

Magdalena Kachniewska
Warsaw School of Economics, Poland

ABSTRACT

The goal of this chapter is to present the application of gamification mechanism and social media tools in the promotion of tourism regions and enterprises as well as the promotion of tourism activity itself. The framework distinguishes between stimulus characteristics of the game (promotion mechanism) that lead to sociological responses toward the game (tourism brand) and actual buyers' (tourists') behaviour. Though the game-like mechanism has been applied in tourism for decades and some funware elements are well known among teens – they hardly deal with competition of computer games. Two popular systems of tourism badges in Poland are thus discussed in order to look for reasons of their falling popularity and teenagers' resistance to participate in the systems. Mobile devices enable teens to combine playing and travelling. The development of mobile applications, integrating social gaming, and location-based technology has led to the growing interest in location-based social network marketing, particularly in tourism and hospitality. The chapter concludes with a proposal how to revitalize an old-school system of tourism badges through the modern gamification mechanism combined with social media tools.

INTRODUCTION

For the past decades we have been living in an era of great changes in the entire world, mostly brought about by technological advances - it is the era of mobile and instant communication. These improvements are reflected in every aspect of life, including consumption and purchase behaviour and, consequently, in marketing practices. One of the most recent marketing practices includes mass-market consumer software that takes inspiration from video games. Usually referred to as "gamification", this trend refers to multiple existing concepts and research in game studies and human-computer interaction (HCI), such as serious games, advergames, alternate reality games or playful design.

The popularity of digital games is considered to be a driver in the adoption of gamification elements in many Internet pursuits. Another primary driver is the rapid uptake of social networks, now used by 70% of Internet users, where reward and status elements are implicitly and explicitly embedded in people's

DOI: 10.4018/978-1-5225-5637-4.ch063

interactions in their online communities' engagement. Game elements and competition are interspersed throughout the platforms that have made social networks like Facebook and Twitter extremely popular.

Parallel with the growing popularity of computer games, teenagers get bored with other activities, not excluding tourism. The idea of tourism badges system – very popular in Poland for over 40 years - proved to be ineffective. The research of tourism badges popularity among teens carried in 12 Warsaw secondary schools shows that only 2% of 5.000 respondents are aware of the tourism badges system and only 96 persons actively participate in the system. In the same group of teens 89% occasionally play the digital games and 32% declared to be addicted to playing. Half of them start the day with logging into their favourite game and checking their rank position. There is no sense to fight the phenomena – it is better to use it. Especially, since the popularity of digital games and their ability to attract attention, has already aroused the interest of marketers.

Like any other consumers, tourists are exposed to an outstanding number of advertising messages every day. As the market has changed to adopt new advertising techniques and consumers' input, marketing faces times of great challenges – and great opportunities. The travel industry has a fine history of leading the way with some highly disruptive innovations such as online review sites, online booking solutions, XML/API and local/community marketplace (Airbnb, Tripbod and Travelmob to name but a few). However the predominance of competition in the tourism market impedes cooperative solutions, as the most brilliant marketing ideas continue to strengthen the biggest players in the tourism market. The overwhelming amount of small and medium sized enterprises (SMEs) with little financial resources stop the industry from a quick adoption of modern marketing techniques.

Cooperation is undoubtedly crucial to the successful marketing of tourism destinations and new technologies offer exciting new opportunities for cooperation among tourism suppliers. The problem of tourism promotion in Poland concerns both: the promotion of tourism regions and enterprises as well as the promotion of tourism activity among teenagers. That very special target group inclines to the adoption of new marketing instruments.

The goal of this chapter is to present the application of gamification and some social media tools (COBRAs, e-WOM) in the promotion of tourism. In the first part, the chapter reviews literature on gamification and offers an insight into the social media opportunity in the field of tourism promotion. In the second part some examples of gamification mechanism being applied in tourism so far are presented (hotel chains' loyalty systems, airline "miles&more" programmes) together with some examples of funware elements well known among teens (scout badges, tourist badges). The section discusses the most popular systems of tourism badges in Poland and looks for the reasons of their falling popularity and young tourists' resistance to participate in the system.

The complexity of tourism destination management and marketing is discussed in order to explain the indispensable role of tourism organisations in the process of tourism promotion.

The chapter concludes with a proposal how to revitalise the systems of tourism badges through the modern gamification mechanism combined with social media tools.

GAME-DESIGN THINKING: SHORT INTRODUCTION TO GAMIFICATION

The word "gamification" has emerged in recent years as a way to describe interactive online design that plays on people's competitive instincts and often incorporates the use of rewards to drive action — these include virtual rewards such as points, payments, badges, discounts, and gifts; and status indicators such as friend counts, leader boards, achievement data, progress bars and the ability to "level up." While some researchers dismiss gamification as a fad, neuroscientists are discovering more and more about the ways in which humans react to such interactive design elements, which can cause feel-good chemical reactions, alter human responses to stimuli — increasing reaction times, for instance — and in certain situations can improve learning, participation, and motivation (Anderson & Rainie, 2012).

The term "gamification" was popularised by Zicherman and Cunningham (2011). It describes the use of video game elements in non-gaming context to improve user experience and user engagement. Gamification as a term originated in the digital media industry. Parallel terms continue being used and new ones are still being introduced, such as "productivity games" (McDonald, Musson, & Smith, 2008), "surveillance entertainment" (Grace & Hall, 2008), "playful design" (Ferrara, 2012) or "behavioural games" (Dignan, 2011). Yet "gamification" has arguably managed to institutionalize itself as the common household term (Deterding, Sicart, Nacke, O'Hara, & Dixon, 2011b).

Gamification is a significant and emerging business practice which the world's top companies are already using in various contexts. Gartner.com (2012) predicts that over 70% of the Global 2000 organizations will have at least one gamified application by 2014, and that more than 50% of the organizations that manage innovation processes will gamify those processes by 2015 (Gartner.com, 2011). Across the world, enterprises are grabbing hold of these constructs to change the way they engage with staff, business partners and customers. In retailing (www.shopkick.com), education (www.mathletics.co.uk) and travel (www.onthebeach.co.uk) the examples abound of how companies are using these dynamics to get ahead of the competition. In financial services, Amex, Barclays, SmartyPig, AXA and ING are all beginning to take the leap into social and gaming. Cisco, Siemens, American Express, Microsoft, Nike, SAP, Salesforce.com, Deloitte, Samsung, Foursquare, LiveOps, Dell, Foot Locker, eBay, Yelp etc. – they all use the marketing power of gamification.

Deloitte cited gamification as one of its *Top 10 Technology Trends for 2012*, predicting: "Serious gaming simulations and game mechanics such as leaderboards, achievements, and skill-based learning are becoming embedded in day-to-day business processes, driving adoption, performance, and engagement." It is really worth thinking, why the game-design elements proved to be so powerful and efficient.

According to Deterding, Dixon, Khalled and Nacke (2011a), the use of game design and game elements in other contexts is an old topic in human-computer interaction (HCI): Attempts to derive heuristics for enjoyable interfaces from games go back to the early 1980s (Malone, 1980, 1982). More recently, researchers have tried to identify design patterns that might give joy of use under the moniker "funology", explicitly drawing inspiration from game design (Blythe, Overbeeke, Monk, & Wright, 2004).

Play has always been important to humankind. With the development of our society into a digital one, it seems no wonder that digital games are prevalent and their dissemination continues to rise (Terlutter & Capella, 2013). Playing digital games is a social phenomenon, given that about two-thirds of gamers play games with others, either in person or online (ESA 2012). Not surprisingly, teens are especially likely to play digital games. According to a representative survey by the Pew Internet and American Life Project, 97% of teens aged 12 to 17 play digital games, with 99% of boys and 94% of girls in the United States doing so. According to that survey, about three quarters of teens play games with others at least some of the time (Lenhart, Sydney, & Macgill, 2008).

Researchers in HCI and management sciences have identified design principles and patterns that enhance the motivational affordances of computer-supported collaborative work (Jung, Schneider, & Valacich, 2010; Zhang, 2008) – principles and patterns which are congruent with research on the motivational psychology of video games (Ryan, Rigby, & Przybylski, 2006). In persuasive technology (Fogg,

2002) video games and game aspects have been studied as potential means to shape user behaviour in directions intended by the system designer (Lockton, Harrison, & Stanton, 2010) or to instil embedded values (Barr, Noble, & Biddle, 2007). The term "gamification" reflects the new phenomenon of games and game technologies transcending the traditional boundaries of their medium.

Gamification techniques strive to leverage people's natural desires for competition, achievement, status, self-expression, altruism and closure. Competition is one of the most important elements of games that can be used in marketing and for promotion purposes. Making the rewards for accomplishing tasks visible to other players or providing leader boards are ways of encouraging players to compete (Reevs & Read, 2009). It perfectly combines with the natural need to be recognised and feel unusual.

Games are not just a jumble of elements that have been stuck together - they are designed systematically, thoughtfully, and artistically for the purpose of being fun (Terlutter & Capella, 2013). "What game designers do is not just a matter of pure engineering. There is an artistic experiential side to game design that involves thinking about problems in a certain way. (...) Game design techniques involve a way of thinking: they are not just a collection of practices but a way to approach the challenges encountered" (von Ahn & Dabbish, 2008, p. 60).

Salcu and Acatrinei (2013) state that the game elements are the "toolbox" of gamification, the pieces necessary to create a service that uses bits and pieces to build a game-like environment - not the game itself, but the regular design patterns that make up the games, common across games as well as gamified services. These elements may include: points, quests, levels, progression, social graphs, badges, avatars and/or resource collections.

Elements of game mechanics are being employed nowadays in training, marketing, education, and wellness initiatives. Some scholars and educators have become interested in harnessing the potential of gaming mechanics and sensibilities as tools for advancing learning. A "serious gaming" movement has arisen to apply gaming techniques to such realms as military and corporate training programs, civilization and environmental ecology simulations, K-12 educational programs on subjects like math and history and the sciences, news events and public policy campaigns, problem-solving strategies in the natural sciences, and even physical exercise programs (*Future of the Internet*, 2013). Gamification has caught the interest of researchers as a potential means to create engaging workplaces (Reeves & Read, 2009). The opportunities for businesses are great – from having more engaged customers, to crowdsourcing innovation or improving employee performance (Salcu & Acatrinei, 2013).

Marketers have come to depend upon the competitive metrics they derive from analysis and implementation of social networks to measure and drive consumer behaviour. According to Norman (2013) "Products were once designed for the functions they performed. But when all companies can make products that perform their functions equally well, the distinctive advantage goes to those who provide pleasure and enjoyment while maintaining the power. It functions are equated with cognition, pleasure is equated with emotion; today we want products that appeal to both cognition and emotion" (p. 65).

Maintaining the proper level of products competitiveness obviously calls for appropriate "hardware" (the thing) and "software" (its application, usability) but also for a huge amount of "funware", intensifying the user's engagement. Gamification is about making existing tasks feel more like games (Deterding, 2010). The main goal of gamification mechanism, while used for marketing purposes, is to gain users/clients attention and loyalty through the incorporation of challenge, risk, fun and other game elements into every stage of consumers behaviour (looking for offers, selection process, booking, assessing, opinion and information sharing etc.). Some techniques used in gamification include adding meaningful choice, increasing challenge (McGonigal, 2011) and adding narrative.

Motivation through gamification may have a social impact, because it is something people want to do (Suits, 2005). The goals of gamification are to achieve higher levels of engagement, change behaviours and stimulate innovation. According to Werbach (2012), there are three main types of categories where gamification can add value: in an external environment, in an internal environment, and in behaviour changing. The external gamification (applied outside the organization) is applied to customers, for the purpose of marketing, sales and customer engagement. The internal gamification refers to the applications of gamification to employees: it can provide productivity enhancement or crowdsourcing (Silverman, 2011). Behaviour change gamification is applied when people need motivation to do something they appreciate the value of (education, sport activities, weighting loss etc.).

The new marketing approach needs new efficiency ratios: the concepts of willingness-to-participate (in place of willingness-to-pay) and return-on-engagement (as opposed to return-on-investment) are proposed as the new measures of success for social media marketing (Frick, 2010; Parent, Plangger, & Bal, 2011). Companies such as Fourscore analyse the competitiveness of local businesses by calculating the number of *check-in* and *mayorship* turnovers of Foursquare users in the establishments. In order to confirm that marketing profession is currently seeing important changes, the ESOMAR Congress (2013) proposed themes such as: identifying the best connection points with consumers and new ROI indicators like Return on Engagement and Return on Customer Experience. The ratios illustrate the marketing power of social media and social gaming.

In fact, the dynamics and popularity of gamification has been strengthened by the rising development of social media environment, especially social networks. Kaplan and Haenlein (2010) define social media as "a group of Internet-based applications that build on the ideological and technological foundations of Web 2.0, and that allow the creation and exchange of user-generated content" (p. 61). Undoubtedly, social media depend on mobile and web-based technologies to create highly interactive platforms through which individuals and communities share, co-create, discuss and modify user-generated content. Internet users continue to spend more time with social media sites than any other type of site.

By applying a set of theories in the field of media research (social presence, media richness) and social processes (self-presentation, self-disclosure), Kaplan and Haenlein (2010) created a classification scheme with seven different types of social media, including: collaborative projects (e.g. Wikipedia), blogs and microblogs (e.g. Twitter), social news networking sites (e.g. Digg, Leakernet), content communities (e.g. YouTube, DailyMotion), social networking sites (e.g. Facebook), virtual game-worlds (e.g. World of Warcraft) and virtual social worlds (e.g. Second Life). The boundaries between the different types of social media are blurred.

Social media is the interaction among people in which they create, share or exchange information and ideas in virtual communities and networks. They introduce substantial and pervasive changes to communication between organizations, communities, and individuals (Kietzmann & Hermkens, 2011). According to Morgan, Jones and Hodges (2010) social media differ from traditional (or industrial) media in many ways, including quality, reach, frequency, accessibility, usability, immediacy and permanence. For content contributors, the benefits of participating in social media have gone beyond simply social sharing to building reputation and bringing in career opportunities and monetary income, as discussed in Tang, Gu and Whinston (2012).

Social media has changed the way people connect, discover, recommend and share. With the internet providing a huge amount of choice, index search is being replaced by recommendations from friends, family and people we trust. It's a self-moderating quality control system that threatens traditional marketing and distribution models whilst simultaneously providing viral means to spread the word (e-WOM), good or bad.

Social psychological studies on contributions in online communities or the motivational uses of recommender systems arrived at conclusions that chime with core design properties of video games (Ling, Beenen, & Ludford, 2005; Rashid et al., 2006). Great gaming dynamics and "fun" are the cornerstones of an active and motivated social community. It is necessary to take into consideration individual factors of the player and social factors surrounding the player. Werbach (2012) enumerates the following conceptual elements that provide the framing for the game: constraints (limitations in the game); emotions and narrative (the structure that pulls together the pieces of the game into a coherent storyline); progression (a sense of having something to achieve – giving the game clear objectives) and relationships (the interactivity and social dynamics that are important to the game experience).

Dynamics are the highest level game elements in the game design system. Apart from the dynamics gamification needs "mechanics" – the elements that move the action forward (Werbach, 2012):

- Challenges (objectives and obstacles),
- Chance (a sense of uncertainty),
- Competition/cooperation (the interactive design of a game),
- Feedback (real time progress report),
- Resource acquisition (ability to acquire tools to progress in the game),
- Rewards (benefits for some kind of achievement in the game),
- Transactions (exchanging with other players),
- Turns (sequences of activity),
- Win state (the final victory).

Last but not least the game design can be easily recognized thanks to "components" such as: achievements, avatars, badges, gifting, leaderboards, levels and rankings, points, quests, teams or virtual goods (Konrad, 2011).

While some would argue that life itself is a game, the social web is certainly turning out to be like a game, as demonstrated by companies like Foursquare and Zynga. Especially the former one has proved the power of badges, when demonstrated in social community. Antin and Churchill (2011) examined the social psychology of badges and noticed that while badges can be fun and interesting; these qualities do not inherently produce social engagement or enhance motivation. They argue that badges can serve several individual and social functions depending on the nature of the activities that a badge rewards and the application of badges in particular contexts. In the tradition of combining HCI and psychology (Olson & Olson, 2003) they presented five primary functions for achievements: goal setting, instruction, reputation, status/affirmation and group identification.

However, Montola, Nummenmaa, Lucero, Boberg and Korhonen (2009) implemented badges in a photo sharing service and found that many users did not appreciate them and were worried that badges would create counterproductive usage patterns. Antin and Churchill's (2011) in-progress research on FourSquare indicates that most users find only some types of badges interesting or motivational, while some badges are even harmful to intrinsic motivation.

Nevertheless badges have become a fixture in many games. Notable implementations of badges in social media include Wikipedia's "Barnstars" which allow users to award each other for doing valued work (Kriplean, Beschastnikh, & McDonald, 2008), StackOverflow's system of badges encourages productive participation, and FourSquare's implementation of badges promotes location-sharing via "check-ins." Salcu and Acatrinei (2013) notice that badges belong to the group of game elements that are more widely used than others. They cover: points, badges and leaderboards (PBL triad). Points are a way of determining how well someone is doing in the game. They can be used to determine win states. They can connect to rewards, display progress, provide feedback for the player, and provide data for the game designer. Badges are representation of achievements. They are flexible, being just a token for the game designer to reward the player. Badges designate the things that are significant in the game and function as credentials. They encourage players to keep collecting them as they convey a certain status or social display. Leaderboards are rankings and feedback on the competition. They encourage the player to achieve a higher score as they enable the players to compare their results (Salcu & Acatrinei, 2013).

Besides the PBL triad, other elements like challenges, puzzles, mastery and community are equally important. What makes the game successful is the way in which all the elements are tied together. Elements themselves do not tell if the experience is fun and engaging. Rewards are not the same thing as fun. Fun can be about interacting with friends, it can be about blowing off steam, and it can be about solving problems or about exploration. The social layer of game design is thus extremely important – the ability to compare the results as well as to cooperate within the teams.

While investigating social network marketing stimuli Tussyadiah (2012) identified two types of social game rewards: system rewards and social rewards. The system rewards can be further divided into application rewards (points, badges, statuses etc.) and merchant rewards (monetary and non-monetary promotional tools) for recommended behaviour. Consumer reward-seeking behaviour associated with merchant rewards (i.e., monetary and non-monetary promotional tools) has been discussed in the marketing literature as consumers' value maximisation strategy (Ong, Ho, & Tripp, 1997; Campbell & Diamond, 1990; Laroche, Pons, Zgolli, Cervellon, & Kim, 2003).

Social rewards range from selfish to altruistic motivations. The users' needs (indigenous and endogenous motivation) are met by different elements of game mechanics: status achieved, contest (rivalry and challenges), self-improvement (level of difficulty, "progress bars", ratings), sense of community and togetherness, contact with other people of the same interests, as well as self-expression (internet forums), altruism (virtual points and items exchange) or even sense of threat ("loss of the crown" or the achieved status) and loss aversion. An old-school gamification takes the form of loyalty cards where the "bingo mechanism" is used: when a player collects the appropriate number of points he/she wins a free accommodation, lunch, spa treatment, voucher etc. An advanced formula of gamification includes the fight for next "level": the player becomes a VIP, gets to a business club etc.

Another element quite commonly used in game-design loyalty programmes is called the "magic of series": an unfilled gap in the collection hurts so much that "players" impatiently look for the missing stamp entitling to a free coffee. The fewer stamps are missing the bigger the determination to get them. The ability to observe the progress of the players' friends (e.g. in social networking) and the realization that they are closer to goal is an additional determinant. The spectacular power of gamification and especially the need for scoreboards might be observed within the social media, where the game ranks and results can be freely published and demonstrated to precisely targeted audience ("friends" and "fans").

Bringing together Fogg's behaviour model; Maslow's hierarchy of needs; Skinnerian conditioning; and Daniel Pink's intrinsic motivators one can create an argument for gamification (Wu, 2011). In parallel companies recognize that the modern customer is a "social customer" - both science and logic bring to the complexity of reputation, relationships and influence in social networks. The problem to be solved is how to motivate and change behaviours; and most importantly, how to create a deeply engage community that will follow the way one wants them to follow.

Social media facilitate the processes of communication and group formation in various social contexts. Mobile technology enables these connected experiences to be pervasive and immediate. In addition, the application of global positioning system (GPS) technology allows social network platform on mobile devices to become context-aware, making it possible to obtain and share real-time, contextual information for various decision-making processes associated with social and general consumption experiences (Tussyadiah, 2012; Kachniewska, 2014b).

The development of mobile phone applications integrating social gaming and location-based technology — such as Foursquare and Gowalla — has led to the growing interest in location-based social network (LSN) marketing and the recognition of its importance for local businesses, particularly in tourism and hospitality. These applications encourage the consumption of places (e.g., dining at local restaurants, shopping at local stores, visiting local salons) by broadcasting relevant social and expert recommendations and offering special rewards for certain accomplishments and/or task fulfilment. Tussyadiah (2012) claims that LSN applications on mobile devices can be used for place marketing as they influence spatiotemporal mobility and the overall patterns of consumption experiences.

Gamification should not be confused with simple marketing neither with advergaming however it demonstrates some similarities to advertising in digital games (in-game advertising, advergames and advertising in social network games). However, thanks to the game-design techniques and dynamics, gamification can drive individual behaviour and can provide excellent promotion. Moreover, when applied properly, gamification can be used to provide the foundation for long term relationship and behaviour management.

Game-Design Techniques in Tourism

Despite all the new marketing tools and components, the fundamental purpose of marketing is and will always remain the same: companies are not interested in what the consumer likes, but in what persuades the consumer to buy products. However, while marketers work to reinvent new ways to reach customers, consumers continue to find new ways to avoid them. As consumers become more resistant, advertisers must become more subtle and subliminal.

Initially, advergaming was coined to refer to the use of games to advertise tourism products and services. Çeltek (2010) identifies that advergaming is successful in branding and integrating cities into the games: companies and tourism destinations are promoting their brands by combining advertisement, online games, and mobile phones. Examples are location-based games that allow users to explore cities such as "Get Lost in Rotterdam" (Rotterdam, The Netherlands) and "Malmö's Mobile Treasure Hunt" (Malmö, Sweden). However, advergaming is ineffective for viral marketing due to the high equipment cost and the lack of connectivity of the players.

Rapid development of social media networks and brilliant results of social gaming brought about gamification as an innovative business tool which is gaining traction in tourism as well. Although the overwhelming majority of current examples of gamification are digital, the term should not be limited to digital technology. Not only are media convergence and ubiquitous computing increasingly blurring the distinction between digital and non-digital: games and game design are themselves transmedial categories (Juul, 2005). The funware concept comes from digital games and it is obvious that it has been readily adapted within e-commerce marketing. However so commonly popularized badges, which are closely associated with online gaming, also have a long history outside of gaming. In ancient times, military heroes were honoured with medals. Closer to home Boy Scouts badges have been used to promote the acquisition of specific skill-sets as diverse as cooking, eastern martial arts and biochemistry.

Gamification is much about competition and winning the prizes/rewards, which can be of merchant or symbolic character. In the tourism industry the humans' inclination to collecting and cumulating has been brought into play for years by the airlines and hotel chains (the "frequent flyer" cards and "miles&more" programmes).

It is worth mentioning that 80% of the programmes' participants are ready to buy at least one redundant ticket in order to collect more airline miles… and never utilize the right to award! (Kachniewska, 2013a) The contest itself occurs to be the sole and sufficient "satisfaction factor" (social reward). On the contrary, Kachniewska (2013a) investigated the participants of a hotel chain loyalty system who seek their rewards, whether valuable (free accommodation) or tiny (free coffee) and being disappointed when the stay was not rewarded with any special.

The symbolic rewards (badges, crowns, points etc.) are the motivating factors that contribute to the personal enjoyment and characterize the social gaming feature of the applications, thus Tussyadiah (2012) called them "application rewards". They are tied to certain tasks that, and in tourism they might constitute some travel challenges, visiting special venues or reviewing hospitality services. Foursquare grants bonus points when a user checks-in to a place before any of his/her friends or be at the same venue at the same time with a mayor. Similarly Tripadvisor App can be used to plug the pins into the virtual map – than the "players" can compare the seized part of the world. The competition-based social rewards signify the power of the application rewards in influencing consumption and mobility as collecting more points places the player in a prominent position on top of the others, and the immediate social reactions and recognition resulting from this, would make the player more inclined to do a task (e.g. to visit a museum, to share a photo, to stay in a hotel etc.). Moreover they allow users to enjoy being mobile and using them makes touristic experiences more playful and fun.

The reward-seeking behaviour associated with social rewards is usually rooted in a motivation to compete with others, whether they were the peers in the social network or people with common interests in a close proximity (Tussyadiah, 2012). Thus nowadays tourism organisations are using gamification techniques to boost consumer engagement and build brand awareness in virtual environment and social networks. "Visit Norway" wanted to drive more traffic to their website, which had links to sponsors and advertisers. Outdoors sports especially winter sports are high up on the agenda in Norway, so they decided to create a game about one of their main attractions namely the Holmenkollen Ski Jump Station. The game can be played online on Facebook and downloaded on mobile devices. Since its first launch in 2006 it has attracted over 800 million jumps (each player gets two jump attempts, so effectively probably half of this amount were individual players). The website 6 million clicks can be attributed directly to the game and the video channel received over 215,00 views where sponsors links were clicked (Coppens, 2013). Similar examples of SmileLand (Thailand) and Nassau Bahamas show evidence that tourism industry is looking into games and gamification.

Aside from the gamification tourism destinations and hospitality firms have started leveraging social media and social game-like applications (FourSquare, Gowalla) for their promotion. Van Grove (2010a, 2010b) gives an example of the City of Chicago (ExploreChicago) and the State of Pennsylvania (VisitPA) in the United States, partnering with Foursquare in order to encourage visitors to uncover the history and culture of the areas, and unlock special badges associated with the city and state's lifestyle.

Rao (2010) examines Disney Parks teaming up with Gowalla to create a branded destination for park-goers to explore Walt Disney World and Disneyland Resorts. These marketing initiatives were developed, based on the idea that location-based social network applications enable tourism destinations to capitalize on the coupling of travellers' motivation and their enthusiasm for participating in the game to suggest and encourage consumption behaviour. Further, the use of such applications also allows tourism destinations to continuously monitor and dynamically respond to visitors' behaviour with customized services and offerings.

Apparently tourism gamification in Poland has been started by the system of tourism badges of Polish Tourist and Sightseeing Society (later referred as PTTK), the successor of the Polish Tatra Mountains Society (founded in 1873) and the Polish Sightseeing Society (initiated in 1906). PTTK is a non-governmental organisation. It gathers tourists and country-lovers, creates conditions which facilitate their hiking and sightseeing activity within the country and abroad, and represents their interests.

PTTK bases its activity on the volunteer work of its members. Its activity covers popularisation of tourism, sightseeing and active recreation, especially hiking and tramping, cruises, horse and canoeing rallies, camps and other activities. It popularizes and protects national traditions, cultural identity and Polish cultural heritage; works to natural protection and health care.

The system of PTTK badges has been developed in 1935 with the first badge called Mountain Tourist Distinction. Nowadays the spectrum of PTTK badges covers two groups of distinctions: qualified tourism badges and sightseeing badges. The former one covers almost all the disciplines of tourists' activities available in Poland: hiking, canoeing, sailing, horse-riding, skiing, motorcycling orienteering and diving. The other group popularizes visiting places listed within the Sightseeing Canon of Poland.

The general rules are the same for all the types of badges: competitors gather the points for the completed tasks (gaining the peaks, riding the distance or visiting places) and the appropriate number of points can be transferred into the adequate level of distinction (gold, silver or bronze medal). Some badges need specialized knowledge: the horse-riding one is not only about horse riding, but also about the basic knowledge of horse anatomy and veterinary. The majority of places of interests, mountain huts and water watchtowers offer a special stamp – usually of the unique design – which confirms the visit to a place and represents a specified amount of points. The stamps are collected in special booklets, designated to different disciplines. The system is adjusted to different age groups (children, teens, adults).

Plenty of elements made the system game-designed: the distinctions symbol correspond to digital games "levelling" and awards. The booklets remind virtual loyalty programmes, however the loyalty is more about travelling in general (tourism activity), than about travelling to a special place.

The majority of badges have been introduced in early 70-ties of the last century – it was also the period of their staggering popularity. The PTTK instructors and guides used to approve some 150 thousands of badges per year. Domestic tourism in Poland was very popular at that time – especially because closed borders definitely separated the country from the rest of Europe. The economic and political reforms of the end of 20th century made the outbound tourism available (both politically and financially). The digital era has blowed away the mass interest in active recreation – especially among young people. The secret lies in faint attractiveness of the PTTK badges system and low power to engage participants. The existing system contains only one typical game element – namely the collecting, which is as exciting to today's youth as collecting the postage stamps. The lack of fun and competition definitely discourages people, raised on video games and addicted to excitement.

The PTTK activists have taken some actions aimed at increasing interest in travelling. New badges have been designed to lure children (characters from fairy tales) and teenagers (new disciplines like survival tourism, shooting camps etc.). One of the most recent areas of activities is geocaching developed in cooperation with Geocaching Poland Society. Geocaching is a worldwide game of hiding and seeking "treasure" - a geocacher can place a geocache in the world, pinpoint its location using GPS technology and then share the geocache's existence and location online. Anyone with a GPS unit can then try to locate the geocache. The geocaching experience proved to be a success – but it promotes only the places with hidden "treasure". Geocaching might also seem too difficult and too dangerous for children and families. However, the system promoting tourism activity in the society and the promotion of different destinations in Poland need some "gamification". It is based on social and digital solutions – tools which are popular among young people, well known and familiar.

Weaving in the value of relationships, the need for trust and the scalable value of "fans" one can formulate the basics for effective gamification system supporting marketing needs of any idea, brand or organisation. The combination of the above mentioned purposes (promotion and gamification of existing tasks) makes the mechanism extremely useful for the purpose of tourism region promotion and tourism education (education for tourism and education through tourism) as well as their mutual support.

Social media characteristics and trends could be very helpful in the promotion of tourism destinations as well as tourism activity itself. The idea has been adapted as a core of two big projects: tourism development strategy of Mazovian District in Poland and the project of revitalising PTTK badge system.

The former one so far has been based on the booklets (similar to those of PTTK) called "Mazovian Passport". Despite a huge amount of the most noble places of interests and activities covered by the "Passport" (e.g. Royal Castle in Warsaw, Vistula River Regatta, traditional cuisine inns) during the last three years less than 100 passports were issued and ... none of them filled with stamps. Neither the participants nor the authorities and enterprises of Mazovian district have any idea of the number of active participants and their results. The development of new mobile application "Mazovian Passport App" seems to be a good starting point, although it needs perfect cooperation of regional tourism enterprises, schools and new technology sector as well as the inventive use of social media.

Rationale for Cooperation in Tourism Destination Marketing

Tourists tend to base their judgments on the satisfaction with a vacation experience on all the components of a complex tourism system. These components are captured by the tourism value chain underlying both the production and consumption of holiday experience (Bieger, 1997). Destinations are amalgams of tourism products, facilities and services which compose the total tourism expertise under one brand name.

The competitiveness of tourism destinations has become a central point of tourism policy. It is vital for their survival and growth in the international market, in the conditions of increasing leisure time and rising levels of disposable income (Echtner & Ritchie, 2003). Given the situation of the world economy, with a decrease in the overall demand for tourist services, the focus of the tourism organizations and destinations has shifted from simply attracting more tourists towards making the tourist destinations more competitive.

According to Ritchie and Crouch (2003) a destination competitiveness is defined by "...its ability to increase tourism expenditure, to increasingly attract visitors while providing them with satisfying memorable experiences and to do so in a profitable way, while enhancing the well-being of destination residents and preserving the natural capital of the destination for future generations" (p. 87). Thus competitiveness in tourism has several dimensions: economic, socio-cultural and environmental. As competition increases and tourism activity intensifies, tourism policy focuses on improving competitiveness by creating a statutory framework to monitor, control and enhance quality and efficiency in the industry and to protect resources (Goeldner, Ritchie & McIntosh, 2000). Tourism destination competitiveness requires combining economic growth with the sustainable use of the destination's resources.

Most studies on tourists' spatiotemporal movements focus their attention on tourism itinerary models (Lue, Crompton, & Fesenmaier, 1993; Mings & McHugh, 1992; Oppermann, 1995) and imply two components, destination and transit components, that make up the total attractiveness of a tourist destination for destination choice consideration. Consequently, destination marketing communication mainly focuses on conveying the totality of destination attractiveness to potential tourists (*i.e.*, why a destination is worth visiting) compared to its competitive sets. While this is important, it is argued that marketing initiatives that direct persuasive recommendations leading to new, creative encounters with the physical and sociocultural characteristics of the destination that enrich the overall tourism experiences (*i.e.*, how to get more out of a visit) can be more powerful in influencing tourist behaviour (Tussyadiah, 2012).

Moreover proper destination marketing is not only about luring mass tourists and tourism expenditure but also about deliberate distribution of tourist flow within the destination. The latter result is usually achieved by discriminatory pricing, while the good system of promoting the less visited places by properly considered distribution of rewards (points and *badges* as well as price discounts and gifts) could deal with that problem more effectively or at least – with more fun! The effective gamification needs different types of rewards and hence a proper organisation (an institution), which will take the responsibility for valuation of activities, ratings and rewarding.

The array of components that make up the destination product (the complexity of the relationships that exist between them and the strengthening of this complexity, due to the tendency for a large number of different stakeholders to be involved) is such that the destination is widely acknowledged to be one of the most difficult products to manage and market. The performance of destination depends on its ability to create value, which is the use of a resource to exploit external circumstances to bring in revenue, or to neutralise external situations likely to keep revenue from flowing in (Coulter, 2002).

Camprubi, Guia and Comas (2008) consider the tourist destination as a network of relations between different actors that, together, create the tourist product. A tourism destination typically comprises numerous autonomous suppliers, yet consumers make purchase and repurchase decisions based on the totality of the experience available at a destination (Williams & Palmer, 1999; Leiper, 1996; Palmer & McCole, 2000). Each tourism organization provides one or several components of the total tourism product that is consumed during the course of the complete tourism experience (Kachniewska, 2006). One week stay in a distant place entails contacts with some 30-50 different entities (tour operator, insurance company, carrier, hotel, restaurant, tourism attraction, exchange office, taxi-driver, souvenir shop, local authorities etc.) - this way a tourist value chain is being constructed (Kachniewska, Nawrocka, Niezgoda, & Pawlicz, 2012). Consequently competition among tourism destinations is not centred on the single aspects of the tourist product (environmental resources, transportation, tourism services, hospitality, etc.) but on the tourist destination as an integrated set of tourism facilities and experiences (Ritchie and Crouch, 2000; Kachniewska, 2013b).

The success of a tourism destination product and its professional marketing depends on a network of independent and inter-dependent organisations (Kotler, Bowen, & Markens, 2006). A frequently used approach to the study of inter-organisational relationships is based on network analysis (Achrol, 1991; Quinn, 1992). The 1990s saw growing interest in a new form of organisation often referred to as the virtual organisation (Davidow & Malone, 1992). The virtual organisation in this context refers to a network of independent companies, suppliers, customers, even erstwhile rivals linked by information technology to share skills, cost, and access to one another's markets. The network rationale is that a single organisation is unable or unwilling to meet the skill and resource demands essential for competing in the global market (Cravens, Shipp, & Cravens, 1993). Members of a network remain independent along certain dimensions of the relationship; however each partner contributes some part of its core competence.

Tourism destinations present an ideal scenario for the development of virtual organisations, linked together by information technology, the more that tourism is an information-intensive industry. Tourist destinations can benefit from the electronic marketing by developing a coherent position in the marketplace; increasing their market share by getting closer to customers (actual and potential); and subsequently by providing greater customer satisfaction (Sussmann & Baker, 1996). The role of information integration and brokerage is especially applicable to destination marketing organisations (DMO) as their role is to match producers with consumers by positioning and promoting a place as a tourism destination brand (Pollock, 1996). Traditionally the planning, management and coordination functions of destinations have been undertaken by either the public sector (at national, regional or local level) or by partnerships between stakeholders of the local tourism industry.

For the last 20 years the development of Destination Management Systems (DMSs) has been one of the most popular solutions to address these issues (Buhalis, 2013). The basic version of DMS consists of Product Database, Customer Database and a mechanism connecting the two. Not only DMSs enable coordination of whole range of products and services offered by the local suppliers and promote them on the global scale but also allow travellers to create a personal destination experience.

The emergence of the Internet and social media has altered dramatically the structure of the travel industry. Overall, consumers benefited the most as their bargaining power increased due to their ability to access accurate and relevant information instantly and to communicate directly with suppliers, while benefiting from lower switching costs. The Internet led to the intensification of rivalry among tourism suppliers (both enterprises and destinations) as it introduced transparency, speed, convenience and a wide range of choice and flexibility in the marketplace (Connolly, Olsen, & Moore, 1998; Millman, 1998).

Transparency enabled buyers to increase their bargaining power by facilitating price comparisons and access to instant, inexpensive and accurate information but reduced the bargaining power of suppliers. Rivalry was further intensified because of lowered barriers to entry and because of the possibility of equal representation of small businesses (Buhalis, 1997). Suppliers need to enhance their direct communications with end consumers and online intermediaries to enhance their efficiency. The visibility and competitiveness of principals and destinations in the marketplace will increasingly be a function of the technologies and networks utilised to interact with individual and institutional customers.

E-Marketing and M-Marketing in Tourism

The use of ICTs in tourism businesses digitises all processes and value chains in the travel, hospitality and catering industries. Sales and marketing, finance and accounting, human resource management, procurement, research and development, as well as strategy and planning for travel, transport, leisure, hospitality, principals, intermediaries and public sector organisations - are influenced by the emerging capabilities of ICTs. Technological solutions are normally incorporated to increase efficiency and reduce the cost and time required for undertaking particular activities and processes.

Information technology and applications used in tourism cover internet/intranets/extranets solutions, office automation, reservation, accounting, payroll and procurement management applications, plenty of internal management tools, databases and knowledge management systems, networks with partners for regular transactions, networking and open distribution of products through the internet, computer reservation systems (CRS) and global distribution systems (GDS, *e.g.*, Galileo, SABRE, Amadeus, Worldspan), switch applications for hospitality organisations (e.g. THISCO and WIZCOM), destination management systems (DMSs), online travel agencies (OTA) and other internet-based travel intermediaries (*e.g.*, Expedia.com, Travelocity.com, Priceline.com, etc.), wireless reservation systems, traditional distribution technologies supporting automated systems (e.g. Videotext), interactive digital TV, kiosks and touch screen terminals as well as the systems of digital signage (Buhalis, 2003; O'Connor, 1999; Kachniewska 2014a).

The nature of tourists' search activity, involving multiple choices of suppliers and comparison of facilities, prices and availability is facilitated by the search capabilities of the Internet, the more that a number of new players have come into the tourism marketplace. Perhaps the most significant change was the proliferation of low-frills airlines that use the Internet as a main distribution mechanism for direct sales. This development educated consumers that they can only find cheap fares if they go direct to the carrier online. The development of Online Travel Agencies (OTA, like: Expedia, Travelocity, Lastminute, Orbitz, Opodo) has created powerful "travel supermarkets" for consumers. They provide integrated travel solutions and value added services, such as destination guides and weather reports. By adopting dynamic packaging, i.e. the ability to package customised trips based on bundling individual components at a discounted total price, they effectively threaten the role of tour operators and other aggregators (Buhalis, 2013; Kachniewska, 2014a).

Increasingly, information intermediaries are able to profile consumers and provide a selection that is based on their needs. E-commerce offers great flexibility for tourism suppliers operating in volatile markets. The promotional message can be changed much more quickly than is the case where the need to print documents leads to long lead times between a policy decision being made and the implementation of that decision. E-commerce is very good at handling clearance of perishable capacity close to the time of use and for managing yields effectively (Wolff, 1997; Connolly et al., 1998). Customers benefit from such channels by gaining immediate gratification of their requests, greater choice, multi-sensory, accurate and up-to-date information and an easy to use interface (Pollock, 1996). Similarly, the costs of obtaining information are reduced and a wide diversity of information can be represented on one terminal, which further reduces the information search costs for potential tourists (Bakos, 1991).

Particularly the Internet has an advantage over any other media in its ability to permanently expose information to a global audience. The Web vastly improves the information availability and user interaction, and makes it possible for companies to improve the service quality at all levels of customer interaction (pre-sale, during and post-sale). Permanent accessibility is especially vital in international tourism, where business spans across different time zones, but it also meets the requirements of the nowadays consumers. Improved access to information has also made it possible for marketers to offer personalized services (Kachniewska, 2014a). Consequently tourism-related services have emerged as a leading product category to be promoted and distributed to consumer markets through the Internet (Connolly et al., 1998; Sussman & Baker, 1996; Millman, 1998; Underwood, 1996).

Technologies changed also dramatically the planning, development and marketing of destinations. To the degree that tourists increasingly research their holidays online, DMOs have already realised the need to have an inspirational web site that can encourage and facilitate tourist visitation. However, the emergence of Web 2.0 with its ideology of openness, sharing and cooperation, proved the limitations of an old-school web site. DMOs are beginning to realise the importance of using the power of social media, however social networks usage among top DMOs is still largely experimental (Buhalis, 2013).

Naturally mobile tourists need mobile information. The trend has been strengthening by new technological means. Notably mobile devices are a communication medium that keeps people connected at any place, wherever they go and any time. Therefore, it is considered to be the most effective tool of direct marketing. Wireless marketing involves reaching and servicing customers and developing relationships with them. Independence and an easy access to information constitute one of the priorities to modern tourists, combining several purposes with travelling, such as business, leisure, entertainment and education (Kachniewska, 2014b). While using the applications customers provide useful information on their interests and preferences thus enabling more precise market segmentation and better targeting. The future competitive advantages for a successful tourism industry will most probably be built around effective mobile value services, but few tourism destinations have already started leveraging customer relationships and building loyalty ties through virtual communities and mobile applications.

Many opportunities to address the destination marketing challenges lay in ICTs integration - providing new marketing tools and empowering consumers who are now more independent, well informed, and look for new experiences. Increasingly, DMOs use ICTs in order to facilitate the tourist experience before, during and after the visit, as well as for coordinating all partners involved in the production and delivery of tourism (Buhalis, 2013). Thanks to mobile devices voluminous information tied to geographic locations is becoming more and more accessible. Using this information, destination marketers are able to tap into micro-segments of tourists' consumption and activities by offering recommendations relevant to space and time that might shape, change, or alter tourists' spatiotemporal movement at the destination (i.e., en route and on site travel decisions). The advancement in mobile technology, specifically in mobile data networks and global positioning system (GPS), makes it possible to extract knowledge from an expert system to generate ubiquitous recommendations for tourists on the move (Gretzel, 2011; Kabassi, 2010), which typically include selection of attractions, restaurants, and other activities.

Mobile value services create customer value with the support of mobile technology. While using the applications, customers provide useful information on their interests and preferences thus enabling more precise market segmentation and better targeting. The future competitive advantages for a successful tourism industry will most probably be built around effective mobile value services, but few tourism destinations have already started leveraging customer relationships and building loyalty ties through virtual communities and mobile applications (Kachniewska, 2014b).

User experience is a multi-dimensional measure that considers the software, the user and the environment. It describes both: how well a system supports users as they try to make sense of a domain space, and the aesthetic experience that results from its use. It combines the functionality of the system, the cognitive, perceptual and psychomotor requirements for using the system, and the psychological and social influences surrounding its use. It also considers the context of use.

Context is any information that can be used to characterise the situation of an entity. In marketing and management, context has been understood as an important aspect influencing consumers' decisions. An entity is a person (e.g. a tourist), place or object that is considered relevant to the interaction between a user and an application (Lau, 2012). *E.g.* modern tourists expect location-aware information about the destination domain, including history, culture, folk, art, economics, environment and nature. They also expect individualised information and services taking into account their own interest and history of their activities. By analysing users' needs and emotional sides organizations can better understand customer demographics, buying patterns and feelings, thus planning so called total experience design (TxD).

The same traveller may adopt different strategies and choose different destinations, accommodations, and activities when facing different travel contexts (traveling with or without children, familiar or unfamiliar with the destination, etc.). Therefore, the capability of mobile recommender systems to integrate the spatiotemporal information in the recommendation generation process is critical to tourism marketing. Context-aware mobile tourism applications are designed to support different context types: location, identity, social and environmental context as well as network and device contexts (Cheverst, Mitchell, & Davies, 2002; Setten, Pokraev, & Koolwaaij, 2004). Adomavicius & Tuzhilin (2011) identify three dimensions of contextual information necessary to deliver consumer experiences in marketing and management: spatial (where), temporal (when), and technological (how). These dimensions of contextual information, when utilized within the mobile application, suggest context-relevant consumption that shapes tourists' mobility.

Social networks are collecting information on everything from events to personal tastes and behaviours. Tourism virtual communities (TripAdvisor, SocialTravel) make it easy for people to obtain information, maintain connections, deepen relationships and meet people they would otherwise never have met. The reach and efficiency of online communities enhance the dynamics of social learning processes relative to exchanges that are face-to-face or facilitated by other media. Thus a professional system has to include all the digital spaces where the users' context might be available and where new services might be offered. The adoption of such marketing techniques in everyday practice remains far beyond the abilities of an average tourism enterprise, and needs the cooperation of all the destination's entities.

The Internet and mobile applications instantly bridge the gap between tourism consumers and enterprises enabling interactive communication and trade. The proliferation of e-commerce and m-commerce enabled electronic trading, both from enterprises to consumers (B2C) and perhaps more importantly between businesses (B2B). Not only did it enable tourism businesses to increase their reach but also intensified online trading and globalised the market of all types of products and services (Beech & Chadwich, 2006). It also enabled consumer-to-consumer (C2C) services and communities to emerge providing a wide range of tourism information services online. Thus, the development of electronic commerce offers new opportunities for collaborative marketing of tourism destinations and tourists' independence in composing their vacation experience. The most obvious method is a kind of virtual cooperation, whereby potential tourists can browse through Websites of individual facilities at a destination and develop a coherent picture of the destination experience on offer. The creative linking of Websites facilitates the profiling of enquiries in a way that allows potential tourists to develop their own package of experiences from a visit to a destination (Palmer & McCole, 2000). Although the method might seem to be a good answer to modern prosumer requirements, it does not take into account important changes resulting from the development of new technologies and m-commerce techniques, nor does it incorporate any engaging elements of social networks.

Tourism marketers much too slowly start to realise that generating emotional attachment and users experience is the key to a long-term consumer-brand relationship. In order to guarantee the effectiveness, the mobile marketing is supposed to offer more than information – it must be a source of new experience and entertainment. The mobile marketplace should cover three dimensions: 1) personalisation according to local position of the holder and the relevance of information to his preferences, 2) localization through the local based services and 3) immediacy (Germanakos, 2008), thus providing users with a value added. All the three dimensions have already been used in GPS tourist guides. The lack of them seems to be one of the most vexing shortages of the Polish tourism badges systems mentioned earlier.

Moreover, the explosive growth in the size and use of the Web may lead in orientation difficulties, as users often lose sight of the goal of their inquiry, look for stimulating rather than informative material, or even use the navigational features unwisely (Kachniewska, 2014b). To alleviate such navigational difficulties, researchers try to identify the peculiarities of each user group and design systems that could deliver a personalized content. Challenges therefore concern not only adapting to the heterogeneous user needs and user environment issues, such as current location and time, but also a number of other considerations with respect to multi-channel delivery of applications. The personalisation of e-commerce and m-services needs a new way of thinking about the user's role in a digital ecosystem. Nowadays they are well connected, very active and conscious of their power. Looking forward, successful tourism organisations will increasingly need to identify consumer needs and to interact with prospective clients by using comprehensive, personalised and up-to-date communication media for the design of products that satisfy tourism demand. Thus, DMO need to utilise innovative communication methods in order to maintain and increase their competitiveness.

"Conversational" Marketing and "Social" Tourists

Nowadays sales are no longer generated by simply saying the right thing at the right time, but by being in the consumer's mind on the long run. According to Grönroos (2008) customers are not predominantly interested in goods or services, but in how these can be used for value creation. Therefore, marketers need to focus on understanding their customers' everyday practices and value-generating processes so that they can assist in customers' value creation. They should not aspire to create value for customers - the focus should be on finding ways to co-create value with customers.

Social media and mobile technology have become important platforms for people's daily experiences. As people are ever more mobile for work and leisure, they increasingly share information and connect with their social network using mobile devices. Thus, the rise in social media forums has reflected the new trend. Many people have their own personal website where they fill out information about themselves, post pictures, upload videos and create their own blogs. Wright, Khanfar, Harrington and Kizer (2010) claim that it is important for advertisers to understand the importance of self-esteem and self-actualization in such highly individualistic societies, and design appeals that satisfy these higher personalised needs.

Real time conversations happen across a range of platforms and media. Social media constitute a substantial part of the search results and therefore traditional providers of travel-related information will have to ensure that they include social media in their marketing strategies. Social gaming is viewed as a hedonic system that offers entertaining and playful services (Shin & Shin, 2011). Hence, Tussyadiah (2012) claims that personal enjoyment and playfulness of gaming are perceived to be of important values to users, aside from the utilitarian values of the technology applications. In the context of advergaming, it is the hedonic value of playing the games that represents an added value to using them as marketing tools. In the context of social gaming, it is the connectivity (and the whole range of social aspects) that provokes people engagement. It is of utmost importance to understand how to embrace the trend for marketing purposes, particularly in the context of tourism and hospitality businesses.

Contemporary consumer, promotional channels and research are greatly different from those described in most classic market theories. The relation between consumer, market and companies moved from completely static – when the consumer was exposed to the information selected by companies and had few to no opportunities to do his own research on products – to absolutely dynamic, when the information that companies present about themselves is only a tiny fraction of the total amount of data available on them. More importantly, companies have little to no control over consumer-generated content, such as electronic word of mouth (e-WoM) and consumer's online brand related activities (COBRAs). The other one covers activities such as uploading pictures of some brands, making comments or sharing the posts concerning branded products or suppliers. Though only 20% of WoM marketing is claimed to happen online (Sernovitz, 2012), this is stored in archives and can be read by other potential clients much later – GfK (2013) showed that online reviews are very important in the purchase decision.

The most promising attribute of "conversational" marketing is the unique ability to influence consumers' decision-making process. Gladwell (2000) identifies three groups of people depending on their ability to support marketers' efforts, namely "connectors", "mavens" and "salespeople". Connectors have a gift of bringing people and ideas together and in a sense connecting people together. They have a prevalent place in social media forums as they move and steer people. Mavens are the ones that essentially soak up information; they want to know the best deal and tell everyone about it. They are credited with having the ability to start word-of-mouth trends with their charisma and social skills (very important in the process of so called buzz marketing). Salespeople in Gladwell's typology are individuals that have the ability to convince and sell people on new ideas. Mavens and salespeople are the most influential customers within branded customer communities that "can increase the effectiveness of WoM marketing programmes by as much as 50 percent" (Wright et al., 2010). Not only does targeting the key people save companies advertising expenses, but it may also dramatically improve their marketing productivity.

However the platform used to introduce marketing messages to the three key movers identified by Gladwell (2000) must be well thought out. Television, radio and even Internet advertising all have the ability to reach large numbers of people but they give no ability to build mutually satisfying long-term relationship neither they give power to customers due to the lack of interactivity.

Barwise and Meehan (2010) relate several examples of social media acting for or against companies, depending on how well they kept their promises. Viral marketing is overall perceived positively, as long as it is informative and entertaining (Zernigah & Sohail, 2012). Another method of increasing ROI through social communication is "to go after existing customers and find their friends", in other words to use the power of actual recommendation through people's social networks (McInnes, 2013). For marketers and market researchers, this implies a shift in customer segmentation, from the traditional demographics to the new sociographics.

The ability for social media to segment the market automatically is one reason why they are so effective. Consumers can customize their networking pages (e.g. Facebook fanpages) so that the information they receive is relevant to them. Social media is all about the conversation and so marketers need to participate in the conversation (Meyer, 2009). Wright et al. (2010) notice that the idea of social, conversational marketing media has been around for decades and did not just emerged with the Internet. Madden (2010) gives an example of the Michelin strategy. When Michelin Brothers wanted to build their car and tire brand they realized that they could engage their potential customers by producing a travel guide, bringing into play independent inspectors that rated the quality of restaurants and hotels. The "conversation" focused on food as it was more relevant to the customers' interests than tires, still the guide promoted both: restaurants and Michelin tires (Madden, 2010).

Similarly nowadays, in new media environment, the importance of two-way communication cannot be overstated and marketers need to maintain relationships with innovative leaders. In the middle of the digital era, consumers still purchase items that make them feel in a particular way: rich, important, fashionable, smart or connected (Barbu, 2013). Adapting the Maslow's hierarchy of needs Bradley (2010) argues that it is analogous to the user experience. Once the availability and basic support needs are satisfied, users move to an experience that gives them significance (connection, growth or personal contribution). E.g. interaction platforms that can successfully address user needs and emotions promote a viral and addictive effect among their users, resulting in higher user satisfaction rates.

Social media is all about answering the basic human question on how we can help one another. They can be powerful media of interconnected social influencers as people, when presented with a choice, refer to the experiences of others to make informed decisions (Wilton, Páez, & Scott, 2011). Hill, Rand, Nowak, and Christakis (2010) affirm that social networks determine interactions and influence the spread of diseases, ideas, and behaviour. Similarly Leenders (2002) argues that people are appropriately taking into account the opinions and behaviours displayed by significant others, combined with the considerations of other constraints and opportunities, to establish their own opinion and behaviour. He labelled this process "contagion" or social influence (Leenders, 2002).

The research on social influence identifies two distinct processes that lead to contagion: (a) communication, when people use others with whom they are directly tied as their frame of reference, and (b) comparison, when people use others they feel similar to as their frame of reference (Leenders, 2002). Consumers with equivalent positions in social networks typically have similar brand preferences (Lee, Cotte, & Noseworthy, 2010). Tussyadiah, Park and Fesenmaier (2011) identify that people tend to follow marketing recommendations from other consumers they can identify with. Therefore, the key to viral marketing using social media is to create a platform of influence enablers where members can influence each other through the processes of communication and comparison (Tussyadiah, 2012).

Notwithstanding the "postmodern tourists" look for the possibility to compose their tourism packages personally and to modify them during the trip, according to their personal needs and interests, thus becoming Toffler defined "prosumers" (Toffler, 1970). As the advanced tourists often change their itinerary during the trip and quite often mix business or education with tourism, they are not likely to invest a great deal of time to pre-plan a travel schedule in detail. That is why they need pragmatic and logistic information within an easy reach (available anytime and anyhow) during their travel. Well-designed location-based social network marketing persuades consumers to stay connected and broaden their social network by nurturing communication and interaction among members of the social network through instant updates and relevant recommendations.

Despite the lack of control, electronic recommendations and appraisals are a convenient manner to have a product promoted via "consumer-to-consumer (C2C) interactions" (Muntinga, Moorman, & Smit, 2011). e-WoM is one of the most important marketing tools in online travel agencies' practices: online hotel reviews strengthen the buyers' decisions to make a reservation or to neglect the offer (Kim, Mattila, & Baloglu, 2011). A good service would result in a positive review which gets the hotel free publicity via social media; however a poor service will result in a negative consumer review which can ruin the company's reputation. Consumer satisfaction is crucial in this context, because "bad is stronger than good", in other words, an unsatisfied customer is more likely to spread the story than a satisfied customer is to spread his (Lax, 2012). Claiming that "Advertising is the cost of being boring", Sernovitz (2012) advocates that companies can cut the cost of advertising if they can spark enough positive word of mouth marketing.

Information and communication technologies (ICT) have created innovative ways for providing value to clients. During the past years, mobile devices and mobile applications have been developed that have high computing power, storage capacity, and graphical and audio capabilities. Many users have deep personal relationships with their smartphones (Feijoo, Gomez-Barroso, Aguado, & Ramos, 2012) and use them to realize a specific lifestyle and to "stay connected". The adoption of mobile devices has grown tremendously and their characteristics of mobility and connectivity support on-demand services that are tailored to users and their specific situations (context). With the advent of Web 2.0 digital systems became collaborative, bringing a social layer to the Web. Wearable sensors are feeding user information to social, medical and edutainment networks - there is no reason why not to use them in tourism marketing. Virtual communities show new opportunities for tourism firms and destinations. Moreover the best way in which companies can still control consumers' discussion is through brand communities.

Tapping into the emotional midbrain to understand desires, motivations and contexts for action lays the foundation for understanding how to drive a user's behaviour. Thus an important approach to personalise tourism services is based on automatic user localisation. The current position of a user can be used to specify the user's request and further filter the relevant information. When tourists are moving in a region, this can be used as a clue to their interests (when they visit palaces – they might be interested in some other historical buildings). Users generate a lot of events when walking around - this can be exploited for the user modelling, to detect and anticipate relevant user interests and to offer individual tourists context-aware recommendations and services based on tourist's geographical location. Being combined with a social game it can offer an additional value of permanent interaction: the users (tourists) feel safe and get more fun (sharing the photos and opinions, suggesting attractions), they can compare their results and status, they can "win a prize".

For tourism destinations, as users rely on social applications for recommendations, it is important to emphasize on stimulating the bundling of attractions and services. For instance, offering themed badges to unlock upon visitation to a number of attractions with the same themes (e.g., historic, movie, or TV scenes, etc.) will encourage tourists with different travel motivations, preferences and styles to experience the destinations in a playful and fun way. Also, since tourists are in a different social competition zone while traveling, it is important to provide opportunities that foster competition among tourists. Tourism destinations can create additional rewards and recognition for tourists upon collecting a certain number of *check-ins* and for writing a number of recommendations. That way, tourism destinations not only facilitate tourists to enjoy the city by competing with other tourists, but also encourage them to spread the information and recommendation to others.

Towards the Gamification of Tourism in Poland

The evolution of tourism as one of the main world-wide trends was characterized by predominance of mass tourism (so called "sun and sea" tourism) throughout the second half of the twentieth century. Overexploitation of numerous destinations paved the way to some new approaches, putting more focus on other types of tourism. Often referred to as niche markets tourism they offered new opportunities, such as adventure and survival tourism, culinary tourism, eco activities, ethno villages, slow tourism etc.

Deeply rooted understanding of tourism only in "sun and sea" terms may cause slow development of tourism in non-traditional tourism countries whereas new consumer trends (individualization of consumption, glocalisation, return to self-development and education, search for tradition and experience) make modern tourists more interested in different elements of the host country culture and nature. Their share in the total tourism activity steadily increases. More and more non-traditional tourism countries are trying to attract visitors by promoting their offer of different cultural and natural resources; however general public often remains reluctant to find the resources attractive.

Tourism activity in Poland has been developing along the path of these processes. The economic transition in the last decade of the 20th century caused sudden economic development and allowed some improvement within the business tourism but very poor climate conditions do not foster the development of leisure tourism. DMOs started to consider new types of tourism as their chance. Especially in the last decade, tourism development efforts have included activities to protect cultural sites, to open new nature sites and to create events which may attract tourists. It has been widely recognised that the main opportunities for tourism in Poland are within the area of cultural tourism (heritage, history, religions, cultural events etc.) and in outdoor offer (wild nature, rivers, bird watching, hiking etc.).

The idea is especially attractive for the Mazovian District situated in central Poland, with no access to the Baltic Sea nor to the mountains, looking for some tourism alternatives. Its flagship tourism product – the city of Warsaw, being the capital of Poland and an important business centre – so far consumed the majority of incoming tourists' expenditures. Although the *per capita* incomes of Warsaw citizens are much higher than in any other part of Poland, very rarely they consider spending their holidays (even the weekend trips) within the district.

One of the most challenging tasks for the Mazovian Destination Marketing Organisation (MDMO) is about encouraging Polish (especially Warsaw) tourists to spend their short-haul travels within the district. Despite its swathes of scenically beautiful countryside, which is quite pristine and unspoilt with few large industrial towns, Mazovian district is not in itself unique, but the access to space and tranquillity within a scenically beautiful and "environmentally clean" setting, particularly when combined with traditional culture, is becoming increasingly rare in Europe.

Among numerous elements of the tourism development strategy, the experts of MDMO developed a long-term marketing plan implying the wide-ranging educational programme for Mazovian teenagers based on the gamification of the old-school Mazovian Passport and a special application enabling the virtual transposition of all the activities to the social layer. The idea of teenagers target group seemed to be obvious: not only that very group creates potential to inexpensive travels within a short distance from Warsaw, but it is also extremely active in social media constituting good e-WOM (viral) effects. Their influence on families should not be underestimated as well.

The system of Mazovian Passport or (at the national level) the system of PTTK tourism badges needs to be gamified and virtualised. The digital native generation cannot content themselves with the paper booklet: they need the virtual scoreboard, where every player can see the results of other competitors. In face-to-face board games the scoreboards are not necessary as the players can see each other's results. In a virtual environment the 3F rule (friends, fun and feedback) is obligatory. A good application needs to help the players select the "friends", this way providing the context of exciting competition and a motivation to self-improvement (like Endomondo application which enables to compare the results of sporting activities). The relevance of information and recommendation results from connection-seeking behaviour and leads to the phenomenon of social influence or social contagion, where members of a social network continue to recommend each other to visit different venues.

Surely the results of the unknown Kowalski cannot impress anybody – but the comparison with "friends" is highly stimulating. It means that the Mazovian Passport application – should be modelled on social networking, where players can "invite" friends from the real world. Every invitation initiates viral thus needs to be remunerated with some extra points. Viral starts multiply when the "friends" from the application start sharing the comments or photos. In order to stimulate COBRA (consumer online brand-related activities) for Mazovian district the players should also be rewarded for being active: at least their comments popularise new tourist routes, new badges and new tourism destinations.

The application is to be based on the system of PTTK badges which deserves maintaining as the virtual world (game-design system) and reality (real badges) should complement each other. PTTK badges have plenty of educational qualities: they organize the process of studying the places, their history and tradition. The well-designed system should enable verification of the players' achievements. It is not enough to designate the routes and mark the must-visit places: every place should enable the geolocalisation-based *check-in* (like in Foursquare). The narrative linking all the places and activities might be an additional value. The story is one of the most important elements of any game. Tourism space (also a virtual one: historic or literary space) offers unlimited opportunities to compose the game story. The more innovative idea the bigger the chance that teenagers will be drawn to the game.

The way tourists are going to move along the routes, the necessity to relieve traffic in the most popular places or during important events needs the good think-over and effective construction of the game dynamics. It should also predict weariness and physical exhaustion of the players (tourists), rejuvenation and time for meals – all the elements should find their place in the story, moreover all of them might be treated as "tasks" and elements of the destination's promotion (culinary tourism, recreation activities, walking in the park, swimming). All the activities can bring the players closer to the goal – even (or especially) if they quit the route or try to arrange a trip on their own.

When tourists quit or miss the "game space" they can multiply their points when they share information on the place which attracted their attention, share a photo of a perfect meal in a local restaurant, which has not been placed on the planned route. This way the invention of players can be awarded and the levelling mechanism can be used to gather information on tourists' likes and dislikes as well as on their creativity (the concept of crowdsourcing). In the most advanced formula this mechanism can help to create a virtual guide in a similar way like on the TripAdvisor portal and in Wikimedia – it is just about humans prone to bragging and sharing their emotions.

Functionality of "Mazovian Passport App" will also include personalised messages showing changes in status, suggesting new destinations and events; relevant offers based on actions and targets; group incentives ("if you and your friends do X, you'll get Y"); limited time offers; progression (the application will show progress towards goals); loyalty, status and awards (the idea of a trophy cabinet); next status action (what the player needs to do to achieve the next award, trophy or status).

Any new application requires promotion – otherwise it perishes among many other game-like applications. MDMO has very good relationships with Mazovian Board of Education. It is a good starting point towards the cooperation on modern educational programmes based on tourism activity. Short-haul, two- or three–day trips can be promoted through the school system: the teachers get "ready-to-use" suggestions of tourist routes and educational trip gets more attractive, as it offers the possibility to collect points, to get rewards, to compete with friends.

In the future the trips should be developed in cooperation with teachers so that to adjust the trips to the education system and differentiated school subjects. Tourism activity can be used to study almost all of them: from history and geography to maths and chemistry. A distinguishing feature of the future "Mazovian Passport App" could include the system of school marks. Depending on the activities during the trip (biology experiments or visits to historical monuments), students will be able to collect points affecting their school marks. It will undoubtedly strengthen the rewards system.

Tourism routes do not need to cover the typical places of interests – the idea is to promote events and places situated away from the most famous monuments. Thus the application should be modelled on dynamic loyalty systems: depending on the season, time of the week or even time of the day, depending on the popularity of a place and difficulty to get there, the number of points for the same activities and visits can be altered thus enabling the most effective distribution of tourism flows. The "badged routes" can be of virtual and fugitive character: they can be marked along the places of interesting events giving the unique opportunity to take part and get extra points. Gamification can be used to promote any visible and invisible tourist attractions (unique dialects, customs, tradition, history); the popular urban games and geocaching can strengthen the tourism offer and make it more attractive. Here again the viral and social communication can serve as additional marketing tools.

The challenges on the route can be more or less difficult and adjusted to the age of tourists. They can require prior individual or group work (*e.g.* to read a paper, to find some information on the Internet), which will make it possible to get better orientation, to find the appropriate objects faster or to answer the question. It constitutes the game element and the basic condition to get to a higher level. This way gamification serves the development of cultural and educational tourism. In the context of very low recreational and sporting activity of Polish teenagers, it is worth including some tasks and challenges of sporting character. It is also worth combining different criteria of evaluation: the number of places visited, the number of kilometres ridden on a horseback, the number of questions answered, etc.

The process of virtualisation (moving some activities to the internet, virtual scoreboards, sharing the posts etc.) increases the attractiveness of the game and the players' engagement. It also strengthens promotion of a place (city) and its attractions thanks to COBRA and e-WOM. In order to achieve this, information and quests can be evaluated by the players and pointed by those competitors who have not visited the place yet. As playfulness and connectivity are key persuasive elements, it is important for tourism and hospitality businesses to concentrate on nurturing the social connection and fostering competition. Hospitality businesses such as restaurants, cafés, and nightlife establishments should strategize their stimuli to target different consumers' behaviour. For example, merchants targeting tourists should focus on encouraging variety behaviour (trying new venues, new services). Thus, the merchant rewards offered should be based on first time *check-ins* (*e.g.*, price discount for first drinks or entrance to the museum). On the other hand, merchants targeting locals and long-term tourists should emphasize on loyalty behaviour by encouraging repeat visitation through status recognition of loyal customers (*e.g.*, badges to unlock after a number of visits).

The players can also contribute (and get extra points) when sharing the unique photos of the destination monuments and landscapes, inviting to visit them or evaluate (the mechanism known from Instagram). The presentation of monuments and places as an element of a bigger whole constitutes a collecting activity itself – the next place to visit, the next photo to share or the next question to be answered remind the missing stamp in a coffee-shop loyalty programme and present higher value than a visit to the same place. Again it helps to distribute tourism flow more effectively.

In a travel context travellers face a series of decision-making processes that entail a combination of different venues (*e.g.*, attractions and services) in different areas of the destination throughout the duration of the trip. Thus, tourism destination game-design marketing requires providing a combination of stimuli that can be transformed into value maximizing strategies within space and over time (selection and bundling, timing and duration, etc.). Consequently the Mazovian Passport App should balance three aspects: context-based recommender system, social influence and social gaming – the set of marketing stimuli. Merchant rewards, which may include monetary and non-monetary promotions, are believed to be one of the driving forces of patronage behaviour due to consumers' value maximizing strategy. While using the application consumers gain personal enjoyment from receiving application rewards upon completion of certain tasks that allow them to compete with others in the social network.

The tasks – especially when we think of teenagers – should be numerous and challenging but achievable, providing the feeling of self-improvement (the "flow"). A very important matter when planning a game is the application of "earning & burning" mechanism (gathering points and their exchange for prizes). The points can guarantee the place on the scoreboard or be utilized (entrance tickets, transportation, snack bar meals etc.). The rewards can be of application character (the tourism badges) or merchant rewards (price discount, free accommodation, dinner in a local restaurant, ticket to a theatre or a possibility to visit a place which normally is not available for tourists). Every reward should invite to compete for the "next level" (the accommodation in an attractive place, which has never been seen before, will probably lure the players, especially when they can solve there a new task and get more points).

The playfulness of collecting points or unlocking badges by *checking-in* to local establishment is magnified by the status recognition from consumers' social network (social reward). Competition-based rewards influence consumers to transform real life into a game, making mobility and experiences more playful and fun. The competition-based social rewards signify the power of the application rewards in influencing consumption and mobility.

The last marketing stimuli made available by the application are the connection-based social rewards. They explain the underlying processes of WoM recommendation as a result of interaction and communication within the social network. Typical tourist consumers stay connected and broaden their social network by nurturing communication and interaction among members of the social network through instant updates and relevant recommendations. From a marketing and sales perspective, the new dimension of using social rewards as promotional tools lies in the immediacy of these rewards made available for consumers. The ability to provide rewards without delay encourages consumers to make instant strategic decisions (Tussyadiah, 2012).

The system of different rewards further stimulate consumers to fulfil certain tasks that lead not only to venue selection, but also to the processes of interaction, direct and indirect communication, and social referencing, making the application a platform of social connection and competition. The marketing stimuli encourage consumers' responses in the form of variety behaviour (*i.e.*, consumers are challenged to try new things and visit new places yet to be discovered) and loyalty behaviour (*i.e.*, consumers are encouraged to visit certain establishments more often).

Moreover, thanks to the virtual character of the system the MDMO can have plenty of information on the tourists' behaviour and their contest results. It will enable the proper management of tourists' flow, both in the low and high season.

The cooperation of hospitality industry, sightseeing societies and educational system seems the natural way to promote tourism activity among teenagers – especially in the context of the heated discussion on the effectiveness of Polish educational system. Strong visual memory of the majority of humans increases the efficiency of learning process, and people's inclination to store in mind nice experiences makes the trips and lessons in the tourism space much more memorable. The diversity of tourism badges provides the opportunity to raise physical fitness and gather different skills: using the map and compass, the group interaction and cooperation, as well as many other skills and competences missing in an educational system. At the same time it can strengthen the promotion of tourism destinations.

FUTURE RESEARCH DIRECTIONS

The functions of badges and gamification elements discussed in the chapter do not represent an exhaustive list. However, there is ample evidence in the literature reviewed, to support the typology of game-design mechanism and its business and education usefulness. Much work remains in order to empirically investigate the individual and social dynamics of gamification in social media contexts.

Although badges are in widespread use in social media, relatively little research has been devoted to understanding how or why they are valuable and useful (Antin & Churchill, 2011). Future research must begin by examining the assumption that game-design mechanism and badging systems are engaging and motivational for all. The research can further evaluate the relationships between gamification and engagement on the ground of tourism activity.

Similarly the location-based social network marketing in tourism is considered a new approach and becomes important to explore. Studies on how to measure the results of social media marketing are also still scant (see Parent et al., 2011; Tussyadiah, 2012). Future research direction is to examine the characteristics of online content and motivations to forward online content. Specifically, a theoretically interesting while managerially relevant question concerns the characteristics of online content which are more readily forwarded by Internet users to others. Since research shows that WOM has greater impact on product decisions compared to more traditional marketing communications such as advertising (Gilly, Graham, Wolfinbarger, & Yale, 1998; Herr, Kardes., & Kim., 1991) and given that source credibility is a major factor influencing WOM behaviour (Richins, 1983) future research should also analyse the impact of source credibility on forwarding of online content.

Gamification is more and more often based on mobile applications. Thus another research direction should cover the analysis of quality characteristics of mobile gaming as well as reasons for consumers to engage in mobile gaming. Okazaki (2008) specified some of them, including intrinsic enjoyment, escapism, efficiency, economic value, visual appeal, perceived novelty and perceived risklessness. Mobile gaming is likely to be characterized by higher playing frequency but shorter playing times with more interruptions and more distractions (*e.g.*, in public transportation) (Choi, Lee, & Li, 2013). It worth examining how the characteristics influence the marketing practices and gamification efficiency.

A special interest of future research needs to be devoted to regulation of gamification. Game-design social media marketing, compared to most other media, is particularly characterized by a blurring of boundaries between advertising and entertainment, and the question whether and how the promotional attempt needs to be made clear to the player is unanswered. The necessity to find solutions to this question is amplified by the fact that numerous gamified applications are used by children and adolescents; many games target children or teenagers. The forthcoming work on "Mazovian Passport App" moves forward very slowly as every aspect of the "game" needs special discussion with psychologists and marketers. A key question that has to be answered is how to strike a balance between protection of children and promotional needs and requirements of tourism industry and tourism destination.

CONCLUSION

In today's global and hyper competitive travel industry tourism destinations are faced with a rapidly changing environment and increasing demands from travellers. In the past, agencies responsible for the development of tourism products and appropriate marketing strategies mainly focused on key marketing activities. Tourists, however, bundle multiple products and services, based upon an assumption that they combine into an overall holistic experience. They became advert-resistant and very individualistic. As a consequence, destinations have begun to focus on building relationships/partnerships supporting the development of a competitive tourism destination. However, traditional marketing tools and activities (tourism fair, outdoor advertisement and vacation catalogues) although more and more beautiful, hardly influence tourists' behaviour and seem useless when shifting the demand from "sun and sea" mass tourism towards the alternative types of travel.

Management guru, Peter Drucker, once said: "There is nothing more wasteful than becoming highly efficient at doing the wrong thing." Thus Polish destinations try to adopt new marketing concepts and tools – namely gamification and mobile applications – which can bring a social layer to the promotion of tourism. They include the set of typical gamification tools (dynamics, mechanics and other components) as well as social and merchant rewords. An outdated system of tourism badges in Poland also needs renovation based on game-design techniques.

Quite complex system of Mazovian Passport App serves at least two purposes: one of them covers the needs of tourism entities and the promotion of destination, while the second one is about promoting tourism and sporting activity among teenagers, more and more often addicted to video games and social networking.

REFERENCES

Achrol, R. (1991). Evolution of the marketing organization: New forms for turbulent environments. *Journal of Marketing*, *10*(4), 77–93. doi:10.2307/1251958

Adomavicius, G., & Tuzhilin, A. (2011). Context-aware recommender systems. In F. Ricci, L. Rokach, B. Shapira, & P. Kantor (Eds.), *Recommender systems handbook* (pp. 217–256). Berlin, Germany: Springer Verlag. doi:10.1007/978-0-387-85820-3_7

Anderson, J., & Rainie, L. (2012). *The future of gamification*. Retrieved April 12, 2014, from http://www.pewinternet.org/2012/05/18/the-future-of-gamification/

Antin, J., & Churchill, E. F. (2011). *Badges in social media: A social psychological perspective*. Vancouver, Canada: CHI.

Bakos, J. Y. (1991). A strategic analysis of electronic marketplaces. *Management Information Systems Quarterly*, *15*(3), 295–310. doi:10.2307/249641

Barbu, A. (2013). Eight contemporary trends in the market research industry. *Management & Marketing Challenges for the Knowledge Society*, *8*(3), 429–450.

Barr, P., Noble, J., & Biddle, R. (2007). Video game values: Human-computer interaction and games. *Interacting with Computers*, *19*(2), 180–195. doi:10.1016/j.intcom.2006.08.008

Barwise, P., & Meehan, S. (2010). *The one thing you must get right when building a brand*. Retrieved February 15, 2013, from http://hbr.org/2010/12/the-one-thing-you-must-getright-when-building-a-brand/ar/1

Beech, J., & Chadwich, S. (2006). *The business of tourism management*. Prentice Hall, Imprint of Pearson Education.

Bieger, T. (1997). *Management von Destinationen und Tourismusorganisationen*. Muenchen, Wien: Oldenbourg.

Blythe, M. A., Overbeeke, K., Monk, A. F., & Wright, P. C. (2004). *Funology: From usability to enjoyment*. Norwell, MA: Kluwer Academic Publishers.

Bradley, S. (2010). Designing for a hierarchy of needs. *Smashing Magazine*. Retrieved March 5, 2014, from www.smashingmagazine.com/2010/04/26/designing-for-a-hierarchy-ofneeds

Buhalis, D. (1997). Information technologies as a strategic tool for economic, cultural and environmental benefits enhancement of tourism at destination regions. *Progress in Tourism and Hospitality Research*, *3*(1), 71–93. doi:10.1002/(SICI)1099-1603(199703)3:1<71::AID-PTH42>3.0.CO;2-T

Buhalis, D. (2003). *eTourism: Information technology for strategic tourism management.* London: Pearson, Financial Times/Prentice Hall.

Buhalis, D. (2013). e-Tourism: Trends and challenges in the social media era. Paper presented at the UNWTO Technical Seminar on Tourism and New Technologies, Costa Rica.

Campbell, L., & Diamond, W. D. (1990). Framing and sales promotion: The characteristics of good deal. *Journal of Consumer Marketing*, *7*(4), 25–31. doi:10.1108/EUM0000000002586

Camprubi, R., Guia, J., & Comas, J. (2008). Destination networks and induced tourism image. *Tourism Review*, *63*(2), 47–58. doi:10.1108/16605370810883941

Çeltek, E. (2010). Mobile advergaming in tourism marketing. *Journal of Vacation Marketing*, *16*(4), 267–281. doi:10.1177/1356766710380882

Cheverst, K., Mitchell, K., & Davies, N. (2002). Exploring context-aware information push. *Personal and Ubiquitous Computing*, *6*(4), 276–281. doi:10.1007/s007790200028

Choi, Y. K., Lee, S., & Li, H. (2013). Audio and visual distractions and implicit brandmemory: A study of video game players. *Journal of Advertising*, *18*(2-3), 219–227. doi:10.1080/00913367.2013.775798

Connolly, D. J., Olsen, M. D., & Moore, R. G. (1998). The Internet as a distribution channel. *The Cornell Hotel and Restaurant Administration Quarterly*, *8*(4), 42–54. doi:10.1177/001088049803900408

Coppens, A. (2013). *Tourism industry is looking into gamification.* Retrieved March 7, 2014, from http://gamificationnation.com/tourism-industry-is-looking-into-games-and-gamification/

Coulter, M. (2002). *Strategic management in action.* Harlow: Prentice Hall.

Cravens, D. W., Shipp, S. H., & Cravens, K. S. (1993). Analysis of co-operative interorganizational relationships, strategic alliance formation and strategic alliance effectiveness. *Journal of Strategic Marketing*, *3*(1), 55–70. doi:10.1080/09652549300000005

Davidow, W. H., & Malone, M. S. (1992). *The virtual corporation.* New York: HarperCollins.

Deloitte Consulting, L. L. P. (2012). *Tech trends 2012: Elevate IT for digital business.* Retrieved January 10, 2014, from www.deloitte.com/us/techtrends2012

Deterding, S. (2010). *Just add points? what ux can (and cannot) learn from games.* UX Camp Europe 28.

Deterding, S., Dixon, D., Khalled, R., & Nacke, L. (2011a). From game design elements to gamefulness: defining gamification. In *MindTrek '11. Proceedings of the 15th International Academic MindTrek Conference: Envisioning Future Media Environments* (pp. 9-15). Tampere, Finland: Academic Press. doi:10.1145/2181037.2181040

Deterding, S., Sicart, M., Nacke, L., O'Hara, K., & Dixon, D. (2011b). Gamification: Using game-design elements in nongaming contexts. In *Proceeding CHI EA'11*. ACM Press.

Dignan, A. (2011). *Game frame: Using games as a strategy for success*. New York: Free Press.

Echtner, C. M., & Ritchie, J. R. B. (2003). The meaning and measurement of destination image. *The Journal of Tourism Studies, 14*(1), 37–48.

Entertainment Software Association (ESA). (2012). *Essential facts about the computer and video game industry*. Retrieved March 16, 2014, from: http://www.theesa.com

ESOMAR. (2013). *ESOMAR congress proceedings*. Retrieved January 4, 2014, from http://www.esomar.org/events-andawards/events/global-and-regional/congress-2013/135_congress-2013.overview.php

Feijoo, C., Gomez-Barroso, J. L., Aguado, J. M., & Ramos, S. (2012). Mobile gaming: Industry challenges and policy implications. *Telecommunications Policy, 36*(3), 212–221. doi:10.1016/j.telpol.2011.12.004

Ferrara, J. (2012). *Playful design: Creating game experiences in everyday interfaces*. New York: Rosenfeld Media.

Fogg, B. J. (2002). *Persuasive technology: Using computers to change what we think and do*. Amsterdam: Morgan Kaufmann.

Frick, T. (2010). *Return on engagement: Content, strategy, and design techniques for digital marketing*. Burlington, MA: Focal Press.

Future of the Internet. (2013). Report of survey by Pew Research Center's Internet & American Life Project. Retrieved February 8, 2014, from www.pewinternet.org

Gartner.com. (2011). *More than 50 percent of organizations will gamify them*. Retrieved March 11, 2014, from http://www.gartner. com/newsroom/id/1629214

Gartner.com. (2012). *Over 70 percent of global organizations will have at least one gamified application*. Retrieved February 15, 2014, from http://www.gartner.com/newsroom/id/ 1844115

Germanakos, P., Tsianos, N., Lekkas, Z., Mourlas, C., & Samaras, G. (2008). Improving m-commerce services effectiveness with the use of user-centric content delivery. *Journal of Electronic Commerce in Organizations, 6*(1), 32–54. doi:10.4018/jeco.2008010101

Gilly, M. C., Graham, J. L., Wolfinbarger, M. F., & Yale, L. J. (1998). Dyadic study of interpersonal information search. *Journal of the Academy of Marketing Science, 26*(2), 83–100. doi:10.1177/0092070398262001

Gladwell, M. (2000). *The tipping point: How little things can make a big difference*. New York: Little, Brown and Company.

Goeldner, R., Ritchie, J., & McIntosh, R. (2000). *Tourism: Principles, practices, philosophies*. New York: Wiley.

Grace, M. V., & Hall, J. (2008). Projecting surveillance entertainment. Paper presented at ETech, San Diego, CA.

Gretzel, U. (2011). Intelligent systems in tourism: A social science perspective. *Annals of Tourism Research, 38*(3), 757–779. doi:10.1016/j.annals.2011.04.014

Grönroos, C. (2008). Service logic revisited: Who creates value? And who co-creates? *European Business Review, 20*(4), 298–314. doi:10.1108/09555340810886585

Herr, P. M., Kardes, F. R., & Kim, J. (1991). Effects of word-of-mouth and product-attribute information on persuasion: An accessibility-diagnosticity perspective. *The Journal of Consumer Research, 17*(4), 454–462. doi:10.1086/208570

Hill, A. L., Rand, D. G., Nowak, M. A., & Christakis, N. A. (2010). Emotions as infectious diseases in a large social network. *Proceedings of the Royal Society, 277*(1701), 3827–3835. doi:10.1098/rspb.2010.1217 PMID:20610424

Jung, J. H., Schneider, C., & Valacich, J. (2010). Enhancing the motivational affordance of information systems: The effects of real-time performance feedback and goal setting in group collaboration environments. *Management Science, 56*(4), 724–742. doi:10.1287/mnsc.1090.1129

Juul, J. (2005). *Half-real: video games between real rules and fictional worlds*. Cambridge, MA: MIT Press.

Kabassi, K. (2010). Personalizing recommendations for tourists. *Telematics and Informatics, 27*(1), 51–66. doi:10.1016/j.tele.2009.05.003

Kachniewska, M. (2006). *Tourism quality management*. Warsaw: WSHiFM.

Kachniewska, M. (2013a). *PlayTourism*. Retrieved January 12, 2014, from http://travelmarketing.pl/play-tourism-czyli-aplikacja-ktorej-jeszcze-nie-ma-cz-i/

Kachniewska, M. (2013c). Towards the definition of a tourism cluster. *Journal of Entrepreneurship Management and Innovation, 9*(1), 33–56.

Kachniewska, M. (2014a). Wpływ digitalizacji kanałów dystrybucji na strukturę rynku usług pośrednictwa turystycznego. [The influence of the digitalization of distribution channels on the market structure of tourism industry]. *e-Mentor, 1*(53), 86-91.

Kachniewska, M. (2014b). Tourism value added creation through a user-centric context-aware digital system. *Zeszyty Naukowe Uniwersytetu Szczecińskiego, 4*(28), 103–118.

Kachniewska, M., Nawrocka, A., Niezgoda, A., & Pawlicz, A. (2012). *Rynek turystyczny [Tourism Market]*. Warsaw: Wolters Kluwer Polska.

Kaplan, A., & Haenlein, M. (2010). Users of the world, unite! The challenges and opportunities of social media. *Business Horizons, 53*(1), 113–118. doi:10.1016/j.bushor.2009.09.003

Kietzmann, H. J., Hermkens, K., McCarthy, I. P., & Silvestre, B. S. (2011). Social media? Get serious! Understanding the functional building blocks of social media. *Business Horizons, 54*(3), 241–251. doi:10.1016/j.bushor.2011.01.005

Kim, E., Mattila, A., & Baloglu, S. (2011). Effects of gender and expertise on consumers' motivation to read online hotel reviews. *Cornell Hospitality Quarterly, 52*(4), 399–406. doi:10.1177/1938965510394357

Konrad, A. (2011). *Inside the gamification gold rush*. Retrieved January 22, 2014, from http:// tech.fortune.cnn.com/2011/10/17/gamification/

Kotler, Ph., Bowen, J. T., & Markens, J. C. (2006). *Marketing for hospitality and tourism* (International Edition). Pearson Prentice Hall.

Kriplean, T., Beschastnikh, I., & McDonald, D. W. (2008). Articulations of wikiwork: uncovering valued work in Wikipedia through Barnstars. In *Proceedings of the 2008 ACM Conference on Computer Supported Cooperative Work*. ACM. doi:10.1145/1460563.1460573

Laroche, M., Pons, F., Zgolli, N., Cervellon, M.-C., & Kim, C. (2003). A model of consumer response to two retail sales promotion techniques. *Journal of Business Research*, *56*(7), 513–522. doi:10.1016/S0148-2963(01)00249-1

Lau, S. L. (2012). *Towards a user centric context aware system: empowering users through activity recognition using a smartphone as an unobtrusive device*. Kassel: Kassel University Press.

Lax, H. (2012). *Bad is stronger than good: Lessons for customer loyalty & experience*. Retrieved April 5, 2014, from http://blog.gfk.com/blog/2012/07/11/bad-is-stronger-thangood-lessons-for-customer-loyalty-and-experience/

Lee, S. H. M., Cotte, J., & Noseworthy, T. J. (2010). The role of network centrality in the flow of consumer influence. *Journal of Consumer Psychology*, *20*(1), 66–77. doi:10.1016/j.jcps.2009.10.001

Leenders, R. T. (2002). Modelling social influence through network autocorrelation: Constructing the weight matrix. *Social Networks*, *24*(1), 21–47. doi:10.1016/S0378-8733(01)00049-1

Leiper, N. (1996). *Tourism management*. Melbourne: RMIT Publications.

Lenhart, A., Sydney, J., & Macgill, A. (2008). *Adults and video games*. Pew Internet and American Life Project. Retrieved April 11, 2014, from http://www.pewinternet.org/Reports/2008/Adults-and-Video-Games/1-Data-Memo.aspx

Ling, K., Beenen, G., Ludford, P., Wang, X., Chang, K., Li, X., & Kraut, R. et al. (2005). Using social psychology to motivate contributions to online communities. *Journal of Computer-Mediated Communication*, *10*(4), 4. doi:10.1111/j.1083-6101.2005.tb00273.x

Lockton, D., Harrison, D., & Stanton, N. A. (2010). The design with intent method: A design tool for influencing user behaviour. *Applied Ergonomics*, *41*(3), 382–392. doi:10.1016/j.apergo.2009.09.001 PMID:19822311

Lue, C. C., Crompton, J. L., & Fesenmaier, D. R. (1993). Conceptualization of multi-destination pleasure trip decisions. *Annals of Tourism Research*, *20*(2), 289–301. doi:10.1016/0160-7383(93)90056-9

Madden R. (2010). Marketing strategy: Stop putting social media cart before content horse. *Marketing Week*, 11.

Malone, T. (1980). What makes things fun to learn? Heuristics for designing instructional computer games. In *Proceedings of 3rd ACM SIGSMALL Symposium*. ACM Press. doi:10.1145/800088.802839

Malone, T. (1982). Heuristics for designing enjoyable user interfaces: Lessons from computer games. In *Proceedings of Conference on Human Factors in Computing Systems*. ACM Press. doi:10.1145/800049.801756

McDonald, M., Musson, R., & Smith, R. (2008). Using productivity games to prevent defects. In M. McDonald, R. Musson, & R. Smith (Eds.), *The practical guide to defect prevention*. Redmond, CA: Microsoft Press.

McGonigal, J. (2011). *Reality is broken: Why games make us better and how they can change the world*. London: Penguin.

McInnes, S. (2013). The social graph & sociographics. *Search Engine Journal, 23*. Retrieved April 2, 2014, from http://www.searchenginejournal.com/the-social-graph-sociographics-how-to-use-friends-to-influence-people/63055/

Meyer, M. (2009). Give more and get more out of social media. *Communication World, 26*(6), 48.

Millman, H. (1998). Online travel arrangements begin to catch on. *InfoWorld, 20*(9), 16–32.

Mings, R. C., & McHugh, K. E. (1992). The spatial configuration of travel to Yellowstone National Park. *Journal of Travel Research, 30*(4), 38–46. doi:10.1177/004728759203000406

Montola, M., Nummenmaa, T., Lucero, A., Boberg, M., & Korhonen, H. (2009). Applying game achievement systems to enhance user experience in a photo sharing service. In *Proceedings of the 13th International MindTrek Conference: Everyday Life in the Ubiquitous Era*. doi:10.1145/1621841.1621859

Morgan, N., Jones, G., & Hodges, A. (2010). *Social media: The complete guide to social media*. Retrieved April 10, 2014, from http://pl.scribd.com/doc/135022820/Complete-Guide-to-Social-Media

Muntinga, D., Moorman, M., & Smit, E. (2011). Introducing COBRAs exploring motivations for brand-related social media use. *International Journal of Advertising, 30*(1), 13–46. doi:10.2501/IJA-30-1-013-046

Norman, D. A. (2013). *The design of everyday things (Revised and expanded edition)*. New York: Basic Books.

O'Connor, P. (1999). *Electronic information distribution in tourism & hospitality*. Oxford, UK: CAB.

Okazaki, S. (2008). Exploring experiential value in online mobile gaming adoption. *CyberPsychology and Behaviour, 11*(5), 619–622. doi:10.1089/cpb.2007.0202 PMID:18785820

Olson, G. M., & Olson, J. S. (2003). Human-computer interaction: Psychological aspects of the human use of computing. *Annual Review of Psychology, 54*(1), 491–516. doi:10.1146/annurev.psych.54.101601.145044 PMID:12209025

Ong, B. S., Ho, F. N., & Tripp, C. (1997). Consumer perceptions of bonus packs: An exploratory analysis. *Journal of Consumer Marketing, 14*(2), 102–112. doi:10.1108/07363769710166747

Oppermann, M. (1995). A model of travel itineraries. *Journal of Travel Research, 33*(4), 57–61. doi:10.1177/004728759503300409

Palmer, A., & McCole, P. (2000). The role of electronic commerce in creating virtual tourism DMO. *International Journal of Contemporary Hospitality Management, 12*(3), 198–204. doi:10.1108/09596110010320760

Parent, M., Plangger, K., & Bal, A. (2011). The new WTP: Willingness to participate. *Business Horizons, 54*(3), 219–229. doi:10.1016/j.bushor.2011.01.003

Pollock, A. (1996). The role of electronic brochures in selling travel: Implications for businesses and destinations. *Australian Journal of Hospitality Management, 3*(1), 25–30.

Quinn, J. B. (1992). *Intelligent enterprise*. New York, NY: Free Press.

Rao, L. (2010). *Welcome to the magic: Gowalla lands location deal with Disney Parks*. Retrieved January 6, 2014, from http://techcrunch.com/2010/11/18/welcome-to-the-magicgowalla-lands-location-deal-with-disney-parks/

Rashid, A. M., Ling, K., Tassone, R. D., Resnick, P., Kraut, R., & Riedl, J. (2006). Motivating participation by displaying the value of contribution. In *Proceedings of CHI 2006*. ACM Press. doi:10.1145/1124772.1124915

Reeves, B., & Read, J. L. (2009). *Total engagement: Using games and virtual worlds to change the way people work and businesses compete*. Boston, MA: Harvard Business School Press.

Richins, M. L. (1983). Negative word-of-mouth by dissatisfied consumers: A pilot study. *Journal of Marketing, 47*(1), 68–78. doi:10.2307/3203428

Ritchie, J., & Crouch, G. (2003). *The competitive destination: A sustainable tourism perspective*. Wallingford, UK: CABI Publishing. doi:10.1079/9780851996646.0000

Ryan, R. M., Rigby, C. S., & Przybylski, A. (2006). The motivational pull of video games: A self-determination theory approach. *Motivation and Emotion, 30*(4), 344–360. doi:10.1007/s11031-006-9051-8

Salcu, A. V., & Acatrinei, C. (2013). Gamification applied in affiliate marketing: Case study of 2parale. *Management & Marketing Challenges for the Knowledge Society, 8*(4), 767–790.

Sernovitz, A. (2012). *Word of mouth marketing: How smart companies get people talking*. Austin, TX: Greenleaf Book Group Press.

Setten, M., Pokraev, S., & Koolwaaij, J. (2004). Context-aware recommendations in the mobile tourism application. In *Proceedings of 3rd International Conference Adaptive Hypermedia and Web-based Systems*. Springer. doi:10.1007/978-3-540-27780-4_27

Shin, D.-H., & Shin, Y.-J. (2011). Why do people play social network games? *Computers in Human Behavior, 27*(2), 852–861. doi:10.1016/j.chb.2010.11.010

Silverman, R. (2011). *Latest game theory: Mixing work and play*. Retrieved January 24, 2014, from http://online.wsj.com/article/SB10001424052970204294504576615371783795248.html

Suits, B. (2005). *The grasshopper: Games, life and utopia*. Broadview Press.

Sussmann, S., & Baker, M. (1996). Responding to the electronic marketplace: Lessons from DMS. *International Journal of Hospitality Management, 15*(2), 99–112. doi:10.1016/0278-4319(96)00013-8

Tang, Q., Gu, B., & Whinston, A. B. (2012). Content contribution for revenue sharing and reputation in social media: A dynamic structural model. *Journal of Management Information Systems, 29*(2), 41–75. doi:10.2753/MIS0742-1222290203

Terlutter, R., & Capella, M. L. (2013). The gamification of advertising: Analysis and research directions of in-game advertising: Advergames and advertising in social network games. *Journal of Advertising, 42*(2–3), 95–112. doi:10.1080/00913367.2013.774610

Toffler, A. (1970). *Future shock*. New York: Random House.

Tussyadiah, I. P. (2012). A concept of location-based social network marketing. *Journal of Travel & Tourism Marketing, 29*(3), 205–220. doi:10.1080/10548408.2012.666168

Tussyadiah, I. P., Park, S., & Fesenmaier, D. R. (2011). Assessing the effectiveness of consumer narratives for destination marketing. *Journal of Hospitality & Tourism Research (Washington, D.C.), 35*(1), 64–77. doi:10.1177/1096348010384594

Underwood, E. (1996). Electronic sky way. *Brandweek, 37*(32), 30.

Van Grove, J. (2010a). *How 5 brands are mastering the game of Foursquare*. Retrieved February 10, 2014, from http://mashable.com/2010/04/02/foursquare-brands/

Van Grove, J. (2010b). *Pennsylvania partners with Foursquare to inspire state tourism*. Retrieved December, 12, 2013, from http://mashable.com/2010/05/26/pennsylvaniafoursquare/

von Ahn, L., & Dabbish, L. (2008). Designing games with a purpose. *Communications of the ACM, 51*(8), 58–67. doi:10.1145/1378704.1378719

Werbach, K. (2012). *Gamification*. Retrieved November, 2013, from https://www.coursera.org/course/gamification

Williams, A. P., & Palmer, A. (1999). Tourism destination brands and electronic commerce: Towards synergy? *Journal of Vacation Marketing, 5*(3), 263–275. doi:10.1177/135676679900500306

Wilton, R. D., Páez, A., & Scott, D. M. (2011). Why do you care what other people think? A qualitative investigation of social contact and telecommuting. *Transportation Research Part A, Policy and Practice, 45*(4), 269–282. doi:10.1016/j.tra.2011.01.002

Wolff, C. (1997). Keeping a tighter rein on information. *Lodging Hospitality, 53*(2), 26–42.

Wright, E., Khanfar, N. M., Harrington, C., & Kizer, L. E. (2010, November). The lasting effects of social media trends in advertising. *Journal of Business and Economic Research, 8*(11), 73–80.

Wu, M. (2011). *The psychology of motivation*. Retrieved January 28, 2014, from https://community.lithium.com/t5/Science-of-Social-blog/Gamification-101-The-Psychology-of-Motivation/ba-p/21864

Zernigah, K. I., & Sohail, K. (2012). Consumer's attitude towards viral marketing in Pakistan. *Management & Marketing, 7*(4), 645–662.

Zhang, P. (2008). Motivational affordances: Reasons for ICT design and use. *Communications of the ACM, 51*(11), 145–147. doi:10.1145/1400214.1400244

ADDITIONAL READING

Anholt, S. (2007). *Competitive Identity – The new brand management for nations, cities and regions.* London: Palgrave MacMillan.

Baltrunas, L., Ludwig, B., Peer, S., & Ricci, F. (2012). Context relevance assessment and exploitation in mobile recommender systems. *Personal and Ubiquitous Computing, 15*(5), 507–526. doi:10.1007/s00779-011-0417-x

Chaffey, D., & Smith, P. (2012). *E-marketing excellence – planning and optimizing your digital marketing* (4th ed.). London: Routledge.

Constantinides E., & Fountain, S. J. (2008). Web 2.0: Conceptual foundations and marketing issues. *Journal of Direct, Data and Digital Marketing Practice*, (9), 231-244.

Destination brands – managing place reputation, 3rd edition, Oxford: Butterworth-Heinemann.

Egger, R. (2010). Web 2.0 in tourism, a look behind the scenes - theoretical concepts and approaches. *Journal of Information Technology & Tourism, 12*(2), 125–138. doi:10.3727/109830510X12887971002666

Fling, B. (2009). *Mobile design and development.* Sebastopol: O'Reilly.

Fotis, J., Buhalis, D., & Rossides, N. (2011). Social media impact on holiday travel: The case of the Russian and the FSU markets. *International Journal of Online Marketing, 1*(4), 1–19. doi:10.4018/ijom.2011100101

Garrett, J. J. (2011). *The elements of user experience – user-centered design for the web and beyond* (2nd ed.). New York: New Riders Publications.

Godin, S. (1999). *Permission marketing: turning strangers into friends and friends into customers.* New York: Simon & Schuster.

Goh, D. H., Lee, C. S., Ang, R. P., & Lee, C. K. (2010). Services for the mobile tourist. *Journal of Computer Information Systems, 5*(1), 31–40.

Govers, R., & Go, F. (2009). *Place branding.* London: Palgrave Macmillan. doi:10.1057/9780230247024

Kalbach, J. (2007). *Designing web navigation – optimizing the user-experience.* Sebastopol: O-Reilly Media.

Kaplan, A. (2012). If you love something, let it go mobile – mobile marketing and mobile social media 4x4. *Business Horizons, 55*(2), 129–139. doi:10.1016/j.bushor.2011.10.009

Keen, A. (2007). *The cult of the amateur: how today's internet is killing our culture and assaulting our economy.* London: Nicholas Brealey.

Kim, H., & Fesenmaier, D. R. (2008). The persuasive architecture of destination websites: The effect of first impressions. *Journal of Travel Research, 47*, 3–13. doi:10.1177/0047287507312405

Laudon, K. C., & Traver, C. G. (2008). *E-commerce, business, technology, society.* New Jersey: Pearson.

Li, C., & Bernoff, J. (2008). *Groundswell: winning in a world transformed by social technologies*. Boston, MA: Harvard Business Press.

Lieb, R. (2011). *Content marketing: think like a publisher -– how to use content to market online and in social media*. Indianapolis: Que Publishing.

Marketing, N. P. V. (2008). How do you measure engagement? Start by defining it in the right context. *Marketing NPV Journal*, 5(1), 3–7.

Osterwald, A., & Pigneur, Y. (2010). *Business model generation – a handbook for visionaries, game changers, and challengers*. Hoboken: John Wiley & Sons.

Pine, B. J., & Gilmore, J. H. (1999). *The experience economy: work is a theatre and every business a stage*. Boston: Harvard Business School Press.

Ricci, F., & Werthner, H. (2002). Case based reasoning for travel planning recommendation. *Information Technology and Tourism*, 4(3–4), 215–226.

Salen, K., & Zimmerman, E. (2004). *Rules of play: Game design fundamentals*. Cambridge, MA: MIT Press.

Schneider, G. P. (2011). *E-Business*. Independence, KY: Cengage.

M. Sigala, L. Mich, & J. Murphy (Eds.). (2007). *Information and communication technologies in tourism. Proceedings of the International Conference in* Ljubljana, Springer, Wien, 109–128.

Solis, B. (2011). *Engage, revised and updated – the complete guide for brands and businesses to build, cultivate, and measure success in the New Web*. Hoboken: Wiley.

Weinberg, T. (2009). *The new community rules – marketing on the social web*. Sebastopol: O'Reilly Media.

Werthner, H., & Klein, S. (1999). *Information technology and tourism - a challenging relationship*. New York: Springer. doi:10.1007/978-3-7091-6363-4

World Tourism Organisation. (2014). *Handbook on e-marketing for tourism destinations*. Madrid: UNWTO.

World Tourism Organization. (2001), eBusiness for tourism – practical guidelines for destinations and businesses, Madrid: UNWTO.

Zhou, Z. (2004). *E-commerce and information technology in hospitality and tourism*. Independence, KY: Delmar Learning.

Zichermann, G., & Cunningham, Ch. (2011). *Gamification by design. implementing game mechanics in web and mobile apps*. Sebastopol, CA: O'Reilly Media Inc.

KEY TERMS AND DEFINITIONS

COBRA: Consumers' online brand-related activities. A concept used as a behavioural construct that provides a unifying framework to think about consumer activity pertaining to brand-related content on social media platforms.

Crowdsourcing: The practice of obtaining ideas, services or content by soliciting contributions from a large group of people (especially from an online community); combining the efforts of numerous self-identified volunteers. Contamination of "crowd" and "outsourcing".

Gamification: The use of game thinking and game-design mechanics in non-game contexts to engage users creativity and activity.

Prosumer: A contamination formed by combining the terms "producer" and "consumer". In business and marketing environment the term describes a market segment between professional and consumer.

Social Media: A group of Internet-based applications that build on the ideological and technological foundations of Web 2.0 and depend on mobile and web-based technologies to create highly interactive platforms through which individuals and communities share, co-create, discuss, and modify user-generated content.

Social Media Marketing: The process of gaining website traffic or attention through social media sites. The resulting electronic word of mouth (eWoM) refers to any statement consumers share via the Internet (e.g., web sites, social networks, instant messages, news feeds) about an event, product, service, brand or company.

Tourism: A social, cultural and economic phenomenon which entails the movement of people to countries or places outside their usual environment for personal or business/professional purposes. These people are called visitors (which may be either tourists or excursionists; residents or non-residents) and tourism has to do with their activities, some of which imply tourism expenditure.

Tourism Sector: The cluster of production units in different industries that provide consumption goods and services demanded by visitors. Such industries are called tourism industries because visitor acquisition represents such a significant share of their supply that, in the absence of visitors, their production of these would cease to exist in meaningful quantity.

This research was previously published in the Handbook of Research on Effective Advertising Strategies in the Social Media Age edited by Nurdan Öncel Taşkıran and Recep Yılmaz, pages 17-51, copyright year 2015 by Business Science Reference (an imprint of IGI Global).

Chapter 64

Digital Resources and Approaches Adopted by User–Centred Museums:
The Growing Impact of the Internet and Social Media

Ludovico Solima
Second University of Naples, Italy

ABSTRACT

Society is experiencing unprecedented changes, largely attributable to the evolution of communication technologies, which are steadily reframing our way of life, and the methods we use to establish and maintain social relations. Museums are therefore facing numerous challenges, in general as a result of these developments: apps, open content, and the Internet-of-things. A complex relationship can be created between visitors and the museum, and this also opens new unexplored opportunities for user involvement in the museum's activities, even during the course of the visit itself. It is worth taking care to identify all the variables involved in the museum-visitor-relationship, which also encompasses the social dimension. Both the museum and the individual are active participants in a gradually expanding relationship, namely the growth of the so-called Web 2.0 and social media. Therefore, we can assume the need for museums to develop a conscious strategy for their social media presence, a real social media strategy, which forms part of the museum's wider digital strategy. The increasingly pervasive spread of e-mobile technology is a foretaste of the moment when museumgoers will radically change both the way of establishing relations with these organisations and the actual ways of using museum services. This chapter focuses on digital resources and approaches adopted by user-centred museums, where there is an increasing impact from the internet and social media.

1. INTRODUCTION

The model of the museum curator or educator who stands in front of an object and interprets meaning for a passive audience is simply no longer realistic in this world of instant access (New Media Consortium, 2012, p. 7).

DOI: 10.4018/978-1-5225-5637-4.ch064

Society today is undergoing unprecedented changes, largely attributable to the recent evolution of communication technologies, which are steadily reframing our way of life, the methods we use to establish and maintain social relations, as well as the way and manner in which we access the information we need everyday.

It is paradoxical in some ways that a careful observation of reality shows us that the only aspect which has remained unchanged is an endless sequence of breaks and profound alterations in our reference context, creating a constant flow of changes in which we are immersed, whether we know it or not, and of which we inevitably form part.

In today's situation – which, based on what has just been said, could be defined in oxymoronic terms, as "stably unstable" – it is particularly difficult to make out what the immediate future holds and what role might be played in that future world by museums and cultural institutions in general. However, this should not put us off making an attempt to identify at least the broad outlines to which we can refer, guidelines which – even if blurred and tentative, because they change over time and space – may help to orient the strategic choices made by such institutions.

Not only are the challenges to be faced numerous but they are also particularly insidious because it is so difficult to identify the boundaries of the "playing field," the rules to be used, let alone the players against whom we will play. But it is precisely this chronic nature of instability that makes it more imperative for museums to establish a plausible, if not certain framework, incorporating growing degrees of flexibility that allow them to react appropriately to changes.

As we will try to explain in the following paragraphs, from now on change must form part of the genetic make-up of museums at every level of their decision-making process (Kelly, 2010), replacing the dangerous, obstinate immobility that is often found there, as if the unchanging nature of their strategic and operative choices can still be a plausible, practicable option, even in a context as variable as the present.

2. WHAT CHALLENGES? WHAT FUTURE?

Museums therefore face multiple challenges, for the most part linked to the development of communication technologies, or more directly to the increasing important of the Internet. The following paragraphs will touch on a number of these challenges, prompted by the recent publication of a series of particularly interesting documents: the Report from the American Association of Museums (2012), the Horizon Report published by New Media Consortium (2012), and the latest edition of the analysis of the relationship between museums and mobile technologies (Tallon, 2013).

The first document is presented as "a summary of the most important drivers of change we have observed over the past years" (American Association of Museums, 2012, p. 3) and identifies a number of aspects that are deemed particularly important for the future of museums. To start with the report focuses on the potential contribution given by those willing to make their own time and knowledge available to museums, over and above the more general and traditional role played by volunteers. In this instance, however, Internet plays a key role because the sharing process – the so-called crowdsourcing – happens online and is therefore much more widespread, heterogeneous and far-reaching.

An individual's contribution can take any number of forms, which range from the provision of contents – in an amateur and/or professional format, using the *wiki* model – to the collection of tips and suggestions, even in the form of rating or tagging works, as will be explained later in this article. The implications of this changing relationship with museumgoers should be seen not only in terms of lower overheads but also as the creation of a community of users who are actively involved in the life of the museum (Sookhanaphibarn & Chatuporn, 2013).

The idea of broadening out the users of a museum to a digital audience can also be adapted to new forms of fundraising (the catchword in this instance is "crowdfunding"), also based on a wider understanding of the museum's relationship with its own public who are prompted to make financial donations – even modest ones – in order to carry out projects and specific activities. A case in point is the Museum of Science in Boston which actively raised funds through Facebook to rebuild its planetarium. However, even in this case, it is worth stressing that that emphasis was not only on the (alleged) primary goal of raising additional funds, but rather on the possibility of forming new relationships with new users and therefore widening the audience of those traditionally reached by the museum.

Another aspect touched on by the AAM Report concerns AR ("Augmented Reality") solutions, which include all those technologies able to enhance the visitor's experience by providing additional information (Kahr-Højland, 2010) whether in audio, video or graphic form, as well tactile technologies in the foreseeable future.[1] The superimposition on the real world of multiple layers of digital information can contribute significantly to improving the visitor's experience, allowing them to access not only a broader range of information but also empowering their ability to observe the real world, as happens, for example, when high-resolution images of works are displayed online which offer a close-up view of details that would not otherwise be visible during the normal course of a visit.

The Horizon Report published by New Media Consortium sets itself a different goal, which can be summarised as follows: to "examine emerging technologies for their potential impact on and use in education and interpretation within the museum environment" (New Media Consortium, 2012, p. 1). In particular, the document uses a more sophisticated approach compared to the one described above and, when outlining the future scenarios for museums, it differentiates between three different time horizons: short-term (with the next 12 months), which includes apps and social media; medium-term (2–3 years), which includes AR and the question of so-called "open content"; and lastly long-term (4–5 years), during which the so-called IoT – "Internet of things" – and natural-type user interfaces are expected to develop.

The term app (or application) has now entered common usage and refers to all those programmes, downloadable free or for a small fee, which can be installed on mobile devices (smartphone, tablet and the new generation of phablets) to provide functions or very specific series of functions that optimise the use of online information resources on smaller displays. A rapidly growing number of museums are providing their own apps, in order to facilitate interaction with their own visitors before, during and after the visit.

With reference to the observations made later in this article on the subject of social media, it might be useful at this stage to dwell briefly on a few other points raised by the Horizon Report. The first of these is linked to the problem of intellectual property rights and the solutions that can be implemented to maximise the circulation of (digital) information in the context of museums. New forms of legal protection – like Creative Commons licences[2] – have opened the way to the use and reuse of digital materials made available by museums or by communities of users focused around a museum, and this encourages a process of sharing and mutual enrichment.

In the longer term it is expected that two additional technologies will become widely established: the first, known as Internet of Things, is closely linked to the growing use of Rfid technology, which enables objects to be automatically identified through a two-way transmission of radio-frequency signals.[3] The new generation smartphones are increasingly adopting the Nfc standard, an even more advanced stage of Rfid technology, mainly with the aim of enabling these devices to make mobile payments simply by holding the device up to a specially adapted reader. In a museum setting this technology would open the way to further interesting uses, for example by making it much easier to access the additional information and content that was mentioned in the context of augmented reality technology: a visitor would only have to hold the mobile device up to the object to order to access this content using automatic identification, and he or she would then have access to whatever digital resources were available. One of the first museums in Italy to develop an experimental use of this type of technology was the Galleria Ambrosiana in Milan. It has developed a pilot project in collaboration with Samsung which will be used at Expo 2015 to allow visitors not only to improve their visit to the gallery but also, at the end of their visit, to purchase items in the gallery shop linked to the works they viewed using the device (Swedberg, 2012).

The second technology refers to natural user interfaces, including all those more innovative methods already available using a variety of devices: one need only consider how, over the course of a few years, we have progressed from the introduction of tactile devices (namely touch-screens) to the development of advanced voice-recognition software (Apple was the first with Siri, quickly followed by Google's Now, etc.) which can not only understand a question asked by the user using normal language, but can also respond with the desired information in voice format. Then, in March 2013, Samsung has developed cutting-edge user interaction functions for its latest model (the "Galaxy S4") which, for example, allow some commands – such as page scrolling – to be given simply using eye movements (Chen, 2013). Further suggestions are offered by the new web-access devices, such as Google Glass, which is due to be launched on the market in 2014, or Apple's so-called iWatch family, fitted with Internet access and touch screens.

Lastly, Tallon's work summarises the key results of a study on the relationship between museums and mobile technologies, thanks to the participation of over 550 museum operators from some thirty countries.

The first question the study posed concerns the reasons underlying the development of projects based on mobile technologies, and in first place it highlights the possibility of attaining the more general aim of involving visitors in the museum's activities, while also offering them a more dynamic and interactive experience. It also emphasises the need to make additional information available to broaden the visitor's interpretation process; this is followed by the desire to attract new visitors and to raise the museum's profile.

The analysis of the relationship between visitors' experience and technology highlights a growing trend to forgo more traditional services (typically the audioguides) in favour of more interactive solutions, in particular those linked to social networks. In this respect, the study in question highlights how current experiments tend to focus most on permanent collections rather than on temporary ones, probably in order to ensure that costs incurred to develop the systems can be amortised over a longer period. The same may be true of the trend for smaller museums to give preference to solutions aimed at optimising mobile access to their websites, thanks to "responsive" web design (RWD) techniques, rather than to developing specific apps for mobile devices (Cooper, 2012; CHIN's TechWatch, 2012).

It is also interesting to note that in most of the cases studied, museums made these new technological solutions available free, despite the fact that high implementation costs are identified as one of the greatest obstacles to their diffusion, together with a lack of personnel.

Finding the necessary financial resources to carry out these trials – both in terms of their design and their realisation – is highlighted as one of the greatest hurdles to overcome, as is the consequent need to update the contents. Another aspect that is far from negligible is the need to ensure that visitors actually use the mobile technologies and this requires specific marketing activities.

In all, the picture that emerges from an analysis of these documents – which look at the general topic of the relationship between museums and technology from different angles – is particularly complex. On the one hand, museums (at least, those that are sensitive to and show a propensity for these trends) wish to explore new technological solutions designed to improve the visitor's experience and to identify those methods that are most compatible with their own organisational and financial resources; while on the other the presence of multiple changes and advances means that these institutions can no longer postpone the need to make strategic, careful and farsighted choices.

3. WHAT VISITORS FOR WHICH MUSEUMS?

All of this has numerous implications for the world of museums. The first point to make relates to the nature of the audience for the museum's activities given that this has gradually evolved over time. The advent of the modern museum is generally traced back to the desire to implement a more democratic access to culture, making it available across the full spectrum of society by creating places – in other words, museums – that could fulfil this aim. For years (and in some cases, still today) these organisations were conceived and run essentially as elitist institutions, reserved to a relatively narrow group of people, namely those who were sufficiently educated and culturally aware to understand and appreciate the information and materials provided by museums (Solima, 2000).

Therefore, many museums completely ignored the fact that their visiting public might instead have been made up of widely different sorts of people, from diverse cultural backgrounds, and they provided a generic form of communication, as if it were indeed possible to identify contents and languages that would suit all visitors without distinction. This short-sighted approach often resulted in a very negative outcome: owing to a sense of unease and intellectual confusion caused by the difficulty of understanding the information made available by museums, many people were put off visiting and preferred to take advantage of the growing number of alternative leisure activities (Solima, 2008).

Even in the case of those museums that were persuaded to take a different approach and fostered a more careful adaptation of contents and languages for individual categories of visitors, the arrival of the Internet has led to the emergence of a very different problem linked to the awareness that the museum-going public, or more correctly, museum-going *publics* now include a new category of users: those online.

While the relationship between a museum and its visitors in the past was created and formed exclusively thanks to the physical presence of visitors inside the museum – those people who were willing, therefore, to incur the costs of the visit, including the costs of getting to and from the museum venue – the spread of Internet has now led to the growth of a completely different group of users, the museum's online users, who stand out for their desire to establish a new sort of relationship with these institutions, based on the remote access of resources and knowledge made available by museums online, and their tendency to share information with other individuals with similar interests.

This means that museums must turn themselves from "acropolises" into "agoras" (from temples into marketplaces; Proctor, 2011a), not only prompting dialogue *with* the various categories of user with whom they come into contact, but also being aware of the various conversations taking place *among* those users who wish to share experiences and personal knowledge.

Museums are therefore addressing an exponentially growing audience, one that includes increasing segments of the community willing to establish a different sort of relationship with these institutions and with other museumgoers/users, overcoming the spatial and temporal barriers linked to physical access[4] (Heritage Lottery Fund, 2011; MTM London, 2010).

Therefore, although it has been possible, until now, to draw a neat line between visitors and non-visitors – and the former were most often included in studies, while the latter represented a completely unknown universe, also because they were difficult to identify (Solima, 2008) – this distinction too seems increasingly less relevant, given that a non-visitor might be an online user of the museum and, moreover, an online user might well be persuaded to become a real visitor.

Indeed, having overcome the initial fear that the presence of museums online might lead to a sort of cannibalisation of real visits, the realisation soon spread that online visitors could actually promote actual *on-site* visitor numbers. This also started to happen once the initial stage of a very simplified online presence had passed. In many cases this took the form of merely transposing traditional type information into digital format, with limited results in terms of communications efficacy.

The growing use of data bases containing digital collections in the creation of museum websites then led to a major improvement in the search functions available to Internet users, especially when they were also offered the opportunity to set up personal accounts to access and store (in sections titled *my museum*, *my gallery*, etc.) those digital resources of particular interest, also with a view to a future visit to the museum. All this led to the creation of online "field trip planning" services capable of automatically generating a map of the museum showing the most appropriate "physical" itinerary through the rooms to view the various works selected online.

But, even this distinction – real visitor versus online visitor – which seems to some extent anchored to the idea of access to a fixed workstation (whether a computer at home or in the office), is destined to be lost in the near future owing to the growing spread of Internet and its increasingly frequent use of mobile devices which allow the visitor to get online using his or her own mobile device, even inside the museum itself.

In this case, direct on-site use will be contextually associated with online use – in the context of what was said earlier regarding the various solutions of augmented reality, accessible simply through Nfc or via the increasingly widespread QR Codes[5] – even leading to an inversion in access times to digital resources: not just before the visit to improve the visit experience, but also after it in order to access additional information on works selected during the visit.

Compared to the actual moment of the visit, access to online resources by a museumgoer can happen at three individual stages, which enormously increase the importance of the museum's communication process:

- **At Any Time Prior to the Visit:** To guide the choice of museum, decide how much time to spend there and choose what itinerary to follow and the works to focus on.
- **During the Visit:** To access any additional information on the works on show in the museum, and to integrate traditional materials, typically of the printed type.
- **At Any Time After the Visit:** To discover more about the works viewed during the visit.

This means that an incredibly rich and complex relationship can be built up between the visitor and the museum using the new online media. It also multiplies the potential access points to the museum's information resources and opens new (and until now unexplored) ways of enabling users to become involved and take part in museum activities, also during the visit itself. One particularly interesting example in this sense is the *I went to Moma and...* project launched by the American museum in 2009 and later reinstated in a more sophisticated version in December 2011. Moma provided small slips of paper on which each visitor could write (or draw) what had most struck them during the visit and share their message using a scanner, which automatically projected an enlarged version of the image onto a wall at the museum entrance, in a sequence of all those made by other visitors. At the same time, the image was also uploaded to a special section of the museum's website where it could be easily found and shared by the user through his or her own social networks.[6] The extraordinary success of the initiative – with over 30,000 cards submitted by visitors – allowed the museum to run a promotional campaign in the daily press and in magazines, as well as on billboards, focused on the most striking cards selected by the museum staff.

Therefore, once again, it is important to identify all the variables that come into play in the relationship between a museum and its visitors, and these include another significant aspect: the social dimension. Both the museum and individuals are at the heart of an ever-expanding web of relations, also as a result of the latest evolution of the Web, namely the advent and spread of the so-called "Web 2.0" and social media (Pett, 2012; Charitonos, 2011; Bonacini, 2010; Proctor, 2010).

4. INTERNET AND SOCIAL MEDIA

The use of the term *Web 2.0* has become increasingly commonplace over the past years and refers to a new way of understanding the use of Internet. The term has been influenced by the language of informatics and now explicitly refers to the custom of numbering the versions of a particular programme, using a progressive and incremental numbering that moves to a higher ordinal when the newly released software contains significantly different features compared to the earlier version, therefore justifying the need for a different numeral.

The term "2.0" therefore marks a paradigmatic shift and one that is also semantic, a transition to a new way of understanding the operating logic of a website.

Indeed, those websites which are described using this term present marked differences compared to the "traditional" ways of being present online. Among these differences, first and foremost, is the central role played by users and by so-called User-Generated Contents (UGC) (Russo & Watkins, 2008; Russo et al., 2007).

Thanks to the use of huge servers, these new forms of website are specially designed to allow users to upload a variety of contents (in the form of text, audio, video, etc.), thus responding to a need for social networking that has been present among Internet users for many years but which, for various reasons, could not be implemented earlier in practical terms (Solima, 2010).

Within a very short time and with increasing frequency, Internet users have shown a marked inclination to share their experiences in "digital format," also thanks to the simplified methods of uploading content, ranging from photos to films, comments and reviews, which can be viewed and read by an expanding number of users, including people they have never met but with whom they share common interests. This propensity to share personal experiences and interests online tends to lead to a gradual intensification of interpersonal relations, resulting in the creation of real communities of users, who frequent the digital fora where they can be present, meet and dialogue with other individuals (Russo et al., 2008; Russo et al., 2006).

The corollary of this changed form of user involvement, which until now was seen as a group of passive recipients of information flowing through the Web, is a radical change in the actual communication process that takes place online: up to now this process could typically be described as "one-to-many," with a clearly identified sender (the website editor) and an audience of varying size, the new Web paradigm falls into the category of "many-to-many," in which an individual's response – say, a comment on a blog post – can spark off a new (and different) discussion and form the starting point for further online debate. Rather like a play of mirrors and multiple refractions, it becomes nearly impossible to draw any clear distinction between sender and recipient, and the production of new contents is constantly fed by a flow of reciprocal references among Internet users.

In this new scenario the so-called social media[7] have enjoyed unprecedented growth within the space of a few years, through innovative websites focusing on the creation, sharing and exchange of user-generated contents and ideas (Gu, 2012; Cui & Yokoi, 2011). The original formats of these websites tended to be very specialised: some concentrated on interpersonal relations (Facebook), others on sharing videos (YouTube), music (MySpace) or photos (Flickr), while yet others enabled a socialisation of knowledge (Wikipedia) or personal experiences, whether for travel (TripAdvisor) or services (Yelp). However, the specialised focus of these social media websites has gradually faded, both because of the changing requirements of social media users in search of more integrated forms of communication and sharing, and because of the arrival of new competitors (Twitter, Google+, Pinterest, Tumblr, etc.) able to combine the multiple functions demanded by users. All this has led to a gradual contamination of the first comers, which as a result have modified their own operating methods and have gradually expanded the range of functions offered.[8]

The reasons for the extraordinary success of social media websites can be attributed not only to their capacity, as explained earlier, to respond to the demand for interaction expressed by Internet users but also to the ongoing changes to methods of accessing digital resources, characterised above all by an increasingly mobile use: users now tend to be *always online*, thanks to the new generation of devices designed to allow users to access and use online content as easily and immediately as possible. As Anderson and Wolff suggested in an article published in *Wired* (September 2010), these changes anticipate the death of the Web in the sense that the website appears condemned to become a residual method of reaching online contents and instead this will become ever more frequently reached through "apps."

In parallel to this, the proliferation of apps – as mentioned earlier – will not only drive the optimisation of ways to use online content, but also new and more effective ways of sharing multimedia contents produced by the users themselves: one need only think of the recent success of Instagram, whose main strength lies in the possibility of sharing a snapshot taken using a mobile device instantly and online.[9]

The next step takes the form of adding the user's geolocation via the mobile device (thanks to the GPS sensors now present even in the cheapest mobile phones) and this has opened the way to the spread of "proximity" services – for example, promotional offers in a store near to the user (e.g. through Groupon or "Google Offers"), or even indicating that a friend might happen to be in the vicinity (via Banjo or "Facebook Friend Finder") – as well as social media like FourSquare or Gowalla based on the user's "check-ins" in a given area and on the benefits of building up points. Brooklyn Museum, for example, uses this formula to offer annual subscriptions and invitations to exclusive events as prizes, while the Ferrari Museum in Maranello offers a discount of 2 euros on the price of admission to anyone who checks-in using FourSquare.

In the future, this development will offer the possibility of identifying a particular object, automatically and without error, thanks to Rfid/Nfc technology, as briefly mentioned earlier. This will simplify both micropayments and also the interchange of information between the museum and its visitors. However, when combined with other Wi-Fi technology, it will also offer visitors the possibility of using their own mobile devices to guide them through the museum spaces, thanks to the spread of indoor navigation solutions (Ijaz & Lee, 2013; Wecker et al., 2013; Möller et al., 2012).

5. THE MUSEUM AS KNOWLEDGE SYSTEM

For museums, the importance of these ongoing changes in terms of digital communications can be attributed, in the first instance, to the role universally played by these institutions, namely that of contributing to the cultural growth of communities.

Here we will refer to a precise interpretation of the museum as institution, using a definition that predominantly sees the museum as a "cognitive system" essentially based on the use of knowledge. Indeed, the cultural activities of the museum can be defined as fulfilling three different functions, all of which are linked to knowledge and interrelated using a non-sequential logic: the conservation, creation and spread of knowledge.

To start with the *conservation of knowledge*, it is worth noting in the first place that each work contains multiple "references," whether artistic, social, historical or cultural: the artist and school; the technique of execution; the person, object or situation represented; the patron, if present; the period during which it was made; the message that the artist intends to convey. In general, the information-related aspects of a particular artefact or work of art can be separated into at least four different levels: the *specific details* of the artist, the title of the work, the date of realisation, etc.; information concerning the *history of the object*, namely the various owners, the different places in which it has been kept, etc.; *iconographical information* relating to the analysis of figurative or symbolic contents; and lastly, *technical information* regarding the style of the work or the methodologies used.

Custodianship of the works therefore guarantees the preservation over time of a rich and stratified wealth of information, which can contribute to the cognitive resources of a museum. This wealth of information can be managed in a structured form (inventories, catalogues, individual files, etc.) and be archived using various forms of support (paper and/or digital), or indeed managed in a de-structured form in those cases where the information is preserved in the individual knowledge systems of particular members of the museum's staff.

The *knowledge creation* function is best understood through the realisation that the pool of information on each work, preserved over time using the conservation function, can be constantly enriched through interpretative activities, namely through study activities and research undertaken by museum staff and, above all, by the scientific community with which the museum interacts. In this sense, one might say that an artwork represents the input of a transformation process during which it is analysed and compared with other works and other knowledge; this process generates an output in terms of knowledge, which throws light on the potential information contained in each work.[10]

Lastly, with regard to the *spread of knowledge*, it should be remembered that museums, as institutions that primarily serve the public, play an important educational role by making available to the scientific community and to the community the wealth of knowledge built up over time.

It is quite clear, therefore, that the transmission of knowledge raises the question of how to select the means of communication. Generally speaking, museums have access to three main categories of media: the "natural" channels, as represented by those museum staff who are in contact with visitors (personnel working at the information desk, room guides, etc.); textual media, in the form of information provided as aids to visitors (labels, panels, etc.); and lastly, the digital media mentioned earlier.

Each museum must therefore find the right combination of media to satisfy its own requirements for the spread of knowledge, within an overall picture of financial compatibility linked to the funds available. It is worth noting, however, that this choice is not only a function of the alternative techniques and technologies available to the museum, but it must also take account – both in the selection of contents and in the choice of media – of the different audiences to whom this spread of knowledge is addressed. As has been stated on numerous occasions, the museum must cater for multiple publics, and it needs to approach each in the appropriate manner.

But the theme of museum demand, based on the observations made in the previous paragraphs, also comes into play if it is analysed from a different viewpoint, namely one that does not associate the user solely with the role of passive recipient of a one-way flow of information but, as is explained more fully in the following paragraph, promotes him or her to the role of co-protagonist in the process of content creation and the circulation of the museum's knowledge.

Thanks to Internet and to the devices that allow mobile Internet access, the museum user can now be involved in a multitude of activities that not only fulfil his or her desire for (greater) involvement and interaction during the visit, but also that of sharing personal knowledge and experience via social networks and contacting other individuals with the same interests.

Therefore, far from being solely a threat to the life of the museum, technology represents a real opportunity to improve the overall quality of the visitor's experience and encourages the creation of a community of users who are actively involved in museum life and who find a space, both real and digital, within the museum in which to develop relations and shared activities.

6. MUSEUMS, SOCIAL MEDIA AND DIGITAL STRATEGY

On the subject of content creation, the first contribution that a user can make to the museum's knowledge system is relatively simple and takes the form of so-called "tagging," namely attaching (digital) tags to an object forming part of the museum's digital collections (Ellis et al., 2012). For example, when looking at an image of Titian's painting *Sacred and Profane Love* some users might decide to highlight the presence of two women, one of whom is partially clothed, rather than a cupid, others might tag the presence of the sarcophagus, the spring, the heated brazier held by one of the women, the bucolic landscape behind them or the castle in the background, and so on.

The tag represents a sort of "meta-datum" which can hugely improve access to the contents of the museum, in that the gradual stratification of these user tags is made available to users of the museum's digital resources as keywords (or tag clouds) and this simplifies access to information and can generate numerous paths for exploring the museum's digital (and real) collections (Smith-Yoshimura & Shein, 2011).

It is quite clear that tagging is not only a time-consuming activity and one that would be difficult for museum staff to carry out owing to objective time limitations, but also it is precisely the variety of opinions – typical of a platform like Internet, which is much broader and more varied compared to the museum staff – that ensures the effective outcome of this operation. One emblematic example of this is "The Commons" Project, which was launched in 2008 by Flickr together with the US Library of Congress and targeted at cultural institutions interested in sharing their own photographic collections.

The aim was not only to improve accessibility but also, and above all, to prompt visitors to the website to add comments and tags. Within a few months of the launch of the project, users had viewed over 10 million images, and had left over 7,000 comments and over 67,000 tags (Freixa-Font, 2011; Prieur et al., 2008; Springer et al., 2008).

Forms of collaborative learning can also be achieved using a more structured approach, by offering museum users the possibility of helping to edit some Wikipedia entries on works or artists represented in the museum, for example, or of joining discussion groups (on Flickr, YouTube or Google). This also has the advantage of encouraging the formation and development of user communities, and as a result adding to the web of relations with the museum.[11]

Another possibility consists of the involvement of online users in the development of activities that the museum plans to carry out (Simon, 2010; Jensen & Kelly, 2009). Generally speaking, jointly planned initiatives not only offer the museum the possibility of identifying themes and/or viewpoints that really interest the potential participants, but also of stimulating a different – and more direct – involvement of users in the life of the museum, with evident positive repercussions in terms of "commitment" (namely, a sense of belonging) and therefore loyalty. From this point of view, social media can represent the means whereby users can be contacted directly, if the museum has no email database to which it can resort.[12]

With regard to the circulation of contents, the "like" and "share" buttons allow users to publicise their interests and preferences to their own networks within the various forms of social media to which they belong (Bocatius, 2012; Kelly, 2008). As in the case of tags, the fact of offering museumgoers the possibility of expressing and publicising their own system of preferences also has the advantage of offering other users highly original pathways with which to explore the museum, as well as fulfilling the need for individual sharing. During the visit to the museum itself, the user can receive suggestions of works or objects to view, in the same way as happens on the more advanced commercial websites (Amazon, for example, for products, or Pandora for music). For several years now, these websites have drawn the user's attention, while surfing, to products purchased by others, or they make recommendations based on preferences shown by the user's own surfing history, which has been analysed using specialised algorithms. These suggestions can therefore prompt the museumgoer to develop his or her own and completely personal way of visiting, which in turn can then be shared with other people and evaluated by them.[13]

The great advantage of a digital communications system compared to more traditional forms lies precisely in the fact that a user is able to express his or her own individuality by personalising the visit and relations with the museum in general (Birkner, 2012).

Social media can therefore be used for broader ends compared to those linked directly to content creation and the circulation of knowledge. These may include, for example, finding human resources with specific skills needed to undertake museum activities (through professional networks, such as Linkedin) or carrying out fund-raising activities to support specific projects, like that recently implemented by the Louvre through the creation of dedicated website (tousmecenes.com).

The contribution of social media can be equally important in promotional terms, offering the museum a different (or alternative) presence online, one that will increase not only its visibility but also awareness of its activities. From this point of view, a service like that offered by Twitter has the advantage of allowing quick updates to announce the start of specific activities – for example, the start of a conference – that might interest both the platform of potential visitors in the vicinity of the museum and those who are already inside its rooms.

The promotional aspect is of course particularly important for a museum which, above all in the case of smaller institutions (Pisu, 2012), often encounters the problem of "primary visibility": it is clear that, from the visitor's point of view, a museum can offer a different view of using free time depending on two things: the extent to which the museum is well known and, possibly, also the renown of its cultural contents. In this respect, social media have the advantage of being much easier to manage, even by the museum's own staff, given that, unlike a website, no specific knowledge of graphics or software is required to create an online presence for the museum.

More generally, one aspect that should not be underestimated is the need for museums to develop a coherent strategy for their presence on social media, namely a proper social media strategy (Martínez-Sanz, 2012; Falkow, 2011; see, for example, Smithsonian Institution, 2011), which will be used to define the levels of sharing their own knowledge systems with different audiences, to stimulate the creation of communities and make the most of user involvement through the joint planning of museum activities.

These choices are just part of the museum's wider *digital strategy*, which in addition to its social media presence must also take into consideration and build up a number of activities, evaluating their organisational implications and financial sustainability. Among these, it is worth mentioning: the use of the institutional website and the creation of apps, the digitalisation of the archives and collections, the creation of multimedia contents, the development of social-tagging solutions, indoor navigation and onsite access to digital contents (using Augmented Reality, Rfid/Nfc, QRcode, etc), the use of podcasts and digital publishing, the activation of open-content licences, the realisation of e-learning projects and gaming, the implementation of e-commerce services and the activation of geolocation information services.

It is important to note, with specific reference to social media, that their functions are evolving over time and new players are appearing on the market and undermining the market share and competitive edge of consolidated sites. One need only think of SecondLife and MySpace, both of which enjoyed extraordinary success to start with, but their competitive space was then progressively invaded by their main rivals or by rival new entrants.

Therefore, given that social media evolve – as is quite natural in a highly and intrinsically dynamic context like the Internet – the museum, like any other institution or company, must be able to identify those sites on which to maintain a presence, as well as when to reduce that presence (and eventually even abandon certain platforms).

In this respect, the underlying principle is to minimise the investment incurred for content creation, broadly speaking based on the (sensible) principle of "Write One, Reuse Often": for example, it is possible to identify ways of making combined use of some types of digital resources on different platforms, thus allowing significant economies of scale that can reduce the relative production costs.

In terms of choosing which social media to use, it should be said that, until a few years ago, this decision was relatively simple owing to the initial specialisation of the individual sites: therefore Facebook would be used for institutional-type communications, alongside the main website; Flickr would be used for images; YouTube for videos and Twitter for micro-blogging, etc. This decision is now much more complex, precisely due to the constant changes to the functions offered by each of these social media, as described earlier.

Therefore, it is important to allow for appropriate monitoring activities, initially for the purposes of internal assessments (Waardenburg & Hekmon, 2012). Thanks to a series of websites and applications that facilitate these activities – such as Facebook Insight, Museum Analytics, SocialMention or Net-Vibes, for example – targets to be attained can be identified and the appropriate operating conditions put in place to ensure that social media function smoothly, for example in terms of updating frequency[14] (Finnis et al., 2011a, 2011b).

On the specific question of targets, these can be set either in absolute terms (namely identifying the reference parameters for each social media website, as shown in Table 1) or in relative terms, by identifying reference benchmarks against which the museum's position can be defined.

In this last instance, useful information is provided by the website Museum Analytic[15] which offers a detailed breakdown, separate for each museum, of activities on Facebook (namely the numbers of "likes," "posts" and "comments") and Twitter (number of followers, new followers, tweets and mentions).

Lastly, it is important to take account of the need to back up the strategic decision-making process with detailed information on the demand (Smith, 2009). While overall studies – like those presented in the introduction to this article – offer the advantage of providing a general picture for reference purposes and outlining the ongoing trends at a global level, it is nonetheless true that a museum must always be able to justify its own choices with regard to its own reference audiences. Studies of museumgoers should therefore be carried out not only in terms of the museum's own visitors (and non visitors), but also – and, looking ahead, to an increasing degree – with reference to digital users whose profiles and models of behaviour are sometimes very different to those visitors who actually visit the museum.[16]

This outcome can be achieved only by dedicating part of the available resources to the *in situ* collection of information about museum visitors and digital users, if necessary enquiring about specific aspects regarding particular topics or particular segments of demand.

The pitfall of "strategic short-sightedness" awaits not only those who fail to draw up a social media strategy but also those who formulate it incorrectly, based on obsolete data and incomplete or wrongly interpreted information.

Table 1. Measuring social media engagement and metrics

Platform	Attachment or Affiliation	Engagement & Metrics
Facebook	Fans	click rate to link volume of comments shares likes traffic to site post views
Twitter	Followers	retweets direct replies mentions traffic to site
Flickr	Contacts	comments gallery additions views traffic to site
YouTube	Subscribers	views embeds shares comments traffic to site

Adapted from "Uses of social media within British Museum and museum sector," by D.E.J. Pett, 2012

CONCLUSION

Museums exist and are constantly interacting with a dynamic and unpredictable world. One of the drivers of this change is technological progress and, particularly in the case of museums, those technologies which are available to back up the creation and valorisation processes for knowledge and collections.

Against this background, Internet and, more especially, social media play a particularly important role both for their extraordinary success on a global scale and for the specific opportunities they offer to museums, as this article has tried to outline.

On the other hand, the increasingly wide and pervasive spread of mobile technologies point to a situation in which museumgoers will radically change both the way in which they relate to these organisations and the actual ways in which they visit them and take part in activities (Wallace et al., 2012; Smith, 2009; Stogner, 2009). As the price of mobile devices falls and free Wi-Fi inside museums continues to spread, visitor activities are likely to be increasingly based on the BYOD ("Bring Your Own Device") model, which will help to abolish for good the boundary between "physical" and virtual visits, and between the online and onsite dimension in terms of access to the museum's real and digital resources (Proctor, 2011b). This will enable visitors to share what they are viewing and enjoying in real time via social media, further extending the process of socialisation and the production of user content.

This process is destined to raise radical and irreversible questions about the role of museums in today's knowledge society and, as a result, about how museums should establish stable relations with an increasingly attentive and dynamic reference audience interested in building dialogues with such institutions and seeking growing levels of interaction and participation.

The abolition of temporal and spatial boundaries brought about by the advent of the digital era applies – and will apply – not only to individuals but also, and above all, to institutions like museums, which have historically made a significant and authoritative contribution to the creation and circulation of learning and knowledge. Precisely with these aspects in mind, museums will have to become increasingly open to the potential input of their own users, developing both an ability to listen that enables them to respond promptly and appropriately to requests from the communities that form their audience and on whom their legitimacy ultimately depends.

It is a challenge that is far from banal, and one that no museum will be able to avoid by resorting – as still happens all too often – to the same old ways of behaving and remaining pretentiously unaware of the changes in progress.

Moreover, it is a challenge that, for those who have not already understood it, calls for a radical change of approach. One that places, above all, at the heart of the museum's activities and as the real target of its activities, the individual and the public as a whole whom the museum serves.

REFERENCES

American Association of Museums. (2012). *TrendsWatch 2012: Museums and the pulse of the future.* Retrieved from http://www.aam-us.org/docs/center-for-the-future-of-museums/2012_trends_watch_final.pdf

Anderson, C., & Wolff, M. (2010). *The Web is dead. Long live the Internet.* Retrieved from http://www.wired.com/magazine/2010/08/ff_webrip/

Beasley, S., & Conway, A. (2012). Digital media in everyday life: A snapshot of devices, behaviours, and attitudes part 1: Mobile device ownership. In *Proceedings of Museums and the Web 2012: The International Conference for Culture and Heritage On-Line*. San Diego, CA: Museums and the Web LLC. Retrieved from http://www.museumsandtheweb.com/mw2012/papers/digital_media_in_every-day_life_a_snapshot_of_d.html

Birkner, C. (2012, September 30). Pointillism in pixels. *Marketing News, 46*(12), 16–23.

Bocatius, B. (2012). *State-of-the-art: German museums on the Social Web. Benefits and effects of social media for museum education and learning.* Paper presented at Museums and the Web 2012: The International Conference for Culture and Heritage On-Line, San Diego, CA. Retrieved from http://www.museumsandtheweb.com/mw2012/papers/digital_media_in_everyday_life_a_snapshot_of_d.html

Bonacini, E. (2010). I musei e le nuove frontiere dei social networks: da Facebook a Foursquare e Gowalla. Retrieved from http://www.fizz.it/home/articoli/2010/302-i-musei-e-le-nuove-frontiere-dei-social-networks-da-facebook-foursquare-e-gowalla

Charitonos, K. (2011). Museum learning via social media: (How) can interactions on Twitter enhance the museum learning experience? In *Proceedings of the Learning, Media and Technology Doctoral Conference* (pp. 1-22). London, UK: Open Research Online.

Chen, B. H. (2013, March 4). *Samsung's new smartphone will track eyes to scroll pages.* Retrieved from http://bits.blogs.nytimes.com

CHIN's TechWatch. (2013). *Search news.* Retrieved from http://www.rcip-chin.gc.ca/sgc-cms/nouvelles-news/anglais-english/?p=4963

Cooper, A. (2013). ARTINFO Reviews 10 Major Museum iPad Apps That You Can Download. Retrieved from http:// www.blouinartinfo.com/print/node/816176

Cui, B., & Yokoi, S. (2011). Enrich knowledge in online museum via social media. In *Proceedings of the Triple Helix IX International Conference* (pp. 1-14). Stanford, CA: Leydesdorff.net.

Ellis, A., Gluckman, D., Cooper, A., & Greg, A. (2012). *Your paintings: A nation's oil paintings go onliine, tagged by the public.* Paper presented at Museums and the Web 2012: The International Conference for Culture and Heritage On-Line, San Diego, CA. Retrieved from http://www.museumsandtheweb.com/mw2012/papers/your_paintings_a_nation_s_oil_paintings_go_onl.html

Falkow, S. (2011). Social Media Strategy. [White paper]. Retrieved from http://falkowinc.com/wp-content/uploads/2010/06/Social-Media-Strategy-Module-Whitepaper.pdf

Finnis, J., Chan, S., & Clements, R. (2011a). *How to evaluate online success? A new piece of action research.* Paper presented at Museums and the Web 2011: The International Conference for Culture and Heritage On-Line, Philadelphia, PA.

Finnis, J., Chan, S., & Clements, R. (2011b). *Let's get real. How to evaluate online success?* New York, NY. *Culture (Canadian Ethnology Society), 24.*

Freixa-Font, P. (2011). Patrimonio fotográfico y web 2.0: La experiencia Flickr The Commons. *El profesional de la información, 20*(4), 1-16.

Gu, M. (2012). Engaging Museum Visitors through Social Media: Multiple Case Studies of Social Media Implementation in Museums. Unpublished thesis dissertation, Graduate Program in Arts Policy and Administration, The Ohio State University.

Heritage Lottery Fund. (2011). *Digital Participation and Learning. 22 Case Studies.* Imagemakers.

Ijaz, F., Yang, H. K., Ahmad, A. W., & Lee, C. (2013). Indoor positioning: A review of indoor ultrasonic positioning systems. In *The 15th International Conference on Advanced Communication Technology, Technical Proceedings, 2013*, 1146-1150.

Jensen, B., & Kelly, L. (2009). Exploring social media for front-end evaluation. *Exhibionist*, 5(3), 19–25.

Kahr-Højland, A. (2010). EGO-TRAP: A mobile augmented reality tool for science learning in a semi-formal setting. *Curator*, 53(4), 501–509. doi:10.1111/j.2151-6952.2010.00050.x

Kelly, L. (2008, February). Museum 3.0: Informal Learning and Social Media. Paper presented at the Social Media and Cultural Communication Conference, Sidney, Australia.

Kelly, L. (2010). How Web 2.0 is changing the nature of museum work. *Curator*, 53(4), 405–410. doi:10.1111/j.2151-6952.2010.00042.x

Li, C., Bernoff, J., Fiorentino, R., & Glass, S. (2007). Social Technographics® Mapping Participation In Activities Forms The Foundation Of A Social Strategy. Retrieved from http://www.forrester.com/ Social+Technographics/fulltext/-/E-RES42057?docid=42057

MTM London (2010, November). Digital audiences: Engagement with arts and culture online. Arts Council England.

Martínez-Sanz, R. (2012). Estrategia comunicativa digital en el museo. *El profesional de la información,* 21(4), 391-395.

Ministero dei beni e delle attivita culturali e del turismo. (n. d.). *Website.* Retrieved from http://be-niculturali.it/mibac/export/MiBAC/sito-MiBAC/Contenuti/MibacUnif/Comunicati/ visualizza_asset. html_648658054.html

Möller, A., Kranz, M., Huitl, R., Diewald, S., & Roalter, L. (2012). A mobile indoor navigation system interface adapted to vision-based localization. In *Proceedings of the 11th International Conference on Mobile and Ubiquitous Multimedia* (MUM'12). New York: ACM.

New Media Consortium. (2012). Horizon Report – 2012 Museum Edition. Retrieved from http://www. nmc.org/pdf/2012-horizon-report-museum.pdf

Pett, D. E. J. (2012). Uses of social media within British Museum and museum sector. In C. Bonacchi (Ed.), *Archaeology and digital communication: Towards strategies of public engagement.* London: Archetype.

Pissard, N., & Prieur, C. (2007). Thematic vs. social networks in web 2.0 communities: A case study on Flickr groups. Paper presentad at Algotel Conference, 2007.

Pisu, C. (2012). I musei italiani nei social networks: relazione preliminare sui risultati dell'indagine promossa dall'Associazione Nazionale Piccoli Musei. Retrieved from http://piccolimusei.com/uploads/ relazione-caterina-pisu-2012.pdf

Prieur, C., Cardon, D., Beuscart, J.-S., Pissard, N., & Pons, P. (2008). The Strength of Weak cooperation: A Case Study on Flickr. Retrieved from http:// http://arxiv.org/ftp/arxiv/papers/0802/0802.2317.pdf

Proctor, N. (2010). Digital: Museum as platform, curator as champion in the age of social media. *Curator*, *53*(1), 35–43. doi:10.1111/j.2151-6952.2009.00006.x

Proctor, N. (2011a). Mobile as Radical Social Media in the Museum as Distributed Network. Retrieved from http://www.docshut.com/rviku/mobile-as-radical-social-media-in-the-museum-as-distributed-network.html

Proctor, N. (2011b). Introduction. Retrieved from http://mobileappsformuseums.wordpress.com/category/introduction

Russo, A., & Watkins, J. (2008). New Literacy New Audiences: Social Media and Cultural Institutions. Paper presented at the EVA (Electronic Visualisation and the Arts) 2008 Conference, London, UK.

Russo, A., Watkins, J., Kelly, L., & Chan, S. (2006). How will social media affect museum communication? Paper presented at Nordic Digital Excellence in Museums (NODEM), Oslo, Norway, 2006.

Russo, A., Watkins, J., Kelly, L., & Chan, S. (2007). Social media and cultural interactive experiences in museums. *Nordisk Museologi*, *1*(1), 19–29.

Russo, A., Watkins, J., Kelly, L., & Chan, S. (2008). Participatory communication with social media. *Curator*, *51*(1), 21–31. doi:10.1111/j.2151-6952.2008.tb00292.x

Simon, N. (2010). The participatory museum. Santa Cruz, CA: Museum 2.0.

Smith, K. (2009). The Future of Mobile Interpretation. In Trant J. & Bearman D. (Eds), Museums and the Web 2009: Proceedings. Retrieved from www.archimuse.com/mw2009/papers/smith/smith.html

Smith-Yoshimura, K., & Shein, C. (2011). *Social Metadata for Libraries, Archives and Museums Part 1: Site Reviews*. OCLC Research.

Smithsonian Institution (2011, November). Social Media Policy, Smithsonian Directive 814.

Solima, L. (2000). *Il pubblico dei musei. Indagine sulla comunicazione nei musei statali italiani*. Rome: Gangemi Editore.

Solima, L. (2008). Visitatore, cliente, utilizzatore: Nuovi profili di domanda museale e nuove traiettorie di ricerca. In A. Bollo (Ed.), *I pubblici dei musei. Conoscenza e politiche*. Milano: Franco Angeli.

Solima, L. (2010). Social network: Verso un nuovo paradigma per la valorizzazione della domanda culturale. *Sinergie*, *82*(1), 47–74.

Solima, L. (2012). *Il museo in ascolto. Nuove strategie di comunicazione per i musei statali*. Roma: Rubbettino editore, Soveria Mannelli.

Sookhanaphibarn, K., & Chatuporn, U. (2013, February). Expanding the Experience of Museum Visitors with a Social Application on Facebook. In ICDS 2013, The Seventh International Conference on Digital Society, Nice, France.

Springer, M., Dulabahn, B., Michel, Ph., Natanson, B., Reser, D., Woodward, D., & Zinkham, H. (2008). For the common good: the Library of Congress Flickr pilot project. Full report and summary. Washington, DC: Library of Congress. Retrieved from http://www.loc.gov/rr/print/flickr_report_final.pdf

Stogner, M. B. (2009, October). The media-enhanced museum experience: Debating the use of media technology in cultural exhibitions. *Curator*, *52*(4), 385–397. doi:10.1111/j.2151-6952.2009.tb00360.x

Swedberg, C. (2012). Milanese Art Museum Uses RFID to Attract a Younger Audience. Retrieved from http:// rfidjournal.com

Tallon, L. (2013). Mobile Strategy in 2013: an analysis of the annual Museum & Mobile survey. Retrieved from http://www.museums-mobile.org/survey/

Waardenburg, T., & Hekmon, E. (2012). Social Media Metrics for the Cultural Heritage Sector. Retrieved from http://crossmedialab.nl/files/Social_Media_Metrics_for_the_Cultural_Heritage_Sector1.pdf

Wallace, H., Tallon, L., James, D., & Cymru, A. (2012). If mobile is the answer, what was the question? Paper presented at Museums and the Web 2012: the international conference for culture and heritage on-line, San Diego, CA.

Wecker, A. J., Kuflik, T., Dim, E., & Lanir, J. (2013). Different Reality Modalities for Museum Navigation. Paper presented at IUI Workshop on Location Awareness for Mixed and Dual Reality (LAMDa). IUI 2013, Santa Monica, USA.

Wikipedia. (n. d.a). Creative Commons. Retrieved May 17, 2013, from http://en.wikipedia.org/wiki/Creative_Commons

Wikipedia. (n. d.b). Creative Commons license. Retrieved from http://en.wikipedia.org/wiki/Creative_Commons_license

Wikipedia. (n. d.c). Near field communication. Retrieved from http://en.wikipedia.org/wiki/Near_field_communication

Wikipedia. (n. d.d). QR code. Retrieved from http://en.wikipedia.org/wiki/QR_code

Wikipedia. (n. d.e). Radio-frequency identification. Retrieved from http://en.wikipedia.org/wiki/Radio-frequency_identification

Wikipedia. (n. d.f). Responsive web design. Retrieved from http://en.wikipedia.org/wiki/Responsive_web_design

KEY TERMS AND DEFINITIONS

Creative Commons License: A Creative Commons license is one of several public copyright licenses that allow the distribution of copyrighted works. A Creative Commons license is used when an author wants to give people the right to share, use, and even build upon a work that they have created. CC provides an author flexibility (for example, they might choose to allow only non-commercial uses of their own work) and protects the people who use or redistribute an author's work, so they don't have to worry about copyright infringement, as long as they abide by the conditions the author has specified (Wikipedia, n. d.b).

Near Field Communication (NFC): Is a set of standards for smartphones and similar devices to establish radio communication with each other by touching them together or bringing them into close proximity, usually no more than a few centimeters (Wikipedia, n. d.c).

Quick Response (QR) Code: Is the trademark for a type of matrix barcode (or two-dimensional barcode); a barcode is an optically machine-readable label that is attached to an item and that records information related to that item. Typically, a smartphone is used as a QR-code scanner, displaying the code and converting it to some useful form (such as a standard URL for a website, thereby obviating the need for a user to type it manually into a web browser) (Wikipedia, n. d.d).

Radio-Frequency Identification (RFID): Is the wireless non-contact use of radio-frequency electro-magnetic fields to transfer data, for the purposes of automatically identifying and tracking tags attached to objects (Wikipedia, n. d.e).

Responsive Web Design (RWD): Is a web design approach aimed at crafting sites to provide an optimal viewing experience – easy reading and navigation with a minimum of resizing, panning, and scrolling – across a wide range of devices (from desktop computer monitors to mobile phones) (Wikipedia, n. d.f).

ENDNOTES

[1] "Soon AR may include haptic feedback (think vibrating cellphones) to simulate handling, such as *touching* a bust of Sophocles" (American Association of Museums, 2012, p. 20).

[2] These licences "allow creators to communicate which rights they reserve, and which rights they waive for the benefit of recipients or other creators" (Wikipedia, n. d.a).

[3] The scenario outlined by the so-called "Internet of things" states that all objects will be connected to the Web, therefore allowing their data to be communicated externally; this possibility presents potentially infinite developmental opportunities, ranging from domotics to surveillance systems, applications in the field of biomedicine to use in the automotive sector.

[4] The theme of museum accessibility – and cultural contents, in general – is approached using completely different ways compared to the past, encompassing a new dimension, the online one, which now joins the three methods known and most frequently analysed in the literature: physical, economic and cognitive (Solima, 2012, ch. 1).

[5] QR Codes (Quick Response Code) are a type of two-dimensional barcode which allow a mobile device fitted with a camera to link automatically to an internet site and, for example, to a digital resource made available by a museum.

[6] www.moma.org/iwent.

[7] To get an idea of the short time between the advent of the first social media websites and their global success, one need only consider that Facebook has been active since February 2004, that the first video was uploaded to YouTube on 23 April 2005 and the first "tweet" was sent on 21 March 2006. It took approximately eight years for these sites to become popular, whereas it took thirty years for mobile phones to gain widespread use and four centuries for printing to become a mass phenomenon.

[8] This is true of Facebook, for example, which recently introduced the so-called "hashtag," along the lines of Twitter, or Twitter itself which introduced the possibility of sharing images.

[9] It is not a coincidence that Instagram was bought out by Facebook in September 2012 for the sum of over 700 million dollars.

[10] See Solima, 2000, ch. 1; research activities and studies must therefore aim at specifying the elements referred to above, exploring the historical and artistic implications of each work (its attribution to an artist or school, understanding the social implications of its creation, etc.), setting it in relation to other works making up the museum's collections or those in other institutions. It should also be added that this activity can also refer to the scientific aspects of the work, the methods of conservation, restoration problems and those relating to the materials used, etc.

[11] For a general overview of this topic, see Pissard & Prieur, 2007.

[12] One such planning activity in which this author recently took part was run by the Museum of Capodimonte in Naples to identify and select participants for the experimental phases of information systems made for a new section of the museum due to be opened shortly. To achieve this the project appealed to residents using, above all, its Facebook page, which was used to signal the existence of the project and to solicit local participation (Ministero dei beni e delle attivita culturali e del turismo, n. d.).

[13] Users can be shown the selections that were most popular among other users in those cases where a rating system has been introduced for the proposals submitted by museum users.

[14] In the case of videos, for example, the British Museum has decided to create two or three high-quality films every month.

[15] museum-analytics.org

[16] An interesting classification of the various online user profiles is offered by Forrester Research, which identifies seven different types of individual, known as the "Social Technographics Ladder," depending on their level of involvement in the use and creation of online contents (Li et al., 2007).

This research was previously published in the Handbook of Research on Management of Cultural Products edited by Lucia Aiello, pages 181-199, copyright year 2014 by Business Science Reference (an imprint of IGI Global).

Chapter 65
Social Media and Social Change:
Nonprofits and Using Social Media Strategies to Meet Advocacy Goals

Lauri Goldkind
Fordham University, USA

John G. McNutt
University of Delaware, USA

ABSTRACT

Technological advances in communications tools, the Internet, and the advent of social media have changed the ways in which nonprofit organizations engage with their various constituents. Nonprofits now have a constellation of tools including: interactive social media sites, mobile applications (apps), Websites, and mash-ups that allow them to create a comprehensive system for mobilizing supports to advocate for changing public policies. From Facebook to Twitter and from YouTube to Pinterest, communicating to many via words and images has never been easier. The authors explore the history of nonprofit advocacy and organizing, describe the social media and technology tools available for moving advocacy goals forward, and conclude with some possible challenges that organizations considering these tools could face.

INTRODUCTION

This chapter explores how social media and related technology tools are used by nonprofit social service organizations to mobilize constituents and drive policy change. Building on a twenty year process of incorporating earlier technology into social change activities, the Web 2.0/Social Media revolution has had an impact on nonprofit organizations who are uniquely suited to reach under-represented communities.

In this chapter, we will look at how nonprofit social services organizations engage in advocacy using the broad range of social media, Web 2.0, and other technological applications. We will explore the available tools and look at how these applications have been used in campaigns and efforts to impact policy change. Finally, we will explore the issues that are involved in using social media in nonprofit

DOI: 10.4018/978-1-5225-5637-4.ch065

efforts to engender social justice outcomes. Social service organizations are not only a substantial component of the nonprofit sector, they represent the part of the sector with immediate exposure to many problematic social conditions as well as a conduit, via the communities they serve, to large populations of under-represented groups of people.

ADVOCACY IN THE NONPROFIT SOCIAL SERVICES SECTOR

Nonprofit social service organizations have historically worked with the poor and oppressed in society (Trattner 2007). They are at the center of hot button issues such as poverty, domestic violence, immigration, health care reform and so forth. While much of this is direct service related, nonprofit organizations also engage in advocacy to change policies and protect the vulnerable (Berry & Arons, 2002; Jenkins, 1987; Libby, 2011; Bass, Arons, Guinane, & Carter, 2007). This means that these organizations have become adept at organizing communities, creating media campaigns, lobbying lawmakers and raising public awareness about issues and problems. This effort dovetails with the efforts of social movement organizations who have broader social change goals.

Advocacy or the constellation of activities which positions individuals and organizations in the public sphere to create dialog and change on behalf of communities and populations of individuals is often thought to be a core activity of the nonprofit social services sector. Yet a growing body of research suggests that nonprofit engagement in policy advocacy activities is often far less than expected (Mosley, 2010; Berry & Arons, 2002; Bass, Arons, Guinane & Carter, 2007).

The broad umbrella of advocacy as a collection of behaviors also includes a range of goals that organizations may wish to achieve. These activities might be characterized as more self-interested organizational advocacy (e.g., advocacy to protect agency funding) in contrast to progressive advocacy, defined as advocacy addressing underlying structural and power inequities (Donaldson, 2008). Progressive advocacy's goal is to advance the interests of a non-profit's constituents, rather than the organization's interests, and fully engages constituents in the advocacy process (Donaldson, 2008).

Many of these activities use traditional social change methodologies: community organization, lobbying, administrative advocacy, judicial intervention and so forth (Berry & Arons, 2002; Libby, 2011; Hoefer, 2oo0; Bass, Arons, Guinane & Carter 2007). In the last two decades, however, the use of information and communication technology has become a staple of nonprofit advocacy (McNutt & Boland, 1999; Hick & McNutt, 2002; McNutt, 2011). Organizations have adapted traditional organizing or advocacy activities to function in the electronic environment, for example, moving letter writing campaigns online or creating online petition drives and more media sophisticated organizations are making use of advanced interactive and networked technologies in attempts to drive social change.

TECHNOLOGY AND NONPROFIT SOCIAL SERVICES ADVOCACY

The use of technology to promote advocacy goals has been around at least since the late 1980s and there is now a substantial literature to draw upon. Early efforts, such as Peace Net and community networking gave form to an activity that has revolutionized political campaigning and transformed the way that nonprofits, throughout the world, have conducted their advocacy activities. Early literature (Downing,

Fasano, Friedland, McCollough, Mizrahi & Shapiro, 1991; Schuler, 1991; 1996; Wittig & Schmitz, 1996; Yerxa & Moll, 1994) looks at the use of pre-Internet and early Internet networking.

The growth of the Internet and other newer technologies has led to a new phase in development, one characterized by websites, e-mail, discussion lists (sometimes called Listservs after the popular software) and related technologies (occasionally referred to as Web 1.0). This might be considered the automation of traditional advocacy, rather than a reinvention. While technology was very much a handmaiden to traditional advocacy (McNutt & Boland, 1999; Hick & McNutt, 2002; Brainard & Siplon, 2002; 2004; Brainard & Brinkerhoff, 2004; Cortez & Rafter, 2007), that was about to change. A study by the Congressional Management Foundation (2005) documented the impact of these technologies on congressional decision making and established that advocacy groups were making substantial use of them.

The growth of Web 2.0 in the first decade of the new millennium promised a sea change in political practice (McNutt, 2011). New technology fused with new organizational patterns to produce a very quick evolution of practice. Part of this was the Web 2.0/Social Media revolution. This combined with new models of political and organizational practice to create a new playing field. Table 1 illustrates the progression from traditional advocacy strategies.

This is the point where technology and organization come together to change practice. In many ways, the technology sets up imperatives that cannot be addressed in traditional practice. It should be noted that while organizations may adopt new technologies, they frequently retain earlier technologies (McNutt & Barlow, 2011) that have proved successful. This suggests that the evolution of technology is less even than we are left to believe.

Social Media and Nonprofit Social Services Advocacy

Social Media and Web 2.0 are terms used to describe technologies that support interaction and networking, user generated content and the pooling of collective intelligence (O'Reilly 2005; Addison, 2006; Germany 2006; Kanter & Fine, 2011; Bryant, 2006). They also tend to be cloud applications where the Internet is used as platform, rather than a device, such as a smart phone or computer.

The major technologies that are part of the Social Media /Web 2.0 constellation are:

- **Blogging:** Blogs are on-line journals that involve of a series of entries or posts and allow blog readers to comment on the posting. Bloggers also frequently comment of each other's posts. Video blogs (called V-Blogs) and Photo blogs are also possible. Blogging is a staple of political action efforts (Davis, 2010; Merry, 2010; Nam, 2012)
- **Wikis:** A wiki is an online site where the pages can be edited by users. Wikis facilitate collaboration and sharing of ideas by allowing multiple authors to work on the same document. While Wikipedia is probably the best known example of a Wiki, they have been used for a variety of collaborative activities (McNutt, 2008).

Table 1. Stages of electronic advocacy

Pre Web Advocacy	Early Web Advocacy	Web 2.0 Advocacy
●E-mail, newsgroups, bulletin boards ●Traditional Advocacy	●Email, websites ●Traditional Advocacy	●Social Media--Older Technology Remains ●Post Traditional Advocacy

- **Social Bookmarking Sites:** Social bookmarking sites collect information about what members are bookmarking and feeds this information back to users making similar searches. This facilitates the search for information by pooling the judgments of other searchers.

- **Social Networking Sites:** These are sites designed to help people network and connect. While Facebook is the primary social network site in the United States, other nations prefer other systems. Many of these sites have combined blogging, video and image sharing, games, location sharing and other systems. Social networking sites give organizations the ability to purchase ads, raise money and organize causes.

- **RSS - Rich Site Summary or Really Simple Syndication:** RSS is a technology that lets users subscribe to an online resource, website, a Blog or some other resource.

- **Podcasting:** Podcasting technology allows the user to create an audio file of a presentation and making it accessible for download on the Web. It can be played on a computer or other device.

- **Image and Videosharing:** These are sites that allow consumers the ability to share their images or videos with other users. Users can create ways to organize the content and display it to others

- **Meetup** (www.meetup.com)**:** Is a system that creates face to face meetings over the Internet. It was used effectively by the Dean Campaign to create face to face political meetings (Teachout & Streeter, 2008; Trippi, 2006).

- **On-line Mapping:** On-line mapping allows users to create or modify maps online and look at maps and map objects created by other users. Mapping can be combined with other programs that collect data.

- **On-line Games/Internet Virtual Worlds:** These are programs that give users access to simulated reality. Users can create a setting and artificial people to represent them and others. Second life is an example. This is program creates an online universe that people can interact with other players (as Avatars) and create a simulated social system. This provides a place where advocates can demonstrate the impacts of social problems within a safe space.

While this list is long and still growing, these applications can be combined to create new applications. This process, called a "Mash Up" results in a new technology tool and shares data between the two applications.

One of the greatest advantages of this technological revolution for the nonprofits is that these social media are available at minimal cost and usable often with minimum skills. The possibilities and uses of this technology are only restricted by the limits of nonprofit organizations' imaginations. Meanwhile governments from the local to the federal level are resorting to cutbacks on welfare and human services. So it is logical to think that crippling resource crunch will increasingly motivate nonprofits to use low cost social media to engage their stakeholders and public policy makers.

One would think that nonprofit social service organizations are already adopting social media, echoing the adoption rates found in politics and industry and the interest shown by the mass media. This is not yet reflected in the research literature. Resource, knowledge and staff constraints all limit the amount of investment organizations may make in digital advocacy strategies. The current literature seems to support the idea that organizations are beginning to adopt social media strategies but that the social service sector has a long way to go before saturation of the media has been reached. For example, among social welfare advocacy organizations, Edwards and Hoefer (2010) found that current Web 2.0 use for advocacy tasks are as low as 3% among a sample of advocacy organizations. A longitudinal study by University of Massachusetts Dartmouth Scholars reported that 89% of from a sample of the 200 largest nonprofit charities in the U.S were using at least one of type of social media (Barnes et al. 2008). While many of these organizations are social service related, others are not. This does not suggest that they are using Web 2.0 for advocacy efforts. Earlier studies of technology adoption in the nonprofit sector suggests that slower adoption of technology characterizes the sector (see Rafter and Cortez, 2007). McNutt and Barlow (2011) found a small but growing use of some social media technologies in their study of child advocacy agencies. McNutt and Flanagan (2007) found similar patterns in a study of environmental groups.

Social media such as Facebook, Twitter, YouTube, have capacity to facilitate interactions among the users through multiple audio and video tools. As a result a few studies on the nonprofit were interested in finding out whether these communication options were employed in a limited manner like traditional news bulletins or were taking full advantage of the interaction capabilities of social media to build dialogic communities (Guo et al, 2013; Lovejoy et al, 2012; Waters, 2009; Greenberg & MacAulay, 2009). Among the nonprofits there is an overarching tendency to limit the communication capabilities of the social media to information sharing with the stakeholders. This is called message control and is an artifact of earlier ideas about political communication. This tendency did not alter even when the social media in study was changed to Twitter (Lovejoy et al, 2012; Guo et al, 2013), Facebook (Waters, 2009), YouTube (Waters & Jones, 2011), and Twitter, Facebook, and other social media together (Greenberg & MacAulay, 2009; Edwards & Hoefer, 2010). These studies also found dialogic communication, collective action, stakeholder engagement, community building, public education, advocacy support and mobilization of the stakeholders were effected though in a limited manner through these social media (Guo et al, 2013; Edwards & Hoefer, 2010; Obar et al, 2012; Lovejoy et al. 2012; Waters 2009).

More problematic is the idea of conflating advocacy outcomes with social media outcomes. While it is possible to evaluate different activities and relate them to social media metrics (such as Tweets, Friends, Retweets and So forth), it is more difficult to associate these with actual advocacy outcomes.

The Use of Web 2.0/Social Media in Nonprofit Social Service Organizational Advocacy Practice

This section will look at the actual application of Web 2.0/Social Media to problems that nonprofits face in advocating for causes and constituencies. We focus on more common applications, but many exciting developments are continuing to present themselves as the struggle for social and economic justice continues.

Social Networking (Facebook, LinkedIn, MySpace)

Social network sites are one of the fastest growing technological arenas in the world today and there are many varieties of social networking sites. Weibo, for example, is popular in China. In the United States, Facebook is most widely used. From a startup created by Harvard student Mark Zuckerberg in his dorm room, Facebook has over a billion users worldwide. It has become an important political tool, regularly used by political campaigns, advocacy groups and social movements. The use of Facebook in the 2012 Arab Spring Demonstrations in Egypt and other places is well documented (Hamdy & Gomaa, 2012; Tufeci & Wilson, 2012; Lim 2012; Castells, 2012).

Perhaps the most frequently used of the social media strategies, social networking sites, function as virtual hubs on the Internet allowing individuals, organizations, and institutions to connect with one another. Social networking sites such as Facebook, MySpace, LinkedIn, Google + and others are defined as those that are driven by user-participation and user-generated content (Tredinnick, 2006). Through interactions with stakeholders such as clients, donors and volunteers on social media sites, organizations are seeking to develop relationships with important publics. Relationships are the foundation for social networking sites.

One mechanism that social networking cites offer that is especially effective for nonprofits interested in activating change comes in the form of gathering and connecting advocates. While the Internet has always done this, social media adds new dimensions. At no time in our prior history has the ability to find and connect with like-minded individuals been more efficient. For organizations interested in creating and sustaining social change the ability to quickly and efficiently identify groups and organizations with common interests and agendas as well as empathic individuals is greatly enhanced by the use of social networking sites[1]. Social networking sites allow organizations and users to rapidly connect and weave together like minded communities which can be leveraged for social change.

Social Networking Example: The Human Rights Campaign

The Human Rights Campaign (HRC) has focused their social media investment on their Facebook profile webpage (http://www.facebook.com/humanrightscampaign). Through data analysis and monitoring of posts, HRC were able to isolate topics and programs that generated the most buzz and fine-tuned their online offering.

As a result, HRC has seen tremendous growth in their fan base—more than 400% over 14 months, jumping from 80,000 to more than 350,000 fans. Facebook also directs 30 to 50% of Web traffic to HRC's blog, consistently making it the top referring site. In the last 12 months, HRC also added more than 23,000 new email addresses to its email list from Facebook users taking action or submitting surveys posted on HRC's profile and signing up through the integrated Convio-driven form on the "Join HRC" tab of the organization's profile ("Going social tapping," 2010).

Image Sharing (Instagram, Flicker, Pinterest; Tumblr)

Distinct from social networking sites are social tools for sharing visual imagery, primarily photograph sharing. Photo sharing sites such as Instagram, Flickr, Pinterest and others allow users to share photographs online. Often linked to other social media infrastructure such as Facebook or Myspace, photo sharing allows users to promote their photographing activities online as well as across more intimate groups of users. Photosharing in the nonprofit space can be used to promote visual images of conditions and causes impacting particular communities. It can also be used to document social functions on behalf of the agency such as events targeted at cultivating donors or new volunteers. Online photo-sharing services allow users to upload photographs, store them, organize them, tag them, share them, discuss them, and explore others' photographs, too.

Image Sharing Example: Operation Smile

Operation Smile is an international children's medical charity that heals children's smiles, and develops medical expertise across sixty countries around the world. The organization offers a mobilized force of medical professionals who provide safe, effective reconstructive surgery and related medical care for children born with facial deformities such as cleft lip and cleft palate. Operation Smile serves as the largest volunteer-based medical charity providing free cleft surgeries in the world. Since 1982, Operation Smile — through the help of dedicated medical volunteers — has provided more than 3.5 million comprehensive patient evaluations and over 200,000 free surgeries for children and young adults born with facial deformities.

Operation Smile uses Pinterest to highlight its successes and drive awareness both of the issue of cleft palate and children's facial deformities. Operation Smile: http://pinterest.com/operationsmile/ The organization has over 614 followers, and uses visual imagery to drive awareness and support for its work. They have a "Before and After" board– showing with incredible clarity how they work to make a difference in people's lives. Their "Creative Fundraising" board posts photos of products or services (read: surgeries) needed by the patients Operation Smile serves–and then adding a price tag for that gift right on the photo. They do the same thing with missions others have taken–and put a price tag on it to give it some context. Finally, their "Our Smile Ambassadors" board highlights the celebrities who support the cause.

Videosharing (YouTube, Vimeo)

Perhaps one of the fastest growing strategies being adopted by political campaigns as well as human services agencies is the use of video for marketing and fundraising as well as for advocacy purposes (see Gueorguieva, 2008). Video, while expensive to produce allows organizations to tell compelling stories quickly, with the potential to reach millions of individuals, should a video clip go viral.

Pearlson (2013) describes the recently-released report "Into Focus: A Benchmark Guide to Effective Nonprofit Video" and how video's potential for unparalleled success in raising awareness and reaching new audiences. Take, for example, the Rainforest Alliance's video *Follow the Frog*, which has over a million views. Although the Rainforest Alliance cannot track the impact of the video on donors, the numbers alone show that the nonprofit has reached a much wider audience than they could have anticipated. Go Red For Women's *Just a Little Heart Attack*, starring and directed by actress Elizabeth Banks, effectively increased awareness about the signs and dangers of heart attacks, achieving over three million views. Similarly, the Invisible Children's Kony 2012 documentary, made international headlines and topped 70 million YouTube hits in a single week. This was considered exceptional for a 30 min. The Kony video dramatized the activities of an African warlord who reportedly used child soldiers (Karlin & Matthews, 2012).

Video activism or using documentary style video to engage audiences and convey messages is not a new strategy, but with the advent of smart phones, video phones and improvements and availability of recording equipment, video production is now more accessible than ever to those in the nonprofit world. Similarly, sites like YouTube, Vimeo and others allow users to have mass exposure for their video messages. One example of cause based video production is the organization Witness (www.witness.org). Witness defines video advocacy as using visual media as a targeted tool that will engage people to create change. Witness provides tools, resources and training for organizations wishing to use video to disseminate their messages.

WITNESS partners with other organizations to curate the YouTube Human Rights Channel—a central repository of citizen created footage on human rights issues. The Human Rights Channel features video from the Arab Spring and uses video to document human rights violations and struggles for justice. The channel provides a showcase for the work that citizens around the world are doing to document issues in their communities.

Microblogging (Twitter)

Twitter is arguably the world's premier message network (Lovejoy & Saxton, 2012). Twitter is a microblogging service, similar to blogging, yet far more brief allows users to send public and private messages which are capped at 140 characters. The site-imposed character limit allows users' updates, or tweets, to be sent to cellular phones and other mobile devises as a text message (Lovejoy & Saxton, 2012). The site has exploded in popularity.

Since its founding in 2006, Twitter has rapidly grown to be one of the most powerful online platforms for connecting hundreds of millions of individuals and organizations around the world. A Pew Research center report (Brenner, 2013) reported that Twitter claims 200 Million active users. The service is experiencing exponential growth and has rapidly changed the Internet. The key feature of Twitter is that it provides a real time means of communicating with the world.

Twitter while serving as a vehicle or platform for nonprofits to catalyze social change has also launched its own proprietary mechanism for creating campaigns and drawing attention to pre-selected causes. Called Hope140, it uses the TwitPay platform to accept donations and intends to serve as an electronic megaphone for launching calls to action. Twitter users participated in World Malaria Day by retweeting and donating $10. The Case Foundation matched donations with a $25,000 grant.

The inaugural campaign, called, #EndMalaria demonstrated that Twitter can be more than an awareness mechanism for nonprofits. Further, Twitter is using its Promoted Tweets feature as public service vehicle, launching with two charities; Room to Read, which is campaigning to promote the building of their 10,000th library, and Partners in Health. Now Twitter's nonprofit offering provides comprehensive capabilities, from click-throughs and retweets to bona fide donations and public service announcements. Hope140 utilizes RT2Give, a service stemming from third-party developer Twitpay. After users donate via the service, the app tweets for them with a campaign-specific hashtag or term soliciting their followers to join them in giving. Currently, Hope 140 is not accessible to all nonprofits, and to be featured, a 501(c)3 organization needs to be selected by Twitter. Twitter says it's exploring how to use Hope140 as a resource for nonprofits, and a way for socially concerned people to connect. But the larger impact on the nonprofit space has yet to be determined.

Short Messages (Text)

Short messaging service (SMS) (a.k.a. text messaging) is a fast, low cost and popular mode of communication, and these advantages can be used in a variety of ways to improve service delivery to clients as well as engage volunteers, donors and other stakeholders. Mobile phone text messaging is a potentially powerful tool for behavior change because it is widely available, inexpensive, and instant. Cole-Lewis and Kershaw (2010) conducted a meta analysis of SMS health and behavior change studies and found that of nine sufficiently powered studies, eight showed evidence supporting text messaging as a tool for behavior change. In the advocacy arena, SMS is being used to mobile constituents on issue campaigns such as immigration reform and same sex marriage (Reform Immigration for America, 2012).

Perhaps one of the most successful SMS campaigns to date has been the Reform Immigration for America campaign, which built the largest bilingual mobile advocacy list in American History (McCarthy, 2012). As of June 2010 this list had 150,000 mobile subscribers and had generated more than 340,000 calls. The campaign went from relying on 300 word emails to 160 character text messages. Messages to their bilingual constituents helped mobilize support for rallies, marches and letter writing campaigns on behalf of immigration reform.

On-Line Mapping (Google Earth, Google Maps)

Nonprofit advocates have taken the available online mapping capabilities of programs like Google Maps and Google Earth to show the relationship between different kinds of data and spatial relationships. Sometimes seeing that the concentration of drug arrests or toxic waste dump is near a school or nursing home is much more powerful than providing figures that provide the same information. The Natural Resources Defense Council (NRDC) has created a number of resources using Google Earth (http://www.nrdc.org/reference/maps.asp) that allow users to see, for example, the effects of climate change on national parks. Other examples of map based advocacy include: The Holocaust Museum's World is Witness blog using Google maps and text updates to document areas where there is risk of genocide worldwide. The map at the top of the page shows trouble reports—text, photo and video—from around the world. As well as the organization Appalachian Voices, who have used Google Maps API to create their "What's my connection to mountaintop removal" map. By entering a US zip code into their site you can discover whether your energy supplier has a connection to mountaintop removal mining.

Blogging (Blogger, Word Press)

Blogging is one of the oldest social media technologies and one that is used by a variety of organizations to communicate with their members and inform the public. Blog post can be created quickly and readers can comment on the posts. Communities of bloggers can help set the agenda for issues and social problems (Davis, 2005).

Share Our Strength is a one example of a nonprofit which successfully uses blogging as part of their social media presence. The organization blogs about topics important to their audience (advocacy, how their partners are supporting SOS and specific programs like Cooking Matters). They include multiple bloggers from across the organization providing a comprehensive vision of the agency's programs. Additionally, they make it easy to subscribe via email so that constituents can stay automatically updated. The blog is searchable and it's easy to share with partners, volunteers and potential donors by simply forwarding a link.

Challenges to Consider

The tools described above are available for nonprofit use either as free or a nominal cost to participate. However, while the tools themselves are free to use, there are resource allocation costs and decisions to be made in terms of an organizations investment in which strategy(s) to pursue. The cost of content production and staff time can be substantial in some cases. While the technologies themselves might be easy to use, applying them in an advocacy context is far more difficult. Most organizations would not be happy, for example, with the type of videos that casual users upload to video sharing sites. Figure 2, above, summarizes the opportunities and challenges inherent in each technological strategy.

Along with technological adaptation and rapid communication of complex messages comes a need to reduce hierarchy in organizational structures. Given the onslaught of messages and communications channels going both in and out of organizations multiple layers of approval and message control are not practical. Traditional organizational leaders who governed in a "command and control" style of management may find themselves confronting the inability to successfully make use of social media and technological tools under a highly centralized communications model. Newer organizational structures are emerging in the start-up community (both in the private as well as the nonprofit sector). Organiza-

Table 2. Benefits and challenges of electronic strategies

Electronic Tool	Benefits	Challenges/Possible Costs
Social Networking (Facebook, LinkedIn, MySpace)	Free (or very low cost) profile raising and marketing to a broad range of constituents	Lack of control with regard to reigning in content
Image Sharing (Pinterest, Flickr, Instagram)	Images can be dramatic way to tell a story Participants can share their images	Constant maintenance Requires compelling content and an individual to manage the upload process
Video Sharing (Vimeo, YouTube)	Free mechanism for sharing video content Can follow similar or sister organizations video streams Free tools for managing video presence Participants can share their videos	Video can be expensive to produce and poorly constructed video can be damaging to organizational brands
Microblogging (Twitter)	Short messages that might be linked to other resources	Requires constant maintenance and updating to maximize effectiveness
Short Message Service (SMS/Text)	By definition forces nonprofit to distill message	Technological knowledge to setup and maintain Requires cultivation and capturing of constituent cell phones and list management of contact list
Mapping	Contextualizes problems/issues/solutions by displaying them geographically	On-going updating and fact checking
Blogging	Allows organization to update content more responsively and quickly than re-designing website Multiple individuals in the organization can present viewpoints Constituents can respond to organizational information	On-going updating, fact checking and comment responses Responses can be damaging

tions characterized by flat leadership structures and high levels of individual autonomy are operating as holacracies characterized by consensus based decision making, a commitment to cultivating and empowering employees and inclusive organizational culture and the ability to rapidly adapt to change (Robertson, 2007). Holacracy has roots in the agile programming movement, which seeks to produce software that adapts and meets customers' needs on an immediate basis. The immediate nature of Internet based communications also imposes a value of agility, immediacy and instantaneousness which may pose challenges to organizations and leaders most versed in highly managing messages and rigid bureaucratic structures.

While organizational leaders may face challenges to their management style should they not be ready to embrace more fluid organizational structures, an additional challenge in the adaptation of technology strategies includes measuring the effectiveness of these new technologies in serving the organizations advocacy goals. Basic outcome evaluation is frequently challenging for nonprofit organizations given the technological, measurement and resource challenges they face. Measuring the outcomes and impacts of their social media and advocacy strategies may be even more complex, given the contextualizing factors involved in trying to measure political and social change (McNutt, 2011).

Promising Practices and Future Directions

Advocacy is an important capacity for the nonprofit sector. It facilitates the protection of the sector, nonprofit organizations and the clients and stakeholders of nonprofit organizations. It is also vital to the protection of the poor, the dispossessed and the powerless in society. Advocates today face challenges that are fundamentally different from those experienced by previous generations of advocates. New tools, particularly those that use technology, are critical to meeting these challenges.

Nonprofits suffer from a dearth of technology expertise and funding for technology projects is often difficult to obtain. Similar to challenges facing the financing of traditional general operating costs, nonprofit executives find themselves forced, in the electronic arena, with a lack of funding and institutional support but oftentimes the additional hurdle of a lack of knowledge and core competencies around communicating their messages effectively. More applied scholarship demonstrating the effectiveness of digital strategies, such as video and photo sharing, as well as how to craft meaningful messaging campaigns will be a welcome addition to the foundational knowledge that leaders need in order to successfully implement these new tools. Developing transferable models of successful implementations will help leaders unfamiliar with this area gain understanding and confidence to implement similar tools and campaigns in their own organizations. This will require an organized and focused effort to create the kind of knowledge base that can sustain advocacy practice.

Technology will continue to advance and the tools of today will seem quaint by the standards of even the near future. We can also anticipate that advocacy will evolve and will allow the sector to meet the challenges of the future.

REFERENCES

Addison, C. (2006). Web 2.0: A new chapter in development practice? *Development in Practice, 16*(6), 623–627. doi:10.1080/09614520600958348

Allen, C. (2004). *Tracing the evolution of social software*. Life with Alacrity Blog.

Bass, G., & Arons, D. Guinane, K., & Carter, M. (2007). Seen but not heard: Strengthening nonprofit advocacy. Washington, DC: The Aspen Institute.

Berry, J. M., & Arons, D. (2002). *A voice for nonprofits*. Washington, DC: Brookings.

Brainard, L. A., & Brinkerhoff, J. M. (2004). Lost in cyberspace: Shedding light on the dark matter of grassroots organizations. *Nonprofit and Voluntary Sector Quarterly, 33*(3), 32S–52. doi:10.1177/0899764004265436

Brainard, L. A., & Siplon, P. D. (2002). Cyberspace challenges to mainstream nonprofit health organizations. *Administration & Society, 34*(2), 141–175. doi:10.1177/0095399702034002002

Brainard, L. A., & Siplon, P. D. (2004). Toward nonprofit organization reform in the voluntary spirit: Lessons from the internet. *Nonprofit and Voluntary Sector Quarterly, 33*(3), 435–457. doi:10.1177/0899764004266021

Castells, M. (2012). *Networks of outrage and hope: Social movements in the internet age*. New York: Polity.

Cole-Lewis, H., & Kershaw, T. (2010). Text messaging as a tool for behavior change in disease prevention and management. *Epidemiologic Reviews, 32*(1), 56–69. doi:10.1093/epirev/mxq004 PMID:20354039

Congressional Management Foundation. (2005). *Communicating with congress: How capitol hill is coping with the surge in citizen advocacy*. Washington, DC: Author.

Cortes, M., & Rafter, K. (Eds.). (2007). *Nonprofits and technology: Emerging research for usable knowledge*. Chicago, IL: Lyceum Books.

Davis, R. (2010). *Typing politics: The role of blogs in American politics*. New York: Oxford University Press.

Downing, J., Fasano, R., Friedland, P., McCollough, M., Mizrahi, T., & Shapiro, J. (Eds.). (1991). *Computers for social change and community organization*. New York: Haworth Press.

Germany, J. B. (Ed.). (2006). Person to person to person: Harnessing the political power of on-line social networks and user generated content. Washington, DC. The Institute for Politics, Democracy and the Internet, George Washington University.

Going Social Tapping into Social Media for Nonprofit Success. (2010). Retrieved from http://www.councilofnonprofits.org/files/Convio_Social-Media-Guide.pdf

Gueorguieva, V. (2008). Voters, MySpace, and YouTube: The impact of alternative communication channels on the 2008 election cycle and beyond. *Social Science Computer Review*, *26*, 288–300. doi:10.1177/0894439307305636

Guo, C., & Saxton, G. D. (2013). Tweeting social change: How social media are changing nonprofit advocacy. *Nonprofit and Voluntary Sector Quarterly*.

Hick, S., & McNutt, J. (Eds.). (2002). *Advocacy and activism on the internet: Perspectives from community organization and social policy*. Chicago: Lyceum Press.

Jenkins, J. C. (1987). Non profit organizations and policy advocacy. In *The nonprofit sector: A research handbook* (pp. 296–320). New Haven, CT: Yale University Press.

Kanter, B., & Fine, A. (2010). *The network nonprofit*. San Francisco: Jossey Bass.

Kaplan, A. M., & Haenlein, M. (2010). Users of the world, unite! The challenges and opportunities of social media. *Business Horizons*, *53*(1), 59–68. doi:10.1016/j.bushor.2009.09.003

Krebs, V., & Holley, J. (2006). *Building smart communities through network weaving*. Appalachian Center for Economic Networks. Retrieved from www.acenetworks.org

KU Work Group for Community Health and Development. (2010). *Conducting a direct action campaign*. University of Kansas. Retrieved January 2, 2010, from http://ctb.ku.edu/en/tablecontents

Libby, P. (2011). *The lobbying strategy handbook*. Thousand Oak, CA: Sage Publications.

Lim, M. S., Hocking, J. S., Hellard, M. E., & Aitken, C. K. (2008). SMS STI: A review of the uses of mobile phone text messaging in sexual health. *International Journal of STD & AIDS*, *19*(5), 287–290. doi:10.1258/ijsa.2007.007264 PMID:18482956

Lovejoy, K., & Saxton, G. D. (2012). Information, community, and action: How nonprofit organizations use social media. *Journal of Computer-Mediated Communication*, *17*(3), 337–353. doi:10.1111/j.1083-6101.2012.01576.x

McNutt, J. G. (2007). Adoption of new wave electronic advocacy techniques by nonprofit child advocacy organizations. In *Information technology adoption in the nonprofit sector* (pp. 33–48). Chicago: Lyceum Books.

McNutt, J. G. (2008). Web 2.0 tools for policy research and advocacy. *Journal of Policy Practice, 7*(1), 81–85. doi:10.1080/15588740801909994

McNutt, J. G. (2011). Is social work advocacy worth the cost? Issues and barriers for an economic analysis of social work political practice. *Research on Social Work Practice, 21*(4), 397–403. doi:10.1177/1049731510386624

McNutt, J. G. (2011). Fighting for justice in cyberspace: The role of technology in advocacy. In *The lobbying strategy handbook*. Thousand Oaks, CA: Sage Publications.

McNutt, J. G., & Boland, K. M. (1999). Electronic advocacy by nonprofit organizations in social welfare policy. *Nonprofit and Voluntary Sector Quarterly, 28*(4), 432–451. doi:10.1177/0899764099284004

Merry, M. K. (2010). Blogging and environmental advocacy: A new way to engage the public? *Review of Policy Research, 27*(5), 641–656. doi:10.1111/j.1541-1338.2010.00463.x

Nam, T. (2012). Dual effects of the Internet on political activism: Reinforcing and mobilizing. *Government Information Quarterly, 29*, S90-S97. O'Reilly, T. (2005). *What is web 2.0.* O'Reilly Media. Retrieved from http://oreilly.com/web2/archive/what-is-Web-20.html

Reform Immigration for America. (2012). *Reform immigration with your cell phone snapshot.* Retrieved March 27, 2013 from http://smsadvocacy.com/Reform_Immigration_With_Your_Cell_Phone-Snapshot_Final.pdf

Robertson, B. J. (2007). Organization at the leading edge: Introducing Holacracy™. *Integral Leadership Review, 7*(3).

Schuler, D. (1994). Community networks: Building a new participatory medium. *Communications of the ACM, 37*(1), 39–51. doi:10.1145/175222.175225

Schuler, D. (1996). *New community networks: Wired for change.* Reading, MA: Addison-Wesley.

Skovdal, M. (2011). Picturing the coping strategies of caregiving children in Western Kenya: From images to action. *American Journal of Public Health, 101*(3), 452–453. doi:10.2105/AJPH.2010.192351 PMID:21307376

Trattner, W. W. (2007). *From poor law to welfare state: A history of social welfare in America* (6th ed.). New York: Simon and Schuster.

Tredinnick, L. (2006). Web 2.0 and business: A pointer to the intranets of the future. *Business Information Review, 23*(4), 228–234. doi:10.1177/0266382106072239

Wang, C., & Burris, M. A. (1994). Empowerment through photo novella: Portraits of participation. *Health Education & Behavior, 21*(2), 171–186. doi:10.1177/109019819402100204 PMID:8021146

Waters, R. D., Burnett, E., Lamm, A., & Lucas, J. (2009). Engaging stakeholders through social networking: How nonprofit organizations are using Facebook. *Public Relations Review*, *35*(2), 102–106. doi:10.1016/j.pubrev.2009.01.006

Waters, R. D., & Jamal, J. Y. (2011). Tweet, tweet, tweet: A content analysis of nonprofit organizations' Twitter updates. *Public Relations Review*, *37*, 321–324. doi:10.1016/j.pubrev.2011.03.002

Wittig, M. A., & Schmitz, J. (1996). Electronic grassroots organizing. *The Journal of Social Issues*, *52*(1), 53–69. doi:10.1111/j.1540-4560.1996.tb01361.x

Yerxa, S. W., & Moll, M. (1994). Notes from the grassroots: On-line lobbying in Canada. *Internet Research*, *4*(4), 9–19. doi:10.1108/10662249410798911

ADDITIONAL READING

Addison, C. (2006). Web 2.0: A new chapter in development practice? *Development in Practice*, *16*(6), 623–627. doi:10.1080/09614520600958348

Andreasen, A. R. (Ed.). (2006). *Social marketing in the 21st century*. Thousand Oaks, CA: Sage.

Avner, M. (2004). *The Nonprofit board member's guide to lobbying and advocacy*. St. Paul, MN: Fieldstone Alliance.

Avner, M. (2010). Advocacy, lobbying, and social change. The Jossey-Bass Handbook of Nonprofit Leadership and Management, 39, 347.

Avner, M., & Smucker, B. (2002). *The lobbying and advocacy handbook for nonprofit organizations: Shaping public policy at the state and local level*. St. Paul, MN: Amherst H Wilder Foundation.

Bernstein, A. (2010). G.O.P. Winning social media battle by a large margin. New York: Headcount. Retrieved fromhttp://www.headcount.org/wp-content/uploads/2010/09/VIEW-REPORT1.pdf

Berry, J. M. (2005). *A voice for nonprofits*. Washington, DC: Brookings Institution Press.

Brainard, L. A., & Brinkerhoff, J. M. (2004). Lost in cyberspace: Shedding light on the dark matter of grassroots organizations. *Nonprofit and Voluntary Sector Quarterly*, *33*(3suppl), 32S–53S. doi:10.1177/0899764004265436

Brenner, J. (2013). Planned Twitter IPO follows years of user growth. Pew Research Center Fact Tank. http://www.pewresearch.org/fact-tank/2013/09/13/twitter-ipo-follows-years-of-user-growth/

Bryant, A. (2006). Wiki and the Agora: 'It's organizing Jim, but not as we know it'. *Development in Practice*, *16*(6), 559–569. doi:10.1080/0961520600958165

Carlson, T., & Strandberg, K. (2008). Riding the Web 2.0 wave: Candidates on YouTube in the 2007 Finnish national elections. *Journal of Information Technology & Politics*, *5*(2), 159–174. doi:10.1080/19331680802291475

Chang, A., & Kannan, P. K. (2008). Leveraging Web 2.0 in government. Washington, DC: IBM Center for the business of government.

Davis, R. (2005). *Politics On-line: Blogs, chat rooms and discussion groups in American democracy.* New York: Routledge.

Davis, R. (2010). *Typing politics: The Role of Blogs in American Politics.* New York: Oxford University Press.

Dunlop, J. M., & Fawcett, G. (2008). Technology-based approaches to social work and social justice. *Journal of Policy Practice*, 7(2-3), 140–154. doi:10.1080/15588740801937961

Feld, L., & Wilcox, N. (2008). *Netroots rising.* Westport, CT: Praeger.

Germany, J. B. (Ed.). (2006). Person to person to person: Harnessing the political power of on-line social networks and user generated content. Washington, DC. The Institute for politics, democracy and the Internet, George Washington University.

Grove, S. (2008). YouTube: The Flattening of politics. *Neiman reports. 62* (2).28-30.

Gueorguieva, V. (2008). Voters, MySpace, and YouTube: The Impact of Alternative Communication Channels on the 2008 Election Cycle and Beyond. *Social Science Computer Review, 26,* 288–300. doi:10.1177/0894439307305636

Guo, C., & Saxton, G. (2012). (Forthcoming). Tweeting Social Change: How Social Media Are Changing Nonprofit Advocacy. *Nonprofit and Voluntary Sector Quarterly.*

Hackler, D., & Saxton, G. D. (2007). The strategic use of information technology by nonprofit organizations: Increasing capacity and untapped potential. *Public Administration Review, 67*(3), 474–487. doi:10.1111/j.1540-6210.2007.00730.x

Hamdy, H., & Gomaa, E. (●●●). Framing the Egyptian Uprising in Arabic Language Newspapers and Social Media. *The Journal of Communication, 62,* 195–211. doi:10.1111/j.1460-2466.2012.01637.x

Hessenius, B. (2007). *Hardball lobbying for nonprofits: Real advocacy for nonprofits in the new century.* Palgrave Macmillan. doi:10.1057/9780230604834

Hick, S., & McNutt, J. G. (2002). *Advocacy, activism, and the Internet: Community organization and social policy.* Lyceum Books, Incorporated.

Hoefer, R. (2000). Making a difference: Human service interest group influence on social welfare program regulations. *Journal of Sociology and Social Welfare, 27*(3), 21–38.

Jansen, B. J., Zhang, M., Sobel, K., & Chowdury, A. (2009). Twitter power: Tweets as electronic word of mouth. *Journal of the American Society for Information Science and Technology, 60*(11), 2169–2188. doi:10.1002/asi.21149

Java, A., Song, X., Finin, T., & Tseng, B. (2007, August). Why we twitter: understanding microblogging usage and communities. In *Proceedings of the 9th WebKDD and 1st SNA-KDD 2007 workshop on Web mining and social network analysis* (pp. 56-65). ACM.

Kanter, B., & Fine, A. (2010). *The Networked Nonprofit: Connecting with social media to drive change*. Wiley.com.

Kanter, B., & Paine, K. (2010). *Measuring the networked nonprofit: Using data to change the world*. New York, NY: Jossey Bass.

Kapin, A., & Sample Ward, A. *Social change anytime everywhere: How to implement online multichannel strategies to spark advocacy, raise money*. Hoboken, NJ: Wiley.

Karlin, B., & Matthew, R. A. (2012). Kony 2012 and the Mediatization of Child Soldiers. *Peace Review, 24*(3), 255–261. doi:10.1080/10402659.2012.704222

Lang, P. (2008). Publicly private and privately public. Social Networking on YouTube. *Journal of Computer-Mediated Communication, 13*, 361–380. doi:10.1111/j.1083-6101.2007.00400.x

Lim, M. (2012). Clicks, Cabs, and Coffee Houses: Social Media and Oppositional Movements in Egypt 2004-2011. *The Journal of Communication, 62*, 231–248. doi:10.1111/j.1460-2466.2012.01628.x

Long, R. (2008, April 7). On no you can't: Amateur propagandists in the YouTube age. *National Review, 60*(6), 22.

Madden, M., & Fox, S. (2006). Riding the waves of Web 2.0. Backgrounder. Washington, DC: Pew Internet and American Life Project. Retrieved from http://www.pewinternet.org on October 13, 2006.

Mathos, M., Norman, C., & Kanter, B. (2012). *101 social media tactics for nonprofits: A field guide*. New York, NY: Wiley.

McNutt, J. G. (2006). Building evidence-based advocacy in cyberspace: A social work imperative for the new millennium. *Journal of Evidence-Based Social Work, 3*(3-4), 91–102. doi:10.1300/J394v03n03_07

McNutt, J. G., Adler, G., Jones, J., & Menon, G. M. (2006). The Cyber commons responds to a major disaster: A Study of On-Line Volunteers in the Face of a Natural Disaster. Paper presented at the 35th Annual ARNOVA Conference, Chicago, IL, and November.

McNutt, J. G., & Barlow, J. (2012). A Longitudinal Study of Political Technology Use by Nonprofit Child Advocacy Organizations. In A. Manoharan & M. Holtzer (Eds.), *E-Governance and Civic Engagement: Factors and Determinants of E-Democracy*. Harrisburg: IGI Books.

McNutt, J. G., & Curtis, K. OBoyle, T., & Fox, S. (2010). Coffee or Tea? An Examination of On-line Organizing Techniques of the Tea Party and Coffee Party Movements. Presented at ARNOVA's 2010 Conference in Alexandria, VA, November 18-20, 2010

McNutt, J. G., & Flanagan, M. (2007). Social Networking Choices and Environmental Advocacy Organizations: Implications for Global Social Justice. Paper presented at the 2007 Meeting of the Association for Research on Nonprofit Organizations and Voluntary Action, Atlanta, GA.

McNutt, J. G., & Quiero-Tajalli, I. (2007). Organizing the digital natives. Paper read at the 2007 Community development society/National Rural Development Society Conference symposium, Appleton, WI, June 17-20.

Mosley, J. (2013). Recognizing New Opportunities: Reconceptualizing Policy Advocacy in Everyday Organizational Practice. Social Work 2013: swt020v1-swt020.

Mosley, J. E. (2010). Organizational resources and environmental incentives: Understanding the policy advocacy involvement of human service nonprofits. *The Social Service Review*, *84*(1), 57–76. doi:10.1086/652681

Naim, M. (2007). The YouTube effect. *Foreign Policy*, *158*, 104.

Obar, J. A., Zube, P., & Lampe, C. (2012). Advocacy 2.0: An analysis of how advocacy groups in the United States perceive and use social media as tools for facilitating civic engagement and collective action. *Journal of information policy, 2*.

Perlmutter, D. (2008). *Blogwars*. Oxford, New York: Oxford University Press.

Proscio, T. (2005). *Advocacy funding: The philanthropy of changing minds*. New York: Grantcraft.

Shirky, C. (2008). *Here Comes Everybody: The Power of Organizing Without Organizations*. New York: Penguin.

Song, F. W. (2010). Theorizing Web 2.0. [Routledge.]. *Information Communication and Society*, *13*(2), 249–275. doi:10.1080/13691180902914610

Suárez, D. F. (2009). Nonprofit advocacy and civic engagement on the Internet. *Administration & Society*, *41*(3), 267–289. doi:10.1177/0095399709332297

Teachout, Z., & Streeter, T. (Eds.). (2008). *Mousepads, shoe leather and hope*. Boulder, CO: Paradigm Publishers.

Trippi, J. (2004). *The revolution will not be televised: Democracy, the Internet and the overthrow of everything*. New York: Reagan Book/Harper Collins.

Tufekci, Z., & Wilson, C. (2012). Social media and the decision to participate in political protest: Observations from Tahrir Square. *The Journal of Communication*, *62*(2), 363–379. doi:10.1111/j.1460-2466.2012.01629.x

Watson, T. (2009). *Causewired*. New York: Wiley.

Williams, A. P., Trammell, K. D., Postelnicu, M., Landreville, K. D., & Martin, J. D. (2005). Blogging and hyperlinking: Use of the Web to enhance viability during 2004 U.S. campaigns. *Journalism Studies*, *6*(2), 177–186. doi:10.1080/14616700500057262

Winograd, M., & Hais, M. (2007). *Millennial makeover: MySpace, YouTube and the Future of American politics*. New Brunswick: Rutgers University Press.

Zuniga, M. M. (2008). *Taking on the system: Rules for radical change in a digital era*. New York: Celebra.

KEY TERMS AND DEFINITIONS

Advocacy: The processes, behaviors and activities engaged in by an individual or group aiming to influence public-policy and resource allocation decisions within political, economic, and organizational contexts.

Civic Engagement or Civic Participation: Has been defined as the individual and collective actions designed to identify and address issues of public concerns. It is the right of the people, citizens, to define the public good, determine the policies by which they will seek the good, and reform or replace institutions that do not serve that good.

Nonprofit: Nonprofit Organizations are generally considered (in the United States) those that serve the public good and do not distribute surpluses to shareholders. Some are incorporated while others are not. The Internal Revenue Service certifies some of these organizations as being tax exempt or tax deductible.

Social Change: An alteration in the social order or fabric of society in the US indicating a change in social policy at the city, state or federal level. Social change may include changes in organizations, social institutions, the governance process or social relations.

Social Media, Web 2.0 and Social Software: This is a set of terms that describe software that is Cloud or Internet Based, Facilitates the development of Collective Intelligence, interactivity and user created content. Examples are Social Networking Sites, Blogging and Microblogging, Image and Videosharing and so forth. This differentiates this set of applications from earlier Web based and Pre Web based systems.

Technology: The making, modification, usage, and knowledge of tools, machines, techniques, systems, and methods of organization, in order to solve a problem, improve a preexisting solution to a problem, achieve a goal, handle an applied input/output relation or perform a specific function. In this chapter technology refers to the computer hardware, software, Internet and Web-based applications that support the use of social media.

ENDNOTE

[1] While some would argue that all things done by the nonprofit sector are for social benefit this isn't always the case. Hate Groups, terrorists and other malefactors have found the Internet useful in identifying potential converts and organizing efforts.

This research was previously published in ICT Management in Non-Profit Organizations edited by José Antonio Ariza-Montes and Ana María Lucia-Casademunt, pages 56-72, copyright year 2014 by Business Science Reference (an imprint of IGI Global).

Section 5
Politics and Government Organizations

Chapter 66
Exploring the Concept of the "Social Media Campaign"

Mary Francoli
Carleton University, Canada

ABSTRACT

On May 2, 2011, Canadians voted in what the news media dubbed "Canada's First Social Media Election." This allowed Canadians to join their neighbours to the south who, arguably, had gone through one national social media election during the 2008 bid for the presidency. Through a theoretical discussion of what constitutes sociality and networked sociality, and a critical examination of social media as a campaign tool, this chapter asks "What makes a campaign social?" It also asks if the term "social media campaign" adequately describes current campaign practices? In exploring these questions, the chapter draws on the 2011 federal election in Canada and the 2008 American election. Ultimately, the chapter argues we have limited evidence that social media has led to increased sociality when it comes to electoral politics. This calls the appropriateness of the term "social media campaign" into question. Such lack of evidence stems from the dynamism of networked sociality, which renders it difficult to understand, and methodological difficulties when it comes to capturing what it means to be "social."

INTRODUCTION

Political campaigns around the world are increasingly being referred to as 'social media campaigns' in electoral politics. On May 2, 2011 Canadians, for example, voted in what the news media dubbed "Canada's First Social Media Election" (Curry 2011). Britain's first social media election was in 2010 (Arthur 2010). Elections in other parts of the world, such as Singapore and Thailand, are also increasingly being called 'social'. This growing phenomenon has followed Obama's successful use of social media during his 2008 bid for the presidency, which has been described as "the watershed moment for social media in politics" (Curry, 2011). But what makes an election campaign a social media campaign? This concept has been ill defined. Too often it is used to capture the simple presence of a party or political candidate in the social media sphere, or any political activity during an election period that engages with social media. As will be demonstrated, this includes identifying and quantifying parties and candidates with a

DOI: 10.4018/978-1-5225-5637-4.ch066

profile on popular social networking sites, such as Facebook or Twitter. The purpose of this chapter is take a step back and to better flush out our understanding of a political social media campaign by asking two main questions. First, what makes a campaign social; is presence on a social networking site sufficient or should they meet additional criteria? Second, does the term social media campaign adequately describe recent election campaigns, such as the 2008 American election or the 2011 Canadian federal election? The answer to this question is more than semantics. Clearly identifying the characteristics of a so called social media campaign has the potential to help us better categorize and discuss the various interactive functions of a campaign as well as the strengths and weaknesses which may be associated with each. Such a nuanced definition or understanding of the concept will be of interest to those studying the intersection between social media and electoral politics as well as those interested in the broader literature related to e-democracy and e-participation which make claims about the potential of technology to enhance democracy and citizen engagement. It also has the potential to help identify gaps in our understanding when it comes to the impact of social media. In doing this it raises interesting questions and issues that might be addressed in the future so that we can have a more concrete understanding of sociality, and networked sociality, which will be discussed below. Perhaps most importantly, having a well-defined understanding of a social media campaign today provides a useful point of departure from which to gauge and discuss future change or deviation.

This chapter is divided into four main sections. The first section starts to explore the above-mentioned questions by building on the concepts of 'social', 'social media' and 'Web 2.0' as well as common understandings political campaigning, to establish criteria for determining what constitutes social media campaigning. The second section offers a brief overview of social media campaigning focusing on the 2008 American election, widely thought of as the first large scale social media election, and the 2011 Canadian federal election as one of the more recent jurisdictions to experience its 'first' social media election. The third section returns to the chapter's original research questions. It explores the elements of the two campaigns discussed here in the context of the definitions offered earlier in the chapter in an effort to construct a better understanding of how a social media campaign might be defined. The fourth, and final, section explores avenues for future research. Ultimately, the chapter argues that we have limited evidence of sociality when it comes to electoral politics, calling the appropriateness of the term social media campaign into question. Such lack of evidence stems from the dynamism of networked sociality, which renders it difficult to understand, and methodological difficulties when it comes to capturing what it means to be social. The goal here is modest. Limitations of length make an in-depth examination of all aspects of the case studies as they relate to Internet technology impossible. They also necessitate the simplifying of the concept of sociality, which has a long, varied and eloquent history. The goal here is to start building a better understanding of social media campaigns and the intersection between the Internet and politics. Future work, building on the discussion offered here, will be both interesting and welcome. It is unlikely to think that social media will cease being a part of the campaign toolbox. Towner and Dulio (2012) forecast continued and growing use of new media, particularly social networking tools, for future campaigns in the United States. Indeed, it wouldn't be farfetched to assume this prediction be fulfilled, not only in the United States, but also much more widely. As such more detailed discussions about what the term means will only continue to gain importance.

BACKGROUND

As an initial step in addressing the chapter's goal to define the term social media campaign, it is useful to take a step back, and first consider what is meant by 'social' and 'social media' and by virtue of that Web 2.0 as it is often use synonymously with the term social media. The concept of social is one that is at the same time inordinately simple, yet tremendously complex. Theorists such as Goffman (1959) and Bourdieu (1977), to just to name a few, focus on the concept of social as it relates to human association. Others still (see Durkheim, 1895 as an example), understand social in terms of structure. Parsons, Turner and Mead explored the idea of social action, which is an interesting point of departure if one thinks of a social media campaign in terms of an action. While the unit of analysis may differ, theorists exploring the social concept share the underlying theme of interactive, or joint, activity. At its simplest it can means association (Dolwick, 2009, p. 21). However, as Dolwick (2009) notes, this might refer to a virtually infinite array of interactions.

The term social media suffers from similarly complicated and varied understandings, but again the idea of interactive or joint activity are key. As noted above, it is not uncommon for social media to be primarily defined as a list of applications or technologies that are considered social. However, some have offered more detailed descriptions of its characteristics and defining features. Danah Boyd (2007), offers one of the early definitions of social networking sites. According to Boyd, they can be defined as "Web-based services that allow individuals to 1) construct a public or semi-public profile within a bounded system, 2) articulate a list of other users with whom they share a connection, and 3) view and traverse their list of connections and those made by others within a system. The nature and nomenclature of these connections may vary from site to site" (2007, p.1).

Boyd's article was written prior to the evolution of the term 'Web 2.0.' However, it is often used interchangeably with the term social media. Social media platforms are a defining feature of Web 2.0. As such, it is interesting to round out our discussion on definitions with one focused on Web 2.0. Here, the work of Matthew Allen is interesting to consider. Allen (2008) builds on aspects of O'Reilly's (2005) original definition of the term Web 2.0. According to Allen, Web 2.0 is "a conceptual frame, within which we can correlate and make sense of diverse events even as we use it as a convenient short-hand" (2008). It is comprised of four distinct features. First, it relates to the interactive design and function of Websites. Second, it relates to a business practice which data about users can be gathered and used in meaningful ways. Third, it relates to services that allow active participation of the user, or 'prouser', in the creation, maintenance and expansion of content. And, fourth, it is a "political statement of a kind of libertarian capitalism" (Allen, 2008). Again, the idea of interactivity is foundational.

Keeping these definitions in mind, it is interesting to reflect on traditional notions of political campaigning. Political campaigns have been described as "organized efforts to inform, persuade and mobilize" (Norris, 2001). An interactive element isn't immediately clear here. In elaborating this model of campaign communication, Norris (2001) states that political campaigns contain four elements: "the messages that the campaign organization is seeking to communicate, the channels of communication employed by these organizations, the impact of these messages on their targeted audience, and the feedback loop from the audience back to the organization." Here one might infer interactivity in the form of the feedback loop from the audience to the campaign. Indeed, this is really the only potential space for interactivity under this somewhat linear model of campaign communication. It does little to capture the more networked sense of sociality underpinning the concepts of social media or Web 2.0. Under such a communicative model, social media platforms would likely be rendered one of many channels of communication employed by campaigns. This implies that the technology be used more to 'push' information from campaigns to the public. Thinking of social media in this way causes one to overlook its nuances and the characteristics that make it unique; namely, its potential for interactivity and its highly networked nature.

Rather than invoking the term social media campaign simply because of the presence of social media as one channel of communication, we need to think about what it means and how it differs from other, more traditional channels and campaign strategies. If we are to think about the linear model outlined by Norris and how it might be changed in light of the development of social networking platforms, we might emphasize the third feature of Web 2.0 outlined by Allen (2008) above which details the active participation of users in the creation, maintenance and expansion of content. Such participation can be reinforced with the notion of interactivity offered by Boyd which underpins our various understandings of the concepts of social and sociality. Thinking about the social media campaign in this non-linear way, it begins to resemble more of a networked model of sociality which is dynamic, chaotic, and unstable at times, but which is interactive with a high potential for participation and sharing. Here we can borrow from Wittel's conceptualization of network sociality as one where "social relations are not 'narrational' but informational; they are not based on mutual experience or common history.....Network sociality consists of fleeting and transient, yet iterative social relations" (Wittel, 2001, p. 51). This, Wittel (2001), is careful to distinguish, differs from concepts of community sociality as the idea of "Community entails stability, coherence, embeddedness and belonging. It involves strong and long-lasting ties, proximity and a common history or narrative of the collective" (p. 51). Network sociality, on the other hand, bares characteristics that are not dissimilar from the attributes of the network society described by scholars such as Manual Castells (1998) and Darin Barney (2004). Here, the network form of organization is dominant and informational. Politically, those whose access to media is non-interactive and limited to "passive consumption of commodified content" are disenfranchised (Barney, 2004, p. 122).

Drawing on these understandings of sociality, networked sociality, social networking and Web 2.0, and thinking of them in the context of political campaigning, we can say that a social media campaign should have three main characteristics. First, and really quite obviously, it needs to have a social media presence. Increasingly, this would mean presence on a variety of the platforms described by Boyd and Allen given the rapidly changing nature of the social media sphere. Second, it requires interactivity. This is the crux of social media and the idea of sociality more generally. Third, it needs to be networked. Keeping these characteristics in mind, we can now start to address the chapter's second question: does the term social media campaign adequately capture or describe recent election campaigns which are commonly referred to as social?

RISE OF THE SOCIAL MEDIA CAMPAIGN

Barak Obama's 2008 presidential campaign is largely thought of as the archetypical social media campaign. According to Joe Rospars, Obama's Head of New Media, "the Obama campaign prioritized the Web because it provided a conduit to the very heart of the organization: the ordinary people" (2010). The iconic status of Obama's campaign and the 2008 presidential election begs the question: what about this particular election made people perceive it as a successful social media campaign? On one level the answer to this question is simple. The 2008 presidential election was the first high profile election in the era of new media. There was a novelty factor. Most social networking sites didn't come on the scene until

2005. Facebook, for example, wasn't made available to the general public until 2006. Twitter emerged the same year. YouTube started a year earlier, but hadn't yet gained widespread popularity. As the first presidential election to engage with these technologies, it, in some ways, was dubbed a social media election simply because the technology was used by the campaigns involved. There was an interest and excitement around this use because it was different. But the simple presence of social media tells us little about its impact or why the 2008 election continues to be described as a good example - the example other campaigns seek to emulate - of a social media campaign?

While Obama's use of social media has gained particular notoriety, in part due to his successful bid for presidential office, it should be noted that the technology was used by other campaigns during that particular election. Barak Obama and John McCain both engaged with Facebook, MySpace, Twitter and YouTube. Those interested in the campaigns carefully followed metrics, such as the number of friends or followers each candidate had and how many videos each posted in the case of YouTube (Towner & Dulio, 2012). This information is interesting, but tells us little about the how those friends, or followers, engaged with the campaigns. The numbers in themselves tell us little about interactivity, which, as was established above is a defining feature of social media and a key measure of a social media campaign.

Smith and Rainie's 2008 study of the election lends a bit more detail into how the technology was used. According to the study, 25% of Obama supporters engaged politically in an online social network, 21% shared photos, video or audio, 18% signed up for election updates, 15% donated money online, 11% volunteered online and 12% signed up for email alerts (Smith & Rainie, 2008, p.11). Comparatively, John McCain lagged in all categories. Given the nascent state of the technology, the significance of such statistics cannot be overlooked, but they do prompt one to again question whether the campaigns should be called social media campaigns. At best, 25% of supporters engaged politically. And, many of the activities outlined by Smith and Rainie are not particularly social. Signing up for email alerts and election updates, for example, aren't particularly interactive activities. Indeed they are reminiscent of traditional push or broadcast styles of communication more than indicators of a new form of networked, social communication.

Beyond the more popular social networking platforms, such as Facebook, Twitter or YouTube, the trend to label the campaigns as social media campaigns might come from the creation of social networking sites that were built specifically for the election. Obama's campaign team, aided by Chris Hughes who cofounded Facebook, created its own social networking platform called MyBO. McCain's campaign followed suit with McCainSpace. As Towner and Dulio (2012) state, both social networking sites "allowed individuals to create their own profiles, interact with others and donate funds, among other things" (p. 99). Effectively, the ability to engage with the technology in these ways satisfies Boyd's (2007) defining criteria for social networking. At first blush the development of MyBO and MCCainSpace would seem logical and solid grounds for deeming the election a social media election. However, there is an argument to be made that the sites, while certainly innovative and potentially useful to their respective campaigns, in some ways ran counter to the spirit of social networking and, as such, couldn't have fostered the sense of sociality required of a truly social campaign. Membership or inclusion on the sites was primarily meant for campaign supporters. They served as means by which to bring together groups of like-minded persons rather than the public at large. This is not a criticism. Innovative means of mobilizing supporters might be seen as an extremely smart campaign strategy. In Obama's case, MyBO proved an effective way to organize supporters and have them engage in 'real world', more traditional campaign activities, such as canvassing. However, the narrow user group of the sites does again prompt one to question their potential for sociality. Indeed, the sites remind us more of the characteristics of a community outlined by Wittel (2001), where users have a common history or narrative of the collective. MyBO and McCainSpace give the sense that they are about coherence, belonging and building a stable base of supporters. Again, this might constitute a sort of community sociality and may be valuable from a strategic perspective, but may not be representative of the sort of networked sociality that we draw from social networking sites that would therefore be reminiscent of a social media campaign.

Where we see more concrete evidence of sociality is with the intersection between the online and offline environments. Those involved with MyBO organized over 200,000 offline events and coordinated volunteers to reach out and engage with the broader community through activities such as canvassing (Vargas, 2008). Here we might say that social media was used as a tool to foster sociality in the real world. Organizationally such use of social media was invaluable and successful. We can identify interaction not only between those using MyBO, but also between those on MyBO and those who may have chosen not to engage with the site, or even with the election.

It has been suggested that while social networking and Internet use more generally, added an element of novelty in 2008, the campaigns were still oriented toward more traditional goals, such as fundraising (Towner & Dulio, 2012), advertising and gathering contact information of potential supporters (Kaye, 2009). It is relatively easy to gauge success when it comes to such goals. And, there is no question that Obama's campaign was successful. His campaign used the Internet to raise half a billion dollars (Vargas, 2008). It spent $16 million on Internet advertising (Towner & Dulio, 2012, p. 97). In addition, the campaign used every opportunity to collect email addresses and cell phone numbers in an effort to build its database of contacts. In total it is estimated that the campaign's database included over 13 million email addresses and a million phone numbers (Vargas, 2008). The database was used to push messages regarding campaign updates and fundraising goals to potential supporters. There is little doubt that the campaign's innovative use of the Internet in these ways contributed to Obama's successful bid for the presidency. However, the degree of sociality associated with such activities is questionable. In spite of this, these are the indicators that are often used as measures of a successful social media campaign.

It is also interesting to consider the role of those outside of the professionally run campaigns. People did engage with the campaign, and the election in general, via the Internet. According to Smith and Rainie "voters in 2008 were not just followers of the political process. They also used a wide range of digital tools and technologies to get involved in the race, to harness their creativity in support of their chosen candidate, and to join forces with others who shared their same political goals and interests" (2008, p.21). While the type of involvement discussed by Smith and Rainie is not specifically nor solely related to social media, they do raise an important point. Citizens were using social media as a mechanism to disseminate content they produced and to share information to a wider audience. The popular 'Obama Girl' videos on YouTube serve as one example among many. Here we see indicators of a social media campaign, but lack evidence regarding the extent of sociality, or the reach of the network. Moreover, citizen led efforts often appeared to be running parallel to the official campaigns. In this case we might characterize an election as consisting of social media campaigns led and sustained by citizens, and perhaps media which reported on their efforts. However, the parallel nature of citizen led campaigns does not automatically point to social media campaigns run by parties or candidates.

Much in the same way that we can question the sociality of the 2008 presidential campaign, we can unpack and scrutinize Canada's first social media campaign, the 2011 federal election. Again, the novelty factor comes into play. However, it is interesting that 2011 was dubbed Canada's first social media election in spite of the fact that it was the country's second federal election in the era of social media. The fact that it wasn't used as widely in the previous, 2008, general election suggests, to some extent, that title of social media election was bestowed in 2011 simply because of increased presence. Much of what we actually know about the use of social media during the recent election is numerical. In the same way that people paid close attention to things such as the number of candidates' friends and followers during the US election, so did those in Canada. The media tracked popularity, number of tweets in the case of Twitter, and number of candidates with accounts on an array of social networking platforms (Canadian Press, 2011a). Such numbers are interesting trivia, but again, they tell very little about use and interactivity, key measures of a social media campaign as defined here. A closer inspection of every candidate's Facebook page for example, showed that while some might host a page, that page was little more than a shell with only bits of information and no opportunity for interactivity. Some simply contained Wikipedia entries, including Gilles Duceppe's, the leader of the Bloc Quebecois (Francoli, Greenberg, & Waddell, 2011).

Another common measure of social media use during the election was number of tweets sent by candidates and parties as well as number of tweets circulating that related to the election. It was estimated that over 99,000 election-related tweets were sent the first week of the campaign alone (Canadian Press, 2011b). Such data might provide more insight into use than counts of Facebook friends, but is still slightly problematic in that it only captures data using specific election related hashtags, determined by the researchers, and tells little of the number of unique users or the content of the messages.

While not all parties followed in the footsteps of Obama or McCain to create their own indigenous social networking sites, it was a tactic emulated by the Conservative Party in the form of ToryNation. ca. As one blogger writes, ToryNation is "a 24/7 virtual campaign office. Apparently if you sign in, you get full access to your own online action centre to help: Spread the Conservative message, Find Events nearby, Raise Money, Connect with other Conservatives, and Recruit Volunteers" (Hamilton, 2011). ToryNation led Hamilton (2011) to declare that Stephen Harper, leader of the Conservative Party of Canada, was "out-Obama-ing" Michael Ignatieff, leader of the Liberal Party. The description of features offered on ToryNation raise the same kinds of question about sociality as MyBO and McCainSpace. It was a tool for supporters, not geared toward engaging the public at large in the campaign. And, unlike MyBO, ToryNation emphasized things such as fundraising over the organization of activities in the off-line environment.

The Canadian Press in conjunction with public affairs strategist Mark Blevis, attempted to study social media beyond individual candidates and parties to see whether it was being used for conversation. Their focus was specifically on Twitter. As they note, such a strategy has its limitations: "The methodology is not scientific; searches are being tailored to try to capture material that is clearly linked to the campaign by using a set of 10 hashtags for Twitter and specific sets of keywords for other media or issues" (Canadian Press, 2011b). Francoli, Greenberg and Waddell (2011) engage in a similar undertaking. They use an analytic tool called *ViralHeat* to gauge influence and reach of each of the leaders and their respective parties in the social media sphere. The analysis encompasses a wider range of social networking tools, beyond Twitter, but it suffers similar limitations as that carried out by The Canadian Press and Mark Blevis. The researchers had to determine what terms to follow and then had to train the software to exclude similar terms that might skew the results. CPC for example, refers not only to the Conservative Party of Canada, but also to a host of other organizations including the Canadian Police College. Accuracy of the findings depends on the researchers' ability to effectively screen for and minimize false or misleading results. While there was definite "chatter" in the social media sphere around the election and the different campaigns, these studies found that the "participants were small in number overall and were most likely already committed partisans or voters who would have been more likely to cast ballots whether the technology existed or not (Francoli, Greenberg, & Waddell, 2011, pp. 241-242). Given this, it was concluded that it might be more accurate to refer to the 2011 general election as Canada's first experimental social media election. The sentiment behind the play on phrase first social media election used by media is one of hesitation and reluctance given the lack of evidence of networked sociality and interactivity.

FINDINGS AND DISCUSSION

Reflecting on the meaning of sociality as it relates to a political social media campaign, and the two elections described above, it is useful to return to the original two questions posed in this chapter. First, what makes a political campaign social? Second, is the term social media campaign an adequate term to describe recent campaign practices?

What Makes a Political Campaign Social?

Drawing on traditional understandings of sociality and common definitions of social media and Web 2.0, this chapter has identified three key and interrelated characteristics of a political social media campaign: technology, interactivity and networks. To be considered a social media campaign, a campaign must engage with technology by incorporating social media tools. As was described by Boyd (2007) and Allen (2008), these are tools that allow users to construct and manage a public profile, to maintain a list of connections, to view the connections made by others, and to allow active participation of users and their connections. Here, indicators such as the quantifying of tweets and friends or followers on social networking sites serve as a good starting point for determining the social media presence of a campaign, but presence alone is not sufficient.

In addition to setting up social media profiles, campaigns must use the technology in an interactive manner. While social media by design allows for interactivity, users have significant control over the way that interactive features are, or are not as the case may be, incorporated. Facebook, for example, allows for features such as discussion boards, polls, video and real time chat. However, it also allows for the most basic of profiles which simply broadcasts information about an individual or group. While this sort of informational, uni-directional use of a social media platform may serve as a sort of electronic campaign pamphlet and as such may have some value, it does not engaging with the technology's interactive or social potential. Rather, it is reminiscent of older, more linear and non-networked forms of campaign communication.

A social media campaign must be networked. Networked sociality, as was discussed by Wittel (2001), is somewhat chaotic and can be unstable. It is informational and stems from the ability to harness the interactive features of social media. It flows from a campaign's willingness to step out of the traditional, linear model of campaign communication and to afford people the freedom to create, maintain and expand content, to draw on Allen's (2008) understanding of Web 2.0. Here, such activities don't simply take place outside of traditional campaign activities and communication; rather they are integrated with campaigns.

Keeping these three criteria in mind while reflecting on the American 2008 presidential campaign, which has been seen as the archetypical social media campaign, and the 2011 Canadian federal election campaign, we can turn to the second question posed in this chapter.

Is the Term 'Social Media Campaign' an Adequate Term to Describe Recent Campaign Practices?

While the campaigns involved in the two elections discussed here fulfilled the first criteria of a social media election by having a presence on a range of social media platforms, evidence of interactivity and network are not quite as clear. In these cases evidence of sociality is somewhat limited. We can speculate that such lack of evidence might be attributed to two phenomena: the failure of campaigns to be interactive and lack of knowledge about sociality. Campaigns may not have used social media to its full potential. Instead of embracing interactivity and the idea of a network, which is chaotic and difficult to control, they may have clung to traditional ideas of campaign communication where feedback and involvement of those outside of the campaign is largely uni-directional and highly controlled. Here, email lists and text alert systems come to mind. Michael Turk, a founder of CRAFT|Media/Digital makes this point arguing that campaigns are "not engaging people. They're still trying to use *social media* as a one-way, top-down message dissemination vehicle" (quoted in Towner and Rainie, 2012, p. 104). The desire to control the message and campaign are likely not the only factors contributing to the lack of interactivity and network. Resources also come into play. Determining how to open lines of communication and continually contribute and respond to the network draws on resources that may not be readily available to all campaigns.

However, it is interesting to think of what we know about campaigns in another way and to consider an alternate possibility: that the campaigns may well be much more social than researchers and those analyzing campaigns realize. The dynamism of networked sociality and election campaigns as they are carried out in social media, render them difficult to understand. Networked sociality is, by its nature, not only interactive, but also chaotic and unstable. This is certainly true of social media. Numbers of friends and followers change with regularity. Users control their own privacy settings and therefore the flow of information on their profiles. This makes it difficult for people to understand the reach and impact of social media. For example, a campaign cannot assume that all of the friends of its followers on a platform such as Facebook, will see messages from the campaign in their newsfeeds. Some may have accounts set so such messages do not appear effectively limiting their reach. This problem is intimately related to questions of methodology.

FUTURE RESEARCH DIRECTIONS

Researchers and those interested in campaigns are struggling to determine what methods to use to capture what it means to be social and to break away from the linear model of campaign communication offered by those such as Norris (2001). The dynamism and nature of networked sociality makes measurement very difficult. As was discussed, the more popular measures of success in the campaigns discussed above were indicators such as numbers of friends or followers, number of tweets sent on Twitter, dollars raised, etc. Such data is easily quantifiable, but again, it tells little of interactivity. If technology has contributed to the complexity of the network, making social media campaigns difficult to understand, it may also serve as the solution to this confusion. Experimenting with technology that helps us to measure the social aspect of election campaigns will be increasingly important as campaign further embrace technology.

Given that social media and its use in political campaigns is still a relatively recent practice, it would not be unfair to suggest that we are witnesses both of the above factors come into play. Campaigns have used social media in interesting ways, particularly to support traditional campaign goals, but have not fully or seamlessly incorporated the technology rendering our recognition of sociality somewhat limited. The Canadian and American elections do show technology being used in innovative ways and in ways that, as was seen with Obama's campaign, contributed to great success when it comes to goals such as fundraising, advertising and building a network of contacts. However, these objectives rely more on communication between individuals and the campaign and really do not tell us much about interactivity or activities among those outside of the campaign. On the other hand, higher levels of networked sociality may exist, but may not have been well captured.

Those studying what have been dubbed social media elections have been, and need to continue to, find new ways to measure sociality. Such an expanded understanding of interactivity would provide a much fuller understanding of a social media campaign and networked sociality. This, in turn, will further inform claims about e-democracy and e-participation which explore the impact of digital media on democracy and citizen engagement. With the incomplete understanding we have of interactivity we may want to reconsider the appropriateness of the term 'social media campaign.' Instead, we might apply other labels that more effectively capture our current state of knowledge. Again, debate over such terms is more than semantics. Different terms evoke a range of realities and carry with them differing assumptions. Naming and defining a practice, such as a social media campaign, provides us with a point of departure for future analyses that can capture deviation and change. While the primary purpose of this chapter is simply to raise question about the definition and appropriateness of the term 'social media campaign', and not to detail to pros and cons of alternative language, two suggestions are offered as starting points for discussion: Internet campaign and social campaign. The first, an older concept, is much more general than social media campaign. It relates to a range of activities that take place in the online environment. While some of these activities may contain potential for sociality, not all do, and indeed the term Internet campaign makes no claim of sociality. This more general term allows us to recognize innovative campaign activities that may not be based on social media. It also fits well with existing knowledge of online campaigning which has focused on data that is easy to identify and quantify.

Alternatively, the term 'social campaign' does lay claims of sociality, but does not limit them to the social media sphere. This allows for greater flexibility to recognize interaction in the real world environment. As discussed above, activities and engagement in the offline world was where sociality can be seen. This was effectively brought about by social media sites such as MyBO or ToryNation, but evidence of interactivity and sociality within the sites themselves was somewhat limited. All terms will have pros and cons and will appeal to some or none. However, as this chapter has argued, it is useful to give the term 'social media campaign' further thought in the future.

REFERENCES

Allen, M. (2008). Web 2.0: An argument against convergence. *First Monday*, *13*(3). doi:10.5210/fm.v13i3.2139

Arthur, C. (2010, May 3). 2010: The first social media election: This is the first British general election in the social media age, but what difference has it made? *The Guardian*. Retrieved January 6, 2012 from http://www.guardian.co.uk/media/2010/apr/30/social-media-election-2010

Barney, D. (2004). *The network society*. Cambridge, UK: Polity.

Bboyd, D. (2007). Social network sites: Definition, history, and scholarship. *Journal of Computer-Mediated Communication, 13*(1).

Bourdieu, P. (1977). *Outline of a theory of practice*. Cambridge, UK: Cambridge University Press. doi:10.1017/CBO9780511812507

Canadian Press. (2011a). *The social media battleground of the 2011 federal election*. Retrieved May 3, 2012 from http://www.marketingmag.ca/news/media-news/the-social-media-battleground-of-the-2011-federal-election-25038

Canadian Press. (2011b). *Social media takes off in first week of campaign*. Retrieved May 3, 2012 from http://www.ctv.ca/servlet/ArticleNews/story/CTVNews/20110402/social-media-election-110402/20110402?s_name=election2011

Castells, M. (1998). *End of millennium*. Oxford, UK: Blackwell.

Curry, B. (2011, March 27). Canada's first social media election is on, but will people vote? *Globe and Mail*. Retrieved January 6, 2012 from http://www.theglobeandmail.com/news/politics/canadas-first-social-media-election-is-on-butwill-people-vote/article1959166/

Dolwick, J. (2009). The social and beyond: Introducing actor-network theory. *J Mari Arch, 4*, 21–49. doi:10.1007/s11457-009-9044-3

Durkheim, E. (1895). *The rules of the sociological method*. New York: The Free Press.

Francoli, M., Greenberg, J., & Waddell, C. (2011). The campaign in digital media. In *The Canadian federal election of 2011*. Toronto: Dundurn.

Goffman, E. (1959). *The presentation of self in everyday life*. New York: Doubleday and Anchor Books.

Hamilton, A. (2011). *How Stephen Harper is out-Obama-ing Michael Ignatieff*. Retrieved May 3, 2012 from http://www.aranhamilton.com/post/4350146223/how-stephen-harper-is-out-obama-ing-michael-ignatieff

Kaye, K. (2009). *Campaign '08: A turning point for digital media*. CreateSpace.

Metzgar, E., & Maruggi, A. (2009). Social media and the 2008 U.S. presidential election. *Journal of New Communications Research, 4*(1), 141–165.

Norris, P. (2001). *Do campaign communications matter for civic engagement? American elections from Eisenhower to G.W. Bush*. Retrieved May 1, 2012 from http://www.hks.harvard.edu/fs/pnorris/Acrobat/Farrell&Schmitt-Beck%20Chapter%209.pdf

O'Reilly. (2005). *What is web 2.0: Design patterns and business models for the next generation of software*. Retrieved January 6, 2012 from oreilly.com/pub/a/Web2/archive/what-is-Web-20.html

Rospars, J. (2010). *Election 2010: New digital battlefield, same old politics none of the parties have leveraged new media in this campaign to build support in the way Barack Obama did*. Retrieved January 10, 2012 from http://www.guardian.co.uk/commentisfree/2010/may/04/new-digital-battlefield-old-politics

Smith, A., & Rainie, L. (2008). *The internet and the 2008 election.* Pew Internet and American Life Project. Retrieved January 10, 2012 from http://www.pewInternet.org/~/media//Files/Reports/2008/PIP_2008_election.pdf.pdf

Towner, T., & Dulio, D. (2012). New media and political marketing in the United States: 2012 and beyond. *Journal of Political Marketing, 11,* 95–119. doi:10.1080/15377857.2012.642748

Vargas, J. (2008, November 20). Obama raised half a billion online. *The Washington Post.* Retrieved May 4, 2012 from http://voices.washingtonpost.com/44/2008/11/obama-raised-half-a-billion-on.html

Wittel, A. (2001). Toward a network sociality. *Theory, Culture & Society, 18*(6), 51–76. doi:10.1177/02632760122052048

KEY TERMS AND DEFINITIONS

e-Democracy: The use of information and communication technology to enhance democratic practice.

e-Participation: The use of information and communication technologies to consult and engage publics in decision making.

Networked Sociality: A model of sociality which is dynamic, chaotic, and unstable at times, but which is interactive with a high potential for participation and sharing.

Political Campaigning: Pippa Norris (2001) describes political campaigning as organized efforts to inform, persuade and mobilize.

Social Media Campaign: A campaign that has a social media presence, is interactive, and is networked.

Social Networking Sites: Digital platforms where users have a profile, a list of connections, and where they engage in content creation and sharing. Interactivity is a defining characteristic.

Sociality: A model of human relations which, among other things, is characterized by an interactive, or joint, activity.

This research was previously published in Transforming Politics and Policy in the Digital Age edited by Jonathan Bishop, pages 133-144, copyright year 2014 by Information Science Reference (an imprint of IGI Global).

Chapter 67
Social Media in Political Public Relations:
The Cases of the Portuguese Social Democratic Party (PSD) and the Socialist Party (PS) in the 2009 Parliamentary Campaign

Sónia Pedro Sebastião
Universidade de Lisboa, Portugal

Alice Donat Trindade
Universidade de Lisboa, Portugal

ABSTRACT

This chapter demonstrates how Web social media can be used in different ways to create more personalized or more impersonal messages in political public relations campaigns. When everyone is awakening to the potential of these social media for political communication campaigns, it is necessary to find alternative strategies to spread our word and distinguish ourselves from our competition. At this point, it is important to define the targets of persuasion and public relations; in addition, the manner in which a public relations campaign can be helpful is yet to be established, as well as the most adequate social media to be used.

INTRODUCTION

A revolution does not happen when a society adopts new tools. It happens when society adopts new behaviors (Clay Shirky, 2008).

The Internet has evolved from a late 20th century information platform, to a 21st century manifold platform that leaves behind models devised at the time of broadcast to enter a time of a two way system of communication.

DOI: 10.4018/978-1-5225-5637-4.ch067

Besides this relevant change, the Internet not only allows ample exchange of thought, but also trade, as an e-commerce tool that provides a new virtual marketplace where users meet online. This means that, additionally, it has turned into a source of easy access to information about products, organizations, public and political issues. Nowadays, web social media have the potential to provide platforms where organizations and individuals can dialogue directly with stakeholders and segmented publics without the traditional mediation of gatekeepers (Phillips & Young, 2009, p. 7). Thus communication became porous and (sometimes) more transparent, reducing inefficiencies and price disparities (Bornheim, 2001, p. 21).

While being recognized as bringing forth the need to inform about everything with transparency and in the right time, the Internet primarily contributes to the availability of an immense volume of information, which can be turned into knowledge, and lead to enhanced freedom of choice, consequently transforming informed consumers into more demanding patrons. This way, and thanks to this platform, it is possible to search for all kinds of information in a quick, constant and selective form. Thus, competition between social actors is getting stronger every day and they are obliged to establish innovative strategies that present fewer costs, high quality, engaging ideas and arguments, and to develop a relation of bigger proximity with each other.

However, the entire world is not online, i.e., web consumption by different generations is not similar (PEW, 2009). On the one hand, prevailing identitarian models of Internet users were early on found to be mainly male white, affluent (Loader, 2011, p. 758). Besides, and thanks to the digital divide, not everyone has access to Internet (income, accessibility, literacy constraints) (Norris, 2001). So we need to know who our publics are, how long they are spending online, what they are doing, and how they interact with web social media, before we define our online communication strategy.

According to Matt Haig, the Internet has changed the activity of the Public Relations practitioner and we are facing a new scenario of e-PR: everything that is communicated online is Public Relations activity and the success of online communication depends on the kind of relations that the organization is able to build with its online audience (2000, p. 1). So the fulfillment of e-PR- is largely chance-related and bets on maintaining close and continuous relations that have been started, managed and kept online, but that can, at any moment, be transferred to a presential situation, for example, to a special event promoted by the organization or brand.

A different opinion has Deidre Breakenridge. Though she agrees that web 2.0 is "putting the public back in Public Relations" (with Brian Solis, 2009), Breakenridge states that the web is only a technological platform, that puts communication together but it will always be the Public Relations' professional job to create messages and interaction with different publics, suiting the former to whatever it takes to get the latter's attention (2008, p. 261). Nevertheless, web social media are amplifying the value and effectiveness of Public Relations as a profession. This opinion is shared by Phillips and Young when they recognize the need for the Public Relations practitioner to define the organization's Internet strategy as more than a presence/absence on a new platform, and more as a discipline in its own right with the benefits of low costing storage, maintenance and distribution of information (2009, pp. 70-71).

In the political area, Public Relations have found a home in the field of political communication (Newman & Vercic, 2002). Public relations have a twofold role in this area; they deal with the communicative needs of political campaigns, candidates' image and reputation management, while simultaneously choosing the adequate tools to transmit those messages to different publics. So Public Relations can be seen as "lubricants that enable political machinery to run smoothly" (Newman & Vercic, 2002, p. 3). As a communication technology, the internet is also being used in political campaigns to spread messages and contribute to inform and engage voters. Web social media, in particular, have been used by Political Public Relations to connect with electorates all over the world (e.g. Haas, 2001; Hermes, 2006; Herrnson, Stokes-Brown & Hindman, 2007; Chadwick, 2009) since they are the sites where people spend most of their online time (e. g. Piombino, 2012).

The main purposes of this research are to highlight the specificities of the online message and structure of the two main Portuguese political parties and to demonstrate how web social media can be used in different ways to create more personalized or more impersonal messages in political public relations campaigns and enhance *eparticipation* among Portuguese citizens who are frequent users of the web. As such, the terms of "user" and "citizen" are mentioned in an interchangeable form.

This chapter has been divided into three main parts. In the first one, previous research on web social media and politics, more specifically citizens' participation and communication campaigns, is introduced. In the second part, methodological approach and data collection are defined, referring they are based on the structural website analysis of the two main Portuguese political parties (PSD and PS). As a complement, the user generated content produced in the private social network of PS, *MyMov*, is also analyzed. The analysis is focused on Computer-Mediated Discourse Analysis (CMDA) of the text messages displayed in the web social network *MyMov* public area, using, as a consequence, participant-based sampling. In the last part, the main results are discussed and some final remarks are made.

WEB, POLITICS AND PUBLIC RELATIONS: LITERATURE REVIEW

The relation between Web and Politics has been studied by several authors, for example: Katz (1997); Coleman (1999); Norris (2000); Wilhelm (2000); Stromer-Galley (2000); Dahlgren (2001); Haas (2001); Lax (2004); Shane (2004); Hermes (2006); Chadwick (2006 and 2009); Herrnson, Stokes-Brown, & Hindman (2007); Mossberger, Tolbert, & McNeal (2008); Park & Perry (2008), who tried to state the importance and limitations of these instruments to deepen the relation between citizens and political actors.

The main concerns of the researchers were: citizens' information; their participation and engagement in political life and debate; and the communication between political actors and citizens. While in early research some optimism could be found and the web was presented as a tool that would motivate and deepen the relationship between citizens and politicians, later ones called the attention to the loss of control over information, the lack of citizens' interest in general politics and the remaining inequalities of access (to web and to political information).

Nevertheless, and according to Phillips and Young, success in politics is now highly influenced by the online activities of political institutions. In this platform, they can exchange views on the latest political developments or hot topics, inviting the public and citizens to comment and adhere to their political programs (2009, p. 88). As a potential way of escaping the "top-down" politics of mass democracy in which political parties make policy with low level participation or citizens' involvement, the Internet provides means for high differentiation of political information and ideas and (at least) theoretical possibilities of participation and high level of involvement in negotiations and feedback between leaders and followers (McQuail, 2000, p. 135). However, a significant limitation to this online involvement is the lack of interest of the electors (Lax, 2004, p. 226). Even if they have access to Internet that does not mean that they will spend time engaging in political debate, because most people simply do not bother (Gauntlett, 2004, p. 21).

Another crucial item in the use of web in political communication campaigns is the interactivity feature. While the low cost and the wide reach of the web to spread messages is important, it may be ineffective if users are not motivated or do not possess the skills to surf in highly interactive pages and contents, that is, if we do not engage users with the political messages or if we are too ambitious with the kind of web design we choose. According to Sundar, Kalyanaraman, & Brown (2003) interactivity is usually associated with positive perception, so the user will only make an effort to search and read the information if he feels engaged with the political party or message. Besides, low interactivity websites have the advantage of departing from the non-interactive nature of the traditional mass media campaign, more familiar and easily consumed by users.

As a whole, it is our belief that the Internet has not fundamentally changed the nature of political action (e. g. Hindman, 2008). It only provides tools that empower people to have a more direct, constant and personal participation in the formal political process – if they want to (e.g. Turkle, 2005; Shirky, p. 2008).

Throughout the last few years and with an increasing penetration of Internet in Portuguese households (58% in 2011 according to the last official survey by Eurostat), political parties seem to have found a new means of communication with their electorate. As a result, political websites and new communication strategies have been developed.

Web social media have become an integral part of modern society. There are web social solutions to just about every need, and Public Relations are not an exception. Through the use of Internet, and specially of web social media, we can access tools that allow and simplify the edition, distribution and storage of information, such as: e-mail, websites, weblogs, RSS (feeds), podcasts, videocasts, instant messaging, voip, forums, wikis, social communities, search engines, social bookmarking and so on. As communication tools, social media are transforming the role and the work of Public Relations practitioners.

In this digital context, the individuals are active and they can produce and manipulate contents in an easy and quick way. Consequently, they stop being dependent on info-communication hierarchy, assuming the control over the contents that interest them. As producers of online contents, the active participants become, consequently, leaders of opinion and creators of noise and buzz, that is, of Word of Mouth.

The possibility of the user to contribute to web-content development, rate, collaboration and distribution, as well as to customize web applications, defines "participative web" and user empowerment. For instance, the effective participation of common web users gives place to user generated content (or user-created content), that is, to content made publicly available over the web, created outside professional routines and practices, using a variable amount of creativity, and shared among Internet users at an increasing speed thanks to broadband availability. Users that generate content are motivated by factors that include: peer interrelation, the pursuit of fame, notoriety and self-expression. As a consequence, the web can be seen as an open platform, enriching diversity of opinion and the free flow of information that otherwise would not be available to citizens. However, "the use of digital network technologies to shape public policy is generally met with incredulity by most politicians, public servants and citizens" (Chadwick, 2009, p. 12).

In addition, and with increasing users' number and diversification of online activities, Public Relations practitioners find the Internet to be another tool that allows them to: know the national and international markets' evolution and environment changes, and to quickly develop secondary inquiries in an easy, quick and efficient way; know the news and activities of the competition; communicate and acknowledge the opinion of publics; test re-styling, new concepts and possible public affairs; fulfill their legal obligations in a quick and simple form, as well as know their legal situation; spread events, news and contents; among many other possibilities. All these tools and online communication potential may allow the identification of a new kind of Public Relations professional: Public Relations 2.0.

Even with this leverage, web social media also present some disadvantages. Namely, it is necessary to take into account that the Internet is not accessible to all individuals and, therefore, information does not reach the whole population, due to the technological and income divides. In addition, we may also pinpoint: the feeling of insecurity toward the new medium (e.g. Wilhelm, 2000; Turkle, 2005); the lack of representativeness of different opinions (e.g. Norris, 2001; Baudrillard, 2007; Hindman, 2008; Chadwick, 2009) and the consequent need to know the profile of the public that expresses those different opinions (e.g. Phillips & Young, 2009; Breakenridge & Solis, 2009). In some situations, available online information is not credible, reflecting the fact that any user can produce contents and alter the already existing ones (e.g. Wilhelm, 2000; Baudrillard, 2007; Chadwick, 2009). So, and as noted by David Philips (2001, p. 6), it is important to take into account the easiness and quickness of the use of Internet to highlight and destroy a reputation. Thus, we must be very careful with the kind of information (text, photos, video, audio) we put online, because this information may be easily distorted, manipulated and reproduced, and be aware of the fact that control over it is fleeting. As stated by Chadwick (2009) "successful e-democracy programs may require a plurality of different sociotechnical values and mechanisms".

In spite of the importance of computer mediated communication and of the available online communicative instruments, the Public Relations practitioner and organizations must not substitute or look down upon face-to-face communication, since publics are composed by people with beliefs, values, attitudes and unpredictable and changeable behaviors. Besides, the Internet does not substitute other social media, but complements them (Park & Perry, 2008).

Despite the advantages of web social media in Public Relations activities, and especially in political campaigns, Public Relations practitioners cannot lose sight of the fact that online communication does not replace offline communication. In a political campaign, the communication strategy must take into account all platforms to ensure and improve the effectiveness of the message in terms of distribution and adhesion.

WEB SOCIAL MEDIA, PSD AND PS IN THE 2009 PARLIAMENTARY CAMPAIGN

In the year 2009, Portuguese citizens went to the polls for three kinds of elections: European Elections; National Government and Parliament Elections; and Municipalities Elections. The two main parties: the PSD – Social Democratic Party (European Affiliation: European People's Party - EPP) and the PS – Socialist Party (European Affiliation: Party of European Socialists) were, once again, disputing victory, using different sorts of messages, mainly due to their roles: the first one as opposition, trying to win power back; the second one as the governmental party that tried to maintain its position.

This chapter focuses the Parliamentary Campaign, where the two main Portuguese parties used web social media and, especially, web social networks in two different ways. The PSD communication strategy seemed to be oriented to global dissemination with the employment of free tools used by the e-community. PSD messages were spread over the most popular global social networks, with heavy use of blogging and micro-blogging.

The PS developed more specific communication, maintaining its historical message and website structure, where its own social network was created, to be accessed by registered members only. This way the party was able to generate consistent, continuous and exclusive relations with its followers.

Bearing in mind the main purpose of this chapter and the computer mediated discourse analysis technique presented by Susan Herring (2004) website analysis of both PSD and PS has been developed.

The main objective is to describe its general content (text, image, video, reports), usability (how easy it is to use the website for those who access it) and interactivity (considering the tools that allow user participation, such as: the option for external users to post comments or contact the site author by e-mail, podcasting, audio and video downloads, user surveys, and the possibility of subscribing) characteristics (Xifra & Huertas, 2008). Considering the general structure of websites1 and our need to understand the use of social media, four main parts in the websites have been acknowledged: header, top menu, main body and social networks' connection. Some elements have been highlighted in each of these parts: the main semiotic elements (leader image, slogan, symbol and colors); web tools (search, syndication, links); multimedia contents (photo and video gallery); interactivity tools (comments form, opinion polls, and so on) and main themes of the messages. After the description of websites, both websites and features have been compared.

The PSD Website (www.psd.pt)

In the process of the 2009 campaign, the PSD institutional website was transformed into a secondary website dedicated to the 2009 campaigns (Parliament and Municipalities) and automatically displayed whenever someone accessed the main website. The main site only became available by pressing the party logo in the secondary website, reversing the natural order of site display.

The secondary website was called "Política de Verdade" ("Truthful Policy") – http://www.politicade-verdade.com/ - the main slogan used by PSD in the campaign propaganda (see Table 1).

The secondary website of PSD can be classified as user-friendly, simple and objective. It reveals coherency of contents and message. The points being transmitted are hard to miss, whether they are institutional or reports or outcomes from third sources (studies, opinion polls), as they are clearly organized. Videos and pictures are grouped in albums systematized by date and place. The contents are introduced by a small text and an available option to change its appearance (increase or diminish the font size) is provided. The users are given the option to share all contents.

The PSD communication strategy seems to be oriented towards global dissemination with the use of free tools familiar to the e-community. PSD messages are spread into the main social networks used in Portugal (*hi5, facebook, youtube, twitter, flickr*), demonstrating not only the nature of a catch-all party but also trying to be visible to everyone. Basically, their message could not be missed.

This strategy can be explained by the need for voters from this opposition party that wishes to conquer power and be elected as the main political force in Portugal. Therefore, their need for a wide-ranging and universal message that may yield the best result on polling day: everyone seeks the truth. PSD political communication is grounded on the value of transparency, present in their online tools, where free information access (especially to statistical data and opinion polls), openness, information sharing, engagement, collaboration (interactivity tools) and user generated content can be found.

Website content management was done by PSD Youth and the webmaster. Moreover, the number of comments or replies from a candidate, at least, from the most publicly known ones, is extremely low.

The PS Website (www.ps.pt)

The political communication of the Socialist Party is quite different from the one of the main opposition party –PSD. PS maintains its institutional website with historical background, affiliations, party members and achievements (see Table 2). Pieces of news are related to campaign moments but also to

Table 1. Secondary website analysis (http://www.politicadeverdade.com/)

Header	
Photography of the Party leader – Manuela Ferreira Leite with slogan	
Symbol of the campaign	
Main logo in the right corner (logo redirected to main website)	
Main colors	White, orange and green
Top Menu	
Search	
RSS	
Main body	
News	With links to videos, speeches, interviews, media appearance, clipping, forum, popular opinions on video and audio streaming
Campaign Agenda	Mostly events with the leader
Donations	With the indication of payment modes
Opinion poll	Electronic form requesting identification
Photo gallery	Link to Flickr
Social Networks	
Weblog «Politica de Verdade» (*Truthful policy*)	With a list of associated blogs (blog network) . same header . propaganda . short text

[1]SAPO: Search engine created and developed by the University of Aveiro and used by a number of Portuguese organizations. Nowadays, one of the main Internet and web providers in Portugal.

Table 2. Secondary website analysis (http://www.socrates2009.pt/)

Header	
Photography of the Party leader – Jose Socrates with slogan	
Main logo in the right corner (the logo redirects to the main website)	
Main colors	Red and white
Top Menu	
MyMov Search	Registration and login
Programme	Important events in the previous government programme (2005/2009) Programme to 2009/2013
Campaign Agenda	
MovTV News	Campaign videos TV spots Of the campaign, but specially focusing the leader
Downloads	Photos Videos Documents Widgets and bottoms Wallpapers and Screensavers Leaflets and other printable elements
MyMov	(see social Network below)
I participate (October 12th)	Forum (not presented in the traditional thread way but as sequencial messages similar to posts on weblogs): . Ambition for Portugal (140 messages)

[1]*Novas Oportunidades* – New Opportunities, a lifelong learning programme launched by a PS government in 2006

government policies and measures. So current information is used as propaganda, but somehow clouded as fact forwarding a posture displaying: "see, we are doing this, it's not only talk".

The main distinguishing features of the PS website are:

1. The use of the leader's image and name in a secondary website that was displayed in a pop-up window - http://www.socrates2009.pt/;
2. The creation of *MyMov*, a private social network, targeted to registered members, either sympathetic to, or followers of the party;
3. Special content generated to mobile devices: Socrates2009 mobile http://m.socrates2009.pt/.
4. The PS slogan ("Avançar Portugal" - *Portugal moving forward*) used in street campaigns (leaflets, outdoor and other print media) can only be found in the Government Program website section.

The secondary website of PS is user-friendly, simple and objective. It reveals coherency of contents and message, mostly related with institutional information. The website is enriched with campaign pictures especially focused on the leader. The contents are introduced with a short text, and users are given the ability to share all of the former.

PS use of the web social network was professional and innovative. It was totally dedicated to its usual supporters who can be classified as active in the search for information and willing to register and supply personal information. After the registration in *MyMov*, members were able to freely discuss their ideas on the website; they received mobile text messages with invitations to dinners, debates, public presentation and other campaign actions and e-mailed newsletters with news and incentives to participate in the campaign.

Then again, there is a latent assumption that the party's web presence would not alter the support given to PS by its steady voters, as they are well aware of its achievements. After all, the PS had a majority of votes in the 2005 elections, and the party bets on maintaining its existing supporters leaving the challenging strategy to the PSD, the party in higher need of more followers and voters.

MyMov: User Generated Content

As mentioned before, the innovative web campaign of PS included a private social network: *MyMov*. The analysis of *MyMov* content has been particularly fruitful within the context of this research. The main questions were: Did *MyMov* enhance the political participation of PS supporters? What kind and quantity of "User Generated Content" was displayed in *MyMov* public area? Was the registered members' discourse one of support or criticism?

Participant-based sampling has been used for the Computer-Mediated Discourse Analysis (CMDA) of the public text messages displayed in the Social Network *MyMov*. According to Herring (2004) what defines CMDA at its core is the analysis of verbal interaction logs (characters, words, expressions, messages, connections, threads, archives, and so on). The analysis has considered:

1. Computer-mediated data sample (*corpus*): text messages in *MyMov* public area (April to October 2009) – see Table 3;
2. Categories and units of analysis: Coded participant; Word count; Named actors: from PS, from the opposition, President of the Republic (PR), other and non-identified actors; General message content: support to PS, criticism to PS, criticism to the opposition, hot issues (from the news), cam-

Table 3. User generated messages in MyMov (April to October, 2009)

Social Network	MyMov	Total messages	Friends
Public Area	Wall messages	<u>260</u>	
	Links (news and weblogs)	53	
	Videos	48	
	Campaign Photos	257	
Groups (private area)	Environment	7	246
	Culture	26	234
	Companies and Jobs	52	312
	Energy	10	166
	Science and Technology	8	217
	Europe and World	13	217
	Defense	5	93
	Security	11	11
	Justice	6	6
	Education and Qualification	20	20
	Health	23	23
	Regional Development	29	29

paign (social networks activity, divulgation, slogans and propaganda), and no clear topic (popular quotes and poems, non-sense).

3. Applied method(s) of analysis to data and interpretation of the results.

CMDA has been used as a basis to verify the following hypotheses, considering the messages posted in the public area:

H_1: *MyMov* did not enhance the political participation of PS followers.
H_2: *MyMov* registered members text messages are mainly supportive to PS.

To verify H_1 quantitative data has been used to compare the number of PS militants with the total number of text, word count, numbers of registered participants and users creating content.

For H_2 verification, the actor(s) referred and the declared subject(s) of the text messages have been considered. All the named individuals and subjects in each message have been identified to avoid the subjectivity of the "most dominant subject" classification.

260 text messages, posted by 110 registered participants, have been examined in the public area of *MyMov* forum. Only registered members were able to post messages even in the public area. The public area was available for reading to all web users that accessed the website (www.socrates2009.pt).

None of these registered participants were PS politicians, only *MyMov* anonymous members. As such, there were no replies to the content created by PS supporters, or candidates or any debate on any posted issue.

47.69% of the posted messages were written by 7 registered members, that is, by 6.36% of the participants in the wall messages of *MyMov* public area. As a consequence, 103 (93.64%) registered members individually posted less than 5 messages in the public area (see Table 4).

Table 4. How many posted messages per participant?

Participant code	Number of posted messages	% (total messages)	% (registered participants)
19	53	20.38	
41	15	5.77	
73	15	5.77	
4	14	5.38	
83	11	4.23	
33	10	3.85	
7	6	2.31	47.69
All the others	Less than 5 (each)		52.31

As regards the length of messages, statistical data has shown a total word count of more than 33 000 words, with an average of 129 words per message (see Table 5).

Considering the actors named in the text messages, the majority are PS members (54.62%) followed by opposition members (30%). About 20.77% of the messages did not identify an author (see Figure 1).

The highest percentage of messages' content has been dedicated to supporting the party (28.85%), political campaign contents favouring PS message (26.92%), the PS leader (24.23%) and criticizing the opposition members (22.31%). Only 3.85% of the messages were critical of PS (see Figure 2).

Discussion

The comparison of the two parties' websites with messages oriented to the Parliament campaign has revealed that their structure and contents are not very different. The main differences are related with menu information and interactivity features (see Table 6). On the PS website, menu information is mainly

Table 5. How many words per message?

Word count	
Total	33294
Minimum	1
Maximum	394
Mean	128,55

Figure 1. Actor(s) identified in the posted text messages (%)
Category "others" contains: Salazar (historical figure); journalists; company president; dead actor (Raul Solnado); head of the Lawyers' Guild (Marinho Pinto).
The same message may have the identification of several actors.

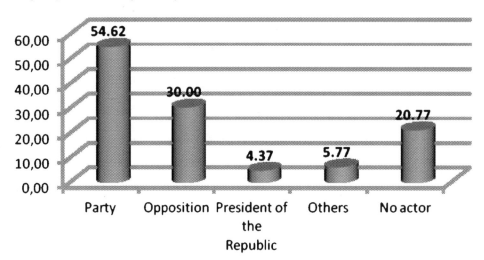

Figure 2. Main themes of the posted text messages (%)
Category "campaign" contains: social agenda, propaganda and slogan divulgation, appeal to vote (including in the reflexion day, when campaign is forbidden).
Category "hot issues" contains: media and politics relation (especially criticism to journalists); conflicts and tensions with the President of the Republic.
Category "other" contains: proposals to improve the campaign; personal divulgation and people's requests (reforms, subsidies). The same message may have up to 3 of the listed subjects.

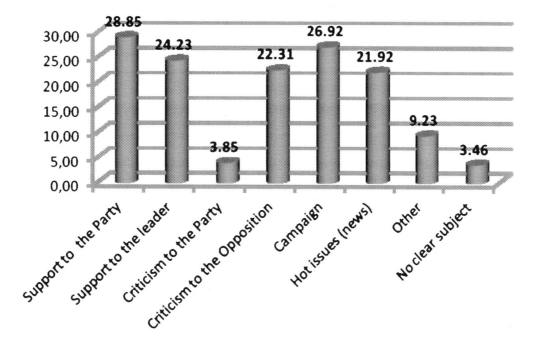

about the party historical and structural existence; while PSD adds data about the country's situation to institutional information, as well as direct links to their web social media profiles. Finally, and regarding interactivity features, the PS offers the possibility of collaboration based on the updating of information about its followers.

Then again, though PSD was promoting its general slogan, providing the country with statistical data that denounced its economic, financial and social situation, in a clear opposition campaign, the PS was spreading information about its policies and main results trying to contradict the opposition campaign and to maintain Portuguese citizens' trust.

On one hand, the PS seemed to have bet totally on its leader – José Socrates – despite the Prime Minister's former attitude, often viewed by the people as arrogant, besides an alleged past involvement in corruption actions. This can be related with his high media profile, with a carefully managed image and presentation, a nice smile and a preachy speech tone. On the other hand, the PSD tried to avoid its less *mediatic* leader's image described by many citizens as an old, austere, rigid, unpleasant, and obsolete lady.

Analyzing data available up to October 11th 2009 (last elections for municipalities) it appears that the PS Social Network did not achieve much success among its followers. On one hand, the general forum had less than one thousand messages posted by less than a hundred followers. On the other hand, only the group of "companies and jobs" in the social network had a few more than three hundred followers and fifty two posts. This fact may have been caused by several reasons, among which might be emphasized: the innovative proposal in the use of social networks which implies new registration, and a rupture with traditional ways in Portuguese political communication; the lack of interest in pre-created groups

Table 6. Comparison PS and PSD website contents and features

		PS	PSD
Structure		Hierarchical	Hierarchical
Party identification		All pages and sections (header)	All pages and sections (header)
Search feature		On top	On top
Content promotion (banner)		Central	Central
News (central and highlighted)		Campaign	Campaign
Menu	Horizontal (top)	Institutional	Institutional
Vertical		Institutional	Outcomes
Horizontal (bottom)		Institutional	Social Media
Visual Identity		Logo. Colors: blue, red, black and white.	Logo and slogan. Colors: orange, blue, black and white.
Speech style		Few and objective words. Low use of images (leader in most of them).	Few and objective words. High use of images (campaign with several candidates)
Interactivity	Direct contact / comment	MyMov / contact form	Comments / contact

(registered members could not create new groups); the overwhelming number of campaign actions and the regular lack of involvement of Portuguese citizens in political campaigns.

From the results of user generated content scrutiny it is possible to appreciate that even PS supporters are not available to participate in its political campaign, in activities involving its private web social network. This conclusion is possible if it is considered that PS has 73,140 militants (February 2009) but, on one hand, only 110 posted text messages in the public area of *MyMov* and, on the other hand, only 7 of these 110 authored almost half (47.69%) of the 260 posted messages. This data allows the confirmation of H_1.

The lack of participation in the online social network developed for the 2009 campaign can be the result of:

- **Apathy:** The general lack of interest in politics;
- **Impact:** The view that individual messages will not make a difference;
- **Alienation:** The view that politics is "not for common people";
- **Knowledge:** Not having technological skills to make the online registration and post messages;
- **Inconvenience:** User generated content is too time consuming, just as much as it is to follow the political campaign on media and on the streets;
- **Wavering:** The citizens' lack of commitment and debt of civic duty.

This data may be evidence to the statement that technological progress does not change the way Portuguese people feel about politics. Supplementary constraints to participation in the political field are in fact added by new possibilities of intervention, as Portuguese citizens, at least in these early days of web social media use in political campaigning, have not used the possibility to engage in debate. Actually, the imbalance between high participation by a few, vs. sporadic intervention by many, seems to give further strength to the thesis that defends alienation by the common people. Following Quan-Haase & Wellman (2002) insight on positive civic engagement, it is not web interactivity, costs, speed, features and "omnipresence" that motivate citizens' political participation, but the message, acts and actors, and previous offline involvement, in the very end, the essence and structure of Portuguese politics or, for that matter, any national politics. Besides, not only the common citizen seems to be estranged from regular participation in online forums: candidates of both parties themselves did not engage in regular activity throughout the campaign on both PSD and PS dedicated sites. As for H_2, most of the messages were positive to the PS campaign. Only 3.85% could be classified as criticism to PS; 3.46% of messages had no clear subject and 9.23% had no direct political content. The remaining categories grouped topics positive to the party even when supporters spent much of the text space talking about the opposition.

All the personalized text messages and e-mail newsletters ceased with the end of the 2009 campaign, suggesting that Political Public Relations are not being used as a continuous activity, but only for time-limited purposes.

CONCLUSION

Although similarities can be found in PS and PSD website contents and features, it seems that PSD generated and controlled all contents spread in its web social media. That eased the burden on journalists and citizens in their search for information but it also uniformized the message of the party, in what can be called a "magic bullet campaign". Centrality of the citizen as displayed by social web media used, that might contribute to further grass roots intervention, did not succeed and, in fact, control exercised over these new media, turned them into an extension of traditional media, and not new media in the fashion put forward by Marshall McLuhan in his 1964 theory, that propounded that the medium is the message. In this case, a new medium divulges an old point; it is merely used as an archive and another venue to disseminate the same message.

Alternatively, the PS has chosen to inspire its campaign messages and actions on an Obama-like campaign model. Consequently, its strategy was based on targeted audiences, voluntary followers, and on the leader's image. Even the slogan used in text messages and e-mail communication is comparable: "I participate" (*eu participo*), "together we can do it" (*juntos conseguimos*).

The PS web-based social networking campaign can be classified as a failure due to the feeble participation of Portuguese citizens and party followers, and therefore as irrelevant to the victory the party achieved in the parliamentary election

In addition, user generated content in political campaign has been taking baby steps in Portugal. PS militants and supporters appeared not to be prepared to volunteer and produce content to a private, dedicated social network as *MyMov* and assume an active role in politics. This may be due to several factors, from alienation and feelings of individual irrelevance, or to a technological divide in face of a new web application. Nevertheless, web social networks cannot be ignored in political communication campaigns, once the web is occupying a definitive role in Portuguese citizens' everyday life.

Finally, web-based social media were used by Portuguese political parties to simply broadcast information and rely on one-side participation of its followers. That is, both PSD and PS politicians have not understood the web-social networking grammar and have not replied to their supporters. In other words, and coming back to the PS strategy, it did not create communication and engagement through the use of web-social media, it only made a new platform available. A platform that the party did not even monitor and that it stopped updating immediately after the electoral campaign.

This study lacks information about web analytics, that is, how many visitors each website and web social network had; when the visits were more frequent. This data would enlighten about the level of participants and passive audience and provide a clearer picture of web social media role in the political campaign. Unfortunately, both websites and web social media profiles did not have counters and the information was not available.

REFERENCES

Baudrillard, J. (2007). In the Shadow of the Silent Majorities or The End of the Social. Los Angeles, CA: Semiotext(e).

Breakenridge, D. (2008). *2.0: New Media, New Tools, New Audiences*. PR: FT Press.

Breakenridge, D., & Solis, B. (2009). *Putting the Public Back in Public Relations: How Social Media Is Reinventing the Aging Business of PR*. FT Press.

Chadwick, A. (2006). *Internet Politics: States, Citizens, and New Communication Technologies*. Oxford, UK: Oxford University Press.

Chadwick, A. (2009). Web 2.0: New Challenges for the Study of E-Democracy in an Era of Informational Exuberance. *I/S: A Journal of Law And Policy for the Information Society, 5*(1), 10-41.

Coleman, S. (1999). New Media and Democratic Politics. *New Media & Society, 1,* 67–74. doi:10.1177/1461444899001001011

Dahlgren, P. (2001). The Public Sphere and the Net: Structure, Space, and Communication. In W. L. Bennett & R. M. Entman (Eds.), *Mediated Politics: Communication in the future of democracy* (pp. 33–55). New York: Cambridge University Press.

Doueihi, M. (2011). *Pour un Humanisme Numérique.* Paris: Éditions du Seuil.

Eurostat. (2011). Retrieved January 13, 2012, from http://epp.eurostat.ec.europa.eu/portal/page/portal/information_society/data/main_tables

Gauntlett, D., & Horsley, R. (Eds.). (2004). *Web Studies* (2nd ed.). London: Arnold Publications.

Haas, G. (2001). *New Tools, New Politics? A Rhetorical Analysis of the Minnesota Fourth Congressional District Campaign Web Sites.* (Unpublished MA Thesis). University of Minnesota.

Haig, M. (2001). *E-PR: the essential guide to public relations on the Internet.* London: Kogan Page.

Hermes, J. (2006). Citizenship in the Age of the Internet. *European Journal of Communication, 21*(3), 295–309. doi:10.1177/0267323106066634

Herring, S. C. (2004). Computer-mediated discourse analysis: An approach to researching online behaviour. In S. A. Barab, R. Kling, & J. H. Gray (Eds.), *Designing for Virtual Communities in the Service of Learning* (pp. 338–376). New York: Cambridge University Press. doi:10.1017/CBO9780511805080.016

Herrnson, P. S., Stokes-Brown, A. K., & Hindman, M. (2007). Campaign Politics and the Digital Divide: Constituency Characteristics, Strategic Considerations. *Political Research Quarterly, 60,* 31–42. doi:10.1177/1065912906298527

Hindman, M. (2008). *The Myth of Digital Democracy.* Princeton University Press.

Katz, J. (1997). The Digital Citizen. *Wired Magazine.* Retrieved December 12, 2009, from http://www.wired.com/wired/archive/5.12/netizen_pr.html

Lax, S. (2004). The Internet and Democracy. In D. Gauntlett & R. Horsley (Eds.), *Web.Studies* (2nd ed., pp. 217–229). London: Arnold Publications.

Loader, B. D. (2011). Networking Democracy? Social media innovations in participatory politics. *Information Communication and Society, 14,* 757–769. doi:10.1080/1369118X.2011.592648

McQuail, D. (2000). *Mass Communication Theory* (4th ed.). London: Sage Publications.

Mossberger, K., Tolbert, C. J., & McNeal, R. S. (2008). *Digital Citizenship: The Internet, Society, and Participation.* Cambridge, MA: MIT Press.

Newman, B. I., & Verčič, D. (2002). *Communication of Politics: Cross-Cultural Theory Building in the Practice of Public Relations and Political Marketing.* London: Routledge.

Norris, P. (2000). *A Virtuous Circle: Political Communications in Post-Industrial Societies.* New York: Cambridge University Press. doi:10.1017/CBO9780511609343

Norris, P. (2001). *Digital Divide. Civic engagement, information poverty, and the internet worldwide.* Cambridge, UK: Cambridge University Press. doi:10.1017/CBO9781139164887

Phillips, D., & Young, P. (2009). *Online Public Relations: A Practical Guide to Developing an Online Strategy in the World of Social Media.* London: Kogan Page.

Piombino, K. (2012, May 16). Infographic: How Internet users worldwide spend time online. *ragan.com news and ideas for communicators.* Retrieved September 11, 2012, from http://www.ragan.com/Main/Articles/Infographic_How_Internet_users_worldwide_spend_tim_44877.aspx

Quan-Haase, A., & Wellman, B. (2002). Capitalizing on the net: social contact, civic engagement and sense of community. In B. Wellman & C. Haythornthwaite (Eds.), *The Internet in Everyday Life* (pp. 291–324). Oxford, UK: Blackwell Publishers. doi:10.1002/9780470774298.ch10

Report, P. E. W. (2009). *Generations Online in 2009.* Retrieved December 2, 2011, from http://www.pewinternet.org/Reports/2009/Generations-Online-in-2009.aspx

Shane, P. (Ed.). (2004). *Democracy Online: The Prospects for Political Renewal through the Internet.* New York: Routledge.

Shirky, C. (2008). *Here comes everybody: the power of organizing without organization.* Penguin Press.

Stromer-Galley, J. (2000). Online interaction and why candidates avoid it. *The Journal of Communication, 50*(4), 111–132. doi:10.1111/j.1460-2466.2000.tb02865.x

Sundar, S. S., Kalyanaraman, S., & Brown, J. (2003). Explicating Web Site interactivity: impression formation effects in Political Campaign Sites. *Communication Research, 30*(1), 30–59. doi:10.1177/0093650202239025

Turkle, S. (2005). The Second Self: Computers and the Human Spirit (20th anniversary Ed.). Cambridge, MA: The MIT Press.

Wilhelm, A. G. (2000). *Democracy in the digital age: challenges to political life in cyberspace.* New York: Routledge.

Xifra, J., & Huertas, A. (2008). Blogging PR: An exploratory analysis of public relations weblogs. *Public Relations Review, 34*(3), 269–275. doi:10.1016/j.pubrev.2008.03.022

ADDITIONAL READING

Bentivegna, S. (2006). Rethinking Politics in the World of ICTs. *European Journal of Communication, 21*(3), 331–343. doi:10.1177/0267323106066638

Blossom, J. (2009). *Content Nation. Surviving and Thriving as Social Media Changes our Work, our Lives, and our Future.* Indianapolis: Wiley Publishing, Inc.

boyd, d. (2005). Sociable Technology and Democracy. In J. Lebkowsky, & M. Ratcliffe (Eds.), *Extreme Democracy* (pp. 198-209). Lulu.com.

Brandenburg, H. (2006). Pathologies of the virtual public sphere. In S. Oates, D. Owen, & R. K. Gibson (Eds.), *The Internet and Politics. Citizens, voters and activists* (pp. 185–198). London: Routledge.

Carpini, M. X., & Keeter, S. (2002). The Internet and an Informed Citizenry. In D. Anderson & M. Cornfield (Eds.), *The Civic Web* (pp. 129–153). Lanham, MD: Rowman & Littlefield Publishers, Inc.

Dahlgren, P. (2003). Reconfiguring Civic Culture in the New Media Milieu. In J. Corner & D. Pels (Eds.), *Media and Political Style: Essays on Representation and Civic Culture* (pp. 151–170). London: Sage. doi:10.4135/9781446216804.n9

Davis, A. (2010). New media and fat democracy: the paradox of online participation. *New Media & Society*, *12*(5), 745–761. doi:10.1177/1461444809341435

Dijck, J. v. (2009). Users like you? Theorizing agency in user-generated content. *Media Culture & Society*, *31*(1), 41–58. doi:10.1177/0163443708098245

Ferber, P., Foltz, F., & Pugliese, R. (2007). Cyberdemocracy and Online Politics: a new model of interactivity. *Bulletin of Science, Technology & Society*, *27*(5), 391–400. doi:10.1177/0270467607304559

Howard, P. N. (2005). Deep Democracy, Thin Citizenship: The Impact of Digital Media in Political Campaign Strategy. *The Annals of the American Academy of Political and Social Science*, *597*, 153–170. doi:10.1177/0002716204270139

Howard, P. N., & Jones, S. (2004). *Society online: the Internet in context*. London: Sage Publications.

Hurwitz, R. (2003). Who needs Politics? Who needs People? The ironies of Democracy in Cyberspace. In D. Thornburn & H. Jenkins (Eds.), *Democracy and New Media* (pp. 101–112). Cambridge, MA: The MIT Press.

Jenkins, H., Purusotma, R., Weigel, M., Clinton, K., & Robison, A. J. (2009). *Confronting the Challenges of Participatory Culture. Media Education for the 21st Century*. Cambridge, MA: MIT Press.

Mirandilla, M. G. (2009, December 8). *Cybercampaigning for 2010: The Use and Effectiveness of Websites and Social Networking Sites as Campaign Platforms for the 2010 Philippine Presidential Election*. Retrieved February 25, 2011, from Social Science Research Network: http://papers.ssrn.com/sol3/papers.cfm?abstract_id=1553724

Susen, S. (2010). The transformation of citizenship in complex societies. *Journal of Classical Sociology*, *10*(3), 259–285. doi:10.1177/1468795X10371716

Thornburn, D., & Jenkins, H. (Eds.). (2003). *Democracy and New Media*. Cambridge, MA: The MIT Press.

KEY TERMS AND DEFINITIONS

Computer Mediated Discourse Analysis: Data analysis technique which uses verbal text displayed in an online page (web social media, email, website, etc.).

Election: When people vote to choose someone for an official position. In this chapter, for a parliamentary position.

Magic Bullet: The dissemination of a message in bulk, to everyone.

Online Strategy: A set of decisions about means and contents that frame the production and dissemination of online messages.

Participation: The act of taking part in an activity, event or debate.

Political Campaign: Strategic design of a series of messages sent to one or more targeted populations, or to the mass, for a discrete period of time (the pre-election time) to promote the ideas and activities of the political candidates.

Political Public Relations: Social, organizational and communicative function which plan and sustain efforts to establish and maintain good-will and understanding between political organizations and their publics.

Targeted Audience: Group of individuals to whom a specific message is directed.

Web Social Media: Web-based tools that allow users to develop a public or semi-public profile, electronically communicate with other users with whom they share a connection, and view and comment on their list of communications with other web users.

ENDNOTE

[1]   A careful observation of the two websites was done in order to choose the common elements to allow the comparison of the content, usability and interactivity characteristics.

This research was previously published in Political Campaigning in the Information Age edited by Ashu M. G. Solo, pages 32-50, copyright year 2014 by Information Science Reference (an imprint of IGI Global).

Chapter 68
The Internet, Social Media, and Knowledge Production and Development of Political Marketing

Nyarwi Ahmad
University of Gadjah Mada Yogyakarta, Indonesia

ABSTRACT

Though the use and development of the Internet, World Wide Web and social media and their impacts on politics have been robustly investigated, specific attention has not yet been paid to explore the impact of adaptation and use of social media by political actors and organizations on the knowledge production and generation of political marketing. In order to fill this knowledge gap, a conceptual framework to explore modes of knowledge production and generation of political marketing has been proposed. The transcendental realism approach postulated by Bhaskar (1998, 2008) and the meta-theoretical assumptions of political marketing proposed by Henneberg (2008) were adopted. A content analysis of 320 articles of Journal of Political Marketing published in between 2002 and 2015 was carried out. This work reveals that the adaptation and use of the Internet and social media have been accounted for in producing and generating the operational or the rudimentary-conceptual or the established-conceptual knowledge of political marketing.

INTRODUCTION

The adaptation and use of Information and Communication Technologies (ICTs), especially the Internet, various websites and social media, have provided various impacts on individuals, society and organisations at large. These developments and their impacts on knowledge management—in general—and knowledge production, and sharing—in particular—have been studied. Nonetheless, such developments and their effects on politics, political communication and campaigning have been robustly undertaken

DOI: 10.4018/978-1-5225-5637-4.ch068

as well. However, a specific research has not yet been undertaken to discuss the impact of the adaptation and use of social media platforms on knowledge production and generation of political marketing.

In addressing this issue, this work postulates following propositions. *Firstly,* the development of media, as a medium of political exchange and interaction and the adaptation and use of ICTs and the Internet by political actors and organisations, as a strategic communication tool and platform in the political sphere, have influenced the knowledge production and generation of political marketing. *Secondly,* there have been two-fold dynamic conditions that determine on how and the extent to which social media have impacted on the knowledge production and development of political marketing. The first one is modes and degrees of the adaptation and use of the Internet, websites and social media by political actors and organizations, while the second one is the ways political marketing scholars have captured and theorised these actors and organisations when they have adopted and used the Internet, websites and social media during the elections and post the elections. *Thirdly,* political marketing scholars whose work has been published in Journal of Political Marketing have been considered to assess the adaptation and uses of social media. The focus was to explore whether they have created and generated the practical or the rudimentary-conceptual or the established-conceptual knowledge of political marketing. However, they have not yet accounted for the various modes of adaptation and use of social media for producing and generating the systemic knowledge of political marketing.

Based on these propositions, the following points will be discussed in this chapter. The first section will examine the media, ICT developments and their impact on political marketing. The second section will propose a conceptual framework that examines modes of knowledge production and generation and its application in the field of political marketing. The third section will spell out the transcendental realism perspective, meta-theoretical assumptions of political marketing and research design. The fourth and fifth sections will explore how, in which ways and the extent to which the Internet and social media has been accounted for in knowledge production and generation of political marketing. The last section will present the conclusions and research recommendations.

THE MEDIA, ICT DEVELOPMENTS, AND POLITICAL MARKETING

The changing landscapes of the media, the development of ICT and the adaptation of the Internet have carved a huge impact on politics, political marketing and campaigning. They have been widely seen of being important as essential factors that determine not only the strategies and practices of political marketing, but also the development of theories and concepts of political marketing (Lees-Marshment, 2001, 2004, 2008; Stromback, 2007; Stromback, et.al, 2012; Ormrod, 2005, 2007, 2009, 2011; Ormrod & Henneberg, 2009, 2010a, 2010b). Some researchers have suggested that they need to be taken into further account practices of political marketing and to develop theories and concepts of political marketing (Harrop, 1990: 227; Lock & Harris, 1996: 21; Henneberg & O' Shaughnessy, 2007: 22; Henneberg, 2008: 171; O'Shaughnessy, 2010: 1050-1051; Temple & Savigny, 2010; Temple, 2013).

Political marketing scholars so far have accounted the development of ICT and the adaptation of the Internet using diverse political marketing perspective. Collins and Butler (1996) and Butler and Collins (1999) have considered the media as a vital element for developing the positioning strategies of political parties in the political market. Moreover, Wring (1997, 2005), and Lilleker (2006) have placed the media as an important element when political parties have followed either the selling-orientation or the market-orientation. Additionally, Lees-Marshment (2000; 2001, 2004, 2008) and Lilleker and Lees-

Marshment (2005) have positioned the media and the Internet as a strategic element of communication and campaigning when political parties have advanced whether it is from a product-orientation, sales-orientation or market-orientation perspective.

In a different vein, Savigny and Temple (2010) and Temple (2013) have highlighted the pivotal roles and powers of the media in shaping political messages and determining whole processes of exchanges and interactions in the political sphere. Moreover, Newman (1994: 12) has placed the media as well as the changing information, communication and technology (ICT) as one of what he called 'environmental-forces' that determine the stages, strategies and processes of political marketing and campaigning of presidential candidates. Furthermore, Stromback (2007, 2009) and Stromback (et.al, 2012) have placed the media as a type of political market arena, while Johansen (2012) has positioned the media as a po-litical sub-market. In addition, Ormrod (2005, 2007, 2009, 2011) and Ormrod and Henneberg (2009, 2010a, 2010b) have considered the media as an external stakeholder.

As evident, these authors have conceptualised the position and role of media and their impact on political marketing and campaigning. However, whilst the landscape of media continues to change, ICT developments and adaptation and usage of the Internet transform modes of political marketing and cam-paigning, these authors have lacked in offering sufficient theoretical frameworks to explain the impact of these developments on knowledge production and generation of political marketing. More importantly, since various forms of social media platforms have been widely adopted in the political spheres soon after Web 2.0, they have not yet specifically discussed on how, in which ways and the extent to which political marketing scholars have considered the uses of these social media platforms by political actors and organizations for the knowledge generation of political marketing and campaigning.

MODES OF KNOWLEDGE PRODUCTION AND GENERATION OF POLITICAL MARKETING

As an emanating study, political marketing has originated from its mother disciplines, which are: mar-keting, political science and communication science (Scammell, 1999; Egan, 1999; Lees-Marshment, 2001a, 2001b, 2001c, 2004, 2008). Political marketing so far has offered the normative, prescriptive and predictive theories, concepts and models, which have been seen of being helpful to understand the whole attitude and behaviour of political actors and organizations within the contexts of policy development in governments or internal organizations or elections (Henneberg, 2004; Savigny, 2004, 2007, 2008; Hennerberg & O'Shaughnessy, 2007; O' Shaughnessy, 2010). Moreover, political marketing has also provided a set of strategies and practices, which have been adopted and developed by political parties, parties' leaders, members, activists and candidates when they have dealt with the changing political environments and addressed the needs, demands and wants of political markets in order to get elected during the elections or be successful in government (Newman, 1999a, 1999b; Lees-Marshment, 2001b, 2004, 2008; Lilleker & Lees-Marshment, 2005; Lilleker, et.al, 2007; Lees-Marshment, et.al, 2012).

So far two-fold elements have determined the development of political marketing. The first one is the ways in which political marketing scholars have realized, captured and understood political marketing and campaigning phenomena and then adopted and constructed the wide or the narrow interpretations of political marketing theories and concepts as they have underpinned and or explored these phenomena (Ormrod, 2012; Ormrod, et.al, 2013). The second one is the way in which political actors and political organizations have considered and adopted concepts, principles and procedures of marketing and advanced a set of practices and strategies of political marketing management when they have dealt with political markets and political market environment (Newman, 1999a, 1999b; Henneberg & O' Shaughnessy, 2007; Butler & Harris, 2009). Whilst such elements have been seen of being closely connected each other (Henneberg, 2002, 2004, 2008; Hennebrg & O'Shaugnessy, 2007; Savigny, 2007, 2008; Butler & Harris, 2009), a specific conceptual framework that explores the relationships between these elements and their impact on knowledge production and generation of political marketing has been still under-developed. In order to untangle this issue, following points would discuss and scrutinize the existing literature that theorise modes of knowledge creation and development.

Generally speaking, knowledge production that has been taking place in modern society in general or groups of (professional) societies in particular are indeed complex and multi-layered processes. Investigations so far have been commonly directed to understand three main sub-topics, which are the knowledge about society, the knowledge of society and the knowledge produced and generated by individual and groups of societies. Although these themes seem closely related to each other, each of them however, typically belongs to a particular field of study. In this respect, the first and the second themes have been recognized as the research domain of sociology of knowledge, while the last theme has been considered as the research domain of knowledge management.

Since 1990s, various perspectives and conceptual frameworks have been introduced to explore diverse issues of knowledge management in general and knowledge creation in particular. Moreover, various terms have been introduced to categorize the types and forms of knowledge (Baskerville & Dulipovici, 2006; Heisig, 2009). Since a specific conceptual lens to understand modes of knowledge creation and generation in the study of political marketing has not yet been advanced, the ideas of other researchers would be adopted in order to tackle this knowledge gap.

Nonaka (1994) has postulated some basic concepts and models of organisational knowledge creation. He has stated that 'knowledge is a multifaceted concept with multi-layered meanings' (Nonaka, 1994: 15). He has clarified the differentiation between knowledge and information. Moreover, as informed by idea of Polanyi (1966), he has outlined two kinds of knowledge, which are *tacit knowledge* and *explicit knowledge*. The first one is a type of knowledge, which is deeply rooted in human skills, mind, ideas, judgments, actions, experiences, commitments and involvements in a specific context, but very hard to be formulated in a formal language and transferred through communication activities. Slightly contrasting, the second one is a type of knowledge, which is much easier to be codified, communicated, reported and transmitted through a formal and systemic language (Nonaka, 1994: 16; Nonaka & Kono, 1998: 42; Chugh, 2013: 25; Chugh, et.al, 2015: 2-3).

Nonetheless, he has proposed four modes of knowledge creation and conversion wherein *the tacit knowledge*, which is produced through socialisation, could be transformed to *the explicit knowledge* through the four types of processes of what he called as socialisation, internalisation, externalisation and combination (Nonaka, 1994: 19-20). Socialisation is a self-transcending process of individuals and involves tacit to tacit knowledge transfer, while externalisation involves converting tacit knowledge into an explicit form. Internalisation focuses on converting explicit knowledge into a tacit form while the combination focuses on organising and integrating explicit into other explicit knowledge forms (Nonaka & Konno, 1998: 43). In types of processes, he has posited that under a certain condition (such as intention, chaos/fluctuation, requisite variety and redundancy), the individual knowledge can be shared, conceptualized, crystalized, justified and generated as the networking knowledge (Nonaka, 1994: 27).

Knowledge production is determined by not only the existing social base of society, but also the dynamic interactions between various agencies and (social) structures that exist in the society (Berger

& Luckmann, 1966; Gidden, 1984). As adopted ideas of Gidden (1984) and Polanyi (1966), Nonaka and Toyama, (2003: 4) have voiced that practical consciousness produces *the tacit knowledge*, while the discursive consciousness generates *the explicit knowledge*. They have also highlighted that knowledge creation is a dialectic process, which is directed by the 'dualistic nature' of interactions between the agents and structures and between the tacit and the explicit knowledge (Nonaka & Toyama, 2003: 9).

Meanwhile, Baskerville and Dulipovici (2006: 91), in line with the ideas of Nonaka and Takeuchi (1995) and Nonaka (et al., 2000), have outlined modes of the knowledge creations wherein four types of knowledge are created and generated. The first one is *sympathized knowledge*, which is realized and approved by the individual and created based on the socialization processes. The second one is *operational knowledge*, which is produced based on the internalization processes. The third knowledge type is *conceptual knowledge*, which is shaped based on the externalisation processes. In addition, the last one is *systemic knowledge*, which is constructed based on the combination processes. They have grouped the first and third types of knowledge as the tacit knowledge, while the second and fourth types as the articulated knowledge.

Based on the work of the previously outlined authors, this work proposes modes of knowledge productions and generations of political marketing as charted in Figure 1. This work assumes that political marketing scholars consider the roles and position of the media, ICT developments and the adaptation and use of the Internet and social media by political actors and organisations as a political marketing phenomenon. This work proposes that these scholars have gradually accounted the adaptations and use of social media for knowledge production and generation of political marketing soon after web 2.0 and various social media platforms have been widely adopted and deployed by political actors and organisations during the elections and post elections.

Social media is a type of web-based service, which is characterized by the controlled-networking activities, the visibility of users' profiles and deliberative discussion and sharing advanced by those who have got connected in various social media network systems. Slightly different from the old fashioned way of web-based services, social media has offered the handiest and the more interesting online communication facilities that provide various advantages for users. They allow individuals to develop a public or semi-public profile located in a bounded system, get connected with a list of other users with whom they possibly share and discuss the information and opinion, evaluate and distribute their list of connections to those who have entered within the system (Boyd & Ellison, 2007; Chugh, 2012). Having offered interactive web-based communication features, social media has been widely embraced by political actors and organizations, including by those who have run, involved in, engaged and participated in policy development in government or elections.

Having realized and accounted these phenomena, they then produce *the tacit-knowledge* and *the articulated-knowledge*. This work conjectures that formulation of *tacit-knowledge* is driven by individual practical consciousness, while construction of *the articulated-knowledge* is directed and stimulated by individual and collective discursive consciousness. Knowledge production is also determined by the 'dualistic nature' of interactions between the *agents* and *structures* and between *the tacit-knowledge* and *the articulated-knowledge*. Five types of knowledge are then produced and generated. As led by practical consciousness, *sympathized knowledge* of political marketing is created. Being directed by discursive consciousness, *operational knowledge* is produced. As followed by practical consciousness, *rudimentary-conceptual knowledge* is constructed. Meanwhile, as stimulated by discursive consciousness, *established-conceptual knowledge* is constructed. In this respect, as formulated from *sympathized knowledge*, *rudimentary-conceptual knowledge* would be considered as *the tacit knowledge*, while as

Figure 1. Modes of knowledge productions and generations of political marketing
Source: Adapted from Nonaka (1994), Baskerville and Dulipovici (2006) and Nonaka and Toyama, (2003).

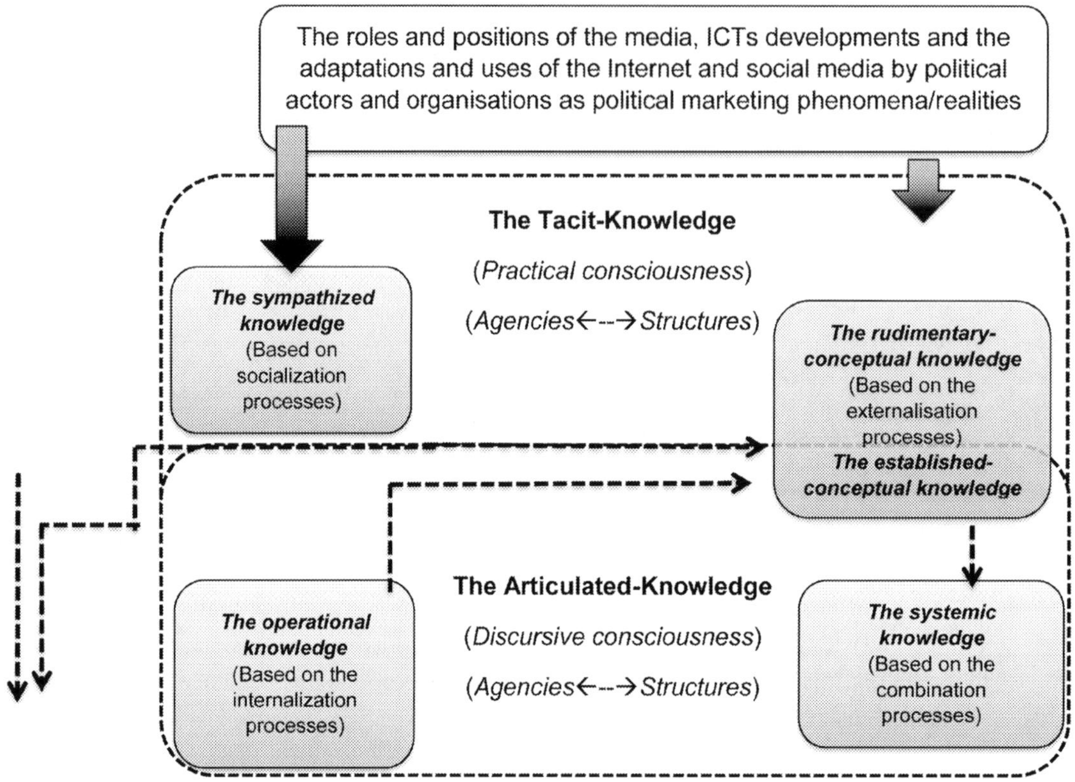

produced from *the operational knowledge, established-conceptual knowledge* would be accounted as *articulated knowledge*. Despite stimulating the production of operational *knowledge*, the discursive consciousness also paves the way for *the systematic knowledge*.

This work postulates that these aforementioned knowledge creation and generation steps take place as a sequential process. As approved, accepted and acknowledged by peer and/or professional groups of people, *the sympathized knowledge*, which is created through the individual practical consciousness, could be leveraged as *conceptual knowledge*. *Conceptual knowledge* could also be modified as *operational knowledge*, as these peer and/or professional groups of people have widely considered this knowledge as the applicable conceptual frameworks or the better role models. As approved, accepted and acknowledged by peer and/or professional groups of people and organisations that exist in society, *the operational* and *the conceptual knowledge* could be possibly produced to *the systemic knowledge*. This work assumes that there would be only a small amount and particular kind of *sympathized knowledge* that could be generated to formulate either *the conceptual knowledge or the operational knowledge*. There would be also only a small amount and particular type of *the operational* and *the conceptual knowledge* that could be advanced to construct *the systematic knowledge*.

In line with this conceptual framework, the transcendental realism perspective introduced by Bhaskar (1998, 2008) would be adopted as a philosophical standpoint. Moreover, the meta-theoretical assumptions of political marketing proposed by Henneberg (2008) would also be considered. Additionally, an appropriate research design would be advanced as well. The next section further elaborates on these issues.

TRANSCENDENTAL REALISM PERSPECTIVE, META-THEORETICAL ASSUMPTIONS, AND RESEARCH DESIGN

Transcendental realism perspective is one of the philosophical school of thought, which is innovative, based on the argument that see there have been *'two-sides of knowledge'* that cannot be simply understood using either the naturalist or the anti-naturalist perspective (Bhaskar, 1998: 16-18, 2008: 11-14). Bhaskar (2008:15-16) highlights that it is the real structures, mechanisms and events which eternally exist and keep existing and evolving independently outside our knowledge and experience on the one hand and how our minds have addressed, defined and understood these structures, mechanisms and events on the other that have really generated the body knowledge of science. Though there is no consensus among social scientists, some called it as 'scientific realism' or 'relational realism' or 'critical realism' or 'empirical realism' perspectives (Sayer, 2000: Moses & Knutsen, 2012).

Bhaskar (1998, 2008) has claimed that this perspective offers a new insight. It ontologically and epistemologically accounts the complexity of the relationships between what Bhaskar (1998, 2008) called as the 'two-sides of knowledge', which are the 'structures and mechanisms that generate phenomena' on the one hand and the 'knowledge' produced in the 'social activity of science' on the other. For realists, they cannot be simplified and being seen as neither the reality that is separable with the human mind (following the *empiricism*) nor the reality that is being constructed by the human mind (following the *idealism*). Rather, being recognized of having the 'categorical distinctness', these 'two-sides of knowledge' have to be ontologically and epistemologically considered as being dialectically existent and eternally transformed within the whole processes of the *'social construction'* of the body of knowledge of science (Hartwig, 2008: xi). The use of realism perspective therefore allows us to avoid of what Bhaskar (1997:40, 2008:30) called as the 'epistemic fallacy' when we have understood the reality. More interestingly, as accounted these intransitive and transitive knowledge dimensions, it would be much more possible for realists for going further into what Bhaskar (1998:xii; 2008: 32) called as the 'trans-factuality (universality) of laws', regardless the complexity and differentiation of the world. It is possibly accomplished because of the existence of what Bhaskar (1998: xix) named as the 'ceteris paribus' condition, which is 'a condition for moving from fact to fact in the open-systemic world to which the laws of nature trans-factually apply as much as it is to moving from fact to value in the practical social world of belief, judgment and action' (Bhaskar, 1998: xix). In addressing these the nature of 'trans-factuality of laws' on the one hand and the 'value in the practical social world of belief, judgment and action' on the other, those who have stood for the philosophical orthodoxy, either the 'naturalist'/'positivist' or the 'anti-naturalist'/'anti-positivist', tend to understand them as the 'radical dichotomies'. Instead, for the realist, they could be seen as the 'exact parallels' (Bhaskar, 1998:xix). This perspective is essentially needed with relevance to the fact that sciences have been created based on the 'imaginative' and 'disciplined work' of scientists. This was determined by *what theories and concepts were given to them* on the one hand and *the ways they have understood the real, the actual and the empirical of levels and forms of reality* on the other (Baskhar, 2008: 176-177).

The transcendental scientific realism perspective would be helpful to tackle the innate weaknesses of the empiricism, positivism and relativism perspectives. Going beyond the naturalist and the anti-naturalist approaches, this perspective has been widely seen of being helpful to understand the multidimensional, multi structure and multi layers of social phenomena (Bhaskar, 1998, 2008; Hartwig, 2008: xi-xv: Moses & Nutsen, 2012:12-14). Since this perspective holistically analyses social phenomena using the methodological approach of natural science on the one hand and the interpretative approach on the other

(Sayer, 2000: 2-3), it allows us to leverage the research paradigm that goes beyond the naturalism and constructivism paradigms (Moses & Knutsen, 2012:12) and resolve the controversial debates between and among those who have followed the behavioralist (positivist) and social constructivist (interpretativist) paradigms (Savingy, 2007:36-37). Therefore, Pavitt (1999) has suggested that this perspective needs to be considered as *the third way* for developing theories and concepts in the field study of communication. Savigny (2007: 36-36) has also echoed this perspective would be useful to develop the theories and concepts of political marketing and formulating models of political marketing. It is utmost ultimate when we want to scrutinize on how far the existing theories and concepts or the new theoretical and conceptual propositions of political marketing can be employed to generate new knowledge in the political sphere (Henneberg, 2008:161). To such ends, we need to consider the ontological and epistemological assumptions of the exchanges and interaction processes of political marketing (Henneberg, 2008: 160-161; Savigny, 2007: 36; Henneberg & Ormrod, 2013: 97).

In specifically addressing the meta-theoretical assumptions of political marketing, Henenberg (2008: 62) has proposed four aspects. They consist of: a) the nature and structure of the exchange and interaction processes of political marketing; b) the conditions of political markets and interactions between political markets and political players of political marketing; c) the social embededness of political system and its relationships with social and the other narrative models of political representation; and d) the structural connectedness of managements of politics and the interdependent of political marketing activities in the political spheres (Henneberg, 2008: 161-163).

Based on the ideas of these authors, a scrutiny of the existing literature published by *Journal of Political Marketing*, which has released articles that cover theories, concepts and practices of political marketing and campaigning would be helpful. To this end, a mixture of qualitative and quantitative methods (Bryman, 2008; Tashakkori, 2009; Tashakkori & Creswell, 2007b; Creswell and Clark, 2007, 2011, Lunde, et.al, 2013) would be deployed. The 'concurrent research design' of these methods (Guest, 2013) would be adopted. Moreover, the quantitative and the qualitative contents analyses would be concurrently undertaken with the thematic analysis (Butler-Kisber, 2010). In this respect, the quantitative analysis using the statistical descriptive analysis would be carried out simultaneously with the thematic analysis. Such analyses are directed to map out how and the extent to which the authors of the articles published in Journal of Political Marketing in between 2002 and 2015 have considered the developments of ICTs and the use of the Internet/new media, websites and various forms of social media and their impact on politics, political marketing and campaigning as a research theme in the field of political marketing. Moreover, the qualitative content and thematic analyses would be utilized together to explore how and in which ways these authors have advanced either the existing or the new theories and concepts of political marketing and campaigning when they have investigated these issues. Further, research synthesis by aggregation and configuration (Sandelowski, et.al, 2012: 324-326) would be undertaken in order to holistically discuss how, in which ways and the extent to which the use of social media and their impact on politics, political marketing and campaigning have been taken into account for knowledge production and development of political marketing. The following section will outline the research findings.

THE ADAPTATION AND USE OF THE INTERNET AND SOCIAL MEDIA AS POLITICAL MARKETING PHENOMENA AND RESEARCH THEMES

The increasing number and forms of social media and the adaptation of social media as interactive communication platforms is closely related with the innovations and developments of the Internet and information and communication technologies (ICTs). For more than two decades, we have witnessed that the Internet has provided a Web platform, which has evolved from Web 1.0 to Web 2.0. Since the Web 2.0 has taken shape, various forms of social media sites have emerged. Such developments have been considered as an interesting theme in the field studies of politics, political marketing and campaigning by those who have published their works in social science and technology journals, including in *Journal of Political Marketing*.

Before this journal was established in 2002, there was potentially no journal that specifically discussed perspectives, theories, concepts, models and practices of political marketing. Scholars interested in such issues have favoured publishing their ideas in the *European Journal of Marketing* and *Journal of Public Affairs* and some edited-books. Most of those who have studied political marketing, released their works in these two journals and disseminated their ideas through various international conferences and edited handbooks since 1996 up to 2010 and have explored either the key concepts used in the political marketing study or boundaries of political marketing research (see Harris and Lock, 2010). Though both of these journals since 2012 up to 2015 have published plenty of articles that cover contemporary issues in political marketing, most of these articles have not yet specifically explored the uses of social media in relations with the knowledge production and development of political marketing.

As *Journal of Political Marketing* established in 2002, a number of authors who have published their works in this journal have gradually considered the development of information, communication and technologies (ICTs) and its impact on politics, political marketing and campaigning. Williams (2012) has run the qualitative content analyses of 214 articles released by this journal in the first five years (2002-2006) and the second five years (2007-2011) to explore how and the extent to which these authors have selected topics of investigation. Williams (2012: 5) has found that following topics such as election campaigns, candidates, political parties and political consultants have emerged as central themes of political marketing research. The uses of the Internet and the adaptations of Web campaigns have been gradually investigated and theorized especially when professionalization of political communication campaigning has taken shape in the US as well as European countries (Williams, 2012: 5-6). Williams (2012), however, has not yet fully detailed on how and the extent to which those who have released their works in this journal have accounted the development and the uses of social media and their impacts on politics, political marketing and campaigning as research themes in the study of political marketing.

Based on this caveat, this work then runs concurrently the quantitative, qualitative and thematic content analyses of 320 articles published by this journal in between 2002 and 2015. The analysis reveals some interesting findings, as displayed by the following figures. As seen from Figure 2 the total number of articles that discuss the development of communication technologies (ICTs) and the use of the Internet and their impact on politics, political marketing and campaigning has gradually rocketed from 2.81% in 2002 to 19.68% in 2015. Moreover, as charted by Figure 3, the percentage of articles that cover such issues has increased from 22.25% in 2002 to 51.21% in 2003. However, it has then dramatically declined from 14.24% in 2014 to 0% in 2007. Though, it escalated from 12.00% in 2008 to 38.09 in 2011, it has then dramatically decreased to 9.52% in 2012. Even though it rose from 14.28% in 2003 to 18.75% in 2014, it has slightly dropped to 17.04% in 2015. Furthermore, these articles cover four main research

Figure 2. A sum of articles (in %) published in Journal of Political Marketing in between 2002 and 2015 that cover the ICTs development and the uses of the Internet and their impacts on politics, political marketing and campaigning
Source: Journal of Political Marketing, 2002-2015.

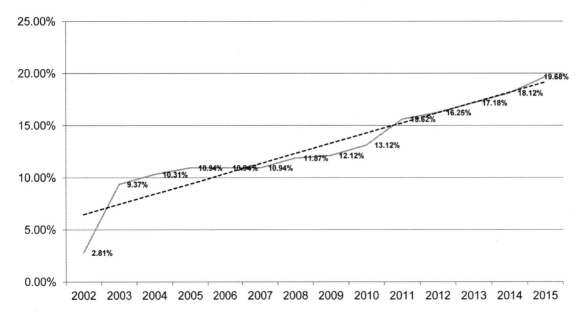

Figure 3. A percent of articles published in Journal of Political Marketing in between 2002 and 2015 (vol 1-14) that cover the ICTs Development and the uses of the Internet and their impacts on politics, political marketing and campaigning
Source: Journal of Political Marketing, 2002-2015.

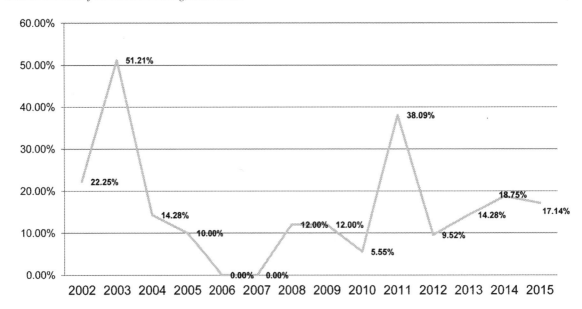

themes, which are: e-government and e-politics (6.87%), cyber-democracy (3.75%), the Internet and new media (5.94%) and the Internet and social media (2.81%), as seen from Figure 4.

Figure 5 then details per cent of a total number of these articles that focus on these themes. As seen, 12.5% of total articles published in 2002, 39.02% of total articles released in 2003 and 4% of articles published in 2008 have focused on e-government and e-politics. Meanwhile, 7.50% of the total articles published in 2002, 7.3% of total articles released in 2003, 4.76% of articles released in 2004, 10% of

Figure 4. A sum of articles (in %) published in Journal of Political Marketing in between 2002 and 2015 that Focus on e-government and e-politics, cyber-democracy, the Internet and new media and the Internet and social media network as a research theme
Source: Journal of Political Marketing, 2002-2015.

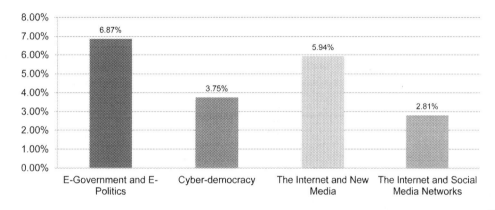

Figure 5. A percent of articles published in Journal of Political Marketing in between 2002 and 2015 that discuss e-government and e-politics, cyber-democracy, the Internet and new media and the Internet and social media network as research themes
Source: Journal of Political Marketing, 2002-2015.

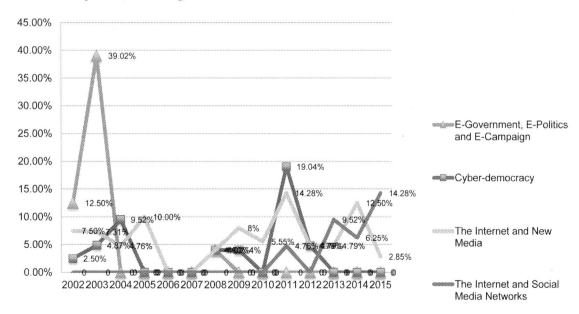

articles released in 2005, 4% of articles released in 2008, or 8% of total articles released in 2009, 5.55% of total articles released in 2010, 14.28% of total articles published in 2011, 4.79% of total articles published in 2012, 4.79% of total articles published in 2013, 12.50% of total articles published in 2014 and 2.85% of total articles published in 2015 have discussed the uses of Internet and the new media as a tool of political marketing and campaigning. In the meantime, 2.50% of total articles released in 2002, 4.87% of total articles published in 2003, 9.52% of total articles published in 2004, 4% of total articles published in 2008, 4% of total articles published in 2009, 19.04% of total articles published in 2011 and 4.79% of total articles published in 2012 have explored the uses of the Internet and the new media and their impact on the practices of political marketing.

A sum of articles, which cover e-government, e-politics and cyber-democracy, is positively correlated with a sum of articles that discusses the Internet/new media and social media uses and their impact on politics, political marketing and campaigning. There is a linear relationship between these articles. As charted by Figure 6, this relationship is numerically significant. Whilst the first one has increased from 6 articles (1.87% of total articles) to 34 articles, the second one has escalated as well stretching from 0.94% in 2002 to 9.37% in 2015. However, while the first one has remained stagnant since 2012 up to 2015, the second one has rocketed dramatically from 18 articles (or 5.6% of total articles) to 30 articles (or 9.37% of total articles). Overall, the first one however, has been higher over the second one.

While those who have published their ideas in this journal in between 2002 and 2010 have shown interest in exploring the ICT developments and the use of the Internet and Web campaigns, as a central theme—in relations with e-government, e-politics, cyber-democracy, e-campaign, web-based marketing

Figure 6. The numerical relationships between a commutative number of articles that examines e-government, e-polititics and cyber-democracy and a sum of articles that assesses the Internet, new media and social media networks
Source: Journal of Political Marketing, 2002-2015.

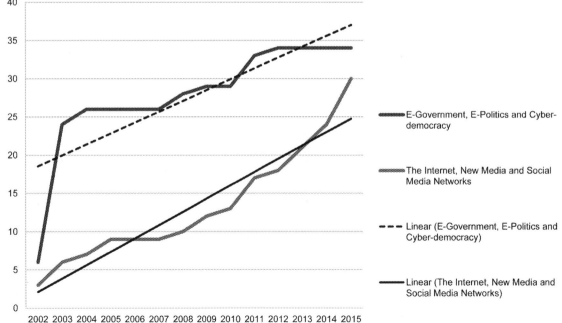

and campaigning and online political marketing, whilst those who have published their works in this journal in between 2011 and 2015 have gradually accounted for the use of the Internet and social media and their impact on political marketing and campaigning as a primary theme. As seen from Figure 5, 4.76% of articles published in 2011, 9.52% of total articles published in 2013, 6.25% of total articles released in 2014 and 14.28% of total articles released in 2015 have explored this issue.

Scholars who have released their works in *Journal of Political Marketing* in between 2012 and 2015 have adopted less of the broad and rudimentary concepts, such as e-government, e-politics and cyber-democracy. Rather, they have favoured adopting and developing the more advanced and specific concepts such as e-campaign, web-based marketing and campaigning, online/e-political marketing and e-branding and interactive political communication. More importantly, some of them have strongly shown interest in exploring social media use and its impact on politics, political marketing and campaigning as primary research. A sum of articles that specifically focuses on social media therefore has substantially increased. As seen from Figure 7, it has been gradually soaring from only 0.87% in 2011 to 7.89% in 2015.

Generally speaking, a total number of those who have published their works in *Journal of Political Marketing* in between 2002 and 2015 and explored the adaptation and the use of Internet, new media and websites in political sphere have substantially increased cumulatively stretching from 2.81% in 2002 to 19.68% in 2015. However, a sum of those who have released their work in this journal and specifically focused on social media use and its impact on political marketing and campaigning has remained at a low level, which is cumulatively only 1.56%. There was no article published by this journal in between 2002 and 2010 that has specifically addressed the adaptation and use of social media as a central theme since social media platforms and the advanced-native social bottoms of these social media, as we see today, were still under-developed.

Figure 7. A percent of articles published in Journal of Political Marketing in between 2011 and 2015 that Specifically focus on the uses of social media networks and their impacts on politics, political marketing and campaigning
Source: Journal of Political Marketing, 2011-2015.

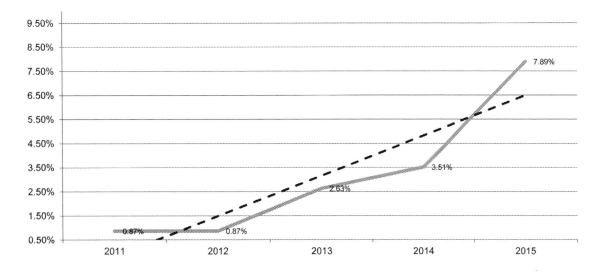

FROM THE SYMPHATIZED AND THE RUDIMENTARY-CONCEPTUAL KNOWLEDGE TO THE OPERATIONAL AND THE ESTABLISHED-KNOWLEDGE

The qualitative and thematic content analyses of 320 articles published in *Journal of Political Marketing* in between 2002 and 2015 reveals the following findings. Led by the practical consciousness, Curtin and Sommer (2003: 108) have come up with *the sympathised knowledge*, which was then transformed to *the rudimentary-conceptual knowledge* as their work was published in *Journal of Political Marketing*. They have proposed that the uses of the Internet and Web Campaigns have taken place in the US politics during 1996 US presidential election. As Bush and Gore campaigns were strongly interested in adopting Web Campaign during the 2000 US presidential election, the development of ICTs and Internet and the use of the Internet and Web Campaign and their impacts on politics have been gradually accounted for to capture transformations of strategies and practices of political marketing and campaigning. Moreover, Sherman and Schiffman (2002) who have released their work in the first volume of *Journal of Political Marketing* have highlighted that the advancement of Web Campaigns not only has transformed the US politics, in general, and practices and strategies of political marketing and campaigning, in particular, but also has opened fertile political marketing research. As directed by the practical consciousness, Sherman and Schiffman (2002) have suggested developing *the established-conceptual knowledge*.

Slightly different to these authors, Johnson (2002a) has advanced a new *rudimentary-conceptual knowledge*, which is *a cyber-democracy*. This conceptual knowledge has been deployed to explore the adaptations and uses of the Internet and Web Campaigns during the 2000 US presidential election. He has optimistically viewed that the Internet uses in political sphere has carried out a similar impact as the television did during the 1960 US election (Johnson, 2002a: 214). Regardless of the existing plenty of pessimistic views related to the impacts of the adaptation of the Internet and Web Campaigns in politics, he has outlined that Websites as new communication and campaign platforms have offered political benefits. He has stated as follows:

…. Electronic campaigns could use their Websites to persuade and inform voters twenty-four hours a day…electronic campaigns could use e-mail; polling could be conducted online, volunteers could be activated and informed, and fundraising could be conducted online. Websites could level the playing field: a campaign, short on funds but with dedicated volunteers, could fight against a well-funded professionally based campaign by hiring a college kid to design a simple Website, and thus get the message out to voters eager for issues papers and persuasion (Johnson, 2002a: 214).

Johnson (2003a, 2003b, 2004a, 2004b) has then advanced this knowledge as *the established-conceptual knowledge*. Johnson (2003a) has deployed this knowledge to examine electronic voting. Moreover, Johnson (2003b, 2004a) has also deployed it to explore the ways members of the US Congress have responded to the online communication environment using the interactive web and e-mail. Jonson (2004b) has scrutinized the development of the Internet uses and its impact on transformation of campaigning during the 2004 US Presidential election. More importantly, as roughly evaluated on how and in ways political parties, parties' candidates and interest groups have harnessed Web Campaigns during this election, Johnson (2004b: 111-112) come up with *operational knowledge* and voiced the following:

Candidates, political parties, and interest groups have come to rely on electronic communications, and there is no going back. But consider this: No successful presidential campaign can function without electronic communications, but no presidential campaign can be successful if it relies solely on it. Campaign websites, blogs, discussion groups, pop-up advertising, instant messaging and e-mail are all vital; but they cannot replace the seemingly old fashioned techniques of grassroots organizing and television campaigning. (Johnson, 2004b: 111-112)

Nonetheless, Johnson (2002b), in addressing the adaptation of Web Campaign by those who have ruled the government, has introduced the subsequent *rudimentary-conceptual knowledge*, which is *e-government*. This conceptual knowledge has also been advanced as *the operational knowledge* to describe several potential advantages offered by State and local government Websites, as follows:

State and local government Web sites, while varying considerably, are now providing an extraordinary amount of information that was unavailable in the pre-online days. But there is still far to go. (Johnson, 2002b: 102)

Likewise Johnson (2002b), the other authors such as Curtin (2002), Curtin (et.al, 2002) and Vis-Sommer (2003) have also advanced this knowledge as *the established-conceptual knowledge* to portray the rise of electronic government in the US politics. Though implicitly hinted that this concept could be furthered especially when voters via the state and local government websites have easily retrievable political information, these authors has detailed less the definition and operationalization of this concept in order to be accepted as *the systematic knowledge*. While Johnson (2002a) has not yet sufficiently explained the extent to which *e-government* has taken shape in the US politics, Curtin (et.al, 2002) has adopted this knowledge to explore on how and the degree of which 223 major American cities populated by 100000 citizens or more have advanced the online services through Websites. This knowledge has been also adopted by Vis-Sommer (2003) as well to explore the development of Web Campaign taken by five ministries of UN members.

Shaw (2002) and Williams (et.al, 2002) have created *the established-conceptual knowledge*, which is 'e-campaign', while Curtin and Sommer (2003) and Sommer and Tavlin (2003) have introduced the rudimentary-conceptual knowledge, which are 'online politics' and 'e-politics'. As used concept 'e-campaign', Shaw (2002) has attempted to explore how and the degree of which: a) voters seek political information from party websites and perceive political information displayed in these websites; and b) political parties and parties' candidates have adopted the Internet/Web Campaign during the 2000 Presidential Election for internal communication and grassroots mobilization. Moreover, Williams (et. al, 2002) has deployed this concept to assess the increasing number of the Website Campaigns of party' candidates those want to get elected as members of US Senate during the 2000 election. Unlike wise to these authors, Curtin and Sommer (2003: 108) have favoured utilizing concept 'e-politics' to portray the emergence and developments of what they called as 'online campaigning' since the 1996 election up to the 2000 election. Though this remains existing as *a rudimentary-conceptual knowledge*, this concept however, has been advanced as *the operational knowledge*. He has stated the following:

The 1996 election cycle was the earliest that anyone can honestly say online campaigning really occurred...During the 1998 election cycle, an increasing number of congressional and gubernatorial candidates, and even a good number of state and local candidates, had moved their campaigns online in one form or another–although in reality one could hesitate to call many of them more than a mere online presence. It was the 2000 presidential election cycle that really sparked the birth of online politics, or e-politics as we now know it...The 2000 election was also noteworthy for a range of online experiments beyond the typical brochure type site, although even then the cost of the more innovative technology was still prohibitive for all but the largest and richest political campaigns. (Curtin & Sommer, 2003: 108)

Likewise, Curtin and Sommer (2003), Sommer and Tavlin (2003) have also deployed this knowledge to assess the emergence of e-politics and its impact on political campaigns in the US politics. They have then also generated this knowledge as the operational knowledge. He has spelled out as follows.

After 2000, we stopped working normal political campaigns to concentrate on and create new, useful alternative Internet political options. We weren't alone. Others were just as smart and had caught the wind. Most of us were betting that sooner or later, citizens might be so energized with their own e-involvement and voter disgust, they might actually use the convenience of the Web to chase away the dominance of fat-cat politics, and help to create confidence in a fair, long overdue, fresh, new grassroots-energized citizen democracy, changing America for the better. (Sommer & Tavlin, 2003: 88)

Unlike these authors, some have favoured the development of American campaign model during the 2000 US presidential election (Espindola, 2002; Holtz-Bacha, 2002). As the Internet and new electronic communication have been vigorously innovative and widely adopted across the globe, Espindola (2002) and Hotz-Bacha (2002) have introduced the new rudimentary-conceptual knowledge, which are 'Americanization' of campaigning and 'professionalization' of political communication and campaigning. Espindola (2002) has favoured using the second concept to assess the changing nature of campaigning in Argentina, Chile and Uruguay during the 1999 elections. Meanwhile, Holtz-Bacha (2002) has utilized this second concept to capture the campaign transformation of Germany political parties. As a rudimentary-conceptual knowledge, 'professionalization' of political communication and campaigning has carried out various interpretations (see Mancini, 1999; Plasser & Plasser, 2002) and entailed disputable debates that need to be sufficiently clarified (see Lilleker & Negrine, 2001, 2002; Negrine, et.al, 2007, 2008). A number of authors have leveraged this knowledge as whether the operational or the established-conceptual or the systematic knowledge by proposing its definitions, indicators and measurements to understand the ways and the degrees of which political parties have adopted the Internet and Web Campaigns during the elections and in between the elections (see Gibson & Rommele, 2001, 2009; Esser & Tenscher, 2005a, 2005b; Stromback, 2007, 2009; Tenscher, et.al. 2012; Tenscher, 2013; Tenscher & Mykkanen, 2013, 2014; Vergeers, et.al, 2013). Unlikewise 'Americanization' of campaigning that remains exists as the rudimentary-conceptual knowledge, 'professionalization' of political communication and campaigning has been advanced not only as the operational knowledge, but also as the established conceptual and the systematic knowledge.

Despite introducing new frameworks, most of those who have published their ideas in *Journal of Political Marketing* in between 2004 and 2014 have also considered the existing theories and concepts of marketing management when political parties and parties' politicians and candidates to gain electorates' support during the elections have gradually harnessed the Internet and Web Campaigns. For example: Demenrtzis (et.al, 2005) have taken into account ideas of Kotler and Kotler (1999) to generate the rudimentary-conceptual knowledge, which are online political marketing and e-political marketing. Moreover, a number of authors have also developed the existing theories of political communication and political sciences to generate the rudimentary-conceptual knowledge, which was then deployed to understand not only the ways American voters have accessed and used the Internet in between 1997-2007 and in between 2004 and 2008 (Hall & Sinclair, 2011), but also how and the degree to which various forms of social media have impacted on political attitudes of American young electorates during the 2008 US presidential election (Towner & Dulio, 2011). Additionally, though advanced, the rudimentary-conceptual knowledge of online political marketing and campaigning, the other authors have investigated various themes, such as the level of adaptation of Web campaign technologies (Foot, et.al, 2009), campaign websites of candidates and endorsement of organizations (Williams, et.al, 2009), the uses of Internet and political blog, online videos and YouTube as campaign platforms during the elections (Wallsten, 2011; Jackson, 2011; Vesnic-Alujevic & Bauwel, 2014) and websites of female candidates and gender-based strategies (Schneider, 2014)

Generally speaking, articles published in *Journal of Political Marketing* in between 2002 and 2011 have discussed the ICTs development and adaptation of the Internet in the fields of politics, political marketing and campaigning, but covered less the uses of social media and their impact on political marketing and campaigning. In slightly contrast, articles published in *Journal of Political Marketing* Vol. 9 (2011) that have focused on this issue have been framed using a broad theme 'money and technology'. In this respect, the emergence of social media networking facilitated by the Internet has been gradually accounted as a leading research theme to produce *the rudimentary-conceptual, the operational knowledge* and *the established-conceptual* of political marketing. *The rudimentary-conceptual knowledge* has taken shape when the 2008 Obama campaign during the 2008 US presidential election has been widely seen of being successfully harnessing the websites (My.BarackObama.com), Facebook and YouTube as a strategic online tool, which is combined with the offline strategies directed either to attract campaign donators or persuade and mobilize some groups of electorates (Hassell, 2011; Lipsitz & Panagopoulos, 2011: 47; Christenson & Smidt, 2011: 24; Garcia-Castanon, et.al, 2011: 33-34). In addressing online campaigning during the 2008 US presidential election, Panagopoulus (2011) has formulated *the rudimentary-conceptual knowledge*. He has stated as follows:

Of the many noteworthy, and even historic, aspects of the 2008 presidential election campaign cycle, developments related to money and technology in political campaigns were especially significant...A wide range of developments in online communications, including but by no means limited to the proliferation of social networking (Facebook) and video sharing (YouTube) Web sites, have essentially revolutionized political campaigns, creating unparalleled opportunities for interaction and information acquisition and helping to make 2008 a watershed year in the trajectory of political campaign history. (Panagopoulos, 2011: 1)

A year later, Towner and Dullio (2012) have strongly called political scholars to further conduct innovative studies that address the developments of technology and new media and their impact on campaigning and relationships among journalists, candidates and citizens. They have implicitly called for developing *the established-conceptual, the operational and the systemic knowledge* that holistically capture and theorise the adaptations and uses of new media and their impacts on political campaigning. In addressing this issue, they have voiced as follows:

These rapid changes in technology and new media require scholars to update the design and direction of future research. Clearly, new media are altering the process of campaigning for political office, changing the relationships among journalists, political candidates, and citizens. Scholars are just beginning to inquire into the empirical links between new media and political attitudes, leaving many questions unanswered and theories untested…In a way, this article is a call to new media researchers to grasp some of these changes and develop innovative research that builds up our empirical evidence and expands our theoretical understanding. (Towner & Dullio, 2012: 112)

Though they advocated the importance of developing these types of knowledge, Towner and Dullio (2012) have not yet specifically suggested to develop the *well-established-conceptual* and *systemic knowledge* that can be deployed to capture and explain the developments and uses of social media and their impact on politics—in general—and political marketing and campaigning—in particular. Political marketing scholars have paid much more attention to social media uses and their impacts on politics when various groups of social media users have successfully triggered political revolution in the Middle East. This has indicated the pivotal roles of social media in shoring up a political movement and campaign against the authoritarian regime. In addressing this issue, Newman (2012) has outlined *the rudimentary-conceptual knowledge*. He has stated as follows:

The world has recently witnessed a series of political revolutions in the Middle East that have resulted in authoritarian leaders who had been in power for decades being overthrown by a coalition of citizens. These revolutions stemmed from political movements and grassroots efforts that relied on the use of social networks and social media tools to organize and plan demonstrations as well as public responses to government initiatives to stop these actions. These tools are one part of the arsenal of hi-tech political campaigns carried out in democracies around the world that are studied by political marketers. (Newman, 2012: 2)

Despite of highlighting the pivotal roles of social media on the Middle East revolutions, Newman (2012) has postulated *the operational knowledge*, which is derived from the uses of social media during the 2008 Obama campaign. He has spotlighted that social media as a campaign tool of Obama to support political movement has led him get elected during the 2008 US presidential election.

The 2008 Obama campaign has been widely seen as a role model of online political marketing and campaigning. Since widely acknowledged on successfully harnessing social media, especially Facebook, this model has been gradually adopted across the globe (Miller, 2013). Further research has been vigorously conducted to explore Web Campaign and social media use within the context of the 2010 UK General Election. For example, in addressing mode of campaigning of parties during this election, Higgins and Smith (2013) have examined on how and in which ways leaders of Conservative and Labour Parties have attempted exploiting various new media platforms that combine official party websites, personal blogs and webcasts. Slightly different with these authors, Lilleker and Jackson (2013) have postulated a new *established-conceptual knowledge*, which is *Obama-ization of e-campaign*. As informed by ideas of O'Reilly (2005), Anderson (2007), Chadwick (2007), Anstead and Chadwick (2008) and Lilleker (et. al, 2010), Lilleker and Jackson (2013) have deployed this conceptual knowledge to understand mode of online campaign strategies of the UK political parties the (main parliamentary parties—Conservative, Labour, and Liberal Democrat—and three non-parliamentary national challengers—Green, UK Independence, and British National) during the 2010 general election. This conceptual knowledge is also advanced as *the operational knowledge*, as it is used to explore the 'Internet selling and campaigning' and the 'marketing communication mix' strategies of these parties during this election.

Meanwhile, since theoretical debates related to political branding have been gradually accounted for, some authors have then considered the importance of social media to develop theories and concepts of political branding (Busby and Cronshaw, 2015; Lilleker, 2015; Rutter, et.al, 2015). Busby and Cronshaw (2015) have simply highlighted that new and social media potentially pave the way for creating a type of *political branding* directed by consumers. Slightly different with these authors, Lilleker (2015) has theorized a conceptual lens to understand how UK parties and these parties' members elected to the House of Commons in the period 2007 to 2010 have harnessed the Internet and social media, such as Facebook, Twitter and YouTube, as interactive platforms for developing of what he called as the *e-branding strategies*. Slightly contrasting, Rutter (et.al, 2015) have favoured adopting idea of Aaker (1997) to explore the ways in which the five UK political parties have differentiated themselves using the *brand personality*, which is constructed through their websites. These new understanding of political branding so far has remained exist as *the rudimentary-conceptual knowledge* and has not yet been properly advanced as whether *the established-conceptual* or *the operational or the systematic knowledge*.

Some authors have specifically addressed developments and uses of social media in the fields of politics, political marketing and campaigning. Cogburn and Espinoza-Vasquez (2011) have created *the rudimentary-conceptual knowledge*, which is called as 'a networked nominee' and 'a networked nation'. The first one has been deployed to understand the role of Web 2.0 and social media in a presidential campaign, while the second one has been deployed to explore the role of Web 2.0 and social media on generating new social movements that shore up the 2008 Obama presidential campaign. Moreover, Cameron (et.al, 2014) has produced the other *rudimentary-conceptual knowledge*, which is *the networks effect of social media on the election results*. It is derived from the types and the degrees of the relationships between the size of candidates' social media on Facebook and Twitter and a total number of voters those who have casting their votes to these candidates during the 2011 New Zealand general election. Furthermore, Bode and Dalrymple (2014) have proposed the effects of Twitter, as a popular social media, on political interest, political knowledge, trust to the media, political engagement and online and offline political participation. While these authors have favoured generating *the rudimentary-conceptual knowledge*, Harris and Harrigan (2015) have been interested in developing *the operational knowledge*. They explored the uses of social media by political parties in the UK politics during the 2010 UK General Election and by the Obama campaign during the 2008 US presidential election, and have scrutinized the extent to which the social media can be considered for establishing the long- or the short-terms online and offline relationship strategy. Similarly, Parsons and Rowling (2015) have also proposed *the operational and the established-conceptual knowledge*, which is called as e-*relationship marketing*. This knowledge discusses the inherent challenges of the uses of social media by politicians when they have favoured an interest in developing political relationship with the electorates.

Generally speaking, either the wider or the narrow interpretations of political marketing (see Ormrod, 2012; Ormrod, et.al, 2013), *the rudimentary-* and *the established-conceptual knowledge* have been introduced to capture and understand the ICTs development and the use of Internet/new media, web campaigns and social media in the fields of politics, political marketing and campaigning. In this respect, those who have published articles in this journal in between 2002 and 2003 have been much more interested in advancing *the rudimentary-conceptual knowledge*, such as *cyber-democracy* (Johnson, 2002a; 2003a, 2003b, 2004a, 2004b), *e-politics* (Curtin and Sommer, 2003), *e-government* (Johnson, 2002b; Curtin, et.al, 2002; Vis-Sommer, 2003) and *e-campaign* (Shaw, 2002; Williams, et.al, 2002). Though widely adopted by political marketing scholars, *cyber-democracy* and *e-politics* have remained existent as *the rudimentary-conceptual knowledge*. Meanwhile, *e-government and e-campaign* as *the rudimentary-conceptual knowledge* have then been advanced as *the established-conceptual knowledge* and modified as *the operational knowledge* since they have been strongly accepted and acknowledged as pivotal and fruitful concepts to explain the ICTs development and the adaptation and use of the Internet and social media by political actors and organisations in political sphere.

Meanwhile, following the narrow interpretation, those who have released their studies in *Journal of Political Marketing* in between 2004 and 2015 have advanced *some conceptual knowledge*—such as *online/e-political marketing* (Demenrtzis, et.al, 2005), *Web campaign* (Yannas & Lappas (2005), *Web campaigning* (Carlson, 2007) and *The Obama-ization of e-campaigning* (Lilleker & Jackson, 2013) and some *operational knowledge* such as *Web-based advocacy* (Williams, et.al, 2007), *Web-based marketing* (Williams, et.al, 2010), *Web-based political campaign* (Wu & Dahmen, 2010), and *e-branding and interactive political communication* (Lilleker, 2014) and *e-relationship marketing* (Parsons & Rowling (2015). The authors however have not yet fully advanced *the systematic knowledge* based on *the operational knowledge* they have proposed. For example, Demenrtzis (et.al, 2005) who have introduced the concept *online/e-political marketing* has not yet further clarified both the similarities and the differences between this concept and the other concepts such as *e-government* (Johnson, 2002b; Curtin, et.al, 2002; Vis-Sommer, 2003), *e-politics* (Curtin & Sommer, 2003) and *e-campaign* (Shaw, 2002; Williams, et.al, 2002). Moreover, Lilleker and Jackson (2013) who have proposed the concept *e-campaigning* have not yet sufficiently discussed this concept with the other concepts such as *Web campaign* (Yannas & Lappas (2005), *Web campaigning* (Carlson, 2007), *Web-based advocacy* (Williams, et.al, 2007), *Web-based marketing* (Williams, et.al, 2010) and *Web-based political campaign* (Wu & Dahmen, 2010). Furthermore, Parsons and Rowling (2015) have advanced the concept *e-relationship marketing* have not yet fully scrutinized the relationships between this concept and the other concepts, such as e-*branding and interactive political communication* (Lilleker, 2014). In addition, Lilleker (2014) who has attempted conflicting concepts of *e-branding* and *interactive political communication* has not yet systematically delineated dimensions and indicators of e-branding and interactive political communication. Nonetheless, though authors of these articles have accounted the developments and the uses of social media by political parties and parties' leaders, candidates and politicians as well as by electorates/voters, most of them however, have much more preferred accounting the social media as part of an extension of Web Campaigns facilitated by the Internet/new media. In this sense, the use, adaptation and development of the Internet and new media have been widely accounted for as a central theme when they have discussed the strategies, practices and activities of online political marketing and campaigning of these parties and parties' leaders, candidates and politicians.

In the meantime, those who have published their works in this journal since 2011 up to 2015 have highlighted the important roles of social media on driving political revolutions and transforming the election campaigning (Newman, 2012) and theorized the uses of social media and their impacts on politics, political marketing and campaigning (Cogburn & Espinoza-Vasquez, 2011; Cameron, et, al., 2014; Bode & Dalrymple, 2014; Parsons and Rowling, 2015; Harris and Harrigan, 2015). Most of them have not yet offered *the established-conceptual knowledge, the operational knowledge* and *the systematic-knowledge* to capture such issues however. For example, though Cogburn and Espinoza-Vasquez (2011) have introduced concepts 'a networked nominee' and 'a networked nation' when they have captured the 2008 Obama presidential campaign, these authors however have not yet fully detailed these concepts. As derived from their subjective views, these authors have offered a less sufficient theoretical explanation and measurements. Such proposed knowledge seems difficult to be adopted and universally accepted and applied as *the systematic knowledge*. Moreover, although some authors have proposed *the rudimentary-conceptual knowledge* to understand the networks effects of social media on the election results (Cameron, et, al., 2014) and the effects of Twitter uses on political interest, political knowledge, trust to the media, political engagement and online and offline political participation (Bode and Dalrymple, 2014), they however have attempted less to develop *the systematic knowledge* that can be used to quantitatively and qualitatively analyse the effects of the social media uses on strategies and practices of political marketing and campaigning of political party and party' leaders, candidates and politicians on the one hand and on political knowledge, engagement and participation of the electorates/voters on the other. Additionally, even though sufficiently constructed, *e-relationship marketing* (Parsons and Rowling, 2015) and the long- or the short-terms of *the online and offline relationship strategy* (Harris & Harrigan, 2015) as the established-conceptual knowledge have not yet been properly advanced as *the systematic knowledge*.

CONCLUSION AND FURTHER RESEARCH RECOMMENDATIONS

Knowledge always takes shape as a multifaceted concept with multi-layered meanings (Nonaka, 1994:15). Knowledge is also produced and generated by scholars from particular point of view and stemmed from particular context wherein the multi dimensions of (social) realities and information have been realized and accounted (Nonaka & Toyama, 2003: 3). As there has always been a social base, the dynamic interactions between the agencies and structures to determine these realities and information that exist in society (Berger & Luckmann, 1966; Gidden, 1984), appropriate conceptual frameworks that can be deployed to holistically understand the knowledge creation and generation are deemed important. Since such frameworks have not yet been advanced within the specific field of political marketing, this work has proposed a specific theoretical framework to capture and explore modes of the knowledge production and generation of political marketing.

The quantitative, qualitative and thematic content analyses of 320 articles published in *Journal of Political Marketing* in between 2002 and 2015, this work highlights the following conclusions. *Firstly,* the quantitative and thematic content analyses of these articles, this work reveals that political marketing scholars who have published their works in this journal have gradually considered the ICTs development and the adaptation and use of the Internet and social media by political actors and organisations in political sphere for the knowledge creation and generation of political marketing. It is indicated by a sum of articles that cover issues related to the Internet/new media, Web Campaigns and social media, which have been substantially increased from 2.81% in 2002 to 19.68% in 2015; though a sum of article that specifically discusses social media use and its impacts on politics, political marketing and campaigning has still been low, at only 1.56% of total articles.

Secondly, the qualitative and thematic content analyses of these articles uncovers that the ICT development and the adaptation and use of the Internet and social media by political actors and organisations in political sphere have stimulated political marketing scholars who have published their works in *Journal of Political Marketing* in between 2002 and 2015 to produce the rudimentary-conceptual or the operational or the established-conceptual knowledge of political marketing. Most of these scholars have advanced the rudimentary-conceptual knowledge; some of them transformed this knowledge into *the* operational knowledge and or the established-conceptual knowledge. There have been a small number of these scholars who have been strongly interested in generating the established-conceptual and the operational knowledge and attempted developing the systematic knowledge. Though acknowledged as a useful conceptual framework to capture and understand the ICT development and the adaptation and use of the Internet and social media by political actors and organisations in political sphere, these kinds of knowledge have not yet been fully advanced as systematic knowledge.

Thirdly, the qualitative and thematic content analyses of these articles indicates that the leading social media platforms, such as Facebook and Twitter, have been gradually accounted for knowledge production and generation of political marketing since the 2008 Obama presidential campaign has succeeded. Harnessing Facebook and Twitter as a campaign platform and strategic tools to raise campaign funds and mobilize electorates have been important for political change in the Middle East revolution. Most of the political marketing scholars who have released their works in *Journal of Political Marketing* in between 2011 and 2015 however have still considered various social media platforms as part of Web 2.0. There have been only some of these scholars who have specifically addressed the adaptation and use of social media by political actors and organisations as a primary research theme to produce either *the rudimentary-conceptual* or *the operational* or *the established-conceptual knowledge*. Though various forms of social media have been robustly adopted in political sphere and vigorously investigated since 2008s, none of them have substantially considered the adaptation and use of social media platforms by political actors and organisations to formulate *the systematic knowledge* surprisingly.

As the research findings presented in this work still entails some innate weaknesses, this work suggests the following further research recommendations. Firstly, this work has strongly relied on articles published in *Journal of Political Marketing* as primary data. Comparative content analyses of articles published in several peer-reviewed journals and edited-book written by scholars those who have different educational background needs to be conducted since these scholars commonly use different philosophical standpoints and meta-theoretical assumptions when they have studied the ICT developments and the adaptation and use of the Internet and social media and their impacts on knowledge production and generation of political marketing.

Secondly, though this study has used the quantitative and the qualitative content analyses, which are combined simultaneously with the thematic content analysis as a mixture of the quantitative and qualitative method, it has taken into account less the other qualitative and quantitative methods. For further research, it is suggested to deploy the other qualitative and quantitative methods, such as survey, in-depth interviews and focus group discussion. These methods need to be properly deployed not only to holistically understand the impacts of social media uses on advancement of political marketing management, but also to explore various views among political marketing scholars on assessing the degrees of importance of the Internet and social media for the knowledge production development of political marketing. These methods would also help in assessing whether the sympathized or the rudimentary-conceptual or the established-conceptual or the systematic knowledge of political marketing is important.

Thirdly, though this work offered a new conceptual framework to understand modes of knowledge production and generation and its application in the field study of political marketing, it has not fully clarified conceptually and empirically demarcated between and among the systematized, the rudimentary-conceptual, the practical-operational and the established-conceptual knowledge. With regards to this limitation, further research needs to be undertaken to examine not only the conceptual boundaries between and among these types of knowledge, but the empirical border and crosscutting lines between and among these types of knowledge. In this respect, a strong theoretical proposition needs to be properly advanced to theoretically define the border and crosscutting lines between and among these types of knowledge. More importantly, an appropriate research method and sufficient data also need to be holistically collated to conceptually and empirically evaluate these border and crosscutting lines.

Fourthly, this article has only focused on how, in which ways and the extent to which political marketing scholars who have published their works in *Journal of Political Marketing* accounted the adaptation and use of the Internet and social media by political actors and organisations as political marketing phenomena to create and generate knowledge production and generation of political marketing. This work has not yet explored the impact of adaptation and use of the Internet and social media on the knowledge production and generation of political marketing among political actors and organisations those who have run in the elections or those who have ruled in the government. Further investigation needs to be conducted to uncover this issue. A holistic research needs to be undertaken to explore the adaptation and use of the Internet and social media on the knowledge production and generation of political marketing among these actors and organisations on the one hand and among political marketing scholars who have studied these actors and organisations on the other. To such ends, a collaborative project involving peer groups of scholars from various disciplines, social science and technology needs to be advanced.

REFERENCES

Baskerville, R., & Dulipovici, A. (2006). The Theoretical Foundations of Knowledge management. *Knowledge Management Research & Practice*, *4*(2), 8M–105. doi:10.1057/palgrave.kmrp.8500090

Berger, P. L., & Luckmann, T. (1966). *The Social Construction of Reality: A Treatise in the Sociology of Knowledge*. London: Penguin Books.

Bhaskar, R. (1998). *The possibility of naturalism: A philosophical critique of the contemporary human sciences* (3rd ed.). London: Routledge.

Bhaskar, R. (2008). *A Realist Theory of Science* (2nd ed.). London: Verso.

Bode, L., & Dalrymple, K. E. (2014). Politics in 140 Characters or Less: Campaign Communication, Network Interaction, and Political Participation on Twitter. *Journal of Political Marketing*. doi:10.108 0/15377857.2014.959686

Boyd, D. M., & Ellison, N. B. (2007). Social network sites: Definition, history, and scholarship. *Journal of Computer-Mediated Communication*, *13*(1), 11. doi:10.1111/j.1083-6101.2007.00393.x

Bryman, A. (2008). *Social Research Methods* (3rd ed.). Oxford, UK: Oxford University Press.

Busby, R., & Cronshaw, S. (2015). Political Branding: The Tea Party and Its Use of Participation Branding. *Journal of Political Marketing*, *14*(1-2), 96–110. doi:10.1080/15377857.2014.990850

Butler, P., & Collins, N. (1994). Political Marketing: Structure and Process. *European Journal of Marketing*, *28*(1), 19–34. doi:10.1108/03090569410049154

Butler, P., & Collins, N. (1999). A Conceptual Framework for Political Marketing. In B. I. Newman (Ed.), *Handbook of Political Marketing* (pp. 55–72). Thousand Oaks, CA: Sage Publications.

Butler, P., & Harris, P. (2009). Considerations on the evolution of political marketing theory. *Marketing Theory*, *9*(2), 149–164. doi:10.1177/1470593109103022

Butler-Kisber, L. (2010). *Qualitative Inquiry: Thematic, Narrative and Arts- Informed Perspectives*. London: Sage Publications Ltd.

Cameron, M. P., Barrett, P., & Stewardson, B. (2014). Can Social Media Predict Election Results? Evidence From New Zealand. *Journal of Political Marketing*, 1–17. doi:10.1080/15377857.2014.959690

Christenson, D. P., & Smidt, C. D. (2011). Riding the Waves of Money: Contribution Dynamics in the 2008 Presidential Nomination Campaign. *Journal of Political Marketing*, *10*(1-2), 1–2, 4–26. doi:10.1080/15377857.2011.540189

Chugh, R. (2012). Social Networking for Business: Is it a Boon or Banes?. In Handbook of Research on Business Social Networking: Organizational, Managerial, and Technological Dimensions. IGI Global.

Chugh, R. (2013). Workplace Dimensions: Tacit Knowledge Sharing in Universtities. *Journal of Advanced Management Science*, *1*(1), 24–28. doi:10.12720/joams.1.1.24-28

Chugh, R., Wibowo, S., & Grandi, S. (2015). Mandating the Transfer of Tacit Knowledge in Australian Universities. *Journal of Organizational Knowledge Management*, *2015*, 297669. doi:10.5171/2015.297669

Cogburn, D. L., & Espinoza-Vasquez, F. K. (2011). From Networked Nominee to Networked Nation: Examining the Impact of Web 2.0 and Social Media on Political Participation and Civic Engagement in the 2008 Obama Campaign. *Journal of Political Marketing*, *10*(1-2), 1–2, 189–213. doi:10.1080/15377857.2011.540224

Collins, N., & Butler, P. (1996). Positioning Political Parties: A Market Analysis. *The Harvard International Journal of Press/Politics*, *1*(2), 63–77. doi:10.1177/1081180X96001002006

Creswell, J. W., & Plano Clark, V. L. (2007). *Designing and Conducting Mixed Methods Research*. Thousand Oaks, CA: Sage.

Creswell, J. W., & Plano Clark, V. L. (2011). *Designing and Conducting Mixed Methods Research* (2nd ed.). Thousand Oaks, CA: Sage.

Creswell, J. W., & Tashakkori, A. (2007). Editorial: Differing Perspectives on Mixed Methods Research. *Journal of Mixed Methods Research*, *1*(4), 303–308. doi:10.1177/1558689807306132

Curtin, G., McConnachie, R., Sommer, M., & Vis-Sommer, V. (2002). American E-Government at the Crossroads. *Journal of Political Marketing*, *1*(1), 149–191. doi:10.1300/J199v01n01_08

Curtin, G. G., & Sommer, M. (2003). Is the Campaign Web Site Really "Dead"? *Journal of Political Marketing*, *2*(1), 107–111. doi:10.1300/J199v02n01_07

Curtin, G.G., Sommer, M.H., & Vis-Sommer, V. (2003) The World of E-Government. *Journal of Political Marketing, 2*(3-4), 1-16. DOI: 10.1300/J199v02n03_01

Demertzis, N., Diamantaki, K., Gazi, A., & Sartzetakis, N. (2005). Greek Political Marketing Online. *Journal of Political Marketing*, *4*(1), 51–74. doi:10.1300/J199v04n01_04

Egan, J. (1999). Political Marketing: Lessons from the Mainstream. *Journal of Marketing Management*, *15*(6), 495–503. doi:10.1362/026725799785045806

Espíndola, R. (2002). Professionalised Campaigning in Latin America. *Journal of Political Marketing*, *1*(4), 65–81. doi:10.1300/J199v01n04_04

Esser, F., & Tenscher, J. (2005a). *The Professionalization Dilemma: Exploring a 'Strategic Approach' for Political Communication Experts*. Paper prepared for presentation to the Political Communication Division at the ICA conference.

Esser, F., & Tenscher, J. (2005b). *Measuring The Professionalization of Political Campaign*. Paper prepared for presentation to the Political Communication Division at the ICA Conference.

Foot, K., Schneider, S. M., Xenos, M., & Dougherty, M. (2009). Candidates' Web Practices in the 2002 U.S. House, Senate, and Gubernatorial Elections. *Journal of Political Marketing, 8*(2), 147–167. doi:10.1080/15377850902813519

Garcia-Castañon, M., Rank, A. D., & Barreto, M. A. (2011). Plugged In or Tuned Out? Youth, Race, and Internet Usage in the 2008 Election. *Journal of Political Marketing, 10*(1-2), 1–2, 115–138. doi:10.1080/15377857.2011.540209

Gibson, R. K., & Rommele, A. (2001). Changing Campaign Communications: A Party-Centered Theory of Professionalized Campaigning. *The Harvard International Journal of Press/Politics, 6*(4), 31–43. doi:10.1177/108118001129172323

Gibson, R. K., & Rommele, A. (2009). Measuring the Professionalization of Political Campaigning. *Party Politics, 15*(3), 265–293. doi:10.1177/1354068809102245

Giddens, A. (1984). *The Constitution of Society: Outline of the Theory of Structuration*. Oxford, UK: Polity Press.

Guest, G. (2013). Describing Mixed Methods Research: An Alternative to Typologies. *Journal of Mixed Methods Research, 7*(2), 141–151. doi:10.1177/1558689812461179

Hall, T. E., & Sinclair, B. (2011). The American Internet Voter. *Journal of Political Marketing, 10*(1-2), 1–2, 58–79. doi:10.1080/15377857.2011.540194

Harris, L., & Harrigan, P. (2015). Social Media in Politics: The Ultimate Voter Engagement Tool or Simply an Echo Chamber? *Journal of Political Marketing, 14*(3), 251–283. doi:10.1080/15377857.2012.693059

Harris, P. (2000). *To Spin or not to Spin that is the Question: The Emergence of Modern Political Marketing*. Westburn Publishers Ltd.

Harris, P., & Andrew, L. (2010). "Mind the gap": The rise of political marketing and a perspective on its future agenda. *European Journal of Marketing, 44*(3/4), 297–307. doi:10.1108/03090561011020435

Harrop, M. (1990)... *Political Marketing. Parliamentary Affairs. Oxford University Press, 1990*, 227–291.

Hartwig, M. (2008). *Introduction. In A Realist Theory of Science* (2nd ed.; pp. ix–xxiv). London: Verso.

Hassell, H. J. G. (2011). Looking Beyond the Voting Constituency: A Study of Campaign Donation Solicitations in the 2008 Presidential Primary and General Election. *Journal of Political Marketing, 10*(1-2), 1–2, 27–42. doi:10.1080/15377857.2011.540192

Heisig, P. (2009). Harmonisation of knowledge management: Comparing 160 KM frameworks around the globe. *Journal of Knowledge Management, 13*(Issue, 4), 4–31. doi:10.1108/13673270910971798

Henneberg, S. C. M. (2002). Understanding Political Marketing. In N. J. O'Shaughnessy & S. C. M. Henneberg (Eds.), *The Idea of Political Marketing*. Westport, CT: Praeger.

Henneberg, S. C. M. (2004). The Views of an Avocatus Dei: Political Marketing and Its Critics. *Journal of Public Affairs, 4*(3), 225–243. doi:10.1002/pa.187

Henneberg, S. C. M. (2008). An Epistemological Perspective on Research in Political Marketing. *Journal of Political Marketing, 7*(2), 151–182. doi:10.1080/15377850802053158

Henneberg, S. C. M., & O'Shaughnessy, N. J. (2007). Theory and Concept Development in Political Marketing. *Journal of Political Marketing, 6*, 2–3, 5–31. doi:10.1300/J199v06n02_02

Henneberg, S. C. M., & O'Shaughnessy, N. J. (2009). Political Relationship Marketing: Some macro/micro thoughts. *Journal of Marketing Management, 25*(1-2), 5–29. doi:10.1362/026725709X410016

Henneberg, S. C. M., & Ormrod, R. P. (2013). The triadic interaction model of political marketing exchange. *Marketing Theory, 13*(1), 87–103. doi:10.1177/1470593112467269

Holtz-Bacha, C. (2002). Professionalization of Political Communication. *Journal of Political Marketing, 1*(4), 23–37. doi:10.1300/J199v01n04_02

Jackson, N. (2011). Perception or Reality: How MPs Believe the Internet Helps Them Win Votes. *Journal of Political Marketing, 10*(3), 230–250. doi:10.1080/15377857.2011.588099

Johansen, H. P. M. (2005). Political Marketing. *Journal of Political Marketing, 4*(4), 85–105. doi:10.1300/J199v04n04_05

Johnson, D. W. (2002a). The Electronic Information Candy Store. *Journal of Political Marketing, 1*(4), 101–102. doi:10.1300/J199v01n04_07

Johnson, D. W. (2002b). Campaign Website. *Journal of Political Marketing, 1*(1), 213–215. doi:10.1300/J199v01n01_11

Johnson, D. W. (2003a). Anthrax and Digital Mail. *Journal of Political Marketing, 2*(1), 113–115. doi:10.1300/J199v02n01_08

Johnson, D. W. (2003b). The U.S. Congress Responds to Online Communication Needs. *Journal of Political Marketing, 2*(3-4), 3–4, 235–254. doi:10.1300/J199v02n03_13

Johnson, D. W. (2004a). the 2004 U.S. Presidential Elections. *Journal of Political Marketing, 3*(4), 111–113. doi:10.1300/J199v03n04_06

Johnson, D. W. (2004b). Rethinking Electronic Voting. *Journal of Political Marketing, 3*(3), 107–109. doi:10.1300/J199v03n03_07

Kotler, P., & Kotler, N. (1999). Political Marketing: Generating Effective Candidate, Campaigns and Causes. In Handbook of Political Marketing. London: Sage Publication.

Lappas, G., Chatzopoulos, S., & Yannas, P. (2008). Parliamentary Candidates Running on the Web for the 2004 Greek National Elections. *Journal of Political Marketing, 7*(3-4), 3–4, 256–277. doi:10.1080/15377850802008327

Lees-Marshment, J. (2001a, September). The Marriage of Politics and Marketing. *Political Studies, 49*(4), 692–713. doi:10.1111/1467-9248.00337

Lees-Marshment, J. (2001b). The product, sales and market-oriented party: How Labour learnt to market the product, not just the presentation. *European Journal of Marketing, 35*(9/10), 1074–1084. doi:10.1108/EUM0000000005959

Lees-Marshment, J. (2001c). *Political Marketing and British Political Parties: The Party's Just Begun.* Manchester, UK: Manchester University Press.

Lees-Marshment, J. (2004). *The Political Marketing Revolution: Transforming the Government of the UK.* London: Routledge Publication.

Lees-Marshment, J. (2008). *Political Marketing and British Political Parties* (2nd ed.). Manchester, UK: Manchester University Press.

Lees-Marshment, J. (Ed.). (2012). *Routledge Hanbook of Political Marketing.* London: Routledge Taylor & Francis Group.

Lees-Marshment, J., & Lilleker, D. G. (Eds.). (2005). *Political Marketing: A Comparative Perspective.* Manchester, UK: Manchester University Press.

Lees-Marshment, J., Stromback, J., & Rudd, C. (Eds.). (2010). *Global Political Marketing.* London: Routlegde.

Lilleker, D. G. (2014). Interactivity and Branding, Public Political Communication as a Marketing Tool. *Journal of Political Marketing.* doi:10.1080/15377857.2014.990841

Lilleker, D. G., & Jackson, N. A. (2013). Reaching Inward Not Outward: Marketing via the Internet at the UK 2010 General Election. *Journal of Political Marketing, 12*(2-3), 2–3, 244–261. doi:10.1080/15377857.2013.781475

Lilleker, D. G., Jackson, N. A., & Scullion, R. (2007). *The Marketing of Political Parties.* Manchester, UK: Manchester University Press.

Lilleker, D. G., & Lees-Marshment, J. (Eds.). (2005). *Political Marketing: A Comparative Perspective.* Manchester, UK: Manchester University Press.

Lilleker, D. G., & Negrine, R. (2002). Professionalization: Of What? Since When? By Whom? *The Harvard International Journal of Press/Politics, 7*(4), 98–103. doi:10.1177/108118002236354

Lipsitz, K., & Panagopoulos, C. (2011). Filled Coffers: Campaign Contributions and Contributors in the 2008 Elections. *Journal of Political Marketing, 10*(1-2), 1–2, 43–57. doi:10.1080/15377857.2011.540193

Lock, A., & Harris, P. (1996). Political marketing – *vive la différence! European Journal of Marketing, 30*(10/11), 14–24. doi:10.1108/03090569610149764

Lunde, A., Heggen, K., & Strand, R. (2013). Knowledge and Power: Exploring Unproductive Interplay Between Quantitative and Qualitative Researchers. *Journal of Mixed Methods Research, 7*(2), 197–210. doi:10.1177/1558689812471087

Mancini, P. (1999). New Frontiers in Political Professionalism. *Political Communication, 16*(3), 231–245. doi:10.1080/105846099198604

Miller, W. J. (2013). We Can't All Be Obama: The Use of New Media in Modern Political Campaigns. *Journal of Political Marketing, 12*(4), 326–347. doi:10.1080/15377857.2013.837312

Moloney, K. (2008). Is Political Marketing New Words or New Practice in UK Politics? *Journal of Political Marketing, 6*(4), 51–65. doi:10.1300/J199v06n04_03

Moses, J. W., & Knutsen, T. L. (2012). *Ways of Knowing: Competing Methodologies in Social and Political Research* (2nd ed.). New York: Palgrave Macmillan.

Needham, C., & Smith, G. (2015). Introduction: Political Branding. *Journal of Political Marketing, 14*(1-2), 1–6. doi:10.1080/15377857.2014.990828

Negrine, R. (2008). *The Transformation of Political Communication: Continuities and Changes in Media and Politics*. New York: Palgrave Macmillan.

Negrine, R., & Lilleker, D. G. (2002). The Professionalization of Political Communication: Continuities and Change in Media Practices. *European Journal of Communication, 17*(3), 305–323. doi:10.1177/0267323102017003688

Negrine, R., Mancini, P., Holtz-Bacha, C., & Papathanossopoulos, S. (Eds.). (2007). *The Professionalization of Political Communication*. Bristol: Intellect.

Newman, B. I. (1994). *The Marketing of the President: Political Marketing as Campaign Strategy*. Thousand Oaks, CA: Sage Publications.

Newman, B. I. (1999a). Preface. In *Handbook of Political Marketing*. Thousand Oaks, CA: Sage.

Newman, B. I. (Ed.). (1999c). *Handbook of Political Marketing*. Thousand Oaks, CA: Sage.

Newman, B. I. (1999b). *The Mass Marketing of Politics: Democracy in an Age of Manufactured Image*. London: Sage Publication.

Newman, B.I. (2012). The Role of Marketing in Politics: Ten Years Later. *Journal of Political Marketing, 11*. DOI: 10.1080/15377857.2012.642697

Nonaka, I. (1994). Dynamic Theory of Organisational Knowledge Creation. *Organization Science, 5*(1), 14–37. doi:10.1287/orsc.5.1.14

Nonaka, I., & Kono, N. (1998). The Concept of "Ba': Building a Foundation for Knowledge Creation. *California Management Review, 40*(3), 40–54. doi:10.2307/41165942

Nonaka, I., & Toyama, R. (2003). The knowledge-creating theory revisited: Knowledge creation as a synthesizing process. *Knowledge Management Research & Practice, 1*(1), 2–10. doi:10.1057/palgrave.kmrp.8500001

Norris, P. (2000). *The Virtuos Circle–Political Communication in Postindustrial Societies*. Cambridge, UK: Cambridge University Press. doi:10.1017/CBO9780511609343

O' Schaughnessy, N. J., & Hanneberg, S. C. M. (2002). *The Idea of Political Marketing*. London: Praeger Series in Political Communication.

O'Cass, A. (2001a). Political Marketing: An Investigation of the Political Marketing Concept and Political Market Orientation in Australian Politics. *European Journal of Marketing*, *35*(9/10), 1003–1025. doi:10.1108/03090560110401938

O'Cass, A. (2001b). The Internal-External Marketing Orientation of a Political Party: Social Implications of Political Party Marketing Orientation. *Journal of Public Affairs*, *1*(2), 136–152. doi:10.1002/pa.59

O'Shaughnessy, NJ. (2010) The marketing of political marketing. *European Journal of Marketing*, *35*(9-10), 1047-1057.

Omrod, R. P. (2011). *Product-, Sales- and Market-Oriented Parties: Literature Review and Implications for Academics, Practitioners and Educators*. Working Paper Series in Management 2011/2 Institute for Economics and Management Aarhus University, Denmark.

Ormrod, R. P. (2005). A Conceptual Model of Political Market Orientation. *Journal of Nonprofit & Public Sector Marketing*, *14*(1/2), 47–65. doi:10.1300/J054v14n01_04

Ormrod, R. P. (2006). A Critique of the Lees-Marshment Market-Oriented Party Model. *Politics*, *26*(2), 110–118. doi:10.1111/j.1467-9256.2006.00257.x

Ormrod, R. P. (2007). Political Market Orientation and Its Commercial Cousin. *Journal of Political Marketing*, *6*(2-3), 2–3, 69–90. doi:10.1300/J199v06n02_05

Ormrod, R. P. (2009). *Understanding Political Market Orientation*. (Doctoral Thesis). Aarhus School of Business, University of Aarhus, Denmark.

Ormrod, R. P. (2012) *Defining Political Marketing*. Management Working Papers. Institut for Økonomi, Aarhus Universitet. 22 Oct 2012

Ormrod, R. P., & Henneberg, S. C. M. (2008). *Understanding Political Market Orientation*. Paper presented at International Conference on Political Marketing, Manchester, UK.

Ormrod, R. P., & Henneberg, S. C. M. (2009). Different Facets of Market Orientation: A Comparative Analysis of Party Manifestos. *Journal of Political Marketing*, *8*(3), 190–208. doi:10.1080/15377850903044742

Ormrod, R. P., & Henneberg, S. C. M. (2009). Different Facets of Market Orientation: A Comparative Analysis of Party Manifestos. *Journal of Political Marketing*, *8*(3), 190–208. doi:10.1080/15377850903044742

Ormrod, R. P., & Henneberg, S. C. M. (2010). Strategic Political Postures and Political Market Orientation: Toward an Integrated Concept of Political Marketing Strategy. *Journal of Political Marketing*, *9*(4), 294–313. doi:10.1080/15377857.2010.518106

Ormrod, R. P., & Henneberg, S. C. M. (2010, February). Understanding voter orientation in the context of political market orientation: Is the political customer king? *Journal of Marketing Management*, *26*(1–2), 108–130. doi:10.1080/02672570903574270

Ormrod, R. P., & Henneberg, S. C. M. (2011). Political Market Orientation and Strategic Party Postures in Danish Political Parties. *European Journal of Marketing, 45*(6), 852–881. doi:10.1108/03090561111119949

Ormrod, R.P., Henneberg, S.C.M., & O'Shaughnessy, N. J. (2013). *Political Marketing: Theory and Concepts.* London: Sage Publication.

Panagopoulos, C. (2011). Introduction: Money and Technology in the 2008 Elections. *Journal of Political Marketing, 10.* DOI: 10.1080/15377857.2011.540188

Parsons, M., & Rowling, M. (2015). Social Media and the Paradox of Fear: An Exploratory Study of Political Relationship Marketing Within South Wales. *Journal of Political Marketing*, 1–23. doi:10.10 80/15377857.2015.1039746

Pavitt, C. (1999). The Third Way: Scientific Realism and Communication Theory. *Communication Theory, 9*(2), 162–188. doi:10.1111/j.1468-2885.1999.tb00356.x

Plasser, F., & Plasser, G. (2002). *Global Political Campaigning: A Worldwide Analysis of Campaign Professionals and Their Practices.* Westport, CT: Praeger.

Polanyi, M. (1966). The Tacit Dimension. London: Routledge & Kegan Paul.

Rutter, R. N., Hanretty, C., & Lettice, F. (2015). Political Brands: Can Parties Be Distinguished by Their Online Brand Personality? *Journal of Political Marketing*, 1–20. doi:10.1080/15377857.2015.1022631

Sandelowski, M., Voils, C. I., Leeman, J., & Crandell, J. L. (2012). Mapping the Mixed Methods–Mixed Research Synthesis Terrain. *Journal of Mixed Methods Research, 6*(4), 317–331. doi:10.1177/1558689811427913 PMID:23066379

Savigny, H. (2004). *Political Marketing: A Critical Assessment-Caveat Emptor.* (Doctoral Thesis). The University of Birmingham.

Savigny, H. (2007). Ontology and Epistemology in Political Marketing. *Journal of Political Marketing, 6*(2-3), 2–3, 33–47. doi:10.1300/J199v06n02_03

Savigny, H. (2008). *The Problem of Political Marketing.* New York: Continuum.

Savigny, H. & Temple, M. (2010). Political Marketing Models: The Curious Incident of the Dog that Doesn't Bark. *Political Studies, 58,* 1049–1064.

Sayer, A. (2000). *Realism and Social Science.* London: Sage. doi:10.4135/9781446218730

Scammell, M. (1999). Political Marketing: Lessons for Political Science. *Political Studies, 67*(4), 718–739. doi:10.1111/1467-9248.00228

Schneider, M. C. (2014). Gender-Based Strategies on Candidate Websites. *Journal of Political Marketing, 13*(4), 264–290. doi:10.1080/15377857.2014.958373

Shaw, D. R. (2002). How the Bush and Gore Campaigns Conceptualized and Used the Internet in 2000. *Journal of Political Marketing, 1*(1), 39–65. doi:10.1300/J199v01n01_04

Sherman, E., & Schiffman, L. G. (2002). Political Marketing Research in the 2000 U.S. Election. *Journal of Political Marketing, 1*(2-3), 2–3, 53–68. doi:10.1300/J199v01n02_05

Sommer, M., & Tavlin, B. (2003). Notes on the California E-Politics Campaign Trail. *Journal of Political Marketing, 3*(1), 87–96. doi:10.1300/J199v03n01_05

Stromback, J. (2007). Political Marketing and Professionalized Campaigning'. *Journal of Political Marketing, 6*(2), 49–67. doi:10.1300/J199v06n02_04

Stromback, J. (2009). Selective Professionalisation of Political Campaigning: A Test of the Party-Centred Theory of Professionalised Campaigning in the Context of the 2006 Swedish Election. *Political Studies, 57*, 95–116.

Stromback, J. (2010). A Framework for Comparing Political Market-Orientation. In Global Political Marketing. London: Routledge Taylor & Francis Group.

Stromer-Galley, J. (2000). On-line interaction and why candidates avoid it. *Journal of Communication, 50*(4), 111–132. doi:10.1111/j.1460-2466.2000.tb02865.x

Tashakkori, A. (2009). Are we there yet? The State of the Mixed Methods Community. *Journal of Mixed Methods Research, 3*(4), 287–291. doi:10.1177/1558689809346151

Tashakkori, A., & Creswell, J. W. (2007a). Editorial: Exploring the Nature of Research Questions in Mixed Methods Research. *Journal of Mixed Methods Research, 1*(3), 207–211. doi:10.1177/1558689807302814

Tashakkori, A., & Creswell, J. W. (2007b). The new era of mixed methods. *Journal of Mixed Methods Research, 1*(1), 3–7. doi:10.1177/2345678906293042

Temple, M. (2013). The Media and the Message. *Journal of Political Marketing, 12*(2-3), 2–3, 147–165. doi:10.1080/15377857.2013.781479

Tenscher, J. (2004, September). 'Bridging the Differences': Political Communication Experts in Germany. *German Politics, 13*(3), 516–540. doi:10.1080/0964400042000287482

Tenscher, J. (2013). First-and second-order campaigning. *European Journal of Communication, 28*, 241.

Tenscher, J., & Mykkänen, J. (2013). Transformations in second-order campaigning: A German-Finnish comparison of campaign professionalism in the 2004 and 2009 European parliamentary elections. *Central European Journal of Communication, 2*, 171–187.

Tenscher, J. & Mykkänen, J. (2014). Two Levels of Campaigning: An Empirical Test of the Party-Centred Theory of Professionalisation. *Political Studies, 62*(S1), 20–41. DOI: 10.1111/1467-9248.12104

Tenscher, J., Mykkänen, J., & Moring, T. (2012). Modes of Professional Campaigning: A Four-Country Comparison in the European Parliamentary Elections, 2009. *The International Journal of Press/Politics, 17*(2), 145–168. doi:10.1177/1940161211433839

Towner, T. L., & Dulio, D. A. (2011). The Web 2.0 Election: Does the Online Medium Matter? *Journal of Political Marketing, 10*(1-2), 1–2, 165–188. doi:10.1080/15377857.2011.540220

Towner, T. L., & Dulio, D. A. (2012). New Media and Political Marketing in the United States: 2012 and Beyond. *Journal of Political Marketing, 11*(1-2), 1–2, 95–119. doi:10.1080/15377857.2012.642748

Vesnic-Alujevic, L., & Bauwel, S. V. (2014). YouTube: A Political Advertising Tool? A Case Study of the Use of YouTube in the Campaign for the European Parliament Elections. *Journal of Political Marketing*, *13*(3), 195–212. doi:10.1080/15377857.2014.929886

Vis-Sommer, V. (2003). Surveying Government Web Sites. *Journal of Political Marketing*, *3*(1), 97–103. doi:10.1300/J199v03n01_06

Wallsten, K. (2011). Many Sources, One Message: Political Blog Links to Online Videos During the 2008 Campaign. *Journal of Political Marketing*, *10*(1-2), 1–2, 88–114. doi:10.1080/15377857.2011.540203

William, C. B. (2012). Trends and Changes in Journal of Political Marketing Titles 2002–2011. *Journal of Political Marketing*, *11*, 1–2, 4–7. doi:10.1080/15377857.2012.642702

Williams, C. B., Aylesworth, A., & Chapman, K. J. (2002). The 2000 E-Campaign for U.S. Senate. *Journal of Political Marketing*, *1*(4), 39–63. doi:10.1300/J199v01n04_03

Williams, C. B., Gulati, G. J., & Foxman, E. R. (2009). What's In an Endorsement? An Analysis of Web-Based Marketing in the 2004 Presidential Campaign. *Journal of Political Marketing*, *8*(3), 173–189. doi:10.1080/15377850903048214

Wring, D. (1997). Reconciling Marketing with Political Science: Theories of Political Marketing. *Journal of Marketing Management*, *13*(7), 651–663. doi:10.1080/0267257X.1997.9964502

Wring, D. (2005). *The Politics of Marketing the Labour Party*. Hampshire, UK: Palgrave MacMillan.

Wu, H. W., & Dahmen, N. S. (2010). Web Sponsorship and Campaign Effects: Assessing the Difference Between Positive and Negative Web Sites. *Journal of Political Marketing*, *9*(4), 314–329. doi:10.1080/15377857.2010.522454

Yannas, P., & Lappas, G. (2005). Web Campaign in the 2002 Greek Municipal Elections. *Journal of Political Marketing*, *4*(1), 33–50. doi:10.1300/J199v04n01_03

This research was previously published in Harnessing Social Media as a Knowledge Management Tool edited by Ritesh Chugh, pages 177-208, copyright year 2017 by Information Science Reference (an imprint of IGI Global).

Chapter 69
Communicating Nation Brands Through Mass and Social Media

Maria De Moya
DePaul University, USA

Rajul Jain
DePaul University, USA

ABSTRACT

Nation branding efforts are the means through which many countries attempt to influence how foreign publics perceive them. However, in a media landscape that now includes not only traditional one-way media but also two-way social platforms, countries undertaking these efforts are presented with a series of new challenges. This environment makes it more difficult to manage the issues associated with a nation brand, challenges countries to better communicate their advantages, and allows the public to create its own, potentially competing, messages about a country. Building on previous work on nation and destination branding, this chapter discusses the changing media environment in which nation-branding efforts are taking place, and—through a combination of DICTION®-assisted, manual, and qualitative content analyses—provides evidence of the new media landscape in which nation branding is taking place. The challenges and opportunities created by this new context are detailed, and potential avenues for further research are discussed.

INTRODUCTION

In the global experience economy, nations compete against each other for the attention of investors, tourists, businesses, consumers, foreign governments, and international media (Anholt, 2006). In an attempt to stand out among competing and contrasting voices, nations use branding and marketing tools to promote a unique and favorable image to their national and international publics (Fan, 2006).

Today, a nation's brand or image has become a valuable asset and a source of competitive advantage (Passow, Fehlmann, & Grahlow, 2005). Thus, many nations are involved in brand-building initiatives, which leverage their image on one or more of the unique economic, cultural, political, and human resources that they possess (Anholt, 2004). Governments engage in these initiatives because they under-

DOI: 10.4018/978-1-5225-5637-4.ch069

stand that public opinion of a nation significantly affects the success of its international business, foreign investment, and tourism initiatives, as well as its diplomatic, cultural, and economic relations with other nations (Anholt, 2006; Nuttavuthisit, 2006). Additionally, these efforts allow nations to communicate a coherent image across different channels and to different publics.

A nation brand is a multidimensional construct reflecting the core values of a nation that should be communicated to home, host, and transnational publics in a clear and consistent fashion (Kotler & Gertner, 2002; Skinner & Kubacki, 2007). One of the most often promoted characteristics of a nation brand is its attractiveness as a tourist destination (Volvic & Andrejevic, 2011). This feature allows for connecting with people all over the world who have an interest in learning more about the country.

Of the various channels that nation branders and country reputation managers use, online media are considered one of the most effective, especially for tourism promotion (Avraham & Ketter, 2012). In particular, social media, which allows for participation and interaction with target audiences, has rapidly emerged as a popular platform for nation branding efforts (Bruell, 2008; Garcia, 2008; Munar, 2011). These new media also allow for two-way communication, contributing to a sense of personal identification with destinations, and transforming users into active participants (Bruell, 2008; Avraham & Ketter, 2012; Garcia, 2008; Pavlik, 2007). While branding through traditional media follows a linear model of communication where end-users are considered passive recipients of information, doing so through social media "is about building a relationship and conversation with your audience" (Drury, 2008, p.275).

Given this new context for nation branding, this chapter focuses on how countries use social media to communicate strong, unique, and favorable nation brands to their various target publics, as well on the challenges that efforts of this type would represent. First, recent literature on nation branding and destination promotion is reviewed. Then, current challenges and opportunities for nation branding are presented through case studies by Mexico, Brazil, Costa Rica and the Dominican Republic (De Moya & Jain, 2013; Jain & De Moya, 2011). Lastly, potential solutions for addressing these challenges are discussed, as well as areas for future research.

BACKGROUND

Nation Brands and Country Reputation

Countries employ a variety of approaches to gain an advantage over competitors for trade, tourism and foreign investment. In their efforts to showcase their uniqueness to foreign audiences, they actively engage in managing their image (i.e. what they project) and reputation (i.e. how they are perceived). Traditionally, a country's image is significantly shaped by the way it is portrayed in the media (Hanan, 2006). Consequently, how the media portray a country affects the way people feel about it; in other words, it affects the country's reputation (Brewer, Graf, & Willnat, 2003; Wanta, Golan & Lee, 2004).

A country's reputation is "the aggregate of stakeholders' images of a country" (Passow, Fehlmann, & Grahlow, 2005, p. 311). The Fombrun–RI Country Reputation Index (CRI) evaluates a country's reputation based on the perceptions that foreign audiences have of its emotional, physical, financial, leadership, cultural, global and political appeal (Passow & Fehlmann, 2005). Similarly, a nation brand is defined as "the total sum of all perceptions of a nation in the minds of international stakeholders, which may contain some of the following elements: people, place, culture / language, history, food, fashion, famous faces (celebrities), global brands and so on" (Fan, 2010, p.98). A key distinction between these concepts is that a country has a reputation in the mind of foreign audiences whether it attempts to manage it or not (Fan, 2008); while a nation brand is the outcome of a strategic effort to identify the aspects of a country's identity that may give it a competitive advantage, and to attach certain images or meanings to them (Anholt, 2004; Skinner & Kubacki, 2007). A favorable country reputation is essential for building a good nation brand, which can influence the public's intention to purchase a country's products or to travel to that country (Anholt, 2006; Gudjonsson, 2005; Nuttavuthisit, 2006).

Public perceptions of a country are based mainly on firsthand and secondhand experiences with the country or its goods and services (Yang et. al, 2008). People obtain firsthand experience by visiting the country, or using its products and services. Those with firsthand experiences often use travel sites, review sites and other social media platforms to express and share their views and opinions about a country and its offerings. The consumption of this information and word of mouth about the country make up the secondhand experience on which others may base their opinion. Therefore, the information that potential tourists or consumers receive via these platforms could be influential in how others feel about a country.

When it comes to forming an opinion about a country, "all transactions and points of contact – whether promoting policies, selling products, or attracting investment— will feed off the general image of a country and reflect back onto it, in both positive and negative directions" (Leonard, 2002, p.49). Therefore, it is in the best interest of a country to actively engage in managing its reputation, given that they are all dependent to a lesser or greater degree on foreign perceptions.

In an effort to gain competitive advantage and manage their reputations, many governments have implemented nation-branding campaigns for their countries. Nation branding is "a process by which a nation's image can be created or altered, monitored, evaluated and proactively managed in order to enhance the country's reputation among a target international audience" (Fan, 2010, p.101). Put differently, nation branding is a way for governments to manage the image that their country shares with foreign audiences, and improve their ability to compete globally for tourism, trade, talent, and investments (Aronczyk, 2008, p.42).

As an ongoing process, nation branding involves employing various marketing and communication tactics to build or manage parts, or the whole, of a country's image. These tactics may include creating a logo or slogan for the nation, placing advertising in international television channels, building unique websites for the nation brand, hosting press tours, etc. (Szondi, 2008).

The Nation Brand Index developed by Anholt (2006), evaluates a nation's image in terms of the perceptions people hold about its tourism, exports, investment, governance, immigration, culture, people and heritage. All of these aspects can have a significant impact on the image of the country and its brand. For example, results of the 2012 Nation Brand Index found that even though the top nation brands remained the same —the U.S. in first place, followed by Germany and the U.K— the contemporary economic and political challenges faced by these countries caused the brand's score for Germany and the U.K. to suffer (GFK, 2012). In other words, even though these brands comparatively remain the ones generating the best overall perceptions, the opinions that international publics have of these brands has declined somewhat.

In fact, one of the main challenges in managing nation brands and reputations today is communicating coordinated and consistent messages to multiple stakeholders about many different aspects of a nation's brand or image (Fan, 2010). Therefore, many nations tend to focus on only one or a few aspects of their country's reputation, and try to affect that image through their nation branding efforts. For example, the most commonly promoted aspect of a nation brand is tourism (Anholt, 2006; Konecknik, 2004).

Similarly, reputation managers are tasked with communicating a certain image of the country that diverse publics can feel connected to. In doing so, they need to ensure that their communication comes through as authentic to the audiences, which matches public expectations to reality. For country reputation managers, communicating the nation's authenticity requires "sharing periodic and accurate information with its consumers and other stakeholders, engaging them in a dialogue by soliciting their feedback, and disclosing its personal values, motives, and beliefs in a manner that enables stakeholders to more accurately assess the identity and integrity of an organization's actions" (Molleda & Jain, 2013 p. 4). Certainly, social media allows for countries to engage key stakeholders in conversations that could aid in communicating the nation's authenticity.

As Internet-based applications "that allow the creation and exchange of User Generated Content" (Kaplan & Haenlein, 2010, p. 61), social media help organizations engage their publics in conversations, and receive immediate feedback. However, this also means that the organization is not always in control of the conversation; publics can just as easily start their own conversation on the country's promotional social media page, as they could follow along the topics proposed by the organization.

In this new communication landscape, existing challenges for contemporary nation branding efforts –i.e the difficulty in successfully managing the diversity of issues or traits associated with a nation brand, and the need to communicate the nation's authenticity– are complicated by the participatory and decentralized nature of communication over social media platforms. Failure to manage these challenges can affect the success of a nation branding campaign, and consequently a country's reputation.

The following sections discuss these challenges in detail, drawing from the authors' research into these areas of nation branding efforts and country reputation of several Latin American countries, as well as other contemporary nation branding and country reputation research.

CHALLENGES IN MANAGING NATION BRANDS AND COUNTRY REPUTATION

The Complexity of Nation Brands

Research in nation branding and country reputation point to the mediated efforts by governments to influence how they are portrayed in foreign media (De Moya & Jain, 2013; Molleda & Roberts, 2008; Rivas, 2011; Volcic & Andrejevic, 2011). Their goal for these efforts is to impact foreign publics' opinions about their country, usually through good media relations or advertising.

Fan (2010) explained that a nation brand is a complex concept, difficult to explain in simple terms. The concept encompasses branding a country's export goods, culture, destinations for tourism, political stances, and other key aspects of its image in order to affect its reputation, competitive advantage, soft power, and even identity. Yet, countries are challenged with communicating "a single image or message to different audiences in different countries" (Fan, 2010, p.101). De Moya and Jain's (2009) analysis of the newspaper coverage of Mexico and Colombia in the United States serves as an example of the way different aspects of a nation brand are communicated to foreign publics, and the challenges that countries face in trying to manage these aspects while communicating a cohesive brand.

As key trade and diplomatic partners for the United States, Mexico and Colombia have long undertaken efforts to influence how they are portrayed in the U.S. media, as documented by previous research (e.g. Avraham & Ketter, 2008; Johnson, 2005; Kiousis, & Wu, 2008; Molleda & Roberts, 2008; Rivas, 2011). However, both countries still face challenges in terms of their country's reputation (Newell, 2011; Sudhaman, 2012).

Because the media are one of the main influencers in how people form opinions about other countries, De Moya and Jain (2009) employed DICTION® to analyze newspaper coverage of Mexico and Colombia. The purpose of the study was to determine how U.S. newspapers, one of the key audiences for these countries, portrayed Mexico and Colombia in terms of trade, tourism, and investment, the three key areas for government branding and communication efforts.

For this study, the authors collected newspaper coverage of both countries' trade, tourism, and investment from five of the largest national-circulating newspapers in the U.S.: USA Today, The Wall Street Journal, The New York Times, Los Angeles Times, and Washington Post. The authors used DICTION's® pre-existing dictionaries, which the researchers operationalized as frames, given that "news frames are constructed from and embodied in the key words" (Saleem, 2007, p.33). Fifteen DICTION® dictionaries were employed in this study, including words related to accomplishment, aggression, ambivalence, blame, centrality, collective, communication, exclusion, hardship, human interest, leveling terms, praise, rapport, satisfaction and self reference.

Operationalizing DICTION'S® pre-existing dictionaries as pre-determined frames, the analysis found 15 frames in the coverage of both countries. The authors categorized these frames as positive, negative, or neutral based on the definition of these categories (DICTION 6, 2012). For example, the blame frame was categorized as negative because it contained terms relate to inappropriateness, unfortunate circumstances, and denigrations; Satisfaction was categorized as positive because it includes words associated with positive affective states, such as "cheerful" or "happiness" as well as terms describing joy or pleasure; and human interest was categorized as neutral, because it groups personal pronouns, family members and relations and generic terms such as "person" or "human." Findings of the DICTION® analysis showed that, for several topics and themes, the scores were outside the software's established normal range, providing evidence of a markedly negative, positive, or neutral valence in the coverage of the country for a given topic (Table 1).

Table 1. Automated frames identified through Diction in newspaper coverage of Colombia and Mexico

Frames and valence	Colombia			Mexico			Diction-established normal range
	Trade	Tourism	Investment	Trade	Tourism	Investment	
Positive							
Leveling terms	4.38	2.03	2.40	2.40	4.28	1.80	5.02-12.76
Satisfaction	2.18	2.94	2.90	1.02	1.47	0.71	0.47-6.09
Praise	0.49	1.50	1.60	2.79	0.96	1.27	2.77-9.59
Accomplishment	15.33	11.08	22.76	13.91	10.09	14.41	4.96-23.78
Rapport	3.25	0.00	2.30	1.51	3.00	1.18	0.42-4.26
Negative							
Ambivalence	9.92	7.26	8.90	9.13	12.11	4.23	6.49-19.21
Blame	2.88	1.09	1.85	1.92	0.90	2.20	0.06-4.16
Hardship	6.05	3.25	3.75	2.58	2.01	2.13	1.26-10.48
Aggression	11.67	2.78	3.47	6.64	0.67	5.31	1.07-9.79
Exclusion	5.60	2.80	3.80	3.03	2.89	1.94	0.0-4.31
Neutral							
Centrality	0.94	1.78	3.17	1.87	4.88	6.08	1.19-7.54
Self-Reference	3.01	0.25	0.60	2.29	1.10	0.70	0.0-15.1
Communication	13.92	5.07	11.01	16.49	11.73	8.70	2.21-11.79
Human Interest	18.52	7.63	6.55	19.91	8.78	4.80	18.13-45.49
Collective	7.35	5.25	8.07	9.22	11.97	10.05	4.04-14.46

For the positive frames, findings revealed that several scores were below the normal range, suggesting that these terms were less present in the stories analyzed than in the thousands of stories contained in the software's libraries. In terms of the negative frames, although most of them where within the normal range, in the coverage of Colombia related to trade, the frames Aggression (which includes terms related to human competition and forceful action) and Exclusion (pertaining to sources and effects of social isolation) were above the pre-established range. From the frames that the authors classified as neutral –i.e. those that in their definition did not contain terms that could be classified as inherently negative or positive— most were within the normal rage. The exceptions were Communication (terms referring to social interaction), which were above the range in the coverage of both countries' trade documents; and Human Interest (including standard personal pronouns, terms for family members and relations, as well as other generic terms related to people), which were below the range in the coverage of Mexico's and Colombia's tourism and investment.

The DICTION analysis was complemented by both quantitative and qualitative manual content analyses of the news stories. These additional analyses offered details about the saliency of the country's trade, tourism, or investment all of which pointed as well as the valence of these stories, to specific parts of the country's image that could be targeted in the country's communication efforts. For example, findings showed that the coverage of Colombia's trade practices included negative stories related to drug trafficking to the U.S., as well as security concerns. Likewise, the manual analyses detailed that the low scores in the coverage of Mexico's trade and tourism, were likely related to themes identified in the qualitative analysis, such as loss of U.S. jobs, rising crime, and democratic instability and corruption. Therefore, it could be concluded that the low scores in positive terms and high scores in negative terms associated with both countries point to problems in managing the image that the U.S. media portrays of the country.

This analysis also evidenced some of the challenges faced by these nations in trying to have a positive impact on managing their reputation through reputation management or branding efforts when using traditional media. Mainly, it pointed to a diversity of issues that both countries need to address in order to project a positive image through U.S. media, and gain a positive impact on their reputations. The low Human Interest scores also suggested a dearth of personal accounts in the coverage. Personal accounts of experience with or in the country in any of these areas (even if secondhand) have the potential to impact a nation's reputation (Yang, et. al, 2008), and, in their absence, readers are left with the (sometimes unfortunate) frames employed by the journalists.

Although the traditional media continue to be an important part of the communication efforts employed in nation branding, they are not the only channel through which countries communicate with foreign audiences about their uniqueness or positive attributes. In fact, they employ a variety of communication channels to influence perceptions of their country. The following sections exemplify how social media are challenging nation and destination branding efforts.

Social Media in Destination Promotion

Just as internet-based media platforms such as Twitter and YouTube have changed the way products are marketed (Dev et al., 2010), so have they altered nation branding, notably in destination promotion efforts. Social media sites are frequent resources for people searching for travel information through search engines (O'Connor, 2008; Xiang & Gretzel, 2010). For those involved in nation branding and destination promotion, social media have facilitated conversations with potential consumers and helped in building relationship with this important audience (Drury, 2008; Hipperson, 2010). At the same time, social media have made consumers active participants in the process of destination and nation branding. Szondi (2010) explained that countries have varied levels of success and professionalism in their attempts to promote their nation brand via social media: "Online nation brand communities are quickly developing via Facebook and blogs, while countries are devoting more resources and attention to their 'country name – dot – com' domains in an attempt to engage with worldwide communities via these websites" (p. 339).

In a recent study of online sources for tourism information about destinations in the United States, Xiang and Gretzel (2010) found that social media (including blogging, social networking, content sharing and virtual community sites) represented 71 percent of the sources available for information about the destinations they studied. A look at top country brand websites suggests that they are currently trying to combine both. Top country brands for 2012 (CBI, 2012), are actively using social media to promote their tourism destinations. In fact, as of January 2013 all of the top ten country brands provided links to two or more social media platforms through their official English-language tourism sites (Table 2).

Because social media allow organizations and consumers to co-create meaning and content, they can have a significant impact on reputation (Owyang & Toll, 2007). O'Connor et al. (2008) found that tourism promotion organizations' use of online tools to promote their destinations had a sizable impact on how potential tourists shop, by giving them access to different opinions. Conversely, Munar (2011) explained that users will contribute content to a country's promotional sites, thereby having a powerful impact on the formation of its image and reputation.

As comparative case studies, Jain & De Moya (2011) conducted a case study analysis of the use of online tools by Costa Rica and the Dominican Republic in their destination branding efforts, also evaluating the content produced and shared by users. The study found that the messages shared by the destination promoters and the tourists (past, present or potential) were not always compatible.

Table 2. Use of social media for destination promotion by top country brands

Top Country Brands[1]	Official Site	Link to Facebook®	Link to Twitter®	Link to YouTube®	No. of links to other social media[2]
1. Switzerland	http://www.myswitzerland.com	√	√	√	1
2. Canada	http://us.canada.travel	√	√	-	1
3. Japan	http://www.japantravelinfo.com	√	√	-	1
4. Sweden	http://www.visitsweden.com	√	√	√	0
5. New Zealand	http://www.newzealand.com	√	√	√	1
6. Australia	http://www.australia.com	√	√	-	0
7. Germany	http://www.germany.travel	√	√	-	0
8. United States	http://www.discoveramerica.com	√	√	√	0
9. Finland	http://www.visitfinland.com	√	√	√	2
10. Norway	http://www.visitnorway.com	√	√	√	2

[1]CBI rankings, 2012
[2]Includes other sites in which user-generated content can be shared, such as Instragram®, Flickr® and Pintrest®

Costa Rica and Dominican Republic's Tourism Promotion Strategy

Costa Rica and the Dominican Republic, two popular tourism destinations in Latin America, have long been involved in nation-branding and destination promotion campaigns and efforts directed to English-speaking publics (Visit Costa Rica, 2011; Go Dominican Republic, 2011a). For both countries, destination promotion is an important part of their nation branding efforts since tourism is such a large part of their Gross Domestic Product (WTTC-CR, 2010; WTTC-DR, 2010).

Costa Rica's destination branding and promotion efforts are led by the Costa Rican Institute of Tourism (Instituto Costarricense de Turismo, ICT). This autonomous governmental institution launched its global tourism branding campaign, No Artificial Ingredients, in 1996 to promote the country as an exotic, but more accessible destination than Thailand. While the campaign's messages have changed over years, the country has continued to use its key tagline. Currently, much of the promotional communication is done through the campaign's official website (www.visitcostarica.com), as well as social media platforms including Facebook®, YouTube®, and Twitter®. In 2010, Costa Rica was named the country with the best destination brand positioning, and its slogan was ranked first in Latin America (Visit Costa Rica, 2011).

Similarly, the Dominican Republic's tourism promotion is led by the Ministry of Tourism, a government institution (Sectur, 2009a). This organization describes the country as offering a leisure destination focused on beachfront tourism. Although the country has been involved in destination branding efforts for decades, its most recent campaign was launched in January 2009 with the Slogan "Dominican Republic Has it All" (Sectur, 2009b). In addition to beachfront tourism, the campaign promotes ecotourism and cultural and historic tourism as alternative getaways in the country. The Ministry communicates with foreign audiences through many media, including a dedicated website (www.godominicanrepublic.com), as well as Facebook® and Twitter® accounts.

In their analysis of these destinations' branding and promotional efforts, Jain and De Moya (2011) explored how they attempt to communicate the authenticity of the countries through their online platforms. Although an elusive term, authenticity has been defined as the quality of being true to oneself (Harter, 2002). Molleda and Jain (2013) explained that authenticity is an experience and perception that is co-created between organizations and their key publics through a process of ongoing negotiation of meaning. The same can be said for reputation, which is formed through the interpretation that publics make of the image communicated by a country. *

Likewise, studying authenticity requires an analysis of how an organization (in this case, a nation) communicates its authenticity, and how the public interpret these claims (Molleda, 2010). Social media platforms allow for the communication and negotiation of meaning to take place on a public platform and therefore provide an opportunity to examine a country's efforts in communicating its authenticity.

Accordingly, Jain and De Moya (2011) analyzed authenticity claims made by both the Dominican Republic and Costa Rica in their campaign materials, using a case study methodology. Media kits, website pages, news releases, videos, images, and the social media pages for both destinations were analyzed. Additionally, in-depth interviews with representatives of the destination promotion offices for both countries were conducted. The authors found that these destinations not only make authenticity claims in their promotional and branding messages, but also consider these claims as key elements of their branding strategy. Both countries attempted to communicate that their destinations are "trustworthy," "legitimate," "honest," "genuine," and "credible," qualities that describe an authentic tourism destination (Molleda, 2010).

Jain and De Moya's (2011) case study did not explore the presence or absence of authenticity claims in the comments posted by past or potential visitors to the countries in their social media sites. However, a later qualitative content analysis of these sites revealed that the posts by their social media friends or followers were not focused on the countries' authenticity claims. Rather, in the case of the Dominican Republic the comments mainly included expressions of nostalgia for the country, such as "I am not a fan of this 20 something degree weather. I wanna go back to @GoDomRep" and "That amazing feeling you get when you land in that Dominican Republic airport and there's that merengue band playing. Feels like home". Other comments, expressed appreciation for the country, such as "A plane ticket to @GoDomRep is better than a golden ticket to a #ChocolateFactory. #JustSaying." Although the tone of these messages is positive overall, the users' comments did not focus on the cultural, natural or historical authenticity that the destination promoters had attempted to emphasize.

Similarly, the users of Costa Rica's social media sites did not make references to the country's natural beauty or unique flora and fauna, but rather asked questions about places to visit ("I'm coming there in may to the guanacaste area what is a must see that we have to do?"), expressed interest to visit ("This is such a beautiful and peaceful place i was told and very therapeutic----hah---maybe one day i will get to go on vacation") and in some cases shared negative perceptions of the country. One Facebook® follower wrote: "Costa Rica is an unsafe country with many, many thieves. The Costa Rican government does nothing to deter the robbers and don't even charge them with the crimes [...]"

Communicating its authenticity to its publics is important for destinations because it is a perception co-created by both the destination promoters and the publics. In other words, the destination cannot be seen as authentic –a highly desirable trait for tourists– if the publics that engage with it do not perceive it as such. The experience of these two countries in communicating with their key publics through social media shows how even though they are successful in engaging with them, they aren't always successful in leading the conversation. Similar results were found in a study of Brazil and Mexico's destination branding efforts through social media. *

Brazil and Mexico's Use of Social Media for Nation Branding

De Moya and Jain (2013) explored the brand identity traits that Brazil and Mexico communicated through Facebook® and those that their friends associated with them. This study of branding efforts by the two most popular Latin American destinations, Mexico and Brazil (UNWTO, 2010), used DICTION 6.0 to analyze the salience of brand personality traits (Aaker, 1997) in the comments posted by the countries and their Facebook® friends.

Brand personality traits are "the set of human characteristics associated with a brand" (Aaker, 1997, p.347). In their study of online destination promotion by 12 nations, Jain & Chan-Olmsted (2009) found that these countries actively attempted to communicate distinct brand personalities via their tourism promotion websites. Therefore, De Moya and Jain (2013) explored whether or not these efforts were also conducted over social media platforms –in this case Facebook®– and whether or not these traits were also present in the messages posted by other users.

The study included messages adding up to 32,000 words posted in Brazil's official Facebook® page (Brazil friends= 10,108; Brazil promotional messages = 22,671), and nearly 21,000 words on Mexico's official Facebook® page (Mexico friends= 11,631; Mexico promotional messages= 9,335). These posts accounted for approximately three months of interactions between the destination promoters and their friends.

Using DICTION's custom dictionaries to identify the words associated with each brand personality trait, the authors found that Mexico and Brazil's destination promoters communicate distinct brand personality traits through their Facebook® page. Most frequently, both countries featured their sincerity, a trait defined by words that reflect being original, cheerful, honest, family-oriented and down-to-earth. The second most occurring trait was excitement, which included terms referring a destination's unique, daring, imaginative, and young nature. Both these traits were found to be the most appealing to tourists (Ekinci & Hosany, 2006; Jain & Chan-Olsmted, 2009); therefore it is not surprising that these would be actively communicated by destination promoters.

However, the messages posted by the destinations' Facebook® friends did not always reflect the brand personalities the promoters were trying to highlight (Figure 1). Although some of the comments from Mexico's friends included mentions of specific brand traits, these were absent from the postings by Brazil's friends.

Additionally, the authors conducted a correspondence analysis to determine whether or not the brand personality traits communicated by the destination promoters and Facebook® friends were in agreement. Similar to the findings of the frequency analysis detailed above, results showed sufficient correspondence between Mexico's promoted and perceived brand personalities, but not for Brazil.

The findings of this study indicate that, although both Mexico's and Brazil's Facebook® friends actively engage with the destination promoters through their social media platforms, this engagement doesn't necessarily lead to a direct favorable influence on their online friends. This is especially surprising since even when Brazil's posts outnumbered the comments by its friends, the country failed to lead the conversation on this important social media platform. Being able to influence such conversations

Figure 1. Frequency of occurrence of brand personality traits on the official Facebook page of Mexico and Brazil

is important for destination promoters because potential tourists use social media to obtain information about tourism destinations (Xiang & Gretzel, 2010).

These cases that demonstrate the lack of agreement between Costa Rica's, Dominican Republic's, Mexico's, and Brazil's social media users and their communication efforts highlight the need to revisit and revise the communication strategies that these nations use on their social media platforms. Our findings also point out the challenges of nation branding on social media, a forum in which target publics have an equal say.

Nation Branding in Challenging Times

Even though the case studies discussed here do not detail the solutions to the challenges presented, they do point to some important aspects of nation branding efforts. In terms of the complexity of branding a nation with many intrinsic and often equally important social, political, cultural and economic dimensions, nation branding leaders need to present segmented images of the brand, while caring for consistent and complementary messaging. On this point, Fan (2010) argued:

One slogan, one campaign, no matter how clever or creative, cannot sell everything to everyone. It would be more meaningful and practical to have nation branding to be conceptualised, measured and executed at one of the sublevels (as a place brand, event brand or export brand) (p.102).

An important element mentioned in this argument is that the nation brand should be measured or, put differently, evaluated before the branding campaign is taken on. Anholt (2006) explained that countries often embark in efforts to fix their image or reputation problems without properly understanding the problem. He argued: "it must surely be the first stage of any responsible nation branding programme to take a good look at the current image of the place, and to make an assessment of exactly how and why it needs to be changed" (p.98). Further, after engaging in nation branding and image repair campaigns, many nations do not evaluate the outcomes of these efforts, thereby losing the chance to inform future initiatives and programs (Zenker & Martin, 2011).

On this point, nation-branding efforts could benefit from adopting a strategic planning process characteristic of public relations campaigns. This process begins with formative research to understand the organization (in this case, the country), the issue or problem, and the publics they are trying to engage, before deciding on the communication channels and tactics that the campaign will employ (Smith, 2011). This process also requires evaluation at many stages of the campaign planning and implementation process.

Along these lines, Szondi (2010) supported a relationship building approach –also characteristic of public relations efforts– to manage a country's image. This would, he explained, allow for a more decentralized approach that could be tailored to specific publics and that would go beyond measuring attitudes to evaluating relationships and behavior.

Although online and social media platforms present a new set of challenges for destination promoters, they also provide opportunities to learn from the publics by evaluating the content they produce. Several theoretical perspectives can serve to understand the potential impact of communication and messaging used by nation branders and the public's response through social media sites. For example, previous studies have employed Aaker's (1997) brand personality framework, framing theory, and authenticity for such types of evaluations (De Moya & Jain, 2009; 2013, Jain & De Moya, 2011). Other theoretical frameworks that might inform nation branding and country reputation management could also be adopted for this purpose.

Social media allow brand managers to "provide better customer service and attain consumer insights" (Lim, Chung & Weaver, 2012, p.199). While traditionally branding experts relied on surveys and focus groups to collect information from their publics, now they can content analyze the readily available user generated content on social media to gauge public opinion. Computer-assisted content analyses can aid in evaluating a large amount of data in a faster and often less costly way.

In terms of the actual planning and implementation of a nation branding campaign, social media also allows for nation branding efforts to reach new publics through word of mouth or, in this case, via connections to their public's contacts on social media sites. In their discussion of the benefits of social media for branding, Lim et al., (2012) argued that content generated by publics can create or shape a brand. The authors explained that social media provide publics with an opportunity to share organizational information with peers (e.g. sharing a video posted on a destination's social media site). Additionally, the information that an organization and its publics share can garner support for the brand. In fact, publics tend to trust the content created by peers more than traditional advertisements or organizational communications (Qualman, 2009).

However, if the information shared by the publics is not favorable, it may have a negative impact on the nation brand and country's reputation. One way in which destination promoters can manage this is by communicating the authenticity of their brand. In other words, they should try to match their messages as closely as possible to the reality of the different aspects of the brand (such as the quality of goods and the top tourism destinations in the country). Similarly, they should attempt to match their authenticity claims to the expectations of the publics with whom they are engaging.

One way in which managers can communicate their brand's authenticity is by highlighting referential authenticity claims. Jain and De Moya (2011) explained that in the context of nation and destination branding, referential authenticity claims can be communicated by including testimonials and comments by other visitors. Ideally, these claims would involve sharing comments by people the intended public could trust or with whom they identify.

Lastly, an important way in which nation brand managers and reputation managers could rise to the challenge presented by social media and the pervasiveness of content created by their publics is to embrace the co-creative nature of nation brands and country reputation. Findings of the case studies discussed in this chapter suggest that even though these brand managers are using social platforms for destination promotion, they seem to be employing one-directional messaging. This is evident in the lack of correspondence between messages from destination promoters for Brazil, Mexico, Costa Rica and the Dominican Republic and their audiences on social media platforms such as Facebook®. The definitions of nation brands and country reputation discussed here emphasize that both are contingent on the interpretation that their intended publics make of them and their communication claims.

Szondi (2010) argued that this issue could be addressed by building relationships rather than by managing images. This approach, he argued, would shift nation branding from a focus on the dissemination of pre-defined messages to the co-creation of meanings and values, "characterised by mutual understanding and dialogue where stakeholder engagement is of paramount importance" (p.342). The authors agree with this assertion, especially if adopting a relationship-building approach placed more emphasis on dialogic engagement with online publics.

In sum, the challenges faced by destination promoters and reputation managers are significant, but not impossible, to address. Conducting targeted rather than all-encompassing branding efforts, careful evaluation of each of the elements of the country's reputation being cultivated through the branding campaign, and a relationship-building approach to engaging foreign publics could address these challenges. Likewise, strategic use of social media that does not treat it exclusively as an information dissemination platform but that also uses it to engage target publics in conversations could help destination promoters overcome some of these challenges. Understanding the value of co-creating meaning with publics in the nation branding process could allow for greater agreement between the projected image and public opinions of a nation, and therefore, contribute to building a more favorable national reputation.

FUTURE RESEARCH DIRECTIONS

This chapter discussed the challenges and opportunities associated with nation branding in an ever-evolving social media environment but more work needs to be done. Although previous research has explored the impact that social media have had on destination branding and tourism promotion (e.g. Munar, 2011; Xiang, & Gretzel, 2010), there is little research on how nations communicate the various aspects of their brand through social media. Likewise, little is known about the publics with whom they engage on these platforms. Therefore, future research could explore the motivations for these publics to become friends or followers of nation brands on social media sites, and the ways in which countries could motivate their continued engagement or reach out to additional publics.

Additionally, most of the research to date on country reputation or nation branding through social media and other online platforms tends to include only textual analyses. Future studies could include videos and photos shared by both the nation brand managers and their publics in their investigation. Lastly, research in the future could delve deeper into user-generated content, and going beyond official social media sites to explore the communities created by fans and other users.

CONCLUSION

Drawing from previous research, this chapter has outlined how existing organizations seeking to manage any aspect of a nation's brand or reputation face important challenges and opportunities, especially in the new social media environment. Because of that nature of the medium, nations will no longer have exclusive control over the information shared about them. However, if managed strategically, social media provide opportunities for nations to gain credibility and reach new publics through third party endorsements and testimonials.

The cases presented in this chapter pointed to both challenges and opportunities for nation branding and tourism promotion employing social media. Most notably, the authors argued for the desirability of a segmented and targeted approach to nation branding whereby each aspect of the brand is addressed and messages are designed for targeted publics, rather than for anonymous masses.

Also, this new environment for nation branding and requires that countries communicate their authenticity and uniqueness to their publics in ways that incorporates their participation. Allowing for sharing experiences and opinions openly could increase the nation's perceived authenticity, and consequently serve to improve, or maintain that country's reputation. Successful nation branding efforts would lead to coherent and complementary messages from both publics and brand managers. However, for this to happen, the latter must engage with the former in open dialogue, acknowledging the public's autonomy when forming opinions about a given country.

Lastly, the authors support Szondi's (2010) push for a relationship-building approach to nation branding, an approach that allows for true engagement with publics and meaning co-creation, something that is inherent in the concepts of authenticity and country reputation management now being studied by scholars.

REFERENCES

Aaker, L. J. (1997). Dimensions of brand personality. *JMR, Journal of Marketing Research*, *4*(3), 347–356. doi:10.2307/3151897

Amis, R. (2007, May). You can't ignore social media: How to measure Internet efforts to your organisation's best advantage. Tactics, p. 10.

Anholt, S. (2004). Branding places and nations. In R. Clifton, J. Simmons, & S. Ahmad (Eds.), *Brands and branding* (2nd ed., pp. 213–226). Princeton, NJ: Bloomberg Press.

Anholt, S. (2006). Why brand? Some practical considerations for nation branding. *PlaceBranding*, *2*(2), 97–107.

Aronczyk, M. (2008). Living the brand: Nationality, globality and the identity strategies of nation branding consultants. *International Journal of Communication*, *2*(1), 41–65.

Avraham, E., & Ketter, E. (2008). Will we be safe there? Analysing strategies for altering unsafe place images. *Place Branding and Public Diplomacy*, *4*(3), 196–204. doi:10.1057/pb.2008.10

Avraham, E., & Ketter, E. (2012). *Media strategies for marketing places in crisis*. New York: Routledge.

Botan, C. (1997). Ethics in strategic communication campaigns: The case for a new approach to public relations. *Journal of Business Communication*, *34*, 188–202. doi:10.1177/002194369703400205

Brewer, P. R., Graf, J., & Willnat, L. (2003). Priming or framing: Media influence on attitudes toward foreign countries. *Gazette*, *65*(6), 493–508.

Bruell, A. (2008, February). The digital effect on agency recruiting. PR Week, 26.

BurellesLuce. (2008). 2008 top newspaper, blogs and consumer magazines. Retrieved June 15, 2008 from http://www.burrellesluce.com/top100/2008_Top_100List.pdf

CBI. (2012). Country brand index 2012-2013. Retrieved January 3, 2013 from http://www.futurebrand.com/wp-content/cbi/pdfs/CBI_2012-13.pdf

De Moya, M., & Jain, R. (2009). Framing partners: A computer-assisted evaluation of how top U.S. newspapers frame business, trade and investment in, and with, two key Latin American partners. Paper presented at the 2009 AEJMC Annual Conference. Boston, MA.

De Moya, M., & Jain, R. (2013). When tourists are your friends: An exploratory examination of brand personality in discussions about Mexico and Brazil on Facebook. *Public Relations Review*, *39*(1), 23–29. doi:10.1016/j.pubrev.2012.09.004

Dev, C. S., Buschman, J. D., & Bowen, J. T. (2010). Hospitality marketing: A retrospective analysis (1960-2010) and predictions (2010-2020). *Cornell Hospitality Quarterly*, *51*(4), 459–469. doi:10.1177/1938965510376353

DICTION 6. (2012). DICTION 6 overview. Retrieved November 10, 2012 from http://www.dictionsoftware.com/diction-overview/

Drury, G. (2008). Social media: Should marketers engage and how can it be done effectively? Journal of Direct. *Data and Digital Marketing Practice*, *9*(3), 274–277. doi:10.1057/palgrave.dddmp.4350096

Ekinci, Y., & Hosany, S. (2006). Destination personality: an application of brand personality to tourism destinations. *Journal of Travel Research*, *45*(2), 127–139. doi:10.1177/0047287506291603

Fan, Y. (2006). Nation branding: What is being branded? *Journal of Vacation Marketing*, *12*(1), 5–14. doi:10.1177/1356766706056633

Fan, Y. (2008). Key perspectives in nation image: A conception framework for nation branding. Retrieved January 13, 2013 from http://bura.brunel.ac.uk/handle/2438/1872?mode=full

Fan, Y. (2010). Branding the nation: Towards a better understanding. *Place Branding and Public Diplomacy*, *6*(2), 97–103. doi:10.1057/pb.2010.16

Garcia, T. (2008, February). The agency business - Social-media know-how crosses practice lines. PR Week, 7.

GFK. (2012). Two-thirds of nations experience reputation decline in 2012 nation brands index. Retrieved December 18, 2012 from http://www.gfk.com/Documents/Press-Releases/2012/20121023_NBI_2012_final.pdf

Go Dominican Republic. (2011). Dominican Republic (DR) frequently asked questions. Retrieved February 1, 2011 from http://www.godominicanrepublic.com/rd/images/files/DR%20FAQ.pdf

Gudjonsson, H. (2005). Nation branding. *Place Branding*, *1*(3), 283–298. doi:10.1057/palgrave.pb.5990029

Gurhn-Canil, Z., & Maheswaran, D. (2000). Cultural variations in country of origin effects. *JMR, Journal of Marketing Research*, *37*, 309–317. doi:10.1509/jmkr.37.3.309.18778

Hanan, A. M. (2006). The media-foreign policy relationship: Pakistan's media image and U.S. foreign policy. (Unpublished doctoral dissertation). York University, Toronto, Canada.

Harter, S. (2002). Authenticity. In C. R. Snyder & S. Lopez (Eds.), *Handbook of positive psychology*. Oxford, UK: Oxford University Press.

Hipperson, T. (2010). The changing face of data insight and its relationship to brand marketing. *Journal of Database Marketing and Customer Strategy Management*, *17*(34), 262–266. doi:10.1057/dbm.2010.25

Jain, R., & Chan-Olmsted, S. (2009). Is your tourist destination sincere, rugged, or sophisticated? An exploratory examination of online brand personality of nations. Paper presented at the annual meeting of the Association for Education in Journalism and Mass Communication. Boston, MA.

Jain, R., & De Moya, M. (2011). Offering an authentic tourism experience: An investigation of nation branding of Costa Rica and the Dominican Republic. In Proceedings of Fourteenth Annual International Public Relations Research Conference, (pp. 339-361). IEEE.

Johnson, M. A. (2005). Five decades of Mexican public relations in the United States: From propaganda to strategic counsel. *Public Relations Review*, *31*(1), 11–20. doi:10.1016/j.pubrev.2004.11.002

Kaplan, A. M., & Haenlein, M. (2010). Users of the world, unite! The challenges and opportunities of Social Media. *Business Horizons*, *53*(1), 59–68. doi:10.1016/j.bushor.2009.09.003

Kiousis, S., & Wu, X. (2008). International agenda-building and agenda-setting exploring the influence of public relations counsel on US news media and public perceptions of foreign nations. *International Communication Gazette*, *70*(1), 58–75. doi:10.1177/1748048507084578

Knight, G. A., & Calantone, J. (2000). A? exible model of consumer country-of-origin perceptions. *International Marketing Review*, *17*(2), 127–145. doi:10.1108/02651330010322615

Konecnik, M., & Go, F. (2008). Tourism destination brand identity: The case of Slovenia. *Journal of Brand Management*, *15*, 177–189. doi:10.1057/palgrave.bm.2550114

Kotler, P., & Gertner, D. (2002). Country as brand, products, and beyond: A place marketing and brand management perspective. *Journal of Brand Management*, *9*(4/5), 249–261. doi:10.1057/palgrave. bm.2540076

Leonard, M. (2002). Diplomacy by other means. *Foreign Policy*, *132*, 48–56. doi:10.2307/3183455

Lim, Y., Chung, Y., & Weaver, P. (2012). The impact of social media on destination branding: Consumer-generated videos versus destination marketer-generated videos. *Journal of Vacation Marketing*, *18*(3), 197–206. doi:10.1177/1356766712449366

McNelly, J., & Izcaray, F. (1992). International news exposure and images of nations. *Journalism & Mass Communication Quarterly*, *63*, 546–553. doi:10.1177/107769908606300315

Molleda, J. (2010). Authenticity and its dimensions in strategic communication research. In S. Allan (Ed.), *Rethinking communication: Keywords in communication research* (pp. 53–64). Cresskill, NJ: Hampton Press.

Molleda, J., & Jain, R. (2013). Testing a perceived authenticity index with triangulation research: The case of Xcaret in Mexico. *International Journal of Strategic Communication*, *7*(1), 1–20. doi:10.1080 /1553118X.2012.725233

Molleda, J. C., & Roberts, M. (2008). The value of authenticity in glocal strategic communication: The new Juan Valdez campaign. *International Journal of Strategic Communication*, *2*(3), 154–174. doi:10.1080/15531180802178679

Munar, A. M. (2011). Tourist-created content: rethinking destination branding. International Journal of Culture. *Tourism and Hospitality Research*, *5*(3), 291–305.

Newell, R. (2011). Restoring Mexico's international reputation. Retrieved January 3, 2013 from http:// www.wilsoncenter.org/sites/default/files/Restoring%20Mexico%20Report.pdf

Nuttavuthisit, K. (2006). Branding Thailand: Correcting the negative image of sex tourism. *Place Branding and Public Diplomacy*, *3*(1), 21–30. doi:10.1057/palgrave.pb.6000045

O'Connor, P. (2008). User-generated content and travel: A case study on tripadvisor.com. Information and Communication Technologies in Tourism, 47–58.

Owyang, J., & Toll, M. (2007). *Tracking the in?uence of conversations: A roundtable discussion on social media metrics and measurement*. New York, NY: Dow Jones Inc.

Passow, T., Fehlmann, R., & Grahlow, H. (2005). Country reputation -- From measurement to management: The case of Liechtenstein. *Corporate Reputation Review*, *7*(4), 309–326. doi:10.1057/palgrave.crr.1540229

Pavlik, J. (2007). Mapping the consequences of technology on public relations. Retrieved on January 2, 2013 from http://www.instituteforpr.org/files/uploads/Pavlik_Mapping_Consequences.pdf

Qualman, E. (2009). *Socialnomics: How social media transforms the way we live and do business.* Hoboken, NJ: John Wiley.

Rivas, C. V. (2011). The rise and fall of Mexico's international image: Stereotypical identities, media strategies and diplomacy dilemmas. *Place Branding and Public Diplomacy*, *7*(1), 23–31. doi:10.1057/pb.2011.4

Saleem, N. (2007). U.S. media framing of foreign countries image: An analytical perspective. Canadian Journal of Media Studies, 2(1), 130, 162.

Sectur. (2009a). Plan estratégico. Retrieved January 30, 2010 from http://sectur.gob.do/Sobre_Mitur/Plan_Estrat%c3%a9gico.aspx

Sectur. (2009b). República Dominicana: Lo tiene todo. Retrieved January 5, 2011 from http://sectur.gob.do/Noticias/Artículo/itemid/286/Repblica-Dominicana-Lo-Tiene-Todo.aspx

Skinner, H., & Kubacki, K. (2007). Unraveling the complex relationship between nationhood, national and cultural identity, and place branding. *Place Branding and Public Diplomacy*, *3*(4), 305–316. doi:10.1057/palgrave.pb.6000072

Smith, R. D. (2011). *Strategic planning for public relations*. Mahwah, NJ: Lawrence Erlbaum Associates, Inc.

Sushaman, A. (2012). Safe and sound: Inside Mexico's fight to reclaim its global reputation. Retrieved January 3, 2013 from http://www.holmesreport.com/featurestories-info/12213/Safe-And-Sound-Inside-Mexicos-Fight-To-Reclaim-Its-Global-Reputation.aspx

Szondi, G. (2008). Public diplomacy and nation branding: Conceptual similarities and differences. Discussion Papers in Public Diplomacy. Retrieved December 10, 2012 from http://ts.clingendael.nl/publications/2008/20081022_pap_in_dip_nation_branding.pdf

UNWTO. (2011). International tourism 2010: Multi-speed recovery. Retrieved February 2, 2011 from http://85.62.13.114/media/news/en/press_det.php?id=7331

Visit Costa Rica. (2011). Retrieved February 2, 2011 from http://www.visitcostarica.com/

Volvic, Z., & Andrejevic, M. (2011). Nation branding in the era of commercial nationalism. *International Journal of Communication, 5*, 598–618.

Wanta, W., Golan, G., & Lee, C. (2004). Agenda setting and international news: Media influence on public perceptions of foreign nations. *Journalism & Mass Communication Quarterly, 81*(2), 364–377. doi:10.1177/107769900408100209

WTTC-CR. (2010). Travel and tourism economic impact: Costa Rica. World Travel and Tourism Council. Retrieved February 2, 2011 from http://www.wttc.org/bin/pdf/original_pdf_file/costarica.pdf

WTTC-DR. (2010). Travel and tourism economic impact: Dominican Republic. World Travel and Tourism Council. Retrieved February 2, 2011 from http://www.wttc.org/bin/pdf/original_pdf_file/dominicanrepublic.pdf

Xiang, Z., & Gretzel, U. (2010). Role of social media in online travel information search. *Tourism Management, 31*(2), 179–188. doi:10.1016/j.tourman.2009.02.016

Yang, S., Shin, H., Lee, J., & Wrigley, B. (2008). Country reputation in multidimensions: Predictors, effects, and communication channels. *Journal of Public Relations Research, 20*(4), 421–440. doi:10.1080/10627260802153579

Zenker, S., & Martin, N. (2011). Measuring success in place marketing and branding. *Place Branding and Public Diplomacy, 7*(1), 32–41. doi:10.1057/pb.2011.5

KEY TERMS AND DEFINITIONS

Brand: Name, term, design, symbol, or any other feature that identifies one seller's good or service as distinct from those of other sellers.

Brand Image: The set of beliefs consumers hold about a particular brand.

Destination Brand: Attributes that represent the core essence and enduring characteristics of a destination.

Destination Management Organization (DMO): Organizations actively engaged in developing, nurturing, and communicated a destination's brand to its national and international publics.

Nation Branding: Applying branding and marketing communications techniques to promote a nation and/or destination.

Nation Brand Index (NBI): A multidimensional measurement of a nation's image as perceived by its target publics.

Social Media: A group of Web 2.0 based platforms that foster and facilitate interaction and conversation among web users.

This research was previously published in Communication and Language Analysis in the Public Sphere edited by Roderick P. Hart, pages 409-425, copyright year 2014 by Information Science Reference (an imprint of IGI Global).

Chapter 70
Wrestling With Contradictions in Government Social Media Practices

Lars Haahr
Aarhus University, Denmark

ABSTRACT

Research in government social media practices highlights expectations of co-creation and progression mirrored in maturity models, but research also documents low deployment degree and thereby points to a discrepancy. The paper suggests that the authors instead of co-creation and progression draw on a dialectical approach and understand the development of government social media practices as a wrestling with contradictions. The case of emerging social media practices in a Danish municipality used to illustrate this framework suggests three main categories of contradictions in emerging social media practices: Contradictions between service administration and community feeling as forms of practice, contradictions in organizing between local engagement and central control, and contradictions in the digital infrastructure between proprietary municipal websites and public social media platforms. The paper discusses if a paradox lens will enhance our understanding of inherent contradictions or the dialectical notion of contradiction serve the purpose. The paper contributes to a dialectical theory of contradictions through an analysis of emerging government social media practices.

INTRODUCTION

The growing investment in social media practices by both private corporations and government organizations has led to increasing research interests. A special issue on social media in *Information Systems Research,* Vol. 24, No. 1, March 2013, points to opportunities for organizational innovation but also to unexpected challenges, for example that involvement of communities in design innovation processes can lead to devaluation of the obtained results. The editorial concludes that many questions are not only unanswered, but unaddressed (Aral, Dellarocas, & Godes, 2013). A special issue on social media in

DOI: 10.4018/978-1-5225-5637-4.ch070

Government Information Quarterly, 29, 2012 includes positive expectations, for example materialized in a typology for citizen co-production (Linders, 2012) and in a maturity model for social media based public engagement (Lee, Kwak, Gwanhoo, & Young Hoon, 2012). However, in the very same issue, empirical data document a low deployment degree of social media in local municipalities in the European Union (Bonsón, Torres, Royo, & Floresc, 2012), and likewise, a low level of activity on a government-run health portal (Andersen, Medaglia, & Henriksen, 2012). The special issue thereby points to a discrepancy between research highlighting expectations and best practices on the one hand, and empirical evidence of low use of social media on the other hand.

The discrepancy between the expectations of co-creation and the low degree of deployment can be explained as an example of what (Andersen et al., 2012) point to in the very same special issue of *Government Information Quarterly*, namely that the first wave of research of emerging phenomena often reflects an enthusiasm for the innovation, while the actual practices lag behind or are never achieved. The fashion aspect of social media (Bergquist et al., 2013) as well as also earlier seen technological determinism (Orlikowski, 1991) is most probably a part of the explanation for the discrepancy.

The paper investigates an alternative route for understanding what is at stake in emerging social media practices by regarding the development of government social media practices less as a matter of progression – for example staged in maturity models – than as a continued wrestling with inherent contradictions. The paper is therefore guided by the research question: *How is contradiction present in government social media practices?*

The paper thereby prolongs the investigation of Andersen et al. (2012) in which the authors point to contradictory effects embedded in social media practices in the healthcare sector. These include among others contradictions between (1) data availability to doctors and violation of privacy due to open exchange of knowledge, (2) widespread information availability, information exchange, and information overload, and (3) the fact that social media, contrary to expectations, is a cost driver rather than a cost saver (Andersen et al., 2012).

According to the literature and dialectical approach that the present study will draw on, contradictions are understood as one possible 'motor' in change processes. To understand how these inherent contradictions are constitutive in the context of emerging government social media practices, the paper traces and analyzes contradictions in a case study of municipal social media practices. The study results in identification of three contradictions: 1.The contradiction between service administration and community feeling as forms of practice. 2.The organizing contradiction between central control and local engagement. 3. The technological infrastructure contradiction between proprietary municipal websites and public social media platforms.

In line with the literature, the paper argues that the future development of government social media practices is dependent on how government organizations wrestle with these contradictions by government organizations.

The study makes two contributions. First, it contributes to research on contradictions as drivers of change by exploring the concept in relation to emerging government social media practices. Because of the elusive nature of the paradox concept, the paper suggests 'wrestling with contradictions' as an alternative analytical lens. Second, the study contributes to our understanding of the opportunities and challenges in emerging government social media practices from an organizational perspective.

CONTRADICTION AND PARADOX

Organizational scholars belonging to a dialectical tradition (Benson, 1977) have used contradictions to explain change and development in organizations (Van De Ven & Poole, 1995). The fundamental assumption in this stream of literature is that organizations exist in a world of colliding forces and contradictory values. Therefore organizational effects of for example emerging IT practices can be described and explained as a result of such contradictory elements and relations. Change is regarded as an effect of the contradictory forces, and the organizational wrestling with these contradictions is regarded as the activity that forms organizational innovation. In the dialectical tradition, the elements and relations in a contradiction are understood as a whole: The contradiction in a change process is inherent or – to use a term more pertinent in the dialectical tradition – immanent. In line with already well-established information systems research that draw on the dialectical tradition and its focus on contradictions (Carlo, Lyytinen, & Boland, 2012; Cho, Mathiassen, & Robey, 2007), this study adopts the dialectical approach in an effort to understand the change processes related to emerging government social media practices.

A stream of organization literature initiated by among others (Poole & van de Ven, 1989) focuses on a special form of inherent contradictions, namely paradoxes. Although not originally conceptualized as a paradox, the conceptual pair of exploitation and exploration (March, 1991) is often regarded as an example of paradox in this stream of literature. This is for example the case in the comprehensive work by Smith and Lewis (2011), where exploitation and exploration is conceived as a paradox within the category of organizational learning. The paradox lens has been applied in a solid stream of organizational studies (Andriopoulos & Lewis, 2009; Berlinger & Sitkin, 1990; Eisenhardt, 2000; Luscher, Lewis, & Ingram, 2006; Lüscher & Lewis, 2008; Poole & van de Ven, 1989; Quinn & Cameron, 1988; Smith & Lewis, 2011; Sundaramurthy & Lewis, 2003).

In information systems research, the dialectical tradition and the focus on paradoxes are also present today (Carlo et al., 2012; Cho et al., 2007). Noteworthy studies of paradoxes in the field of information systems research include studies of how technological affordances are always already paradoxical (Arnold, 2003), how nomadic technologies have an embedded paradox of empowerment and enslavement (Jarvenpaa & Lang, 2005) and how the most significant paradox of virtual teamwork is that between physical and virtual presence (Dubé & Robey, 2009).

Relevant for the present study is also an analysis of the emerging digital infrastructures through a dialectical approach (Tilson, Lyytinen, & Sørensen, 2010). The emergence of an all-encompassing digital infrastructure is regarded and named as 'infrastructure turn', thereby alluding to 'linguistic turn' and 'literary turn'. The authors hereby imply that it is not merely a matter of a faster and more widespread digital infrastructure, here under the 'social' Internet, but also a new infrastructure condition. The authors therefore argue that this emerging or new condition necessitates a rethinking within the information systems research community, and it is to that end the authors employ a dialectical approach and a paradox lens. Important in relation to the present study are two contradictions or paradoxes as they are named. The first paradox is that of change. The paradox of change exists between the opposing logics of stability and flexibility and plays itself out across the infrastructural layers and elements. The second paradox is that of control. The paradox of control exists between the opposing logics around centralized and distributed control, and it includes the strategic actions of heterogeneous actors and their control preferences in relation to change processes.

Despite the interesting contributions from the stream of literature using the paradox lens, it is relevant to ask whether the trending focus on paradox is pertinent, or the more mundane term contradiction suffices. If the definition of paradox alone is 'inherent contradiction' (Smith & Lewis, 2011), then it is difficult to distinguish paradox from contradiction as this concept is used in the dialectical tradition. Often the terms are used interchangeably and as synonyms: "The paradox invites us to adopt a fresh stance on how change in digital infrastructures is driven by the dialectic of stability and flexibility and how it affects uses of IT in corporate environments" (Tilson et al., 2010, p. 754). Furthermore, paradox as a special type of inherent contradiction is elusive because of its linguistic nature. The verbal phrasing is very important for obtaining the paradoxical quality. If what is perceived as a paradox, for example the paradox of centralized and distributed control (Tilson et al., 2010), is explained straight forward, the paradoxical quality melts into air.

The present study will draw on both the fundamental dialectical tradition for focusing on immanent contradictions as drivers of change and innovation, and also include the studies that focus on paradoxes, but only use the term contradiction. The use of the metaphor of wrestling is inspired by Barley and Kunda (1992).

RESEARCH SETTING, DATA COLLECTION AND ANALYSIS

The study followed the principles for interpretive field research (Klein & Myers, 1999) in the investigation of social media practices in one of the five largest municipalities in Denmark. This empirical ground for the analysis was chosen because Denmark, according to (Bonsón et al., 2012), is among the countries in the European Union with the most active municipalities in social media. However, an initial contextualization revealed that there is no dedicated social media department or functions in the municipality, nor is there a special social media strategy or social media code of conduct. As one of the five largest municipalities in Denmark, one could expect that there was at least a formalized and central function to manage and govern the social media activities. But there was not even one person with the title of social media manager in the municipality. This basic field observation pinpoints the emerging and contradictory practices at stake. Although there was no formalized central organization in place, the directors of the six municipal departments did have social media as a focus area. During the period of the interviews, the directors had also formed a special tasks force, and the directors prioritized networking with other municipalities around social media practices. Historically the municipality has a long tradition for prioritizing citizen dialogue. Already back in the 1990s, it had web-based citizen dialogue initiatives. The city of the municipality has a high percentage of young inhabitants and students and has an innovative IT culture and industry.

Following the principles of interaction between researchers and participants (Klein & Myers, 1999), the empirical material was provided by interviews with directors tasked with social media activites in the municipality and by online observations of the municipality's online social media activity. The interviewees were selected to ensure sensitivity to possible differences in interpretations among the directors of the different municipal departments and followed the principles and guidelines for qualitative interviews (Kvale, 1996; Myers & Newman, 2007). First, to establish a historical perspective and an overview of the practices within the municipality, we interviewed the director of communication in the mayor's office and at the same time made online observations of the municipality's social media practices. Next, to ensure variance and a deeper understanding in prolongation of the insights from the first interview, we interviewed the directors from the six main departments of the municipality. Finally, to test and saturate our analysis, we interviewed the director and manager responsible for one of the most active social media sites within the municipality. The interviews and observations were conducted from February 2013 to April 2013 and took place in the town hall of the municipality. The interviews lasted between forty five minutes and hundred and fifty minutes. The progression of the interviews were designed to facilitate a saturation of the analytical findings in observations and interviews and to clarify unclear issues.

The analysis of the interviews and observations took place as an iterative process of working with the empirical material combined with the focus on contradictions to tease out analytical insights (Golden-biddle & Locke, 1993; Klein & Myers, 1999) . The analysis followed three steps: First, we listened to the interviews, took notes, and went through the original notes from our online observations. The aim was to establish a general understanding of the case and to identify tentative focus points for the following iteration of interview and observation. Second, after the second and third iteration of interviews and observation, we carefully read through the transcribed interview data and conducted a coding of contradictions. This general coding resulted in a list of unordered contradictions found in the municipal's social media practices. Third, we drew on literature to sharpen our analytical understanding of the empirical material and considered the interdependent meaning of parts and wholes. To finalize the analysis with a parsimonious set of categories and elements, we classified only the most robust and relevant contradictions in our data. This resulted in three categories of contradictions (See Table 1).

Table 1. Contradictions in municipal social media practices

Category and Elements	Description of Contradiction	Illustration From Interview and Observation
Form of practice Contradiction between community feeling and service administration.	Social media facilitate personal community feeling, but is intervened and exploited by professional service administration in a process where local social media actors in turn become dependent on municipal service administrators.	Interview quote # 1 "The Clean-City project has a Facebook site with more than thousand likes. A person here offered a sofa for free and got serveral hundred likes. Such spontanous municipal projects occur and function very well due to a professional effort. And the agenda of our task force is to ask: How can the municipality prolong and profit from this activity?" Online observation # 1 Posts and comments by citizens on the Facebook site for 'Clean City' is intervened by a municipal moderator who posts news and responds to questions, and direct citizens to municipal service functions on a proprietary municipal website.
Organizing Contradiction between local initiatives and central governance.	Local social media actors foster initiatives and engagement and thereby organizational autonomy, but are still subject to central governance and control which in turn depend on the local social media actors.	Interview quote # 2 "If we don't do something on the municipal level pretty fast, then the traffic department will go solo" Online observation # 2 Indication of many Facebook sites for local or specific activities. No evidence of any social media sites that officially represent the municipality or any of the six main departments. Indication of temporary project sites and municipal campaign sites, for example 'bicycle city' and 'Clean City'.
Digital infrastructure Contradiction between public social media and proprietary municipal IT.	Public social media functions as driver of change and challenger of proprietary municipal controlled IT, but are also met with imperatives about business directed IT integration from central municipal actors.	Interview quote # 3 "It is important that we can build on top of the initiatives of the engaged citizens and dedicated unsers [of the local social media sites], to the advantage of the whole business of the municipality." Online observation # 3 Photos, comments and questions by citizens on Facebook site for 'Bicycle City'. Self-service forms and official public information relevant for 'Bicycle City' is only placed on municipal website. Visible traffic from Facebook site to municipal website, but not the reverse.

Findings

The analysis identified three categories of contradictions in municipal social media practices, each with its specific set of mutual relations and contradictory elements. The identified categories are 'form of practice', 'organization', and 'digital infrastructure' (See Table 1).

Form of Practice: The first contradiction concerns the modality or form of the social media practices. Online observations indicate the existence of Facebook sites that evolve around a community feeling, for example local municipal schools where participants share photos and personal experiences in relation to specific events and daily life in school. Other Facebook sites, for example 'Clean City', have a municipal administrator who responds to questions and comments and thereby enters a professional administrative service discourse in the midst of the community feeling that also exists on the Facebook-site (See observation #2 in Table 1).

Interviews indicate that the central actors are aware of the local actors being the drivers of community experience, and that the central actors would like to match and integrate this dimension as a part of the municipal service affairs. Interviews indicate this when the director of communication for the mayor's office expresses recognition for local engagement and success, but in the same sentence also says that it would be valuable for the central municipality to exploit this further (See interview quote #2 in Table 1). On the basis of such contradictory relations of community feeling and service administration, the analysis constructed the category 'form of practice'.

Organizing: The second finding concerns the organizing of the social media practices in the municipality. There is one striking finding concerning the organizing. On the one hand there is a presence of local initiatives and engagement, but often in unofficial forms. On the other hand there is a lack of central presence and activity, but large concerns about control and exploitation of social media. Online observations indicate that Facebook facilitates many sites for local or specific educational, cultural and city infrastructure activities. However, we have not found any indication of one single social media site that represents the municipality as an integrated or official whole. Nor does an official website exist for any of the six main departments (See online observation #1 in Table 1).

Interviews confirm that local Facebook-actors are the initiators and are regarded as successful, while central municipal actors express that they are concerned about municipal integration of the diverse local initiatives. For example, a central director expresses that local initiators are proactive and the central administration is lagging behind. Thereby local social media activities gain autonomous or 'solo' status within and beyond the organization (See interview quote #1 in Table 1). Grounded in such contradictory and interdependent elements of central control and local engagement, the analysis constructed the category 'organizing'.

Digital Infrastructure: Online observations indicate activity of posts, photos, and comments on municipal social media sites, for example the Facebook site for 'Bicycle City'. However, when it comes to administrative service functions, for example self-service forms and official public information about road repair and bicycle lanes, these functions are under proprietary control from a municipal website. The municipal website is fueled by a Facebook site, but the reverse is not the case (See observation #3 in Table 1).

Interviews indicate a central municipal recognition of the value of engaged participants on local social media sites, but also an imperative to integrate this activity into a proprietary digital infrastructure as a municipal 'business' project (See interview quote # 3 in Table 1). Grounded in such contradictory relations of public social media and proprietary municipal information and communication technology, the analysis constructed the category 'digital infrastructure'.

DISCUSSION

The emergent interactions between social media and government administration are an intriguing phenomenon that calls upon theoretically and empirically based investigation. Grounded in a case study, the purpose of this paper was to discuss the pertinence of dialectical theory to understand the contradictions present in municipal social media practices.

The analysis identified three categories of contradictions in municipal social media practices, each with their specific set of mutually related and contradictory elements. Figure 1 has been developed in order to better illustrate how the three categories are related and each one embeds contradictory elements: First, contradictions in forms of practices between service administration and community feeling. Second, contradictions in organizing between local initiatives and central control. Third, contradictions in the digital infrastructure between proprietary municipal IT and public social media (See Figure 1).

Concerning the contradictions inherent in practice forms, the present study detected a significant field of practices evolving around community presence, engagement and feeling. This stream of practices was mainly apparent in very local social media practices, for example in a Facebook group for a local municipal primary school. These social media practices in some aspects resemble "Do It Yourself Government" type in Linders (2012) classification of citizen co-production in the age of social media. Linders (2012) specifies that the "Do It Yourself Government" type of social media practices take place with little or no interference. However, Linders (2012) understands the activity within a service concept, for example when using the term 'self-service', and in general also uses the term 'co-production'. In the present study, many local activities happened exactly as Linders' "Do It Yourself Government" without interference from central municipal authorities. However, the form of the practices was also in many aspects outside the 'service' or 'co-production' logic, and rather to compare with a conversation for its own sake. We have named this practice form 'community feeling' to stress the difference to any production or service logic.

However, we also observed social media practices that had a professional tone and approach, and therefore named service administration. This stream of social media practices was mostly apparent in relation to municipal institutions that directed their activity to a broader audience and market and were managed by employees who had it as a part of their professional portfolio of activities. Noteworthy about this stream of activity is that it often did not manage to address the citizens as citizens, but only as professional actors in the related industry. By being simply a professional service administration executed on social media platforms by municipal employees, these cases of municipal social media practices go beyond the other end of the scale of Linders' typology for citizen co-production (Linders, 2012). In comparison with Linders' interesting typology, the social media practices indicated in the present case study thereby falls outside both poles of citizen engagement; 'citizen sourcing' as well as 'Do It Yourself Government'. In other words, the current municipal wrestling with contradictions in social media only involves citizen engagement to a very little degree.

The present study has only a few indications of 'citizen engagement'. The most evident examples are incidents related to activity on the 'Clean City' or 'Bicycle City' Facebook sites where spontaneous or 'self-organizing' citizen activity is staged or intervened by professional municipal service administrators. Thereby the present study points to a context of contradictions that differs considerably from the typology by Linders (2012) and the maturity model by Lee et al. (2012).

Concerning the contradictions between the local initiatives and the central control, the study revealed that there exists a diverse landscape of local social media engagement. A part of the local activity is very visible and recognized by the central authorities. In these situations, the central authorities express that

Figure 1. Wrestling with contradictions

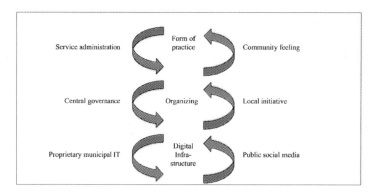

it is desirable that the official municipality can benefit from these local activities. Other local activities are almost invisible or not recognized by others than the local community itself. In both situations, a dialectical approach, that focuses on contradiction, demonstrates its analytical pertinence by being attentive to how the municipality is wrestling with its own inherent contradictions, and how this wrestling plays a central role in the organizational change process (Van De Ven & Poole, 1995). Compared to studies of the deployment degree of government social media practices (Bonsón et al., 2012), the dialectical approach in the present study is capable of observing both the formal and official organizing and the tentative and informal activities of which the latter are not captured by the radar of the municipality itself.

As mentioned before the municipality despite being one of the five largest in Denmark, lacks a formal social media department. Never the less it acts as an organization that in certain ways is very attentive to and active in social media practices. Instead of understanding this situation as a lack of progression within a maturity scheme (Lee et al., 2012), the present paper suggests that it is more adequately understood as an example of municipal wrestling with contradictions. It is outside the scope of the present study to evaluate the wrestling itself, but it could turn out to be an example of resilience (Cho et al., 2007) or collective minding (Carlo et al., 2012).

The present study has also pointed to the fact that the municipality as an organization incorporates a wide variety of social media practices that are not officially recognized or even known. If these social media practices are not included in investigations, we are perhaps in a situation where the deployment degree of social media practices are considerably higher than current research points out (Bonsón, 2012), and may also include a wider variety of practice forms than anticipated so far.

Concerning the contradictions inherent in the digital infrastructure, the dialectical approach in the present study has most importantly implied the inclusion of both proprietary municipal platforms and social media platforms as the adequate object of analysis. In line with Tilson et al. (2010), the present study regards the digital infrastructure as one whole 'affordance' that includes contradictory or paradoxical logics. We found indications of contradictions between the proprietary municipal 'part' of the digital infrastructure and the public social media 'part' of the digital infrastructure. This identification is in line with studies that also identified the relation between an existing organization and an emerging community being central for understanding the change process (Castello, Etter, & Morsing, 2012; Harri, Kalle, & Youngjin, 2010; Paramewaran & Whinston, 2007). What the present study highlighted is the digital infrastructure per se, for example by pointing to how social media platforms become a natural working environment for municipal administrators in certain situations and municipal service functions, including integrating questions posted on Facebook via a form on the proprietary municipal website.

CONCLUSION

The paper took its point of departure in the discrepancy between current research in government social media practices that highlights expectations of co-creation and progression mirrored in typologies for citizen co-production (Linders, 2012) and maturity models (Lee et al., 2012) on one hand, and on the other hand research that documents low deployment degree of social media in local municipalities in the European Union (Bonsón et al., 2012). Extant literature on social media practices in both private and public contexts have detected inherent contradictions (Andersen et al., 2012; Aral et al., 2013) and the objective of the paper therefore becomes to prolong this literature. To this end, the paper draws on the dialectical tradition (Benson, 1977; Bjerknes, 1991) and the literature in which contradictions are understood as possible drivers of change and innovation (Poole & van de Ven, 1989; Smith & Lewis, 2011; Tilson et al., 2010) and asks how contradiction is present in government social media practices.

To theorize how contradiction is present in emerging government social media practices, the paper used a case study of social media practices in one of the five largest municipalities in Denmark. As the findings of the case study, the paper analyzes three related categories of contradictions in municipal social media practices, namely 'form of practice', 'organizing' and 'digital infrastructure'. In the category 'form of practice' the contradiction exists between community feeling and service administration. In the category 'organizing' that contradiction exists between local initiatives and central governance. In the category 'digital infrastructure' the contradiction exists between public social media and proprietary municipal information and communication technologies. The analytical findings are discussed in relation to extant literature on government social media practices (Bonsón et al., 2012; Lee et al., 2012; Linders, 2012).

The main theoretical contribution of the paper is therefore to theorize how emerging government social media practices are driven via three related categories of contradictions. More specifically the theoretical contribution of the paper is a conceptualization of the inherent contradictions of each category and how the organization in question copes with these contradictions. The paper hereby contributes to extant literature on contradictions in government social media practices (Andersen et al., 2012) and to theory on contradictions as drivers of change and innovation in organizations (Poole & van de Ven, 1989).

The practical contribution of the paper is the focus on social media practices as constitutively contradictory and organizational practice therefore a matter of coping with these contradictions. The dialectical approach of the paper suggests that practitioners understand this ambidextrous coping (Andriopoulos & Lewis, 2009; Smith & Lewis, 2011) less as a matter of progression – for example staged in maturity models – than as a continued wrestling with inherent contradictions.

The study acknowledges its limitations. First, despite single cases can provide a rich understanding of the studied phenomenon (Walsham, 1995), the studied case might have special characteristics. Future case studies can clarify this through comparison. Second, the study is also limited in only interviewing directors from the municipality administration and not citizens or groups of citizens. Future studies that include more relevant participants can establish a more complete material ground and critical context of interpretation (Klein & Myers, 1999). Third, the dialectical lens and the focus on contradictions might have become a part of what it describes and thereby constrained the attention to conflicting aspects in the empirical data (Golden-biddle & Locke, 1993; Klein & Myers, 1999). Future research in the contradictions of social media practices that employ alternative theoretical lenses are therefore desirable.

As a final critical reflection (Klein & Myers, 1999), it is worth noting that on the one hand the study found social media practices that bridge service administration and community feeling and thereby indicate a dawn of an 'integrated information environment' (Orlikowski, 1991), but on the other hand observations and interviews also point to social media as a digital infrastructure (Tilson et al., 2010) that can be used to exploit citizen engagement for municipal 'business' purposes. It is therefore pertinent to ask if municipal social media practices as part of an all-encompassing digital infrastructure will facilitate citizen co-production (Linders, 2012) or rather will become a 'matrix of control'. However, drawing on a dialectical tradition and understanding emergent social media practices as constitutively contradictory, the situation is rather to be understood as a both-and: social media practices will result in both citizen co-production and municipal matrix of control. Such a contradictory nature of social media practices can perhaps explain the lack of citizen participation in current municipal social media practices and perhaps exactly reflects a dialectics of collective mindfulness (Carlo et al., 2012). The paper therefore suggests a collective mindfulness in government social media practices as highly relevant for both researchers and practitioners.

ACKNOWLEDGMENT

I thank the reviewers and editors for insightful comments as this paper has evolved significantly through the review process.

REFERENCES

Andersen, K. N., Medaglia, R., & Henriksen, H. Z. (2012). Social media in public health care: Impact domain propositions. *Government Information Quarterly, 29*(4), 462–469. doi:10.1016/j.giq.2012.07.004

Andriopoulos, C., & Lewis, M. W. (2009). Exploitation-exploration tensions and organizational ambidexterity: Managing paradoxes of innovation. *Organization Science, 20*(4), 696–717. doi:10.1287/orsc.1080.0406

Aral, S., Dellarocas, C., & Godes, D. (2013). Social media and business transformation: A framework for research. *Information Systems Research, 24*(1), 3–13. doi:10.1287/isre.1120.0470

Arnold, M. (2003). On the phenomenology of technology: The "Janus-faces" of mobile phones. *Information and Organization, 13*, 231–256. doi:10.1016/S1471-7727(03)00013-7

Barley, S. R., & Kunda, G. (1992). Design and devotion: Surges of rational and normative ideologies of control in managerial discourse. *Administrative Science Quarterly, 37*(3), 363–399. doi:10.2307/2393449

Benson, J. K. (1977). Organizations: A dialectical view. *Administrative Science Quarterly, 22*(1), 1–21. doi:10.2307/2391741

Bergquist., et al. (2013). Social media as management fashion – A discourse perspective. In *Proceedings of the 21st European Conference on Information Systems.*

Berlinger, L. R., & Sitkin, S. B. (1990). Paradox and transformation: Toward a theory of change in organization and management. *Administrative Science Quarterly, 35*(4), 740–744. doi:10.2307/2393523

Bjerknes, G. (1991). Dialectical reflection in information systems development. *Scandinavian Journal of Information Systems, 3*, 55–77.

Bonsón, E., Torres, L., Royo, S., & Floresc, F. (2012). Local e-government 2.0: Social media and corporate transparency in municipalities. *Government Information Quarterly*, *29*(2), 123–132. doi:10.1016/j.giq.2011.10.001

Carlo, J. L., Lyytinen, K., & Boland, J. R. J. (2012). Dialectics of collective minding: contradictory appropriations of information technology in a high-risk project. *Management Information Systems Quarterly*, *36*(4), 1081–A3.

Castello, I., Etter, M., & Morsing, M. (2012). Why stakeholder engagement will not be tweeted: Logic and the conditions of authority corset. [Boston, MA.]. *Academy of Management Journal*, 2012.

Cho, S., Mathiassen, L., & Robey, D. (2007). Dialectics of resilience: a multi-level analysis of a telehealth innovation. [Palgrave Macmillan]. *Journal of Information Technology*, *22*(1), 24–35. doi:10.1057/palgrave.jit.2000088

Dubé, L., & Robey, D. (2009). Surviving the paradoxes of virtual teamwork. *Information Systems Journal*, *19*(1), 3–30. doi:10.1111/j.1365-2575.2008.00313.x

Eisenhardt, K. M. (2000). Paradox, spirals, ambivalence: The new language of change and pluralism. *Academy of Management Review*, *25*(4), 703–705. doi:10.5465/AMR.2000.3707694

Golden-biddle, K., & Locke, K. (1993). Appealing work: An investigation of how ethnographic texts convince. *Organization Science*, *4*, 595–617. doi:10.1287/orsc.4.4.595

Harri, O.-K., Kalle, L., & Youngjin, Y. (2010). Social networks and information systems: Ongoing and future research streams. *Journal of the Association for Information Systems*, *11*(2), 61–68.

Jarvenpaa, S. L., & Lang, K. R. (2005). Managing the paradoxes of mobile technology. *Information Systems Management*, *22*(4), 7–23. doi:10.1201/1078.10580530/45520.22.4.20050901/90026.2

Klein, H. K., & Myers, M. D. (1999). A set of principles for conducting and evaluating interpretive field studies in information systems. *Management Information Systems Quarterly*, *23*(1), 67–93. doi:10.2307/249410

Kvale, S. (1996). *Interviews: An introduction to qualitative research interviewing*. Thousand Oaks, CA: Sage.

Lee, G., Kwak, Y. H., Gwanhoo, L., & Young Hoon, K. (2012). An open government maturity model for social media-based public engagement. *Government Information Quarterly*, *29*(4), 492–503. doi:10.1016/j.giq.2012.06.001

Linders, D. (2012). From e-government to we-government: Defining a typology for citizen coproduction in the age of social media. *Government Information Quarterly*, *29*(4), 446–454. doi:10.1016/j.giq.2012.06.003

Luscher, L. S., Lewis, M., & Ingram, A. (2006). The social construction of organizational change paradoxes. *Journal of Organizational Change Management*, *19*(4), 491–502. doi:10.1108/09534810610676680

Lüscher, L. S., & Lewis, M. W. (2008). Organizational change and managerial sensemaking: Working through paradox. *Academy of Management Journal*, *2*(2), 221–240. doi:10.5465/AMJ.2008.31767217

March, J. G. (1991). Exploration and exploitation in organizational learning. *Organization Science, 2*(1), 71–87. doi:10.1287/orsc.2.1.71

Myers, M. D., & Newman, M. (2007). The qualitative interview in IS research: Examining the craft. *Information and Organization, 17*(1), 2–26. doi:10.1016/j.infoandorg.2006.11.001

Orlikowski, W. (1991). *Integrated information environment or matrix of control? The contradictory implications of information technology.* Accounting, Management and Information Technologies.

Paramewaran, M., & Whinston, A. (2007). Research issues in social computing. *Journal of the Association for Information Systems, 8*(6).

Poole, M. S., & van de Ven, A. H. (1989). Using paradox to build management and organization theories. *Academy of Management Review, 14*(4), 562–578. doi:10.5465/amr.1989.4308389

Quinn, R. E., & Cameron, K. S. (1988). *Paradox transformation: Toward a theory of change in organization and management.* Cambridge, UK: Ballinger.

Smith, W. K., & Lewis, M. W. (2011). Toward a theory of paradox: A dynamic equilibrium model of organizing. *Academy of Management Review, 36*(2), 381–403. doi:10.5465/AMR.2011.59330958

Sundaramurthy, C., & Lewis, M. (2003). Control and collaboration: paradoxes of governance. *Academy of Management Review, 28*(3), 397–415. doi:10.5465/AMR.2003.10196737

Tilson, D., Lyytinen, K., & Sørensen, C. (2010). Digital infrastructures: The missing IS research agenda. *Information Systems Research, 21*(4), 748–759. doi:10.1287/isre.1100.0318

Van De Ven, A. H., & Poole, M. S. (1995). Explaining development and change in organizations. *Academy of Management Review, 20*(3), 510–540. doi:10.2307/258786

Walsham, G. (1995). Interpretive case studies in IS research: Nature and method. *Organization Science.*

This research was previously published in the International Journal of Electronic Government Research (IJEGR), 10(1); edited by Vishanth Weerakkody, pages 35-45, copyright year 2014 by IGI Publishing (an imprint of IGI Global).

Chapter 71

Amplification and Virtual Back–Patting:
The Rationalities of Social Media Uses in the Nina Larsson Web Campaign

Jakob Svensson
Uppsala University, Sweden

ABSTRACT

This chapter explores the rationalities of politicians' social media uses in Web-campaigning in a party-based democracy. This is done from an in-depth case study of a Swedish politician, Nina Larsson, who with the help of a PR agency utilized several social media platforms in her campaign to become re-elected to the parliament in 2010. By analyzing how and for what purposes Larsson used social media in her Web-campaign, this chapter concludes that even though discourses of instrumental rationality and of communicative rationality were common to make her practices relevant, Nina primarily used social media to amplify certain offline news media texts as well as to commend and support other liberal party members. Hence, from this case, the authors conclude that Web-campaigning on social media is used for expressive purposes, to negotiate and maintain an attractive political image within the party hierarchy.

INTRODUCTION

There is hype around social media, not least when it comes to election campaigning. Politicians are no doubt turning to social media in increasing numbers when campaigning today (Anduiza, 2009; Jackson & Lilleker, 2009; Montero, 2009; Zafiropoulos & Vrana, 2009; Goldbeck et al., 2010; Grusell & Nord, 2011; Jackson & Lilleker, 2011). However the reasons for this are not explored to any great extent, especially not in party based democracies, even though theories of how and why to use social media often are implicit as background assumptions and normative lenses to frame studies of political participation on social media. There is a black box to be uncovered here. We know that politicians use social media even though most studies have revealed that the effect on electoral participation and opinion formation is small (Gibson et al., 2008; Jackson & Lilleker, 2011; Larsson & Moe, 2011). The question then arises

DOI: 10.4018/978-1-5225-5637-4.ch071

for what purposes do candidates use social media? Such inquiry is especially intriguing in a party-based democracy where election lists and voting behavior to a large extent still depend on political parties rather than on individual candidates.

To explore rationales for election campaigning on social media I have conducted an in-depth case-study of Nina Larsson, a young Swedish politician in her 30s, representing *Folkpartiet* (the Liberal Party) in the region of Värmland (midwest of Sweden) in the 2010 general elections. By contracting a communication agency, *Hello Clarice,* for professional input and coaching in her social media endeavors, she is most untypical of Swedish politicians. However by her conscious and ample use of social media for campaigning purposes, she is suitable for an explorative study into the rationales of social media campaigning practices. I will attend to Nina and the design of the study more thoroughly in the forthcoming sections. I begin with outlining the analytical framework for this study, starting with definition of social media.

SOCIAL MEDIA, INDIVIDUALIZATION AND WEB-CAMPAIGNING

Social media is a contested term since it implies that traditional media would not encompass social dimensions. What is often referred to when talking about social media are online communication platforms were the *social* seems to refer to the possibility of users to influence and *interact* with the content and each other in some way or another. O'Reilly (oreilly.com/web2/archive/what-is-web-20.html, retrieved 16ᵗʰ April 2006) claims that for a website to be defined as *social* the user him/herself should be able to participate and contribute to the content of the site. The user should be able to take control over his/hers information and the overall design should be interactive and user-friendly. The more elaborate definition of Social Network Sites (SNS) focuses on the possibility for users to articulate their social networks and make them visible to others (Ellison & boyd, 2007, p. 2). SNS are defined as web-based services that allow users to construct a public, or half-public profile, tie this profile to other users, sometimes self-selected, whose contacts in turn are made available by the service. In this chapter I will attend to Nina's uses of Facebook, Twitter, an interactive campaign website and two blogs. Since neither the blogs nor the interactive campaign website would fit the SNS definition by Ellison & boyd, I will use O'Reilly's more encompassing definition of social media.

The rise of social media is interlinked with heightened processes of individualization. The experience of increased personal autonomy and expressions of this are among the most debated trends in our time (see Lasch, 1979/1991; Giddens, 1991; Bauman, 2001). In accounts of the late modern era, processes of individualization are given priority over collectively shared cultural frames of references that dominated social spaces and their organization in modernity (such as family, nation, class, party affiliation et cetera). With an increase of use of online social media platforms, processes of individualization tend to become more networked in character (Castells, 2001, pp. 122-125). Hence, managing your identity on social media platforms largely revolves around connecting yourself to other nodes in the network (users, fan pages, groups et cetera). Since we lack bodily cues in computer mediated communication, connections to others are essential in the management and negotiation of ourselves online (Miller, 2008). It would therefore be wrong to conceive of late modern individualization and a sense of collectiveness as mutually exclusive. Individualism could very well be considered a form of collective identity (see also Lasch, 1979/1991). Here I find the concept of networked individualism particularly illuminating for understanding the practice of linking the individual to different groups online (see also Castells, 2001, pp. 129-133).

The emergence of social media and online networking in digital and late modernity coincided with lower participation in elections (Coleman & Blumler, 2009, p 143; Dahlgren, 2009, p. 159). It seems like citizens are increasingly dissatisfied and estranged from the processes and people of representative democracy (Loader, 2007; Coleman & Blumler, 2009). Since representative democracy has its roots in an era marked by modernization and industrialization, contemporary withdrawal from its institutions and new forms of political participation may be understood in tandem with new individualized and networked forms of sociability (Coleman & Blumler, 2009, p. 84). Nevertheless the internet and social media are increasingly used by politicians and discussed as political tools within the field of political communication (Bimber & Davies, 2003; Gulati, 2004; Foot & Schneider, 2006; Gibson et al., 2008; Stanyer, 2008; Anduiza, 2009; Costa, 2009; Jackson & Lilleker, 2009; Montero, 2009; Goldbeck, 2010; Schweitzer, 2010; Dimitrova et al., 2011; Grusell & Nord, 2011; Jackson & Lilleker, 2011; Larsson, 2011; Karlsson et al., 2012). Within these discussions I have discerned three different rationales for politicians to use social media; 1) to strategically target voter groups 2) for communicative deliberations with their constituency and 3) to negotiate their image as politicians. I will attend to them separately next, even though they might blur and not so easily be separated.

Obama's presidential campaign 2008, where much of his support and electorate engagement was initiated and staged with the help of social media, has served as an inspiration and example for numerous politicians, campaign workers and theorists of political communication (Costa, 2009; Montero, 2009, p. 30). Within the field of strategic political communication social media platforms are discussed out of their potential for fast circulation of large amounts of information that could be targeted to particular groups and networks and hence win their support (Anduiza, 2009), and as a way for politicians to keep in touch and communicating directly with constituents (Zafiropoulos & Vrana, 2009, p. 78; Schweitzer, 2010; Jackson & Lilleker, 2011). In these accounts it is especially underlined that traditional media and its logics can be bypassed online. In the domain of political communication, the theory of media logics have drawn attention to how political life in its broadest sense has become situated within the domain of media (Street, 1997). Politicians have to adhere to the dramatization style in media discourses, the increasing prominence of short sound bites, visuals and entertainment formats et cetera in order to be picked up by traditional broadcast media (Kepplinger, 2002; Altheide, 2004, p. 294; Hjarvard, 2008). With the advent of social media it has been argued that traditional media and its logic can be circumvented.

A theoretician most influential for research on social media and political participation is Habermas. In sharp contrast to strategic political spin his theories focus on what procedures and qualities should persist communication within democratic fora. Habermas (1996, pp. 114-115) outlines a communicative rationality, a rationality he bases on peoples' inherent strive for enlightenment through listening to each other's arguments and being willing to change ones opinions according to the best argument. In this way consensus is supposed to be reached and more informed decisions are made (Habermas, 1996, p. 140). Deliberative democrats have attempted to apply Habermas' normative philosophy in real life politics, and to evaluate democratic procedures according to ideas of an ideal public sphere where everybody is heard, may voice their concerns and consensus can be obtained when agreeing on the best arguments (Fishkin, 1991; Dryzek, 2000; Fenton, 2010). Rational conversations (i.e. deliberations) are considered to have a democratizing effect because participants are supposed to become more attuned to the common good of all rather than to negotiate between predetermined personal interests (Coleman & Blumler, 2009, p. 17). However the largely normative theories of deliberative democracy have often been used for participatory democratic experiments as if the citizenry already possessed the rather demanding qualities necessary for successful deliberations (see Svensson (2008) for an example of such an experiment as well as Stokes (2005) for a discussion on the likelihood for actual deliberative democracy). Recent research has also questioned the potential of online platforms for engaging citizens in deliberations with representative institutions, and questioned whether online communication platforms really are governed by communicative rationality (Calenda & Mosca, 2007, pp. 87, 92; Dahlgren & Olsson, 2007; Vromen, 2007, p. 97, 113; Anduiza, 2009, p. 8). The promise of deliberation online continues to excite researchers and practitioners though, not the least because of the interactive potential of, and increasing usage of, social media.

Perhaps the closest to theories of late modern individualization is the use of social media as a way for politicians to negotiate an attractive image in front of their constituency. Only by being online politicians wish to convey a message, especially to younger segments of the electorate, that they are up-to-date (hence a kind of *jump-on-the-bandwagon* mentality, see Jackson & Lilleker, 2011). The rise of electronic media is thus intertwined with personalization of politics. Today it is argued that politicians are scrutinized for authenticity and style by an electorate that is increasingly visually and emotionally literate (Stanyer, 2008, p. 415), hence a need for politicians to manage an attractive image online. Many political communication researchers have translated Goffman's well-known work on how individuals seek manage what impression they give to others into motivations for politicians to use social media (see Gulati, 2004; Stanyer, 2008; Jackson & Lilleker, 2011). Studies from the US and the UK have shown how the internet presents a front region for politicians to present themselves to the electorate (Stanyer, 2008), to negotiate different images (Gulati, 2004) and to promote themselves (Goldbeck et al., 2010). Through selective disclosures about their private lives politicians have used the internet and social media to show themselves as ordinary and like-able persons (Jackson and Lilleker, 2009, 2011), in this way carefully managing the information they reveal online to influence the impressions the audience construct (Stanyer, 2008, p. 418). In Sweden, Gustafsson (2012) found that Facebook groups are used to build group identity among members of political parties. In many of these studies impression management are rather linked to instrumental purposes of winning votes than to heightened processes of individualization. Hence it is arguable whether politicians are mostly motivated by identity/ preference expression, indicating a kind of expressive rationality (see Brennan & Lomasky, 1993; Engelen, 2006; Svensson, 2011) or by becoming elected, indicating an instrumental rationality. Studies of Twitter use among politicians have shown though that neither early adoption nor high usage is correlated with electoral success (see Jackson & Lilleker, 2011; Larsson & Moe, 2011). Still politicians use it indicating that there are more than purely instrumental reasons for doing so.

To sum up lets return to the question this chapter seeks to answer; for what purposes did Nina use social media in her election campaign? As this section has shown, such question can be approached with different theoretical lenses. Social media could be used as strategical instruments to target certain voter groups and circumvent traditional media and their logics. This would suggest a more instrumental rational approach. Social media could also be used to increase the quality of democracy by promoting deliberations. This would imply a communicative rational approach. But social media could also be used for image negotiation. This would point to a more expressive rational use of social media. Before analyzing the rationales of social media uses in the Nina Larsson web-campaign, I will next attend to the setting in which the campaign took place, the different social media platforms she used in her election campaign 2010, and describe the methods for empirical data gathering.

THE SETTING AND CASE

Sweden is a party-based democracy with very high ICT usage. In the election year of 2010 broadband penetration reached 92,5 percent of the population (World Internet Stats, www.internetworldstats.com/ eu/se.htm, retrieved April 17th 2012), 68 percent of the population between 9-79 used the internet daily and 35 percent used social media (Nordicom Internet Barometer). The use of internet and social media in Värmland, where Nina Larsson campaigned, reflects the nation at large. 70 percent use internet daily or several times a week and 35 percent of the respondents claim to use social media daily or several times a week (compared to 46 percent who claim not to have used social media at all during 2010).

But is social media used for political purposes? A recent panel study on social media usages in Sweden up to the elections found that reading blogs about politics or current affairs were the most common social media used with 8 percent (Dimitrova et al., 2011). 4 percent followed a politician on Facebook and only 1 percent used Twitter to follow a politician or political party. These numbers are further confirmed in Värmland. Only 35 percent of those that used social media several times a week had participated in an online campaign/ petition through e-mail or social media in 2010 (17 percent of the total sample), and less than 14 percent have discussed politics at all on an online debate forum during the election year (7 percent in the total sample). These numbers should be related to that 53 percent of the respondents in Värmland state that they are very or quite interested in politics in general and also related to that 53 percent claimed to have discussed politics during the last month, but apparently not on social media platforms. Hence even though social media use is rising in Sweden, the low numbers for using them for political participation should be discouraging for any social media campaigner.

If we now return to politicians and their uses of social media in campaigning, there are some studies of individual candidates using social media especially from the US and the UK (see for example Gibson et al., 2008; Goldbeck et al., 2010; Jackson & Lilleker, 2011). However, I have found no such studies in Sweden. Gustafsson (2012) made focus groups interviews with party members 2009 (among other groups) in order to study the effects of social media on political participation. Studies from the 2010 Swedish elections have either been focusing on political parties' (Grusell & Nord, 2011; Karlsson et al., 2011; Larsson, 2011), or the electorate's uses of social media (Dimitrova et al., 2011; Larsson & Moe, 2011). Karlsson et al. (2012) made a longitudinal study of parties usage of social media and found that all ten parties in the study had social media presence on Facebook, Twitter and YouTube, but that the activities on them were heavily concentrated to the weeks running up to the elections (see also Larsson, 2011). Grusell & Nord's (2011) study of the political parties use of social media in the 2010 elections concludes that social media are generally not yet mastered by politicians and political parties, and not yet integrated in parties overall communication strategies (see also Karlsson et al., 2012).

So why then study Nina Larsson's campaign on social media? The decision was made because her explicit focus on social media platforms as tools for web-campaigning was rather unique in Värmland, and as it seems exceptional in Sweden as a whole. Nina contracted a communication agency, *Hello Clarice,* to help her with her social media presence, and both Nina and Hello Clarice agreed on to co-operate in an academic study of the web-campaign. The research project was deemed particularly interesting since Karlstad University had entered an agreement with the SOM Institute and would gain access to data on Nina's constituents usages of social media to compare her campaign usages with (presented previously). Hence a study would provide an in-depth insight into one instant of a candidate's election campaign in one constituency. She is not a typical case since she did integrate social media into her campaign and she did attempt to master them with the help of professionals (as compared to the study by Grusell & Nord, 2011). But even though a deviant case her conscious use of social media makes her suitable for an in-depth explorative study into the rationales of social media campaigning practices. In this way we could even consider her as a *pathway case* (Gerring, 2007, pp. 44, 122) since the study of her aims at elucidating causal mechanisms behind politicians' social media uses. Nina is an early adopter and other politicians might follow her example since social media is likely to continue playing an increasing role in web-campaigning. This study is thus explorative and hypothesis generating in its aims rather than hypothesis testing, looking to spread light into causal mechanism rather than causal effects (Gerring, 2007, pp. 37-39). Nina is an example of a future generation of politicians and her web-campaign in Värmland provides us insights into the rationales of campaigning on social media platforms in a party-based representative democracy and with professional input.

Which social media did Nina Larsson use? During the election campaign she was active on Twitter (http://twitter.com/NinaLarsson), Facebook (http://www.facebook.com/ninalarsson), a campaign website (www.kryssaninalarsson.nu) and on two blogs, one connected to the regional newspaper VF (Värmlands Folkblad, http://blogg.vf.se/ninalarsson) and one personal blog Ninalarsson.se tied to her as politician representing Folkpartiet (the Liberal Party, http://www.Ninalarsson.se). Ninalarsson.se has been up and running since 2006, and is used to communicate ideas with more apparent political angles. The months prior to the elections Nina posted approximately four posting a week (135 postings in total in 2010 up to the Election Day September 19th). On the blog there are links to Nina's Twitter and Facebook account, her campaign website as well as the VF blog.

On the regional newspaper Värmlands Folkblad (VF), Nina had a blog since 2008. Her aim was one posting a day, however, postings here were more rare than on Ninalarsson.se, approximately two posting per week. During 2010 she posted 20 times in January but then less and less up with only four postings the election month of September (87 postings in total 2010 to the election day). Nina decided herself what to post on the VF blog, the newspaper only provided the domain. On the VF site there were also other blogs from other politicians and regional celebrities to follow. Nina stopped using this blog after the elections. October 11th she posted the last time.

The campaign website was launched May 26th and was active up to the Election Day September 19th. Here visitors could practice in voting for Nina through an interactive application, donate money, pose her questions, as well as reading about her political agenda, watching and listen to campaign material. There were links to her Facebook profile on the front page, and further inside the site there were also links to Ninalarsson.se and her twitter-feed. The campaign website was completely controlled by Nina and *Hello Clarice*. They decided which questions should be answered to and be made visible on the website. This makes it questionable whether the website could be considered a social medium at all, and is hence less interesting for this study.

Nina Larsson uses Twitter since spring 2009. The months up to the elections Nina used Twitter practically several times every day. The month of January 2010 she tweeted 139 tweets and then, as with the VF blog, less and less as she was increasingly busy with offline campaigning (the last 30 days up to the elections she tweeted 74 times). Twitter was used more for personal networking than the two blogs tweeting updates on her whereabouts, plans and situations. A majority of the tweets were addressed to someone with an @tag. However she did use the platform, especially the months prior to the elections, for stating political opinions especially by directing traffic to Ninalarsson.se, as well as to newspaper articles suitable for her political agenda. The same goes for her Facebook page and here her network was made visible even more with friends and acquaintances posting encouraging postings and shows their support. On Twitter, Nina had a link to her campaign website. On her Facebook page there were also links to Ninalarsson.se, her twitter account and her personal page on the liberal party website.

METHODOLOGICAL CONSIDERATIONS

The study of Nina Larsson has been inspired by nethnographic methodology (ethnography being a good methodology for case study research (Gerring, 2007, pp. 68-69)). The aim of nethnographic research is to understand the social interaction taking place online, hence a focus on the interaction and user-generated information flows (Berg, 2011, p. 120; Kozinets, 2011). The nethnographic approach thus suits the aims of this paper since I am studying how Nina used social media and the information flow she initiated and/ or took part in. Doing nethnography I followed Nina Larsson on all her five social media platforms took field notes and screenshots when I observed something I deemed particularly interesting. I have followed Nina since 2009 but the main period of study for this chapter started January 2010 and continued to the elections September 19th. Screenshots have been selected every week from all five social media platforms. All postings on Twitter, the VF blog and Ninalarsson.se were saved for the studied period and later used for different content analyses. In this sense I used her social media platforms as archives of information (see also Berg, 2011, p. 126), but I have also created my own archive with weekly screenshots since data and interactions on social media are instantaneous and may be changed or disappear. In addition I have used the Politometer, a widget that measures in-, and out-links to and from Swedish political blogs (see www.politometerns.se).

For better understanding of the online interactions, I have participated on some of the debates on Ninalarsson.se as well as twittered and face-booked with her. My interventions with Nina followed a simple plan; when I reacted on, or felt I wanted to get clarification, information or just agreeing on something she posted, I interacted with her (wrote on the wall, retweeted a tweet, commented on, or liked a posting et cetera). My interventions most often concerned statements on education policies and infrastructure (since I work at a university and used to commute between Karlstad and Stockholm). Examples of interactions on her Facebook was giving thumbs up when she posted her train was on time, or posting comments about my train delays and asking for her ideas of improving the railway tracks in Värmland. Our twittering mostly revolved around when to meet, or asking for quick information on liberal politics, or sending condolences when she twittered she had a cold et cetera.

Nethnography works well in combination with a more traditional ethnographic method, especially when inquiring into what considerations are behind (inter)actions online. Hence online observations and interventions were complemented with continuous and open ended interviews online and offline with both Nina Larsson herself and Olle Nilsson and Gunnar Bark at *Hello Clarice*. Besides online chatting and e-mailing shorter questions and requests for clarifications, I conducted one more structured interview with Olle Nilsson and Gunnar Bark offline and one with Nina. Interview data have also been used from David Kvicklund and David Samuelsson's essay for bachelor degree. I also followed Nina offline during two weeks in September before the elections. Being close to her I often took the opportunity for posing questions and discussing her social media use (in the car to different events for example).

It is difficult to say whether conducting this study influenced her behavior. On the one hand the mere fact that she was part of this research project indicates that she conceived of her campaign as novel and of interest. And since I continuously asked her questions, participated on her social media platforms and followed her offline, she was constantly reminded of my interest in her social media uses. On the other hand it was my impression that she was too independent and too focused on the campaign to let me distract or influence her. After a while I also became such a natural part of her network, to the extent that I believe she conceived of me more as an acquaintance among others rather than as a researcher.

HOW NINA USED SOCIAL MEDIA AND MADE IT RELEVANT

What rationalities governed Nina Larsson's uses of social media in her web-campaign? Nina explains that she uses the internet as a complement to personal face to face meetings which she means is the best way of communicating with citizens. Through social media she comes in contact with her voters, can discuss and listen to the different sentiments in her constituency. Nina looks down on other politicians that she claims still use social media as megaphones, as yet another channel to broadcast their statements in (see also Bimber & Davies, 2003; García & Lara, 2009; Jackson & Lilleker 2009). She, on the other hand, conceives of them more as platforms for dialogue rather than as megaphones and in this way she believes they will reinforce representative democracy. Talking to Nina it becomes obvious that she uses discourses of communicative rationality to frame her web- campaign and to provide meanings to her social media practices. Communication did however not take place on most of social media platforms. The exception is Facebook and especially Twitter. 60 percent of her tweets were addressed to someone with the help of @tags. However the discussions on Twitter rather seemed to take place among friends and party colleagues than with constituents. Studying the positing on Facebook it also becomes underlined that the ones that posted on her wall and the ones she engaged in discussion with, were rather friends from before than constituents.

It is hardly surprising that Nina as a professional politician when talking to me underlines the purpose of her online social networking to come closer to her constituency and to dialogue with potential voters. But if I go beyond what seems to be a discursive façade of deliberation, I soon discern more strategic and instrumental purposes with Nina's social media practices, such as being visible, becoming re-elected, get new voters to her and her political party. Nina says that she conceives of social media as channels to come in contact with new voters and to broaden her web of contacts. However, the interactions she establishes and participates in are mainly on her terms and around the topics she herself puts on the agenda. It is Nina who decides what will be discussed, even if she cannot completely govern the commentaries she gets. Here there are differences between the different platforms she use. The campaign website for example was completely controlled by her and *Hello Clarice,* deciding which questions should be answered to and made visible on the website, whereas on Ninalarsson.se all comments to her entries were made visible right away (most of the time). Hence it does not seem that she really used social media to deliberate with her constituents, and it does not seem that what she labels as dialogue should bring about the type of consensus underlined in theories of deliberative democracy. For example, Nina defines a good posting on Ninalarsson.se as something that not everyone agrees upon and something that is "a little bit provocative" (all quotes translated from Swedish by author). Through coaching by *Hello Clarice* Nina confirms that she have become more daring in her postings. Olle Nilsson at Hello Clarice explains that they give Nina feedback on her postings on the two blogs in forms of thumps up or thumbs down with the purpose of getting her to mediate certain kinds of emotions and to get her to "think right" about online communication. When asking Olle what this thinking right implies, he explains that they coach her to become more personal, to dare to be more provocative and direct in the communication with her constituency. Nina on her hand claims that she has noticed that this tone attracts more readers. I thus conclude that being exposed to a large amount of readers that might not always agree with her is of greater importance when posting than communication towards agreement upon an issue. This is pointing to an instrumental rational, rather than a communicative rational use of social media in her campaign.

A closer study of the postings on the blog Ninalarsson.se indicates that the more provocative and personal tone have not led to more comments (Kvicklund & Samuelsson, 2010) which I would take as an indication on whether she had succeeded in attracting more readers or not. Looking at the postings 30 days before election day on Ninalarsson.se, she attracted on average 1,1 comment. In January the average was 3,8 comments per post, but this is especially due to two postings, one on the pricing of electricity (21 comments) and one on wolf hunting (24 comments) which is a particularly controversial issue in Värmland. One comment was especially interesting. Someone invited Nina to his/her own blog instead of "fighting" in the commentary section of Nina's blog (Kvicklund & Samuelsson, 2010). When asking Nina about this she says herself that communication tends to become unpleasant rather quickly online even if not really meant to. Hence, the overall picture emerging of her social media use is that it is framed in a mix of a deliberative democratic discourse of increasing dialogue with citizens, and a more strategic purpose of being exposed to as many potential voters as possible though provoking debate with people with diverging opinions. However, when such a debate finally is happening it seems not a priority to maintain it.

Both discourses of communicative as well as instrumental rationality are utilized by Nina and people at *Hello Clarice* to make her social media practices meaningful and relevant for election campaigning. Here it is interesting to compare these discourses to the uses of social media for political purposes in the Värmland constituency. As revealed in the SOM survey, only a small segment of the population actually discusses politics online and hence could be targeted on social media platforms or engaged in deliberations. In talks with Nina it seemed that she was aware of that not everyone was online and she also had difficulties to give more than one or two examples of successful deliberations and new voters being attracted to her through her social media presence. Still, she continued with the web-campaign. Therefore we need to go beyond these initial explanations given by Nina and people at *Hello Clarice* and have closer look at the actual interactions taking place on the social media platforms she used.

AMPLIFICATION AND VIRTUAL BACK PATTING

Let's turn to theories of increasing possibilities of image management online. If we look closer at Nina's postings on the VF blog, the use of social media as expressive tools for image management is clearly underlined. The postings there were more personal, dealing with her feelings about her life and job as a politician, and she also discloses selected parts of her private life, such as renewing her apartment for example. According to Gunnar Bark at *Hello Clarice* the strategy for the VF blog is for the reader to get to know Nina on a more private level. The VF blog reader should more easily embrace Nina as person, through shorter postings and more pictures. Approximately half of the postings (43 out of 87) contained primarily information about her as a person (even though she often ended a posting with a link to Ninalarsson.se or an opinion piece in a newspaper) and one third (32 out of 87) posting had pictures or videos that Nina herself had recorded (sometimes even acting in front of the camera interviewing a researcher, blogger, musician, sportsperson she liked or reporting from an event such as car race or a meeting with local interest groups). This illustrates the shift towards greater individualization in late modernity and personalization of politics. Nina herself defines a good posting on the VF blog if she succeeded with a good picture of an exciting meeting, or an entertaining story. Nina says that the image she wants transmit on the VF blog is as engaged and hardworking, both at work and at home. Hence, she used the VF blog to promote and manage the image of herself in front of the constituents (see also Gulati, 2004; Stanyer, 2008; Goldbeck et al., 2010).

When interviewing Nina she underlines several times the possibility for her to put forward "her own version in her own media channels". This statement is interesting since within political communication it has been discussed whether the online communication platforms contributes with ways for politicians to circumvent the media logic that established and commercial offline-media have set up (see Altheide, 2004). Social media give Nina a possibility to use other channels she has greater control over than established media channels. However, in relation to the media logic argument, traditional news media still seems to be the center of attention for Nina. She used her social media channels to rather position herself in relation to traditional news media text, whose stories and angles she has no influence over, than to circumvent them all together. For example in one posting on Ninalarsson.se she comments on an investigative journalistic TV program scrutinizing the presence of Members of Parliament during voting in the chamber, in which she was portrayed as a politician being absent from many parliamentary votes. In another posting she comments the editorial of leading national newspaper et cetera. It seems that established media channels are setting the agenda for her social media postings. Up to 56 percent of the postings on Ninalarsson.se (76 of 135) referred to media texts initially broadcasted offline (newspapers, TV or radio) by either commenting on, or spreading texts initiated in traditional offline news media (35 percent in the VF blog). If Nina for example writes a debate article in a daily newspaper, or appears on TV or radio, this will almost automatically generate a blog posting, a Facebook posting and a tweet – all with links to the original appearance. In this way her uses of social media have the function of *amplifying* selected texts originating in traditional offline news media. This resonates with Goldbeck et al. (2010) content analysis of members of US Congress using Twitter who found that a majority of the tweet was information such as position on an issue, opinions, facts et cetera. And a vast majority of these informational tweets contained links to other media texts (ibid.). And if we look at her social media practices, Ninalarsson.se was at the center with almost all her postings there amplified with tweets, Facebook posting and mentions on the VF blog with a link redirecting the readers/ followers to Ninalarsson.se.

Nina's interactions with regional news journalists are worth a mention here. They are part of each other's Facebook- and Twitter-networks and there are numerous examples of connections between them. She sometimes addressed them especially on Twitter with @tags when for example visiting a company or a school for example, to get them to come and cover the event. In 4 percent of all her tweets I could identify @tags to traditional broadcast media and journalists. Journalists also contacted Nina directly a couple of times during the two weeks I followed her offline, to get her quickly to the radio studio to comment on an event, to ask for clarifications on liberal policies or commenting on an opponent's proposals. However during all the time I have followed Nina, there was only one time that a blog posting originating from Nina online that made it into the offline news. This makes it questionable if we can talk about a new media logic in Nina's case. The high circulation of broadcast news media texts suggests that appearances in offline media and texts originating in traditional mass media are of prime importance in the negotiation of her political persona. The importance of offline media, such as televised debates, is also underlined in other studies of the 2010 elections. For example the amount of tweets among followers of the hashtag #val2010 (Swedish for election2010, see Larsson & Moe, 2011) and among political parties (see Grusell & Nord, 2011) increased notably during televised debates.

Communicating and commenting stories from traditional news media as well as disseminating media appearances of herself, stand out as a substantial part of Nina's social media practices. It is not only her own media appearances that get amplified in her online social networks. She also links to, retweets and comments on news stories and other politicians' debate articles. She clearly used her social media platforms to promote the Liberal Party, to reinforce, retweet, and "like" political messages that other liberals have been communicating both in traditional offline media, as well as on their social media platforms. Data from the Politometer confirms that during the months up to the elections more than 90 percent of both links in to, and out of Ninalarsson.se were from/to other liberal party members. In more than 50 percent of the postings in Ninalarsson.se (68 of 135) and 32 percent of the VF blog (28 of 87) I could identify links to other liberal politicians or liberal party websites. Hence a virtual patting the backs of fellow liberal party comrades seems to take place in Nina's social media networks in form of multiplying and commending each other's appearances. This result resonates in Gustafsson's (2012) study where he found that party members mostly obtained a Facebook account in order to discuss politics with other party members and to receive information from the party. It is perhaps not surprising that the political party is important for candidates' image management in a party-based democracy (see Stanyer, 2008). But the extent to which this is done on Nina Larsson's social media platforms surprised me. This is pointing to the fact that it is rather in front of the party and fellow party colleagues she is managing her image than in front of her constituents, further underlining an expressive rather than an instrumental rational use of her social media platforms.

We can understand the practices of amplifying own and others media performances in light of increased possibilities for image management on social media. Studying Nina it becomes obvious that it actually revolves around negotiating the image of her as a liberal politician. Contrary to Sey & Castells (2004, p. 366) who claims that it is more difficult for politicians to control the information flow on social media, I argue this is precisely the reason why Nina is using social media platforms in her campaign (see also Stanyer, 2008, p. 418; Zafiropoulos & Vrana, 2009). And it is not primarily the information she seeks to control, it is rather the image of herself as a politician and her liberal network of political contacts. This illustrates the kind of networked individualism discussed previously. We can clearly observe contemporary tendencies towards greater personalization of politics in Nina's campaign. However the party political network is very present in this personalization. It is her political contacts within the liberal party that are used, made visible and most often referred to in her social media practices. These connections, these nodes in her network, seem to be of particular importance in the negotiation of her political self on social media platforms, to relate her image to other liberals and to maintain her party political network through linking to, and commenting on selected others postings

CONCLUSION

In conclusion Nina uses social media primarily to negotiate and express her political persona, to control the image that is broadcasted of her in established media. Readers may comment on the postings that Nina chose to put on the agenda, but they hardly have any influence over this agenda. The strategic purpose to stand out and be seen through provoking debate is not compatible with striving for consensus through deliberation. And debate does not to take place at great length on the social media platforms she uses. Rather, observing the exchanges online I witness calm and friendly interaction between what seems to be a rather familiar and party political network. This is pointing to expressive use of social media in her campaign, to negotiate herself as a politician through amplifying the messages and the performances she has participated in herself in other channels, comment on current affairs and not least to tie her political persona to other liberals. This suggests that politicians campaigning online in a party-based democracy may not only use social media strategically (in order to gain more voters) or normatively (for a better communication with the electorate), but as the study of Nina has shown, politicians may also use social media reflexively, in order to express and promote themselves and to negotiate their image within the party political network. It would be interesting to study this quantitatively across a population of all candidates in a party based-democracy in an upcoming election.

The aim of this paper is to contribute to the discussion of social media and how they are used in a web-campaign. Social media platforms may certainly be used as tools for better and more direct communication with the electorate as well as for circulating large amounts of tailored political messages for specific target groups. However among the inhabitants in Värmland almost half of the electorate never use social media and among the people who use social media weekly less than 14 percent discussed politics on debate forums at all during the election year of 2010. Hence we should not neglect expressive rationality as a potential perspective for understanding uses of social media in an election campaign.

An interesting observation from this study is the many rationalities referred to and the different approaches among the different actors in Nina's web-campaign in Värmland. Nina herself tended initially to lean towards a communicative rational approach when describing what she wants to do with social media in her campaign. The communication agency Hello Clarice rather departs from instrumental rationality when coaching her to be provocative in order to be seen and attract followers to her social media platforms. The constituents did not seem to use social media much at all, at least not for communicating with politicians. And then there is the actual use by liberal politicians to build and maintain a party political network and to manage their image within this network.

So what happened to Nina after the elections? She was not immediately re-elected by the Värmland voters, but eventually she got to keep her seat in the Parliament due to a so-called adjustment mandate (my translation; utjämningsmandat) that was awarded the Liberal Party in the Värmland constituency. After the elections she also promoted to the Liberal's Party Secretary, maybe because of her strong position the Liberal Party political network.

ACKNOWLEDGMENT

This chapter comes out of a research project where Karlstad University cooperated with communication agency Hello Clarice and Nina Larsson. The project has been supported from the Wahlgrenska Foundation and the Lars Hierta Memorial Foundation. Some empirical data has been used from David Kvicklund and David Samuelsson's essay for Bachelor's degree that under the supervision of the author.

REFERENCES

Altheide, D. (2004). Media Logic and Political Communication. *Political Communication, 21*(3), 293–296. doi:10.1080/10584600490481307

Anduiza, E. (2009). The internet, election campaigns and citizens: state of affairs. *Quaderns del CAC*, *33*, 5–12.

Bauman, Z. (2001). *The Individualized Society*. Cambridge, MA: Polity Press.

Beck, U. (1998). *Risksamhället: På väg in i en annan modernitet (Risk Society. Towards a New Modernity)*. Göteborg: Daidalos.

Berg, M. (2011). Netnografi (Nethnography). In G. Ahrne & P. Svensson (Eds.), *Handbok i kvalitativa metoder* (pp. 118–130). Malmö: Liber.

Bimber, B. A., & Davis, R. (2003). *Campaigning online: The Internet in U.S. elections*. New York: Oxford University Press.

Brennan, G., & Lomasky, L. E. (1993). *Democracy and Decision: The Pure Theory of Electoral Preference*. Cambridge, UK: Cambridge University Press. doi:10.1017/CBO9781139173544

Calenda, D., & Mosca, L. (2007). Youth online: researching the political use of the internet in the Italian context. In B. D. Loader (Ed.), *Young Citizens in the Digital Age: Political Engagement, Young People and New Media* (pp. 82–96). London: Routledge.

Castells, M. (2001). *The Internet Galaxy: Reflections on the Internet, Business and Society*. Oxford, UK: Oxford University Press. doi:10.1007/978-3-322-89613-1

Coleman, S., & Blumler, J. G. (2009). *The Internet and Democratic Citizenship: Theory Practice and Policy*. New York: Cambridge University Press. doi:10.1017/CBO9780511818271

Costa, P. O. (2009). Barack Obama's use of the Internet is transforming political communication. *Quaderns del CAC*, *33*, 35–41.

Dahlgren, P. (2009). *Media and Political Engagement*. New York: Cambridge University Press.

Dahlgren, P., & Olsson, T. (2007). Young activists, political horizons and the Internet: adapting the net to one's purposes. In B. D. Loader (Ed.), *Young Citizens in the Digital Age: Political Engagement, Young People and New Media* (pp. 68–81). London: Routledge.

Dimitrova, D. V., Shehata, A., Strömbäck, J., & Nord, L. (2011). The Effects of Digital Media on Political Knowledge and Participation in Election Campaigns: Evidence from panel data. *Communication Research*. Retrieved from http://crx.sagepub.com/content/early/2011/11/02/0093650211426004.abstract

Donath, J., & boyd, d. (2004). Public displays of connection. *BT Technology Journal*, *22*(4), 71–82. doi:10.1023/B:BTTJ.0000047585.06264.cc

Dryzek, J. (2000). *Deliberative Democracy and Beyond: Liberals, Critics, Contestations*. Oxford, UK: Oxford University Press.

Ellison, N., & boyd, d. (2007). Social Network Sites: Definition, History and Scholarship. *Journal of Computer-Mediated Communication*, *13*(1), 210–230. doi:10.1111/j.1083-6101.2007.00393.x

Engelen, B. (2006). Solving the Paradox: The Expressive Rationality of the Decision to Vote. *Rationality and Society*, *18*(3), 419–441. doi:10.1177/1043463106066382

Fenton, N. (2010). Re-imagining Democracy: New Media, Young People, Participation and Politics. In P. Dahlgren & T. Olsson (Eds.), *Young People ICTs and Democracy: Theories, Policies, Identities and Websites* (pp. 19–34). Göteborg: Nordicom.

Fishkin, J. S. (1991). *Democracy and Deliberation: New Directions for Democratic Reform*. New Haven, CT: Yale University Press.

Foot, K., & Schneider, S. M. (2006). *Web campaigning*. Cambridge, MA: MIT Press.

Gerring, J. (2007). *Case Study Research: Principles and Practices*. Cambridge, UK: Cambridge University Press.

Gibson, R. K., Lusoli, W., & Ward, S. (2008). Nationalizing and normalizing the local? A comparative analysis of online candidate campaigning in Australia and Britain. *Journal of Information Technology & Politics*, *4*(4), 15–30. doi:10.1080/19331680801979070

Giddens, A. (1991). *Modernity and Self-Identity: Self and Society in the Late Modern Age*. Cambridge, MA: Polity Press.

Golbeck, J., Grimes, J. M., & Rogers, A. (2010). Twitter use by the US Congress. *Journal of the American Society for Information Science and Technology*, *61*(8), 1612–1621.

Grusell, M., & Nord, L. (2011). *Twitter: Small talk, huge impact?* Paper presented at IAMCR. Istanbul, Turkey.

Gulati, G. (2004). Members of Congress and Presentation of Self on the World Wide Web. *The Harvard International Journal of Press/Politics*, *9*(1), 22–40. doi:10.1177/1081180X03259758

Gustafsson, N. (2012). The Subtle Nature of Facebook Politics: Swedish Social Network Site Users and Political Participation. *New Media Society*. Retrieved from http://nms.sagepub.com/content/14/7/1111.short

Habermas, J. (1996). *Kommunikativt handlande: Texter om språk, rationalitet och samhälle* (2nd ed.). Göteborg: Daidalos.

Hjarvard, S. (2008). The mediatization of society: A theory of the Media as Agents of Social and Cultural Change. *Nordicom Review*, *29*(2), 105–134.

Jackson, N., & Lilleker, D. (2009). MPs and E-representation: Me, MySpace and I. *British Politics*, *4*(2), 236–264. doi:10.1057/bp.2009.2

Jackson, N., & Lilleker, D. (2011). Microblogging, Constituency Service and Impression Management: UK MPs and the Use of Twitter. *Journal of Legislative Studies*, *17*(1), 86–105. doi:10.1080/13572334.2011.545181

Karlsson, M., Clerwall, C., & Buskqvist, U. (2012). *Digital Political Public Relations and Relationship Management, The Swedish Case*. Paper presented at the 62nd ICA Conference. Phoenix, AZ.

Kepplinger, H. M. (2002). Mediatization of Politics: Theory and data. *The Journal of Communication*, *52*(4), 972–986. doi:10.1111/j.1460-2466.2002.tb02584.x

Kies, R. (2010). *Promises and Limits of Web-deliberations*. New York: Palgrave MacMillan. doi:10.1057/9780230106376

Kozinets, R. V. (2011). *Netnografi (Nethnography)*. Lund: Studentlitteratur.

Kvicklund, D., & Samuelsson, D. (2010). *Nina på Nätet. En Netnografisk Studie av Politisk Kommunikation i de sociala medierna (Nina on the Net. A Nethnographic Study of Political Communication in Social Media). Unpublished essay for Bachelor Degree*. Karlstad, Sweden: Karlstad University.

Larsson, A. O. (2011). Extended infomercials or Politics 2.0? A study of Swedish political party Web sites before, during and after the 2010 election. *First Monday*, *16*(4). doi:10.5210/fm.v16i4.3456

Larsson, A. O., & Moe, H. (2011). Studying Political Microblogging: Twitter Users in the 2010 Swedish Election Campaign. *New Media Society*. Retrieved from http://nms.sagepub.com/content/14/5/729.short

Lasch, C. (1991). *The Culture of Narcissism: American Life in an Age of Diminishing Expectations*. New York: W. W. Norton and Company.

Loader, B. D. (2007). Introduction: young citizens in the digital age: dissaffected or displaced? In B. D. Loader (Ed.), *Young Citizens in the Digital Age: Political Engagement, Young People and New Media* (pp. 1–18). London: Routledge.

Miller, V. (2008). New Media, Networking and Phatic Culture. *Convergence: The International Journal of Research into New Media Technologies*, *14*(4), 387–400.

Montero, M. D. (2009). Political e-mobilisation and participation in the election campaigns of Ségolène Royal (2007) and Barack Obama (2008). *Quaderns del CAC*, *33*, 27–34.

Nordicom. (2011). *Internetbarometer 2010* (Internet Barometer 2010). MedieNotiser. Göteborgs Universitet 2: 2010, Göteborg: Nordicom.

Schweitzer, E. J. (2010). *Mediatized Politics on the Internet: Evidence from a Multi-Level Analysis of German Online Campaigns in State, National, and European Parliamentary Elections*. Paper presented at the 3rd European Communication Conference of the European Communication Research and Education association (ECREA). Hamburg, Germany.

Sey, A., & Castells, M. (2004). From media politics to networked politics: the Internet and the Political Process. In M. Castells (Ed.), *The Network Society: A Cross-Cultural Perspective* (pp. 363–381). Cheltenham, UK: Edward Elgar Publishing. doi:10.4337/9781845421663.00030

Stanyer, J. (2008). Elected Representatives, Online Self-preservation and the Personal Vote: Party, Personality and Webstyles in the United States and the United Kingdom. *Information Communication and Society*, *11*(30), 414–432. doi:10.1080/13691180802025681

Stokes, G. (2005). *Critical Theories of Deliberative Democracy and the Problem of Citizenship*. Paper presented at the Institute for Citizenship and Globalisation seminar. Burwood, Australia.

Street, J. (1997). Remote Control? Politics, Technology and Electronic Democracy. *European Journal of Communication*, *12*(1), 27–42. doi:10.1177/0267323197012001003

Svensson, J. (2008). *Kommunikation, medborgarskap och deltagardemokrati: En studie av medborga-rutskotten i Helsingborg*. Lund: Lund Studies in Media and Communication 10.

Svensson, J. (2011). The Expressive Turn of Citizenship Digital Late Modernity. *JeDem – eJournal of eDemocracy, 3*(1), 42-56.

Thompson, J. B. (2001). *Medierna och Moderniteten. (Media and Modernity)*. Göteborg: Daidalos.

Vromen, A. (2007). Australian young people's participatory practices and internet use. In B. D. Loader (Ed.), *Young Citizens in the Digital Age: Political Engagement, Young People and New Media* (pp. 97–113). London: Routledge.

Zafiropoulos, K., & Vrana, V. (2009). The impact of political events on blog conversational patterns: two cases from Greece. *Quaderns del CAC, 33*, 77–85.

KEY TERMS AND DEFINITIONS

Communicative Rationality: To establish loci for the electorate in election campaigning.

Deliberations: Communicative rational conversations.

Expressive Rationality: To negotiate a political image in front of voters during election campaigning.

Image-Management: Selective disclosure by politicians about their private lives on different media platforms to convey the image of them as ordinary and likeable people.

Individualization: The experience of increased personal autonomy and expressions of this experience.

Instrumental Rationality: To strategically target specific voter groups during election campaigning.

Social Media: Media that users are able to participate in by creating new media content.

This research was previously published in Political Campaigning in the Information Age edited by Ashu M. G. Solo, pages 51-65, copyright year 2014 by Information Science Reference (an imprint of IGI Global).

Chapter 72

The Use of Social Media and Online Petitions to Achieve Collective Change for a Sustainable Future

Vannie Naidoo
University of KwaZulu-Natal, South Africa

ABSTRACT

Scandals of corruption in government and mismanagement in business and government departments has made us rethink of what the world is becoming and what should be done to steer it on the right track. Brilliant policy and law makers have tried to put in place laws and governing statutes that can assist in ethically governing businesses and governments so that they can sustain themselves and maintain a healthy respectful and transparent relationship with all their stakeholders and communities. The failure by certain governments and businesses to adhere to policy, statutes and laws has frustrated good people and their only podium left standing is social media and online petitions. On websites worldwide communities are getting together to discuss and defame businesses and governments that are perpetuating unethical behaviour. This has changed the face of marketing as marketers and the public relations departments are in change of maintain and promoting a company or governments image. The face of marketing has changed as social media has introduced itself into the mix.

INTRODUCTION

Waste and water pollution, depletion of the ozone layer and global warming affects everyone on the planet. Responsible and sustainable business practices are the only way for society to sustain itself. Business and governments have a responsibility to maintain good ethical conduct and maintain good business practice with the stakeholders and communities they do business with. It is no longer about limiting one's carbon foot print or showing solidarity towards democracy within society. Many corporates are

DOI: 10.4018/978-1-5225-5637-4.ch072

involved in shocking ethical misconduct yet they hide behind cleverly manipulated public relations and marketing campaigns that portray them as pillars of corporate society.

Corporate Social Responsibility should be the cornerstone of business practice worldwide. In order for a company to be a well-respected or good corporate citizen in the business world it needs to be socially responsible and ethical in its business practice. People in society want assurance by business and government that they will comply with the laws and regulations to maintain and sustain resources and prescribe to a body of conduct that is honest and instils confidence in society. Marketing has changed in this contemporary era. A marketer now has the responsibility to ensure their company or organisation is producing and selling products/ services that are safe, value for money and not harming the community or environment. Communities who fail to be heard by irresponsible businesses and governments are now using social media to champion their cause and be heard. Social media is a powerful tool that has grown in awareness in the business and social communities worldwide. Social media has changed the manner in which businesses and governments interact with their target audiences, distributors, suppliers, employees and communities.

In this age where resources are scarce, businesses and governments need to keep abreast of their ethical and social obligation to their customers and communities in which they reside in. Businesses and governments have an obligation to the public they serve or the services or goods they provide. The main theme in this chapter is to highlight how social media can serve as an excellent way to bring online communities together to name and shame organisations that are socially irresponsible, unethical or unsustainable.

This chapter will explore the following key themes:

1. Background into social advocacy
2. What is social media?
3. Online petitioning
4. Various theorists views on social media
5. Irresponsible behaviour by businesses
6. Cultural jamming a new concept to be taken seriously in marketing
7. A way Forward: The use of social media and online petitions to name and shame irresponsible governments and businesses.
8. Direction for future research

The chapter will start with providing a background into social advocacy and linking it to social media and online petitioning of big businesses who are corrupt and are perpetuating unethical behaviour.

Background Into Social Advocacy

Activists are now using social media and on-line petitioning to gather much needed support to change the way big businesses and governments are doing things. They want to make a difference by creating awareness of the unethical practices and corruption perpetuated by big business and governments. Baron (2003) argues that through boycotts, protests, and civil suits, activists can force firms to comply with their demands or make a change to how businesses are conducting themselves. Davis, McAdam, Scott & Zald (2005) adds that neoinstitutional theorists are increasingly treating social movements as motors of institutional change.

Big businesses have an obligation to the public and its consumers. They need to take into account their behaviour before they fixate on profit margins. Research indicates that many customers in the world prefer not to purchase products from big businesses that destroy the rain forest, pollute the natural habit of animals and the environment at large and exploit poor workers. The following authors Crossley (2002); Raeburn (2004) and Schurman (2004) argue that the targeting of Nestlé, Chevron, and The Home Depot for environmental degradation, to animal rights protests against Procter & Gamble and General Motors, to the battle between gay rights proponents and opponents for sway over Disney and AT&T, activists have made corporate change a key part of broader social change agendas. While activists continue to target states and international organizations, "naming and shaming" corporations has become a signature piece in many social movement repertoires.

According to research, 30% of U.S. consumers claimed to have avoided purchasing products made by companies that pollute the environment (Cambridge Reports, 1989) and over 65% asserted that they would pay more for products that protect the environment (Pew Research Center,2003). Consumers according to surveys conducted in U.S have indicated that they would pay more in order to deter sweet-shop labour practices. According to PIPA (1999) surveys reported that consumers indicated even higher "willingness to pay" for "sweat-free" garments, with 76% of respondents in one survey asserting they would pay 25% more for a $20 garment if it were certified not to be made in a sweatshop). Respondents in another survey claiming they would pay 28% more on a $10 item and 15% more on a $100 item if they were not made in sweetshops (Elliott & Freeman, 2000).

O'Rourke (2005) argues that NGOs usually begin their campaigns by conducting an exposé on a leading firm. Campaigns are framed to challenge or undermine a company's brand reputation, targeting how it sells itself, and raising questions or highlighting hypocrisies within the brand (e.g., Nike empowering women consumers but exploiting women workers, Dell trumpeting a recycling program that turned out to involve prison labor, etc.). The media is key to these information campaigns and brand attacks. According to Sen, Gurhan-Canli & Morwitz (2001) evidence does indicate that information on firm practices and product impacts can sway consumers. Co-operative Bank (2003) added that consumers used the disclosure of negative information to help screen out and avoid socially or environmentally irresponsible companies. It is quite common now for consumers to boycott bad companies. In the UK, over 50% of respondents in a poll claimed they had punished a firm by boycotting it in the last year. Vogel (2005) argued that the "market for virtue" among individual consumers is slight but that shareholder responses to naming and shaming campaigns have sometimes proven powerful. King and Soule (2007) also indicated in their study that protest activity sends signals to shareholders regarding future market trends, stakeholder discontent or new costs for the firm.

Khondker (2011) argues that the most famous of politically-fuelled examples of online activism involved a wave of riots and demonstrations during the Arab Spring, where social media were used to organise action despite state attempts to censor the Internet. Activists can now use technology like social media and on-line petitioning to reach a broader audience in their plight to make a difference and sustain the world as we know it. According to Shellenberger (2003) NGO market campaigns first identify a specific problem that resonates with consumers (e.g., shoes made with child labor, phonebooks made out of old-growth forests, computers made with toxic chemicals) and then connect these to larger issues (e.g., labor rights, sustainable forest management, toxic use reduction). NGOs then work strategically to frame these problems in a way that supports the consumers understanding and action and places responsibility on specific corporations. Successful NGOs strategically reframe existing problems to present both specific culprits and consumer alternatives.

Since social media is relatively new in marketing the next section in this chapter will un-wrap the concept of what social media is all about.

What Is Social Media?

There are various definitions and views on social media. The definitions of social media provided by different authors contain some similarities yet each definition has a unique approach to explaining this technology. To the marketer, social media offers a different approach to traditional marketing. The marketer in today's world should understand that social media provides a platform for his business. If used correctly, social media can assist the marketer to create long lasting relationships with its consumers. Taken a step further the social media can assist marketers in getting to know how consumers feel about their product, service and brand.

The social media are electronic tools that enable communication between people in which they exchange knowledge, experience and information in virtual networks. They allow people to source and share information as well as to promote existing and new products effectively. This new technology makes it easy to convey text, photos, audio, video and information between internet users, (Thackeray *et al*, 2008).

Social media is "a group of internet based applications that builds on the ideological and technological foundations of Web 2.0, and it allows the creation and exchange of user-generated content" (Kaplan & Haenlein,2010).

Shettleworth (2010) mentioned that applications like social media networks permits operators to create individual web sites available and that are easily reached for conversation of individual content and message. Social media can be considered as stages, online applications and broadcasting which purpose is to enable, simplify and assist communications and interfaces to share information.

Dewing (2012) indicates that social media refers to the wide range of Internet-based and mobile services that allow users to participate in online exchanges, contribute user-created content, or join online communities".

Xie and Stevenson (2013) argues that "Social media is a means of communication through the internet that enables social interaction".

Social media is defined by Salt (2011) "as a services, tools and platforms such as Twitter, Facebook, LinkedIn and others that allow users to share information with each other".

After looking at the various definitions of social media and what it means to different theorists, the next section will elaborate on on-line petition.

On-Line Petitioning

Much of the activist space today is dominated by online petitioning. An on-line petition is a petition that is signed online on a website. Another name for an on-line petition is an e-petition. People who are in support of such petitions add their names online so that they can make a difference to society.

Romano (2010) indicates that the rise in the use of social network platforms has produced a new breed of citizen or deliberative journalism, which puts the power to disseminate ideas, and to champion causes, in the hands of the public. Stassen (2010) adds that online social networks support the democratisation of knowledge sharing because they are about listening to the ideas of others and offering a response.

Looking specifically at the motivations behind online protest action, Yang (2009) outlines social activism as that which is concerned with corruption, the environment, and human rights.

Briassoulis (2010) argues that "Online petitions cover all conceivable matters of interest, from the global to the local to the individual level. They are created and promoted by specialized international groups and online communities, professional or occupational organizations, special interest groups and individuals. Most petitions include some text that presents the issue at stake and the associated request for resolution. Depending on the author(s) of the petition, these texts may be very informative, offering historical documentation and facts, explanations of the issue and justification for the cause of the petition. Supporting material may be provided such as videos, photographs or important documents"

Online activism has close ties with online petitioning. According to Yang (2009) Online activism is a new form of popular contention in that is spreading worldwide. In some cases, the Internet serves to mobilize street protest. More often, protest takes place online. The most common forms include online petitions, the hosting of campaign websites, and large-scale verbal protests. The most radical is perhaps the hacking of websites. These forms of contention may be found in blogs, Internet bulletin boards, online communities, and podcast and YouTube-type web sites.

After discussing online petition, in the next section various views by different theorists on social media will be put forward and discussed. This will help to further contextual the area of social media.

Various Theorists' Views on Social Media

Perceptions by different theorists on social media are often varied. This has created a debate as some theorists advocate strongly for business's and governments' to actively use social media in the marketing and promoting of their organisations whilst other theorists believe that social media can lead to the ultimate downfall of a business or government.

If we have to look at what has occurred in industry. Companies have used social networks to support car launches for example. Chevy and Dodge were among the first to use Facebook and Twitter in their marketing objectives. Employees and target members are often used in social network campaigns. Companies are avoiding social sites and are inserting a social component to their own site. Companies have incorporated Twitter and Facebook as a means of direct interaction with their customers, these networking environments have been chosen due to their high success rate (Blakeman, 2013).

Web strategist Jordan Raynor (2013) is reported to have said "it has never been easier to be as influential as you can be today. Information is cheap. Information is easier to produce, and if you have a quality message, it's never been cheaper to get out." This surely explains the growing phenomena of social media. Through the social networking site of Twitter, 64% of its users are more likely to purchase a product from a brand they follow online, whilst Facebook users spend an average of 405 minutes per month communicating and interacting with friends and following their favourite brands, services, outlets, sport personalities, etc (Zeevi, 2013). Vinerean, Cetina, Dumitrescu & Tichindelean1 (2013) argues that in particular, peer communication through social media, a new form of consumer socialization, has profound impacts on consumer decision making and thus marketing strategies.

According to Edosomwan, Prakasan, Kouame, Watson & Seymour (2011), social media is best for the following situations:

- Promoting open communication between employees and management.
- Enabling employees to share project ideas and work in teams effectively, which helps in sharing knowledge and experiences.

- Social media also promotes better content, such as webcast and videos, than just simple text.
- Helps to communicate collaboratively between current and potential customers, in receiving feedback, product definition, product development, or any forms of customer service and support.
- Encouraging members, or part of the company's employees, to become members of a well-recognized community.
- Social media becomes a good venue for discussions and becomes a classic goal of marketing and communications, but the companies must ensure that the employees are adhering to the rules and etiquettes of social media.

Edosomwan, Prakasan, Kouame, Watson & Seymour (2011) added that many social networking sites were created in the 1990s. Some examples included Six Degrees, BlackPlanet, Asian Avenue, and MoveOn. These were, or have been, online niche social sites where people could interact, including sites for public policy advocacy and a social network based on a web of contacts model. In addition, blogging services such as Blogger and Epinions were created.

Edosomwan, Prakasan, Kouame, Watson & Seymour (2011) further added that Facebook was a social networking website launched in February 2004. In January 2009, Facebook was ranked as the most used social network worldwide. Facebook network is on the rise on a daily basis. According to Stone (2007) Facebook is also the top social network across eight individual markets in Asia—the Philippines, Australia, Indonesia, Malaysia, Singapore, New Zealand, Hong Kong and Vietnam.

Social media in marketing is a new contemporary issue being explored by theorists.

Since Facebook is so popular worldwide, the discussion below will highlight how it ties in with marketing.

Ramsaran-Fowdar & Fowdar (2013) has indicated that popular Facebook tools via which marketing objectives can be achieved are:

- **Facebook Profile:** A strong profile of the organization can be established on Facebook with its vision and mission statement stated and clearly defined.
- **Facebook Groups:** The following are the most important aspects that can be used to attract consumers: the name of the group, the group topic and image of the group.
- **Business/Fan Pages:** Fans will receive updates from the company as new information is posted. The organization can regularly post information on the business/fan page on upcoming events, articles, games, blogs, podcasts, videos and links.
- **Sharing Events:** The organization can advertise its upcoming events on Facebook.
- **Social Ads and Polls:** Social ads can be placed on Facebook according to the age, sex, location, workplaces and education level of the users. Polls can also be organized on Facebook to obtain valuable feedback from users.
- **Facebook Messages:** Can be tailored and sent to individual users.

It is interesting to note that despite its popularity social media cannot replace traditional communication methods. Carter (2012) argues that social media will not replace traditional communication methods such as print media (newspaper, magazine,), broadcast (radio and television), but believes that social media is intended to complement by creating long term relationship with current and potential customers.

It is important for marketers to bear in mind the disadvantages associated with social media. Negative feedback can be expressed and generated on-line by customers via social media. Customers here can express their disregard for the company's poor ethics or complain about its poor quality product, service or brand. Sandilands (2014) argues that unless a company has someone in charge to check their social media accounts several times a day, dissatisfied consumers can publish comments which may not always be removable. The social media application of Twitter is a public platform and companies have no control over what people say, thereon bad news can get viral as easily as good news can, doing the business irrevocable harm.

Marketers have to understand that social media can be very problematic if not understood and handled properly within the company. Sandilands (2014) also added that in June 2010, the IT governance group and Control Association released a report which revealed that brand high jacking, lack of control over content, viruses, unrealistic consumer expectation and non- compliance with record management was listed as the top five threats associated with social media that marketers need to be aware of.

Szabo and Barefoot (2010) indicated that if a company's product or service experiences negative publicity it is not wise to use social media as a tool to change that negative publicity. A good example is what happened to BP. In 2010 BP had an oil spill in the Gulf Mexico and its public relations department tried to use social media to fix its image and do damage control. This was a disaster and a media nightmare as social media just served to make the whole media debacle more talked about worldwide. The company was very hard hit by this incident. The lesson learnt by BP and other big companies is that they cannot use social media to clean up a major media disaster. Edosomwan, Prakasan, Kouame, Watson & Seymour (2011) argued that the major challenge for social media is that it should be a reliable source for communication as it is not for damage control.

Governments can and have also used social media. However Kamwaria, Kamau, Githaiga, Guantai, Mugwe, Makin & Dida (2015) cautions governments from using social media and argues that "Since social media is relatively accessible and cheaper; it is the best and versatile publicist tool that the government can utilize to engage the public on policy and development issues. However, social media is a double-edge sword; it can build as well as destroy. As such, there is need to exercise caution in its use."

According to Langley & van den Broek (2010) various internet communities have been set up by a range of individuals, social entrepreneurs, NGOs and others to stimulate the sustainable behaviour of individuals and organisations. They range from making individual CO2 footprints more transparent (e.g. MakeMeSustainable and Treemagotchi) to micro funding websites supporting entrepreneurs in third world countries (e.g. Kiva and MicroPlace). Most of these communities are part of a whole new range of internet applications, known as social media applications, in which on-line social communities with a strong bottom-up and user-friendly character play the key role and where the mobilisation (aggregation and syndication) of content generated by users is the main function.

Assaad & Gómez (2011) argues that although Social networks can help companies spread good news fast, it can also spread bad news just as quickly. Moreover, if customers want to vent their anger about your product or service, they can use your social network account. Managers need to understand how to handle those situations quickly and effectively.

After an extensive discussion on social media and how it is contextualised by various theorists the next theme seeks to explore irresponsible behaviour by businesses as activists often use social media to target such businesses.

Irresponsible Behaviour by Businesses

Over the years as watch dog organisations in society have begun to name, shame and penalise big business who have been involved in irresponsible, unethical or corrupt dealings with its various stakeholders, many companies and governments have been brought forward and in some instances charged for their poor, disgraceful and unacceptable business practices. These businesses are named, shamed and penalised because they have been guilty of crimes, corruptions or irresponsible behaviour. If we read the newspaper headline world-wide many companies have been guilty of irresponsible or unethical behaviour in recent years. Under this section irresponsible behaviour by businesses and big companies will be outlined.

In the discussion below various irresponsible and unethical companies scandals are discussed.

Enron was a company that filled the headlines of newspapers in its management's unethical behaviour and corruption scandals that rocked the business world. According to Johnson (2003), he advocated that top officials at Enron abused their power and privileges, manipulated information, engaged in inconsistent treatment of internal and external constituencies, put their own interests above those of their employees and the public, and failed to exercise proper oversight or shoulder responsibility for ethical failings.

Nestlé, maker of Kit Kat, a chocolate know by many South African's as well as Europeans was also involved in a bad scandal a few years ago. Greenpeace (2010) argued that Nestlé used palm oil from companies that were trashing the much threatened Indonesian rainforests. This resulted in threatening the livelihoods of the Indonesian local people and pushing orang-utans towards extinction.

In July 2013, labor groups protested against health and labor violations committed by Dynamic Precision Industry Corp., a Taiwanese adidas supplier with a factory in Guangzhou, China. Incidents of Benzene poisoning, hearing loss, pneumoconiosis, and hand-arm vibration syndrome (HAVS) were reported at the factory (Facing finance, 2013).

The well-known giant Anglo American was also involved in a recent scandal. Anglo American's expansion plans in the Brazilian Amazon endangered its' environment and its'

Indigenous population. The Brazilian government, motivated by the prospect of economic stimulation, had accelerated construction of necessary infrastructure (roads, railways, dams,

etc.) in the Amazon in order to make the area more suitable for mining activities. The government of Brazil had also attempted to amend certain laws to allow mining companies to operate on designated indigenous lands. Despite Anglo American receiving concessions from the federal government, Brazil's environmental regulator in northern Amapa fined Anglo American $10 million following an incident at the company's port terminal that left three people dead and three missing (Facing Finance, 2013).

South African was also rocked by a corporate scandal. In mid-November 2007 Tiger Brands was fined 98.8 million rands (roughly equivalent to US$12,8 million) by the South African Competition Commission for colluding with other bread producers to raise the price of bread by 30c and 35c per loaf (Wikipedia, 2015).

The list below developed by Global exchange (2015) was placed on-line for all the world to see which listed the top 10 corporate criminal companies. They are as follows:

1. Alpha Natural Resourcesfor pollution of rivers, streams, and groundwater; violation of the Clean Water Act; destruction of forest and wildlife habitats; and devastation of Appalachian communities.
2. Felda Global Ventures Violation of basic worker and human rights, withholding worker pay, wage manipulation, insufficient screening of work contractors company that it is affiliated with, and the use of toxic pesticides that are harmful and dangerous to both the environment and people.

3. FIFA for forced evictions from homes and stores, damaging local business, tax evasion, labor abuse, corruption, and violating human rights including: right to adequate housing, right to free movement, right to work, right to protest, and right to labor protection.

4. Gap Inc. for refusal to sign "Accord of Fire and Building Safety in Bangladesh," refusal to compensate victims' families, workers' rights violations, and unsafe building conditions.

5. Koch Industries for thwarting public policy; forcing policies on funded politicians, judges, and organizations; working to destroy minimum wage, unions, and social security; re-segregation of public schools and toxic pollution.

6. McDonald's Corporation for limited (and relatively non-transparent) environmental policies; unethical marketing to children; and lack of willingness to reform worker wages.

7. Nissin Foods Holdings Co., LTD for weakly defined palm oil sourcing practices; compliance in conflict palm oil related human rights and environmental violations and absence of public commitment to protect the environment from unsustainable expansion of palm oil plantations.

8. The Ralph Lauren Corporation for unsustainable sourcing of raw materials in viscose fibers; deforestation; environmental damage; human rights abuses; lack of consumer transparency; increasing CO_2 foot-print and cultural appropriation.

9. TransCanada for plans to construct Keystone XL Pipeline.

10. Vattenfall for destruction of the environment and communities; political manipulation and legal abuse of international treaties.

The discussion above has clearly brought to light the extent of corruption by big businesses. In the discussion that follows the theme to be explored is cultural jamming. Cultural jamming is a concept that has transformed the marketing arena. Cultural jamming and its implications on marketing is another contemporary marketing issues. In the discussion below cultural jamming would be outlined and discussed in great detail.

Cultural Jamming: A New Concept to Be Taken Seriously in Marketing

Cultural jamming is where activists seek to aggressively target businesses that are socially irresponsible or are engaging in unethical behaviour. In cultural jamming the activist/s aims to inform consumers about the reality of a company's intentions. Cultural jamming came about because activists were fed up with big companies that tried to sell the world lies about their image. These companies used the media to portray themselves as socially responsible, honest, transparent and ethical when in fact they were involved in unethical business practices to increase their market share at the risk of communities, the environment and hardworking employees. These companies cared only about profits and did not spare expense to indigenous communities, endangered animals or plant life and rain forest and poor communities who work for them under unsafe labour conditions and for very little basic wages. They disregarded human life and the environment and never once saw the error of their bad ways.

In this new age of technology, activists both human rights and consumer have taken the forefront in using social media to name and shame these unethical greedy corporate giants who have destroyed so much of the world and its natural resources. These activists work timeously to name and shame companies that say one thing and do another in their business practice. These cultural jammers often hijack unethical company's advertisements and change the context of the message. Companies like Nike were targeted as they use slave labour to produce their products. It has been brought to light that the factories used to make Nike shoes have been reported to have very poor health and safety regulations. This was not known to the international community who only saw what Nike let them see, as they were always in the media for engaging in social upliftment programs when in actually fact they were engaged in cost cut backs that lead to the use of slave labour. McDonalds is also under attack by activists who claim that the fast food restaurant is promoting an unhealthy lifestyle of obesity for its customers. Coca-Cola, another well-known international company has been cited by cultural jammers as being only profit motivated. These are but a few examples of companies who have been targeted by activists/ cultural jammers. These activists have used cultural jamming to defame companies by distorting their advertisements.

Harold (2004) argues that culture jamming is usually described as a kind of "glutting" of the system; it is an amping up of contradictory rhetorical messages in an effort to engender a qualitative change. In this sense, jamming need not be seen only as a damming, or a stopping of corporate media. Rather, it may be more useful to consider jamming as an artful proliferation of messages, a rhetorical process of intervention and invention, which challenges the ability of corporate discourses to make meaning in predictable ways.

It is interesting to note that consumers boycotted companies that were unethical or involved in corporate scandals. Becchetti and Rosati (2007) indicated that "the 2003 Corporate Social Responsibility Monitor findings revealed that more consumers looked at social responsibility in their choices of purchases. The results indicated a jump from 36 per cent in 1999 to 62 per cent in 2001 in Europe. Also, more than one in five consumers reported having either rewarded or punished companies based on their perceived social performance and more than a quarter of share-owning Americans took into account ethical considerations when buying and selling stocks. The Social Investment Forum also reported that in the US in 1999, there was more than $2 trillion worth of assets invested in portfolios that used screens linked to the environment and social responsibility."

According to Carducci (2006) to be truly effective as a cultural, media and social practice, it appears that culture jamming must be tied to a larger purpose and not be taken as an end in itself. The most effective tendencies seem to be those that link with broader social concerns about global ecology and human rights. As a result of consumer activism, Nike, to take one example, now offers PVC-free products packaged in recycled boxes and has established a code of ethics for offshore suppliers.

Harold (2004) argues that cultural jamming examples include everything from rewording conversations between popular comic strip characters, to reworking the sign on a storefront, to making subversive collages out of familiar commercial and government images.

After the discussion on cultural jamming the next section would discuss a way forward: the use of social media and on-line petitions that name and shame big businesses.

A Way Forward: The Use of Social Media and Online Petitions to Name and Shame Irresponsible Governments and Businesses

Social media has been used by activists to place online petitions or shame companies that are selling unsafe products or that are engaging in unfair or unethical business practices. Activists have a role to play in educating the public to the wrongs perpetuated by big corporates. Information is now readily available to customers and they have a right to know about the brand or company they support. According to Boulianne (2015) Social media has skyrocketed to popularity in the past few years. The Arab Spring in 2011 as well as the 2008 and 2012 Obama campaigns have fuelled interest in how social media might affect citizens' participation in civic and political life.

Political consumerism has been around for a long time. Political consumerism and its implications on marketing is very important to take note of. de Zúñiga, Copeland & Bimber (2014) have argued that political consumerism is a tool through which people can articulate social or political preference and it can take one of two forms. Firstly, people can avoid (i.e., boycott) specific products or brands to punish companies for undesirable policies or business practices. For example, people may avoid purchasing clothes and accessories made in sweatshops to promote fair labor practices. Secondly, people can purchase products from companies whose production practices or values are consistent with their own (i.e., buycott). For instance, people may purposefully buy organic fruits and vegetables because organic farms do not produce pesticide runoff that harms soil and water. The use of purchasing power to express political preferences is not new, but it is only recently that researchers have attended to consumerism.

According to Bartley and Child (2014) Wal-Mart was an early and frequent target, beginning with an exposé of child labor in its suppliers in Bangladesh, which aired on NBC's *Dateline* in early 1993. The campaign to get Wal- Mart (and to a lesser extent, Sears and Kmart) to end the employment of children, and a threatened boycott of apparel from Bangladesh, raised public awareness in the United States. Armbruster-Sandoval (2005) adds that campaigns focused on Central American factories did link local organizing with pressure on companies like The Gap, Kohl's, and Phillips-Van Heusen (PVH). UNITE, Guatemalan Unions, and international unions cooperated to build a solidarity campaign to support unionization of a PVH factory. Bartley and Child (2014) indicated that this led to demonstrations targeting PVH, as well as JC Penney, which sold many PVH goods.

Consumer activism can be seen on-line in social media across the world. Taki and Coretti (2013) posits that through the spread of information online, internet activists were able to establish networks of resistance within Egyptian political society. And, despite the relative weakness of the ties between members of these networks, it still emerged as an effective tool to facilitate collective action. Perpetual connectivity of activists enabled them to have access to an infinite number of networks of trust and multiply the impact of social protest through the creation of an insurgent community. Internet activism made political action easier, faster and more universal in Egypt.

Environmental activists such as Green peace are actively using social media to name and shame big business. They are an NGO that believes the world is worth sustaining for generations to come and companies need to be part of this or they should be taken to task for their poor business practice that can lead to the destruction of our world. Greenpeace and Friends of the Earth are two NGO's that have used social media to get their message across borders. Their message is simple the world is in trouble and it is up to all of us in the world to saved it. The hole in the Ozone layer, the devastation of the rainforests in the Amazon, the indigenous tribes of the different countries in the world, the animals, the plants and trees and the bird and insect life are humanities responsibility. They must be saved at all cost to sustain the world.

The examples below are of companies that are named and shamed by Greenpeace because they are unethical and are involved in the destruction of communities. Facing Finance (2013) indicated that a 2012 Greenpeace report accused Adidas, along with several other big garment industry names, of contaminating water systems through chemical residues left on clothing sold to consumers worldwide, even in areas where chemical use was restricted. Greenpeace appealed to the adidas Group again in a more recent report for condoning the PT Gistex Group's repeated contamination of the Citarum River in West Java, Indonesia. The region hosts several clothing factories that dye, print, and finish polyester fabrics.

While adidas admits to having business ties to the factory, the company refused to reveal the extent of those ties. The factory, like many others in the region, uses the river as a dumping ground for waste.

Facing Finance (2013) posits that several of Gazprom's gas and oil projects are criticized for having serious ecological and social impacts. For example, Greenpeace and other organizations have criticized Gazprom's risky oil drilling activities in the Arctic Sea. The use of fossil fuel energy exacerbates the melting of arctic ice. Less ice makes it easier for oil and energy companies like Gazprom to operate and exploit the area's resources. Greenpeace asserts that Gazprom endangers the region's marine ecosystem because it is not prepared to handle a potential spill in such an extreme climate region. Greenpeace recently carried out several protests hoping to raise awareness for the issue of arctic drilling and to prevent Gazprom from drilling in the area.

Facing Finance (2013) Jindal a UN Global Compact participant, meaning that the company has committed to supporting, respecting, and protecting internationally proclaimed human rights. Jindal is widely criticized in Mozambique for partaking in human rights violations, environmental destruction, and corruption. In the Tete province of North-western Mozambique, Jindal Mozambique Minerals operates the Chirodzi Coal Project. Jindal is one of only three companies with mining rights in the coal-rich Moatize region located in the Tete Province. Since its arrival in the country, Jindal has been responsible for violating community rights, damaging the environment through open-pit mining, and abusing Mozambican workers. Over 2,500 people still reside near the Chirodzi Coal Project's open-pit mine. Despite the company's promise to resettle communities before mining commenced, resettlement has not taken place. Further, the communities did not receive any form of compensation or substitute land for their sacrifices. Jindal continues to extract coal from land that is vital to the survival of residents and their families. The food insecurity that has resulted from Jindal's operations makes people vulnerable to poverty and hunger.

Environmental, labor, religious and GLBT activists have waged campaigns to "name and shame" and otherwise pressure numerous firms in the United States and Europe. Firms have responded with a dizzying array of codes of conduct, "corporate social responsibility" policies and certification and labeling schemes. Among social scientists, scholars of strategy are increasingly portraying activism as a game-changing challenge for firms (Baron & Diermeier, 2007; Lenox & Eesley, 2009). The world as we know it is changing and technology can help the people of the world in their fight to sustain it.

The might of social media has grown. It is a platform that can be used by social activist to get their message across about greedy and unethical businesses. The people of the world need to be aware of the companies they buy products from. As a marketer in the new millennium it is important to understand that a good corporate image and being a social responsibility company go hand in hand in sustaining the business in the long term.

DIRECTION FOR FUTURE RESEARCH

Social media and online petitioning is an important contemporary issue in marketing. If used properly NGO's can develop marketing campaigns to expose corrupt businesses on social media. Future research needs to be done in areas that explore social media and online petitioning and its impact on big business. The impact of social movements on corporate social responsibility is another interesting area for future research since social movements can cause consumers to boycotts products that can result in affecting stock market returns.

Online petitioning of governments and its implications on sustainable can also be researched. Other areas like online petitioning of child advertising and its implications to marketers also bear future research investigation. Lastly, online petitioning on unethical business practices can be another area for future research to be explored.

CONCLUSION

Social and consumer activists have changed the landscape of marketing as activists are now using Facebook and other social media platforms to name and shame companies and large corporations that are unethical or adopting socially irresponsible business tactics. Protests can come in the form of boycotts, public demonstrations, "naming & shaming" on social media, protest tactics and forms of cultural jamming. Activists have a right to help protect the planet against big companies that want to destroy it for the sake of larger profit margins. Customers have a right to know the companies they buy from or the brands they use. In the past, big businesses hid behind their advertisements and the public was not privy to their business ethic or their social irresponsibility. Now with information being so freely available the veil has dropped on corrupt, greedy and unethical businesses do anything to increase their market share at the expense of good values or the sustainability of our world. The social media is a platform that can be used by human and consumer activists to bring about social change. The main advantage of using social media is that it offers activists a fast easy and cheap way to spread their message to millions of people worldwide. At the end of the day it is about bringing about social change.

This research was previously published in Collective Creativity for Responsible and Sustainable Business Practice edited by Ziska Fields, pages 261-277, copyright year 2017 by Business Science Reference (an imprint of IGI Global).

REFERENCES

Aronczyk, M. (2013). Market(ing) Activism: Lush Cosmetics, Ethical Oil, and the Self-Mediation of Protest. *Journal Media Studies,*1-22. Available at: www.cf.ac.uk/jomecjournal

Assaad, W., & Gómez, J. M. (2011). Social Network in marketing (Social Media Marketing) Opportunities and Risks. *International Journal of Managing Public Sector Information and Communication Technologies, 2*(1), 13–22.

Baron, D. P. (2003). Private Politics. *Journal of Economics & Management Strategy, 12*(1), 31–66. doi:10.1162/105864003321220724

Becchetti, L., & Rosati, F. C. (2007). Global Social Preferences and the Demand for Socially Responsible Products: Empirical Evidence from a Pilot Study on Fair Trade Consumers. *World Economy, 1*(1), 807–836. doi:10.1111/j.1467-9701.2007.01012.x

Bennett, W. L. (2008). *Civic Life Online Learning How Digital Media Can Engage Youth.* London: Mitt Press.

Blakeman, R. (2013). *Nontraditional Media in Marketing and Advertising*. SAGE Publications.

Boulianne, S. (2015). Social media use and participation: A meta-analysis of current research. *Information Communication and Society*, *18*(5), 524–538. doi:10.1080/1369118X.2015.1008542

Brennan, L., & Binney, W. (2010). Fear, guilt and shame appeals in social marketing. *Journal of Business Research*, *63*(2), 140–146. doi:10.1016/j.jbusres.2009.02.006

Briassoulis, H. (2010). Online petitions: New tools of secondary analysis? *Qualitative Research*, *10*(6), 715–727. doi:10.1177/1468794110380530

Cambridge Reports. (1989). *National omnibus survey*. Storrs, CT: Roper Center for Public Opinion Research, University of Connecticut. July.

Carducci, V. (2006). Culture Jamming A Sociological Perspective. *Journal of Consumer Culture*, *6*(1), 116–138. doi:10.1177/1469540506062722

Carter, B. (2012). *The like economy: How businesses make money with facebook* (1st ed.). Indianapolis, IN: Que Publishing.

Co-Operative Bank. (2003). *The ethical consumer report*. London: Co-Operative Bank.

Crossley, N. (2002). Global Anti-corporate Struggle: A Preliminary Analysis. *The British Journal of Sociology*, *53*(4), 667–691. doi:10.1080/0007131022000021542 PMID:12556289

D'Amato, A., Henderson, S., & Florence, S. (2009). *Corporate Social responsibility and sustainable business a guide to leadership tasks and functions*. Center for Creative Leadership.

Davis, G., McAdam, D., Scott, W. R., & Zald, M. (2005). *Social Movements and Organization Theory*. London: Cambridge University Press. doi:10.1017/CBO9780511791000

de Zúñiga, H. G., Copeland, L., & Bimber, B. (2014). Political consumerism: Civic engagement and the social media connection. *New Media & Society*, *16*(3), 488–506. doi:10.1177/1461444813487960

Dewing, M. (2012). *Social Media: An introduction*. Library of Parliament.

Edosomwan, S., Prakasan, S. K., Kouame, D., Watson, J., & Seymour, T. (2011). The History of Social Media and its Impact on Business. *The Journal of Applied Management and Entrepreneurship*, *16*(3), 1–13.

Elliott, K., & Freeman, R. (2000). *White hats or Don Quixotes? Human rights vigilantes in the global economy*. Cambridge, MA: NBER.

Erdogmus, E. I., & Cicek, M. (2012). The Impact of Social Media Marketing on brand loyalty. *Journal of Procedial Social and Behavioral Sciences*, *58*(2), 1353–1360. doi:10.1016/j.sbspro.2012.09.1119

Europeana Creative Cultural Jam. (2015). Available at: https://www.google.co.za/search?q=examples+of+cultural+jamming&biw=974&bih=734&tbm=isch&tbo=u&source=univ&sa=X&sqi=2&ved=0ahUKEwig7t-wns_KAhWBQhQKHY7lDIAQsAQIOQ&dpr=1.25

Facing Finance. (2013). *Dirty Profits II: A Research Paper Prepared for Facing Finance*. Amsterdam: Facing Finance Organisation.

Globalexchange.org. (2015). Available from: http://www.globalexchange.org/corporateHRviolators

Greenpeace.org. (2010). Available from: http://www.greenpeace.org/international/en/campaigns/climate-change/kitkat/

Harold, C. (2004, September). Pranking Rhetoric: "Culture Jamming" as Media Activism. *Critical Studies in Media Communication, 21*(3), 189–211. doi:10.1080/0739318042000212693

Johnson, C. (2003). Enron's ethical collapse: Lessons for leadership educators. *Journal of Leadership Education, 2*(1), 45-56.

Kamwaria, A. N., Kamau, J. M., Githaiga, A. J., Guantai, P. M., Mugwe, R., Makin, K. R., & Dida, G. B. (2015). Socialising Government: Evaluating the Role of Social Media in Governance and Ethics in Kenya. *International Journal of Humanities and Social Science, 5*(1), 17–122.

Kaplan, A. M., & Haenlein, M. (2010). Users of the world, unite! The challenges and opportunities of socialmedia. *Business Horizons, 53*(1), 59–68. doi:10.1016/j.bushor.2009.09.003

King, B., & Soule, S. (2007). Social Movements as Extra-institutional Entrepreneurs: The Effect of Protest on Stock Price Returns. *Administrative Science Quarterly, 52*(3), 413–442.

Langley, D., & van den Broek, T. (2010). *Exploring social media as a driver of sustainable behaviour: case analysis and policy implications.* Internet Politics and Policy Conference 2010, Oxford, UK.

Lenox, M., & Eesley, C. (2009). Private Environmental Activism and the Selection and Response of Firms Targets. *Journal of Economics & Management Strategy, 18*(1), 45–73. doi:10.1111/j.1530-9134.2009.00207.x

O'Rourke, D. (2005). Nongovernmental Organization Strategies to Influence Global Production and Consumption. *Journal of Industrial Ecology, 9*(1-2), 115–128. doi:10.1162/1088198054084608

Pew Research Center. (2003). *Values update survey. Roper Center for Public Opinion Research.* University of Connecticut.

PIPA (Program on International Policy Attitudes). (1999). *Americans & the world: International labor standards.* Available from: www.americansworld.org/digest/global issues/intertrade/laborstandards.cfm

Raeburn, N. C. (2004). *Changing Corporate America from Inside Out: Lesbian and Gay Workplace Rights.* Minneapolis, MN: University of Minnesota Press.

Ramsaran-Fowdar, R. R., & Fowder, S. (2013). The Implications of Facebook Marketing for Organizations. *Contemporary Management Research, 9*(1), 73–84. doi:10.7903/cmr.9710

Raynor, J. (2013). *First Edelman "Last Thursday" Breakfast Seminar is a Great Success - Irish Centre for Cloud Computing and Commerce.* Available from: http://www.ic4.ie/first-edelman-last-thursday-breakfast-seminar-is-a-great-success/

Salt, S. (2011). *Social Location Marketing: Outshining Your Competitors on Foursquare, Gowalla, Yelp & Other Location Sharing Sites.* New York: Library of Congress Cataloguing.

Sandilands, T. (2014) *Advantages and Disadvantages of Social Media Marketing.* Available from: http://smallbusiness.chron.com/advantages-disadvantages-social-media-marketing-21890.html

Schurman, R. (2004). Fighting 'Frankenfoods': Industry Opportunity Structures and the Efficacy of the Anti-Biotech Movement in Western Europe. *Social Problems, 51*(2), 243–268. doi:10.1525/sp.2004.51.2.243

Sen, S., Gurhan-Canli, Z., & Morwitz, V. (2001). Withholding consumption: A social dilemma perspective on consumer boycotts. *The Journal of Consumer Research, 28*(3), 399–417. doi:10.1086/323729

Shellenberger, M. (2003). *Race to the top—A report on ethical business campaigns.* Portland, OR: Ethical Business Campaigns Network.

Shettleworth, S. J. (2010). Cognition, Evaluation and Behavior (2nd ed.). New York: Oxford.

Simon, B. (2011). Not going to Starbucks: Boycotts and the out-scouring of politics in the branded world. *Journal of Consumer Culture, 11*(2), 145–167. doi:10.1177/1469540511402448

Slot, M., & Frissen, V. A. J. (2007). Users In The 'Golden' Age Of The Information Society. *Observatorio Journal, 1/3,* 201–224.

Soar, M. (2002). The first things manifest to and about the politics of cultural jamming: towards a cultural economy of graphic design and advertising. *Cultural Studies, 16*(4).

Stone, B. (2007). Microsoft to Pay $240 Million for Stake in Facebook. *The New York Times,* p. 1.

Szabo, J., & Barefoot, D. (2010). *Friends with benefits: A social Media Marketing Handbook* (1st ed.). New York: William Pollock.

Taki, M., & Coretti, L. (2013). The role of social media in the Arab up-rising past and present. *Westminster Papers in Communication and Culture, 9*(2), 1-115.

Thackeray, R., Neiger, B. I., Hanson, C. L., & McKenzie, J. F. (2008). Enhancing promotional strategies within social marketing programs. Use of Web 2.0 social media. *Health Promotion Practice, 9*(4), 338–341. doi:10.1177/1524839908325335 PMID:18936268

Vinerean, S., Cetina, J., Dumitrescu, L., & Tichindelean, M. (2013). The Effects of Social Media Marketing on Online Consumer Behavior. *International Journal of Business and Management, 8*(14), 66–79. doi:10.5539/ijbm.v8n14p66

Vogel, D. (2005). *The Market for Virtue: The Potential and Limits of Corporate Social Responsibility.* Washington, DC: Brookings Institution Press.

Wikipedia.*org.* (2015). Available from: https://en.wikipedia.org/wiki/Tiger_Brands

Xie, I., & Stevenson, J. (2013). Social media application in digital libraries. *Online Information Review, 38*(4), 502–523. doi:10.1108/OIR-11-2013-0261

Yang, G. (2009). Online Activism. *Journal of Democracy, 20*(3), 33–36. doi:10.1353/jod.0.0094

Zeevi, D. (2013). *What Makes Social Media So Influential?* Retrieved from http://www.socialmediatoday.com/daniel-zeevi/1246736/infographic-what-makes-social-media-so-influential

KEY TERMS AND DEFINITIONS

Activists: These are people involved in transformation in society that are driven by political or social ideology.

Consumers: These are people who purchase and consume goods or services.

Cultural Jamming: A form of subvertising, used to expose questionable business practices perpetuated by big businesses and is used to name and shame them.

Government Scandals: Disgraceful, shocking behaviour perpetuated by government officials that can give the government a bad name in public.

Online Petitions: It is a petition that is a way of bringing a grievance or an issue of public concern to the attention of the public that is signed online.

Social Media: A combination of electronic tools that enables communication between different online users to exchange ideas, knowledge and information in virtual networks.

Unethical Business Practices: Where management or employees of the business are involved in irresponsible behaviour, corruption or collusion that can results in bringing the business practices name into disrepute.

Chapter 73
Social Media's Role in Alleviating Political Corruption and Scandals:
The Philippines During and After the Marcos Regime

Cecilia G. Manrique
University of Wisconsin-La Crosse, USA

Gabriel G. Manrique
Winona State University, USA

ABSTRACT

This chapter is an attempt to show how the use of social media in one country, the Republic of the Philippines, has grown and has been used to encourage political awareness and participation among the Filipino masses. The country is ranked among the most technologically savvy in the world but ironically is also considered one of the most corrupt countries as well. The authors believe that, as a result of the showings Filipinos have made when called upon via social media to oust corrupt officials, there is a method whereby such knowledge can be harnessed for the good thus alleviating scandals and ultimately corruption in the country. This research points to the direction the country, and various other countries in the world in similar situations, may take in order to combat corruption through greater citizen participation.

INTRODUCTION

Data indicate that the Philippines is among the first countries to have rapidly embraced the use of social media via the Internet and cell phones. It ranks among the top countries when it comes to cell phone, Internet and social media usage. At the same time, the Philippines has been plagued by decades of political corruption and scandals which accelerated during the regime of Ferdinand Marcos and continues

DOI: 10.4018/978-1-5225-5637-4.ch073

to the present. It ranks as one of the most corrupt countries in the world based on its placement in the Corruption Perception Index.

It is also true that historically, the Philippines has been able to effect regime changes in a relatively peaceful and non-violent manner as shown by the overthrow of Ferdinand Marcos in 1986 after more than 20 years of his "benevolent dictatorship" via the Epifanio de los Santos Avenue (EDSA) People Power Revolution/Movement from February 22-25, 1986. This led to the eventual installation of Corazon (Cory) Aquino as the legitimate president of the country after a much contested election. People Power 2 or the second EDSA revolution also known as EDSA II (or EDSA 2) led to the ouster of Joseph "Erap" Estrada, the corrupt president who succeeded Fidel Ramos, the successor to Aquino. Gloria Macapagal-Arroyo (GMA), who succeeded Estrada and is rumored to have exceeded Estrada's corruption, was herself driven from office by widespread unrest and protests.

A case may be made that the quick and widespread use of social media in the Philippines and the success of Filipinos in getting rid of corrupt regimes are related phenomena. Political mobilization is made possible by social media, along with the spread of relatively cheap communications like texting. Aside from facilitating the flow of information among the population, the logistics of deploying the masses once the movement for the overthrow of regimes begins is made easier by social media.

However, it is ironic and even tragic that the forces of social media that contribute to the overthrow of corrupt regimes have not yet been able to alleviate the high level of corruption that continues to plague the Philippines. The chapter proposes to examine the extent of the relationship between social media and corrupt regime change in the Philippines during the last three decades. This chapter also proposes to explore the possible ways that social media can alleviate corruption in a country, and the reason why these have not been effective in the Philippines. It is hoped that through the examples and suggestions proposed herein some semblance of domestic policy and even international policy can be effected that can help transform the politics of individual nations and maybe even the international system.

A note of optimism surrounds our initial assessment of the Philippines. Even with such a poor record of corruption, the authors consider the Philippines as a case of a Third World country that, partly through the spread and increasing sophistication of social media, is starting to be transformed during the past 30 years from a highly corrupt country into one that is making great political and economic strides that could still erase its reputation for corruption and economic malaise. In the recent past, it has performed among the best in Asia in two measures – economic growth and stock market returns. Authors thus consider what factors may be responsible for its continuing transformation.

BACKGROUND

The Republic of the Philippines has been called the "promise of Asia" and the "sick man of Asia" alternately ever since its search for stability, prosperity and development began in the 1940s. After centuries of Spanish rule and half a century under American tutelage, the Philippines has struggled with its attempts at political and economic development since 1946. Right after the Second World War and independence from the United States, it was thought that the democratic institutions that had been installed during American colonization would lead the country to the road to economic prosperity as well. And by the 1960s, it seemed that she would be on the right path because at that time the country was considered one of the fastest growing economies in Asia.

However, the ambition of one man, Ferdinand Marcos, aided and abetted by his cronies would lead to a pernicious though seemingly benevolent authoritarianism that would impede political and economic development and would setback the country for decades. A culture of governing primarily for one's personal gain festered and spread leading to the characterization of the Marcos regime as a "Kleptocracy" – a government that exists primarily to plunder a country. It would not be until the Marcos dictatorship was dismantled that the institutions required to rebuild the nation would be re-instituted. By then, so much had already been done to institutionalize corruption which in turn stymied economic development and legitimate business transactions. And as the authors have previously indicated in a paper on the "Digital Divide," there are times when development requires a stimulus for a nation to take off (Manrique & Manrique, 2009). In the case of countries like Singapore, South Korea and Taiwan, it was sparked by the infusion of information technology within the economy in the latter part of the 20th century that spurred economic growth and which continues until today. In the Philippine case, it should have been the massive infusion of foreign direct investment (FDI) that would act as the catalyst for take-off. But such investment would be squandered by Marcos cronies and its promised path to economic growth would not come to fruition. This time as it plays catch up in the early 21st century, the Philippines, like its Asian neighbors, may have to rely on innovations in information technology to sustain its take off but only if accompanied by an improved business climate.

DIGITAL PHILIPPINES

Current data and information about the state of social media worldwide puts the Philippines at the very top of every list. As of January 2015, it was estimated that there were 44.2 million active Filipino Internet users (out of a total population of 101M as of July 2015) 90% of whom have active social media accounts. Since 2010, the Philippines has ranked as the fastest growing country when it comes to Internet access. In fact when it comes to social media visits by country the Philippines ranks first on Facebook (FB) and in the top five on YouTube, Twitter and Google+ (Chaffey, 2016).

Filipinos spend a lot of time on the Internet through their laptop and desktop but more so in terms of their mobile device (cell phone) usage, averaging 6.3 hours per day on the laptop and 3.3 hours on their mobile devices (Revesencio, 2015). Over 40% of Filipinos also own active social media accounts surpassing the South Koreans and Japanese in that respect. It was likewise named the "Selfie Capital of the World" by Time Magazine in 2014.

Much of the growth of social media penetration in the Philippines has been attributed to several factors. Foremost among them is the influx of low-priced mobile devices such as smart phones that has encouraged even the poorest of the poor to be in possession of these devices. Social media penetration has also been spurred by the economic growth that has been experienced by the country over the past few years and the stability brought about by peaceful political transition from one leader to another since Corazon Aquino came into power. It also helps that the Philippines is one of the countries that has encouraged the use of the Internet and social media without blocking content or engaging in censorship unlike a country like China (Barone, 2015). More importantly, the digital lifestyle that Filipinos now adopt in terms of a reality which is "powered by apps, sites and gadgets" is clearly supported by a young, dynamic population (Revesencio, 2015).

RELEVANT LITERATURE

A good summary of what is taking place in the Philippines today can be obtained from the work of Bertelsmann Stiftung which provides an update as to where the Philippines is in terms of political and economic development (Bertelsman, 2016). Its value lies in tracing not only the economic indicators that have accounted for the optimism about the economy over the past few years but also the focus on the political characteristics of the transformation that is taking place in the democratic institutions of the country starting from the peaceful uprising that ousted Ferdinand Marcos and installed Corazon Aquino as president after 21 years of dictatorial rule to the current peaceful transition from the Presidency of Noynoy Aquino to that of Rodrigo Duterte.

It is widely recognized that despite economic successes such cannot be sustained unless the weak and ineffective political leadership and institutions are converted into efficient and effective ones. Gridlock between the legislative and executive branches of government will need to be alleviated. Much of the country's problems stems from the inability to formulate reasonable and attainable long term policies instead choosing expedient solutions to short term problems. Expediency coupled with a large bureaucracy leads to systemic problems such as red tape, corruption and low quality service.

Political scientists in the realm of political communication literature continue to delve in debates regarding the Internet and social media in regards to the extent to which they can open up communication lines; foster grassroots mobilization and greater political activism and participation; give voice to the voiceless by providing access to political communication channels; and maybe even eventually modify, disrupt or replace the dominance of the politically advantaged in a country (Margolis, Resnick, & Wolfe, 1999; Bimber, 2003; Chadwick, 2006; Hindman, 2009). Some political scientists fall on the side of supporting the notion that the Internet does not do more than just reinforce the already existing political communication power structures (e.g. Margolis, Resnick, & Wolfe, 1999; Hindman, 2009). However, there are those of the belief that "some of the most important examples of how information technology affects politics involve marginalized groups overcoming resource limitations and other more serious barriers to gain political power" (Bimber, 2003, p. 235). This is where a discussion of the Philippine people power movement with the help of social media comes into play.

The literature seems to indicate that with the rise in the use of Facebook, Twitter and blogging sites people anywhere and everywhere are able to continually replay, analyze and discuss issues ad nauseam. The Internet has created an atmosphere where it seems that everything is publicly displayed and no issue can be hidden from the people's eyes. Thus the behavior of government officials, political figures or individuals in positions of power which causes shock and gets people upset because the action is morally or legally wrong is the classic definition of a scandal. Some scandals can be sexual in nature. Some can be illegal in nature such as the workings of a kleptocracy in which leaders steal from their constituents once they assume power. Some can be abuse of power such as the corrupting influence of those who maintain dictatorships so that they can do all of the above as in the case of the Philippines (Fitz, 2014).

Scholars who have researched the new technology within the context of Philippine democracy seem to be divided regarding the role that social media plays in political mobilization, participation and activism. Some like Brisbin, Rafael and Rheingold are of the view that the ouster of Ferdinand Marcos during the first EDSA revolution constituted the first successful revolution facilitated by the electronic media. Likewise, the use of texting to get protestors out into the streets during EDSA 2 re-enforced the belief that the new media has taken politics in the Philippines to a new height in fostering political activism and bringing about change (Brisbin, 1988; Rafael, 2003; Rheingold, 2002). There are scholars who are more skeptical of the transformative nature of social media in the Philippines and other settings. They contend that the role of social media in encouraging political action has been exaggerated (Pertierra, et al., 2002). Others indicate that the ability of the new media to bring about political action is still at a very early stage (Aguirre, 2009). Regardless, it seems that the following can be said about the role of the new media in the Philippines: 1) the new media is just another venue used by those who are already politically motivated and active and heavily into social media anyway (Mirandilla, 2009); 2) the new media has the ability to initiate political controversy but then is picked up by the traditional media to make it more accessible; and 3) whether the new media is able to reflect popular discontent or actually fuel it is still unknown with the direction of the correlation still difficult to determine, but regardless the new media is capable of making the discontent towards an issue or its unpopularity better known to the general public. There is no denying that it has some impact on political reporting and maybe even political action, but its long term effect remains to be seen (Pertierra, 2012).

It cannot be denied that the recent history of the Philippines relied strongly upon social media in leading the Filipino towards transformative participation in the ouster and change in political personalities ruling the country. Accounts of how people were brought out to the streets and communicated with each other via text messaging are rampant (EDSA, 2016; Perral, 2016). And there continue to be stories of how social media has led to the unveiling of corruption, the shaming of politicians and their eventual ouster from power.

Because political corruption remains a major issue in the domestic politics of most developing countries in the world including the Philippines, the material from Ahmed rings true when he posits that the media in general act as the indirect deterrent of corruption in his country of study, Bangladesh. Although the focus of attention is traditional media like newspapers and television, the findings could very well apply to today's social media. They try to assert social responsibility and work towards social accountability by keeping an eye on the powerful, guarding the public interest and protecting it from incompetence, corruption, and misinformation. It can be engaged in uncovering misdeeds of political parties and politicians as well as in educating the masses against the adverse impacts of corruption. Moreover, people can realize the pervasiveness of political corruption from the material that is disseminated through social media (Ahmed, 2013).

THE PHILIPPINES: SOCIAL MEDIA AND CORRUPTION

The Philippine notoriety for being a corrupt country is reinforced by the 20 year data shown in Table 1 below which describes the Philippines and its Corruption Perception Index ranking from the years 1995 to 2015. It ranks among the lowest in terms of clean government and being highly corrupt. In fact from 2003 to 2007 data in Table 1 show that it is stuck at a 2.5 value in terms of the index and the next three years after that showed a decline in the index. If the data is not affected by the change in range valuation which took place in 2012, improvement for the Philippines based on the index has only taken place over the last 4 reporting periods (2012-2015).

The perception of the Philippines being a corrupt country based on the evaluations of businesses and visitors to the country is very difficult to overcome. When coupled with stories of politicians, the elite and prominent personalities engaged in scandalous activities one begins to wonder whether there is hope for the country. The scandals are not only sexual and pornographic in nature such as the sordid affair of Ferdinand Marcos with Dovie Beams which was recorded and disseminated using old traditional media

Table 1. Corruption Perception Index Ranking: Philippines

Year	RANK	OUT OF	TI Index*
1995	36	41	2.77
1996	44	54	2.69
1997	40	52	3.05
1998	55	85	3.3
1999	54	99	3.6
2000	69	90	2.8
2001	65	91	2.9
2002	77	102	2.6
2003	92	133	2.5
2004	102	146	2.5
2005	117	159	2.5
2006	121	160	2.5
2007	131	179	2.5
2008	141	180	2.3
2009	130	180	2.4
2010	134	178	2.4
2011	129	178	2.6
2012	105	176	34**
2013	94	177	36
2014	85	175	38
2015	95	168	35

*0-10 range with 0 as highly corrupt and 10 as very clean

**In 2012 the index was changed to a 0-100 range with 0 as highly corrupt and 100 as very clean

Source: The Corruption Perception Index Retrieved June 13, 2016 from http://www.transparency.org/research/cpi/overview

since the newer social media were not yet available then. One can argue that it was a precursor of postings that had gone viral then on various media – radio, newspaper, and television. Nor are the scandals limited to the excesses of those in power such as the infamous shoe collection of Imelda Marcos, although it would have been a favorite of today's social media "fashionistas". Such scandals are not the concern of this chapter. The scandals that have provided the greatest amount of the exhibition of people power are those that are economic and political in nature.

Another useful measure of the Philippine environment for business is the "Doing Business Index" (2015) published by the World Bank. The Philippines ranks poorly on many such measures. In 2016, it ranked 103 in doing business (out of 189). This is worse than in 2015 when it was ranked 97. Oftentimes there is a correlation between the low ranking and the level of corruption.

By documenting processes associated with business practices in various countries, Doing Business rankings are broken down into different categories and these help to illustrate the opportunities for corruption and areas for improvement in a country. For example, the Philippines ranks 165th in the category "Starting a Business" which attests to the difficulties encountered by companies that wish to make inroads in business in the Philippines. It takes more than 3 times as long to start a business compared to advanced countries and relative to a country's income, it is 5 times more expensive to start a business. Likewise, it takes so many days to register property (2016 rank – 112) because of the inordinate number of steps and paper work involved. The point is that long, often unnecessary and duplicate steps in any of the doing business categories give rise to opportunities for corruption to hasten the startup process. It is not uncommon for businesses, both domestic and international, to simply give up on starting businesses because of the unneeded complexity and delay and because many simply refuse to take part in the bribery and corruption that is so prevalent. The authors strongly suggest that the monitoring and reporting of such bottlenecks and corruption traps can improve business conditions.

The judicial system can also be improved by social media monitoring. In the latest Doing Business rankings, the Philippines is 140th in the enforcement of contracts. The difficulty of enforcing contracts entered also serves as a powerful deterrent for doing business. It has been reported repeatedly that some members of the judiciary and the bureaucrats that work in the judiciary have been corrupted. For this reason, the enforcement of contracts suffers from delay or worse it leads to the dependence of ultimate outcomes on the willingness and ability to give bribes and find the right connections. The posting of actual problems with the judiciary on social media and even calling attention to specific locations and personnel via social media can result in a more impartial judiciary and a fairer enforcement of contracts (Doingbusiness.org, 2016).

It should come as no surprise that in the Doing Business ranking for "Trading across Borders," the Philippines ranks 95th and even more telling is that in the Philippines, it costs 4 times as much as in high income Organization for Economic Co-operation and Development (OECD) countries to pass import border compliance procedures. The cost ratio for export border compliance is only slightly lower. That is because the Bureau of Customs (BOC) is considered to be among the most corrupt offices in the Philippines rivaled only by the Bureau of Internal Revenue (BIR) (Gonzales, 2010). It follows that it imposes additional costs to cross-border trade, further retarding an economy that is heavily dependent on international trade. Numerous well-meaning non-political appointees have tried to break through the wall of corruption of this agency to no avail. Perhaps the ubiquitous presence of social media can break through the infested labyrinth that is the Philippine BOC.

The specific listing of some of the political scandals that have plagued the country from the 1990s to the present can be found in Table 2.

Based on the Table 2, corruption and scandals are not only on the national scale but also in the provincial and local level as evidenced by mayoral and gubernatorial cases. The case of Mayor Antonio Sanchez of the city of Calauan in the province of Laguna is an example of the abuse of power of a local official. President Joseph Estrada's nefarious activities have impacted current and former governors such as Richard Gordon and Chavit Singson. Philippine Generals and national artists have had their own share of scandals. And the role of a businesswoman, Janet Napoles in the PDAF pork barrel scam was covered in Facebook and the Twitterverse. There have also been instances of Twitter wars involving the children of former President, now Manila Mayor Estrada.

The Philippines became the texting (SMS) capital of the world with the encouragement of the proliferation of social media devices under the Fidel Ramos and Joseph Estrada administrations. This was before Facebook and Twitter would take to the airwaves when Filipinos found the use of texting as the most effective way of mobilizing their friends and neighbors. This practice played an important role in the ouster of President Estrada in 2001. When the Senate impeachment trial was suddenly adjourned without verdict, the text message went around to "meet at EDSA (Epifanio de los Santos Avenue)" the same venue which led to the ouster of Ferdinand Marcos. Thus this would be dubbed as People Power

Table 2. Philippine Scandals

YEAR	INVOLVED	BRIEF DESCRIPTION
1993	Mayor Antonio Sanchez	Rape of a student and murder of her boyfriend
1998	Subic Bay Leadership	President Joseph Estrada removes Richard Gordon as chair of the Subic Bay Metropolitan Authority
	President Joseph Estrada	Nepotism exhibited by appointing relatives to government positions
	President Joseph Estrada	Assigned vehicles seized by the Bureau of Customs to Cabinet secretaries and favored political allies
2000	President Joseph Estrada	Profited from stock manipulation scheme
	President Joseph Estrada	Engaged in drinking and gambling sessions in Malacanang Palace
	President Joseph Estrada	Receivedjueteng (Philippine illegal numbers game) payoffs and bribes
2004	President Gloria Macapagal-Arroyo (GMA)	Involved in electoral fraud during 2004 elections
	Jocelyn Bolante	Undersecretary of Agriculture who diverted fertilizer funds to 2004 election campaign of GMA
2008		Government Service Insurance System (GSIS)-Meralco bribery case
		NBN/ZTE deal(or NBN/ZTE mess) involved allegations of corruption in the awarding of a US$329 million construction contract to Chinese telecommunications firm ZTE for the proposed government-managed National Broadband Network (NBN)
	Philippine Generals	Involved Eliseo de la Paz and several Philippine National Police officials who went to Russia on October 2008 to attend the Interpol conference. De la Paz was detained for carrying a large sum of undeclared money.
2009		GMA used presidential prerogative to proclaim four individuals as National Artists without prior nomination by a selection committee
2013	Janet Lim-Napoles	A businesswoman who is allegedly the mastermind of a controversial pork barrel scam involving the misuse of Priority Development Assistance Funds (PDAF)

Source: Wikipedia, 2016

II or EDSA 2. Crowds gathered in the middle of the night and refused to leave the main Manila thoroughfare until "Erap," (Estrada's nickname) left the presidential palace.

Today Facebook is being used by more than 25 percent of the Philippine population, sometimes ranking the country 8th in the world in FB use and sometimes even #1. Other social media networks (such as Twitter) are rapidly growing in popularity. In September 2011, the Philippine Trust Index, commissioned by EON The Stakeholder Firm, was released. The study revealed that 68 percent of the respondents view online news sites as the most trusted sources of news and information while 49 percent trust social networking sites.

During the 2011 Philippine State of the Nation Address, some attendees initiated the use of the hashtag #WeWantPnoyTo, a call to make President Benigno (NoyNoy) Aquino aware of the different concerns of advocates. This spread among Expanded Digital Activism participants, as well as among members of their organizations. It became one of the 10 most trending hashtags in the Philippines during that week. We can take this as evidence that there is a hunger for change that can perhaps be harnessed into social pressure to end corruption.

Clearly, development workers saw this avenue as an inexpensive yet effective way to instill advocacy into the stream of public consciousness. The civil society organizations that were trained knew that social media is most effective when it supplements the traditional mode of campaigning to encourage collective action against human rights abuses. As mobile phones reach even the most remote citizens and as Internet penetration – and along with it social media usage – widens its reach in the Philippines, these tools will become potentially more valuable to civil society, citizens, and officials in their advocacy efforts. As skills in these tools are acquired and greater education about the potential of these tools are disseminated, careful attention needs to be paid to how much impact social media is making on the daunting development challenges facing the country (Tapnio & Rood, 2011).

ANALYSIS

Even though the Philippines has been dubbed a major social media country in the world as exhibited by the number of Filipinos who own cell phones; are part of Facebook, Twitter and Instagram; and who engage in blogging the examples of the past few years may not be enough to definitively conclude that social media can be the answer to alleviating corruption in the Philippines. Analysts have gone on both sides of the argument with those who have seen in EDSA 2 and the reporting on the abuses of Gloria Macapagal-Arroyo that mobilizing using the new media has worked and led to greater political awareness, involvement and participation by the Filipino people. On the other side are those who are skeptical about the role of social media in a struggling economic system. The new media is seen as still an instrument of the educated political and economic elite whose role is to reinforce what the traditional media has already uncovered. Thus, the new media is viewed as just another venue to vent discontent but it will still require the support of the traditional media, newspapers, radio and television, to move the rest of the population along.

SOLUTIONS AND RECOMMENDATIONS

The point is that entrenched corrupt ways of doing things can be brought to light much easier with the use of social media. Of course the use of social media to monitor corruption can lead to abuse as well. It may lead to the posting of false accusations, cyber bullying by advocacy groups, and extortion as well. That is the reason why the researchers suggest that countries intent on eradicating a culture of corruption can learn some lessons from sites that have a well-developed verification system and broad participation. Tripadvisor.com and yelp.com are useful examples of such sites. These popular sources of reviews of establishments, services, etc. can provide countries with lessons on how to balance the free flow of information on social media with the need for verification and veracity. It would put the onus on citizens to inform their fellow countrymen of the existence of both good and bad government agencies thereby challenging the "old" ways of doing business.

But for such social media sites to work, certain conditions must be present. It would first need the broad participation of a citizenry committed to improving government who are willing to share personal experiences for the purpose of improving government. Second, it would need an independent overseer to monitor and filter social media postings for their veracity because it is easy to flood such sites with "fake" reviews, both favorable and unfavorable which in turn creates social media noise that negates the usefulness of these sites. Third, there should be some assurance of freedom from retaliation and retribution among those who responsibly participate and publish reviews.

A fourth condition necessary for social media sites to succeed in helping to transform a corrupt society concerns sanctions. Sites such as yelp.com rely on the sanctions and rewards of the marketplace. Consistently poor reviews beget fewer sales. Consistently good reviews can beget greater sales and profits. Unlike such market-driven sites, government-agency monitoring sites (which can be called transparency sites) must be accompanied by a system of sanctions and rewards imposed by the responsible authorities. Here again, it would require further social media pressure to ensure that such proper sanctions and rewards are meted out.

We should also point out that whatever uses of social media develop for transparent government, the traditional media must retain its role as a watchdog and an unbiased source of information. The different media complement each other in any effort to improve governance and to reduce corruption.

Given such scenarios, it should be clear that the Philippines is ripe for people taking politics in their hands. Digital Activism which is the harnessing of the power of online social media for human rights advocacy can also be used for all types of political activism and advocacy. The following specific examples of the use of texting, Facebook and Twitter should provide the reader with a fairly good idea of the shape and importance of their role in Philippine politics today.

FUTURE RESEARCH DIRECTIONS

On May 6, 2016, the Philippines elected a new president for a 6-year term beginning on June 30, 2016 when Rodrigo Duterte was inaugurated. As in the past, the election of a new president brings high hopes that the new regime will be able to tame the corruption that has plagued the Philippines. The new president's approach to improve government and society has admittedly been on the unconventional side, relying on very heavy-handed applications of the law. It is too early to say where such governing tactics will lead or how long it will be effective and be accepted by the people and tolerated by the international community.

While social media has been able to help topple regimes, the more salient question about social media is how it can be effectively used to battle corruption at the retail level. For example, if the driver's license agency extracts bribes before it issues licenses, social media can be used to inundate the agency with protestors as well as a social media campaign can be launched to "shame" the agency. Such timely mobilization can be effective especially if the new president and his lieutenants react as they promised. How the people and government officials react under a new regime will be an interesting follow up to this study.

Aside from Twitter, Facebook and texting, Filipinos in the past have been known to populate other social networks such as Flickr and MySpace. It would be an interesting comparative study to see the role played by such networks which are less popular in other countries because of the different demographic profiles of those who tend to use such social media.

And of course, this study would be enhanced by the more detailed investigation of individual sites like Facebook and Twitter for more specific material on the use of that medium for political activism/participation in the Philippines. Going into specific Philippines sites on FB and using Twitter hashtags relevant to Philippine politicians, events and activities could reveal useful insight into the viability of Filipinos to use "trip-advisor-like" or "yelp-like" sites to encourage political awareness and eventual greater political participation.

CONCLUSION

There are clearly instances when social media has spurred political participation and political change in the Philippines as evidenced by the examples of the ouster of President Joseph Estrada and the million people protest. The big question is can it alleviate political corruption? When politicians know that the people have some semblance of power through social media they may be more reluctant to engage in obvious activities that will get the people out into the street to protest their nefarious activities.

But more importantly the authors suggest that the use of social media has a huge monitoring potential. By setting up systems where people can provide input on people, places and events that border on scandals and corruption and reporting such as those found in, and obtained from, a site like, TripAdvisor. com and Yelp.com greater awareness ensues. People become part of the process and are able to feel that they have an input on the system. In some small ways, they are able to have an impact on alleviating the corruption that may exist in the country. Such can apply not only to the Philippines but all countries that experience the political and economic impact of being in the lowest ranking of the Corruption Perception Index and which are tagged as countries difficult to do business in.

Another issue that seems to come up as in the case of the Philippines is whether such political participation through social media can be sustained? Filipinos have a tendency to be faddish and may not give social media transparency efforts the long-term seriousness it deserves. However, the examples and the data from 1993 to 2013 show the public has staying power and that vigilance on the part of the people in reporting scandals can lead to change. So long as mobile devices remain cheap and accessible especially to the masses, so long as the people feel that such devices help them provide input to the system, and so long as concrete results emanate from such digital activities, political participation using social media can be deemed to be sustainable. Finally, the authors recognize that the powerful and ruling class can co-opt social media and use it to their advantage. After all, ownership of the communication infrastructure lies with oligarchic powers in the Philippines who may choose to use the power of social media to protect the power of their cronies and themselves.

REFERENCES

Aguirre, A. (2009). *ICT and Social Movements in the Philippines: From Estrada to Arroyo*. Philict Research Group.

Ahmed, F. (2013). Role of Media in Uncovering Political Corruption in South Asian Perspective. *Asian Journal of Public Affairs*, 5(1), 20–37.

Barone, E. (2015, November 23). Which countries censor the Internet? *TIME*.

Bertelsman. (2016). *Shaping Change – Strategies of Development and Transformation: Philippines*. Retrieved from http://bti2006.bertelsmann-transformation-index.de/122.0.html?L=1

Bimber, B. (2003). *Information and American Democracy: Technology in the Evolution of Political Power*. New York, NY: Cambridge University Press. doi:10.1017/CBO9780511615573

Brisbin, D. (1988). Electronic Revolution in the Philippines. *Journal of Popular Culture*, 22(3), 49–63. doi:10.1111/j.0022-3840.1988.2203_49.x

Chadwick, A. (2006). *Internet Politics: States, Citizens, and New Communication Technologies*. New York, NY: Oxford University Press.

Chaffey, D. (2016). Global social media research summary 2016. *Smartinsights.com*. Retrieved from http://www.smartinsights.com/social-media-marketing/social-media-strategy/new-global-social-media-research/

Doing Business. (2015, October 27Index. Retrieved from http://www.doingbusiness.org/reports/global-reports/doing-business-2016

EDSA People Power Revolution (2016, January 10). Philippine History. Retrieved from http://www.philippine-history.org/edsa-people-power-revolution.htm

Fitz, P. (2014, February 21). Social media and political scandals. *Miami.edu*. Retrieved from http://students.com.miami.edu/reporting/social-media-and-political-scandals/

Global Voices. (2013, August 27). *Million People March Against Corruption in the Philippines*. Retrieved from https://globalvoices.org/2013/08/27/million-people-march-against-corruption-in-the-philippines/

Gonzales, I. C. (2010, October 6). *Philippine Public Transparency Reporting Project Too Corrupt to Change? The Battle to Reform the Bureau of Customs*. Retrieved from http://peranatinito.net/index.php?option=com_content&view=article&id=135:too-corrupt-to-change-the-battle-to-reform-the-bureau-of-customs&catid=44:stories&Itemid=94

Hindman, M. (2009). *The Myth of Digital Democracy*. Princeton, NJ: Princeton University Press.

Manrique, C. G., & Manrique, G. G. (2009). The Global Digital Divide: What the Indices Reveal. *Paper presented at the American Political Science Association Meeting*, Toronto, Canada.

Margolis, M., Resnick, D., & Wolfe, J. (1999). Party Competition on the Internet in the United States and Britain. *The International Journal of Press/Politics*, 4(4), 24–47. doi:10.1177/1081180X9900400403

Mirandilla, M. P. (2009). *Cyber campaigning for 2010: The Use and Effectiveness of Websites and Social Networking Sites as Campaign Platforms for the 2010Presidential Election in the Philippines*. Canada: IDRC.

PerralD. (2016). *EDSA 2*. Retrieved from https://www.scribd.com/doc/61265052/edsa-2

Pertierra, R. (2012). *The New Media, Society & Politics in the Philippines*. Berlin: Fesmedia Asia.

Pertierra, R., Ugarte, E., Pingol, A., Hernandez, J., & Dacanay, N. (2002). *Texting Selves: Cellphones & Philippine Modernity*. Manila: De La Salle University Press.

Rafael, V. L. (2003). The Cell Phone and the Crowd: Messianic Politics in the Contemporary Philippines. *Public Culture*, 15(3), 399–425. doi:10.1215/08992363-15-3-399

Revesencio, J. (2015). *Philippines: A Digital Lifestyle Capital in the Making?* Retrieved from http://www.huffingtonpost.com/jonha-revesencio/philippines-a-digital-lif_1_b_7199924.html

Rheingold, H. (2002). *Smart Mobs: The Next Social Revolution*. Cambridge: Perseus.

Tapnio, E., & Rood, S. (2011, October). Social Media in the Philippines is Widespread, but what is its Impact? *Asia Foundation*. Retrieved from http://asiafoundation.org/2011/10/12/social-media-in-the-philippines-is-widespread-but-what-is-its-impact/

Transparency.org. (2016The Corruption Perception Index. Retrieved from http://www.transparency.org/research/cpi/overview

Wikipedia. (2016). List of Political Scandals in the Philippines Retrieved from https://en.wikipedia.org/wiki/List_of_political_scandals_in_the_Philippines

Wilson, C. (2014, March). The Selfiest Cities in the World: TIME's Definitive Ranking. *Time*. Retrieved from http://time.com/selfies-cities-world-rankings/

KEY TERMS AND DEFINITIONS

Corruption Perception Index (CPI): The index measures the perception of the corruption exhibited by politicians and the bureaucracy in a particular country. It is an annual ranking produced by Transparency International.

Digital Activism: Commonly used to refer to the use of digital technology in order to being about political, economic and social change.

Digital Divide: Is a measure of the inequalities that exist between those who have and do not have access to technology and its commensurate peripherals such as computer hardware and software, Internet access, social media connectivity, etc. Such divide is said to exist between developed and developing countries.

Doing Business Index: A World Bank ranking that takes a look at the ease of doing business in various countries of the world including such factors as the ease of obtaining permits, getting credit, getting electricity, paying taxes among others.

EDSA Revolution: Epifanio de los Santos Avenue is the main thoroughfare used by the hundreds of thousands of Filipinos who gathered together in popular demonstrations against the Marcos regime and eventually ousted him.

Kleptocracy: A political system that is ruled by individuals who literally rob their constituents of government funds.

People Power Movement: Also known as the EDSA Revolution. This is a grassroots movement which overthrew Ferdinand Marcos from political power in the Philippines in 1986 and installed Corazon Aquino to the Presidency.

Selfie Capital: TIME Magazine's designation of a city that has the most people taking and posting pictures of themselves using their mobile device specifically their phones (selfies). Makati, a city in the Philippines, has been ranked #1 as such.

TripAdvisor: This is the world's largest website that caters to individual's travel needs including flights, hotels and eating places. Reviews are entered by those who have had experiences with these businesses.

Yelp: A website that helps people find the best businesses in a specific location especially geared towards restaurants and places to dine.

This research was previously published in Political Scandal, Corruption, and Legitimacy in the Age of Social Media edited by Kamil Demirhan and Derya Çakır-Demirhan, pages 205-222, copyright year 2017 by Information Science Reference (an imprint of IGI Global).

Index

N

O

P

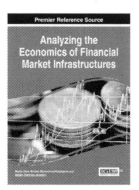

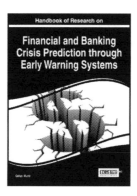

Stay Current on the Latest Emerging Research Developments

Become an IGI Global Reviewer for Authored Book Projects

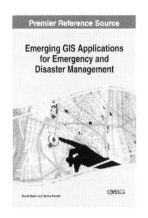

Premier Reference Source

Emerging GIS Applications for Emergency and Disaster Management

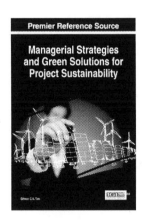

Premier Reference Source

Managerial Strategies and Green Solutions for Project Sustainability

Premier Reference Source

Comparative Approaches to Using R and Python for Statistical Data Analysis

Premier Reference Source

Solutions for High-Touch Communications in a High-Tech World

The overall success of an authored book project is dependent on quality and timely reviews.

In this competitive age of scholarly publishing, constructive and timely feedback significantly decreases the turnaround time of manuscripts from submission to acceptance, allowing the publication and discovery of progressive research at a much more expeditious rate. Several IGI Global authored book projects are currently seeking highly qualified experts in the field to fill vacancies on their respective editorial review boards:

Applications may be sent to:
development@igi-global.com

Applicants must have a doctorate (or an equivalent degree) as well as publishing and reviewing experience. Reviewers are asked to write reviews in a timely, collegial, and constructive manner. All reviewers will begin their role on an ad-hoc basis for a period of one year, and upon successful completion of this term can be considered for full editorial review board status, with the potential for a subsequent promotion to Associate Editor.

If you have a colleague that may be interested in this opportunity, we encourage you to share this information with them.

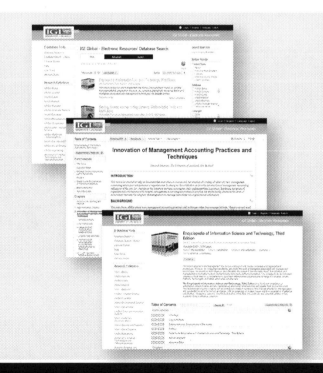